DATE DUE			

THE PAPERS OF

FREDERICK LAW OLMSTED

CHARLES CAPEN McLAUGHLIN

Editor in Chief

CHARLES E. BEVERIDGE

Series Editor

THE PAPERS OF
FREDERICK LAW OLMSTED

VOLUME IV

DEFENDING THE UNION

The Civil War and
the U.S. Sanitary Commission
1861–1863

JANE TURNER CENSER

Editor

THE JOHNS HOPKINS UNIVERSITY PRESS
Baltimore and London

This book has been brought to publication with the generous
assistance of the National Historical Publications and
Records Commission.

The Johns Hopkins University Press
701 West 40th Street
Baltimore, Maryland 21211
The Johns Hopkins Press Ltd., London

∞ The paper used in this publication meets the minimum
requirements of American National Standard for Information
Sciences—Permanence of Paper for Printed Library Materials,
ANSI Z39.48-1984.

Library of Congress Cataloging-in-Publication Data

Olmsted, Frederick Law, 1822–1903.
    Defending the union: The Civil War and the U.S. Sanitary Commission,
1861–1863

    (The papers of Frederick Law Olmsted; v. 4)
    Includes bibliographies and index.
       1. United States—History—Civil War, 1861–1865—Health aspects.
2. United States Sanitary Commission—History.   3. Olmsted, Frederick
Law, 1822–1903—Contributions in public health.   I. Censer, Jane Turner,
1951–.   II. Title.   III. Series: Olmsted, Frederick Law, 1822–1903.
Papers of Frederick Law Olmsted; v. 4.
SB470.05A2   1977   vol. 4   [E621]   973.7'77   85-24044
ISBN 0-8018-3067-2 (alk. paper)

CONTENTS

CONTENTS

CONTENTS

CONTENTS

ILLUSTRATIONS

ACKNOWLEDGMENTS

The research for this volume began when the late William Quentin Maxwell, modern biographer of the U.S. Sanitary Commission, allowed Charles C. McLaughlin, then a graduate student, to make copies of manuscript letters microfilmed from the archives of the U.S. Sanitary Commission, in the New York Public Library. We owe a special debt of gratitude to Dr. Maxwell for sharing with us in the spirit of scholarly cooperation the letters he had found most valuable in this massive collection. We are also particularly grateful to Terry Niles Smith for allowing us to publish family letters which belonged to her grandmother Bertha Olmsted Niles.

Preparation of this volume was made possible by both public and private donors. Funds from the Andrew W. Mellon Foundation, which has generously underwritten our efforts, enabled us to obtain a WANG OIS word processor, which has proven invaluable in our editing and control of documents. We are also grateful for matching grants from the National Endowment for the Humanities. Gifts from the late Eleanor Murdock have been extremely helpful in times of need. The Hubbard Educational Trust has kindly underwritten our procuring of maps and illustrations. Grants from the National Historical Publications and Records Commission have assisted us in bringing this volume to publication and in upgrading our word-processing system; an editing fellowship provided by NHPRC supported the initial research.

The editors especially wish to thank Richard Sommers at the U.S. Army Military History Institute for helping us to use Olmsted's own valuable collection of books, pamphlets, and photographs relating to the U.S. Sanitary Commission (presented by Olmsted to the Massachusetts Commandery of the Loyal Legion in 1890 and later transferred to the Rare Book Room of the Institute at Carlisle Barracks). Sara Jackson and Mary Giunta of the National Historical Publications and Records Commission gave us the benefit of their extensive knowledge of the Civil War records in the National Archives and Records Service. We are grateful to Lucinda Kester for aiding our search for illustrations at the National Library of Medicine in Bethesda, Maryland. We have received helpful comments and suggestions from our advisory board and from other historians, including Jack R. Censer, Joseph L. Harsh, and James C. Turner. Arleyn Levee provided important documents, and we were again fortunate to have the skillful services of Stephen Kraft in the preparation of the maps.

We are grateful to the following institutions for providing important research materials: the Archives of the New York Times, New York City; the Department of Rare Books and Special Collections, Princeton University Library, Princeton, N.J.; the New England Historical Genealogical Society, Boston, Mass.; the New-York Historical Society, New York City; the Department of Special Collections, University of California at Los Angeles, Los Angeles, Ca.; and the University of Cincinnati, Cincinnati, Ohio.

We wish to thank the following repositories for allowing us to publish documents or photographs in their possession: Butler Library, Columbia University, New York City; the Historical Society of Pennsylvania, Philadelphia, Pa.; Houghton Library, Harvard University, Cambridge, Mass.; the Massachusetts Historical Society, Boston, Mass.; the National Archives and Records Service, Washington, D.C.; the National Library of Medicine, Bethesda, Md.; the National Park Service, Frederick Law Olmsted National Historic Site, Brookline, Mass.; the Society for the Preservation of New England Antiquities, Boston, Mass.; and the Union League Club of New York, New York City. In particular we wish to thank the New York Public Library for the courtesy extended while we explored many boxes of the U.S. Sanitary Commission records in the Rare Books & Manuscripts Division, Astor, Lenox and Tilden Foundations. We are grateful to the staff of the Manuscript Division of the Library of Congress, which has graciously continued to aid and assist our work.

Many past and present workers here at the Papers have contributed to this volume. Charles E. Beveridge and Charles C. McLaughlin accomplished the preliminary letter search in the course of their own researches about Olmsted. Barbara Lautman and Maureen Miller typed drafts of the texts and annotation. Archivist Duncan McCollum not only helped locate valuable texts and materials, but also played an important role in overseeing the introduction of word processing to our project. Research associate Kenneth T. Stringer, Jr., skillfully completed difficult research tasks and clarified many obscure references. Mary Sykes Wylie and Tina Raheem helped with the proofreading and checking. Carolyn F. Hoffman oversaw valiantly questions of consistency and brought her expertise in word processing to numerous problems of formating.

THE PAPERS OF

FREDERICK
LAW
OLMSTED

INTRODUCTION

The Civil War brought change and upheaval to Frederick Law Olmsted's life, but it also marked the culmination of important prewar ambitions and projects. Describing himself at the beginning of the war as "pining to find" a "mission," he searched for it during the next two years in areas that long had interested him. Throughout this period he undertook a new activity—guiding the growth and development of the U.S. Sanitary Commission, a voluntary organization that by the end of the war had spent funds and dispensed supplies totaling fifteen million dollars to benefit the Northern soldiers.

The "mission" of the Sanitary Commission was to aid in the care of the large volunteer Union army until the army's small, antiquated Medical Bureau could better do so on its own. The Commission soon became renowned for its work in the hospitals and camps as well as on the battlefields, and Olmsted met the challenge of creating an administrative apparatus which would allow quick response to the medical needs of the army, wherever it was stationed. Because he and the other commissioners believed that primary responsibility for the care of the soldiers must lie with the Medical Bureau, they waged a successful campaign to reorganize and expand it and secure a more energetic surgeon general. Although Olmsted directed most activities from his desk in Washington, he also spent two and one-half months with the Army of the Potomac supervising the hospital ships staffed by Commission workers.

At the Sanitary Commission Olmsted was involved in strife that, to him, paralleled in drama and importance the North's struggle to subdue the secessionist South. Despite its authorization from the national government, the Sanitary Commission was forced to compete for supplies and money with numerous organizations that were intent on aiding the soldiers in their own manner. From the autumn of 1861 the Western Sanitary Commission, headquartered in St. Louis, became a rival for influence with the Western armies, and by late 1862 the U.S. Christian Commission was successfully appealing for funds from pious Americans. But the rivalry that Olmsted found most disturbing came from organizations that emphasized their local orientation by aiding only troops from their own area. He reacted even more angrily when the auxiliary society of the Sanitary Commission in Cincinnati demanded more autonomy and a part of a large special contribution the central body had received. In his struggle to ensure the Sanitary Commission's preeminence among aid societies, Olmsted believed that he was fighting against the petty localism and destructive selfishness that, through secession, threatened the nation's very existence.

During the war Olmsted also found time for other interests related to his war aims of destroying slavery and discrediting the ideology of states' rights. Longing for the abolition of slavery and the reconstruction of Southern society, he hoped that the war would present an opportunity to implement the plan of gradual emancipation and cotton cultivation by free labor which he had first advocated in the 1850s. After drawing up legislation to create a governmental agency to supervise blacks on the federally occupied South Carolina sea islands in 1862, Olmsted lobbied to receive a post there. Although unable to obtain it on terms he deemed satisfactory, he nevertheless strongly endorsed the Emancipation Proclamation and remained committed to ending slavery. During the winter of 1862–63 he and Oliver Wolcott Gibbs outlined a plan for a patriotic and educational organization which took form as the Union League Club of New York. That spring, with Edwin L. Godkin, Olmsted began to take steps toward founding a weekly newspaper of political and intellectual opinion intended both to strengthen public support of the government and to influence the kind of reconstruction policies that the administration would undertake.

At the same time Olmsted was also able to pursue some of his prewar interests. Long a proponent of sanitary reform, he saw his work at the Sanitary Commission as offering an opportunity to educate the common soldiers, who in turn would propagate such ideas among the American people. He also retained his keen interest in understanding American national character and the influence that immigration had played upon it. While he gathered statistical information about the background of the American soldier, he also took advantage of a journey in the Midwest and South to write a series of sketches (published for the first time in this volume) about the distinctiveness of American life and the progress toward attaining the sort of "domestic amenities" which he believed essential for civilization. Finally, as an indication of the significance that urban design had already assumed for him, he remained greatly concerned about the development of New York City. The post of street commissioner, which Mayor George Opdyke twice offered to Olmsted, attracted him, but the city's aldermen, who no doubt were aware that Olmsted, as the administrator of Central Park, had not paid attention to political patronage in his hiring, did not approve the nomination. Central Park continued to be important to Olmsted, and he frequently traveled to New York City to supervise the ongoing construction of the upper park.

During the Civil War Olmsted shared interests common to many Republican Northern gentlemen: the military progress of the war, the nation's war aims, the fostering of loyalty, the medical care of the soldier, and the issues of emancipation and educational and urban reform. His writings—over one thousand letters, newspaper articles, circulars, and reports—illustrate these concerns with great immediacy. The approximately one hundred fifty documents presented here describe the policies, development, and institutional life of the Sanitary Commission, give detailed observations about the fighting power and medical care of the Union army, and present Olmsted's opinions on major questions and controversies of the day, whether slavery and emancipation, national politics, or urban and park design.

In the spring of 1861 Frederick Law Olmsted closely watched the gathering clouds of war. The conflict between North and South had long concerned him, and he had come to believe that the social and economic systems of the two sections of the country were incompatible. When he had first traveled to the South in the early 1850s, he had been sympathetic to the problems that had to be faced if slavery were to be abolished. But the time spent in the Southern states convinced him that their citizens were not making a sincere effort to eliminate slavery. Instead, he had come to believe that the South, as an expanding slave power, threatened the political and civil liberties of Americans. By December 1860 Olmsted had already steeled himself for Southern secession and also for resisting it. In a letter to his old friend Charles Loring Brace he resolutely claimed, "my mind is made up for a fight. The sooner we get used to the idea, the better, I think." Olmsted was even ready to take part in combat, despite his almost forty years and his lameness, the result of a carriage accident in 1860. In April 1861 he considered joining the navy and thought his sixty-nine-year-old father also might wish to serve.[1]

The war probably increased Olmsted's sense of frustration with his increasingly circumscribed position as architect-in-chief and superintendent of Central Park. During the early months of 1861 he had rebelled against the growing power exercised by the comptroller of the park, Andrew H. Green. Accordingly, Olmsted delivered an ultimatum to the Board of Commissioners. He declared that he would not continue to exercise general superintendence unless he regained his former power over appointments and dismissals. The board took him at his word and in June 1861 limited his role to overseeing the finishing touches on the design that he and Calvert Vaux had drawn up.[2]

But even had his position with Central Park been less troubled, the war brought an opportunity which Olmsted had long desired—to shape the transition of blacks from slavery to freedom. In May 1861 at Fortress Monroe, Virginia, Gen. Benjamin F. Butler had decided not to return runaway slaves to disloyal masters but to designate them "contraband of war" and set them to work in the Union camp. Learning that this course had been approved by Secretary of War Simon Cameron, Olmsted realized that such a policy would require superintendence of the blacks at a crucial stage. On June 1, 1861, he asked Henry W. Bellows, a New York City Unitarian minister then in Washington, to help him obtain the post of superintendent of contraband labor. Because the minister had written an article in *Atlantic Monthly* praising Central Park and Olmsted's administrative achievements there, he appeared well suited to argue the case.[3]

But Bellows had a different role in mind for Olmsted and wanted him to be the secretary of the U.S. Sanitary Commission, a benevolent organization then being formed. Since late April, when genteel women had chosen Bellows to be a member of the executive committee of the newly formed Woman's Central Association of Relief, an organization to coordinate soldiers' aid in the New York City area, he had become increasingly involved in the relief effort. A journey to Washington in mid-May with physicians Jacob Harsen, Elisha Harris, and William Van Buren led to an effort to form a broader organization, a commission recognized by the government and similar to the British Sanitary Commission that had been created during the Crimean War.

By June 19, when Bellows asked Olmsted to become the Commission's secretary and chief executive officer in Washington, the struggle to gain official recognition for an organization to gather and disseminate statistical and medical information had succeeded. Olmsted was probably only dimly aware that the consent wrung by Bellows from Acting Surgeon General Robert C. Wood in May had been countermanded in early June by Clement A. Finley, the newly appointed surgeon general. Finley finally agreed to approve the Commission if it restricted its activities to the volunteer army. On June 9 Secretary of War Simon Cameron had given his approval, and on June 13 a hesitant Lincoln, who characterized the Commission as a "fifth wheel" to the coach of state, had signed the executive order bringing it to life.[4]

The organization as Olmsted found it on June 19 was skeletal, consisting only of a board of commissioners. In addition to the founders—Bellows, Harris, and Van Buren—the other original members included: Alexander Dallas Bache, who as long-time director of the U.S. Coast Survey was wise in the ways of official Washington; noted reformer Samuel Gridley Howe of Boston; three New Yorkers—physician Cornelius R. Agnew, lawyer George Templeton Strong, and chemist Oliver Wolcott Gibbs; and the scientist and physician John S. Newberry from Cleveland. As a conciliatory gesture to the Medical Bureau, three army officers—George W. Cullum, Robert C. Wood, and Alexander Shiras—were appointed to the board. On June 20 Olmsted became one of the commissioners as well as their executive agent.

The early civilian members of the Commission would be the men with whom Olmsted would work most closely in determining policy. By and large, they came from wealthy, privileged backgrounds and were related by familial and educational ties to the elites of their areas. They were highly educated—Olmsted was the only one without a college degree—and many had had professional or postgraduate training. By and large, they were not men who had been prominent in prewar benevolent or reform organizations. Only Bellows, Howe, and Olmsted had been active in reform movements, and most of Olmsted's efforts had been confined to the free-soil struggle. Despite their ties to old social elites, however, the most common characteristic shared by these men was a commitment to a "professional ethic." Not a single early member was a businessman. Instead, their careers were in medicine, science, law, religion, and government. A concern for rationality, "expert opinion," meritocracy, and efficiency united the group.[5]

Olmsted shared these concerns; moreover, he brought experiences and convictions to the position of secretary that would enormously influence the organization of the Sanitary Commission and the direction it would take. Though weak eyes and poor health had limited his formal education, he had attended a semester of chemistry lectures at Yale College. Training and practice as a scientific farmer and later as superintendent of Central Park had further reinforced his respect for and interest in applied sciences, particularly those related to public health. Both at his farm on Staten Island and at Central Park, Olmsted had studied and applied the principles of thorough-drainage, the drainage of swampy lands using underground tile pipes. In 1850, as a representative of the Richmond County Agricultural Society, he had purchased an English machine which manufactured tile drain pipes. Later, in his report on the need for a system of thorough-drainage at Central Park, he had demonstrated his technical knowledge of its installation. Aware of the unhealthy consequences of stagnant water (though unaware, like others of his day, that these consequences came about through disease-bearing parasites such as mosquitoes), he argued that the "sanitary influence" of thorough-drainage was of paramount importance to the park. To support this claim, he noted that almost one-seventh of the laborers on the park had contracted intermittent fevers (malaria).[6]

Olmsted also came to the Sanitary Commission with considerable administrative experience, gained mainly on Central Park. There he had found great scope for his supervisory abilities as well as his creative skills. In his first position, that of superintendent, he oversaw the work of thousands of men. After 1858, when he assumed the additional post of architect-in-chief, Olmsted supervised four thousand laborers and a department that was expending millions of dollars. His great pride in his administrative achievements at the park was evident in a later discussion with Vaux about their respective contributions to the design of Central Park. Olmsted then expressed the belief that the "Administration & management of the public introduction to and use of the Park" was his own most valuable contribution to it and added: "I have taken more interest in it, given more thought to it, had greater satisfaction in it than in all else together." Olmsted had considerable cause for satisfaction. He had instituted a new, more accurate system of time keeping for workers, and many of his other accomplishments were directly relevant to his position at the Sanitary Commission. Believing both in the delegation of authority and the accountability of workers, he had ordered his ten engineers to report regularly to him about the progress of construction. At the same time, he had overseen the creation of the special police force, a group that, according to the regulations he issued, adhered to military discipline while introducing the people to the proper use of the park.[7]

Despite these achievements, various incidents at Central Park and at the publishing firm Dix & Edwards, in which Olmsted had earlier been a partner, did not augur well for his tenure at the Sanitary Commission. At Dix & Edwards a heated argument over whether the firm should pay royalties to foreign authors revealed Olmsted's stubbornness in what he believed to be matters of principle. Later, at Central Park he sometimes found it difficult to achieve the results he desired within the financial constraints imposed, and he also proved himself a difficult subordinate. Carrying out a considerably more sophisticated plan than he and Vaux had originally proposed for separating pedestrian and vehicular traffic in the park, he incurred large cost overruns. In the financial retrenchment that followed, he lost much of his authority over park spending to Comptroller Andrew H. Green. Olmsted resented the curtailment of his powers and frequently argued that discretionary spending and power over hiring were necessary to the successful completion of the park.[8] At the Sanitary Commission he would repeat these patterns of hostility to superiors and lavish spending to achieve his goals.

Also important for Olmsted's years at the Sanitary Commission would be his sense of commitment. The responsibility for organizing and guiding the Commission, while not the "mission" he had originally envisioned, was important to him for several reasons. Through its emphasis upon relaying the latest medical and scientific knowledge to army doctors and upon educating the soldiers and their officers to their proper duties, the Sanitary Commission would be uplifting and civilizing the American people—a role that Olmsted had earlier seen himself playing as an editor of *Putnam's Monthly* and in his work on the park. Olmsted also believed that service on the Commission was part of his patriotic duty. It would strengthen the fighting power of the nation by assuring the health of the soldiers and by making the best use of goods and money contributed by the public.

When in late June 1861 Olmsted left New York City to begin his job in Washington, he expected to play a major, though short-term, role in the Commission. Even though he foresaw a long war, he thought that six weeks of work would organize the Commission's executive service and allow him to return to his post at Central Park. Instead, both the war and the Sanitary Commission greatly expanded during that summer, and so did his role in each. In Washington, Olmsted found the Sanitary Commission with no other salaried employee and indeed an all-but-empty treasury. Bellows had devised the first system of organization by dividing the Commission into two main parts, one concerned with inquiry, the other with advice, both containing several subdivisions. For the first month or so, these committees, composed of the board members, carried out the daily tasks of the Commission. Joining in the projects already under way, Olmsted lobbied Congress and the War Department for such measures important to the health and well-being of the army as the construction of modern general hospitals and the creation of a system that would allow soldiers to forward their military pay to their families. Some days he waited for hours in governmental reception rooms to meet with officials.[9]

Despite these time-consuming responsibilities, Olmsted's most pressing duties were the hiring of a professional staff and the creation of an organizational structure. By late June he had begun to recruit workers. First he chose inspectors to study the sanitary conditions of army camps and hospitals and to cooperate with military doctors in the distribution of donated supplies. With a few exceptions, these inspectors were physicians, and a high proportion were graduates of the prestigious Eastern medical schools. There were several reasons for this. The professional and school ties of his fellow commissioners were to young medical men educated at schools such as Harvard, the University of Pennsylvania, the College of Physicians and Surgeons (today a part of Columbia University), and University Medical College in New York. No doubt Olmsted and the other commissioners believed these graduates to be particularly well qualified to instruct the army surgeons on the best medical and hygienic practices. Moreover, the rapid expansion of the volunteer army and the large number of physicians gaining commissions in it meant that in that competitive situation, Olmsted needed to rely on the commissioners' ties in order to secure able men.[10]

While inspectors formed a large part of the work force during the Commission's first year, Olmsted also employed men to perform office work and other nonmedical tasks. For these positions, he first called upon those known to him or recommended by close friends or the other commissioners. Two of the first men he hired had worked for him at Central Park: Alfred J. Bloor, a young architect, became assistant secretary; and Joseph Bridgham Curtis, a young engineer and the half-brother of George William Curtis, accepted a temporary position. Later Olmsted employed other former Central Park employees, including John Y. Culyer and Howard Martin. As the Commission grew, the number of its nonmedical employees greatly expanded. By the summer of 1862 its roster of employees included more clerks and many quartermasters, teamsters, cooks, watchmen, warehousemen, and servants.[11]

During the early months the few employees of the Commission carried out a variety of duties. The inspectors, and even Olmsted himself, spent considerable time answering the stacks of mail—primarily inquiries or letters accompanying donations—that arrived. But this was a temporary situation that existed only until Olmsted was able to put his ideas of organization into practice. From the beginning, he wished to employ a permanent staff in specialized positions that would fully utilize the expertise and experience of these workers.

By mid-September 1861 Olmsted had created the basic organizational structure that would serve the Commission. His goal had been to divide responsibilities and power so that he would not have to make numerous routine decisions. On September 18 he announced to his wife, "I have completed a *large* organization which leaves me only matters of the first importance to personally attend to." In this system the inspectors served as the intermediaries between the Commission and the army. The inspectors and their helpers, the agents, were responsible for distributing medical and hospital supplies to the army doctors, educating them in the best medical and hygienic practices of the day, and gathering information through questionnaires on illness and death in the army. From July to September 1861 the inspectors reported directly to Olmsted. In September the three newly appointed associate secretaries (J. Foster Jenkins, John H. Douglas, and John S. Newberry) began to supervise the inspectors according to geographical location. The associate secretaries received and reviewed regular returns by the inspectors and agents and in turn presented both periodic and special reports to the secretary, who drew up a comprehensive annual report as well as special reports.[12]

Olmsted also sought a clear delineation of responsibilities among the other workers in the central office. In part the emerging role of the Sanitary Commission as a central agency to disburse contributions to the soldiers shaped clerical duties. By the autumn of 1861 the Commission was acquiring branches—subsidiary societies that would solicit, receive, store, and ship supplies according to the Commission's orders. The Woman's Central Association of Relief, the New York City organization which had given birth to the Commission, became its principal branch and then acquired numerous auxiliaries of its own in other towns and cities of New York, Connecticut, and New Jersey. As this important substructure developed, the Commission no longer had to answer letters from the numerous people whose contributions and inquiries had formed such a large part of its correspondence during the summer of 1861. Instead, for the most part the branch societies mediated between individuals and the Commission. Olmsted assigned Assistant Secretary Bloor to oversee the Commission's correspondence with the auxiliaries, one of the most important clerical tasks. Olmsted also instituted specific procedures for filing and answering all the Commission's mail. Upon its receipt, each incoming letter was dated and assigned a number. The clerk then logged it in an index, prepared and inscribed a precis of its contents, and indicated the person who would reply to it. Similarly, all official correspondence from workers in the Washington office was copied into books or duplicated by the letterpress method. Although formalized in a circular of 1862, these practices apparently began during the summer of 1861. Agents were expected to file reports of their own *per diem* and traveling expenses promptly, and associate secretaries were to file monthly estimates of expenditures in their sections.[13]

In the structure of the central office defined by Olmsted, there would be no need for him to participate in the normal duties of the inspection, collection, and distribution of supplies, or in the administrative correspondence with the tributary societies. His advice to his stepmother, Mary Bull Olmsted, about how she, as president of the Hartford Soldiers' Aid Society, should use her time, set out his ideas of his own duties:

> Your first business is to read the newspapers, the whole aim & object of your organization being with regard to matters of which you can only get early and sufficient information from them. You can deputize any responsibility

9

better than that as a general rule. If, in an emergency, it is otherwise & you are obliged to give personal attention to matters of detail, your first duty is to remedy the imperfection of your organization which makes this necessary—meantime employing father, Mary, Bertha, or someone as clerk to read the newspapers & furnish you, verbally or in writing, with an abstract of all matters bearing upon soldiers, directly or remotely.

His conception of his own role at the Commission can be further understood by the distinction he later made between an administrator and an executive. In his view the administrator was a supervisor, while the executive actually carried out the task: "The further (i.e. the more distinctly) removed an administrator is from pure execution the better. I am the Commission's executive, but with reference to my executives, I am a pure administrator, and it is just as absurd & as fatal for me to take my executives' business, or if you please, other executives' of the Commission's business out of their hands as it is for the Exec. Com. to take my business out of my hands."[14]

Although Olmsted attempted to delineate duties and responsibilities clearly, there remained two murky areas that were to cause numerous quarrels within the Commission. Both he and Associate Secretary John S. Newberry were members of the Commission's board and at the same time its employees. As commissioners the two men were equals; in the executive service, Olmsted was Newberry's supervisor. Moreover, Olmsted and the board had not clearly determined what would be the extent of his independent powers of decision. When a subdivision of the board, the Executive Committee, began to play a greater administrative role in 1862, numerous clashes with Olmsted resulted.

Despite these problems, this organizational structure emphasizing clearly defined duties, specialization, and the delegation of powers probably was Olmsted's greatest achievement at the Sanitary Commission. The combination of a professional staff and tributary local societies provided both an expertise and a flexibility that at the time were nearly unique. By relying upon local contributions but using central coordination, the Commission had an extraordinary ability to respond in times of crisis, such as major battles. Such an organization, and indeed such a large specialized cadre of employees, was unheard of in a benevolent organization. Most of the national agencies of reform—whether the American Tract Society or the American Missionary Society—depended upon their executive board and a secretary obedient to its wishes. The local societies oversaw the work in their own villages as they saw fit.[15]

The bureaucratic organization of the Sanitary Commission, with its emphasis on professional management, appears to have been more sophisticated than that of most businesses. In fact, only two other bureaucracies—the railroad system and the U.S. government—offered comparable systems. During the 1850s the railroads had pioneered the introduction of modern middle management to American business. The coordination of a specialized and wide-ranging enterprise in which precision was absolutely necessary had led to the creation of a hierarchy of professional managers.[16] Although the Sanitary Commission did not demand the extent of coordination that a major railroad did, the operations of both were geographically complex.

How did Olmsted come to develop an organizational structure akin to the most sophisticated systems of that day? It is tempting to speculate that he was influenced by two leading railroad men—Thomas A. Scott, vice-president of the Pennsylvania Central, and John Murray Forbes, builder and financier—whom he came to know very well during the fall of 1861. There is no indication, however, that Olmsted ever discussed principles of management with either man. It is possible that his association with some of the best organizers in government, such as Quartermaster General Montgomery C. Meigs and Surgeon General William Hammond, was important. Most likely, Olmsted came to his bureaucratic organization in much the same way as had the railroad managers and governmental officials. The tasks of the Sanitary Commission—to study and care for a widely dispersed army and to be able to react quickly and efficiently to its wants—suggested its organization. Indeed, Olmsted's background may have prepared him especially well to arrive at such a conception. Alfred D. Chandler has pointed out the predominance of civil engineers among the managers of the railroads in the 1850s. While not formally trained in engineering, Olmsted at Central Park had been in close contact with young engineers such as George Waring, Joseph Curtis, and William H. Grant. More important, the actual creation of Central Park demanded the traits that Chandler has found in the engineer-managers who responded to new demands in "the same rational analytical way as they solved the mechanical problems of building a bridge or laying down a railroad."[17]

Numerous historians have recognized the Sanitary Commission as a well-administered organization. Allan Nevins in his magisterial study of the Civil War pointed to the Commission as one of the harbingers of what he called the "organized war" of the North. To him the achievements of the Commission suggested the reforms that were to come in the War Department and the quartermaster's, ordnance, medical, and commissary bureaus. But neither contemporaries nor later scholars have realized that it was the administrative apparatus devised by Olmsted that made possible the expertise, flexibility, and efficiency of the Commission. In its internal organization as well as the national scope of its work, the bureaucratically staffed and managed Sanitary Commission was much in tune with the centralizing, rationalizing tendencies that Nevins, Morton Keller, and

11

Stephen Skowronek have found in other aspects of American life during the war.[18]

But at midsummer 1861 these organizational achievements still lay in the months ahead. In late June and early July Olmsted and Elisha Harris undertook the Sanitary Commission's first inspections of material conditions in the camps of the volunteer soldiers. Olmsted's report disclosed many problems. The soldiers rarely swept their crowded and poorly ventilated tents, and their latrines frequently became disgustingly filthy. While Olmsted found the food and clothing supplied to the troops to be generally ample, he argued that changes such as the addition of fresh or dried vegetables to the army ration would clearly produce greater healthfulness and comfort. Both in this report and in his letters, Olmsted reserved his strongest criticisms for the personal habits and grooming of the soldiers, whom he described as "really much dirtier than it can be believed they have been accustomed to be in their civil life." Concluding that the army was in great danger from an epidemic of contagious disease, Olmsted blamed the officers and their ignorance of military regulations. To remedy these problems, he proposed using inspectors of the Sanitary Commission, who, under the guise of inquiry, would "without special effort or intention, really be the best possible missionaries of sanitary science to the army." But these men, Olmsted argued, needed the power to enforce their suggestions, a power that was never granted by the War Department.[19]

To Olmsted, the importance of sanitary reform extended beyond the immediate problem of preventing the spread of contagious diseases in the army. Long an admirer of cleanliness as one of the virtues of civilization, he believed slovenliness to be a national vice. By educating the soldiers to the importance of healthful living and by demonstrating the means to achieve it, he hoped to propagate these notions among the public at large. "If five hundred thousand of our young men could be made to acquire something of the characteristic habits of soldiers in respect to the care of their habitations, their persons, and their clothing, by the training of this war," he later posited, "the good which they would afterwards do as unconscious missionaries of a healthful reform throughout the country, would be by no means valueless to the nation."[20]

While he hoped for an ultimate general uplifting of all classes in America to genteel standards of domestic tidiness and taste, Olmsted saw a more pressing need for sanitary reform. He and the other commissioners believed it bore a close relation to discipline, which they held to be absolutely essential to a successful army. On July 21, 1861, the battle of Bull Run added strength to these convictions. While the Union force fought creditably much of the day, Confederate reinforcements broke the Union right flank late in the afternoon. Part of those troops retreated in a disorganized manner, some running in headlong flight back to Washington.

When Olmsted, in New York at the time of the battle, returned to Washington the following day, he was aghast at the grimy, sullen, and disheartened soldiers who thronged the streets. Even more disturbing to him was the sight of their officers cheerfully and lazily drinking in the hotel bars. Thoroughly depressed, Olmsted wrote his wife, "The demoralization of a large part of our troops is something more awful than I ever met with."[21]

Olmsted immediately undertook an investigation of the causes of the soldiers' failure in battle. Armed with questionnaires that he had drawn up, the inspectors of the Commission began to interview the regiments involved in the battle. But even as this inquiry began, the Sanitary Commission passed resolutions urging the importance of stringent military discipline upon George B. McClellan, the newly appointed commander of the army at Washington. To Olmsted, the need for discipline and for officers and soldiers to know their duties and fulfill them, went hand in hand with the sanitary reforms he had already advocated. He saw the demoralized soldiers as frightened savages. Discipline, in his view, meant not only their subordination to rules but, in return, their right to the respect of their superiors. Later he clearly stated these ideas when he declared that authority commensurate with responsibility was the ruling principle of military authority because it "implies entire respect for the personal responsibilities of those subject to it." In the system that Olmsted envisioned, mutual duties and respect were essential; a private could have an officer court-martialed for refusing to return a salute.[22]

Olmsted believed that this discipline, growing as it did out of self-respect and respect for superiors because of their greater responsibilities, was consistent with the kinds of arrangements in diet, clothing, hygiene, and housing that the Commission had advocated. Studying the questionnaires in August, he noted that the regiments that had performed most poorly at Bull Run had had little sleep, had not eaten, and were short of water. On the other hand, the best regiments not only were well fed, well clothed, and well drilled but had comfortable quarters, martial music, and amusements to maintain their morale. For Olmsted, teaching the soldier how to cook healthful foods for himself and his messmates, as well as how to maintain personal hygiene and a clean, comfortable camp, would reinforce discipline and help sustain morale. Moreover, keeping the soldier as comfortable and as healthy as was consistent with the army's need for mobility was also part of the obligation the government owed the soldier in return for his service. Throughout the war Olmsted found disheartening the attitude of many army officers—physicians among them—that anything more than crude living conditions and bare necessities pampered the soldier and spoiled him as a fighting man.[23]

As Olmsted sought reasons for the Union defeat at Bull Run, he increasingly blamed the leadership of the country. Believing that the military officers were more culpable than those they commanded, Olmsted and his fellows at the Sanitary Commission applauded when McClellan, shortly after he replaced Irvin McDowell, demanded drills, appointed provost marshals to close the Washington bars to officers and soldiers, and began to enforce military regulations. But Olmsted found no similar solace when he surveyed the current political leadership.

During the summer and fall of 1861 Olmsted believed the Lincoln administration to be totally unequal to the enormous tasks of organizing and fighting the war. Shaken by the experience of Bull Run, some Republicans, including Olmsted, feared that their government was tottering on the brink of disaster. But even among those who shared such fears, responses differed. Henry W. Bellows and Charles Eliot Norton discussed the need for rule by a new "committee of safety" modeled on the American Revolutionary precedent but composed of the nation's "best men"—such as themselves. Olmsted, who was more skeptical that the social elite possessed any special capabilities of leadership, did not advocate that solution. Instead, he, like his close friend Charles Loring Brace, believed briefly in late summer 1861 that a temporary military dictatorship might be necessary to mobilize more effectively for war and to put an end to slavery. In Olmsted's view the South in its bid for independence was showing a flexibility and determination unequaled by the North. But even as he was considering the possible need for a dictatorship, his support for civil liberties and representative government appeared strong. In the summer of 1861 Anglo-Irish journalist William Howard Russell described Olmsted as ready to lay down his life in defense of free speech. This commitment to liberty coupled with an acceptance of possible military rule was not as contradictory as it might appear. For several years Olmsted had believed that the South advocated despotic government and in its zeal to protect slavery threatened personal liberties. In the introduction that he wrote in 1857 to *An Englishman in Kansas*, a travel account by Thomas Gladstone, Olmsted analyzed Southerners' recourse to violence and brutality. He concluded that the South's disregard of constitutional guarantees of liberty was so great that force might be necessary if Northerners were to protect themselves and their rights. "Shall we hereafter exercise our rights as citizens of the United States, which are simply our natural rights as men, only by favor of Sharps rifles and in entrenched villages?" he asked. It was this stark vision of a South uninterested in guaranteeing personal safety and bent on suppressing freedom of speech, petition, and the press which led Olmsted to support a military dictatorship to organize the North for military combat. In his eyes an interim authoritarian government appeared preferable to defeat by the South and a subsequent permanent abridgment of liberties. After Olmsted's despair over the defeat at Bull Run had passed, however, he did not again express any belief that a dictatorship might be necessary.[24]

The report on the causes of the demoralization of soldiers at Bull Run that Olmsted finished in early September was a scathing exposé of the administration's lack of leadership. Although the first version of this report has not survived, it apparently placed clear blame for the defeat upon governmental incompetence that had left the troops emotionally and physically unprepared for battle. The government's inability to quell open support for the Southern cause, even in Washington, combined with its failure to provide proper care of the soldiers, produced a disaster at Bull Run. Olmsted's presentation of his findings to the Commission created a storm of opposition. Although he believed that the objections came primarily from members serving in the government—Bache and the army officers—others were dismayed. George Templeton Strong privately noted that the report could not be released, for fear its grim picture of army life would hinder recruiting. Even after Olmsted revised and softened his criticism, others on the Commission considered the report too strong for public consumption. Their solution was a confidential printing of the document, with circulation limited to the commissioners themselves.[25]

Although Olmsted in his report blamed the government in general for the defeat at Bull Run, he and the Sanitary Commission thought the army's Medical Bureau especially inept. They believed that only through an efficient Medical Bureau could the soldiers receive adequate care. The Commission's small treasury and reliance upon public donations limited the amount of work it could undertake on its own. If the Commission tried to supply all demands, its expenses would rise so dramatically that its funds would soon be exhausted. Faced with these conditions, Olmsted concluded that the only remedies were "a general reform, enlargement and vitalization of the Medical Bureau" through the appointment of a new surgeon general, one who would be "big hearted and energetic."[26]

Given the Commission's official status as a subordinate adviser of the Medical Bureau, discretion appeared necessary in its attempts to secure a new surgeon general. Confidential letters to Secretary of War Cameron and to McClellan in early September asked for the retirement of Finley and increased power for McClellan over the medical care of his troops. On September 11 Olmsted and Bellows met with McClellan and Cameron, probably to explain the Commission's requests, and received the encouragement they desired. The "Napoleon of the Union army" told them to find him a "Larrey" (the medical director of Napoleon's Grand Armée) for the Army of the Potomac. Cameron assured Bellows that he had never made a request that had gone unfulfilled and never would. Though the future looked bright, neither Cameron nor McClellan actually lived up to his promise. Moreover, the secretary of war placed the Commission in an extremely embarrassing position when he forwarded the confidential request to Surgeon General Finley, whose dislike of the Sanitary Commission thereafter increased.[27]

Olmsted, who had long argued the necessity of revealing the need for improvement in all departments of the government, saw that the more diplomatic efforts of his fellow commissioners produced few results. In mid-October President Lincoln rebuffed the Sanitary Commission's suggestions that Finley be removed. With some asperity, he asked the presumptuous commissioners if they wanted "to run the machine." By this time the Commission had fixed upon its own candidate for the post of surgeon general—William Alexander Hammond, a thirty-three-year-old physician who in 1859 had resigned his commission because the army would not assign him to a sedentary position. Although he reenlisted at the outbreak of the Civil War, Hammond had lost his seniority and was a low-ranking assistant surgeon.[28]

As its attempts at reform using official channels failed, the Sanitary Commission moved toward Olmsted's position. In late September Olmsted had chafed at McClellan's censorship of an appeal for blankets and argued that the public would donate many blankets if it knew that some soldiers slept with only straw to cover them. "I am so well convinced that it is necessary to the safety of the country that the war should be popularized that I can hardly be loyal to the Commission and the government, while it is required of us to let our soldiers freeze & our armies be conquered for the sake of maintaining a lie," he fumed. "Our men are dying and are losing strength, spirit and morale already for want of clothing," he pointed out, "and there is not one family in a hundred at the North, that wouldn't use bed-quilts & quilted petticoats & send their flannels & blankets here if this was known." To Olmsted, it appeared that the administration, through its desire to appear fully in control of the situation, was allowing soldiers to suffer unnecessarily and was losing an important opportunity to rally the full support of the Northern people behind the war effort.[29]

Olmsted also worried that supplies contributed through the Sanitary Commission only disguised the failures of the Medical Bureau. The extent to which the Sanitary Commission's efforts, by muting any public outcry against the Medical Bureau, might thus allow greater suffering in the future was of particular concern. Olmsted had rather bravely and even callously declared at one point, "Government should be forced to do better for the disabled, even at the expense of some temporary cruelty." But that was a position that he and the other commissioners proved unwilling to put into effect. Instead, they continued to seek solutions to the many shortcomings in the care of soldiers: the need for modern pavilion hospitals; for a separate, independent ambulance corps; and for sufficient clothing, bedding, and medicines for the military hospitals. But on November 2 the commissioners adopted a new strategy they hoped would clear them of any complicity in the failures of the Medical Bureau. Anonymously they began to take their cause to the people through a newspaper campaign aimed at revealing the inadequacies of the army doctors. Cornelius R. Agnew enlisted his friend Manton Marble, publisher of the *New York World*, to run highly critical articles about Finley. Marble, later a vociferous critic of the Lincoln administration but still a loyal Republican in the autumn of 1861, printed Agnew's exposés and also wrote editorials praising the work of the Sanitary Commission.[30]

This approach backfired badly, however, when in December other prominent newspapers rushed to Finley's defense. At the *New-York Times*, Henry J. Raymond, who in 1853–54 had published Olmsted's observations about the South and slavery, strongly supported the surgeon general. In December 1861 Raymond published articles by Elizabeth Powell, a young nurse of whom he was enamored. Writing under the pseudonym "Truth," Elizabeth Powell praised Finley's abilities and argued that the meddlesome Sanitary Commission attacked him because it was powerhungry. Olmsted's attempts to convince Raymond that "Truth" did not accurately describe the Sanitary Commission were unsuccessful.[31]

Olmsted did, however, manage to silence much of the criticism with his report to the secretary of war, a ninety-six-page history of the activities and observations of the Sanitary Commission. He included a thorough analysis of the physical condition of the volunteer troops as derived from questionnaires and also described the Commission's distribution of supplies and its recommendations for changes. Implicitly he criticized the Medical Bureau for not providing better care for the soldiers. The report was ready by December 21, but only after an enormous exertion of time and energy. Olmsted drove himself hard, staying up late and then rising and dictating portions of the report during his breakfast. He also pushed his staff to the point of exhaustion. In fact, only partly joking, he told of having to watch actuary E. B. Elliott, who if left alone would immediately fall asleep.[32]

Even as Olmsted attempted to protect the Sanitary Commission from the consequences of its attack on the Medical Bureau, he and the other commissioners sought reform by other means. When John H. Douglas heard that McClellan would support the Sanitary Commission if it could offer evidence that Surgeon General Finley was incompetent, Bellows immediately drew up a bill of particulars and left that memorandum for McClellan. Moreover, the Commission attempted to promote legislation to restructure the Medical Bureau. On December 10 Henry Wilson introduced Senate Bill 97, which William A. Hammond had drawn up for the Sanitary Commission. This bill contained the innovations the Sanitary Commission believed necessary for a revitalized Medical Bureau: creation of a new group of medical officers (an inspector general and eight inspectors), who would assume responsibility for the sanitary condition of quarters, camps, and military hospitals; and conferral of higher rank upon the surgeon general. It also provided mandatory retirement with a pension for officers over sixty-five and required that merit, not seniority, be the primary criterion for appointments, for which officers aged sixty or older would not be eligible.[33]

Olmsted, with the advice of the board, began a carefully orchestrated campaign in support of the bill. He arranged for the bill to arrive at the War Department at a time when Cameron was absent and Assistant Secretary of War Thomas Scott, who supported it, could act as his deputy. Olmsted and Hammond, who had some important political acquaintances, also began to lobby selected congressmen. Further encouraged by the appointment of Edwin M. Stanton as secretary of war in January 1862, Olmsted then sought to bring public influence to bear upon him. Under this plan, delegations of prominent citizens from such strongholds of Commission support as New York City, Philadelphia, and Boston visited Stanton and their congressmen to urge passage of the bill reorganizing the Medical Bureau. In New York City the associate members of the Sanitary Commission chose these delegations in a meeting presided over by Mayor George P. Opdyke (who was not then acting in his official capacity).[34]

Several reasons led Olmsted to use public opinion as the motive force behind the medical bill. The presence of governmental officials on the Commission meant that it did not unanimously hold a single concept of the nature and scope of the Medical Bureau. Not only did Olmsted, Bellows, Van Buren, and others disagree with Wood about the kind of reorganization necessary, but the latter's own position as second in seniority in the Medical Bureau made him a strong candidate for surgeon general, were Finley to be retired. Further, Olmsted perceived that some members of the Sanitary Commission, such as Elisha Harris and Bishop Thomas Clark, were sympathetic to Wood and his desire to become surgeon general. Only if the Sanitary Commission did not take an official position concerning the medical reform bill, would it be able to prevent the dissension among its members from becoming apparent. Moreover, the severe criticism directed against the Commission late in 1861 probably influenced Olmsted to avoid provoking further attacks.[35]

The fate of the medical reform bill seemed to become yet more uncertain in late January when Henry Wilson proposed a compromise bill, which he formally introduced in February. Olmsted believed that another alternative measure drawn up by Congressman Francis P. Blair, Jr., was favored by members of the Medical Bureau and even the surgeon general himself. Hammond worried that Wilson's new bill would leave seniority as the guiding principle for selecting the surgeon general, even though it might retire Finley and some of the other older surgeons whom the Sanitary Commission considered the most inflexible.[36]

Early February brought little legislative action on medical reorganization and consequently increased Olmsted's frustration. He distrusted Henry Wilson and believed that only the support of McClellan and Stanton could bring about passage of the bill. With reform seeming no closer, the Sanitary Commission began to consider whether its continued existence was justifiable or even possible. The commissioners, including Olmsted, fretted that they had achieved much less than they had intended. Even after months of requests, McClellan and the secretary of war had not issued a general order recognizing the Commission's right of inspection in hospitals and camps. While funds had always been limited, the Commission's treasury had become so depleted by mid-February that Bellows and Strong were considering ways of winding up the organization's affairs. At a meeting of the New York members a week later, Olmsted single-handedly opposed and defeated the resolution that the Commissioners submit their resignations to the government.[37]

By the end of the month, however, there were signs of victory. The Senate passed Henry Wilson's compromise measure, but so amended its wording that it deviated even further from the original bill. Economy-minded legislators deleted any increase in pay or rank for the surgeon general and inspectors. Another amendment allowed the surgeon general to be chosen from the volunteers as well as from the regular army physicians. At that point, Surgeon General Finley's handling of a complaint by one of Stanton's friends so angered the secretary of war that he removed Finley from his post and exiled him to Boston. In March the House of Representatives began to consider Senate Bill 188. Somewhat to Olmsted's surprise, Congressman Blair reported a substitute bill which required the president to appoint the surgeon general from the ranks of the medical staff on the basis of merit rather than seniority. Blair also argued successfully in favor of increased rank for the surgeon general and the new inspectors.[38]

Thus, in April 1862, when the House of Representatives passed the medical reform bill and, in conference, managed to carry most of its provisions over those of the Senate, the Sanitary Commission believed it had fulfilled its major mission. Olmsted himself considered the reorganization of the Medical Bureau his most important achievement. To him, the Commission's distribution of goods to the soldiers was of small importance compared to its "great benefaction": "I refer to the reform and enlargement, and to the popular support of the reform and enlargement of the Medical Department of the army and to the wonderful suppression which

19

in the midst of this period of intense popular excitement, we have witnessed, of Quackery, Pedantry and the conservatism of ignorance."[39]

Although the medical reform bill was accepted, the Sanitary Commission still had to lobby to install the "best men" in the surgeon generalship and the newly created medical inspectorships. In mid-April Olmsted hurriedly summoned Bellows and Van Buren to Washington. Van Buren convinced Stanton that Hammond was the man for the job, while President Lincoln replied to Bellows's harangue about the young physician's qualifications, "Shouldn't wonder if he was Surgeon-General already." In actuality the nomination had to win the approval of the Senate, where some members supported Wood, who had continued to press his claims to the post. Still other senators questioned whether Hammond, who had earlier resigned from the army for reasons of health, would be physically able to handle the demands of the office.

The Senate confirmed Hammond as surgeon general on April 25, but the commissioners continued to demand appointment of the candidates they believed most qualified to fill the inspectorships. Olmsted and his fellows were dismayed when Stanton, impatient with the importunings of the Sanitary Commission, quarreled with Bellows on May 13. Doubtless the secretary of war believed that the commissioners were interfering in political decisions; conversely, they believed it their duty to promote the candidacies of the best-qualified physicians. Thus, ironically, as the Commission won the victory that would establish closer relations with the Medical Bureau, it infuriated the surgeon general's superior, the secretary of war. That rift would never be mended.[40]

By the end of January 1862, as the campaign to reform the Medical Bureau slowly proceeded, Olmsted returned to a subject that had long interested him—the transition of blacks from slavery to freedom. The superintendence of contraband laborers had been the area in which he had first seen the possibility of making a contribution to the war. His interest remained keen: in conversations with Cameron and McClellan during the summer and autumn of 1861 he described a role the army might play in undermining the institution of slavery in the South.[41]

The capture of the South Carolina sea islands (commonly known collectively as Port Royal) in the vicinity of Port Royal Sound by a joint army-navy expedition in November 1861 confronted the Lincoln administration anew with the problem of how to deal with Southern slaves. Suddenly, some of the largest and richest plantations of the South, deserted by their white owners, had come under the control of the Union army. The army's first actions gave the slaves more problems than aid. It seized their corn and work animals for its own uses and spread such contagious diseases as smallpox among them. Some soldiers even physically assaulted the slaves. Secretary of the Treasury Salmon P. Chase, probably the strongest antislavery man in Lincoln's cabinet, saw in events at Port Royal not only a chance to increase the government's revenues by the sale of confiscated cotton but also an opportunity to strike a blow against slavery. Under the laws governing abandoned property, he was able to send treasury agents to the sea islands. Among those he appointed in January 1862 was Edward L. Pierce, an idealistic young man who had read law in Chase's office and had supervised contraband laborers at Fortress Monroe. Wishing to make the sea islands an experiment in freedom for blacks, Pierce opposed plans to lease plantations and their black workers to private individuals. He received aid from antislavery workers in Philadelphia, Boston, and New York, who created societies early in the spring of 1862 to provide teachers for the Port Royal blacks.[42]

But Chase's activity was not enough to satisfy Olmsted as he began to study Port Royal in January 1862. He viewed the federal occupation of the sea islands as an unparalleled opportunity to put into effect his long-held views about how slaves should be guided to freedom. By demonstrating the superiority of free labor, he dreamed of showing that the South's advocacy of slavery and secession had been and continued to be an economic mistake. Worried by descriptions of increasing want among the blacks on the sea islands and by the failure of the government to announce any policy toward them or the captured plantations, Olmsted took action late in January 1862. Accompanied by Bellows and A. D. Bache, he called upon Secretary Chase on January 27 to urge comprehensive measures. Chase, harried by the government's pressing financial problems, took little notice of Olmsted's suggestions and simply informed him that Pierce would take care of matters at Port Royal. Undeterred by this reception, Olmsted on the following evening visited Lafayette S. Foster, a Republican senator from Connecticut. On that very day, Foster had requested the secretary of the treasury to report whether any legislation would be necessary for the cultivation of the captured cotton fields and the care of the blacks at Port Royal. Olmsted easily won Foster over to his views: within a week he had drawn up the bill and on February 14 the senator introduced it.[43]

The bill prepared by Olmsted set up a general framework for administering the plantations on the federally occupied sea islands and for creating a system of work for the blacks there. He first attempted to define the obligations of the government—to protect the blacks from exploitation and assure them a minimal level of subsistence—and to ensure that these were met. He also argued that the slaves must be taught certain basic duties of citizens, namely, the need to support themselves and their families and to understand and abide by the laws of the nation. While Olmsted wanted the slaves to receive both education and religious instruction, he expected that this would come from private benevolence rather than from

21

the government. According to his plan, a three-member board of commissioners would either lease the lands on an annual basis or cultivate them directly. Referring to the blacks only as "indigent persons," the bill drawn up by Olmsted provided for advances of necessary provisions to them and for their compensation on a task or piece-work basis. Such a form of payment was essential to Olmsted's purpose: he wanted to give blacks a system of incentives which would illustrate the superiority of free labor.[44]

Foster's bill reflected Olmsted's long-term views on the necessity of training slaves for freedom and giving them careful guardianship during the transition from slavery to freedom. He strongly believed that the damage done to the minds and morals of the slaves could be repaired, but he expected the process to be gradual rather than immediate. Earlier, in his book *A Journey in the Seaboard Slave States*, Olmsted had put forth a plan for the gradual emancipation of slaves that would allow them to purchase freedom over an extended period of time as they learned the value of hard work and thrift. Now he saw an opportunity to put some of these same ideas to the test.[45]

The Senate bill also reflected Olmsted's desire to secure the immediate adoption of a plan that would provide an auspicious beginning for the experiment in free labor. It was already February; preparations for planting would have to begin immediately if a cotton crop were to be produced that year. With this in mind, Olmsted tried to make the provisions of the bill as simple and uncontroversial as possible. Deliberately avoiding the question of the actual legal status of the blacks, Olmsted confided to James R. Spalding:

> The Bill is drawn with especial care to avoid all issues of a radical character. Neither slave-holder nor abolitionist would be compromised in voting for it—and, as it will not stand in the way of more thorough measures, one way or the other, when the policy of the country with regard to slavery is determined, it may be hoped to unite all who do not wish to establish at Port Royal, another evidence of the folly of ever hoping to see negroes usefully employed in any other condition than that of abject slavery.[46]

Olmsted also attempted to aid Foster's bill by using some of the techniques he had employed in the reform of the Medical Bureau. First, he sought favorable publicity in the *New York World*, which had already praised him as the kind of man exactly suited for the management of slaves under government control. In the hope that public opinion, especially that of influential businessmen, would strengthen the resolve of legislators supporting the bill, he drew up a petition asking Congress to provide superintendence and protection for the sea-island blacks. This he sent to his father, who secured seventy-five signatures in Hartford alone. To prepare and circulate a petition in the Boston area, Olmsted looked to Edward

Everett Hale, an old comrade in free-soil ventures, while Charles Trask, a Yale classmate of his deceased brother John Hull Olmsted, assumed the task of gathering signatures from "well known capitalists and bankers" in New York City.[47]

In late February, as the bill came before the Senate, Olmsted was optimistic about its passage. Resolved, if appointed, to accept a post as a commissioner, he hoped that Frederick Knapp and George Templeton Strong would be selected for the other two positions called for in the pending legislation. But even as the bill was being debated in the Senate in early March, Francis George Shaw, a prominent abolitionist and father-in-law of Olmsted's close friend George William Curtis, wrote him about another position—that of general agent for the private relief organizations that had been formed in New York, Philadelphia, and Boston. Secretary of the Treasury Chase also showed a new interest in appointing Olmsted: the two men met sometime between March 3 and March 10, and Chase then requested him not to press Foster's bill (which the Senate had earlier passed). On March 13 Chase formally offered Olmsted the position.[48]

At the same time, Olmsted received an offer of still another post— that of street commissioner for New York City. When on March 14, 1862, he returned from a two-day visit to the old battlefield of Bull Run, he found not only Chase's letter but also a message from George Opdyke, mayor of New York City. At a meeting the following day, Opdyke asked him to become the city's street commissioner, a position which to Olmsted offered an opportunity to shape and direct the growth of New York City. The duties of the commissioner included administering the system of gas lighting and wharves as well as the oversight of street construction and maintenance. To be sure, a plan for laying out the street system already existed in the grid map of 1811. But while that map indicated where the streets should run, the form of the avenues was still a matter for debate. Olmsted may have hoped that in the course of extending the avenues he would be able to determine their width and the use of plantings and medians. Thus, he might be able to transform some of these avenues into parkways similar to those he later designed. Whether or not his ideas were so fully developed, Olmsted probably believed that the extension of the avenues northward would allow him to put into practice some of his views concerning urban design. Two years earlier, when he and Calvert Vaux had served as consulting architects to a commission laying out northern Manhattan, Olmsted had described his alternative to the grid plan of streets. He had then argued that stable residential communities could be created by laying out side streets in a curving, indirect manner that would make them unsuitable for main thoroughfares. This pattern, he argued, rather than narrow or hilly streets, would discourage commercial development that might otherwise change the character of the neighborhoods.[49]

Olmsted demonstrated his intense interest in urban planning by the preference he gave the street commissionership over the superintendency at Port Royal. In his reply to Chase's note, he indicated that, as a gentleman, he would do nothing to advance his candidacy as street commissioner but that he could not accept the Port Royal position until the aldermen had decided for or against him. Even though the secretary of the treasury was offering a position in a field of endeavor that had interested Olmsted for a decade and that he had earlier believed to be his "mission," he held back. Since the two offers came virtually at the same time, Olmsted's statements do not appear entirely candid. Although he later declared that he had no intimations before April 1862 of how limited Chase believed his own authority over the sea islands to be, he must already have had misgivings about the position the secretary of the treasury offered. Even if he did not yet realize that Chase construed all of his authority in relation to Port Royal to be derived from a section of the commercial code governing areas in rebellion, Olmsted knew that the government's policy—largely determined by Chase—did not measure up to his ideas in system or scope.[50]

Despite his willingness to risk the post superintending blacks on the sea islands, Olmsted was not at all sanguine about his chances of being confirmed as street commissioner by the city's board of aldermen, still dominated by Democrats. After all, the street commissioner controlled a large department with many jobs subject to political patronage. Given Olmsted's objections to patronage appointments when he was superintendent of Central Park, he could not reasonably expect the aldermen to welcome—or even approve—his nomination. Moreover, he was willing to do little to allay their fears. At Opdyke's request, Olmsted journeyed to New York City in late March. He earlier truthfully asserted that he had given no political pledges, except to reassure the mayor that he would not be "an *impracticable*, wholly" in appointments, but he did not mention the pressure already being brought to bear upon him. In his later reminiscences, Olmsted recalled that at least two politicians—one a former congressman and a "man of wealth and social position"—called upon him to discuss the distribution of positions. According to Olmsted, "When one of the mayor's friends in the city-hall understood that I seriously meant to be my own master, or defeated, he exclaimed, 'Why, the man must be a fool!'"[51]

As it became apparent that Opdyke could not secure the aldermen's approval and would not formally nominate Olmsted, the latter again turned his interest toward a position at Port Royal as the agent of the union of aid societies there. Even though he had argued that combining governmental and charitable functions in one person might confuse the blacks at Port Royal, he told John W. Edmonds, the representative of the aid societies, at the end of March that he would consider their offer. Early in April Olmsted again met with Chase. Only Olmsted's vague account of this meeting has survived, but it was obviously unsatisfactory to both. At last Olmsted was certain that his and Chase's conceptions of the governmental role at Port Royal could not be reconciled. He also learned that Pierce had derived much of his authority from a letter written by the secretary of war. Within the next ten days Olmsted decided that only Stanton could empower him to carry out his plan at Port Royal. Accordingly, he then revised his earlier proposal to Chase, adding new sections that explained the significance of the slaves and plantations to the military effort, and on April 13 presented it to Stanton. The secretary of war's reaction is not known, but Olmsted was not awarded the post. Instead, on April 29, 1862, Stanton appointed Rufus Saxton, then chief quartermaster of Thomas W. Sherman's troops in South Carolina, as brigadier general with authority to make and enforce rules and regulations concerning the sea-island plantations and their inhabitants. Chase and Stanton, like Olmsted, had come to believe that a military officer whose high rank would guarantee power and respect should direct the Port Royal experiment in free labor. But, unlike Olmsted, they probably thought such a brigadier general could be most expediently selected from the already swollen ranks of the army's officers. Stanton may also have been unwilling to choose Olmsted because of the latter's disagreements with Chase. By April 19 Olmsted could see that the post at Port Royal was slipping away, although he bravely told his father, "I suppose that if I was determined to have it, and could neglect other matters to devote myself to it, I could get myself appointed Brigadier General, and assigned to duty as Military Governor of the islands, and then have absolute dictatorial control of it." Still, Olmsted rationalized, "I believe it paid, though the study and energy I gave to the matter, did not accomplish the precise result, nor anything like as good a result as I meant it should."[52]

And so in April 1862 Olmsted discarded one of his fondest dreams. Although his Western journey during the spring of 1863 would demonstrate a continued concern with the position of blacks, never again would he actively seek a position supervising their transition from slavery to freedom. In the spring of 1864 Francis George Shaw began to promote Olmsted's candidacy for the commissionership of the proposed Freedman's Bureau. While Olmsted praised the merits of a bill to establish such a bureau, he showed little interest in overseeing it. Pleading poor health as his reason, Olmsted enigmatically added: "This consideration is at the present moment so strong as to leave me under no necessity of enquiring what my duty would otherwise be. What my inclinations are I need not tell you." The following year when he learned that John Murray Forbes and George William Curtis wanted him to receive the superintendence of the

25

Freedman's Bureau, Olmsted gave a franker, more pessimistic assessment to his friend Godkin: "I do not much incline to it, because I do not believe the government would allow me to do what I should think best to be done. It would be, I fear, not only a vexatious, aggravating and thankless duty but a puerile pretence & fizzle." Believing the government's commitment to any comprehensive measures to be far too tenuous, and aware that Stanton's dislike made it highly unlikely that he could be appointed, Olmsted was not particularly interested in the position. Nor did he appear tempted by offers from private aid organizations. When J. Miller McKim, president of the American Freedman's Aid Union, asked him in the fall of 1865 to be its secretary, he quickly and decisively declined. Olmsted's role in proposing plans for the transition of Southern blacks to freedom had come to an end.[53]

In time, his pessimistic assessment of the government's intentions at Port Royal would be borne out, and there seems little question that he would have encountered the same difficulties that hampered Pierce and Saxton. In addition to those problems, Olmsted's own presuppositions might have hindered him. Firmly convinced that free labor was economically as well as morally superior to slave labor, he was optimistic—probably unduly so—about the increased financial benefits that would immediately become available to the freedmen. To be sure, he believed that the sea-island blacks would have to be educated to the new social and economic order. But because he was confident that his system of piece-rate compensation would encourage industriousness and the gradual accumulation of money and property, Olmsted did not find it necessary to confront—or even consider—the question of land for Port Royal blacks.[54]

While Olmsted wanted a rigorous, though benevolent, guardianship to guide blacks from slavery to freedom, he was generally optimistic about what they would be able to achieve. Still, like many other white Americans of his day, he quite often made disparaging remarks about blacks. In his proposal to Edwin M. Stanton, Olmsted appeared willing to allow blacks, because of their peculiar history, to be made liable to discriminatory laws; he also alluded to special vices and character flaws. Yet some of his other writings present less harsh views and suggest that in that presentation, as in the bill he drew up for Senator Foster, Olmsted put forth his minimal demands for the treatment of blacks. In the 1850s he had criticized the discriminatory treatment accorded free blacks in the North and had called for that region to show "that the negro is endowed with the natural capacities to make a good use of the blessing of freedom; by letting the negro have a fair chance to prove his own case, to prove himself a man, entitled to the inalienable rights of a man." At that same time, Olmsted demonstrated his own respect for many blacks by the praise he showered upon the Rochester Convention: "It may be doubted if there has ever met a Convention of white men in our country in which more common sense, more talent, more power of eloquence, a higher civilization, more manliness, or more of the virtues and graces of the Christian and the gentleman, were evidenced than in that Convention of the despised Northern negroes." A decade later in testimony before the American Freedmen's Inquiry Commission in 1863, Olmsted indicated that his opinion of the innate abilities of blacks had not diminished. He admiringly described the former slaves as workers and argued that, given equal treatment, they would be good soldiers. Again that same year, a letter to Samuel Gridley Howe further indicated Olmsted's skepticism about current racial thought, which held the mulatto to be a hybrid, weaker and less fertile than either black or white.[55]

In the spring of 1862, as the Medical Bureau came under new management and the possibility of a post supervising freedmen dimmed, Olmsted found himself with a new responsibility: equipping and overseeing hospital ships that would transport the sick and wounded of McClellan's army. These were not the first floating hospitals of the war, but the Peninsula campaign marked the first use of such hospital transports in the war on a daily basis.

The full-scale involvement of the Sanitary Commission with hospital ships came about as the result of a fortuitous conversation between Stanton and William Van Buren. After Stanton admitted that few plans had been made for the medical care of McClellan's army, Van Buren volunteered to supply sufficient nurses and stores to fit up a hospital ship chartered by the government, an offer that was quickly accepted. Objections by Quartermaster General Meigs, who controlled all transportation, temporarily suspended the project. He soon relented, however, and on April 25, after a week's wait, the Commission received an old steamboat, the *Daniel Webster No. 1*. Together, Olmsted and Knapp supervised Sanitary Commission employees and volunteers who a few days later embarked for Ship's Point on Cheeseman's Creek.[56]

Upon his arrival on the Peninsula, Olmsted could scarcely have foreseen what the next eleven weeks would bring. He thought he had come to organize a transport service in cooperation with the Medical Bureau: he little dreamed that he would remain to run a system that did not at all meet his ideas of organization and efficiency. While he was obliged to assume great responsibility, his actual power remained severely circumscribed.

Although at first optimistic that an efficient system of care and transportation would quickly be devised and put in place, he soon discovered the difficulties of cooperating with the various branches of government. On May 4 the Sanitary Commission was given the use of the *Ocean Queen*, a large, spacious steamship ideally suited to transport up to one thousand patients. But the *Queen* arrived stripped of its furniture and stores, and the Confederate evacuation of Yorktown delayed Olmsted's plans to refit it. On May 6 Olmsted learned from J. Foster Jenkins that Quartermaster General Meigs was going to reclaim the *Queen* in order to provide stores to Benjamin Butler's troops in New Orleans. This was only the first instance of what would become a major problem confronting both the Sanitary Commission and the Medical Bureau: the lack of independent medical transportation. Steamers could be—and were—diverted at a moment's notice from hospital duty. Later that month, the *Elm City*, a ship frequently used by the Sanitary Commission, was withdrawn from hospital service and stripped of its berths, only to be returned to the Sanitary Commission two days later. While Olmsted found it difficult to obtain and keep ships for hospital transport duty, he soon discovered other problems as well. Crews, hired and paid by the government, feared the contagion of hospital ships and were often ready to desert or to mutiny. And since many of the workers on the Sanitary Commission ships changed between voyages, it was difficult to enforce a consistent system among short-term volunteers of varying ability.[57]

Olmsted's pleas for the use of the *Ocean Queen* in early May 1862 proved futile, but he soon assembled a small fleet equipped and manned by Sanitary Commission workers. In addition to the *Webster*, he received the *Elizabeth*, a small storeboat, and the *Wilson Small*, which served as headquarters for Commission workers remaining on the Peninsula. By the middle of the month the quartermaster's department replaced the *Queen* with the *S. R. Spaulding*, a seaworthy vessel which could carry many soldiers. On occasion, the Sanitary Commission also staffed river steamers such as the *Knickerbocker*, *Elm City*, *State of Maine*, and the *Daniel Webster No. 2*, and later that summer it equipped two fine sailing vessels, the *Euterpe* and the *St. Mark*, to be used as receiving hospitals. All these vessels carried sick and wounded soldiers to locations—usually Fortress Monroe, Annapolis, or Washington—specified by the medical director.[58]

By early May, Olmsted was assembling the staff that would undertake the Sanitary Commission's work on the Virginia Peninsula. The Commission employed physicians, female superintendents of nursing, male and female nurses, dressers (usually medical students), stewards or quartermasters, apothecaries, baggagemen, and servants. There often was considerable turnover among the workers who were hired or accepted as volunteers by Sanitary Commission members or branch organizations in the Northern ports. Thus, many of the workers who accompanied a ship back to the North were then replaced by other employees or volunteers. But Olmsted, who thoroughly disapproved of short-term service, was able to assemble a dedicated staff which stayed on the Peninsula through much of McClellan's campaign. Knapp shared the administrative chores involved in fitting up ships, and though a gentle, emotional man, often proved resourceful and tough. At one point he shot a cow to obtain beef; on other occasions he pushed the Sanitary Commission's claims to the point of irritating Charles S. Tripler, medical director of McClellan's army. Olmsted also valued physicians James M. Grymes and Robert Ware, neither of whom would survive the war. Whether caring for soldiers on the ships or on shore, both men were untiring and unflinching. But, perhaps the most steadfast workers came from a somewhat unlikely group—the genteel women who had volunteered their services as superintendents of nursing. Despite their generally sheltered and privileged backgrounds, women such as Katharine P. Wormeley, Georgeanna Woolsey, and Christine Kean Griffin worked long hours to provide comfortable quarters, clean clothing, and nourishing food for sick and wounded soldiers. The organizational skills of the ladies impressed Olmsted, who said of them: "They beat the doctors all to pieces. I should have sunk the ships in despair before this if it had not been for their handiness and good nature."[59] Shared experiences under emergency conditions placed these women among Olmsted's strongest admirers.

During most of May few battles occurred. Although McClellan's troops captured Yorktown and Williamsburg, a relatively small number of soldiers were wounded. Still, the list of sick steadily increased. The water supply in a swampy area was easily contaminated, especially by an army that seemed to consider keeping wastes away from its drinking water an unnecessary nicety. Typhoid flourished, and by the time Olmsted and the Sanitary Commission arrived, the Peninsula was teeming with sick soldiers with whom the Medical Bureau was ill equipped to cope. Tripler had ordered tents and other supplies, but they had arrived mixed with the quartermaster's stores in ships yet to be unloaded. Again, the supplies furnished by the Sanitary Commission proved vital.[60]

Throughout much of May, Olmsted and his staff constantly met emergencies that testified to the poor care the army doctors were able to provide. Because doctors at the front shipped out typhoid victims unaccompanied by any attendants, Sanitary Commission workers often rescued seriously ill men, too weak to sit or walk, who had been dumped on the creek banks to await a hospital ship. Olmsted was aghast at the management of the hospitals and hospital ships by the military physicians. Since they, too, wished to be rid of the sick and wounded as promptly as possible, they unsystematically hustled men onto hospital ships regardless of the severity of their illnesses. In contrast, the Sanitary Commission sought to provide care to the many soldiers who merely needed rest, nourishing food, and more healthful surroundings. Olmsted believed that these soldiers should be nursed on the Peninsula so that after a few days' convalescence they could return to their units. He further argued that sending any but the seriously ill to the North discouraged men from protecting their health and encouraged shirkers to feign illness.[61]

In mid-May, while the Sanitary Commission's boats were stationed on the Pamunkey River at White House (the Custis family plantation which then belonged to William Henry Fitzhugh "Rooney" Lee, one of Robert E. Lee's sons), Olmsted tried to systematize and improve the care of the soldiers there. On May 18 he convinced Tripler to join in a request that the surgeon general equip a hospital depot for six thousand men at White House. He also urged Tripler to adopt a systematic plan for the evacuation of sick and wounded in case of a major battle. Seeking the most efficient and humane use of the boats at the Commission's disposal, he proposed that the *Elm City* serve as a receiving hospital until a battle occurred, at which time it would become a surgical receiving hospital. At that time the *S. R. Spaulding*, assisted by the *Daniel Webster No. 1*, would evacuate four hundred seriously ill soldiers from the *Elm City* and the shore hospitals. The *Knickerbocker* would daily transport surgical patients only as far as Fortress Monroe. By May 20 Olmsted had received Tripler's assent to this proposal. But a message from Surgeon General Hammond, curtly informing Tripler that he already possessed the independent authority to set up such a depot and should have done so if it were necessary, made the old soldier nervously revert to shipping away as many sick men as possible.[62]

By the end of his first month on the Virginia Peninsula, Olmsted was thoroughly worried and depressed about the transport service and the hospital facilities thus far provided. Any large battle would, he believed, immediately overwhelm both the floating and the field hospitals. Despite the high cost of their daily charter, some vessels, he urged, should be held in reserve in case of a major battle. All his worst forebodings about the adequacy of the system of transporting and caring for the wounded suddenly appeared justified when on May 31 Joseph E. Johnston's Confederate army attacked part of McClellan's forces north of the Chickahominy River near Fair Oaks (Seven Pines), inflicting heavy losses on the Union troops. By the following day, the wounded began to pour into White House via the railroad connecting it with McClellan's army. Tripler had gone to the front, leaving his old medical school friend Henry Hollingsworth Smith, surgeon general of the state of Pennsylvania, in charge at White House. Olmsted found that the plan earlier agreed upon by Tripler for the use of ships fitted up by the Sanitary Commission was being completely disregarded. Instead, ships were filled and sent on their way as quickly as possible. When Olmsted saw wounded soldiers being loaded onto a ship that had not yet been cleaned or fitted up, he attempted unsuccessfully to determine who was in charge. But Dr. Smith was nowhere to be found, while Tripler, unaware of the movements of the hospital ships, sent telegraphic orders that could not be carried out. Thus, in the confused aftermath of the battle of Fair Oaks, Olmsted loaded and dispatched the boats controlled by the Sanitary Commission, paying little attention to the conflicting and even impossible orders that occasionally arrived from Tripler. For example, on June 2 Olmsted felt obliged to send the *Daniel Webster No. 1* to Boston, even though a directive from Tripler had stated that no wounded soldiers were to be sent to Northern cities for five days.[63]

The government's medical response to the battle of Fair Oaks disheartened Olmsted. During those busy days of early June, only one surgeon, Thomas T. Ellis, claimed and exercised authority over the numerous wounded—and he later proved to be a shady character temporarily working for the government and not the commissioned officer he represented himself to be. Never did Olmsted find the Sanitary Commission's position to be more anomalous or more open to conflicting interpretations. After his constant struggles with Tripler and other military officers, he was enraged to find that Surgeon General Hammond, much like the Sanitary Commission board and staff in New York and Washington, wrote and acted as though Olmsted indeed commanded the hospital ships supplied and staffed by the Sanitary Commission. These problems of a poorly defined status persisted through Olmsted's tenure on the Peninsula, but he found the change welcome in late June when Hammond replaced Tripler with Jonathan Letterman, a young physician who shared Olmsted's emphasis on hygiene and sanitary regulations and could also cut bureaucratic red tape.[64]

In June, while awaiting McClellan's march upon Richmond, Olmsted attempted further to improve preparations for caring for the wounded that would inevitably result. He prodded Hammond to provide more stewards, contract surgeons (civilian doctors serving the Medical Bureau under short-term contracts), and shelter and sustenance for as many as ten thousand wounded. When, late in the month, Robert E. Lee attacked the Union forces, Olmsted and the Sanitary Commission participated in shifting the Union army's base of operations from the Pamunkey to the James River.[65]

During these Seven Days' battles, the transport service functioned far more efficiently than it had a month earlier, and Olmsted's thoughts turned to what he saw as the more urgent problem of reinforcements. Thrown into close contact with McClellan's officers, he had come to accept their inflated estimates of the enemy's numbers. At the same time, the fierce fighting of the Union soldiers renewed Olmsted's faith in them. At last, he exulted, the North had an army in which it could take pride. By letters and in person he pleaded with government officials to reinforce McClellan's army or remove it from its unhealthy location on the Virginia Peninsula. In the course of a short visit to Washington he met with Quartermaster General Meigs, Assistant Secretary of War Peter H. Watson, and Assistant Secretary of the Navy Gustavus Vasa Fox, but gained little satisfaction from these interviews. To obtain the eighty thousand additional men, Olmsted urged President Lincoln to appeal personally for volunteers. He also tried to convince Senator Preston King that conscription—probably administered by the federal government—would be necessary. At the same time, Olmsted was arguing McClellan's case with Sydney Gay, the influential editor of the *New-York Daily Tribune*, and was insisting that Stanton was responsible for the failures of the Peninsula campaign.[66] Ironically, even as Olmsted sought to convince governmental officials, newspapermen, and others to come to McClellan's aid, the Peninsula campaign had already ground to a halt, since neither McClellan nor the Confederates assumed the offensive.

In early July Sanitary Commission officials noted that the gaunt, sunburned Olmsted looked tired and worn, and Bellows again urged him to give up superintendence of the Commission's work on the Peninsula. Finally, on July 16 Olmsted relinquished his post in the field and sailed to New York. In trying to assess the Commission's achievements on the Peninsula, he could reach only ambivalent conclusions. Undoubtedly it had accomplished valuable work in obtaining contributions and in saving lives; still, this task properly belonged to the government, not to a voluntary organization. Olmsted further reasoned that changes in the Medical Bureau during the spring and summer had brought forth men of such organizational talent that they should be able to offer a better service than the Commission had provided, hamstrung as it was by a lack of clear authority.[67]

Olmsted's return from Virginia gave him little respite from work. After a few days on the Staten Island farm belonging to his stepchildren, he plunged into Sanitary Commission business once again. Meetings with the Executive Committee (composed of New York members Bellows, Agnew, Gibbs, Strong, and Van Buren) brought before him some of the problems he would be facing that fall. Unknown to Olmsted, a shift in power had taken place during his absence. As Olmsted's deputy, J. Foster Jenkins had overseen the daily work in the Washington office, but he had assumed little initiative in decision making. The Executive Committee, organized in the fall of 1861 to deal with matters that arose between meetings of the board, had filled this vacuum by meeting on almost a daily basis. Upon his return Olmsted discovered this group handing down decisions and intervening in areas that formerly had been the preserve of the Washington office. The Executive Committee now expected him to be accountable to it and also demanded that he exert close supervision over all Sanitary Commission affairs. Moreover, in late July the Executive Committee chided him for a lack of knowledge about the Commission's operations in the West, overlooking the fact that John S. Newberry, associate secretary for the West, had not submitted a single report to the Washington office during the summer.[68]

In August 1862 as Olmsted resumed charge of the central office and direction of Commission affairs, the strain of the months on the Peninsula, combined with continuing overwork, undermined his health. His condition steadily deteriorated, and by the end of August he was jaundiced (possibly from hepatitis), had developed a severe skin disorder which itched incessantly, and was on the verge of nervous collapse. Accordingly, Agnew ordered him to Saratoga Springs, where he was convalescing when the large number of casualties suffered by John Pope's army at the second battle of Bull Run once again gave the Sanitary Commission an important role to play.[69]

Arriving back in Washington on September 17, Olmsted found the Commission already in session and critical of the operations of the central office over the summer. Although he had only a few days to prepare his report instead of the month he had planned, Olmsted presented a cogent, persuasive defense of the Commission's activities on the Peninsula and elsewhere. Once again by force of will and tightly constructed arguments, he was able to convince Bellows and the other commissioners that his oversight and direction of the Commission's affairs had been most prudent.[70]

Olmsted's return to the central office again brought to the fore many of the questions that his ill-health had only postponed. Not only did he need to report on past activities and oversee relief efforts after the bloody battle of Antietam, but he also had to assume charge of the new activities planned by the Commission. Meetings with the surgeon general early in August 1862 had convinced the commissioners that they should press the government to provide the trained independent ambulance corps they had unsuccessfully advocated a year earlier. But though their efforts were ineffective against the opposition of General-in-Chief Henry W. Halleck, Olmsted and the Sanitary Commission could point to other achievements during the autumn of 1862. After the battle of Antietam, when medical officers in the Union army had left behind or used most of their supplies, those rushed to the battlefield by the Sanitary Commission assumed major importance. The Commission also successfully introduced two new services: a volunteer special inspection corps of distinguished physicians to visit the military hospitals and recommend changes, and a hospital directory (planned by Olmsted) to aid persons wishing to learn the location of sick or wounded soldiers. By late November the Commission had established a directory for military hospitals in the Washington area and was prepared to answer inquiries. In 1863 this system was extended to cover all military hospitals.[71]

In addition to his numerous responsibilities at the Washington office, Olmsted was also faced with the worsening of a persistent problem—the activities and claims of state and local soldiers' aid associations. Societies that were unwilling to become tributaries of the U.S. Sanitary Commission had long worried the commissioners, and St. Louis produced the most formidable rival. In the autumn of 1861, a group of philanthropists led by Unitarian minister William Greenleaf Eliot and businessman James Erwin Yeatman founded the Western Sanitary Commission. Organized to aid soldiers in Missouri, the Western group gained an endorsement that fall from John C. Frémont, the local commanding general. Only vociferous protests by the national Commission convinced Simon Cameron to countermand Frémont's order. Spurred to greater efforts in the Mississippi Valley, the national Commission sent an inspector to St. Louis, but in the absence of specific orders from Newberry, he took little action. Although Olmsted recognized that the Western Sanitary Commission wished to retain nominal independence, he hoped that the national organization could maintain its dominant position and convince the St. Louis association to become one of its branches. In this he was mistaken, and the already strained relations between the rival aid organizations worsened during the spring of 1862 as the Western Commission began to solicit funds in New England, the area that had contributed most generously to the treasury of the national Commission.[72]

The Western Sanitary Commission, however, did not represent the form of localism in relief services that Olmsted found most alarming. While the Western Commission sought to aid all soldiers within its restricted area of operation, some local and state organizations directed their efforts toward, and reserved their supplies for, only their native sons. In a letter of February 1862 to the secretary of the Iowa State sanitary commission, Olmsted set forth the practical and philosophical reasons that lay behind the Sanitary Commission's policy of aiding the soldiers most in need, regardless of their place of origin. In the work of the Commission, he admonished, "no state is known, all contributions to it are to a common stock for the army of a common country." Should state and local prejudices be given rein, Olmsted argued, both goods and money would be wasted in shipping supplies long distances when they could be better obtained where the soldiers were stationed. Such a narrow view would also ensure that some regiments would receive far more than they could use while others would be severely deprived. But the question of localism in aid was far more than just a matter of practicality to Olmsted. To him it represented selfish pettiness and the states' rights doctrine that had directly given rise to secessionism and that threatened to destroy the American nation. He told the Iowa secretary, "There seems to me to be a stain of the very soil, out of which the monster Secession has grown, when such a complete machinery as you have formed in Iowa is confined in its operations by State lines."[73]

In the fall of 1862 the spirit of localism appeared to be on the increase everywhere. Midwestern and Eastern states empowered their agents to channel aid and supplies to troops from their own localities, and Olmsted found similar tendencies even in his hometown of Hartford, where the local soldiers' aid society, of which his stepmother was an officer, wished to reserve a portion of its contributions for soldiers from Connecticut. The national Commission, while resenting the criticism of its large, salaried staff by the independent state and local societies, denounced localism primarily because it believed that such an attitude weakened the war effort and undercut the very Union that soldiers were fighting to restore. Thus, in the fall of 1862 Olmsted and his associates were only partly joking when they referred to localism as the "boss devil" or "old boss devil."[74]

In October 1862 Olmsted wrote a circular, "What They Have to Do Who Stay at Home," to stimulate contributions and to demonstrate the advantages that a centralized professional organization, constantly in readiness to meet emergencies, possessed over any other form of relief. He later described his argument as "an appeal for an improved organization of those who stay at home, to the end of obtaining a more secure supply, to the distributing depots of the Commission, urged by a presentation of the essential rightness, justice, and beauty of its federal or fraternal purpose, in distinction from any merely local or sectional purpose of benevolence." In this pamphlet Olmsted also spelled out the duties of branch organizations of the Commission to channel money and supplies to the central organization. Although these were views which he had long held, they would later contribute to the growing disagreements between the Commission and its Western auxiliaries.[75]

The immediate cause of worsening relations between the national Commission and the local organizations, however, was a sudden windfall of two hundred thousand dollars from California. In mid-September Thomas Starr King, a Unitarian minister and a former protégé of Bellows, persuaded the Committee of Thirteen in San Francisco to contribute most of the funds it had raised to the national Commission. But, predictably even in far-off California, the boss devil of localism was present, and King warned Bellows that the Sanitary Commission must share the money with the St. Louis Commission. California was part of the West, King cautioned, and its citizens wanted their money to aid Western soldiers.[76]

Nevertheless, the California contribution did have many positive effects. For one, the national Commission, which had always operated on shaky financial footing, suddenly found itself with a large reserve fund. This was especially helpful since the hospital transport system had consumed most of the funds that had been raised by publicizing it. Moreover, the second battle of Bull Run and the battle of Antietam had required large expenditures for supplies and transportation.

Even before the California donation, Olmsted had encountered difficulties with the Sanitary Commission's Western branches, where the activities of Newberry had long been a matter for concern. Newberry had created a strong branch society at his headquarters in Cleveland and had also encouraged the development of branches of the Commission in Chicago, Cincinnati, and Louisville. But early in 1862 the organization in Cincinnati—and to a lesser extent that in Chicago—were showing a great deal of independence. They preferred to raise and disburse their own funds and hire their own "inspectors" rather than contribute to the central organization's system. Newberry, in Olmsted's view, had not sufficiently countered that parochial view. Despite Olmsted's frequent admonitions to spend whatever sums were necessary, Newberry tended to work by himself or with only a skeleton crew.[77]

Under any circumstances, the California contribution would probably have increased local jealousy of the national Commission, but it came with the specific stipulation that it be shared with the Western Commission and with "other branches, too, if there are still other subsidiary organizations whose cash treasury is distinct from yours." The national Commission was unsure how much of the contribution should be turned over to the St. Louis Commission, and Bellows suggested that the gift be divided proportionately, based on the amount of money expended and supplies distributed by each. This plan would have severely limited the share of the Western Commission since, in Olmsted's estimation, it had received by this time only one-tenth as much in contributions as had the national organization. In October, King instructed Bellows to give fifty thousand dollars to the Western Commission, but by late November he had raised another two hundred thirty thousand, which he forwarded to the national Commission without any conditions.[78]

By far the largest problem raised by the California contribution came from within the Sanitary Commission itself: this was the demand of the branch at Cincinnati that it receive a share of the funds, an action that marked the culmination of its drive for autonomy. From the beginning of the war, the Cincinnatians had displayed a penchant for running their own show. Newberry had never successfully harnessed this organization, which on occasion had shown suspicion and hostility to at least two of his inspectors.[79]

Olmsted set little of the early policy toward the Cincinnati branch. The first reaction to these demands was an unofficial attempt by Bellows to pacify George Hoadly, the leader of the Cincinnati dissidents. Proposing the creation of a Western council to advise Newberry about expenditures in the West (an idea that Olmsted had already been considering), Bellows also tried to make peace by offering Hoadly a seat on the board and by suggesting that the U.S. Commission might allow Cincinnati to direct the expenditure of over fifty thousand dollars in the West. But Bellows's plan only made the demands more peremptory: if it did not receive its rightful share of the California contribution, the Cincinnati branch threatened to declare its independence or to affiliate with the St. Louis Commission. In his letters of early November, Hoadly detailed a series of charges that were later used as Cincinnati's justification for its claims. He depicted the U.S. Commission as a self-constituted body of Eastern men with little knowledge or understanding of conditions in the West, where an adequate staff had never been maintained. To be sure, the national Commission had inspected a few Western army camps, but the work of raising and distributing supplies and of providing battlefield relief had fallen to local organizations such as the Cincinnati branch, whose use of volunteer agents was superior to the national Commission's reliance upon salaried workers. Only after it received the contribution from California, Hoadly claimed, had the national Commission begun to assert that the branches were agencies of collection and that it alone distributed supplies.[80]

Olmsted took a more unyielding position than Bellows. As these charges were reiterated in November and December of 1862, he became increasingly angry and disgusted with the Cincinnati branch, whose claims represented to him but another form of the contemptible spirit of states' rights and secessionism. Believing the allegations to be largely lies designed to procure part of the donation from California, he characterized the Cincinnatians as swindlers or confidence men who were trying to extort money from the national Commission to finance their self-aggrandizing ventures in soldiers' relief. To counter the Cincinnatians' claims, Olmsted prepared a detailed exposition—138 printed pages in its final form—of the organization and methods of supply used by the U.S. Sanitary Commission. While he depicted an organization which included both a central and local bodies, the concentration of power that he envisaged in the central office could hardly have appealed to the Cincinnatians.

Olmsted's report, completed in early December, attempted to meet the objections raised by the Cincinnatians point by point. Carefully marshaling his evidence, he argued that the national Commission, far from being self-constituted, had in fact been commissioned by the president and was therefore directly responsible to the government. For this reason the Commission could not delegate any of its powers to the branch societies. The disbursement of funds and supplies entrusted to the Sanitary Commission must be by agents directly responsible to it. Olmsted then proceeded to illustrate how the Commission had carried out its trust without regard to state or local boundaries. From the beginning of the war, it had stationed its employees with the Western armies, where they had furnished needed supplies and had provided battlefield relief. Indeed, the national Commission had established a receiving depot in Cincinnati even before the branch society there had been organized, a fact Olmsted did not allow to go unnoticed.[81]

By cogently putting forward the ideas that had guided him for the past one and one-half years in the organization and direction of the Commission, Olmsted built a compelling case. Still, this battle made him realize that the organization in the West had never really conformed to his vision. Although his views of the duties of the branch societies and of the associate members—to assist primarily in relations with the public and in the raising of money, supplies, and workers—had remained unchanged, these responsibilities had not been clearly defined in Sanitary Commission publications before the autumn of 1862. Newberry used only a few inspectors and had tacitly permitted the Western branches to hire their own agents and distribute their own supplies. Even as Olmsted was composing his account of the operation of the Sanitary Commission, he was taken aback by a letter from Newberry which referred to supplies dispensed by the "state agents" of the Sanitary Commission.[82] Nowhere could the general secretary in his careful description of the Sanitary Commission's policies find a basis for many of the Cincinnati branch's past actions. His version—that the Commission expected the branch societies to use their own resources in local hospitals and camps and to join in the general relief operations after major emergencies—could only partly explain the independent action the Cincinnati group had always taken.

In its handling of the demands from the Cincinnati branch the Sanitary Commission attempted the contradictory task of upholding the position Olmsted had articulated while at the same time conciliating the Westerners. Although the board adopted the resolutions offered by Olmsted, asserting responsibility for all contributions to its treasury and the need to supervise expenditures, the commissioners had indicated a willingness to spend fifty thousand dollars in the West. In January 1863 they offered fifteen thousand of this amount to the Cincinnatians, who remained a grumbling and dissatisfied part of the national Commission, although they accepted the money and ceased their demands.[83]

While Olmsted sought to combat separatism and factionalism within soldiers' aid societies and the Sanitary Commission itself, he also tried to foster a similar spirit in political affairs. The situation appeared very dark to him during the autumn of 1862. His exchange of letters with Charles Loring Brace illustrated his pessimism as well as the differing views of two lifelong friends who shared Republican politics, a deep commitment to the war effort, and a dislike of slavery. In common with the Radical Republican critics of the conduct of the war, Brace believed that an overly timid McClellan had mismanaged the Peninsula campaign.

Olmsted, on the other hand, continued to view McClellan as the organizer of victory for the Union army and to blame Secretary of War Stanton for the government's failure to supply all the reinforcements the general had requested. Moreover, a year in Washington had generally soured Olmsted's view of the leading Republican officeholders. Although Lincoln had risen in his estimation, he feared that the president did not sufficiently control his generals and his cabinet officers. But despite a growing disenchantment with leading Republicans and his admiration for McClellan, Olmsted continued to dislike the Democratic party because of its emphasis upon limiting the powers of the central government and its failure to criticize slavery or seek its containment. The proposals for a negotiated peace with the South that came from some Democrats in the fall of 1862 further increased his distaste for that party.[84]

Though he was far from satisfied with the Republican administration, the triumph of the Democrats in much of the North during the autumn elections led Olmsted to seek increased support for the war by helping to found the Union League Club. Even before November 5, when the Democrats swept the elections in New York, he and Wolcott Gibbs had discussed the need for an organization composed of men who supported the war and the national government. Although this was to be a secret, apparently social, club, Olmsted proposed that it should be based on what he believed to be the cardinal idea of the American republic, and one that separated it from the European countries: namely, that the only aristocracy should be one of talent (although he thought that members of old, distinguished families would be quite likely to belong to such a natural elite). He disparagingly described what he saw as the efforts by such *nouveau riche* as August Belmont to institute an American hereditary aristocracy modeled upon the European example. In addition to a social goal, Olmsted also believed the projected club should promote important political ideas. Above all, it should foster loyalty to the national government and stimulate national unity by combatting the doctrine of states' rights in all its forms.[85] Gibbs generally agreed with Olmsted's aims but proposed to extend these notions of nationalism and national unity still further. Not only should the club foster political ideals by elevating the *New York Evening Post* to a position of national leadership among newspapers, it should also increase ties among American intellectuals.

To bring such an organization into being, Olmsted proposed that a steering committee, or "ante-club," should be carefully chosen to consider goals and aims; it would create the framework and begin to select a somewhat socially diverse membership. While the club should include some worthy men from families of outstanding patriotism and social standing, its dues should be low enough to attract those who lived by their own labor—such as Olmsted's émigré friend Friedrich Kapp. Men in both of these

39

categories would then set a good example for the third group to be re-cruited: well-to-do young men who otherwise might be tempted by the twin devils of dissipation and states' rights. Olmsted was even more certain about the sort of people that should not be asked to join the club. These included such former Democratic antagonists as August Belmont and Henry G. Stebbins, who should not be allowed in the club even though they professed to support the war and, in Stebbins's case, agreed that slavery should be abolished. Though they may have held some of the necessary beliefs, Olmsted believed that these men were not sufficiently anti-aristocratic; nor did their conception of patriotism sufficiently repudi-ate states' rights.[86]

As the war and the Lincoln administration came under increasing criticism, Olmsted and Gibbs were not alone in their desire for some kind of loyalists' club, or union league, that would stimulate patriotism and aid the government. In Philadelphia a similar move was afoot to form a patri-otic society which also would be called the "Union League Club." And though of differing political persuasions, at least two other groups in New York City sought to organize more popularly based clubs. The plan offered by Olmsted and Gibbs differed from these others by containing social aims and stressing the explicit rejection of states' rights while it similarly empha-sized loyalty to the national government. Olmsted wanted the proposed society to serve as the model for others. As he told Gibbs in January 1863, "Your league ought to be extended over the whole country before Con-gress adjourns."[87]

Though Olmsted and Gibbs early conceived the idea for a Union League Club and encouraged its formation in New York, the actual organi-zation, even as it first took shape, diverged considerably from their ideal. Early in 1863 Gibbs, guided by his exchange of letters with Olmsted, drew up a charter which circulated among the organizers of the club. Although this document has not survived, it apparently described the aims of the "National," as it was then known, to be the fostering of loyalty and national unity. Included at first was an explicit repudiation of the doctrine of states' rights; but as the organizers met and discussed it, they began to alter the tone of the club they envisioned. In February, Gibbs foresaw that others did not share the "white heat" of patriotism for which he and Olmsted had hoped, and the first meeting of the Union League Club later that month fulfilled his pessimistic predictions. Led by Bellows, some of the members proposed to substitute the platform of the Union League of Philadelphia for that drawn up by Gibbs. The Philadelphia club required only unquali-fied loyalty to the national government and support of the war. George Templeton Strong derided it as a "vague, unsubstantial 'platform,'" and Olmsted expressed his displeasure when he told Gibbs that everyone who had been detained on suspicion of disloyalty could subscribe to that oath:

40

"Loyalty means lickspittle to save the Union with some men," he sneered. The New Yorkers also departed from Olmsted's aims when, at an early meeting, they raised the annual dues for their club from ten to twenty-five dollars.[88]

Thus, the Union League Club that came into existence in New York City in the spring of 1863 met neither Olmsted's social nor his political goals. The organization adopted what he believed to be a weak political platform, and it did not assume the educational role that he had desired. Gibbs and Olmsted had shown themselves to be more hostile to localism and the belief in states' rights than were other Republican gentlemen of New York during the war years. As it turned out, the founders of the Union League Club were more interested in aiding the Lincoln administration than in promoting other forms of national unity or in providing an institution that would educate the nation's natural aristocracy to its responsibilities. Early in February 1863 Gibbs had resigned himself to the kind of organization that was emerging, and he used the comparison between a whistle and a trumpet to indicate how far short of his ideal it had fallen.[89] This disparity between their vision and the reality explains in large part why Olmsted and Gibbs participated little in the Union League Club during 1863.

Although the Union League Club did not develop according to Olmsted's hopes and plans, he took an interest during late 1862 and 1863 in other activities intended to bolster the war effort and to show support of the national government. He used the Sanitary Commission's network of agents and local societies to distribute such pamphlets supporting the Union cause as Charles J. Stillé's *How a Free People Conduct a Long War*, whose publication had been financed by private contributions. Despite his worries about his own financial situation, Olmsted paid for at least one hundred tracts. He also supported the Loyal Publication Society, which wealthy philanthropist John Murray Forbes organized to duplicate the success that religious tract societies had enjoyed in disseminating information.[90]

As Olmsted sought to aid the Union cause during the dark days that followed the disastrous Union defeat at Fredericksburg, he clearly set out his version of loyalty and his war aims. As his letters to Wolcott Gibbs indicate, loyalty meant more to him than mere support of the Lincoln administration: it also held important social and political implications. Consistent with his republicanism and belief in representative institutions, he envisioned himself as loyal to a nation whose distinguishing trademark had long been a hostility to any kind of hereditary aristocracy. Moreover, the issuance of the Emancipation Proclamation, which pledged the government to a war against slavery, had strengthened his attachment. Although the proclamation applied to slavery only in the areas still in open rebellion, he saw it, coupled with the administration's support for compensated emancipation in the loyal slave states, as the death knell of a hated institution. While he believed that slavery had degraded blacks by increasingly breeding a habit of dependence and lessening their efficiency as workers, he had not called for the government to move against slavery earlier in the war. Probably his hesitance to make emancipation a war aim sprang from the belief that Union victories would free slaves before the government was willing and able to assist them in their difficult transition from slavery to freedom. By 1863 Olmsted was adamant that the Emancipation Proclamation was essential to a reconstituted nation. Vowing to live by it throughout his life and to teach his children to fulfill its aims in theirs, he declared, "I shall be for continual war, or for Southern independence rather than go back one step from it."[91]

The Emancipation Proclamation played such an important role in Olmsted's war aims because he believed that by its degradation of labor, slavery had harmed the white community as well as the black. Many nonslaveholding whites were mired in poverty and illiteracy. Moreover, by encouraging a wasteful system of agriculture that destroyed the land and pushed Southerners ever westward to virgin lands, slavery brought about a frontier society east and west, one that possessed few of the institutions of community and culture that Olmsted had prized since his boyhood in the towns of Connecticut. To him, it seemed that slaveholders, intent only on buying more land and slaves, possessed few of the domestic amenities essential to civilized life, while the necessity of guarding against slave revolts had produced a violent society in which the rule of law was broken with impunity. Fear of insurrection had often led Southerners to abridge such essential civil liberties as freedom of speech and of the press.[92]

Believing that slavery had brought about a backward, violent society, Olmsted held that its abolition was necessary to ameliorate Southern life, to reconstitute the Union, and to safeguard the political life of the nation. He expected the war to regenerate the South by destroying the old social order, whose cornerstone had been slavery: "I do want the dissolution of Southern Society," he informed Bellows, "and I mean, as one part of the people, to have it." In this view no compromise could be possible; the South must be subjugated and slavery destroyed before any reunion could be attempted. Only the introduction of the free institutions that characterized the North would prevent the South from again attempting to bend the political process to its own selfish ends.[93]

For Olmsted the war offered extraordinary opportunities, though purchased at great cost, to remake American society. From the beginning, he had soberly assessed Southern resistance and had been more astute than many of his contemporaries in predicting the probable course of the war. In June 1861 he was expecting it to cost six hundred million dollars and to last two or three years. But even with this relatively clear-sighted estimation of what the war might be, he thought it worthwhile because it offered a chance to vanquish the ideological enemy, states' rights, and to free the slaves and begin their integration into American society. Since the war had come, he wanted it to last long enough to bring about the disintegration of the slave regime in the South. Moreover, the war gave him the opportunity to educate and uplift Americans—to create a greater awareness of hygiene, cleanliness, and self-discipline among the soldiers, who, in turn, would propagate these beliefs among their friends and relatives. Finally, the war could expand the functions of the government by making it active in many new areas.[94]

To accomplish these aims, Olmsted was perhaps more adamant than most of his peers concerning the necessity for dogged determination in the war. Still, like both Northerners and Southerners of that day, he saw the patriotism shown in the current struggle as akin to that of their colonial ancestors; like their forebears who persevered during a six-year war for independence, the "respectable middle-class people" of the North "were setting their teeth in the old revolutionary way." He possessed no tolerance for disloyalty and argued that it should be dealt with sternly. "Seven years, if necessary," he vowed, "and the gallows in every town, if necessary, but the business is to be done." Only when the North presented a united front in favor of the war and showed itself unwilling to consider any compromise with the South would the war cease, Olmsted concluded. The North's vastly superior resources meant that in a war of attrition it could endure far longer than the South. Therefore, it need only convince the South of its determination for the war to be "largely over."[95]

Olmsted was far from sanguine, however, about what the end of the war would bring. As warfare ceased, peace would return only gradually, for the intransigence of white Southerners would ensure that guerrilla warfare continued in isolated areas. In Olmsted's own words, "the leaders and desperate men, and those whom they could control, would keep together as armies as long as they could, afterwards as bands in the mountains and swamps, and a large part of the population would continue, while nominally submissive, to give them all the aid, and the civil officers of the nation, all the embarrassment possible." Complete peace in the South would therefore require many years and would be achieved only "by the gradual wearing out, dying off, and killing off—extermination of the rebels." Despite this grim view of the probable course of the war, Olmsted was heartened in 1863 to see slavery breaking down in the areas occupied by Union troops. In April 1863 he asserted that if the war continued one more year, and blacks continued to work for wages and fought steadfastly as soldiers, slavery would be doomed. "Thank God, we live so close upon it," he exulted to Charles Eliot Norton. "It is more than I had expected a hundred years would bring the world to."[96]

But even as he sorted out and made explicit his war aims, Olmsted faced a worsening situation at the Sanitary Commission. As 1862 drew to a close, he was confronted by a growing problem that would not be fully resolved until his resignation in late summer 1863. Increasingly, he and the Executive Committee disagreed about his role, his responsibilities, and the amount of power he should exercise. Although he had silenced the Committee's criticisms in September 1862, new confrontations had arisen and an ideological disagreement had become apparent. Ironically, the large contribution from California, which had both increased financial stability for the Commission and given rise to quarrels with other aid societies, also contributed to the growing tension between Olmsted and the Executive Committee. As a conservative Wall Street lawyer, treasurer George Templeton Strong wanted to ensure that no questions could be raised concerning his handling of the Commission's finances. Strong's background in business also led him to demand a systematic way for handling all matters and one that would allow for few exceptions. This meant that Strong and Olmsted soon were at loggerheads over various issues of administration.

Disagreements with the Executive Committee, which had begun when Olmsted returned from the Virginia Peninsula, became more intense early in October. Believing at that time that both his decisions and his general management were increasingly under attack, Olmsted spelled out his philosophy of administration to Bellows and defended his powers as absolutely essential. The Sanitary Commission's special mission meant that its chief executive officer must have discretion to act quickly and decisively in emergencies. Because the Commission intended to supplement the deficiencies of the Medical Bureau—usually after battles or when supplies were otherwise unattainable—agents of the Sanitary Commission needed to be able to spend money freely. This purpose, Olmsted argued, meant that the Commission could not be governed by the same kind of regulations as the Medical Bureau. "You can't have red-tape when your object is to get clear of red-tape," he lectured Bellows. "You can't have the ordinary securities here against waste and extravagance and petty peculation. You can't have your cake and eat it." If the usual safeguards were instituted, Olmsted continued, they would only waste money and hamper the work of the Commission. Ridiculing the chain of command that Strong advocated, Olmsted later asserted that such a system would be far less flexible than that of the Medical Bureau.[97]

Olmsted's solution to the problem—which was already in effect—was to hire workers who saw their positions as trusts rather than merely as jobs. The Commission already depended upon the honesty and faithfulness of its employees; it must continue to inspire their loyalty and dedication. It need not be overly concerned about public appearances; the probity and high moral standards of its members should form the major guarantee that funds would be properly used. This argument built upon beliefs that had guided Olmsted for the past ten years. As a partner in the publishing house of Dix & Edwards he had argued that adherence to principle—in that case royalty payments to foreign authors who had only a moral, rather than a legal, claim—was not only right but also practical and sound business. Later, as superintendent of Central Park, he similarly had wished to make the service of the engineers, draftsmen, and other professionals a labor of love.[98]

While defending his conception of his own role at the Commission, Olmsted also outlined his view of the proper functions of the Executive Committee. Specifically, he proposed to place its work of local relief under a separate committee and to reduce its autonomy significantly in relation to the Commission's Washington office. Under this plan, the Executive Committee would be a decision-making body on questions referred to it by the central office. Implicit in this view was Olmsted's assumption that he, as the person supervising the Washington office, would retain authority over numerous issues that he did not believe merited or required the attention of the Executive Committee. That is, the general secretary, rather than the Committee, should determine what issues came before it. Olmsted also sounded another theme in October 1862 that would constantly recur in his wrangles with the Executive Committee: the need for a clearer demarcation of areas of responsibility. He complained about the actions of the Executive Committee on the questions of establishing a Western council to aid Newberry and of reorganizing the supply service with the Army of the Potomac. Olmsted himself had been devising plans for both areas, and he argued that it wasted time and duplicated effort for them to be considering the same matter.[99]

In October 1862 a more emotional tone began to appear in Olmsted's correspondence with the Executive Committee. The restrictions upon his power and the new demands of the Executive Committee increasingly recalled to Olmsted his unhappy experience as superintendent and architect-in-chief of Central Park. There he had not only been obliged to account to an exacting board of commissioners, but after the autumn of 1859 his accounts had been scrutinized for even the smallest errors and his every expenditure called into question. Eventually Olmsted had found such conditions intolerable, but when he demanded that the Central Park commissioners either increase his authority or relieve him of the responsibility of general management, his powers had been sharply curtailed.[100] This former debacle must have increased the emotional turmoil to which his increasing conflicts with the Executive Committee gave rise.

45

Disagreements between Olmsted and the Executive Committee continued during November and December. In November the Committee decided to lessen the amount of discretionary power it would allow him in financial matters. For the past year he had occasionally given raises in salary, usually after consultation with Bellows, in order to hold valuable employees who considered leaving the Sanitary Commission for financial reasons; now the Executive Committee demanded that it approve all such increases. Although Olmsted formally protested and asked that the board reconsider the issue, the Committee remained firm about this new procedure. Olmsted continued displeased, despite Strong's attempt to conciliate him by arguing that in the future the Committee would be likely to grant all his requests as it was then in the habit of doing.[101]

A resolution by the Executive Committee in early December requiring Committee approval for all expenditures of over one thousand dollars led Olmsted to believe his authority was further diminished. Even the addition of an amendment that gave him full power of spending during emergencies did not mollify him. He and Strong continued to dispute about good business practices and the effect of the new rules on the efficiency of the Commission.[102]

John S. Newberry also became a complicating factor in the growing rift between Olmsted and the Executive Committee. Tempers flared over Newberry's duties and responsibilities and his adherence to the rules promulgated by the Executive Committee. In part, this was not a new problem. Newberry's position both as a member of the Commission and as an associate secretary had given him anomalous standing. While not denying Olmsted's authority, he had never really conformed to the latter's system. Unlike their Eastern counterparts, inspectors and agents in the Western department did not submit weekly reports to the central office, and Newberry had been notoriously lax in writing general reports. Some disagreements about the relations between the Western and central offices had already occurred. Although Olmsted believed the Western department should have autonomy in its own affairs, Newberry often felt neglected. In the fall of 1862 a clash of personalities occurred. Newberry protested that Olmsted was issuing peremptory commands in a dictatorial manner. In a long, angry reply Olmsted demonstrated that the Executive Committee had, in fact, issued these orders, against his own advice. Moreover, he pointed out that he had consistently urged that Newberry receive all the funds he requested and that he be permitted to inspect the military hospital at Evansville, Indiana, at his own discretion. These actions were consistent with Olmsted's belief that the discretionary powers he claimed should similarly be exercised by subordinates.[103]

Olmsted remained troubled over his relations with Newberry and believed that the Executive Committee was aggravating the situation.

Newberry would not recognize that a private letter to Olmsted or Bellows did not constitute the required general report. At the same time as the Executive Committee was demanding that Olmsted tighten control over operations, Newberry still received considerable latitude. To be sure, during its meeting in January 1863 the Sanitary Commission resolved that Olmsted held responsibility for the Western department and that Newberry should send to him all official communications, including the required reports. But the Commission softened these resolutions by specifically complimenting Newberry on his management and declaring that the Western department needed more flexibility in its system of administration than did the central office. Despite Olmsted's protestations, the Executive Committee also ordered him to visit and inspect the operations of the Western department.[104]

As his disagreements with the Executive Committee persisted, Olmsted became increasingly distraught. Late in December 1862 he complained to Bellows that constant anxiety made it impossible for him to concentrate upon his work. "My brain simply vomits all the business that I bring to it," Olmsted exclaimed. "I can lay hold of nothing right end foremost. I have my way of carrying on business, and it plainly is not your way." Part of this increasing sensitivity doubtless resulted from prolonged overwork. Two months earlier Olmsted had attempted to explain to his wife how even the ordinary daily tasks confronting the Commission required great energy to meet, and "from this plain rise constantly mountains of the steepest sort, and no sooner do I feel that I have got things prepared to overcome one than another arises over topping it beyond." Such an atmosphere of constant crisis had continued. Even though he moved his family to a rented house in Washington in November 1862, he continued to spend the same long hours at the office. In January 1863 George Templeton Strong observed with some distaste the "most insanitary habits of life" that led Olmsted to work until four in the morning, sleep in his clothes, and breakfast on coffee and pickles. By February 1863 stresses, past and present, had brought Olmsted close to the breaking point and had already led him to consider resigning from the Commission.[105]

At that point Olmsted acceded to the demands of the Executive Committee; he, accompanied by his trusty lieutenant Knapp, began a six-week tour of the Western department. This visit resulted in part from Newberry's conviction that the Eastern officers needed to observe the Commission's work in the West. Sharing the common Western belief that the government and the Sanitary Commission neglected its armies, Newberry for some time had urged the Commission to hold a meeting in the Midwest. Alarmed by growing sick lists and reports of poor health in Grant's army, the commissioners themselves wanted Olmsted's firsthand account of the Western soldiers. Intended to conciliate the Western branches and to produce a report on the care of the soldiers, Olmsted's visit also held the promise that a plan of union, or at least of closer cooperation, could be adopted with the independent Western Sanitary Commission. At no time since the autumn of 1861 had the union of the two organizations seemed so possible.[106]

Olmsted's itinerary was designed to combine inspections and friendly visits. After meeting with local societies in Altoona, Pittsburgh, and Cincinnati, Olmsted and Knapp continued on to Louisville, where Newberry had established new headquarters. After an interview with William S. Rosecrans and a survey of the Army of the Cumberland at Murfreesboro, the two returned to another round of meetings at Louisville, then visited Cairo and Memphis. A tour of Grant's Army of the Tennessee, stationed near Vicksburg, preceded a series of conferences with aid society officials in St. Louis, Chicago, Cincinnati, Cleveland, and Buffalo.[107]

The Western trip was almost as barren of results for the Sanitary Commission as Olmsted had anticipated. He reported ineptitude and inefficiency in some of the Commission's operations to Newberry and the Executive Committee, but his principal contribution was a limited one. Finding that some enterprising soldiers and civilians had used the free shipment of donated articles to soldiers as a means to carry on illegal trade, Olmsted persuaded Grant to restrict the activities of local and state societies and to require that such shipments pass exclusively through the Sanitary Commission. To accomplish this, the government would furnish the Commission with a steamer. But the exclusion of the Western Sanitary Commission, which Grant mistakenly believed to have independent transportation, meant that this order could not stand without modification.[108]

Although the Executive Committee had planned the Western tour, in Olmsted's words "to cultivate a friendly feeling amongst all concerned by a little white lying," he actually was unable to conciliate the Western branches. To be sure, the meetings were so cordial that Newberry asserted that he and the general secretary could resolve their differences. But no real basis for compromise existed. Although the Western tour confirmed Olmsted's belief in the correctness of his system of organization, the Executive Committee's increasing unwillingness to accept his views undercut his position in the West. Even while Olmsted was in Louisville, Bellows wrote letters to Newberry and to John H. Heywood, president of the Kentucky branch, which were highly critical of Olmsted. Bellows also indicated that the Executive Committee would uphold Newberry's course and did not favor the plan of reorganization that Olmsted had drawn up in January. An entry that Strong made in his diary at this time strongly suggests that Bellows was indeed speaking for the Executive Committee, not just for himself.[109]

Though undertaken for the business of the Sanitary Commission, the journey to the Midwest and South acquired another meaning for Olmsted: it provided his first opportunity since the Southern journeys of the 1850s to evaluate American manners and mores. Two well-known British men of letters, the journalist William Howard Russell and the novelist Anthony Trollope, had just published accounts of their travels in America that included assessments of national character. Olmsted felt that neither of these men really understood American civilization, although he deemed Trollope—who did not share Russell's antidemocratic views—the fairer. Inspired by these books, Olmsted produced a series of vignettes from his observations.

In these sketches Olmsted developed a theme that had long concerned him—the condition of domestic amenities and taste in American life. In public life he found little that was encouraging; he excoriated hotels in Cincinnati, Nashville, and Memphis for their lack of concern for the comfort of the traveling public and indicted the railroads for their delays, misrepresentations, and the filthy state of their passenger cars. Americans bore such conditions too patiently, he charged, and his solution was complaint and exposure.

But it was in private domestic life that Olmsted found what he believed to be the character of the nation. While Russell saw only crudeness and vulgarity in frontier villages, Olmsted argued that, despite a rude style of life, the small farmer was hardy, self-sufficient, and had "not the smallest particle of servility." Moreover, according to Olmsted, this life was more comfortable and economically secure than that of the English farm laborer. The cities of the Midwest revealed even more meaningful progress in domestic life. Olmsted argued that Cincinnati, St. Louis, and Cleveland—all solid, well-built towns—reflected a middle-class respectability that the English travelers had too often overlooked. On two streets in Cleveland he found that every house "was a villa in a garden, and every one looked comfortable, as if inhabited by a fore-handed man, with a family of sociable habits and some impulses of taste." Pronouncing Euclid Street in Cleveland to be a finer street than New York City's fashionable Fifth Avenue, Olmsted also declared, "It is a thousand-fold more a distinctively American sight."[110]

To be sure, not all aspects of the Midwestern cities were equally encouraging. At St. Louis and Chicago an excessive concern with commerce hampered the development of institutions meant to educate and uplift all the people. The building of parks and libraries, in particular, tended to depend on their direct importance to the business community, while the pitifully low salaries paid to public school teachers in Chicago formed a marked contrast to the wages of railroad superintendents or steamboat pilots. Olmsted believed that commerce in Chicago too much engrossed the time and energies of wealthy men who, under other circumstances, might be making larger cultural contributions to their community. A case in point was Ezra McCagg, who agreed with Olmsted about the need for public parks in Chicago, but who pleaded his inability to campaign for them because of pressing business.[111]

Despite these limitations, Olmsted believed that he had discovered strong evidence of civilization in the Midwest. Surely a traveler such as Trollope, who stressed the taciturnity of Americans, or Russell, who emphasized the aristocratic pretensions of a Fifth Avenue soirée, had misjudged the people. They particularly misunderstood American women, who often exemplified what was best and most distinctive in the American character. An evening with Sarah Elliott Perkins, the widowed sister of his friend Charles Wyllys Elliott, was a bright spot in Olmsted's visit to Cincinnati. She and a neighbor both had sons in the army, and their patriotism, as well as the simple domestic comforts of the Perkins cottage, deeply impressed Olmsted. His experience in Cleveland similarly confirmed his opinion that the "cheerful, quiet, deep, patient, religious patriotism" of the women was "purely American in character." Although earlier in the war he had worried that "vulgarity and poverty of intellect" ruled in the North, he perceived in 1863 a growth in taste and character among the people of the Midwest that corresponded to his long-held desire for a general elevation of all classes to the "mental & moral capital of gentlemen."[112]

In the South, however, Olmsted found little positive change. In 1853 a long, heated discussion with Samuel Perkins Allison, a lawyer in Nashville, had forced Olmsted to reevaluate Northern and Southern society. While the North had not then measured up to his goals, he had been even more sharply critical of Southern gentlemen and their conception of honor. Similarly in 1863 Olmsted recounted the experiences of Northern army officers with Southern hospitality and "high-toned" Southern gentlemen—all of which confirmed his earlier opinions. Moreover, his own conversations with black and white Southerners supported his earlier criticisms of slavery.[113]

During his tour of the Mississippi states, Olmsted also came to view the leadership of the Union army there as indicative of the best American virtues. Throughout the war he had tended to sympathize with the Northern generals, who, he believed, faced an enormous task in producing disciplined soldiers from the highly individualistic American volunteers. The "journey in the West" introduced him to generals who eclipsed his former hero, McClellan. "In Grant, Sherman & Rosecrans," he told Edwin L. Godkin in April 1863, "we have three who may well be great Generals." In his account, intended for publication, Olmsted presented William S. Rosecrans, who had publicly praised the Sanitary Commission, as a patriotic leader who approached his task with religious fervor and a belief in the fundamental justice of the Union cause. These sketches barely mentioned Grant, but he also deeply impressed Olmsted. After visiting the army at Memphis, Milliken's Bend, and Young's Point, Olmsted was convinced of the health and vigor of the troops and of Grant's virtues as an officer and a man. While doubting that the current operations could bring about the capture of Vicksburg, Olmsted described Grant as "par excellence, a *gentleman,* a modest, good hearted, self-sacrificing, resolute common-sense gentleman."[114]

The "journey in the West" provided a further opportunity for Olmsted to continue his speculations about the effect of immigration on the American character. In his interest in this subject, he probably had been influenced by Horace Bushnell, the renowned Congregational clergyman who was also the Olmsted family's pastor in Hartford. In his famous sermon *Barbarism the First Danger,* Bushnell had described the decivilizing aspects of westward movement for the individual who left home and community. In the course of his own Southern travels in the 1850s Olmsted had noted the sparse settlements and lack of domestic amenities, and now in 1863 he implicitly—and at times explicitly—compared the South and Midwest with the South he had seen ten years earlier.[115]

Olmsted had also earlier been interested in gathering statistics pertaining to the working classes and European immigrants and their families. In 1859 he had written John Jay about the "excellent opportunity" Central Park offered for "obtaining statistics of the poorest class of American working-men, or of New York working men." Olmsted had speculated that for less than ten dollars, one could gather answers to six or so questions from three thousand men. He then continued, "I have already taken the height & size of 1000, with the nationality, and I should be glad to receive suggestions from you for as extended a census as could be made without exciting unpleasant feeling among the men." There is no indication, however, that Olmsted took any further steps with regard to the workers on the park. In 1863, as he prepared the vignettes from his journey, he also began to obtain information about the nativity of Union soldiers. Building upon the Commission's work in amassing statistical medical data, he devised a questionnaire as part of his own systematic investigation designed to ascertain the "social statistics" of the soldiers; and he compensated Commission agents for completing it. Especially interested in determining the proportions of immigrants and first- and second-generation Americans among the soldiers, Olmsted also planned to use this statistical evidence as a base for "a sort of treatise on the established tendencies of the European races in the United States." This intention lasted well past the war. In 1867 he offered to pay his friend Knapp to tabulate some of the data into general categories and remarked: "If I

51

should be moderately successful in business, it is my hope to complete this book & of course I should like to be able to incorporate the results of your discussion of these returns, if you should undertake it, in this book." Olmsted, however, never completed this project.[116]

The journey in the West, though suggesting numerous reflections on issues that had long interested Olmsted, formed only a brief respite in the storm that was building at the Sanitary Commission. The rift between Olmsted and the Executive Committee steadily widened, and the increasing competition that the Sanitary Commission faced by December 1862, as rival soldiers' aid groups began to gain ground, doubtless aggravated this problem. Already enriched by fifty thousand dollars from the California fund, the Western Sanitary Commission gained yet another benefit when Secretary of War Stanton extended formal governmental recognition by reviving Frémont's order of September 1861 and further extending its scope to include all Western armies. This came as an unexpected blow to the Sanitary Commission, and Olmsted and the other commissioners viewed it as yet another manifestation of Stanton's hostility. He had already canceled their privileges at the government printer's office that August, and his relations with Hammond had become so strained that the commissioners feared the surgeon general would soon be removed from his post.[117]

But the challenge that most alarmed the members of the Sanitary Commission came from the rapidly expanding U.S. Christian Commission. Founded by the Young Men's Christian Association in the autumn of 1861, the Christian Commission suddenly became far more active toward the end of 1862. Although Olmsted then issued a circular urging Sanitary Commission agents to cooperate with agents from the Christian Commission, he personally disliked the Christian Commission's principles and methods. Whereas the Christian Commission used unpaid volunteer labor, generally clergymen who had donated a month or six weeks of their time, Olmsted argued that only by employing a trained, experienced staff, one accustomed to system and rules, could battlefield relief and the other duties of inspectors and agents be adequately accomplished. With paid employees, responsibility for the large amounts of money and supplies entrusted to the Sanitary Commission could be enforced. In contrast, the Christian Commission argued that its unpaid labor, freely donated, enabled it to use all its resources directly for the soldiers.

Philosophical differences other than those of method also separated the Christian and Sanitary commissions. Although some of its major officers, contributors, and workers were religious leaders, the Sanitary Commission was determinedly secular in its orientation and its appeals. Thus, to some partisans of the Christian Commission, the Sanitary Commission represented the threat of godlessness or the religious heterodoxy of Unitarians such as Bellows. Priding itself on bringing God to the battle-field, the Christian Commission emphasized ministering to the spiritual as well as the physical needs of soldiers. In contrast, the Sanitary Commission's philosophy, as set forth by Olmsted, was to secure for each soldier the care that his nation owed to him, and this aid was to be bound by no special conditions except need. With its promise of aid and religious consolation by devoted volunteers rather than by the "hirelings" used by the Sanitary Commission, the Christian Commission could appeal powerfully to the pious, benevolent men and women of the small towns and rural areas who had formerly contributed freely to the Sanitary Commission. The touching testimonials and sentimental appeals of the Christian Commission deeply moved many and forced the Sanitary Commission to work harder for contributions.[118]

This competition with the Christian Commission, as well as with local soldiers' aid societies, appears to have further added to the disagreements between Olmsted and the Executive Committee. Some members of the Sanitary Commission almost instinctively sought to preempt and use the same appeal to sentiment that had been employed so successfully by other organizations. To help counter this competition, the Executive Committee proposed in late 1862 to offer its supporters a monthly bulletin which would recount the Commission's achievements. Opposed to such a publication on principle, Olmsted argued that it could present only a partial and misleading picture of the Commission's activities. Unable to carry his point, he offered as his reason for not implementing this proposal a lack of reports from the Western department.[119]

The example of the Christian Commission probably also influenced the nature of the quarrel that occurred between Olmsted and Cornelius R. Agnew, the most evangelically oriented member of the Sanitary Commission's Executive Committee. Late in April 1863 Agnew attacked Olmsted's management of the Sanitary Commission's work force. This was not the first indication of Agnew's dissatisfaction: the previous February he had demanded the dismissal of a Sanitary Commission agent accused of binges of drinking. Olmsted had referred the matter to his subordinates Jenkins and Knapp, who decided that the worker deserved a second chance and reassigned him to a position in the central storehouse, where he no longer worked with the soldiers. Although Agnew had acquiesced in this decision and had even praised the Christian magnanimity it showed, peace prevailed for only a short time. A visit, in the company of Bellows, to the agents stationed with the Army of the Potomac at Acquia Creek led Agnew to launch a second attack upon Olmsted's personnel policies. After talking with Isaac N. Kerlin, the rather strait-laced chief inspector, Agnew concluded that at least four employees should immediately be fired for character flaws. He further held Olmsted responsible for the agents' alleged dereliction of duty and argued that more time should be given to direct supervision and less to constructing plans of organization. Agnew also praised the Christian Commission's operations and despaired of the Sanitary Commission's regaining a commensurate amount of influence with the Army of the Potomac.[120]

Angered by Agnew's charges, Olmsted complained bitterly to Bellows about their injustice but nevertheless discharged three of the men criticized. He also sent an icily polite note to Agnew stating that responsibility for correcting defects in management would henceforth lie with the Executive Committee. In effect, Olmsted chose a course similar to the one he had pursued at Central Park two years earlier. Pleading the necessity of mulling over what he had recently observed in the West, he refused to resume general superintendence of the Sanitary Commission's central office.[121]

The quarrel with Agnew was only one of several major upheavals affecting Olmsted in the spring of 1863. That February Calvert Vaux had indicated that he soon intended to resign the position of consulting architect of Central Park, which he and Olmsted had held jointly since April 1862. Olmsted had not been able to give any time to the park for almost a year, but Vaux's growing dissatisfaction evoked conflicting emotions. Although aware of the problems that Vaux encountered with the comptroller and the Central Park board, Olmsted also expressed his own deep attachment to the park and his sense that he was losing an important opportunity. He had always hoped to return to the park; now that door was closing to him. Olmsted and Vaux remained consulting architects until the park commissioners adopted their revised plan for the upper park, including the new addition extending the park to 110th Street. In early May Vaux submitted his and Olmsted's joint resignation.[122]

About this time another new, even more distressing difficulty arose in Olmsted's family relations: this was a quarrel with his father. John Olmsted, who had patiently underwritten his son's farming and publishing ventures, apparently proposed to lend two thousand dollars—and perhaps to give another thousand outright—to make capital improvements on the Staten Island farm that belonged to Olmsted's stepchildren. This offer came in response to Olmsted's suggestions in July 1862 that such changes could significantly increase the value of the farm. Olmsted, however, declined the loan upon the grounds of his probable inability to repay it and rambled on at length about the possibility of leaving the Commission's service and about other jobs that might be open to him. The likelihood that his forty-one-year-old son, who had a wife and four children to support, might embark upon yet another career alarmed and dismayed the elder Olmsted. In a letter that has not survived he reproached his son for not attempting in the spring of 1861 to secure his position at Central Park by mobilizing public opinion. Olmsted angrily retorted that his father must not expect success of him in all ventures; such opinions about Central Park not only were mistaken but did him an injustice. Despite John Olmsted's attempts to smooth over their disagreement, relations remained strained until late that summer. For Olmsted this was a new experience—made doubly trying by other problems. While John Olmsted had offered advice, he seldom praised or blamed. His opinion was very valuable to his son, who had become dependent on that constant support through his many changes of career and direction. For Olmsted the quarrel cut deeply.[123]

During the spring of 1863 the Sanitary Commission was rapidly becoming unbearable for the increasingly overwrought Olmsted, but one project appeared to offer an attractive alternative. He and his friend Edwin L. Godkin, a talented young Anglo-Irish journalist living in New York City, had often discussed the kind of weekly paper that they believed America needed. By the spring of 1863 Olmsted expressed his willingness, upon a month's notice, to collaborate in a weekly newspaper. Elated by this interest, Godkin began to lay plans for such a venture. During a visit by Olmsted to New York City in June, the two men hammered out a prospectus that presented both the rationale for establishing the journal and a strategy for supporting it. They expected their proposed publication to fill an important gap in American political and intellectual reporting. Its appearance on a weekly basis would mean that it could discuss events in a more reflective manner than a daily paper, while at the same time retaining more immediacy than the monthly or quarterly periodicals. Although they believed that the audience for such a journal was growing, they also argued that its limited appeal meant that it must possess secure financing. Only then would there be time to establish its reputation for thoughtful political and cultural articles. Olmsted had good cause to insist upon a financially stable journal. His first venture into publishing, a partnership in the firm Dix & Edwards, had lost his father's initial investment of five thousand dollars and had left him with a large debt for which he felt responsible; and he wished at all costs to avoid a similar fiasco.[124]

The proposed weekly newspaper appealed to Olmsted's desires to encourage patriotism and undertake reforms at a time when other opportunities such as Port Royal and the Union League Club had proven unrealizable. And while it posed an alternative to his increasingly painful position at the Sanitary Commission, the journal could also provide a "mission" in its education of the thoughtful reading public. The role of a man of letters had long interested Olmsted, who earlier had attempted a literary career in New York City. In fact, for over ten years Olmsted had dreamed of publishing a high-quality weekly paper. Late in 1853 he wrote about the need for "an organ of a higher Democracy and a higher religion than the popular." Less than two years later he drew up an outline which he entitled "Plan of

Weekly Magazine," presumably to convince his partners at the publishing house Dix & Edwards to establish such a journal. This early prospectus, which also called for thoughtful analyses of politics and for articles from informed correspondents on topics such as science, philosophy, social reform, and cultural affairs, was quite similar to the one which Godkin and Olmsted wrote in 1863. In the midst of civil war, however, the two men chose to stress the political importance of their proposed journal. For Olmsted the weekly paper would combine his goal of instructing and uplifting all classes in society with his increasingly urgent desire to nourish patriotism and national unity. His suggestions for an appropriate name for the newspaper illustrate his vision of its role. While some names were drawn from this long-held belief in popular education (the Householder, Yeoman's Weekly, the Work of the Week), he chose others because of their relation to nationalism (the Loyalist, the National, the Holdfast).[125]

The prospectus drawn up by Olmsted and Godkin was given an encouraging reception on June 25, when a group of New Yorkers met at the Union League Club to discuss the proposed publication. George Griswold pledged one thousand dollars, and others agreed to canvass to establish a capital fund. In particular, Bellows agreed to talk to several of his prosperous parishioners. But despite Olmsted's enthusiasm, the weekly newspaper project languished after June. Bellows wrote the men on his list rather than talking with them, and as the summer continued, more and more of the city's wealthy businessmen retreated to vacation homes and resorts. The battle of Gettysburg called Olmsted away in early July, first to oversee the shipping of supplies from Baltimore, then to inspect the battlefield and the Sanitary Commission lodge and feeding station in Gettysburg. He remained optimistic that the money for the paper could be raised, and the draft riots which occurred in New York City in mid-July only strengthened his conviction about the necessity for such a journal. "What a pity it is not in existence now," he told Bellows. "Never was there so favorable a season for planting good seed, especially in New York."[126]

At this time Olmsted's mounting dissatisfaction with the Sanitary Commission reached a new peak. During the period when he declined to exercise general superintendence, he had been busily drawing up yet another plan of organization to resolve some of his difficulties with Newberry and the Executive Committee. In January 1863 Olmsted had presented a plan to rename the Western department and to appoint an assistant who would oversee record keeping there. When Newberry objected to that arrangement, Olmsted presented an alternative plan. In June he proposed to divide the Commission by function and by geographical area: included were a financial section; a research department, which would also dispense advice; and a supply department, the regional subdivisions of which Newberry would supervise. This second plan drew a storm of protest; Newberry rejected such a radical change, and the Chicago branch objected to cooperating with the Western Sanitary Commission. These protests induced Bellows to suspend putting the new plan into operation.[127]

Stung by this rebuff, Olmsted was also exhausted from overwork. In June he discovered that the manuscript of *Hospital Transports*, a compilation of letters written by Sanitary Commission workers describing their activities during the Peninsula campaign, was in such a disorganized state that he needed to read the proofs and make numerous last minute corrections. Then, overseeing relief efforts after the battle of Gettysburg demanded much time and energy. In this atmosphere of crisis, Olmsted was brought to the verge of resignation by several events that were petty in themselves but indicative to him of a pattern. In May the publication of the *Sanitary Reporter*, a bulletin issued by the Commission's Western department, greatly annoyed him. Generally opposed to the Commission's publication of a periodical, Olmsted had further reason to find this one particularly offensive. Newberry's use of testimonials and sentimental congratulatory letters seemed little short of self-advertisement and "puffery." Furthermore, the Western publication symbolized how Newberry had undercut Olmsted's position, inasmuch as only Newberry's failure to submit reports had prevented the central office from beginning its own periodical. Two public letters further exacerbated Olmsted's anger. An effusive letter of thanks from Newberry for lemons donated by policemen in New York City seemed to contradict the guiding principles of the Sanitary Commission. Olmsted had long discouraged special donations of perishables which had to be shipped long distances. Moreover, Newberry's letter undermined the Commission's claims that its officials were able to determine the needs of all parts of the army and could supply them promptly from the most advantageous locations. Similarly, a notice by Bellows praising the work of the Christian Commission at Gettysburg also appeared to contradict all the earlier strictures against volunteer workers and sensational appeals for miscellaneous goods to be rushed to the battlefield. To Olmsted, the final insult was a sarcastic remark by Bellows about the agents who had been fired at Agnew's insistence and then temporarily rehired for emergency service. Hampered in his ability to act and to compel Newberry to acquiesce in the Commission's system, Olmsted found his position to be untenable. As had been the case at Central Park, he felt that he had responsibility without authority—a condition that contradicted his ideal of administration. Even more distressing to him was his perception that the Sanitary Commission was moving away from the ground it ought to occupy. Too much emphasis had been placed upon its role as a dispenser of donated medical supplies, and not enough on its role as the agent of scientific and medical innovation. In a long, aggrieved letter of July 25 Olmsted presaged his resignation.[128]

Rapidly moving toward a break with the Sanitary Commission, Olmsted viewed the proposed weekly paper as his best alternative and sought the necessary capital by sending Knapp to Boston with a list of possible donors. But early in August a chance meeting with his old friend Charles A. Dana, then an assistant secretary of war, produced yet another possibility. In refusing the position of superintendent of the large Mariposa gold mining estate in California, Dana had suggested Olmsted to the New York capitalists who had recently acquired the estate. When on August 10 they offered Olmsted the position with its generous compensation—an annual salary of ten thousand dollars in gold and shares of company stock—he believed it a godsend for his increasingly precarious financial position. All the men of business he consulted, including his father, Howard Potter, and George Templeton Strong, agreed that the California position was an attractive one. Moreover, Olmsted's efforts to place the weekly newspaper on a firm financial footing and to clarify his position at the Sanitary Commission were meeting with little success. Bellows disapproved of Olmsted's new scheme, which would not obligate Olmsted to repay any of the starting capital, even if the journal were successful. Despite Bellows's attempts to induce Newberry to submit the required reports, the minister did not understand that in Olmsted's eyes, failing to send the reports constituted only one instance—though the most flagrant—of a more general insubordination. The debate that Olmsted and Bellows waged in their August letters over the proffered California position ultimately referred more to the past than to the future. While Bellows argued that the reputation Olmsted had built with the Sanitary Commission would make him indispensable to the reconstruction of the South, the latter put forward his pessimistic view of the little he believed he had accomplished.[129]

In early September Olmsted composed his resignation letter and probably read it to the assembled Executive Committee. This contained a more balanced interpretation of his tenure at the Sanitary Commission. The Commission's great success during this period had been the reform of the Medical Bureau, and its great tasks, the collection of data about the soldiers and the transmission of the latest and best medical and hygienic knowledge to the army physicians. He claimed less credit for the supply service of the Commission because, as he put it, there was reason to believe that had the Commission not undertaken it, some other group would have. Again, perhaps implicitly criticizing his foes at the Christian Commission and the localistic societies, he proclaimed his pride in the way supplies had been distributed to benefit the soldiers most in need, regardless of their state of origin or their religious affiliation.[130]

By September 1863 wartime experiences had left their mark on

Olmsted. One effect, though short term, was severe: chronic overwork and anxiety had greatly undermined his physical and psychological health. At the end of 1863 he somberly reflected upon the death of a friend: "The war makes us all old, it seems to me. I feel toward death as an old man myself." In California he would also complain of "pen-sickness" and depression, much of which appeared to be a delayed reaction to the years at the Sanitary Commission. Although Olmsted's experiences in Washington had not disillusioned him about the role that government could play, they had profoundly disenchanted him about the possibility that he might directly or indirectly influence its policies. The Republican administration had adopted one of his major goals, emancipation, but his experiences with the secretary of the treasury and the secretary of war seemed to indicate that the national government was not committed to the kind of measures he advocated and would neither appoint him to high positions nor listen to his views. While believing that the war would be continued and the Union reconstructed, he—realistically enough—did not expect to play an important role.[131]

In September 1863 Olmsted sailed for his new position in California, and the Sanitary Commission quickly chose J. Foster Jenkins as his replacement. Never again did the Commission have a general secretary so powerful or so forceful as Olmsted. The trends that he had decried continued: the branch societies continued to display considerable independence, and the Executive Committee retained its primacy in decision making. From Brooklyn to Cincinnati to Chicago, a series of "Sanitary fairs" featuring displays, bazaars, and the auctioning of donated memorabilia raised millions of dollars during the last two years of the war, but little of this money found its way into the coffers of the central organization. In October 1863, in an attempt to better define the relationship between the general secretary and the Executive Committee, the board of the Sanitary Commission made Jenkins a member of that committee and moved his office to New York City. Without Olmsted's strong leadership, factionalism soon erupted among the supervisory employees at the Washington office. The disaffection of the self-important and suspicious Alfred Bloor was not particularly surprising, but even the usually gentle Knapp participated in the recurring quarrels. Moreover, the Commission's relations with the Medical Bureau again worsened as Hammond was convicted by court-martial and dismissed as surgeon general in 1864. The Commission, while undertaking some new endeavors, such as its army-navy claims office to aid soldiers seeking pensions or back pay, largely continued along the lines Olmsted had laid out early in the war. Throughout the remainder of the war, it played an important supplemental role and stood high in public esteem. Olmsted's part in its work was recognized by Harvard College, which in 1864 conferred the honorary degree of Master of Arts upon him in recognition of "the remarkable energy & success with which you have lent yourself to good & noble works in the service of humanity."[132]

Yet it was a tragedy for Olmsted and the Commission he served that it proved unable to transmit its organizational achievements to a successor. Self-conscious about its place in history, the Commission slowly wound up its affairs after the war. It put its archives in order and commissioned its own authorized histories—some of which, like Knapp's manuscript on the special relief service, were written but never published. In 1866 Bellows became president of the American Association for the Relief of the Misery of Battlefields, an organization that wished to gain American ratification of the Geneva Convention (which called for granting protection and the privileges of neutrality to wounded soldiers and medical workers on the battlefield) and cooperation with the International Red Cross Committee. These efforts proved fruitless, and the organization disbanded in 1872. Ironically, the participation of the United States in the Red Cross would result from the promptings of Clara Barton, a heroic Civil War worker, who then had operated independently of organizations such as the Sanitary Commission. Her novel conception of the role such an organization could play—providing peacetime civilian disaster relief as well as battlefield aid—helped to gain governmental recognition and ratification of the Geneva accords in 1882. Several months earlier she had requested and received a letter of support from Bellows, who was near death. But the early American Red Cross did not benefit from the organizational innovations of the Sanitary Commission: not until 1905 did it create a bureaucratic structure which clearly designated the responsibilities belonging to the auxiliaries and to the national society. Unmarked and unmourned, the Sanitary Commission had gone out of existence in 1878.[133]

Searching for a mission at the outbreak of the Civil War, Olmsted found it, but not in the areas he expected. Although he tried to influence the transition of blacks from bondage to freedom, he ultimately left little mark on the experiment at Port Royal. His efforts to nurture nationalism and unity of purpose in the North in general, and among intellectually inclined gentlemen in particular, through the Union League Club of New York and a weekly paper were only a little more successful. The Union League Club did not adopt the explicitly nationalistic and educational platform he had advocated. Realization of the *Nation* lay with Godkin in the future, although the statement of purpose that he and Olmsted drafted in 1863 described the periodical that began publication in July 1865. It was the Sanitary Commission that provided Olmsted with a chance to fulfill his yearnings. His two years with it yielded concrete achievements in aid of both the Union war effort and the soldiers. He played a major role in forming both policy and organizational structure at the Commission during its first year. He built a cadre of dedicated, experienced workers and fashioned a system that emphasized the efficient distribution of supplies to the soldiers most in need, regardless of their area of origin. He fought within the Commission to avoid parochialism and to recognize no state or municipal rivalries in its procurement or distribution of stores. Olmsted also assumed an important part in setting goals and deciding on tactics in the successful campaign to reform and enlarge the army's Medical Bureau. Moreover, his close supervision of the evacuation of the sick and wounded from the Virginia Peninsula in the summer of 1862 helped bring some order to the chaotic conditions there. Ultimately, his accomplishments did not measure up to his lofty aspirations for the Sanitary Commission. Still, the Commission must be seen as one of the great voluntary, nationalistic, and bureaucratic achievements of the war.

While Olmsted saw many of his hopes disappointed during his two years at the Sanitary Commission, his writings provide insights in a number of areas. Residence in the nation's capital made him a witness and frequent critic of the government's operations. His position at the Sanitary Commission gave him the opportunity, unusual for a civilian, to scrutinize the volunteer army in the field, in its camps, and after battle. That post also made him a participant in the Commission's internal debates about goals and methods. Olmsted's letters, articles, and reports present the views that one Northern intellectual and reformer held about the political, medical, social, and intellectual life of the wartime North.

1. FLO to CLB, Dec. 8, 1860, and FLO to JO, April 17, 1861 (*Papers of FLO*, 3: 287, 342).
2. FLO to the Board of Commissioners of the Central Park, Jan. 22, 1861 (*Papers of FLO*, 3: 297–319); New York City, Board of Commissioners of the Central Park, *Minutes of Proceedings of the Board of Commissioners of the Central Park* (New York, 1858–69), June 6, 1861, pp. 24–25.
3. Louis S. Gerteis, *From Contraband to Freedman: Federal Policy toward Southern Blacks, 1861–1865* (Westport, Conn., 1973), pp. 11–16; FLO to HWB, June 1, 1861, below.
4. There are numerous accounts of the formation of the U.S. Sanitary Commission. Consult, for example, Robert H. Bremner, *The Public Good: Philanthropy and Welfare in the Civil War Era* (New York, 1980), pp. 37–46; William Quentin Maxwell, *Lincoln's Fifth Wheel: The Political History of the United States Sanitary Commission* (New York, 1956), pp. 4–9; Charles J. Stillé, *History of the United States Sanitary Commission: Being the General Report of Its Work during the War of the Rebellion* (Philadelphia, 1866). See also Henry W. Bellows's reminiscences in HWB to Charles J. Stillé, Nov. 15, 1865, Henry Whitney Bellows Papers, Massachusetts Historical Society, Boston, Mass.
5. USSC, *Minutes*, pp. 5, 6; HWB to FLO, [June 19, 1861]; doc. nos. 1 and 2 in USSC, *Documents*. This is an analysis only of the first group of commissioners, even

though the Sanitary Commission added new members, primarily from Western cities, until 1863. The newer members were less likely to attend meetings; moreover, after the summer of 1862 the Executive Committee assumed increasing importance in policy making. Only Charles J. Stillé, who in 1863 joined the board and became the only member of the Executive Committee from outside New York City, would ever exercise power commensurate with that of the original members; but even his influence was slight before late in 1863. A different interpretation of the commissioners is found in George M. Fredrickson, *The Inner Civil War: Northern Intellectuals and the Crisis of the Union* (New York, 1965), pp. 23–35, 98–112.

6. *Papers of FLO*, 1: 121, n. 13; FLO to the Board of Commissioners of the Central Park, Oct. 6, 1857 (*Papers of FLO*, 3: 94–100).

7. *Papers of FLO*, 3: 27–29; FLO to CV, Nov. 26, 1863.

8. FLO to Arthur T. Edwards, Aug. 7, 1855 (*Papers of FLO*, 2: 357–61); *Papers of FLO*, 3: 25–30, 35–36.

9. USSC, *Minutes*, pp. 3–5, 10–44, *passim*; FLO to MPO, July 2, 1861, below.

10. George Worthington Adams, *Doctors in Blue: The Medical History of the Union Army in the Civil War* (New York, 1952), pp. 15–19, 47–54, 152–53. For representative biographies of inspectors hired early in 1861, see the biographical sketches of J. Foster Jenkins and John H. Douglas, and FLO to William Cullen Bryant, July 31, 1861, n. 4, below.

11. Consult FLO to JO, Aug. 3, 1861, n. 8, below; Roster of U.S. Sanitary Commission Employees, Oct. 1, 1862, USSC-NYPL, box 642.

12. FLO to MPO, Sept. 18, 1861; *New-York Daily Tribune*, Sept. 25, 1861, p. 6. Over time Olmsted continued to refine this organizational structure. According to Lewis Steiner, chief inspector for the Sanitary Commission with the Army of the Potomac, "After the battle of Gettysburg, Mr. Olmsted prepared the outline of the Field Relief Corps of the Army of the Potomac, which served afterwards as a species of model for similar Relief Corps in the other armies." The formation of this corps further elaborated the organization of Sanitary Commission agents and assistants in the field. Lewis H. Steiner, A *Sketch of the History, Plan of Organization, and Operations of the U.S. Sanitary Commission* (Philadelphia, 1866), p. 8.

13. FLO to Lewis H. Steiner, Aug. 12, 1861, below; doc. nos. 24², 52, and 53 in USSC, *Documents*.

14. FLO to Mary Bull Olmsted, Feb. 3, 1862, in the possession of Terry Niles Smith; FLO to HWB, Feb. 4, 1863, below.

15. Clifford S. Griffin, *Their Brothers' Keepers: Moral Stewardship in the United States, 1800–1865* (New Brunswick, N.J., 1960), pp. 23–43, 61–98.

16. Alfred D. Chandler, Jr., *The Visible Hand: The Managerial Revolution in American Business* (Cambridge, Mass., 1977), pp. 79–121.

17. Ibid., p. 95; FLO to William H. Hurlbert, Jan. 31, 1863, below. For information on the education and training of engineers in the early nineteenth century, see Daniel Hovey Calhoun, *The American Civil Engineer: Origins and Conflict* (Cambridge, Mass., 1960).

18. *War for the Union*, 1: 414–16 and 3: 317–23; Morton Keller, *Affairs of State: Public Life in Late Nineteenth Century America* (Cambridge, Mass., 1977), pp. 1–13. Although Stephen Skowronek, in *Building a New American State: The Expansion of National Administrative Capacities, 1877–1920* (Cambridge, Mass., 1982), pp. 3–18, 24–31, 50–59, focuses upon the post-Reconstruction period, he sees the Civil War as an episode in state development which involved only one-half the nation and was tied to the Republican party.

19. Doc. no. 17 in USSC, *Documents*.

20. Doc. no. 40, ibid.

21. FLO to MPO, July 29, 1861, below; FLO, "Draft Report on Demoralization," n.d., USSC-NYPL, box 735: 2453. G. W. Adams, *Doctors in Blue*, pp. 169–91, discusses

hygiene and disease extensively and argues that discipline and hygiene were related among Civil War soldiers.

22. USSC, *Minutes*, pp. 29–31; FLO to the Board of Trustees of the College of Agriculture, and the Mechanic Arts, of the State of Maine, Jan. 22, 1867, Raymond H. Folger Library, University of Maine, Orono, Me.

23. "Report on the Demoralization of the Volunteers," Sept. 5, 1861, below.

24. G. M. Fredrickson, *Inner Civil War*, pp. 108–9; Eliza H. Schuyler to HWB, Sept. 10, 1861, Henry Whitney Bellows Papers, Massachusetts Historical Society, Boston, Mass.; William Howard Russell, *My Diary North and South* (Boston, 1863), p. 514; Frederick Law Olmsted, "American Editor's Introduction to *The Englishman in Kansas*" (*Papers of FLO*, 2: 416); FLO to MPO, Sept. 28, 1861, below. For an illustration of Olmsted's skepticism about government by the elite, see FLO to Edwin L. Godkin, Feb. 20, 1865, Edwin Lawrence Godkin Papers, Houghton Library, Harvard University, Cambridge, Mass.; and for a helpful account of the political views of Olmsted and his friends, consult Geoffrey Blodgett, "Frederick Law Olmsted: Landscape Architecture as Conservative Reform," *Journal of American History* 62 (March 1976): 869–89.

25. "Report on the Demoralization of the Volunteers," Sept. 5, 1861, below; *Diary of the Civil War*, p. 180; FLO to JO, Sept. 12, 1861, below.

26. FLO to William E. Boardman, Jan. 16, 1862, USSC-NYPL, box 833, 2: 406–12; FLO to HWB, Sept. 25, 1861, below. For detailed information on the army's Medical Bureau during the Civil War, consult G. W. Adams, *Doctors in Blue*; Percy M. Ashburn, *A History of the Medical Department of the United States Army* (Boston, 1929); U.S. Office of the Surgeon General, *The Medical Department of the United States Army from 1775 to 1873* (Washington, D.C., 1873); Thomas Marshall Hunter, "Medical Service for the Yankee Soldier" (Ph.D. diss., University of Maryland, 1952).

27. HWB to Simon Cameron, Sept. 12, 1861, USSC-NYPL, box 638; FLO to JO, Sept. 12, 1861, below; W. Q. Maxwell, *Lincoln's Fifth Wheel*, pp. 96–97.

28. *Diary of the Civil War*, pp. 186–88.

29. FLO to HWB, Sept. 29, 1861, below.

30. FLO to HWB, Aug. 16, 1861, below; FLO to John S. Newberry, Nov. 5, 1861, box 909, 1: 45; *New York World*, Nov. 8, 16, and 27, 1861.

31. *New-York Times*, Dec. 4, 1861, p. 3; ibid., Dec. 6, 1861, pp. 2–3; John H. Douglas to FLO, Dec. 11, 1861, USSC-NYPL, box 731: 1319.

32. FLO to HWB, Dec. 20, 1861, and Dec. 21, 1861, below.

33. John H. Douglas to FLO, Dec. 7, 1861, USSC-NYPL, box 731: 1279; HWB, Memorandum for General McClellan, n.d., [Dec. 7, 1861], Record Group 393, Records of U.S. Army Continental Commands, 1821–1920, Army of the Potomac, Scrapbooks of Telegrams and Letters Sent and Received, vol. 32, National Archives and Record Service, Washington, D.C.; *Congressional Globe*, 37th Cong., 2nd sess., 1861–62, 40: 37; William A. Hammond to HWB, Nov. 26, 1861, USSC-NYPL, box 640; "An Act for the Reorganization of the Medical Department of the Army," n.d., [c. Nov.–Dec., 1861], Alexander Dallas Bache Papers, Library of Congress, Washington, D.C.

34. FLO to Thomas A. Scott, Dec. 9, 1861, USSC-NYPL, box 833, 2: 85; William A. Hammond to FLO, Dec. 13, 1861, USSC-NYPL, box 731: 1343; FLO to HWB, Jan. 18, 1862, below.

35. FLO to HWB, Jan. 18, 1862, USSC-NYPL, box 641.

36. Ibid.; William A. Hammond to FLO, Jan. 29, 1862, USSC-NYPL, box 738: 258; *Congressional Globe*, 37th Cong., 2nd sess., 1861–62, 40: 172, 364.

37. FLO to Edward Hartshorne, Feb. 5, 1862, USSC-NYPL, box 833, 2: 560–62; HWB to FLO, Feb. 17, 1862, USSC-NYPL, box 739: 427; GTS to FLO, Feb. 17, 1862, USSC-NYPL, box 739: 424; FLO to HWB, Feb. 7, 1862, below.

38. *Congressional Globe*, 37th Cong., 2nd sess., 1861–62, 40: 1166, 1193, 1268–73, 1583–88; HWB to FLO, March 4, 1862, USSC-NYPL, box 739: 525.

39. FLO to HWB, Sept. 1, 1863, below.

40. FLO to Charles J. Stillé, April 18, 1862, USSC-NYPL, box 834, 1: 277–79; *Diary of the Civil War*, p. 218; W. Q. Maxwell, *Lincoln's Fifth Wheel*, pp. 137–38; HWB to William Van Buren, May 13, 1862, USSC-NYPL, box 638.

41. FLO to Manton M. Marble, Feb. 16, 1862, below; FLO to Edwin M. Stanton, [April 13, 1862], below.

42. Willie Lee Rose, *Rehearsal for Reconstruction: The Port Royal Experiment* (Indianapolis, Ind., 1964), pp. 17–44.

43. FLO to Bertha Olmsted, Jan. 28, 1862, below; FLO to Lafayette S. Foster, Feb. 3, 1862, USSC-NYPL, box 833, 2: 547–53; *Congressional Globe*, 37th Cong., 2nd sess., 1861–62, 40: 505, 815.

44. U.S. Congress, Senate, *Index to the Bills and Resolutions of the Senate of the United States, for the Thirty-Seventh Congress. 1861-'62-'63* (Washington, D.C., 1863).

45. Frederick Law Olmsted, *A Journey in the Seaboard Slave States, With Remarks on Their Economy* (New York, 1856), pp. 443–44.

46. FLO to James R. Spalding, Feb. 15, 1862, below.

47. FLO to Manton M. Marble, Feb. 16, 1862, below; *New York World*, Feb. 19, 1862, p. 4; FLO to JO, Feb. 19, 1862; [FLO], "Petition of John Olmsted & 75 Other Citizens of Hartford Conn.," Feb. 22, 1862, Record Group 46, Records of the House of Representatives, HR 37A, 68.18, National Archives; FLO to Edward E. Hale, Feb. 18, 1862, Edward Everett Hale Papers, New York State Library, Albany, N.Y.; Charles Trask to FLO, March 5, 1862.

48. FLO to HWB, Feb. 25, 1862, USSC-NYPL, box 641; Francis G. Shaw to FLO, March 7, 1862; FLO to Edwin M. Stanton, [April 13, 1862], below; Salmon P. Chase to FLO, March 13, 1862.

49. FLO to HWB, March 15, 1862, USSC-NYPL, box 641; FLO to Henry H. Elliott, [Aug. 27, 1860] (*Papers of FLO*, 3: 259–69); FLO to Edwin M. Stanton, [April 13, 1862], below.

50. FLO to Salmon P. Chase, March 15, 1862, below; FLO to Edwin M. Stanton, [April 13, 1862], below.

51. FLO to HWB, March 15, 1862, USSC-NYPL, box 641; *Papers of FLO*, 3: 15, 89; *Forty Years*, pp. 125–26. Although in his reminiscences Olmsted did not give the date of these incidents, they must have occurred when he visited New York City late in March 1862. Although the mayor again nominated him for the post of street commissioner in the autumn of 1862, Olmsted did not visit New York City at that time.

52. J. W. Edmonds to FLO, March 22, 1862; FLO to Edwin M. Stanton, [April 13, 1862], below; W. L. Rose, *Rehearsal for Reconstruction*, pp. 36–42, 152–54; FLO to JO, April 19, 1862, below.

53. FLO to F. G. Shaw, May 5, 1864, William P. Palmer Papers, Western Reserve Historical Society, Cleveland, Ohio; Edwin L. Godkin to FLO, April 2, 1865, and FLO to Edwin L. Godkin, [c. May 1–8], 1865, Edwin Lawrence Godkin Papers, Houghton Library, Harvard University, Cambridge, Mass.; FLO to J. M. McKim, Sept. 7, 1865. During the postwar years Olmsted served as an officer of the Southern Famine Relief Commission, but this was a humanitarian effort to alleviate hunger among blacks and whites in the South.

54. The connection between the civil rights and political independence of the freedmen and their acquisition of land has long interested historians. See, for example, LaWanda Cox, "The Promise of Land for the Freedmen," *Mississippi Valley Historical Review* 45 (Dec. 1958): 413–40; Herman Belz, "The New Orthodoxy in Reconstruction Historiography," *Reviews in American History* 1 (March 1973): 106–13.

55. FLO to Edwin M. Stanton, [April 13, 1862], below; "The South no. 48" (*Papers of FLO*, 2: 264, 265); FLO, "Testimony before the Special Inquiry Commission," April 22, 1863, below; FLO to S. G. Howe, Aug. 13, 1863, below. For a more optimistic assessment of Olmsted's plans for Port Royal, see Laura Wood Roper, "Frederick Law Olmsted and the Port Royal Experiment," *Journal of Southern History* 31 (Aug. 1965): 272–84.

56. Hospital ships had been provided by the Western Sanitary Commission or by branch societies of the U.S. Commission after the battles of Fort Donelson and Shiloh. Jacob Gilbert Forman, *The Western Sanitary Commission; A Sketch of Its Origins, History* . . . (St. Louis, Mo., 1864), pp. 24–25, 42–45; John Strong Newberry, *The U.S. Sanitary Commission in the Valley of the Mississippi, during the War of the Rebellion, 1861–1866* (Cleveland, Ohio, 1871), pp. 28–29, 34–38; JFJ to George B. McClellan, March 29, 1862, Record Group 393, Records of U.S. Army Continental Commands, 1821–1920, Army of the Potomac, Letters Received (S-400-1862), National Archives; FLO to Montgomery C. Meigs, April 19, 1862, Record Group 92, Records of the Office of the Quartermaster General, entry 20, Letters Received, box 86 (960-s-1862), National Archives; FLO to Charles J. Stillé, April 25, 1862, USSC-NYPL, box 590: 61; FLO to Edwin M. Stanton, April 26, 1862, USSC-NYPL, box 742: 1228.

57. FLO to HWB, May 4, 1862, USSC-NYPL, box 641; JFJ to FLO, May 5, 1862, USSC-NYPL, box 741: 940; FLO to Jedediah H. Baxter, May 28, 1862, USSC-NYPL, box 741: 1172; FLO to HWB, May 2, 1862, USSC-NYPL, box 641; FLO to JFJ, May 29, 1862, below.

58. FLO to HWB, May 15, 1862, below; FLO to HWB, June 18, 1862, below; *Hospital Transports*, p. 132.

59. *Hospital Transports*, pp. 36–37, 45–48, 61–67; FLO to JFJ, May 25, 1862, below. For general overviews of women's nursing service during the Peninsula campaign, see Marjorie Latta Greenbie, *Lincoln's Daughters of Mercy* (New York, 1944), pp. 124–88; and Mary Elizabeth Massey, *Bonnet Brigades* (New York, 1966), pp. 43–66.

60. FLO to JFJ, May 3, 1862, below.

61. FLO to HWB, May 15, 1862, below; FLO to JFJ, May 21, 1862, below.

62. FLO and Charles S. Tripler to USSC, May 18, 1862, USSC-NYPL, box 741: 1066; FLO, "Plan of Action Approved by Dr. Tripler," May 20, 1862, USSC-NYPL, box 741: 1096; William A. Hammond to Charles S. Tripler, May 19, 1862, Record Group 112, Records of the Office of the Surgeon General, letterbook 30, pp. 467–68, National Archives; FLO to JFJ, May 20, 1862, below.

63. FLO to HWB, June 3, 1862, below; Charles S. Tripler to FLO, June 2, 1862, Record Group 393, Records of the U.S. Army Continental Commands, 1821–1920, Army of the Potomac, Letters and Telegrams Sent and Received, vol. 36 (old bk. 37), National Archives.

64. FLO to HWB, June 3, 1862, below; FLO to HWB, June 18, 1862, below; FLO to HWB, June 30, 1862, USSC-NYPL, box 743: 1685.

65. FLO to William A. Hammond, June 17, 1862; FLO to CLB, [June 29, 1862], below.

66. FLO to MPO, July 3, 1862, below; FLO to HWB, July 5, 1862, USSC-NYPL, box 744: 1894; FLO to Abraham Lincoln, July 6, 1862, below; FLO to Preston King, July 9, 1862, below; FLO to Sydney H. Gay, July 12, 1862, below.

67. A. D. Bache to HWB, July 7, 1862, USSC-NYPL, box 640; HWB to FLO, July 19, 1862, USSC-NYPL, box 744: 1940; GTS to HWB, July 17, 1862, USSC-NYPL, box 642; FLO to HWB, July 13, 1862, below.

68. FLO to JO, July 25, 1862; FLO to JFJ, Aug. 6, 1862, USSC-NYPL, box 743: 1776; FLO to JSN, Aug. 21, 1862, below.

69. FLO to MPO, Aug. 30, 1862; FLO to JFJ, Aug. 31, 1862, USSC-NYPL, box 744: 2093.

70. USSC, *Minutes*, pp. 98–99; FLO to MPO, Sept. 21, 1862, below.

71. FLO to MPO, Aug. 4, 1862; FLO to HWB, Aug. 20, 1862, USSC-NYPL, box 641; FLO to MPO, Sept. 21, 1862, below; *Diary of the Civil War*, pp. 256–59; doc. no. 56 in USSC, *Documents*; FLO to HWB, Oct. 13, 1862, USSC-NYPL, box 641.

72. J. G. Forman, *Western Sanitary Commission*, pp. 10–11; Robert Collyer to FLO, Oct. 24, 1861, USSC-NYPL, box 729; FLO to JSN, Nov. 16, 1861, below.

73. FLO to George F. Magoun, Feb. 6, 1862, below.

74. Louisa L. Schuyler to FLO, Dec. 22, 1862, USSC-NYPL, box 667: 1–5; FLO to HWB, Oct. 7, 1862, below; FLO to HWB, Nov. [24], 1862, below.

75. Doc. nos. 50 and 60 in USSC, *Documents*.

76. T. S. King to HWB, Sept. 18, 1862, Henry Whitney Bellows Papers, Massachusetts Historical Society, Boston, Mass.; C. J. Stillé, *History of the United States Sanitary Commission*, pp. 214–23.

77. J. S. Newberry, *U.S. Sanitary Commission*, pp. 218–29, 251–81, 299–310; see, for example, FLO to JSN, Oct. 11, 1862, below.

78. Henry Teschemacher to HWB and GTS, Sept. 19, 1862, Henry Whitney Bellows Papers, Massachusetts Historical Society, Boston, Mass.; HWB to James Yeatman, Sept. 28, 1862, USSC-NYPL, box 608: 390; T. S. King to HWB, Nov. 24, 1862, Henry Whitney Bellows Papers, Massachusetts Historical Society, Boston, Mass.; C. J. Stillé, *History of the United States Sanitary Commission*, pp. 201–3, 214–23.

79. Doc. no. 60 in USSC, *Documents*; George Hoadly to HWB, Nov. 5, 1862, USSC-NYPL, box 640.

80. HWB to George Hoadly, Oct. 28, 1862, USSC-NYPL, box 638; George Hoadly to HWB, Nov. 5, 1862, USSC-NYPL, box 640.

81. Doc. no. 60 in USSC, *Documents*.

82. FLO to JSN, Feb. 24, 1862, below; Oct. 16, 1862, USSC-NYPL, box 914, 1: 154; and Dec. 8, 1862, USSC-NYPL, box 914, 1: 295.

83. JSN to FLO, Feb. 10, 1863, USSC-NYPL, box 756: 380; USSC, *Minutes*, pp. 117–18, 130–31. For an account of later activities of the Cincinnati branch, consult Charles Brandon Boynton, comp., *History of the Great Western Sanitary Fair* (Cincinnati, 1864).

84. FLO to CLB, Aug. 25, Sept. 20, and Oct. 4, 1862, below; CLB to FLO, Sept. 12 and Oct. 1, 1862, below.

85. For related information on how governmental officials and congressmen viewed the problem of loyalty and sought to punish disloyalty within their departments, see Harold M. Hyman, *Era of the Oath: Northern Loyalty Tests during the Civil War and Reconstruction* (Philadelphia, 1954), pp. 1–32; and idem, *To Try Men's Souls: Loyalty Tests in American History* (Berkeley, Ca., 1959), pp. 139–66.

86. FLO to Oliver W. Gibbs, Nov. 5, 1862, below.

87. Guy Gibson, "Lincoln's League: The Union League Movement during the Civil War" (Ph.D. diss., University of Illinois, 1958), pp. 37–50; FLO to Oliver W. Gibbs, Jan. 31, 1863, below.

88. G. Gibson, "Lincoln's League," pp. 37–50; Oliver W. Gibbs to FLO, Feb. 8, 1863, USSC-NYPL, box 756: 357; Henry W. Bellows, *Historical Sketch of the Union League Club of New York, Its Origin, Organization, and Work, 1863–1879* (New York, 1879), pp. 21–26; *Diary of the Civil War*, p. 302.

89. Oliver W. Gibbs to FLO, Feb. 8, 1863, USSC-NYPL, box 756: 357. An account which sees a greater connection between Olmsted's plans and the actual organization of the Union League Club is found in Laura Wood Roper, *FLO: A Biography of Frederick Law Olmsted* (Baltimore, 1973), pp. 214–15.

90. Oliver W. Gibbs to FLO, Feb. 8, 1863, USSC-NYPL, box 756: 357; FLO to Oliver W. Gibbs, Jan. 31, 1863, below; FLO to Charles E. Norton, April 30, 1863, below; George Winston Smith, "Broadsides for Freedom: Civil War Propaganda in New England," *New England Quarterly* 21 (Sept. 1948): 292–97.

91. FLO to Charles J. Stillé, Feb. 25, 1863, below.

92. See, for example, *Papers of FLO*, 2: 6–8, 13–16, 29–30.
93. FLO to HWB, July 4, 1863, below.
94. Alfred Field to Charlotte Field, June 2, 1861.
95. FLO to William H. Hurlbert, Jan. 31, 1863, below; FLO to Charles E. Norton, April 30, 1863, below.
96. FLO to Charles E. Norton, April 30, 1863, below.
97. FLO to HWB, Oct. 3, 1862, below; FLO to GTS, Dec. 6, 1862, below.
98. FLO to HWB, Oct. 3, 1862, below; FLO to Arthur T. Edwards, Aug. 7, [1855] (*Papers of FLO*, 2: 357–60).
99. FLO to HWB, Oct. 7, 1862, below.
100. FLO to HWB, Oct. 3, 1862, below; FLO to the Board of Commissioners of the Central Park, Jan. 22, 1861 (*Papers of FLO*, 3: 297–319, 34–36).
101. FLO to HWB, Nov. [24], 1862, below; HWB to FLO, Nov. 29, 1862, USSC-NYPL, box 747: 2886; GTS to FLO, Dec. 6, 1862, USSC-NYPL, box 747: 2951.
102. FLO to HWB, Dec. 10, 1862, below; HWB to FLO, Dec. 9, 1862, USSC-NYPL, box 747: 2973.
103. FLO to JSN, Nov. 5, 1862, below.
104. FLO to HWB, Oct. 7, 1862, below; USSC, *Minutes*, p. 134.
105. FLO to HWB, Dec. 27, 1862, below; FLO to MPO, Oct. 11, 1862, below; *Diary of the Civil War*, p. 291; FLO to HWB, Jan. 13, 1863, below.
106. FLO to HWB, Feb. 4, 1863, below; Cornelius R. Agnew to FLO, Feb. 15, 1863; HWB to FLO, Feb. 11, 1863.
107. FLO to USSC, March 4, 1863, USSC-NYPL, box 757: 657; FLO to MPO, Feb. 28, 1863; FLO to MPO, March 8, 1863, below; FLO to JO, April 1, 1863, below; FLO to Mark Skinner, April 24, 1863.
108. FLO to Ulysses S. Grant, April 21, 1863; FLO to James E. Yeatman, April 21, 1863; FLO to JO, April 1, 1863, below.
109. FLO to HWB, Feb. 4, 1863, below; HWB to JSN, March 10, 1863, USSC-NYPL, box 611: 1744; HWB to John H. Heywood, March 10, 1863, USSC-NYPL, box 611: 1740; *Diary of the Civil War*, pp. 304–5. Like Bellows, Strong compared Olmsted to Gregory VII, the eleventh-century pope who emphasized the superiority of the papacy over the state and asserted his own omnipotence in church affairs.
110. "Journey in the West, Cincinnati," March 1, 1863; "Journey in the West, Nashville to Murfreesboro," March 7, 1863; "Journey in the West, Memphis to Young's Point," March 16–24, 1863; "Journey in the West, Louisville toward Cairo," March 13, 1863; "Journey in the West, St. Louis, Chicago," April 4–11, 1863; all below.
111. "Journey in the West, St. Louis, Chicago," April 4–11, 1863, below.
112. "Journey in the West, Cincinnati," March 1, 1863, below; FLO to MPO, Sept. 28, 1861, below; "Journey in the West, St. Louis, Chicago," April 4–11, 1863, below; FLO to CLB, Dec. 1, 1853 (*Papers of FLO*, 2: 235).
113. FLO to CLB, Dec. 1, 1853 (*Papers of FLO*, 2: 235); "Journey in the West, Memphis to Young's Point," March 16–24, 1863, below.
114. FLO to Edwin L. Godkin, April 4, 1863, below; "Journey in the West, Nashville to Murfreesboro," March 7, 1863, below; "Journey in the West, Memphis to Young's Point," March 16–24, 1863, below.
115. *Papers of FLO*, 1: 72–74; 2: 15–16, 20, 26, 34.
116. FLO to John Jay, June 30, 1859, Jay Family Papers, Rare Books and Manuscripts, Butler Library, Columbia University, New York City; FLO to Frederick N. Knapp, July 7, 1864, and Dec. 13 and Dec. 16, 1867. None of these statistical forms—completed or uncompleted—has survived, although Olmsted kept them until his death. In 1904 his son Frederick Law Olmsted, Jr., gave them to a renowned library, which then declared them worthless and, after gaining the family's permission, destroyed them.

117. *Official Records*, ser. 3, vol. 2, p. 947; FLO to JSN, Dec. 27, 1862, below; *Diary of the Civil War*, p. 306.
118. *United States Christian Commission, Facts, Principles and Progress* (Philadelphia, 1863), pp. 7–13; FLO to the Executive Committee of the USSC, July 9, 1863, below. The poet Walt Whitman perhaps best summed up this dislike of the paid workers of the Sanitary Commission in a letter to his mother: "You ought to see the way the men, as they lay helpless in bed, turn away their faces from the sight of those agents, chaplains, etc (hirelings as Elias Hicks would call them—they seem to me always a set of foxes and wolves). They get paid, and are always incompetent and disagreeable; as I told you before, the only good fellows I have met are the Christian commissioners—they go everywhere and receive no pay." Walt Whitman, *The Wound Dresser: A Series of Letters Written from the Hospitals in Washington During the War of the Rebellion*, ed. Richard Maurice Bucke (Boston, 1898), pp. 86–87. This distaste for professional "hirelings" was widespread among nineteenth-century Americans, who sometimes viewed professional men, such as doctors and lawyers, in such a light. However, the anti-aristocratic bias toward the latter groups may not have existed toward relief agents. See Daniel Hovey Calhoun, *Professional Lives in America: Structure and Aspiration, 1750–1850* (Cambridge, Mass., 1965), pp. 1–19, 178–197.
119. GTS to FLO, Dec. 5, 1862, USSC-NYPL, box 747: 2944; FLO to GTS, Dec. 6. 1862, below; FLO to HWB, May 25, 1863.
120. Cornelius R. Agnew to FLO, Feb. 10, 1863, USSC-NYPL., box 756: 382; Cornelius R. Agnew to FLO, Feb. 15 and April 24, 1863.
121. FLO to HWB, April 25, 1863, below; FLO to Cornelius R. Agnew, April 25, 1863; FLO to HWB, April 25, 1863, USSC-NYPL, box 641.
122. FLO to CV, Feb. 16, 1863, below; CV and FLO to the Board of Commissioners of the Central Park, May 12, 1863; *Papers of FLO*, 3: 37–38.
123. FLO to JO, July 25, 1862; April 18, April 25, May 2, and May 22, 1863; all below. After his father's death, Olmsted wrote Frederick Kingsbury on January 28, 1873:

> I am glad to think that the real loveliness of his character had not been unrecognized though so much veiled by the habits into which his extreme diffidence led him. He was a very good man and a kinder father never lived. It is strange how much of the world I feel now gone from me with him. The value of any success in the future is gone for me.

124. FLO to Edwin L. Godkin, April 4, 1863, below; Edwin L. Godkin to FLO, May 9, 1863; FLO and Edwin L. Godkin, "Prospectus for a Weekly Journal," [c. June 25, 1863], below; *Papers of FLO*, 2: 23, 350–51. The maneuverings in 1865 that led to the actual publication of the *Nation* that year under Godkin's editorship may be followed in William M. Armstrong, "The Freedmen's Movement and the Founding of the *Nation*," *Journal of American History* 53 (March 1967): 708–26.
125. FLO to CLB, Dec. 1, 1853, and FLO, "Plan of Weekly Magazine" (*Papers of FLO*, 2: 236, 350–51); FLO to MPO, July 2, 1863; FLO to Edwin L. Godkin, July 19, 1863, below.
126. FLO to MPO, June 26 and July 7, 1863, below; HWB to FLO, July 23, 1863; FLO to Edwin L. Godkin, July 19, 1863, below; FLO to HWB, July 28, 1863, below.
127. Doc. nos. 61 and 66 in USSC, *Documents*; USSC, *Minutes*, pp. 138–39; FLO to MPO, June 26, 1863, below; John H. Heywood to HWB, June 23, 1863, USSC-NYPL, box 640; HWB to JSN, June 24, 1863, USSC-NYPL, box 710, 1: 10–17.
128. FLO to James T. Fields, June 13, 1863, James Thomas Fields Papers, Huntingdon Library, San Marino, Ca.; FLO to HWB, May 25, 1863; John H. Douglas to Executive Committee of USSC, June 3, 1863; FLO to HWB, July 25, 1863, below.
129. FLO to Edwin L. Godkin, Aug. 1, 1863; FLO to JO, Aug. 10, 1863; FLO to MPO, Aug. 12, 1863; FLO to HWB, Aug. 15 and Aug. 16, 1863; all below.

130. FLO to HWB, Sept. 1, 1863, below.
131. FLO to CLB, Dec. 21, 1863; FLO to Edwin L. Godkin, Dec. 25, 1863, Edwin Lawrence Godkin Papers, Houghton Library, Harvard University, Cambridge, Mass.
132. USSC, *Minutes*, pp. 149–54; W. Q. Maxwell, *Lincoln's Fifth Wheel*, pp. 224–27; *Diary of the Civil War*, pp. 490, 492–93, 535, 567–68, 590; Thomas Hill to FLO, July 20, 1864, University Archives, Harvard University, Cambridge, Mass.
133. Foster Rhea Dulles, *The American Red Cross: A History* (New York, 1950), pp. 6–21; Walter Donald Kring, *Henry Whitney Bellows* (Boston, 1979), pp. 463–64; W. Q. Maxwell, *Lincoln's Fifth Wheel*, pp. 224–27.

EDITORIAL POLICY

The purpose of the Frederick Law Olmsted Papers project is to publish, in annotated form, the most significant of Olmsted's letters, unpublished writings, professional reports, and articles for newspapers and periodicals. The letterpress edition will consist of twelve volumes: ten volumes arranged chronologically, one volume containing major documents on park design and city planning, and one large-format volume of plans and views of landscape designs.

Document Selection Although the process of choosing documents for a selected edition of papers is to some extent subjective, the editors require every document published to meet at least one of three criteria: that it provide insight into Olmsted's character, present valuable commentary on his times, or contain an important statement on landscape design.

Annotation Since Olmsted's most revealing letters in this period were usually written either to colleagues or family members conversant with Sanitary Commission affairs and the course of the Civil War, annotation is frequently needed to explain to the modern reader what was obvious to Olmsted's correspondents. In general the editors give only skeletal outlines of major events such as the battles of Bull Run and Gettysburg and of major figures such as Charles Sumner or William Tecumseh Sherman, since further information is readily available elsewhere for the reader. When, however, Olmsted or the Sanitary Commission had a significant relationship with such an important figure or event, the relationship is discussed. For lesser-known people and events, the editors provide basic information and cite the relevant sources. Annotation of this sort is fullest for Olmsted's close friends or collaborators, other Sanitary Commission workers, and Sanitary Commission policies and activities. Such information, available in the Olmsted Papers, the numerous publications of the Sanitary Commission, and the one thousand boxes of the Commission's papers in the New York Public Library, is difficult for either the experienced scholar or interested reader to retrieve, and the editors believe discoveries in these vast collections should be shared with our audience. The fact that the only book-length study of the Sanitary Commission, William Quentin Maxwell's stimulating *Lincoln's Fifth Wheel*, does not provide citations for most of its information and interpretations increases our sense of obligation to explain such references. The editors also provide annotation explaining elliptical comments and obscure references.

Treatment of Text The intent of the editors is to provide a text as close to the original as possible without causing undue difficulty for the reader. This means that we reproduce most of Olmsted's inconsistencies of spelling, capitalization, and punctuation. We occasionally alter the original text in the interest of clarity: in such cases, we furnish guides to our alterations that permit recovery of the original text.

The complete existing text of each document is published. All of the words that Olmsted wrote and did not cross out are presented, with the exception of inadvertently repeated words. The treatment of illegible and missing words is as follows:

> [. . .] indicates illegible words or words missing because of mutilation of the manuscript.
> [*italic*] indicates the editors' reading of partially missing words.
> [roman] indicates a word supplied by the editors.

Where needed, these brackets are supplemented by an explanatory endnote. In those rare instances where Olmsted himself used brackets, they are so identified in an endnote.

In the occasional instance where a passage does not make sense without substitution of a word or words for those in the original version, the editors make the needed substitution and supply the original wording in an endnote. When the word that Olmsted wrote appears not to be the one he meant to write and the correct word cannot be discerned, the editors suggest, in an endnote, an alternate word or phrase that seems closer to Olmsted's meaning. Where the document is not in Olmsted's hand and what appears to be incorrect wording may be due to the error of a transcriber or typesetter, one of these two approaches is also used.

The published texts include words and phrases deleted by Olmsted only when they add material that does not appear at some other point in the document. If they are integral to the document, such deleted words are presented in the text in italics and in brackets. If the deleted words are less directly relevant to the theme of the document, they are given in an endnote.

The principles of transcription stated here are applied by the editors to all kinds of documents, including drafts of articles and lectures that exist in "fair copy" as well as fragmentary drafts. When preparing a text from manuscript fragments that have no clear order, the editors construct a text, adding such indications as endnotes, extra spaces between lines of text, dividing lines, ellipses, and editors' headings, to mark the transition from one segment of the original text to another. When a document exists in both printed and manuscript form, and (as with park reports) Olmsted wrote the document for publication, the most complete version is used as the basic text. If the other version or versions contain significant variations from that text, the differences are described and quoted in notes added at appropriate places in the document. The first, unnumbered endnote to the document explains the textual treatment in such cases.

For manuscripts that were published at a later date, the original version is used as the basic text. Differences between the two versions that appear to be printer's or transcriber's errors are noted in endnotes, as are changes apparently made by Olmsted for the published version; obvious typographical errors, such as wrong, missing, or transposed letters, are silently corrected when a published version of a document is being used as the text.

At the end of this volume the editors provide a list of textual alterations, giving the original form of texts or quoted material where a change has not been indicated in endnotes or by brackets in the text. The list indicates the original form of contractions that have been expanded. It gives each deleted or altered punctuation mark with the word preceding and the word following it, and indicates added punctuation by giving the words preceding and following it. The list indicates the original form of misspelled words that have been corrected in the text, except as noted below.

Spelling   Olmsted consistently misspelled words with double consonants (as "dissapoint" for "disappoint"). He frequently misspelled words with double vowels (consistently writing "lose" as "loose"), and he misspelled words with the diphthong "ie" (as "cheif" for "chief"). The editors silently correct these three kinds of Olmsted's misspellings. All other misspelled words are presented in the text as Olmsted wrote them. If the misspelling makes a word particularly difficult to interpret, however, it is corrected and its misspelled form is presented in the list of textual alterations.

Paragraphing   The editors follow Olmsted's indications of internal paragraphing. Where he indicated a paragraph by a long dash or a large space between sentences, we silently make a new paragraph. We do the same when he inserted a paragraph symbol or where a change in subject matter between two pages of manuscript indicates that he used the page change as a paragraph. Sections of conversations are silently rendered as paragraphs. Other paragraphing introduced by editors is indicated in the list of textual alterations.

Contractions The editors present the original form of abbreviations and contractions. Superscripts are reproduced. Apostrophes are silently added if they are missing from the contraction "nt" (for "not"), from conjugations of the verb "to be," and from possessives. Particularly awkward or unclear contractions are expanded and the original form is indicated in the list of textual alterations.

Punctuation The editors do not regularize Olmsted's punctuation or make it consistently grammatical; but we do make changes in his punctuation when it would be time-consuming for the reader to work out the meaning of a passage in its original form. In long and convoluted sentences, or where the original text is likely to cause the reader to misread phrases, the editors alter punctuation. We occasionally delete punctuation where it unnecessarily complicates already difficult passages, and we add punctuation in order to clarify basic sentence structure. These changes are not indicated in the text itself by brackets or other symbols, since that would introduce new distractions and complexity at the very place where they would be most troublesome. Instead, the changes are given in the list of textual alterations. We silently supply periods where the end of a line served for Olmsted as the end of a sentence.

Marginalia Material that Olmsted added in the margins is inserted at the point where he indicated that it belongs. If such material has no clear place within the text, it is printed at the end of the document with an explanatory note. Notes or jottings on a document by other persons are not included in the text, but if informative are given in an endnote. Olmsted's infrequent footnotes are presented at the bottom of the page.

Place and Date of Documents Dates for documents are given as they appear in the original. If that information is partial, incorrect, or missing, the probable date or time period is supplied in brackets, with an explanatory endnote if needed. Printed letterheads that are misleading are not reproduced but are noted in the first, unnumbered endnote of the letter.

Arrangement of Documents Documents are presented in chronological order except for occasional pieces such as autobiographical fragments or reminiscences written at a later time than the period covered in the volume. Such pieces are presented with the documents from the period they describe.

Citation of Sources Full bibliographical information is provided in the first citation of a source in each chapter, except for sources that appear in a volume's list of "Short Titles Used in Citations." These are cited consistently by short title throughout the volume. A full listing of sources about an individual is given in the note accompanying the first mention of that person in the documents of a volume. In subsequent references, sources are given only for additional information supplied. Birth and death dates for persons mentioned in the text of the documents are given in the first note identifying them and, for selected persons, in the index.

If no repository is given for a manuscript, this means that it may be found in the Frederick Law Olmsted Papers, Manuscript Division, Library of Congress, Washington, D.C.

SHORT TITLES
USED IN CITATIONS

1. Correspondents' Names

   CLB   Charles Loring Brace
   CV   Calvert Vaux
   FLO   Frederick Law Olmsted
   GTS   George Templeton Strong
   HWB   Henry Whitney Bellows
   JFJ   John Foster Jenkins
   JO   John Olmsted
   JSN   John Strong Newberry
   MPO   Mary Perkins Olmsted
   USSC   United States Sanitary Commission

2. Standard References

   BDAC   *Biographical Directory of the American Congress, 1774–1971*
   DAB   *Dictionary of American Biography*
   DNB   *Dictionary of National Biography*
   EB   *Encylopaedia Britannica*, 14th ed.
   NCAB   *National Cyclopaedia of American Biography*
   OED   *Oxford English Dictionary*

3. Books by Frederick Law Olmsted

   Back Country (BC in citations)   *A Journey in the Back Country* . . . (New
      York, 1860).

Cotton Kingdom   *The Cotton Kingdom; A Traveller's Observations on Cotton and Slavery in the American Slave States. Based upon Three Former Volumes of Journeys and Investigations by the Same Author. Edited, with an introduction, by Arthur M. Schlesinger* (New York, 1953).

Hospital Transports   *Hospital Transports. A Memoir of the Embarkation of the Sick and Wounded from the Peninsula of Virginia in the Summer of 1862* (Boston, 1863).

4. Other Published Works

Appleton's Cyc. Am. Biog.   *Appleton's Cyclopedia of American Biography*, ed. James G. Wilson and John Fiske (New York, 1887–89).

Diary of the Civil War   George Templeton Strong, *Diary of the Civil War, 1860–1865*, ed. Allan Nevins (New York, 1962).

Notable American Women   *Notable American Women, 1607–1950: A Biographical Directory*, ed. Edward T. James, 3 vols. (Cambridge, Mass., 1971).

Official Records (O.R. in citations)   U.S. War Department, *The War of the Rebellion: A Compilation of the Official Records of the Union and Confederate Armies*, 70 vols. in 128 (Washington, D.C., 1880–1901).

Olmsted Genealogy   Henry K. Olmsted and George K. Ward, comps., *Genealogy of the Olmsted Family in America Embracing the Descendants of James and Richard Olmsted and Covering a Period of Nearly Three Centuries, 1632–1912* (New York, 1912).

Papers of FLO   *The Papers of Frederick Law Olmsted*, ed. Charles C. McLaughlin et al. (Baltimore, 1977–).

USSC, *Documents*   *Documents of the U.S. Sanitary Commission*, 2 vols. (New York, 1866).

USSC, *Minutes*   *Minutes of the U.S. Sanitary Commission* (Washington, D.C., 1865).

War for the Union   Allan Nevins, *The War for the Union*, vol. 1, *The Improvised War, 1861–1862*; vol. 2, *War Becomes Revolution, 1862–1863*; vol. 3, *The Organized War, 1863–1864*; vol. 4, *The Organized War to Victory, 1864–1865* (New York, 1959–71).

Yale Obit. Rec.   Yale University, *Obituary Record of Graduates of Yale University* (New Haven, [1860–]).

5. Unpublished Sources

Bloor Diary   A manuscript diary by Alfred Janson Bloor from 1848 to 1867, in the Alfred Janson Bloor Papers, New-York Historical Society, New York City.

JO Journal   A manuscript journal and domestic account book kept by John Olmsted from 1836 to 1873 and continued until 1888 by his widow, Mary Ann Bull Olmsted. Three volumes, in the Frederick Law Olmsted Papers, Manuscript Division, Library of Congress, Washington, D.C.

USSC-NYPL   United States Sanitary Commission Records, a series of approximately 1,180 boxes, in the Manuscripts and Archives Division, Rare Book & Manuscripts Division, The New York Public Library, Astor, Lenox and Tilden Foundations, New York City.

BIOGRAPHICAL DIRECTORY

CORNELIUS REA AGNEW (1830–1888) was a member of the Executive Committee of the U.S. Sanitary Commission and one of Olmsted's chief critics. The son of a wealthy New York City merchant, Agnew graduated from Columbia College, studied medicine in the office of well-known physician J. Kearney Rogers, and received his medical degree in 1852 from the College of Physicians and Surgeons in New York. After studying abroad in Dublin, London, and Paris, he practiced medicine in New York City and served as surgeon to the eye and ear infirmary there. In 1858 the governor of New York appointed him surgeon general of the state militia, a position he held through the war.

Upon his election to the Sanitary Commission in the summer of 1861, Agnew quickly became a dedicated and hard-working member. That fall he wrote articles critical of the surgeon general and convinced his friend Manton Marble, editor of the *New York World*, to publicize the inadequacies of the army's Medical Bureau. In 1862 Agnew sailed to the Virginia Peninsula in the first hospital ship staffed by the Sanitary Commission. He also helped supervise the Commission's aid to soldiers wounded during the battle of Antietam.

For well over a year, relations between Olmsted and Agnew were amicable. When Olmsted became seriously ill during the summer of 1862, Agnew accompanied him to the resort of Saratoga Springs and was "most kindly & closely attentive."[1] However, as Olmsted's management came under closer scrutiny by the Executive Committee in the fall and winter of 1862–63, Agnew was among those who questioned his methods. At the

CORNELIUS REA AGNEW

January 1863 meeting in which the Commission passed resolutions praising Newberry's work and ordering Olmsted to undertake a trip to the
Western department, Agnew apparently was among the members favoring
those measures. He attempted to mollify Olmsted:

> Have I offended you? If so, consider the act as having been unintentional, in
> fact as not having been done. I yield to no one in the Commission in
> personal affection for you, & am therefore greatly grieved on learning from
> Doctor Bellows that there lingered in your mind some painful recollection of
> my official behavior. If you come to New York en route for the West, remem-
> ber that my house is open for you.[2]

Despite this attempt at reconciliation, relations between the two
worsened. An allegation of drunkenness against a Sanitary Commission
employee which Agnew received from a "confidential" correspondent and
communicated to Olmsted in early February created new difficulties.
Olmsted had already learned of the problem, but because Knapp and
Jenkins believed that the offending employee deserved another chance,
had assigned him to different duties rather than fire him. Although Agnew
praised the "Christian magnanimity" that Olmsted had displayed in that

case, he continued to have doubts about whether the Commission's employees were being managed effectively. A visit to the Army of the Potomac in April 1863 convinced him that four of the Sanitary Commission employees there lacked the requisite moral character and should be discharged. He also lectured Olmsted on principles of management: "I believe, as I have always believed, that you should be a locomotive Secretary, instead of spending so much time in office work upon theoretical plans of organization. While we are theorizing at Washington about organization our agencies in the Potomac Army are rotting from neglect."[3] Although Olmsted believed Agnew's demand for the dismissal of the employees to be unfair, he submitted to the request. But it no doubt influenced his decision not to resume general superintendence of the Commission's activities.

Another difference of opinion separated Agnew and Olmsted in 1863. The physician, though urging Olmsted to assume a more direct superintendence of Sanitary Commission workers, was quite satisfied with John S. Newberry's work in the Western theater of the war. In June, Agnew credited Newberry with helping the Sanitary Commission gain ground steadily "in the respect & confidence of the western people & the best men of the army."[4] Agnew believed that Newberry's failure to file regular reports with the central office was regrettable but not particularly important. Indeed, that September he favored Newberry as Olmsted's replacement but concluded, "I shall ask Olmsted what he thinks of Newberry & purge my crude opinions by a grain or two of his ripe wisdom."[5]

In the postwar years when both Olmsted and Agnew lived in New York City, they again resumed friendly relations. Occasionally they dined together. Each also sought the other's professional advice—Agnew treating Olmsted's ocular problems and Olmsted drawing up a plan for the design of a summer colony at Montauk, Long Island, in which the physician was interested.

1. FLO to MPO, Aug. 30, 1862.
2. C. R. Agnew to FLO, Feb. 2, 1863, USSC-NYPL, box 755: 98.
3. C. R. Agnew to FLO, April 24, 1863.
4. C. R. Agnew to HWB, June 30, 1863, Henry Whitney Bellows Papers, Massachusetts Historical Society, Boston, Mass.
5. C. R. Agnew to HWB, Sept. 7, 1863, USSC-NYPL, box 638.

Additional Sources

Atkinson, William B., *The Physicians and Surgeons of the United States* (Philadelphia, 1878), pp. 485–87.
DAB.

ALEXANDER DALLAS BACHE

ALEXANDER DALLAS BACHE (1806–1867) belonged to a distinguished Pennsylvania family and was a descendant of Benjamin Franklin. Active in scientific research, he became in 1843 the superintendent of the United States Coast Survey, a position he held for the rest of his life. He served as a regent of the Smithsonian Institution and was the first president of the National Academy of Sciences. Bache also had military credentials to add to his stature: he graduated from West Point at age nineteen and spent three years in the U.S. Army.

Bache's position as vice president of the Sanitary Commission brought him into close communication with Olmsted, and a friendship eventually developed between them. In the early months of the Commission they were sometimes on opposite sides. Bache was one of the Commission members unwilling to allow publication of Olmsted's report on the demoralization of the Union soldiers at the battle of Bull Run. Moreover, Olmsted thought Bache overly sympathetic to Surgeon General Finley and Robert C. Wood in the struggle to reorganize the Medical Bureau. But in time Bache came to admire Olmsted strongly. In January 1862 he expressed this to Bellows, saying: "What a grand heart he has. Is not good-ness after all the bestest of qualities."[1] During Olmsted's campaign in 1862 to become superintendent of plantation labor at Port Royal, he called upon Bache's knowledge of Washington politics. Similarly, it was Bache who in July 1862 presented Olmsted's views of what was necessary to win the Peninsula campaign to President Lincoln.

By the end of Olmsted's tenure as secretary of the Sanitary Com-mission, Bache was one of the few members with whom his relations had not become strained. A flourishing friendship between Mary Perkins Olmsted and Nancy Bache, who summered together in 1863, and Bache's strong support for Olmsted's position, gave Bache a special place in Olmsted's estimation. The farewell letter that he sent to Bache upon resigning from the Commission has not survived, but it was so effusive that the latter rather embarrassedly replied: "Truly your note of good bye is one of the most gratifying documents that I have ever received & within this year I was made Pres^t of our National Academy of Sciences by our associates. Let me say in great sincerity—in all truth—that I did not know you cared so much for me—."[2] Although Bache had earlier declared that he too would resign if Olmsted left the Sanitary Commission, he did not take that step; but he was clearly dissatisfied with operations of the Sani-tary Commission after Olmsted resigned. "How much I miss you! The Sanitary is not the same to me anymore," Bache wrote Olmsted in 1864. Later in that letter he exclaimed, "But you see I am grumbling, & that is because Olmsted is not here to lead, & I do not see the profound ability & sagacity & consistency wh. I was perfectly willing to follow, and loyal to, to an excess *perhaps*."[3]

In 1867 and 1868 Olmsted performed one last service for his then deceased friend Bache. C. P. Patterson of the Coast Survey asked him to suggest a designer for a memorial monument for Bache's grave. Olmsted agreed and persuaded the young architect Henry Hobson Richardson to draw up the design for the memorial that was erected in the Congressional Cemetery in Washington, D.C.

1. A. D. Bache to HWB, Jan. 17, 1862, USSC-NYPL, box 638.
2. A. D. Bache to FLO, Sept. 30, 1863.
3. A. D. Bache to FLO, Feb. 26, 1864.

Additional Sources

DAB.
Henry, Joseph, "Memoir of Alexander Dallas Bache, 1806–1867," in National Acad-emy of Sciences, *Biographical Memoirs* (Washington, D.C., 1877), vol. 1, pp. 181–212.

Kowsky, Francis R., "The William Dorsheimer House: A Reflection of French Suburban Architecture in the Early Work of H. H. Richardson," *Art Bulletin* 62 (March 1980): 136.

U.S. Coast and Geodetic Survey, *Centennial Celebration of the United States Coast and Geodetic Survey, April 5 and 6, 1916* (Washington, D.C., 1916), pp. 91–95.

HENRY WHITNEY BELLOWS (1814–1882) was the founder and only president of the U.S. Sanitary Commission. He recruited Olmsted to be the Commission's general secretary and was Olmsted's main ally and confidant on the board.

Born into a wealthy old New England family (though his father's mercantile business was bankrupted in the 1830s), Bellows attended Round Hill School, the famous experimental school, and Harvard College. After graduating from Harvard Divinity School in 1837, he spent six months on a temporary pastorate in Mobile, Alabama. In 1838 he declined offers from Cincinnati and Mobile and became instead the minister of the First Congregational Church (Unitarian) in New York City.

The pastorate at the First Church, which Bellows held for over forty years, was just the position for a man of his tastes and disposition. His congregation consisted of prosperous and influential members of New York society: it included Peter Cooper, William Cullen Bryant, the George Schuyler family, and merchants Moses H. Grinnell and Jonathan Goodhue. The young minister soon courted and married Eliza Townsend, the daughter of a wealthy merchant. Bellows was an invigorating force for the New York Unitarians: under his leadership his congregation financed and erected two new edifices, the "Church of the Divine Unity" in 1845 and "All Souls Church," uptown at Union Square, in 1855, designed by Jacob Wrey Mould. Bellows also sought to steer a middle course among the various Unitarian factions, which ranged from transcendentalists to conservatives. He wished to keep Unitarianism on its reforming course but to resist the secularizing and anti-institutional aspects of the transcendentalists. One of his most famous sermons, "The Suspense of Faith," delivered in 1859, criticized malaise in his denomination and called for the creation of a sense of community. In addition to emphasizing liturgy and institutional coherence, Bellows also wished to create a national movement that would link all the liberal Christian denominations. Although during the postwar period Bellows redoubled his efforts, ultimately he achieved little success in uniting Unitarians or forging a liberal Christian alliance.

From his post at the First Church, Bellows took an active interest in the reform movements of the day and in the intellectual life of New

HENRY WHITNEY BELLOWS

York City. A founding member of the literary Century Club, he occasionally wrote articles and travel accounts and delivered public lectures. Bellows supported causes ranging from the Women's Protective Association, which helped unemployed young women emigrate to the West, to postwar civil service reform. In 1857 he presented a series of twelve Lowell Lectures in Boston entitled "The Treatment of Social Diseases," speaking on such social problems as poverty, crime, and alcoholism. While admitting that these problems sprang in part from personal weaknesses, he still emphasized the role society could play in ameliorating them. He declared:

84

"The true view of poverty is that which considers it as an evil to be extinguished. The true charity of a nation, therefore, lies in equal laws, social rights, popular education and protective legislation." Linking crime and alcoholism, he further argued that "better wages, cheap food, cheap fuel and light are enormous lesseners of crime."[1] And in 1865, when he foresaw "one year of terrible suffering" for blacks and whites in the South, Bellows hoped that the federal government would take an active role in combatting hunger. "Of course it will be cheated & bamboozled, & idleness & dependence will be encouraged," he wrote. "But in a flood it won't do to think that sending boats to the relief of millions will prevent some thousands from *learning to swim*."[2]

The prominence of both Bellows and his congregation in such benevolent efforts in New York City set the stage for his activities during the Civil War. Late in April 1861 he chanced to attend an organizational meeting held by prominent women in New York City (including some of his parishioners) and offered his aid in creating the Woman's Central Association of Relief, the goal of which was to coordinate the numerous soldiers' aid societies. Because military authorities in New York gave only grudging cooperation, Bellows became the emissary to Washington for the Woman's Central. There his efforts produced a larger organization modeled upon the British Sanitary Commission. Almost single-handedly he maneuvered the appointment of the U.S. Sanitary Commission through government officials who, by and large, were indifferent or hostile. He set up the Commission's first organizational framework, and his energy in publicizing and raising funds played a major role in its continued success. In fact, it was Thomas Starr King, a Unitarian minister and one of Bellows's protégés, who secured the enormous donations in California that financed so much of the Commission's work. Throughout the life of the Commission, Bellows recruited many of its best workers. He brought in members of his own family, as well as acquaintances from school, church, and other activities, to play important roles in the Commission. He himself chose the two major candidates for the secretaryship—Edward Everett Hale, a reform-minded Unitarian minister, and Olmsted, whose administration of Central Park and whose writings on slavery Bellows knew well.

Bellows and Olmsted had much in common. Both were staunch Republicans interested in politics, intellectual life, and reform. They were sons of the New England town who shared a belief in the civilizing and uplifting nature of institutions, whether parks, schools, churches, or the family. But some important differences of temperament separated them. Olmsted had little of the breezy optimism, self-possession, and self-confidence that characterized Bellows and allowed the latter to harangue high public officials such as Lincoln and Stanton. Bellows also had an easy fluency in the sentimental idiom of the day which was foreign to Olmsted.

The two men further differed in their attitude toward power: Bellows loved its trappings and welcomed the possibility of becoming the mentor of generals and presidents, while Olmsted wanted its substance and disliked relinquishing any authority. Although Bellows could stand by his principles—he once refused to retract antislavery declarations that had offended his most powerful conservative parishioners—he generally wished to be a mediator. In 1863 he prefaced one of his more controversial sermons: "I deliberately strive to be on both sides of every great question, whether in theology, politics, social ethics, or philanthropy, because Truth is on both sides of them."[3] In the same way that the minister attempted to unite Unitarianism, he tried to smooth over differences with political antagonists, other members of the Sanitary Commission, and rival aid commissions such as the U.S. Christian Commission. Not only at the Sanitary Commission, but also in the formation of the Union League Club and the weekly newspaper proposed by Olmsted and Godkin, Bellows attempted to make changes and concessions that did not fit Olmsted's views. In time, Olmsted came to view Bellows as overly compromising. For his part, Bellows found Olmsted too rigid. By August 1863 he declared: "I don't believe any Body of Directors could get along two years with you. And this because your own notions are so dominant & imperative, & enlist conscience, heart, will & body & soul in a way, to make concessions to ordinary judgments—which are none the less valuable for being instinctive & the result of contact with average people—utterly impossible."[4]

The friendship between Bellows and Olmsted was an intellectual one, important to both men. They exchanged ideas and read and candidly critiqued each other's writings. Bellows's description of his own speech at the Philadelphia Academy of Music in 1863 illustrated well his respect for Olmsted's intellectual prowess: "Olmsted, a severe judge, seldom pleased & whose presence I dreaded more than every body else's said, 'He wd not have altered a word.'"[5] Admiring and perhaps somewhat envious of Bellows's Harvard education, Olmsted used his few Latin tags and rather rusty French in their correspondence. Even in California, when his distaste for writing was rapidly increasing, Olmsted still desired Bellows's opinions so strongly that he declared, "There is scarcely a day that I do not have a strong impulse to write to you, in spite of the habit of refraining from it."[6]

The time and place of the first meeting between Olmsted and Bellows has not been ascertained, but they had met as early as March 1855, when Olmsted tried to secure Bellows as a contributor to *Putnam's Monthly Magazine*. When in 1860 Bellows wrote an admiring article about the superintendence of Central Park, Olmsted had already guided him around the park. The choice of Olmsted for the post of secretary of the U.S. Sanitary Commission began an intense partnership and friendship that was documented in the exchange of approximately two hundred letters over a twenty-seven-month period. Long visits and consultations whenever both men were in New York City or Washington supplemented this correspondence. During the Commission's first year, Olmsted generally reported directly to Bellows when the board of the Sanitary Commission was not in session. As the Executive Committee came to assume increasing importance in the autumn of 1862, Olmsted relied upon Bellows to present his case to the other four members. While Olmsted directed some formal protests to the Committee and some informal ones to George Templeton Strong, he primarily sought to convince Bellows of the correctness of his position. But that became increasingly difficult to do as Bellows, who did not consider himself particularly acute in business concerns, tended more and more to defer to "practical" fellow Committee members such as Strong. Bellows later revealed his own conflicting feelings to Olmsted: "I could not desert the Board & go with *you*, without the greatest peril to the cause, & I have not been able to go with the Board, for fear of losing your talents & devotion—which I feel, & always have felt, to be invaluable to our cause."[7]

In 1863 the relationship between the two men became strained as Olmsted's difficulties with the Executive Committee increased. Bellows actually undercut Olmsted's position in the Western department by assuring Newberry and his supporters that the board understood his problems and would support him against Olmsted. Perhaps Bellows's opinion of Olmsted was lowest in March 1863, when in a letter to the president of the Kentucky branch he noted Olmsted's "glorious & invaluable qualities"— "his integrity, disinterestedness & talent for organization, his patriotism & genius"—but went on to refer to Olmsted's "impracticable temper, his irritable brain." In terms strikingly similar to those Strong was then using in his diary, Bellows characterized Olmsted as an "unconscious *tyrant*" with "an indomitable pride of opinion, habit of self-reliance, and passion for uniformity" and declared, "If he were a priest, he would be worse than Hildebrand or Laud; if a monarch he would rule with a rod of iron."[8]

Despite these reservations about Olmsted, Bellows retained a great deal of respect for his abilities and during the spring and summer of 1863 again became convinced that Olmsted was correct about some of Newberry's failings. When the Mariposa Company offered Olmsted a position in August 1863, Bellows attempted to convince him to stay with the Commission by instructing Newberry on the necessity for filing reports with the central office.

In August 1863 the discussion of Olmsted's future produced an open exchange of views about his abilities, duties, and responsibilities, and what the achievements and shortcomings of the Sanitary Commission had been. Stating that the country was at a critical moment in its history, Bellows told Olmsted that the nation would need men like themselves in the reconstruction of the Union that would follow the war. "I think you are gradually but surely gaining a place of confidence & respect as a man of statesmanlike mind & character—that you have already become known in a way to give your future words & works, great efficacy. I don't know a half-dozen men in the whole North, whose influence in the next five years I should think more critically important to the Nation," he wrote. "I have counted on working with you & a few others in this grand patriotic arena— where perhaps we may yet have a chance or a necessity of laying down our lives."[9] Olmsted emphatically rejected Bellows's estimation by recounting two years of snubs from officials in Washington. Unconvinced, Bellows argued, "I still think you greatly under-rate the feelings of respect & confidence felt towards you by the best people of this country, & your chances of influence here within the next five years."[10]

Only through this debate did Bellows finally come to a clear understanding of Olmsted's dissatisfaction with the course of the Commission. Somewhat shocked at Olmsted's low estimate of the Commission's achievements and the depth of his bitterness, Bellows rather sharply replied:

> Not being able to understand clearly *what* you have aimed to make the Commission—or what its ideal in your own mind is—of course I can have little sympathy with your declarations about its failure. It has failed to realize *your* ideal for it. It has not failed to realize that of the Board, or that of the Nation, or that of its contributors. It has effected ten times over all I ever had in view in starting it.[11]

Despite their differences, the two parted friends. On August 19 Olmsted ended a long letter about his plans: "Honestly, I can treat nothing you say with indifference, and I want to have your approval of my decision."[12] And he did gain Bellows's blessing as well as a special letter of introduction to Thomas Starr King. "I part with you with a painful reluctance, yet with a great satisfaction," Bellows declared, "for I am sure that under very trying relations, in which utter frankness has marked our intercourse, we have done nothing & we feel nothing that in the least degree clouds our mutual esteem & affection."[13] The shared experience seems to have held them together through the rest of the Civil War, for they continued to correspond and Olmsted promoted the Commission and educated the people in California about its work. On his journey to California in 1864, Bellows visited Olmsted's home on the Mariposa Estate and traveled with him to the Yosemite Valley.

The following year, Bellows best summed up his opinion of Olmsted when James Miller McKim asked for an evaluation of Olmsted as a candidate for the post of general secretary of the American Freedman's Aid Union. Bellows told him: "Mr. F. L. Olmsted is, of all men I know, the most comprehensive, thorough & minutely particular organizer. He is equally wonderful in the management of principles & of details. His mind is patient in meditation, capable & acute, his will inflexible, his devotion to his principles & methods, confident & unflinching." Bellows's assessment also alluded to the problems between Olmsted and the Executive Committee of the Sanitary Commission:

> He looks far ahead, & his plans & methods are sometimes *mysterious*. Consequently, he is not an easy person for an ordinary Board of shrewd, worldly-wise, self-opinionated Managers to get along with. They think him impracticable, expensive, slow—when he is only long-headed, with broader, deeper notions of economy than themselves, & with no disposition to *hurry* what, if done satisfactorily, must be thoroughly. My feeling is that Olmsted is an admirable *Governor*, altho' an uncomfortable *Subject*. He loves power & is fit to hold it.

In his summation Bellows declared, "I won't guarantee you peace, comfort, daily satisfaction, if you harness in as a Board, with O, but I will promise you larger, better & nobler results (with whatever amount of friction in getting them) than you can secure under any other General Secretary."[14]

Even though Olmsted was back in New York City by 1865, the end of the Civil War had dissolved the principal ties that bound him and Bellows; and their other interests took them in different directions. Olmsted was busy with his landscaping projects, Bellows with his congregation, Unitarian affairs, and local reforms. In 1879 Bellows wrote a history of the Union League Club of New York and related the efforts by Olmsted and Gibbs that led to the club's creation. Bellows also described Olmsted in glowing terms and sent him a copy in proofs. Obviously touched by the memories of past shared endeavors, Olmsted began his reply, "My dear friend," and concluded: "I am more than grateful that you can have had it in your heart to so deal by me. And I don't repine that the fact of my life falls so very far short of what you have wished to think it."[15]

1. *New-York Times*, Feb. 3, 1858, p. 4, and Feb. 20, 1858, p. 3.
2. HWB to James Miller McKim, Aug. 18, 1865, Henry Whitney Bellows Papers, Massachusetts Historical Society, Boston, Mass.
3. Henry W. Bellows, *The National Instinct Our Guide Through the War: An Address Given on Occasion of the National Thanksgiving, November 26, 1863* (New York, 1863), Department of Rare Books and Special Collections, Princeton University Library, Princeton, N.J.
4. HWB to FLO, Aug. 18, 1863.
5. HWB to Eliza Nevins Bellows, n.d. [Feb. 25, 1863], Henry Whitney Bellows Papers, Massachusetts Historical Society, Boston, Mass.
6. FLO to HWB, March 4, 1865.

7. FLO to JO, March 13, 1855 (*Papers of FLO*, 2: 347); HWB to FLO, Aug. 18, 1863.
8. HWB to John H. Heywood, March 10, 1863, USSC-NYPL, box 611: 1740.
9. HWB to FLO, Aug. 13, 1863.
10. HWB to FLO, Aug. 20, 1863.
11. HWB to FLO, Aug. 18, 1863.
12. FLO to HWB, Aug. 19, 1863, Henry Whitney Bellows Papers, Massachusetts Historical Society, Boston, Mass.
13. HWB to FLO, Sept. 11, 1863.
14. HWB to James Miller McKim, Aug. 18, 1865, Henry Whitney Bellows Papers, Massachusetts Historical Society, Boston, Mass.
15. FLO to HWB, Dec. 22, 1879, Henry Whitney Bellows Papers, Massachusetts Historical Society, Boston, Mass.

Additional Sources

Clark, Clifford E., Jr., "Religious Beliefs and Social Reforms in the Gilded Age: The Case of Henry Whitney Bellows," *New England Quarterly* 43 (March 1970): 59–78.
DAB.
Fredrickson, George, *The Inner Civil War: Northern Intellectuals and the Crisis of the Union* (New York, 1965).
Kring, Walter Donald, *Henry Whitney Bellows* (Boston, 1979).
Wright, Conrad, *The Liberal Christians: Essays on American Unitarian History* (Boston, 1970).

ALFRED JANSON BLOOR (c. 1828–1917) served as assistant secretary of the U.S. Sanitary Commission from 1861 until 1864. Born in England, he was educated primarily by private tutors. He also studied with the architect Frederick Diaper, and in 1861 was elected a fellow of the American Institute of Architects. Bloor, who first met both Olmsted and Vaux in 1859, worked for them on Central Park that year as an assistant.

Bloor began to work for the Sanitary Commission after the battle of Bull Run in July 1861. Calvert Vaux, Olmsted's partner in landscape design, was aware how desperately the Commission needed clerical assistance, and he convinced Bloor to leave New York for Washington. At the Commission Bloor immediately began to work long hours and was dedicated and efficient, though self-important and censorious. As assistant secretary he corresponded about supplies with the women's auxiliary societies, supervised the local supply department and the publication of Commission documents, approved hospital requisitions, and generally managed the clerical work of the Washington office.

Bloor enjoyed the camaraderie of the Sanitary Commission's central office at 244 F Street in Washington. He prized the friendship of Olmsted, Knapp, and Douglas and resented any perceived slights to them. This cast of mind made it difficult for him to remain in the Commission's

ALFRED JANSON BLOOR

service after Olmsted's resignation. He disliked the members of the Executive Committee because of their opposition to Olmsted's plans, but he also held a more personal grudge: upon Olmsted's resignation he had hoped to receive a higher position. Although the decision in the autumn of 1863 to make New York City the home base of the Commission's general secretary left Bloor nominally in charge of the Washington office, his ambitions were not satisfied. In the autumn of 1864 his request for promotion and an increase in salary were denied. In response Bloor wrote a letter which was so insulting that the Executive Committee voted to dismiss him unless an apology were forthcoming. Perhaps in a parody of Bloor's pretentious style, George Templeton Strong declared in Latin in his diary that Bloor was a bad egg ("*Malum Ovum*"). Strong also presciently predicted that Bloor would seek revenge by writing about the Commission but concluded, "whatever he writes is so verbose, polysyllabic, and obscure that it will do us no great mischief."[1] Indeed, the Commission had not heard the last from Bloor. In 1867 he submitted a claim for additional payment for travel he had undertaken on behalf of the Commission, which it rejected despite his numerous letters and representations. In 1871 he published a pamphlet of over forty pages filled with charges and animadversions. Unlike the other employees and members of the Sanitary Commission, who put aside their differences after the war, Bloor still clung to the old antipathies. In 1891, over twenty-five years after his service to the Sanitary Commission had ended, he admonished Olmsted not to allow the latter's secretary to address letters to him as "Dr" Bloor: "Long before I got through with Drs Bellows, Agnew et hoc I had to give up attaching any true claim to consideration in the initials D.D. or M.D. or any other D's after a name."[2]

In 1865 Bloor again began to practice his profession of architect. For over two years he worked as an associate at 110 Broadway, which served as the office of the architectural firm Vaux, Withers, and Company and of the landscape architectural firm Olmsted and Vaux. He became unhappy with the arrangement and, by the summer of 1867, believed that the relations of those firms with him were "unjust." That August, Bloor wrote an angry letter to Olmsted that gave his complaints in detail. He charged that Vaux had obtained several sizable loans from him by intimating that "within reasonable time" he could become a principal in the firm Vaux, Withers, and Company. He also declared his "contempt" for Vaux, which arose from the "violation of all actual or implied agreements with me."[3] Olmsted, who was attempting to stay out of the quarrel, told Bloor that the only conclusion that he could draw was that "you entertain feelings toward Mr Vaux which render it painful for you to remain longer in the office of the firm of which he is partner. This is clear enough, & as a friend, I can not object or feel grieved at your taking measures to free yourself."[4] Olmsted also declared that while he would lose by Bloor's departure, he did not wish him to stay even one day with feelings of having been the victim of injustice.

After Bloor's quarrel with Vaux, Olmsted saw the young architect more infrequently but continued to offer assistance. In 1868 Bloor became very interested in photosculpture, a process that promised to make low-cost three-dimensional representations available to the public, and he sought Olmsted's aid in securing the secretaryship of the American company that was to be formed. Olmsted, probably from his prior unhappy experiences in business, was wary of any involvement, but he did attempt to promote Bloor's candidacy. When that enterprise failed, he also offered Bloor an opportunity to work as his assistant in landscape architecture—an offer that Bloor did not accept. In 1876 Olmsted had a more unpleasant encounter with Bloor, who as secretary of the New York chapter of the American Institute of Architects, savagely attacked a revised design for the New York state capitol proposed by an advisory committee composed of Henry H. Richardson, Leopold Eidlitz, and Olmsted.

In 1882 Bloor offered to repay money lent to him by Olmsted in 1868 in a note so friendly that Olmsted passed it along to Frederick Knapp with the comment, "I suppose you like to think charitably of Bloor and his loose screw. The enclosed may help you to."[5] But in the letters that followed, Bloor again brought up the subject of his ill-treatment by Vaux. Bloor also aimed some barbs at Olmsted by vaguely referring to "weaknesses" that he had observed during their time at the Sanitary Commission.[6] He further stated that Olmsted had not always thought well of Vaux. These charges deeply angered Olmsted. Although he admitted some "incompatibilities for close association" with Vaux, he avowed, "You are wrong in supposing that you have at any time 'heard or seen in print' anything from me or caused by me reflecting on Mr Vaux's integrity, or giving the least countenance to any charges or slurs against him or claims in behalf of others at his expense, professionally or otherwise." Moreover, Olmsted declared with some asperity that he could find no justification for Bloor's charges. "In all I read at the time of your voluminous notes there was [not] a line that came near to proving his insincerity or that he had ever had an unfriendly intention toward you." He closed the note, "I am sorry that the wretched matter comes up again but as it does there must be no question as to where I stand in it."[7] Unabashed, Bloor replied: "But you waste your time in writing—& mine in reading—your remarks on Mr Vaux & your relations to him. They have not a particle of effect on me one way or the other—." Bloor then proposed that they drop the subject and concluded, "I think rather poorly of Mr V. and quite well of yourself, but of what possible consequence is it to anything except our own amour propre what I think of either of you, or what either of you think of me?"[8] This exchange ended their correspondence for eight years, and it was reopened only by Bloor's efforts to set up a fund to support John H. Douglas, who had become poor and infirm.

Despite his quarrels and problems, Bloor did make his mark in the world. Although he designed few buildings, he gave invaluable service to the American Institute of Architects (the national professional organization of architects) and its New York chapter. He became the Institute's librarian in 1867, edited its publications, and for over ten years served as its secretary. From 1898 until his death in 1917 Bloor lived primarily in retirement.

1. *Diary of the Civil War*, p. 493.
2. A. J. Bloor to FLO, Sept. 5, 1891.
3. A. J. Bloor to FLO, Aug. 30, 1867.
4. FLO to A. J. Bloor, Sept. 19, 1867, Alfred Janson Bloor Papers, New-York Historical Society, New York City.
5. FLO to Frederick N. Knapp, Sept. 18, 1882.
6. A. J. Bloor to FLO, Sept. 27, 1882.

7. FLO to A. J. Bloor, Oct. 4, 1882.
8. A. J. Bloor to FLO, Oct. 6, 1882.

Additional Sources

"A. J. Bloor," *Architecture and Building* 28, no. 7 (Feb. 1898), pp. 61–62.
Bogart, Michele, "Photosculpture," *Art History* 4 (March 1981): 54–65.
"Obituary. Alfred J. Bloor," *Journal of the American Institute of Architects* 5 (Dec. 1917): 640.

JOHN HANCOCK DOUGLAS (1824–1892) was one of Olmsted's closest and most trusted associates on the staff of the U.S. Sanitary Commission. From July 1861, when Douglas joined the Commission as an inspector, until his resignation in the autumn of 1864, he capably carried out his duties and ardently supported Olmsted's policies.

Born in Waterford, New York, Douglas graduated from Williams College in 1843 and later received his medical degree from the University of Pennsylvania (where J. Foster Jenkins was a fellow student). Douglas also studied in Europe. After a brief period in New Orleans, he moved his medical practice to New York City. There he edited the *American Medical Monthly* from 1856 until 1862 and served as an examining physician for the New England Life Insurance Company. In 1861 that firm suggested that the Sanitary Commission appoint him as one of its associate members.

Douglas began work with the Sanitary Commission after the battle of Bull Run and in the autumn of 1861 was appointed one of three associate secretaries. After he assumed superintendence of the Commission's activities in the St. Louis area in December 1861, Douglas organized relief efforts for the wounded of the battles of Fort Donelson and Shiloh. Returning to the East in the spring of 1862, he worked with the hospital transports on the Virginia Peninsula from late June until August. In addition to his service in the Commission's Washington office, Douglas was employed in the field after the battles of Fredericksburg, Gettysburg, and the Wilderness.

From the beginning, Olmsted and Douglas admired each other and generally agreed about aims and methods in Sanitary Commission work. Douglas described Olmsted in September 1861 as one of the excellent men of the Commission. Olmsted, for his part, recognized that Douglas was exceptionally able—although sometimes temperamental and impatient with those he believed impractical. In the autumn of 1862, when women from the town and city aid societies were frequently visiting the Washington office and pressing their views upon the higher-ranking employees, Douglas found it difficult to use the necessary diplomacy and tact. Olmsted reported that, "office work does not agree with Douglas and he is very freaky."[1] To pacify such a valuable worker, Olmsted promised him duty in the field. Douglas, who had earlier clashed with John S. Newberry, also supported Olmsted in the latter's disagreements with the Executive Committee in 1863. Douglas, like Olmsted, believed that the bulletin published by the Western department did not properly reflect Sanitary Commission aims and policies and futilely sought to convince the Executive Committee to suppress it. In 1865, after his resignation from the Commission, he wrote Olmsted, "You must permit me to say that I have missed your hand at the helm from the moment you left, and never more so than during the last summer when I was placed in charge of operations in the Army of the Potomac from May to Aug."[2]

Douglas returned to the private practice of medicine in 1864. During Ulysses S. Grant's final illness, of almost one year, Douglas served as his personal physician. The constant attendance upon the former president apparently undermined Douglas's own health, and he suffered a debilitating stroke not long after Grant's death. In financial straits, Douglas thereafter lived with a married daughter. Alfred J. Bloor solicited contributions from former colleagues on the Sanitary Commission to aid him, and Olmsted was among the contributors.

1. FLO to HWB, October 1, 1862.
2. J. H. Douglas to FLO, January 3, [1865].

Additional Sources:

Appleton's Cyc. Am. Biog.
Douglas, John Hancock, Papers, Manuscript Division, Library of Congress, Washington, D.C.
Douglas, John Hancock, *Three Years in the Sanitary Commission, with Service in the Field, West, East and South, and Attendance for Nine Months upon Gen. Grant* (n.p., n.d.).
McFeely, William S., *Grant: A Biography* (New York, 1981).
Parsons, E. B., *Obituary Record of the Alumni of Williams College, 1892–1893* (Williamston, Mass., 1893), pp. 185–86.

WILLIAM ALEXANDER HAMMOND

WILLIAM ALEXANDER HAMMOND (1828–1901) was the physician whom the Sanitary Commission successfully recommended for the post of surgeon general. Born in Annapolis, Maryland, he grew up in Pennsylvania. He attended St. John's College, studied medicine in William Van Buren's office, and in 1848 received his medical degree from University Medical College of New York. That summer Hammond was commissioned as an assistant surgeon in the U.S. Army, a rank he would hold for the next eleven years.

Although most of Hammond's military assignments were to isolated frontier posts, he took great interest in medical and scientific inquiry. He conducted laboratory experiments, wrote two essays (one prize-winning) on physiology, and gathered specimens for his friends at the Philadelphia Academy of Science and at the Smithsonian Institution. During this period he suffered two attacks that were diagnosed as stemming from a heart condition. Although he repeatedly asked for duty in an Eastern city, and, after his second attack, sought a sedentary post, Surgeon General Lawson refused these requests. As a result, Hammond left the army in 1859 and accepted a teaching position at the University of Maryland. At the outbreak of the Civil War, he reenlisted in the army. His

96

resignation, however, had cost him all his seniority, and his rank was that of a beginning assistant surgeon.

During the autumn of 1861, Hammond quickly gained the attention of the Sanitary Commission. A former protégé of Van Buren and a friend of John H. Douglas, he was one of the few military physicians sympathetic to the aims of the Sanitary Commission and willing to criticize the actions of fellow officers in the Medical Bureau. No doubt, Hammond's wide-ranging interests, forceful personality, and openness to innovation further impressed the commissioners. In late September 1861 Olmsted said that he wished he had the power to appoint Hammond medical director of the Army of the Potomac; by mid-October the Sanitary Commission was recommending that Secretary of War Simon Cameron select Hammond as the new surgeon general. For the next six months the Commission steadfastly supported Hammond for that position, which, despite the rivalry of Robert C. Wood, he received in April 1862.

As surgeon general, Hammond began to reform and revitalize the Medical Bureau. To be sure, problems with supply and transportation, both under the control of the quartermaster's department, continued. From his vantage point with the Army of the Potomac during the summer of 1862, Olmsted still believed the medical care of soldiers to be inadequate. But Hammond brought innovation and a new attitude toward spending to the Medical Bureau. He liberally disbursed funds to employ civilian physicians temporarily and to obtain badly needed supplies. He tried to ensure the competence of all military physicians by extending the army's examination system to the volunteer medical officers, and he encouraged army doctors to obtain training in military surgery. Hammond established many new military hospitals, some of which concentrated upon specific injuries, and he created the Army Medical Museum. He also laid the groundwork for the publication of the *Medical and Surgical Memoirs of the War of the Rebellion*, an important medical reference work. In short, he oversaw the expansion of the Medical Bureau to meet its enormous wartime task and also tried to apply the standards and findings of professional medicine of the day to this growth.

Despite his considerable achievements, Hammond made numerous enemies. Foremost among these was his immediate superior, Secretary of War Edwin M. Stanton. Hammond's ties to and sympathy for George McClellan probably worsened the personality conflict between himself and Stanton, both being proud and tactless. In the spring of 1863 Hammond removed calomel, a widely used mercury-based purgative, from the army's supply list of medicines: this meant that army surgeons wishing to prescribe that remedy had to place a special order for it. This action, though medically sound, caused a great outcry among physicians, especially in the West, and diminished his popularity.

During the summer of 1863, Stanton ordered Hammond to make a trip of inspection in the West and relieved him of the duties of the surgeon general's office. The secretary of war also appointed a commission—whose chairman, Andrew H. Reeder, was an old political enemy of Hammond's—to investigate the Medical Bureau. The Reeder Commission's report recommended that Hammond be dismissed. The surgeon general, however, demanded and secured a court-martial, which began in January 1864. The charges against Hammond were not particularly grave: he had acted improperly by personally buying overpriced blankets for the Medical Bureau rather than ordering the medical purveyor to make such purchases, and by lying to another officer concerning the reasons why an army doctor had not received a promotion. Although the trial lasted through the summer of 1864, the court-martial deliberated only two hours before finding Hammond guilty. He was dismissed from the army in August 1864. In 1878 Hammond secured passage of a congressional bill annulling that verdict and placing him on the list of retired army officers.

Hammond's conviction by court-martial did little to injure his high professional standing, and he enjoyed a long, successful postwar career as a specialist in the newly emerging field of neurology. He combined a lucrative private practice with editing professional journals and teaching at prominent medical schools in New York City: the College of Physicians and Surgeons (1866–67), Bellevue Hospital Medical College (1867–74), and University Medical College (1874–82). He was also a founder of the New York Postgraduate Medical College, which attempted to improve the qualifications of the physician who already held a medical degree, and the American Neurological Society. During the 1880s, however, Hammond became increasingly out of step with others in his specialty. In 1888 he moved to Washington, D.C., where he erected a sanitorium in which injections of extracts from animal organs such as the heart, liver, or ovaries were used to treat nervous disorders. Hammond also separately marketed these expensive products. Although failing health led him to sell the sanitorium in 1894, he retained one-half interest in it until his death, of a heart attack, in 1900.

Olmsted's relationship with Hammond was cordial though never particularly intimate. The two men worked together in August 1862 planning a campaign to secure an independent ambulance corps. In 1863, when Olmsted consulted Hammond about the weekly journal that he and Edwin L. Godkin proposed to edit, the surgeon general immediately promised to write articles and secure financial backers. In 1864, while in California, Olmsted complained to Bellows that no one had written about Hammond: "I retain an interest in his fortunes & know absolutely nothing, since I left you, of them except that he is to be court-martialed, has returned from his Southern tour & has met with a serious accident."[1] After the Civil War, when both Hammond and Olmsted were living in New York City, they apparently saw each other occasionally at meetings. In 1868 both served on a committee to organize a national institute of arts, sciences, and letters. In 1878, when Olmsted's position at Central Park was under attack, Hammond sought to use his influence with the mayor and with George McClellan to rally support for him.

1. FLO to HWB, March 5, 1864, Henry Whitney Bellows Papers, Massachusetts Historical Society, Boston, Mass.

Additional Sources

Adams, George Worthington, *Doctors in Blue: The Medical History of the Union Army in the Civil War* (New York, 1952).

Blustein, Bonnie E., "A New York Medical Man: William Alexander Hammond, M.D. (1828–1900), Neurologist" (Ph.D. diss., University of Pennsylvania, 1979).

Pilcher, James Evelyn, *The Surgeon Generals of the Army of the United States of America; A Series of Biographical Sketches* . . . (Carlisle, Pa., 1905), pp. 47–57.

Zeidenfelt, Alex, "The Embattled Surgeon General, William A. Hammond," *Civil War Times Illustrated* 17 (Oct. 1978): 24–32.

John Foster Jenkins (1826–1882) served as associate secretary and later as general secretary of the U.S. Sanitary Commission. Born in Massachusetts, Jenkins attended Brown University and Union College. He studied medicine with a physician in Schenectady, New York, and received his medical degree from the University of Pennsylvania in 1848. To this training he added a year's study at Harvard Medical School and an eight-month tour of England and France which included attendance at lectures and clinics in Paris. Jenkins then practiced medicine in New York City until 1856, when he moved to Yonkers, New York.

Jenkins joined the staff of the Sanitary Commission in 1861, probably at the suggestion of William Van Buren. Originally an inspector, Jenkins soon became associate secretary for the East. During Olmsted's extended absences (whether supervising hospital transports on the Pamunkey River in 1862 or traveling in the Midwest in 1863) Jenkins served as acting general secretary. By the autumn of 1862 he feared that his absence from Yonkers had seriously damaged his medical practice there, and he contemplated resigning his position with the Commission. Olmsted convinced the Commission to pay the rent for a furnished apartment so that Jenkins could move his family to Washington, D.C. Nonethe-

John Foster Jenkins

less, Jenkins left the Commission in April 1863; but he returned as successor to Olmsted as general secretary in September 1863. The following year Jenkins offered his resignation to the Commission, asserting that he did not have the necessary administrative abilities. Although the members of the board assured him of their support, they soon came to the same conclusion. In April 1865 Jenkins returned to his private practice in Yonkers, where he was also active in local and state medical societies.

Olmsted considered Jenkins an invaluable employee. In 1862 he commented: "His services are almost indispensable here. We can not all together supply his place."[1] Jenkins's talents lay in his medical skill and his capacity for hard work. Mild mannered and not innovative, as general secretary he tended to carry out the policies adopted by the board and the Executive Committee and, unlike Olmsted, seldom questioned them.

Jenkins and Olmsted remained on friendly terms after 1863 but seldom corresponded or saw each other. While in California, Olmsted consulted him about a diagnosis he had received from a doctor there, and when in 1873 Olmsted desired a family physician, he asked Jenkins for a recommendation. The two men do not appear to have otherwise visited or corresponded after Olmsted's return to New York in 1865.

1. FLO to HWB, Oct. 2, 1862, USSC-NYPL, box 641.

Additional Sources

Diary of the Civil War.
Fisher, George Jackson, "A Memorial Sketch of the Life and Character of the Late John Foster Jenkins, A.M., M.D., of Yonkers, N.Y.," *Transactions of the Medical Society of the State of New York*, 1884, pp. 369–87.

FREDERICK NEWMAN KNAPP (1821–1889) became Olmsted's most valued associate and closest friend in the Sanitary Commission. Knapp, like his first cousin Henry W. Bellows, was a Unitarian minister and a graduate of Harvard College and Harvard Divinity School. Poor health led him to resign from two pastorates—one of eight years in Brookline, another in East Cambridge, Massachusetts—and he returned to his native town of Walpole, New Hampshire, where he was living at the beginning of the Civil War.

Knapp was one of the Sanitary Commission's first workers and remained in its service through the Civil War. Invariably kind and compassionate, he was appalled by suffering. His reaction to the sight of soldiers discharged from the service but too ill to proceed home from Washington led to the creation of a lodge to feed, shelter, and care for them. During most of his tenure with the Commission, Knapp supervised its division of special relief, which generally aided sick soldiers who had been discharged or temporarily separated from their units.

Although Olmsted and Knapp worked together in the Commission's central office in Washington over two years, the shared experience of the hospital transport service during the Peninsula campaign in May and June 1862 deepened their relationship. The emergencies they encountered there revealed a strength and resoluteness in Knapp of which Olmsted had been only dimly aware. He came to regard Knapp as one of the most competent men to care for patients requiring emergency treatment. The closeness fostered by work under such harrowing conditions was probably increased by their six-week journey together in the Midwest and the lower Mississippi Valley during the spring of 1863.

Even after Olmsted's resignation from the Sanitary Commission, his friendship with Knapp remained strong. In November 1863 he told Knapp that he expected him to come to California after the war ended. When the Mariposa Company was failing in the spring of 1865 and Olmsted's prospects appeared especially bleak, it was to Knapp that he

101

Frederick Newman Knapp

turned in two remarkably revealing letters. Only to Knapp was Olmsted able to give a stark self-appraisal and reveal the depths of his depression.

In the postwar period the two men continued to aid and encourage each other. Olmsted was a financial supporter of the school that Knapp briefly operated in Eagleswood, New Jersey, and he became a partner in the cranberry farm that Knapp ran in Sutton, Massachusetts. When in 1869 Knapp was offered a pastorate in Plymouth, Massachusetts, he sought Olmsted's counsel—a situation that the free-thinking Olmsted humorously likened to a drinker asking a teetotaler's opinion.

During these postwar years, other members of Olmsted's family maintained ties with Knapp. Olmsted sent his stepsons John Charles and Owen to Knapp's schools for at least six years. Mary Perkins Olmsted and the children also occasionally visited the Knapp family. Although the men continued to exchange letters, Knapp seldom saw the increasingly busy Olmsted, and by 1880 he was saying that he wished that they could meet even for an hour or two, "Not that there is any thing special to talk about, but I want to see you on the ground of general refreshment, (being the best special treatment I know of for neuralgia)."[1] Even after Olmsted moved to Brookline, he and Knapp visited only occasionally. When Knapp died suddenly in 1889, Olmsted was among the many mourners at the funeral. The following month he gave his own final assessment of Knapp in an oblique reference in a speech mentioning his regard for his adopted home of Brookline. Recalling a man in his office in Washington in 1861 who often mentioned Brookline proudly and affectionately, Olmsted observed, "He was the best man that I ever had so near me as he was."[2]

1. F. N. Knapp to FLO, Jan. 21, 1880.
2. FLO, "The History of Streets" (unpublished lecture to the Brookline Club, Brookline, Mass., February 1889).

Additional Sources

Peck, Thomas Bellows, *The Bellows Genealogy* . . . (Keene, N.H., 1898), pp. 348–54.
"A Public Sorrow" (obituary), *Old Colony Memorial*, Jan. 17, 1889, Frederick Newman Knapp Papers, Massachusetts Historical Society, Boston, Mass.

JOHN STRONG NEWBERRY (1822–1892) was a member of the Sanitary Commission and the associate secretary responsible for activities in its Western department. Although he and Olmsted clashed over policies, methods, and organization, Newberry retained this post throughout the Civil War.

Born in Connecticut, Newberry as a youth moved to Cuyahoga Falls, near Cleveland, Ohio. After attending Western Reserve College, he graduated from the Cleveland Medical School in 1848. He then spent two years in Paris attending medical lectures and clinics. From 1851 until 1855 he practiced medicine in Cleveland. Greatly interested in the natural sciences, and especially in fossils, Newberry then received the commission of assistant surgeon in the U.S. Army in order to accompany the Williamson expedition as its physician and geologist in the exploration of the area between San Francisco Bay and the Columbia River. He similarly participated in two other explorations sponsored by the U.S. government—the Colorado expedition of 1857–58 and the San Juan expedition in 1859. When the Civil War began in 1861, Newberry was in Washington, D.C., preparing his report on the latter. Joseph Henry, director of the Smithsonian Institution, suggested to A. D. Bache that Newberry would be an ideal member of the Sanitary Commission. In June 1861 Newberry was elected a member and that August he was appointed associate secretary for the region lying between the Alleghenies and the Mississippi.

JOHN STRONG NEWBERRY

Newberry's task of overseeing the Commission's activities and dealing with the auxiliary societies of the Midwest was, in truth, a most difficult one. In his soft-spoken way he tried to build support for the national organization. He made first Cleveland, and later Louisville, his base, and the aid societies in those cities became pillars of the Commission. He was less successful with the highly independent branches in Cincinnati and Indianapolis. During the first two years of the war, when supply problems were especially acute and bloody battles were fought in the Western theater, he also found caring for the wounded to be an enormous challenge. Though constantly prodded by Olmsted to increase his expenditures and hire additional agents, Newberry tended to supervise personally the relief operations after major battles. In order to retain the support of the local societies, he allowed them to operate freely and commended them for their achievements.

Newberry's position in the Sanitary Commission was always somewhat anomalous. As a member of the governing board he was Olmsted's equal, but as an associate secretary he reported to the general secretary. In the early months of the Commission, he sometimes seemed unsure of just how much authority he possessed. In November 1861 Olmsted attempted to delineate responsibilities. He declared that Newberry was autonomous in regard to Western affairs and continued: "You are dependent on us only for supplies and information. You are authorized to employ and discharge all agents, to determine remunerations for service; to collect and disburse money and supplies."[1] Only in policy questions that concerned the entire army should Newberry defer to the judgment of the Washington office. Although Olmsted intended an equitable division of responsibilities, Newberry feared that he was being set adrift without advice. "I can do as I please in all things, but if I err, the Comm. suffers and the board is compromised," he complained. "Bear with my importunity: it is but an exponent of my high estimate of your executive capacity."[2] Perplexed by Newberry's reluctance to assume responsibility, Olmsted replied: "Is it or is [it] not a mark of that executive capacity which you do much honor, that I am slow at letter-writing and so loth to assume business that would otherwise be done by men far better able to do it than I am? Of what earthly value is my advice to you in the case in question?"[3]

The most persistent problem between the two men was Newberry's failure to ensure that his own and his inspectors' reports were filed promptly, as the Commission's system required. By early November 1861 Olmsted was bewailing a lack of Western camp reports and asking that Newberry do all he could to supply statistical information for the report being prepared for the secretary of war. Instead, Newberry was writing his own report of activities in the Western office—which was not completed until the end of December, after Olmsted's report had been printed. The lack of accurate information from Newberry's department became an even greater problem when battles began to occur frequently there. In February 1862 Olmsted reminded Newberry that inspectors should be told to report after a battle as quickly and as fully as possible. Newberry soon came to resent these repeated demands for liberal spending and regular reports. In May 1862 he complained that Olmsted's most recent letter had given him "a going over for not obeying instructions never received." He continued: "I think you do me considerable injustice. I have a great deal more to do than you are aware of—simply to carry the US Sanitary Commission on my shoulders, in the Valley of the Miss." Listing his many activities—such as coordinating efforts with the branch societies, raising money, publicizing the Commission through newspaper articles and talks, establishing depots, and detailing inspectors and agents to duty—Newberry declared, "It makes my head swim to think of all that I have said and done & written the past month—and it was too much for me."[4]

During the last half of 1862, relations between Newberry and Olmsted worsened. That summer Newberry became very upset about the Washington office's failure to send him instructions and information, while he did not once report to it. Olmsted, spurred by the criticism of the

Executive Committee, again forcefully reminded Newberry of the necessity of regular reports and passed on various instructions from the Executive Committee. These orders prompted another outburst from Newberry, but the two secretaries were able to collaborate well in drawing up the Commission's response to the Cincinnati branch's demand for a part of the donation from California. But even as Newberry was placating Olmsted by noting that the Cincinnatians had received copies of all Commission publications and should have been conversant with Sanitary Commission policies, he was also, much to Olmsted's chagrin, speaking of "state agents"—that is, inspectors provided by the local societies.[5]

The year 1863 brought even greater strain to the relationship between Olmsted and Newberry. Although Olmsted's trip to the West was intended to conciliate Newberry, who wished Commission members to visit his department, it may actually have increased tensions between the two men. Always sensitive to criticism, Newberry resented some of Olmsted's disparaging remarks. "Your letter," he wrote, "gave a terrible blow to my vanity as it showed me how little attention you paid to all the things I said to you when you were here."[6]

Olmsted was also grappling with a problem that greatly concerned him: what reorganization of the executive service would remove his responsibility for obtaining reports from Newberry. In February 1863 Olmsted drew up a new plan of organization that would delegate record keeping to one of Newberry's subordinates, whom the Washington office could, in turn, hold responsible for such paperwork. Olmsted argued privately to Bellows that his own position was untenable; in actuality, he could neither dismiss nor even reprimand Newberry, who was a member of the Commission. When the Executive Committee failed to approve the proposed reorganization, Olmsted suggested at least one alternative in June that would have placed Newberry in charge of a new supply department with divisions to cover all the Commission's operations. But Newberry vehemently objected to the plan as increasing his own responsibility while decreasing his power. At the same time, he continued to report only irregularly. In May 1863 he declared a full report to be impossible because he was sick, in the process of moving to new office space, and without his principal assistant.

During the months that followed, Olmsted became more exasperated with Newberry. In May 1863 Newberry began publishing a regular bulletin in the Western department. Olmsted was affronted because a paucity of information from the West had hindered the central office's publication of a periodical. Moreover, he believed that Newberry had disclaimed in March any intention of issuing a Western publication. Still, Olmsted declared in May, "I have the best opinion of Dr. Newberry as a well-meaning man and a warm friendly regard for him."[7] But the Western secretary's next action—a letter effusively thanking New York City policemen for fifty boxes of lemons (just the kind of donation that for two years the Sanitary Commission had been discouraging) enraged Olmsted and caused him to lose all confidence in Newberry. Bellows's attempt in August to solve the problem by ordering Newberry to make the requested reports did not at all appease Olmsted, who argued that the letter did not address Newberry's other forms of insubordination: "It leaves entirely out of view what is of infinitely more influence on my convictions—the constant manners and language of friendly confidence and Christian & manly truthfulness, concealing purposes & plans which he knew to be revolutionary." Olmsted refused to be conciliated. "I will have nothing more to do with him," he stormed. "It is not possible that I can have more to do with him except fighting."[8]

For his part, Newberry seemed unaware that the controversy entailed anything other than policy questions. In July he assured Bellows that "while entertaining notions of policy differing widely from those of the General Secretary, I have ever entertained the kindest feelings personally for him and every member of the Board."[9] Although Olmsted was able to convince the members of the Executive Committee that Newberry would not be a good choice for his replacement, the Western secretary continued to be an important member of the Commission. In 1865, when J. Foster Jenkins resigned as general secretary, the position was offered to Newberry, who declined it.

After the war, Newberry accepted a chair in the newly created School of Mines at Columbia University and taught there the remainder of his life. From 1869 until 1874 he directed the state-sponsored geological survey of Ohio. He also wrote numerous articles on paleontology and geology. His and Olmsted's paths crossed briefly when he undertook some geological work for the survey for the improvement of Staten Island, on whose advisory board Olmsted served.

1. FLO to JSN, Nov. 12, 1861, below.
2. JSN to FLO, Nov. 19, 1861, USSC-NYPL, box 918, 1: 4–9.
3. FLO to JSN, Nov. 21, 1861, USSC-NYPL, box 909, 1: 53.
4. JSN to FLO, May 1, 1862, USSC-NYPL, box 640.
5. FLO to JSN, Dec. 8, 1862, USSC-NYPL, box 914, 1: 295½.
6. JSN to FLO, April 2, 1863, USSC-NYPL, box 758: 1042.
7. FLO to HWB, May 25, 1863.
8. FLO to HWB, Aug. 16, 1863, below.
9. JSN to HWB, July 20, 1863, USSC-NYPL, box 640.

Additional Sources

DAB.

Newberry, John Strong, *The U.S. Sanitary Commission in the Valley of the Mississippi, during the War of the Rebellion, 1861–1866* (Cleveland, Ohio, 1871).

White, Charles A., *Biographical Memoir of John Strong Newberry, 1822–1892. Read before the National Academy of Sciences April 17, 1902* (Washington, D.C., 1906).

GEORGE TEMPLETON STRONG (1820–1875) was treasurer of the U.S. Sanitary Commission. Born into a prominent New York City family, he graduated from Columbia College and read law in his father's law office, Strong and Bidwell, on Wall Street. In 1845 he became a partner in the firm. As a junior in college he began a diary, and during the next forty years he filled it with pithy anecdotes and frank, often acerbic, comments about his friends, relations, and public figures and events of the day.

The Sanitary Commission's selection of Olmsted as secretary introduced him to Strong, and each was favorably impressed with the other. Immediately after that first meeting, Strong wrote in his diary, "I like him much."[1] Indeed, they shared some important traits: they valued rationality during an era when sentimentality was rife, enjoyed poking fun at the foibles and self-delusions of others, and were earnest though skeptical. Despite their emphasis on rationality, both possessed an aesthetic sensibility. Olmsted expressed his primarily in a love of nature and its beauty, Strong in an appreciation of music and literature.

Strong, however, differed from Olmsted in several ways. The temperaments of the two were little alike. Unlike Olmsted, who gave vent to anger and frustration in long, impassioned, and animated arguments or letters, Strong, though often irritated and sometimes indignant, was outwardly reserved and rarely showed anger except in his private diary. He also valued a peaceful life at home and the elegant dinners and entertainments given by his wife and others of their social circle. Though no dilettante himself, he was appalled by the headlong manner in which Olmsted flung himself into his work. When Olmsted began to quarrel frequently with the Executive Committee in 1863, Strong somewhat fastidiously speculated that "perhaps his most insanitary habits of life make him morally morbid." He continued: "He works like a dog all day and sits up nearly all night, doesn't go home to his family (now established in Washington) for five days and nights together, works with steady, feverish intensity till four in the morning, sleeps on a sofa in his clothes, and breakfasts on *strong coffee and pickles*!!!"[2]

GEORGE TEMPLETON STRONG

Strong tended to be more localistic than Olmsted and moved in a social and intellectual world largely bounded by New York City. There he accepted many responsibilities in civic life and genteel society. A High Church Episcopalian in religious sentiments, he long served as a vestry-man of Trinity Church. He also faithfully worked hard as a trustee of Columbia College.

Strong also tended to be more conservative than Olmsted in politics. Never a reformer, he distrusted democracy and the common people and believed that universal suffrage had caused many of the North's problems. He often tended to be contemptuous of the working classes, blacks, and immigrants—whether Irish, German, or others. Consistent with this skepticism about egalitarian principles, he did not attack slavery in principle, but had come to dislike the institution in the South and had come to resent the increasingly shrill rhetoric of proslavery Southern politicians. Like Olmsted, he believed slavery injurious to Southern economic development and was appalled by the lack of protection afforded the slave family, the prohibitions against teaching slaves to read and write, and their disabilities in courts of law. Strong's fervent support for the Civil War pushed him much closer to Olmsted's views for that period, and the two agreed on the kind of organization the Union League Club of New York should take.

Because Strong was more conservative in financial matters, his greatest problems with Olmsted arose over differing conceptions of how the Sanitary Commission should be managed. Their difficulties began in the autumn of 1862, after the Sanitary Commission had received large gifts of money from California. Strong, as treasurer of the Commission, had always worried that his reputation might be compromised by any irregularities in the accounts, and his fears appear to have grown proportionately with the treasury. Thus, he suggested that the Executive Committee formulate policies that would require the Committee's approval of large disbursements and of increments in salary. Olmsted disliked the new policies, which tended to limit his authority, and bitterly criticized them as decreasing the flexibility of the Commission both in Washington and in the field. Strong attempted unsuccessfully to convince Olmsted that the policies were simply good business practices.

Not surprisingly, these disagreements strained relations between the two men. Moreover, they came to affect unfavorably Strong's evaluation of Olmsted's talents. In December 1862 Strong had wished that Olmsted were secretary of war, saying, "I believe that Olmsted's sense, energy, and organizing faculty, earnestness, and honesty would give new life to the Administration were he in it."[3] Though Strong continued to admire Olmsted, he would never again speak in such glowing terms of his organizational talents. By March 1863, when Strong gave his most thorough appraisal of Olmsted, he had become more critical:

> He is an extraordinary fellow, decidedly the most remarkable specimen of human nature with whom I have ever been brought into close relations. Talent and energy most rare; absolute purity and disinterestedness. Prominent defects, a monomania for system and organization on paper (elaborate, laboriously thought out, and generally impracticable), and appetite for power. He is a lay-Hildebrand.[4]

While increasingly doubtful of Olmsted's practical abilities, Strong dreaded his impending resignation, noting in August 1863 that "we can ill spare him."[5]

At the end of Olmsted's tenure with the Sanitary Commission, Strong and Olmsted parted ways. They dined together upon Olmsted's return from California in the autumn of 1865 but appear to have met seldom thereafter. Strong was a dedicated member of the Sanitary Commission and its Executive Committee until his death, and he wrote a chapter on the financial history of the Commission for its authorized history. He remained a lawyer on Wall Street until 1872, when he became comptroller of Trinity Church.

110

1. *Diary of the Civil War,* p. 160.
2. Ibid., p. 291.
3. Ibid., p. 276.
4. Ibid., p. 304.
5. Ibid., p. 350.

Additional Sources

Aaron, Daniel, *The Unwritten War: American Writers and the Civil War* (New York, 1973).

Bender, Thomas, *Community and Social Change in America* (New Brunswick, N.J., 1978).

Fredrickson, George, *The Inner Civil War: Northern Intellectuals and the Crisis of the Union* (New York, 1965).

Strong, George Templeton, Manuscript Diary, New-York Historical Society, New York City.

Strong, George Templeton, *The Diary of George Templeton Strong,* ed. Allan Nevins and Milton Halsey Thomas, 4 vols. (New York, 1952).

KATHARINE PRESCOTT WORMELEY (1830–1908), a volunteer worker for the Sanitary Commission from Newport, Rhode Island, became an admirer and close friend of Olmsted. Born in England of American parents, she was educated there and in France and Switzerland. Living in Newport, Rhode Island, in 1861, she quickly assumed a position of leadership in the Newport Women's Union Aid Society. In May 1862 she volunteered for duty with the Sanitary Commission in Virginia as a lady superintendent of nursing. There she formed friendships with fellow workers Georgeanna Woolsey, Harriet Douglas Whetten, and Olmsted. Katharine Wormeley left the Virginia Peninsula in July 1862 but continued to work in military hospitals. For a year, she served as superintendent of nursing at the military hospital in Portsmouth Grove, Rhode Island, near Newport. In 1863 she also wrote a history of the Sanitary Commission, *The United States Sanitary Commission. A Sketch of Its Purposes and Its Work,* as a means of raising funds for the Commission. She retained an interest in nursing and in 1873 considered accepting a position at the training school for nurses at Bellevue Hospital in New York City.

After the war, Katharine Wormeley continued to live in Newport, where she cared for her elderly mother. She became a founder of the Newport Charity Organization and was a leader in its activities. In the 1880s she also began to translate French novels, most notably the work of Honoré de Balzac, and gained considerable acclaim in that field.

KATHARINE PRESCOTT WORMELEY

The year 1862 marked the beginning of an intense correspondence between Olmsted and Katharine Wormeley. They discussed books, travel, their activities and personal lives, and argued occasionally about politics. The high opinion each held of the other's abilities lent mutual support in times of frustration. Katharine Wormeley's attitude toward Olmsted bordered upon idolatry; she believed him largely responsible for the achievements of the Sanitary Commission. Her telling description of him in 1862 also indicates how important he was to her:

He is small, and lame . . . but though the lameness is decided, it is scarcely observable, for he gives you a sense that he triumphs over it by doing as if it did not exist. His face is generally very placid, with all the expressive delicacy of a woman's, and would be beautiful were it not for an expression which I cannot fathom,—something which is, perhaps, a little too severe about it. . . . He has great variety of expression: sometimes stern, thoughtful, and hag-gard; at other times observing and slightly satirical (I believe he sees out of the back of his head occasionally); and then again, and not seldom, his face wears an inspired look, full of goodness and power. I think he is a man of the most resolute self-will,—generally a very wise will . . . born an autocrat, however, and, as such, very satisfactory to be under. His reticence is one of his strong points: he directs everything in the fewest possible words; there is a deep, calm thoughtfulness about him which is always attractive and sometimes—provoking.[1]

Over the years this unflagging devotion must have proven most welcome to Olmsted, for at one point she wrote, "You say *truly* (though I thank you for saying it) that I am one of the few (*if* few they be) who understand, believe, & sympathize with you."[2]

Still, they disagreed strongly over politics. While disliking slavery, Katharine Wormeley hated abolitionists and blamed extremists both in the South and in New England for the Civil War. Somewhat aghast at the extent of Olmsted's antislavery fervor, she reproached him in August 1863: "How *can* you say that you would prefer Anarchy to slavery—the one is an Evil—with hope—the other is Destruction."[3] He reacted to her comments by defending the tendency of New Englanders to advocate reforms: "I am sure," he asserted, "that the evils of our government and which result from our government are not evils of democracy so far as democracy is a matter of choice and plan, nor are they evils of what you would call New England-ism, so far as what you might call so, is a vice of intellect or morality." He then criticized what he saw as the unwarranted detachment of genteel people like herself from reform movements:

You—your class—perceive your superiority in certain respects to the mass of the people but because they think too well of themselves, are too original, self-sufficient, and too much inclined to recklessly busy themselves in mat-ters with which they have no natural concern, and because they have not made arrangements politically and socially, as in England, with special refer-ence to the convenience with which superior talent, tact and taste may be exercised for the benefit of the community, you assume to yourselves the right to live quiet, scholarly, secluded and selfishly domestic and aesthetic lives. The difficulties, annoyances and embarrassments, which gentlemen and gentlewomen of any talent have to meet in doing their duty with their talent are certainly very great, and talent is not to be exercised here with the preordained quiet, grace and decorum which may be associated with it in a country of thoroughly well established and congealed civilization. The greater is the need, however, that it should be exercised courageously, resolutely and perseveringly.[4]

Despite such occasional quarrels over their divergent political philosophies, the two generally skirted such subjects and continued to correspond frequently.

After seventeen years, however, the friendship soured. The cause of the rupture cannot be determined, but the well-known physician Mary Putnam Jacobi told Olmsted that his description of Katharine Wormeley's behavior suggested that she was suffering from hysteria. It was probably at this time that Katharine Wormeley destroyed all the letters that Olmsted had written to her. In 1893 a reconciliation of sorts occurred. In answer to a letter from her, Olmsted wrote a chatty account of his work on the World's Columbian Exposition and signed it, "your old friend."[5] Whatever the difficulty between them had been, it does not appear to have dimmed her regard for him or his for her. She later recalled that his last words to her were: "Remember, whatever comes in life, nothing can ever make me lose my perfect confidence in you." To her, his death was the loss of one of "the two men I had loved best in life out[side] of my own family."[6]

1. Katharine Prescott Wormeley, *The Other Side of War; with the Army of the Potomac. Letters from the Headquarters of the United States Sanitary Commission during the Peninsular Campaign in Virginia in 1862* (Boston, 1889), pp. 62–63.
2. K. P. Wormeley to FLO, Jan. 15, 1874.
3. K. P. Wormeley to FLO, Aug. 17, 1863.
4. FLO to "Miss W.," n.d. [c. late Aug. 1863].
5. FLO to K. P. Wormeley, Dec. 10, 1893, Olmsted Associates Records, Library of Congress, Washington, D.C.
6. K. P. Wormeley to Emma Brace, Feb. 20, 1904.

Additional Sources

Notable American Women.

DEFENDING THE UNION

UNION

1861–1863

CHAPTER I

ORGANIZING THE
U.S. SANITARY COMMISSION

THE LETTERS IN THIS CHAPTER present Olmsted's first experiences with the Civil War and with the U.S. Sanitary Commission. His letter of June 1, 1861, to Henry W. Bellows expresses his desire to play a meaningful role in the war—a role that he believed would lie in working with the escaped slaves of Confederate masters. Bellows, however, found another role for Olmsted—that of secretary of the newly organized Sanitary Commission. Olmsted's letters of late June and early July 1861 demonstrate how unformed and indefinite his early position with the Commission was. These letters give his first, unfavorable impressions of the nation's volunteer soldiers and of the governmental machinery in Washington. The letter of June 28, 1861, details with striking imagery the bravado and unconcern for detail that he believed was prevalent among the Union soldiers.

To HENRY WHITNEY BELLOWS

Central Park, June 1st 1861.

My Dear Doctor Bellows:
The opinion you have so often done me the honor to publicly express of my talent in organization and my executive ability,[1] justifies me in disclosing to you an ambition with which I am fired.

117

As the government has determined to hold slaves in certain cases, and as those cases are likely to be numerous,[2] there must arise a responsibility of an unusual character for the administration of which I suppose myself somewhat peculiarly prepared. This not alone because I have studied the usual slave management of the South carefully,[3] nor because I have had the superintendence of near 15,000 working-men & have been very successful in my dealings with them,[4] but also because I have, I suppose, given more thought to the special question of the proper management of negroes in a state of limbo between slavery & freedom than anyone else in the country. I think, in fact, that I should find here my "mission" which is really something I am pining to find, in this war.

This being my confession, my petition is that, if you can while in Washington, without going out of your way or in the slightest degree embarrassing your great object,[5] you would ascertain if I should be likely to get a hearing for an offer of my services as a Commissioner of contraband goods of this kind—superintendent of slaves in the custody of government.

Mr Sumner[6] is the only man who knows me in Washington, though I imagine Mr Seward[7] & Mr Chase[8] will both have heard something of me.

Yours Very Respectfully

Fred. Law Olmsted.

The original is in the Henry Whitney Bellows Papers, Massachusetts Historical Society, Boston, Massachusetts.

1. Henry W. Bellows, pastor of All Souls Unitarian Church in New York City, had publicly commented favorably on Olmsted's work on Central Park on at least two different occasions. In a letter to the publisher James T. Fields in October 1860, Olmsted mentioned Bellows as a candidate to write a review of the park for the *Atlantic Monthly*, remarking that the minister, "as he preached about it (so I am told) would, no doubt, write con amore, if he wrote." This prediction was borne out by Bellows's article, which lauded Olmsted's executive as well as artistic abilities. Bellows called Olmsted "equally competent as original designer, patient executor, potent disciplinarian, and model police-officer," and praised him for enforcing "a method, precision, and strictness, equally marked in the workmanship, in the accounts, and in the police of the Park."

   Then, in a private letter informing Olmsted of his appointment as a director of the Woman's Central Association of Relief, Bellows wrote: "Your acknowledged administrative talent is much needed in the methodizing of this business. And if your pursuits and health do not permit you to give more than two or three attendances at the Board, your services will still be very great, & in my judgment cannot easily be dispensed with" (FLO to James T. Fields, Oct. 21, 1860 [*Papers of FLO*, 3: 269]; [Henry W. Bellows], "Cities and Parks: With Special Reference to the New York Central Park," *Atlantic Monthly* 7 [April 1861]: 422; HWB to FLO, [April 29, 1861]; see also *Papers of FLO*, 3: 330, n. 9).

2. A reference to the policy instituted by General Benjamin F. Butler at Fortress Monroe, Virginia, in late May 1861. When three slaves belonging to Confederate army officer Charles Mallory sought refuge at the Union installation on May 23, Butler received them and refused to return them. According to the general, the use of slave labor on Confederate fortifications made slaves belonging to disloyal masters contraband of war, and he confiscated them as property rather than free them.

      Olmsted probably believed that Butler's policy would increasingly place slaves under governmental control. Probably he had read the articles of May 30 and May 31, 1861, in the *New-York Daily Tribune* reporting that Secretary of War Simon Cameron approved of Butler's actions and that 135 slaves were then working within the Union lines (Louis S. Gerteis, *From Contraband to Freedman: Federal Policy toward Southern Blacks, 1861–1865* [Westport, Conn., 1973], pp. 11–16; *O.R.*, ser. 1, vol. 2, pp. 649–50; *New-York Daily Tribune*, May 30, 1861, p. 4; ibid., May 31, 1861, p. 4).

3. Olmsted here refers to the fourteen months that he had spent traveling in the South and to his three books of observations on slavery and Southern agriculture and society: *A Journey in the Seaboard Slave States* (1856), *A Journey Through Texas* (1857), and *A Journey in the Back Country* (1860).

4. This reference is to Olmsted's past experience as superintendent and architect-in-chief of Central Park. He gives here the total number of workmen (approximately 15,500) employed directly by the park between 1857 and 1861 rather than the number employed at any one time—which does not appear to have exceeded 3,700 (New York City, Board of Commissioners of the Central Park, *Third Annual Report, January 1860* [New York, 1860], p. 25; idem, *Fourth Annual Report, January 1861* [New York, 1861], p. 7; idem, *Fifth Annual Report, January 1862* [New York, 1862], p. 7).

5. A reference to Bellows's attempt to launch the Sanitary Commission. Although the Commission did not gain official recognition until June 9, Olmsted probably knew of their activities from his position as a member of the board of the Woman's Central Association and from an admiring editorial in the *New York Evening Post* on May 30 (*New York Evening Post*, May 30, 1861, p. 2).

6. Charles Sumner (1811–1874), U.S. senator from Massachusetts and an ardent opponent of slavery. How and when he and Olmsted became acquainted has not been determined by the editors. Possibly the introduction came through acquaintances in Boston such as Charles Francis Adams, Jr., with whom Olmsted had corresponded about the free-soil cause. In the spring of 1861 Olmsted wrote to Sumner in support of the candidacy of Charles N. Riotte, an antislavery German friend, for the post of minister to Costa Rica. At that time Sumner urged Olmsted to give a more searching, private appraisal of Riotte, who did receive the appointment. In December 1861 Sumner thanked Olmsted for sending him a copy of *Cotton Kingdom* and added, "I have already read carefully & gratefully yr two vols in the American edition; & am now proud to possess them in this new form from the author" (*DAB*; FLO to Charles Sumner, April 5, 1861, Record Group 59, Letters of Application and Recommendation, . . . 1861–1869, Diplomatic Branch, Civil Archives Division, National Archives and Records Service, Washington, D.C.; Charles Sumner to FLO, Dec. 18, 1861; *Papers of FLO*, 2: 75–77).

7. William Henry Seward (1801–1872), secretary of state in the Lincoln administration and a former U.S. senator from and governor of New York. Seward probably had heard of Olmsted through Henry J. Raymond, a political ally who as editor of the *New-York Daily Times* had commissioned and published Olmsted's travel letters about the South and slavery. On at least two occasions Olmsted had contemplated meeting Seward. After Olmsted's return from the South in 1854, Seward had invited him to call. Again in the spring of 1861, as Olmsted was completing *Cotton Kingdom*, he considered calling upon Seward to gain access to the recently completed federal

census (*DAB*; FLO to JO, Nov. 7, [1854] [*Papers of FLO*, 2: 332]; FLO to JO, March 22, 1861 [*Papers of FLO*, 3: 328]).

8. Salmon Portland Chase (1808–1873), Lincoln's secretary of the treasury and an anti-slavery politician. Olmsted probably expected Chase to have heard of him, not only because of his writings on slavery, but also because of a brief correspondence. In August 1857 Olmsted had written to Chase, then serving as governor of Ohio, to inquire about the feasibility of growing tobacco in that state. Chase referred the letter to the secretary of the Ohio board of agriculture and forwarded the secretary's report to Olmsted in December, remarking, "I now send you what I hope may not come to [*sic*] late for your purposes" (*DAB*; S. P. Chase to FLO, Dec. 19, 1857; John H. Klippart to S. P. Chase, Dec. 5, 1857).

To John Olmsted

C. Park, June 26th [1861]

Dear Father,

You know nearly as much as I know myself of my appointment & of its duties; I have, indeed, to shape the latter in a great measure for myself. There is at present not a dollar in the Treas[y] of the Commis[n] and I go without any definite arrangments. The duty will, I apprehend, be an ungrateful one & hard for me but being called unanimously by the highly honorable men who compose the Commis[n] I felt obliged to accept it.[1]

I have made no definite arrangment with C.P. Com.[2] I presume it will result in my accepting an advisory connection with the park at a reduced salary.

I am just leaving for Washington—& very glad to have had this visit from you & the girls & Fanny[3] before going.

Owen[4] has unmistakable signs of a malarious virus & I want him to have a complete change of air for some time as soon as it is safe for him to travel. I have asked Mary O[5] to take him to Conne[ct]. It is the only medicine in which I have any faith.

Your affectionate son

Fred. Law Olmsted.

1. Olmsted was elected resident secretary of the Sanitary Commission on June 20, 1861, at the Commission's second session. At its first meeting six days earlier, the Commission's committee on the appointment of secretaries recommended that the New York

members undertake the appointments. Elisha Harris was then elected recording secretary, a post abolished later that year when Olmsted's title was changed to general secretary. At the first session, Olmsted and Edward Everett Hale, the Unitarian minister who had married Olmsted's former fiancée, Emily B. Perkins, and who had collaborated with Olmsted in free-soil activities, were recommended as candidates for the post of resident secretary.

        Olmsted appears to have been Bellows's choice. He arranged to meet Olmsted before the meeting at which the election would occur, probably to ascertain whether Olmsted would accept the position if elected. Although Olmsted called the election "unanimous," there is no indication that it was. The minutes of Sanitary Commission meetings usually applied that term to their elections of members or officers, but it did not do so concerning Olmsted's selection. This suggests that at least one member may not have voted for Olmsted (USSC, *Minutes*, pp. 3, 5, 6, 9; HWB to FLO, [June 19, 1861]).

2. Although Olmsted had not reached any agreement with the Board of Commissioners of the Central Park, in July he was able to secure a resolution granting him two weeks' leave of absence (MPO to JO, July 9, 1861).

3. Olmsted's half-sisters Mary Olmsted (1832–1875) and Bertha Olmsted (1835–1926), his father John Olmsted, and probably his cousin Frances Maria Coit (b. 1852), went to New York on June 11 to visit him. John Olmsted returned to Hartford on June 17 (JO Journal; *Olmsted Genealogy*, pp. 60, 109, 155; *Papers of FLO*, 2: 270).

4. Olmsted's stepson, Owen Frederick Olmsted (1857–1881) (*Olmsted Genealogy*, p. 109).

5. That is, Olmsted asked his half-sister Mary to take Owen to their parents' home in Hartford. Mary apparently remained in New York after John Olmsted's departure, perhaps returning with Bertha on June 27, the day after this letter was written (JO Journal).

To Mary Perkins Olmsted

Washington
Friday June 28th 61

Dear Wife,

        I came in good order, arriving here at 6 P.M. yesterday. It was very hot but not excessively dusty until this side Baltimore & the discomfort less than I anticipated.

        The farm-houses in Jersey frequently show the flag. South of Phila^{da} they do not, but at Wilmington & other towns there is an abundance of them. Approaching Havre de Grace, the first war sign is seen in a shantee with a charcoal sign. "Bloody 11th Camp C." and a dozen or more fellows in shirt sleeves and dirty Havelocks[1] with muskets, and so afterwards at every bridge, and south of the long one which was burnt, off the road in a wood, a quiet camp of perhaps a regiment with the flag. In

ANNAPOLIS JUNCTION, 1861

Baltimore nothing. Fort McHenry[2] only seen with half a doz. tents outside; but South of Bat[o], just beyond the outskirts, a large camp on the right & beyond it another on the left, shirt sleeves & motley; a broad meadow with a regiment resting on their arms; hospital tents close to the road with sun struck fat men, being fanned. No more soldiers till we reach the Relay House,[3] & few seen there, but a camp on the hill. At the Annapolis junction[4] a crowd of these uniforms & no uniforms & mixed. Lots of men lying at full length on the grass, dirty and loaferish. Arms stacked near by and sentinels in shirt sleeves & straw hats; a deserted camp-ground which I presume to be the 20th's which went to Balto[e] yesterday.[5] Occasional stations of one or two tents & lounging fellows in shirt sleeves beyond & nearer Washington every mile a bell-tent[6] and squad of men. In the suburbs of Washington several regimental camps are seen at a distance. About the station, Vermont soldiers with their coats unbuttoned but belted over, & with muskets, dozen of baggage waggons with four mules each. In the streets more than half have some military insignia, but none are complete.

I get my room & Waring[7] comes in dressed in a blue flannel jacket with regulation buttons, worn open, army old regulation cap, and drab corduroy panteloons, strapped and spurred. After tea—I called at Prof[r] Bache's[8] who was not at home, and went on to Waring's camp which is two miles East of the Capitol. He gave me a pass. Regularly brought to at an outpost & the pass sent to a lighted guard tent near by for examination. "All Right" and we drove on, coming on lines of tents and a babel of sounds: the camp has a flanking of brush wood hovels. When we stop, a crowd of men talking various languages surrounds us, very polite and very stupid & uncomprehending. I got out & settled with the driver & a very very polite man conducted me to Waring's tent. A wall tent 8 or 9 ft sq. with a few boards for a floor,[9] a rough table covered with oil cloth, a narrow bed 12 inches high, wash-stand, books on the table & lots of all sorts of uniforms & equipments not grouped picturesquely, but hung along the ends & down the middle on clothes lines. The Col. & Lt Col were absent & he in charge. Took me to the Col's tent, which I find should have been a hospital tent, & which is a big affair, on a pole in the centre the colors & the Col's uniforms & traps. A set of embroidered silver tea service on a packing case; a large table with books & papers, an orderly in shirt sleeves, whom W. orders to get ice-water & "a bottle of wine." W. is called out, and a man tall & rude, in dirty white shirt & brown trowsers, strolls in, & another—the adjutant or clerk, who looks an Italian military clerk under difficulties, the white shirt walks up & down. "It's a fine night" he says without looking at me but as nobody else answers I do; the orderly says something about vino; "Isn't a bottle of wine in the camp" says the shirt, "get some brandy." And the orderly sets a champagne bottle before me with three small silver cups, and the shirted man says it's good brandy & I ask him to drink & he does; then Waring comes in, and another red faced man in a blue flannel shirt worn outside & a sword, who is the officer of the day—the white shirt being the officer of the guard, both capitans. Then there is a talk of Capt[n] Takats'[10] company intending to call on the Col in the morning with muskets loaded to demand that Capt[n] T's resignation shall not be accepted and W. says Capt[n] ___, your company can be relied on? "Oh yes, My God, yes, Major—& soon." "Well have you got cartridges—get some cartridges & have them here loaded at 4 o'ck & when the Takats Company comes up, tell them to keep the other side of the police lines & if a man comes over the police lines, shoot him. If all come over, fire at em!" &c. &c. all boyish, weak and Italian playing soldier & I know it means nothing and take Waring's bed after the brandy & sleep pretty well; though waked often by the camp-noises, and challenges of sentinels & a visit of a field officer & escort on grand round duty I believe.

In the morning I visited the hospital & talked with all the surgeons & saw all their kit & food & learned something—but this was much the best part of the camp. Breakfasted with the Col[11] & staff; of whom the best seemed the priest.[12] Though I think well of Rappetti;[13] of the Col[l] I do not. Nobody was dressed, except Rappitti arriving fresh from New York. The men on duty were more or less dressed according to individual caprice, but generally in caps with Havlocks and straw hats & red shirts, though some wore the full dress, dirty & slouched.

Have done nothing else & train's off.

Quite well.

Fred.

1. The havelock, named after English general Sir Henry Havelock, was a cloth attachment to the cap to shield the soldier's neck from the sun.
2. Fort McHenry at Whetstone Point in Baltimore was erected in 1794 and named in honor of George Washington's secretary of war, James McHenry (John Thomas Scharf, *History of Maryland from the Earliest Period to the Present Day*, 3 vols. [Baltimore, 1879], 2: 582–83).
3. A way station of the Washington Branch of the Baltimore and Ohio Railroad, located in Baltimore County, Maryland, near the west branch of the Patapsco River.
4. Another, more southern, way station located in Anne Arundel County at the junction of the Washington Branch of the Baltimore and Ohio Railroad with the Annapolis and Elkridge Railroad, which served Annapolis.
5. Most likely the 20th New York State Militia, a regiment enlisted for three months' service and stationed first at Annapolis, later at Baltimore (Frederick Phisterer, comp., *New York in the War of the Rebellion, 1861–1865*, 3rd ed., 6 vols. [Albany, N.Y., 1912], 1: 608).
6. Shaped like a large bell, this tent was better known as the Sibley tent. Henry H. Sibley, a career army officer who had accompanied John C. Frémont on a Western expedition, patented this tent, which probably was inspired by the Indian tepee, in 1857. The Sibley tent was large—eighteen feet in diameter and twelve feet high—and could comfortably house twelve men, but its bulkiness made it unsuitable for field service (Francis A. Lord, *Civil War Collector's Encyclopedia: Arms, Uniforms, and Equipment of the Union and Confederacy* [Harrisburg, Pa., 1963], pp. 279–80).
7. George E. Waring, Jr. (1833–1898), was employed from 1857 to 1861 as an agricultural engineer to supervise the drainage of Central Park and earlier had rented Olmsted's Staten Island farm. After the Civil War, Waring became an important sanitary engineer. He oversaw the installation of a new sewerage system for yellow fever–ravaged Memphis, Tennessee, and served as New York City's street-cleaning commissioner. He and Olmsted collaborated on several projects, most notably the suburb Riverside, near Chicago.

    In the spring of 1861 Waring joined the 39th New York, also known as the Garibaldi Guard, and served as a major. He must have come to share Olmsted's low opinion of the regiment, for after being transferred west in the fall of 1861, he told Olmsted: "The immense, immense difference between this Regt and the Garibaldi Gd. is a source of daily delight to me. . . . When we take a walk through the camp we have the satisfaction of meeting gentlemen—with clean collars, shaven faces and trim moustaches." Although in 1863 he sought Olmsted's aid to be named brigadier general, Waring remained colonel of the 4th Missouri Cavalry from 1862 through 1864 (F. Phisterer, *New York in the War*, 3: 2189; *DAB*; G. E. Waring, Jr., to FLO, Oct. 31, 1861 and Jan. 23, 1863; *Papers of FLO*, 3: 105, n. 5).
8. Alexander Dallas Bache.

9. The wall tent had four upright sides and was commonly used by commissioned officers. It was also known as the hospital tent because large wall tents frequently served as field hospitals (F. A. Lord, *Civil War Collector's Encyclopedia*, pp. 276, 279).
10. Francis Takats (b. c. 1826) was captain of the Garibaldi Guard from May 1861 until his discharge in November of that year. He was a Central Park employee, and before his departure from New York he reminded Olmsted of a promise to take care of the families of the men from the park who volunteered for military duty. Olmsted replied that although he had been unable to secure funds for that purpose, the city's Union Defense Committee would aid Takats's family should his military salary prove insufficient. Olmsted also promised that occasionally he would have someone check to see that Takats's family was not neglected (Francis Takats to FLO, May 20, 1861; FLO to Francis Takats, May 21, 1861; F. Phisterer, *New York in the War*, 3: 2211).
11. Frederick George D'Utassy (b. c. 1827), colonel of the Garibaldi Guard. He was dishonorably discharged in May 1863 (F. Phisterer, *New York in the War*, 3: 2200).
12. Theodore Kruger (b. c. 1827), chaplain of the Garibaldi Guard from May until late August 1861 (ibid., 3: 2204).
13. Alexander Repetti (b. c. 1822), lieutenant colonel of the Garibaldi Guard, served in the Union army until June 1862 (ibid., 3: 2207).

To Mary Perkins Olmsted

> Sanitary Commission, Washington, D.C.
> Treasury Building,[1] July 2[d] 1861

My Dear

It is cool and pleasant here and I am well.

I have your note of the 29th.

I have not yet wanted anything of all that you omitted. You can send some cards by mail to Willard's Hotel,[2] when convenient.

I do not get on very well; do not accomplish much & shall not I fear. The army men on the Commission[3] can not be seen at an average expense of less than five hours & it is hard to get their pretence of attention for five seconds when you get access to them. They do nothing but discourage & obstruct, & so of all officials. The official machinery is utterly and absurdly inadequate for the emergency & there is no time to think of enlarging it. I feel that the whole business is exceedingly uncertain & should not be much surprised to get up & find Jeff Davis in the White House. There is a great lot of fine material for soldiers here but no army. Seventy disjointed regiments of infantry under canvass. I can not comprehend it and fear there is no policy or meaning in it.

ROBERT CROOKE WOOD

There is to be some movement, I think, soon after the 4th, probably only a reconnaissance in force on Fairfax C.H.[4]

I have seen a good many camps & have a better opinion of the soldiers & a little better of the officers.[5]

I am inclined to regret at present that I accepted the post. I can hardly give it up. I am afraid it will cost us $2000 a year.[6]

Give me some good news of yourself, please, and of the park. I can not get on long without you here.

I saw the President this morning walking hastily with two or three other loafers to the War Department.[7] He looked much younger than I had suppos'd, dressed in a cheap & nasty French black cloth suit just out of a tight carpet bag. Looked as if he would be an applicant for a Broadway squad policemanship, but a little too smart and careless. Turned & laughed familiarly at a joke upon himself which he overheard from my companion *en passant.*

I have commissiond Dunning[8] for Fort Monroe.

The present minor curse of Washington is flies. It is far worse than Staten Isl[d] in fish time.

Yours

Fred.

1. The Sanitary Commission had by late June been given office space in a government building, as was provided in the resolution recognizing the Commission. George Templeton Strong described the room as a "very grand official room in the Treasury Building, with its long, official, green-covered table and chairs ranged in official order around it, and official stationery in front of each chair." He then added, "One could not sit there a moment without official sensations of dignity and red-tapery" (*Diary of the Civil War*, p. 164).

2. Olmsted was staying at Willard's City Hotel, located on the corner of 14th Street and Pennsylvania Avenue. In 1850 the Willard brothers had bought several contiguous houses and had remodeled them into a four-story, one-hundred-room structure that became very popular (Garnett Laidlaw Eskew, *Willard's of Washington: The Epic of a Capital Caravansery* [New York, 1954], pp. 12–13).

3. A reference to the three members of the Sanitary Commission—George W. Cullum, Alexander E. Shiras, and Robert C. Wood—who were career army officers.

    George Washington Cullum (1809–1892) entered the army's engineer corps after graduating from West Point in 1833. He supervised the construction of various fortifications and taught military engineering at West Point. In 1861 he served as an aide-de-camp to General Winfield Scott and was promoted from captain to major in August. Commissioned as brigadier general of volunteers in November 1861, he held various engineering posts in the Western departments until late 1864, when he became superintendent of the U.S. Military Academy. Cullum is best remembered as the compiler of biographical registers of graduates of the U.S. Military Academy.

    Alexander Eakins Shiras (c. 1812–1875), a West Pointer who before 1861 taught there, served in an artillery unit and in the subsistence bureau. Promoted to the rank of major in April 1861, he remained on the staff of the commissary of subsistence in Washington. Shiras became a colonel and assistant commissary general of subsistence in 1863 and headed the bureau shortly before his death. Although George Templeton Strong scornfully called Shiras an "inveterate red tapist," Olmsted was more admiring and early in 1863 listed him among the few really competent administrators in Washington.

    Robert Crooke Wood (d. 1869) served as acting surgeon general during the last illness of Thomas Lawson in 1861 and gave initial approval for the formation of the Sanitary Commission. Wood's career in the army had been long: he was named an assistant surgeon in 1825. Stationed first at Western outposts, he also served in the Mexican War. Wood had important political connections. In 1829 he married Ann Mackall Taylor, oldest daughter of then Lieutenant Colonel Zachary Taylor. Wood and his father-in-law were close friends and political confidants. Stationed in Baltimore during Taylor's presidential term, Wood was next assigned to Washington, D.C., from 1854 until 1862. There the Wood family lived a pleasant life. Olmsted called their house "the best . . . I have seen in Washington, with some pictures & things."

    Wood never favorably impressed members of the Sanitary Commission. Although George Templeton Strong called him "warm-hearted" and "our excellent old colleague," he also believed that "Wood is far too old and too far gone in the ossification of routine to be fully fitted" to become surgeon general. Bellows was even less complimentary; he called Wood "grey and impassive, unsmiling and cold."

    None of the "army men" on the Commission was active in its affairs after December 1861. Late in 1861, when George W. Cullum was transferred to the Army of the Missouri, he offered his resignation to the Commission, which did not accept it. Although Shiras remained in Washington, he never attended a Commission meeting after December 1861. Wood also stayed away from meetings during the Commission's drive to reform the Medical Bureau in the winter of 1861–62, and he too was transferred to St. Louis after William A. Hammond became surgeon general in the spring of 1862 (George Washington Cullum, *Biographical Register of the Officers and Graduates of the U.S. Military Academy at West Point, N.Y.* . . . , 3rd ed., 3 vols.

[Boston, 1891], 1: 550–51; *DAB*; FLO to William Henry Hurlbert, Jan. 31, 1863, below; *Appleton's Cyc. Am. Biog.*; Brainerd Dyer, *Zachary Taylor* [Baton Rouge, La., 1946], p. 96; *Diary of the Civil War*, pp. 181, 186, 204, 218; FLO to MPO, Dec. 8, 1861; USSC, *Minutes*, p. 80).

4. This reconnaissance in force upon Fairfax Courthouse, Virginia, does not appear to have taken place (Frederick H. Dyer, *A Compendium of the War of the Rebellion . . . ,* 3 vols. [1908; rpt. ed., New York, 1959], 2: 894).

5. A reference to the visits Olmsted was then making to the camps of the volunteer troops. He wrote in his report of July 9, 1861, that the "Resident Secretary has inspected twenty of the volunteer camps during the last ten days." For his first impression of volunteer soldiers, see FLO to MPO, June 28, 1861, above (Frederick Law Olmsted, "Report of a Preliminary Survey of the Camps of a Portion of the Volunteer Forces near Washington," doc. no. 17 in USSC, *Documents*).

6. Exactly how Olmsted arrived at this figure is not clear. Even though he assured his wife that he believed that he could retain his post as superintendent of Central Park, he probably expected a reduction in his annual salary of five thousand dollars from the park. In fact he may have anticipated that the commissioners would cut it in half, as they did in a resolution of January 1862 that was retroactive to July 1861. He probably also expected that the expense account accompanying his annual salary of two thousand dollars from the Sanitary Commission would not cover the additional cost of maintaining a second household (FLO to MPO, July 9, 1861; New York City, Board of Commissioners of the Central Park, *Minutes of Proceedings of the Board of Commissioners of the Central Park* [New York, 1858–69], p. 73; MPO to JO, July 17, 1861).

7. That is, Olmsted saw President Abraham Lincoln walking to the War Department building at 17th Street and Pennsylvania Avenue, only a short distance from the White House.

8. Edwin James Dunning (1821–1901), a dentist and one of the first inspectors for the Sanitary Commission. Born in Camillus, New York, he studied in the office of a Syracuse dentist. From 1844 until 1856 he worked as an assistant to Dr. Eleazar Parmly, a renowned dentist in New York City. Dunning then began his own practice in New York City. Living on Staten Island, he became acquainted with Olmsted through their mutual interest in the Richmond County Agricultural Society.

Dunning served with the Sanitary Commission during the summer and fall of 1861 and again, despite poor health, during the Antietam campaign. After the war he briefly taught at the New York College of Dentistry, and he practiced dentistry until partial blindness led to his retirement in 1874 (Charles Otis Kimball, "A Biographical Sketch of Edwin James Dunning," *International Dental Journal* 22 [1901]: 808–12; HWB to FLO, Oct. 8, 1862, USSC-NYPL, box 746: 2434; "Appeal to the Citizens of Staten Island, by the Board of Managers of the Richmond County Agricultural Society" [Dec. 1849]).

CHAPTER II

THE UNION DEFEAT
AT BULL RUN

THE BATTLE OF BULL RUN, which ended in defeat and the flight of part of the Union army, dominated Olmsted's thoughts and writings during the late summer and early fall of 1861. His letters of late July display an intense reaction to the defeat and an insistence upon admitting the fact that some of the Union volunteer forces had performed badly under fire. His letter of August 15, 1861, arguing that the Sanitary Commission should explode myths of Confederate atrocities against wounded Union soldiers during that battle, also illustrates his view that truthfulness and a dispassionate analysis of the facts were necessary to the North's cause.

Olmsted's writings during this period show his disillusionment with the leadership and administrative ability of officials of the federal government. His report upon the demoralization of the Union troops at Bull Run, which is presented here, focuses on the underlying causes for the soldiers' dissatisfaction—the government's failure to provide healthful food, clothing, and shelter and to equip, pay, and command the volunteer regiments adequately. This report and his letters to Henry W. Bellows indicate Olmsted's increasing criticism of the Medical Bureau's response to its greatly expanded tasks. A letter to Alfred Field reveals that Olmsted also believed the federal government was incompetent in meeting the wartime needs of the nation and in dealing with the problem of slavery.

Despite his general gloom, Olmsted saw one encouraging sign: the accession of George B. McClellan to command of the Army of the Potomac. In his letter to his father of September 12, 1861, Olmsted sketches a vivid portrait of the young, self-assured military leader. Olmsted's other letters of this period also show his conviction that McClellan was bringing necessary system and order to the drilling of troops, as the Sanitary Commission was seeking to do in the care of the volunteer soldiers. Olmsted's correspondence with the agents and inspectors of the Sanitary Commission stresses the importance of teaching the new army officers proper measures for preserving the health of their men. It also emphasizes the Commission's obligation to use its resources to meet any shortages of medical or hospital supplies.

To Mary Perkins Olmsted

Sanitary Commission, Washington, D.C.
Treasury Building, July 29, 1861

Beloved!

We are in a frightful condition here, ten times as bad as anyone dare say publickly. I think we are getting better, but are also growing nearer a crisis—an attack. Why Beauregard[1] does not attack I can not imagine unless he be—no general. I have not been to bed since I have been here without a strong apprehension that I should be waked by cannonading. The demoralization of a large part of our troops is something more awful than I ever met with.

There is but one Sanitary measure to be thought of now & that is discipline. We want numbers of fresh men for the moral effect on ourselves and on the enemy; but practically, for action, numbers will only increase confusion, until they are a thousandfold better disciplined than the most of those now here or than those who were spoiled for soldiers at Bull Run.

I will have a Report on the subject soon.[2]

Write to me and make the best of our affairs. I could not flinch from this now if it starved us all to stay.

Yours.

Tell all our friends to stiffen themselves for harder times than we have yet thought of. Unless McLellan[3] is a genius as well as a general & unless he becomes a military dictator & rules over our imbecile government, we should & must have a revolution before we can do anything with the South.[4]

You will see from this that I am overwhelmed. I have suffered intense humiliation. Our Commission can do something and I from my

THE STAMPEDE FROM BULL RUN

position in it can do something to set public opinion in the right direction & to overcome in some details the prevailing inefficiency & misery. You would not have me do less than I can.

I remain pretty well, having got off my cold. I need not confess that I am working harder & longer than is good for me & have been in want of sleep. I am doing well under the circumstances. Many regiments are not a mob; they are parts of a disintegrated herd of sick monomaniacs. They start and turn pale at the breaking of a stick or the crack of a percussion cap—at the same time they are brutal savages. That is the meaning of "demoralization." It is a terrific disease. They are fast recovering. Most may now be called recoverd of those that remain. Thank God, McIntee[5] escaped the disgrace of Bull's Run. What it was will never be told publickly. Human nature has seldom showed itself so degraded.

1. Pierre Gustave Toutant Beauregard (1818–1893), a career army officer who very briefly served as superintendent of the military academy at West Point. Appointed a Confederate brigadier general, Beauregard commanded the troops that captured Fort Sumter in April 1861. In June he took command of the Confederate army in northern Virginia near Washington, and he drew up the orders for the battle of Bull

Run. In the spring of 1862 he was transferred to the Western department, but his later service during the war was primarily in Virginia and South Carolina.

In March 1861 Mary Perkins Olmsted met Beauregard when, upon his departure to his native Louisiana, he visited her to learn about the qualifications of Miss Centayne, the governess of the Olmsted children, as a teacher for his daughter. Mary described Beauregard as "a stiff, tall, thin, grey haired youngish man—precise and positive" and sardonically added that he "took a fancy to me so I hope to be well treated when we are conquered" (*DAB*; MPO to JO, March 22, 1861).

2. Olmsted and the Sanitary Commission workers began an investigation into the behavior and condition of Union troops at Bull Run almost immediately after that battle took place (July 21, 1861). See "Report on the Demoralization of the Volunteers," September 5, 1861, below.

3. George Brinton McClellan (1826–1885) was called from military successes in western Virginia in late July 1861 to take command of the Union troops near Washington, D.C. A graduate of West Point, he had served in the engineers corps and the cavalry before resigning his commission in 1857. By 1860 he had become president of the Ohio and Mississippi Railroad, but he returned to military duty in 1861 as a major general. Removed from command of the Army of the Potomac in November 1862, McClellan returned to civilian life and became the Democratic party's unsuccessful candidate for president in 1864.

In the summer of 1861 McClellan immediately impressed the members of the Sanitary Commission by his attention to order, drill, and discipline. They also found him willing to listen to their suggestions about hygiene and other aspects of camp life. By mid-September Bellows and Olmsted believed they had found the man who would put the Commission's recommendations into effect. Their confidence in McClellan's vigor and receptivity to new ideas led Bellows to request that the medical director of the Army of the Potomac report only to McClellan, not to the surgeon general. In the fall and winter of 1861–62, however, McClellan did not prove as willing to force through reforms as he had first appeared to be. Olmsted fretted over the failure to issue a general order extending official recognition to Sanitary Commission agents inspecting the military camps.

But in the spring of 1862, while critics chafed at McClellan's lack of activity, Olmsted and the other commissioners remained among the general's supporters. Eleven weeks with the Army of the Potomac during the Peninsula campaign further convinced Olmsted that McClellan had built a splendid fighting force and that only the failure of the government to send sufficient reinforcements kept him from victory. Through the fall of 1862 as McClellan was removed from and then restored to command of his old troops, Olmsted's faith in the general remained steadfast. Olmsted angrily quarreled with his longtime friend Charles Loring Brace over McClellan's abilities and the wisdom of his military strategy during the Peninsula and Antietam campaigns. Only in 1863 as McClellan, who again had been removed from command, began to assume an active role in Democratic politics did Olmsted's admiration flag. By July 1863 he saw no reason for McClellan to be reinstated, even were the Union army to be defeated by the invading Confederates. By then Olmsted believed McClellan to be the pawn of his powerful Democratic friends S. L. M. Barlow and August Belmont; he also argued that McClellan's continued support of his court-martialed general, Fitz-John Porter, indicated a serious weakness (*DAB*; HWB to Simon Cameron, Sept. 12, 1861, USSC-NYPL, box 638; FLO to JO, Sept. 12, 1861, below; FLO to HWB, Feb. 7, 1862, below; FLO to CLB, Aug. 25 and Sept. 30, 1862, below; FLO to HWB, July 4, 1863, below).

4. Olmsted was disgusted with the inability of the government to cope with the monumental task of creating a bureaucracy capable of supplying and training a newly raised army. Apparently he wondered if the republican system of government was equal to the task. Such pessimism over the failures of the Lincoln administration

seemingly led him temporarily to consider the use of revolutionary measures to secure the organization necessary to subdue the South. His friend Eliza H. Schuyler commented in early September 1861, "It is interesting to see how the younger generation, represented by sincere, earnest men like Olmsted & Brace & others, of radical & extreme views, all tend *now* towards centralization, unconstitutional & illegal, or despotic measures—a National act of Emancipation to begin with, or a revolution at home, & a Dictator" (E. H. Schuyler to HWB, Sept. 10, 1861, Henry Whitney Bellows Papers, Massachusetts Historical Society, Boston, Mass.).

5. Jervis McEntee (1828–1891), the brother-in-law of Calvert Vaux, Olmsted's collaborator on the design for New York's Central Park. McEntee, an artist who had studied under Frederick Church, had opened his own studio in New York in 1854. At the outbreak of the Civil War, McEntee volunteered for service in the 20th New York State Militia. The 20th New York was not stationed in the Washington area and thus did not participate in the battle of Bull Run (*NCAB*; Frederick Phisterer, comp., *New York in the War of the Rebellion, 1861–1865*, 3rd ed., 6 vols. [Albany, N.Y., 1912], 1: 608, 610).

To William Cullen Bryant[1]

Private

Sanitary Commission, Washington, D.C.
Treasury Building, 31st July 1861

My Dear Mr Bryant,
    I have just observed an article in the Post of the 29th on the character of the Retreat from Bull's Run.[2]
    It is best we should all look the truth in the face, and although it is not best to say it publickly, you should know, at least, that this retreat was generally of the worst possible character, and is already in its results most disastrous.[3] We have had six educated, careful men engaged in a systematic visitation of the regiments which were engaged in the fights,[4] (where regiments could be found, of the disorganized materials of regiments, in some cases), and with their detailed reports in my hands, and with the evidence before my eyes of a different character, I must assure you that a large portion of our forces were stricken with a most terrible mental disease, under which all manliness was lost and the utmost cowardice, unreasonableness and fiendish inhumanity were developed. From this disease, a large part are yet but slowly recovering. The condition of things here now is simply appalling. With very few exceptions, the men, even of the better regiments, represent their officers to be cowards and fools. And that many officers and even medical officers did act in the most dastardly manner

there can be little question. One who stood upon the long bridge[5] says that of the first three hundred of those heading the retreat, two hundred were officers, and a large part of these were in the ambulances; while scarcely any of the wounded were brought in. A large part of those in hospitals are men who walked in, in spite of their wounds.

A vast improvement in the character of our officers, and a complete reformation in respect of discipline, is a matter of vital necessity. This was evident to most of us before the battle; it is demonstrated now. We never shall succeed without it.

This conviction is [so] strong in my mind that I could not resist expressing it to you. I feel that it is of the utmost importance that the facts should be understood and that the whole strength of the good men of the country should be immediately directed to the remedy.

Yours Truly & Respectfully,

Fred. Law Olmsted.

The original is in the Bryant-Godwin Collection, Rare Books & Manuscripts Division, The New York Public Library, Astor, Lenox and Tilden Foundations, New York City.

1. William Cullen Bryant (1794–1878), poet and editor of the *New York Evening Post*. An acquaintance from Olmsted's years in the literary world, Bryant was also an early advocate of a New York City park and had signed Olmsted's petition in 1857 for the superintendency of Central Park. The editor was a close friend of the Perkins family, and his wife had been Mary Perkins Olmsted's godmother (*DAB*; *Papers of FLO*, 1: 18–19; Laura Wood Roper, *FLO: A Biography of Frederick Law Olmsted* [Baltimore, 1973], p. 58).
2. The editorial of July 29 to which Olmsted refers inspired this letter by its interpretation of the Union retreat from Bull Run, which began:

    The day after the fatal reports of the rout of our army at Bull Run the *Evening Post* denied that any of our soldiers who had been engaged in the conflict ran. We did so on the strength of evidence furnished us by more than one eyewitness of the whole scene. We said that the disorderly part of the movement was confined to the straggling troops to the rear, to the teamsters and civilians, and to the reserves at Centreville, who being without a sober commander, were set in motion by the fearful stories of defeat carried to them by the fugitives.

    The article then discussed new reports that the retreat had been a rout and used an official report and further eyewitness testimony to dismiss such stories as uninformed hearsay. The newspaperman concluded, "All this confirms our original view of the disaster, which was founded upon what we deemed such good authority that we shall adhere to it until the official reports tell another tale" ("The Character of the Retreat," *New York Evening Post*, July 29, 1861, p. 2).
3. Olmsted worried that what he perceived as the lessons of Bull Run concerning the need for discipline among the troops were not being learned by either men of influence or the general population. He contemplated sending a "private circular" to "our friends" because "it seems to me that by common consent, for the sake of weak

minds, the terrible truth of our situation is being ignored. But there are men who should know what we know." Obviously he saw Bryant as such a man (FLO to Alfred J. Bloor, July 27, 1861, USSC-NYPL, box 727: 205).

4. Olmsted's old friend Charles Loring Brace (1826–1890), and five Sanitary Commission employees: John Hancock Douglas, Frederick Newman Knapp, Godfrey Philip (or Philip Godfrey) Aigner, William Peter Buel, and Robert Tomes.

Godfrey Philip Aigner was a German-born physician from New York City. A graduate of University Medical College in New York, he served as an inspector, primarily in the Sanitary Commission's Western department, until the spring of 1862. Poor health then led to his resignation, but he again worked for the Commission in 1864. In 1865 he practiced medicine in New York City and was the house physician of the New York Dispensary.

William Peter Buel (1807–1888), a New England–born physician who was a graduate of Yale College and the College of Physicians and Surgeons in New York. He practiced medicine in New York City for twenty years and then served as physician for two steamboat lines plying the Panamanian route between New York and San Francisco.

Buel served as an inspector for the Sanitary Commission from the late summer of 1861 until 1862. Stationed in Missouri, he found his position difficult to define because of the work that the local organization, the Western Sanitary Commission, was undertaking in St. Louis. His response to a lack of instructions was to do nothing, and the U.S. Sanitary Commission voted in December 1861 to relieve Buel of his duties. In January 1862 Bellows apparently had second thoughts about the case and expressed the fear that the Commission had "unwittingly wronged" Buel "in the implied censure of our recall." The minister then suggested to Olmsted that if an inspectorship with specific duties were open, it should be given to Buel. No such post was forthcoming, and in 1862 Buel was appointed surgeon of the 131st New York. He remained an army physician until 1871.

Robert Tomes had studied medicine at the University of Edinburgh. He had also attended Washington College in Hartford, Connecticut, where possibly he first met Olmsted. When Tomes planned to visit London in 1857, Olmsted gave him a letter of introduction to his friend Henry Stevens, a prominent book dealer there. In June 1861 Olmsted recruited Tomes to serve as an inspector for the Commission, but the physician resigned in the late autumn of that same year (USSC, *Minutes*, pp. 48, 83, and 173; William Quentin Maxwell, *Lincoln's Fifth Wheel: The Political History of the United States Sanitary Commission* [New York, 1956], p. 317; John H. Douglas to JFJ, April 26, 1862, USSC-NYPL, box 740: 855; Guido Furman, ed., *The Medical Register of the City of New York, for the Year Commencing June 1, 1865* . . . [New York, 1865], pp. 133, 247; *Yale Obit. Rec.*, 3rd ser., 8 [June 1888]: 421–22; W. P. Buel to FLO, Aug. 10, 1861, USSC-NYPL, box 728: 338; HWB to FLO, Jan. 14, 1862, USSC-NYPL, box 738: 131; Robert Tomes, *My College Days* [New York, 1880], pp. 21, 73, 210; FLO to Henry Stevens, March 19, 1857, Henry Stevens Papers, Department of Special Collections, University of California at Los Angeles, Los Angeles, Ca.; FLO to Robert Tomes, June 25, 1861, USSC-NYPL, box 833, 1: i).

5. The long bridge was the principal north-south bridge spanning the Potomac River to link the city of Washington with Virginia.

To Alfred T. Field[1]

To Field.

July 31ˢᵗ 1861.

To what President or Congress or General, to what individual wisdom political or military shall we ascribe the final eradication of the vices of slavery. One and all our "leaders" are contemptible. The people is far above & beyond them always.

How, with the ideas we have had, could slavery be destroyed & that infernal state [of] society nurtured—there & here—by slavery? We shall do it of no direct intention, but as an incident of other purposes—or rather of the outworking of a principle of virtue incident of popular freedom. When we no longer think of slavery, but only of the duty which is next before us, and every man goes forth with his life in his hand & property & all that property represents, made of no more account than it is to a man with his head under the axe, what chance then for slavery is left, in the character of the regenerate nation. Slavery has rested for years on broken laws—laws broken in detail.[2] It now rests on defiance of the same laws at wholesale. What is called secession is the organization & dignification of anarchy. Either with or without a bayonet I am going to speak my mind of the economy of slavery in Virginia—going to offer my books for sale there.[3] This is my right under our compact, and I don't care what the obstruction to this right is called, mob or government, it's going to be put down. If slavery goes with it, down with slavery. This is not my business & will not be[4] my war cry, but down it goes all the same.

(We couldn't see that slavery was inconsistent with Law, demonstration in detail was not enough. The leaders would therefore organize wholesale & complete that rebellion which had been partial & therefore more ruinous to our liberty & Law than direct & avowed enmity.)

The original is a fragment of a draft.

1. Alfred T. Field (1814–1884), an English hardware merchant and manufacturer. He and Olmsted became friends while they were neighbors on Staten Island in the 1850s. Although Field moved back to England in 1854, he continued to visit the United States and was in New York in June and July 1861.

    The letter presented here was one of Olmsted's attempts to convince Field of the correctness of the Northern response to secession. The Englishman's doubts about whether the North should or even could defeat the South and reestablish the Union angered Olmsted and temporarily strained their friendship. In 1862 he complained to Field that while English opinion in general might be dismissed, "when I know that a man, for whom I have the respect & regard and something more, that I have for you, expresses no other than the popular view of the case, to which the Times administers as above, I must say that I am shocked and grieved, and feel it as a more melancholy thing than all that occurs at home" (FLO to A. T. Field, Jan. 30, 1862; A. T. Field to FLO, Nov. 14, 1862; A. T. Field to Charlotte E. Field, June 2 and July 9, 1861; *Papers of FLO*, 1: 342, n. 11).

2. Most likely Olmsted refers here to at least two different kinds of laws being broken in support of slavery. The first would be those fundamental laws protecting people from violence and murder. Olmsted believed that the maintenance of the slave regime required a resort to personal violence against slaves. In 1857 he wrote, "Any symptoms of rebellion on one side, or of treachery on the other, cannot safely be left to the slow process of civil law; every white man is expected to deal summarily with them, and in such a manner as to pervade with terror, cowardice, and hopelessness all the possibly disaffected." He argued that this extralegal violence was also used against whites, and that it allowed assassinations and attacks like that of Preston Brooks upon Charles Sumner.

   Olmsted also believed that constitutional guarantees of free speech were flouted. He proclaimed indignantly that in the South,

   > Books, periodicals, and newspapers, are interdicted, if they maintain the faith which was universal among its Friends in the South when our Union was formed. However calm and respectful their manner, they are denied the service of the United States mails; those who receive them are denounced as abolition traitors; gentlemen who acknowledge themselves to privately hold similar opinions, and who are on terms of friendship with their authors, feel obliged to 'discountenance' them.

   Olmsted's view of events in Kansas in 1856 and 1857 held that both kinds of fundamental laws, those protecting against violence and those allowing the free circulation of ideas, had been ruthlessly broken by the proslavery men. Not only had free-soilers been murdered, but civil liberties had been severely abridged by laws such as one that made the proclaiming of antislavery views a felony (Frederick Law Olmsted, "American Editor's Introduction" to *The Englishman in Kansas* [*Papers of FLO*, 2: 412, 418]; idem, "Supplement by the American Editor" to *The Englishman in Kansas* [*Papers of FLO*, 2: 424–28]).

3. At this time Olmsted was particularly concerned about the South's abridgment of civil liberties. William H. Russell, a British journalist, described Olmsted in August 1861 as "prepared to lay down his life for free speech over a united republic, in one part of which his freedom of speech would lead to irretrievable confusion and ruin."

   Earlier in the year Olmsted had pondered Southern censorship. He praised an article written by Charles Francis Adams, Jr., and remarked: "If a few hundred thousand could be distributed now in a pamphlet form in the Slave States, it would be invaluable. It is one of their curses that this cannot be." Olmsted then suggested the formation of a group to "stimulate, aid and cooperate with an organized rebellion against the Cotton King, within the South itself." He himself had personally encountered at least one instance of Southern censorship. In May 1857 a Mobile, Alabama, bookseller requested his publisher to allow the return of seven copies of *A Journey Through Texas*. The bookseller noted "considerable objection" in Mobile to Olmsted's opinions and observed, "We are obliged to be very cautious with regard to selling any books at all impregnated with [the] abolition principle" (William Howard Russell, *My Diary North and South* [Boston, 1863], p. 514; FLO to C. F. Adams, Jr., March 25, 1861 [*Papers of FLO*, 3: 330–31]; Middleton & McMaster to Dix, Edwards & Co., May 6, 1857).

4. By a slip of the pen, Olmsted here wrote "by."

137

To John Olmsted

Washington, August 3^d 1861.

Dear Father,

It is a sweltering, calm, noxious, tropical night, and I rise for relief, after having rolled on a bed in a closet of a room at Willard's, not able to sleep, till 3 o'clock, and write on what I find by chance at hand. It has been dreadful here since my return. To the humiliation of the defeat and the terrible humiliation of the mad flight, which transformed what we had been calling a grand army of gallant men, into a miserable collection of dejected wild animals, there has been added the appalling conviction that our rulers were utterly unable to comprehend, far less to cope with, the emergency. How terrible is the trial of our country, how weak, how unprepared to meet it, we are, it is impossible to find terms to express. Lincoln has no element of dignity; no tact, not a spark of genius. This is almost true of all his cabinet. He is an amiable, honest, good fellow. His cabinet is not that. There is the greatest conceivable dearth of administrative talent. The rabble armies of Garrabaldi[1] were not half as badly provided for. The best material for an army in the world has been ruined by bad management, inefficiency. There are few armies that would not have mutinied before the battle, so badly fed and cared for. There was no discipline, and the pretence and form of discipline, kept up in some particulars of outside show, only made the want of it the more dangerous, the disaster more certain. We have now to reorganize; we have the sickly season of the Potomac at hand. We are hurrying more thousands of green men, badly prepared, totally undisciplined, and are to undertake the drilling and formation of an army of them within sight of the smoke of the camp-fires of a victorious enemy.

Now, if I can do anything to strengthen the hands of McLellan, upon whom for the present all depends; anything to give him greater confidence to enforce discipline, anything to help the men to resist the coming pestilence, as well as the threatening army, will you not justify me in neglecting the park; neglecting everything else for a time?

So much for that aspect of it—confessing that it occupies and drives me so much that I need to give you my justification. There are things more deplorable than loss of health or life. However, I do not mean to give up the park, nor to lose my health, nor do I make life of no value.

I spent half the day out yesterday, visiting the hospital at Alexandria which is under the charge of (Ed?) Sheldon M.D.U.S.A. (of Hartford)[2] a capital fellow, who has done himself great credit in its management; the wounded are all doing very well. We have provided them all with shirts, sheets &c, have a barber going round, provide ice, ad libitum,[3] face covers,

WILLIAM HOWARD RUSSELL

bed tables, backgammon boards, paper & pens &c. &c. This afternoon I dined with Russell[4] of the Times; Visetelli,[5] the coresp[t] of Illustrated news, formerly of Garrabaldi's suite, and Ritchie, Maj. Wordsworth's son-in-law,[6] himself aid to Col Miles in the engagment. We had a long & very jolly evening, full of Indian, as well as Crimean & Italian reminiscences. I have dined with a party, and had all the champagne I wanted, four days in succession; and, as you know, that always agrees with me. The doctors of the Commission prescribed champagne for me, and as they must foot the bill, I don't think I shall spare it, hereafter.

I am holding out very well, and am gradually getting the work organized—the difficulty being that the field enlarges, to this time, so rapidly that no system holds adequate from day to day. I have sent off three inspectors for the other army columns today; all of them excellent men, talented surgeons.[7] I have seven gentlemen employed hereabouts, in & out the office.[8] I have a large correspondence with Woman's Societie[s] & on hand a stock of hospital stores more than sufficient for the present. More

139

than 200 tons of ice. Several casks of spirit & wine. The Commission adjourned last night, after an important session of a week. All the old members here except one.[9] (We elected Bishop of R.I.[10] a member.) Why don't the girls[11] write to a fellow—I suppose Bertha does, but I'm none the better for it. I was delighted with your account of Owen,[12] I wish I could see him. Don't let him forget his daddy if I do sometimes neglect mine too long. None the less in constant affection,

Your Son,

Fred.

1. Giuseppi Garibaldi (1807–1882), military leader in the struggle to unify Italy, had commanded ill-clad and poorly supplied troops during campaigns in 1848, 1849, 1859, and 1860 (George M. Trevelyan, *Garibaldi's Defence of the Roman Republic*, new ed. [London, 1908], pp. 48, 88–90; idem, *Garibaldi and the Thousand* [London, 1909], pp. 85–87, 218–23).
2. Henry Lawrence Sheldon of Connecticut was an assistant surgeon in the United States Army. Olmsted's question mark indicates his uncertainty about the surgeon's first name (Francis Bernard Heitman, *Historical Register and Dictionary of the United States Army . . .* , 2 vols. [Washington, D.C., 1903], 1: 879–80).
3. A Latin phrase that can be translated as "at their pleasure," probably meaning that the Sanitary Commission supplied these services when the patients desired them.
4. William Howard Russell (1820–1907), war correspondent and journalist. Born in Ireland, Russell was educated in Dublin and attended Trinity College there. He joined the staff of the *Times* of London in 1843 as a reporter. His series of articles from the Crimea in 1854-55 exposing the inadequate provisions made for British soldiers won fame and acclaim for him. Russell then journeyed to India, where he reported on the campaign to quell the native mutineers. Such past experience reporting upon world crises made him an obvious choice of the *Times* to describe the American secession crisis and Civil War to its readers.

   When Russell arrived in the United States on March 16, 1861, he carried a letter of introduction to Olmsted from the editor of the *Times*, John T. Delane, with whom Olmsted, in the 1850s, had discussed the prospects for cotton grown by free labor. Russell was very impressed by Olmsted. After they attended a press breakfast together in March, Russell described Olmsted as "the indefatigable, able, and earnest writer, whom to describe simply as an Abolitionist would be to confound with ignorant if zealous, unphilosophical, and impracticable men." The two men also breakfasted together in Washington in early April, and Olmsted probably advised Russell about the journey in the Confederacy that the reporter intended to make.

   Upon Russell's return from the South and Olmsted's acceptance of the position of secretary of the Sanitary Commission, the two men entered the period of their greatest intimacy. In July and August 1861 they visited each other and dined together several times. Russell left Washington on September 18, and although he returned and remained there from October through December and from March to April 1862, there is no indication that he and Olmsted had any further social encounters. Only one other meeting between the two was reported, and it resulted from Olmsted's wish to obtain some information about the British government's actions. Neither man commented on the apparent cooling of their friendship, but a remark by Olmsted in January 1862 imputing "inordinate prejudice" to "the stuff which Russell & others write from here, about the President, Congress & Mr Seward's being afraid of the mob of New York" suggests that the newspaperman's criticisms of the North angered him. He may also have become increasingly dismayed by Russell's aristocratic and antirepublican biases. Moreover, the press of Sanitary Commission business probably left Olmsted with less time for socializing.

Russell's opinions of American life, however, continued to interest Olmsted. When he began his journey through the Midwest in the spring of 1863, he used Russell's accounts, published in book form that year, as a reference point for his own observations (*DNB*; J. T. Delane to FLO, Feb. 28, 1861; William Howard Russell, *My Diary North and South* [Boston, 1863], pp. 7, 28, 55, 390–91, 482, 485, 514, 589–90; FLO to Alfred T. Field, Jan. 30, 1862; *Papers of FLO*, 2: 32, 446).

5. Frank Vizetelly (1830–1883?), artist and war correspondent for the *Illustrated London News*. Born in London of Italian ancestry, he had accompanied Garibaldi's troops in the campaign of 1860. Vizetelly met a tragic end, however: he was either killed or imprisoned and enslaved in the crushing defeat of General Hicks's army in the Sudan (*DNB*).

6. Montgomery Ritchie (d. 1864) of Boston, who in 1857 had married Cordelia Wadsworth, eldest daughter of Olmsted's third cousin James S. Wadsworth of Geneseo, New York. Ritchie served informally as the aide of General Dixon Miles at the battle of Bull Run. During August 1861, the Bostonian, while attempting in vain to obtain an army commission, spent much time with Olmsted. Ritchie finally entered military service in early 1862, serving first as a commissary of subsistence and later as a captain in the 1st Massachusetts Cavalry. He resigned from the army in May 1864 and died in November of that year (F. B. Heitman, *Historical Register and Dictionary*, 1: 833; *Olmsted Genealogy*, pp. 112–13; Henry Greenleaf Pearson, *James S. Wadsworth of Geneseo, Brevet Major-General of United States Volunteers* [New York, 1913], pp. 31, 78–80; see also FLO to MPO, [Aug. 9, 1861] and [c. Aug. 11–17, 1861]).

7. Sanitary Commission inspector William P. Buel left Washington on July 31 to join the army in Missouri, and Godfrey P. Aigner and John H. Douglas, whose destinations respectively were Cairo, Illinois, and Hagerstown, Maryland, departed on August 1 (FLO to Ellen Collins, Aug. 1, 1861, USSC-NYPL, box 654: 77; FLO to JSN, Aug. 6, 1861, USSC-NYPL, box 909, 1: 2).

8. The seven gentlemen probably included Frederick N. Knapp, Robert Tomes, Assistant Secretary Alfred Janson Bloor, Joseph Bridgham Curtis (1836–1862), George J. Pinckard, and two employees identified only as Mr. Cleary and Mr. Barnard. Curtis, younger half brother of Olmsted's friend George William Curtis, graduated from Lawrence Scientific School at Harvard and was an engineer on Central Park in New York. His friend Alfred J. Bloor recruited him to work briefly for the Sanitary Commission in the late summer of 1861 between stints in the army. In September 1861 he joined the 4th Rhode Island as a second lieutenant and was almost immediately promoted to first lieutenant. He was killed at the battle of Fredericksburg in December 1862.

Pinckard, Cleary, and Barnard also were short-term employees. Cleary was a young clerk recommended to Elisha Harris by the superintendent of the U.S. Treasury building. In November 1861 Pinckard, then serving as a storekeeper, was dismissed because he had shown a lack of "judgment and discipline" by misrepresenting his position with the Commission (FLO to GTS, Aug. 1, 1861, USSC-NYPL, box 608: 408; *NCAB*; *Appleton's Cyc. Am. Biog.*; A. J. Bloor to G. J. Pinckard, Nov. 24, 1861, Alfred Janson Bloor Papers, New-York Historical Society, New York City; Bloor Diary, July 26, 1861; Elisha Harris to FLO, July 24, 1861, USSC-NYPL, box 727: 108).

9. The one "old member" of the Sanitary Commission not attending any meetings in its fourth session (from July 27 until August 1) was John Strong Newberry of Cleveland, Ohio. He had been elected a member on June 14, 1861 (USSC, *Minutes*, pp. 5, 28–43).

10. Thomas March Clark (1812–1903), Episcopal bishop of Rhode Island. Olmsted was not certain of Clark's name and first wrote "Dr. Wells," then crossed it out. Clark, a Massachusetts native, was educated at Yale College and Princeton Theological Seminary. Reared as a Presbyterian, he left that church as an adult to enter the Episcopal ministry. After pastorates in Boston, Philadelphia, and Hartford, he was elected Bishop of Rhode Island, a post he held for almost fifty years.

   Clark was an urbane, witty man who thoroughly enjoyed life. When Olmsted wrote an anecdote to his stepson John Charles, he used one supplied by the bishop. George Templeton Strong pronounced Clark a "brick" and noted that his love of pleasure never ran to excesses (*DAB*; *Diary of the Civil War*, pp. 178, 297; FLO to John C. Olmsted, Oct. 17, 1861).

11. Olmsted's half-sisters Bertha and Mary Olmsted.

12. Owen Frederick Olmsted, Olmsted's stepson, was then on a visit to the John Olmsted family in Hartford, Connecticut (see FLO to JO, June 26, 1861, n. 5, above).

To Lewis Henry Steiner[1]

August 12th [1861]

My Dear Sir,

Your proposal to aid the Commission as a Sanitary Inspector was duly received and is gratefully accepted. Enclosed you will receive a certificate of appointment, countersigned at the Office of the Lieutenant General.

Having received an offer of similar service from the Reverend D[r] Winslow,[2] chaplain of a New York regiment now in Baltimore, I have requested him to cooperate with you. Will you oblige me by calling on him and arranging with him a proper division of duties. His regiment is known as Duryea's Zouaves, I do not know the number. It is camped on Federal Hill.[3] As D[r] Winslow is liable to be ordered to move with his regiment, it is desirous that you should comprehend the whole field.

The duties to be performed are properly divided under three heads:

1st The visitation of regimental camps, the object and method of which you will find indicated in a proof-sheet of instructions enclosed.[4] These instructions are imperfect and incomplete, but your own judgment will supply their deficiency. It is only necessary to say that the main object

LEWIS HENRY STEINER

is not to obtain a record but to facilitate and insure the giving of instruction and advice where needed.

2nd   The visitation of Hospitals:—the object of which is to stir up the surgeons and nurses by an exhibition of watchfulness and interest in their doings; to observe the wants of the patients and administer to them as far as possible. (See Resolutions 37 & 41, and 43, enclosed).[5]

3rd   To look after troops arriving, departing, or passing through by rail: The arrangement may be more perfect at Baltimore than here, where a man is most usefully employed in and around the station, giving information and advice, setting stragglers right, conveying word to friends, and making the sick comfortable amidst the confusion, disorder, and ignorance which prevail with new comers.

As our purpose is prevention rather than cure, the most important duty is that of suggesting, advising, and instructing the officers in camp. The record of their condition is of less importance, very much, but is conveniently made the medium of instruction.

The Commission is highly honored by your offer and will be grateful for your aid. I enclose a proper certificate of authority to engage in your duty.

It is desirable that you make a weekly report of your doings in behalf of the Commission. The printed form should be filled up but once for each regiment; subsequently changes, only, should be noticed.

When you see occasion, you will report directly to Gen. Dix[6] or to the Governor of any state suggesting any action which you may think to be urgently needed.

You will please return an account of expenses at least monthly: a detailed account is not required unless they should exceed $4. per diem. In any emergency, for the relief or transportation of the sick, & the like, you are expected to make any moderate expenditure on account of the Commission which you may deem to be required by humanity.

I am dear Sir
Your very obe't Servant

Prof. Steiner.
Baltimore Md.

The original is a letterpress copy in box 833, volume 1, pages 96–99, in USSC-NYPL. The first four paragraphs of the letter are in Olmsted's handwriting, the remainder in that of a copyist.

1. Lewis Henry Steiner (1827–1892), a native of Frederick County, Maryland, who had studied medicine at the University of Pennsylvania. Interested in natural science, he gave up the practice of medicine to teach chemistry at the Maryland College of Pharmacy. He also assisted John H. Douglas in editing the *American Medical Monthly*. Steiner's career after 1865 also was varied. In 1865 he presided over the Frederick County school board and took a special interest in the education of black children. In the 1870s he served in the state senate and became an editor of the *Frederick Examiner*. When Enoch Pratt established a free library in Baltimore in 1884, he persuaded Steiner to become its first librarian, a post he held until his death eight years later. Steiner wrote numerous articles and pamphlets on medical, historical, chemical, and religious topics.

   It is likely that Steiner's acquaintance with John H. Douglas and A. D. Bache brought him into the employ of the Sanitary Commission. On August 8 Steiner offered his services to Bache, who highly recommended him to Olmsted. During Steiner's three years of service with the Sanitary Commission, he inspected camps and hospitals and took charge of the relief effort at Antietam in 1862. In May 1863 the Commission appointed him chief inspector of the Army of the Potomac, and he served briefly as acting associate secretary after Olmsted's resignation. Relations between Olmsted and Steiner appear to have been friendly but not particularly intimate (DAB; L. H. Steiner to A. D. Bache, Aug. 8, 1861, Alexander Dallas Bache Papers, Library of Congress, Washington, D.C.; FLO to Gordon Winslow, Aug. 12, 1861, USSC-NYPL, box 833, 1: 85–88; L. H. Steiner to John S. Blatchford, Sept. 21, 1866, USSC-NYPL, box 1086).

2. Gordon Winslow (1803–1864), an Episcopal clergyman from Staten Island. Born in Vermont and educated at Yale College and Yale Divinity School, he held pastorates at Troy and Elmira, New York, and Annapolis, Maryland. Serving as chaplain of the

quarantine station on Staten Island and as rector of St. Paul's at Edgewater, he knew Elisha Harris, who, without consulting Olmsted, enlisted Winslow's services for the Sanitary Commission. During the Civil War, Winslow was both a Sanitary Commission inspector and chaplain of the 5th New York (also known as the Duryeé Zouaves or the National Zouaves), in which two of his sons also served. In June 1864 Winslow drowned in the Potomac River while caring for his wounded son (*NCAB*; F. Phisterer, *New York in the War*, 2: 1751, 1768; FLO to Gordon Winslow, Aug. 12, 1861, USSC-NYPL, box 833, 1: 85–88).

3. Located southwest of the basin of Baltimore's harbor, Federal Hill received its name after a parade celebrating the ratification of the U.S. Constitution concluded there in 1788. Duryeé's Zouaves, who had been transferred to Baltimore on July 27, were stationed at Fort Federal Hill, whose guns could defend all approaches and fire upon the city (John Thomas Scarf, *History of Baltimore City and County . . .* [Philadelphia, 1881], pp. 116, 131–32; F. Phisterer, *New York in the War*, 2: 1751).

4. Olmsted probably enclosed a pamphlet he had written, "General Instructions to Sanitary Inspectors," which was later published by the Sanitary Commission; see USSC, *Documents*, doc. no. 24.

5. These three resolutions were passed by the Sanitary Commission to increase the comfort of wounded and sick soldiers. Resolution 37 called for a system to enable wounded soldiers to write to their relatives or friends and to allow them to read or be read to. Resolution 41 requested that publishers of newspapers and magazines donate copies of their journals to the hospitals. Resolution 43 appropriated money for washing the clothing of soldiers in the hospitals ("A Record of Certain Resolutions of the Sanitary Commission," doc. no. 21 in USSC, *Documents*).

6. John Adams Dix (1798–1879), commander of the Department of Maryland. A prominent free-soil Democratic politician, he had served as U.S. senator from New York and secretary of the treasury during the last days of the Buchanan administration (*DAB*).

To Henry Whitney Bellows

Sanitary Commission, Washington, D.C.
Treasury Building, August 15 1861

To the Revd H. W. Bellows D.D.
President of the Sanitary Commission
Sir:

A statement was some time since published in the newspapers, to the effect that evidence had been presented to the Sanitary Commission of acts of savage brutality on the part of our enemies toward prisoners and wounded left on the field of battle.[1] This statement was not authorized from this office. It is true that evidence of the nature referred to was presented to the Commission, but it is also true that a careful examination of the circumstances under which the outrages were alledged to have been witnessed, and of other evidence, led to the conclusion, that these statements were greatly exaggerated, and that in the few instances where wounded men were known to have been attacked, it was under circumstances of great excitement by individual soldiers; without the approval of the officers. There is some reason to think also that in these cases the wounded in view had been firing with revolvers upon the approaching enemy, making it necessary for the latter to dispatch them for their own safety.

There are two reasons why if possible all misrepresentations on this subject should be corrected.

First: We recognize in the conduct of General Beauregard most conclusive evidence of a consciousness of the desperate chances of an essentially weak cause, when he seeks to vindicate and stimulate the fanaticism of his army by scandalous misrepresentations of our own.[2] We are under no necessity of resorting to similar temporary and fallacious means of strengthening our cause. The time will come when we shall be the stronger for having avoided all false grounds of martial ardor, and the enemy will be the weaker for having had resort to them.

Secondly, the belief that the enemy uses a savage method of warfare, is calculated to foster a spirit of retaliation in our men, and this is not favorable to habits of order, calmness, and discipline in the battle field. According to the degree in which our soldiers are established in such habits, they will be successful. Whatever interferes with these habits, prolongs the war; whatever tends to strengthen them, tends to lessen the cost and shorten the period of the rebellion.

In this view, it may be thought best that reports which I have just received from several of the surgeons, who in the gallant performance of their duty, were taken prisoners after the battle of Bull's run, should be immediately made public.[3]

It is not of course possible for these gentlemen to say how the wounded were treated in parts of the field, which did not come under their observation, but their opportunities of observation were so extended, that their evidence may be considered to conclusively establish the custom of the enemy. Except that the wounded of our forces were at first mainly left to the care of our own surgeons (who surrendered with them) while their surgeons were chiefly occupied with their own wounded, no difference was known between friend and enemy. Our wounded men were as tenderly treated as was practicable under the circumstances. Prisoners were subjected to no more inconvenience or discomfort than prisoners of war must expect with any civilized people. Whatever might be considered an unnecessary hardship in their experience was to be accounted for, by attributing it, not to a vindictive spirit, but to the necessities of the policy,

which is so thoroughly and successfully carried out in the strategy of Beauregard, of not letting his right hand to know what his left hand doeth.[4]
> Respectfully

Fred. Law Olmsted.
Secy

The original, in a copyist's hand but signed by Olmsted, is in box 641 of USSC-NYPL. On the back of the letter Olmsted scrawled, "Submitted with doubt."

1. Olmsted here is probably referring to an article published in the *New-York Daily Tribune* on July 27 that claimed that Dr. Norman Barnes, surgeon of the 28th New York left thirty wounded men and upon his return found that they had been bayonetted to death. The article concluded, "Dr. Barnes has given his testimony to the Sanitary Commission, and it will doubtless appear in an official form, in connection with a large amount of other evidence of a similar character." Other reports of Confederate atrocities in shooting, bayonetting, or cutting the throats of wounded Union soldiers were appearing elsewhere in the *Tribune* and other newspapers (*New-York Daily Tribune*, July 27, 1861, p. 4; ibid., July 24, 1861, p. 4; *New-York Times*, July 24, 1861, p. 1; ibid., July 28, 1861, p. 2; Norman S. Barnes to J. McDougal, July 28, 1861, USSC-NYPL, box 727: 212 [Barnes's testimony to the Sanitary Commission]).
2. Stories of Union army atrocities in the treatment of wounded and captured Southern soldiers and of civilian noncombatants were frequently featured in the Confederate press (J. Cutler Andrews, *The South Reports the Civil War* [Princeton, N.J., 1970], p. 527).
3. During the Civil War, medical officers were not officially recognized as noncombatants, and Union surgeons were captured at the battle of Bull Run when their temporary hospitals were overrun by the enemy. Some of the captured Union physicians were released by parole before Olmsted wrote this letter.
   Bellows replied to Olmsted's recommendation that the captured surgeons' reports be published:

   > I must doubt, however, whether in our present state of information, such *a correction* as your letter to me furnishes, does not overstep our information, & would not ultimately recoil upon us. . . . I feel a little wary of taking the testimony of those returned Doctors, for law & gospel. . . . I can't help being wicked enough to think that leaving the *sick behind* them, these men have a selfish motive for representing that they were well taken care of—for what else could authorize their leaving them?

   (HWB to FLO, Aug. 20, 1861, USSC-NYPL, box 728: 408; Thomas Marshall Hunter, "Medical Service for the Yankee Soldier" [Ph.D. diss., University of Maryland, 1952], pp. 33, 38–39.)
4. Possibly a reference to Beauregard's seemingly contradictory attitudes toward the Union army. In August Beauregard paroled captured Union surgeons although he was under no obligation to do so. Two months earlier, however, he had issued a proclamation to northern Virginians which declared the Union soldiers there to be "abolition Hosts" who "are murdering and imprisoning your citizens, confiscating and destroying your property, and committing other acts of violence and outrage too shocking and revolting to humanity to be enumerated." According to the Confeder-

147

ate general, "All rules of civilized warfare are abandoned, and they proclaim by their acts, if not on their banners, that their war-cry is 'Beauty and booty' " (O.R., ser. 1, vol. 2, p. 907).

To Henry Whitney Bellows

> Sanitary Commission, Washington, D. C.
> Treasury Building, August 16th 1861

My Dear Doctor,

I have just received your note of the 13th.

Three persons whose assistance I had expected to have in one way or another this week have failed me and I have been trying to carry along too great a variety of matters to accomplish much of consequence in any one. I have depended on Mr. Knapp to keep you informed, having more of essential matters for my pen than I could accomplish.

I still believe that we are in a very critical condition here—ill prepared to resist such a general advance as it may be possible for the enemy to make. Many regiments are in a mutinous condition.[1]

I have been putting off, from day to day, for a week, going to New York. I think I must go to-morrow morning, and I will then discuss the time for meeting with our friends there.

I quite agree with you as to our policy.[2] It seems to be working successfully, so far. We are gaining the confidence of the stronger heads, but the time is approaching to use this. I am making up my mind to a policy different from that of "the Departments", and also from that of "the people"—more savage than the one, more broadly comprehensivly humane than the other. We must force a more liberal policy upon the Surg[n] Gen[l].[3] There must be something equivalent to a large contingent fund. And the contingent fund of charity which we represent, must be superceded by something more systematic & warlike. Even the care of the sick & wounded in war is not a feminine business. It must have a masculine discipline, or as a system, as a sustained & "normal" arrangement, it must have a bad tendency. We have gone far enough to see this and to be justified in stating it strongly and plainly to the Secretary[4] at our next session. This hospital *system* is simply disgraceful, & I think we must, if necessary, tell the country so. And at the same time take the ground that our intervention is not the proper remedy. We are far too much engrossed with cure: our main business should be prevention. Government should be

CLEMENT ALEXANDER FINLEY

forced to do better for the disabled, even at the expense of some temporary cruelty.

I am tolerably well, thank you—& most cordially yours

Fred. Law Olmsted.

The original is in box 641 of USSC-NYPL.

1. A reference to the insubordination of regiments such as the 79th New York and the 2nd Maine (see "Report on the Demoralization of the Volunteers," Sept. 5, 1861, nn. 28 and 44, below).
2. On August 13 Bellows had outlined what he believed should be Sanitary Commission policy: "We must gradually convince the Government that we are discreet and *necessary*. When any serious sickness comes they will find it so. Meanwhile we must bide our time" (HWB to FLO, Aug. 13, 1861, USSC-NYPL, box 728: 254).
3. Clement Alexander Finley (1797–1879) became the surgeon general of the U.S. Army and headed the Medical Bureau from May 1861 until April 1862. Educated at Dickinson College and the medical school of the University of Pennsylvania, Finley entered the army in 1818. He saw extensive field service during the Black Hawk and Mexican wars. Upon the death of long-time Surgeon General Thomas Lawson in 1861, Presi-

dent Lincoln promptly appointed Finley, the most senior medical officer in the department, to be Lawson's successor.

Finley's appointment almost immediately led to a clash with the Sanitary Commission which presaged the whole of his relationship with that group. Acting Surgeon General Robert C. Wood had during Lawson's final illness consented to the government's creation of the Sanitary Commission as an organization of inquiry and advice. Suspicious of such civilian meddling, Finley was induced to consent to the creation of the Commission only by the explicit concession that its activities would be limited to the volunteer troops. Finley also disliked innovations such as the use of female nurses, and angered the Sanitary Commission by failing to address the hygienic problems of the army. By the time of this letter, Olmsted was convinced that the Medical Bureau under Finley's leadership had not shown sufficient interest in conserving the health of the soldiers. Olmsted complained, "It is the army theory that soldiers are tough animals, sick or well, and the regular officers including the medical department seem determined to do all they can to make them uncomfortable and unsuccessful till their theory is consistently adopted."

Neither Olmsted nor the Sanitary Commissioners came to view Finley more positively during the autumn of 1861. They sought his removal and lobbied both Cameron and McClellan, neither of whom was willing to join in the campaign. Lincoln similarly did not act upon the Commission's request in October 1861 for a new, more effective surgeon general. Failing in these attempts to convince officials of Finley's incompetence, the Commission anonymously launched a public attack upon him in the *New York World* and the *New-York Daily Tribune*. But Finley also possessed an important friend in Henry J. Raymond, editor of the *New-York Times*. The battle over the surgeon general became somewhat of a stand-off, as Raymond published editorials that lauded the surgeon general's skill and expertise while criticizing the Sanitary Commission for its lust for power and government funds.

While the medical reform bill containing a provision for the retirement of elderly medical officers was being debated in Congress, Finley made a powerful enemy in Secretary of War Stanton. After a quarrel with the surgeon general, Stanton assigned him to Boston. There the old soldier, unable to win Lincoln's support, ended his military career of almost forty-five years by choosing retirement (W. Q. Maxwell, *Lincoln's Fifth Wheel*, pp. 96–100; James Evelyn Pilcher, *The Surgeons General of the Army of the United States of America: A Series of Biographical Sketches* . . . [Carlisle, Pa., 1905], pp. 40–46; Charles J. Stillé, *History of the United States Sanitary Commission, Being the General Report of Its Work during the War of the Rebellion* [New York, 1868], pp. 53–60; FLO to Samuel G. Howe, Aug. 10, 1861, USSC-NYPL, box 833, 1: 75–76).

4. Simon Cameron (1799–1889), U.S. secretary of war in 1861. A former U.S. senator from Pennsylvania, Cameron also controlled the Republican party machine there. Corruption and mismanagement marked his tenure at the War Department. Although Cameron does not appear to have enriched himself, some of his friends and political associates made enormous profits through government contracts.

Olmsted and the Sanitary Commission generally found it difficult to work with Cameron. To be sure, there was a brief honeymoon. In early September 1861 Cameron assured Bellows, "You have never asked anything of me yet that you have not got—and you never will." But soon the Commission asked for more than the secretary was willing to grant. Cameron refused to second its pleas in September and October for the removal of Surgeon General Finley. Still less was he amenable to replacing Finley with William A. Hammond, a fellow Pennsylvanian with whose family Cameron had apparently disagreed politically. The Sanitary Commission and the secretary of war parted ways on other questions as well. Cameron declined to use the ambulance corps offered by the surgeon general of Pennsylvania and put into effect only a weak version of the allotment system (allowing soldiers' wives to draw their husbands' pay) championed by the Commission. His protection of the commissioners' rights and privileges also did not satisfy them. Although Cameron at first revoked General John C. Frémont's order recognizing the Western Sanitary Commission, he later reversed himself and allowed the St. Louis organization to remain independent.

Increasing criticism of the War Department, and irritation over a published report by Cameron that went beyond administration policy and advocated the arming of slaves, led Lincoln in January 1862 to replace his secretary of war. To soften the blow, the president named Cameron minister to Russia. Few in the Sanitary Commission mourned Cameron's departure, but Bellows did note that the former secretary had believed the Sanitary Commission to be his own handiwork and had taken pride in its accomplishments (*DAB*; W. Q. Maxwell, *Lincoln's Fifth Wheel*, pp. 46–47, 76–77, 96–104, 117; FLO to JO, Sept. 12, 1861, below).

To William Peter Buel

Aug. 31st [1861]

My Dear Doctor,

I wrote you last week from New York with regard to hospital supplies.

Touching ambulances &c. the statement of your letter of 19th inst, which came into my hands yesterday seemed to be important,[1] and I called at once on the Quarter Master Genl [2] who informed me that to this time no requisition or intimation of a wish for ambulances from the west had been received at his office, consequently he had sent none. He was surprised that no requisition had been made, and had nearly 300 ready to be sent when they should be wanted.

Had you not better state this to the General?

I apprehend from the negligence which you report in this particular that there must be a general deficiency of articles necessary for the comfort of the wounded & sick. You are expected to exercise a liberal discretion in overcoming all difficulties on this score. Address yourself zealously to the commanding General in the name of the Commission; purchase moderately and telegraph if you deem it necessary to employ extraordinary means or incur large expenses to secure the exercise of an efficient humanity in this particular.

Very Respectfully

Fred. Law Olmsted

Wm. P. Buel M.d.
U.S. Sanitary Inspector
Burnam's Hotel, St. Louis, Mo.

The original is a letterpress copy on pages 199–202 of volume 1 of box 833 in USSC-NYPL.

1. On August 19 Buel had written Olmsted from St. Louis about "a very important deficiency" existing in the Western department: "the entire absence of Ambulances, Field Stretchers, or any provision whatever for the transportation in the Field of the Sick & wounded" (W. P. Buel to FLO, Aug. 19, 1861, USSC-NYPL, box 728: 406).

2. Montgomery Cunningham Meigs (1816–1892), quartermaster general of the Union army. Educated at the University of Pennsylvania and at West Point, he entered the army corps of engineers. He was stationed at various fortifications and spent nine years constructing Fort Wayne in Detroit. In 1853 Meigs was promoted to the rank of captain and given superintendence of three important projects in Washington, D.C.: the construction of the Washington Aqueduct and the extensions of the U.S. Capitol and the federal post office building. Both the Capitol and the Aqueduct demanded innovative engineering and considerable ingenuity. Meigs successfully laid the groundwork for the replacement of the Capitol's dome with Thomas U. Walter's larger one and for the Aqueduct's Cabin John bridge. Although a Democrat with powerful friends in Congress, including Jefferson Davis and William H. Seward, Meigs clashed with Buchanan's secretary of war, John B. Floyd, over hiring practices and the extent of his authority. In 1860 that feud led to the transfer of Meigs to the Dry Tortugas. In February 1861 he returned to Washington and resumed supervision of the Capitol and Aqueduct construction projects. That June he was appointed quartermaster general.

   Meigs brought a scrupulous honesty and an attention to detail to his new post, qualities noticeably lacking in many employees of the War Department under Simon Cameron. Meigs was also willing to complain—sometimes vociferously—about abuses, and he demanded accountability from employees. Although his greatest accomplishments in the quartermaster general's department came in the last two years of the war, with the reorganization of the department and the successful supply of the far-flung Union armies, Meigs's energy and determination were always evident. Olmsted may have found him especially admirable because as superintendent of the Capitol and Aqueduct projects, Meigs had faced problems similar to those encountered by Olmsted in his own superintendence of Central Park. Then too, Meigs, like Olmsted, had great confidence in his own abilities and expected to be able to wield considerable authority.

   From their first meeting, Olmsted and Meigs each found the other congenial. Meigs later recalled Olmsted's "joyful expression" when "comparing our opinions and views as to the manner in which the [Sanitary] Commission could best fulfill its objects of usefulness": "he said that I had given him new hope and confidence, and that he then, for the first time, felt as though he had 'touched bottom,' and had found firm ground to stand upon." Olmsted, for his part, declared that the Sanitary Commission from its inception found the quartermaster's department the branch most willing to cooperate with it, and he added, "The hospitality of no other single man was worth as much to our undertaking as that of Major-General M. C. Meigs."

   The professional relationship between Meigs and Olmsted continued after the war. In 1866 the quartermaster general encouraged Olmsted to apply for the position of commissioner of public buildings in the District of Columbia as a step toward securing a public park for Washington. He sought Olmsted's advice about suitable landscaping of the national cemeteries and also helped secure his services for such projects as the grounds of the Jeffersonville Depot in Indiana and the Schuylkill Arsenal in Philadelphia (*DAB*; Russell Frank Weigley, *Quartermaster General of the Union Army: A Biography of M. C. Meigs* [New York, 1959], pp. 28, 37, 62–85, 98–108, 162–68, 180–95, 235; M. C. Meigs to John S. Blatchford, July 19, 1865, in John Strong Newberry, *The U.S. Sanitary Commission in the Valley of the Mississippi . . .* [Cleveland, Ohio, 1871], p. 187; FLO to Arnold A. Rand, Dec. 30, 1890, in Frederick Law Olmsted, *Books and Printed Papers Relating to Concerns of the United States Sanitary Commission in the War of the Rebellion . . .* [n.p., 1890], p. xi; M. C. Meigs to FLO, June 23, 1866, and July 23, 1870; M. C. Meigs to FLO, May 6, 1875, Record Group 92, Office of the Quartermaster General, Consolidated Correspondence File 1794–1915, Fred'k L. Olmstead [*sic*], 1875–, National Archives and Record Service, Washington, D.C.).

REPORT ON THE DEMORALIZATION
OF THE VOLUNTEERS

WASHINGTON, *Sept.* 5, 1861.

TO THE SANITARY COMMISSION:

GENTLEMEN:
    As soon as practicable after the battle of Bull's Run, a series of seventy-five enquiries was prepared, intended to elicit information as to the condition of the troops before, during, and after the engagement, and as to the defects in the mode of providing for the necessities of the army which had been manifested in the series of movements which were connected with it. These questions were placed in the hands of the seven inspectors of the Commission, who were then employed in visiting the regiments which had been engaged, for the purpose of ascertaining and administering to their wants, and they were instructed to obtain answers to them, which would represent as nearly as possible the knowledge and judgment of the most intelligent officers and surgeons of these regiments with whom they were able to confer. They were to present themselves for this purpose in their official capacity, with authority from the Secretary of War to obtain information in all respects with regard to the sanitary condition of the forces, and were to make their return to the Secretary of the Commission, with such expressions of their own judgment as to the credibility of the statements, and such record of their own observations, and of other information obtained, as would aid him in arriving at the truth.
    The returns received comprise about two thousand items of evidence with reference to the history of the battle, and have a certain value otherwise than from a medical or sanitary point of view. The largest part of them were collected by physicians and examiners of life insurance companies, accustomed to an exact and searching method of inquiry.*

*Messrs. Robert Tomes, M.D., J. H. Douglas, M.D., Philip Aigner, M.D., Wm. P. Buel, M.D., C. L. Brace, Frederick N. Knapp, and E. B. Elliott.

These items, after having been carefully studied and culled of those which bore internal evidence of error or carelessness, have been digested and tabulated by E. B. Elliott,[1] Esq'r, a gentleman recently employed by the Boston Life Insurance Companies, as an actuary for scrutinizing and arranging evidence with regard to the laws of mortality, and author of several papers on this subject published by the American Association for the Advancement of Science, and the American Academy. The complete tables are on file in the office of the Commission.

The following are the results which have the most obvious, immediate practical bearing:

Extent of the Field of Observation.

Portions of each of the twelve brigades under the command of Major General McDowell, at the time of the general advance of July 16, were visited by the inspectors.

The entire number of bodies of troops visited was thirty.

Of the twelve brigades comprising the army of the Potomac, seven only crossed the stream known as Bull Run, on the occasion of the engagement of Sunday, July the 21st, and took any active part in the main action with the enemy.

Certain regiments that crossed the stream and took important part in the action of the 21st, (as, for instance, the 69th and the 71st, New York State Militia,) were removed from Washington to be mustered out of service so soon after the battle, that no reports were obtained from them.[2]

Concerning several of the regiments visited, replies were obtained to the entire series of seventy-five questions proposed; concerning others, replies were obtained to but a portion of the series—the defect being due in some instances to neglect on the part of inspectors, in others, to inability on the part of the regimental officers consulted to give the information desired.

Skirmish of the 18th.

From the reports of the inspectors, confirmed by the official reports of officers commanding, it appears that of twenty-nine bodies of soldiers visited, four were actively engaged in the "demonstration" of the 18th of July, (Thursday,) at Blackburn's Ford, (across the Bull Run,)[3] three others were engaged, but not actively, and twenty-two were not engaged.*

---

*The thirtieth body, previously referred to, was Blenker's Brigade,[4] which also was not engaged, and which is for the present disregarded, because the returns from it are more imperfect than the average.

154

Engagement of the 21st.

Of the same twenty-nine bodies of troops, twenty were actively engaged in the battle of the 21st of July, (Sunday,) seven were engaged, but not actively, and two were not engaged.

Camp Guard.

The average number left as camp-guard at the time of the general advance, previous to the engagements of the 18th and 21st, from each of nineteen regiments reporting on this point, was sixty-eight, (more exactly, 68.2.) From ten of the twenty-nine regiments visited, no report was made as to the number so left. The smallest number so left behind by any regiment was thirteen; the largest number so left, one hundred and fifty-one.

Strength of Regiments.

The average number of troops that marched for the battle field at the time of the general advance, from each of twenty regiments reporting on this point, was (as stated by their officers) eight hundred and two;* nine of the twenty-nine bodies of troops visited not reporting. The smallest number so marching was six hundred, the largest number nine hundred and fifty-one.

Last Meal.

The last meal before the battle of the 21st, of sixteen of the twenty-nine regiments, was on the evening of the day before; that is, on the evening of the 20th. Six regiments had a regular breakfast early (that is, before 2½ o'clock) on the morning of the day of the battle; two regiments breakfasted at six, and the battalion of United States infantry is reported to have enjoyed a regular meal in the woods about eleven A.M. The time of the last regular meal of three regiments is not reported, but there is reason for stating it to have been about 6 A.M.

First Movement on the 21st.

The troops, except those in the reserve, were aroused from sleep between the hours of one and two o'clock on the morning of the battle of July the 21st, the march being ordered to commence with some at two, with others at half-past two.†

*This is believed to be somewhat over estimated.
†Those regiments which breakfasted at six were of the reserve.

155

The Commissariat.

The troops had all been supplied at about 3 P.M., on the 16th of July, with three days' rations in their haversacks, "which should have lasted them to the afternoon of the 19th." (See Report of Captain Clarke,[5] Commissary of Subsistence.) And again, in a circular from headquarters, dated at Centreville, July 20th, 1861, an equal distribution of the subsistence stores on hand was required to be immediately made to the different companies of each division.[6] In accordance with this last-mentioned order, "160,000 complete rations were received by the army at and in the vicinity of Centreville—sufficient for its subsistence five days." (Hence there appears to have been a short interval unprovided for.)

According to the reports made to the inspectors, few companies complied fully with these orders: twenty-six of the twenty-nine regiments visited took at least a partial supply, say from one to three days' rations, under the former order; two regiments, it is said, taking "no supply," depending for food upon "forage." An insufficient supply in one case was accounted for by the statement that "they had no expectation of being called to march;" (that is, therefore did not obey the order.) In several instances it is stated that the supply of three days' rations taken by the troops was "exhausted before the close of the second day;" that is, the rations were wasted. These confessions of neglect or improvidence on the part of the volunteers are confirmed by the report of Commissary Clarke, in which it is stated that after the distribution had been properly made to the several divisions, he (Captain Clarke) knew "of several instances in which subsistence stores remained in possession of division and brigade commissaries, and of others in which provisions were left on the ground of the encampments on the morning of the 21st of July."[7]

Distance Marched before the Battle.

The distance marched to the field of battle on the morning of the 21st by those who became actively engaged, varied from four to twelve miles; of those in the vicinity of the field but not actively engaged, the distance generally was from two to four miles, (Richardson's brigade remaining in the position it held on the 20th, menacing the enemy at Blackburn's Ford.)[8]

Double Quick.

The portion of this march to the battle field which was at double-quick,[9] was, in the case of fifteen of the regiments, from one and one-half to three miles—generally from two and a half to three miles; in the case of thirteen of the regiments there was no portion of the march at double-quick. During the battle a few of the companies, and but a few, moved at double-quick for one or two miles.

It seemed to be generally considered by the volunteers that their strength was unnecessarily and injudiciously wasted by the extent of the double-quick advance. To a certain extent this appears to be true, yet the result could hardly have been affected by it if the men had been in tolerable condition.

DEGREE OF VIGOR AT COMMENCEMENT OF BATTLE.

As to the physical condition of the troops on reaching the field of battle, it is reported that eight of the regiments visited were in "fair," "excellent," "good," "best" condition;

That in eight others "the men were somewhat exhausted," "partially exhausted," "evidently suffering;"

That in twelve of the regiments visited, the troops were said to be "much exhausted," "generally fatigued," "many considerably exhausted;" in six of the regiments from one to twenty were "giving out," "giving completely out," &c., one or two instances of "sun stroke" being specified.

In eight regiments none "gave out" before the battle; in from nine to eleven regiments some gave out before the battle; and concerning the remaining regiments there is no report.

(There was an evident disposition to regard the exhausted physical condition of the men as a chief cause of the defeat.)

CAUSES OF EXHAUSTION BEFORE THE BATTLE.

As to the causes assigned for the exhaustion, it appears that of the regiments visited it was stated that three had not suffered at all from fatigue or heat, or want of food or drink, or sleep; in seventeen of the regiments "fatigue" was assigned as a cause of exhaustion; in eleven the march at "double-quick" was specified as peculiarly fatiguing; in eight of the seventeen the exhaustion is attributed more to the double-quick than to want of food and drink; in sixteen of the regiments want of food was assigned as a cause of exhaustion; in eleven want of drink was assigned as a cause; and in a few cases, the exhaustion was attributed, in part at least, to want of sleep, and to a bivouac of three or four nights in the open air, with insufficient clothing, as was the case with the Fire Zouaves,[10] who left their blankets and rubber cloths in camp.

So much as to the condition and movement of the troops before the battle.

TIME IN THE BATTLE.

The time during which the troops taking part in the battle of the 21st were actively engaged (pushing toward the enemy, or being temporarily on retreat, after first coming under fire,) appears to have varied from twenty-five minutes to six hours, being in most cases from five to six hours.

To the regiments most actively engaged the time was thought to be much shorter than actually elapsed, the five or six hours in which they were engaged seeming to the men, as they state, scarcely one hour. The time during which men stood under fire without being actively engaged themselves is, on the other hand, found to be over-estimated by them.

DEGREE OF VIGOR DURING THE BATTLE.

It is claimed that in eight of the twenty-nine regiments visited, there were no symptoms of exhaustion manifest during the battle; that in eight there was evident suffering and fatigue evinced by men lagging behind, and by companies breaking up, especially after double-quick, few or none giving completely out; that in ten regiments, many (in some instances stated as high as one-fourth or one-third of the number constituting the regiment,) gave completely out, "some few dropping down in convulsions," or suffering from "sun stroke." The evidences of exhaustion in other regiments are not assigned.

CAUSES OF EXHAUSTION DURING THE BATTLE.

In explanation of the alleged excessive exhaustion of the men toward the close of the battle, the officers consulted in twenty-six of the twenty-nine regiments referred to, attribute it to fatigue and heat, twenty-one to lack of food and drink. All the reports which assigned insufficiency of food and drink as a cause, also assigned excessive fatigue. Six of them assign fatigue, and especially the march at double quick, as the main cause of the exhaustion which was manifest during and just after the battle.

CAUSE OF RETREAT.

The proximate cause of the retreat is variously assigned—to the attack of fresh reserves of the enemy upon our right—to the rapid and apparently wild return of the caissons for ammunition—to the appearance of a retreat of our cavalry, who were thought by some to be riding over our own infantry, the rear guard, at the same time, mistaking them for secession cavalry, &c. Certain more organic causes of the defeat are frequently stated.

By some the defeat is attributed to the condition of the men, exhausted by excessive fatigue, and by want of sufficient food, drink, and sleep; by others to "a feeling," on the approach of the fresh reserves of the enemy, "of the total inadequacy of a small force to compete with superior numbers supported by masked batteries." By others the defeat is attributed to "causes involving the whole command;" "to the inefficiency of the general commanding;" "not due to previous exposure and fatigue, but to the bad conduct of the battle on the part of the leaders." By others (regulars) the defeat is attributed to "inefficiency of volunteers;" by one (German) to "bad strategy and want of discipline."

Through all the regiments there appears to have prevailed the false idea of the vast superiority in point of numbers possessed by the enemy, together with a lack of confidence in the military skill of the leaders of the army of the Union as compared with that of the leaders on the part of the rebels; also combined to a certain extent with a dread of meeting an invisible foe.

Officers Leaving Their Commands.

In thirteen of the regiments the officers are said not to have been much separated from their commands, except in the case of wounded officers; in eleven regiments it appears that the officers were, to a considerable extent, separated from their commands, the regiments being "much scattered," "badly disorganized," "broken into fragments," the men being, in certain cases, "left entirely to themselves." Concerning five of the regiments visited, no information was given on this point. (The above report is that of the officers themselves in most cases.)

Throwing Away of Arms and Equipments.

Of the twenty-nine bodies visited, twenty-two threw away or laid aside blankets and haversacks before engaging in battle. Some placed them in a pile under guard, others threw them aside carelessly, either before arriving on the field, while approaching it at double quick, or immediately before engaging with the enemy. Three regiments threw off their blankets during the battle and the march at double quick on the battle-field; one regiment threw aside blankets only, retaining haversacks; and three only of the twenty-nine bodies of troops visited retained possession of their blankets and haversacks during the engagement.

During the retreat, it appears from the reports of the inspectors that the men of ten regiments did not throw away any of their arms or accoutrements: that the men of nine regiments did throw away portions, no report being made relative to the course of the remaining ten regi-

THE PAPERS OF FREDERICK LAW OLMSTED

ments. There is no reason to believe that these latter averaged better in discipline than the former, and it is probable that there was some loss of arms in, at least, half of them. Colonel Keyes, of 1st brigade, 1st division, reports that his brigade bivouaced on the night of the 23d near Fort Corcoran, "every man with his firelock."[11]

The number of muskets thrown away during the retreat was stated, in some cases, to be about fifty; generally the number is not mentioned. (A considerable portion of one regiment are reported to have exchanged their smooth-bore muskets for those of a superior kind left behind by regiments preceding.)

The blankets and haversacks of many of the regiments, especially of those actively engaged in the conflict of the 21st, were lost, being left on the field of battle wherever they were deposited before the engagement. A small number of the regiments, and a few individuals and companies in each regiment, possessed themselves again of their blankets and haversacks, it is stated, before leaving the field.

Overcoats do not appear to have been so generally lost, as many of the regiments left their camps at the time of the general advance, (July 16,) equipped in "light marching order," that is, with blankets, haversacks, and canteens, leaving overcoats in their camps. Certain of the regiments, as for instance the Connecticut regiments and the 2d Maine regiment[12] in the brigade under the efficient command of Col. Keyes, recovered much property of other regiments, including arms and other equipments thrown aside in flight, and also including the abandoned tents and camp equipage of two regiments, (of another brigade,) this latter property being secured by his troops during the continued drenching rain of the 22d. Companies in certain other regiments (as in the Massachusetts 1st)[13] halted on retreat, and picked up blankets, camp kettles, &c., which they found thrown aside on the road. (The loss of blankets at this time led in certain regiments to a good deal of subsequent sickness and increased demoralization.)

Bad Arms.

One regiment complained of the bad condition of their smooth bore muskets (the altered muskets of 1840,) nipples breaking, cartridges too small, so as to drop in, or too large, so as to require to be forced in by pressing the ramrod against trees, &c., &c.[14] This complaint does not seem to have been general, with certain regiments the smooth bores working efficiently.

Distance Traveled.

The distance traveled by the several regiments on the night of the retreat varied from twenty to thirty-five miles, generally it was about twenty-seven. The average distance of the day's advance and retreat, including movements on the field, was about forty-four miles.

Physical Condition after the Retreat.

The next morning, (the 22d,) according to the almost universal report, there were few, if any, able men in the infantry. Blistered feet, rheumatic pains, aching limbs, diarrhoea, and nervous debility being prevalent.

The physical condition of three of twenty-nine bodies of troops when visited a few days later, was reported "unaltered by exposure and retreat," "not exhausted;" the men of four regiments were reported to be not much exhausted; those of fifteen were reported to be much exhausted, "physically prostrated," "prostrated," "exhausted and worn out," "greatly affected by exposure and retreat," "terribly fatigued, could not get rested," &c. The physical condition of seven of the regiments was not stated.

Causes of Exhaustion.

The physical exhaustion of the troops was attributed to excessive fatigue, to heat, and to want of food and drink.

Extent and Degree of Demoralization
after the Battle.

At the time of making the inquiries, from the 25th to the 31st of July, inclusive, it appeared that of the twenty-eight regiments visited, eight were considered by their officers not to be essentially demoralized;* one was described as "not discouraged;" another "full of courage and ready for an engagement;" (1st. Mass.) *morale* good," (2d R.I.) "in good spirits," (2d N.H.)—eight were reported to be not much demoralized, "some few dispirited, but generally cheerful and animated," "somewhat depressed and disgusted with needless(?) exposure, otherwise not much demoralized," (there is reason to think that the exposure to rain, complained of as needless, was far from needless, was in fact essential to the protection of property;) "not much disheartened" "will re-enlist, &c.;" twelve were reported "as much demoralized," "much disheartened and discouraged," "morally prostrated by the rout," "low spirits," "one-half of the regiment demoralized, majority wish to go home," "wish to be disbanded and return to fight under other leaders," "completely demoralized, discontented, unwilling to serve, because, as they allege, ill-fed and unpaid."

*Subsequent reports have sometimes been less favorable.

The degree of demoralization does not appear to be coincident with the degree of physical and nervous exhaustion.

As a rule, the best officered, the best disciplined, and the best fed regiments, were obviously the least demoralized.

Causes of Demoralization.

The demoralization was attributed, by those making answer to the inquiry, generally, in each case, to several causes combined. Among these, in fifteen cases physical and nervous prostration was mentioned; in seven cases, discouragement on account of the result of the battle, accompanied sometimes with a feeling of inadequacy to compete with superior numbers; in two cases the great mortality attendant upon the late engagements was assigned among the causes; in three cases, dissatisfaction with armament—smooth bore muskets; in three, dissatisfaction with and lack of confidence in officers; in five, dissatisfaction with food; in one case, dissatisfaction on account of failure to receive from Government pay promptly for services; in two dissatisfaction in consequence of supposed needless exposure to storm.

General Summary.

From these investigations, combined with information derived from official reports of the generals commanding; from published statements in rebel as well as loyal journals; from previous investigations of the inspectors of the Sanitary Commission as to the condition of the troops, and from other sources, it is manifest that our army, previous to and at the time of the engagement, was suffering from want of sufficient, regularly-provided, and suitable food, from thirst, from want (in certain cases) of refreshing sleep, and from the exhausting effects of a long, hot, and rapid march, the more exhausting because of the diminution of vital force of the troops due to the causes above enumerated. They entered the field of battle with no pretence of any but the most elementary and imperfect military organization, and, in respect of discipline, little better than a mob, which does not know its leaders. The majority of the officers had, three months before, known nothing more of their duties than the privates whom they should have been able to lead, instruct, and protect. Nor had they, in many cases, in the meantime, been gaining materially, for they had been generally permitted, and many had been disposed, to spend much time away from their men, in indolence or frivolous amusement, or dissipation.

It appears that many were much exhausted on reaching the field of battle, but that, supported by the excitement of the occasion, they rallied fairly, and gradually drove the opposing forces from Sudley Spring to the lower ford, and from the lower ford to beyond the Stone bridge and the Warrenton road;[15] that, at this time, (half-past three,) when congratulated by superior officers, and congratulating themselves on having achieved a victory, and when having repulsed reinforcements sent from the extreme right of the enemy to support their retreating columns, they were just relaxing their severely-tried energies, there appeared in the distance "the residue" of the forces of General Johnston, (see McDowell's report, Dr. Nott's letter to a Mobile paper, and correspondence of Charleston Mercury,)[16] a single brigade (Elsey's) coming up from the Manassas Gap Junction railroad, marching at double-quick to engage our troops at the right who had been hotly fighting unrelieved by reserves during the day. This brigade, joined with the two regiments of Kershaw and Cash,[17] "turned the tide of battle." (See in Richmond Dispatch, July 29, statement "of a distinguished officer who bore a conspicuous part on the field of battle on the 21st of July.")[18]

Our troops, ignorant of the fact that they had been contending against and repulsing the combined forces of Beauregard and Johnston; and believing that this inconsiderable remnant of Johnston's forces, which they now saw approaching, to be his entire column; and feeling their inability, without rest or refreshment, to engage an additional force of fresh troops nearly equal in number to those with whom they had been contending during the day,—commenced a retreat, not very orderly, but quite as much so, at first, as had been the advance in which they had driven back the forces of the enemy. Their (nominal) leaders, who too often had followed them in battle, were, in many cases, not behind them on retreat.

As they retired, however, a sense of disintegration began to pervade their ranks; each ceased to rely on his comrade for support, and this tendency was augmented by the upturned wagons blocking the road, which served to completely break the imperfect columns.*

The reports of the inspectors give no evidence that the panic infected the extreme left, or the reserves, to any sensible degree. It was uncontrollable only with the troops on the extreme right, among whom it

---

*From a consideration of all the evidence, Mr. Elliott states that he has himself formed the following opinion:

"The *retreat* was immediately due mainly to *delusion*, on the part of the troops of the Union, respecting the force of the enemy, especially of the reserves advancing from the railroad to engage our forces, combined with extreme physical exhaustion; that the *rout* was due, in part at least, to the too near approach of the wagons of the volunteers to the field of battle, thereby dividing their columns on retreat; and that the sense of disintegration, and consequent *panic*, (so far as it existed,) was due to want of discipline, to physical exhaustion, and to want of all provision for securing an orderly retreat, combined."

originated. Many at the centre and the left were surprised when the order came to retreat, and for a time considered it as merely an order to change position in view of a still further general advance. Some officers state that they "warmly remonstrated"—"too warmly, perhaps"—when they received the order to retire.

The returns of the inspectors are not conclusive on this point; but from the result of subsequent specific inquiries by Mr. Elliott and the Secretary, it can be stated with confidence that indications of terror or great fear were seen in but a comparatively very small part of the retreating force. Most trudged along, blindly following (as men do in any mob) those before them, but with reluctance, and earnest and constant expressions of dissatisfaction and indignation, while no inconsiderable number retained, through all the length of the privation and discomfort of their dreary return to Washington, astonishing cheerfulness and good humor, and were often heard joking at their own misfortunes, and ridiculing the inefficiency of their officers. The Germans of the reserve were frequently singing. None of the reserves were in the slightest degree affected by the panic, and their general expression with reference to the retreat was one of wonder and curiosity.

The reserve, nevertheless, suffered much from fatigue, and subsequently exhibited most decided demoralization.

The Commission met in Washington on the 26th of July, and most of its members suffered the pain of witnessing something of the general condition of the army at that time.[19] As there are no means of recording it with exactness, it is important to the purpose of this report that the impression then received should be in a measure recalled, analyzed, and traced to its foundations.

A victorious enemy was known to be within ten miles of the capital, and was presumed to be cautiously advancing. Never could the occasion for military vigor, energy, promptitude, and thoroughness of action seem to be greater. It was the belief that the utmost and best directed efforts of every one who had to do directly or indirectly with the army should be concentrated at Washington; that, without previous concert, brought the majority of the Commission thither. Arriving, as they did, soon after daybreak, and passing from the railroad station toward the President's House,[20] the aspect of the streets was in the strongest possible contrast to that which would be imagined of a city placed by a stern necessity under the severe control of an effective military discipline. Groups of men wearing parts of military uniforms, and some of them with muskets, were indeed to be seen; but, upon second sight, they did not appear to be soldiers. Rather they were a most wo-begone rabble, which had, perhaps, clothed itself with the garments of dead soldiers left in a hard-fought battle-field. No two were dressed completely alike; some were without caps, others without coats, others without shoes. All were alike excessively dirty, unshaven, unkempt, and dank with dew. The groups were formed around fires made in the streets, and burning boards wrenched from citizens' fences. Some were still asleep, at full length in the gutters and on doorsteps, or sitting on the curbstone, resting their heads against the lamp-posts. Others were evidently begging for food at house-doors. Some appeared ferocious, others only sick and dejected; all excessively weak, hungry, and selfish. They were mainly silent, and when they spoke, it humiliated a man to hear them. No pack of whining, snarling, ill-fed, vagabond street dogs in an oriental city ever more strongly produced the impression of forlorn, outcast, helpless, hopeless misery. There was no apparent organization; no officers were seen among them, seldom even a non-commissioned officer. At Willards' hotel, however, officers swarmed.

They, too, were dirty and in ill-condition; but appeared indifferent, reckless, and shameless, rather than dejected or morose. They were talking of the battle, laughing at the incidents of the retreat, and there was an evident inclination among them to exaggerate everything that was disgraceful. Since they had not a victory to boast of, they made the defeat as dramatic and notable as possible. They seemed to be quite unconscious of personal responsibility for the results of the battle.

"Where is your regiment?" one was asked.

"Completely demoralized, sir; completely demoralized."

"Where is it now?"

"All disorganized—all disorganized."

"But where are the men?"

"I'm told that there are two or three hundred of them together somewhere near the Capitol, but I have not seen them yet since the battle."

A captain sat with his feet on the window grating, smoking; a man outside said to him, "Captain, there are two hundred of our men just beyond the Long Bridge, and they have not had anything to eat to-day."

"Where's the Quartermaster?"

"I don't know: there isn't any officer there."

"They don't want me, do they?"

"They have not had anything to eat to-day, and there's no officer to get it for them."

"Well, it's too bad;" and the Captain continued smoking, and ten minutes afterward had not put his feet to the floor. It was not till a Provost Guard of regulars drove these officers out of the town, almost at the point of the bayonet, that they seemed capable of entertaining any purpose of duty.[21] As to the men, it was nothing but starvation, in many cases, that brought them back to their's. In how many ways the humiliating confession of cowardice was heard; how piteously the desire was expressed to go

165

home; how distrustful the officers were of the men; how universally those who did not acknowledge cowardice and home-sickness were disinclined to resume duty, or to continue under the same officers as before, cannot be statistically told. It was enough to establish the conviction that the army was, for the time being, quite broken up and useless. For a time it seemed as if there was no government, civil or military, at the seat of government. The newspapers re-echoed the words of the Secretary of War, "the Capital is safe;"[22] because, as every one understood, the Capital could be defended with no spirit, confidence, or resolution, even by the large body of soldiers in it who had not directly participated in the battle. To re-establish in them some degree of confidence was the first necessity. With this the Capital would be safe. But this was wanting. All power of exercising confidence, all respect, every social sentiment seemed to have been for the time lost to them. This but feebly indicates the nature of that condition of the government forces which was generally denominated their "demoralization," and which was considered the direct result of the battle of Bull Run.

It did not seem sufficiently accounted for by the simple facts of the battle as generally related; that is to say, by an advance against the enemy, which was everywhere successful, until a check to the right wing caused with some a panic, and led to a general discontinuance of the aggressive movement, both armies resuming the position held previously, the enemy having suffered much the most, as was then generally believed, and, so far as yet appears, truly.

Considering that it was desirable that its real causes should be more clearly ascertained and defined, the investigation was set on foot, the results of which, to the present time, have now been laid before the Commission. Regarded as an attempt to find in the minor circumstances attending the battle adequate causes for the condition of the army which succeeded it, the investigation has not succeeded. Should it warrant the conviction, however, that no sufficient cause of the demoralization was to be found in the circumstances immediately attending the battle, it may be that a further investigation would be induced, which would yield results even more important than were originally anticipated.

The Secretary has executed the duty which he had proposed to himself, in the analysis of the facts of the battle directly bearing on the question. The duty of a complete exploration of the causes of the demoralization of the army in July he trusts will be assumed by a committee of the Commission.

That there is a broad field for such an exploration yet remaining to be entered, and that it will involve the consideration of many questions, a satisfactory decision of which will have a direct and important bearing upon the welfare of the country, the Secretary is prepared to give his reasons for believing. In doing so, he will not attempt to reserve an expression of his own judgment upon the questions which naturally arise, because it will be found that some of these involve questions of his official duty, and in regard to which it is proper that the Commission should be informed how he is impelled to act; for which reason also he desires, as a constituent member of the Commission, to be allowed to present views to which he has no assurance that the Commission is prepared to assent.

———————————

Where the phenomena are the most distinct, the causes should be the most obvious.

The most distinct and notable example of demoralization after the battle of Bull Run is found in the regiment known as the New York Fire Zouaves.[23] It so happens that the circumstances of the battle, to which the general demoralization is commonly ascribed, could have had very little effect on this regiment. It was dispersed as a regiment long before the reserves of the enemy, which led to the general retreat, and which immediately induced the panic, were brought into action.[24]

Whatever the circumstances were which more immediately preceded its disorganization, the officers and members of it were not found disposed to lay much stress upon them, but rather to refer their demoralization to the bad terms on which the men had previously been with some of their officers, to their having been obliged to sleep for several nights without the protection of tents or blankets, to excessive fatigue and exhaustion before they came under fire, and to the fact that they had never been paid. It is observed that more of this regiment than of others fell out, apparently from physical exhaustion, but certainly exhausted in courage, before the battle opened.

This explanation is less unsatisfactory than most which were offered by the various officers of other regiments examined by the inspectors. Yet to one who knows the habits of the class from which this regiment was recruited; how frequently they voluntarily pass night after night without sleep, and under circumstances most unfavorable to health; to one who has seen them at daylight of a winter's morning pressing forward, and with no possible mercenary motive, struggling for the privilege of dragging a soaked hose up a ladder to the roof of a tall warehouse in a biting northerly wind, and this after they have been standing all the night in freezing water, and when their clothing is covered as with a mail of ice,—

167

this explanation of the condition in which they were found a week after the battle of Bull Run, can hardly be sufficient. The sudden tap of a drum caused numbers of them to start and turn pale. They were confessed cowards; and whatever else they were, when they left New York, cowards they were not. No one in Washington called them cowards during the fire at Willards' hotel.[25]

Statements which have been made publicly, attribute the numerous desertions and subsequent mutinous condition of this regiment mainly to certain alleged special causes of complaint against its officers.[26] But why should a disgraceful imputation, which in a large measure others share with this regiment, be ascribed to causes special to it? There were the men of Varian's battery, for instance, whose conduct was even more cowardly, but who, after sneaking off, on a paltry excuse, before the battle, instead of complaining of their officers, had the assurance to come before the public with a testimonial of their satisfaction with them.[27] Weeks after the battle, the New York 79th—a regiment which has since had an opportunity to show itself really brave—was in actual mutiny, under circumstances which led General McClellan to apply the term "dastardly" to their conduct.[28] The same was, in fact, the case, at that time, with many other regiments, the mutinous disposition in these being only more readily and completely concealed.

Thus, though there was some difference of symptoms, the essential disease of the Fire Zouaves seems not to have been peculiar to them, but general. Is it not probable that its causes were also general? And if the disease of the Fire Zouaves existed before the battle, must we not look for the causes of the general disease also in circumstances which existed before the battle?

As the reverse extreme, the Second Rhode Island may be taken. This was one of the regiments mentioned by the Secretary in his report of July 9th, as under exceptional sanitary conditions.[29] It was so in the following respects: it was better lodged than others; it was better clothed than others; it was better fed. The men had fruit, soft-bread, butter, and a variety of condiments, regularly and constantly, which was the case with scarcely any other than the Rhode Island troops. They frequently had roast meats, baked meats, puddings, and pies. They had an excellent band of music, which played frequently for the pleasure of the regiment, and not merely as a military ceremony, as was the case with most of the regimental bands. They had dancing and social and athletic recreations; they had an industrious chaplain, and regular daily religious services conducted with good taste, the strictest decorum, and real solemnity. They were famous for their singing. They had singing societies, and various other social organizations. They received more visitors, including members of the Cabinet and others of distinction, and especially they were more visited by ladies than others.*

Their march to the battle-field was as fatiguing as that of others; they were as badly off for food as others, having nothing but a few crackers to eat for more than thirty-six hours. They were the first to engage; were severely engaged, and as long as, or longer than, any others; they were badly cut up, losing their colonel and other officers, and sixteen percent. of the ranks in killed.[30] They stood firm under fire while the panic-stricken crowd swept by and through them, and until they received the order to retreat. They then wheeled steadily into column, and marched in good order, until the road was obstructed by overturned wagons. Here they were badly broken up by a cannonade, scattered and disorganized, but afterwards, having mainly collected at Centreville, reformed and marched the same night, under such of their officers as remained alive, to and through Washington to a position several miles to the northward—a post of danger—where they at once resumed regular camp duties. When visited by the inspector, a few days afterwards, he was told and was led to believe that the men had only wanted a day's rest to be ready and willing to advance again upon the enemy. He reported the regiment not demoralized.†

How is this to be accounted for on the supposition that the general demoralization of the volunteers was caused by the failure of the battle? Is it not more rational to believe that pre-existent circumstances had produced a latent general demoralization, and that the Fire Zouaves had suffered under an excess of these, while the Rhode Island Second had been so fortunate as to entirely escape their action?

Let us, then, glance for a moment at the pre-existent circumstances of the volunteers.

They had hurried to Washington, in April, to offer their services to government to defend the country against secessionists and traitors. They

---

*Baron Larrey[31] says: "To prevent this sort of cerebral affection (nostalgia) in soldiers who have lately joined their corps, it is necessary to recruit their strength exhausted during the day, to vary their occupations, and to turn their labors and recreations to their own advantage as well as to that of society. Thus, after the accustomed military exercises, it is desirable that they should be subjected to regular hours, gymnastic amusements, and some mode of useful instruction. It is in this manner especially that mutual instruction, established among the troops of the line, is beneficial to the soldier and the State. Warlike music during their repasts, or at their hours of recreation, will contribute much to elevate the spirits of the soldier, and to keep away those gloomy reflections which frequently produce the effects which have been traced above."

†This regiment is now in admirable condition, physically and morally. Its sick list is less than one to a hundred. On one occasion, on an order to advance against the enemy, every man presented himself as fit to undertake a forced march.

169

had done this with a generous and manful neglect to inquire on what terms the service was to be rendered, and with little regard to their own comfort or pecuniary interest. All such considerations, if they occurred to them, were, at least, made secondary to the consideration of the first importance, the secure defence of the country against secessionists and traitors.

Under a military organization, the country is represented by the government. To the volunteer at the seat of government, the country and government were soon interchangeable terms. It was no confusion of ideas by which the volunteer came to regard himself as serving the government; nor is it entirely a confusion of ideas which regards government as a personality. It is an organization of persons. It is not to be expected of the volunteer that he should comprehend this organization, nor that he should distinguish between that for which the laws are accountable and that for which those who administer the laws have to answer. He presumes the government to be much obliged to him for the aid which he is so ready to give in its emergency, and he understands that government is only too glad to assume certain duties in return toward him. To provide for him suitable food and lodging, and to take care of him when sick or wounded, are perhaps the best defined of these.

That so much was undertaken by government, and that he was to immediately risk his life in the defence of government against the secessionists and traitors, was about as far as the volunteer, on an average, had thought, as in April he walked out of the railroad station, with thousands of others, to stand in the dreary streets of Washington, patient for hours in the strength of his great new nobleness of purpose, waiting for the country to find something for him to eat, and to get some place ready where he could be allowed to rest. Sometimes he waited, standing in the rain, all night for this; but at that time, though he may have sickened bodily under it, he did not get soul sick.

But two and three months after this it was an every-day occurrence for the agents of the Commission to find the volunteer in a camp hospital very sick; his only sustenance fresh bread and salt pork; his only drink, green coffee. He lies on the damp ground, with no covering but a blanket, which cannot properly be called a blanket. He wants kind and constant attention, and delicate food, such as from childhood, in his northern home, he has been accustomed to when sick. But the regimental surgeon, who may or may not be properly called a surgeon,[32] is too much absorbed in learning the intricate history of official requisitions, and in waiting for a personal interview with the government man on the other side of town, who can supply an ambulance, to see him often. His comrades, who might be supposed to be ready to tend him to the best of their imperfect ability, have got tired of doing chambermaid's work for the doctor, and at last have refused to do it any longer, because it is not what they volunteered for, and they think it's time government made other arrangements; and then it may very likely be that he has just heard that his wife was, a week ago, on the point of being turned out of doors, because she could not pay her rent—that he had promised to send her his pay, but has failed to do so, and is yet unable to do so, because, after nearly three months' service, he has not seen the first dollar of his pay. Many cases like this came to the knowledge of the Secretary. They were extreme cases, it is true; and if it was the object of this report to arraign the government, it might not be just to cite them. But the purpose now in view is to ascertain what influences were acting on the character of the volunteers, and it cannot be said that extreme cases do not affect character. It may be that the ignorance of the surgeon was the only cause of the apparent neglect of the sick volunteer; but that does not diminish the neglect, nor the effect which that neglect will exercise upon his feelings, and which will be radiated from him, when he recovers, upon others. It may be that it is entirely owing to the neglect of his colonel to render his muster-roll that he is not paid; but he will hardly know this, and, if he does know it, it will but little diminish his disappointment and sense of neglect. The Secretary recollects that one colonel told him in June that, if his regiment did not soon get their pay, it would be impossible to prevent many desertions—difficult to prevent mutiny; and he distinctly remembers hearing a company of sick men curse a government which provided so inefficiently for its sick servants. The government responsibility in the matter may have been no greater than it is for an overturned government mail-coach; but the irresponsibility of the government does not lessen the pain of the man who has his leg under the wheel, nor help in the least to cheer up the sick volunteer lying neglected on the ground, disgusted with salt pork and acrimonious coffee, and heart-aching with appeals from home, to which he thinks he is unjustly prevented from responding. Let the skill of the surgeon at length set him on his feet again, and he becomes a centre of influence for his comrades. What is that influence likely to be?

But if this was an unusual condition, what was the usual condition of the volunteer early in July, and what effect was this condition producing?

His air, diet, drink—his habits in all respects—had been for some time quite different from what they ever were before. His original excitement had all been exhausted. He came fully expecting an immediate battle with the traitors. There had been some assassination of pickets, but nothing more. He had no experience of anything so simply tiresome as this war. It was from no want of traitors that it dragged so slowly. In every bar-room where volunteers were daily drugged in Washington there were traitors. He was told that they were yet in every ship and fort and public office—that the clerks of the departments and of the congressional committees, and the President's servants themselves, were traitors. Female traitors looked disdainfully down from windows and out of carriages upon the ragged and hungry and dirty volunteer. Secessionists were common enough; but any fighting of secessionists was very uncommon. Sumter[33] had been yielded to them, and Harper's Ferry,[34] and the forts at Savannah, at Mobile, and the Balize.[35] They had taken the navy yard at Norfolk, and that at Pensacola;[36] the pirates had been let out, and scores of resigned officers let in,[37] and the army in Texas parolled;[38] and, while the blockade was made game of, the secessionists were actually allowed to establish batteries between the navy yard at Washington and the sea.[39] And yet he saw no sign of fighting them. Would it be strange if the volunteer began at length to feel that when he "rushed to arms" he had been imposed upon? That he began to suspect that the talk of war was all for "buncomb?"[40] War? War without artillery and without cavalry? Without shoes? With these antique smooth-bores?[41] With that crazy bridge over the Potomac,[42] and that slab-sided old wood scow, to keep up a communication with Fort Corcoran? And when he has never yet seen a general officer, and when nothing is ever found for him to do, but in guard duty over his own camp and the eternal manual of arms? If he had been a less intelligent soldier, he would have known and cared less about these things. As it was, he talked of little else, except his personal grievances.

Did the government really care at all for the "brave volunteer?" If so, why did he sometimes have food that he could not eat, and sometimes none at all, for days together? Why should he be left to sleep in rotten straw and shoddy blankets, and sometimes for months with nothing at all, on the bare ground? Why should he be required to stand for an hour at noon, exposed to the sun of the hottest day of the year, in Pennsylvania avenue, while his colonel takes a drink with his friends at Willards', and there is the shade of brick walls, forty feet in his rear? Why should his captain be allowed to insult him with impunity, when, if he speaks a word for himself, he may be sent to the guard-house, and put to work in filth?

Did it answer this satisfactorily to say to him that his officers were of his own selection?—that his captain was a blackguard and a petty tyrant, his colonel a politician, his surgeon a quack, and his quartermaster a knave? He did not know them for this when he chose them. Now he does, he would choose to be rid of them. Why should not the government remove them and appoint better men? Is the difficulty in the laws? But here are the law-makers in session: why not make better laws?

All who were intimately associated with the volunteers about Washington in the early part of July will bear witness that their conversation was mainly of the tenor above indicated. It is not at all improbable that there were agents of the secessionists among them to encourage such conversation.

If the volunteer could have found precisely where and with whom rested the responsibility of that which offended him: if he could have been made sure that the present administration had nothing to do with it, and was doing its best to remedy it, it is doubtful if it would have averted the effect of the continued disappointment and humiliation of his patriotism. It is certain that this effect was none the less because, to the volunteer, the difficulties of the case were "all a muddle."

There was, at the same time, a growing want of confidence between the men and the more immediate representatives and agents of the Government—the officers—because the men were naturally disposed to hold their officers, in the first place, responsible for the causes of their discontent. To a certain extent, but not altogether, justly so. They, however, could not distinguish between that for which the officers were justly to blame, and that which lay behind them. The consciousness of this had its effect on the officers. The company officers, especially, were acquiring habits of treating their men, some with familiarity, others with an apologetic manner, others with an insolent affectation of sternness, each according to his character, responding to the ill-will of the men in their duty to him.

Thus, while the larger and nobler purposes of the army had no opportunity of action, but were rather constantly being frustrated, of the smaller, the everyday wants, the appetites, there was also nothing but disappointment. Drill and the dress parade was no longer an amusement. The only obvious general resort for recreation was the dram shop, and this only made the volunteer feel the more angrily the want of his pay. The Commission will remember that some officers presented it as a reason why it might not be best to urge measures to secure the more prompt payment of the men; that no recreation was open to them, except such as would demoralize them, and they were as well without it.

The better men were tired of this sort of soldier's life; were disgusted with it, and yet were ashamed to acknowledge this, and strove to resist and suppress a natural and truthful manifestation of it.

But there really had been pervading all classes in most regiments a sense of disappointment, of annoyance, humiliation, and vexation. Consider that co-existent with this there was the effect of an entire change of air and of habits, of food and drink; irregular sleep, and exposure to excessive heat, alternating with exposure to cool, damp, and malarious night-air, or the mephitic atmosphere of crowded and unventilated tents.*

---

*In June the director of one of the general hospitals called attention to the fact that a remarkable proportion of his patients were from Maine, and that they seemed to

The volunteer was in a transitional state physically. He was distinctly undergoing the process of acclimation. Was he not, only as much less distinctly, as all diseases of "the moral faculties" being complicated with those of the body are more beyond human comprehension than those of the body simply, undergoing a demoralizing process? Was he losing confidence only, or was he losing something of the "faculty" of confidence—the power of exercising confidence?

A sick man is expected to be peevish, timid, weak, and wilful. Insist that he shall not be, demand of him the usual exercise of his mental and moral faculties, and you aggravate his disease. To the soul-sick volunteer came, at length, a demand to advance towards the enemy. With some the disease was even then so deeply seated that they threw away the rations provided for the advance, so little were they able to believe of the actual fact of war—so little confidence could they exercise in the judgment of those placed over them. But actual war it was, not demanding merely the usual exercise of the virtues of courage and faith and perseverance of the volunteer, but putting these to the severe trial—for severe it always is with every man—of his first battle. The strong excitement overrides the moral sickness as it does fatigue, and hunger, and thirst, during the stormy advance; but then comes the check, the repulse, the retreat; obstacles breaking column; final dispersion and military disintegration. And here must come the relapse; with some, as, quite generally, with the Fire Zouaves, it will have come earlier; but with all, there at length comes a relapse, and with the relapse a frightful aggravation of the malady.

Thus, by accepting, as a condition in the case, the essential deep-seated demoralization of the volunteers before the battle, the degree of

---

be suffering under no distinct disease, but from general debility and depression of spirits. He attributed this to the fact of their having experienced a greater change of air than any of the others. The regiments in which demoralization has since been most obvious are from Maine, Minnesota, and that class of the population of New York who would be selected as peculiarly subject to the sweep of an epidemic. Nostalgia seems more evident in one of the Maine regiments than elsewhere. A private of this regiment, a few days since, placed a check for $150 in the hands of his surgeon, as an inducement to him to obtain his discharge.

Baron Larrey says:

"The inhabitants of moist and cold climates, as Holland, or mountainous regions, as Switzerland and Brisgau, are very susceptible of the moral impressions which produce nostalgia; a remark which has been already made by many celebrated physicians. The troops of these nations, in consequence of susceptibility, suffered most from the cruel vicissitudes to which we were exposed during the campaign of Moscow."[43]

Since this note was written, above 100 men of the Maine regiment referred to have thrown down their arms, and demanded to be sent home. They are under arrest.[44] The Minnesotans, who are the finest men, physically, in the army, seem to have recovered, and are now "ready for anything."

their demoralization after the battle becomes less extraordinary, because more analogous to a common experience.

If this view be not adopted, then we seem left to accept it as a fact that thousands of men, as enthusiastic, and, the Secretary believes, as brave by nature, as any that can ever be drawn from among a civilized people, became, practically, good for nothing for any warlike purpose, under a trial of battle and of campaigning such as would have had scarcely the least depressing effect upon soldiers proper; which, in fact, did have no perceptible depressing effect upon the regular soldiers taking part in it,* and which really was but little more severe than the dangers and fatigues, and privations and hardships that, as seamen and whalers and fishermen, and lumbermen and miners and quarriers, thousands of these very men had been accustomed to undergo without discomposure or complaint; which was not at all more terrible than the dangers and privations and hardships that men of delicate nurture frequently encounter in following a mere purpose of recreation, and which, beyond a day, has no other effect upon them than to cheer and invigorate their spirits.

If not in the nature of a disease, that is to say, if not assignable to special local causes, which can be traced out, defined, and in future guarded against, but a condition natural, normal, and always to be reckoned upon in dealing with volunteers, is it not the duty of the Commission to apprise the nation upon what a game of chance its liberty is staked?

The Commission had abundant personal observation of the volunteers a fortnight after the battle of Bull Run, and will judge whether regiment upon regiment of them, whose losses had been in less proportion to their numbers than the average losses of the Massachusetts fishing craft in every heavy easterly gale, would have been of the smallest value in the practice of the science of war as an exact science.

There is every reason to believe that a parallel state of things existed, it is true, in the rebel army. That man for man, the force of the nation is now stronger, less liable to panic, and less liable to demoralization, under similar circumstances, than that of its enemy's;† but this fact affords but insufficient assurance of safety. If properly presented to them, the people will not allow that the subjugation of this land to the purposes of the dealers in a certain kind of property and its products shall be hazarded on a game of cards, even if their generals hold the better hand.

Must the nation, which depends mainly on volunteers for a defence of its liberties and independence, be at the mercy of any powerful enemy? Certainly no man of military experience would have considered it

---

*See, in Appendix, a comparison of regulars and volunteers in and after the battle.

†See a comparison in the Appendix.

175

impracticable to have compelled an early surrender of the capital, with all the heads of the nation, and its central legislative bodies, together with the whole volunteer army, with all its equipments and stores, to form which the energies and patriotism of the loyal States had been for three months devoted, if he could have occupied the position of the enemy at that time with but a score of regiments of the disciplined soldiers of any European army. It is mortifying to acknowledge it, but the Commission will hardly find reason to refuse to do so. And unless it can be seen that there were circumstances preceding this affair of Bull Run, peculiarly calculated to undermine the strength of a volunteer army, which circumstances may, in future, be surely guarded against, the Commission cannot too soon or too earnestly protest against the further waste of the national resources in the attempt to maintain a system so inherently weak and worthless. That it is and must be weak and worthless, is well known to be the judgment of nearly all the officers of the regular army who had experience of the volunteers in the Mexican war. Whatever the result of the present war, it can hardly reverse the judgment of the regular officers, inasmuch as the final success of the volunteers, however complete it is, must be a success only against volunteers, not against a regular army. Yet it is extremely doubtful if the American people will submit, however strongly advised to do so, to the maintenance of a standing army as large as the regular officers would deem to be adequate for the protection of the country in all contingencies. The volunteer system is, in truth, a part of our system of government, and when we wholly give it up, we surrender with it something of our distinctive national life. It is obvious that every hour this war continues, intensifies our national life, and increases the devotion of the people to whatever is essentially distinctive in it. The volunteer system is not, then, likely to be wholly given up in any case; but it may be, and it must be, placed upon a firmer and more trustworthy foundation than it has hitherto had.

If, therefore, the volunteer army at Washington, in June last, was undergoing a process of gradual but sure demoralization, it is of the first importance that this should be distinctly established and made known, and the causes defined as fully as possible, in order that they may be forever hereafter avoided. The Commission at that time formally called attention to certain dangers which it recognized, and suggested remedies for them. Informally, in interviews of the members of the Commission with the leading persons of the military administration, many such suggestions were made. A few can readily be recalled, together with the substance of the answers which were received.

1st. A general order requiring a stricter physical examination of recruits? Answer. The volunteers would not submit to it.

2d. A general order placing a limit on the number of absences to be allowed from the camp of each regiment? Answer. The colonels ought to know enough not [to] grant leave injudiciously.

3d.   A general order limiting the hours during which officers and men should be allowed leave of absence from their camps? Answer. It could not be enforced.

4th.   An order to prevent men from purchasing intoxicating liquor, and from bringing it into the camps? Answer. It could not be enforced.

5th.   A general order calling attention to various infractions of the army regulations and of the articles of war, which were then constantly witnessed, and which passed without rebuke? Answer. Nothing better is to be expected of volunteers.

6th.   The issue of detailed instructions to captains, with regard to certain duties which were almost universally neglected by them? Answer. It is the duty of their colonels to instruct them.

7th.   The issue of instructions to colonels as to certain duties almost universally neglected by them? Answer. If they don't know the duties of their office, they have no business in it.

8th.   The modification of certain rules to meet the special difficulties of officers ignorant of their duties? Answer. These rules work well in the regular army.

In fine, while the volunteer officers were nearly all ignorant and inexperienced in military affairs, and were known and acknowledged to be so, scarcely the slightest variation, abatement, addition, or explanation was thought practicable to be made, in their favor, to the laws, regulations, rules, and customs applicable to the carefully prepared, thoroughly trained, and well-tried officers of the regular army. But one important exception is recollected. Absolute physical starvation of the volunteers could not be permitted; and as this would have inevitably resulted to thousands from the ignorance of the captains of their duty, if the officers of the Subsistence Department had refused to go beyond the requirements of the regulations, this part of the duty of the captains was anticipated and in a measure executed for them. Unquestionably, it was still executed imperfectly, and not nearly as well or as economically as it would have been had it been left to captains who had enjoyed the benefit of a West Point education, or who, by any other means, had been able and willing to perform the full service required of captains, under the regulations. For all that, it was much better than if it had been entirely neglected. But various other services little less important to the vigor and spirit of the army were also entirely neglected by the captains, and were not in the least provided for by higher authority. The result has been less tangible and obvious, perhaps, than would have been the result of neglect to distribute food to the men, but it has scarcely been less calamitous to the nation.

These remarks are not made with a fault-finding purpose toward the regular officers as a body. They generally performed all their duty, and more than all the duty required of them by the laws, under the circumstances. It was their duty to be governed by the army regulations, and the army regulations did not require of them to become the schoolmasters of the volunteer officers, nor to interfere to obviate the natural results of their ignorance and neglect. They believed (and, perhaps, they were right) that it was necessary that the volunteers should be made to understand their duty through an experience of the inconvenience which a neglect of it would occasion. At all events, with the opinion they had always had and been ready to express of the fatuity of the nation in depending so entirely upon volunteers, and in maintaining so small a regular force, it was hardly in common human nature to make the best they could under the circumstances of that which they deemed incorrigibly wrong and weak from its very starting point, viz: the organization of companies by an election of officers.

The sagacity and courage of two very uncommon men, General McClellan and General Meigs, cutting through, over-riding, and superseding the old traditions and customs of the army wherever the interests of the nation made it necessary, yet using ten times the rigor of enforcement in regard to the regulations that had been previously used with volunteers, has, since July, made the best of an ineffective system, and shown what might have been done with volunteers before July. Even the demoralized regiments, with but very few exceptions, are now in better condition, in better spirit, in better health, than they were when they received the order for the advance to Bull Run. The very measures which the Commission urged, which it was said could not be enforced, would not be submitted to, and would be useless with volunteers, are now rigidly enforced, are submitted to with manifest satisfaction by volunteers, and are obviously producing the most beneficent effects, and this equally in the new and the older regiments. It is found not impracticable to attempt discipline with volunteers. On the contrary, the most thorough enforcement of discipline leads to the best results. The most exact disciplinarians are the favorites of the volunteers; the best disciplined regiments are the most contented regiments.

All that it was possible, under the laws, for good generalship to do in the time which has elapsed since General McClellan assumed command of the army of the Potomac, has been done to make the best of the national military system; but the great improvement that has been effected must not lead us to shut our eyes to that which is still reprehensible, or prevent us from asking how far this is due to inefficiency of administration, and how far to inherent vices of the system.

To revert again to the hypothesis of disease, there is still room for the inquiry, Has it been entirely eradicated? The Secretary suspects that

certain regiments are hardly yet convalescent. In one of those which suffered most, and most unaccountably, on the theory that the demoralization was the result of the battle, a medical inspector of the Commission
reported this week that fully one-half the extraordinary number of men
reported as sick, were sick, in his judgment, in no otherwise than home-
sick. Even the nominally well men, though in the presence of the enemy, it
was confessed, had no stomach for fighting;—in this respect being in
remarkable contrast to others camped adjoining them, who were impa-
tiently anticipating an immediate order to engage.

If the disease is thus deep-seated, we can hardly imagine that its
causes have been destroyed at a blow. Let us look the facts fairly in the face
without fear or flattery.

The volunteers are now abundantly, yet far from wholesomely fed;
they are lodged as well as the laws provide that soldiers shall be lodged, yet
no sensible farmer lodges his beasts nearly as unwholesomely—the government lodges its own horses in some respects better. They are beginning to
be well clothed; but some regiments are yet objects of charity in this
particular. With typhus increasing, no means are available—at least none
at all adequate—to keep them clean; and many of the camps are yet really
in a filthy condition. It would be a poor farmer who would offer the same
invitation to vermin and cutaneous diseases to enter his stables that are
offered in some of our volunteer regiments. The sick frequently suffer
for want of proper medicine, food, attendance, shelter, and professional
advice.

Congress did, in its extra session, in some sort recognize the fact
that volunteers were not as regulars.* The volunteers were badly fed, and
therefore Congress increased the ration. But was not the ration abundant
in quantity before? Did not this Commission most satisfactorily ascertain
in June, that there was food enough provided by the law, and the only
difficulty was that the volunteer could not get it, and that when he got it
he could not cook it?†[45]

These, the real defects of the army system in its application to
volunteers, Congress did nothing to remedy. The agents of this Commission verbally and by printed documents[46] have labored to make commanders of companies acquainted with their functions (as established for

---

*In the revised army regulations, issued since this report was written, two
pages, out of two hundred and fifty, are devoted to *"volunteers and militia in the service
of the United States."* They relate exclusively to the recruiting, mustering in and mustering out, and payment of volunteers and militia.

†The Prince Napoleon[47] is said to have observed, after visiting a camp at
Washington, "What is here wasted would feast a French regiment." A considerable part
of the food is, in fact, literally thrown away in most regiments.

the regular army) in respect to the subsistence of the men; and in some measure by these means, and probably much more by the gradual teaching of necessity, in experience, a considerable and quite general improvement is believed to have occurred both in the distribution and in the cooking of food. It has been, however, by adapting the knife to the case, not the case to the knife.

Some improvement in the method of payment, by which volunteers could meet their special obligations at home, was also authorized by the last Congress, at the suggestion of the Commission.[48] It has not yet gone into operation, and has probably been found impracticable to be carried out with the present organization of the volunteers.* Something was done by Congress also about the grand difficulty with the volunteers, their alleged disposition to take the most unfit men for officers.[49] To this time, however, no method has been put in operation for subjecting either candidates or officers already elected, to an examination by those competent to judge of their qualifications; and officers who are not only notoriously ignorant, but who are notoriously bad men—bad men among bad men—are allowed to retain responsible commands. Are the difficulties in the way of remedying these evils of the volunteer system insurmountable?

The Secretary is every day called upon to give information to the surgeons of volunteer regiments, as to how they shall proceed in order to obtain the simplest medicines and other supplies necessary for the treatment of the commonest cases of camp disease.†

This constant experience as to a matter which must be considered of vital importance to volunteers who are in the field, and exposed to all the vicissitudes of a life in the field, illustrates the grand fact of danger which everywhere presents itself.

If, at this period of the war, it is a necessary danger attending the employment of volunteers, then the conviction is irresistible that the present should be the last volunteers to be employed by the United States. If a remedy, if an alleviation of the evil can be found, its application is surely too long delayed.

Some reference must, in justice, here be made to the complaints received at this office from the volunteer surgeons, of the inadequacy of the government supplies for the sick. The Secretary admits that the volun-

---

*Inquiry was made, and such was the answer. There is now reason to hope, however, that the practical difficulties will be overcome, and the law go [in]to effect.

†According to the reports of the surgeons themselves to the Commission's Inspectors, 21 per cent. of the volunteer surgeons received their appointments and entered upon their duties without having been subjected to any official inquiry as to their medical qualifications or their knowledge of the army medical regulations.

teer surgeons are generally too much inclined to make inordinate requisitions and to keep cases under field-treatment which ought to be transferred to general hospitals; but if, as is stated, the force in the medical purveyor's warehouse is so small that, at this period of the war, the delay of a fortnight occurs in answering a surgeon's requisition for medicines—and this statement is understood to be admitted to be true—and if the supply of medicines in store is so limited that, without any inquiry as to the peculiar circumstances to meet which each requisition is made, he arbitrarily reduces the quantities, and varies the assortment of medicines supplied in each case, the Secretary cannot but think the Commission has a duty before it of a different kind to that with which it has hitherto occupied itself.

Another matter of complaint constantly addressed to the Secretary must be alluded to. It is, that patients far too ill to be properly kept in camp are often refused admittance to the general hospitals. Regimental surgeons being, as they assert, thus forced to keep a certain class of patients under canvas, call for various articles—wine, for instance—which otherwise it would not be thought proper to supply for camp use. In the majority of cases of this kind which have been investigated by the Secretary, the failure to get the patient into the general hospital has been owing to ignorance of the proper forms to be observed for that purpose. In not a few, however, it appears to have been because the hospitals were full. Considering the rapid increase of severe illness, which is liable to occur in an army; considering, too, the liability to battles, is it right that, under ordinary circumstances, the hospital accommodations of the army should become anywhere near exhausted? The Secretary feels it his duty to say that, regarding the question from an unprofessional point of view, but regarding it as he is confident ninety-nine in a hundred tax-paying citizens would regard it, the hospital preparations are yet manifestly inadequate and unsuitable for the volunteer army. Can it be right, for instance, that there should be but one surgeon and two young assistants to attend to from 160 to 180 patients, a large part of these being surgical cases or illness of a typhoid character? This is the case at Alexandria, with the disadvantage of buildings not intended for hospital purposes, and without the ordinary modern conveniences of even citizens' dwellings in northern towns.

The occasional very great unfitness of the surgeons for their posts is an evil which will be the subject of a special report to the Commission. It is alluded to here as being the chief cause of another great evil—the want of confidence in the regimental surgeons by their superior medical and other officers. This, at the present time, is painfully illustrated by the measures to which it has given rise to prevent improper discharges of invalids. A statement on this subject, just received, is as follows:

181

There are men in this camp who, to my knowledge, have been held in suspense for weeks, and are dying by inches, because they cannot be released. They are unfit for duty, and have the surgeon's certificate that they are unfit for service, and probably ever will be, and yet the papers that have been forwarded have been held back. There is some clog in the wheel; what it is we do not know.

Some of the men have been summoned before the medical board at Alexandria, but what can they know about the man I pointed out in the tent, who is made blind by the rush of blood to the head. In a short interview they can learn nothing. Yet he has been lying in the tent for weeks, perfectly unfit for duty.

(Signed by a Chaplain of Volunteers)

Is not the existence of this Commission based on an assumption of the insufficiency of the regular army organization to meet the wants of the volunteers; and if so, is it not the first duty of the Commission to inquire what those wants are, and advise the government how they can be regularly, systematically, and adequately provided for directly by government?

The Secretary confesses that it does not appear to him to be right that certain offices for the volunteers, undertaken by the Commission, should rest on the uncertain means upon which the Commission is obliged to depend. When a man who has, through a patriotic impulse, volunteered to serve his country in the field of battle, falls dangerously ill, or has a leg shot off, he cannot feel that it is right that an adequate supply—a generous supply—of proper clothing, delicate and nourishing food, wine, surgical attendance, nursing, or of anything else which will materially contribute to a reasonable assurance of saving his life, should be dependent on the success of any number of persons who are obliged to solicit the means to procure these articles and these services as if for charity.

This is precisely the way in which the case stands at present. If it is not, the Commission is spending a great deal of energy, and a great number of benevolent persons throughout the country are laboring with it, for an unnecessary purpose.

In the judgment of the Secretary, the Commission should not be content with leaving this business where it is. Either the government should do a great deal more or the Commission should do a great deal more. To illustrate the matter as it stands:

The Commission, at its last session in Washington, had its attention called to the case of a man in one of the general hospitals who had just suffered amputation of a leg. As it was thought that his chances of recovery would be enhanced if he could be placed on a water-bed, an article not included in the government hospital supplies, the Secretary was directed to procure one for him, which was done, by ordering it from New York.

182

The surgeon in charge lately reported that, in his judgment, the man's life was saved by the water-bed. What constitutes a necessity of a military hospital, if this was not an instance of it? Six other water-beds have since been called for by different surgeons, each being required for special cases. Through the generosity of certain noble women in New York and on Staten Island, the Secretary has been able to promptly supply four of them. On telegraphing for the fifth, an answer was received that it would be necessary to wait for it to be manufactured, as the stock in store was exhausted.[50]

Should such cases be dealt with only in this retail way?

The Secretary may be misinformed as to the value of water-beds. He may be equally mistaken as to [the] intrinsic value of the thousands of other articles which he has supplied, at the request of the hospital surgeons, for the wounded and sick, during the last month. In that case the Commission is imposing upon the public in asking to be supplied with these articles, and in soliciting funds to purchase them. But if water-beds, for instance, are ever a necessity in a military hospital, then, in the judgment of the Secretary, it was a national sin that there should have been not one such thing in the government stores at the breaking out of the war; and he can, at this period of the war, in no way justify a neglect to put hundreds of them within easy reach of the headquarters of every column of the army.

The proper function of the Commission, appears to the Secretary, in this case, to have been, on discovering the need of a water-bed, to procure it by the most ready means available, but to provide for future cases, by calling upon the government to at once supply not only this but every other proper appliance of the best of civil hospitals abundantly to every medical purveyor of the army.

The Secretary, with the greatest possible respect for the Commission and for the government, feels it necessary to urge this suggestion. If the government fails in its duty toward the volunteers, he is convinced that it is from no want of disposition to thoroughly execute their duty on the part of those who administer the government. Government is in the predicament which the master of a small craft would be, were he suddenly forced to take command of a ship-of-the-line,[51] with a crew of green-horns, and no officers but those he had had on his little trader to assist him. There is great danger that habits formed on the coaster, and which were excellent habits for the coaster, will bring the liner to grief. Government depends for information and advice about the army, and the wants of the army, almost entirely on a class of gentlemen who have, for the greater part of their lives, been under a systematic training deliberately intended by the nation to make them adapt themselves to that which should be given them, and not to look out for that which would be best for them; deliberately intended to confine the energies of each of them to his own special responsibility. This has been the time-honored and much boasted policy of the country towards the army. An officer of the army or of the navy is disqualified for every legislative and administrative duty, except with reference to his own command; and for that, the limits within which his ambition may range have been more closely defined than those of a shop-boy's. For instance, a lieutenant colonel of the regular army is restricted by law in making his official memorandums and reports to the use, annually, of "one piece of red tape, the quarter of an ounce of wafers, the quarter of a quire of envelope paper, 12 quills, or, in lieu thereof, 12 steel pens, and one pen holder," etc. The same close calculations and parsimonious spirit rule the medical regulations;[52] and when you propose to a surgeon who has adapted his habits to them, that he shall call for the same degree of comfort for a sick soldier which you are accustomed to see offered a sick laborer in every respectable civil hospital, you will learn from his answer what the effect has been. No member of the Commission is without a sufficient experience of this kind.

To make the government dependent on the information that will be transmitted to it by regular officers, of the wants of the volunteer army, and to suppose that it will thus be able to anticipate these wants, and to make such timely and abundant provision for them, as the people expect at this time, is to depend on the fleetness of a horse that has been kept in fetters since he was a colt. These gentlemen—the Secretary says it with the most sincere and unqualified respect for them—these gentlemen cannot get over the habit of putting off every demand upon the government to the last moment, and of reducing every demand upon government to the least possible amount which will meet the immediate imperative necessities of carefully selected and thoroughly trained soldiers. The nation has always insisted that in that way they should do business, or not at all.

This the Secretary deems to be the true explanation of the false economy which had so manifestly been practised before the battle of Bull Run, and, so far as the army now suffers from maladministration rather than bad laws, this still explains the most of it—this, and not an indisposition to provide adequately for the suppression of the rebellion on the part of the government. And hence he deems it proper, hence he deems it the first duty and the most important service which a body constituted as this has been, representing the feelings, the plans, the temper, and the demands of the people; constituted by government, and yet independent of the favor of government, and constituted by government for the express purpose of inquiry and advice, that it should freely consider and determine the wants of the army, and freely and frankly represent them to the government and to the people—to the government, that it may be led to endeavor to supply them; to the people, that they may the more heartily sustain the government in its efforts to supply them.

But if the Commission is not disposed to take this wide view of its duty, then the Secretary begs leave to urge, as the practical conclusion of this Report, that at least it is within its duty to advise the Government to adopt a much more liberal, thorough, and effective policy with reference to the medical department of the army; and if, finally, the Government cannot be induced to act what seems to the Secretary to be the proper part of a civilized Government towards its sick soldiers, then, he further urges that, unless the Commission has been going all wrong heretofore, it will unquestionably become its duty to undertake a far larger business than its present organization is adapted to meet; and measures should at once be initiated to canvass the country for subscriptions to establish its treasury on a much stronger basis.

If, however, the Government, upon the representations of the Commission, shall be found ready to abundantly provide for the care of its sick and wounded soldiers and sailors, then the field of duty of the Commission may be correspondingly curtailed; its functions being mainly reduced to that of procuring statistics which will be of service to the world with reference to disease and mortality in war, and that of the preparation and distribution of information and advice calculated to improve the sanitary condition of the forces engaged.

It may be asked, why should not these duties be undertaken also by Government under its paid agents?

The answer is, with regard to procuring information, that a certain class of facts may be desirably investigated and classified by the Commission, which it does not necessarily come within the duty of a government to deal with. It is considered a part of the contract which government enters into with the soldiers that it shall provide water-beds and such like articles, if these are necessary for the saving of their life. Government is under no obligations to procure statistics, which would only have a general philanthropic value; and at such a crisis as the present, the heads of Government are supposed to be too much needed in meeting its immediate essential duties to undertake the responsible superintendence of measures of general philanthropy.

And with reference to the dissemination of information, the whole system of government in dealing with the army is based on the assumption that its officers are well informed in certain respects, and its privates in the main well drilled and disciplined. As has already been said, the Secretary questions if this system is not a mistaken one, where the volunteer army is concerned; but though it may be gradually somewhat modified, it cannot be entirely changed in a day nor a month; probably not during the present war. There is then, and there is to be, a large number of officers in the

employment of government, who have had no means of informing themselves of the conditions of health of soldiers in camps, and a vast army of
men, the preservation of whose health depends far more on their own
prudence in certain respects than upon those safe-guards for which government relies solely upon discipline and acts of routine. Hence a field of
operations exists which can only be entered in co-operation with government, and yet which cannot be fully occupied by government.

The Secretary has been thus particular in defining what he deems
to be the possible duties of the Commission, because he considers it is no
longer right for the Commission to proceed on the supposition that it is
meeting a wholly temporary emergency.

It should be determined, at this session of the Commission, if
practicable, what duties shall be undertaken for the war; and the organization of the Commission, for all other purposes than these, should be
wound up. Measures should also be taken to establish the organization of
the Commission for the duties which it shall undertake for the war on a
firm basis.

If the Commission is to undertake to meet the deficiencies of the
government supply for the care of the sick and wounded, the government
supply not being assuredly enlarged in its scope and variety, it should
establish depots for this purpose at various points in the country, and
should be prepared to use for this purpose a capital stock of at least
$50,000, and to be assured of a monthly revenue also for this purpose of
$5,000.

For the efficient performance of the other duties which have been
indicated, it should be assured of a monthly revenue to continue without
abatement during the war, of about $4,000. This is on the supposition that
the accommodations at present afforded the Commission by the Government continue to be enjoyed.

The Secretary respectfully requests determinate action, if practicable, at this session, upon these suggestions, and recommends the passage
of the following resolutions:

Resolved, That the Committee of Inquiry be requested to prepare
a report to the Commission on the moral and sanitary influences resulting
in the demoralization observed among the troops of this department in the
latter part of July.

Resolved, That the Committee of Inquiry be requested also to
report how far the causes contributing to the demoralization of the troops
still exist, and how far and in what way they may be modified or removed.

Resolved, That a special committee be appointed to visit the Surgeon General, the Medical Director, and the Medical Purveyor of the
department of the Potomac, and report to the Commission what, if any,

additional provisions of any kind are needed for the proper care of the sick and wounded of the army.[53]

Respectfully,

FRED. LAW OLMSTED,
Secretary.

The text presented here is from a pamphlet entitled "Report of the Secretary with Regard to the Probable Origin of the Recent Demoralization of the Volunteer Army at Washington, and the Duty of the Sanitary Commission with Reference to Certain Deficiencies in the Existing Army Arrangements, as Suggested Thereby," which is on file at the Library of Congress, Washington, D.C. The title page also bears the notations "[Confidential]" and "[Printed for Members Only]" and carries this explanation: "Read before the Commission September 5th. Referred to the Committee of Enquiry, and ordered to be printed for members only, September 11th, 1861." Internal evidence— Olmsted's reference to the bravery of the 79th New York Infantry—suggests that Olmsted was revising this report as late as September 11. An extremely abridged version of this report, one that included none of its conclusions, was printed as an appendix to Sanitary Commission document number 40, issued in December 1861.

1. Ezekiel Brown Elliott (1823–1888), a statistician and the Sanitary Commission's actuary until 1864. A graduate of Hamilton College in Clinton, New York, Elliott provided statistical studies for the state of Massachusetts and private insurance companies during the 1850s. In July 1861 Elisha Harris urged Henry W. Bellows to hire Elliott, calling him "the most competent man who can be found" to prepare and carry out plans to gather statistical data on illness and death among the soldiers.

     During his tenure with the Sanitary Commission, Elliott prepared statistical materials and tables for documents such as the Commission's report to the secretary of war in December 1861. He also worked on a more thorough statistical survey of the troops. At times Elliott's enthusiastic immersion in his subject and his manner of organizing data did not appear very practical to some members of the Commission. In August 1862, after a presentation by Elliott, Olmsted noted that the Executive Committee "got out of patience with Elliott, very thoroughly." Alfred J. Bloor conjectured in February 1864 that were the Commission to dismiss Elliott, "All he has done in the last three years would be valueless. Only himself holds the clue his labyrinth." Olmsted, however, apparently had great confidence in Elliott and paid for his assistance in compiling data for a never-completed study of the social statistics of Union volunteer soldiers during the war.

     Elliott eventually lost his position with the Sanitary Commission. In the summer of 1863 he attended an international statistical meeting in Berlin and at its end did not return to the United States or give the Commission any reason for his absence. After the Civil War, Elliott entered government service. In 1865 he served as secretary to the U.S. Revenue Commission, and in 1871 he became chief clerk of the Bureau of Statistics in the U.S. Department of the Treasury. At the time of his death, Elliott had been a government actuary for seven years (*NCAB*; Elisha Harris to HWB, July 19, 1861, USSC-NYPL, box 640; FLO to JFJ, Aug. 6, 1862, USSC-NYPL, box 743: 1776; A. J. Bloor to JFJ, Feb. 24, 1864, USSC-NYPL, box 618; FLO to F. N. Knapp, July 7, 1864).

2. The 69th and 71st regiments, New York State Militia, as troops enlisted for only three months of government service, were mustered out in New York City on

August 3 and July 31, 1861, respectively (F. Phisterer, *New York in the War*, 1: 674, 690–91).

3. The demonstration mentioned here by Olmsted was a skirmish that occurred on July 18, 1861, at Blackburn's Ford, an eastern ford of Bull Run, as part of the Union army's general advance. Gen. Irvin McDowell had ordered Daniel Tyler, commander of the 1st Division, to move upon Centreville and the Manassas road, showing force but avoiding an engagement with Confederate troops. After taking Centreville, evacuated by the Southern troops, Tyler proceeded to Bull Run. At the creek he used his 4th Brigade, commanded by Israel B. Richardson, to test the strength of the Confederate forces deployed there under the commmand of James Longstreet. The four bodies of troops to which Olmsted refers were probably the four regiments composing that brigade: the 1st Massachusetts, the 12th New York, and the 2nd and 3rd Michigan. After indecisive fighting, Tyler ordered his troops to retreat back to Centreville (William C. Davis, *Battle at Bull Run: A History of the First Major Campaign of the Civil War* [Garden City, N.Y., 1977], pp. 102, 112–24).

4. Blenker's Brigade was the 1st Brigade of the 5th Division, but Olmsted here appears to be referring to a smaller body of troops, perhaps the 8th New York, sometimes known as Blenker's Rifles (O.R., ser. 1, vol. 2, p. 315; F. Phisterer, *New York in the War*, 3: 1815).

5. Henry Francis Clarke (1820–1887), an army captain who was the chief commissary in McDowell's command at the battle of Bull Run. A graduate of West Point, Clarke served as chief commissary of subsistence for the Army of the Potomac until January 1864 (*Appleton's Cyc. Am. Biog.*).

6. This circular, issued by Assistant Adjutant General James B. Fry, can be found in *Official Records*, series 1, volume 2, on pages 325–26.

7. Olmsted here quotes directly from Henry F. Clarke's report, reprinted in *Official Records*, series 1, volume 2, pages 336–38.

8. During the battle of Bull Run, Richardson's Brigade, the 4th Brigade of the 1st Division, was positioned near Blackburn's Ford, where the skirmish of July 18 had occurred (W. C. Davis, *Battle at Bull Run*, pp. 240–41).

9. A military term applied to the fastest step next to the run. The U.S. Army defined the double-quick as 165 steps, each of thirty-three inches, per minute.

10. The 11th New York Infantry (see n. 23 below).

11. Erasmus Darwin Keyes (1810–1895) commanded the 1st Brigade of the 1st Division at Bull Run. Fort Corcoran, where these volunteer troops bivouacked, was located on Arlington Heights in Virginia. Keyes's report can be found in *Official Records*, series 1, volume 2, pages 353–56. See also *DAB*.

12. The 2nd Maine was the first regiment to leave Maine in 1861. At the battle of Bull Run, it acted as a rear guard and was among the last regiments to leave the field (William Edward Seaver Whitman and Charles H. True, *Maine in the War for the Union: A History of the Part Borne by Maine Troops* . . . [Lewiston, Me., 1865], pp. 37, 43).

13. The 1st Massachusetts, composed in large part of members of the state militia's 1st Regiment, was among the first regiments enlisting for three years' service. It participated in both the skirmish at Blackburn's Ford and the battle of Bull Run (Warren Handel Cudworth, *History of the First Regiment [Massachusetts Infantry]* . . . [Boston, 1866], pp. 14, 26–27, 40).

14. The altered muskets of 1840 were old smoothbore (nonrifled and muzzle-loading) flintlocks, which were then the standard arms for United States troops. In 1842 the decision was reached to discontinue manufacture of flintlock firearms for the army and to convert many existing flintlocks to percussion firing. The nipple on the altered musket was the metal piece that served as the striking point to set off the paper percussion cap. Since the nipple was usually made of copper, a ductile metal, it was susceptible to the breakage to which Olmsted here refers (Robert M. Reilly,

United States Military Small Arms, 1816–1865: The Federal Firearms of the Civil War [Baton Rouge, La., 1970], pp. xx–xxii, 18–20).

15. Olmsted here describes the fighting on the right of the Union line involving brigades from the 1st, 2nd, and 3rd divisions, and extending east from Sudley Spring, the northwesternmost ford of Bull Run, to the turnpike leading to Warrenton.

16. Gen. Irvin McDowell's report on the battle of Bull Run appeared in the *New-York Daily Tribune* and *Washington Intelligencer* on August 9, 1861. The *Tribune* also reprinted "Dr. Nott's letter to a Mobile paper" on August 4 and published during late July and early August numerous reports that originally appeared in the *Charleston Mercury*.

17. When Confederate general Joseph E. Johnston's army in the Shenandoah Valley eluded the forces of Union general Robert Patterson and reinforced Beauregard near Manassas, Johnston's 4th Brigade, under the command of Gen. Edmund Kirby Smith, was among the last of the troops to be sent by train to Manassas Junction. The 4th Brigade arrived there after three on the afternoon of the battle. Kirby Smith was almost immediately wounded, and Gen. Arnold Elzey led the brigade into action at about four o'clock. Slightly earlier, the 2nd and 8th South Carolina, commanded respectively by Col. Joseph B. Kershaw and Col. E. B. C. Cash, had reinforced Confederate troops at the front (W. C. Davis, *Battle at Bull Run*, pp. 139, 224–27).

18. Olmsted is perhaps referring to an article from the *Richmond Dispatch* reprinted on page 8 of the *New-York Daily Tribune* of August 2, 1861.

19. The Sanitary Commission met in its fourth session beginning July 27 in Washington. Olmsted and treasurer George Templeton Strong issued the call for the meeting.

20. That is, the White House.

21. A reference to the activities of the provost marshal, Col. Andrew Porter, in imposing curfews and requiring all soldiers absent from their units to have written passes. According to one account, the provost marshal's troops "penetrated 'the bar-rooms and restaurants and lug[ged] out the officers in the hotels as well as the men in the streets.'" Before the outbreak of the Civil War, regimental officers policed the men from their own units. After George McClellan assumed command of the troops at Washington in late July, he extended the rudimentary provost-marshal system instituted by Irvin McDowell. McClellan appointed Porter of the 16th United States as provost marshal with the regular army troops (numbering about one thousand) that had been stationed in Washington to serve as his provost guard. The provost marshal also instituted patrols, closed saloons, and required civilians to obtain permits to visit the military camps (Wilton P. Moore, "The Provost Marshal Goes to War," *Civil War History* 5 [March 1959]: 62–65; *War for the Union*, 1: 275).

22. Probably the message from Secretary of War Simon Cameron, published on July 23, 1861, in the New York newspapers, that "there is no danger of the capital or the republic" (*New York Evening Post*, July 23, 1861, p. 2; *New-York Times*, July 23, 1861, p. 1).

23. The 11th New York, commonly known as the Fire Zouaves or Ellsworth's Zouaves, was recruited largely from the New York City volunteer fire department by Elmer E. Ellsworth. Ellsworth gained fame in 1860 by commanding and touring with an Illinois militia company known as the United States Zouave Cadets. Patterning themselves after distinguished French troops who had adopted the name and costume of fierce Algerian tribesmen, Ellsworth's cadets dressed in distinctive loose fitting, brightly colored uniforms and practiced the Zouave drill, which was noted for its emphasis on precision and gymnastic feats.

After the fall of Fort Sumter, Ellsworth raised the regiment of Fire Zouaves and was elected its colonel. In Washington the regiment acquired the ironic nickname of "pet lambs" because of Ellsworth's intimacy with the Lincoln family and his men's rambunctiousness. In late May as Union troops occupied Alexandria, Virginia, Ellsworth met a tragic end. As he boldly hauled down a Confederate flag flying over a local inn, he was fatally shot by its proprietor, who in turn was killed by one of the Fire Zouaves. The command of the 11th New York then devolved upon Noah L. Farnham, the regiment's lieutenant colonel and a member of the fire department (Ruth Painter Randall, *Colonel Elmer Ellsworth: A Biography of Lincoln's Friend and First Hero of the Civil War* [Boston, 1960], pp. 8, 44–47, 118, 177, 230–31, 243–45, 257–60; Charles Anson Ingraham, *Elmer E. Ellsworth and the Zouaves of '61* [Chicago, 1925], pp. 7, 24).

24. Olmsted probably exaggerates how early the Fire Zouaves were incapacitated for battle. The attacks that demoralized the Zouaves that afternoon and left them unwilling to provide the necessary support for a Union battery came after two o'clock from Confederate general Thomas J. Jackson's 1st Division and from J. E. B. Stuart's 1st Virginia Cavalry (W. C. Davis, *Battle at Bull Run*, pp. 203–12).

25. In Washington on the evening of May 9, 1861, a fire broke out at a building adjoining Willard's Hotel. The Fire Zouaves obtained the city's fire engines and reached the blaze before the local fire department did. The *New-York Times* praised the Zouaves' "wonderful feats of agility and bravery": "They formed pyramids on each other's shoulders, climbing into windows, scaling lightning-rods, and succeeded in two hours in saving the whole structure. . . . For want of a ladder, two Zouaves held another down from the eaves, while he, with his head down, played water into the burning building" (*New-York Times*, May 10, 1861, p. 1; R. P. Randall, *Colonel Elmer Ellsworth*, pp. 241–42).

26. One example of such public statements was the article in the *New-York Daily Tribune* which argued that the Fire Zouaves became demoralized after the battle of Bull Run because of a delay in paying the soldiers that arose from the ineptness of the regimental disbursing officer. In addition, the article questioned the adequacy of the Zouaves' clothing and provisions for personal hygiene, which similarly were the responsibility of regimental officers (*New-York Daily Tribune*, Aug. 3, 1861, p. 5).

27. Varian's Battery was Company I of the 8th New York State Militia, mustered out in New York City on August 2, 1861. On Saturday, July 20, these artillerymen, who had volunteered for only three months' duty, asserted that their time of service had expired. Despite the entreaties of General McDowell and Secretary of War Cameron, the soldiers refused to participate in the battle scheduled for the following day. The testimonial to which Olmsted refers may have been a declaration in the *New-York Daily Tribune* by members of Varian's Battery that a report in the *New-York Times* about the company's refusal to serve at Bull Run was "totally devoid of truth, and without the slightest foundation in fact, unjustly reflecting on Capt. Varian" (F. Phisterer, *New York in the War*, 1: 556–58, 566; *O.R.*, ser. 1, vol. 2, p. 325; *New-York Daily Tribune*, Aug. 1, 1861, p. 8; *New-York Times*, July 31, 1861, p. 1).

28. On August 14, 1861, eight companies of the 79th New York, known also as the New York Highlanders, refused to obey an order to dismantle their tents in preparation for moving their camp. McClellan characterized their conduct as "disgraceful" and termed it "decided insubordination, if not open mutiny." He demanded and received compliance to earlier commands, but thirty-five leaders of the revolt were arrested and twenty-one were sentenced to the Dry Tortugas. The 79th New York's rebellion appears to have been related to disorganization after the battle of Bull Run. There the regiment suffered great losses—its colonel, James Cameron, brother of Secretary of War Simon Cameron, was killed, and casualties totaled almost two hundred. The general belief that the regiment would return to New York to recruit new volunteers and elect new officers was suddenly dashed when on August 10, Col. Isaac Stevens, a West Pointer, assumed command.

Olmsted must have added the remark about the regiment's bravery to his final draft of this report, as the incident occurred on September 11, 1861, the day the Commission ordered the report reprinted. Several companies of Highlanders served as skirmishers and as a rear guard for the reconnaissance in force near Lewinsville in northern Virginia. Olmsted himself observed the soldiers' return from that expedition. McClellan praised the regiment and returned its colors, the regimental flag that had been removed at the time of the mutiny (William Todd, *The Seventy-Ninth Highlanders, New York Volunteers in the War of Rebellion, 1861–1865* . . . [Albany, N.Y., 1886], pp. 48, 55–66, 77, 80; see FLO to JO, Sept. 12, 1861, below).

29. The 2nd Rhode Island, raised in May and June 1861, was composed of men enlisting for three years' service. Olmsted, in his report of July 9, 1861, stated, "The camps of the Rhode Islanders, and of the 71st and 12th New York militia have not been visited, because it has been understood that their condition was exceptional" (Augustus Woodbury, *The Second Rhode Island Regiment: A Narrative of Military Operations* . . . [Providence, R.I., 1875], p. 24; Frederick Law Olmsted, "Report of a Preliminary Survey of the Camps of a Portion of the Volunteer Forces near Washington," doc. no. 17 in USSC, *Documents*).

30. Among those killed at the battle of Bull Run were the colonel of the 2nd Rhode Island, John S. Slocum, and three of the regiment's other officers. Olmsted, however, appears to be badly misinformed about the other losses of the regiment. His estimate of those killed far exceeds the correct proportions. The casualties—killed, wounded, and missing—of this regiment numbered 104, including commissioned officers. The number of casualties among the enlisted men (excluding all commissioned officers and the artillery company) barely reached 12 percent of the total enlisted force, and at most the fatalities among them were 3 percent of the total (A. Woodbury, *Second Rhode Island Regiment*, pp. 19, 38–39).

31. Dominique-Jean Larrey (1776–1842), surgeon-in-chief of Napoleon Bonaparte's Grand Army. During his tenure with the French Army of the Rhine during the Revolutionary Wars, Larrey set up an ambulance service which, unlike earlier ones, did not wait until the end of a battle to transport the wounded. He subsequently organized ambulance service for all the French armies and served in numerous campaigns directed by Napoleon in Egypt, Spain, Austria, and Russia. Larrey also wrote many books and articles drawn in large part from his experiences as an army surgeon.

    Olmsted's quotation here appears to have come almost verbatim from pages 177–78 of John Revere's translation of Larrey's *Surgical Essays*, published in Baltimore in 1823 (*Biographie universelle [Michaud] ancienne et moderne* . . . [Paris, 1854–65]).

32. Although the U.S. Army required an examination for appointment to its medical corps, the surgeons of the volunteer troops did not have to meet many formal qualifications. The appointment of surgeons for volunteer regiments lay in theory with state governors, but in practice the regimental colonels often put forth their own candidates. These had then to pass the scrutiny—widely varying in its intensity from state to state—of an examining board. Thus, surgeons had differing abilities, training, and experience (George Worthington Adams, *Doctors in Blue: The Medical History of the Union Army in the Civil War* [New York, 1952], pp. 9–11).

33. Fort Sumter, located in the harbor of Charleston, South Carolina, yielded to Confederate fire on April 14, 1861. That attack signaled the beginning of the Civil War.

34. Confederate troops captured the federal armory and arsenal at Harper's Ferry, located at the confluence of the Shenandoah and Potomac rivers in northwestern Virginia, on April 17, 1861. Although it contained twenty thousand rifles and manufactory works, fewer than fifty Union soldiers were defending it. The Union troops destroyed the munitions, but the valuable armory machinery fell into Confederate hands (*War for the Union*, 1: 156–58).

35. A reference to the bloodless takeover of federal forts by state troops in the South. On January 3, 1861, Forts Jackson and Pulaski in Savannah and Fort Morgan in

Mobile were seized. The forts at "the Balize" were probably Forts Jackson and St. Philip, which were surrendered to Louisiana officials on January 10. The latter, approximately seventy miles south of New Orleans on the Mississippi River, guarded that city from attacks coming upriver from the Gulf of Mexico. Although the Balize was actually a small settlement and old fortification built on stilts at Pass de l'Outre, one of four Gulf entrances to the Mississippi River, the name had come to be used as a synonym for the greater New Orleans area (*New-York Daily Tribune*, Jan. 4, 1861, p. 5; ibid., Jan. 11, 1861, p. 5; Harold Sinclair, *The Port of New Orleans* [Garden City, N.Y., 1942], p. 267; Sarah Searight, *New Orleans* [New York, 1973], pp. 283–84; John D. Winters, *The Civil War in Louisiana* [Baton Rouge, La., 1963], pp. 10–11).

36. Confederate state forces captured the naval yards at Pensacola, Florida, and Norfolk, Virginia. In neither case had adequate measures been taken to protect the naval yard or to destroy its munitions in case of such a seizure. Although local authorities took possession of the Pensacola naval yard on January 12, the large naval yard at Norfolk remained under Union control until April 21. The Norfolk base remained unfortified that spring for fear of giving offense to the state of Virginia, which did not secede until after the assault upon Fort Sumter. Despite the last-minute attempts of the newly appointed commodore to destroy war materials, much ordnance and machinery and many other supplies then fell into Confederate hands (*War for the Union*, 1: 155–56; John E. Johns, *Florida during the Civil War* [Gainesville, Fla., 1963], pp. 26–30).

37. The "pirates let out" were privateers operating under the auspices of the Confederate government. President Jefferson Davis proclaimed on April 17, 1861, that his government would issue official letters of marque, which empowered private shipowners to act against hostile nations such as the North. In May the Confederate Congress enacted legislation that granted practically the entire proceeds of captured merchant ships to the privateer and provided bounties for the destruction of Union warships. The Union fleet began to blockade Southern ports in May 1861, but some Southern privateers, such as the *Calhoun* from New Orleans, had already put to sea. Others, such as the *Dixie* and *Savannah*, soon followed and harassed Northern shipping. To Olmsted and other patriotic Northerners, these privateers were pirates because the Confederate government did not represent a legitimately constituted nation and thus could not commission privateers.

The "scores of resigned officers let in" probably refers to the numerous Southern officers in the U.S. Army and Navy who gave up their commissions and returned to the South to fight for the Confederacy. Nearly one-third of the commissioned officers resigned (*War for the Union*, 1: 106–8, 208–10).

38. Gen. Daniel E. Twiggs surrendered all United States military posts and troops in the state of Texas to Confederate state officials there on February 18, 1861. Then dismissed from the Union army, Twiggs promptly joined the Confederate service. Most Union soldiers in Texas, faced with possibly indefinite imprisonment as prisoners of war, chose the proffered alternative of signing letters of parole pledging them to leave Texas. By June 1861 most United States troops had left the state ([Edwin D. Phillips], *Texas and Its Late Military Occupation and Evacuation . . .* [New York, 1862]).

39. Probably a reference to Confederate batteries located on the Aquia and Potomac creeks in Virginia, near Washington (Everette B. Long and Barbara Long, *The Civil War Day by Day: An Almanac, 1861–1865* [Garden City, N.Y., 1971], pp. 111, 193–99; U.S. Department of the Navy, Naval History Division, *Civil War Naval Chronology, 1861–1865*, 5 vols. [Washington, D.C., 1961–65], 1: 1–11).

40. An American expression describing an empty political speech springing not from conviction but a desire to please the public. Its origin allegedly lay in the determination of the North Carolina representative from Buncombe County to give a speech

to satisfy his constituents during the congressional debate on the Missouri Compromise, even though men on both sides of the issue were clamoring for a vote (OED).

41. A reference to the problems of supply and organization encountered by the Union army early in the war. In some cases, shoes and clothing were not distributed to soldiers needing them. In other cases, shoes and uniforms made of cheap imitation materials by unscrupulous contractors quickly fell apart. The "antique smoothbores" were old, nonrifled muskets, many of which had been altered from flintlock to percussion firing. In July 1861 the Army of the Potomac possessed "an infinitesimal portion of cavalry, and a few batteries of artillery" (Fred Albert Shannon, *The Organization and Administration of the Union Army, 1861–1865*, 2 vols. [1928; rpt. ed., Gloucester, Mass., 1965], 1: 85–98, 112–14, 183).

42. The "crazy bridge" over the Potomac was probably the long bridge, which in 1861 was composed of "half earth embankments, half rotten timbers and broken planks" (Margaret Leech, *Reveille in Washington, 1860–1865* [New York, 1941], pp. 11, 109; see FLO to William Cullen Bryant, July 31, 1861, n. 5, above).

43. This quotation appears to have been taken almost verbatim from John Revere's translation of Baron Larrey's essays (D.-J. Larrey, *Surgical Essays*, pp. 159–60).

44. Olmsted is referring to the mutiny among the men of the 2nd Maine that occurred on August 14, 1861. Originally enlisted for only three months, members of that regiment then claimed that their time of service had expired and refused to serve further. Over sixty soldiers from the 2nd Maine were sentenced to the Dry Tortugas, but their penalty was commuted to military service (W. E. S. Whitman and C. H. True, *Maine in the War*, p. 44; *War for the Union*, 1: 276).

45. In its special session the Thirty-seventh Congress enacted a law signed by the president on July 31, 1861, to increase the army's ration. Olmsted had earlier noted in his preliminary report on the army camps around Washington that

> where there is not a most incredible ignorance, incapacity, or neglect on the part of officers, the regiments are supplied with an over-abundance of the raw material of food, excellent of its kind. . . . The raw materials furnished are generally atrociously cooked and wickedly wasted. In consequence of waste, complaint is sometimes made of inadequate supplies, but this is remarkably rare, proving that with care the supply would in all cases be overabundant.

The Sanitary Commission in its third session sought to alleviate this problem by encouraging Congress to make legal provision for the employment of a "competent cook" in every company of the volunteer regiments (John F. Callan, *The Military Laws of the United States Relating to the Army, Volunteers, Militia, and to Bounty Lands and Pensions* . . . [Philadelphia, 1863], p. 484; doc. nos. 17 and 21 in USSC, *Documents*).

46. See, for example, "Rules for Preserving the Health of Soldiers," a pamphlet by William H. Van Buren published as Sanitary Commission document number 17^2 on July 13, 1861.

47. Napoleon-Joseph-Charles-Paul Bonaparte (1822–1891), usually known as Jerome Napoleon, was the son of Jerome Bonaparte and Catherine of Württemberg, and a cousin of French emperor Napoleon III. In 1861 Prince Napoleon, who was strongly sympathetic to the North, visited the United States from late July through late September (Camille Ferri-Pisani, *Prince Napoleon in America, 1861: Letters from His Aide-de-Camp*, trans. Georges J. Joyaux [Port Washington, N.Y., 1973], pp. 5–10, 17; François Berthet-Leleux, *Le Vrai Prince Napoleon [Jerome]* [Paris, 1932], pp. 25, 105–13, 311).

48. An act approved on July 22, 1861, provided that the secretary of war introduce among the volunteer troops "the system of allotment tickets now used in the navy, or some equivalent system, by which the family of the volunteer may draw such portions of his pay as he may request." For over a month the Sanitary Commission

had been suggesting such a measure. In its second session, on June 21, the Commission passed a resolution that its secretary inquire of the secretary of the treasury whether some way existed for the soldiers to send their pay to their families. In early July Olmsted wrote to Henry Wilson, chairman of the Senate Committee on Military Affairs, to urge that the volunteer soldier "be provided with some simple and safe means of making a portion of his wages (not less than 10$ at a time), due payable to his family, and if, as I understand, the chief objection to this is that it would require a great increase of force in the paymaster's department, I submit that such increase however great would be economical in its results to the country." At its meeting on July 10 the Sanitary Commission also decided to arrange for a committee to call on the army's paymaster general to discuss this question (John Scroggs Poland, *A Digest of the Military Laws of the United States* . . . [Boston, 1868], p. 34; USSC, *Minutes*, pp. 10–11, 17; FLO to Henry Wilson, July 1861, USSC-NYPL, box 833, 1: v-vi).

49. Probably a reference to the law enacted on July 22, 1861, providing for the removal of unfit officers among the volunteers. It authorized the commanding general of an army or a department to appoint a military board consisting of three to five officers "to examine the capacity, qualifications, propriety of conduct, and efficiency of any commissioned officer of volunteers within his department or army." An unfavorable report by the board would, with presidential consent, result in the removal of the officer so examined (J. F. Callan, *Military Laws of the United States*, pp. 470, 488–89).

50. A reference to water beds supplied by the Woman's Central Association of Relief. Olmsted told a member of the W.C.A.R. on August 27 that according to the medical director of the Department of Washington, "your water-bed has undoubtedly saved the life of the man at the Union Hotel hospital for whom it was first asked. I have requested you to send four more" (FLO to Susan Shaw, Aug. 27, 1861, USSC-NYPL, box 833, 1: 170).

51. The largest warship of that era, the ship of the line contained three or more decks of guns and formed the principal "line of battle" in naval engagements.

52. Under the direction of Surg. Gen. Thomas Lawson from 1836 to 1861, the Medical Bureau had been noted for its parsimony. Lawson himself disapproved of any unnecessary expense and included under that rubric the purchase of medical books or an army post's possession of two sets of surgical instruments (G. W. Adams, *Doctors in Blue*, pp. 4–5; James Evelyn Pilcher, *The Surgeon Generals of the Army of the United States of America: A Series of Biographical Sketches* . . . [Carlisle, Pa., 1905], pp. 35, 39).

53. Olmsted offered the first two resolutions listed here at the Sanitary Commission meeting of September 11, 1861, and both were approved. There is, however, no indication that the Committee of Inquiry ever presented—or even prepared—either report requested. The Sanitary Commission does not appear to have considered the third resolution, which asked for the appointment of a special committee to meet with the surgeon general and the Army of the Potomac's medical director and medical purveyor (USSC, *Minutes*, p. 58).

To John Olmsted

Sanitary Commission, Washington, D.C.
Treasury Building, Sept[r] 12th 1861

Dear Father,

The Commission met a week ago. I brought before them a long report on conditions of demoralization (military). It was received with great interest, and as first appeared, with great applause. But the government members[1] considered it an attack on government and objected to its being printed. It was recommitted to me & modified. Still the gov[t] members could not suffer it to be printed and threatened to resign if the other members insisted upon it—for the rest all approved of it & were willing to endorse it. It went to committees & returned & was three times made the special order. I finally tonight asked for a committee to be appointed on the subject to whom the report is to be committed & for whom, confidentially it is to be printed.[2] So it will become a historical document. Meantime the practical measures which I urged have practically been all adopted and we have started a pretty row, which brings us at once to the side of McLellan.[3]

We had then several appointments with him before, but unexpected calls—skirmishes—took him away at the time we were to call, till ten this morning & then we found him taking his breakfast like a sensible man. He kept us waiting below till he was well through with it, & then we saw him in his private office. He is a more refined and less extraordinary looking man than the published portraits would indicate. A very fine animal. Graceful from perfection of muscles. A good honest eye with the slightest possible tenderness; power without fierceness, unpoetic. A low forehead, compact brain, bull-dog tenacity of lip and strength of jaw. Reflection, decision, confidence, prudence, tenacity. Dressed carelessly & not in good taste; careless & Western in style, though graceful and moderate. A good voice without being very musical. He received us (D[r] B, the Bishop[4] & myself) quietly, enquiringly, gracefully. He has a good deal of "self consciousness," though not enough to make him indirect in his dealings. He soon took our measure, said to himself, these are men to be trusted, and became as frank with us and commanded our frankness as fully as if we had been familiar friends, (as far as the matter in hand). We were in conversation with him, (smoking) for about an hour, and he disclosed to us a great deal that is not public, about himself & his relations to others and also about the troops. He gave us his estimate of the number of the enemy & told us on what data it was based; also what the enemy's idea of us now was. (He did not give us the slightest clue to our own force.) His strength lies in his abnegation of self—or rather in his consciousness that he is indispensable & everything must give way to his will, and in his faith. He said: "it does not seem unnatural to me. It does not excite me." His brother[5] told us that he fell asleep immediately when he wished & was never in better health. He agreed with us in the matter of business we had with him and appointed another interview this evening.

Last evening, we drove, some of us, to the "chain-bridge."[6] The right river-bank is a steep wooded bluff. The bridge is well guarded—howitzers raking it, the foot path planks all taken up, and 200 ft from the West end a barricade of plank with guard house, & gates with loopholes, all lined with sheet-iron & arrangements for dismantling and breaking up the W. end of the bridge. A steep, crooked, rocky road, full of baggage waggons going up and down, & soldiers guarding them. At the top there was the most of war that I have seen; a considerable fort[7] on a knoll to the left of the road, a considerable fort of fresh earth work, with heavy timber palisades and gate; and abbatis of fresh cut trees, and fresh cut timber all about for a mile opening ranges for the guns, of which there are several heavy pieces & some rifled guns already mounted and trained up the road, Virginia-ward—it is, of course, in Virginia. All this has been done since last Wednesday. Baggage-waggons, moving; baggage waggons standing still, baggage waggons unloading before a hut & tent, & piles of Quarter master & subsistence stores, mountain howitzers; field forge, tumbrils, artillery & baggage horses picketted along the road-side; and men, dirty half uniformed volunteers lying about in every position: a squad drilling: regimental band a little [to] one side practicing, no tents, but lots of little bivouac shelters of boughs and blankets laid on poles &c.—finally as the road comes straight out on something of a plain, a trifling barricade, only half across the road, of felled trees, and about 100 feet on the hither side of it, two brass field pieces commanding the road beyond the barricade. Here a few regulars with the volunteers. We got out & talked with them. They had been out in the morning & had a slight skirmish, took four prisoners, one a major. The regulars spoke well of the volunteers here; said they were good respectable men, farmers' sons, "none of that city skum we had at Bull's Run."

Tonight when we met an appointment at McLellan's, he had just got in & we waited talking with his aids an hour. There had been a reconnaissance in force—1700 men from this Chain bridge fort, and another skirmish with artillery, the same battery & the same men we saw, being engaged. The officers all said the men (of 79th N.Y., 2[d] Vermont & another) behaved exceedingly well, standing firm in rank when shells were bursting over & among them—two were killed & some wounded.[8] McLellan, when we saw him, seemed greatly pleased with this—said he began now to feel that he had an army. He had been out as soon as the guns were heard & met them coming in. We went with him to the Secretary of War's[9] & heard him report it all to the Sec^y, report sitting lolling on a sofa with a cigar. We were several hours with the Secy & once all retired with McL. & his brother for consultation. He was throughout, with the Secy as well as with us, as direct, frank and familiar as if he never saw a politician or heard of rank. The degree of his independence of political considerations, of red tape & circumlocution, was magnificent. To us his attitude and in effect his words were, "We are working for the same ends. I have entire confidence in you: you know more of medical and sanitary matters than I do. Tell me what ought to be done & it shall be done. I do not care who is in the way nor what. He and it shall be over-ridden." We accomplished then & there, at least in the promise of the Secy of War, the most wonderful revolution in medical affairs of the army. McLellan said: "Find me a Larry[10] and he shall be at the head of everything & have everything he can ask for, to-morrow." And to me—personally, he said, "I will do anything you will ask for your Commission, anything that you say will increase your usefulness in this department." I replied that I must reflect before replying & he told me to come & see him whenever I had anything to ask, he would always see me when it was possible. The Secretary said nearly the same to me & to Doctor B. he said: "You have never asked anything of me yet, that you have not got it—and you never will." We left at 12, after taking a drink of Penn'a whiskey.

Now I must go to sleep.

12th I am quite well & getting on fairly well. I have not heard from you since you went toward New Hampshire.

Your affectionate son

Fred. Law Olmsted.

Although Olmsted dated this letter September 12, internal evidence—his reference to a reconnaissance taking place on the 11th and his dating of a postscript as September 12—suggests that it was actually begun on September 11.

1. Army officers George W. Cullum, Alexander E. Shiras, and Robert C. Wood; and A. D. Bache, head of the U.S. Coast Survey.
2. A recounting of the history of Olmsted's report on the demoralization of the volunteer troops at the battle of Bull Run. On September 5 he first presented his findings and conclusions to the Commission. To his wife he recounted the members' reaction:

> My general Report somewhat startled them. I traced the disaster—demoralization of the troops which was the real disaster—not to Bull Run but to the imbecility of the government & the poorness of our system of government for this purpose. They all admit that I carry their convictions, but they dare not have it published—saying that it would be the severest & most effective attack ever made on the government.

That day the Commission referred the report to a special committee composed of Henry W. Bellows, Thomas M. Clark, William Van Buren, Wolcott Gibbs, and Cornelius R. Agnew. On Saturday, September 7, Olmsted requested that his report be recommitted to him, and the following Monday he presented a revised version which tended to blame the disaster more upon the laws than upon the administration in power. The revised report was again committed to the special committee, to which A. D. Bache was added. Although the report was made the Commission's special order of business on September 9 and 10, it was only on September 11 that the Commission resolved its dilemma by ordering that the report "be confidentially printed forthwith, for the use of the members of the Commission" (USSC, *Minutes*, pp. 45, 51, 53–54; FLO to MPO, Sept. 7, 1861).

3. Probably a reference to the requests made by Henry W. Bellows in a letter of September 12, 1861, to Secretary of War Simon Cameron. Not only did Bellows call for the removal and replacement of Surgeon General Finley, but he also asked that McClellan be given the power to appoint the medical director for the Army of the Potomac, who would then be accountable only to McClellan and not to the surgeon general. Furthermore, Bellows requested that McClellan receive authority to organize an ambulance corps for the Army of the Potomac. The Sanitary Commission had gained the general's approval of these two requests that sought to augment and extend his powers (HWB to Simon Cameron, Sept. 12, 1861, USSC-NYPL, box 638).

4. Henry W. Bellows and Thomas M. Clark.

5. Arthur McClellan (1842–1895) served as his older brother's aide-de-camp (Janetta [Wright] Schoonover, ed., *The Brinton Genealogy* . . . [Trenton, N.J., 1925], p. 245).

6. The chain bridge spanned the Potomac River northwest of Georgetown and connected the District of Columbia to Virginia.

7. Probably either Fort Marcy or Fort Ethan Allen in Virginia.

8. A reference to a reconnaissance to Lewinsville, Virginia, on September 10 and 11, 1861. Participating regiments included the 79th New York, the 2nd Vermont, the 5th United States Artillery, and also the 65th New York, the 19th Indiana, the 5th Wisconsin, the 3rd New York Battery Light Artillery, and the 5th United States Cavalry. There were fourteen Union casualties: six killed and eight wounded (Frederick H. Dyer, *A Compendium of the War of the Rebellion* . . . , 3 vols. [1908; rpt. ed., New York, 1959], 2: 895).

9. Simon Cameron.

10. Dominique-Jean Larrey (see "Report on the Demoralization of the Volunteers," Sept. 5, 1861, n. 31, above).

CHAPTER III

REFORMING THE MEDICAL BUREAU

In the Fall and Winter of 1861 Olmsted worked diligently to improve the hygiene and medical care of Union soldiers. The letters presented in this chapter illustrate the importance that he and the other members of the Sanitary Commission placed upon revitalizing the army's Medical Bureau. Olmsted's writings detail his own low opinion of Surgeon General Finley and his outrage at the inadequate and short-sighted policies of the surgeon general's office. Olmsted's correspondence describes the campaign that the commissioners waged to procure a new, more vigorous surgeon general. Despairing of convincing President Lincoln and Secretary of War Cameron to replace Finley, they tried to influence public opinion and thereby achieve legislative reform of the bureau. Olmsted's letters of December 1861 and January 1862 outline this strategy and the series of damaging attacks on the Sanitary Commission that it in turn inspired.

During this period Olmsted also set forth his theory of the Sanitary Commission's purposes and operations. His letter to Sarah Shaw of November 29, 1861, explains the Commission's system for distribution of supplies and its safeguards against waste. Letters to his half-sister Mary Olmsted and to George Magoun, secretary of the Iowa Army Sanitary Commission, show Olmsted's desire to aid soldiers according to need, without regard for state or local origin, and describe his efforts to halt wasteful duplication of effort. The letter to Magoun and that of November 16, 1861, to John S. Newberry also present Olmsted's early views on the role of auxiliary societies and his desire for an effective department of the Sanitary Commission in the West.

During this period Olmsted continued to criticize the inactivity and lack of vision of politicians and public officials. His letters of September 29 and October 3, 1861, lament the failure of the government to rouse public opinion, and the former unfavorably contrasts the poor showing of the North in this respect with that of the South. His letter of November 8, 1861, shows his disappointment with the autumn elections and, with his article "How to Reason with the South," indicates his interest in the role the Southern slaves might play in the war. Letters to his wife and to his half-sister Bertha also present humorous sketches of President Lincoln and give frank assessments of leading politicians of the day.

To Henry Whitney Bellows

Sanitary Commission, Washington, D.C.,
Treasury Building, Sept[r] 25th 1861

My Dear Doctor,

Another letter from D[r] Van Buren[1] this morning, mildly hinting that "documents"[2] are wanting in New York. Upon reflection—the unnecessary delay in the printing of the "Collection" has been greater than I stated it. The printer apologizes for it on the ground of pressure from other government quarters, more imperative upon him. But if you have printed—as you certainly must have done—many pamphlets in New York, you surely know that there are often the most unaccountable difficulties in keeping printers up to time. My own experience of it has been such that I have, when it was of great consequence, actually lived in the printing office to guard against an "overslaugh."[3] In any job proof reader's office, you may often see several day's work behind hand. In all cases where it was important to be as quick as possible I have employed the civil offices—because more accessible and not held to as rigid rules of time, having, in the first place, taken pains to ascertain what office had the reputation of working fastest, here.

Now will you oblige me by considering my letter of yesterday & this on this subject "confidential" and not let the rest know, that I am so easily annoyed—and consider that after catching it most politely from each member daily during all the late session I have receivd written rowellings since from yourself, Agnew,[4] Gibbs,[5] Van Buren and Harris![6] All writing as

WILLIAM VAN BUREN

if I didn't know that there had been anything wrong. I suppose the imme-diate cause for your action is the delay of the documents of the last session. D[r] Newberry's MS.[7] was not given to me till a week after the Commission adj[d] and I got the proofs yesterday only. Mr Knapp only completed his,[8] day before yesterday. D[r] Bache's[9] I haven't yet received, though I infer from a telegram that he has sent it since he left here.

The display of our work in the letter of the Tribune,[10] from Wash-ington, of yesterday is excellent, and almost worth reprinting for gen'l circulation. It answers so many enquiries. If you should think so, there are a few mistakes to be corrected. There were over 100 regiments instead of 50 reported. Over 50,000 instead of 30,000 articles received—the 30,000 was of "made up" articles.

27th   Still unsuccessful in reaching the Secretary.[11] There are daily cabinet meetings now, upon, I suppose, the Fremont matter.[12] I am to call at the Secy's house tomorrow morning at 9 o'clock and shall then leave the paper whether I see him or not.

Knapp will have seen you before this and have told you the last word from McClellan.

We spent the night at Suckley's[13] hospital, as a severe engagment was expected this morning. The rains prevented it.

201

I learn with great satisfaction, in a letter from Mr Strong[14] tonight, that you propose to come here next week. I am very glad of it. I have been extremely anxious to get [to] the park[15] every day for the last three weeks, but day after day have not been able to make up my mind to leave things in their present condition. I hope you will not think it wrong for me to leave when you come. I confess that I am in the greatest anxiety and fear for the national cause. I can't lose the slightest chance of using any hair's weight of influence I possess or can apply, to the strengthening of the army. I am not satisfied with the way things are going in any direction—least of all, perhaps, in the medical. I believe men are dying daily for the want of a tolerable Surgeon Gen[l]. The whole business is miserably bad from the start. I constantly see more & more evidence of it. With such radical errors, it is paltry business to be trying to remedy or palliate only details. This morning at daylight, the surgeon of a regiment which was under orders for an attack came to Suckley to report that he had no ambulance and no stretcher and so on. He had made his requisitions a week before & in answer to a later special requisition, in view of the prospect of an immediate engagement, had been answered that when news of an engagement reached Washington, everything required would be at once sent him. Suckley has no bedsteads & would have no beds and no anything, if his General & himself were not rich men and able to supply the most necessary articles independently of government—partly by confiscation. A gentleman with us gave him ten dollars for the sick. To what luxury do you think it is devoted? Old Madeira? Aromatic vinegar? No, but potatoes. "There's nothing they so long for & nothing does them so much good." And today I heard of four men carted down to Alex'a being very sick with typhus, and then carted several miles back again to lie in the wet camp again—the journey & the disappointment was enough to kill them.

Miss Dix[16] held me for an hour today, and told me such a series of frightful stories, that I must believe her crazy to get any sleep to-night. Of one thing, I must confess to you, she well nigh convinces me. That female nurses, in her, and our, plan, are under the present Military Regulations, not practicable. Miss Dix reports but one doctor who really does well with the nurses, and he, she thinks, is a Secessionist. The others are satisfied in some cases each with one or two of the nurses, but these nurses are women of bad character—are in fact the mistresses of the doctors & this is the only reason they are retained. Poor Miss Dix. I really am distressed for her, as well as on my own account. I am very much inclined to think that only religious sisterhoods should be admitted to these hospitals—whom the odour of sanctity might be hoped to preserve from scandal. There is not a woman in all the hospitals of Washington, unless she be of the Sisters, who is not constantly watched for evidences of favor to individuals and for grounds of scandalous suspicion and talked of & probably often talked to, with a double meaning. And this is true not only of the patients & the doctors & the stewards, but of the women toward each other, very much. I am led to this opinion by what I hear & see every time I walk through the hospitals as much as from Miss Dix's own unconscious confessions. Even at Suckley's hospital where a poor woman had come, bringing her child with her, to look after a husband who had been near dying, the behavior of the men to her, & their talk about her, was as if she had been a convicted strumpet & so was even—from atmospherical influence—the doctors' own.

But how can you expect this evil to be less, when you are told by a respectable surgeon that four men have killed themselves while in his hospital by masturbation?[17] I hate to speak & hate to write the truth, in fact the whole truth in all these matters can't be generalized, & therefore my convictions sometimes boil up in exaggerated statements of what can be said. Everything leads me along however, as it were instinctively, but really only by a generalization—the process of which & the minute facts at the bottom of which can not be expressed or circumstantially recollected—to strike lower and deeper—and I really think I would die satisfied with my life, tomorrow, if I could put a live strong man with a humane big heart also—at the head of the Medical bureau—& give him a clear swing.

Hoping that you will be on and really get that thing done, next week, I shall be more patient with the nothing that I seem to be doing. I really never have felt from the outbreak of the war, so anxious and aching to do something—to have something done. I believe that my humor is a good barometer of the morale of the army, and I *feel* that we are now at the zenith & if we don't do something soon, we shall be on another ebb of the tide.

Pray pardon if it is a fit of the blues I have been expending on you. I don't think it is. At any rate I am delighted that you are coming here, and that I can feel it right to go home for a few days.

With deep respect,

Fred. Law Olmsted.

The original is in box 641 of USSC-NYPL. Internal evidence—the reference to the article in the *Tribune* and to a letter written on September 25—suggests that Olmsted misdated this letter and it was actually written on September 26, 1861.

1. William Holme Van Buren (1819–1883), physician and member of the Sanitary Commission and its Executive Committee, was the descendant of a Dutch family of physicians. He attended Yale College and received his medical degree from the University of Pennsylvania. He then spent five years as an army surgeon before

entering private practice in New York City. From 1852 until 1867 he was professor of anatomy in the medical department of the University of the City of New York, and he later taught at Bellevue Hospital Medical College.

Van Buren was a particularly valuable member of the Sanitary Commission because of his wide professional experience and circle of acquaintances. His own reputation and his marriage to a daughter of the renowned physician Valentine Mott made him well known and well respected among elite doctors in New York. Similarly, his past service in the army added credibility to his suggestions for reform. His experience as a teacher had introduced him to promising young doctors like George L. Andrew, who became a Sanitary Commission inspector, and William A. Hammond, the future surgeon general. Van Buren's relationship with Olmsted was cordial. Olmsted admired the physician's abilities and wished in September 1861 that he were surgeon general. After the war Olmsted visited Van Buren's country home in Shrewsbury, New Jersey, and advised him about laying out its grounds. Several years later Van Buren invited him to visit again and assured him, "I am slowly but surely carrying out your plan, & prize it more & more; it has served as a sort of gospel to me" (*DAB; Yale Obit. Rec.*, 3rd ser., no. 3 [June 1883]: 134–35; FLO to HWB, Sept. 25, 1861, USSC-NYPL, box 641; W. H. Van Buren to FLO, Nov. 7, 1871).

2. That is, copies of the publications of the Sanitary Commission.

3. The loss of one's turn, being skipped or omitted (*OED*).

4. Cornelius Rea Agnew.

5. Oliver Wolcott Gibbs (1822–1908), a member of the Sanitary Commission and a scientist. He graduated from the College of Physicians and Surgeons in New York and spent three years studying in France and Germany. In 1863, after teaching at the Free Academy of New York for fourteen years, he was appointed Rumford Professor of Chemistry at Harvard, where he remained until his retirement in 1887.

Wolcott Gibbs became one of Olmsted's lifelong friends. The two found each other's company congenial, and Olmsted probably especially enjoyed the chemist's lively sense of humor. Gibbs once playfully cautioned Olmsted not to stay at the Cambridge home of the latter's friend, the quite proper Charles Eliot Norton: "You should know what dreadful things have happened in his house. How many guests have mysteriously disappeared and what frightful suspicions there are in Cambridge in regard to him. Come therefore to my house & I will ask Norton to meet you & watch him closely." Gibbs and Olmsted found themselves in close agreement when they collaborated in laying out the ideological foundations for the organization that became the Union League Club of New York. Gibbs then told Olmsted, "I feel that you and I are one in political opinion and feeling." Still, Gibbs, like other members of the Executive Committee, probably disagreed with and criticized Olmsted's managerial principles and organization in 1863. Several years later Gibbs reminded Olmsted, "Do you remember how I used to abuse you & caricature you in the Commission?" Though the two men only occasionally visited with each other in later years, their friendship continued. In 1879 Gibbs summed up their relationship, "I see but little of you my dear old Olmsted as we grow older as our paths in life are so different but I always keep you in cherished remembrance and your old mug often smiles at me from my album" (*DAB*; O. W. Gibbs to FLO, Feb. 8, 1863, USSC-NYPL, box 756: 357; O. W. Gibbs to FLO, March 5 and Aug. 5, 1867, and Aug. 11, 1879).

6. Elisha Harris (1824–1884), a physician, sanitarian, and member of the Sanitary Commission. Born in Vermont to a farm family, Harris received his medical degree from the College of Physicians and Surgeons in New York. After practicing medicine in New York City, he became superintendent of the quarantine hospital on Staten Island. By 1861 he had overseen construction of a floating hospital and had helped draw up the code that guided quarantine practices at the port of New York.

One of the founders of the Sanitary Commission in 1861, Harris also designed the hospital car that in 1863 greatly improved the rail transportation of the wounded. After the war he remained active as a sanitarian and public health official. The report that he drew up after a sanitary survey of New York City in 1865 helped give rise to the Metropolitan Board of Health. Serving as New York City's sanitary superintendent, he inspected tenements and organized a program of free vaccinations. He was also one of the organizers of the American Public Health Association.

Despite his expertise in hygiene and public health, Harris never was fully appreciated by his colleagues on the Sanitary Commission. He was the only original member from New York City who did not serve on the Executive Committee. The other commissioners doubted Harris's executive ability; they also believed him impractical and overly voluble and excitable. Olmsted fully shared these reservations; he once characterized Harris as an "open mouthed white whiskered man" and described a communication by him as "one of Harris's everlasting four volume letters." When Harris arrived to aid the Commission after the battle of Antietam, Olmsted bitterly complained to Bellows, "I can't allow him to take charge, but it will be hard to enforce a general direction that his requisitions shall not be honored or his advice taken."

Olmsted's opinion of Harris's abilities, at least in his specialty of hygiene and public health, may have improved over time. In 1870 the two men worked together on a four-member "board of experts" to prepare a report about Staten Island and a general plan for its improvement (*DAB; Journal of the American Medical Association* 2 [1884]: 194–95; FLO to Alfred J. Bloor, July 27, 1861, USSC-NYPL, box 727: 205; FLO to HWB, Sept. 25, 1862, USSC-NYPL, box 641; Nicholas C. Miller to FLO, Oct. 14, 1870).

7. Newberry's manuscript, entitled "Report on the Sanitary Condition of the U.S. Troops in the Mississippi Valley during the Month of August," was published as document number 27 by the Sanitary Commission.

8. Frederick N. Knapp's manuscript, entitled "Special Relief Report—No. 1," was dated September 23, 1861, and was issued as document number 29 by the Sanitary Commission. (Later it and a second report by Knapp were combined as document number 35.) In the first report, Knapp described the operations of the "Soldier's Home," a lodge located near the railway station. Sponsored by the Sanitary Commission, it provided food and shelter for soldiers passing through Washington.

9. A. D. Bache's paper, an untitled four-page report about the examination of officers, was printed by the Sanitary Commission as document number 30. Bache, as chairman of the Committee on the Examination of Officers, recommended that a system of examinations be instituted in which a board composed of former officers and graduates of the U.S. Military Academy would thoroughly question all officers in new regiments and those officers in old regiments who were adjudged by their commanders to be performing unsatisfactorily. The report also called for the formation of training schools for both commissioned and noncommissioned officers and requested McClellan to begin this program in the Army of the Potomac.

10. On September 25, 1861, the *New-York Daily Tribune* published a two-column article that approvingly described the organization, aims, contributions to, and achievements of the Sanitary Commission (*New-York Daily Tribune*, Sept. 25, 1861, p. 6).

11. Olmsted attempted on September 25 and 26 to give a letter written by Bellows about Western affairs to Secretary of War Simon Cameron. Bellows called for the replacement of the "old & inadequate" army medical director at St. Louis, whose retention, he charged, "only more distinctly proves the inefficiency of the Chief of the Medical Bureau." Bellows also addressed the problem of the rival Western Sanitary Commission, which had been organized in St. Louis and had received offical recognition from Gen. John C. Frémont. Characterizing the Western Sanitary Commission as a body which, "without experience or resources, can only

embarrass the general plan adopted by us and approved by you," Bellows called for Cameron either to rescind Frémont's order recognizing that commission or to have Frémont instruct it to work under the U.S. Sanitary Commission's authority (FLO to HWB, Sept. 25, 1861, USSC-NYPL, box 641; HWB to Simon Cameron, Sept. 26, 1861, USSC-NYPL, box 833, 1: 338a).

12. On August 30, 1861, John Charles Frémont (1813–1890), noted Western explorer, Republican presidential candidate in 1856, and commander of the Department of the West, issued a proclamation that declared martial law in Missouri, ordered a court-martial of any person found with firearms within much of Missouri, and confiscated the property of and freed slaves belonging to disloyal masters there. Lincoln was alarmed that the proclamation might strengthen secessionist sentiments in the slave state of Kentucky. In early September he asked Frémont to modify—in effect, rescind—the clauses concerning confiscation, emancipation, and courts-martial in the proclamation. Upon Frémont's refusal, Lincoln changed his request to a direct command. At this time Frémont was also quarreling with his old friends and former political allies, the Blairs, about military appointments and patronage. Since Montgomery Blair was Lincoln's postmaster general, the Blairs could easily tell the president their grievances with Frémont. This dispute came to a head on September 18, 1861, when Frémont arrested Francis P. Blair, Jr. (Allan Nevins, *Frémont, Pathmarker of the West*, 2nd ed. [New York, 1955], pp. 499–525; *War for the Union*, 1: 338–39).

13. George Suckley (1830–1869), a physician who entered the U.S. Army in 1853. A graduate of New York's College of Physicians and Surgeons, he was a brigade surgeon in 1861 (*Appleton's Cyc. Am. Biog.*).

14. George Templeton Strong.

15. That is, Central Park. Olmsted was anxious to return to oversee the autumn tree planting.

16. Dorothea Dix (1802–1887), a humanitarian reformer who had successfully crusaded for better treatment of the insane and of prison inmates. In June 1861 the secretary of war appointed Dorothea Dix to be superintendent of army nurses, and she moved to Washington, D.C. There she carefully scrutinized the qualifications of the volunteer women nurses and issued her famous rules requiring them to be at least thirty years old, plain, and willing to dress unfashionably.

In 1861 friction soon arose between Dix and the men of the Sanitary Commission. In both temperament and orientation, she and they differed markedly. She was too much the sentimentalist and too little the organizer to suit them. George Templeton Strong recorded that she interrupted a Commission meeting to tell them about a cow dying of heat stroke on the Smithsonian grounds, and "she took it very ill that we did not adjourn instantly to look after the case." During the fall of 1861, hostility increased on both sides. Because Dorothea Dix and the founders of the Western Sanitary Commission were close friends, the U.S. Sanitary Commission suspected her of helping establish that rival group. Since she had publicly begun to request supplies for the hospitals, she was offended in turn when a Sanitary Commission circular written by Olmsted suggested that it provided the only safe way of conveying donations to the soldiers. After her complaint to the Commission, Olmsted wrote a rather pained letter of apology that claimed he did not know she had been soliciting supplies and promised that the offending clause would be omitted in subsequent editions of the circular. Dorothea Dix, however, found his letter "strange" and asserted that her storeroom was not a "new thing" and that the Sanitary Commission should have directed more energy to the reform of the army hospitals. Although she remained superintendent of nurses, her interaction with the Sanitary Commission appears to have been limited after the fall of 1861 (*Notable American Women*; *Diary of the Civil War*, p. 182; FLO to Dorothea Dix, Oct. 24,

1861, USSC-NYPL, box 833, 1: 439; JFJ to FLO, Nov. 1, 1861, USSC-NYPL, box 609: 871).

17. Physicians and moralists in mid-nineteenth-century America theorized that by concentrating all the body's energy upon the sexual organs, masturbation could overexcite and debilitate. Thus it was believed that in extreme cases it could lead to insanity or death (G. J. Barker-Benfield, *The Horrors of the Half-known Life: Male Attitudes toward Women and Sexuality in Nineteenth-Century America* [New York, 1976], pp. 163, 180–81).

To Mary Perkins Olmsted

Sanitary Commission, Washington, D.C.,
Treasury Building, Septr 28th 1861.

Dearest:

I am disheartened. I can see nothing but humiliation & the destruction of every patriotic hope and pride before us, except a miraculous man such as does not now show his head in the least, soon appears. The chances of war are open to us and at the worst we may throw doublets,[1] but the North certainly is not & never can be what we had hoped of it. Vulgarity & poverty of intellect rule. We have no greatness; no heroism; no art. Dear me! I am ashamed of myself for talking to you so, but I am sick of it. Last night W^m K Strong[2] told me that the Secy of War had promised him a Brigadier Generalship, he had he said, enthusiasm if no other quality for it. But W.K. did not feel so sure of the Secy's keeping his word but that he wanted me if I saw him to remind him of it. "Strong's the man! tell him, Strong's the man." And he is: the man of the day, Ecce homo![3]

I just now walked after dinner into the President's grounds where on the lawn the Marine band, (Germans) were playing exquisitely, I really thought better than Dodworth, a duet from Nebuchadnezer,[4] it really took me down as music does sometimes. It was all very fine: the people grouped very well about on the lawn only some very dirty dragoons—as dirty and as rowdy dirty as you ever saw any laborers after a muddy day on the park— made it uncomfortable until was pointed out to me on the grand semicircular portico, looking down in a queenly way upon it, Mrs. Lincoln, with no other lady and no man but that insufferable beast Wycoff.[5] One could endure the want of tact & dignity of such an exposure if there were any sign of talent or any success or thoroughness in any direction. But in fact Wm K. Strong or Andrew H Green or Tom Fields[6] are in my judgment

207

either of them better fitted to rule the land & would rule it with more dignity than those who now occupy the seat of Washington & Adams. I think Millard[7] would carry himself with more dignity & propriety. Wykoff sat right in the centre of the portico, the only man seen at the house, & Mrs L. turned constantly and nodded to him, evidently interested in his conversation. If he had been the king he could not have carried it off better. He is one of this kind of beast, stout, ponderous and with evidently no humbug, his self-conceit & stolidity accounting for everything. You see at once that it is all real, it is impossible for him to doubt that the Englishwoman is infatuated with him and that Lord Palmerston neglects to reply to his notes only from some[8] deep diplomatic policy & overruling jealousy of his abilities. At the same time the most perfect picture of stupidity and dullness: a great ass and nothing else. And why in March last he published a "pamplet" addressed to Lord Palmerston, & stated to have been at first "intended only for his lordship's private perusal," in which he argued that the election of such a vulgar fellow as Lincoln was a sufficient justification for rebellion. Upon my word, I begin to have a sympathy with him and what will become of *me*. I'm getting sicker of it all every day.

The original is unsigned, though probably complete.

1. The same number turning up on each of a pair of dice. Olmsted may have been thinking of a specific kind of doublets, double ones, the lowest and worst throw in many games.
2. William Kerly Strong (1805–1868), a New York merchant and a member of the Central Park commission. Olmsted appeared even more contemptuous of Strong's military credentials when he remarked to Bellows on September 29: "What do you think of W. K. Strong for a Brigadier General? He told me that it was promised him & the *Chronicle* announces it this morning. (He does not know a platoon from a battalion)." Strong did receive a commission as brigadier general of volunteers dated September 28, 1861; he resigned from the army in October 1863 (*Papers of FLO*, 3: 325, 327; FLO to HWB, Sept. 29, 1861, USSC-NYPL, box 641; Francis Bernard Heitman, *Historical Register and Dictionary of the United States Army* . . . , 2 vols. [Washington, D.C., 1903], 1: 933).
3. That is, "behold the man."
4. Harvey B. Dodworth (1822–1891), a noted musician, orchestra conductor, and concert band leader in New York City. Verdi's opera *Nabucco* [*Nebuchadnezzar*] was first performed in 1842 in Milan and in 1848 in New York City (J. P. Wearing, *American and British Theatrical Biography: A Directory* [Metuchen, N.J., 1979], p. 315; Julius Mattfeld, *A Hundred Years of Grand Opera in New York, 1825–1927* [New York, 1927], p. 66).
5. Henry Wikoff (c. 1813–1884), an American who gained notoriety by his political and personal escapades in Europe. He spent much time abroad and briefly worked as an

agent for the British foreign office. Olmsted's remark about Wikoff's certainty of the Englishwoman's infatuation refers to Wikoff's abduction of Jane C. Gamble, a wealthy American who lived in London, in 1851. When she, as Wikoff's fiancée, called off the wedding, he kidnapped her in Genoa in an attempt to change her mind. She appealed to the British authorities, who helped secure his imprisonment for over one year. The affair received much publicity, partly because Jane Gamble regretted her part in his jailing. Wikoff himself wrote a book about it entitled *My Courtship and Its Consequences.*

The "pamplet" mentioned by Olmsted was *A Letter to Viscount Palmerston, K.G, Prime Minister of England, on American Slavery,* published in 1861. Wikoff's preface read, in part: "This letter was originally intended for the private perusal of the Noble Lord to whom it is addressed; but it was suggested to me that its publication here might possibly be beneficial." Strongly proslavery and pro-Southern in tone, Wikoff's essay claimed that Northern aggression (in its toleration of abolitionists) justified Southern secession. Although he did not specifically refer to Lincoln as a vulgar fellow, Wikoff declared that the Illinoisan, though chosen to be a presidential candidate, had "no apparent claim to so great a distinction" (*DAB*; Henry Wikoff, *A Letter to Viscount Palmerston, K.G., Prime Minister of England, on American Slavery* [New York, 1861], p. 52).

6. Andrew Haswell Green (1820–1903) and Thomas Craig Fields (1825–1885), two of the men connected with Central Park whom Olmsted liked least. Both belonged to the Democratic party, an organization for which Olmsted had only contempt. They also clashed often with him over his plan for and superintendence of the park. Green, as comptroller of the park, was extremely frugal and scrutinized Olmsted's every voucher. He and Olmsted argued about what constituted reasonable expenditures necessary to carry out Olmsted and Vaux's Greensward design for the park. Thomas C. Fields was the only member of the Central Park commission to vote against Olmsted's appointment as superintendent. Fields constantly opposed the course taken by Olmsted, who in turn dubbed him "the best partisan I ever knew" (Frederick Law Olmsted, "Passages in the Life of an Unpractical Man" [*Papers of FLO*, 3: 85]; *Papers of FLO*, 3: 27, 30–35, 43, 55–59; *New-York Times*, Jan. 26, 1885, p. 1).

7. Unidentified, perhaps a servant.

8. By a slip of the pen, Olmsted here wrote "seem."

To Henry Whitney Bellows

Sanitary Commission, Washington, D.C.,
Treasury Building, Septr 29th 1861.

My Dear Doctor,

I have bored you enough, you may think, in the last two or three days to find better business for Sunday, but I am thoroughly sick of this humbug and if you don't look after me, I shall get off the handle some day and run you into a scrape.

I am so well convinced that it is necessary to the safety of the country that the war should be popularized that I can hardly be loyal to the

Commission, and the government, while it is required of us to let our soldiers freeze & our armies be conquered for the sake of maintaining a lie. Let the people know that we are desperately in want of men, desperately in want of arms, desperately in want of money, desperately in want of clothing, desperately in want of medicines and food for our sick, and I believe we should be relieved of our difficulties as a suffocating man is relieved by opening a window. That we are so in fact, I have not a doubt. The South by adopting a thoroughly republican and popular system of carrying on the war is miraculously successful.[1] We are losing everything to maintain the pretence of a strong government. Our men are dying and are losing strength, spirit and morale already for want of clothing and there is not one family in a hundred at the North, that wouldn't use bed-quilts & quilted petticoats & send their flannels & blankets here if this were known. We have several thousand soldiers here without guns—500,000 rifles could be had for the asking. We have 10,000 cavalry horses here without saddles. We could have 50,000 saddles in a week if we'd ask for them.

There will be a grand explosion one of these days and when the truth is suddenly told, will not it be too late: hope lost, and the republic wrecked. It is yet possible to stir the whole North by a confession that we need to put forth a revolutionary strength to resist a revolutionary strength.

This is all suggested by reading an advertisement in its emasculated form according to McClellan.[2] It is a piece of childish sentimental nonsense to which I am sorry to have my name attached—that's the fact. Moreover, it is essentially a lie—a statement in the interest of a lie, & I can't help being ashamed of it & ashamed of the position in which it places the Commission.

Yours bluer than ever

Fred. Law Olmsted.

The original is in box 641 of USSC-NYPL.

1. Olmsted no doubt overestimated the success of Southerners' efforts to care for their soldiers. He probably was impressed by the outpouring of money and supplies such as uniforms, blankets, and hospital stores from the Southern population and from soldiers' aid societies. He may also have mistakenly believed that the Confederate government was taking larger steps than the Northern government to systematize relief efforts. Although two laws enacted by the Confederate Congress in August 1861 authorized the secretary of war to arrange for the forwarding of donations of supplies and hospital stores to the soldiers, no central agency was ever formed (Edwin B. Coddington, "Soldiers' Relief in the Seaboard States of the Southern Confederacy," *Mississippi Valley Historical Review* 37 [June 1950]: 17–22; Francis Butler

Simkins and James Welch Patton, *The Women of the Confederacy* [1936; rpt. ed., Richmond, Va., 1971], pp. 18–24).

2. Probably a reference to a circular drawn up by Olmsted and censored by McClellan. The printed version read, in part: "It has been ascertained from the Quartermaster General that a short supply of suitable woolen goods for the army is to be apprehended during the next two months, and it is proposed by the Commission to furnish the hospitals with light cotton quilts and other suitable articles, by which means it is thought that fifty thousand blankets might be set free for the comfort of the fighting men." This indirect way of soliciting blankets particularly disgusted Olmsted because the need for them was so great. He told McClellan: "The men are already complaining much of cold at night and severe colds and coughs are becoming prevalent. . . . The Quarter Master General believes that it will be impossible to supply all the Army with blankets of any kind. There will be for some time to come a deficiency of body-clothing. Under these circumstances, it is respectfully suggested that an allowance of straw be ordered for the men in camp" ([FLO], untitled Sanitary Commission circular, Sept. 26, 1861; FLO to George B. McClellan, Sept. 30, 1861, USSC-NYPL, box 833, 1: 350).

To HENRY WHITNEY BELLOWS

Sanitary Commision, Washington, D.C.,
Treasury Building, Octr 3^d 1861.

My Dear Doctor,

I am very sorry you have such sad reason for remaining.[1]

Of course my letters justified the view you take of me. I am one of those men who work best with a strong head of steam on. Waiting in the War Office five hours with a lot of contractors is calculated to generate steam too fast even for my case however, when nothing is accomplished by it, and I don't know that I could do a safer thing than lift the valve in a letter to you, to get me into working order. There was "lots" of rosin to my fires, that I didn't tell you of. Wykoff tete à tete with Mrs Lincoln, on the portico of the White House was a heavy barrel full,[2] for instance. Then there were two persons who kept poking me up—Dr Gibbs and Miss Dix.[3]

I don't know what I may have said to you in a paroxysm but I think that I have not intended to change the policy of the Commission, adopted before I came into it. If I am not mistaken I have heard you and have heard Dr Van Buren and Doctor Agnew and Mr. Strong utter some revolutionary sentiment—some of you talk of resigning if government refused to do something. But I have always been conservative, impetuoso in modo perhaps, conservative in res.[4] If my towering ambition leads me to neglect the humbler duties then you are right, I never meant it should, and if I told you so, I take it back.

But when I recollect the Secretary's promises & McClellan's promises, and now—three weeks afterwards—find not the first thing done—the Surgn Genl as Molochish[5] as ever and as powerful, men dying every day—as I am told & am inclined to believe on account of their forgetfulness or neglect, I do want to stir you up to come and stir them up. I don't think that it was dissatisfaction with the opportunity offered me of doing something that I was impelled to impress upon you, as you seem to have supposed, but I won't fill another sheet with egotisms to prove it.

Bloor[6] has just showed me Meigs' card in the Tribune,[7] now I don't mean to say any more about I, but don't you think I have a right to be mad. With McClellan for excising my circular, I mean. I have burned the midnight oil not a little lately to know how we could have the face to ask for blankets without letting the recruits know we wanted them. Do you believe Meigs was as conservative as I was? I don't believe he submitted it to McClellan at all. If I had not done so, we should have *got* the blankets. He won't.

But you see I was not behind time in my intentions, for all I burst my boiler just a little. I really don't feel as if I could leave things just as they are but may see you Friday night. The convert[8] will be turned to good account. Begging you to pardon my flurry, I am with most sincere respect

The Secretary of the Sanitary Commission.

The original is in box 641 of USSC-NYPL.

1. Charles Davis, a relative of the Bellows family, was fatally ill in New York City (HWB to Russell N. Bellows, Sept. 29 and Oct. 29, 1861, Henry Whitney Bellows Papers, Massachusetts Historical Society, Boston, Mass.).
2. See FLO to MPO, September 28, 1861, above.
3. Olmsted probably meant that Dorothea Dix and Wolcott Gibbs were telling him stories that increased his anger at governmental inefficiency.
4. That is, impetuous in manner, conservative in substance.
5. Moloch was a Canaanite idol to whom children were allegedly given as burnt offerings. Thus, to be Molochish would be to demand horrible sacrifice of lives (OED).
6. Alfred Janson Bloor, assistant secretary of the Sanitary Commission.
7. A reference to the advertisement, written by Quartermaster General Montgomery C. Meigs, which began: "The troops in the field need Blankets. The supply in the country is exhausted. Men spring to arms faster than the mills can manufacture, and large quantities ordered from abroad have not yet arrived. To relieve pressing necessities, contributions are invited from the surplus stores of families." Meigs then described the weight of regulation blankets and offered to pay the full market value to those with extra blankets who could not afford to donate them (New-York Daily Tribune, Oct. 2, 1861, p. 4).

8. Edward Alexander, a new employee of the Sanitary Commission. Bellows had referred to Alexander in a letter of introduction as a "converted Jew." According to the minister, Alexander had received a partial medical education and would be a good hospital steward, physician's assistant, or nurse (HWB to FLO, Sept. 28, 1861, USSC-NYPL, box 729: 624).

To Mary Perkins Olmsted

U.S. Sanitary Commission, Washington, D.C.
October 19th 1861.

My Dearest Love,

I hope this silvery weather is with you and is brightening you. We have had thus far a very interesting and harmonious session. Fuller than ever before; every member proper except Bache & the Philadelphian[1] & the two militaires Shiras & Cullom[2] which latter are no loss; but we have also had Revd Dr Vinton of Trinity[3] who turns up a trump, and though an associate takes hold as a member & having been in the army when a young man is useful.

We have had also in session with us, Mr Beekman of N.Y. & Mr Rogers[4] of Boston. Dr Howe[5] has been constant for the first time. When we called on the President,[6] Mr Minturn and Mr Sturgis of New York & Bishop McIlvaine[7] joined us as associates. I gave you my impressions of the President in a letter to Charley, truly.[8] He appeared older, more settled (or a man of more character) than I had before thought. He was very awkward & ill at ease in attitude, but spoke readily with a good vocabulary, & with directness and point. Not elegantly. "I heerd of that," he said, but it did not seem very wrong from him, & his frankness & courageous directness overcame all critical disposition. We all called on the Asst Secy of War, Col Scott,[9] last night. He showed the same characteristics—tho a quite young and small man. He lost no time in words but [went] straight to it. We demanded the immediate getting out of our way of the Surgeon General. I wonder if & think we shall accomplish it, though I can't see how.

Bellows, Bloor, Knapp & myself all sleep in this house now; I have the lower & best room, & am quite comfortable. It is a nice house for our purpose, with stables & all.[10] The Commission goes into session after dinner, now, at 5 o clock & has tea served without breaking up, at 7 to 9. Then at about 12, we of the house & who stays so late take a drink.

Bloor is very lame from a collision with a baggage waggon & didn't leave his room yesterday, but will probably soon get well.

244 F Street, the Central Office of the U.S. Sanitary Commission

Those who must, quit today, but the session will continue next week & Bellows stays over. It is a great good fortune to be so intimate with so many good and respectable men. There is but one member of the Commission & but one of the whole concern of us—20 or more—who is not a really respect-worthy man.[11] I am only ashamed to be enjoying it away from or without you—but let it not be without you.

God strengthen & cheer you, darling.

Fred.

I enclose draft for $200.

1. Horace Binney, Jr. (1809–1870). A lawyer in Philadelphia, as was his more famous father, Binney graduated from Yale in 1828. He was elected to the Sanitary Commission in August 1861 and later also served as president of its Philadelphia branch. He helped found the Union League Club of Philadelphia and was one of its early

presidents (*NCAB*; FLO to Horace Binney, Aug. 8, 1861, USSC-NYPL, box 833, 1: 65–66).
2. Alexander E. Shiras and George W. Cullum.
3. Francis Vinton (1809–1872), Episcopal minister and associate member of the Sanitary Commission. Vinton's training and interests were exceptionally broad. Graduating from the United States Military Academy in 1830, he served in the army until 1836. During that period, he also studied law and was admitted to the bar. After attending the General Theological Seminary in New York, Vinton entered the Episcopal ministry and served parishes in Rhode Island. For eleven years he was pastor of Emmanuel Church in Brooklyn, New York, and in 1859 he moved to Trinity Church in New York City (*DAB*).
4. James William Beekman (1815–1877), heir to a large fortune. He had studied law but did not follow a profession. He served as president of the Woman's Hospital, director of the New York Dispensary, and vice-president of the New York Hospital.

      Henry Bromfield Rogers (1802–1887) was, like Beekman, an associate member of the Sanitary Commission. A graduate of Harvard College, Rogers practiced law in Boston and had served on the board of aldermen there and in the state senate. In 1861 and 1862 he gave freely of his time to the Sanitary Commission. He remained in Washington from the fall of 1861 until the summer of 1862 to collaborate with Frederick N. Knapp in the work of special relief. Knapp called him "my most constant and valued coadjutor." Rogers also served the Sanitary Commission in the Peninsula campaign and presided over the New-England Women's Auxiliary Association, a branch of the Sanitary Commission, in 1864 and 1865 (*NCAB*, s.v. "Beekman, James William"; *Boston Evening Transcript*, March 31, 1887, p. 5; Frederick N. Knapp, "Third Report Concerning the Aid and Comfort Given by the Sanitary Commission to Sick Soldiers Passing Through Washington," doc. no. 39 in USSC, *Documents*; USSC, New-England Women's Auxiliary Association, *Third Annual Report . . .* [Boston, 1865]).
5. Samuel Gridley Howe (1801–1876), noted reformer and a member of the Sanitary Commission. A physician by training, he had directed the Perkins Institute for the Blind in Boston since 1831. He also supported numerous causes, such as prison reform, public education, the free-soil movement in Kansas, and better care for the insane.

      Olmsted's remark about Howe's being "constant" refers to the doctor's attendance at Sanitary Commission meetings. The sixth session, from October 15 to 19, was the first full set of meetings at which Howe had been present since the formative gathering back in June. Ill health and his Boston residence brought about his absence; his attendance in late 1861 and in 1862 became more regular. Howe was most active in the Commission in 1861, when he wrote pamphlets, inspected camps, solicited donations, and attempted to win the support of influential friends, such as Senator Henry Wilson, for the Commission.

      By early 1862 Howe had come to have serious reservations about the Commission's provision of medical and hospital supplies. In a pamphlet to "loyal women" published in February 1862, he urged them to send money rather than supplies to the Sanitary Commission. His objection was that the sending of provisions would degrade the soldier by making him an object of charity and would reduce the medical officer's accountability for the soldier's health. In November 1862 Howe found the Sanitary Commission's role intolerable and told Bellows, "I believe that, but for you, the Govt would now be as much blamed for lacking hospital sheets, as it would be for lacking percussion caps." In Howe's opinion, the Commission had sheltered the Medical Bureau from public criticism that would force it to reform. He then refused to help raise further contributions of clothing or supplies.

Howe also disliked and resented the enlarged role that the Executive Committee (composed of the New York City members of the Commission) began to play in 1862. That August, George Templeton Strong reported Howe "a little aggrieved . . . by the course of the Exec. Com. in exercising all the power of the Commission without consulting its members generally." The increasing importance of the Executive Committee continued to concern Howe, who in June 1863 bitingly called the Sanitary Commission "de facto, a very *sub* Commission to a New York Commission, of three or four very worthy and zealous gentlemen." Howe complained that his resolution binding the Commission to hold at least one formal meeting each quarter had been disregarded and added, "I am bound to respect the powers that be; & to recognize *de facto* revolutions; & though I do not know whence the Executive Committee derived its power, it has got it." In fact, Howe, who had given up attendance at meetings, even attempted to resign from the Commission, but Bellows told him that it had no power to accept a resignation.

During their years together on the Commission, Olmsted could count Howe among his supporters. In May 1863, even as Howe was considering his own work with the Commission to be finished, he told Olmsted, "I consider you to be essential to the Commission, for you strive continually to keep things in *order*, and that is the great law of business." Referring to his own appointment to the three-man American Freedmen's Inquiry Commission of March 1863, Howe continued, "Most heartily do I wish you were on *this* Commission for Freedmen; and even in my place" (*DAB*; Samuel Gridley Howe, *Letters and Journals of Samuel Gridley Howe*, ed. Laura E. Richards, 2 vols. [Boston, 1909], 2: 496–501; S. G. Howe to FLO, Aug. 4, 1861, USSC-NYPL, box 727: 285; S. G. Howe to HWB, Nov. 5, 1862, box 640; doc. no. 60, p. 96, in USSC, *Documents*; GTS to HWB, Aug. 12, 1862, USSC-NYPL, box 642; S. G. Howe to FLO, May 29, 1863).

6. On October 17, 1861, the Sanitary Commission was granted an audience with President Lincoln from nine until eleven in the morning. The commissioners called for the removal of Finley as surgeon general, but Lincoln questioned their motives and asked if they wanted "to run the machine" (*Diary of the Civil War*, p. 188).

7. Robert Bowne Minturn (1805–1866), merchant and philanthropist. As a partner with Moses and Henry Grinnell in the firm Grinnell, Minturn and Company, he was part of a successful shipping firm with farflung interests. He was also an early member of the Association for Improving the Condition of the Poor. Republican in political persuasion, Minturn served as the first president of the Union League Club of New York in 1863.

Jonathan Sturges (1802–1874), New York merchant and philanthropist. He was a partner in the firm Sturges, Bennett and Company, prominent in the tea and coffee trade, and also served as a director of the Bank of Commerce and Illinois Central Railroad. A strong supporter of the Union, Sturges helped organize the Union Club in New York and served as its president.

Charles Pettit McIlvaine (1799–1873), Episcopal clergyman. A former professor and chaplain at the United States Military Academy, McIlvaine became Bishop of Ohio in 1831. After the federal seizure of Confederate commissioners John Slidell and James M. Mason on the steamer *Trent* late in 1861, McIlvaine visited England at President Lincoln's suggestion in an effort to conciliate the English clergy. Minturn, Sturges, and McIlvaine were all associate members of the Sanitary Commission. Sturges and Minturn also served from June 1861 on the Commission's Central Finance Committee, which collected funds from Commission branches and audited the Commission's accounts (*DAB*; *NCAB*; doc. nos. 6 and 74 in USSC, *Documents*).

8. In a letter to his nine-year-old stepson, John Charles Olmsted (1852–1920), Olmsted described Abraham Lincoln: "He is a very tall man. He is not a handsome man. He is not graceful. But he is good. He speaks frankly and truly and straight out just what

he is thinking. Commonly he is very sober but sometimes he laughs. And when he laughs he laughs very much and opens his mouth very deep. He said he was glad to see me and shook hands with me. It seemed as if he was. He did not look proud nor cross but a good sort of fellow" (FLO to John C. Olmsted, Oct. 17, 1861).

9. Thomas Alexander Scott (1823–1881), assistant secretary of war. Although of limited education (since he began working at age ten), he had by 1860 risen in the employ of the Pennsylvania Railroad from station agent to first vice-president. Secretary of War Cameron called on Scott's services as an adviser in April 1861. From August 1861 until June 1862 Scott served as assistant secretary of war supervising government transportation. After his return to private life, he continued to be successful. In the 1870s he was president of the Pennsylvania Railroad and of the Texas and Pacific Railway Company.

During the first year of its existence, the Sanitary Commission found Scott its most valuable ally in the War Department. When in December 1861 a bill that the Sanitary Commission supported, to reform and enlarge the Medical Bureau, was introduced in Congress, Olmsted was careful to see that it arrived at the War Department when Cameron was absent since Scott would—and did—give his approval for it. Moreover, in January 1862, as Olmsted was planning tactics to lobby for the reforms the Commission advocated, he met with Scott to discuss them (*DAB*; FLO to T. A. Scott, Dec. 9, 1861, USSC-NYPL, box 833, 2: 85; FLO to HWB, Jan. 18, 1862, USSC-NYPL, box 641).

10. A reference to the new Sanitary Commission headquarters in Washington at a house owned by the Adams family on 244 F Street. Olmsted called it "a fine old house occupied once by Madison, John Q. Adams &c." and described his second-floor room as "freshly prepared, carpeted and bedded, ready for me, opening into a fine board room, which when Board not in session will be my private office or parlor." General offices of the Commission were located on the first floor, and Knapp, Bloor, and Bellows each had a bedroom on the third floor (FLO to MPO, Oct. 15, 1861).

11. Perhaps this was Elisha Harris, whose religiosity, verbosity, and excitable temperament appear to have irritated Olmsted.

To Mary Olmsted[1]

Central Park.
Office of Construction & Superintendence.
Mt. St. Vincent, 104th St., near Fifth Avenue.
Nov[r] 6th 1861.

Dear Mary,

I don't know what the date was of the baby's birth, but it was sometime last Tuesday. No. Monday, 28th says M.C.O.[2]

We want to call her Content, but Vaux[3] makes such a fuss about it, that it's like to be Contention unless you can settle it. He says that we ought to have some regard for her opinion. *Do* folks whose name is Content don't like it? Ask father.[4]

Sorry to hear Fanny[5] is not right well. Mary's well enough, only she's so everlasting lazy. She never gets up till after breakfast and she goes to bed as soon as it grows dark and then sits up and reads official reports by candlelight and is ever so bad.[6]

The baby's well enough too, but I think she's a regular Tom-gal, she pouts & makes faces at me, horrid, every time I go near her. Mrs. Lucas[7] says it's only wind, but it [is] what they used to call spunk when I did it, and didn't make light of it that way.

Why does mother send boxes to Cairo?[8] We have got a hundred boxes waiting between here and there & it only doubles the freight to send them from here. When brigade or other surgeons write to you, refer them to the Sec'y of the Sanitary Commission, either of the Sec'ys, according to vicinity. We have a very extensive organization in Illinois, as well as Wisconsin, Michigan & Ohio. It is wrong in my judgment for you to send directly to any soldiers. What is the use of our organization unless it is to save you from possible[9] waste & imposition?

As for the mitts: if the Quartermaster really wants them, he ought to have a contract for a million of them.[10] No doubt the soldiers would like each a present of a pair, but to furnish them to a regiment is just the same as voting that your society will raise the wages of that regiment. Certainly *you* should supply nothing to well-men. There are exigencies where we may do so, as for instance to men who threw off their clothing to swim the river at the Ball's Bluff battle[11] but we should not do it, even then without the evidence of our own inspector on the ground that there was no other way in which the men could be supplied with what was necessary to their health.

We have a good sensible zealous inspector at Cairo,[12] with a large stock of supplies always on hand, and a much larger stock within reach. We pay him fairly to do a certain business and you ought to let him do it.

At present there is not a tenth part of the *hospital clothing* ready which would be required to keep the wounded from freezing to death, if there should be a well contested battle between the two armies now face to face in Virginia. If mitts and socks should be given to men in the field, those who have been sick & wounded & are going to their tents from the warm hospitals, surely need them most. We have not enough for them yet.

Your affectionate brother,

Fred. Law Olmsted.

P.S. *"given* to men in the field." These men are all as well able to pay for their socks & mitts & havelocks & all that, as any other citizens. You degrade them by unnecessarily treating them as objects of charity. I hear of societies sending shirts and drawers to soldiers in the field—furnishing regiments with them, at the request of their Colonels. Now the Quarter Master Genl told me a month ago, he had a great plenty of shirts & drawers & could supply all demands. If this is so, the Colonel that calls on women to supply them to his men gratuitously ought to be cashiered. It is simple robbery[13] in the guise of beggary. You doubtless have thousands of people in Connecticut who stand more in need of your charity. In the first place if the officers have done their duty, these regiments cannot be wanting these articles at present unless there has been the most reckless waste & improvidence; secondly there's no regiment that couldn't save enough out of its rations to clothe itself anew if it needed it; thirdly, the soldiers are very generally wasting their money in the most absurd manner on pies and cakes & bad whiskey, and can just as well buy their clothing instead as not. Fourthly, if they are in want of ready money, government has provided means for their getting all their clothing & everything they want on the easiest possible credit.

There are extraordinary circumstances when it is important soldiers should be at once & liberally assisted with these things, but what they want never can be sent them from Hartford under these circumstances. They must be ready nearer by. We sent three waggon loads to Ball's Bluff immediately after the battle & they were of great use. Sent there a week afterwards they would have been wasted—would have been a useless encumbrance.

My love to Owen,[14] mother's love to Owen & Content's love to Owen. Charly & Charlotte[15] are down at the island and if they are not in the house they must be wet, for it's raining hard. I have not had a letter from Charly in a long time, tho I've written him three times. There's a fox over at Captain Renwick's[16] & a muskito on the top of my head. I killed him. There are a great many muskitoes, I counted over 80 on my ceiling. The leaves are all getting off the trees. We've got a new horse, another one, a red one, & we haven't got the old one any longer. The baby's got fuzz on her head.

I go to Philadelphia tomorrow for a general Pennsylvania meeting for organization & conference. Shall return Friday & go to Washington early next week. I'm afraid I can't get up to Thanksgiving & it's quite a disappointment to me not to do so. I will try for Christmas & shall hope to see Mr Niles.[17]

I have not got a perfect copy of the Book[18] yet. It is well reviewed in the Atheneum[19] with a funny misapprehension. I have an application to authorize a translation to be published at Leipsic.[20]

P.P.S. It strikes me I've given you a pretty good blowing up, take it altogether, & that you will not be much the wiser for it all. Well, the facts are too complicated to admit of much instruction in a letter. But, to repeat: it is safe to make & send anything that will be useful to sick men & wounded men, and if it is of a sort to be good for well men too, so much the better. If we have a surplus, we can supply well-men, judiciously, which you can not. Brigade Surgeons, you must know, are often exceedingly green & easily imposed upon. All our inspectors at the present moment, and our Secretaries, with one exception, are qualified as Brigade Surgeons.[21] Several of them have been appointed & resigned because they could do more good as Inspectors under us, and they all are better qualified to judge where supplies can be most economically and usefully directed than any Brigade Surgeons or Colonels or Generals can be, because they look over a wider field & have a more complete knowledge of all the conditions of the cases.

The Woman's Central[22] is a very sagacious body and does its business most admirably. You may be sure that what you send them goes as nearly right where it is most wanted as it is practicable to have it. But I don't think they send anywhere but to Washington now, because the Western States are quite as well able to provide for the Western armies as the East for the combined armies in the East. If not however, a telegram can, any hour, switch off all supplies on the way to Washington at Philadelphia, and send them by Express wherever they are more wanted. We are in daily correspondence with all parts of the West & with each of the armies.

We have distributed over 40,000 of the appeal to Loyal Women,[23] & I hope there is not a hamlet in all the free West where the women are not at work. (I don't say much about the mitt[n] question, because I don't feel very sure of what I think.)

Did Mother receive a little parcel from Mary last week?

---

1. Olmsted, who returned to New York City by October 31, wrote this letter to his half-sister Mary Olmsted in Hartford.
2. Mary Perkins Olmsted, who used her middle name, Cleveland, had corrected her husband about the birth of their daughter, who was later named Marion (*Olmsted Genealogy*, p. 108).
3. Calvert Vaux (1824–1895), Olmsted's friend and collaborator on the design for New York City's Central Park.
4. Olmsted referred this question to his father because John Olmsted's mother had been named Content Pitkin Olmsted (*Olmsted Genealogy*, pp. 35–36; *Papers of FLO*, 1: 111, n. 16).
5. Frances Olmsted Coit (1829–1907), Olmsted's cousin, who on October 12 gave birth to her fourth child (*Olmsted Genealogy*, p. 109).
6. Olmsted is jokingly attributing his own habits to his wife.
7. Mrs. Lucas was the "good nurse" that Mary Perkins Olmsted obtained (FLO to Mary Olmsted, Nov. 13, 1861).
8. Mary Bull Olmsted (1801–1894), Olmsted's stepmother, was active in the Hartford Soldiers' Aid Society, which was apparently sending supplies to soldiers stationed in Cairo, Illinois (see *Papers of FLO*, 1: 84–85, 399).

9. Olmsted originally wrote "such," but then crossed it out and interlined "possible."
10. Here Olmsted softened his original statement, "he doubtless has a contract for a million of them."
11. The engagement at Ball's Bluff, Virginia, approximately forty miles from Washington, D.C., on October 21, 1861, was a debacle for Charles P. Stone's brigade of Union soldiers, which had been ferried across the Potomac River from Maryland. Confederate fire trapped Union troops on the bluff overlooking the river, there were too few boats for the crossing, and many desperate soldiers attempted to escape by swimming the river (*War for the Union*, 1: 298–99).
12. Godfrey Aigner was the Sanitary Commission's resident inspector at Cairo in the autumn of 1861 (John Strong Newberry, *The U.S. Sanitary Commission in the Valley of the Mississippi, during the War of the Rebellion, 1861–1866* [Cleveland, Ohio, 1871], p. 21).
13. Olmsted first wrote "mendicity," then crossed it out and substituted "robbery."
14. Four-year-old Owen F. Olmsted was still on a visit to his grandparents in Hartford (see FLO to JO, June 26, 1861, above).
15. John Charles Olmsted and Charlotte Olmsted (1855–1908), Olmsted's stepchildren, were visiting on Staten Island, probably at their great-grandmother Perkins's house (*Olmsted Genealogy*, p. 155).
16. Alexander Renwick, captain of the Central Park keepers (*Papers of FLO*, 3: 278, n. 2).
17. William Woodruff Niles (1832–1914), the fiancé of Olmsted's half-sister Bertha (ibid., p. 343, n. 2).
18. Olmsted's book, *Cotton Kingdom*, a condensation of his three earlier books about the South, had just been published.
19. A review of *Cotton Kingdom* appeared in the October 12, 1861, issue of the *Athenaeum* on pages 474–76. The "funny misapprehension" possibly was the reviewer's assertion that Olmsted was deliberately producing as many books on Southern economy and slavery as possible since he had the "ear of the public." The reviewer noted: "Mr. Frederick Law Olmsted's books on slavery follow each other thick and fast. Only the other day we had occasion to notice his 'Journey in the Back Country,' and now lies before us his present work in two volumes, based on *three former* volumes. How long are we to wait ere he presents us with another work on the same subject based on *five former volumes?*" Olmsted considered such remarks a misapprehension because he had produced *Cotton Kingdom* only after Sampson Low, Son & Company had proposed to publish such an edition (*Papers of FLO*, 3: 329, n. 1).
20. The editors have found no evidence that a German translation of *Cotton Kingdom* was ever undertaken. A Leipzig publishing house, however, printed a German translation of Olmsted's *A Journey Through Texas* in 1857, and it was subsequently reissued in 1865 and 1874.
21. All three associate secretaries possessed medical degrees, but Olmsted and Assistant Secretary Alfred J. Bloor had no medical training.
22. The Woman's Central Association of Relief for the Army and Navy, organized in April 1861, was both the parent and the most important auxiliary of the U.S. Sanitary Commission. It was at the urging of the women of the W.C.A.R. that Bellows, who was a member of its executive committee, made the journeys to Washington which resulted in the formation of the Sanitary Commission. During the war, the Woman's Central was among the branches most active in providing supplies for the Commission.

Although its officers—President Valentine Mott, Secretary George F. Allen, and Treasurer Howard Potter—were male, and its major committees included both sexes, the Woman's Central both depended upon and trained women for leadership and benevolent work. And it, like the Sanitary Commission, drew upon its own auxiliary societies, mainly in upstate New York and in communities in adjacent states. The central office of the W.C.A.R. was governed primarily by committee: although the names and functions of these committees changed over time, the Subcommittee (later Committee) on Correspondence, headed by Louisa L. Schuyler, and the Executive Committee were the most important. Olmsted was chosen during the spring of 1861 as a member of the Executive Committee but did not serve after he became secretary of the Sanitary Commission. The Woman's Central not only played an important role in raising and forwarding supplies but through a program supervised by the noted female physician Elizabeth Blackwell also provided the first trained female nurses for the war. Unlike the Sanitary Commission, the W.C.A.R. quickly closed its offices and went out of existence on August 12, 1865 (USSC, Woman's Central Association of Relief, *Second Annual Report of the Woman's Central Association of Relief . . . May 1, 1863* [New York, 1863]; idem, *Third Semi-Annual Report of the Woman's Central Association of Relief . . . November 1, 1863* [New York, 1863]; William Quentin Maxwell, *Lincoln's Fifth Wheel: The Political History of the United States Sanitary Commission* [New York, 1956], p. 288; doc. no. 32 in USSC, *Documents*).

23. A reference to the circular "To the Loyal Women of America," which Olmsted composed for the Sanitary Commission. This document, issued in October 1861, described the Commission's policies and achievements in inspecting camps, advising officers, and systematically distributing the contributions received. The circular included a list of most-wanted articles, and it also called upon the women of the North to organize and work to support the Union effort:

It is, therefore, suggested that societies be at once formed in every neighborhood where they are not already established, and that existing societies of suitable organization, such as Dorcas Societies, Sewing Societies, Reading Clubs, and Sociables, devote themselves, for a time, to the sacred service of their country; that energetic and respectable committees be appointed to call from house to house and store to store, to obtain contributions in materials suitable to be made up, or money for the purchase of such materials; that collections be made in churches and schools and Factories and shops, for the same purpose; that contribution boxes be placed in post offices, newspaper offices, railroad and telegraph offices, public houses, steamboats and ferry boats, and in all other suitable places, labelled, "FOR OUR SICK AND WOUNDED;" and that all loyal women meet at such convenient times and places as may be agreed upon in each neighborhood or social circle, to work upon the materials which shall be so procured. (Frederick Law Olmsted, "To the Loyal Women of America," Oct. 1, 1861.)

To CHARLES LORING BRACE

New York, Nov. 8th 1861.

My Dear Charley,

I am not competent to give an opinion as to the comparative merit of a light edition of the New Haven, and the French regulation, mule-litter.

I think it very desirable that an article of this kind (the French has been well tried in actual service, answers required purposes and can be advocated far more effectively than anything at all new) should be extensively employed in our service. If we had an enlightened, efficient and influential surgeon general, I presume that a large number of them would be got at once.

Glad to hear of your success.[1] We have a girl,[2] which though not what the country wants now is to me personally more agreeable than a man-child would have been. Your uncle[3] and I proposed to call it Charles Brace but her mother thinks it would be irrelevant.[4] Then we were going to make it Content but since Lynch's election[5] and Gov[r] Andrews' proclamation,[6] we conclude to have her regularly baptized in Potomac water, "ThankGodthingscan'tbemuchmeanerinmytimes." But congratulations, thankfully, in sincerity & truth to Letitia.[7]

Some folks think it was I, & some that it was another man more closely intimate with the Secy of War. It's generally understood that Cameron has bought up the Tribune. There no doubt is a feud between Cameron & Seward.[8]

Well, really I don't know what I think is to happen. But I know that it is not that the army of the Potomac is to rest idly all winter before Washington.[9] I guess that either the larger part of it will be transported to South Carolina before long;[10] or when the rebels are once in winter-quarters,—thus establishing what point or points are most important in their line of defence. We shall approach them carefully with counter-works, and dislodge them by heavier artillery and more unlimited supplies of gunpowder. They can not possibly keep up a great cannonade all winter. We can. When they shall be exhausted of powder, they must give way. I think we are getting on very well, and that the slaves will get emancipated long before we are in a condition to deal with them decently in any other way than as slaves. What are you in such a frightful hurry, for? You are no better than an infidel. "Not succeed in the Gulf States", "Potomac our boundary"?[11] You are as bad as those damned fools of Englishmen.[12] You and I won't live to see Peace on those terms. In my humble judgment there'll be a battle in Broadway and your bones and mine will help the grass to grow there before any such disgrace comes upon us.

I can not take sides on the Fremont question.[13] The country and the administration stands stronger for his removal I am inclined to think.

As for stirring up the Slaves—why do you want to be so savage with the Southerners? If I thought they were worse or more truly our enemies than the New Yorkers who did not vote against Lynch, I don't know as I should object very strenuously to setting niggers or bloodhounds on them. But I shouldn't be in a hurry about it. I don't really think that the fact of Slavery is nearly as degrading to the race as the fact of Lynch's election. I think the slaveholders stand higher in the rank of civilization and Christianity to-day than English merchants or New York politicians. I declare that nothing in the progress of the war has been half so discouraging to me as the evidence of an insanity of meanness in England, and of imbecility in the people of New York, which it has evoked.

I think I have more respect for the slaveholders and less for the slaves thus far, on account of the rebellion. On the other hand, I care less for our own "institutions." Slavery does not seem so very bad a thing along side of us. Do you think Lynch could have been elected to anything but the gallows, either by the slaves or their masters? Do you think that there are any men at the South whose intellects could be so completely obfuscated by their selfishness, as we see the case with thousands of "Liberty loving Englishmen"! Gov. Andrews ought to have included this lesson in charity in his enumeration of the blessings of war.

The San. Com. is doing a good deal. I don't know where the army would be without it. You are greatly mistaken if you mean that you think that the distribution of *supplies* is its "great work". It is a mere incident of its work and if it had left it alone entirely, the army would not be perceptibly weaker than it is. I believe it is many brigades stronger for what it has done otherwise—supposing that what it has done would otherwise have been left undone.[14]

Tell Neill[15] he ought to bring his wife and child away from England before the rotten old shop[16] sinks. If he wants to know where the flood of Almighty wrath at cowardice, hypocrasy & meanness is going to leave any of the civilized human race, I think it must be either in South Carolina or Massachusetts.[17]

Yours in a very mixed up sort of faith but bound to fight it through

Fred. Law Olmsted.

1. A reference to the birth of Brace's son Robert N. Brace on October 3, 1861 (John Sherman Brace, *Brace Lineage . . .* , 2nd ed. [Bloomsburg, Pa., 1927], p. 105).
2. Olmsted's newly born daughter Marion (see FLO to Mary Olmsted, Nov. 6, 1861, n. 2, above).
3. Possibly Dr. Abel Brace, who lived in Catskill, New York (*Papers of FLO*, 1: 297, n. 2).
4. Here Olmsted probably meant to write "irreverent."
5. James Lynch was elected sheriff of New York City in a three-man contest in November 1861. This election was so distasteful to Olmsted because Lynch had been a member of Varian's Battery of the 8th New York State Militia in July 1861. Olmsted earlier characterized as cowardly this artillery company's refusal to serve at the battle of Bull Run. Lynch, according to the scathing editorials in the *New-York Daily Tribune*, had headed the delegation of soldiers that insisted on the eve of battle that its term of service had expired. Olmsted therefore probably saw him as most culpable for the behavior of Varian's Battery (*New-York Daily Tribune*, Oct. 30, 1861, p. 4; ibid., Nov. 4, 1861, p. 4; "Report on the Demoralization of the Volunteers," Sept. 5, 1861, n. 27, above).

6. A reference to the Thanksgiving proclamation issued on October 31, 1861, by John Andrew, Republican governor of Massachusetts. Olmsted probably was offended by Andrew's view of the war as a positive good. The proclamation read, in part: "With one accord let us bless and praise God for the oneness of heart, mind and purpose in which He has united the people of this ancient Commonwealth for the defence of the rights, liberties and honor of our beloved country. . . . Let our souls arise to God on the wings of praise, in thanksgiving that He has again granted to us the privilege of living unselfishly and of dying nobly, in a grand and righteous cause" (*New-York Times*, Nov. 10, 1861, p. 4; Historical Records Survey, Massachusetts, *Proclamations of Massachusetts Issued by Governors and Other Authorities, 1620–1936* . . . [Boston, 1937], p. 251).

7. Letitia Neill Brace (1822?–1916), Charles Loring Brace's wife (*Papers of FLO*, 2: 52, 335).

8. Faced with the enormous task of mobilizing for war, Simon Cameron turned to William H. Seward for advice. Cameron soon found the secretary of state too domineering in his instructions, and a rift between the two developed. The secretary of war then increasingly relied on Salmon P. Chase as his adviser. Olmsted's reference to Cameron as having "bought up" the *New-York Daily Tribune* may have been prompted by a highly laudatory article on Cameron which that newspaper published on November 5 (Erwin Stanley Bradley, *Simon Cameron, Lincoln's Secretary of War: A Political Biography* [Philadelphia, 1966], pp. 176–78; *New-York Daily Tribune*, Nov. 5, 1861, p. 4).

9. Olmsted's prediction was inaccurate, and the Army of the Potomac remained inactive near Washington until March 1862.

10. Olmsted mentions South Carolina as a possible destination of the army because on November 4 a Union naval expedition under the command of Samuel F. DuPont successfully attacked Confederate forts Beauregard and Walker at Port Royal Sound in South Carolina. Confederate soldiers and local whites quickly evacuated the area, and Union forces took control of the South Carolina sea islands (*War for the Union*, 1: 372–73).

11. Olmsted here is quoting from a letter by Brace which has not survived. In September 1862 Brace reiterated his pessimistic assessment: "I hoped a year ago for the boundary of the Potomac, the Mts of W. Va, Ken. & Tenn. & the Mississ. River. Now I think Jeff Davis will proclaim himself Pres't of the U.S. at Harrisburg!" (CLB to FLO, Sept. 12, 1862, below.)

12. Probably a reference to the belief, often expressed in the English press in 1861, that the North would be unable to reconstitute the Union. Some English writers declared that even if the North could defeat the South, it would not be able to govern such a hostile area (Donaldson Jordan and Edwin J. Pratt, *Europe and the American Civil War* [Boston, 1931], pp. 12–21; Ephraim Douglass Adams, *Great Britain and the American Civil War*, 2 vols. [London, 1925], 1: 174).

13. On October 24, 1861, Abraham Lincoln removed John C. Frémont from command of the Department of the West. Frémont's emancipation proclamation, though abrogated by Lincoln, won great popularity for the general among antislavery Republicans and abolitionists who believed the war should be fought against slavery as well as to preserve the Union. Frémont's removal from command unleashed a storm of protest from these groups. Charles Loring Brace probably shared that sense of outrage and disappointment and communicated it to his friend Olmsted (A. Nevins, *Frémont*, pp. 539–49).

14. Olmsted meant that the primary contribution of the Sanitary Commission lay in inquiry and advice. To him, its inspection of camps, instructions to army surgeons, and efforts to revitalize the Medical Bureau were the measures that were saving soldiers' lives.

15. Probably William Neill (b. c. 1823), Brace's brother-in-law and a British cotton mer-

chant who in 1857 had collaborated with Olmsted in a scheme to encourage the production of cotton by free rather than slave labor. Since Neill was visiting the United States in the autumn of 1861, he may have been visiting the Braces (*Papers of FLO*, 2: 440–48; FLO to MPO, Nov. 19, 1861).

16. Olmsted here wrote "shop" but probably intended "ship."
17. Probably a reference to the extreme positions of Massachusetts and South Carolina on slavery. The citizens of Massachusetts were generally more antislavery, those of South Carolina generally more proslavery, than those of other states. Thus these states, representing two clear-cut though radically opposed views, would not share in the hypocrisy Olmsted attributed to other areas, mainly other states still in the Union.

To CHARLES HANDY RUSSELL[1]

Central Park, November 12th 1861.

My Dear Sir,

I think it right to state to you the conviction which led me to use certain expressions, in our conversation today, which you heard with surprise. I do not like to have said that of a man in his absence which I might avoid saying in his presence, or which I might prefer not to have repeated to him, without giving a reason for it. Nor do I like to seem to deal in innuendo.

My conviction is—and it certainly has been acquired with reluctance and deliberation enough—that the limits within which it might have been possible for me to effectually serve the Central Park Commission, have been gradually, skillfully, carefully and circumspectly curtailed. From the day when Mr Green[2] received the first instalment of a salary larger than that of the Architect in Chief and Superintendent, there has been a constant effort not only to assume more important responsibilities and more valuable duties, but to include all other duties and responsibilities within his own, and to make those of the inferior office not only completely and servilely subordinate but to make them appear of a temporary value only and unimportant even temporarily. How successful this policy has been, the fact that I could be absent from the park four months, without giving occasion for the slightest action on the part of the Commission, demonstrates, as possibly it has been intended that it should, very effectually. What part, may I ask, have you, my dear Sir, supposed that I bore in the economy of the park, when, (yourself the only arboriculturist of the Commission), you drove through the park in the heart of the planting-season without ascertaining my presence and without enquiring how, supposing me absent, the responsibility to the Board for the planting could be assumed by anyone else? Since I first went to Washington, I have, in fact been six weeks on the park.[3] But I have never had reason to think that I was wanted there by the Commission or its representative. My advice has not been asked when present, any more than it has by letter when absent. When in New York, I have never been asked how long I should stay, nor when I should come again. I have no reason to believe and I do not believe that my taste, judgment and skill in the laying out and management of the work, was any more wanted, *or was of any more use* last year than this. For the means of performing what duties were then yet nominally allowed me I was made so absolutely and to the last detail dependent on Mr Green's pleasure—not possessing the smallest right by which I could employ my judgment otherwise than in subjection to his, that I feel, though relieved of an immense weight of anxiety and humiliation, that I have no less impressed my own taste on the work this year, than the last.

Mr Green's services as a politician have been perhaps essential to the Commission. The power he has may be the proper price of these services. Cooperation with Mr. Green, while he thus controls the park, so far as I can hope to yet influence it, is essential. I can not counter-plot him. To charge upon him individually that for which the Commission is finally responsible, is unnecessary. To do so, to his face, would be to stimulate enmity and to establish a quarrel. To quarrel with him, while I am his official subordinate would be undignified and impolitic, and would be playing into the hands of the enemies of the park. I said to you once before, "I will not remain on the park to quarrel with Mr Green." I will not, if I can avoid it, quarrel, or give occasion for quarrel with him while I remain in the service of the park. But, conscious that my devotion to the park has forced me to patience, he has continued to pursue a course toward me of which no honest man could know himself to be subject without occasionally giving more or less articulate vent to feelings such as I was so unfortunate as to betray to you.

Yours Very Respectfully

Fred. Law Olmsted.

C. H. Russell Esq[r]

The original is a draft copy.

1. Charles Handy Russell (1796–1884), a New York merchant and member of the Central Park commission from 1857 until 1870. In February 1861 Olmsted remarked, "Russell, as Chairman of the Finance Committee, works well with Green and has

been very useful—has done more for the park than anyone else, although during all the important part of the year he is at Newport" (*New-York Times*, Jan. 22, 1884, p. 5; FLO to John Bigelow, Feb. 9, 1861 [*Papers of FLO*, 3: 324]).

2. Andrew H. Green became comptroller of Central Park on October 6, 1859 (*Papers of FLO*, 3: 30).

3. Olmsted first wrote "five" then changed it to "six" weeks. Through visits of one week in July, nearly two weeks in November, and approximately ten days each in August and October, he had spent almost six weeks in New York.

To John Strong Newberry

November 16ᵗʰ 1861.

To Dʳ Newberry.
My Dear Doctor,
　　I learn, on arriving here, that a letter to Dʳ Bellows from St. Louis has crossed me on the way from New York, in which the Western Sanitary Commission declines, formally, the proposition of the U.S. San. Com. but expresses a desire to cooperate and aid in all its operations.[1] My own impression is that it is still practicable to virtually make it an auxiliary Society, granting them the distinctive name of the Western San. Com. which may be interpreted "Western [branch of] San. Com."[2]

　　But in any case we should now do *well*, whatever they leave undone. I suggest that Douglas and Andrew,[3] who is now our best Inspector here, should be sent to Missouri, and should go over the ground as thoroughly as possible, before we have any further unnecessary intercourse with the St. Louisans.

　　Your letter to Bloor, of the 12ᵗʰ, is just received. It seems to me that there is some misunderstanding between you. In this note of the 12ᵗʰ you say that you had never authorized the reference of the question of Mrs Bell to this office. Bloor says that the letter of Mrs Bell, was addressed to us, in your handwriting.[4] He had no intention of offering you instructions in your duty, but merely to suggest that you gave yourself no unnecessary trouble. To remove any doubt as to the understanding "of this office," as the Surgeon General would say, it is this: that when the *Board* is not in session you have no superior as to affairs of your department. You are dependent on us only for supplies and information. You are authorized to employ and discharge all agents, to determine remunerations for service; to collect and disburse money and supplies. Matters of the whole army as the Surgeon General, the allotment Question,[5] only, belong in strict etiquette to this office. The governing purpose of the organization is to avoid delay and circumlocution for the purpose of accomplishing efficiency and directness of action. All practicable checks and method consistent with and subsidiary to this are to be observed. None are to be cared for which essentially interfere with it.

I write this, and will have it copied that you may be sure that Mr Bloor and all hands here understand it.

As to the mere question of trouble, the solution is in this rule: one man can only do so much. So long as our funds hold out, we are to do all we see occasion to do as well as we can. What one man can not do, two must. It is immaterial whether the work is done here or there. The only question is one of time—not of trouble, for money is in our hands wherewith to save trouble. Whether it goes through your hands or mine is no matter. When the money gives out, we are to scuttle and go down all standing. Till then do our work thoroughly.

Yours Cordially

Fred. Law Olmsted.

The original is letter 46 in volume 1 of box 909 in USSC-NYPL. A letterpress copy is in box 833, volume 1, pages 589–92. Olmsted wrote this letter on old stationery that carried the printed heading, "Sanitary Commission, Washington, D.C. Treasury Building," which had become incorrect when the Commission moved to new quarters at 244 F Street.

1. In a letter of October 31, 1861, James E. Yeatman, president of the Western Sanitary Commission, notified Bellows that the "deliberate and unanimous" decision of that organization and one "not likely to be changed" had been to retain its separate identity. Yeatman reasoned:

   Whatever we could do as a sub-committee or branch of your Commission, we can do equally well, or better, retaining our present organization, and co-operating with you . . . while we gain special advantage for doing an important local work in our district, by immediate commission from the Commanding General of the Department. At all events, we cannot work heartily and well in any other way, under the circumstances in which we are placed, and our only object is to do the greatest possible good, in the best possible manner, with the limited means at our command. (J. E. Yeatman to HWB, Oct. 31, 1861, USSC-NYPL, box 735: 2434.)

2. The brackets here were used by Olmsted.
3. George Lafferty Andrew (1822–1911), physician of La Porte, Indiana, and Sanitary Commission inspector. A graduate of Miami University and the Ohio Medical College in Cincinnati, he also studied medicine in New York City from 1849 to 1851 and served on the staff of Bellevue Hospital there. His friendship with William Van Buren probably dated from that period. After offering his services to Van Buren in August 1861, Andrew became an inspector of the Sanitary Commission in late September. Despite Olmsted's suggestion to Newberry, Andrew did not accompany John H. Douglas to St. Louis. Instead he served with the Port Royal expedition in South

Carolina from December 1861 through April 1862, when illness forced him to resign. Andrew returned to the Commission's service in the fall of 1862 and aided the wounded at the battle of Antietam. Although hampered by poor health, he continued to work for the Sanitary Commission through 1863 and accompanied Grant's army during the Vicksburg campaign. He then returned to his private practice in La Porte.

Olmsted found Andrew a valuable inspector and in 1862 called him the Commission's "most experienced and trustiest" man. Although he suspected Andrew of being "wanting in enterprize," he also recognized that the doctor was "methodical and very sure and careful." The relationship between the two men did not come to an abrupt end when Olmsted left the Sanitary Commission. In 1864, when Bear Valley, California, needed a physician, Olmsted tried to recruit Andrew for the post. Each man also occasionally sought the other's expert opinion. In 1864 Andrew expressed skepticism—probably justified—about a medical diagnosis that Olmsted had recently received. In turn, when Andrew began to build a house in 1866, he asked Olmsted to suggest books that would help him lay out its grounds. Olmsted not only furnished a reading list but also suggested changes and modifications and finally even drew up a plan. Although Olmsted and Andrew did not correspond in later life, Andrew sent a note of condolence to Mary Perkins Olmsted upon Olmsted's death in 1903 (A *Biographical History of Eminent and Self-Made Men in the State of Indiana* . . . , 2 vols. [Cincinnati, Ohio, 1880], 1: 2–3; G. L. Andrew to William Van Buren, Aug. 15, 1861, USSC-NYPL, box 728: 366; G. L. Andrew to John S. Blatchford, Oct. 17, 1866, USSC-NYPL, box 1086; FLO to JSN, Dec. 27, 1862, USSC-NYPL, box 914, 1: 320; FLO to GTS, Dec. 26, 1862; FLO to G. L. Andrew, July 3, 1864; G. L. Andrew to FLO, Aug. 8, 1864, Aug. 6, 1866, and April 2, April 15, and July 10, 1867; G. L. Andrew to MPO, Sept. 2, 1903).

4. A reference to a misunderstanding between Newberry and Alfred J. Bloor over a letter from M. L. Bell, a Cleveland lady who wished to give public dramatic readings whose proceeds would go to soldiers' aid societies and the Sanitary Commission. Assuming that Newberry had referred the matter to the Washington office, Bloor answered her letter and sent him a copy of the reply. But Newberry had not directed M. L. Bell to write to the Washington office and, as he told Bloor, "had never authorized" referral of the matter to the central office.

Olmsted attempted in this reply of November 16 to draw up a reasonable division of responsibilities among the Sanitary Commission's offices. He seems to have thought that Newberry feared that Bloor and the central office were trying to usurp authority. But Newberry apparently believed that Olmsted's discussion of the Western office's independence rebuked him for referring too many matters to the central office. Newberry protested to Bloor on November 19: "I have made no reference of any matter to the Washington office, which did not legitimately demand its action—I was therefore naturally surprised and somewhat hurt by a request, in substance, that I would keep my own affairs to myself and not trouble you with them" (M. L. Bell to FLO, Nov. 5, 1861, USSC-NYPL, box 730: 900; JSN to A. J. Bloor, Nov. 12, 1861, USSC-NYPL, box 730: 1001; JSN to A. J. Bloor, Nov. 19, 1861, USSC-NYPL, box 730: 1075).

5. A reference to the Commission's attempts to have the paymaster's department forward part of the volunteer soldier's pay, at his request, to his family. Although the Commission campaigned successfully in July 1861 for a law enacting a system similar to that used by the U.S. Navy, the army had not yet instituted such measures. A committee from the Sanitary Commission met with the army's paymaster general in September and learned that he considered the navy's allotment system impracticable. In October the Commission formed another committee, composed primarily of associate members, to "bring in a scheme for the promotion of remittances of sol-

diers' pay." In mid-November the allotment question still weighed heavily on Olmsted's mind. He told Henry W. Bellows:

> I am more and more established in the belief, I have before expressed to you, that the Naval System should be the model. All things considered I have concluded that it will be useless to take any further action with regard to it until Congress meets, being chiefly moved to this conclusion by the improbability that any of the Secretaries or High functionaries can be got, at this time, to give the necessary attention to it, and to decide and take measures for effecting what would be necessary.

(USSC, *Minutes*, pp. 56, 71; FLO to HWB, Nov. 17, [1861], USSC-NYPL, box 833, 1: 597; see also "Report on the Demoralization of the Volunteers," n. 48, above.)

To Sarah Blake Sturgis Shaw[1]

Nov[r] 29th [186]1.

Dear Mrs Shaw,

I have just received your letter of yesterday.

You will readily see that there must be some check placed upon an injudicious and dishonest distribution of the stores which we receive. We must have the assurance in some form of a responsible person that the goods are not misused. The goods are placed in our hands for the benefit of soldiers in the military hospitals. The responsible person and the only officially responsible person in any hospital under the government is the surgeon (with his deputies, the assistant surgeons.) Every surgeon and every assistant surgeon in all the hospitals about Washington is informed of the character of the stores we have and is urged to call upon us [for any] thing that any of his patients may want which the hospital stores supplied by government, and constantly on hand in the hospital, do not furnish. The slightest memorandum with the surgeon's initials, or a specific verbal message from the surgeon or any of his assistants (trusting to obtain his voucher subsequently) would be immediately honored by our store-keeper. Our own inspectors when, in visiting a hospital, they see that a patient would be better from anything which we could supply, ask leave of the surgeon to supply it and get his signature to a memorandum for that purpose. The members of the Commission when visiting hospitals adopt the same rule. You will see that it would be improper and wrong to do otherwise. The surgeon being responsible, no one has a right to administer anything to a patient without his knowledge and approval. We supply

231

however, large stocks in advance of any immediate want to the hospitals, taking a surgeon's receipt for them.

If Mrs Fales[2] sees a real need for anything we have, and which is not already in the stores of any hospital she is visiting, she has only to make a note of it on any bit of paper and before she leaves the hospital get the surgeon's approval expressed by writing his name or initials on the same paper, and to send or call with this at our store-room. Mrs Fales has repeatedly done this and she never failed to get anything she wanted without the least delay.

If you can suggest any simpler process under which waste and injustice would not be sure soon to prevail, I should be glad to adopt it.

There are no stores spoiling in our hands and there is not one-hundredth part of the accumulation of any kind of stores here that there should be.

I am, dear Mrs Shaw, most sincerely yours

Fred. Law Olmsted.
Secy.

The original is a letterpress copy on pages 7–10 of volume 2 in box 833 of USSC-NYPL.

1. Sarah Blake Sturgis Shaw (1815–1902), a Staten Island resident and wife of the wealthy philanthropist Francis George Shaw, who was also her cousin. The mother-in-law of Olmsted's friend George W. Curtis, Sarah Shaw was also the mother of Robert Gould Shaw, who in 1863 became colonel of the 54th Massachusetts, a black regiment that distinguished itself at the assault upon Fort Wagner, where he was killed. Sarah Shaw strongly approved of Olmsted's labors upon Central Park and for the Sanitary Commission. In August 1861 she told him, "If we can re-make the Government, abolish Slavery & get the Central Park well under weigh for our descendants, we shall have done a work worthy of the 19ᵗʰ century" (*Appleton's Cyc. Am. Biog.*; Robert Faxton Sturgis, ed., *Edward Sturgis of Yarmouth, Massachusetts, 1613–1695, and His Descendants* [Boston, 1914], p. 53; S. B. S. Shaw to FLO, Aug. 14, 1861, USSC-NYPL, box 728: 360).
2. Almira Fales, a volunteer nurse to the Union troops. She personally distributed hospital stores to many sick or wounded soldiers and ministered to the wounded after the battles of Corinth, Shiloh, Second Bull Run, and during the Peninsula campaign. Her relations with the Sanitary Commission, however, were not particularly amicable. She believed that its inspectors used insulting language toward her, and one Sanitary Commission employee characterized her as "not a very judicious or reliable person" (Linus Pierpont Brockett and Mary C. Vaughn, *Woman's Work in the Civil War: A Record of Heroism, Patriotism, and Patience* [Boston, 1867], pp. 279–83; Alfred J. Bloor to FLO, May 18, 1862, USSC-NYPL, box 638: 405).

New-York Times, December 4, 1861

THE REBELLION.

How to Reason with the South—How to Deal with the Slavery Question.

Washington, Thursday, November 29, 1861

To the Editor of the New-York Times:

Those who say that the people of the South can never be made to submit to the Government are either repeating a cant phrase without meaning anything more than that their personal sympathies are with the rebels, or they forget what a different thing is the submission of a people struggling against a cruel despotism, from the submission of a people merely unwilling, as a matter of feeling, to return to an old habit of self-government, under a few general laws, in the making of which they themselves were consulted, and had a fair and honest part, and under which they have for many years enjoyed great freedom and light taxation. The case of the Irish, the Hindoos, the Poles, and the Hungarians,[1] was very different from this, and if, after long years of desperate resistance, their submission to a foreign force seems to have been somewhat reluctant and imperfect, it forms not the slightest ground for assuming that our own misguided citizens will never accept peace under their old and honored flag, as soon as certain delusions by which they are still influenced have been dispelled.

The rebellion is justified at the South under the name of revolution. Thousands of men are fighting for it now, who, a year ago, denounced the movements which initiated it, as criminal.[2] What justifies a revolution, and what makes rebellion criminal? Success, or the prospect of success. It was confidence in the military force of the Slave States, as compared with the Free, then, that turned the scale, and alone made rebellion formidable. "Revolution" sinks to "rebellion" again when this confidence is destroyed, and thousands now fighting for it will then again denounce persistence in it as criminal.

One of the delusions which has led to the false estimate of the comparative power of the rebels and of the Government, which prevails at the South, is that of the anarchical condition of the Free States, and the military feebleness of the Government so far as it is dependent on them. The habit of using arbitrary authority reduces the capacity of sympathy, and our power of understanding men's motives and characters is proportionate to our ability to sympathize with them. The state of society in the

Free States is very different from that in the South, and there is nothing to which men adapt their habits of thought with more difficulty than social conditions to which they are unaccustomed. Of this, the English writers, in their comments on our affairs, give no infrequent evidence in their habitual assumption that there necessarily must be something in this country corresponding, though in a diluted form, to their gentry and peasantry, with an intermediate stratum, poor relation to the one, and jealous, contemptuous, timorous neighbor to the other. They cannot get the notion out of their minds, that, in some way, class interests are acting one against another, or, one in combination with another, in all our politics. Much less easily can the Southerners be freed from the idea that where there is so much industry there must be a master class and a servile class, the one more or less wisely caring for government as the safeguard of property, the other regarding government inimically, as a social power by means of which they are kept under control, and which it is consequently their interest to weaken as much as possible.[3] The intelligent slaveholder appreciates even less than the Englishman, therefore, that deep-seated, unconscious and instinctive conservatism, formed in the habits of a people where the status of a man is never felt to be fixed, which in moments of peril places a sudden feminine strength at the disposal of the agents of Government, such as no mere ruler over a land ever possessed, and which is the natural compensation of that very dependence of the government upon the will of the governed, that renders it powerless for many purposes readily assumed by rulers of weaker nations, more pompously powerful and ostentatiously dignified.

The thick habit, however, under which the slaveholders have been led to doubt and defy the strength of the gathering tempest of our Northern loyalty, is already worn with a conscious awkwardness under their recent experiences. This is plainly shown in the disgraceful falsehoods to which Davis, Beauregard, and others who labor to control public opinion at the South, are driven; in their efforts to maintain the impression that the Union army has been mainly formed of hireling foreigners, and that it is incited only by lust and greed.[4] This new delusion, if it prevails at all, is far less formidable than that which it is intended to fortify, namely: that diffusion of power is absence of power; diffusion of patriotism, want of patriotism; and that weakness of the agents of Government is equivalent to weakness of Government itself.

The cupidity and baseness of England is another delusion which is being slowly relinquished at the South. England has ever talked little and done much. Now she talks much because, though the necessarily slow process of our war costs her some, she has the heart to do nothing to establish a nation on a basis which, above all other things, she hates.[5] The blockade is no longer laughed at in the South.

A minor delusion has been that ships could do little against shore batteries. Hatteras and Port Royal have effectually dispelled that, as the evacuation of Tybee satisfactorily informs us.[6]

The grandest delusion of all, industriously fostered by many public teachers of the South, and discountenanced during the last twenty years by few, until, absurd as it may seem to us, a generation has almost grown in its habit, is, that slaves are a source of military strength to those who possess them.[7] Till now, the war has been mainly carried on by Government as if it had been for our interest, as perhaps it has been, to strengthen this delusion. While thousands of negroes have been employed to resist the enforcement of the laws, all use of them in sustaining their supremacy has been as much as possible avoided.[8]

In the conduct of the slaves at Port Royal, if our information can be trusted, the South is presented with the first tangible evidence of the *essential weakness of this main prop of the rebellion.* Government had offered no inducement for the slaves to desert, had offered them no protection. There is in all the South no other district in which the slaves were less likely to be intelligently informed, or where they could as easily have been deceived as to the motives of the attacking force.[9] The fact, therefore, that when the forts were taken, the slaves refused to withdraw from the vicinity with their masters, and that numbers of them were shot down in the vain attempt to prevent their falling into our hands, is of more value in demonstrating to the people of the South the futility of the struggle into which they have been inveigled than all else that has been as yet accomplished by our arms.

Negroes in the rebel States are property, and, as property, are the very sinews of the rebellion. The occurrences at Port Royal indicate that, at least whenever our forces penetrate the rebel States, it is in our power to sever these sinews, and by so much destroy the strength of the rebellion. For the sake of our friends in Kentucky and Maryland, we may spend a few hundred millions before we systematically use this power, but we cannot avoid estimating its value and availability. Nor can the rebels flatter themselves that we shall yield them independence before we have made use of it.

The use of slaves as property depends on the degree in which their services are controllable. This control is never perfect; if it was, there would have been no need of the whip, no need of the Fugitive Slave law, no need of discountenancing the instruction of slaves in the common arts of writing and reading. There is always more or less of what the overseers call "ugliness," or resistance to control, to be overcome and to be guarded against. On a large plantation some of "the people" are almost always "out," or "in the swamp;" that is to say, they have, through insubordination, carelessness, or sheer indolence, or disinclination to work, incurred

235

the prospect of punishment and have hid themselves away to avoid it. In doing this they have no hope before them of attaining permanent freedom, but only a respite from Slavery. They reason, as has often been explained to me, that whenever they are caught or choose to return, the punishment they will receive for running away cannot be much heavier than that they would have received for the previous offence, without injuring their value as property. They would use the proverb, "It is as well to be *paddled* for a sheep as for a lamb." If even a remote chance of escaping punishment altogether is seen by the slave, he often seizes it with a spirit, which, in a slave, is wonderful and admirable. It not unfrequently appears in the advertisements of Mississippi, that a runaway is supposed to be "making for the Free States," hundreds of miles distant; and I have seen a fugitive in Mexico who had felt his weary way thither, at what enormous risks I need not say, clear from Louisiana.[10] If Government should take possession of certain districts of the South, or even mere fortified points at convenient distances around the planting region, as at Wilmington, Hilton Head, Fernandina, Pensacola, Bayou Calcasieu, Galveston, San Antonio, Fort Smith and the mountain passes of Kentucky and Tennessee,[11] and should offer at all of these a safe harbor for all negroes, there can be no doubt that slave property throughout the South would become rapidly less controllable than it is at present and as rapidly less valuable.

That a knowledge of these asylums would soon reach every plantation is quite certain. I have often been told by planters in the interior that information of important National events had reached them through the negroes long before it came by mail.[12]

It is not to be supposed, however, that all the slaves would at once run to obtain the protection of these sanctuaries of freedom, but while thousands would do so, all would have such a resort in view and be affected by it in their daily conduct, and thus sensibly deteriorate in value. Not only would they fail in their accustomed tasks in the fields; they would, while still remaining on the plantations, pilfer and waste and carelessly and mischievously damage much other property besides that of their own labor. A hostile force would thus invade the enemy in his very stronghold. With every negro who ran away and escaped immediate pursuit, the tendency to disregard control among those remaining would increase in strength.

The need to call back from the army every active, strong, and resolute man would be less imperative for the pursuit of the actual fugitive than for the overseeing of those of feebler enterprise who remained behind.

Organized insurrections and St. Domingo massacres[13] are not, in my judgment, to be apprehended under any circumstances. The slaves are neither as savage, nor as civilized as those who entertain this fear suppose.

But, whatever danger of this kind there may be, there will be less, if a prospect is offered those more discontented, of escaping from their masters by flight, and the measure that will present such a prospect to them will set on foot a quiet and inactive method of exhausting the effective resources of the rebellion, which will increase and become more and more irresistible, the longer all other methods of attack are incompletely successful.

It is unquestionably in the power of our Government to do all that I have suggested; and probably at a tenth of the cost of our present operations, such posts could be constantly held, and the fugitives reaching them be safely and humanely cared for. Suppose we are unsuccessful in our advances into the interior of the South, while this depleting and demoralizing process continued, and only otherwise successful in resisting invasion of the Free States and in maintaining the blockade, with what confidence of success would the rebellion continue? Where would be the military strength founded in Slavery?

But the instigators of the rebellion say, that they can make their slaves fight for them, and several negro regiments are reported to be now enrolling.[14] In the construction of their earthworks, military roads, &c., it is known that the rebels employ many slaves. The African nature inclines to the pomp and circumstance of war, and yields more readily and completely to discipline than any other in this country. By taking advantage of the disposition of the negro to imitate, and where practicable, to emulate, the whites, and by working upon his vanity and love of approbation he can doubtless be rapidly brought to a high condition of drill and discipline. But he would be a far better soldier on our side than on theirs. On theirs it is impossible that he should not be affected by the constant assertion of the Southern camps, that the Lincolnites are fighting for the negro. On ours it is equally impossible that he should not be affected by the knowledge that to surrender would be to him death, or hopeless Slavery. Placing him under martial discipline, is not offering encouragement to the horrors of a servile war, but exactly the contrary. It is preventing a servile, by substituting a civilized war. There are many military duties to be undertaken in which negroes, properly trained and officered, would be far better than white soldiers. Even if the rebels had not set us the example of them, the provision against which they hypocritically cry out in advance, for forming regiments of their black deserters to be turned back threateningly upon them, is not merely a justifiable act of war, but is in all respects a humane and honorable one.

The best reason for it, however, is the effect it would have in aiding the removal of the delusion out of which the war has partly grown, namely: that the peculiar property which the South holds gives the right of revolution to a wicked rebellion, by supplying peculiar means of offence and defence. Whatever will prove to the Southerners that the advantages they suppose themselves to hold are common to all who enter their territory in arms, will not merely tend to make the war shorter and cheaper, but will also tend to enforce the necessity for a policy in peace upon them, the neglect of which hitherto has been the foundation of all their political troubles.

YEOMAN.

The text presented here is taken from the *New-York Times*, December 4, 1861.

1. A reference to rebellions staged by subject peoples in order to secure self-government. Insurrectionary attempts among the Irish against English rule were of long standing and had occurred as recently as 1798, 1803, and 1848. The other uprisings were the Polish Revolution of 1830–31 against Russian rule, the Hungarian Revolution of 1848–49 against the Austrian Empire, and the Sepoy Mutiny of 1857 in India against British domination (James Cumlin Beckett, *A Short History of Ireland*, 5th ed. [London, 1973], pp. 126–27, 136).

2. Some Southerners who had been conservative Whigs denied that any state possessed the constitutional right to secede from the national Union but supported the formation of the Confederacy as an exercise of the natural right of revolution (Henry McGilbert Wagstaff, *State Rights and Political Parties in North Carolina, 1776–1861* [Baltimore, 1906], pp. 122–24, 150–52).

3. A belief that the North was composed of capitalists and wage slaves, more servile than black slaves and antagonistic to the government of the wealthy, was common among Southern defenders of slavery such as John C. Calhoun, James Henry Hammond, and George Fitzhugh (Richard Hofstadter, *The American Political Tradition and the Men Who Made It* [New York, 1948], pp. 78–82, 86–91).

4. Olmsted was probably thinking of P. G. T. Beauregard's assertion in June 1861 that Northern soldiers were bent on obtaining "beauty and booty." Olmsted may also have seen the text of Jefferson Davis's July message to the Confederate Congress, which included the statement: "Mankind will shudder to hear the tales of outrages committed on defenseless females by soldiers of the United States now invading our homes." According to Davis, such actions and pillaging sprang from "inflamed passions and the madness of intoxication" (Jefferson Davis, *Jefferson Davis, Constitutionalist, His Letters, Papers and Speeches . . .* , ed. Dunbar Rowland, 10 vols. [Jackson, Miss., 1923], 5: 114; see also FLO to HWB, Aug. 15, 1861, n. 4, above).

5. An allusion to the importance of slavery in the formation of the Southern Confederacy. Slavery had been abolished in 1833 throughout the British Empire, and English ships had been singularly important in efforts to suppress the African slave trade (E. D. Adams, *Great Britain and the American Civil War*, 1: 8–9).

6. Joint army-navy expeditions captured the forts at Cape Hatteras Inlet, North Carolina, on August 28–29, 1861, and Port Royal, South Carolina, on November 7. On November 24, 1861, a naval party landed at Tybee Island, located in Savannah harbor, which had been abandoned by Confederate forces alarmed at the Union navy's earlier successes (U.S. Department of the Navy, Naval History Division, *Civil War Naval Chronology, 1861–1865*, 5 vols. [Washington, D.C., 1961–65], 1: 23, 31, 37).

7. In the last three decades before the Civil War, some Southerners began to assert that slaves, rather than becoming a liability in time of war, would be a source of strength. Chancellor William Harper of South Carolina argued that slavery would allow almost all able-bodied free men to join the army without decreasing agricultural or industrial production and that slaves themselves could be armed to repel invaders (John Hope Franklin, *The Militant South, 1800–1861* [Cambridge, Mass., 1956], pp. 92–95).

8. A reference to the Confederate government's extensive use of slaves, mainly as laborers in the construction of fortifications. As Olmsted points out, the Union army made little use of slaves, and some officers returned runaway slaves to their masters (Bell Irvin Wiley, *Southern Negroes, 1861–1865* [New Haven, Conn., 1938], pp. 110–13).

9. Olmsted is referring to the peculiar conditions of slavery on the South Carolina sea islands. Plantations were large, and the few white people, other than overseers, who lived there spent only part of the year on their estates. Blacks were culturally as well as physically very isolated from whites. Most sea island slaves spoke Gullah, a dialect that included thousands of African words (Willie Lee Rose, *Rehearsal for Reconstruction: The Port Royal Experiment* [Indianapolis, Ind., 1964], pp. 96–100).

10. In *A Journey Through Texas*, Olmsted reported seeing two runaway slaves in Mexico. The fugitive with whom he talked at length was, however, described as born in Virginia, "brought South by a trader and sold to a gentleman who had brought him to Texas, from whom he had run away four or five years ago" (Frederick Law Olmsted, *A Journey Through Texas; Or, a Saddle-Trip on the Southwestern Frontier* . . . [New York, 1857], pp. 323, 327, 338–39).

11. Olmsted probably believed these locations to be particularly accessible, geographically or ideologically, to the U.S. armed forces. Wilmington, North Carolina; Hilton Head, South Carolina; Fernandina and Pensacola, Florida; Bayou Calcasieu, Louisiana; and Galveston, Texas, all were coastal settlements and thus open to capture by the U.S. Navy. Fort Smith was a frontier outpost on the Arkansas River. Olmsted considered San Antonio, Texas, and the mountains of Kentucky and Tennessee to be areas peopled by many with strongly Unionist sentiments.

12. Early in 1853 Olmsted wrote:

> The spread of intelligence of all kinds among the slaves is remarkable. . . . Another [planter] told me that he had been frequently informed by his slaves of occurrences in a town forty miles distant, where he spent part of the year with his family, in advance of the mail, or any means of communication that he could command the use of. Also, when in town, his servants would sometimes give him important news from the plantation, several hours before a messenger dispatched by his overseer arrived. ("The South" no. 9 [*Papers of FLO*, 2: 122].)

13. When slaves revolted in the French colony San Domingo (Saint Domingue) in 1791, they killed many white residents there.

14. Olmsted probably read reports, reprinted from Southern newspapers, of free blacks in states such as Louisiana, Tennessee, Alabama, and Virginia enrolling for military duty in support of the Confederacy. Although some black troops like the Louisiana Native Guards of New Orleans were mustered into service, they did not take part in any important engagements (Horace Greeley, *The American Conflict: A History of the Great Rebellion* . . . , 2 vols. [Hartford, Conn., 1864–66], 2: 521–22; Mary F. Berry, "Negro Troops in Blue and Gray: The Louisiana Native Guards, 1861–63," *Louisiana History* 8 [Spring 1967]: 167–68).

To John Murray Forbes[1]

December 15th [1861]

J. M. Forbes Esq[r]
My Dear Sir,

I have just received your favor of the 12th and am exceedingly glad there is so good a prospect of financial aid to the Commission from Massachusetts.[2] Your contributions of goods have astonished me and overrun all my calculations. You have done in a month nearly four times as much as the New York association—of which we had been quite proud—in six months! If the present rate of supply continues, I shall soon be in concern to know where to put it.

I shall refer that portion of your letter which relates to the Surgeon General to D[r] Bellows. The simplest statement of the case would be perhaps that with an army of 600,000 fresh men with impromptu officers, it is criminal weakness to entrust such important responsibilities as those resting on the surgeon general to a self-satisfied, supercilious, bigoted blockhead merely because he is the oldest of old mess-room doctors of the old frontier-guard of the country. He knows nothing and does nothing and is capable of knowing nothing and doing nothing but quibble about matters of form and precedent and sign his name to papers which require that ceremony to be performed before they can be admitted to eternal rest in the pigeon holes of the bureau. I write this personally rather than as the Secretary, and from general report rather than personal knowledge. But if it were not true, is it[3] not certain that as Secretary of the Sanitary Commission, after six months' dealings with these poor green volunteer sawbones, I should have seen some evidence of life in and from their chief?

You may contradict the report, to which you refer, that the contributions made to the Sanitary Commission for the benefit of the soldiers sick, have been diverted to the aid of the exiles of the rebellion. To this date, no funds of the Commission have been disbursed in St. Louis. Probably the local Commission there has done something which has given rise to the report.[4]

I have directed D[r] Ware,[5] in visiting Fort Monroe, to ascertain the condition of the refugees there and report, but to give them no aid except under advice or in an emergency.

Very Respectfully Yours

Fred. Law Olmsted.

The original is a letterpress copy in box 833, volume 2, pages 142–45, in USSC-NYPL. A printed version also appears in Sarah Forbes Hughes, editor, *Letters and Recollections of John Murray Forbes*, 2 volumes (Boston and New York, 1900), volume 1, pages 265–66.

1. John Murray Forbes (1813–1898) was a prominent businessman and railroad builder. A resident of the Boston area, he made his fortune in his family's trading ventures in China but also became a major figure in the financing and construction of Midwestern railroads, including the Michigan Central.

    Although more hostile to abolitionism than Olmsted, Forbes was a fellow Republican and had been a free-soiler. The two men may have met during the 1850s through the New England Emigrant Aid Company. Forbes had contributed both money and transportation for men and rifles to the free-soil cause in Kansas. During the Civil War, he was active in several areas that greatly interested Olmsted. The businessman was a member of the Boston branch of the Sanitary Commission and tried to enlist support for the reform of the Medical Bureau. Concerned about the blacks' transition from slavery to freedom in the Union-occupied sea islands, he traveled to Port Royal early in 1862 and remained there for several months. He also shared Olmsted's commitment to mobilizing popular support for the war and organized the Loyal Publication Society for that purpose. An early member of Boston's Union League Club, Forbes served as an adviser to state and federal officials, especially on naval affairs.

    Forbes described Olmsted's Southern travel books as the "best books ever written upon the slavery economic question" and in 1891 he expressed the wish to have a condensed version of Olmsted's *Cotton Kingdom* published. Olmsted dismissed the idea because he thought that no commercial demand for the book existed and that the omission of material would destroy its historical value (*DAB*; Henry Greenleaf Pearson, *An American Railroad Builder, John Murray Forbes* [1911; rpt. ed., New York, 1972], pp. 109–21, 135; J. M. Forbes to FLO, June 19, June 23, and July 1, 1891; FLO to J. M. Forbes, July 2, 1891).

2. Probably a reference to ten thousand dollars given by the people of New England through J. Huntington Wolcott of Boston. This contribution formed a large part of the nineteen thousand dollars received by the Commission in December. Before November 1861 the Commission's receipts totaled only about fourteen thousand in monetary gifts (Charles J. Stillé, *History of the United States Sanitary Commission, Being the General Report of Its Work during the War of the Rebellion* [New York, 1868], pp. 470–75).

3. The editors have here altered Olmsted's original word order, "it is."

4. Olmsted was correct that the Western Sanitary Commission was aiding the Unionist refugees in St. Louis who had been displaced from other sections of Missouri by Confederate guerrilla activities. The Western Commission opened a home for the refugees and solicited money and clothing for them (Jacob Gilbert Forman, *The Western Sanitary Commission; A Sketch of Its Origins, History* . . . [St. Louis, Mo., 1864], p. 124).

5. Robert Ware (1833–1863), a Sanitary Commission inspector who arrived at Fortress Monroe on December 7, 1861. He was the grandson and nephew of the well-known Unitarian clergymen Henry and William Ware. Robert, like his father, John, graduated from Harvard College and Harvard Medical School. In 1857 the younger Ware was chosen district physician of the Boston Infirmary.

    The Peninsula campaign of 1862 gave Olmsted the opportunity to know Ware much better and deepened his appreciation of the younger man's skill and dedication. When Olmsted had to cope with the embarkation of typhoid patients who had been left lying in the rain, he was relieved by the arrival of Ware, for in his estimation Ware and Frederick N. Knapp were "the two very best men I ever saw for such an emergency." Ware's unfailing energy impressed his fellow workers, and Georgeanna Woolsey believed that ill and wounded soldiers transported from the front would have been poorly cared for had it not been for "the sleepless devotion of Dr. Ware, who, night after night, works among them, often not leaving them till two or three o'clock in the morning."

In the fall of 1862, after approximately nine months' service with the Sanitary Commission, Ware was appointed surgeon of the 44th Massachusetts. He died of typhoid fever with his regiment in North Carolina in April 1863. That year, when the Sanitary Commission published *Hospital Transports*, its memoir of the Peninsula transport service, it dedicated the book to Ware and other "martyrs" (Emma Forbes Ware, *Ware Genealogy* . . . [Boston, 1901], pp. 158–59; *DAB*, s.v. "Ware, John"; *Hospital Transports*, pp. iv, 33, 110).

To Henry Whitney Bellows

U.S. Sanitary Commission, Washington, D.C.
Dec. 20th 1861.

My Dear Doctor,

I received yours of the 19th last night. Am very sorry to hear of your illness.

We have constant evidence of the harm the Times articles[1] are doing. If however the Report[2] does what I expect of it, they will simply serve as a means of advertisement. I saw Raymond[3] yesterday and told him that each and every statement made in the editorial of the previous day was specifically false.[4] I then wrote him a note, denying in detail his information and telling him that his informant[5] was an imposter. I concluded it best to say nothing publickly however & marked it private. It was intended for the perusal of the Surg[n] Gen[l] however. Raymond says the Surg[n] Gen[l] is his friend; the attempt to throw him out by the Bill before the Senate[6] is unjust—mean, & he will fight it. If he is incapable & inefficient, let him be proceeded against legitimately. I insisted that the San. Com. had taken precisely the course which he demanded & no other.

To the Report, as our grand coup in reserve—to justify not only our course but our silence under attack, I have given myself wholly. There has not been a minute's delay that could be avoided. The city has been searched for printers, other offices have been applied to [for] aid, and we have had night gangs of compositors. It will be a bigger volume than you think for & will be worth something if it justifies the labor put on it the last week. I have worked Elliott[7] up in recalculating all the figures & comparing and verifying, so that during the last two days it is not safe to leave him alone, as he topples off asleep. I am in prime condition having been in my natural way of living, having taken my clothes off to sleep for the first time last night. I have discovered that pale ale is an admirable prophylactic of nervous exhaustion, and I believe that Knapp, Elliott & I have consumed about seven dozen of it this week. Some brewing friend of Douglas sent us a barrel full just in time.

You will understand that editing has not stood for a minute in the way of printing. I have been personally twice a day to the printers & they have never waited for copy, proof or revise an instant. Nevertheless if you don't say the thing has been well edited, I will turn Methodist & keep early hours the rest of my life.

I have had to let everything else slide, to get it *done well, in time*.
Yours faithfully

Fred. Law Olmsted.

The original is in box 641 of USSC-NYPL.

1. In late November 1861 the *New-York Times* began its defense of the surgeon general in response to attacks by the *New York World*. The Sanitary Commission came under steady fire in the columns of the *Times* for its criticism of Finley. On November 25 an editorial charged that the *World* articles were written to further the Sanitary Commission's "ambition of superseding, or at least remodeling the established Medical Bureau of the regular army." The editorialist for the *Times* further averred that the surgeon general possessed "a high professional standing" and "a degree of experience in the medical care of armies to which none of the gentlemen composing the Sanitary Commission can for a moment pretend." To the *World*'s charge that neglect of sanitary precautions led to loss of life in the general hospitals, the *Times* replied that such deaths from unsanitary conditions actually occurred in the camps and were the responsibility of the Sanitary Commission. "The Sanitary Commission, which has assumed the special care of the camps, has it in its power to prevent a very large proportion of these deaths, by increasing its vigilance in urging sanitary precautions there, and especially by causing the removal of the sick to the general hospital before all hope of their recovery has fled."

This editorial was only the *Times*'s opening salvo. In December the newspaper began to publish the letters of "Truth," the pseudonym used by Elizabeth Powell, who mounted a more vitriolic attack on the Commission. On December 4 she asserted that the Commission's plans for model hospitals were ill-advised and that it knew little about hospital management. She further alleged that the Commission's agents "have a very slipshod way of doing their little bit of work of distributing jellies, &c., though the secretaries, operatives, agents, and all that are engaged, get rather good salaries for the times, and all out of the pockets of the 'generous public.' Has any one ever thought of appointing a 'Board of Inquiry' as to whether the labors of the Commission really pay for supporting it?" Her final allegation in that letter was, "[The] Government provides every needful comfort for the sick and it is the fault of the head Surgeon in any Government hospital if he lacks such," a comment implying that the Commission performed no vital service there. In a second letter published on December 6, "Truth" reiterated her praise of the surgeon general and her criticism of model hospitals and of the Sanitary Commission.

Stung by "Truth's" criticisms, Olmsted attempted to rebut them in a short article published by the *Times* on December 7. He noted that the Commission had fifteen qualified men "engaged in the duty of inspection" of camps. Moreover, he stated that the Commission and its branches had provided contributions valued at over one thousand dollars daily to the military hospitals, over twenty thousand articles in November alone. "Truth," however, remained obdurate, asserting on December 14 that she had never seen Olmsted visiting the hospitals and that he could "easily learn that the general hospitals in the City of Washington and vicinity have received but little, very little, of this 'thousand dollars a day' contributions" (*New-York Times*, Nov. 25, 1861, p. 4; Dec. 4, 1861, p. 3; Dec. 6, 1861, pp. 2–3; Dec. 7, 1861, p. 3; and Dec. 14, 1861, p. 3).

2. A reference to the paper published as document number 40 of the Sanitary Commission and entitled "A Report to the Secretary of War of the Operations of the Sanitary Commission and upon the Sanitary Condition of the Volunteer Army, Its Medical Staff, Hospitals and Hospital Supplies, December 1861." In this eighty-page report Olmsted gave the results of and conclusions drawn from the Commission's inspections of the camps of the volunteer soldiers. The report covered such areas as the cleanliness, clothing, and food of soldiers, and it discussed such topics as recreation for soldiers, drunkenness, and arrangements for soldiers to remit their pay to their families. Also presented were the statistics of sickness and death for the army and a discussion of the staffing, supply, and construction of military hospitals. A final section focused on the Sanitary Commission's own accomplishments.

3. Henry Jarvis Raymond (1820–1869), the editor of the *New-York Times* and a Republican politician. Olmsted wrote his first and second series of newspaper articles about the South for Raymond between 1852 and 1854 (*DAB*).

4. An unsigned editorial in the *New-York Times* on December 18 charged that the proposed act reorganizing the Medical Bureau was "a device of the Sanitary Commission, to get rid of Dr. Finley, whose bureau they have been unable to control, who has declined to surrender control of his department of the service to them, and against whom, nevertheless, they are unable to substantiate any charge involving inefficiency or dereliction of duty in any respect." According to the anonymous writer, the Sanitary Commission was attempting to "clamor" Surgeon General Finley out of office "by whispered insinuations which nobody ventures to make specific, by charging upon him faults and shortcomings which belong to others and by imploring Congress to embody their hostility in a public law" (*New-York Times*, Dec. 18, 1861, p. 8).

5. Elizabeth Powell (b. c. 1835), a resident of New York City and a volunteer superintendent of nurses in a Washington military hospital. In 1858 she and unhappily married Henry Raymond met and developed a close relationship which she later characterized as a "silly platonic friendship," though she admitted that he was in love with her. Thus in 1861 Raymond, a friend of Surgeon General Finley, promised to publish Elizabeth Powell's letters defending the surgeon general.

When Finley visited the hospital where Elizabeth Powell worked, she was impressed by both his ability and his "solicitude for the comfort of the soldiers." Her encounter with the Sanitary Commission was not so pleasant; she claimed that its agents were unwilling to issue any shirts or socks to her hospital or to answer her questions about how they spent their money. Her view of the Commission was also strongly influenced by her opinion of Olmsted, whom she believed to be the major impetus behind the movement to oust Finley. She called Olmsted a man of "consummate ability," but thought that he "loved power and the handling of millions." In her view Olmsted wished to replace Finley with Hammond in order that the Sanitary Commission might receive funds from the U.S. Treasury.

Olmsted and his associates soon discovered that Elizabeth Powell was "Truth." On January 11, 1862, Olmsted told Henry W. Bellows, "Miss Powell is doing much mischief propagating falsehood and slander very industriously. It is very desirable to squelch her." And she was silenced, she believed by the Sanitary Commission. In her version:

> Mr. Olmsted after a useless personal appeal to Mr. R. employed surer tactics. He had it committed to the ears of Mrs. Raymond thro' some lady officer of Clubs organized to send supplies to the San. Com. that there was a girl in Washington who had "an undue influence" on the Editor of the Times and was using it to hurt the San. Com. and trying to harm its benificent work. . . . Raymond appealed to me to release him from his promise for the sake of "escaping hell" within his own doors.

According to Elizabeth Powell's later reminiscence, she gave up her defense of Finley as well as her friendship with Raymond after the latter's wife insulted her at a party. Contemporary accounts were racier. In May 1862 George Templeton Strong gossiped to Olmsted, "I hear that Miss P. is found out, and that Raymond has had a grand scene with that lady which culminated in intervention by the Police, who coerced the lady to quit Mr. Raymond's premises." In 1867 Elizabeth Powell married a Mr. Deleschaze (or Delescluze) (FLO to HWB, Jan. 11, 1862, USSC-NYPL, box 641; Elizabeth Powell Deleschaze to Adolph Ochs, Feb. 15, March 12, and Aug. 25, 1901, and n.d. [c. 1901], Archives of the *New York Times*, New York City; GTS to FLO, May 18, 1862, USSC-NYPL, box 741: 1068).

6. On December 10, 1861, Senator Henry Wilson of Massachusetts introduced Senate Bill 97, which was drawn up by William A. Hammond for the Sanitary Commission and which survives only in a manuscript version. The bill embodied the major reforms sought by the Commission. It would provide increased rank for the officers of the Medical Bureau, promoting its director general (the proposed new title for the surgeon general) from colonel to brigadier general. It would also create a new group of medical officers—an inspector general and eight inspectors—who would be responsible for the sanitary condition of camps and hospitals—a task the Sanitary Commission had been performing. The bill's most controversial sections, however—and those that had angered Finley's supporters—related to the selection of the director general and inspectors and the retirement of officers. The bill called for the president to appoint these officers from the ranks of the career army physicians according to their "peculiar fitness for such positions" rather than their seniority. Furthermore, medical officers aged sixty and older would not be eligible for those positions, and all of them would retire with a military pension at age sixty-five. These provisions reflected the Sanitary Commission's view that the Medical Bureau needed more youthful, vigorous leadership chosen on the basis of merit. A compromise measure, rather than this original, was enacted into law in April 1862 ("An Act for the Reorganization of the Medical Department of the Army," n.d. [c. Nov.–Dec. 1861], Alexander Dallas Bache Papers, Library of Congress, Washington D.C.; *Congressional Globe*, 37th Cong., 2nd sess., 1861–62, 40: 37; William A. Hammond to HWB, Nov. 26, 1861, USSC-NYPL, box 640.

7. Ezekiel Brown Elliott, the Commission's actuary.

To Henry Whitney Bellows

U. S. Sanitary Commission, Washington, D.C.
Decr 21st 1861.

My Dear Doctor,

You will receive with this an advanced copy of the Report. In the regular issue the dead paper will be filled & there will be an appendix (not much).[1]

I want that as soon as practicable after this is out, there should be a grand simultaneous expression of confidence in the Commission, which shall completely counteract the effect which has unquestionably been mischievous of the Times' & other attacks upon us. There is a *systematic* war on the Commission organized and before any further progress is made, we must overwhelm them. Get the editors *committed* against them as generally as possible.

Ask Agnew to look after the World.[2] I will write Dana.[3] I want someone to write an editorial for the Post[4] and get it adopted. The Post is important. Mr Rogers[5] is strenuous upon this point. I shall hope that you will do it, or get someone to do it.

What I think should be the cue to all the newspapers I have given in the concluding ¶¶ of the Report—(Shame on making such a question *personal*).[6]

Insist that it shall not be personal and refuse to notice the allegations against the character of the Commission, further than that they are accomplishing nothing, & that there is nothing to be done outside of the present government arrangments.

Excuse these suggestions, but if anything is to be done I want it comprehensive and united—and all at once. So I hope next week we shall all do our best with the press. Our letters from every quarter, show need for a demonstration to reassure the public that we [are] attending our business well & not going beyond it.

Yours faithfully

Fred. Law Olmsted.

The original is in box 641 of USSC-NYPL. A letterpress copy also appears in volume 2, pages 221–23, of box 833.

1. A much-shortened version of Olmsted's controversial "Report on the Demoralization of the Volunteers" was appended to the report to the secretary of war. In this new version the results of inspections were briefly summarized, but Olmsted's recommen-

dations and criticisms of government were omitted. Two new sections—one concerning ambulances, the other the patriotic efforts of Northern women to aid the soldiers—also were published in this appendix.

2. Cornelius R. Agnew and Manton Marble (editor of the *New York World*) were friends. Some of the attacks upon the efficiency of the surgeon general published by the *World* came from Agnew.

3. Charles Anderson Dana (1819–1897), the managing editor of Horace Greeley's *New-York Daily Tribune*. Olmsted and Dana were friends and had collaborated on *Putnam's Monthly* in the 1850s. Dana had also solicited Olmsted's article "Park" for an encyclopedia that he was editing with George Ripley (*DAB*; *Papers of FLO*, 2: 348, 349; ibid., 3: 360).

4. William Cullen Bryant's newspaper, the *New York Evening Post*.

5. Henry B. Rogers.

6. In the concluding paragraphs of the report to the secretary of war, Olmsted declared that in order to secure the proper care of the sick and wounded soldiers, "a higher place needs to be accorded the medical staff in the organization of the army. Its relations with all departments and all ranks, as well as with the Government itself, needs to be more intimate, confidential, and influential." He then proceeded to justify the Commission's actions and motives:

> Whatever and whoever stands in the way of this, the Commission wants put out of the way. But if an impression prevails in any quarter that the members of the Commission, in their devotion to this purpose, have been over-zealous, or sought, individually or collectively, to bring it about by action not absolutely within their assigned duty, or that they have used any indirect or unworthy means therefor, that impression is without the smallest foundation in truth. Whoever seeks to promulgate it, narrows to a personal issue a question of the broadest humanity, and is without provocation or excuse for so doing, in any action of the Commission.
>
> The one point which controls the Commission is just this: a simple desire and resolute determination to secure for the men who have enlisted in this war that care which it is the will and duty of the nation to give them. That care is their right, and, in the Government or out of it, it must be given them, let who will stand in the way.
>
> The Commission has no fear that its motives will be misconstrued, or its words perverted. In the life-struggle of a nation, soft speaking of real dangers and over considerateness is a crime. (Frederick Law Olmsted, "A Report to the Secretary of War ...," doc. no. 40, pp. 70–71, in USSC, *Documents*.)

To James Russell Lowell[1]

Washington. Jany 12th 1862.

My Dear Lowell,

I write at the request of Prof.r Bache, who but that the critical position of the Coast Survey appropriation so fully occupies him, would write you himself—to ask you to address the Atheneum on the subject of

Maury,[2] apropos to his letter published therein, December 21st.[3] The game, personally, is contemptible but the probable success of the imposture is too great, and the opportunity it affords of riddling the general imposition with which it is associated, is too good a one to be neglected while, in the judgment of the Professor and others who have been talking of it here, no one has a weapon as well adapted to the work as yourself.

If you are not familiar with the numerous tricks, assumptions, and downright falsehoods by which this charlatan has gained his European reputation, Prof[r] Peirce[4] can readily boost you up; those of the letter itself, beginning with the "price set on his head," are obvious enough.

I know that you will gladly undertake the business if it commends itself to you as a favorable occasion to serve the Country—we must all use the tools we can, now—if it does not, it is no trouble to neglect it, so no apology is necessary for proposing it to you & the wish that you may think well of it.

Very Cordially Yours

Fred. Law Olmsted.

Prof[r] J. R. Lowell

The original is in the James Russell Lowell Papers, Houghton Library, Harvard University, Cambridge, Massachusetts.

1. James Russell Lowell (1819–1891), poet and man of letters. Lowell won acclaim in the 1840s for his humorous poems collected as *The Bigelow Papers*, which criticized the federal government's involvement in slavery and the Mexican War. Active in the antislavery movement, he was appointed a professor of foreign languages at Harvard in 1855 and was also a popular public lecturer. In 1857 he became the first editor of the *Atlantic Monthly* magazine, a position he held until 1861.

   In 1855 Olmsted's activities as managing editor of *Putnam's Monthly* led to his introduction to Lowell, who wrote several travel pieces for the magazine. That June, Olmsted gave one of the luncheons in honor of Lowell, who was then preparing to depart for a year in Europe. Relations between the two men were never close, but Lowell appears to have reciprocated some of Olmsted's admiration. In his answer to the letter presented here, the poet warmly praised Olmsted's "rare merit as observer & reporter" and further commented:

   > I have learned more about the South from your books than from all others put together, & I valued them the more that an American who can be patient & accurate is so rare a phenomenon. . . . Most of our writers in all departments, & it is even worse in politics, instead of being *rare* (if I may dip into my Yankee inkstand for a pun) are *under done*. I was particularly impressed with the compactness & quiet power of the introduction to the new volumes [i.e., the two-volume *Cotton Kingdom*, just published].

   (*DAB; Papers of FLO*, 2: 21, 345, 349; J. R. Lowell to FLO, Jan. 25, 1862.)

2. Matthew Fontaine Maury (1806–1873), naval officer and scientist. He joined the U.S. Navy in 1825 and in 1842 became superintendent of the depot of charts and instruments, a position which included oversight of the naval observatory. As an oceanographer, Maury undertook research on winds and currents and was a leader in gathering systematic data. The charts that he drew up using these data allowed shipping companies to shorten considerably their sailing times.

   Born in Virginia, Maury took a keen interest in Southern commerce and its development. Olmsted was familiar with Maury's proposal in the 1850s to establish a line of steamships between Norfolk and Brazil—a plan that Olmsted had criticized in his writings on the South. When Virginia seceded in April 1861, Maury resigned his post and was appointed a commander in the Confederate Navy. In the fall of 1862 he became a special representative of the Confederate government in England and spent most of the remainder of the war there (*DAB*; *Papers of FLO*, 2: 144–47, 151).

3. The article "Capt. Maury on American Affairs," published in the December 21, 1861, issue of the London *Athenaeum*, was primarily a letter from Maury to Adm. Robert Fitzroy of the Royal Navy. Maury passionately defended Southern secession and denounced Northern actions throughout the nineteenth century as prompted by the desire to take advantage of the South economically. He also claimed that through the tariff, the North forced the South to pay more than its share of taxes but gave it few of the benefits of the federal government's expenditures.

   The imposture to which Olmsted refers is the letter's introduction, which described Maury, who had frequently championed the extreme Southern rights position, as "a scientific man who is neither a partisan nor a politician." By "downright falsehoods" Olmsted means Maury's declaration that "the Yankees . . . have shown themselves vindictive to a degree; they have vilified me; they have set a price upon my head, and intercepted all my foreign correspondence, so that I have not been able to get a hearing in any part of Europe, or to communicate, since April last with any friend there."

   Although Olmsted was proposing that Lowell write a reply—perhaps in a satirical vein—to Maury's letter for the same magazine, the poet apparently thought that Olmsted wished him to give a public lecture about Maury, presumably at the Boston Atheneum. In his reply of January 25 Lowell declined the opportunity to "crack such a flea as Maury" and included a Latin verse which he translated as "I save my shafts for game less sorry/than charlatan & fussy Maury." Disappointedly, Olmsted scrawled on the back of Lowell's reply, "a misapprehension of my proposal" (*Athenaeum: Journal of English and Foreign Literature, Science, and the Fine Arts*, no. 1782 [1861], pp. 846–48; J. R. Lowell to FLO, Jan. 25, 1862).

4. Benjamin Peirce (1809–1880), professor of mathematics and astronomy at Harvard College for over thirty-five years. One of the best-known and most respected American mathematicians of his day, he published extensively in the fields of pure mathematics, astronomy, geodesy, and mechanics. Not only was Peirce a colleague of James Russell Lowell, but his role in the founding of the Harvard Observatory and his position as director of longitude determinations for the U.S. Coast Survey meant that part of his scientific expertise lay in areas similar to Maury's. Olmsted's first meeting with Peirce apparently occurred in January 1862 while the mathematician was staying at A. D. Bache's home in Washington (*DAB*; FLO to MPO, Jan. 19, 1862).

249

To John Strong Newberry

Jan. 15th [1862].

My Dear Doctor,

There is no change in the drift of our affairs here and the machinery is working steadily. Evidences of virulent opposition and hatred increase. Slander and libels float and lodge in the majority of uninformed minds to which they get access but the favor of substantial appreciation from knowledge also increases and the Commission becomes respected and cherished as it becomes feared and hated. Legislation is simmering, Bills preparing and no obvious progress. I have written the President, that I think the meeting of the Commission here had better be postponed, but that members should come here to influence legislation in their individual capacity.[1] As I asked him to telegraph if he did not agree with me, I think the meeting will be postponed to February. I will let you know as soon as possible when decided.

The clothing issued here of late has been of scandalous quality. The waste from the excessive ration is abominable. Horses are shockingly treated—starving in hosts. The army is far from what it ought to be for an advance. I hope that an advance from this point will not be necessary before the ground is settled in the spring.

I believe that a very strong tax bill is being prepared with the deliberation it needs to have.[2]

Cameron's retirement and Stanton's[3] nomination are generally satisfactory. Stanton and McClellan work together.[4] All that I hear of Stanton is good, unless perhaps that he represents Kentucky ideas too much.[5]

Bloor writes you today about supplies for St. Louis. Douglas seems working along quietly to good results.[6]

Will you please settle all open accounts in your department to the 1st of January, paying all balances due, as soon as practicable, and, hereafter, do so on the first of each month, estimating in advance the amount necessary and obtaining it from Mr. Strong, or making the Commission debtor to your sub-treasury for it, if you collect it at the West, so that all accounts with the Commission may be settled monthly. I will send you blank vouchers.

Yours Very Cordially

Fred. Law Olmsted

P.S. 16th   The meeting is indefinitely postponed. Dr B. will come here Monday, with some of the associate members. The faculty, I hope, later in the week.[7]

Dr J. S. Newberry,
Cleveland, Ohio.

The original is letter 185 in volume 1 of box 909 of USSC-NYPL. Olmsted wrote this letter on old stationery with the printed heading "Sanitary Commission, Washington, D.C.   Treasury Building" and the printed date "1861."

1. In his letter of January 11 Olmsted suggested to Bellows that the Commission should not hold its scheduled meeting, since divisions within the organization over the proposed bill to reorganize the Medical Bureau would then become apparent. According to Olmsted, Commission members Robert C. Wood, Alexander E. Shiras, and Samuel Gridley Howe would oppose the bill, and Thomas M. Clark and A. D. Bache were uncertain allies. Olmsted also believed that in a crisis, Elisha Harris would lean toward compromise. As an alternative to the meeting, Olmsted proposed that the Commission members from New York come to Washington either to lobby individually or with a citizens' committee appointed by the New York associate members of the Commission at a recent meeting (FLO to HWB, Jan. 11, 1862, USSC-NYPL, box 641).
2. Although an income tax and an increase in the tariff had been approved by Congress in its special session during the summer of 1861, it was evident when Congress reconvened in December 1861 that these measures would not generate enough revenue to meet the growing expenses of the war. Olmsted's expectation of a new and stronger tax bill mirrored the concern expressed in both letters and editorials of the *New-York Times* in early January (Leonard P. Curry, *Blueprint for Modern America: Nonmilitary Legislation of the First Civil War Congress* [Nashville, Tenn., 1968], pp. 154–63).
3. Edwin McMasters Stanton (1814–1869) was appointed U.S. secretary of war on January 14, 1862. A Democrat and former U.S. attorney general in the Buchanan administration, Stanton was generally regarded as an extremely hard-working and able lawyer. He greatly improved the efficiency of the War Department and eliminated much of the fraud and mismanagement that had characterized Cameron's tenure.

     A controversial figure from 1862 until his death, Stanton was by most accounts conscientious and careful but also irascible, rude, and vindictive. Although the vigor that he brought to the War Department first pleased the Sanitary Commission, this satisfaction did not last long. Within six weeks of his appointment, the Commission was chafing at his failure to carry out promised reforms and to increase its power. In a more personal matter Olmsted was disappointed when Stanton failed in April 1862 to give him superintendence of the Port Royal experiment in free labor. When in May 1862 Bellows attempted to influence Stanton's appointments in the Medical Bureau, he found the secretary abrupt in his unwillingness to be counseled. By the time of the Peninsula campaign, Olmsted vehemently declared: "I thoroughly hate that canting small politician, the Secretary of War. . . . He is more a fool than a knave, however, I believe, yet he is a big knave." And Olmsted came to detest Stanton even more as that military campaign unfolded. As an admirer of McClellan's generalship at that time, Olmsted blamed all failures of the Army of the Potomac upon the administration in general and Stanton and the War Department in particular.

     Olmsted's and the other Sanitary Commission members' opinions of Stanton never grew more favorable. When Stanton and William A. Hammond, both strong-willed men, clashed late in 1862 and in 1863, the commissioners' sympathies lay with the reforming surgeon general they had helped elevate to office. They also viewed petty attacks by the War Department upon the Commission's privileges, such as the free printing of documents by the government printing office, as continued evidence of Stanton's rancor. The court-martial and conviction of Hammond in 1864 upon charges based on scanty evidence further confirmed the commissioners in their dislike of Stanton. To George Templeton Strong, Hammond's conviction appeared "a base tyrannical outrage on law and right effected by the vast power of the man at the head of the War Department who hates Hammond, and whose hates are as unscrupulous as they are bitter and dangerous" (*DAB*; FLO to JSN, Feb. 24, 1862, below;

HWB to William H. Van Buren, May 13, 1862, Henry Whitney Bellows Papers, Massachusetts Historical Society, Boston, Mass.; FLO to JFJ, May 25, 1862, below; *Diary of the Civil War*, p. 476).

4. As fellow Democrats, Stanton and McClellan had met and become friends in Washington during the summer of 1861. After Stanton helped McClellan write an official report that November, some newspapers described Stanton as the general's "confidential advisor." These cordial relations between the two men vanished in the spring of 1862 as Stanton grew impatient at McClellan's failure to advance decisively against the enemy (Benjamin P. Thomas and Harold M. Hyman, *Stanton: The Life and Times of Lincoln's Secretary of War* [New York, 1962], pp. 126–27, 130–31, 182–88).

5. It is not clear why Olmsted believed that Stanton, a native of southern Ohio, represented "Kentucky ideas." Possibly Olmsted thought that Stanton, like many prominent Kentuckians and Democrats, would be loyal to the Union but would continue to support slavery. Actually, the new secretary of war held antislavery views but had neither made them public nor broken with the Democratic party over the issue of slavery (ibid., pp. 4, 99–107, 140).

6. Associate Secretary John H. Douglas arrived in St. Louis on December 16, 1861, to oversee the Sanitary Commission's activities west of the Mississippi River (J. H. Douglas to FLO, Dec. 16, 1861, USSC-NYPL, box 731: 1382).

7. The "faculty" to which Olmsted refers was that part of the citizens' committee (nominated by the New York associate members of the Sanitary Commission) which was meant to represent the medical schools there. This committee, which also represented life insurance companies and the relatives of the volunteer soldiers, with similar groups from Boston and Philadelphia, formed an important part of the Sanitary Commission's lobbying activities in favor of the reform of the Medical Bureau (FLO to HWB, Jan. 18, 1862, USSC-NYPL, box 641; *Diary of the Civil War*, pp. 201–3).

To Henry Whitney Bellows

U.S. Sanitary Commission, Washington, D.C.
January 18th [1862].

My Dear Doctor,

I've no doubt that a more or less vague impression prevails quite generally with careless people—and everybody is careless until forced to care—that there is a personal quarrel between the members of the Sanitary Commission and the Medical Bureau. The Medical Bureau has endeavored to produce that impression. That impression is very unfavorable to a fair hearing of our charges against the Medical Bureau. For that reason the Medical Bureau fosters it. Dr Finley's friends, instead of replying to our charges, distract attention from them by counter charges, by charging us with interested motives, with impertinent meddling, &c.

STAFF BUILDINGS OF THE U.S. ARMY MEDICAL BUREAU

I am trying to account for my wish to keep the Commission in the back-ground in the approaching assault, which was indicated in the last sentence of my letter to you sent by Wood this afternoon. There are other reasons but I have said enough to indicate the controlling one.[1]

You must be prepared to encounter an entire indifference to the whole subject on the part of every member of Congress, only here and there, sometimes politely concealed. Whatever is done—mark this—will be done to oblige the surgeons or to oblige the gentlemen who oppose the surgeons and be rid of their importunity. I do not believe there is a single exception to this. And no bill stands the least chance of passing unless we force ours through, or force the surgeons to force theirs against the inclination of Congress.

And more, I believe, after a talk with Wilson and Forster,[2] tonight, that both the military Committees are opposed to us—not actively but passively at least. Wilson, by the way, said that his committee would not give audience to your citizens' Committee, or to the Sanitary Commission, and that there was no use in my asking it. Not very decidedly, but he thought so. He said nothing would or could be done about the Med. Bureau for two or three weeks, at any rate. And though he did not quite say so, I know that he thought that nothing would be done about it, this session, and he don't mean to waste his time, energy and spend his influence, in trying to carry a thing which very likely can't be carried, and which is not considered of first rate importance. He can be worked up to it, but against his inclinations and without much heart.

253

All that we can hope to do next week, as far as Congress is concerned, is to make reconnaissance in force, and then hold a council of war, with reference to approaches, and a final assault some weeks afterwards.

If we can carry the Committees we can probably carry Congress: if not, not. Therefore your lobby agent should be appointed solely with reference to the Committees, & mainly on account of a known social advantage with certain members of the Committees.[3]

I have little hope that, do our best, we can carry anything thro', till after the Surg[n] Gene[l] has been changed.

Therefore let the business be, first, to prevail upon the Secy of War, to *act*, at once, next Thursday, to remove Finley. Then, if that can be done, feel Congress, make a demonstration with individuals, and leave D[r] Hammond[4] to plan the final battle. If you don't succeed with the Secy of War—Troy was. I fear our usefulness is ended.

Yours Very Cordially &c

Fred. Law Olmsted.

P.S. Sunday morning: I have prepared a formal request to the Secy of War to receive a Committee[5] (naming the members) of the citizens of New York, with Committees of similar character from Phil[a] & Boston, with the President & Exec. Com. of the San. Com.[6] on Thursday morning. They wish a confidential interview to present a proposition of importance affecting the efficiency of the army. I shall try to see Marcy[7] tomorrow. My impression is that there should be two addresses to the Secy. One from a representative of the citizens—the people—(Ruggles)[8] complaining *in general terms* of the *inefficiency and inadequacy* of the medical care of the volunteers, demanding a much higher standard of care for them than has been felt to be sufficient in old times for hireling armies. The impression being that our army medical system compares fairly with that of some of the old despotic armies, but that something much better is wanted under present circumstances, without specifying very distinctly what. Then in a second address from the Pres[t] of the San. Commission, let the specific facts be stated, the necessity for a sweeping reform and radical remedy expounded, and a history given of what has been done and promised, and neglected and delayed. Then urge instant decision and action, and get this promised, contingent upon Gen[l] McClellan's approval. That will have been already secured.

The original is in box 641 of USSC-NYPL. Olmsted wrote this letter on stationery that carried the printed date "1861" and he did not correct it.

1. Olmsted, in an earlier letter that day, had proposed a new strategy after he learned that Francis P. Blair, Jr., chairman of the Committee on Military Affairs in the House of Representatives, had introduced a bill which Robert C. Wood had drawn up to reorganize the Medical Bureau. Olmsted worried that this bill might further impede passage of the measure favored by the Sanitary Commission and was pessimistic about the Commission's ability to influence him. Olmsted offered a new plan: "Would it not be better that instead of acting immediately on Congress, we return to our original program &c, and that these delegations, representing the Medical faculty and the Life Insurance Companies, and the relatives of the volunteers, in Boston, New York *and* Philadelphia, wait on the new Secretary of War and ask of him to retire Dr Finley and appoint Dr Hammond Acting Surgeon General."

    His final sentences read: "If you adopt it, I want Dr Van Buren to prepare a sharp, distinct Bill of Indictment against Finley which can be signed by the delegations—not the Sanitary Commission. I propose that the San Com. shall, officially, have nothing more to do in the matter. It has done its work in investigating the facts and presenting the result" (FLO to HWB, Jan. 18, 1862, USSC-NYPL, box 641).

2. Henry Wilson (1812–1875), U.S. senator from Massachusetts, and Lafayette Sabine Foster (1806–1880), U.S. senator from Connecticut. Wilson was a self-made man who had been prominent in Massachusetts politics successively as a Whig, a Know-Nothing, and a Republican. As chairman of the Senate Committee on Military Affairs, he worked tirelessly to improve the nation's army. During the campaign to reform the Medical Bureau, Olmsted came to distrust Wilson and in September 1862 classed him among the Republican leaders who were "liars, pettifoggers and sneaks." Olmsted further declared, "He lies and jumps the fence faster and more freely than any man I ever knew except one."

    Foster, a lawyer, had represented Norwich in the Connecticut General Assembly and had also been an unsuccessful Whig candidate before his election as a Republican in 1854 to the U.S. Senate. An invaluable ally of Olmsted's, he introduced in the Senate the bill that Olmsted proposed on the Port Royal question. After failing to gain the Republican nomination during his quest for a third term in 1866, Foster subsequently received an appointment to a state court judgeship (*DAB*; *BDAC*; FLO to Edward Hartshorne, Feb. 5, 1862, USSC-NYPL, box 833, 2: 560–62; FLO to CLB, Sept. 20, 1862, below).

3. On January 17 Bellows had told Olmsted, "The Committee of Associates strongly advise the employment of some able *lobbyist*, at an expense, if necessary $500, to be raised by private subscription, for a continued pressure on the Senate & House" (HWB to FLO, Jan. 17, 1862, USSC-NYPL, box 738: 162).

4. Dr. William Alexander Hammond, the choice of the Sanitary Commission for the post of surgeon general.

5. That day Olmsted wrote to Stanton asking that he meet with a New York citizens' committee consisting of Samuel B. Ruggles; prominent businessmen Moses H. Grinnell, Robert B. Minturn, Frederick Winston, and Stewart Brown; and physicians Alonzo Clark, William Van Buren, and Cornelius R. Agnew (FLO to Edwin M. Stanton, Jan. 18, 1862, Record Group 107, Off. of Sec. of War, Letters Recd., 0–17 [102], box 263, National Archives and Records Service, Washington, D.C.).

6. In October 1861 George Templeton Strong had proposed

    that an executive and finance committee be appointed, to consist of five members, who shall meet at least once in each week in the city of New York, when the Commission is not sitting, and that all bills exceeding twenty dollars in amount (except freight and telegraph expenses, and except payments to officers of the Commission,) as hereinafter provided, be certified by each committee before payment by the Treasurer.

    Henry W. Bellows, Cornelius R. Agnew, Wolcott Gibbs, William Van Buren, and

Strong were then appointed to this newly formed committee. It was relatively inactive until the summer of 1862, but after that time played an increasingly important role in the formation of policy and the direction of activities for the Commission (USSC, *Minutes*, pp. 72–73).
7. Randolph Barnes Marcy (1812–1887), colonel and chief of staff for his son-in-law, George B. McClellan (*DAB*).
8. Samuel Bulkley Ruggles (1800–1881), a prominent New York City civic leader and father-in-law of George Templeton Strong. Ruggles had been a successful lawyer and a member of the state legislature and had served for eighteen years as president of the state board of canal commissioners. He also wrote numerous articles on economic topics. As an associate member of the Sanitary Commission, Ruggles took part in the meeting that passed resolutions calling for reform of the Medical Bureau; and he was appointed to the committee that visited Washington (*DAB*; *Diary of the Civil War*, p. 201).

To Bertha Olmsted

> Sanitary Commission, Washington, D.C.
> 28th January 1862.

Dear Bertha,

I was glad to get your note last week, not having heard from father or any of you for a long time. I ought to write oftener, but I have so much hard writing to do, that all writing has got to be a task to me, and it is not natural to task one's self with going home. I am always grateful to hear from you and ought to know that you want to hear from me.

It is a good big work I have in hand, giving me absorbing occupation and that sort of connection with the work of the nation without which I should be very uncomfortable. I am rather close, morally and materially, to Head Quarters. We had McClellan and the new Sec'y of War in our office a few days ago.[1] The latter makes a most satisfactory impression—so much better than Cameron, that I wonder we could ever have hoped to be successful while he remained. He is strong, energetic and careful. McClellan shows the wear and tear very much, being not nearly as well as when I last saw him closely. I had some personal conversation with him and Stanton, each—but nothing was said of interest. My ideas of McClellan do not change. He is a splendid general for the field—not the man for a cabinet office at all. As Cameron was not & Stanton is, in my judgment; McC. will, now, I hope, have a better chance.

I believe people here are coming more generally to the opinion which I have held, that we must succeed by a slow, tedious, patient process—not by a grand coup. I don't believe in the immediate advance,

GEORGE BRINTON McCLELLAN AND HIS WIFE, ELLEN MARCY McCLELLAN

(the everlasting immediate advance) and don't want it.[2] The volunteers won't fight a grand battle and it's simple stupid recklessness which would make them try for it. They will want years of preparation before they will be soldiers—much longer time than other people—not because themselves unadapted, but because wanting officers able to discipline & instruct them.

We have had here the last week, to help get some regeneration of the Medical Bureau, a Committee of solid men of New York & Philad[a]— Stewart Brown (Brown Bro.),[3] Aspinwall,[4] Minturn[5] & so on. D[r] Bellows & others of the Commiss[n] also, though it is not a Commission meeting. We

257

were before the Committee of military affairs of the House yesterday (Blair, Chairman) & today before Committee of the Senate, Wilson, Chairman.[6] D[r] B. addressed them at some length & then we had a general talk. Blair impressed me very favorably. Wilson we thought the worst of his Committee, a slippery clever fellow—Preston King[7] the best man on it. We shall help to other important improvements besides in the Med. bureau.

Called on Chase last night, to talk about Port Royal and urge something done to have niggers put to work & crops planted in February. Couldn't do much, he is so overwhelmed with the main financial problem.[8] Can't think of matters of a few million. Miss Chase,[9] a nice girl; sensible young lady at that. Called on Forster[10] tonight on same matter seeing he called for information today. He bites better. Noble woman his wife[11] is. Really the finest in Washington, I guess. She is working well in hospitals—& with poor Mrs. Lincoln, who is a thin specimen of a Western woman.[12] Old Abe, on the other hand, grows in our respect. A straight forward, shrewd, quaint, ready and rough old codger. There are no great men here—(Stanton & Chase nearest to it) & the low, obscure, mysterious strength of the free and unenlightened people bears all along and is to carry us through this grand period without heroes or philosophers. So it now seems. What a great humiliating lesson will it be to those miserable infidels of democracy and lusters after strange gods of despotism—if we do by & by walk them down.

I think we shall; all our difficulties strengthen us for it—for thorough work.

I live—board at Willard's—work all night & sleep half the day, at my office—after the manner of the Olmsteds—and am very well.

The reason I haven't sent for Ally[13] is that since father spoke of it, we have always had an overplus of volunteer, gratuitous aid, for such work as he could be useful in—therefore it wouldn't be right to pay his expenses.

The San. Com. by the by is in good financial condition—$10,000 at least in hand, & more promised when we shall need it.

Love & good cheer to you all

Fred.

P.S. I have just been calling on Mrs McClellan[14] who receivd me at once with great cordiality, as the brother of her friends in Hartford, and sent her love to you both. She is very pretty, and seems soundly amiable & good. They live apparently in good & not at all grand style.

1. George B. McClellan and Edwin M. Stanton called at the Sanitary Commission's offices on the afternoon of January 23, 1862 (Thomas A. Scott, memorandum, Jan. 22, 1862, written on the back of FLO to Thomas A. Scott, Jan. 22, 1862, USSC-NYPL, box 748: 3256).
2. A reference to public clamoring for the Army of the Potomac to attack Confederate troops in northern Virginia (*War for the Union*, 2: 395, 404–8).
3. Stewart Brown (d. 1880), son of the Stewart Brown who, with his brother Alexander Brown, founded the banking firm Brown Brothers & Company with branches in New York, Philadelphia, Baltimore, and Liverpool. The younger Stewart Brown worked in the family business in New York. He was very active in humanitarian and religious organizations such as the American Bible Association, the Association for Improving the Condition of the Poor, and the Young Men's Christian Association (*New-York Times*, Feb. 1, 1880, p. 5).
4. William Henry Aspinwall (1807–1875), a wealthy New York merchant who had increased his already considerable fortune by building the Panama Railroad across the isthmus and securing a monopoly of the shipping and passenger trade between the East and California. A prominent patron of the arts and a supporter of Lincoln's policies, he helped found the Union League Club of New York (*DAB*).
5. Robert B. Minturn.
6. In January 1862 the Senate Committee on Military Affairs was chaired by Henry Wilson and included Preston King of New York, Henry Smith Lane of Indiana, James Henry Lane of Kansas, Milton S. Latham of California, Henry M. Rice of Minnesota, and James W. Nesmith of Oregon. Wilson, King, and both Lanes were Republicans. At that time the House Committee on Military Affairs was chaired by Francis P. Blair, Jr., of Missouri, and its members included William A. Richardson of Illinois, James Buffinton of Massachusetts, Abraham B. Olin of New York, William Allen of Ohio, Hendrick B. Wright of Pennsylvania, Gilman Marston of New Hampshire, and William McKee Dunn of Indiana. Blair, Buffinton, Olin, Marston, and Dunn were Republicans (*Congressional Globe*, 37th Cong., 1st sess., 1861, 39: 2, 22; ibid., 2nd sess., 1861–62, 40: 9, 19).
7. Preston King (1806–1865), U.S. senator from New York. A member of the free-soil wing of the Democratic party, King in 1846 supported the Wilmot Proviso, which would have prohibited the extension of slavery to any territory acquired as a result of the Mexican War. He left the Democratic party after passage of the Kansas-Nebraska Act and supported Frémont's candidacy for the presidency in 1856. After service in the House of Representatives, he was elected to the Senate in 1857 but did not seek reelection in 1863.

   During the Civil War, King was a supporter of Lincoln's policies, and members of the Sanitary Commission considered him sympathetic to their viewpoint. In May 1862 Bellows thanked King for his role in the passage of the bill reorganizing the Medical Bureau and asked his aid in influencing the appointments that were to be made according to the provisions of that bill. When Olmsted became convinced in July 1862 that conscription was necessary to sustain the Union war effort, he conveyed his views to King (*DAB*; HWB to P. King, May 9, 1862, USSC-NYPL, box 638; HWB to P. King, May 27, 1862, USSC-NYPL, box 741: 1165; FLO to P. King, July 9, 1862, below).
8. The "main financial problem" troubling Salmon P. Chase in January 1862 was the state of the nation's currency. Although in 1861 Congress authorized the U.S. Treasury to issue fifty million dollars in paper money, only specie (gold and silver coin) was legal tender. Whether additional paper money should be issued and whether it should be legal tender were questions under debate in Congress (L. P. Curry, *Blueprint for Modern America*, pp. 181–96).
9. Catherine (Kate) Chase (1840–1899), Salmon P. Chase's attractive and vivacious daughter. Gifted with great charm and ambition as well as a keen interest in politics,

she served as her widowed father's hostess during the Civil War and gave some of Washington's most glittering parties. In 1863 she wed William Sprague, a wealthy industrialist and former governor and U.S. senator from Rhode Island. The marriage was not happy and ended in divorce (*Notable American Women*).

10. Senator Lafayette S. Foster had indeed become more interested in the Port Royal question. On the day Olmsted met with him, Foster introduced a resolution, unanimously approved by the Senate, which directed the secretary of the treasury to report whether any legislation would be necessary to take charge of and cultivate cotton lands at Port Royal or to "provide suitably" for and employ the blacks there (*Congressional Globe*, 37th Cong., 2nd sess., 1861–62, 40: 505).

11. Martha Lyman Foster (c. 1822–1903), Foster's second wife, who was from Northampton, Massachusetts, and had married him in 1860 (*DAB*, s.v. "Foster, Lafayette Sabine"; "Mrs. L. S. Foster Dies," *New York Times*, Jan. 21, 1903, p. 9).

12. A joking reference to Mary Todd Lincoln's plumpness.

13. Albert Henry Olmsted (1842–1929), Olmsted's younger half-brother (*Papers of FLO*, 1: 143, 399).

14. Ellen Marcy McClellan (1835–1915), daughter of army officer Randolph Barnes Marcy, had married George B. McClellan in May 1860. Her acquaintance with Olmsted's half-sisters Mary and Bertha presumably dated from the period when she attended school in Hartford (William Starr Myers, *A Study in Personality: General George Brinton McClellan* [New York, 1934], pp. 124–26, 153, 512).

To George Frederic Magoun[1]

6 February [186]2

To the Rev. Geo. Magoun:
Secy Iowa Army Sanitary Commission
Sir:

I yesterday received your favor of January 28th, in which you suggest that a connection should be formed between your Association and the Sanitary Commission. You do not state the object to be gained by the connection, nor indicate any advantage which would arise from it. As there will be sufficient time for letters to be exchanged between us before the next meeting of the Commission, at which it will give me pleasure to propose any plan of connection which you may think desirable, I should be glad to hear further from you on this point.

You will excuse me for reminding you of a few circumstances which must influence the Commission in whatever action it may conclude to take.

Our loyal fellow countrymen in Tennessee are suffering persecution, their crops and cattle have been taken for the support of the rebel hordes, their houses burned, their stores plundered.[2] Sick and weary, thousands hide in the mountains biding their time. How they support life, God knows. They certainly have nothing to spare, and though many of them have broken through the defensive lines of the enemy, if they had to spare, it would not be possible to send their goods where they are more wanted than they are at this moment in Tennessee. But of those who have escaped, the strong and healthy men to the number of two or three thousand, are fighting our battles in Kentucky[3] side by side with your Iowan heroes. Those who are not strong and well fill the homes of our noble and hard tried brethren of "the dark and bloody ground," and these have enough to do to provide for their necessities.

Virginia, in like manner ravaged by War, furnishes seven thousand men to fight the battles of our common country.

This Commission received the other day seventeen thousand dollars in hard cash, collected in one of the states of New England. It has received within two months in hospital stores, from the same state, sufficient supplies for ten times as many men as that state has sent to the field. The troops of Iowa and Virginia and of Tennessee have received within two months at least as great advantages from these contributions as those of that state.

Do you wish Iowa troops to be dependent on the contributions of New England? On the other hand, do you wish to spurn for Iowan volunteers the patriotic offerings of New England? Would you at such a time as this say to New England: "Mind your own business," would you say to Virginia and Tennessee, "Take care of your own sick folks and we will take care of ours"?

Suppose that in the next battle in Kentucky the brunt should be borne by Iowans and some thousand of them should be thrown on the Surgeons' hands—do you wish that the Surgeons should refuse all assistance for them until it can be sent from Iowa? Would you be unwilling that they should be dependent for a time on the provision for such an emergency to which the women of New England have contributed so liberally? Whether you would or not; they will be so dependent: they have been so dependent; and at this moment some of your Iowan sick, I do not doubt, rest on beds sent from New England, and their strength is sustained by wine sent from New-York.

This being so, are you willing that when in the next battle in Virginia the husbands and fathers and sons and brothers of the women of New England are brought low, Iowa shall have contributed nothing (except in the form of a tax) by which their lives also can be cherished?

Of course I do not ask these questions reproachfully; upon their answer seems to me to depend the answer which should be made to your proposal. In the work of this Commission no State is known; all contributions to it are to a common stock, for the Army of a common country. It has received, as it happens, by far the most from those states for whose men it has done least. Whether aided by Iowa or not, it will be as ready to aid Iowa, as to aid New York, New England, Ohio, or Tennessee.

You may ask how far it has done so? I do not know because I have never thought of asking how far it has aided one or another. I know that its agents, under their orders, can never regard one and disregard another.

To be more explicit, however, I will give the outlines of the arrangements of the Commission for collecting and supplying hospital stores.

Dépôts for hospital supplies are established at different points, with reference to accessibility for different columns of the Army. Four of these are at the four largest seaports; one at Washington, for the Army of the Potomac; one at Wheeling for Western Virginia and Kentucky; one at Louisville; one at Cairo, and one at St. Louis for the columns operating in the Mississippi valley and Missouri. Another will probably be established soon further West. There is also one at Port Royal; one at the Tortugas, and one at Ship Island.[4] At each of these dépôts it is intended to keep a stock of hospital goods in reserve. A further reserve is also usually maintained at Cleveland intermediate between those of the East and West, and which is intended to be drawn upon both from the East and West upon occasion.

There are three associate secretaries of the Commission, one of whom is responsible that the goods given in charge to the Commission are distributed as far as possible to those most in need of them on the Atlantic. The second is in like manner responsible for the necessary distribution to the Armies between the Alleghanies and the Mississippi, the third for those west of the Mississippi.[5] The duty of the latter is however complicated and embarrassed somewhat by the existence of a Commission[6] organized by General Fremont, which has undertaken to do the same work in the same field, believing that it can do so harmoniously without being in subordination to the same rules. The national Commission has thought best, while it regards the arrangement as a bad one, to yield to the wishes of the excellent men at St Louis, who under official sanction, have established a local institution which they are perhaps, natura[lly] indisposed to make merely auxiliary to the national system. This local institution however, while it has an independent dépôt and makes independent collections therefor, and exercises duties other than those undertaken by the Commission, is perfectly national and catholic in its purpose. Although its members all live in St Louis it takes thought as much for the sick Illinoisian or Ohioan, as for the sick [St.] Louisian or Missourian. It can therefore work harmoniously with the Commission. The Commission is, however, obliged in order to carry out its plan completely, to maintain an independent dépôt at St Louis free of any provincial control, and always ready like those in New York, Cleveland, and Washington, to serve any demands of the sick and wounded of the Army or Navy anywhere they may arise. At any of these dépôts contributions are received from the various societies of patriotic women throughout the land counting by hundreds in every state [east] of Iowa and north of Kentucky, and including some in Kentucky as well. It is not known, and it never will be known, how much the women of one state have given, and how little those of another. All who contribute, contribute freely according to their means, to a common stock.

The advantage of this common stock thus divided is almost daily illustrated. For instance:

A considerable force has been recently massed and placed in movement in the mountain region of Virginia, west of the field previously occupied by the Army of the Potomac and east of that occupied by the Army of Western Virginia. Owing to the difficulty of transportion, this force was without tents, and being obliged to bivouac in bad weather at mid-winter in a highland region, a large sick list was rapidly formed. An inspector of the Commission had been sent a week ago to look after it,[7] but it was not till the day before yesterday that information of its wants was received by the Associate Secretary of the Commission for the army of the Potomac to which the column was subordinate. To send goods to the position in question from Washington, or any of the Eastern dépôts, it would have been necessary to move them several days' journey by waggon, and with considerable hazard. A supply of hospital stores for a thousand patients was consequently ordered by telegraph from Wheeling whence, although needed for the Army of the Potomac, it was sent by Railroad at least sixty miles nearer to the point of demand, than it could have been by any Railroad from the East. At the same time, the agent at Wheeling was advised by telegraph that if his supply ran short it would immediately be replenished from Cleveland and those in charge of the dépôt at Cleveland were advised that although the dépôts at New York and Philadelphia had been drawn low to supply Naval Expeditions, a considerable reserve existed at Boston, upon which, if they were not amply provided for all probable demands from Kentucky and Missouri, they should immediately make requisition. This, however, was found to be unnecessary, the industry of the women of Michigan, Western New York, and Ohio, having at this time supplied a very large accumulation at Cleveland.

There has been no time to my knowledge during the last six months when any demand made upon any one of the dépôts of the Commission has failed to be met, and yet the Commission has been during all that time giving out to hospitals nearly two thousand articles of clothing every day, and no Surgeon has allowed a want of hospital clothing in his regiment to become known to the Commission or to any of its twenty Camp Inspectors, or other agents, that a supply has not been immediately placed at his disposal. Since our dépôts were fairly established at Cleveland, Wheeling, Cairo, and St Louis, I am not aware that any demand upon any one of them has failed to be met at once. Nevertheless, urgent appeals have been frequently made by ignorant persons to New England, New York, New Jersey, and Pennsylvania for goods immediately needed for a regimental hospital within fifty or a hundred miles of those dépôts and many tons of freight have been conveyed unnecessarily and at great cost from the Atlantic to the Mississippi in answer to such appeals.

The Commission cannot engage that its dépôts always will be fully supplied, it cannot engage that all proper demands upon it shall be met. This will depend upon what is supplied to it. It can engage, having better means of information than any organization of a local character, or any not in immediate communication with the War department can have, that what it receives shall as far as possible be so distributed as to be of the greatest good to the greatest number of soldiers of the Union, come whence they may, go where they may.

At each dépôt where goods are received to a considerable amount by direct contribution, there are local organizations auxiliary to the Commission, composed of its Associate Members and other men, with a body of women, and young people, who undertake the onerous labor and expense of opening, assorting, packing and accounting for goods, and of the necessary correspondence. These auxiliary organizations also frequently purchase articles needed by the sick, which they fail to [receive] as contributions in kind, in sufficient quantity. They pay the local rents, &c. A large working staff is constantly required and is maintained for these purposes. An expenditure of many thousand dollars in each case has thus been saved the Treasury of the Commission.

There are many hundred sub dépôts maintained in the same manner, again auxiliary to these, no one of which however is expected to be constantly ready to meet a sudden demand as is the case with the regular directly auxiliary dépôts of the Commission among which besides those already named, there is a very important one at Chicago, for the State of Illinois: another at Cincinnati for Southern Ohio, &c.

If the good people of Iowa believe that they can best serve the common cause by directing their energies exclusively to the supply of their own neighbors and relatives gone to the War, it is no part of my duty, nor am I disposed to argue against that conviction. At the same time, I cannot conceal that my own judgment is led to a different conclusion, and it is within my duty to fully explain and justify the plan of the organization I represent, which plan would certainly fail if none should take a different view of their duty, from that which I find indicated in your letters and publications.[8] There seems to me to be a stain of the very soil, out of which the monster Secession has grown, when such a complete machinery as you have formed in Iowa is confined in its operations by State lines.

But if you contribute to the common stock, it may be asked what assurance will you have that Iowans will not be neglected? I might ask in reply what assurance has Massachusetts, New York, or Ohio? But a better answer is found in the fact, that no Surgeon from Iowa or anywhere else, has for months past asked for a single article which it was not in his power to get, as a right directly from a Government source, that it has not been supplied to the full extent of the entire resources of the Commission, and as soon as possible.

That the Iowan hospitals have nevertheless wanted much is to be accounted for

1st By the constant movements and frequent changes in the plan of the campaign in Missouri[9] which for a time rendered all attempts at systematic supply abortive.

2nd The failure of the arrangements instituted under General Fremont to relieve the national Commission of duty in Missouri, it having been understood that these would render unnecessary if not impertinent any undertaking on its part to provide systematically for the wants of the forces within the field of the St Louis organization.

3rd The neglect of the Surgeons to call upon the Commission,— excusable when it is considered what a variety of sources they are invited to resort to for the same articles, as for instance, first the government stores, second, the Sanitary Commission, third, the St Louis Sanitary Commission, fourth, the Iowa Army Sanitary Commission, fifth, various village Sanitary Commissions, which, as I observe by your report, supply directly as well as through your state organization, sixth, Eastern Local Societies, seventh, Church Societies &c. in St Louis, eighth, individual benevolence.

I am advised that an impression prevails with you that our organization has chiefly confined its operations to the East. On the contrary, the very first action of the Commission after its complete organization, before it looked at the Army in Maryland was to send its president along with a special resident Western Secretary to look after the Troops then beginning to concentrate in Illinois and Missouri. The first Iowa Volunteers were visited by the President of the Commission and Dr Newberry in June last and before the Commission had met in Washington except in part for the purpose of organizing.[10]

You observe in your own report of a visit to the hospitals at Mound City, on the Mississippi, the largest Military hospital in the United States: "The Surgeons assured us that they could not possibly carry it out, but for the Sanitary Commission. Said one, 'You will find a hundred articles here from the Sanitary Commission where you will find one from the Government.'" By reference to our report of operations in the West for the three months ending 30th November, you will see that these supplies were from our dépôts at New York and Cleveland, and that at that time upwards of 90,000 articles had been sent from the Cleveland depot alone, to Western hospitals. In the first report of the Chicago branch of the Commission p. 4, you will find reference to "repeated visits of the members of the U.S. Sanitary Commission to the camps and hospitals at Cairo."[11]

The meetings of the Commission are held at Washington, because Washington is the headquarters of the Army, and the seat of Government, with whom it is a part of the duty of the Commission to constantly advise. A majority of the members of its central board reside in the East, because it is necessary that they should be frequently and quickly assembled. For the same reason its Central Office is established at Washington.

If the army of the Potomac has been better supplied than that of Missouri, it is because the former has been closely concentrated and at rest. Systematic provision for it has therefore been more practicable. But precisely the same machinery of supply has been extended throughout the West. And as soon as it became apparent that the Commission should re-assume the duty of providing for the forces in Missouri, one of its Secretaries, familiar with all the details of its operations in Maryland, was sent to reside in Missouri, and all the resources of the Commission placed at his command.[12] Obviously however, if other organizations undertake the supply of the hospitals in Missouri, obtaining their supplies from the neighboring sources, our Secretary for Missouri must either enter into a competition with them for these supplies, or obtain supplies at greater and unnecessary cost from other sources, which he can have no certainty will be required.

The explanation I have thus given of the existing arrangements of the Commission will, I trust enable you the more readily and definitely to determine in what manner your very efficient State organization can be honorably and advantageously brought into connection with it.

The Commission will probably meet at Washington about the 20th inst.

Reciprocating your assurance of sympathy in the cause and the work

I am most respectfully yours

(Signed) Fred. Law Olmsted
General Secretary

The text is taken from a letterpress copy in a copyist's handwriting in volume 2, pages 548–601 of box 833, in USSC-NYPL. A printed version appears as part of document number 60 published by the Sanitary Commission.

1. George Frederic Magoun (1821–1896), Congregational clergyman. A Maine native who studied theology at Andover and Yale, he held pastorates in Illinois and Wisconsin before moving to Iowa. In 1862 he was pastor of the Congregational Church in Lyons, Iowa. Magoun, who was a Republican in politics, worked for antislavery and temperance reform. He later served as president of Iowa College (today known as Grinnell College) for twenty years (*DAB*).
2. Much of East Tennessee was strongly Unionist in sentiment, but the Confederates were willing to take strong measures to control that area. By November 1861 Confederate officials were imprisoning Unionist leaders, disarming Unionist followers, and confiscating crops. Guerrilla warfare between Confederate and Unionist sympathizers added atrocities on both sides (James Welch Patton, *Unionism and Reconstruction in Tennessee, 1860–1869* [Chapel Hill, N.C., 1934]; Ellis Merton Coulter, *William G. Brownlow*, [Knoxville, Tenn., 1971], pp. 162–74).
3. Approximately two thousand Tennesseans slipped into Kentucky through the mountain passes and joined the Union army at Camp Dick Robinson near Lexington. Before January 1862 the battles in Kentucky, a state which had long been known as "the dark and bloody ground," were little more than skirmishes. On January 19, 1862, Union troops commanded by Gen. George H. Thomas defeated Confederate forces under the command of Gen. George B. Crittenden at Mills Springs (Logan's Cross Roads) near the Cumberland River in southeastern Kentucky (E. M. Coulter, *William G. Brownlow*, p. 166; Frederick H. Dyer, *A Compendium of the War of the Rebellion*, 3 vols. [1908; rpt. ed., New York, 1959], 2: 731; *War for the Union*, 2: 12).
4. The "four largest seaports" here mentioned by Olmsted are Boston, New York, Philadelphia, and Baltimore. The Dry Tortugas are islands lying west of the Florida Keys and north of Havana, Cuba; and Ship Island is located south of Biloxi, Mississippi, in the Mississippi Sound of the Gulf of Mexico.
5. J. Foster Jenkins was associate secretary for the Atlantic region, John S. Newberry for the central region, and John H. Douglas for the region west of the Mississippi (doc. no. 40 in USSC, *Documents*, p. 72).
6. The Western Sanitary Commission.
7. On January 29, 1862, Olmsted ordered Gordon Winslow, a Sanitary Commission inspector, to inspect troops under the command of Gen. Frederick W. Lander in the western Virginia mountains near Cumberland, Maryland. Lander's division, actually a part of the Army of West Virginia rather than the Army of the Potomac as Olmsted reports, was being ravaged by illness. Even before Winslow's report arrived, Olmsted learned from the general's wife that one thousand soldiers from that division were ill in Cumberland. Olmsted immediately telegraphed Sanitary Commission depots at Cleveland and Wheeling to send nurses and hospital supplies to Cumberland (F. H. Dyer, *Compendium of the War of the Rebellion*, 1: 335; Gordon Winslow to FLO, Jan. 29, 1862, USSC-NYPL, box 728: 252; FLO to JSN, Feb. 3, 1862, USSC-NYPL, box 909, 1: 213; FLO to Mary Bull Olmsted, Feb. 3, 1862 (in the possession of Terry Niles Smith); FLO to JSN, Feb. 8, 1862, USSC-NYPL, box 909, 1: 265).
8. In his letter of January 28, 1862, Magoun noted that he had sent a circular of the Iowa Army Sanitary Commission and a report on sick and wounded Iowan soldiers which presumably was the document that Olmsted later in this letter to Magoun refers to as "your own report of a visit to the hospital at Mound City" (G. F. Magoun to HWB, Jan. 28, 1862, USSC-NYPL, box 738: 247).
9. A reference to the series of advances and retreats by the Union army in western Missouri. Defeats at Wilson's Creek and at Lexington drove out Union troops in September 1861. As commander of the department, Frémont then moved west in October to reoccupy Springfield. When he was relieved of command early in November, his successor, Gen. David Hunter, ordered yet another retreat eastward.

Gen. Henry W. Halleck assumed command in mid-November and sent Gen. Samuel R. Curtis to recapture Springfield and southwest Missouri (James Monaghan, *Civil War on the Western Border, 1854–1865* [Boston, 1955], pp. 181–83, 191–94, 203–8).

10. Henry W. Bellows and John S. Newberry visited Cincinnati, Cairo, and St. Louis in late June and early July 1861. Bellows's only reference to the 1st Iowa in his report was the statement that "General Lyon has also an Iowa regiment with him." The 1st Iowa volunteered for only three months and after service under Gen. Nathaniel S. Lyon, it was mustered out on August 21, 1861 (Henry W. Bellows, "Notes of a Preliminary Sanitary Survey of the Forces of the United States in the Ohio and Mississippi Valleys, near Midsummer, 1861," doc. no. 26 in USSC, *Documents*; F. H. Dyer, *Compendium of the War of the Rebellion*, 1: 141).

11. A paraphrase of the statement on page 3 of "Report on the Condition of Camps and Hospitals at Cairo and Vicinity, Paducah and St. Louis . . . October 1861," written by William W. Patton and R. N. Isham of the Sanitary Commission's Chicago branch and published by the Commission as document number 38.

12. Associate Secretary John H. Douglas arrived in St. Louis on December 16 to oversee the Sanitary Commission's work in Missouri (J. H. Douglas to FLO, Dec. 16, 1861, USSC-NYPL, box 731: 1382).

To Henry Whitney Bellows

United States Sanitary Commission,
7ᵗʰ Febry 1862

My Dear Doctor,

As you will see, I have written a very long reply to the letter of the Secy of the Iowa Army Sanitary Commission,[1] which you directed me to "attend to." The reason for doing so is this: Having re-read all his papers here,[2] I was conscious of an odor of dishonesty in them—an under-tone of special-pleading, and I wanted, if we were to have anything to do with them, to clear this away first. Then I thought it best that the business should not all be left to the Secretary who certainly has given out, whether intentionally or not, that the Sanitary Commission does not want to bother with the relief work, and I thought that if I sent him a formidable document like this, he couldn't so well have it all to himself. Besides I thought they were wrong—working in a mean way—and if I could get them to see that it appeared so, I might bring them right. And I think if we had them right, it would give us a great leverage to right the St. Louis business.

I send the document, however, for your approval.

If you approve, I have half a mind to print it, so that it may be laid before the constituency of the Secretary—and others who need to be told the value of the Union in matters concrete as well as abstract.

Senator Harris,[3] by the way, remarked yesterday, that the expulsion of Bright,[4] was the end of States' Rights.

It is, as I anticipated it would be, when you all left, not a step is made toward the reform of the Med. Bureau. I do not think it will do any good for me to stir them. Give them a fortnight more and then march in full force again.

By the way, it is time, the next meeting should be arranged for. When shall it be.

They are calling in Phil[a] for the General Order.[5] So is Newberry. Neither the Department nor the General have done anything yet to right things, and they evidently feel annoyed in Philad[a]. Did you notice that Clymer[6] had been appointed Brigade Surgeon? I suppose he takes it as a step to one of the Inspectorships.

Three days ago, I wrote the Gen[l] reminding of his promise about the General Order, and telling him of the Philadelphia call, and of Rogers' having been told in effect, by Aberdie that he could not inspect the Columbia hospital, under authority of the Commission—which happened last Saturday.[7] I have seen one of the officers who is to enquire into the alledged starvation at Alexandria hospitals, and given him my views of the facts, which are simply that Sheldon[8] ran the Hospital fund $200 in debt to get what he thought indispensible, and that the new doctor has been working off that debt by bringing the volunteers down to old fashioned army hospital diet.

How strange it is nothing more is heard from Burnside?[9]

The mud grows daily deeper and liquider and dark, damp weather continues.

Yours sincerely

Fred. Law Olmsted.

The original is in box 641 of USSC-NYPL. The last three paragraphs (comprising two manuscript pages) had mistakenly been appended to a letter of May 4, 1862, from Olmsted to Bellows, but the references to the letter to George McClellan and the Burnside expedition clearly show that they instead belong to this letter.

1. See FLO to George Frederic Magoun, February 6, 1861, above.
2. Ibid., note 8.
3. Ira Harris (1802–1875), a Republican elected to the U.S. Senate from New York in 1860 (BDAC).
4. The expulsion of Jesse David Bright (1812–1875), a proslavery Indiana Democrat, from the U.S. Senate. On February 5, 1862, the Senate voted by a margin of 32 to 14 to expel Bright, who had addressed Jefferson Davis as president of the Confederacy and also had opposed coercion of the seceding states, for disloyalty. In 1863 Bright

unsuccessfully attempted to regain the Senate seat he had held for seventeen years (*BDAC*; *Congressional Globe*, 37th Cong., 2nd sess., 1861–62, 40: 644–55).

5. The Sanitary Commission had been endeavoring for some time to persuade George B. McClellan to issue a general order giving official approval of and authority for its inspection of military camps and hospitals. As part of the Commission's campaign, a Philadelphia delegation of associate members called for the conferral of this authority (Edward Hartshorne to FLO, Feb. 3, 1862, USSC-NYPL, box 739: 302).

6. Meredith Clymer (1817–1902) was appointed surgeon of volunteers in December 1861. Educated at the University of Pennsylvania, he had practiced medicine in Philadelphia and had taught at Franklin Medical College; Hampden-Sydney College, near Farmville, Virginia; and the College of Physicians and Surgeons in New York (F. B. Heitman, *Historical Register and Dictionary*, 1: 312; Howard Atwood Kelly and Walter Lincoln Burrage, *Dictionary of American Medical Biography: Lives of Eminent Physicians of the United States and Canada . . .* [New York, 1928], p. 236).

7. On February 5 Olmsted had asked McClellan for "the immediate issue of the proposed General Order defining our right of Enquiry." Olmsted argued that the Philadelphia associate members of the Commission (in which McClellan's older brother, a physician, was active) wanted "a definition of their proper relation to the army." As further justification for his request, Olmsted related a problem encountered by Sanitary Commission agent Henry B. Rogers when he wished to inspect a military hospital whose chief surgeon was Eugene H. Abadie, a career army physician (FLO to G. B. McClellan, Feb. 5, 1862, USSC-NYPL, box 833, 2: 557–58; Guy V. Henry, *Military Record of Civilian Appointments in the United States Army*, 2 vols. [New York, 1870], 1: 51).

8. Henry Lawrence Sheldon, a career army physician who in 1861 had been stationed at the military hospital in Alexandria, Virginia.

9. A reference to the Union amphibious expedition commanded by Ambrose Everett Burnside and aimed at Roanoke Island, North Carolina. Even as Olmsted wrote, Union forces were capturing the Confederate defenses at Roanoke (*War for the Union*, 2: 90; *DAB*).

CHAPTER IV

PLANNING FOR FREEDOM: THE PORT ROYAL EXPERIMENT

EARLY IN 1862 Olmsted focused his attention on the cotton plantations held by Union forces in the South Carolina sea islands and the thousands of blacks who lived on them. The letters presented in this chapter detail his keen interest in the federal government's approach to the problems posed by its custody of Southern slaves. Letters to Manton Marble, James R. Spalding, and Henry W. Bellows indicate both his impatience with the nature and scope of governmental activity and his lobbying efforts for the congressional bill that he had drawn up. These documents also illustrate Olmsted's emergence in February 1862 as a candidate for superintendent of the Port Royal experiment in free labor and freedom for the slaves. As he was considering the possibility of overseeing this project, his letters to Abraham Lincoln and Charles Eliot Norton, and his presentation to Edwin M. Stanton, provide the clearest statements of his conception of the government's relation to and obligations toward the sea-island slaves. They also describe how the transition from slavery to freedom could be accomplished.

During this period, Olmsted also searched for another career. His letter of March 15 to Salmon P. Chase declining the post at Port Royal because of his candidacy for the commissionership of streets in New York City foreshadows Olmsted's later choice to work again in the field of urban design. The letter of March 25 to his father gives an assessment of the post of New York City's commissioner of streets, while that of April 19 presents a dispassionate accounting of his own talents and prospects for employment. But even as Olmsted looked beyond his work with the Sanitary

Commission, he was still coping with the difficulties it encountered. The letters in this chapter reveal that while other members of the Commission talked of winding up its work, he was opposing such a move and attempting to spur John S. Newberry to greater activity in the West, where important battles of the war were occurring. Moreover, Olmsted's letter to James E. Yeatman indicates that the Western Sanitary Commission was becoming a great annoyance and a formidable rival by soliciting contributions in the East.

To Henry Whitney Bellows

Washington, 15th Feby [1862].

My Dear Doctor,

I see by the papers of today that you are expected to take a prominent part in the meeting to be held next week in New-York with regard to the Contrabands at Port Royal.[1] I shall try to have a copy of Forster's Bill[2] sent you. I have studied the whole business carefully and discussed it with Pierce and two other sensible men from Port Royal,[3] and have confidence that the Bill can not be materially improved without decreasing the chances of its passing.

I hope the time-serving, shilly shally, disjointed, incoherent, lazy, cowardly disposition which prevails at Washington, will not fail to be denounced, and the urgency of immediate, *comprehensive* governmental action in the premises, will be insisted on.

I understand the gov[t] agents[4] promise to send from the plantations in our possession, cotton to the amount in value of considerably over a million dollars! Yet Governor Chase is dickering and hesitating about spending a few hundred dollars for efficient superintendence of the contrabands whose labor produced the crop.

Would it not be proper to present a memorial to Congress asking for *instant* action? The whole crop of next year will be lost if it is not had.

The business must be kept out of the hands of speculators.

How incredibly blind these men are! That such an opportunity should be deliberately neglected—carelessly put away with a lazy half-way botch of an arrangment—it does make my soul ache.

We are getting our Sanitary decks cleared up and everything into fine, fair, steady-going sailing order. We must let them dilly dally another week over the Medical Bills, and then go in with all the force we can command and keep up a steady hard fire without rest or intermission for a single day until we get something actually *done*. We have certainly paid respect enough to their promises.

We sent Dr Parrish[5] & shipped about 70 cases from Balt^o for Roanoke Island direct, within a day after the official account was received.[6] All our depots at the West are abundantly supplied. Dr Newberry is in Kentucky himself & I have urged a large and generous policy upon him.

He will establish a home at Louisville & employ several special relief agents.[7]

Yours Very Cordially

Fred Law Olmsted

Revd Dr Bellows

The original is in box 641 of USSC-NYPL. A copy is also misfiled as letter 1894 in box 744. Olmsted originally dated this letter January ("Jany") but realized his mistake and altered it to "Feby."

1. A reference to the meeting held on February 20, 1862, at Cooper Institute in New York City, for the benefit of contrabands at Port Royal and Fortress Monroe. Bellows was one of the meeting's featured speakers (*New-York Daily Tribune*, Feb. 21, 1862, p. 8).
2. On February 14, 1862, Lafayette S. Foster introduced Senate Bill 201, "A Bill to provide for the occupation and cultivation of the cotton and other lands in possession of the United States lying along the southern coast of the United States." This measure, which was drawn up by Olmsted but never enacted into law, called for a three-member board of receivers and guardians to be appointed by the president with the consent of the Senate. The board would have authority to lease the lands in South Carolina for up to one year or to divide them into tracts of from one thousand to three thousand acres for direct cultivation.

   Foster's bill provided salaried employment and minimal care for the sea-island slaves, who were designated only as "indigent persons." Although lodging, food, and other necessities might be advanced to them, the bill set the maximum allowance for food at fifteen cents per person per day. Expenditures for medical care could not exceed fifteen cents per person per month, and medical facilities and equipment were to be capitalized at a per-capita rate of one dollar. The emphasis of the bill lay upon work rather than care. The slaves could work upon either leased or directly administered lands at a task or piece rate (averaging fifty cents per day) under the watchful eye of a supervisor who would receive either one hundred dollars per month (not to exceed one thousand dollars annually) or a share of the proceeds of the crop produced. The bill declared it to be the duty of the board of guardians to induce the indigents "to support themselves, and live in an industrious, orderly and respectable manner." Members of the board also were empowered to use "decent and humane means of constraint against idleness, dishonesty, and vice, in accordance with the most enlightened policy of dealing with vagrants which has obtained in civilized societies" (U.S. Congress, Senate, *Index to the Bills and Resolutions of the*

Senate of the United States, for the Thirty-Seventh Congress. 1861-'62-'63. [Washington, D.C., 1863]).

3. Edward Lillie Pierce (1829–1897), a Massachusetts native who was supervisor of contraband labor at Port Royal. Chase had several reasons for selecting Pierce for this post in December 1861. He knew Pierce well, since the young man had studied law in his Cincinnati law office and had served as his confidential secretary. Charles Sumner also was a friend and influential backer of Pierce. Moreover, Pierce had supervised the contraband workers at Fortress Monroe during his three months of military service.

Pierce was determined to make the areas of the sea islands controlled by the Union army an experiment in freedom for the former slaves and a demonstration of the superiority of free labor. He sought governmental approval of the project from President Lincoln and aid from philanthropic groups. Early in 1862, however, he expressed the wish to return to the more lucrative practice of law and requested that Chase name Olmsted as his successor at Port Royal. The secretary of the treasury, however, repeatedly asked Pierce to remain in the sea islands and offered him several different positions there. Pierce was adamant nonetheless and left in June 1862. In later life he served in the Massachusetts legislature and in other public offices.

Probably one of the other "sensible men from Port Royal" was Edward S. Philbrick (1827–1889), whom Olmsted met sometime before April 1862. Also from Massachusetts, Philbrick was an engineer who had donated his services to the Port Royal experiment. In 1863 he headed a group which with the financial assistance of Boston philanthropists purchased several sea-island plantations as a free-labor experiment (George F. Hoar, "Edward Lillie Pierce," *Proceedings of the American Antiquarian Society*, n.s., 12 [Oct. 1897]: 197–201; Willie Lee Rose, *Rehearsal for Reconstruction: The Port Royal Experiment* [Indianapolis, Ind., 1964], pp. 49–50, 152–55, 212–16; E. L. Pierce to FLO, March 29, 1862).

4. Olmsted probably obtained this information from Edward L. Pierce, who in his report of February 1862 stated that agents of the Treasury Department expected to be able to obtain two and one-half million pounds of ginned cotton from the sea islands that spring (U.S. Treasury Department, *The Negroes at Port Royal. Report of E. L. Pierce, Government Agent, to the Hon. Salmon P. Chase, Secretary of the Treasury* [Boston, 1862], p. 7).

5. Joseph Parrish (1818–1891), a physician and inspector for the Sanitary Commission. A graduate of the medical school of the University of Pennsylvania, he superintended the Pennsylvania School for Feeble Minded Children. From 1863 through 1865 Parrish served the Sanitary Commission in several different posts. In 1863 he traveled through Pennsylvania, raising funds and supplies. The following year he superintended the Department of Canvassing and Supplies until he became the editor of the *Bulletin*, a Commission publication. His wife, Lydia, also was a volunteer worker for the Commission. After the war Parrish's life work centered upon the treatment of alcoholism (Howard Atwood Kelly and Walter Lincoln Burrage, *Dictionary of American Medical Biography: Lives of Eminent Physicians of the United States and Canada* . . . [New York, 1928], p. 887; USSC, *Minutes*, pp. 128, 202; *Diary of the Civil War*, p. 487; Linus Pierpont Brockett and Mary C. Vaughan, *Woman's Work in the Civil War: A Record of Heroism, Patriotism, and Patience* [Boston, 1867], pp. 362–73).

6. A joint Union army and naval expedition captured Roanoke Island, North Carolina, on February 8, 1862, after two days' fighting (U.S. Department of the Navy, Naval History Division, *Civil War Naval Chronology, 1861–1865*, 5 vols. [Washington, D.C., 1961–65], 2: 19–20).

7. On February 1, 1862, the Sanitary Commission opened its first shelter in the West, the Louisville Soldiers Home, located near the Louisville and Nashville Railroad in a shed furnished by that railroad company. The home provided food and lodging for furloughed soldiers who were in transit (John Strong Newberry, *The U.S. Sanitary*

Commission in the Valley of the Mississippi, during the War of the Rebellion, 1861–1866 [Cleveland, Ohio, 1871], pp. 361–68).

To James Reed Spalding[1]

Private.

U.S. Sanitary Commission, Washington, D.C.
15th February 1862

My Dear Sir,

The advantage which I happen to possess for dealing with the Port Royal problem, from having some years ago, made a careful study of the rural economy of that district, to which you allude in a manner so complimentary to me in the World of today,[2] authorizes me to call your especial attention to the Senate Bill of Mr Forster, in the preparation of which I had the honor to be consulted,[3] and which I believe to be altogether the best bill which would have any chance to be acted upon favorably at present.

The urgent importance of the earliest possible action, and of adopting some thoroughly comprehensive, and at the same time *elastic*, scheme can not be too strongly stated.

We have on our hands, from fifty to a hundred of the most valuable plantations on the continent, with on an average, the full complement of working hands for their cultivation. The Treasury agents estimate that they will be able to gather and send from these plantations the value of a million and a half of cotton. During the months of January and February the operation of *listing*[4] the cotton fields, in preparation for planting is performed. In March and April cotton is planted. Not the first stroke of work has yet been done in the cotton-fields. If there should be another month's delay, nothing can be done this year, and we have on our hands 12,000 paupers to be supported in the main at public expense.

Mean-time, I am already informed that our soldiers are suffering for want of a due supply of vegetable food, and Commodore Dupont[5] has sent home one of his best ships to recruit the crew, in which the fearful scourge of scurvy had begun to rage. As the weather grows warmer the want of a proper diet will become a more serious evil.

But a decent regard for the national honor, a decent respect to the science of social economy, a decent reverence to the demands of Christianity, should forbid our dealing any longer with these people in a desultory, stingy, temporizing, penny-wise, pound foolish, way. The Bill is drawn with especial care to avoid all issues of a radical character. Neither slave-holder nor abolitionist would be compromised in voting for it—and, as it will not stand in the way of more thorough measures, one way or the other, when the policy of the country with regard to slavery, is determined; it may be hoped to unite all who do not wish to establish at Port Royal, another evidence of the folly of ever hoping to see negroes usefully employed in any other condition than that of abject slavery.

The opportunity of proving to the South, the economic mistake of Slavery, which is offered us at Port Royal, is indeed invaluable. It has for months engaged my profoundest attention, and I am heartsick at the listlessness, indifference and utter childish cowardice with which it is regarded by controlling minds at Washington.

Hoping that you will agree with me as to the urgency of the case, and excuse me for intruding so long upon your valuable time.

I am, dear Sir, yours most Respectfully,

Fred. Law Olmsted.

Mr. Spaulding.

The original is in the Grenville H. Norcross Papers, Massachusetts Historical Society, Boston, Massachusetts.

1. Although Olmsted addressed this letter to a "Mr. Spaulding," internal evidence indicates that the recipient was James Reed Spalding (1821–1872), a newspaperman employed by the *New York World*. His journalistic career began at the *Morning Courier & New-York Enquirer*, where he was a colleague of Richard Grant White, a literary acquaintance of Olmsted who in 1858 had defended the Greensward design for Central Park in that newspaper. A founder and editor-in-chief of the *World* in 1860, Spalding was not a good manager, and the newspaper's trustees removed him from the editorship in April 1861. He resigned from the *World* in October 1862 when the paper both opposed the Emancipation Proclamation and supported Democratic candidates for office. He then worked for his old friend and former college classmate Henry J. Raymond at the *New-York Times* until illness cut short his career (Phineas Spalding, *Spalding Memorial and Personal Reminiscences* . . . [Haverhill, N.H., 1887], p. 56; *New-York Times*, Oct. 12, 1872, p. 7; George T. McJimsey, *Genteel Partisan: Manton Marble, 1834–1917* [Ames, Iowa, 1971], pp. 21–27, 41; J. R. Spalding to Manton M. Marble, Oct. 6, [1862], Manton Malone Marble Papers, vol. 3, pp. 559–60, Library of Congress, Washington, D.C.; *Papers of FLO*, 3: 191, n. 1).

2. An editorial in the *New York World* of February 15, 1862, called for the appointment of a commission to devise a plan for the government's management of the slaves at Port Royal. It suggested that commissioners should be men "who have faith in the character and capacity of the Negro race, but who are at the same time free from crotchets, fair-minded, practical, and one or two of whom should possess a faculty for philosophical observation." Of the three men proposed (including antislavery activists

John Jay and Gerrit Smith), Olmsted received the highest praise: "Mr. Fred. Law Olmsted probably combines more qualifications for such an office than any other man in the country." Olmsted first believed James R. Spalding to be the author of this editorial but discovered that, in fact, Manton Marble had composed it (*New York World*, Feb. 15, 1862, p. 4; see also FLO to Manton M. Marble, Feb. 16, 1862, below).

3. A more modest reference to Olmsted's part in the drawing up of Senate Bill 201 than he elsewhere made. At about the same time, he told his father, "I drew the Bill entire & it was adopted by Foster without changing a word." Lending credence to this claim is Olmsted's opening statement to Foster in the letter accompanying it: "I herewith hand you the draft of a bill to provide for the cultivation of a portion of the land held by the United States forces in South Carolina & Georgia & for the care & management of the negroes thereon—which I have prepared at your request" (FLO to JO, Feb. 19, 1862; FLO to Lafayette S. Foster, Feb. 3, 1862, USSC-NYPL, box 833, 2: 547–53).

4. Listing or bedding was part of the preparation of the fields in January and February for cotton planting. The worker used a hoe to throw up ridges of dirt to form the rows of beds in which the cotton would be planted; these rows were separated by vacant "alleys" (U.S. Treasury Department, *Negroes at Port Royal*, p. 21).

5. Samuel Francis DuPont (1803–1865), a career naval officer who in 1861 commanded the South Atlantic blockading squadron. He headed the Union naval expedition that in cooperation with the Union army captured Port Royal (*DAB*).

To Manton Malone Marble[1]

Private

U.S. Sanitary Commission,
Adams House, 244 F street,
Washington, D.C.,
16th Feby 1862.

My Dear Sir,

A very hastily written letter, which I yesterday addressed to "Mr. Spaulding" at the World office,[2] should have been addressed to you. I hope that you may have received it and have found in it a sufficient answer to the enquiries of your note of the 13th which has just reached me.

The contingency which has arisen at Port Royal was one which I had anticipated at an early period of the war, and even before I was appointed upon the Sanitary Commission, I tried to have a plan initiated by which the slaves of rebels seeking the protection of our arms should be rationally taken care of.[3] Again in August I drew up a scheme for this purpose and made an effort to get it adopted by Genl McClellan.[4] Since then I have endeavored to act on Mr Chase, but I have found nowhere any real appreciation of the opportunity or of the danger of neglecting it and I now look to nothing before us with as much apprehension as to the consequences of neglecting to adopt a broad, comprehensive and efficient method of dealing with the question it involves.

Mr. Forster's Bill, as you will have observed, entirely meets your suggestion. It proposes to appoint three Commissioners, whose duty with reference to the management of the Agricultural property shall be that of Receivers of a bankrupt estate, and with reference to the negroes shall be that of Guardians of the Poor and of orphans. A generous and enlightened view of their duty in the latter function is, however, insisted upon. They are required not merely to encourage, but, if need be, to enforce industry, their responsibility being the same as that of masters to apprentices and their means of enforcing authority the same. No expenditure from the national treasury is authorized for education, or for the moral and religious training of the negroes except incidentally, but it would be in the power of the Commissioners to control, direct and aid the disposition of the negroes to help themselves in this respect as well as any efforts in this direction of the public benevolence. Limits to expenditure are carefully fixed in every direction and the Commissioners would be held to a very exacting responsibility, yet the arrangment would have sufficient elasticity to accommodate a business tenfold greater than is at present anticipated.

For myself, I should not be willing to be completely cast off from the Central Park, because I know that nobody else, without occasional assistance from me, can do justice to that work. It is not possible to place another mind completely in rapport with the detail of the design. But, presuming that I could continue to hold an official relation to that enterprise, I should be very glad to devote myself to a business which I feel to be so vastly important.

I am, dear Sir,
Very truly & Respectfully Yours,

Fred. Law Olmsted.

Manton Marble, Esq[r]

The original is in volume 2 of the Manton Malone Marble Papers, Library of Congress, Washington, D.C.

1. Manton Malone Marble (1835–1917), managing editor and later publisher of the *New York World*. After beginning his journalistic career in Boston, Marble worked for the *New York Evening Post* from 1858 until 1860. Appointed night editor of the *World* in 1860, he became managing editor in July 1861 and set the paper's editorial policy. In April 1862 Marble would purchase the controlling interest in the *World*.

Marble proved to be an important ally for the Sanitary Commission and Olmsted in 1861 and early 1862. His editorials favored the bill to reorganize the Medical Bureau, and he supported Foster's bill for Port Royal. On February 19 Marble combined and printed as an editorial much of this letter and the letter that Olmsted addressed to Spalding. But in the summer of 1862 the newspaper, which had supported Lincoln's candidacy in 1860, increasingly advocated the Democratic policies favored by the group of investors that had rescued it from financial problems (*DAB*; Bernard A. Weisberger, *Reporters for the Union* [Boston, 1953], p. 253; *New York World*, Feb. 19, 1862, p. 4; G. T. McJimsey, *Genteel Partisan*, pp. 31–42).

2. See FLO to James Reed Spalding, February 15, 1862, above.

3. Probably a reference to Olmsted's desire in early June 1861 to be appointed commissioner of contrabands (FLO to HWB, June 1, 1861, above).

4. The editors have not been able to find a copy of any plan proposed by Olmsted to McClellan about contrabands; most likely it was an oral proposal made during one of their meetings. McClellan later claimed that during 1861 he believed that "emancipation should be accomplished gradually, and that the negroes should be fitted for it by certain preparatory steps in the way of education, recognition of the rights of family and marriage, prohibition against selling them without their own consent, the freedom of those born after a certain date, etc." Probably Olmsted would not have disagreed with those views. However, McClellan, as a Democrat, would most likely have doubted that he himself held the necessary authority to undertake any of the measures Olmsted advocated (George B. McClellan, *McClellan's Own Story: The War for the Union* . . . [New York, 1887], p. 34).

To John Strong Newberry

U.S. Sanitary Commission,
Adams House, 244 F street,
Washington, D.C.,
Feby 24th 1862.

My Dear Doctor,

I returned from New York, this morning,[1] and find here your note of the 16th.

At the meeting of the Exec. Com.[2] in New York D[r] Bellows read a letter which he had prepared to be sent immediately to the Secy of War, resigning the Commission, to take effect from 1st of April, being moved thereto by the strange neglect of the Secy and of McClellan to keep their several promises to us,[3] and by the condition of the Treasury which does not contain enough to carry us, at our present rate of expenditure, through March. Each of the members present, except myself, approved of the letter and of the proposition. My judgment and statements had sufficient weight to induce a delay and at a subsequent meeting, it was determined to make another effort to increase our fund, and to still further postpone decisive action. I think, however, that a definite plan for winding up our operations in a gradual manner is likely to be adopted, and I shall propose some scheme of reduction, as an alternative of a more abrupt termination of our work. This can be done justly and appropriately, if the new Medical Bill passes. And some new Medical Bill, I think, must pass, which will provide for inspection, hygenic precaution and a better system of supply.

I enclose an extract of a letter (in copy) received by one of our ladies in New York from a friend in Louisville.[4] Urgent appeals for aid, backed by similar statements, have been received by others from Louisville. I, of course, would not allow them to send anything and requested them all to inform their correspondents that they should apply to you. Mr Burnet[5] has also applied to the W.C.R.A. of New York, for assistance to the Cincinnati depot, and the article which you have sent me, appealing to the public and manifesting great want and anxiety, was sent to the Woman's C.R.A. apparently for the same reason—viz. to induce them to send goods to Cincinnati from New York. I would not allow them to do so however, until you should be heard from. We are well supplied here without much superfluity, but could easily quadruple our rate of supply, I have no doubt, if it were thought best. I should have no reluctance to send you 500 boxes, if you were in need of them, and as you seem likely to have all the fighting for a while, of course, you will not fail to call if you have reason to apprehend the exhaustion of your western resources, in any temporary emergency.

Douglas writes that they have a large overstock in the W. San. Com. dépôt at St. Louis.

Be good enough to send your Feby accounts as early as possible—in advance if you can—and a liberal, battle-month estimate for March, so that I can make up accounts and full estimates before the meeting on the 4th.

Please furnish me also full estimated accounts of the Western supply business to March, as soon as you can.

The London Times has had two leading articles based on the Report to the Secy of War, treating us with great respect.[6]

Yours very faithfully

Fred. Law Olmsted.

J. S. Newberry M.D.

The original is letter 294 in volume 1 of box 909 of USSC-NYPL. A letterpress copy is on pages 21–26 of volume 1 of box 834 there.

1. Olmsted went to New York City February 17, 1862, and worked mainly on Central Park and Port Royal affairs there (FLO to JO, Feb. 19, 1862).
2. At the urging of George Templeton Strong, the Sanitary Commission on October 18, 1861, had created a five-member "executive and finance committee" which would meet at least weekly in New York City when the board was not in session. The members, though not listed by name in the resolution, were: Strong, Agnew, Bellows, Gibbs, and Van Buren. Although Strong apparently intended the major duty of the Executive Committee to be certifying the payment of bills, it assumed a greater supervisory and policy making role in the summer and fall of 1862 (USSC, *Minutes*, pp. 72–73).
3. Most of these "promises" concerned the reform of the Medical Bureau and the enforcement of rules of hygiene in the Army of the Potomac. One specific "promise" from both McClellan and Stanton was the proposed general order recognizing the right of the Commission to inspect military hospitals. Stanton endorsed such an order on March 7, 1862 (Clement Finley, Printed Order of Surgeon General Making Hospitals Subject to Inspection by the Agents of the Sanitary Commission, March 7, 1862, Frederick Law Olmsted Collection, Rare Book Room, U.S. Army Military History Institute, Carlisle, Pa.; see also FLO to HWB, Feb. 7, 1862, nn. 5 and 7, above).
4. A reference to a letter probably addressed to Ellen Collins of the Woman's Central Association of Relief and written by Harriet Staples Douglass Smith. Her husband, Benjamin Bosworth Smith, was the Episcopal Bishop of Kentucky, and she had numerous friends and acquaintances among the well-to-do and wealthy of New York City and Connecticut. In this letter, which Ellen Collins gave to Olmsted on February 21, Harriet Smith claimed that there were nearly two thousand sick soldiers in Louisville and that the hospitals there were begging for shirts so that soldiers suffering from typhus might have a change of clothing (Ellen Collins to JSN, Feb. 22, 1862, USSC-NYPL, box 909, 1: 322).
5. Robert Wallace Burnet (1808–1898), president of the Cincinnati branch of the U.S. Sanitary Commission. A graduate of West Point in 1829, Burnet returned to his native Cincinnati after serving in the army for four years. At the beginning of the Civil War, he raised and equipped an army company known as Burnet's Rifles. He presided over the Sanitary Commission's Cincinnati branch until its final dissolution in 1880. According to the branch's historian, Burnet was "judicious and temperate, and more than anyone else, it was he who set the tone for the organization" (Charles T. Greve, *History of Cincinnati and Hamilton County, Ohio, Their Past and Present* [Cincinnati, Ohio, 1894], p. 479; Francis Bernard Heitman, *Historical Register and Dictionary of the United States Army . . .* , 2 vols. [Washington, D.C., 1903], 1: 264; William J. Jacobs, "Quiet Crusaders: A History of the Cincinnati Branch of the United States Sanitary Commission" [M.A. thesis, University of Cincinnati, 1956], pp. 39–40).
6. Although an article of January 28 mentioned the Sanitary Commission, the principal article in the *Times* of London that was based upon the Sanitary Commission's report to the secretary of war appeared on January 25, 1862. The writer commented upon the voluminousness of the Commission's publications and declared about the range of subjects covered in inspections: "We must say that we never met with a more exhaustive report. The Commission appears to have been of great benefit to the army, and it will now enable the world to observe how that singular army has been constituted" (*Times* [London], Jan. 25, 1862, pp. 8–9).

To John Olmsted

U.S. Sanitary Commission, Washington, D.C.
24th Feb[y] 1862

Dear Father,

Thanks for your prompt action.[1] I shall go to Port Royal, if I can, and work out practically every solution of the Slavery question—long ago advocated in my book.[2] Forster's Bill is drawn up in accordance with it. Negroes are to be treated simply as other vagrants. If they are fools, so many as are—like other fools. If savages, like other maniacs. If idle, like other idlers.

I have talked it over with Mary[3] and she agrees that I ought to be glad to take it, if I am asked. I have no reason to think I shall be except that it would be right & natural that some body should think to so advise the President. But in any case I hope the Bill and the system I have advised will be adopted.

Have you seen the London Times articles on the San. Com. Report?[4] They are in the no's of Jan 25th & 28th. I think you will be interested to see them if in at the Reading Room (editorials). The military men here are much interested in them.

I am very glad to hear your account of Owen.[5] I found the girl[6] quite shapely, lively, human & pretty. We shall probably have to move off the park in the spring, the house being to let for a restaurant.[7]

It is high spring weather here.

Your affectionate Son

Fred. Law Olmsted.

---

1. Olmsted is thanking his father for sending a petition concerning the slaves at Port Royal to Congress. On February 19 Olmsted requested that he try to drum up support in Connecticut for Senator Foster's measure: "I want somebody in Hartford & somebody in Norwich to immediately prepare and send a petition or Memorial to Congress to sustain Senator Foster's Bill for the management of the Port Royal Cotton lands." Apparently Olmsted himself drew up a more general petition a few days later and mailed it to his father for circulation in Hartford. Addressed to the U.S. House of Representatives and Senate, the petition, written in Olmsted's hand, requested them to "take such immediate measures, as, in your wisdom, may be most effectual to the end of providing employment, superintendence, discipline and support for the negro population, now under the protection of the arms of the United States at and near Port Royal in South Carolina, and to prevent the scandal and disgrace to our nation which is liable to occur from their being left to a desultory method of management or uncertain and possibly ill-directed benevolence." John

Olmsted procured the signatures of seventy-five other citizens of Hartford and forwarded the petition to the House of Representatives (FLO to JO, Feb. 19, 1862; [FLO], "Petition of John Olmsted & 75 Other Citizens of Hartford Conn.," Feb. 22, 1862, Record Group 46, Records of the House of Representatives, HR 37A, 68.18, National Archives and Records Service, Washington, D.C., courtesy of the Freedmen and Southern Society Papers Project, University of Maryland).

2. A reference to the plan for gradual, compensated emancipation with preparation for freedom which Olmsted advocated in his first book about the South, A *Journey in the Seaboard Slave States*. This plan called for a system of bookkeeping that would allow slaves, over time, to purchase their freedom. Although in 1862 he probably believed that recompense of slaveholders would take place only in cases involving loyal masters, Olmsted thought that a variant of his old plan of incentives to labor could be instituted. In this case the government would stand as guardian of the slaves. Olmsted had earlier declared:

> Let, for instance, any slave be provided with all things he will demand, as far as practicable, and charge him for them at certain prices—honest, market prices for his necessities, higher prices for harmless luxuries, and excessive, but not absolutely prohibitory, prices for everything likely to do him harm. Credit him, at a fixed price, for every day's work he does, and for all above a certain easily accomplished task in a day, at an increased price, so that his reward will be in an increasing ratio to his perseverance. Let the prices of provisions be so proportioned to the price of task-work, that it will be about as easy as it is now for him to obtain a bare subsistance. When he has no food and shelter due him, let him be confined in solitude, or otherwise punished, until he asks for opportunity to earn exemption from punishment by labor.

His plan also required the black community to care for all dependents:

> Oblige them to purchase food for their children, and let them have the benefit of their children's labor, and they will be careful to teach their children to avoid waste, and to honor labor. Let those who have not gained credit while hale and young, sufficient to support themselves in comfort when prevented by age or infirmity from further labor, be supported by a tax upon all the negroes of the plantation, or of a community. Improvidence, and pretense of inability to labor, will then be disgraceful.

(Frederick Law Olmsted, A *Journey in the Seaboard Slave States, With Remarks on Their Economy* . . . [New York, 1856], pp. 443–44.)

3. Mary Perkins Olmsted.
4. See FLO to JSN, February 24, 1862, note 6, above.
5. Olmsted's four-and-one-half-year-old stepson, Owen Frederick Olmsted, was at his grandparents' in Hartford on an extended visit that had lasted eight months (see FLO to JO, June 26, 1861, above).
6. Olmsted's infant daughter, Marion.
7. Olmsted opposed transforming a building of the former Mount St. Vincent Convent in Central Park, where his family lived, into a restaurant. In a letter to Central Park Comptroller Andrew H. Green, Olmsted admitted the need for a restaurant but argued that one located in the lower park, rather than the upper park, where Mount St. Vincent lay, would be more useful and more likely to be successful because so many of the park's visitors came only to the lower park. Green replied, "I quite concur with you that what is done should be done well & successfully done & I shall not act hastily in the matter." He apparently kept this promise to act deliberately, and a military hospital rather than a restaurant was established at the Convent in June 1862 (FLO to A. H. Green, Feb. 26, 1862; A. H. Green to FLO, March 17, 1862; *Boston Medical and Surgical Journal* 66, no. 19 [June 12, 1862]: 404).

To Charles Eliot Norton[1]

Sanitary Commission, Washington, D.C.,
March 3[d] 1862

My Dear Sir,

I have been in hopes that some definite comprehensive plan of dealing with the negroes at Port Royal, would be determined on ere this, and have delayed replying to your note of the 22[d] in order that my reply might have reference to such a plan.

At present, under the law, I suppose that money deposited in a Savings Bank by a Port Royal negro,[2] would really belong to his *owner*, would it not?[3] To get the negro to deposit, he must first be persuaded to think that it will be of use to him to save, and that he can trust his savings with the representative of the Savings' Bank with safety. And if a good man can readily persuade him of this, a bad man can as readily persuade him to evil, can cheat him and in every way impose upon him.

The first necessity then is something in which he can have confidence, and some strong and assured protection against imposition. The negro is not a gentleman and a Christian, whatever the reverend Mr French[4] may think. He is little better than a cunning idiot, and a cowed savage. He does not on this account need an owner but he does need a guardian and he knows that he does. He would rather have an owner than no guardianship.

Nothing can be well done in my opinion, on the present temporizing, desultory plan. Little can be done by philanthropy as philanthropy. The extension of civilized law and social polity so as to include the negro among other human beings, is what is wanted. And for any organized work, there must be some few, distinct, large purposes clearly in view, and some central will and power to which all details must be subordinated in their proper order. Without this, I do not feel sure that anything can be done that may not be mischievous.

Very Truly & Cordially Yours

Fred. Law Olmsted.

C. E. Norton Esq[r]

The original is in the Charles Eliot Norton Papers, Houghton Library, Harvard University, Cambridge, Massachusetts.

1. Charles Eliot Norton (1827–1908), critic, scholar, and later a professor at Harvard College. The son of Andrews Norton, the controversial professor of theology at

Harvard Divinity School, Charles received an excellent classical education and graduated from Harvard College. At the time of this letter, he had been pursuing a literary career for some years. In 1855, at the behest of his friend George W. Curtis, Norton enthusiastically reviewed Walt Whitman's *Leaves of Grass* for *Putnam's Monthly*. He was also a sporadic contributor to the *Atlantic Monthly* while James Russell Lowell served as its editor. In 1863 John Murray Forbes convinced Norton to edit patriotic pamphlets for the New England Loyal Publication Society. During the war Norton and Lowell became editors of the *North American Review*.

A humorous letter of introduction by Curtis and the letter presented here began a correspondence which lasted over thirty years. Olmsted found much to admire in Norton and once called him a "perfect gentleman." Norton moved easily in literary circles in England and New England: Lowell, Elizabeth Gaskell, and Robert and Elizabeth Barrett Browning were among his friends; while John Ruskin, though much his senior, considered him his mentor. As well as intellectual attainments, Norton possessed exquisite manners and a patrician Boston background. Even more important in Olmsted's estimation, Norton combined urbanity with a social conscience. Concerned with the plight of the urban poor, in the 1850s he had drawn up a plan to provide better cheap housing and had taught at a night school. Moreover, Norton shared Olmsted's desire to raise the general level of American culture and taste. While initially more optimistic than Olmsted about the possibility of the Civil War sparking a regeneration of the nation, Norton ultimately became more disillusioned with democratic society. During their friendship Olmsted enjoyed Norton's dry wit and found the latter's moral earnestness and religious skepticism much more congenial than the piety of other close friends like Charles Loring Brace.

Through Olmsted, Norton met Edwin L. Godkin and helped in 1865 to found the journal the *Nation*. In the 1870s and 1880s Norton collaborated with Olmsted in the struggle to preserve Niagara Falls from development, and he remained a steadfast supporter of Olmsted's numerous professional works, such as the New York state capitol and the Boston parks (Kermit Vanderbilt, *Charles Eliot Norton: Apostle of Culture in a Democracy* [Cambridge, Mass., 1959], pp. 18–21, 26–31, 48–51, 68, 77, 84–88, 96; G. W. Curtis to FLO, Feb. 22, 1862; Katharine P. Wormeley to FLO, Feb. 15, 1867).

2. In his letter of February 22 Norton enclosed a note from his friend Samuel G. Ward, Boston banker and brother of Julia Ward Howe, which advocated the organization of a savings bank for the blacks at Port Royal. Olmsted's copy of this plan has not survived, but Norton's promise suggests that Ward's plan was general, rather than specific, in its recommendations: "If you think the project one worth being carried into effect, and can suggest any suitable person to take the matter in charge at Port Royal, or elsewhere where freed slaves are collected and working for wages . . . the details of the plan will be arranged here, and suitable provision for the security of the deposits be made" (C. E. Norton to FLO, Feb. 22, 1862).

3. Olmsted's point here was that a slave, as property, could not be the legal owner of money or property.

4. Mansfield French (1810–1876), a Methodist minister and friend of Salmon P. Chase. In February 1862, after a visit to the sea islands, French became the general agent of the New York-based National Freedman's Relief Association and headed the New York delegation of teachers and "missionaries" that arrived in South Carolina in March 1862. A former president of female colleges in Ohio, French had also owned and edited a small religious magazine. He became a leader in fighting for the right of blacks on the sea islands to purchase confiscated land there at nominal cost, and he remained in South Carolina until 1872.

Most likely Olmsted's remark about French was a reaction to reports about French's high opinion of the character of sea-island blacks. Henry W. Bellows and French had been featured speakers together at the February 20 meeting at Cooper

Institute, and Olmsted may have learned about French's views from Bellows (*Appleton's Cyc. Am. Biog.*; W. L. Rose, *Rehearsal for Reconstruction*, pp. 26–27, 272–96, 393–94; *New-York Daily Tribune*, Feb. 21, 1862, p. 8).

To ABRAHAM LINCOLN

U.S. Sanitary Commission
Adams House, 244 F. St.
Washington, DC   March 8th 1862

Dear Sir

At the request of several gentlemen—I mention D[r] Howe, Prof[r] Bache, D[r] Bellows and G W Curtis[1]—I shall offer you my thoughts about the management of the negroes at Port Royal. That I can suppose it worthy of a moment of your time is to be accounted for simply by the fact that it chances to be more mature than most men's thoughts on this subject can be, the occasion which has arisen having been practically anticipated by me several years ago.[2]

Aside from military considerations, the duty and function of government with regard to the negroes is included in and limited by these two propositions:

1. To save the lives of the negroes, except possibly as death may be a natural punishment of neglect of duty.

2. To *train* or *educate* them in a few simple, essential and fundamental social duties of free men in civilized life: as, first, to obtain each for himself the necessities of life, independently of charity; second, to regard family obligations; third, to substitute for subordination to the will of their former owners, submission to Laws—or rules of social comity with the understanding that these are designed to correspond to the natural laws of their happiness; 4th, to discriminate between just authority under the Laws as above, and despotic authority—between the duty of obedience to administrators of law and obedience to masters by might.

I do not know that there are any more than these: if there are, they should be clearly defined before they are sought to be inculcated by the use of the money or agents of government.

Whoever is entrusted with the administration of the duty of government to these negroes should be under no necessity or temptation to engage in purely philanthropic, benevolent or charitable duties toward them.

If the two classes of duties (governmental and charitable) are not absolutely inconsistent one with another, the exercise of the latter by the same person with the former will do much to maintain a confusion of ideas which exists in the minds of the negroes and from which it is [a] large part of the duty of government as an economic operation to free them. It should be laid down as an absolute rule that government will do nothing merely for charity. The negroes are not to be in the least fed & clothed for charity but because either they are expected to be valuable to the state, and for that purpose their lives must be conserved, or because it is tacitly agreed upon between every civilized man and the community to which he attaches himself that in dire extremity of misfortune he shall not want protection against the coup de grace of cold & hunger. To accomplish these points, the agent of gov^t should have the means within his control beyond all peradventure:

1   To place within the reach—upon proper conditions—of each negro, what is barely necessary for the support of his life. The limit of expenditure for this purpose should be strictly defined and the agent should be rigidly and accurately held within it, but within it there should be nothing left doubtful.

2   To offer employment and wages to each negro which will enable those who are diligent to provide something more than what is barely necessary for the support of life; which will, for instance, at least enable parents to provide for their children's necessity.

A very moderate sum to be attainable by each laborer daily will suffice for this; but the sum however large in the aggregate should be provided beyond any possibility of failure; otherwise the second proposition will fail and the unsuccessful attempts to realize it will accomplish results precisely the opposite to those required.

It would be better for the state, and more merciful to the negroes to guillotine them at once, than to educate them by any means in beggary, distrust of themselves and cowardly hatred of the first duties of freedom.

sgd. Fred. Law Olmsted.

The text presented here is from a copy signed by Olmsted.

1. Sanitary Commission members Samuel Gridley Howe, A. D. Bache, and Henry W. Bellows, and Olmsted's old friend George William Curtis (1824–1892), a literary man who was the son-in-law of the influential philanthropist and abolitionist Francis George Shaw. Curtis and Olmsted collaborated on *Putnam's Monthly Magazine* and were also partners in the publishing firm Dix, Edwards & Company in 1856–57 and

in its successor firm Miller & Company. Curtis's father-in-law settled the firm's debts after its failure in 1857. In 1862 Curtis still wrote a regular column for *Harper's Monthly* and took great interest in the government's treatment of slaves falling into its hands. He was among those urging Salmon P. Chase to put Olmsted in charge of the government's activities at Port Royal (*Papers of FLO*, 2: 53–56; G. W. Curtis to FLO, Feb. 23, 1862).

2. A reference to the plan for educating slaves for emancipation which Olmsted presented in A *Journey in the Seaboard Slave States* in 1856 (see FLO to JO, Feb. 24, 1862, n. 2, above).

To Salmon Portland Chase

Washington, 15th March, 1862.

My Dear Sir,

Absence from town has prevented an earlier acknowledgment of your favor of the 13th inst. enclosing a Report of Mr. Pierce's, which I herewith return.[1]

I regret to say that I am precluded at present from accepting the appointment with the offer of which you have honored me.

I have just been most unexpectedly informed by the mayor of New York[2] that he should—probably on Monday next—present my name to the Common Council as his nomination for the office of Street Commissioner of that city.[3] The work committed to Mr Pierce is one much more to my liking than that intended for me by the mayor, but the reasons which he assigns for his determination are such as to give him a right to claim my acceptance of the nomination.[4]

I do not propose to visit New York while the nomination is pending and it will not be urged in any way, nor will any inducement be offered for its adoption beyond what is presented in my previous management of a public trust of that city.[5] It is hardly probable under these circumstances, that the nomination will be confirmed, but until it shall have been rejected, I can not undertake any responsibility which would be incompatible with the acceptance of the appointment. The question can not be decided in less time than a fortnight.

I trust that, in the meantime, you will find a man much better qualified than myself to relief Mr Pierce, and, most sincerely grateful for the opportunity offered me,

I am, dear Sir, most respectfully Yours

Fred. Law Olmsted.

Hon S. P. Chase,
Secy of the Treasy.

The original is in Record Group 56, Records of the Department of the Treasury, Miscellaneous Correspondence, Unbound, O—Feb 1862–Apr 1878 (box 104), entry 179, National Archives and Records Service, Washington, D.C.

1. Olmsted returned on Friday, March 14, from a two-day visit to the battlefield at Manassas, Virginia, to find a letter from Salmon P. Chase, which enclosed Edward Pierce's report on the blacks at Port Royal and offered the supervisory position there to Olmsted by the simple question, "Have you not made up your mind to be 'designated as his successor'?" (S. P. Chase to FLO, March 13, 1862.)
2. George Opdyke (1805–1880), a wealthy Republican businessman who in 1861 had been elected mayor of New York City. Born in New Jersey, Opdyke had laid the basis of his fortune by the manufacture and sale of clothing in New Orleans. In 1832 he moved to New York City, where he continued to be successful and changed his business to that of wholesale dry goods. During his term as mayor, Opdyke was confronted with the Draft Riots of 1863. One of his political rivals, Thurlow Weed, charged that Opdyke gouged the government by inflating the value of his munitions factory that was burned by the rioters. Opdyke sued Weed for libel, but the sensational trial ended in a deadlocked jury. After the war, Opdyke became a banker.
      After Opdyke agreed to serve on the Sanitary Commission's Central Finance Committee in the autumn of 1861, he probably met Olmsted. He and Olmsted shared some interests and views. Opdyke, a self-educated man who had written on political economy, believed as did Olmsted that slavery was injurious to the master as well as the slave. He probably was impressed by Olmsted's administration of Central Park and the Sanitary Commission, since he tried in both the spring and autumn of 1862 to appoint him commissioner of streets. Although not able to convince the city's aldermen to approve that nomination, Opdyke became involved with yet another offer of a position to Olmsted. In August 1863 the mayor, who was a shareholder in the Mariposa Company, helped persuade Olmsted to become superintendent of the estate and its mining operations in California (*DAB*; Melvin G. Holli and Peter d'A. Jones, eds., *Biographical Dictionary of American Mayors, 1820–1980: Big City Mayors* [Westport, Conn., 1981], pp. 274–75; Charles Wilson Opdyck, *The Op Dyck Genealogy* . . . [New York, 1889], pp. 375–87).
3. The office of street commissioner was one of the most important posts for patronage in the municipal government, and its responsibilities included oversight "of opening, altering, regulating, grading, flagging, curbing, guttering, and lighting streets, roads, places and avenues; of building, repairing and lighting wharves and piers, the construction and repairing of public roads, the care of public buildings and places, and the filling up of sunken lots under the ordinances of the Common Council." The office included eight bureaus, two of whose heads were not appointed by the street commissioner. Olmsted elsewhere described the position as "a sort of associate mayor's office, appointing and controlling a number of the civic bureaus, very few of them being really street matters—Street paving and street cleaning are not under the Commiss^r—Lamps & gas and wharves and piers are so."

289

    While the street commissioner was nominated by the mayor, the Board of Aldermen of the Common Council could accept or reject candidates. Before Opdyke submitted Olmsted's name to the aldermen, he wished to have a good chance of securing the appointment. Thus he delayed making the nomination. On March 28 Olmsted still expected to be considered for the post. "The Mayor proposes to nominate me Monday night, & hopes to carry the nomination that night," he wrote Jenkins. "It is very doubtful if he succeeds. If he does not, he does not intend to give it up at once, & I think my chances are fair of getting the appointment in the end." Opdyke, however, did not formally propose Olmsted for the post that spring (FLO to HWB, March 15, 1862, USSC-NYPL, box 641; New York City, Common Council, *Manual of the Corporation of the City of New York* [New York, 1862], p. 18; FLO to JFJ, March 28, 1862, USSC-NYPL, box 740: 644).

4. In a letter to Bellows of March 15, Olmsted declared that "the one thing" Opdyke wanted was "an efficient superintendence." According to Olmsted, Opdyke "believed that three or four hundred thousand dollars might be saved in a year in that Department and that I was the man to do it" (FLO to HWB, March 15, 1862, USSC-NYPL, box 641).

5. Despite these claims, Olmsted was aware that he would have to make some effort to conciliate the aldermen whose support would be necessary to confirm the appointment. That same day Olmsted more fully described to Bellows the political aspect of this possible appointment:

> He would expect me to turn out most of the present incumbents—because they probably are not the best men—and in filling their places, he would expect to nominate a considerable number of those to whom he owed his election. He declares that he would not expect me to appoint his nominees, however, unless I was satisfied they were as good men as I could get. He would also presume that I should pay especial regard to the wishes of those who voted for me in the Common Council in respect of appointments, but I would be under no pledges.

Olmsted declared himself willing to make only a small nod to political patronage. He would accept Opdyke's nomination "on the terms indicated—that is, without the slightest pledge or promise on my part, but only an understanding that I shall not be an *impracticable*, wholly."

    Despite Olmsted's intention not to go to New York, he did travel there and probably met with some of the aldermen. On March 19 Opdyke wrote Olmsted: "It is desired by a few of our friends to confer with you. They think your nomination would not be confirmed without some understanding with the Democratic members of the Board, and that it would be unfortunate to send in your name without some assurance of your confirmation." The following day, Thursday, March 20, Olmsted took the train to New York City (FLO to HWB, March 15, 1862, USSC-NYPL, box 641; G. P. Opdyke to FLO, March 19, 1862; Bloor Diary, March 20, 1862).

To John Olmsted

New York, March [25] 1862[1]
Tuesday.

Dear Father,

I came here last Thursday. The Sanitary Commission is half disposed to resign. The Mayor has offered me the nomination to the office of
Street Commissioner. I have accepted it on condition that I am not to be
trammelled in appointments, or to make or keep any political bargains.[2]
The Mayor, is apparently very anxious that I should have it on those terms
& is very frank, direct and generous about it. He thinks the aldermen will
not dare reject it—but of course there is a desire to arrange with me about
the patronage before they commit themselves. I think it very doubtful and
shall not want the nomination made—& it will not be made—without a
fair prospect of success. The duties are very complicated and the responsibility very onerous—the patronage is the largest of any of the civic offices
& rightfully belongs to the Mayor's office. It includes the appointment of
eight heads of bureaus with salaries of two to three thousand each &
several hundred clerks, inspectors &c, some fee offices, one said to have
been worth $10,000 last year. The Salary is $5,000. It would be a hard office
& I am not over anxious to get it—but shall be glad to if I can have it on my
own terms. The offer from the mayor is at any rate very gratifying to me
and to my friends.

Mary is quite ill, with a severe protracted feverish cold—keeps her
bed. Marion, fine, fat & jolly. The others doing well. Give my love to Owen
boy. I must manage to see him before long. I shall probably return to
Washington on Friday. The nomination if made, will go in on Monday.

My friend Dana,[3] who has never been backward in helping me,
wants to borrow $3,000 for a year or more—I should think a very safe man
to trust. He is a salaried man—steady employment, & extra work, as editor
of the Am. Cyclopedia &c. He offers [as] security shares of the Tribune
stock, which I believe is always of ready sale, but is very rarely in market. (I
should like very much to own a few). Could you get it for him in Hartford?

Your affectionate Son

Fred. Law Olmsted.

---

1. Although Olmsted dated this letter "Tuesday March 1862," the editors have chosen
the date March 25 because Olmsted traveled to New York City on March 20, the "last
Thursday" here referred to as his arrival date (Bloor Diary, March 20, 1862).

2. See FLO to Salmon Portland Chase, March 15, 1862, above.
3. Olmsted's friend Charles A. Dana. Then managing editor of the *New-York Daily Tribune*, Dana lost his job three days later. On March 28, 1862, Horace Greeley demanded his resignation because the two had come to differ on editorial policy. Although Greeley still strongly supported the war, he had come to oppose the vigorous war policy epitomized by the slogan, "Forward to Richmond," which Dana had been advocating. Dana then entered the employ of the War Department and became an assistant secretary of war, serving in that position until the end of the Civil War (*DAB*).

To Edwin McMasters Stanton [April 13, 1862]

In the stubborn refusal of the people of the slave states to entertain any proposition favorable to the abolition of slavery, there doubtless is much of selfishness, much of cowardice, and much of willfully blind and deaf prejudice and passion, but it can hardly be that there is not also some element of common sense to which it is the part of wise statesmanship to accommodate itself. Such an element as well as the relation to it which the dealings of government at this time with the negroes of the Sea islands must have, it is my purpose to demonstrate.

[*Because slavery is essentially unjust, it is commonly said that there can be nothing in it compatible with common sense.*]

The man whose twenty first birth-day comes on the fourteenth of November will be allowed to cast his vote at an election on that day when he will not be allowed to do so on the thirteenth. Why is it his right tomorrow and not today? Nature knows no such line. It is an artificial boundary arbitrarily fixed by law. And on this ground I have heard a proposition to abolish it gravely made and argued, it being forgotten that human government can proceed not a single step without classifying men, and dealing with them differently, each after his class. Is not this truth too much lost sight of in the advice commonly given the people of the slave states?

There are some men under twenty one years of age of much more mature intellect than others who are above that age. Yet common sense acquiesces in the law which receives the vote of the latter class and rejects that of the former. There are negroes in slavery who have attained to a higher civilization, and a purer morality than some white men, who are, nevertheless, neither confined in the madhouse, nor the penitentiary. The distinction of classes established by law, has, in all such cases, a certain *basis* in nature. There is equally a basis in nature for a *distinction* between the negro class of the South and all other classes of its society.[1] It is true that if we examine the most obvious grounds of this distinction—those of form and color—we find them in reality of no importance [*whatsoever*] *except* as of marks of historical peculiarities. But do not these historical peculiarities necessarily involve mental and moral peculiarities? Unquestionably. We know that whoever possesses them must have inherited whatever congenital idiosyncrasy would naturally result from the circumstance that his stock during some five or six generations had one after another been condemned for life to hard, unrequited labor upon a crude, monotonous diet. He is also very sure to be in direct descent, and but a few generations removed from a completely savage and heathen people.

Being thus [*naturally*] distinguished from all other classes in the republic, and the distinction being thus marked and defined, there can be nothing essentially unreasonable or unrepublican in the idea that special enactments of law *may* be required with reference to this class.*[2]

If we concede this, [*that a proposition to place the African race under special provisions of law is neither essentially absurd nor essentially inconsistent with the foundation of our system of law*] we must also concede that a majority of the citizens of any state may rightly *demand the enactment* of such provisions.

Concede this, and we may, at any moment, be brought face to face with the question: To *what* peculiar liabilities or disabilities, temporary or otherwise, in their requirements, shall Africans residing in the state be *made* subject?

To this question, what to the citizen of a slave state will always be, while it remains a slave state, the simplest and readiest answer? Obviously this: "Those already on our statute books."

"I know these Africans," says the citizen of the South, "and in my judgement they demand different supervision and requirements of law from those which are necessary for the rest of our community; a supervision which it would be expensive, and, in the main, useless to maintain with the races of Europe; police requirements which it would be irksome and equally useless to have forced upon me and my family. There is an existing system which meets this demand. You propose to abolish it. What substitute do you offer? Will it raise cotton? Will it prevent vagabondism? Is it compatible with my dignity and interests? Is it likely to be satisfactory

---

*The Hon. Charles Sumner, in an address to the people of New York at the Metropolitan Theatre, 8th of May, 1855, says: "While discountenancing all prejudice of color and every establishment of caste, the Antislavery Enterprise—at least so far as I may speak for it—does not undertake to change human nature, or to force any individual into relations of life for which he is not morally, intellectually and socially adapted; nor does it necessarily assume that a race, degraded for long generations under the iron heel of bondage, can be lifted at once into all the political privileges of an American citizen."

293

in my household? Where can I see it at work? Where is all you assert of it, demonstrated? Nowhere,—no demonstration? A mere theory that something might be done? [*Away! Away!*] I'll hear no more of this idle talk. The evils of Slavery I know and can bear with; the evils of an untried system of dealing with these savages, who are but just now well broken in to a useful part in our social economy, I will not think of venturing upon."

Mr. Secretary, I shall be excused for observing before proceeding to what must be necessarily a matter of opinion, that my opinions upon this subject are not closet opinions, and they have not been hastily formed. I some years since spent considerably more than one whole year in daily personal intercourse with the citizens of the slave states for the express purpose, constantly in view, and I believe, constantly with a sincere and honest endeavour, to gain a trustworthy knowledge, and to form trustworthy opinions, upon it.[3] And I have long entertained the opinion, that, for the security and permanence of our government, nothing was so much needed, as an opportunity of demonstrating to the citizens of the South upon their own soil that there was another alternative to the Slavery of this class of their population besides that of merging it in the existing classes, which might be adopted with reasonable certainty of satisfactory results. We now have such an opportunity, and with it we have an administration which was elected by the people with a distinct understanding that, within just, reasonable and constitutional limits, it would favor freedom. It has gone so far as to declare its disposition to offer a compensation to the owners of Slaves, as an inducement to them in favor of freedom.[4] It has not declared, but, it is about to demonstrate, what it thinks should be done by the states with and for this class in its first step of freedom.

There are three courses, one of which this administration must and will take, concerning the opportunity to which I refer:

1st   It may neglect it altogether:

2nd   It may use it in such a way as to give grounds for the assertion that it has found the African inhabitants of the Sea Islands freed from the liabilities of slavery;[5] that it acknowledges its duty as a government toward them; that it has taken out of their reach the products of their last year's labor, that it has allowed its highest military and financial representatives on this ground to solicit charitable donations for them, that it has encouraged and co-operated with a system of eleemosynary supply for their wants, and that it has thus presented to the citizens of the Slave States[6]

ORGANIZED BEGGARY

as the only alternative to slavery which it is able to adopt when it undertakes the duty of dealing directly with the Africans upon the soil, and in the climate of the South. Assertions of this character are already publickly made. Can it be said that they are entirely without foundation?

3^d It may use it in a way to make as complete and consistent a trial as is practicable of the abolition of slavery in the South, with twelve thousand plantation negroes, for the most part upon their plantations; securing to them for this purpose every reasonable legal advantage and requiring of them all just and proper service. It may thus not only demonstrate the good faith with which it has professed to regard slavery as an evil, but at the same time demonstrate that there may be a just alternative to slavery, to the willing adoption of which there can thereafter be no obstacle except ignorance and passion, which the declaration already made at the suggestion of the administration will not go far to remove.

Of these three courses the first, that is to say, an entire neglect of these negroes by government, would have simply the objection that it might cause much privation and suffering to an innocent people. This however is but a common and unavoidable contingency of war, and might[7] be much more merciful than the second which in aiding to fix a demoralizing and wasteful policy upon the country would be entirely inhumane, unwise and disasterous. Doubtless there will be found occasion for cavilling in any case but I speak now with regard to men who mean to be honest and reasonable, and who yet sustain slavery. These men in my judgement will not fail to be told that what shall have been done with and for these twelve thousand plantation negroes was what this administration, what Lincoln and the northerners, would have done if they could, with all the Slaves upon all the plantations of the South. And I think that there will be some reason for them to believe it. Therefore I think that the larger the amount of assistance which these negroes have forced upon them of a merely charitable character, or of what may seem to be of a fortuitous character, without order, system or responsible return of the results, such as the army may incidentally throw to them, as a hunter throws the offal of his game to his dogs—the larger the amount of all such assistance they get, the stronger will be the hold of that old prejudice [*which exists in the mind of every citizen loyal and disloyal of the South, and of many also loyal and disloyal in the north,*] against which the plan initiated by this administration, and against which every plan for relieving the country of this terrible Old Man of the Sea[8] of Slavery, will have to contend in the forum of popular discussion.

But there remains the third course; namely, to establish a policy of dealing with the negroes on the Sea Island plantations in which the primary duty of government toward such a class of its population shall appear to have been recognized; which shall be in substantial accordance with the principles of law which this administration would be willing to see the governments of the Slave States adopt, and to so carry out that policy as to present a real vindication of those principles and demonstrate to the honest common-sense of the citizens of the South when this excitement shall be overpast, the sufficiency of such a policy for all the purposes of just dealing, with all the negro class in their midst.

[*And now Sir, I have to ask what is the true republican plan of dealing with the negro class of the South? It may be said that the Administration has no precedents to govern it.*] Precedents involving the principle applicable in the case, do not seem to be entirely wanting. Sir, what do the peculiarities—the idiosyncracies of the class in question amount to? The negro has, it is said, but an imperfect intelligence; he is childish; he is improvident; he is sensual and exciteable, and his temper is to be distrusted. [*Is this not the worst that can be said of him?*] Have we no precedents for special legislation as to men possessing such peculiarities? What then is the matter with the inmates of your District workhouse, and of your five and twenty institutions, State and National, for the treatment of lunatics and weak minded persons? And are there not special enactments of law for the supervision and provision of minors? [*Or are these human beings made chattels and sold away from their parents to the highest bidder, on account of these peculiarities? Are the Governors of our Workhouses, and the Superintendents of our Insane Retreats, and the Guardians of our orphan children owners of human property? Far from it.*]

Suppose that a Governor or Superintendent or Guardian should be appointed for these negroes, who like the insane of the Army and Navy can properly be regarded as under no state government, and who consequently have at this time got to be looked after, if they are adequately looked after at all, by the National Government,[9] what in accordance with these precedents of our laws, will be his first duty? Unquestionably it will be to see that his wards are provided with the means of supporting life. Let it be assumed that for this purpose the use of the abandoned plantations on which they are found living is entrusted to him, and that until these are available for their entire support, government will make the necessary advances afterwards to be returned out of the proceeds of the sale of their surplus productions, or in fresh provisions to be supplied to the Army. Then his second duty will be to guard against their peculiar vices or frailties, so far at least as they would otherwise cause inconvenience or expense to the community, that is, to the nation. For this purpose it is essential that he possess all necessary legal authority, and power to enforce legal authority, to prevent them from becoming an unnecessary burden upon others, or upon the Treasury. This authority will be of the same character as that of a Tradesman with an idle apprentice, or as that of the master of a Merchant Ship with a truculent seaman.

And his third and most important duty will be to make the Negroes comprehend that this authority is not the same as that by which a master compels a slave to work for his own purposes, namely that of ownership; and again, that it is not merely the natural authority of a superior intellect over an inferior, or of a good man over a bad man. But that it is *the sacred authority of Government* to enforce a natural duty of each man to all other men; an authority before which all white men are expected and required to bow equally with black, an authority to which their Governor or Guardian is himself subject equally with them. In other words he must be to them the representative and the instrument of that Common law to which they in common with white men are hereafter to hold themselves subject and their loyalty to which, especially in this particular of industry, it is to be hoped will demonstrate that their slavery or subjection to the merely private interests of another man has been heretofore unnecessary.

It may seem to be too nice a distinction to be comprehended by such people—this between subjection to the authority of an owner backed by statute law, and subjection to the authority of a guardian backed by Common Law—but if the guardian is armed with the authority of government to be to them not merely its instrument to compel them to their duty, but equally and at the same time its instrument to protect them in the rational exercise of their just and proper rights, to secure to them the natural reward of their labor, and to guard them against the lazy rapacity of other men, there need be no fear that they will long remain without a wholesome and happy respect for the corresponding exercise of authority by which he protects the nation against their inclination to indolence and other vices. It will then be essential to success that he possess means of controlling all the dealings which others may need to have with the negroes so far at least as to prevent violence and frauds upon them. For this purpose he must either be clothed with the authority of a magistrate himself, or he must have a ready and efficient appeal to someone else who is clothed with this authority. Thus only will he be able to command the confidence of the negroes as their true governor, guardian, superintendent or legally appointed protector and friend.

To properly execute his trust, therefore, he must be possessed beyond all question of the following endowments from government

1st   Means of securing to the Negroes temporarily, at least, protection against hunger, cold, &c. (conditionally it may be upon their good order and industry)

2nd   Means of offering them some sort of wages for work;

3rd   Means of entailing upon them a sure punishment for indolence and other vice;

4th   Means of securing them against unlawful violence and the impositions and tyranny of others.

[There is in my mind no question that] All this is nothing less than it is the simple *[decent]* duty of the administration to offer and secure to them, and *[I repeat that]* unless this much can be attempted, I can not but gravely doubt if it would not be better for me and for all good citizens, in view of the great interests of our race which are involved, to refrain from aiding or taking part with the administration in carrying out a plan which will necessarily cause so large a body of our brethren hereafter to offend, and that upon a point so vital to our national existence.[10] They will die then, says the Secy of the Treasy. Let them die. What are ten thousand lives longer or shorter in a question of this magnitude? Four millions of Negroes here today to be eight millions tomorrow. What shall we do with them?

In its relations to that question, the importance of the business of Government with this insignificant ten or twelve thousand unfortunate men, women and children, wrecked by process of War, on the Sea Islands, is very far from being limited by the measure of its mere duty to them.[11]

Yet as regards these Negroes alone, what is the duty of government?

You have taken their corn; you have taken their mules and horses and wagons; you have prevented them from preparing the soil for their only staple crop;[12] you have through the criminal negligence or more criminally contracted judgement of duty of your Medical Bureau introduced small pox and have propagated other diseases among them.[13] Can you say that what is being now done, is all the duty that government owes them?

I know, Sir, that the Secy of the Treasury is doing what he can in his own department and that he is willing to stretch[14] his authority to the utmost to meet the more important demands of humanity, but with how little confidence, Sir, can [it] be possible for his agent to proceed in the attempt to realize a consistent policy of executing the duty of government, I ask you to judge after hearing the statement of the Secretary himself addressed to that agent & which thus defines and limits his authority in the case:

"The whole authority of the Department over the objects of your report is derived from the 5th Sec. of the act *to provide for the collection of duties*, approved July 13, 1861, by which the President is authorized to permit *Commercial intercourse*, with any part of the country declared to be in a state of insurrection, under such rules and regulations, as may be prescribed by the Secy of the Treasury."

"As incidental to this authority alone have I any power to sanction any measures for the culture of the abandoned estates in the Port Royal or other districts."[15]

Under the administration of your predecessor, Sir, I endeavored to induce your Department to adopt a comprehensive plan of dealing with these plantations and with this people, which had come under its control and were held and used under its control as an incident of War.[16] It had not occurred to me, Sir, nor did it occur to the gentleman long connected with government,[17] with whom I then consulted about it, that the necessity which existed for government to take action in the premises, *was* a necessity incident to the collection of duties.

Such, however, was, I think, Sir, owing only to its preoccupation of mind by more imperative duties, preventing deliberation, the conclusion adopted by the administration, and accordingly I was then unable to obtain the attention of the Department. Without knowing the reason therefor, I cheerfully submitted to its wisdom.

Learning however, from the Inspector of the Sanitary Commission that no measures were being taken at all adequate to the demands of the case; sometime subsequently I called upon the Secy of the Treasury, in company with two other gentlemen who had a benevolent interest in the matter, to represent the importance of such measures.[18]

The Secretary informed us that he had employed a person[19] whom he believed to be fully competent to superintend the business and that he possessed all requisite authority of action.

Though I did not feel authorized to occupy his time in argument, from my own knowledge of the circumstances I could not with all respect for his judgment agree with him, and I felt obliged in my conscience to act in another channel.

I consequently drew up the Bill, sometime afterwards presented by the Honble Mr Forster to the Senate. I have been informed that the Secy of the Treasy did not wish that Bill to pass, it did however at length pass the Senate by a vote of 24 to 14. And I have reason to believe that it would have passed the House, some of the ablest and most conservative minds of the House having assured me that it would receive their active support in debate.

At this time however the Secy of the Treasy sent for me and let me know that he did not wish the Bill to pass; at the same time, he proposed that I should myself take entire charge of the negroes and the superintendence of the government duty to them.

Never doubting that the authority of such an agent would be adequate for the duties which I deemed it necessary governmt should undertake, I requested the gentlemen who had most interested themselves in the Bill in the House to let it sleep while I took the proposition of the Secy into consideration.

It is only within a few days that I have fully understood the state of the case—having learned from the Secy of the Treasury that he had never read the Bill in question, that he entirely misapprehended its scope and purpose, and that he regards himself as having no power to confer any authority upon an agent which would have the slightest practical value.

In fact, Sir, I understand that really the only authority which is pretended to be exercised, as a legal authority, over this population, *is* a military authority and so far as this is exercised with any regard to any of the objects—whether of state or of charity, to which I have had the honor to be allowed to ask your attention—it is by reason of a letter borne by the Agent of the Treasury Department addressed by *you*, Sir, to the *Military* authorities, recommending him to their countenance and such assistance as—incidental to the operations of *War*—they may find it convenient to give him.

I respectfully submit, Sir, that this is a complicated arrangment— that it has the inherent fault of all unnecessarily complicated arrangments of government, the creation of undefined responsibilities and imperfect duties.

I do not feel willing[20] Sir, to accept a responsibility which is morally so great, and legally so questionable in its scope.

It may seem to you, Sir, immodest in me to tender my services to your department in a manner which implies that I consider that tender as an inducement to you to undertake the duty of government in the premises. [*I hope that*] You will believe my assurance, however, Sir, that I do so simply because I trust that you regard it as important that some man possessing certain qualifications which I suppose myself to possess, and who is thoroughly imbued with a sense of the responsibility resting on the administration in the premises, should be appointed for this purpose, and it is because I wish to testify to the administration in the most emphatic manner the fact, that it is very doubtful if a man so imbued will assume that responsibility with only such means of executing it satisfactorily to his conscience, as the Secy of the Treasury can offer, while he will readily do so, if you desire it and will give him the support morally and materially which I suppose it to be in your power to do.[21]

Mr Secy, I have endeav^d to show you that the administration has a duty to those negroes, which is incident to the operations of war. This duty, Sir, will meet every imperative requirement of the case which can properly be made upon government. There is another Class of duties, Sir, which it is important should not be confused with those of gov^t. If gov^t will attend to the economical demand of the case, I am authorized to pledge the faith of the leading citizens of Boston, New York & Phil^a that the religious and educational demand which it presents, shall be also generously met—generously and in an orderly, quiet, respectable and systematic way. I refer, Sir, to the gentlemen composing the associations organized at the instance of the Secy of the Treasy, committees from each of whom are now here. They are willing to undertake this—are not willing to be responsible for the duty which the Secy of the Treasy has been disposed to leave to them.[22]

But, Sir, if I have not succeeded in impressing you with the conviction which I possess that it is the proper duty of your department of this administration, as a consequence of the incident of war, which deprived these innocent people of their usual means of subsistence, to provide for their government in the only proper way they can be governed, then I wish to put it on another ground which I deem conclusive as to the question of your authority.

As Secy of the Sanitary Commission, Sir, I have received much evidence that the army on the Southern Coast is already suffering from a lack of sufficient provision of fresh vegetable food. In that climate a larger quantity of vegetable food than is provided for in your rations is an absolute necessity of health. I do not exaggerate the case when I state that your army can not live without it.

This necessary provision can in no way be obtained with any regard to economy except by the cultivation of those plantations, and those plantations can in no way be cultivated for this purpose so efficiently, so economically, as [*by a system of piece-work or of tasks*] under the direct superintendence of your depart[ment].

I only ask, Sir, that you give me the authority to employ precisely those agencies which would be most economical for this purpose, and I will engage to accomplish all the duty of government so far as that is practicable by any means from this time henceforth, until the final adjudication of this whole great question of the government of the rebellious districts.

The text presented here is from a manuscript copy of Olmsted's oral presentation to Secretary of War Edwin M. Stanton, probably on April 13, 1862. The editors have chosen that date because Alfred J. Bloor noted in his diary that Olmsted visited the secretary of war that evening. Moreover, in a letter headed April 12 but actually written on the 14th, Olmsted told Bellows that he had argued his case for Port Royal with Stanton on the preceding evening. The correspondence of Salmon P. Chase for April 1862 also indicates that Chase was then ready to relinquish authority over the abandoned plantations and slaves to Stanton and allow him to appoint a military governor.

A copyist wrote on an envelope that accompanied this manuscript, "Argument addressed to the Secy of the Treasury and afterwards to the Secy of War, after the former had asked me to take charge of the negro population of the Sea Islands, February 1862. Sgd Fred. Law Olmsted." The assigned date is incorrect, but the manuscript is what the note indicates: an argument intended first for Salmon P. Chase, and later revised for Edwin M. Stanton. Olmsted added corrections and interlineations to his first version and presented his case to Chase sometime between March 10 and March 13. Later Olmsted took his presentation and further revised it by adding eight manuscript pages in his own handwriting on a different kind of writing paper. Most likely it was at this time that he discarded the first four pages of the original argument.

The speech to Stanton is presented here. The text of the presentation to Chase can not be recovered, since that part of the document was subsequently rewritten at least twice and possibly three or four times. Only the final revision, made in pencil, can be said with certainty to have been made for Stanton. The editors have, however, included in italics within brackets or as notes, any crossed out words, phrases, or passages of substantive content. With this presentation Olmsted filed several other pages in his own handwriting on the same paper as the addition written expressly for Stanton. One page is a draft of the appointment of a military governor; the others appear to be part of a fragmentary general order that Olmsted probably intended for Stanton to issue with his appointment. Since those pages are not integral to this presentation, they are not published here (FLO to HWB, April 14, 1862, below; Bloor Diary, April 13, 1862).

1. Olmsted first framed this statement as a question: "Is there not a certain basis in nature for a legal distinction between the negroes of the South and all other classes of its society?"
2. Similarly, Olmsted first expressed this thought as a question: "Is there anything essentially unreasonable, or unrepublican . . . ?"
3. A reference to the fourteen months between October 1852 and August 1854 that Olmsted spent traveling through the South.
4. On March 6, 1862, President Lincoln asked Congress to pass a joint resolution authorizing financial assistance to any state adopting a plan for the gradual emancipation of slaves within its limits (*War for the Union*, 2: 31–32).
5. Olmsted's first version read: "It may use it in such a way as to manifest and place on record the fact that it has found the African inhabitants of the Sea Islands freed from slavery."
6. Olmsted's original statement was more tentative: "It may thus present to the citizens of the Slave states . . ."
7. Here Olmsted first used "would."
8. A reference to the character in *One Thousand and One Arabian Nights* who clung to Sinbad the Sailor and could not be dislodged. Thus the expression describes any tedious burden that is difficult to shed.
9. Olmsted refers to a congressional act of 1855 establishing the Government Hospital for the Insane to care for and treat the mentally ill of the army, the navy, and the District of Columbia (John F. Callan, *The Military Laws of the United States Relating to the Army, Volunteers, Militia, and to Bounty Lands and Pensions* . . . [Philadelphia, 1863], pp. 437–38).
10. Olmsted originally cast the last part of this sentence quite differently. He wrote:

> Unless this much can be attempted, I am convinced that it would be better for me and for all good citizens, in view of the great interests of our race which are involved, to refrain from giving the smallest ground for the allegation that with all the aid which could be given them by the theoretical advocates of the abolition of Slavery, under the advice and patronage of an administration elected and pledged to do all which the Constitution would permit it to do, to justify freedom, these negroes miserably failed to prove themselves worthy of it.

He then continued this argument directed at Salmon P. Chase in a paragraph that he also deleted:

> I protest in the name of Truth and Justice, now in advance, and with as full a knowledge of all the circumstances as it has been possible for me with your aid to obtain, against this allegation. But I know that such protest is in vain, and I therefore beg most respectfully to repeat that unless this first, simplest, plainest duty of all civilized Government can be undertaken toward these people, I for one dare undertake no responsibility in behalf or in the name of government in

regard to them. And to a similar conclusion must advise all to come who respect my judgement in this matter.

11. The phrase originally read, "far from being one of its duties toward them."
12. Here Olmsted had inserted a footnote to Chase that read, "You will remember that I called upon you with Prof Bache & Dr Bellows two months ago to urge that this wrong should be repaired while there was yet time." In his revision of the presentation for Stanton, Olmsted slightly recast his account of that meeting and probably forgot to line through the footnote (see n. 18, below).
13. Several different sources informed Olmsted about the situation at Port Royal. Edward L. Pierce in his report, a copy of which Chase had lent to Olmsted, stated that large amounts of corn had been taken by the army from the plantations, almost none of which had enough grain to feed its inhabitants until April. Pierce also noted that the army had impressed horses, mules, and oxen for transportation, and that foraging soldiers and the military authorities had slaughtered cattle to obtain beef. George L. Andrew, a Sanitary Commission inspector who arrived at Port Royal in late December 1861, had informed Olmsted that through the Medical Bureau's failure to quarantine all soldiers exposed to smallpox, there had been twenty-eight cases of the disease and eight deaths. Andrew had included the vaccine in his stores, and he supplied enough to vaccinate both the soldiers and the black inhabitants of the sea islands. In the redrafting of this presentation for Stanton, Olmsted at one point intended specifically to blame former Surgeon General Finley with the phrase, "or more criminally contracted judgement of duty of the late head of your Medical Bureau," but then lined through the words "the late head of" ("From Port Royal," *New-York Daily Tribune*, Jan. 21, 1862, pp. 6, 7; U.S. Treasury Department, *Negroes at Port Royal*, p. 34).
14. The original version in the copyist's hand, first intended for Chase, ends at this point.
15. Olmsted correctly synopsized the law, which gave the secretary of the treasury the power not only to set rules and regulations for such commercial intercourse but also to appoint officers to carry out such regulations (*The Statutes at Large of the United States of America* [Washington, D.C., 1863], 12: 255–56).
16. The editors have been unable to discover any letter from Olmsted to Simon Cameron advocating such measures. Most likely Olmsted informally suggested such a course of action to Cameron during a meeting on another issue.
17. Probably A. D. Bache, who had headed the U.S. Coast Survey since 1843 (*DAB*).
18. A reference to the visit that Olmsted, Bellows, and Bache paid to Chase on January 27, 1862 (HWB to Eliza Bellows, Jan. 28, 1862, Henry Whitney Bellows Papers, Massachusetts Historical Society, Boston, Mass.; FLO to Bertha Olmsted, Jan. 28, 1862, above).
19. Edward L. Pierce.
20. Olmsted first wrote, "I cannot."
21. Here Olmsted softened his original statement, "which it is in your power to do."
22. On March 20, 1862, the Educational Commission (Boston), the New York National Freedmen's Relief Association, and the Port Royal Relief Committee (Philadelphia)—all three organized to aid the blacks at Port Royal—had signed an agreement of cooperation. Two days later they asked Olmsted to become their general agent. At the time of this presentation, Olmsted was still considering their offer (W. L. Rose, *Rehearsal for Reconstruction*, pp. 36–42; J. W. Edmonds to FLO, March 22, 1862).

To Henry Whitney Bellows   [April 14, 1862][1]

U.S. Sanitary Commission,
Adams' House, 244 F street,
Washington, D.C., 12th April 1862.

My Dear Doctor,
Your note of the 12th duly arrived; I think there is no point upon which Jenkins[2] will not have given you more true impressions than any I can convey by letter, as to the affairs you write of,[3] except as there has been advance since he left. I saw the Secy of War last night and by my advice that he would come if called for, he telegraphed for D[r] Van Buren and for D[r] Hammond simultaneously. This indicates his intention. Wood is, however, entrenching himself as strongly as possible.[4] I had quite a talk with him this morning; he is doing his best to provide for Yorktown wounded[5] he says: clearing the hospitals here. I offered him our stock and he seemed very glad to learn how large it was. He was "down on" Hammond and went thro' the same charges that you heard.[6] They do not in the least affect my conviction that he is the best man.
I saw Vollum[7] also, last night. He is working like a beaver against the Bill—[was] urgent that I should say that I thought it best to give up the increased ranks and let the Inspectors be "assigned" surgeons, without rank or sanitary specialty, rather than open the doors to volunteer surgeons to compete with regulars. I could offer him no comfort.[8] We have had a fine illustration of the way the assigning would work, in the case of a regular surgeon, sent to inspect Winchester, who went there, took a friendly drink with his bretheren and reported that they were good fellows and everything going along smoothly—as it was, to the devil. I have some hope of the Bill's passing today. If it does, I strongly advise you to come on at once, to influence the appointments.
The Port Royalists are at work with the President.[9] I argued the case with the Secy of War last night,[10] and I think they are both convinced that Mr Chase's plan is wrong. I don't know that I told you my final answer to him. It was—the business can never be properly managed under your authority. I cannot accept a responsibility under you in the matter. If the Secy of War will offer it to me, I will take it. My impression is that he will do so—in which case I shall go. I presume that it will be decided today.
Yours Most Cordially

Fred. Law Olmsted.

The original is letter 16 in box 636 of USSC-NYPL.

1. Although Olmsted dated this letter "April 12th," all evidence points to April 14 as the day it was actually written. On April 13 Alfred J. Bloor recorded in his diary that Olmsted had met with the secretary of war that evening. William A. Hammond wrote Olmsted on April 13 but gave no indication of having received a telegram from the secretary of war—a telegram that by Olmsted's dating here would have been sent on April 11. Internal evidence from the letter presented here also suggests that it was written later than April 12. Olmsted refers to the possibility of the bill reorganizing the Medical Bureau passing Congress "today"; indeed, the conference committee agreed to it on April 14. Moreover, Bellows's letter of April 12, to which Olmsted refers, was unlikely to have reached him before April 14 since the 13th was a Sunday (Bloor Diary, April 13, 1862; W. A. Hammond to FLO, April 13, 1862).

2. J. Foster Jenkins, associate secretary of the Commission, was visiting in New York City.

3. Bellows in that letter anxiously queried Olmsted: "What bill has passed the House? When is it likely to come up in Senate? Has the Secy of War said anything? When is it very desirable for the Comn to be in Washington? What is doing for the wounded at Pittsburg Landing by us?" (HWB to FLO, April 12, 1862, USSC-NYPL, box 740: 728.)

4. Robert C. Wood, who became acting surgeon general after Secretary of War Stanton assigned Finley to duty in Boston.

5. McClellan moved the Army of the Potomac to the Virginia Peninsula in late March, and the men marched overland from Fortress Monroe to lay siege to Yorktown. By April 14 only a handful of Union soldiers had been wounded in skirmishes. Wood's efforts were in anticipation of a battle at Yorktown (Frederick H. Dyer, *A Compendium of the War of the Rebellion . . .* , 3 vols. [1908; rpt. ed., New York, 1959], 2: 879–98).

6. A letter written by Hammond to Bellows in February 1862 suggests that these allegations, promulgated by members of the Medical Bureau, were that Hammond's low rank, questionable loyalty to the North, and poor health all rendered him unfit to be surgeon general. In his letter Hammond defended his patriotism and noted that his length of service as an army officer was comparable to that of numerous career soldiers holding high rank. The most serious charge questioned Hammond's physical ability to carry out the surgeon general's duties, and he addressed it at length. In 1852, while stationed in New Mexico Territory, Hammond suffered chest pains and fainting spells. His condition was diagnosed as a cardiac problem, and he received a six-month leave. A year later a similar attack felled him in Florida, and the problem, complicated by a knee injury, recurred again in 1858. He then received another leave, visited Europe, and applied for sedentary duty in 1859. After that request was denied, he resigned from the army to accept a teaching post at the medical school of the University of Maryland. According to Hammond, his heart condition had been diagnosed as not stemming from any organic impairment, and by 1862 he declared himself free of attacks for the past five years, a slight exaggeration. When upon the outbreak of the Civil War he reenlisted, Hammond also pledged to resign should his ailment recur (W. A. Hammond to HWB, Feb. 24, 1862, USSC-NYPL, box 640; Bonnie E. Blustein, "A New York Medical Man: William Alexander Hammond, M.D. [1828–1900], Neurologist" [Ph.D. diss., University of Pennsylvania, 1979], pp. 36–38, 55–63).

7. Edward Perry Vollum (d. 1902), a surgeon in the U.S. Army who was among the members of the Medical Bureau most sympathetic to the Sanitary Commission's aims and activities. He received one of the new appointments as medical inspector in June 1862. He collaborated with Olmsted during the Peninsula campaign and later gratefully recalled that the Sanitary Commission had provided him with a "cargo of stimulants, foods, anodynes, dressings, fruit &c, . . . to take to Harrison's Landing, June '62 on my steamer, 'Arrowsmith,' which I distributed freely to the

worn out troops, when they came in there after the seven days fights, destitute of everything needed for the sick and wounded." In 1863 Olmsted endorsed a proposal by Vollum, which was not adopted, to create a culinary department as part of the Medical Bureau.

  After the Civil War, Vollum spent the remainder of his career in the army. In 1890 Olmsted wrote a letter supporting Vollum's candidacy for the post of surgeon general, which he did not receive (E. P. Vollum to FLO, March 3 and July 30, 1890; FLO to USSC Executive Committee, Jan. 4, 1863; F. B. Heitman, *Historical Register and Dictionary*, 1: 988–89).

8. That is, Vollum believed that the Sanitary Commission should give up its attempts to secure higher ranks for some officers of the Medical Bureau and should concentrate upon defeating a provision that would allow volunteer army surgeons to compete with regular army surgeons for appointments to those offices. The bill favored by the Sanitary Commission would raise the surgeon general in rank from colonel to brigadier general and would provide that the offices of assistant surgeon general and medical inspector general carry the rank of colonel of cavalry. It would also create the office of medical inspector with the rank of lieutenant colonel of cavalry. Although the Sanitary Commission wished to abolish the awarding of offices by seniority and to institute a system of selection by merit, it did not favor including the volunteer surgeons in this competition. The Commission, unlike the regular army officers of the Medical Bureau, however, did not consider this an important issue (*Diary of the Civil War*, pp. 217–18).

9. On April 13, 1862, a committee from New York, Boston, and Philadelphia societies to aid the sea-island blacks met with President Lincoln to urge Olmsted's appointment as military governor of that area. The committee included the wealthy abolitionist Francis George Shaw and physician Robert W. Hooper, both from Boston; and from Philadelphia, Philip P. Randolph and lawyer Stephen Colwell. The committee members soon discovered that their efforts were in vain, however, for Lincoln told them that Salmon P. Chase had already offered the job to Edward Pierce. While some members of the committee remained longer in Washington and met again with Chase, they found him adamant about his commitment to Pierce, even though Pierce did not want the position (William Rhinelander Stewart, *The Philanthropic Work of Josephine Shaw Lowell* . . . [New York, 1911], pp. 24–25; Stephen Colwell to FLO, April 29, 1862).

10. See FLO to Edwin M. Stanton, April 13, 1862, above.

To James Erwin Yeatman[1]

17th April [1862]

My Dear Sir,

  I find it difficult to reply to such letters as the one which I enclose without expressing an opinion that your association is pursuing an objectionable method of benevolence. It is obvious that if Chicago, Nashville, Louisville, Memphis and other cities of the West and South, as they come to contain Union hospitals, should think best to pursue the same course with St. Louis, some would receive and have to spare, while others less fortunate than St Louis has been in possessing men of earnestness, energy and eloquence, might, although their needs were greater, obtain little or nothing. If you say that you send of your superfluity where need exists, I must ask what is the need of these two machines? We have an organization designed for the express purpose of sending the contributions of the benevolent—of Boston for instance—where they are most wanted. If you think we neglect St. Louis, why not call upon us? If, on the other hand, you undertake to supply the wants of the Mississippi valley, why should we have a receiving depot at Chicago, and you one at Boston? Surely the present arrangment is calculated to create distrust and unnecessary expense. Is it possible that a competition such as now practically exists between us in the Eastern fields of supply can be for the advantage of the cause to which we are both devoted? If the West thinks it best that there should be two "Commissions," can not the field both of supply and of distribution be fairly divided?

I write with a sincere desire to preserve not only harmony but if possible to secure unity of purpose, among good men with common ends to serve, and am, Sir,

Most Respectfully, & Cordially Yours;

Fred. Law Olmsted

Jas. E. Yeatman, Esquire,
Pres^t W. San Comm.
St Louis, M^o

The original is a letterpress copy on pages 381–84 of volume 1 in box 834 of USSC-NYPL. Since the letters preceding and following it were written on April 24, 1862, it is possible that it too was written then and was antedated to April 17.

1. James E. Yeatman (1818–1901), the Tennessee-born president of the Western Sanitary Commission. He moved to St. Louis in 1842, ran a commission business there, and became a founder and president of the Merchants' National Bank. Long active in civic affairs, Yeatman also helped establish the Mercantile Library Association and was the first president of the city's institution for the blind.

    When the Civil War began, Yeatman devoted his efforts to the Union cause. An army surgeon stationed in St. Louis in early 1862 described Yeatman as the most prominent Union man in the city. Like his counterparts in the U.S. Sanitary Commission, Yeatman took an interest in the condition of slaves as well as that of soldiers. In 1863 he compiled an invaluable report upon freedmen in the Mississippi River valley.

    Relations between Olmsted and Yeatman were always somewhat strained because of the competition between the two commissions. During Olmsted's visit to St. Louis in 1863 he and Yeatman worked on a plan, never implemented, to unite the rival organizations (*DAB*; James Cox, *Old and New St. Louis* [St. Louis, Mo., 1894], pp. 188–89; John Hill Brinton, *Personal Memoirs of John H. Brinton, Major and Surgeon U.S.V., 1861–1865* [New York, 1914], p. 109; FLO to J. E. Yeatman, April 21, 1863).

To John Strong Newberry

April 18th 1862

My Dear Doctor,

Dr Bellows & Dr Van Buren are here, and we are all very anxious to hear from you, having had nothing but your fatigue note from Nashville since the battle of Pittsburg Landing.[1]

It is obvious that you need a larger organization at the West. It is not practicable to carry the West along so independently of the East. After receiving various letters and telegraphic messages reproving my reticence as to our operations, I telegraphed for information to you at Cleaveland, and got next day a reply from your wife that you were at Nashville, but of what was doing, or wanted, not a word.[2] Meantime the Western Sanitary Commission was plowing our field so successfully with its floating hospitals and special appeals, based upon what it was doing, as to get $5000 in New York alone in one week.[3] It was equally active in Boston and our agents there also address me in earnest anxiety and bewilderment. Last night I received another request from Agnew and Strong that I would send them without delay specific statements of what our agents did and what our auxiliaries, at and after Pittsburg Landing. I have not received a specific statement of any kind from all the West, of anything which has been done during the last month.

I certainly ought to have at least weekly reports of all that is occurring within our organization. The idea that we did nothing for the West has cost us at least a thousand dollars a day during the last week. We combat it as well as we can, but you know of how little value general statements of plans and intentions are, compared with [narrations] of experience. Moreover, I am constantly obliged to say, I have not heard from the West, and the natural inference is that I have nothing really to do with the West. The Western Sanitary Commission is getting all the glory and all the dimes.

Yours Cordially,

Fred Law Olmsted.

Dr Newberry

The original is a letterpress copy on pages 287–90 of volume 1 in box 834 of USSC-NYPL.

1. The battle of Pittsburg Landing, better known as the battle of Shiloh, occurred in southern Tennessee on April 6 and 7, 1862. Confederate forces under the command of Albert Sidney Johnston surprised Union troops commanded by Ulysses S. Grant. On the second day of fighting, federal reinforcements from Don Carlos Buell's army and the absence of Johnston (mortally wounded on the first day of fighting) helped turn the tide of battle for the Union soldiers, who forced a Confederate retreat to Corinth, Mississippi. Both Union and Confederate casualties were high in this bloody battle: approximately thirteen thousand for the North, eleven thousand for the South (*War for the Union*, 2: 76–87).
2. On April 10 Olmsted telegraphed Newberry: "Can the East do nothing for Pittsburg wounded? Telegraph what is doing" (FLO to JSN, April 10, 1862, USSC-NYPL, box 834, 1: 242).
3. After the Western Sanitary Commission used steamboats in February 1862 to transport the wounded from the battle of Fort Donelson, the army's medical director at St. Louis suggested fitting up ships as floating hospitals complete with medical personnel and stores. The *City of Louisiana* was readied as a hospital ship by March 20. After the battle of Shiloh, the assistant quartermaster placed five other vessels under the direction of the Western Sanitary Commission to be used to transport the wounded (Jacob Gilbert Forman, *The Western Sanitary Commission; A Sketch of Its Origins, History* . . . [St. Louis, Mo., 1864], pp. 24–25).

To JOHN OLMSTED

Confidential.

U.S. Sanitary Commission
Adams' House, 244 F street
Washington, D.C. April 19th 1862.

Dear Father,

     I was very glad to hear from you last week. As long as I keep my health, I suppose that you don't care how hard I work. From an observation of yours which Mary quotes in a letter received this morning, I understand that you know what I have been doing about the Sea Islands. I believe it paid, though the study and energy I gave to the matter did not accomplish the precise result, nor anything like as good a result as I meant it should. I suppose that if I was determined to have it, and could neglect other matters to devote myself to it, I could get myself appointed Brigadier General, and assigned to duty as Military Governor of the islands, and then have absolute dictatorial control of it. But it is now too late to accomplish one grand object I should have had in view, could I have got such vantage ground before the cotton-planting season.[1]

As to the Sanitary Commission, our success is suddenly wonderfully complete. The Medical Bill after having been kicked about like a football, from House to Committee & Committee to House and House to Committee & Committee to subCommittee & back to House & thro' similar processes in Senate & from Senate to House & over & over again, at each kick losing on one side & gaining on another, until it was so thoroughly flabbergasted that nobody knew where or what it was, and a new one had to be started—this process repeated several times—all of a sudden a bill which is just the thing we wanted quietly passes thro' both houses the same day and before we know it is a law,[2] and this occurs at the moment the Secy of War kicks the old Surgn Genl out of his seat,[3] and all the staff, which, through esprit du corps has been regarding the Sanitary Commission as its enemy, suddenly opens its eyes to the fact that the San. Com. is its best friend and that Finley's obstinacy and stupid bigotry has well-nigh ruined it. The President yesterday promised to nominate for Surgeon General, Hammond, the very man whom, eight months ago, we picked out as the best man in the corps for that office,[4] and, who, this having been discovered, has since been regarded as a rebel and rancorously hated accordingly. Our advice will probably be taken also, as to most of the appointments, especially of Sanitary Inspectors, of which there are to be eight, each of rank and pay equal to that of the Surgeon Genl himself under the old law. We place first on our list A. K. Smith[5]—"Seed Smith" of the Grammer School, and it is [a] great pleasure to me to thus serve an old school mate, and friend of John's. Lyman[6]—brother in law of Sen Forster, is our candidate for Inspector General, which gratifies Foster very much.

As you will see by the papers, I am getting up floating hospitals. I shall probably take command of the first in person and expect to bring 500 wounded men in her to New York. I have got the bedding, dressings, instruments and medicines secured, to be ready Monday night. Have appointed my chief officers and assigned them their duties. I expect to have Parker,[7] and all the best surgeons of New York assigned me, as volunteers.

Yet it may all slip up, so don't talk of it.

I just received $1000 in a letter from San Francisco, which strengthens my hands for the Yorktown job.[8] It runs our Treasury up plump to $20,000 I believe.

If the Bill passes constituting a Bureau of Agriculture and Statistics, would you advise me to get the appointment of Commissioner if I can? One of the Bills give it all the Census business & this is most likely to pass. Another makes it an independent Department of Government, reporting direct to Congress.[9] Salary $3000, & no other emoluments. It would be respectable, comparatively quiet and might be exceedingly useful, leading all the industry of the country and even greatly aiding banking & finance. I am much better qualified for its organization & the more important part of its superintendence, & for the editing of its results, than anybody else who is yet talked of for it—& could get I guess, if I tried. It would require residence in Washington, I suppose $3000 in Washington is nearly as good as $4000 in New York, and there would be some chance of making it permanent. The Patent Coms[r] does not change with the administration nor the Head of Coast Survey—nor did the Census Coms[r] last time. The distance it would keep me from Hartford is a serious objection with me, for tho' I don't see you very often, it is uncomfortable not to feel able to.

The alternative is going in & trying to build up a landscape gardening business—an alternative that even at forty, I am not likely to follow very steadily, I fear. "Wherever you see a head, hit it" is my style of work, & I have not yet sowed my wild oats altogether.

I am reckoning on being in at the wedding,[10] so keep me[11] informed of the latest improvements on the programme.

Love to them all.

Your affectionate son,

Fred.

John Olmsted Esq[r]
Hartford, C[t]

If I go on the steamer, I will telegraph for Ally[12] to come on as a volunteer nurse, or as my aid. Will pay his expenses after arriving here, if you send him. If inconvenient to come, he need not regard the telegram.

---

1. Most likely Olmsted's one grand object was the establishment of a comprehensive model program to work the abandoned cotton plantations and aid the slaves in a transition from slavery to freedom. Olmsted believed that the cultivation of the cotton crop under his system would help blacks demonstrate their capacity to work as freedmen and would further enlarge and extend their capabilities. Moreover, he thought that the cultivation of cotton under his program would illustrate the superiority of free labor to slave labor and would, as he elsewhere phrased it, prove "to the South, the economic mistake of Slavery" (FLO to James R. Spalding, Feb. 15, 1862, above).
2. Olmsted's description of the course of the medical reform bill through Congress, though exaggerated, does indicate some of the difficulties it encountered. The original measure, Senate Bill 97, languished, and on February 7 Henry Wilson introduced a substitute, Senate Bill 188, which passed on the 27th in a greatly amended version that did not give increased rank or pay to the surgeon general and other officers of the bureau. In March, after the bill reached the House of Represen-

tatives, Francis P. Blair's committee reported back a substitute measure, much closer in form to the original. On April 10 the House passed this bill. A conference committee was necessary to compromise the differences, and on April 14 it reported a bill similar to the version passed by the House. This measure, immediately agreed to by both bodies, provided increased rank and pay for officers of the Medical Bureau, but retained a few of the Senate's amendments: one that opened competition for the offices to surgeons in the volunteer as well as the regular army, another that limited the bill's provisions to the duration of the war. By April 16 the bill had been signed into law (William Quentin Maxwell, *Lincoln's Fifth Wheel: The Political History of the United States Sanitary Commission* [New York, 1956], pp. 122–29, 135–37; *Congressional Globe*, 37th Cong., 2nd sess., 1861–62, 40: 911, 995–98, 1166, 1193, 1268–73, 1583–88, 1603).

3. On April 14, 1862, Surgeon General Finley was placed, at his own request, on the army's list of retired officers, but he had not willingly given up his office. Finley was forced out more because he had offended Secretary of War Stanton than because of the Sanitary Commission's criticisms. Stanton had forwarded to Finley a private letter written by a friend and containing allegations about the conduct of the physician supervising the army's general hospitals in Philadelphia. The secretary of war expected Finley to investigate the charges and report to him. The surgeon general, however, copied an extract from the letter and sent it to the accused physician, who promptly filed a suit for libel against Stanton's friend. The secretary of war demanded an explanation from Finley, and upon learning what the latter had done, ordered him to Boston to await further assignment. There the old soldier campaigned hard to regain his old post but, despairing of that result, chose retirement (F. B. Heitman, *Historical Register and Dictionary*, 1: 420; James Evelyn Pilcher, *The Surgeon Generals of the United States of America: A Series of Biographical Sketches* . . . [Carlisle, Pa., 1905], pp. 44–45).

4. By late September 1861 William Alexander Hammond, an assistant surgeon in the army, had attracted favorable notice from the Sanitary Commission. Olmsted on September 25 complained to Bellows, "I wish that he [Charles Tripler, medical director of the Army of the Potomac] could be shipped off to Missouri, Hammond put in his place, Van Buren made S. Genl." During the following month Hammond became the Commission's candidate for surgeon general. He combined ten years' experience as an army physician, extensive medical research and publication in scholarly journals, and a willingness to criticize and to try to change the practices of the Medical Bureau and its doctors—all qualities that recommended him highly to the Commission (FLO to HWB, Sept. 25, 1861, USSC-NYPL, box 641; Charles Janeway Stillé, *History of the United States Sanitary Commission, Being the General Report of Its Work during the War of the Rebellion* [New York, 1868], pp. 128–31).

5. Andrew Kingsbury Smith (d. 1899), a native of Hartford, Connecticut, whom Olmsted here identifies as a friend and former classmate of his deceased brother, John Hull Olmsted, at the Hartford Grammar School. Smith was appointed assistant surgeon in the U.S. Army in 1853 with the rank of captain and was promoted to surgeon and major in 1862. He remained in the army until his retirement in 1890 (F. B. Heitman, *Historical Register and Dictionary*, 1: 894; *Hartford Daily Courant*, Aug. 16, 1899, p. 10; *Papers of FLO*, 1: 392).

6. George Hinckley Lyman (d. 1891) was not appointed inspector general but was named a medical inspector on June 11, 1862. Commissioned a surgeon of volunteers in August 1861, he served in the army until November 1865 (F. B. Heitman, *Historical Register and Dictionary*, 1: 648).

7. Willard Parker (1800–1884), a distinguished physician who was professor of surgery at the New York College of Physicians and Surgeons from 1839 until 1870. Before John Hull Olmsted's health failed, he studied medicine in Parker's office (*DAB*; *Papers of FLO*, 1: 8, 362).

8. That is, the hospital transport ships at Yorktown, Virginia.
9. President Lincoln signed into law a bill creating the U.S. Department of Agriculture on May 15, 1862. The bill provided for the appointment of a commissioner of agriculture who would collect and disseminate information about agricultural statistics, experiments, and important new varieties of seeds and plants. The census office remained a separate governmental body (Edward L. Schapsmeier and Frederick H. Schapsmeier, *Encyclopedia of American Agricultural History* [Westport, Conn., 1975], p. 13).
10. The marriage of Bertha Olmsted to William W. Niles, which would take place on June 5, 1862, at St. John's Church in Hartford, Connecticut (JO Journal).
11. Olmsted here wrote "my."
12. Olmsted's nineteen-year-old half-brother, Albert Henry Olmsted, who briefly served as a volunteer with the Sanitary Commission. In late April 1862 he worked as purser, commissary, and baggageman for the hospital steamer *Daniel Webster* on its voyage from Virginia to New York (A. H. Olmsted to Mary Bull Olmsted, April 26, 1862; A. H. Olmsted to JO, May 2, 1862).

CHAPTER V

HOSPITAL TRANSPORTS IN THE PENINSULA CAMPAIGN

As GENERAL MCCLELLAN moved the Army of the Potomac to the Virginia Peninsula in the spring of 1862 for an attack upon Richmond, Olmsted and the Sanitary Commission acquired a new responsibility—the transportation of sick and wounded soldiers to Northern hospitals. The letters and reports presented in this chapter describe Olmsted's supervision of the Sanitary Commission's "floating hospitals." During his eleven weeks behind the lines, Olmsted's position permitted him to observe the general care of the Union soldier in the field as well as the horrors of the aftermath of battle.

Olmsted's letters in early May show optimism that a working system could soon be established for the hospital ships. They also indicate a mounting frustration with the military authorities, who, at short notice and capriciously, removed ships from hospital duty. But it was the medical men of the army who received Olmsted's most scathing criticisms. In May, even before the bloody battles began, his letters tell how the Sanitary Commission provided sorely needed shelter, food, and medical care to ill soldiers neglected by their medical officers. Numerous anecdotes, such as that in his report of May 15 about the dying soldier Corcoran, portray official callousness and lack of system. Olmsted's letters after the battle of Fair Oaks graphically describe the inadequacies of the medical care of the Union wounded.

Through this period Olmsted's letters indicate the increasing problems caused by the ambiguous position of the Sanitary Commission. Olmsted grew increasingly touchy as Medical Director Charles S. Tripler

314

and other staff officers permitted him little independent authority, while the surgeon general and Sanitary Commission acted as though he were, in fact, in charge of operations. The letters of June 13 and 19 highlight the difficulties of Olmsted's position.

As the Seven Days' battles occurred in late June, Olmsted's writings illustrate his increased pride in McClellan's army. They also reflect his growing desire that McClellan receive large reinforcements. Appeals to President Lincoln and Senator Preston King present Olmsted's solution to the problem: new enlistments and expanded conscription enforced by the federal government. Olmsted's private letters in July also reveal his conviction of the necessity for influencing public opinion toward patriotic action and for replacing Secretary of War Stanton. The letter of July 13, written as Olmsted prepared to leave the Virginia Peninsula and as McClellan's campaign to capture Richmond faltered, gives a disheartened assessment of the extent of the Sanitary Commission's accomplishments during the preceding weeks.

To John Foster Jenkins

May 3[d] 1862

My Dear Doctor,

I have just received your favor of yesterday with enclosures, by the Nurse Reverend Doolittle to be surnamed of Harris.[1]

You are right about the Hospital Inspection paper.[2]

Tell Douglas there is no shadow of disposition to do without him to my knowledge.[3] We shall pretty surely want you both for a month or two to come, if not to the end of the war.

We are taking sick aboard the Webster.[4] (I don't mean taking sick but taking sick.) Have 50 in the bunks and are promised a hundred and fifty tomorrow. When complete, I shall send her off to New York in charge of D[r] Charly J. Smith[5] and D[r] Grymes.[6] Knapp & I will remain to fit up the Ocean Queen[7] which is now aground about five miles off in the offing. By that time things will be working smoothly on the Webster, but it has been a more tedious job to shake the men and things into their respective places than I had anticipated.

I suppose Agnew and the rest of us have acquired a sympathy for Tripler[8] and would be glad to know that he was appointed Inspector General. Wood's appointment[9] does not give unalloyed discomfort, though

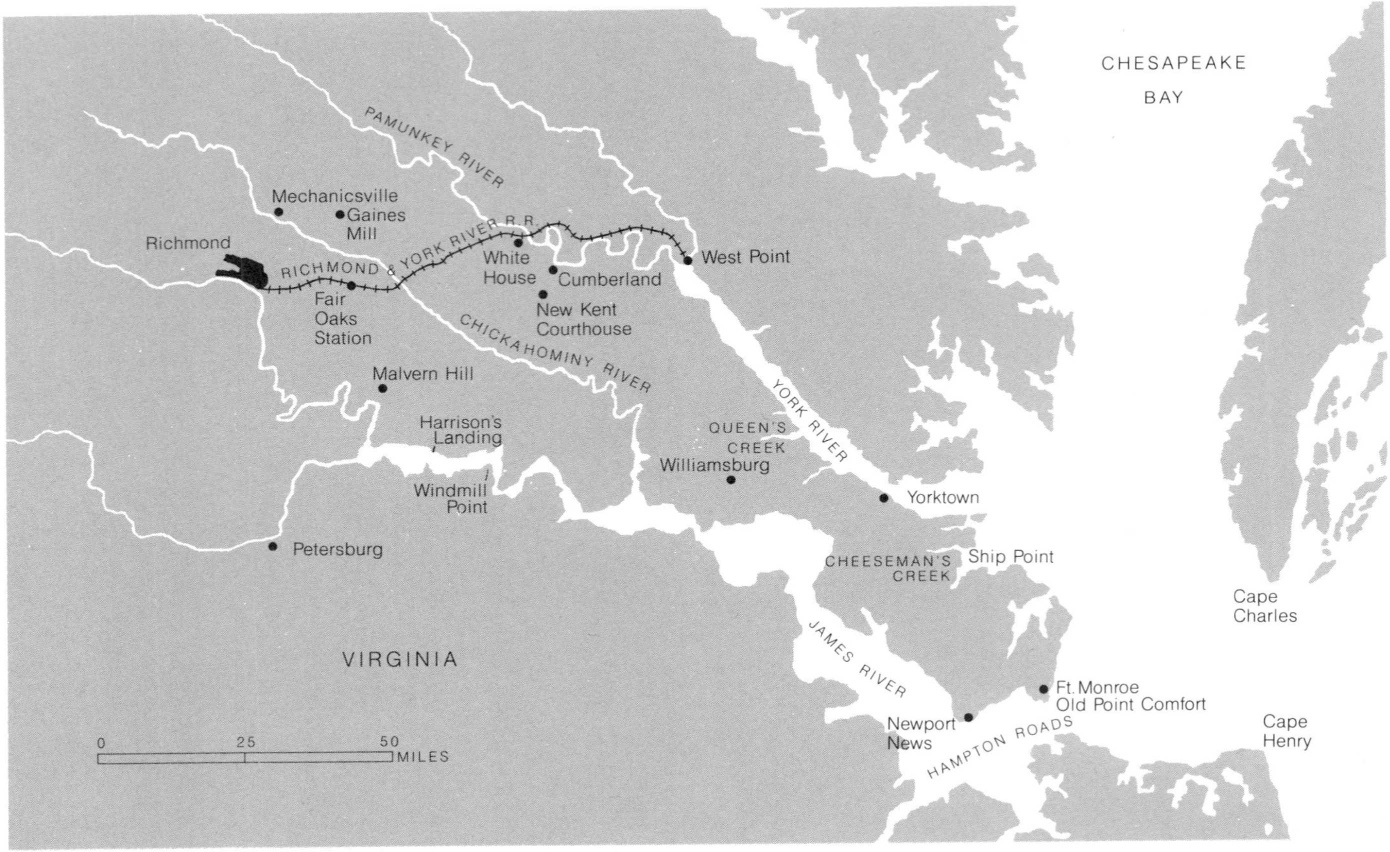

THE VIRGINIA PENINSULA, 1862

CHESAPEAKE BAY

Cape Charles

Cape Henry

Ft. Monroe
Old Point Comfort

HAMPTON ROADS

Newport News

JAMES RIVER

Ship Point

CHEESEMAN'S CREEK

Yorktown

YORK RIVER

QUEEN'S CREEK

Williamsburg

West Point

PAMUNKEY RIVER

Cumberland

New Kent Courthouse

White House

RICHMOND & YORK RIVER R.R.

CHICKAHOMINY RIVER

Mechanicsville

Gaines Mill

Fair Oaks Station

Malvern Hill

Harrison's Landing

Windmill Point

Richmond

Petersburg

VIRGINIA

0   25   50
MILES

comfort hardly predominates. I would have preferred—someone else. Trip-
ler seems to have been very badly used by Finley and by the Q. M. Dept.
He is not responsible for the present most notable deficiencies.[10] I wish D[r]
Hammond could come here, before the appointments are made. I hope
Smith[11] & Cuyler[12] will not be crowded out.

The captain of the Queen assures me that she can carry 2000 sick,
easy, cool & comfortable. My requisitions on you & New York have been
for 400 on her. Remember this if you are sending more in time for her.

We know nothing of the army doings here—our news from before
Yorktown is all by the papers you send. We hear much firing tonight and
see the flashes of the guns.

Yours Very Cordially,

Fred. Law Olmsted.

Knapp has telegrap[d] you for some supplies for the Queen since the above
was written.

The original is letter 925 in box 741 of USSC-NYPL. For this letter, written at Ship
Point, Virginia, Olmsted used stationery with the printed heading "Sanitary Commission, Adams House, 244 F street, Washington, D.C."

1. A sarcastic reference to Elisha Harris, who was overseeing the recruitment of nurses
   by the Sanitary Commission in New York. In his letter of May 2 Harris informed
   Olmsted that most of the male nurses whom he had asked in April to be ready to
   serve were still willing to go to Virginia when requested (Elisha Harris to FLO, May
   2, 1862, USSC-NYPL, box 741: 911).
2. Jenkins in his letter had enclosed what he called "an excellent code of rules for
   hospital inspection" by Dr. Carson of Philadelphia, and he proposed to ask the
   physician to send "more," presumably more copies (JFJ to FLO, May 2, 1862,
   USSC-NYPL, box 742: 1249).
3. In a letter of April 26, 1862, to Jenkins, John H. Douglas had suggested that the
   Sanitary Commission might believe itself overstaffed in the West and that he would
   voluntarily retire from service if reductions of personnel were needed (J. H. Douglas
   to JFJ, April 26, 1862, USSC-NYPL, box 740: 855).
4. On April 25 the quartermaster general's department assigned the *Daniel Webster
   No. 1*, described as "an old Pacific Coast steamer of small capacity," to the Sanitary
   Commission. It left Alexandria, Virginia, on April 27 and arrived at Ship Point at
   Cheeseman's Creek the following day. On the evening of May 2 the *Daniel Webster*
   received its first patients, thirty-two sick soldiers from the Ship Point hospital. Its
   total cargo of patients soon reached 184. The steamer departed for New York on
   May 5, because Olmsted believed it best to start while the weather remained favorable (Albert H. Olmsted to JO, May 4 and May 6, 1862; Albert H. Olmsted to Mary
   Bull Olmsted, April 29, 1862; FLO to HWB, May 2 and May 5, 1862, USSC-NYPL,
   box 641; *Hospital Transports*, pp. xiv, 18–19, 25, 26).
5. Possibly Charles J. Smith, M.D., who practiced medicine in Philadelphia during the
   1860s. Olmsted first wrote "Dr. Stephen G. Smith," then corrected himself. On May

4, Olmsted claimed that the evacuation of Yorktown had "apparently disordered" Smith's brain: "Dr Smith (Chas) who was yesterday appointed the responsible surgeon of the Webster by Dr Tripler, and whom I this morning ordered to be respected and obeyed as such, went ashore without leave or warning and has since made no report" (*McElroy's Philadelphia City Directory for 1863* . . . , 26th ed. [Philadelphia, 1863]; FLO to HWB, May 4, 1862, USSC-NYPL, box 641).

6. James M. Grymes (c. 1828–1863), a physician who before working for the Sanitary Commission had a private practice in Washington, D.C. Late in the summer of 1861, as Frederick N. Knapp set up "The Home," a lodge to care for sick and invalid soldiers passing through Washington, he arranged for Dr. Grymes to be its attending physician. Grymes also carried out the normal duties of a regimental surgeon for parts of regiments sent to Washington without a physician. During the summer of 1862 he was one of the Sanitary Commission's most tireless workers on the Peninsula. Despite rapidly worsening health, he returned to his post at "The Home" in the fall of 1862. Early in 1863 he died of tuberculosis.

    Grymes was one of the Sanitary Commission's most valued employees. In the fall of 1862 the Commission unanimously passed a resolution tendering its "warmest thanks" to Grymes for his "self-sacrificing, devoted, and heroic exertions . . . in the care of sick and wounded soldiers, in the transports and in the Soldiers' Home." Olmsted himself regarded Grymes highly and possibly wrote the posthumous tribute in *Hospital Transports*, which read, "Wherever he served his labors were singularly wise and efficient; with exceeding gentleness and quietness of manner he combined much energy of will, and to thorough skill was added a loving heart, and a rare devotedness of purpose" (*Washington Evening Star*, Feb. 6, 1863, p. 3; doc. nos. 35, 39, and 59a in USSC, *Documents*; USSC, *Minutes*, p. 107; *Hospital Transports*, p. 48).

7. The *Ocean Queen* was a 327–foot sidewheel steamer of 2,802 tons. It belonged to Cornelius Vanderbilt, who had commissioned it in 1857 for his transatlantic service.

    Olmsted described the *Queen* to Bellows: "She is a magnificent vessel, the noblest merchant-vessel I ever saw, and perfectly clean and sweet in every deck. She has berths fitted for somewhere near four hundred, and at an expense of five hundred dollars could be fitted to carry a thousand wholesomely" (FLO to HWB, May 4, 1862, USSC-NYPL, box 641; William A. Fairburn, *Merchant Sail*, 6 vols, [Center Lovell, Me., 1945–55], 2: 1353).

8. Charles Stuart Tripler (1806–1866), medical director of the Army of the Potomac from August 1861 until June 1862. A graduate of the College of Physicians and Surgeons, he received his commission as an army surgeon in 1830. Among his assignments were posts in Michigan, California, and Kentucky. While in Kentucky, Tripler lectured at the Cincinnati Medical College nearby and wrote the manual *A Handbook for Military Surgeons*. He also served in the field during the Mexican War.

    The Sanitary Commission and Tripler became increasingly at odds in 1861 and 1862. At first the commissioners admired Tripler, probably because he shared their belief in the importance of hygiene for preserving the health of the soldiers and because he was willing to consult with them. When Bellows confidentially wrote to McClellan about the need for a new surgeon general, the minister specifically mentioned Tripler as the kind of man "of zeal, administrative power & adequacy to great emergencies & new times" who should be given greater power. During the fall of 1861 Tripler met with the Commission and discussed building plans for new military hospitals. But his rigid adherence to rules and accepted military procedures probably limited his accomplishments. Although Tripler believed that an ambulance corps was needed, he argued that existing laws and regulations did not allow it.

    The Peninsula campaign marked the period of Olmsted's closest contact with Tripler and the growth of an unfavorable opinion of the medical director among the commissioners. Although sympathetic to the problems of supply and transportation faced by the medical director, Olmsted became increasingly impatient at Tripler's unwillingness to set up and operate a system to select medical cases to be sent north. Olmsted also resented the conflicting and peremptory orders that Tripler issued to ships staffed by the Sanitary Commission. For his part, Tripler was suspicious of civilian meddling and was not pleased with the Commission's role on the Peninsula. In particular, Olmsted's sending of the *Daniel Webster No. 1* to Boston in defiance of orders indicated to Tripler the kind of insubordination one could expect from nonmilitary workers. The medical director described the incident in his official report but did not specifically identify Olmsted as the culprit: "I do not doubt that the agent thought it made no difference where he went, but he was none the more excusable for that. However, if civilians are allowed to have anything to do with military matters, confusion can not be avoided. They see things only from their own limited standpoint, will form and act upon their own opinions, and in ninety-nine cases in one hundred go wrong." Significantly, Tripler's later suggestions for improving medical care in the Army of the Potomac called for more career military surgeons to be assigned to the field.

In June 1862 Tripler's nomination to the new post of medical inspector was not confirmed by the Senate. Hammond then removed him from the position of medical director of the Army of the Potomac and, at his request, assigned him to duty in Detroit. In 1865 Tripler was breveted brigadier general for faithful and meritorious service (HWB to G. B. McClellan, Sept. 11, 1861, USSC-NYPL, box 638; Eunice Tripler, *Some Notes of Her Personal Recollections* [New York, 1910], pp. 83–87, 117–19, 163–68; O.R., ser. 1, vol. 11, pt. 1, pp. 177–96; ibid., vol. 5, pp. 77–113; Francis Bernard Heitman, *Historical Register and Dictionary of the United States Army* . . . , 2 vols. [Washington, D.C., 1903], 1: 971; W. A. Hammond to C. S. Tripler, June 19, 1862, Record Group 112, Records of the Office of the Surgeon General [Army], letterbook 31, p. 170, National Archives and Records Service, Washington, D.C.).

9. On April 30 Jenkins had relayed to Olmsted information obtained from Hammond about appointments to be made under the provisions of the bill reorganizing the Medical Bureau. According to Hammond, Stanton had given an order for Robert C. Wood to be nominated assistant surgeon general and for Jonathan Letterman to be inspector general, but had later refused to sign the letters of nomination. Jenkins ended this section, "So as yet no nominations are sent to the Pres't" (JFJ to FLO, April 30, 1862, USSC-NYPL, box 742: 1242).

10. At this time Olmsted still believed that the mistakes of others had caused the difficulties encountered by Charles S. Tripler. In a later report Tripler blamed problems of supply on medical officers who left their stores behind in Washington. The supplies Tripler ordered from New York were first delayed at Fortress Monroe and then were difficult to unload because they were mixed with other goods (O.R., ser. 1, vol. 11, pt. 1, pp. 182–83).

11. Andrew Kingsbury Smith.

12. John M. Cuyler (c. 1810–1884), a career physician in the army. Appointed an assistant surgeon in 1834, Cuyler was at this time the senior medical officer at Fortress Monroe. In June 1862 he received one of the newly created posts of medical inspector. He remained in the army until his retirement in 1882 (*Appleton's Cyc. Am. Biog.*).

To Henry Whitney Bellows

"Ocean Queen," off Yorktown,[1]
May 7th night. [1862]

My Dear Doctor,

When we reached the ship on our return from Fort Monroe yesterday,[2] we found two steamboats along side shovelling sick men aboard of her. There were already 300 on her. Knapp and the ladies & all of ours[3] had done the best possible under the circumstances. Knapp was then ashore trying to get Commissary stores. To this time they had been able to give them only their corn-meal gruel, and the cook with his limited utensils was necessarily far behind hand in preparing this. The surgeons immediately distributed themselves over the ship, prescribing for the worst cases—there were several men dying or near it—one dead—but it was daylight the next morning before our medicines could be made fully available. The men had swarmed into every part of the ship, and she was necessarily a pig stie in filth and stench. Nobody knew who or exactly how many were on board. To further complicate matters, a surgeon with straps[4] came with an order from Tripler to take charge of the vessel and go with her to New York. I managed to keep the question of authority in abeyance and proceeded as well as I could[5] to organize order in some degree, out of the chaos. It was noon today before, being constantly interrupted by urgent demands for instructions in matters requiring immediate attention, I was able to give any general orders.

The watch system of the Webster is simplified and improved:[6] There are five wards of very sick patients—mostly typhoid, averaging now about 65 in each. The sixth ward is the deck and the steerages of the ship in which men who can live on the "house diet" and who do not require close medical attention are placed. Doctor Watts Jr.[7] who came as a dresser has charge of this. I have ordered tea for four hundred tonight in it, and estimate that we have 730 on board. There are two boats waiting with more near us. I shall take no more till I see these comfortably resting. Three hundred bed sacks have just arrived and we are filling them with hay in the Elizabeth[8] along side. I shall probably drop down the river tomorrow morning with what we have on board—perhaps a few more.

Greenleaf[9]—Tripler's assistant has just been on board. He says he is left to take care of 5000 sick with orders to ship them off as fast as they can be carted to Yorktown and got on Transports. He has at Yorktown *one* assist[ant] surgeon of volunteers—expects some volunteers to arrive and has authority to arrest them if they refuse to stop. The regimental surgeons are generally or frequently deserting their sick and going on to the fighting ground. They are mad with *surgical* fever. Tripler has himself gone

320

U.S. SANITARY COMMISSION STOREBOAT *ELIZABETH*

to the front. I have made a preliminary treaty with Greenleaf and shall stay here with Knapp to do what we can.

(P.S.) Have just been thro' the ship and though there is much that is painful, some delirious, some dying and one just dead, the condition of the whole is, under the circumstances, satisfactory. With perhaps some exceptions among the last fifty who have been put on board, there are none who have not had needed sustenance, or who are not provided with a tolerable resting place for the night. The surgeons are all but Watts and Ware[10] ashore, where, in fact, I fear they are more needed than here. I am glad to say also that the ship is essentially clean, far cleaner and purer in every ward than any of the transport steamers—or than some of the division hospitals. What the labor has been to secure this you can never imagine.

Your ladies arrived this P.M.[11] I need not say this is no place for them. I slept what little I slept last night on deck. I had no time to see or advise with them. Even the servants would at the present do more harm than good, for those having duties are just learning them and would be disarranged and delayed by the introduction of new elements. Knapp reports that they are in comfortable quarters, the guests of some New York Colonel and being sumptuously entertained on a clean steamboat.

We have several officers—a colonel and a Lt. Col. among them, on board.

I have several times sent for a detail of men for guard duty, but don't get them. The men behave very well, in general, are indeed wonderfully patient, reasonable and even grateful. It is in this respect the most satisfactory exhibition of respectable human nature I ever experienced.

I am sorry to say that some of the nurses evidently came for a pleasure excursion. Most are doing very well and the students nobly. They are a fine lot of true gentlemen and I fairly love them. As for the women, Mrs Howland, Miss Woolsey and Mrs Bradley[12]—if every man in the ship was their brother, I should have said that such untiring industry, self-possession and tranquil cheerfulness was incredible. It beats all I ever imagined of women or experienced except for my wife when I was down last year.[13]

I must keep the best men and women not necessary to the organization, to help what now is to be done here. There are many patients without descriptive lists or any kind of accounts and there will be a great deal of trouble on arriving at New York about their baggage & where they will go. The only excuse is we had to take them in this way or leave them in a much worse plight. We were under military authority and were required to take them as we have. I have resisted it all that I could.

I want a gang of sail-makers put on board the ship at New York at once, with canvas, ropes &c. to make an awning from stem to stern. I estimate that it will cost $1500. If we had it on tonight I have no doubt it would save some lives. The captain understands about it and what else she most wants. I have carpenters aboard who will return in her. There should be a gang of scrubbers & whitewashers ready to go to work as soon as she can be cleaned. Send her back with the best lot of surgeons, dressers and nurses you can, as quickly, as by working night & day, is possible. I think she will arrive on the 9th before night.

Yours Respectfully,

Fred Law Olmsted.

Dr H. W. Bellows
Presidt

The original is in box 641 of USSC-NYPL.

1. On May 4 Olmsted gained possession of the *Ocean Queen* after promising Tripler that it would be ready to receive patients within forty-eight hours. That morning Olmsted telegraphed Tripler that he could transport six to eight hundred on the *Queen* as soon as they were sent aboard.

The Confederate evacuation of Yorktown on May 4, however, surprised Olmsted and threw all his plans into disarray. On May 5 he moved the small steamer *Wilson Small* and the *Ocean Queen* to Yorktown. That evening, before any preparations had been made, two steamboats arrived with sick soldiers to be transferred to the *Queen*. Olmsted described the incident:

> There was no surgeon on board, and I refused to receive them until I could get one. Borrowed Dr Hodges from the Pennsylvania State hospital. When I returned from the Pennsylvania boat, I found the surgeon had contrary to my injunctions turned as many of the sick as he could loose upon the deck, with no record or account of baggage. He told me that he was under orders to get two hundred more on board the same night & couldn't wait. I put a man in the gangway with orders to prevent by force any more coming on board until I authorized it.
>
> As soon as possible I got all who could walk into the ship's dining room, & then got the very sick aboard and put to bed; then got beds prepared for the remainder, and taking them one by one from the saloon, each with his baggage, got a proper record, and put them to bed.

(FLO to HWB, May 4, 5, and 6, 1862, USSC-NYPL, box 641.)

2. Since Olmsted found the telegraph offices removed from Ship Point on May 5 he hoped to be able to wire the Sanitary Commission offices at Washington and New York from Yorktown. There he found no office yet set up. On the morning of May 6 he took the *Wilson Small* to Fortress Monroe, where he sent telegrams, secured supplies, and met a party of Sanitary Commission workers from New York who had been sent for duty on the *Ocean Queen* (FLO to HWB, May 5, 1862, USSC-NYPL, box 641; ibid., May 6, 1862, USSC-NYPL, box 742: 1252).

3. Olmsted here is referring to those Sanitary Commission workers who came from Washington, D.C., on the *Webster* but remained on the Peninsula after it sailed to New York on May 5. This staff included physicians, male nurses, servants, and lady superintendents of nursing.

4. That is, the shoulder straps that indicated an army officer's rank.

5. Here Olmsted wrote "good" instead of "could."

6. Olmsted meant that he had improved the method of assigning shifts of duty, which he had first designed for the *Webster*. He divided the work force on the *Queen* into two watches (A and B), which alternated service, each working a six-hour shift at morning and at night and one of three hours during the afternoon. Each watch was divided into squads, consisting of nurses, servants, and wardmaster, corresponding to the number of wards. As part of the system, Olmsted also assigned times for the surgeons to make rounds and for the watches to take their meals ([FLO], "Papers Relating to the *Ocean Queen*," May 4, 1862, USSC-NYPL, box 742: 1207).

7. Robert Watts (b. 1837), son of a prominent physician, graduated from the New York College of Physicians and Surgeons in 1861. He served briefly as a volunteer dresser for the Sanitary Commission and in June 1862 was appointed surgeon of the 133rd New York (John Shrady, ed., *The College of Physicians and Surgeons, New York, and Its Founders, Officers, Instructors, Benefactors, and Alumni: A History*, 2 vols. [New York, c. 1903–4], 1: 448).

8. The *Elizabeth* was a small steamer which the Sanitary Commission used as a storeboat (*Hospital Transports*, p. 23; FLO to HWB, May 4, 1862, USSC-NYPL, box 641).

9. Charles Ravenscroft Greenleaf (1838–1911) was commissioned as a surgeon in the U.S. Army in August 1861 after serving as assistant surgeon of the 5th Ohio. As assistant to Medical Director Tripler, Greenleaf superintended the army hospital at Yorktown during the Peninsula campaign. He remained in the army until 1902 and served with distinction during the Spanish-American War (Howard A. Kelly and

Walter L. Burrage, *Dictionary of American Medical Biography: Lives of Eminent Physicians of the United States and Canada* . . . [New York, 1928], p. 428.

10. Dr. Robert Ware.

11. Olmsted is referring to a party of genteel women volunteer workers from New York City and their servants which Bellows had accompanied as far as Baltimore. Bellows's wife, Eliza Townsend Bellows, and Ellen Ruggles Strong were part of the group. The other ladies were Harriet Douglas Whetten, Mary B. Gardner, Mrs. Joseph Allen, Mrs. Balestier, and Mrs. Devill. Since the Commission had a sufficient number of workers on the *Ocean Queen*, the ladies from New York were housed on the *Knickerbocker* until another ship was ready for them (HWB to FLO, May 6, 1862, USSC-NYPL, box 742: 1252; Mary B. Gardner, "Minutes from Memory of Six Weeks Service with the San Comm," [c. July 1862], USSC-NYPL, box 741: 942).

12. Eliza Newton Woolsey Howland (1835–1917), her unmarried sister Georgeanna Muir Woolsey (1833–1906), and Amy Morris Bradley (1823–1904) were three of the Sanitary Commission's most dedicated and capable "lady superintendents of nurses" during the Peninsula campaign. The Woolsey sisters belonged to a large New York family that was active in the Union cause and were also cousins of Theodore Dwight Woolsey, the president of Yale College. Georgeanna was among the select group of women admitted to the nursing course conducted by Dr. Elizabeth Blackwell for the Woman's Central Association of Relief. During the winter of 1861–62 she worked in army hospitals near Washington, where her sister Eliza's husband, Joseph Howland, was stationed. When his regiment was transferred to Virginia for the Peninsula campaign, Eliza and Georgeanna welcomed the opportunity offered by the Sanitary Commission to go there as nursing supervisors. Both women served on the hospital ships until early July 1862. Although Eliza Howland did not undertake any further nursing assignments, Georgeanna remained active in army nursing through 1864. Bubbling with high spirits yet coolly efficient, "Georgy" was one of the most popular nurses. Olmsted was among those who recognized and appreciated her administrative abilities, and almost thirty years later he declared that he believed that she "would, upon orders, take command of the channel fleet; arm, equip, man, provision, sail and engross the enemy, better than any other landsman I know." After the Civil War, Georgeanna Woolsey married Francis Bacon, a professor at Yale's medical school. She retained her interest in nursing and benevolent organizations and helped found the Connecticut Training School for Nurses in 1873.

      Amy M. Bradley was a schoolteacher from Maine who in 1861–62 was a lady superintendent at the hospital for Slocum's brigade of the Army of the Potomac. After serving on hospital ships throughout the Peninsula campaign, she worked for the Sanitary Commission at various hospitals and convalescent camps for the remainder of the war. She later organized and taught in schools for poor white children in Wilmington, North Carolina, and began a school to train local teachers. Although Olmsted here refers to her as "Mrs Bradley," she never married (*Notable American Women*; Anne L. Austin, *The Woolsey Sisters of New York: A Family's Involvement in the Civil War and a New Profession [1860–1900]* [Philadelphia, 1971], pp. 37–68, 93–106; FLO to Elizabeth Baldwin Whitney, Dec. 16, 1890).

13. Despite his mention of "last year," Olmsted is referring to the carriage accident of August 1860 which badly fractured his leg and left him an invalid for several months (*Papers of FLO*, 3: 34).

New-York Times, May 24, 1862

LABORS OF THE
SANITARY COMMISSION

Its Attentions to the Wounded and Sick Soldiers in Eastern Virginia—

REPORT OF MR. OLMSTED, THE SECRETARY,
TO DR. BELLOWS, THE PRESIDENT, OF THE COMMISSION.

Steamboat Wilson Small,[1]
Off Yorktown, Thursday, May 15, 1862.[2]

My Dear Sir:

The Commission is throwing itself into so many gaps that I not only cannot find time to make full reports to you, but it is impossible to recollect much detail, of more or less importance, determined and acted upon at the instant of necessities, even of only day before yesterday. I think you are fairly well informed of the outline of our work till then. We had on our tender, the *Small*, twenty-five severely wounded men, two dying and one or two dead; we had the night before sent two portions of our company, with such stores as could be at a moment's notice sent with them, to two vessels conveying wounded from the battle of Williamsburgh to Fortress Monroe; another portion was with the wounded of West Point, on the *Star*.[3]

These drafts had left us no more on the *Small* than was necessary for the care of those on board of her. Yet the boat was crowded, and for a week, most of the men have slept, when they could, out on deck, the cabins being occupied by the wounded. Early in the morning the *Webster*[4] arrived. We ran alongside and took from her some much-needed stores. We breakfasted on board, and were delighted with her arrangements and the good order which prevailed on her, contrasting so favorably with the impromptu ill-considered arrangements and disorder of everything else of which we have had recent observation. I immediately reported her ready to receive two hundred patients to the surgeon in charge of the Yorktown hospitals,[5] and having received your telegram announcing the definite withdrawal of the *Ocean Queen*,[6] I went on board the *S. R. Spaulding*,[7] and finding her, though lamentably inferior to the *Queen* for our purposes, the best, in fact, the only available vessel for outside service, I obtained an assignment of her to the Commission from the Quartermaster's Department, and took measures to have her at once [given] coal and water.

325

THE HOSPITAL STEAMER *DANIEL WEBSTER NO. 1*

Arranged also for the coaling of the *Knickerbocker*,[8] and put a company on board, to fit her for a surgical hospital. Got a wharf-berth for the *Webster*, near the hospitals; but, finding that she could not get in, on account of spiles[9] broken off near it, got an order to take any small steamboat for lighterage, and secured a tug, and running this alternately with the *Small*, until near eleven o'clock at night, took off, and put safely and comfortably to bed on her, 240 sick and wounded men. After this, rearranged her hospital service, so as to transfer from her all who could by any means be spared, and to put on her such of our company as it was necessary to part with. Had an estimate of stores necessary for her return trip made, and at daylight sent what she could spare, on the *Small* during the night.

I found everything working beautifully on the *Webster*, every man knowing his place, and not trying to do the duty of others. I cannot speak too highly of the service of Dr. Grymes. He is just the man for the duty. At 9 A.M. the *Webster* weighed anchor, and we turned our attention to the other vessels which were being fitted. We had a company at work on the *Elm City*, another on the *Knickerbocker*, and were supplying stores to the *State of Maine*.[10] We found them getting on as well as possible with the limited force we could spare on the *City*, but the *Knickerbocker*, after twice running through the fleet in search of her, we had to conclude was missing. Going to the Quartermaster's,[11] we learned that, at 11 the night before, a requisition had been made upon him for the *Knickerbocker* to go to our advanced position on the Pamunkey, and forgetting that she had been assigned to the commission, he had given a written order to the

Captain to take her there. Four of our company, including two ladies, were on board of her.[12] The only relief to our anxiety for them was the assurance that she would undoubtedly return at once.

After considerable other business at the Quartermaster's office, we got from the Military Governor[13] a detail of carpenters and other privates, and an order to destroy a platform erected by the rebels, which would furnish lumber for the fitting up of the *Spaulding.*

We left the *Small* to take this on board, and went to the shore hospital, where after considerable debate with D^r W, Surgeon in Charge,[14] we agreed to have the *Elm City* ready by 2 o'clock to take on the sick, and see the *State of Maine* immediately fully supplied to follow the *Elm City* without delay. Returning to the *Small*, were met by a note from the Quartermaster, enclosing a telegram from the Medical Director, at Williamsburg,[15] demanding a boat provided with straw and water to take on two hundred sick within two hours at Queen's Creek. "This is of the utmost urgency—see Mr. Olmsted," concluded the dispatch. The only boat in the fleet that had a fair supply of water on board, and which could be otherwise made anywhere near ready in less time than a half a day, was the *Elm City*, and she had no provision of food.

We had a day's supply on the *Small*, and I at once wrote to Dr. Greenleaf, that to meet an order of the Medical Director I had to withdraw the *Elm City* but we would send supplies to the *State of Maine* at once, so that she could take her place. We then ran near the *Elm City*, hailed her to fire up and be ready to go up the river in half an hour; ran alongside the *Spaulding*, threw the lumber and carpenters on board of her, arranged plan of berths and set them to work; then steamed off to the *Alida*,[16] and sent her with the supplies for *State of Maine* and others; returned past the *Elm City* and ordered her to follow us; ran up to the mouth of Queen's Creek and anchored by the side of the *Kennebec*,[17] which was being loaded with wounded secession prisoners, brought out of the creek by the lighter steamers. Went up the creek in our yawl[18] to Bigelow's Landing, and saw the process of embarkation, which was rude, shiftless and painful, the poor wretches being made to climb a plank set at an angle of forty-five degrees, which they could only do by the aid of a rope thrown to them from the deck.

There was a small guard to carry up those who had suffered amputation or other severe injury. You can imagine, perhaps, what a cruel process it was by which they accomplished this. There being no officer to whom we could report, and nothing apparently for us to do at this place, we went (Knapp, Ware, Wheelock[19] and myself) in a couple of returning ambulances to Williamsburgh, to report to the Medical Director. We had in this drive a sufficient experience of the abomination of two-wheeled ambulances. Our road, for a mile or more, lay through the midst of the field of

327

battle, of which we saw many marks. On inquiring for the hospital at Williamsburgh, the reply was, "Every house on the main street is a hospital." We found the Medical Director surprised at our promptness. Not having supposed such a literal compliance with his orders possible, he was unable to take advantage of it, but promised to send us two hundred sick and wounded in the morning. We returned late in the evening, and at five the next morning all hands were again up to complete as far as possible the preparations of the *Elm City*, for we were very short-handed, and an imperfect make-shift organization and arrangement was alone possible.

At the first step I was met by a brigade surgeon from the *Kennebec*, who said: "No, this shall be so and so; I shall take charge here." As he persisted, after I showed my authority, and refused to compromise, I said that I should allow no sick to come on board. He then said he should go to the Medical Director. "The very thing I wanted, and I will go with you. Meanwhile the sick, if any arrive, shall come on and Dr. Ware will see that they are cared for temporarily."

We then went to the landing and saw the lighter loaded with sick in the same manner as yesterday. When the lighter was full, the surgeon told me that he should return and see the sick properly disposed of on the *Elm City*.

"But I thought we were to appeal to Dr. Tripler."

"I have concluded not to go to him, and have *written* to inform him that my authority is questioned." I deemed it best, upon this, to make sure of a written order from Dr. Tripler, and after a tedious delay got passage on a forage wagon, loaded with oats.

This was a hard ride—a continuous atmosphere of thick yellow dust, and the jar of the heavy wagons over execrable roads. I found Dr. Tripler—got a copy of an order which the Brigade-Surgeon should have received but had not, and the failure of which justified officially his assertion of authority over any transport for the sick at that anchorage. Returned to Bigelow's Landing, and, the lighters having grounded, waited there on the banks of the creek, along with a hundred sick men, being devoured by mosquitoes and sand flies. On returning, at length, to the *Elm City*, found that, owing to the conflict of authority, and the insufficient number of attendants, the sick were, with difficulty and slowness, taken care of.

After the hundred brought off with me had been taken on, the count was over four hundred, or twice as many as the Medical Director had estimated, or I had calculated on, in considering the supply of water, medicine and stores.

After sunset, I went again up the creek, and found eight men on the beach, left there sick—some very sick—without a single attendant or friend within four miles, while only the night before two of our teamsters had been murdered in the woods near by.[20] After they were on board, I asked who was in charge of the party, wishing to make sure that no stragglers were left. A man was pointed out, who, because he was stronger and more helpful than the rest, seemed to have been regarded by them as their leader, though he had no appointment. He was able to answer my inquiries satisfactorily, and then told me his own story. His name was Corcoran. After the battle of Williamsburgh he was sick for three days. Then there was an order to march. His Captain said, "Good God! Corcoran, you are not fit to march; go into the town and get into a hospital." He walked three miles, carrying his knapsack, and when he came to a hospital, the surgeon told him he must bring a note from his Captain, and refused to receive him. He went out, and as he was very sick he crawled into something like a milk-wagon and fell asleep.

He was awakened by a man who pulled him out by his feet, and he fell on the ground and was hurt. He begged the man—a Secessionist, he supposed—for some water, and he brought him some, and said he would not have done it, only he wanted his wagon. He tried to walk away, but pretty soon fell down and fell asleep. By-and-bye a negro man woke him up and asked him if he shouldn't help him to a hospital. The negro man was very kind, but when he came to a hospital (it was in a church) the doctor said he couldn't take him because he hadn't a bit of a note. Then he said, "For God's sake, give me room to lie down here somewhere; it's not much room I'll take any how, and I can't keep up any longer." It was then three days since he had tasted food. Then the doctor told him he could lie down, and he had not been up since till to-day. I have told the whole of this story, simply because the man, as I just now chanced to learn, died a few hours afterwards, kindly attended, in his last moments, by our sisters of mercy. He has been buried to-day at Yorktown. A letter to his mother was found in his pocket, and one of the ladies has written to her.

The weather being unfavorable, we laid at anchor off Queen's Creek during the night, and by midnight had got all our affairs in pretty good trim. Knapp had been to and returned from Yorktown in the *Small*, with stores for the *Elm City*, and reported the arrival of the *Knickerbocker*, and that the *State of Maine* was loading with sick.

This morning we returned to Yorktown, and took on thirty more sick from a steamboat which had brought them from Cumberland on the Pamunkey. At 10, the *Elm City* left for Washington. Knapp went ashore to carry telegrams, and get some more lumber, and I went to bed. After noon I went ashore; called on the surgeon in charge and the Military Governor; made our arrangements for a trip up the river to collect sick from the advance, and to tow our *Wilson Small* up to West Point for repairs; for she has become completely disabled. Were met by an officer with a telegram, begging that a boat should be immediately dispatched to Bigelow's Landing, where an ambulance train master had reported that a hundred sick had been left on the ground in the rain without attendance or food, "to die." Bigelow's Landing is up a narrow, shoal, crooked creek, and we ran about the harbor looking in vain for a boat that could be expected to get there. At length we determined to take our whole fleet there, and leaving the *Knickerbocker* and *Alida* outside, to try to get up with the storeboat *Elizabeth,* she being the shortest.

We ran to the *Knickerbocker,* but before we could get her under way, a steamboat came alongside, and a letter was handed me begging that I would take care of one hundred and fifty sick men on it, who had been taken on at West Point early in the morning, and who had had no nourishment during the day. It was at sunset, and stormy-cold. I at first refused, on the ground of the greater need of those at Bigelow's Landing, but the surgeon in charge induced me to take a look in the cabin, and I changed my mind. The little room was as full as it could be packed of sick soldiers sitting—not lying—on the floor; there was not room for that. Only two or three were at full length; one of these was dying—was dead the next time I looked in.

We immediately began taking them on the *Knickerbocker.* It is now midnight. Knapp started with Dr. Miller[21] and a part of our company, and the two supply-boats, five hours ago for Queen's Creek, with the intention of getting to the sick at Bigelow's Landing if possible; if not, to go up in the yawl and canoe with supplies and firewood, and do whatever should be found possible for their relief. Two of the ladies are with him.

The rest are giving beef-tea and brandy and water to the sick on the *Knickerbocker.* These have all been put into clean beds, and are about as comfortable as it is possible to make them. But, to take decent care of 150 sick fellows at such short notice, on a steamboat, is not so easily accomplished as you might imagine. Dr. Ware and Dr. Swann[22] are in attendance, aided most efficiently by Wheelock and Haight.[23] Mr. Collins[24] is the executive officer of the *Knickerbocker,* and Mr. Woolsey, clerk,[25] taking charge of the effects of the soldiers. I am quite at a loss to know what I shall do to-morrow. Unless reinforcements arrive, we certainly cannot meet another emergency.

It will not be surprising if you find this report somewhat incoherent for I have several times fallen asleep while writing it. We have a cold northeast storm and thick weather, and I conclude that Knapp's expedition is unable to get down to-night. I have just been through the *Knickerbocker,* and find nearly all the patients sleeping quietly, and (a few typhoid murmurers excepted) with every indication of comfort.

May 16.—I was so soundly asleep fifteen minutes after I finished writing you last night, that it had to be several times repeated to me before I could comprehend what it meant, that the supply boats were coming alongside with over a hundred more sick. Anchoring the *Alida* outside, Knapp had attempted to get up the creek with the *Elizabeth*, but as I had feared would be the case, she went aground. Going on with the yawl, he found one of the steam lighters at anchor, with over a hundred sick lying on the deck, who were not only soaked with rain, but who had been obliged to wade out to her in knee-deep water. We learned that, further up the creek, a few men too sick to stand, and who, of course, were unable to wade off to the boat, had been left behind. No persuasion could induce the Captain to return for them, but a distinct assertion of authority in the case by Knapp, which he had from Gen. Van Vliet, and a threat to report him to headquarters, at length forced him to fire up and go back for them. There were eight of them, some in a nearly dying condition. These having been brought on board, and stimulants furnished them, the whole party was brought down and transferred to the supply-boats, the freight-rooms of which had, in the meantime, been as well as possible prepared for them. The ladies were ready with hot tea; there were plenty of blankets, and before the boats got down to us the larger part of the company were sound asleep. Those who were awake when I visited them were very ready to say that they wanted for nothing, and that they had not been as comfortable since they left Washington. We concluded to let them remain where they were for the night. They had been on the creek shore from ten to fourteen hours without a physician or a single attendant, a particle of food or a drop of drink. A cold, foggy day, with rain and mist after nightfall. With half a dozen exceptions, they appear marvelously well this morning and profoundly grateful for the kindness, which I need not say the ladies are extending to them. I am yet unable to make up my mind what to do with them. There is a hard northeasterly storm, with heavy rain, to-day.

Yours respectfully,

Fred'k Law Olmsted,
Gen. Sec.

H. W. Bellows, D.D., President San. Com.

The text presented here is taken from the *New-York Times* of May 24, 1862. An incomplete original, which was transcribed by several different copyists, is document 998 in box 741 of USSC-NYPL. The editors have chosen to present here the more complete text, but have incorporated the changes that Olmsted scrawled on the manuscript copy and have corrected printer's errors.

1. The Sanitary Commission used the side-wheel steamboat *Wilson Small* as its headquarters for much of the Peninsula campaign. Built in 1851, the *Small* weighed 258 tons. Sanitary Commission workers nicknamed it the *Collida* because it was so often

struck and damaged by other ships in the harbor (William M. Lytle and Forrest R. Holdcamper, *Merchant Steam Vessels of the United States, 1790–1868*, rev. ed. [Staten Island, N.Y., 1975], p. 233; Katharine Prescott Wormeley, *The Other Side of War; With the Army of the Potomac. Letters from the Headquarters of the United States Sanitary Commission during the Peninsular Campaign in Virginia in 1862* [Boston, 1888], p. 42).

2. Internal evidence from this letter indicates that Olmsted's dating of it as May 15 and of its postscript as May 16 is incorrect. The letter's general chronology suggests that it was begun on May 14. More specific evidence further bolsters this conclusion since the *Elm City*, a ship that Olmsted here reports as having departed for Washington "this morning," left the Peninsula on May 14, according to a telegram that he sent (FLO to USSC, May 14, 1862, USSC-NYPL, box 741: 1036).

3. Union casualties at the battle of Williamsburg on May 5 numbered about fifteen hundred. During the engagement at West Point on May 9, over one hundred Union soldiers were wounded. The *Knickerbocker* and *Daniel Webster No. 2* conveyed the wounded of Williamsburg to Fortress Monroe on May 10. Georgeanna Woolsey and Rosalie Butler were superintendents of nurses on the *Knickerbocker*, and Eliza Howland and Harriet Douglas Whetten held that position on the *Webster*. The Medical Bureau controlled the *Star*, probably an old side-wheel steamer (Frederick H. Dyer, *A Compendium of the War of the Rebellion . . .* , 3 vols. [1908; rpt. ed., New York, 1959], 1: 898–99; K. P. Wormeley, *The Other Side of War*, p. 31; W. M. Lytle and F. R. Holdcamper, *Merchant Steam Vessels*, p. 202).

4. The *Daniel Webster No. 1* arrived at Yorktown on May 11, and Olmsted sent it back to New York the following day (FLO to USSC, May 11, 1862, USSC-NYPL, box 741: 1002).

5. Probably Frank L. Wheaton, a surgeon of the 2nd Rhode Island, whom by May 8 Charles R. Greenleaf had placed in charge of the hospital at Yorktown (C. R. Greenleaf to FLO, May 8, 1862, Frederick Newman Knapp Papers, Massachusetts Historical Society, Boston, Mass.).

6. On May 10 Bellows, then in Washington, D.C., had telegraphed Olmsted that the *Ocean Queen* had arrived in New York and had been withdrawn from transport service under the Sanitary Commission. He also informed Olmsted that Quartermaster General Montgomery C. Meigs had ordered that the Sanitary Commission be provided with "the best and most capacious steamer" that could be spared by the government (HWB to FLO, May 10, 1862, USSC-NYPL, box 834, 1: 4–5).

7. The *S. R. Spaulding* was a large side-wheel steamer of 1,090 tons. Built in 1859 for ocean travel, it was the boat that Olmsted wished to use to transport the sick and wounded to cities outside the Chesapeake Bay area (W. M. Lytle and F. R. Holdcamper, *Merchant Steam Vessels*, p. 190).

8. An 858-ton steamboat built in New York in 1843. According to Olmsted, "The K. is a very old boat, low between decks in the hull, with no means of ventilation under the main deck and consequently of scarcely more than half the capacity of other boats of not much greater length and with which she would by a careless observer be classed" (ibid., p. 122; FLO to HWB, June 3, 1862, below).

9. That is, long stakes or pilings used to construct wharves or docks.

10. The *State of Maine*, built in 1858, was an 806-ton steamboat, and the *Elm City*, built in 1855, was a 760-ton steamer (W. M. Lytle and F. R. Holdcamper, *Merchant Steam Vessels*, pp. 63, 203).

11. Stewart Van Vliet (1815–1901), a West Pointer and career officer, was chief quartermaster of the Army of the Potomac from August 1861 until July 1862 (George Washington Cullum, *Biographical Register of the Officers and Graduates of the U.S. Military Academy at West Point, N.Y. . . .* , 3rd ed., 3 vols. [Boston, 1891], 2: 30–31; Ezra J. Warner, *Generals in Blue: Lives of the Union Commanders* [Baton Rouge, La., 1964], p. 524).

12. Georgeanna Woolsey and Rosalie Butler were still aboard the *Knickerbocker* when it was sent up river (K. P. Wormeley, *The Other Side of War*, p. 31).
13. James Henry Van Alen (1819–1886), a wealthy New Yorker who financially underwrote the recruiting and arming of the 3rd New York Cavalry. Promoted to brigadier general of volunteers in April 1862, he received command of Yorktown after its capture by Union troops (*O.R.*, ser. 1, vol. 11, pt. 1, p. 316; E. J. Warner, *Generals in Blue*, pp. 520–21).
14. Frank L. Wheaton.
15. Charles Tripler had accompanied the army on its advance (*O.R.*, ser. 1, vol. 11, pt. 1, pp. 184–86).
16. A small steamer not under the control of the Sanitary Commission.
17. A side-wheel steamer of 480 tons built in 1845 (W. M. Lytle and F. R. Holdcamper, *Merchant Steam Vessels*, p. 120).
18. A small boat.
19. George Gill Wheelock (1838–1907), a dresser for the Sanitary Commission and Henry W. Bellows's second cousin. Wheelock graduated from Harvard College in 1860 and received his medical degree in 1864 from the College of Physicians and Surgeons in New York (Thomas Bellows Peck, *The Bellows Genealogy* . . . [Keene, N.H., 1898], pp. 399–404; Harvard University, *Quinquennial Catalogue of the Officers and Graduates* . . . [Cambridge, Mass., 1925], p. 237).
20. Here Olmsted crossed out a fragmentary sentence that read, "This is what they call the guerrilla warfare in Virginia, in other parts of the Anglo-Saxon world."
21. Perhaps the Dr. Miller who, according to John H. Douglas in July 1862, remained at White House after its evacuation by Union troops and was captured by the Confederates. After Miller's release by the Confederates, Union officials imprisoned him at Berkeley. Douglas skeptically remarked about him, "He tells big & strange stories" (J. H. Douglas to FLO, July 20, 1862, USSC-NYPL, box 744: 1945).
22. Probably Wilson C. Swann (d. 1876), a wealthy physician who resided in Philadelphia. Born to a Southern slaveholding family, he emancipated approximately forty slaves he owned. He was also an art collector, president of the local Society for the Prevention of Cruelty to Animals, and an early member of the Union League Club of Philadelphia (*Biographical Encyclopedia of Pennsylvania of the Nineteenth Century* [Philadelphia, 1874], pp. 113–14).
23. David Lewis Haight (1839–1918), a medical student serving as a dresser on the Sanitary Commission's hospital boats. He graduated from Yale College in 1860 and received his medical degree from the College of Physicians and Surgeons in 1864 (*Yale Obit. Rec.*, 7th ser., 4 [Aug. 1919]: 866).
24. Benjamin Collins became the superintendent of the New York office of the Sanitary Commission and Bellows's chief assistant in 1862. In 1864 the Commission appointed Collins assistant treasurer. George Templeton Strong considered him "cross-grained and crotchety" but of "unquestionable honesty and reliability" ("Roster of Persons Employed by the Sanitary Commission," Oct. 1, 1862, USSC-NYPL, box 642; USSC, *Minutes*, p. 180; *Diary of the Civil War*, p. 519).
25. Charles William Woolsey (1840–1907), the younger brother of Eliza Woolsey Howland and Georgeanna Woolsey. In October 1862 he was commissioned first lieutenant in the 164th New York and served until May 1865 (A. L. Austin, *Woolsey Sisters*, pp. 1, 79–80; Frederick Phisterer, comp., *New York in the War of the Rebellion, 1861–1865*, 3rd ed., 6 vols. [Albany, N.Y., 1912], 5: 3920).

To John Foster Jenkins

On board Stm^r "Spaulding"
below White House, Pamunky river,
Sunday, May 18th 1862

My Dear Doctor,

After sending off the Knickerbocker yesterday[1] and making some transfers of stores, we removed our station from the Wilson Small to this fine ocean steamer, in which at breakfast time this morning we reached this point and found here a heap—being in Virginny speak the Virginny tongue—a heap of letters from you and others, some dating so far back as 28th ultimo. The $50 check from Hartford was among them.[2] I can not answer them. I can scarcely look beyond the immediate scene of our special work here. I hope you fully occupy the position of General Secretary and accept its responsibilities. Please write or ask Dr Bellows to write to Newberry and to Mr. Yeatman whose letter pains me, it so entirely misconceives the purpose and spirit of mine to which it is a reply.[3] This can only arise from a false idea of my character received in some other way than from the letter itself.

I telegraphed you this morning about the needs of this place.[4] During the half hour that I was in Tripler's tent, three persons reported their arrival at Head Quarters with sick and were informed that there was no accommodation for them. Tents had been received and a detail called for the day before, to pitch them. It was supposed that something would be done before night. The tents being placed, there are no beds, no bed pans, and no surgeons, I suspect, to attend them. Sickness is increasing rapidly and every case shows the influence of malaria. The number sent home "sick," who were merely fatigued, is very large, and the knowledge that a slight indisposition gives a man a good chance to go to see his friends is having a very demoralizing influence. The reason they are packed off in the reckless, undiscriminating way they are is that nothing can be done for them here. They are unfit for the heavy marching required of the fighting men and must be got rid of. Establish dépôt hospitals as often as may be necessary to have accommodation for all who may fall sick within accessible distance of the front, and I believe that three fourths of those who otherwise are to be sent off would be restored to their regiments within a fortnight, in good order. The reduced number could be transported in a decent manner.

Tripler says, and apparently with justice, that he anticipated all this and had made ample provision but that almost none of his ordered supplies reach him. The minor surgeons say the same thing. Chamberlain[5] tells of having found a detail of men digging roots for a regimental surgeon

WHITE HOUSE, ON THE PAMUNKEY RIVER, 1862

as a means of supplying substitutes for drugs which he had ordered five weeks ago. Our own draft on the Medical Purveyor's boat made today, for this ship, discloses important defects in the supply.

It is said that Richmond is already crowded with the sick of the rebels. Their army of the Peninsula left it in very bad health. It will not do, at any rate, to depend on the accommodations which the enemy will provide or leave for our sick.

The want of surgeons—or rather of physicians—is becoming serious. I saw at Tripler's a report from the Brigade Surg[n] of the 3[d] of Porter's,[6] showing that he had in the whole brigade but one surgeon and three assistant surgeons, others being dead, sick or left at hospitals in the rear. The civil surgeons who have recently come here have been on the whole of no use. They do not come to do good wherever they may be needed but to distinguish themselves in battlefield surgery, at least such is the idea of the army surgeons, and the civilians, if they are not sent to the front or to surgical hospitals, attribute it to professional jealousy, and go home in disgust.

We had no sooner arrived this morning than Dr. Tripler wrote a peremptory order that we should be ready to take sick on at once. You can see the reason for this in what I have told you of his necessities. I went to his tent prepared to refuse to regard his order—to tell him that I was not under his orders. But I found him, as I always do, when I came to reason with him, very sensible. I told him that the Spaulding was not in any condition to receive sick, but that by tomorrow morning I could accommodate 200 on the Webster, and by tomorrow night 400 on the Elm city. This rejoiced him and he yielded at once to all I had to propose, and I sent Knapp down this afternoon to bring up our whole fleet from Yorktown with all stores which can be spared from there.[7] I shall do all I can to carry out the plan I have always wished to pursue, namely to have a receiving hospital from which at intervals those who need to be sent away may be deliberately transferred to proper vessels properly equipped. I shall use the Elm city for the receiving hospital. But all this may again be upset by unexpected necessities in the next twenty four hours.

The ladies continue to work nobly and we are with one or two unimportant exceptions quite well. I constantly urge the use of Quinine as a prophylactic,[8] and today's rest will bring us all up straight I think. We are doing nothing but fitting up the apothecaries' shop & seeing friends—and enemies.

Yours faithfully

Fred. Law Olmsted.

The original is letter 1067 in box 741 of USSC-NYPL.

1. The *Knickerbocker* departed for Washington at 5:00 A.M. on May 17 (FLO to USSC, May 17, 1862, USSC-NYPL, box 741: 1061).
2. A donation of fifty dollars to the Sanitary Commission from the Hartford Ladies Soldiers' Aid Society addressed to Olmsted by Sarah S. Cowen on April 28. In his letter of acknowledgment of May 21 Olmsted gave a short account of the Commission's activities on the Peninsula and solicited further contributions (FLO to S. S. Cowen, May 21, 1862).
3. A reference to James E. Yeatman's reply to Olmsted's letter of April 17. Yeatman argued that the U.S. Sanitary Commission had earlier ignored the Western Sanitary Commission's offer to receive and distribute supplies free of charge and instead had sent "high salaried" agents there, and for a short time only, to perform those tasks. When the U.S. Sanitary agents left St. Louis, the Western Commission then had to assume all responsibility and thus had to supplement its limited supplies. Yeatman further defended his association's appeal to Eastern citizens:

> We made the demand and nobly have the patriotic people of the North responded—they did not have to give unless they were willing to do so. We cannot see how in doing this our association pursued an objectionable mode of benevolence—on the contrary had we not done so, we would have been highly reprehensible. I am surprised and humiliated in this enlightened age and in times like these that there should be one man found to object, to have others take hold and assist in doing what they themselves deemed worthy of doing.

Yeatman also intimated that the U.S. Sanitary Commission's objections sprang from jealousy and contrasted to it the Western Commission's willingness to cooperate:

> We have had no feeling of rivalry or jealousy of any association. We felt that our work was a peculiar, and to some extent a local one, but still a mammoth one, and that it could be best done by us, and this I had supposed was fully understood by

you, so was unprepared for your letter objecting to our course of proceeding. We have a work to do, and we have a will and a heart to do it, it is a labor of love, and we all feel that we cannot labor too much—it is grating to have those engaged in the same good cause to come forward and object to what we are doing, and to produce suspicion and distrust in the minds of those who contribute. Should this be, would it not be far better for you to say to them that our store Houses are full, send to our brothers in the West, who are doing all the fighting and who consequently have all the wounded to take care of. Why must everything pass through your channels. God waters the earth with many streams and there are many channels for the benevolence of his people, and it is useless to try and dam them up. If you have supplies for the West and desire to send them to us we can make good use of them and will not object to receive them from any source from which they may come.

(J. E. Yeatman to FLO, May 4, 1862, USSC-NYPL, box 642.)

4. A telegram jointly signed by Olmsted and Tripler urged that a hospital depot for six thousand men be established as soon as possible at White House, with "tents, stores, physicians, nurses and everything complete" sent from Washington or New York (FLO and C. S. Tripler to USSC, May 18, 1862 [misdated 1861], USSC-NYPL, box 741: 1066).

5. William Mellen Chamberlain (1826–1887) received his bachelor's and medical degrees from Dartmouth College. After completing an internship at Charity Hospital in New York City, he practiced medicine at Astoria on Long Island until 1860. During 1861 he briefly served as a brigade surgeon for volunteer troops, then became a Sanitary Commission inspector with the Army of the Potomac, a position he held through the summer of 1862. In December 1862 he was appointed an examining physician for the U.S. Pension Bureau and in 1863 he began to lecture on obstetrics at the New York Medical College. Retaining his private practice, Chamberlain was also active in professional societies and published a number of articles.

At the Sanitary Commission, Chamberlain's superiors and fellow workers came to dislike him. In August 1862 Bellows observed that the physician had "grown brusque and presumptuous and wants a serious caution." Chamberlain alienated others by his report on his activities during the aftermath of the battle of Antietam. Not only Douglas and Bloor, but even kindly Frederick Knapp, complained that Chamberlain had overstated his own role. Sanitary inspector George L. Andrew accused Chamberlain of shirking less-interesting though essential duties. Thus, when after a leave of absence Chamberlain wished to reenter the Commission's service, he was not accepted (John S. Warren, "A Biographical Sketch of Dr. William Mellen Chamberlain," *Transactions of the Medical Society of the State of New York for the Year 1888*, 1888, pp. 564–68; HWB to C. R. Agnew, GTS, and W. H. Van Buren, Aug. 13, 1862, USSC-NYPL, box 638; FLO to HWB, Sept. 29, 1862, USSC-NYPL, box 641; HWB to FLO, Oct. 8, 1862, USSC-NYPL, box 746: 2434).

6. A reference to the 3rd Brigade in the 1st Division, commanded by Gen. Fitz-John Porter, of the III Corps of the Army of the Potomac (F. H. Dyer, *Compendium of the War*, 2: 294–95).

7. That is, after the *Spaulding* had arrived at White House, Olmsted sent Knapp back to Yorktown to bring upriver the Sanitary Commission's supply ships and to leave orders that the Commission's hospital ships, upon arrival from the North, should proceed to White House (K. P. Wormeley, *The Other Side of War*, pp. 55–56).

8. Long before the Civil War, quinine was known to be effective in treating malaria, and some physicians also believed the drug to be useful in preventing the disease. William Van Buren summarized these opinions in a paper entitled, "Report of a Committee . . . to Prepare a Paper on the Use of Quinine as a Prophylactic Against Malarious Diseases." In October 1861 the Sanitary Commission approved a resolution to print

that report and circulate it among the army physicians ("Quinine as a Prophylactic," no. D in U.S. Sanitary Commission, *Medical and Surgical Monographs* [New York, n.d.]; USSC, *Minutes*, p. 76).

To John Foster Jenkins

Sanitary Commission Floating Hospital,
"S. R. Spaulding," off White House,
on the Pamunkey, Va.   May 20ᵗʰ 1862.

"This is to be considered as in my "private book".[1]

F.L.O.

My Dear Doctor,

I have today received your favor of the 18ᵗʰ. I wrote you yesterday. I went up with the Webster this morning to the railroad bridge and after a deal of trouble in getting her a berth began at once taking on sick. Tripler was on the shore with the ambulance train, and as soon as I came off it [to] him, handed me the Surgn Genl's despatch in answer to my telegram of yesterday to you. "Now see how they misunderstand me." Frightened by the mild reproof administered, he had entirely lost sight of the plan of yesterday and was only anxious to get the sick off as fast as possible.[2] Wanted to fill the Spaulding up at once &c. He had telegraphed for leave to go to Yorktown, having an idea that there was a grand snarl there. Also thought he ought to go to the point.[3] I went on the purveyor's boat and while there, came Knapp with a favorable report of Yorktown & Williamsburg—Greenleaf, following our advice at last, was making the best of the means at his disposal, and these were not, it proved, entirely inadequate. Greenleaf sent a cheering message. At the same time arrived large supplies—medical & hospital furniture—what was most needed—what was deficient we now had ready to offer in great part, and I had little difficulty in getting him to recur to the plan of yesterday—as far at least as we were a part of it. To relieve myself of further responsibility in case of another change of plan, (in not being prepared for it) I wrote a memorandum of what we expected to be able to do and got him to sign an approval of it.[4]

He told me yesterday that he meant to have those who were to take ship very carefully selected and he did not believe that there were half a dozen who ought to go from here. I saw, among those going on board, the

CHARLES STUART TRIPLER

usual proportion of merely "sick in quarters" men and told him of it. He said it was because the volunteer surgeons would not obey orders—he could not depend on them. I found Smith[5] and told him it would not do and he went to the hospital and, as he said, found that the surgeon had heard a report that the Sanitary Commission was going to have a receiving hospital ship here and was sending men without any reference to the gravity of their cases. He also said that he found that ambulances coming in from the country had entered the train after it left the hospital and the men they brought had gone on board. I asked him to go on board and send off such as he found of these interlopers. Finally, instead of half a dozen, two hundred and fifty six (256) were put on board. Smith said the old gentleman was mightily flustered and he wished that I could induce him to go to the front and leave him to manage the business here. He seemed to think they might get on very well now, if it were not for the folly of some of these "Albany" gentlemen,[6] one of whom complained bitterly that he actually had not been able to change his shirt for two days.

Except to meet the results of a heavy engagement, my impression is that we have now in our hands fully all the boats that are needed. In addition to those mentioned in the Memorandum, a copy of which I mean to enclose, we have, ready to fit up, the D. Webster No. 2. I presume that you will send me physicians to supply the place of those on the Elm City, who—as they *must* return in so many days—are only encumbrances to my plans. I have telegraphed to Parker[7] and Watts[8] offering them our surgical

339

hospital if they will come here to take it—in reserve for an engagement. I have persuaded Draper[9] to remain and have one other besides Ware. (Chamberlain is to the front). These I reckon upon for at least a week. We should still be, by Thursday or Monday at furthest without any surgeon for the D. Webster No 2.[10] One, a stranger, has just come on board to offer his services & I shall hold him. Tripler says he is pestered with surgeons who come for a few days and expect to be put in a deadly breach at once. He has not tents, horses, forage, nor table room for them. Don't let any more *surgeons* come here if you can help it. We try to be polite to them, but all, ashore and afloat, feel like kicking a man the moment he graciously proposes to be entertained and sent to the front because, you understand, he is not one of your physicians but a surgeon and not afraid of taking a gunshot case in hand, though everybody else declines it. If there is anything the regimental surgeons hate, it is to let these magnanimous surgical pretenders get hold of their pets. For this reason I hope Parker, who has a name, will take the responsibility of our surgical hospital.

I must caution you all, again, if I have done so, as I probably have before, not to form theories of what I am to do and expect me to do it. We are liable to occurrences every day, which make a new disposition of all the forces necessary. In fact new and previously unexpected dispositions are made daily and these involve a continual modification of all plans. All that can be done is to be as fully prepared as possible for whatever can occur, or, to speak more practically—*you*, at that end, can only see that our boats are as well equipped, manned and womanned as practicable, not for special service but for any service for which it would be proper to have them used. You must trust to my perceptions of what is most needed, with the light which I get, as I can, here at the centre. I must act a little blindly sometimes—at all events can't readily give my reasons for what I determine upon. Twice I have come up the river from hardly anything more than a general idea that it was prudent to lay our anchor that way and would cost but little, and in each case, it proved to be, what they call a grand, good Providence, and led to a complete change of our tactics.[11]

I adopt Dr Bellows' advice[12] without understanding the occasion for it, and will, as a rule direct all telegrams to you—you to forward to those concerned. This is what I believe I have always done except there was special occasion to send to some *individual* direct. You will have observed that my telegrams go with no regularity. Probably some miss you entirely. I have been several times advised to telegraph more freely and explicitly. There has been good reason for not doing so. The telegraphers complain and threaten and it is important to put & keep them in good humor. (It is not a question of pay, there is no pay.)

Our hired women, of all classes, except Mrs Redding & Mrs Johnson,[13] have proved either useless or worse. The ladies are all, in every way, far beyond anything I could have been induced to expect of them. They never fail in anything wanted of them. The dressers are generally ready for anything and work heroically. The male nurses are of all sorts. I believe the details of soldiers have been the most satisfactory, because there was not among them the slightest taint of the prevailing sentiment of the nurses that they were going upon an indiscriminate, holiday scramble of Good Samaritanism. There can not be too much care, in future, that, whoever comes here on our business, comes not to do such work as he thinks himself fit for, but such as he will be assigned to, and under such authority as will be assigned him. He or she must come as distinctly under an obligation of duty in this respect as if he or she were paid, and must be expected to be treated with the same discipline. I particularly don't want anybody on any other terms, and will not have them. If anybody comes, therefore, not prepared for this, they may as well be prepared to take care of themselves in a Virginia river swamp—for they will incontinently go ashore wherever I happen to be when I discover it, probably. I have had very little trouble of this sort, however, and in all respects am surprised at the good sense and working quality of companies made up as ours have been.

> Yours Very Faithfully

> Fred. Law Olmsted
> General Secretary

Dr J. Foster Jenkins,
Secy San. Com.

The original is letter 1098 in box 741 of USSC-NYPL.

1. Olmsted is here distinguishing between two kinds of business correspondence: in the first, he conveyed his own opinions; in the second, he merely stated or carried out official policies of the Sanitary Commission. In the autumn of 1862 he attempted to explain that difference to Bellows:

    > Please understand that when I write *private* over letters, I mean only private as in distinction from purely official. Such letters go into my *private* copybook (if any) and *are not the property*, as one sixteenth undivided portion, of Dr Harris, for instance. For closer confidence if ever needed I will write *personal*.

    From mid-June 1862 through mid-May 1863 Olmsted used at least two different letterpress books for copies of his letters relating to Sanitary Commission affairs. One was marked "private," the other "official" (FLO to HWB, Oct. 6, 1862, Henry Whitney Bellows Papers, Massachusetts Historical Society, Boston, Mass.).
2. On May 19 Surgeon General Hammond replied to Tripler's and Olmsted's suggestion for a hospital depot by chiding Tripler with these words: "If a depot is necessary at Yorktown for 6000 patients why do you not establish it? You have been given full

powers to act altogether independently, and must be your own judge of what is best to be done." Hammond also pointed out that although Tripler was asking for large amounts of additional supplies, the medical purveyor for the Army of the Potomac was reporting that he had sufficient stores. Finally, Hammond met complaints about transportation by suggesting that Tripler consult with General McClellan, who "surely would not refuse his assistance" (W. A. Hammond to C. S. Tripler, May 19, 1862, Record Group 112, Records of the Office of the Surgeon General [Army], letterbook 30, pp. 467–68, National Archives).

3. Probably Ship Point.
4. This agreement was a plan to use the transports for specific purposes. The *Elm City* would become a receiving hospital for ill soldiers, and the *Spaulding* would be held in reserve until a battle occurred. After a battle, the *Elm City* would receive only wounded men and the *Knickerbocker* would transport 250 of them each day to Fortress Monroe. Ill soldiers earlier housed on the *Elm City* would be transferred to the *Spaulding*, which, with the *Daniel Webster No. 1*, would transport them to hospitals either in Washington or in Northern cities. Olmsted believed that neither the *Spaulding* nor the *Webster* was properly ventilated to accommodate or transport wounded soldiers (FLO, "Plan of Action Approved by Dr. Tripler," May 20, 1862, USSC-NYPL, box 741: 1096).
5. Andrew K. Smith.
6. A slighting reference to a contingent of at least four physicians from Albany, New York, who were serving as volunteer surgeons at White House during the third week of May (*Boston Medical and Surgical Journal* 66, no. 20 [June 19, 1862]: 416–17).
7. Willard Parker.
8. Robert Watts (1812–1867), professor of anatomy at the College of Physicians and Surgeons in New York. A founder and past president of the New York Pathological Society, he was also a fellow in the New York Academy of Medicine (J. Shrady, *College of Physicians and Surgeons*, 1: 115–18).
9. William Henry Draper (1830–1901), a New York City physician. He had graduated from Columbia College and the College of Physicians and Surgeons and had studied in London and Paris. Draper was an active member of the Woman's Central Association of Relief and served on its Executive Committee and Board of Managers. During the summer of 1861 he and Olmsted had corresponded about hospital supplies (*NCAB*; "Report Concerning the Woman's Central Association of Relief at New York to the U.S. Sanitary Commission at Washington. October 12, 1861," doc. no. 32 in USSC, *Documents*, pp. 16–17).
10. The *Daniel Webster No. 2*, built in 1853 or 1854, was much smaller than the other side-wheel steamboat of that name (W. M. Lytle and F. R. Holdcamper, *Merchant Steam Vessels*, p. 51).
11. Olmsted is probably referring to his voyages upriver that changed the base of operations for the hospital ships. On May 5 the *Ocean Queen* and *Wilson Small* sailed up the York River to Yorktown, and on May 18 the *S. R. Spaulding* reached White House on the Pamunkey. The first trip enabled the Sanitary Commission to aid many soldiers ill with typhoid fever who would otherwise have gone uncared for. Most likely Olmsted saw the second trip as a "grand good Providence" because it appeared to be leading to a change of tactics through the establishment of a system that would assign each soldier to a hospital ship by the nature of his illness or injury (see FLO to JFJ, May 7, 1862, above; FLO to JFJ, May 18, 1862, above).
12. On May 16 Bellows wrote Olmsted: "We have a good deal of perplexity about telegrams. Could you not adopt a rule to telegraph in all cases either to New York, or to Washington, so that no conflict of purposes might exist. . . . Adopt one rule & let it be the shortest & swiftest way." The problem had arisen when Olmsted requested supplies and nurses both from Washington and New York, and the Commission

officials were unsure whether he wished both branches or only one to fill his request (HWB to FLO, May 16, 1862, USSC-NYPL, box 742: 1280; GTS to FLO, May 18, 1862, USSC-NYPL, box 741: 1068).

13. Ellen Cheney Johnson (1829–1899), a former schoolteacher, was a member of the executive and finance committees of the New England Women's Auxiliary Association, a branch of the Sanitary Commission. After the war she served on the Massachusetts state prison commission and became superintendent of the state prison for women. Under Florence Nightingale's supervision Mrs. Reading had nursed soldiers during the Crimean War. Katharine P. Wormeley considered her an "excellent surgical nurse" (Robert McHenry, ed., *Liberty's Women* [Springfield, Mass., 1980], pp. 211–12; K. P. Wormeley, *The Other Side of War*, p. 85).

To John Foster Jenkins

Sanitary Commission,

White House, Va   Floating Hospital,

May 21st 1862.

My Dear Doctor,

I think that the enclosed sheet, in pencil, may have been omitted from the ms copy sent you yesterday. It should be inserted, if I recollect rightly, after the Hours of Meals.[1]

I wrote you yesterday that things looked more promising ashore, except for the want of hands. Drs Ware, Draper and Armstrong,[2] spent the greater part of the day, with some of the young men, in the hospitals, and their report at night was far far from favorable. The sick are coming in very rapidly, much more rapidly than the accommodations for them can be increased. The record is said to show a total of 1600. I suspect this includes the 256 taken on the Webster and all who have been discharged, as there certainly is not tent room for that number. There are five surgeons and assistants, one steward, no apothecary, and *no detail*. No nurses except those selected from the patients themselves. Two wells have been dug but the water of neither has been as yet fit to use for drinking. Water is brought from the White House well—nearly quarter of a mile distant—and until yesterday, the whole supply was brought by hand. It is now waggoned in casks. We sent up three casks of ice from the Webster's stock, which was found of great value. The greater part of the men are not very ill; with nice nourishment, comfortable rest, and good nursing, would be got ready to join their regiments in a week or two—but this is just what they are not likely to have. They have but two soup-kettles to cook for the whole

BOATS AT WHITE HOUSE LANDING, 1862

number and the surgeon in charge, Baxter,[3] seemed to think this enough—
and, apparently, that they were doing well enough for soldiers altogether.
He was nevertheless eager to throw them on board our boats.

I am in a quandary as to the best policy to be pursued. The
weather is growing excessively hot and we are pushing forward in a malarious country in the face of the enemy. We have taken on one or two
wounded men from the skirmishes yesterday.[4] There is obviously great
danger that they will be altogether overwhelmed with sick and wounded in
a few days. If the recommendation of my telegram of Sunday is adopted—
a complete hospital for 6000 sent here from Washington—there will be
reasonable provision for the contingency.[5] But I believe that the Surgeon
General is wrong when he says that Tripler can accomplish this himself.
He is dependent on the Quartermaster's department of the army, I suppose, and I have no idea that the Quartermaster's Department will listen to
anything at present but getting forward rations and forage for the fighting
Divisions. If I am wrong as [to] the means at his disposal I still do not
believe that he can have faith enough in his power to be ready to exercise
it. He does not, and can not be made to, believe it possible that when the
Army is advancing, anything but very moderate and modest propositions
will be listened to from the Medical Staff. There is no doubt that we can
take care of three or four hundred or more on our boats—probably save
the lives of some among them who will otherwise die from the inadequacy

344

of the accommodations ashore—but considering what a week, or, for that matter, a day, may bring forth, I feel it right to throw them, still, on their resources—force them to enlarge their shore accommodations, believing that they are not doing half what they might, nor quarter what they ought to be able to do, in this respect. I have therefore patiently submitted to the delay of the Quarter Master's Department, in getting a wharf ready for the Elm city. Nor shall I be disposed to hasten the disposal of the sick on her. I shall endeavor to prevent any but serious cases from coming on. Then, as to the removal of the sick North, it is plain that the facilities so far offered in this respect have been greatly abused, and that serious evils have come of it. Those responsible for the care of the sick here,—I mean the military administrative as well as medical officers—have been encouraged to ne-glect all proper local provision for them, and to depend entirely on hurry-ing them on board vessels with the idea that they thus relieve themselv[es] of responsibility about them. I saw this at our first freight, and have, (I wish the Surgeon General and our friends to be sure of this), constantly done all that I could to counteract it—not only by verbal protest—but by a habit of action, which I know that Knapp and other friends here, who have not had the duty to look at the matter so largely as I, have not been able always to regard as justifiable. But there is a greater evil than this. There is a great deal of home-sickness in the army, and among a hundred thousand men, there must always be a great many shirks. This is really the first experience of nearly all of our officers in active campaigning. They are learning to [take] care of their men as a matter of self-interest. The men themselves need to learn to make themselves content—of contented habit—to be away from home, to understand that this is in the bargain. It is obvious from the remarks we hear that the rumor that sick men are to be sent home has a demoralizing effect, encouraging neglect of precaution and provision against sickness with the officers and the surgeons; distracting the minds of the men from their business—their duty—by leading them to think of the chances of their getting home on sick leave. I find this appreci-ated by Gen'ls Williams, Van Vliet and Franklin,[6] with whom I have con-versed. It was one of many reasons for my sending the Webster to Boston, that, as no selection of New England men had been made for her, it would be seen that we did not study to send men near their homes. (It was suspected too that there might have been some management to get New York men on her, who wanted to go home, without regard to their neces-sity).

The Knickerbocker has arrived while I have been writing, thus I have all the elements of my plan approved by Tripler, on Monday.[7]

The quandary is this: If they have several hundred more patients on shore than they have tents for, or beds, and among them all several hundred seriously ill—such as would properly be sent North—shall I break up my reserve and have no provision for the avalanche of suffering which a great battle before Richmond would send down upon us? I have more than fifty idle hands here—and the boats I hold, cost government three to four thousand dollars a day. I am afraid that I stand alone in my resistance to the demands of the present, and I may be induced to modify my plan.

I have just bought what is left of a cargo of ice—probably sixty tons—at $12., having been authorized by my own suggestion to do so, on acct of gov[t] by Tripler. We are now very well supplied at all points I think; thanks to your good judgment and energy. There are doctors enough here, for the present, and if necessary, we could even man the D. Webster No. 2., which is clean, and which we shall have ready as a reserve sick transport, inside. Keep us informed of the accommodations at Washington, Annapolis and Baltimore. I am determined not to send sick people in any of these outguard boats outside.[8] The only vessels we have, that I shall ever send out, of my own will, are the Webster No 1. & Spaulding.

As Dr. Bellows knows Warriner;[9] suppose you refer the matter of Mrs Harlan[10] to him, assuring Mr Harlan, that justice will be done. It is quite incomprehensible. Of course Mrs Harlan is in some way mistaken. I entirely approve the course you have taken. The immediate difficulty will be to satisfy Mr Harlan that there is no unnecessary delay in dealing with the matter.

night—We began taking sick on the Elm city the P.M. I am sorry to say that D[r] Fisher[11] proves good [for] nothing. He is excessively fussy, slow and without any authority or efficiency. I telegraphed you about the crowded state of the hospitals and about our feeding sixty men who had been turned away from them. I wrote to the surg[n] in charge about it & Knapp called on him with my note.[12] He merely denied that there could have been as many as sixty turned away. He had a detail of ten men who were four hours getting their dinner, while sick men were being almost drowned in a very heavy rain. The water stood several inches deep in some tents of the hospital and the men brought on the Elm city had evidently been lying in a puddle which nearly came over them. These were selected by Ware as the sickest men, and their clothing was soaking wet. Ware helped to put up tents to protect men before the storm, and said that he saw half a dozen tents yet remaining not put up at night-fall, though men were constantly arriving and were left in their ambulances. If an engagement occurs this side of Richmond, my opinion is that we shall have all the horrors of Pittsburg landing[13] in an aggravated form. I have tried in vain to awaken some of the Head Quarters officers to a sense of the danger, but while they admit all I say, they regard it as a part of war, and say "there *never* was a war in which the sick were so well taken care of"; "England does no better by her wounded",—"true they will suffer a good deal for a time, but that is inevitable in war", &c.

The only comforting circumstance in our present situation is the fact that the prevalent sickness is not of a very serious character. Of the men we relieved today not more than six of the sixty, seemed to require anything more than rest and good diet for a few days, and half of them, after having had a little brandy and water, bread and tea, were inclined to walk about and amuse themselves. It was nearly twenty four hours since they had had anything to eat, except a few ginger nuts bought of a sutler.[14]

The sutler nuisance, by the way, is dreadful here. I met a dozen boys peddling pies within a hundred yards of the Elm city today.

Yours Very Truly

Fred. Law Olmsted.

The original is letter 1101 in box 741 in USSC-NYPL. Although Olmsted dated it May 21, internal evidence indicates that it was written on the following day, May 22.

1. In a letter of May 21 Olmsted sent a version of what he called "Instructions for floating hospital service on the Atlantic coast" and requested that Jenkins have the list printed and posted in the hospital ships. Olmsted noted that any suggestions from the surgeon general or other workers in the Sanitary Commission could be incorporated into the final draft. These instructions, which have survived only in final published form, set forth fully the organization of each hospital ship, including its chain of command, hours of duty, time of meals, and the proper procedure for the reception and care of patients. In general, these instructions were a longer, more detailed exposition of rules that Olmsted first drew up for hospital service in early May (*Hospital Transports*, app. B, pp. 143-50; see FLO to HWB, May 7, 1862, n. 6, above).

2. Possibly Robert Armstrong, a New York City physician (*Trow's New York City Directory... For the Year Ending May 1, 1862* [New York, 1861]).

3. Jedediah Hyde Baxter (1837-1890). A graduate of the medical school of the University of Vermont in 1860, Baxter was commissioned surgeon of the 12th Massachusetts in 1861 and became a brigade surgeon in April 1862. After the war he served as medical purveyor and was appointed surgeon general in 1890 (F. B. Heitman, *Historical Register and Dictionary*, 1: 200; H. A. Kelly and W. L. Burrage, *Dictionary of American Medical Biography*, p. 76).

4. Probably the operations of the Union army that occurred at Bottom's Bridge from May 20 until May 23 (F. H. Dyer, *Compendium of the War*, 1: 899).

5. See FLO to JFJ, May 18, 1862, note 4, above.

6. Seth Williams (1821-1866), Stewart Van Vliet, and William Buel Franklin (1823-1903) were graduates of West Point, veterans of the Mexican War, and brigadier generals of volunteers in May 1862. Williams was adjutant general for the Army of the Potomac, while Franklin commanded the VI Corps and in July 1862 was promoted to major general (*DAB*, s.v. "Franklin, William Buel"; G. W. Cullum, *Biographical Register*, 2: 30-31, 130-32; F. B. Heitman, *Historical Register and Dictionary*, 1: 984).

7. That is, Olmsted then had possession of all the boats to be used in the plan for receiving hospitals that Tripler had approved (FLO to JFJ, May 20, 1862, n. 4, above).

8. Olmsted meant that he would send sick patients no farther than the cities and towns on the Chesapeake Bay when they were transported by the steamboats designed for river rather than ocean travel.

9. Henry Augustus Warriner (1824–1871) taught zoology and physiology at Antioch College in Yellow Springs, Ohio, at the beginning of the Civil War. In November 1861 Warriner, who possessed a medical degree, offered his services to Henry W. Bellows for the Sanitary Commission. The two men knew each other through Bellows's extensive fund raising for Antioch.

    As an inspector for the Commission, Warriner was stationed in the Western department, first in Missouri, later in Kentucky and Tennessee. In 1862 he married Fanny Swan, who aided him in his work but died less than a year later. Ill health also cut short his own service to the Commission. After the Civil War he briefly edited a newspaper and began a never-completed history of the Sanitary Commission. He died at Frederick Knapp's school in Plymouth. Knapp eulogized Warriner for his "*genuineness* & simplicity & hearty sympathy, and his faith (in God & man, & law, & truth, & right)" (Edwin Warriner, *The Warriner Family of New England Origin* . . . [Albany, N.Y., 1899], pp. 185–86; H. A. Warriner to HWB, Nov. 12, 1861, USSC-NYPL, box 642; Walter Donald Kring, *Henry Whitney Bellows* [Boston, 1979], pp. 204–5; F. N. Knapp to FLO, Nov. 20, 1871).

10. Ann Eliza Peck Harlan, the wife of James Harlan (1820–1899), who was a U.S. senator from Iowa and a friend of Abraham Lincoln's. The matter in question was Ann Harlan's assertion that Sanitary Commission agents Henry Warriner and John H. Douglas had insulted her. According to her husband, the two men blocked the delivery of supplies that she had solicited and intended to distribute among wounded Iowan soldiers after the battle of Shiloh. When she protested, they used "gross and threatening language." The senator lodged his complaint on May 16, and Bellows on May 28 assured him that the incident was being investigated. Upon hearing Warriner's and Douglas's accounts, Bellows chose to believe them and dropped the investigation, much to Harlan's chagrin (*DAB*; James Harlan to FLO, May 16, 1862, USSC-NYPL, box 640; HWB to James Harlan, May 28, 1862, USSC-NYPL, box 741: 1040; James Harlan to HWB, June 26, 1862, USSC-NYPL, box 640).

11. George Jackson Fisher (1825–1893) was a surgeon from Sing Sing, New York. A bibliophile and a friend of J. Foster Jenkins, Fisher wrote about the history of medicine as well as on specialized medical topics. He later served as president of the state medical society (H. A. Kelly and W. L. Burrage, *Dictionary of American Medical Biography*, pp. 408–9).

12. Olmsted's letter of protest to Jedediah H. Baxter, the surgeon in charge, described the incident as involving sixty men "who reported they had come fourteen miles since midnight & had had no sustenance since yesterday; that they went to the hospital & were refused entrance, shelter or food & were advised to look along shore for a hospital boat." Assuring Baxter that the report "no doubt" was exaggerated, Olmsted reminded him about the agreement with Tripler that the Sanitary Commission, after the sailing of the *Webster*, would remove no sick soldiers until a battle occurred (FLO to J. H. Baxter, May 22, 1862, USSC-NYPL, box 742: 1300).

13. The Union wounded at the battle of Shiloh (Pittsburg Landing) received little immediate medical care. Because the Union forces were not expecting a battle, medical officers had not made preparations for it. Even before the battle, Union surgeons had few medical supplies, and the Confederate capture of regimental hospitals further depleted this store. Moreover, because of the breakdown of the brigades' ambulance service, many of the wounded were left on the battlefield for a

day or more (George Worthington Adams, *Doctors in Blue: The Medical History of the Union Army in the Civil War* [New York, 1952], pp. 75–76).
14. An army follower who sold provisions to the soldiers.

To John Foster Jenkins

Spaulding, White House
May 25th 1862.

My Dear Doctor,
I have today received your favors of 22[d] with enclosures.

I am sorry that Newberry is disappointed by my absence; far more sorry that there has been a disagreement with some feeling between him and Douglas. My verbal instruction to Douglas was that he should always yield on any question of policy to Newberry. My instructions to Newberry were that he should advise with Douglas, yield as far he thought right to his wishes and finally divide the field of duty according to his own judgment—leaving the responsibility of division finally with Newberry. The lines of their respective duty necessarily cross each other as the army moves, and there can be no exact division of responsibility; hence the necessity of making Douglas subordinate. Newberry errs in assuming too much personally, obviously, if he finds it necessary to directly superintend floating hospitals, he must give temporarily into other hands his general and ordinary duty, or that must be intermitted entirely. As he is your superior you can only—as acting general secretary—refer the matter with such suggestions, as you think proper to offer, and with all the information in your possession which facilitate a fair understanding of it, to the President.[1]

The suggestion of sending young Stetson[2]—a very good fellow— to relieve me, is a little startling. I have the strongest possible desire to get home for many reasons, but it would be far easier for me to step into D[r] Bellows' pastoral shoes, some fine morning and let him go to Europe than for the best man in the world to step into mine here. I don't think any of you begin to comprehend the difficulties of the position. It is damming a river with sand. All our vessels are from the nature of engagement and intentions of those on board in a constant state of pre-organization and disorganization. Our relations to the crews, upon whom we are dependent, differ on every vessel. Scarcely a day passes in which there is not a real

GEORGEANNA MUIR WOOLSEY, IN HER NURSING COSTUME

mutiny to meet, in which we have no rightful authority to interfere, but which it is necessary we should manage to control. We have scarcely any established rights and are carrying on a very large business by the favor of a multitude of agents, whose favor in each case hangs upon a separate string. Every hour brings its own difficulty, which must be met by itself, and to meet which successfully, requires a knowledge that no man can acquire, except by experience on the ground. Hence I have not sent for you or for Mr Rogers. The whole service is only adapted to an emergency; it is excuseable only on that ground. It is all spasmodic from beginning to end, and, on this voluntary, gratuitous basis, with borrowed boats, which may be taken away any moment, with crews bound only to sail those boats, entirely subject to the whims of surgeons, quartermasters, harbor masters & commissaries, it can not be anything else. It certainly can not be managed without system, but that system can only rest on individual experience. It can not be defined and communicated. I often surprise and alarm Knapp by my decisions, but I believe I have always been able to justify them by reference to facts which he had forgotten or never known—or they have been justified by immediate results.

Except in the results accomplished, I need not say that the whole duty is exceedingly unpleasant from the amount of dependence without rights, and of command without authority.

Of course this sort of thing can't last long. There can not be a chronic emergency, and I am anxiously waiting to see some signs of a rising Surgeon General.

The list of nominations[3] which you send me, is enough to make a saint swear. I thoroughly hate that canting small politician the Secry of War. I think, really, it is time the Sanitary Commission resigned and spoke its mind of him. He is more a fool than a knave, however, I believe, yet he is a big knave.

We have a stormy day. Are loading the Spaulding from the Elm city. Shall send tomorrow to New York. Mrs Strong[4] goes home. Her tact and energy has saved the poor souls on the Elm city from the direct consequences of the narrow incompetence of the surgeons—not as surgeons, but as hotel keepers. Mrs Strong can keep a hotel. So can Mrs Griffin[5] and Miss Woolsy & Miss Wormley[6] and perhaps some of the others. They beat the doctors all to pieces. I should have sunk the ships in despair before this if it hadn't been for their handiness and good nature.

I am exceedingly sorry to receive your intimation that there is danger of your losing Mr Rogers.[7] I don't know how you can get along without him. No one else can do the work half as well. I can only advise, if he does leave, that you should curtail the business preparatory to a general windup. For, if the Surgn Genl does not begin pretty soon to take up our business, I, for one, have no idea of going much further with it.

Yours Faithfully,

Fred. Law Olmsted.

The original is letter 1143 in box 741 of USSC-NYPL.

1. That is, the president of the Sanitary Commission, Henry W. Bellows.
2. Either Charles A. Stetson, Alexander McCulloch Stetson, or Prince Redington Stetson, the sons of Charles A. Stetson, who was the proprietor of the Astor House in New York City. Bellows had considered sending young Stetson to "quartermaster & commissary" the hospital ships, and Jenkins relayed the suggestion to Olmsted (*DAB*; John Stetson Barry, *A Genealogical and Biographical Sketch of the Name and Family of Stetson . . .* [Boston, 1847], p. 61; JFJ to FLO, May 22, 1862, USSC-NYPL, box 742: 1302).
3. Jenkins had informed Olmsted that, according to Hammond, Stanton intended to nominate Robert C. Wood as assistant surgeon general, Jonathan Letterman as inspector-in-chief, and John M. Cuyler, Richard H. Coolidge, Charles C. Keeney, Edward P. Vollum, Joseph R. Smith, Roberts Bartholow, George H. Lyman, and John L. LeConte as inspectors. This list upset Olmsted because those mentioned were

generally regular army surgeons in the Medical Bureau. In Olmsted's view, they would not be able to bring either sanitary expertise or administrative innovation to the Medical Bureau (JFJ to FLO, May 22, 1862, USSC-NYPL, box 742: 1302).

4. Ellen Ruggles Strong (1825–1891), the daughter of Samuel B. and Mary Rosalie Ruggles, had married George Templeton Strong in 1848. Her desire to serve on the hospital transports somewhat surprised and alarmed her husband, who nevertheless acceded to her wishes. She left New York on May 5, 1862, and later undertook a second tour of duty on the hospital ships from June 15 until July 11. Ellen Strong's hardiness and administrative abilities drew plaudits not only from Olmsted but also from her devoted husband, who wrote: "The little woman has come out amazingly strong during these two months. Have never given her credit for a tithe of the enterprise, pluck, discretion, and force of character she has shewn" (*Diary of the Civil War*, pp. 223, 230, 239; George Templeton Strong, *The Diary of George Templeton Strong*, ed. Allan Nevins and Milton Halsey Thomas, 4 vols. [New York, 1952], 4: 602).

5. Christine Kean Griffin (c. 1826–1915), the widow of naval officer William Preston Griffin, served on the Board of Managers of the Woman's Central Association of Relief and was active in its work. She served as a lady superintendent on the Pamunkey from early May 1862 until illness forced her to return to New York on June 19. In less than a month she returned to her work on the hospital ships. Katharine P. Wormeley believed Christine Griffin combined efficiency with great aplomb and described her as a "magnificent" worker. Olmsted too admired Christine Griffin's abilities. When he drew up a plan to stimulate army enlistments by hiring female store clerks to replace young males, who could then enlist, he first submitted it to her for advice (*New York Times*, July 31, 1915, p. 7; K. P. Wormeley, *The Other Side of War*, pp. 15, 29, 158, 202; FLO to C. K. Griffin, July 12, 1862, USSC-NYPL, box 655: 562).

6. Katharine Prescott Wormeley.

7. Jenkins in his letter of May 22 told Olmsted that he had hired a new employee because of Henry B. Rogers's imminent departure. Olmsted apparently did not realize that Rogers was not planning to leave the service of the Commission, but simply to leave Washington to join the other workers on the Virginia Peninsula (JFJ to FLO, May 22, 1862, USSC-NYPL, box 742: 1302).

To John Foster Jenkins

> Sanitary Commission,
> Floating Hospital.
> May 29th 1862.

My Dear Doctor,

Yours of 27th is received.

Dr. Newberry arrived on Sunday and left on Monday in the "Spaulding".[1] Mr Rogers, we have not seen or heard from. I am very glad you have so satisfactory an assistant in Mr Fowler.[2] I have placed Dr Griscom[3] in charge of the Elm city and have refitted her. We are now taking sick on her—probably for Yorktown. I should send her to Washington if I could. I have no nurses for her and have called for a detail of soldiers. The Knickerbocker remains under charge of D[r] Swann, who for that purpose is good for nothing. I have been, since the Spaulding sailed, trying to get her in order, but she is still in a disgraceful state: dirty, stinking and disorderly. The reason under all is that we have no working force which feels under any obligations to obey disagreeable orders. More than one third of the nurses on this boat avoid all duty on the ground of illness; a considerable number of the rest, the doctor reports as insubordinate and some are insolently so. One came to me this evening and said he must leave the boat immediately because the doctor's tone of voice was "disrespectful" to him.

They sent me a queer fellow from New York, recommended as a good organizing business man. The students have at once seen his quality and happily express it in the soubriquet of Pickwick which is fastened upon him.[4] He is appointed Administrative Agent under Griscom and if he were suddenly appointed Secy of War, he could not be more nervous or dumbfounded.

We have had a number of orders and counter-orders today, the net result of which will be, probably, the departure of the Elm city with sick (and the Commodore[5] with wounded) to-morrow, and the Knickerbocker, Daniel Webster nos 1 & 2 left free of patients, two manned after a fashion; the other entirely unmanned. The hospital ashore was too full to take the sick who came yesterday afternoon and they slept in the rail-cars. The Elm city's freight will make room for another day or two—of the 200 thus far arrived, not more than half a dozen are unable to walk aboard. A large proportion have all the appearance of well-men, though perhaps, of a rather mild sort. It is raining hard this evening, and this will probably postpone the attack on Richmond again for a few days.

I wish I could see some end to this work. Our whole undertaking is so obviously wrong and unjustifiable in its present shape and with the means at our command, except to meet an emergency, that it is most unsatisfactory to continue the battle for it, day after day, hopeless of victory and with no end to the line of retreat in view.

Has anyone a clear idea of what we are attempting? I have never heard the faintest attempt to express it. We are piecing out, as we best can, the deficiencies of the Medical Department in respect to the accommodation for the sick and the transportation of the sick, during the time the Surgeon General is getting ready to manage the business. Is that it? I confess, if it is, I can not understand the slowness of the Surgeon Gener[l]. All that we supply, so far as the business which keeps Knapp and myself, here is three or four indifferent surgeons, twenty to thirty cadets, and a respectable boarding place for a dozen or twenty sisters of charity. As for the nurses, I don't count them anything. An average soldier from the ranks has all the time been better than three of them. What ought to be done? The Surgeon Genl can not at once do our sea transport business as well as we can. By recruiting deficiencies at each trip, we can for the present continue to employ the Webster & the Spaulding advantageously. We can continue the boarding house with advantage. We can continue the supply business as it was before we came, with advantage for a while longer. We want also a dépôt at this end for our transports. For the rest, the Sgn Genl[6] can *at once* have it done a great deal better than we, if he can place two steamboats under Dr Tripler's orders, (in addition to the Commodore & Vanderbilt[7]), equip them, or take them equipped from us, put one good, authoritative surgeon on board each, with two to four assistant surgeons and six to ten dressers & stewards, and twenty to thirty privates, and require certain rules for the decent treatment of the sick to be observed on them.

If the Surgeon General can not secure as much as this by this time, he ought to go to the country. But I won't grumble any more. But— well, I won't. What I mean, with regard to the Sgn Gnl, is that Inspectors and all are not necessary so far as I see to some control of these matters. It is nearly a fortnight since I telegraphed the immediate need of establishing by intervention and not by permission, a full rigged hospital at this point. I have since repeatedly explained the necessity—the continued necessity, and yet the hospital is so small and is managed with such improvident consideration that it [will be] entirely swamped by any train that brings down a handful of sick men. Any considerable skirmish would crowd all the boats [that] there are here. Half these boats are managed by the Sanitary Commission & the San. Com., having no authority and no rights, can never manage things decently.

I have seen but one man since I came to the peninsula who seemed to have the slightest aptitude for a comprehensive and large management of the army medical business: I refer to Smith, A.K. who was our first candidate for inspector and whose name does not appear at all in any recent surmises of appointments.[8] I have no hope of anything from the inspectors, as they will be appointed. I don't think much of Smith, he is too much habituated to the present rule, but he has capacity.

I don't think I can continue the attempt to carry on our present business, in the present way, a week longer. I shall probably surrender the Elm city, Knickerbocker and Webster no 2, unless by the arrival of the Spaulding, I get a force for which I must provide quarters.

It is ludicrous to see the enthusiasm of the men who come here— on their arrival—about details, cleanliness, numbering, records of disease, pure water etc. and their entire forgetfulness and ineptness for more essential matters, food, bed-pans, and water of any sort. We don't want doctors & nurses & philosophers, we want a man or two who could keep an oyster

ROBERT WARE

cellar or a barber's shop—I am not so ambitious as to say, who could keep a tavern.

Griscom, with immense pretensions is lazy, careless and deceptive. He shirks whatever he does not fancy to attend to personally.

I said I wouldn't grumble.

I may as well stop then, for, as it wouldn't do to grumble here, I can't keep my discomfort to myself when I turn to you.

For whatever has been accomplished here thus far under the flag of the San. Com., credit is almost wholly due—at this end—to two men, Knapp and Grymes. Ware honors all demands. So do the women, with a surplus, and generally the medical students. Peverly[9] & Wood[10] are all that is wanted in their places. But governors or Lieut[t] governors, there are none.

There is nothing for the Webster to do here at present. Neither she or the Spaulding are well adapted for the transportation of the wounded. If there should be another move without a battle here, had they not—or one of them—best go to Port Royal or New Orleans?[11]

Yours Cordially

Fred. Law Olmsted.

The original is letter 1180 in box 741 of USSC-NYPL.

1. The S. R. *Spaulding* departed on Monday, May 26, for New York, where it arrived on May 28 (GTS to FLO, May 27 and 29, 1862, USSC-NYPL, box 741: 1157).

2. Francis Fowler (b. 1822) was from Stockbridge, Massachusetts. In May 1862 Jenkins hired Fowler, who carried a letter of recommendation from Charles Loring Brace. During the absence of Frederick N. Knapp and Henry B. Rogers from Washington, Fowler oversaw the work of special relief there, and he continued to work in that department through the fall of 1862. In December 1862 he became the Sanitary Commission's chief clerk, and by 1865 he was serving as an assistant secretary. In 1867 he became a professor of English language and literature at Pennsylvania State College (JFJ to FLO, May 22, 1862, USSC-NYPL, box 742: 1302; F. N. Knapp, "Fourth Report Concerning the Aid and Comfort Given by the Sanitary Commission to Sick Soldiers Passing Through Washington," USSC doc. no. 59a, pp. 1, 7; Christine Cecilia Fowler, comp., *The History of the Fowlers* [Batavia, N.Y., 1950], p. 574; Wayland Fuller Dunaway, *History of the Pennsylvania State College* [State College, Pa., 1946], p. 67).

3. John Haskins Griscom (1809–1874), a prominent New York City sanitarian who had received his medical degree from the University of Pennsylvania. A physician at the New York Hospital, he had also overseen the care of ill immigrants for the Commission of Immigration and had briefly served as head of New York City's health department. Griscom wrote numerous pamphlets on topics in medicine and hygiene (H. A. Kelly and W. L. Burrage, *Dictionary of American Medical Biography*, pp. 501–2).

4. Olmsted likened this Sanitary Commission worker, whom the editors have not been able to identify, to Samuel Pickwick, the naively self-important founder of the Pickwick Club, in *The Posthumous Papers of the Pickwick Club*, by Charles Dickens.

5. Probably a 984-ton steamer built in 1848. The *Commodore* was directly controlled by the Medical Bureau (W. M. Lytle and F. R. Holdcamper, *Merchant Steam Vessels*, p. 43; *O.R.*, ser. 1, vol. 11, pt. 1, pp. 179–81, 184).

6. That is, Surgeon General.

7. A spacious, 3,360-ton ocean steamer, built in 1857 and bought by the U.S. Navy in March 1862 (W. M. Lytle and F. R. Holdcamper, *Merchant Steam Vessels*, p. 220).

8. Andrew K. Smith.

9. Thomas Everett Peverly (b. c. 1824), a civil engineer from Boston who served the Sanitary Commission as a "documents director" and quartermaster during the Peninsula campaign. In December 1862 he was one of the Commission's relief agents stationed with the Army of the Potomac. Most likely Peverly knew of the Commission through his stepfather, William Hobart Hadley, a Unitarian minister who canvassed for funds for the Commission in 1862 (Henry Winthrop Hardon, *Peverly Family . . .* [Boston, 1927], p. 25; "Roster of Persons Employed by the Sanitary Commission" [Oct. 1, 1862], USSC-NYPL, box 642; FLO to Mr. Hill, Oct. 4, 1862, USSC-NYPL, box 609: 769; FLO to W. H. Hadley, Dec. 29, 1861, USSC-NYPL, box 833, 2: 493–95; FLO to HWB, May 2, 1862, USSC-NYPL, box 641; doc. no. 57 in USSC, *Documents*).

10. Willard Stanard Wood, an agent employed by the Sanitary Commission for special duty in 1861 and 1862 (doc. nos. 40 and 57 in USSC, *Documents*).

11. On April 24, 1862, Union forces had captured New Orleans (*War for the Union*, 2: 99–102).

To Henry Whitney Bellows

White House on the Pamunkey,
June 3[d] 1862.

My Dear Sir,

Sick men arriving Friday (30th May) night by the Railroad, could not be provided for in the crowded field hospital ashore, which still remains but one fifth the capacity, in tent room, which I urged it should be made three weeks ago. To make more room, on Saturday morning (31st ulto.) we were ordered to take four hundred upon the Elm city. They were sent to her by smaller steamboats and the last load, which brought the number up to four hundred and fifty, arrived so late that she could not leave 'till Sunday morning. The orders were to deliver them at Yorktown and return immediately.

We had previously sent out two parties to look for straggling sick and visit the hospitals in the rear of the left wing. One of these returned at noon at Friday, having been by Cumberland to New Kent Court House. From D[r] Allen[1] who was in charge of the other I received a dispatch about sunset, stating that his party were assisting the surgeons in a field hospital to which wounded were crowding from a battle then in progress. Soon after midnight the party arrived on board, having come from the front with a train of wounded, and we then had our first authentic information of the fierce battle in which our whole left wing had been engaged, and which still continued, our forces losing ground, when the party left the field. We were left in painful anxiety as to the result.[2]

Early in the morning an order came for the Knickerbocker to come immediately to the Rail Road landing. Before she could get steam up, she was twice again visited by a tug to repeat the order and hasten compliance with it. These orders came from the Surgeon General of Pennsylvania,[3] only one of them was written; it was upon a sheet headed "Surgeon General of Pennsylvania"; was addressed "to the Surgeon in Charge of U.S. transport boat Knickerbocker", and was signed "by order of the Medical Director", with the signature of D[r] Smith. The Knickerbocker had, with the written approval of D[r] Tripler, been arrang[d] for a *receiving* surgical hospital,[4] and by permission of the Quarter Master, she had been especially exempted from the requirement made of others to keep her fires going. I did not feel at liberty to disregard the order, however, and all possible speed was made in firing up, but before she could move, a small steamboat came alongside with a hundred and fifty wounded men. As these came on board, they were duly registered, cleaned and dressed and each man's personal effects so disposed of that when taken from the boat they would go with him. I preceded the Knickerbocker to the landing, and

THE ARMY OF THE POTOMAC AT CUMBERLAND LANDING, 1862

finding Dr Smith in the tent of the Quarter Master & Provost Marshal, Captn Sawtelle,[5] I reported to him the condition of the Knickerbocker and of our other boats. I then stated what our original orders had been from the Surgeon General and what had been agreed upon between myself and the Medical Director as to the use of the boats, and proposed in accordance therewith to assort the patients which should be placed on the Knickerbocker sending such as could be properly removed by sea to the Webster No. 1, which had been waiting two days for a load, and holding the rest for the Elm city to be conveyed to any point not outside the capes,[6] all being dressed, and operations, so far as immediately necessary, being performed on the Knickerbocker. He said that each boat would be filled up as rapidly as possible and then anchored off to await orders, these being his instructions from the Medical Director. Having said this, he left the tent and I asked Captn Sawtelle, if Dr Smith had been given charge of all the boats to be used for hospital purposes on the river. He had not till now been aware he said that Dr Smith had any authority over them, but he had assumed it and seemed to be justified in doing so by a telegraph dispatch, which he had just exhibited, from the Medical Director. Captn Sawtelle seemed perplexed[7] and said that he should call for distinct information on the subject. In the meantime, it was obvious that [*Dr Smith had the control of*

358

our boats and] nothing could be done with our boats except in compliance with the orders of Dr Smith. I give you these details in order that you may understand why we have been diverted from our original plan of operations and somewhat embarrassed in our disposition to meet the emergency most effectually.

Passing over other incidents of the day—about five o'clock a train arrived with five hundred wounded. At the landing, next [to] the cars was a scow; next the Pennsylvania hospital boat Whillden[8] the Hd. Q. of Dr Smith; outside of her the Commodore; outside the Commodore, the Knickerbocker. Doctor Smith had also ordered up the Webster No 2 and the State of Maine, on neither of which was there any hospital company or proper arrangments for the care of wounded or their sustenance. I again proposed to Dr Smith to so classify the patients that proper use could be made of the Webster and the graver cases be placed on our well-provided boats for stillwater transportation. He answered that Richmond was being evacuated, that there would be more patients than all the boats could hold, and that there was no time to pick them out. He should put as many as possible on the Knickerbocker as fast as he could, as ordered by the Med. Direc. The K. is a very old boat, low between decks in the hull, with no means of ventilation under the main deck and consequently of scarcely more than half the capacity of other boats of not much greater length and with which she would by a careless observer be classed. The Surgeon of the Commodore told me that if necessary he could stow 700. I knew that half that number would [*in a single night*] soon breed a pestilence on the Knickerbocker, and I asked leave again, after filling her, to transfer as many from her, as the surgeon in charge of her might think best, to the Webster. He said that he should need the Webster to be filled up at once to her utmost capacity, in the same manner as the Knickerbocker. I replied that the Elm city would arrive the next morning & the Spaulding probably before the next night and between them they would take seven to eight hundred. At this moment Knapp reported to me that the Elm city was coming up. Five minutes afterwards she was made fast outside the Knickerbocker. She had been to Yorktown, landed her 450 patients and returned within the day. Dr Smith, however, declined any other arrangment than that already ordered, and the wounded were presently brought across the scow, the Whillden and the Commodore to the Knickerbocker; up and down, a hard road. Knapp suggested and urged some improvement but was answered: Our arrangments are already made and can not be changed. We began registering them as usual, but this caused delay and by Dr Smith's orders it was discontinued and those who could walk were turned in like sheep, no record being taken and no attention to the personal effects of the men. I had the captain prepared to move the boat with rapidity and directed the surgeon in charge to report to me when she should seem to have[9] received as many as could possibly be taken *with safety*, allowing that one hundred should be removed within twelve hours. As soon as he did so, D[r] Smith not being present to direct in the matter, I took the responsibility of taking in the gang-planks and pushing the boat out. I ran her a mile down the river and anchored near the Webster No 1, (to which next morning—as no orders to sail were received—I had the hundred removed). She had—by estimate—three hundred & fifty on board; the night being fine, many were disposed of on the outer decks, and before I left at eleven at night, nearly all had been washed, dressed and put to bed decently and as comfortably as possible. All had received needed nourishment and such surgical and medical aid as was immediately required.

I came up in a small boat to the landing again where I found the Elm city with nearly five hundred wounded on board. D[r] Smith had not been seen since they commenced taking them on. I ordered her to run down and anchor near the Knickerbocker. There had been a special order in her case from the Medical Director to run to Washington; I judge that this was given under the misapprehension that she had failed to go to Yorktown and had her sick still on board. She was unable to go at once, for want of coal, which could not be furnished her till the evening of the next day, (Monday). [*The Commodore got away before noon of Monday. Complaints having been made of the crowded condition of the Commodore and of the stench which prevailed in her, the Provost Marshal took the responsibility of ordering her to run to Fortress Monroe, there to receive orders for the disposal of the wounded. She only ran as far as the lower anchorage, however, that night, and by order of D[r] Smith, I believe—waited for the Whillden, in company with which she left next day. The Medical force seemed inadequate on board her, many patients, at least on the main deck, being in a very filthy condition and not having had their wounds dressed. The surgeon seemed industrious but the amount of surgical attendance for the number of wounded was lamentably inadequate. Assistance of a surgeon and dressers was offered from the Webster, but I know not for what reason, was declined without thanks. While she lay at the wharf landing she had, at the request of the Surgeon in charge, been largely supplied from our stores.*] The State of Maine was filled up with wounded in great haste immediately after the Elm City. The ladies on the Elm city sent some supplies on board of articles of immediate necessity and some of our men from the Webster [were] aiding in distributing them. We also put on board bedding and various stores of which there was evident need, from our supply boat without waiting to be asked, and without finding anyone to receive them, the surgeons being no doubt fully engrossed with pressing surgical duties. [*I do not know who was placed in charge of her.*] The battle had been renewed in the morning of this day (Sunday) and we had sent a party with supplies of stimulants, lint &c. to the battlefield hospitals. This party re-turnd about midnight with another train of wounded. All our force that could possibly be withdrawn from duty on the boats was employed in supplying drink to the wounded on the cars and in carrying them from the railroad to the boats. [*The State of Maine, I think, took all who arrived that night. After the State of Maine, the Vanderbilt was filled. This on Sunday night.*]

The next morning, Monday, when I first went on shore, I found that a train had just arrived, and the wounded men were walking in a throng across the scow to the Webster No 2. I knew that she was not properly prepared, and I tried to stop them, and sent for Dr Smith. Dr Smith could not be found. I asked for the medical officer in charge of the Webster. The captain said there was none, and that he had had no orders but to come to the landing to take wounded. I sent for the surgeon in charge of the train and the answer was that there was no surgeon—there was no one in charge of the wounded. Meantime, they were being taken out of the cars and assisted toward the landing by volunteer by-standers until the gangways of the boat, the scow and the landing were crowded. I finally concluded that Dr Smith must have ordered them to go on board, although I could find no one in the crowd who professed to have received his orders. At all events as I had no authority to stop them and as many of them seemed fainting in the sun, I advised the Captain to let them on board. He did so and they hobbled in till the boat was crowded in all parts. The Small was outside the Webster No 2, and our ladies administered as far as was possible to their relief. Going on shore, I found still a great number, including the worst cases, lying on litters, gasping in the fervid sun. I do not describe such a scene. Then and frequently since I saw more appalling things than were ever imagined in the wildest mania of delirium tremens. There were many volunteers busily doing what little could be done with-out any order or system or materials of relief, to mitigate the suffering of individuals. As is always the case under such circumstances, the greater number were giving orders and advice and grumbling because they were not regarded. Two or three men were working effectively and being ac-cepted as leaders, Knapp & Ware among them. There were a few soldiers, engaged in carrying those on litters. I soon saw that these got their orders chiefly from and were working effectively under the orders of an active man, breezing about in his shirt sleeves, but with a stripe on his pante-loons. As I was leading and ordering too, we soon, of course, ran foul. "May I ask who you are, Sir, & what is your authority?"

"I am Surgeon Ellis,[10] lately post surgeon at New York, and am ordered by the Sgn Genl to take charge of wounded at White House."

"Thank God, but what has become of Dr Smith?"

"Dr Smith? I saw a man here last night who told me that he was D^r

Smith; he was looking for Pennsylvania officers. He has not been about here today."

We had receivd several telegrams from the Medical Director, which indicated a great misapprehension on his part of the state of things. He could not understand my replies or would not believe my statements. For instance, one of his orders was to fill up the Knickerbocker, which I had already reported to be full; one of his messages ran in this way. "I was informed on Sunday that the Elm city had four hundred and fifty sick upon her, and that the Knickerbocker was empty. I have depended upon these statements. If the Elm city had four hundred and fifty sick on Sunday, how can she now [Monday][11] have four hundred and seventy wounded? The Elm city must discharge her sick and the Knickerbocker take on wounded." The climax was a message from the Medical Director to the Quarter Master saying that the boats held by the Sanitary Commission must be turned to use for the conveyance of the wounded. Before this I had dispatched a messenger with a letter explaining the actual condition of things, showing that every order has been followed to the letter, and that as far as possible we had pursued his intentions. Assuring him that, however incredible[12] it might appear to him the Elm city, [*if human testimony could be trusted,*] had been here on Sunday morning with four hundred and fifty sick upon her, had proceeded to Yorktown, discharged them, returned and taken on four hundred and seventy wounded before eleven o'clock the same night. That the Knickerbocker had been empty the same morning and loaded the same night, and that as, at the time of writing, one was halfway to Washington and the other halfway to Newport News, according to the latest previous orders, it was not possible to comply with the last order of all, which was to immediately fill them (specifying these two boats) with wounded at White House.[13] I telegraphed more briefly to the same purport and begged that Dr Ellis or Dr Watson,[14] at the camp hospital, might be clothed with some discretionary power as to the transportation of the wounded at this landing, using the means which from hour to hour, might be most available. Dr Ellis telegraphed his orders from the Sgn Gnl at the same time and made a similar request. The reply was that 'till Dr Ellis reported to the Medical Director in person, he could not be recognized; this to Dr Ellis—to my suggestion of Dr Watson, no reply. It has got to be Thursday[15] since I commenced writing and I have just now received another order from the Medical Director to fill up either the Knickerbocker or the Vanderbilt and send them to Portsmouth. Neither boat has been here during the last two days, and the Vanderbilt has never been under my orders. The telegraph has broken down since this order was transmitted and I can not reply or ask other instructions. Dr Tripler now explains to me (June 6th) that my telegraphic reports have not reached him,

BRINGING THE WOUNDED TO THE RAILROAD CARS AT FAIR OAKS STATION,
AFTER THE BATTLE

not until in some cases several days after they were sent and in irregular sequence.[16]

At the time of which I am now writing, Monday afternoon, wounded were arriving by every train, entirely unattended or with at most a detail of two soldiers to a train of two or three hundred of them. They were packed as closely as they could be stowed in the common freight cars, without beds, without straw, at most with a wisp of hay under their heads. They arrived, dead and alive together, in the same close box, many with awful wounds festering and alive with maggots. The stench was such as to produce vomiting with some of our strong men, habituated to the duty of attending the sick & wounded of the army. How close they were packed you may infer from the fact which one of our company who was present at the loading of a car reported. A surgeon was told that it was not possible to get another man upon the floor of the car. "Then," said he, "these three men must be laid in across the others for they have got to be cleared out from here by this train." This outrage was avoided, however.

Shall I tell you that our noble women—true nobility, no empire was ever blessed with nobler—were always ready and eager, and almost always the first, to press into these places of Horror, going to them in torrents of rain, groping their way by dim, lanthorn light, at all hours of night, carrying spirits, ice and water, calling back to life those who were in the despair of utter exhaustion, or catching for mother or wife the priceless, last faint whispers of the dying. Dr Ellis was the only man who, at this time, claimed to act as a medical officer, he was without instructions and without recognized authority. Dr Ware was, for a time the only other physician on the ground. Before night however, the Spaulding opportunely arrived—not in a condition to be made directly useful [. . .] being laden unfortunately with government stores, which could not be removed for twenty four hours. The physicians and students could never have been more welcome. I put one half her whole company on duty for the night on the Webster no 2. Captain Sawtelle, at my request, pitched a hospital tent for our ladies on the river Bank by the rail-road, behind which a common camp-kitchen was established. To this tent quantities of stores were conveyed, and soup and tea, prepared in camp-kettles, kept hot. Before this arrangment was complete, and until other stores could be landed, bread and molasses and iced molasses, vinegar and water were dealt out to all who needed. Many of the slightly wounded seemed almost famished, and the assertion that they had eaten nothing for three days was frequent. Before Tuesday night, Captn Sawtelle had got up for us a dozen Sibley tents[17]—since then a much larger number—into which, after the boats at the wharf had been crowded, the wounded were conveyed, not before, however, several score of them had been exposed to the rain for some time. The vicinity of the landing was a very inconvenient and every way bad place, for all this. Dr Ware took the main, medical charge ashore, besides doing much else. Dr Ellis and the two surgeons of the Spaulding, with their company, took the boats. I can not disentangle, now, the events of the two days, nor have I a very exact idea of the numbers we took care of. We put two hundred and fifty on the Webster No. 1, on Monday; among them were General Devin and Col. Briggs of Massachusetts,[18] and fearing that all intermediate hospitals were full, in the absence of orders, I sent her to Boston.[19] The same day the Vanderbilt was filled and sent. After her the Kennebeck. Today the Spaulding has been filled and sent and the State of Maine is filling a second time. [*The Vanderbilt and State of Maine were sent off, the former had government surgeons on board; the latter was put in charge of a contract surgeon, who was pressed into the service as he was passing on to Head Quarters.*] The number of wounded thus far brought here this week is between two and three thousand. At least 9/10^ths of these have been cared for exclusivly while here, by the Sanitary Commission, with the constant aid of Dr Ellis and for some time that of the surgeons of the gun boat Sebago,[20] Mr Odell,[21] a member of Congress, the Revd Mr May,[22] [*who staid in our boat*] of Syracuse, and one or two others, who chanced to be here. We have sent away on our boats since Sunday morning seventeen hundred and seventy (1770) patients. These, after having been got upon our beds, have been all methodically and tenderly cared for. The difficulties which have had to be overcome in accomplishing this were enormous, and perhaps the greatest of them were of a nature which it would be ungrateful to describe. We have in these four days also distributed a large amount of hospital stores to the government hospitals and boats.

The text presented here is composed of two fragments from USSC-NYPL. The first part is filed as letter 1351 in box 742, and the second part is letter 4681 in box 752. Olmsted wrote on the first, "Dft of Rept to Dʳ Bellows." The second half ends at the bottom of a page and may be incomplete. The editors present in italics within brackets substantive material that Olmsted lined through.

1. Charles M. Allin (1827–1880), a physician who, like Cornelius R. Agnew, had graduated from the College of Physicians and Surgeons. Allin practiced medicine in Flushing, New York (Brown University, *Historical Catalogue of Brown University, Providence, Rhode Island, 1764–1894* [Providence, R.I., 1895], p. 153).
2. In late May 1862 McClellan had sent two of his corps, commanded by Erasmus D. Keyes and Samuel P. Heintzleman, across to the south side of the Chickahominy River while the other troops remained on the north side to retain communications with White House. On May 31 Confederate commander Joseph E. Johnston seized the opportunity of fighting a divided army when he attacked Keyes's and Heintzleman's position in the battle of Fair Oaks. Only a desperate crossing of the rainswollen Chickahominy by Edwin V. Sumner's corps in the late afternoon held the Union lines. Casualties in the Union army were approximately forty-four hundred; Confederate losses exceeded fifty-seven hundred (*War for the Union*, 2: 121–23; Thomas L. Livermore, *Numbers and Losses in the Civil War*, 2nd ed. [Boston, 1909], p. 81).
3. Henry Hollingsworth Smith (1815–1890), a physician and professor of surgery at the University of Pennsylvania, served as the surgeon general of the state of Pennsylvania in 1861 and 1862. During the Peninsula campaign, he directed a corps of eighteen surgeons and dressers on the hospital ships *Wilmon Whillden* and *Commodore*. Charles S. Tripler thoroughly appreciated Smith, whom he implicitly compared to the fault-finding Sanitary Commission when he wrote in a later report that Smith "entered into . . . [my plans] with hearty good-will, and seconded them with an earnest zeal and a refreshing intelligence." On May 30, 1862, Tripler placed Smith in charge of the transportation of the sick and wounded from White House (H. A. Kelly and W. L. Burrage, *Dictionary of American Medical Biography*, p. 1127; *O.R.*, ser. 1, vol. 11, pt. 1, p. 181).
4. See FLO to JFJ, May 20, 1862, note 4, above.
5. Charles Greene Sawtelle (1834–1913), a captain in the Union army and assistant quartermaster during the Peninsula campaign. He later became quartermaster general of the army (G. W. Cullum, *Biographical Register*, 2: 597–99; *New York Times*, Jan. 5, 1913, p. 17).
6. Cape Charles and Cape Henry, which marked the entrance to the Atlantic Ocean from Chesapeake Bay.
7. Here Olmsted first wrote "annoyed."
8. The 241-ton *Wilmon Whillden*, built in 1845 (W. M. Lytle and F. R. Holdcamper, *Merchant Steam Vessels*, p. 233).

9. Letter 1351 in USSC-NYPL, box 742, ends here.

10. Thomas Thompson Ellis (b. 1816) arrived at White House as the wounded from the battle of Fair Oaks began to congregate there. Although Ellis supposedly carried orders from the surgeon general, Charles Tripler demanded to see them before granting any official recognition to him.

Tripler's caution in this case was probably wise, for the scanty autobiographical information that Ellis provides in his book, *Leaves from the Diary of an Army Surgeon*, leaves little doubt that he was the same physician who had been convicted of grand larceny in New York City in 1860. Born Thomas Thompson in England, he had studied medicine and had served as a British military surgeon at the Cape of Good Hope in South Africa. Immigrating to the United States in 1846, he set up practice in Boston and later in New York City. The elegant and handsome Ellis allegedly defrauded numerous female patients by first wooing them, then borrowing their jewelry or large sums of money. In February 1860 he was sentenced to three years' imprisonment but apparently was released early.

Despite his checkered career, Ellis obtained a position as post surgeon at Camp Washington and other Staten Island camps for New York State volunteers in the fall and winter of 1861–62. Apparently his reports led Surgeon General Hammond to employ him as a contract surgeon during May and June 1862. Ellis, however, sought—with at least some success—to create the impression that he was a regular army officer. In fact, it was in that guise that he obtained credit from at least two unsuspecting merchants who later tendered his bills to the office of the surgeon general.

In June 1862 Olmsted harbored few suspicions about Ellis. After the battle of Fair Oaks, he commended Ellis to the surgeon general's attention, saying, "I have never before seen a man, in the same space of time, perform so much labor as he has done, and that of a kind involving such grave responsibility and anxiety with such unflagging energy and vivacity." On June 22 Olmsted told Bellows that he was "very well satisfied" with Dr. Ellis as the surgeon in charge of the *Elm City*. "You will probably have seen him before this reaches you," Olmsted continued. "He is only too modest." No further contacts between Ellis and Olmsted occurred until the physician in early April 1863 sent Olmsted a prospectus for his forthcoming book on the military campaigns of 1862 and asked permission to dedicate it to him. Olmsted was then traveling in the Midwest and did not personally answer the request. But Ellis was not at a loss, for he secured George B. McClellan's permission and dedicated the book to the general (*New-York Times*, Feb. 21, 1860, p. 3; ibid., Feb. 25, 1860 [suppl.], p. 2; Thomas T. Ellis, *Leaves from the Diary of an Army Surgeon; or, Incidents of Field, Camp, and Hospital Life* [New York, 1863], pp. 5–28; John Shaw to W. A. Hammond, July 22, 1862, J. M. Brown to W. A. Hammond, July 21, 1862, and FLO to W. A. Hammond, June 6, 1862, all in Record Group 94, Records of the Adjutant General's Office, Records of Physicians and Medical Officers, "Thomas T. Ellis, Volunteer and Post Surgeon," National Archives; FLO to HWB, June 22, 1862, USSC-NYPL, box 743: 1751; T. T. Ellis to FLO, April 2 and May 5, 1863).

11. These brackets were used by Olmsted.

12. Olmsted here first wrote "miraculous."

13. Tripler's telegrams of June 2 did indeed give orders that were impossible to carry out. Olmsted resented the peremptory nature of the orders and the implication that the Sanitary Commission had failed to meet its obligations and had not obeyed orders. He replied to Tripler on June 3:

There must be some frightful misunderstanding at the bottom of what is occurring here, in your department. It is obvious from the tenor of your telegraphic orders that you are altogether wrongly informed. The Sanitary Commission, let me say at once, has not only obeyed every order, no matter how irregular or disrespectful the mode of its transmission, but has in good faith endeavored to carry out at every point it could reach what was judged to be your intention, supplying the absence or neglect of other agents on whom you appeared to depend as it best could. (FLO to C. S. Tripler, June 3, 1862, USSC-NYPL, box 743: 1740.)

14. Alexander T. Watson was appointed a surgeon of volunteers in April 1862 and served through the war (F. B. Heitman, *Historical Register and Dictionary*, 1: 1009).

15. Thursday was June 5, 1862.

16. In a telegram that Olmsted probably received on June 5, Tripler explained his actions of the preceding week. He had not answered Olmsted's request that Watson or Ellis be given discretionary powers because he had not received that telegram. Not having met Ellis or received any information about him from the surgeon general, Tripler believed it necessary that the physician report to him and show him his orders before being recognized (C. S. Tripler to FLO, June 4, 1862, Record Group 393, vol. 36 [old bk. 37], Letters and Telegrams Sent and Received, Army of the Potomac, Records of the U.S. Army Continental Commands, National Archives; a copy dated June 5 is in USSC-NYPL, box 742: 1375).

17. Also known as bell tents (see FLO to MPO, June 28, 1861, n. 6).

18. Charles Devens (1820–1891), a lawyer from Massachusetts, was breveted brigadier general after the capture of Yorktown and was seriously wounded during the battle of Fair Oaks. Henry Shaw Briggs (d. 1887) was colonel of the 10th Massachusetts (F. B. Heitman, *Historical Register and Dictionary*, 1: 244, 370; *Encyclopedia of Massachusetts, Biographical—Genealogical . . .* , 5 vols. [Boston, 1916], 2: 55–56).

19. Olmsted appears to have acted in defiance of orders rather than in the absence of them when he sent the *Daniel Webster No. 1* to Boston on June 2. Tripler had already informed Olmsted by telegram, "The Surg. Genl. has forbidden me to send any more men North for 5 days." That same day another of Tripler's telegrams reiterated the prohibition as being in effect until "next Thursday." Olmsted clearly had received these telegrams, since he mentioned them in the above letter, begun on June 3. He probably referred to the sending of the *Webster* when he told Bellows on June 18: "I have only been able in one instance to select the patients for the vessel or to control the destination of a vessel with wounded on board; and in this instance I acted in disregard of orders. Taking advantage of a storm, which broke down the telegraph to do so . . ." Olmsted most likely justified his disregard of orders by asserting that if the telegraph had been in service, he would have asked for and received new orders for the *Webster*. He perhaps revealed the state of mind that governed his actions when, in the draft of a letter to Tripler on June 2, he wrote that Drs. Watson and Ellis should be given discretionary power and concluded, "If this is not done I suppose it will be right for me to disregard orders which seem to have been made without knowledge of the means available if I act in harmony with their ruling intention" (C. S. Tripler to FLO, June 2, 1862, Record Group 393, Records of the U.S. Army Continental Commands, vol. 36 [old bk. 37], Letters and Telegrams Sent and Received, Army of the Potomac, National Archives; FLO to HWB, June 18, 1862, below; FLO to C. S. Tripler, June 2, 1862, USSC-NYPL, box 742: 1345).

20. The gunboat U.S.S. *Sebago* was a wooden side-wheel steamer launched in November 1861. In late May and early June 1862 it was stationed at White House (O.R., ser. 2, vol. 1, p. 204; ibid., vol. 7, p. 728).

21. Moses Fowler Odell (1818–1866), a Democratic congressman from New York from 1861 to 1865 (BDAC).

22. Samuel Joseph May (1797–1871), a Unitarian minister, abolitionist, and noted reformer for peace, temperance, education, and women's rights. He held a pastorate in Syracuse, New York, for over twenty years (DAB).

To Mary Perkins Olmsted

Sanitary Commission,
Floating Hospital.
White House, June 11th 1862.

Dear Wife,

We have got through with a terrible week's work, and now that we have an opportunity to catch breath again, my dear good friend Knapp, having worked a greater deal harder than anybody else, and accomplished more, proves to have made the worst expenditure for himself; and the doctors have ordered him to be turned out to pasture for a week at least.[1] He promises to find and bring me word of you. It is more than a month since I have heard of [or] from you, and, knowing that you must have moved from Mt St Vincent,[2] and that much must have happened, I need not say that my anxiety has become painful almost beyond endurance. I have written you six or eight times to the usual address. It is useless to speculate on the cause of my not getting letters from you. I find one or two others suffering in a similar way and as unaccountably. I should have been driven to go to you, if Bellows had not given me reason to believe that you and Marion were well and you in your usual condition—as you would not have been if anything very bad had happened [to] us, and if it would not have been the meanest sort of desertion of my post. I felt as if it were a post of some importance before the battle; since then—let Knapp tell you what it has been. It is worth while to have seen such awful suffering to have also the recollection of such relief and such gratitude. If we had not been just where we were and just so well prepared as we were, I can not tell you what a horrible disgrace there would have been here to our country. It will not be known in history but I want you to share the satisfaction of my consciousness that I am not playing an unworthy part—spite of my crippled body—in the great tragedy, consequently that you, left forlorner, if not as lonely, are doing your share, carrying your share, of the great weight under which the nation is staggering. It can not be equally distributed as you would know, had you seen the noble men, as I have seen them, in these last days, smiling in their last cruel struggle with death, or had you part in the crowd of those who are now coming here, eager to know how fell this or that son, brother or father, reported among the dead or missing. Thank God this comes not to us. Pray God it come not again in our time or with our children. The horror of war can never be known but on the field. It is beyond, far beyond all imagination. One of our most efficient men, who worked through all with untiring nonchalance, today, being the first day of rest, broke out in hysterics, and for hours afterwards, was in a swooning state. We send him home with an attendant tomorrow, if he is well enough.[3] It is wonderful how the women not only retain their senses but their strength and spirit. I do hope you will think it right to come to me with Knapp. Do we not both need it? It will go far to break me down, if I can not at least be sure of hearing of you often hereafter.

  Your husband.

1. Frederick N. Knapp, ill with malaria, left the Virginia Peninsula about the time this letter was written. His recovery took much longer than the one week Olmsted here anticipated. Knapp remained in New York for several weeks and then traveled to his parents' home in Walpole, New Hampshire. When he wrote to Olmsted in late July, Knapp believed himself *almost* well" but noted that Van Buren had advised that he not return to work for another three or four weeks (HWB to Anna Bellows, June 14, 1862, Henry Whitney Bellows Papers, Massachusetts Historical Society, Boston, Mass.; HWB to A. J. Bloor, July 4, 1862, USSC-NYPL, box 743: 1726; F. N. Knapp to FLO, July 22, 1862, USSC-NYPL, box 744: 1960).
2. By June 6 Mary Perkins Olmsted had moved from the residence furnished to the Olmsted family at Mount St. Vincent's (A. J. Bloor to FLO, June 10, 1862, USSC-NYPL, box 742: 1438).
3. A Sanitary Commission worker from Philadelphia whom the editors have been unable to identify (FLO to Charles J. Stillé, June 10, 1862, doc. no. 44 in USSC, *Documents*).

To Henry Whitney Bellows

Sanitary Commission,
Floating Hospital.
White House, June 13th 1862

My Dear Doctor,

  I have flung my impatience and anxiety upon two sheets of paper, (besides this fine writing which I did in a tent this morning about Harris[1])—and now getting a good natured turn I throw it overboard. I think you & the Sgn General are made a little sick by the atmosphere of Washington. Finley[2] has been kicked out and the lion has been in his place these two months and I see that things are worse than they were before and that nothing is done until it would be as well it were not done, and you say he is just the man for the place and the Sanitary Commission was never more powerful or useful.[3] Yet if these armies keep their promises to-night, tomorrow ten thousand men will bleed to death and starve to death whose lives could have been saved if proper measures had been taken. Perhaps nobody is to blame for this but the Secy of War, but I would not like to stand in Hammond's shoes. I don't think his apology is a bit better than Tripler's. I don't think your own alledged grounds of condemnation of Tripler any stronger against him than against Hammond. Prima facie—both have been tried & found wanting.[4]

Hammond must be made to do something at once to revolutionize the policy of the Medical Department. New offices and changes of persons are not needed for this and will not in themselves accomplish it. That the business, the duty of the surgeons high and low is not to cure but to provide against, not to overtake but to meet,—that must be said loud and strong. He has no right to scold Tripler, as he did in a telegram which he directed should be shown me, for not doing what until now Tripler would have been snubbed for attempting or proposing to do.[5] Let him issue a manifesto. And don't let him wait another hour.

I am vexed and saddened to hear that he can, in a moment, at the suggestion of Mr Barclay,[6] order the abandonment of Yorktown. Yorktown should have been summarily suppressed or summarily multiplied & improved weeks ago. Now it has grown into a decent establishment—just now, another day's sun will bring it up to the condition of affording a large amount of very tolerable hospital accommodations within eight hours of the Chickahominy. I would sooner cut the throats of a hundred men in a deliberate way than put this out of the way at this moment.

The Webster goes to Boston and returns with an entirely new company;[7] all the surgeons in mutiny; the Sgn in Charge reports certain "passengers", and two ladies for duty beyond his complement. I assign these ladies to duty on the Elm City which is filled with wounded and needs them. They open their eyes in mild surprise and "do not understand". It turns out that the whole company wish to attend church in Boston next Sunday unless it should be convenient to do so in Richmond, and that most of them confound the Sanitary Commission with the Institution for the Blind.[8] (However, they are sensible Boston folks and soon readily shake down to their proper places).

Tripler has ordered a contract surgeon[9]—a poor Jew whom he evidently wanted to lay on a shelf—to go on duty on the Knickerbocker: he is not ordered to report to anyone. The K. has surgeons enough. He can not assume charge and he can not take a subordinate position. He comes and goes as he pleases. No one can define any responsibility or be held to any responsibility; orders come from various quarters about the same thing to various persons, and are obeyed or not, according to the wisdom or cowardice of the ordered.

I should have resigned long ago, if I could see what I had to resign and to whom, except the opportunity of administering large means in a desultory way to the relief of the sick & wounded which come to me.

370

I naturally like, as the Secesh say, exact lines of responsibility, organized official relations, clearly defined, and it is intolerable to me this chaos into which the Sgn General is now beginning to put a stick and stir three ways. I had two additional telegrams[10] from him yesterday each knocking the previous one in the head, while as often as he throws sugar, Tripler dashes in pepper.

Will you please engage a pleasant room for me in Brown's Bloomingdale Hotel[11] and see that there is a grating in the chimney that Harris can not squeeze through.

Confectionately,

Fred. Law Olmsted.

This letter is composed of two different parts from USSC-NYPL. The first three paragraphs comprise letter 1490 in box 742. The second part (the last pages of number 1384 in box 742) was mistakenly cataloged as part of a rough draft of a letter of June 6, 1862, to William A. Hammond. These pages cannot have been intended for Hammond—they are not included in the final draft of the letter he received, and they refer to him in the third person. Moreover, the joking remarks about the Institution for the Blind and Elisha Harris and the playful complimentary closing suggest an easy informality that did not exist between Olmsted and the surgeon general. Olmsted, however, often adopted such a tone in his correspondence with Henry W. Bellows. The events mentioned in this second part—most notably the return of the *Daniel Webster No. 1* from Boston on June 13—give it the same date as that of the fragment to Bellows. The letter paper and the slope and size of Olmsted's writing (which often varied greatly among documents) are identical in both fragments. For these reasons, the editors have combined these two parts into one letter (FLO to W. A. Hammond, June 6, 1862, Record Group 94, Records of the Adjutant General's Office, Records of Physicians and Medical Officers, "Thomas T. Ellis, Volunteer and Post Surgeon," National Archives).

1. Elisha Harris, who had arrived on the Peninsula. Bellows had told Olmsted on June 9: "You will of course make such use of Dr. Harris, as you can. I think he may be truly & largely serviceable under your guidance. He has more administrative faculty than our Brethren give him credit for" (HWB to FLO, June 9, 1862, USSC-NYPL, box 742: 1428).
2. Clement A. Finley, the former surgeon general.
3. Olmsted is responding to the florid praise that Bellows in a long letter heaped upon Hammond and the Sanitary Commission. On June 9 Bellows noted, "I think our reputation and influence were never so good and great as now." He also commented about Hammond: "I am more and more pleased with Dr. Hammond. His views are large, his mind active & prompt—his action at present embarrassed by almost insuperable difficulties. But he is cutting his way out." Here Olmsted seems to have confused the order of the pages in this letter and thus to have misread a partial sentence about a new employee that ended "just the man for his place" as the ending of the sentence about Hammond (HWB to FLO, June 9, 1862, USSC-NYPL, box 742: 1428).
4. Olmsted is referring to Bellows's assessments in earlier letters. On May 29 he told Olmsted that the Sanitary Commission, while trying to secure the nominations of

inspectors under the new medical bill, had protested against Tripler and Robert C. Wood as candidates because they were "men who have been tried and found wanting." A few days earlier Bellows had commented on the "tremendous folly in Tripler's management" and had asked: "But how long is this shiftless, hand to mouth policy to go on? Is it not time to come to some order & system." At the same time that Bellows treated as evidence of incompetence Tripler's inability to retrieve medical supplies from the government transport ships, where they were mixed with other cargo, the minister excused Hammond's inability to improve medical care of the army as a result of the failure of the secretary of war to appoint medical inspectors (HWB to FLO, May 25 and May 29, 1862, USSC-NYPL, box 742: 1319 and 1336).

5. Most likely a reference to Hammond's communication of May 19, 1862, to Tripler (see FLO to JFJ, May 20, 1862, n. 2, above).

6. Clement Biddle Barclay (1817–1896), a well-to-do Philadelphian who was active in hospital work and who had politically powerful friends. Bellows had told Olmsted about an interview with Barclay in which the latter personally claimed to be able to obtain more supplies for the sick and wounded than the Sanitary Commission could. Bellows also recounted how Hammond had, at Barclay's request, ordered the abandonment of both the Hygeia Hospital at Fortress Monroe and the Yorktown Hospital (HWB to FLO, June 9, 1862, USSC-NYPL, box 742: 1428; "Clement Biddle Barclay Dead," *Philadelphia Record*, Aug. 11, 1896, p. 1; R. Burnham Moffat, *The Barclays of New York: Who They Are* . . . [New York, 1904], p. 229).

7. The *Daniel Webster No. 1* arrived at White House from Boston on June 13 (FLO to C. S. Tripler, June 13, 1862, USSC-NYPL, box 743: 1502).

8. Probably a humorous reference to the Perkins Institution for the Blind, whose director, Samuel Gridley Howe, was a member of the Sanitary Commission.

9. Unidentified.

10. These telegrams apparently have not survived.

11. Rather than referring to a hotel, Olmsted was joking that he was becoming insane. David Tilden Brown was resident physician at the Bloomingdale Asylum in New York City from 1852 until 1877. Olmsted and Vaux had drawn up the plan for laying out the grounds of that institution in 1861 (H. A. Kelly and W. L. Burrage, *Dictionary of American Medical Biography*, p. 150; *Papers of FLO*, 3: 32, 454).

To Henry Whitney Bellows

Sanitary Commission
Floating Hospital
June 17th 1862.

My Dear Doctor,

The reason I do not write to you is because it is not possible to communicate what is most concerning me any day without leading you astray. The status of everything changes continually. It is necessary to live in the moment and act for the moment, and whatever facts of an organic sort I communicate to you, will surely not be facts by the time they reach you. I sent you, last night, a copy of a letter addressed to the Surgn General which sets forth the skeleton-facts perhaps of the disorder.[1] But there are a lot of sub-trunks besides. I am now acting under at least nine different commissions. 1 Sanitary Commission (Secy of War); 2 Surgeon General; 3 Medical Director; 4 Quarter Master General, 5 Commandant of the Post, 6 Genl McClellan (by his aid de camp), 7 Surgeon of the Post, 8 Sgn Sup't of Transportat[n] under Med. Director; 9 Provost Marshal of the Post. Each one of these offices holds me in some way subordinate, responsible and responsive to it; and except as certain of them are united in the same individual, each can give me an order at any moment with regard to the same matter, independently of all the rest. No two individuals have the same understanding of my duty or priviledges; no two expect the same thing of me; no two look in the same direction for the remedy for any abuse, in the supply of any organic deficiency to which I call attention. A line of policy vindicated at 9 o'clk by the Sgn in Chg of Transportation of Wounded is changed by the Quarter Master at ten; and again by the Medical Director at eleven, by a telegraph from the Sgn General at twelve. Not one is acting in any correspondence or accord with any other. The Sanitary Commission in Boston, Philadelphia and New York each acts independently upon some ideas received I know not how, with as much confidence and assurance, as if they were Medes and Persians' laws. People come consigned to me for whom I have not asked and those who are promised me and for whom I make arrangments, upon whom I depend for carrying out engagements, do not come and I get no explanation of their absence. I completely organized the Spaulding—I take the case because it is referred to in the letter to Sgn Gnl—personally instructed the various officer[s] in fact practically educated them, as well as I could and sent her off with a small cargo to be broken in (for the third time), my printed instructions [posted] prominently in her wards. She comes back with a "Medical Director", two "Assistant Medical Directors", sundry surgeons; assistant surgeons; cadets, etc. etc. (several are in uniform). The medical directorship with a delegation of the inferior surgery, come up to the landing and announce that they want their patients sent at once on board as they must be back to open hospitals and deliver lectures and friends' wives on Monday morning at ten o'clock. And when, after some explanations, I happen to refer to the rules of the Commission, I am asked "what is this Sanitary Commission and what has it got to do with it", and two thirds of the directory, presently finding that it can not immediately proceed to ex sections,[2] produces commissions from the Sgn Genl to rove through the Army of the Potomac and goes off to Hd Quarters where each man presents himself with the title of Medical Director, rousing old Tripler who tells them that they are "under his thumb," and when they fall back on the Sanitary Commission of Philadelphia, informs them that that

373

nuisance is also under his thumb, and that he puts surgeons to boats and boats to surgeons without regard to the Sanitary Commission. Thereupon a new tangle commences.

The original is letter 1543 in box 742 of USSC-NYPL. It is unsigned and may be incomplete.

1. The editors have been unable to discover this letter to Hammond. Telegrams exchanged by the two men at this time, however, indicate that the letter probably addressed the question of how much authority the Sanitary Commission could and did exercise over the transport ships. On June 14 Hammond had telegraphed Olmsted: "The Hospital transports are under charge of the Sanitary Commission: if they cannot manage them I will take charge. I understand that the Sanitary Commission undertake to transport the sick and wounded. I turned the matter over to them and I hold them responsible till they resign the charge. I will furnish all stores of any kind on application."

Replying by telegraph on June 16, Olmsted queried the surgeon general: "Have I any authority or responsibility over transports except as derived from Tripler. Both he and I understand not. The San. Com. now complicates and prevents general improvement. Should be withdrawn entirely or put in charge of all and all brought to one system. There is no time to be lost. I have written you for tomorrow's mail" (W. A. Hammond to FLO, June 14, 1862, Record Group 112, Office of the Surgeon General [Army], letterbook 31, pp. 123–24, National Archives; FLO to W. A. Hammond, June 16, 1862, USSC-NYPL, box 743: 1534).

2. A surgical term referring to the action of cutting out or away.

To Henry Whitney Bellows

On board "Wilson Small",
White house, June 18th 1862

My Dear Doctor,

I enclose copy of a letter addressed today to the Sgn General.

If he does not immediately adopt this suggestion,[1] I think that you should do so, so far at least as to send shelter for 4000 men, to be used at two or three points on the rail-road, and kettles altogether of a capacity of 250 gallons, with soupstock in proportion. If you do this, send also fifty laborers and a few good rough carpenters with some light joist[s]: Also two or three good beef-tea cooks.

The general impression now is that the rebels have concentrated a vast force at Richmond and are very determined and confident. We hope that they will attack; and if they do not, that some important advantages will be gained by the gun-boats and the cooperation of Burnside, before we attack.[2] We think therefore that at least a week will elapse before the grand battle—time enough to do something if we have the means wherewith to work. We look with awe and dread to the prospect of a battle—of the battle on which so much hangs. If, as is probable it becomes a pitched battle of one or two days, engaging the whole lines, it is morally certain that thousands will unnecessarily bleed to death—other thousands starve to death.

Suppose 20,000 fall; half of them, on the fourth day, will be still on the bare ground, without shelter, and such as remain alive just getting their first sustenance in the shape of hard biscuit and salt-beef. This is a fair deduction from our experience at Fair Oaks. Not half our force was then engaged and the wounded of both sides exceeded ten thousand.[3] Richmond is said to be already crammed with sick & wounded.

I feel sure that we shall lose more by neglect to provide for the succour of the wounded than we shall by[4] the necessarily fatal results of the battle. Our preparations really amount to nothing. They are a mockery.

Send all the medical students of the sort that we have thus far chiefly had who can be got to come. We can't have too many, if they will be content to live cooped up in idleness on an old steamboat until the work begins again.

Chamberlain gives me his resignation; Ware thinks he can not stand it much longer, Mrs Griffin is hors du combat. All suffer from persistent mild diarrhea. Most of the officers & clerks have it. McClellan himself is greatly bothered with it.

I am quite well, having no trouble but an occasional headache, and, having reestablished communication with my wife, can be reckoned on to hold here till we enter Richmond, subjugators or subjugated.

Yours Very Cordially,

Fred. Law Olmsted.

P.S.

Sanitary Commission,
Floating Hospital.
June 19th

Here is a telegram signed "Draper,[5] Medical Director": the St. Marks[6] has arrived at Fortress Monroe and awaits my orders.

Now, my dear doctor, this is too bad. I know nothing of the "St Marks", her capacity, draft of water, whether with or without a tug (as proposed in the only reference which has been made to her in my letters from the Commission), whether designed (as then seemed to be the case) for a transport, or as Jenkins and my own judgment of what is best, supposes, for a stationary hospital for special cases of some sort. I hear through the letters recvd by the ladies that she has been expensively fitted and prepared. I wonder if any assurance has been obtained that she will not be seized and used for other purposes than those for which you design her, as the boats of the Sanitary Commission have three times been at Fortress Monroe, the good luck of an assistant Secy of War falling present and under persuasion overruling the Quarter Master's order, only preventing the total loss of all that had been done for them.[7] I wonder—but I will not give you further evidence that I have a wandering mind.

But how can the St Marks be under my orders—at Fortress Monroe? I have no more control over her movements than any other citizen. All I can do is to report to Tripler or Cuyler that she is waiting orders from one of them, and see that she is kept in decent order.

You surely do not understand it so, but what ground you have for any other understanding I am entirely at a loss to suspect. Until the startling telegram of the Sgn General[8] was received the other night, I have never had any intimation that I had any authority over these or any transports except as permitted from day to day by the local military & medical authorities. I am a mere aid de camp with reference to them—in respect of authority. Whatever else I have done since I have been here, has been by persuasion, argument, management and assumption.

I want you to see this clearly, because I feel that if I had possessed the authority you evidently suppose me to have had, I could have prevented a vast deal of wretchedness, pain and death that I have had to witness powerlessly. I would have given my life to be able for one week to exercise the authority which the Sgn Genl has the assurance to tell me that I have had, and which you apparently suppose that I have had.

Here comes a letter from the New York Agency of the Sanitary Commission coolly informing me that a number of compound fractures of the thigh & gunshot wounds of the joints have recently arrived in New York from Whitehouse—obviously with the idea that I am blameable for it.[9] Not a single vessel has gone from here to New York with any previous knowledge on my part of her destination. I have not been authorized to choose to have go or to save from going a single individual. My wishes in this respect, repeatedly and strongly expressed, have not been in the slightest degree regarded. I have only been able in one instance to select the patients for the vessel or to control the destination of a vessel with wounded on board, and in this instance, I acted in disregard of orders,[10] taking advantage of a storm, which broke down the telegraph, to do so. And now Hammond mocks me with the assertion that I am responsible for all the horrors of murder by inefficiency, the mere memory of which sometimes sweeps my brain as a night-mare.

F.L.O.

P.P.S. I am really very well, tranquil & comfortable, and can stand the racket as long as you think it serves a good purpose. But, in my judgment, I am only pumping to keep the water a little lower than it might otherwise be. It is at your end the leak must be stopped.

The original is letter 1564 in box 743 of USSC-NYPL. The postscript was filed separately in that box as letter 1576. Both its date and internal evidence indicate that it is an addition to this letter of June 18 to Bellows.

1. In a letter of June 17 Olmsted thanked Surgeon General Hammond for sending large quantities of vegetables to combat the outbreak of scurvy among the troops and also suggested new measures to aid the wounded:

> I therefore urge that tarpolins, old sails, felt, or canvas in bolts, with means of putting it together, be sent here immediately in quantity sufficient to form a shelter for ten (10) thousand wounded men. The materials for extending and supporting it in the form of sheds can be found in the woods immediately in the rear of the line of operations before Richmond where the shelters should be placed. I should propose that at least one dépôt for wounded should in this way be prepared for each army Corps. Water should be secured in its vicinity and means for providing large quantities of beef tea or soup.

   Olmsted further requested the surgeon general to send all materials and personnel to build, staff, and supply such depots (FLO to W. A. Hammond, June 17, 1862).
2. Gunboats of the U.S. Navy had been on the Pamunkey River since mid-May, and in late May, a joint army-navy expedition had ascended the Pamunkey twenty-five miles above White House. Ambrose E. Burnside commanded the Union forces at New Bern, North Carolina, and Olmsted had probably heard rumors that McClellan meant to obtain reinforcements from Burnside's command (U.S. Department of the Navy, Naval History Division, *Civil War Naval Chronology, 1861–1865*, 5 vols. [Washington, D.C., 1961–65], 2: 64, 66).
3. The Confederate and Union wounded at the battle of Fair Oaks totaled approximately eighty-three hundred (T. L. Livermore, *Numbers and Losses*, p. 81).
4. Olmsted here wrote "be."
5. Probably Dr. William H. Draper.
6. A "splendid clipper East Indiaman" fitted up by the Sanitary Commission as a special surgical hospital. According to Olmsted, it could transport 250 at sea or could hold 450 as a stationary hospital. The *St. Mark* drew too much water to sail up the Pamunkey and was stationed at Yorktown (*Hospital Transports*, p. 132; FLO to C. S. Tripler, June 18, 1862).
7. On three occasions the Sanitary Commission was, with the aid of Assistant Secretary of War John C. Tucker, able to retain the *S. R. Spaulding* for hospital service after the quartermaster's department had ordered the ship to be used to transport troops. Twice in late May and again on June 13, Tucker overruled the orders of the

quartermaster's department (*Hospital Transports*, pp. 85–86; Charles G. Sawtelle to FLO, May 24, 1862, and J. C. Tucker to FLO, May 25, 1862, both in the Frederick Newman Knapp Papers, Massachusetts Historical Society, Boston, Mass.; FLO to J. C. Tucker, May 27, [1862], USSC-NYPL, box 741: 1146; FLO to C. S. Tripler, June 13, 1862, USSC-NYPL, box 743: 1503).

8. The telegram of June 14, 1862, in which Hammond asserted that the Sanitary Commission held authority over and responsibility for the hospital transport ships (see FLO to HWB, June 17, 1862, n. 1, above).

9. A letter of June 11 from Thomas H. Faile, Jr., superintendent of the New York agency, and written by "order of the Executive Committee," informed Olmsted that these "wounded men have suffered greatly and incurred fatal risks" during the voyage to New York. Faile then requested Olmsted to "use your best efforts as far as possible to retain such wounded men in Hospital at Yorktown or Fortress Monroe & send convalescents or less seriously wounded in their stead as far as circumstances will permit" (T. H. Faile, Jr., to FLO, June 11, 1862, USSC-NYPL, box 742: 1455).

10. A reference to his sending the *Daniel Webster No. 1* to Boston on June 2 (see FLO to HWB, June 3, 1862, n. 19, above).

To Henry Whitney Bellows

White house, June 22ᵈ 1862.

My Dear Doctor,

The grand work before the Commission, yet to be entered upon, is the nationalization of the care of the invalids of the war, guarding them from humiliation and fostering among them the spirit of independence and self support. You have studied the principles upon which this work should be based more carefully than any other man in the country and I think you should soon lay down the main lines of the plan to be had in view.[1] It has got to be brought before the public, adroitly, cunningly. Perhaps the first move could be made on the coming 4th of July. Have you any opening ready wherein to insert a wedge? The first thing is to head off by a concerted movement all provincial poor-house arrangments. Then we must be careful not to excite a jealousy of New York, and a suspicion of a concealed local purpose. New York and other large cities offer the best field for cultivation because only in dense communities can there be such division of labor as will afford employment for men deficient in important members. One legged men can collect fares and take tickets and keep tally as well as any others, and one armed men can run errands, carry telegraphic messages, watch against fires and ring alarm bells.

The idea has hardly taken any definite shape in my mind. I will try to give a provisional shape to it. Suppose we should prepare matters so that we could after a time advertize as follows:

"The Sanitary Commission has established offices—(in all the principal cities) at which soldiers of the Union army who have been seriously wounded in the performance of duty can secure the following advantages:

    1st   Information, advice and assistance in procuring back-pay, head-rights, pensions, &c. without payment of lawyers' fees.

    2d   Assistance in obtaining such employment as they are fitted to undertake.

    3d   Assistance in making the most of their means.

    4th   Insurance against the necessity of begging for a livelihood.

These benefits will be offered upon 1 condition, that the services of the applicant shall be at the disposal of the Commission, and that they shall be given with honesty & industry.

Each applicant will be examined by the local board of the office at which he applies. This board must, before the Commission is obliged to assist him, be satisfied of his good character and be willing to recommend him for any employment which he is fitted to undertake.

If accepted, he will be furnished with a book which will contain a careful statement of his qualifications and a certificate that he is entitled to the protection of the Commission and its agents and associates, wherever he may go. In the same book, a record will afterwards be kept of the duties in which he shall have been employed and of his ability and fidelity in the performance of them.

Immediately after having been accepted by the local board as entitled to the benefits of the Commission, measures will be taken to find, wherever possible throughout the whole country, employment adapted to his particular case, and for which his wound will not disable him, and by which he can live usefully and independently of charity.

The Commission will thereafter, watch over and guard him against imposition and tyranny, and whenever employment shall fail, will, if necessary temporarily maintain him and use every proper means to again obtain for him the opportunity of independent self-support."

The above does not satisfy me. There should be more of the element of mutual insurance, and more of apprenticeship. The beneficiaries—or shareholders—should be under surveillance and discipline, should maintain and grow in soldierly, orderly, prompt and correspondent habits. They should be uniformed and numbered, and wherever seen should be recognized and assured as trusty, orderly men, proud of their fraternity and its badges and obligations. I will try again:

"National Invalid Corps
of the Sanitary Commission

Notice. An examiner of the Sanitary Commission will visit _____ on the _____ and will receive applications for admission to the National Invalid Corps which must be made by applicants in person at _____ St. between the hours of 9 A.M. & 1 P.M. daily till _____. Applicants, to be successful, must satisfy the examiner that they have suffered severe bodily injury in defence of the Union, that they are disposed to earn their living by faithful service in whatever situation it is practicable for them to be useful, that they are not likely to disgrace and injure the corps by drunkenness, falsehood or eyeservice, but that they will regard it as their highest interest to gain for it and maintain for it a reputation for fidelity, truthfulness, trustworthiness, precision and punctuality.

Each member of the corps will be instructed, if necessary, in how it is possible for him to be useful to others in spite of the injury which he has received. After proper instruction the members will be organized in squads or companies, each of which will be stationed under a proper officer in some town or place where its members will be likely to obtain employment. Arrangments will be made by which lodgings, rations and uniforms will be supplied them at low rates of cost and by which they may by small savings lay by a provision for old age or for the benefit of their families.

Members accused of acts of dishonesty, habitual indolence, or conduct calculated to seriously impair the confidence of the public in the good character of the corps, will be brought before a Court of Enquiry, and upon conviction, will be liable to dismissal and forfeiture of" &c.

I don't know that I am any better satisfied with that. I think the true thing lies somewhere between—but there should be special provision for all necessary surgical attendance, for dispensing with lawyers and lobbyers, and for wooden legs etc. when necessary to usefulness.

It does not seem to me that something like what I have sketched would be impracticable. We should keep up on Ladies—Woman's Relief Associations—and get them to furnish the clothing for instance. By selecting and putting a mark—uniform—on all the temperate, honest, deserving men, we should do much to put down the beggary of the other sort. But I need not pursue it further. Please let me know how it strikes you.

Yours faithfully

Fred. Law Olmsted.

Dr Bellows

The original is in box 641 of USSC-NYPL, and a letterpress copy is on pages 28–34 of Olmsted's official letterbook.

1. Olmsted's allusion to Bellows's having studied the principles upon which assistance should be provided to disabled soldiers probably refers to the minister's earlier interest in and writings on social problems. In 1857 Bellows delivered a series of twelve lectures at the Lowell Institute in Boston entitled "The Treatment of Social Diseases." According to Bellows, his preparation for the lectures, which dealt with topics such as drunkenness, pauperism, and crime, acquainted him "with the best works in English & French, upon this general class of subjects" (HWB to Charles J. Stillé, Nov. 15, 1865, Henry Whitney Bellows Papers, Massachusetts Historical Society, Boston, Mass.; W. D. Kring, *Henry Whitney Bellows*, pp. 177–79).

To Charles Loring Brace   [June 29, 1862][1]

On board the "Wilson Small";
Hampton Roads, 1st Sunday,
after the skedaddle of the Pamunkey, 1862

My Dear Charley,

I employ three classes: surgeons, nurses and women—the first and last of two grades but in neither of either would you yoke. For nurses, I find that any not very sick common soldiers, Yankee, Irish or German, are better than any volunteers; also that mercenaries are better than gratuitous volunteers. I have therefore abandoned volunteers—don't want them, consequently, in the way of business, I don't want you—for any man without a clearly defined function about the army is a horrid nuisance, and is treated as such unless he comes with a peremptory edict from the Secy of War that he shan't be; when aside swearing becomes the substitute for kicks and cold shoulders. I have seen enough of it & it's not an entertainment to which I would invite a friend. There were about forty men and five women arriving daily at White house, who desired to make themselves generally useful. They commonly lay around over one night and concluded to go back next morning—sour, and seedy. There is just one thing which a man can usefully bring to the army of the Potomac: reinforcement of sturdy musket bearers. There is but one other service to which a true patriot and Christian could as well devote his energies—the guillotining of the aforesaid Secretary of War.

I have always thought Chase[2] and Wordsworth[3] and the Tribune & Post wrong in their policy with regard to McClellan.[4] I have done my best, in a humble way, to oppose it. Stanton I should say, I know is an infernal,

"The Skedaddle of the Pamunkey"

ınfidel scoundrel—with the others it is simply an error of judgment. Because I respected those people individually—morally and common sensically—I did not till lately feel much in opposition to them, lacking confidence in my own judgment, but lately, here, as I know the business better & better, I feel hotly and bitterly. I don't think McClellan a great man, certainly not a genius of a general; I think we might find a better one; I think he makes a great many mistakes, and is altogether unworthy of the hero-worship which he commands from the army, as a whole; but as between him and his enemies, I am a McClellan man to the backbone. Everything depended on him. To begin cutting the ground from under him, if it had been never so carefully and considerately, was desperate folly.

I do not doubt this interference has cost us millions on millions of money and lives worth tenfold more than all the millions—if in God's mercy it has not cost us our country, and it is clear to me that if the original plan had been strictly adhered to,[5] we should before this have been nearer the end of the rebellion than I think we are now likely to be this time twelve month.

The impatient folly—the improvident impatience and the reckless confidence of people who come here, fresh from New York & Boston, is very shocking and frightful. I can't tell you how heartless and flippant it sounds.

> Thursday July 3ᵈ
> Harrison's landing up James River.
> Boat just leaving.

I wrote the above before any body suspected the disaster of the army. God has saved us from immediate destruction by the rain of yesterday.[6] I hope we shall entrench and be able to hold our position till you can send us a fresh army. But every man who arrives here now till we get 50,000 is worth millions. The artillery is yet safe, and the men have lost no pluck or confidence in McClellan; he can not move even now without cheers; but they are awfully worn out.

F.L.O.

1. After heavy Union losses at Gaines' Mill, where the second of the Seven Days' battles was fought on June 27, a Friday, McClellan hurriedly decided to move his base from White House on the Pamunkey to the James River. Captain Sawtelle on June 26 privately advised Olmsted to leave White House, and the *Wilson Small, Wissahickon,* and *Elizabeth* proceeded to West Point. The mechanical problems of the *Small* were repaired there, and Olmsted returned to White House on June 27 only to find transports and other hospital steamers evacuating the area (*War for the Union,* 2: 134; *Hospital Transports,* pp. 132–35).
2. Salmon P. Chase, who by the time of the Peninsula campaign had lost faith in McClellan's ability.
3. James Samuel Wadsworth (1807–1864), a wealthy farmer and politician from Geneseo, New York, who was appointed brigadier general of volunteers in August 1861. Wadsworth took command of the Union forces that were left in Washington, D.C., in the spring of 1862 when the Army of the Potomac moved to the Peninsula. Responsible for the defense of Washington, he criticized McClellan for leaving too few troops to protect the capital adequately. Wadsworth was assigned to field command late in 1862, after his defeat in the New York gubernatorial race, and was fatally wounded during the battle of the Wilderness in 1864.
    Some personal and family ties existed between Olmsted and Wadsworth. The latter was a friend of Mary Perkins Olmsted's family and had served as trustee of her real estate in western New York. Wadsworth was also Olmsted's third cousin, and the two men occasionally met while in Washington. On September 18, 1861, Olmsted described a tour of Wadsworth's brigade and concluded, "He looked very well and is seemingly a capital commander" (*DAB*; FLO to MPO, Sept. 18, 1861; *Olmsted Genealogy,* pp. 24, 39, 64, 112; Henry Greenleaf Pearson, *James S. Wadsworth of Geneseo, Brevet Major-General of United States Volunteers* [New York, 1913], pp. 118–21).
4. The *New-York Daily Tribune* and *New York Evening Post* had criticized McClellan for his failure to attack the Confederate army during the fall and winter of 1861, and the *Tribune* had then called for his removal from command. During the Peninsula cam-

383

paign, however, both newspapers refrained from criticizing McClellan until after the Seven Days' battles. In July 1862 both began to call for his removal (Allan Nevins, *The Evening Post: A Century of Journalism* [New York, 1922], pp. 288–92; J. Cutler Andrews, *The North Reports the Civil War* [Pittsburgh, Pa., 1955], pp. 206–17).

5. Olmsted here probably is not speaking of McClellan's original plan early in 1862 to move his entire army toward Richmond via the Rappahannock River; rather, he is most likely referring to the deployment of troops as planned in April and May. Since Wadsworth convinced Lincoln and Stanton that too few troops were then guarding Washington, they ordered McDowell's corps of thirty thousand, an important unit in the Army of the Potomac, not to join McClellan as originally planned. Although McDowell was to reinforce McClellan in May, Confederate activity in the Shenandoah Valley led Lincoln to send that corps there (T. Harry Williams, *Lincoln and His Generals* [New York, 1952], pp. 56–84, 87–100; FLO to Sydney H. Gay, July 12, 1862, nn. 7 and 9, below).

6. Olmsted was mistaken about the outcome of the battle of Malvern Hill. Union troops did not suffer a disaster that brought them to the edge of destruction; instead, they severely punished Confederate forces on July 1. Only two thousand Union soldiers were among the day's casualties, while Confederate losses exceeded five thousand. Probably the Union army's retreat to Harrison's Landing in the rain that began early on July 2 led Olmsted to these erroneous conclusions. Although McClellan believed his army needed a safe base of operations, some of his generals believed, and historians have since argued, that the Union troops could have held a more advanced position or could have pushed Lee's battered army farther back toward Richmond (*War for the Union*, 2: 135–37).

To Mary Perkins Olmsted

Harrison's landing, James' River
July 3ᵈ 1862.

Dear Wife,

I write in my stateroom on the Wilson Small, which lies two hundred feet East of the long pier of what we call, with some doubt if it is not another, Harrison's landing. The shore is like that of Staten Island at Redbank[1]—or along near there. Immediately in front, it rises with a rapid slope for a distance of 1000 feet, and beyond is a table land or gentle slope northward. There are slight undulations right and left, about as on the Leveridge farm,[2] and from half a mile to a mile distant are open country in each direction, then irregular skirts of woods. At the highest point of the swell in front is a fine old brick mansion (the central hospital).[3] The beach below the broken bank is filled with soldiers, some bathing, some washing clothes, many reading newspapers which have just arrivd from New York; some and I hope most are wounded—I can see arms in splints. About the head of the pier there is a dense crowd of wounded, being led and carried one by one down to the hospital-boats at the end. From the edge of the bank, on the right for a short distance, there are rows of waggons, drawn up as "in line of battle"—that is, not in column—teamsters in their saddles, row after row, at right angles to the river; more are forming in the rear, and still further to the right, columns of them are moving this way. More to the left and along the crest of the hill, artillery is forming and moving off on a walk, till out of sight; over the next swell to the right, a body of cavalry is moving off—to the right. Further to the left, through the low trees & bushes on the bank there, is a city of tents to be seen. Out of them, we catch glimpses of infantry columns in movement toward the front and right. Head Quarters are a little to the left on swampy ground, and this is not far from the military centre of our position. There is a large fleet of transports in our rear and up and down the river, and at the extreme right and left are the gun-boats, with their heavy guns. The boat has swung since I commenced writing and I see down the river the turret of the Monitor[4]—a puff and cloud of white smoke rises and is blowing away a large white gusty cloud, a heavy, shaking report and hoarse screech of shell (the sound is nearest like that of a violent steam escape, a rush, a buzz and a metallic ring combined, but with a varying, wavering intensity); then a duller one from another gun-boat, and another; something oftener than once a minute these, the heaviest reports; up the river a little further off, another set; from the front the reports, sharper but not as loud, come irregularly from one to twenty seconds apart (field artillery). Now we hear loud cheering, long and multitudinous and excited, caught up from one to another body, and then again by others more distant and then louder by those nearer again. The Hero[5] comes up with six hundred, not more than six hundred, fresh troops, who cheer as they pass us, and we wave back their salutation with feeling, for though but a drop, we hope it is the drop of a coming shower, and we know how every drop brings its special relief to the parched and haggard heroes who have fought five battles in five successive days[6] and each night after repulsing the attacks of double their number, made a forced march to gain a new position, who have had but two days' rations of uncooked food during these five days, who had their first night's rest last night, sleeping on their arms, without tents, blankets or fire, the rain falling in torrents, and who are now again advancing in line of battle, and who have tonight again to find strong picket guards.

Col. Howland's[7] servant (Col. Howland is wounded, and on board) has just come off, and says their division has just been moved off; they were told it was for a special and important duty and they were expected to do their very best.[8] Whereupon they cheered. The excitement keeps them up wonderfully, but I don't believe that braver, pluckier men were ever

McClellan's Headquarters, Harrison's Landing, July 1862

gathered in as large a number before on the same space of ground, as now within a radius of a mile and a half of this boat.

Letterman[9] the new Medical Director has been on board and I am to go with the Small as quickly as possible to Washington to tell the Surgn General more fully than he can write what the condition & the medical needs of the Army are, and to bring back direct what it most urgently wants.

Wounded are arriving from the battle of today;[10] which is now ended or suspended, though our line of battle is maintained. By climbing a mast, we can see it.

Our grand army is very nearly destroyed. I wonder whether they will let you know it. It is striving bravely and cheerfully—heroically to the last, but there is an end to human endurance, and if the enemy with his double force, keeps pushing upon it, it can not hold out much longer, unless reinforcements of considerable strength arrive.

Letterman estimates our loss in the last week at 30,000; our present force—effective—at 60,000; the enemy's at 150,000 to 200,000.[11] The majority of our men have lost tents, knapsack and blanket, have saved only musket and cartridge box. Many in the line of battle are bareheaded and barefooted. Think what their condition will be in this shadeless plain when the July sun comes out tomorrow. I am going to get if possible, first, tents, or something that will cast a shade for the wounded.

Chesapeake bay, 4th July.

We were all night feeling our way without a pilot down James river.
We have met no reinforcements.
Your affectionate husband,

1. Redbank lies on the southeastern coast of Staten Island.
2. The Leveridge family owned a farm near the Olmsted family's Tosomock Farm on Staten Island (FLO to JO, [March 20, 1848]).
3. Berkeley, the manor house of the Harrison's Landing plantation and birthplace of former president William Henry Harrison (Virginia Navigation Company, *Afloat on the James* [New York, 1897], pp. 31–32, 34).
4. The U.S.S. *Monitor*, built by John Ericksson and launched in January 1862 as the first Union ironclad, was a turreted, steam-powered gunboat. Its most famous engagement was the drawn battle with the C.S.S. *Virginia* (formerly known as the U.S.S. *Merrimac*) off Hampton Roads on March 9, 1862. During the Peninsula campaign the *Monitor* was part of the James River flotilla stationed in the waters of the Peninsula (*O.R.*, ser. 2, vol. 1, p. 148; Rowena Reed, *Combined Operations in the Civil War* [Annapolis, Md., c. 1978], pp. 178–79).
5. A steamboat used for the transportation of Union troops (*O.R. [Naval]*, ser. 1, vol. 7, p. 191).
6. The Seven Days' battles of Mechanicsville (Beaver Dam Creek) of June 26, Gaines' Mill of June 27, Savage's Station of June 29, Frayser's Farm (Glendale) of June 30, and Malvern Hill of July 1.
7. Joseph Howland (1834–1886), who had married Eliza Woolsey and was colonel of the 16th New York Infantry. Wounded during the battle of Gaines' Mill, he left with his wife for New York on July 5 on a hospital boat. Howland resigned from the army on September 29, 1862. The servant to whom Olmsted refers probably was Stanislaus Moritz, who attended Eliza Woolsey Howland on the hospital transports and was himself a tireless worker on behalf of the wounded (A. L. Austin, *Woolsey Sisters*, pp. 1, 47, 64, 67; F. B. Heitman, *Historical Register and Dictionary*, 1: 549).
8. The 16th New York, as part of the 1st Division of the VI Corps, commanded by William B. Franklin, probably played a part in dislodging Confederate general J. E. B. Stuart's cavalrymen from Evelington Heights above Harrison's Landing (John W. Thomason, Jr., *Jeb Stuart* [New York, 1930], p. 205).
9. Jonathan Letterman (1824–1872), Hammond's appointee as the new medical director of the Army of the Potomac. A friend of Hammond, Letterman had graduated from Jefferson Medical College in Philadelphia and had served in the army's Medical Bureau since 1849. As medical director, he was capable and innovative. His greatest achievement was the establishment of an efficient ambulance service, but he also took great interest in other aspects of the health of soldiers in the field. From the first, Letterman very favorably impressed Olmsted, who wrote on June 30, 1862: "I like him at first sight better than any Surgeon U.S.A. whom I have seen. He asks & offers cooperation, and will have it with all my heart, so far as it is worth-while to give it." The two shared many of the same concerns: like Olmsted, Letterman worried about the diet and hygiene of the troops, believed that medical ships should be used exclusively for that purpose, and argued that the indiscriminate transporting of sick and wounded lowered both troop morale and effectiveness.
    In January 1864 Letterman resigned as medical director of the Army of the Potomac. In December 1864 he resigned his commission in the army. Probably

the removal from office and subsequent court-martial of Hammond influenced Letterman's decision. He then moved to California, where he entered business (*DAB*; Jonathan Letterman, *Medical Recollections of the Army of the Potomac* [New York, 1866], pp. 8–9, 20–24, 185; FLO to HWB, June 30, 1862, USSC-NYPL, box 743: 1685).

10. Probably the shelling of Harrison's Landing from Evelington Heights by J. E. B. Stuart's 1st Virginia Cavalry. Union troops forced Stuart to withdraw and fortified that area (Joseph P. Cullen, *The Peninsula Campaign, 1862: McClellan & Lee Struggle for Richmond* [Harrisburg, Pa., 1973], pp. 164–65).

11. These figures, though reflecting McClellan's belief that his army was fighting against much greater numbers, were not accurate. Immediately after the Seven Days' battles, the number of fighting men probably stood at seventy-five thousand for both the Union and Confederate armies on the Peninsula. The Union army's losses from those battles totaled approximately ten thousand killed or wounded and eight thousand missing; the Confederate loss was approximately twenty thousand killed or wounded but less than one thousand missing (T. L. Livermore, *Numbers and Losses*, pp. 82–86).

To Henry Whitney Bellows

On board Steamboat "Wilson Small",
Chesapeake bay. July 4th 1862.

My Dear Doctor,

I left our anchorage off Head Quarters of the Army of the Potomac—where I wrote you last—about 4 o'clk yesterday afternoon, and am running for Washington, by request of the Medical Director, to advise the Surgeon General of the sanitary condition of the army and secure the immediate supply, as far as possible of its most urgent surgical and medical wants. As the rebels have put out the lights and we could get no pilot, we were all night feeling our way down the river, and shall not be able, with all we can do, to get to Washington till late tonight. I hope to get what is most necessary and leave on our return before night to-morrow. I telegraphed from Old Point to have everything advanced.

There is one want of the army, which on Sanitary grounds as well as every other, is so extremely urgent, that all other wants become insignificant, and I can think and care for nothing else, while it seems possible for me to use the smallest influence favorable to its supply. Why, in the name of God, if our public servants at Washington know the condition of the Army of the Potomac, do we, on this fourth of July, meet not a solitary boat load of re-inforcements going to it? Surely, they do not know it—the people do not know it—how anxiously those exhausted heroes, facing the enemy, who as they believe, presses still upon them with double their numbers, look over their shoulders, as they advance, to see if the help they have fought so hard to secure the chance of receiving, will not arrive in time to give them rest, before they faint with fatigue. No men ever deserved better of their country. They know it. They exult in it. They die exultant. But it is because they believe that by the sacrifice of their lives they have secured an opportunity to their country, of which it will now be eager and quick to take advantage.

Whatever is the truth, the Army of the Potomac believes this and lives in this belief: That its General has comprehended better than anyone else, the military opportunity, the military resources and the military cunning of the enemies of the country; also that better than anyone else he has seen how these could be successfully overcome in one blow; that the government had hitherto not seen the opportunity of the rebellion; had underestimated the value, in this opportunity, of its resources, and had failed to comprehend the motive of its moves. It has consequently refused to believe that the Army of the Potomac could not advance without reinforcements, it has not suspected that it could be threatened by overpowering numbers of the enemy upon whom it was called upon to advance, and it has attributed to an excessive caution, allied to cowardice, or to a weak ambition which it would be dangerous to gratify, the continued entreaty of its General to be supplied with the additional force, which he had from the first asserted to be essential to the sure success of his undertaking. This is suddenly ended by the enemy, who all at once throws upon three sides of this Army, with a vehemence and recklessness and prodigality of life which was calculated to overcome it as by a deluge, forces, which they believe to have been more than double their own in number. They are on low ground, untenable for prolonged defence; and they are hopelessly cut off from their base, and the enemy, again and again repulsed, reforms on the hills his broken lines and brings over fresh troops, and day after day renews with unabated confidence the purpose of overwhelming them. Every day they stand up in resistance, and every night they toil through the swamp roads, till at length on the sixth day, they have established a new base, and hold for the country the opportunity of remedying its mistake, and of yet ending the life of the rebellion at a blow.[1] They believe the country appreciates this now and will throw everything else aside to avail [themselves] of it. They can not hold it long in their exhausted condition, and they believe that every hour will bring the beginning of the stream which is to flow in to stay, and, in its turn, to set back and finally to overwhelm the foe who still desperately renews the effort on which his all is staked.

Whatever measure of misapprehension of facts there may be in this, I am sure that not far differently from this believes nine tenths of the Army of the Potomac; and in this belief—this faith—that the country will regard them as having, by unparalleled exertion, endurance and heroism, saved it from a blow which would have established the confederacy, and as now holding, with even greater endurance and heroism, the forlorn hope of the battle against the Confederacy, and [that the country] will press forward to their rescue and the rescue of the opportunity of which they hold the key—in this faith it sustains the contest, looking every hour for large reinforcements to arrive.[2]

I have seen and conversed freely with many staff officers and been among the men, wounded and well—if any can be called well where all are feverish with six days and nights of frightful fatigue and exhaustion and starvation and excitement. One, a Major General said, "I have not been asleep nor have I tasted food in five days—I have only sustained myself with coffee and segars."[3] As to the men, the common and average statement is; "My regiment has had for the last five days before arriving here, two days' rations: what has been eaten of this has been eaten uncooked; during that time it has made five forced marches, and fought five battles; one third of it has fallen in killed or wounded and not one man has been shot in the back. One third of what remains is now on picket duty in the woods, which the enemy is shelling; the other lies yonder in the mud, sleeping on its arms." This was during the rain, which fell in torrents day before yesterday. Yesterday the enemy was attacking again,[4] and when we left, the whole army was in line of battle, cheering the general, wherever he presented himself. The common saying was: "He knows now, that he can depend upon us for anything he wants, and we know that he can save us, if any man can." But still, there was a constant looking down the river for reinforcements from Washington, and looking across the river for Burnside.[5]

The exultant confidence of the army in itself is beyond all verbal expression. It has grown out of the experience of the ability of its Generals to resist and foil and terribly punish with it, desperate assaults made upon it with forces greatly superior in numbers. It says, proudly and joyfully: "All that men can do, we can do", but there is also, the consciousness of a terrible strain upon their energies, of an unnatural strength, and the reflection is frequent that there must be a limit to every man's endurance.

Rest and recuperation, how are they to be had? The first, only by the relief of reinforcements; the second by good diet and favorable hygienic circumstances. Eastern Virginia is all malarious; the banks of James river notoriously so; the army is chiefly upon a moderately elevated, slightly undulating table-land; the river on the south side, swampy land at no great distance on the other sides. It is open, airy, dry, a healthful point,

U.S. Mail Dock, Harrison's Landing, July 1862

on the whole, as any that could be selected East of Richmond. But the sun will be exceedingly fierce upon it, and it is supposed the army has lost two thirds of its tents. Probably a majority of the men have lost also their knapsacks and blankets. Many were without caps or shoes. The area held is small and will be crowded. If the enemy is active as it would appear to be his policy, the officers will be too much occupied with the immediate military necessities of the position to give much attention to police duties. And if they should be disposed to guard against the great dangers which will arise if they are neglected, the excessively fatigued and exhausted condition of the men and the necessity of reserving their strength, from day to day, for the struggle with the enemy, will forbid the constant labor which would be necessary to prevent a terrible accumulation of nuisances, until at least reinforcements shall arrive so large that no more than the ordinary quotas will be required for guard and picket duty.

After such tension and trial, a rapid reduction of force must also occur from sickness, and those not on the sick list will suffer from the lassitude of reaction from excitement. Under these circumstances, all our experience shows that it will be hardly possible to enforce requirements, the observance of which must be essential to a healthy camp.

Unless large reinforcements speedily arrive, then, not only must the army feel that its heroism is unappreciated, and the object, for which it struggled, is to be lost by the neglect of others, and thus become dejected,

391

dispirited and morally resistless to the dangers of disease, but it will be physically impossible to establish such guards against these dangers as are most obviously and directly called for.

(Private)   Letterman thinks our loss may be 30,000, our present force 60,000—our net loss of artillery is probably about 50 pieces—mostly small field pieces; one battery(?) of 20 pounders. There is a general large degree of confidence that with the aid of the gun-boats which are throwing shell on the flanks at frequent intervals, we can hold the position, till sufficient reinforcements come to place it beyond question, but, no one speaks with entire confidence, and the nearer to the head, the graver seems to be the apprehension—though with all, there is that strange exultation—ready to break out in laughter like a crazy man's. There are some few—Casey's[6] old officers chiefly—who are utterly despondent and fault-finding. One in an important position for his rank, predicted openly that McClellan would surrender today. But there is less of this than ever before, and fewer stragglers and obvious cowards. Nothing like what was seen by Douglas, he says, after Pittsburg landing.[7] Of what we saw after Bull Run there is not the slightest symptom. In short we have then a real grand army, tried, enduring, heroic: worth all we can give to save it.

Yours Respectfully,

Fred. Law Olmsted.
General Secretary

H. W. Bellows. D.D. Pres't. San Com.

The original is in box 641 of USSC-NYPL.

1. McClellan's new base, established at the end of the Seven Days' battles, was Harrison's Landing, on the north bank of the James River.
2. Olmsted here is describing the achievement and potential, if properly reinforced, of the Army of the Potomac. He is probably using the phrase "forlorn hope" in its older meaning to refer to a part of the Army of the Potomac as a detachment sent to lead the attack.
3. Probably William B. Franklin, commander of the VI Corps. On July 1 Olmsted wrote, "Gen'l Franklin said he had eaten nothing in four days" (FLO to HWB, July 1, 1862, USSC-NYPL, box 743: 1704).
4. See FLO to MPO, July 3, 1862, note 8, above.
5. On June 28, 1862, Lincoln ordered Ambrose E. Burnside at New Bern, North Carolina, to send McClellan any reinforcements that could be spared. Although this order was reiterated, Burnside with eight thousand soldiers did not arrive at Fortress Monroe until the afternoon of July 7 (O.R., ser. 1, vol. 11, pt. 3, pp. 270-71, 290-91, 305).

6. Silas Casey (1807–1882), a graduate of the U.S. Military Academy and a career army officer, had been breveted lieutenant colonel for his gallantry in the Mexican War. Appointed a brigadier general of volunteers in August 1861, he commanded the 3rd Division of the IV Corps in the Army of the Potomac from March 1862 until June 6 of that year, and the 2nd Division of that corps from June 6 to June 24 (G. W. Cullum, *Biographical Register*, 1: 383–85).
7. John H. Douglas had arrived on the Peninsula in late June or early July. His comment about Pittsburg Landing referred to his experience while supervising the embarkation of wounded soldiers after the battle of Shiloh.

To ABRAHAM LINCOLN

Chesapeake Bay,[1] July 6th 1862

M[r] President,

After having been for three months in the rear of the army of the Potomac, superintending the business with it, of the Sanitary Commission, I have just spent a day in Washington, where I had the honor of conversing with several gentlemen who are your advisors, or in your confidence.[2] What I learned of the calculations, views and feelings prevailing among them, causes with me great apprehension.

In the general gloom, there are two points of consolation and hope, which grow brighter and brighter,—opening my eyes suddenly, as I seem to have done, in the point of view of Washington, I may see these and their value, more clearly than those about you. One, is the trustworthy, patriotic devotion of the solid, industrious, home-keeping people of the country; the other, the love and confidence constantly growing stronger, between these people and their president.

Here is the key to a vast reserved strength, and in this rests our last hope for our country.

Appeal personally to the people, M[r] President,—Abraham Lincoln to the men and women who will believe him, and the North will surge with a new strength against which the enemy will not dare advance. Then, can not fifty thousand men, now doing police and garrison duty, possibly be drawn off with safety, and sent within a month to M[c]Clellan? Add these to his present seven times tried force and he can strike a blow which will destroy all hope of organized armed resistance to the Law. Without these, the best army the world ever saw must lie idle, and, in discouragement and dejection, be wasted by disease.

393

I am, Mr. President, most Respectfully, Your obt. servant,

Fred. Law Olmsted.
General Secretary
San. Com.

Abraham Lincoln,
President of the United States.

The original is in the Abraham Lincoln Papers, Library of Congress, Washington, D.C. The heading, salutation, and text are in a copyist's hand, the closing, signature, and address in that of Olmsted. During his visit to Washington, Olmsted was unable to see the president. Anxious to express his views, he addressed this letter to Lincoln, sent it to Bache, and wrote: "I feel more and more that he is the man to bring us right if anyone. I have very slim excuse for addressing him a letter, but if you think it will do, perhaps you will think it worth while to give yourself the trouble to send the enclosed so that it will be likely to reach him." Lincoln's visit to the Army of the Potomac in early July greatly cheered Bache, but he decided to forward the letter. He described it to John G. Nicolay, the president's private secretary, as "showing the ideas of a true hearted loyal man whose time & talents are given up to the country" and requested him, "Will you with your knowledge & tact decide the question & if you agree with me present Mr. Olmsted's letter to the President at a suitable time" (FLO to A. D. Bache, July 8, 1862, William Jones Rhees Collection, Henry E. Huntington Library and Museum, San Marino, Ca.; A. D. Bache to J. G. Nicolay, July 11, 1862, Abraham Lincoln Papers, Library of Congress, Washington, D.C.).

1. Olmsted was en route from Washington to the Virginia Peninsula.
2. During his visit to Washington on July 5, Olmsted, aided by A. D. Bache, attempted to influence several men holding high governmental posts. He talked with Peter H. Watson, assistant secretary of war; Gustavus Vasa Fox, assistant secretary of the navy; Montgomery C. Blair, postmaster general; and Montgomery C. Meigs, quartermaster general of the army. These officials were not favorably impressed, and Bache described Olmsted as "in depressed spirits at the little impression he had made of the necessities of the case" (FLO to HWB, July 5, 1862, USSC-NYPL, box 744: 1894; A. D. Bache to HWB, July 7, 1862, USSC-NYPL, box 638).

To Henry Whitney Bellows

Berkeley—Harrison's landing—
James River. July 7th 1862.

My Dear Doctor,

We arrived here at 10 A.M. today, not having stopped except in the river, a few hours after moon setting last night, after coaling at Alexandria.

JONATHAN LETTERMAN AND HIS STAFF

We were warned by a gun-boat that the rebels had artillery opposite Wind-mill point but ran by without a shot; the Juniata[1] which preceded us received several. I studied the shores very carefully, and could see easily enough that the gun-boats would have their hands full to keep the river open. In fact I do not see how they can do it—and the honest truth is I do not believe they will. No more ladies or female nurses should be sent here. I have just learned that the Arrowsmith[2] which followed us received ten bullets from rifles fired simultaneously from both banks. I have been ashore and visited Head Quarters. Reaction from the excitement of last week is apparent; the guards march with their eyes on the ground, and there is general grumbling and criticism. Many officers are behaving shamefully, having an irresistable desire to go home, like that we witnessed after Bull Run with the men. They sneak or bully their way onto the hospital boats and disguise themselves, hide, and lie, and when confronted and threatened say plainly that they don't care for their commissions, they care for nothing, they want to go home at the price of anything and everything. This is Vollum's[3] report. Gen. Williams said that if the exodus of officers on sick leave continued at the rate of today, there would be none left in a week or two.

The wounded have been mainly sent away; a sick camp is being started with considerable enterprise and Dr Letterman takes hold vigorously. But as I anticipated, no attention is given to police of camp, and already at 1000 feet from the shore, we have the smell of a sewer opening wafted to us. Within 150 feet of McClellan's Head Quarters there is a small swamp to which thousands, literally, must already have resorted and from which the smell is frightful. There is, I am afraid, a good deal of marshy land within the lines, from the surface of which the water has just disappeared.

Oh! I do so hope the army will not remain here—it will be destroyed morally and physically. If 50,000 men cannot be already seen on their way here, I would far rather see it return to Washington than remain here a week. There ought to be no delay in accepting this alternative at Washington. Recall or reinforce, at once.

Nothing is heard of the enemy, he has strong pickets and picket reserves but does not show in force. Is he bound for Washington?

I think that no considerable number of sick or wounded will be sent from here for some time.

All our company seem pretty well. I think that I seem to be the least vigorous, and there's not much wrong with me except excessive indolence of brain & body. The slightest exertion tires me "ridiclus."[4] It is very hot. Ther'o. 96° & calm, on the river.

Yours Cordially & Respectfully

Fred. Law Olmsted.

The original is letter 1836 in box 744 of USSC-NYPL.

1. A 231-ton side-wheel steamer built in 1848 (W. M. Lytle and F. R. Holdcamper, *Merchant Steam Vessels*, p. 118).
2. Capable of transporting 750 uninjured soldiers, the *Arrowsmith* served as a hospital steamer under the command of Dr. Edward P. Vollum of the Medical Bureau (*O.R.*, ser. 1, vol. 11, pt. 3, p. 262; E. P. Vollum to FLO, March 3, 1890).
3. Edward P. Vollum.
4. Probably an attempt to render a Southern pronunciation of "ridiculous."

To Preston King

Office of the Sanitary Commission,
Army of the Potomac, Berkely,
James River, July 9th 1862.

My Dear Sir,

As one of your constituents, observing this army from a peculiar point of view, may I tell you what I think of the duty of government to it?

If it remains here, the usual dangers of crowded encampments in a hot and malarious climate being aggravated by disappointment, idleness and home-sickness from hope of home hopelessly deferred, it will lose half its value. And its value as an army, culled by hardship and disease of its weaker constituents, and disciplined and trained by three months' advance in the face of a strong, vigilant, watchful, wiley and vindictive enemy, is at the present market price of soldiers fully equal to its enormous cost. By one means or another, government must save and use it. To this end the army of the Potomac should be withdrawn, at once, entirely from James river or it should be so rapidly and constantly strengthened that the men will have the utmost confidence that in a month at furthest, they will [be] able to advance on Richmond with certainty of success. For this purpose 50,000 men in regiments already disciplined should be transferred here from localities which can be abandoned, where they can be dispensed with, or where raw regiments will be able to safely supply their place, and thirty thousand men should be added to the regiments already here and greatly reduced in force by losses in battle.

The latter should be carefully inspected sturdy conscripts.

Conscription would greatly hasten volunteering. It would force a large class of men to serve the country in the only way they can be effectually made to do so. It would not withdraw men from their usual pursuits who are of more value to the community in those pursuits than they would be in the ranks, because the measure of their value is their earnings and these must be sufficient to enable them to enter successfully into competition with government in offering premiums for volunteers—as substitutes.[1]

Thirty thousand fresh men, each placed between two veteran volunteers, three weeks hence, would add greatly to its strength and diminish but imperceptibly its mobility and efficiency. They would be welcomed by the volunteers because they would bring to each regiment so much relief in guard and fatigue duties.

The chief objection to conscription will be the supposed appearance of weakness which it will exhibit to foreign powers. Does not hesitation to adopt conscription at a crisis like this, illustrate and demonstrate an

397

essential weakness in our form of government for purposes of war, which already is overestimated, and much to our damage and danger abroad?

Will it be wholly unpopular? It will convince the people that their government is in downright earnest in its purpose to overcome the rebellion whatever it costs, and that it realizes the fact—spite of the vain-glorious boastings of its newspapers, its orators and its generals—that this is not to be accomplished by ordinary small politicians' small politics, nor without a sacrifice which every citizen, patriotic or otherwise, must have a part in. Whatever does this, in my judgment, will be popular.

Yours Most respectfully,

Fred. Law Olmsted.

Hon. Preston King.

The original is in the Abraham Lincoln Papers, Library of Congress, Washington, D.C. After reading this letter, Preston King forwarded it to Abraham Lincoln and wrote Olmsted, "I think the Government has determined to act with vigor and energy and promptly—What you say is so just and reasonable that the simple statement is stronger than argument—" (P. King to FLO, July 14, 1862, USSC-NYPL, box 743: 1508).

1. At the time Olmsted wrote this letter, the individual states which had carried on recruiting had encountered serious problems in attracting soldiers. Each state had prepared its own laws offering bonuses for enlistments and allowing the purchase of substitutes by men otherwise subject to military service. The central government took a large step toward national conscription in mid-July 1862 when it assigned each state, based upon its population, a quota of soldiers it must supply to the government. That Olmsted addressed his letter to his senator rather than a state official suggests that he envisioned an even larger role for the central government in conscription than the new laws provided (Fred Albert Shannon, *The Organization and Administration of the Union Army, 1861–1865*, 2 vols. [1928; rpt. ed., Gloucester, Mass., 1965], 1: 271–76, 281–86, 291–92).

To Sydney Howard Gay[1]

Berkeley, July 12th 1862.

My Dear Gay,
(as if he had an impersonal responsibility
for the Tribune:)

You will recollect the last conversation I had with you perhaps—four or five months ago in the Tribune Office, just after the evacuation of

Manassas.[2] It was the last time that I was in New York, and I went to all my friends who were pushing on the Secretary of War, and undermining Mc-Clellan, to relieve my own uneasiness by a quiet and modest remonstrance mainly addressed to the assertion that it was impossible to suppose that any sufficient apology or justification could be found for the dilatoriness of the McClellan policy. I imagined a possible plan of a campaign, by which I conceived that everything to which you objected so strongly and confidently might be explained and justified. I see now, as I think, that my hypothetical plan had been *the* plan, and I see that had it not been for the precipitation at the West, for which I have reason to believe Pope to have been responsible as the secret & indirect adviser of the government—and the subsequent sub-division of McClellan's reduced command, it would long before this have brought the organized armed rebellion to an end.[3] If you recollect what that hypothesis of the proposed campaign was, I think that you, with the experience we have had, will agree with me, that it would almost certainly have been successful, comprehensively and completely so.

I have not the slightest amount of hero-worship for McClellan— he does not seem to me to be a great man, but his plan of conducting the war, has from his first taking hold commended itself to my instinct thoroughly, while your policy, as opposed to it, has always seemed to me unsound, reckless, careless, and in the highest degree, hazardous and expensive. I don't think you have treated him, I'm sure you have not treated his policy, fairly. I don't think you are treating him, or his policy fairly now. I think you are prejudiced and under the influence of prejudice are going on, making and sustaining and nourishing terrible, fatal mistakes. I am devoted to the same ends that you (Tribuners) are, my prejudices should disassociate me from those you oppose and hold me to you. You know that I am an honest man and no fool, and you may guess that I write to you in the bitterest sadness, simply again to make my one individual protest against the policy which you have helped to form, still sustain, defend and apologize for, and the responsible (morally between you & I) head of which you are trying to bolster up yet again in his war-horse saddle.[4]

I have not any hypothesis about Stanton. I know that he is the meanest kind of small, cunning, short sighted, selfish politician, that he is the worst kind of a hypocrite, that he trades in prayer and devotion and is habitually the grossest possible blasphemer; that he is a bully and a liar. He is, I judge, a political confidence-man, a black-leg of large stakes, an imposter,—but no matter about judgments—what I say I know of him, I know, mainly from personal experience—all at not further than second-hand, and such a hand as Dr Bellows[5] or equally as responsible [a] man. I believe him capable of any crime even of deliberately plotting the destruction of the republic with a view of his personal elevation upon its ruins. Ah, well, you don't know him, and you don't think so, and I can't help it.

I can't often get a Tribune nowadays, the newsboys have had nothing here for a week but the accursed Herald,[6] but tonight, I got Thursday's of a friend, and I can't read the article on Stanton[7] and rest easy without bearing my testimony against him, to your private ear—not but that I would gladly say it publickly & stand by it if it were worth anything. Am I so intolerably prejudiced or are you? All I can say is, I am conscious of no prejudice against you, but the contrary, yet I see nothing but special pleading & quibbling in your argument, and when I have read it all, I go back and read the quotation from the World[8] and I declare, it is to me, in a broad sense, justice & truth. I trust in God it will prevail. As to the minor question which you so confidently settle in these words: "We know not who is responsible for the grave mistake involved in the approach to Richmond by way of Yorktown rather than the Rappahannock—but this has not ever been charged upon Secy Stanton," I beg to assure you that I most fully believe that Secy Stanton is responsible for that mistake and that, when the proper time comes, he will be charged with & convicted of it.[9] I sincerely hope he will be hanged for it, if a hangman's rope is necessary to swing him out of office and into the infamy I know he deserves.

With sincere respect & regard.

Fred. Law Olmsted.

Sydney Gay.

The original is in the Sydney Howard Gay Papers, Rare Book and Manuscript Library, Columbia University, New York City.

1. Sydney Howard Gay (1814–1888) was managing editor of the *New-York Daily Tribune* from April 1862 until 1866. A steadfast opponent of slavery, he had been a lecture agent for the American Antislavery Society and had edited the *National Anti-slavery Standard* for over ten years. Gay later became managing editor of the *Chicago Tribune* (NCAB; DAB).

2. The Confederates retreated from Manassas in early March 1862. Olmsted was in New York City from March 20 until April 3. Since in a letter of March 25 he mentioned having met with Charles A. Dana, then managing editor of the *New-York Daily Tribune*, most likely he had visited the newspaper office and talked with Gay by that date (See FLO to JO, March 25, 1862, above).

3. Probably a reference to military operations in western Virginia. Olmsted probably considered the Union army's efforts during late May 1862 to entrap and defeat the Confederate army commanded by Thomas J. "Stonewall" Jackson to be precipitous and unwise, especially since they utilized soldiers who might otherwise have reinforced McClellan. Most likely Olmsted also disapproved of the creation on June 26 of the Army of Virginia, commanded by John Pope, to unify what had been the com-

mands of Irvin McDowell, Nathaniel P. Banks, and John C. Frémont (T. H. Williams, *Lincoln and His Generals*, pp. 96–105, 119–21).

4. An allusion to the anti-McClellan and pro-Stanton tone of the *Tribune*'s editorials. The "responsible head" to whom Olmsted here refers is Secretary of War Stanton (J. C. Andrews, *The North Reports the Civil War*, pp. 206–17; see FLO to CLB, June 29, 1862, n. 3, above).

5. On May 13, 1862, Henry W. Bellows recorded in great detail the very unpleasant interview he had had with Stanton the preceding day. Bellows had gone to the secretary of war's office to urge the immediate appointment of inspectors as provided in the recently enacted legislation reorganizing the Medical Bureau. He questioned the reason for the delay and also reminded Stanton that the Sanitary Commission had sent a list of the men it considered best qualified for the new positions. Stanton's answer to these importunings was that he could not be thus harangued, the government would act when it was ready, and he saw no reason for the Sanitary Commission to be concerned in the matter. Bellows then recalled the Commission's role in passing the reorganization act and received the same reply: that the government would act at the proper time. Bellows disliked Stanton's answers but especially resented what he perceived as a lack of respect shown toward himself (HWB to William H. Van Buren, May 13, 1862, Henry Whitney Bellows Papers, Massachusetts Historical Society, Boston, Mass.).

6. The sensationalistic *New York Herald*, published by James Gordon Bennett, tended to support Democratic politics. Olmsted also had special reason for disliking the newspaper: it had frequently criticized Central Park and had endorsed the changes in the park's plan that Commissioners August Belmont and Robert J. Dillon had unsuccessfully proposed. In 1860 Olmsted had characterized one such unfavorable piece as an example of the *Herald*'s "peculiar playful slang-whang articles" (*Papers of FLO*, 3: 24, 193–99, 259, 267).

7. The *Tribune* article of July 10 defended Stanton from charges that he deliberately divided the command of troops in Virginia to withhold reinforcements from McClellan. That division, according to the editorial, by necessity sprang from the plan to capture Richmond using the Peninsula as a base rather than using the overland route from Washington, D.C., via Fredericksburg ("Secretary Stanton," *New-York Daily Tribune*, July 10, 1862, p. 4).

8. The *Tribune* article quoted a long section from an editorial of the *New York World* which argued that many people believed Stanton had intrigued against McClellan and that the withholding of necessary reinforcements from the general was evidence of such a plot. The *World* then called for Stanton's resignation or removal ("Secretary Stanton," *New-York Daily Tribune*, July 10, 1862, p. 4).

9. Apparently Olmsted is arguing here that McClellan retained his base on the Peninsula only because McDowell's army, stationed in late May at Fredericksburg on the Rappahannock River, was ordered to move to the Shenandoah Valley rather than toward Richmond via Urbanna to reinforce McClellan. In the clearest statement of this position, Olmsted told Charles Loring Brace in August:

> Upon the question you put—"Is not the great fault of the campaign—the making of the peninsula the base—his? (McClellan's)" I answer, no. I am convinced it is Stanton's. That is, if McC.'s plan of landing all of McDowell's corps at Urbanna, marching it across to West Point & then cutting off the enemies' peninsula army from its base, had been carried out, it would not have been a mistake.

Olmsted believed Stanton responsible for this decision not to send McDowell to reinforce McClellan, even though the order was actually given by Lincoln (T. H. Williams, *Lincoln and His Generals*, pp. 92–101; FLO to CLB, Aug. 25, 1862, below).

To Henry Whitney Bellows

Berkeley, James River,
July 13th 1862.

My Dear Doctor,

To what work does the raising of 300,000 new troops call the Commission?

Can we, in the first place, do anything to aid and hasten recruiting—not as the Sanitary Commission but as patriots using the organization of the Commission? For there are, to my mind, just two things to which every patriot should address himself and to which he should devote every opportunity he possesses by which he [can] accomplish anything—1st the deposition of [the] canting imposter who is Secretary of War; 2d the effective reinforcement of the army. If we could help to hang Stanton by resigning & posting him as a liar, hypocrite and knave, I think we should render the country a far greater service than we can in any other way—save more lives than we can in any other way. Think of the first time we saw him with McClellan; what a business he made of taking us in.[1] Do you doubt that ten times more he made a business of taking in McClellan,—that he makes a business of taking in the President—the abolitionists,—the country? I really doubt if we could serve the country better than by calmly stating the conclusions to which our intercourse with him has led us. By the way, Mr. President, would it be in order for me to withdraw my apology for having expressed the conviction, at a meeting at Dr Van Buren's, that his devout letter to the Tribune[2] was a piece of outrageous cant, justifying an approach to profanity, when referred to reverentially before a man with an empty stomach? If so, I would move the reading of the said letter before supper, and that a vote of reverence be taken upon it.

As to the second point, I have written to Mrs Griffin, on the Euterpe[3] at Old Point, suggesting that the good women (Woman's Central, as a centre,) might perhaps publish a request to the shop-keepers and others to send their "young men" to the war, employing young women instead.[4] If the women took hold of this in the smaller towns, where competition is excessive, and everybody knows everything of everybody, I think it would set free several thousand men, but chiefly it would aid in developing a healthy public sentiment, shaming those who staid at home, and leading on to other devices for encouragement of enlistment and the discouragement of furloughs, desertions & lukewarmness. The public sentiment is shamefully and dangerously low, I fear. The desperation of some of the officers here in their attempts to go home, their contemptuous disregard of appeals to their honor or their fear of punishment, and their evident confidence that political influence will relieve them of any danger, has sometimes been melancholy. Can we with advantage urge our associates and contributors to aid in working up a more vigorous public opinion?

Shall we, through our associates endeavor to secure more thorough inspection of recruits,—by inspectors, or by correspondence with officers civil & military—or shall we only suggest this to the Sgn General? All former attempts to do anything through our associates have completely failed of their object but have seldom failed to get us into hot water.[5]

Either by ourselves, or the Sgn General or both, advice to officers as to their administrative & parental duties, based on experience of the war, should be given. Instructions to surgeons as to matters of Red Tape, should be given by Hammond, & soon, without fail.

I am inclined to think we should reserve our "relief," hereafter, for the new regiments, assuming that the older surgeons & Q. Masters have learned their business & have complete & sufficient organization. If they have not, demand that they have.

The Surgn General should be induced to request the good people not to encumber the new regiments with loads of useless or unnecessary stores; stating what they can get from government and how much better it is to trust the Sanitary Commission—if we are going to be necessary.

Yours Very Respectfully

Fred. Law Olmsted.

The original is letter 1882 in box 744 of USSC-NYPL. A letterpress copy is on pages 28–33 of Olmsted's private letterbook.

1. The meeting of January 22, 1862, soon after Stanton had been confirmed as secretary of war (see FLO to Bertha Olmsted, Jan. 28, 1862, above).
2. Most likely a reference to the letter that Stanton wrote to the *New-York Daily Tribune* on February 19 after the newspapers had ascribed the Union triumphs at Forts Henry and Donelson to his achievements in revitalizing the War Department. He argued in that letter, published the following day, that the "glories" of those battles belonged to the soldiers who had fought them. In the section that probably especially disgusted Olmsted, Stanton questioned how any leader could successfully organize for victory, and then continued:

> We owe our recent victories to the spirit of the Lord that moved our soldiers to rush into battle and filled the hearts of our enemies with dismay. The inspiration that conquered in battle was in the hearts of the soldiers and from on high; and wherever there is the same inspiration there will be the same results. . . . We may well rejoice at recent victories, for they teach us that battles are to be won now by us in the same and only manner that they were won by any people, or in any age, since the days of Joshua—by boldly pursuing and striking the foe.

Olmsted was in New York at the time this letter appeared in print, and he criticized it at an informal meeting of the Commission (Frank Abial Flower, *Edwin McMasters Stanton, the Autocrat of Rebellion, Emancipation, and Reconstruction* . . . [Akron, Ohio, 1905], pp. 129–30).

3. The *Euterpe*, like the *St. Mark*, was a new clipper ship fitted up as a model hospital ship by the Sanitary Commission. Because the Pamunkey River was too shallow to accommodate it, the *Euterpe* lay at anchor at Yorktown between its trips to New York (*Hospital Transports*, p. 132).

4. On July 12, 1862, Olmsted had written Christine Kean Griffin:

> Would it not help to two good ends if a few hundred good women of New York should address a public letter to the shopkeepers, mechanics, manufac-turers and merchants, requesting them to send their young men to the war and to employ young women, as much as possible in their place? Would not the many disadvantages of this substitution, so far as it would be at all likely to be influenced by such a proceeding, be fully compensated? It is not in shops with which ladies deal that the gravest objection to the employment of girls is strongest. Young women are not as good shop-attendants as young men, but they will answer the purpose, they will cost less, and they will not answer the purpose as would many of the young men whom they would displace, of the country as soldiers. . . . The two best regiments which New York has sent to the war are those which enlisted the largest number of this class, the Fifth and the Ninth.

Christine Griffin replied that she highly approved of Olmsted's plan and would arrange for it to be proposed at the next meeting of the W.C.A.R. (FLO to C. K. Griffin, July 12, 1862; C. K. Griffin to FLO, n.d. [c. July–Aug. 1862]).

5. Olmsted refers to such earlier efforts as the New York associates' campaign in January 1862 to bring pressure upon the secretary of war to reform the Medical Bureau and the lobbying by Philadelphia associates to convince McClellan to issue a general order giving increased recognition to Sanitary Commission inspectors (FLO to JSN, Jan. 15, 1862, nn. 1 and 7, above; FLO to HWB, Feb. 7, 1862, nn. 5 and 7, above).

To HENRY WHITNEY BELLOWS

Berkeley, James River,
July 13th 1862.

My Dear Doctor,

I am quite sure that our special transport service no longer pays what it costs, and that our position is not a dignified one. The Medical Department is either adverse to our work—to our having any active part in its business or the business of providing for the sick and wounded of the army, or it is not treating us with proper respect. I have repeatedly inti-mated to you that these convictions were growing in my mind; they are now dead ripe. The thought, labor and money which you have bestowed on the St Mark and the Euterpe, have thus far met with not the smallest reward. All our labor and pains for the transport service for the last month has been of questionable utility. The results of our experience should be of the greatest value to the Bureau; they are in a great measure, thrown away. I see no reason for and no evidence of an unfriendly or disrespectful disposition toward us and am inclined to infer that it is not practicable for government agents, in the tumult and occupation of war, to avail themselves of assistance and instruction offered by anyone to whom they are not officially responsible. Whatever the reason, the fact is established in my mind, that we have utterly failed in the purpose which has been uppermost in my mind, in our work of the last four months in these waters, the substantial building up of a good hospital transport system for the army. I see no reason why the sick and wounded should be removed with any less assured comfort and safety than they are, if a week ago all the past had been brushed away. Anything lacking which is now had, would I am sure be evidence of gross incompetency or carelessness—would have been so six months ago.

Our own vessels are exceptional. Are they valued by government? We are flattered a good deal, but my belief is that no man wearing shoulder straps who knows anything about them wouldn't be glad never to hear of them again. If any discrimination is made between them and the slipshod government transports, it never indicates a preference for employing them. It is a constant struggle to get an opportunity to make them useful. The reason is obvious. You will not use another man's horse when you have your own ready saddled. And if your neighbor presses his horse upon you, he will soon be regarded as a bore. He will be avoided until his horse is really very much wanted and then you will take him with a determination to drive him at your own pace and with very little regard to his wishes as to where or how he shall go. Profuse thanks and protestations of profound obligation, no doubt you will offer with sincerity, but you will pick up the whip at the first corner, nevertheless, and will forget to have the wheels greased.

The summer's work has paid splendidly in lives saved and pain alleviated; it is valueable also negatively as indicating what our function is not.[1] But as to improving the service—upon my conscience, I believe the average transport service would be better than it is, if we had never touched it. With Hammond as Surgeon General, Vollum as Inspector and Letterman as Director, I can't think it possible that it would be worse.[2] Do I think it very bad, then? I think there is much that is certainly bad about it, and really nothing that is certainly good. From end to end, it is a slipshod, temporizing business, and I fear that we work with a tendency to keep it so. I know that if I were Surgeon General, there should be no such classification as "Sanitary Transports," and—insanitary? All should be under the same rules and government.

Yours Respectfully,

Fred. Law Olmsted.

The original is in the Frederick Newman Knapp Papers, Massachusetts Historical Society, Boston, Massachusetts.

1. Probably Olmsted meant that the work of the Sanitary Commission was not to perform tasks that the government could and should be undertaking.
2. That is, these three members of the Medical Bureau were so competent that they should be able, at the least, to organize as good a hospital transport service as the Sanitary Commission had provided.

CHAPTER VI

SUSTAINING THE WAR

As Olmsted Returned to supervision of Sanitary Commission affairs late in July 1862, he found both new and old problems awaiting him. During his absence from Washington, affairs at the central office had limped along, and the Executive Committee in New York had begun to assume greater powers. As the New York members became more interested in the routine workings of the Commission, they demanded that Olmsted account to them more completely. Olmsted's chagrin that he could not sum up the Commission's activities at the West because of a dearth of reports from John S. Newberry and his Western agents is evident in the letter of August 21. Similarly, Olmsted's letter of October 3 describes his conception of what his own role on the Commission had been and how the new limits on his discretionary powers would hamper the efficient operation of the Commission. The letter of October 7 to Henry W. Bellows further elaborates Olmsted's ideas of organization and sets forth his notion of what the Executive Committee should and should not be.

As Olmsted grappled with these new questions of the distribution of power within the Sanitary Commission, he resumed work on numerous projects. His letters of September and October indicate his and the Commission's efforts on behalf of an ambulance corps; they also describe the creation of the Commission's hospital directory, a guide that listed the location and condition of hospitalized or recently discharged soldiers. Although the Sanitary Commission had gained the support of Surgeon General Hammond and the Medical Bureau, it still battled against the resistance to change evinced by General-in-Chief Henry W. Halleck and the War Department.

During this period Olmsted retained his interest in the political and military events of the day. This chapter presents both sides of his heated exchange with his old friend Charles Loring Brace in the fall of 1862. The two men debated McClellan's abilities and tactics, the conduct of the Peninsula and Antietam campaigns, and the merits of Republican politicians. These letters as well as those to Henry W. Bellows reveal Olmsted's deep pessimism about the political leadership of the period and the extent of the political commitment to the war. The letters of the early autumn of 1862 also reflect the problems and uncertainties of his personal life. During this entire period his health was precarious. A week at Saratoga Springs in late August removed his worst symptoms, but his writings show how he continued to push himself to the point of exhaustion. The serious illness of his partner in landscape design, Calvert Vaux, described here, added to his worries. Olmsted's letters to his wife discuss his ambivalence about remaining with the Sanitary Commission, while a letter of October 3 to Bellows expresses his relief at his second failure to receive the post of commissioner of streets in New York City. Amid all the perplexities, his sprightly account of a visit to Walpole, New Hampshire, illustrates his continuing interest in landscape design and domestic amenities.

To Mary Perkins Olmsted

Walpole,[1] August 12th 1862

Dear Mary,

I came easily to Springfield, in the mail smoking car, the Sunday passenger cars being full, spent the night quietly at the Hotel by the Station, had a walk on the main St at Springfield in the morning, breakfasted, and then came to Westminster by the train, easily, alone,[2] finding the scenery interesting, the scale being smaller but more fresh and attractive than I had expected. A native farmerig acted as station master at Westminster & brought me to Knapp's house in a one hoss wagging for 30 cts.

Knapp's house is over the river and someway up a hill East of the town. It is a very nice Anglo-Swiss cottage, very dark brown in color, and has an original quality in the roughness of its cottage carpentry—unplaned boards, etc—which is agreeably congruous with the style. It is on a narrow terrace between the road and a ravine, thro' which a little mountain stream, liable to become a deep and furious torrent, ripples most musically

about this profile. There are lots of elms and some other trees with ferns and other small stuff down in the channel of the brooks on the rocks. Over the other side with a bridge & path to get to it, is old Man Knapp's, a brick mansion with an old gentleman near 90 & his wife, farming son & daughter[3]—beyond is Bellows' & a brother in law's house,[4] a comfortable sort of common farm house fixed up by Knapp for him. Knapp's father was his foster father & guardian. All the Bellowses are there & live very comfortably & quietly, only Mrs B[5] bores him with ambitious schemes of doing something with the ground & the garden & he says women never can understand how much these "little things" cost, nor how much it costs to get what they cost, and he don't want to begin, wants to be quiet & careless here, and is right about the ground as it is quite in keeping with the house as it is.

Gibbs[6] came this morning & we had a long session—nothing quite concluded & some talk of telegraphing for other members who are detained by professional duties & sickness. I think I shall go to Washington last of week taking Litchfield[7] on the way.

Your affectionate husband

Fred. Law Olmsted.

Mrs Olmsted.

1. Walpole, where Henry W. Bellows spent his summers, is on the east bank of the Connecticut River in southern New Hampshire.
2. Olmsted's railroad route via Springfield, Massachusetts, and Westminster, Vermont, ran parallel to the Connecticut River.
3. Jacob Newman Knapp (1773–1868) and his wife, Louisa Bellows Knapp (1785–1872), the parents of Frederick N. Knapp and the uncle and aunt of Henry W. Bellows. Jacob, a graduate of Harvard College, had taught school before his move in 1824 to Walpole, where he became a farmer. Olmsted is mistaken, however, about Knapp serving as Bellows's foster father and legal guardian: John Bellows died in 1840, when his son Henry was twenty-six years old. Olmsted's misconception may have arisen from Bellows's accounts of his close relationship to the Knapp family: his Aunt Louisa had cared for two-year-old Henry and his siblings after their mother's death. Moreover, he had spent two years, from age seven until nine, at Jacob Knapp's school.
   The Knapps' only other child was Francis Bellows Knapp (1820–1896), a bachelor who managed their farm. The "daughter" to whom Olmsted refers was

probably Jacob's niece, Susan Knapp (1799–1876), who lived with the family (Thomas Bellows Peck, *The Bellows Genealogy* . . . [Keene, N.H., 1898], pp. 158–63; Walter Donald Kring, *Henry Whitney Bellows* [Boston, 1979], pp. 1–2, 42).

4. Joseph Goldthwaite Dorr (1804–1867) was the husband of Henry W. Bellows's older sister, Eliza Eames Bellows Dorr (1804–1872). In 1855 he took charge of Bellows's farm in Walpole. His family resided in the house all year round, while the Bellows family also lived there during the summers (T. B. Peck, *Bellows Genealogy*, p. 279).

5. Eliza Nevins Townsend Bellows (1818–1869), Henry's wife and the daughter of a wealthy New York merchant (ibid., p. 319).

6. Wolcott Gibbs.

7. Mary Perkins Olmsted and her children were visiting relatives in Hartford, and she and Olmsted planned to meet in Litchfield, Connecticut, where she earlier had been boarding. The children's illness, however, detained her in Hartford, and Olmsted stopped there on August 18 before his return to New York City (FLO to JFJ, Aug. 6, 1862, USSC-NYPL, box 743: 1776; FLO to HWB, Aug. 20, 1862, USSC-NYPL, box 641).

To John Strong Newberry

Washington, August 21st 1862.

My Dear Doctor,

I yesterday received your letter of the 12th inst[t] and hasten to comply with your request to write you "once more before I die". I have been in such a disgusting condition of ill-health for two or three weeks past that unless I get better soon, I think I should prefer to die.[1] I arrived here yesterday, having been North, since I withdrew from my post on the James river. I am confident that my personal superintendence of the Atlantic Transport Service was essential to its success, and it is almost entirely owing to its success that we have now $25000 in our Treasury. Yet I was roasted most cruelly by the Executive Committee because I could give them no definite information about our work in the West.[2] I was obliged to take the ground that I was under no obligations to report to them, that my records were at Washington and in due time would be presented to the Commission. In my general instructions to you for the summer's work I called for specific reports from each inspector to be forwarded to this office weekly or oftener, and more general occasional reports. I am somewhat shocked on arriving here to find not a single report directly or indirectly received from any Western Inspector since February 7th, nor anything like a comprehensive report even from yourself since May last. You will remember I wrote you shortly before I went to Yorktown entreating

410

you to report to me more systematically and explaining the exceedingly embarrassing position in which your neglect to do so placed me, as well as the great loss which it occasioned to the Commission.[3] I hold myself primarily responsible to the Commission for the doings or the non-doings of all who are in its employment. I hold you primarily answerable to me for all employed in your department. I must answer to the Commission, you must answer to me; your inspectors and agents must answer to you. That is the theory of our organization. We need not be inconveniently nice about it, but it certainly ought not to be suspended for months altogether. Your "very grumbling letter to Dr Bellows,"[4] of which you were good enough to send me a copy, perhaps explains all this, but as the copy has not reached me I can't help feeling as if the West had seceded and that I may be looked upon as having played the part of Buchanan.[5] Moreover, if any part of my official duty to you has been neglected I think you should have informed me personally. I have been obliged to perform most of the duties of my office by deputy. A special provision was made at the outset of our work to enable me to do so.[6] You could have no cause of complaint if I availed myself of it and if my arrangments failed to accomplish their purpose and you suffered any embarrassment in consequence, I think official duty as well as friendship should have led you to advise me of it, before going to the President. But no neglect on the part of this office relieves you from your responsibility to it.

I don't doubt that there are good and sufficient reasons for your not reporting, or forwarding reports from the inspectors, but if so, I ought to have been informed of them before this, so that I, in my turn, could satisfactorily account to the President or Executive Committee for the inability of this office to report of the work of the Commission at the West.

I have fully and frankly showed you how I look at it because if there is any difference between us, it either arises from some mistake of one of us or it is an honest difference. In either case, it ought to be cleared up and settled. Whether I was bound to meet the demand of the Executive Committee or not, I am to blame for not being *able* to meet it at very short notice. Have I not a right to blame you that I am not so?

I telegraphed you from Walpole, when the Committee met, to send me before 1st Sep. all the materials I should require from the West, for a general review or report of all the summer's work of the Commission and its auxiliaries. The Commission will meet here on the 16th September.

Most of our force in the East has been ill lately. Bloor has been off duty for a month & is now at the North convalescing. Jenkins has been ill but is now fairly well. I have not been very seriously ill, but for some time in a half nauseated condition, with frequent sick headache &c. Jenkins is going [to] put me in dry-dock tonight & treat me with mercury.

411

The Surgn Genl is doing well. We have not much confidence in Pope,[7] and await the shock of the gathering hosts on the Rapidan with much anxiety.

Yours Very Cordially

Fred. Law Olmsted.

D[r] Newberry.

The original is letter 44 in box 914 of USSC-NYPL.

1. Olmsted's physical condition was steadily deteriorating. Approximately one week later he traveled to Saratoga Springs, New York, with Dr. Cornelius R. Agnew to recoup his health. At that time Olmsted described his appearance:

> I grew daily more yellow, until I could have passed for rather a dark mulatto; the whites of my eyes gave place to a queer glistening saffron colored substance, and my skin became flabby leather, dry and dead. I itched furiously and where I plowed the surface with my fingerends, it presently became purple, and a purple maculation began to grow on my arms. A little exertion or excitement shook me so that my voice trembled. (FLO to MPO, August [30], 1862.)

2. The Executive Committee presumably reprimanded Olmsted during a three-day meeting in late July because the central office in Washington had not been receiving regular reports from John S. Newberry. The committee then expected Olmsted to obtain the necessary information from Newberry and to report at the September meeting of the Commission on the general work as well as on the activities on the Virginia Peninsula (FLO to JFJ, Aug. 6, 1862, USSC-NYPL, box 743: 1776; HWB to C. R. Agnew, W. H. Van Buren, and GTS, Aug. 13, 1862, USSC-NYPL, box 638).
3. See FLO to JSN, April 18, 1862, above.
4. This letter, which apparently has not survived, probably complained about a lack of instructions and aid from the central office during the summer of 1862.
5. A reference to the failure of President James Buchanan to intervene against seceding Southern states during the winter of 1860–61.
6. That is, Olmsted delegated the duties of his office as general secretary to his subordinate, Associate Secretary J. Foster Jenkins. When Jenkins joined Olmsted on the Peninsula, the position went virtually unfilled.
7. John Pope (1822–1892), a graduate of West Point who during the war had won distinction in its Western theater. In June 1862 Lincoln appointed Pope to command the newly created Army of Virginia. At the time this letter was written, Pope had begun to retreat behind the Rappahannock River, and Confederate forces under Robert E. Lee and Thomas J. "Stonewall" Jackson were assembling along the Rapidan River to the south (DAB; War for the Union, 2: 171–76).

To Charles Loring Brace

Washington, Aug. 25th 1862

My Dear Charley,

I came back to Washington last week; I have been ill, and still am far from well, being very deeply jaundiced, but avoiding acute illness by every dodge to which with the best medical advice, I can from hour to hour, resort.

In looking over my trunk full of postponed letters, I find yours of July 9th in which you ask me for the grounds of my strong judgment of Stanton. They are chiefly personal. I mean that my personal intercourse with him leaves me with a strong "instinctive" conviction that he is a bad man, a coward, a bully and a swindler. My judgment of the facts of his dealing with McClellan, agree with those of the enclosed paper from "the World" which I only just now met with.[1]

Upon the question you put—"Is not the great fault of the campaign—the making the peninsula the base—his? (McClellan's)" I answer, no. I am convinced it is Stanton's. That is, if McC.'s plan of landing all of McDowell's corps at Urbanna, marching it across to West Point & then cutting off the enemies' peninsula army from its base, had been carried out, it would not have been a mistake. I have lost my respect for Lincoln since he assumes the responsibility of the order which prevented that.[2] Whoever is responsible for that ought to be hanged, it seems to me.

McClellan is not a Napoleon and he has the great merit of not thinking himself a Napoleon. He has got to be successful, if at all, by wise and considerate action, not by audacity or strokes of genius. If you like to have very common intellects undertake to fight in the method of very great military geniuses, I commend you to Pope. But Pope is said to have always been a notorious liar, as well as profligate ass. He and Fremont bear the worst reputations of all men who have been in the army and escaped being kicked out with official infamy by a court-martial, and there is no doubt in the mind of any regular officer I know, that Fremont would have been if Benton had not intrigued to save him.[3] I believe them both to be great scoundrels, intriguers, just fit to plan with Stanton.

We have not any genius. We may hope, but we have no right to expect to succeed by genius. What we want is conscientious, *industrious*, *studious* men, who will do their duty, carefully, thoroughly. We want them in all ranks and this is our great want, our most urgent want. The inefficiency, the want of men who can be depended upon to be energetic and thorough in the execution of any trust committed to them, is the appalling circumstance of our case. It is equally apparent in all departments. I see it most directly in surgeons & chaplains, but I also see it in sergeants &

captains & colonels and Generals. Men with great responsibilities are careless about them, will not take the trouble—apparently can not—[to] study carefully & thoroughly how they can be best executed, but *get along somehow & guess it will do*. Damn them. *Guess it will do* when the life of the nation & much more may depend on it. I have seen hundreds of lives lost which would have been saved by half as much expenditure of brain-power as would be needed to comprehend the simplest problem of Euclid. What is our Educational System worth, if this is the result? But the worst of all are these lazy loafers trained in your Theological seminaries. They could not step out of their ruts to save their own lives. Our strength & merit is cheerful or sullen endurance. In stupid British, blind lumbering momentum we beat the British themselves. By the way, why do you not come as a chaplain? It seems exactly what you have always wanted & you could be immensely useful.

Let me hear from you.

My love to Letitia.

Yours affectionately

Fred. Law Olmsted

1. Olmsted may be referring to an editorial in the *New York World* of July 7 which was highly critical of Stanton. Calling for the dismissal of the secretary of war, the article blamed all McClellan's failures upon Stanton's decisions. The removal of McClellan from his position as commander in chief of the Union armies at the beginning of the Peninsula campaign, the editorialist argued, had undermined the general's ability to launch a fully coordinated attack. Moreover, Stanton had further wronged McClellan, first by failing to provide the necessary troops and later by refusing to send essential reinforcements. In consequence, his army was almost overwhelmed by a Confederate force allegedly twice or thrice its size ("A New War Secretary," *New York World*, July 7, 1862, p. 4).

2. On May 24, 1862, Lincoln suspended an earlier order for Irvin McDowell's troops to reinforce McClellan's army on the Peninsula. Stanton came under increasing criticism during the summer of 1862, and on August 9 Lincoln claimed responsibility for the withholding of reinforcements from McClellan (Benjamin P. Thomas and Harold M. Hyman, *Stanton: The Life and Times of Lincoln's Secretary of War* [New York, 1962], pp. 213–14; T. Harry Williams, *Lincoln and His Generals* [New York, 1952], pp. 95–98; see FLO to Sydney H. Gay, July 12, 1862, n. 9, above).

3. A reference to the sensational court-martial of John C. Frémont in 1847 and early 1848. Frémont, aided by his father-in-law, Sen. Thomas Hart Benton of Missouri, had demanded a trial after his clash with Gen. Stephen W. Kearny in California. The dispute originated from vague orders and centered about whether Kearny or Commodore R. F. Stockton of the U.S. Navy was Frémont's rightful superior there. The charges against Frémont, who had defied Kearny's orders, were mutiny, disobedience to lawful command, and conduct prejudicial to good order. Although the court-martial, in January 1848, found Frémont to be guilty of all three charges, President James K. Polk declared that he believed Frémont innocent of mutiny (though guilty

of the other offenses) and remitted the penalty of dismissal from the army. Frémont then resigned his commission (Allan Nevins, *Frémont, Pathmarker of the West*, 2nd ed. [New York, 1955], pp. 305–42).

Charles Loring Brace to Frederick Law Olmsted

Hastings on the Hudson[1]
Friday Sept 12 [1862]

My dear Fred,

I was so much struck with your last of Aug 23[d2] that I sent it to Howard Potter,[3] who liked it so much that he asked permission to show portions of it to Mr James Brown[4]—the last thoughts on *Thoroughness vs. Genius* have got into print.[5]

I am glad there is one honest well-informed man who believes in Gen McLellan. It is a ray of light at this midnight. Since I wrote you, Chandler's *expose*[6] & the course of events have made up my mind on him. I believe his honest constitutional well-intentioned defects have nearly broken the heart of this Nation. It is Caution become a chain or a nightmare.

What has been, will be. Such a man never can beat those fiery rebels—& they would play all around him.

But now, if we get the right accounts, he acted most disgracefully & wickedly in not helping with more re-inforcements Pope's army, & in forcing himself by military influence & power on the Pres't for Commander in Chief in the field.[7]

I hoped a year ago for the boundary of the Potomac, the Mts of W. Va, Ken. & Tenn. & the Mississ. River. Now I think Jeff Davis will proclaim himself Pres't of the U.S. at Harrisburg![8]—& we shall have a chaotic war—& a devilish pro-slavery McLellan compromise party, trying to patch up—and all other forms of infernal evil. *If* only Washington could be taken & Lincoln, Halleck & McLellan carried off south, then we might find a Leader.

The last days of the Republic are near. The popular mind would prefer a tyrant like Andrew Jackson, who could carry us through, to the President, as he is.

But to be delivered up to military dictatorship as we are now—& that of such a weak & cautious kind that success *never* can follow it!

Stanton is rousing against himself deep & bitter hate for his causeless & atrocious attacks on civil liberties.[9]

415

We have passed hope here—hope in leaders.

Nothing but a divine *ictus*[10] can save us.

Do tell me your impressions about the slaves. Have they not behaved better than you thought?—more discreetly & christianly.

Can they ever be used for us—do you think?

What is your outlook for the future of the Republic?

We are truly rejoiced that you still keep well, for it must have been a most perilous & arduous task you have had.

You drop a hint about a Chaplain. Can you tell me what Chaplains do? Is there really much chance for moral influence? I should not like to leave our charities or a good position for putting muscle in the Times which I have,[11] without some very definite & some range of good. Can a Chaplain do much sanitarily. Is he not a tool of the Colonel? Letitia remains in the Adirond. Mts to improve health.

Yours affectionately

C. L. Brace

Keep this Letter of Allen's[12] as long as you like.

1. The town in which Brace lived. Hastings lay on the Hudson River, north of Yonkers, in Westchester County, New York. After the Civil War, Olmsted and Calvert Vaux drew up a plan for a suburban community to be located there (see Jacob Weidenmann, *Victorian Landscape Gardening: A Facsimile of Jacob Weidenmann's Beautifying Country Homes. With a New Introduction by David Schuyler* [Watkins Glen, N.Y., 1978], plate 19).
2. Brace is mistakenly citing the date of Olmsted's letter of August 25 (see FLO to CLB, Aug. 25, 1862, above).
3. Howard Potter (1826–1897), lawyer and banker. The son of Alonzo Potter, Episcopal bishop of Pennsylvania, Howard had married a daughter of the wealthy banker James Brown. Potter and Olmsted became friends and cooperated in 1863 in the effort to found the magazine that became the *Nation*. During the 1870s they also collaborated in the fight to protect Niagara (Marguerita Arlina Hamm, *Famous Families of New York: Historical and Biographical Sketches* . . . , 2 vols. [New York, 1902], 2: 56; "Howard Potter Dead," *New York Times*, March 25, 1897, p. 1).
4. James Brown (1791–1877) founded Brown Brothers in 1825 as the New York branch of the Baltimore banking firm Alexander Brown and Sons. He successfully directed Brown Brothers during the Civil War period, steadfastly supporting the Union cause. Active in charities in New York, Brown also contributed generously to churches and the Union Theological Seminary (*DAB*).
5. The editors have been unable to discover the periodical in which this excerpt from Olmsted's letter of August 25 was published.
6. A reference to the speech by Zachariah Chandler (1813–1879) of Michigan in the U.S. Senate on July 16, 1862. The Joint Committee on the Conduct of the War, of which Chandler was a member, had voted the previous day to allow the testimony given before it in secret session to be made public. Chandler, a Radical Republican

and ardent opponent of Southern secession, used that testimony as evidence in a stinging attack upon McClellan's abilities as a general. The senator criticized Mc-Clellan's inaction during the winter of 1861–62 but reserved his most blistering comments for the general's direction of the Peninsula campaign. He accused Mc-Clellan of dividing his forces, keeping his soldiers digging trenches in malarious swamps, and refusing to follow up his victories. Chandler further charged, "Human ingenuity could not have devised any other way to defeat that [Union] army; divine wisdom could scarcely have devised any other way to defeat it than that which was adopted" (Zachariah Chandler, *Conduct of the War. Speech of Hon. Z. Chandler of Mich., Delivered in the Senate of the United States, Wednesday, July 16, 1862* [Washington, D.C., 1862], pp. 13–15; Mary Karl George, *Zachariah Chandler: A Political Biography* [East Lansing, Mich., 1969], pp. 63–65).

7. McClellan's withdrawal of the Army of the Potomac from the Peninsula to unite it in northern Virginia with Pope's Army of Virginia had proceeded very slowly during August 1862. On the eve of and during the second battle of Bull Run (August 28–30), McClellan had further delayed, in spite of numerous requests from Halleck, in sending William B. Franklin's corps to reinforce Pope. Brace's comment about McClellan's forcing himself upon the president as commander in chief in the field refers to Lincoln's consolidation in early September 1862 of the Army of Virginia into the Army of the Potomac under McClellan's leadership because neither officers nor troops would fight under Pope (*War for the Union*, 2: 170–88).

8. That is, Harrisburg, Pennsylvania.

9. Brace is reacting to the increased number of arrests and detentions on suspicion of disloyalty which occurred late in the summer of 1862. Authority over political prisoners had been transferred from the State Department to the War Department in February 1862, and numerous people were then released. But as protests against the war mounted, Stanton's policy became sterner. In August 1862 the War Department issued rules that restricted the travel of men eligible for the renewed draft of militia and that also suspended the writ of habeas corpus for those suspected of disloyal offenses such as discouraging volunteering. Arrests of Midwestern Democrats were especially numerous at this time (*War for the Union*, 2: 313–17; Wood Gray, *The Hidden Civil War: The Story of the Copperheads* [New York, 1942], pp. 85, 88).

10. A blow or stroke.

11. Since 1853 Brace had headed the Children's Aid Society, which sought to aid and uplift the poor and abandoned children of New York City. His mention of the *New-York Times* refers to his friendship with its editor, Henry J. Raymond. This relationship allowed Brace to publish articles written or selected by him, such as the editorial on emancipation which appeared on September 28, 1862. Thus Brace could help swing the paper's editorial position toward the abolitionism he favored (*Papers of FLO*, 2: 9, 50–51, 204; CLB to FLO, Oct. 1, 1862, n. 16, below).

12. A letter written by George Featherstone Allen (d. 1863) which described the effects of emancipation in Jamaica and which Brace had promised in July to send to Olmsted. At that time Brace commented that Allen's opinion was not favorable but that "he has not been among the mountains"—that is, Allen did not share the lofty vision of the abolitionists.

Allen, a graduate of Columbia College in 1829, was a lawyer, associate member of the Sanitary Commission, and secretary of the Woman's Central Association of Relief. He had married Grace Brown, daughter of wealthy financier James Brown. In 1854 Allen was one of the few passengers who survived the wreck of the *Arctic*, a luxury steamship that sank with his wife, infant son, and other relatives aboard. At Allen's death, his close friend George Templeton Strong wrote, "It seems hardly credible that George Allen's face and form, so familiar and so welcome in this house for many years, so full of geniality and sympathy, sagacity, keenest intelligence, high culture, appreciation of art, devotion to the nation and to the church, should now be lying under six feet of earth" (Columbia University, *Catalogue of Officers and Graduates of Columbia University from the Foundation of King's College in 1754* [New York, 1906], p. 97; HWB to Salmon P. Chase, Aug. 13, 1862, Henry Whitney Bellows Papers, Massachusetts Historical Society, Boston, Mass.; Alexander Crosby Brown, *Women and Children Last: The Loss of the Steamship Arctic* [New York, 1961], pp. 36, 87–91, 204–5; *Diary of the Civil War*, p. 353; CLB to FLO, July 9, 1862).

To Charles Loring Brace

Sanitary Commission,
Adams' House, 244 F street,
Washington, D.C., Sept[r] 21st 1862.

My Dear Charley,

Most of the Chaplains seem to be very poor stuff, about such men tho' I suppose as could be got in the market for the ordinary wages of country parsons for any other business—[*New York*][1] policeman for instance. They are about what you say: creatures of their Colonels just as a policeman would naturally be expected to be the creature of a Police Commissioner. But sometimes for the love of Christ or something else, you may find men of ordinary respectability taking the position and in all such cases, I think their light shines as it never shone before. D[r] Winslow[2] has been worth more since he has been Chaplain to the Duryee Zouaves than he would be in 90000000+ years as pastor of an average sleepy church. So of Post[3] the Protest[t] Chaplain of McLeod Murphy's regiment. Both of these men influence their colonels I suspect more than he overtakes them.

I never saw the Devil so rampant before as he is now—I can't say that I have lost faith to the extent you say you have done, but I am astonished beyond expression by the stupidity & folly I see. I must say that your talk about McClellan seems to me to be as wild as anything I have heard. I don't see the smallest ground for it. My opinion of McClellan has fluctuated a little but on the whole rests now almost precisely where it did one year ago—or ten months ago. He is a respectable general, as generals go in this & the old world. I think he is an infinitely better General than Lincoln is President, Seward Secy of State or Chase Secy of Treasury, better as General than Greely or Dana or Gay or Bryant or Raymond as editors.[4] He is a man of more than the average talent of "great men" in history. He is an honest, true, simple, loyal gentleman—far more so than any member of the Cabinet or any leading member of Congress with whom I have come in contact. He is a simple stupid Christian, which is hardly the case of any other man of eminence. He is industrious, brave, patient. I can not see that he has not accomplished all that could have been reasonably asked of him. I do not see where he has made a single great mistake. I do not see that he has ever been behind time or out of his place. I can not see one single complaint that has been made against McClellan which is not founded, in my judgment, on falsehood or misapprehension of facts. McC. has from the first estimated the difficulties of overcoming the rebellion somewhat higher than most other men. Higher than I have perhaps and I have, much higher than my friends. But if McC. erred in his estimate he erred in underestimating the force of the rebellion. McC. thought it desirable probably that the army should be thoroughly disciplined before it undertook the invasion of the South, more so than it was last October—perhaps even more so than it was last spring. For myself I always said, repeatedly said; said in the office of the Tribune & the Post, at the time they were asserting that he had a thoroughly disciplined army of 200,000, that there were but four of the sub divisions of that army that had begun to be disciplined, that more than half of it, was utterly unfit for a campaign. Two days ago the President complained that the army was good for nothing; that it couldn't be depended on; that if it started 100,000 strong to march against the enemy, in two days it would be not more than 80,000 strong. He was asked if this was the case with the four corps of the oldest of McClellan's organization, the Secy of War was appealed to & after hemming over it, he confessed it was not; that is, that where McC. had been allowed to take his time in preparation he had formed soldiers who could be depended on and these were the only soldiers the President had whom he could depend on to do their duty.[5] And I tell you that with small exceptions we have as yet no disciplined army beyond this. The rebel force is far better disciplined than ours, far more trustworthy.

What have our generals been doing? They have been intriguing and fighting intrigues with these infernal gamblers, the Abolition politicians at Washington. I write now not for Mr Brown,[6] but privately & confidentially. The damnedest fools and rascals out of asylums and prisons in this or any other country are our republican leaders. They are liars, pettifoggers and sneaks. I have taken the measure of some of them with tolerable accuracy and I have been in Washington long enough & sufficiently behind the curtains to judge the others pretty well. I mean for instance, Chase[7]—he is contemptible, a mere ward politician with a clean face. I mean Wilson[8]—he lies and jumps the fence faster and more freely than any man I ever knew except one. I have been on intimate terms with him & have seen a good deal of Chase. McDowell is Chase's nephew &

Pope is the son in law of Chase's neighbor & friend Horton, M.C. of Ohio.[9] Chase six months ago at his own dinner table stated his purpose to depose McClellan & put McDowell in his place. If this had not been his purpose & if similar purposes had not ruled others, we should have been in Richmond, Raleigh and Charlestown long before this. But of all the damnd infernal scoundrels that the Almighty for our sins' sake curses us with, Stanton is the hardest to bear. In all Dixie there is not so wicked a man. Lord deliver us! If the nation can't see through his veil of godliness & patriotism, no wonder it can't through the weaker ones.

I have seen Halleck.[10] Heaven help us. He is no more to be compared with McClellan than Geo Francis Train is to Wendell Phillips.[11]

The Tribune & Post and Independent[12] abound with the most outrageous lies. There is a great deal of carelessness in them & recklessness and prejudice, but there is also, I am sure, a great deal of imposition, intentional falsehood, designed to deceive & hoodwink the public. Whose is it? Not Gay's nor Godwin's nor Beecher's[13] I am sure. Whose then? Some of these damnd rascals here in Washington who take advantage of the prejudices and strong desires for emancipation of those simple men to deceive them. The President is a poor whining broken-down idiot at such a time as this.

Looking back I fear you think me unjust with the rest to McDowell. He is a loyal gentleman & tolerable general—a bad tempered, well educated but not well disciplined man. He suffers for the sins of Chase & Stanton. The common reports about him are false.[14] One of the best generals & one of the truest & most loyal gentlemen in our army, I believe to be General Stone.[15] I never saw him. I formed my judgment of him before he was arrested & I hold it still. Time may show, in spite of Bully Stanton. I hope to see Stanton's head roll with many others for that crime.

Yours affectionately

Fred. Law Olmsted.

1. Olmsted lined through these words.
2. Gordon Winslow, chaplain of the Duryeé Zouaves and a Sanitary Commission inspector.
3. George E. Post (b. c. 1839) served as the chaplain of the 15th New York Engineers (Veteran) until February 1863. In September 1862 that regiment's colonel was John McLeod Murphy (Frederick Phisterer, comp., *New York in the War of the Rebellion, 1861–1865*, 3rd ed., 6 vols. [Albany, N.Y., 1912], 2: 1650–52, 1666).
4. New York City newspaper editors Horace Greeley and Sydney H. Gay of the *Tribune*; William Cullen Bryant of the *Evening Post*; and Henry J. Raymond of the *Times*. Olmsted here grouped Charles A. Dana with the editors of the *Tribune*, even though Dana no longer held a position at that paper.

5. The editors have been unable to confirm Olmsted's account of Lincoln's and Stanton's remarks or to discover who his informant was.

6. A reference to Brace having shown Olmsted's letter of August 25, 1862, to James Brown (see CLB to FLO, Sept. 12, 1862, above).

7. Salmon P. Chase.

8. Henry Wilson.

9. John Pope was married to the daughter of Valentine Baxter Horton (1802–1888), a Republican U.S. congressman from eastern Ohio. Olmsted's belief that McDowell and Chase were close relatives was, however, erroneous (NCAB, s.v. "Pope, John"; BDAC).

10. Olmsted had seen and talked with Henry W. Halleck on September 17 when the general met with the Sanitary Commission (USSC, Minutes, pp. 99–101).

11. Wealthy merchant and entrepreneur George Francis Train (1829–1904) had recently returned from England, where as a defender of the Union he had battled public opinion. Although Train, like the noted abolitionist Wendell Phillips (1811–1884), had written and lectured widely on controversial subjects, Olmsted probably disliked the former's brash nationalism, eccentric behavior, and proslavery views (DAB; Willis Thornton, The Nine Lives of Citizen Train [New York, 1948], pp. 66, 78–88, 108–34).

12. Three New York City newspapers whose editorial policies were anti-McClellan and strongly antislavery (Frank Luther Mott, American Journalism: A History of Newspapers in the United States through 250 Years, 1690–1940, rev. ed. [New York, 1950], p. 378).

13. Parke Godwin (1816–1904), an editor of the Evening Post, and Henry Ward Beecher (1813–1887), editor of the Independent (DAB; Papers of FLO, 2: 63).

14. After Irvin McDowell's poor performance at the second battle of Bull Run, various rumors held that he was disloyal, drunken, and incompetent. Early in 1863 a military court of inquiry cleared McDowell of all such charges (DAB; O.R., ser. 1, vol. 12, pt. 1, pp. 33, 323–32).

15. Charles Pomeroy Stone (1824–1887), a graduate of West Point and veteran of the Mexican War, commanded the special corps of observation of the Army of the Potomac in the autumn of 1861. Blamed for the rout of Union troops at Ball's Bluff that October, Stone, who was a Democrat and had required his soldiers to return fugitive slaves to their masters, was arrested on suspicion of disloyalty in February 1862. Although no formal charges were ever filed against him, he remained in prison for more than six months. He later served under Nathaniel P. Banks in Louisiana and during the Red River campaign.

Soon after Stone's arrest, Olmsted gave his opinion about the case:

> I think intelligent men generally believe it a mistake. No man in the army has more and warmer friends and it is their universal conviction, as far as I learn, that he is a man of the highest honor and integrity. If there is treason in his case, it is more surprising and melancholy than was [Benedict] Arnold's. If there is not distinctly treason, the manner of his arrest and his incarceration in Fort Lafayette would seem to be very unjust and bad policy.

(Appleton's Cyc. Am. Biog.; FLO to JSN, Feb. 11, 1862, USSC-NYPL, box 909, 1: 272.)

To Mary Perkins Olmsted

U.S. Sanitary Commission,
Adams' House, 244 F Street,
Washington, D.C.   Sept. 21ˢᵗ 1862.
Sunday

Dear Wife,

You know I wanted a month to arrange a report so the Commission when it met could take a comprehensive view of things & not go off half-cocked on seeing some one or two sides of our many sided work. Vaux's illness[1] kept me, so I finally got here (after a fatiguing *twenty* hours passage in poor stinking day cars from New York, missing connections all the way & bothered with military trains) after the third meeting of the session was well in progress and everything going at sixes & sevens just as I apprehended.[2] I rushed to the rescue with all my might & for two days was busy eno' heading off all sorts of mistaken impressions, theories & projects. I couldn't help getting the Governor[3] quite red in the face sometimes, in resisting the strong set of his will. He had for instance three times up a peremptory order for immediately undertaking the weekly publication of a Hospital Directory & if I couldn't do it, getting some Antioch professor[4] put in charge of it. I "cuss'd and swore", so about it, that they yielded to my will until I got half an hour to deliberate upon it, when I demonstrated that instead of a small newspaper it would be equal in letter-press to two large quarto volumes of 240 pages each & would require several hundred clerks and the largest steam-printing establishment in the U.S.[5] This was a sockdolager.[6] After three days, I got up my papers & went in for a "field-day". I had Knapp to help me, and beginning at 10 A.M. gave them a sort of familiar history of our more important work of the summer & how things stood. They were (really) intensely interested & didn't want to break up until I got quite through about 4 P.M. I carried their convictions & sympathies & regained their entire confidence. Dʳ Bellows immediately afterwards retracted all his doubts, apologized for them & expressed his strong conviction of the wisdom with which everything had been managed during the summer. And I think I stand better with the whole Commission than I ever did before—I mean that [they] are more disposed to trust my judgment and leave the business to me untrammelled with specific instructions.

In the midst of all this, were the exciting telegrams of the great battles finally culminating in that of Antietam,[7] and we were rushing to the rescue. I sent agents & $3500 into Pennsylᵃ to purchase & push thro' stimulants from the North; got on six "quarter masters" (old hospital transport men) from New York; sent all we could by rail, but fearing the trains would choke the road, bought, hired & borrowed waggons & horses and sent them through by the turnpike, ("National road"). The Rail Road did get choked, and all the government medical stores as well as ours were held back somewhere in twenty miles of cars, behind ammunition & subsistence, so that our waggon trains passed them & were twenty four hours ahead of anything else on the battle fields. Agnew is there with half a dozen of our best inspectors and a score of distributory assistants.[8] We have sent 20 or 30 tons of soup, wine &c. & are constantly yet pushing it.

Of course I have been working my brain like fury & my blood boils.

Jenkins, ordered off by the doctors to save his life, goes home today with three weeks' leave of absence with pay & a present of $250.

All the world comes to our office now, to enquire about hospitals, wounded men &c.

I have your collection of letters from Aug 4 to Septr 14th & have enjoyed them very much as a cool breeze in the battle. By the way have you read the Tribune correspondent's report of the battle of Antietam?[9] If not, do so, it's reprinted in most of the papers & is the most extraordinary literary production as well as the best possible large loose sketch of this great battle that you will see in the next ten years.

I wrote "Mrs Vaux[10] is alone" they put [for] alone, alive. This gives you the key to all I said & did. It was for you to judge how much she needed you & how well you could come considering the children's health & your own. You know he has gone to D[r] Brown's.[11] I am greatly perplexed and perhaps not in a position or state of mind to consider healthily & with confidence, what I ought to do. I wish you would advise—I don't mean tax your energies but give me your impressions from your superficial general view. The park & Vaux's interests pull me toward New York; I am intensely held here. It don't seem as if I could do justice to both. Which shall be paramount? Self interest says the park I think. Benevolence, duty(?) & gratitude say San. Com. The San Com. are gentlemen, liberal, generous, magnanimous.

I have rather favorable intelligence regarding Vaux, but shall be surprised if he gets out for work this fall. Poor fellow, how it will annoy & depress and perplex him that he has been liable to go crazy & may be again.

I enclose check for $100. I had to borrow $300 of father, to pay Vaux's office rent &c. & make sure they did not suffer for money.

Write a word daily if you can.

Fred.

Didn't you get a letter from me when in New York about Vaux & about Masons?[12]

My impression is we can best live, especially if Vaux is going to be in poor trim, in one of the houses of Cook's[13] block in 78th St, rent probably $400, he says they are comfortable small houses & the situation is as nearly right for me as possible.

1. Calvert Vaux was seriously ill with what had been diagnosed as a remittent fever. Delirious for several days, he had required a professional nurse to restrain him. His doctors feared that this condition might become a brain fever and lead to permanent mental illness. On September 15 Olmsted described Vaux as "incessantly philosophizing about glass and colors and drapery" and added that he "insists on a floating capacity—tries to repose on air &c." (FLO to MPO, Sept. 15, 1862).
2. Olmsted returned to Washington, D.C., on September 17. The Sanitary Commission had begun its meetings on the preceding day (USSC, *Minutes*, pp. 98–99).
3. That is, Henry W. Bellows.
4. That is, a professor at Antioch College in Yellow Springs, Ohio. The board probably was considering hiring a professor from Antioch because Bellows, as a trustee of the college, was aware that its collegiate program, for lack of funds, had been suspended in July 1862 for the remainder of the war and that its professors needed employment. In 1861 the Sanitary Commission had hired Henry A. Warriner, a physician who had been teaching at Antioch (W. D. Kring, *Henry Whitney Bellows*, pp. 135–36, 256–58; FLO to JFJ, May 21, 1862, n. 9, above).
5. At the September 1862 meetings, the Sanitary Commission passed resolutions calling for the secretary to establish a hospital directory. At first Bellows and the other commissioners envisioned this directory as a publication that would appear weekly. Olmsted, as he relates in this letter, believed that such a periodical would necessarily be larger and more expensive than anyone else realized. In late September he discussed publication size and costs with a printer and reported to Bellows that, even using as many abbreviations as possible, the directory would be nine pages long and that a press run of five thousand copies would cost one thousand dollars a week. The Executive Committee, already alarmed at the burgeoning costs of the Washington office during recent months, resolved on October 3 that Olmsted present the plan of registration to the surgeon general and the War Department and offer to carry it out if the government would defray most of the expenses. Unless government support could be secured, the Commission intended to shelve the plan.
   In early October Olmsted met with Surgeon General Hammond and Jonathan Letterman, medical director of the Army of the Potomac, and learned about the system the army already used to compile a register of the soldiers in Washington hospitals. In mid-October John Bowne of the Commission assumed superintendence of the project and a month later had completed an index to the almost twenty thousand patients of the Washington army hospitals. The hospital register as Bowne organized it was able to give up-to-date information in answer to questions, directed to it either by letter or in person, about the location and condition of sick and wounded soldiers. By the end of December 1862 the Commission was compiling at Louisville, Kentucky, a similar directory of soldiers in the western hospitals. In June 1863 the directory (with two other offices in Philadelphia and New York) covered all the army's general hospitals (USSC, *Minutes*, pp. 100, 102, 104, 110; FLO to HWB, Sept. 29, 1862, USSC-NYPL, box 641; FLO to HWB, Oct. 2, 1862; HWB to FLO, Oct. 3, 1862, USSC-NYPL, box 745: 2393; FLO to HWB, Oct. 13, 1862, USSC-NYPL, box 641; JSN to FLO, Dec. 27, 1862, USSC-NYPL, box 641; [Katharine Prescott Wormeley], *The United States Sanitary Commission. A Sketch of Its Purposes and Its Work . . .* [Boston, 1863], p. 235).

6. A slang expression meaning a "knockdown blow" (*OED*).
7. The battles at Turner's Gap and Crampton's Gap of South Mountain, near Sharpsburg, Maryland, on September 14 preceded the battle of Antietam (Sharpsburg) that occurred on September 17 (Frederick H. Dyer, *A Compendium of the War of the Rebellion* . . . , 3 vols. [1908; rpt. ed., New York, 1959], 2: 760).
8. Among the Sanitary Commission inspectors working in that area in the aftermath of the battle were: C. W. Brink, Edward A. Crane, T. Blanch Smith, William M. Chamberlain, Edwin J. Dunning, Jesse W. Page, and Lewis H. Steiner (FLO to Cornelius R. Agnew, Sept. 18, 1862, USSC-NYPL, box 835, 1: 35; C. W. Brink to FLO, Sept. 27, 1862, USSC-NYPL, box 752: 4752; FLO to E. A. Crane, Sept. 24, 1862, USSC-NYPL, box 745: 2297).
9. The report, "The Great Battle of Wednesday," was written by George W. Smalley and published on pages one and eight of the *New-York Daily Tribune* of September 19, 1862. Smalley, who had been in the thick of battle, wrote his article while taking the night train back to New York. Others have shared Olmsted's high opinion of Smalley's account, and one authority has called it "finer than any other writing of the kind during the whole four years of the conflict" (J. Cutler Andrews, *The North Reports the Civil War* [Pittsburgh, Pa., 1955], pp. 64–65).
10. Mary McEntee Vaux (d. 1892), was the wife of Calvert Vaux and a friend of Mary Perkins Olmsted's. On September 14 Olmsted telegraphed his wife about Vaux's illness and Mary Vaux's need for a companion. Although Olmsted left the decision to his wife, he asked her to consider coming to stay with Mary Vaux during the illness. Apparently the telegraph operator garbled this message (FLO to MPO, Sept. 15, 1862).
11. Probably David Tilden Brown, a physician at the Bloomingdale Asylum.
12. A reference to the letter that Olmsted had written to his wife on September 13. In it, he referred to Vaux's illness and to the impending bankruptcy of Mason Brothers, the firm that had published his book *A Journey in the Backcountry* in 1860. According to Olmsted, the firm hoped to be able to pay him the one hundred dollars in royalties due him and was attempting to save the copyright and printing plates of his book from a forced sale.
13. Presumably Clarence Chatham Cook (1828–1900), a literary acquaintance of Olmsted's, who either lived in or owned a house on 78th Street in New York City. A graduate of Harvard, Cook had studied architecture with his brother-in-law Andrew Jackson Downing. Cook had written art criticism for *Putnam's Monthly* until Olmsted, then an editor of that periodical, had secretly procured his dismissal. Cook had also studied with Calvert Vaux and, according to Olmsted, visited the sick man twice a day "heated with sympathy, but he can be of no use to Mrs. Vaux" (FLO to MPO, Sept. 15, 1862; *DAB*; *Papers of FLO*, 2: 54).

To Henry Whitney Bellows

Sanitary Commission,
Adams' House, 244 F street,
Washington, D.C., Septr 22[d] 1862.

My Dear Doctor,
I write to urge the immediate preparation and extensive publication of the proposed communication to the President urging energetic and

persistent, sustained, measures for improving the discipline of the army and for an ambulance corps.[1] I think under cover of the first, you may, if you choose, give the President some home thrusts and the people some enlightenment. I would refer to the old excuses—the impracticability of having court-martials—and say they won't do, I would allude to Halleck's private complaints and McClellan's public confessions of straggling[2] and I would tell him that the people suspect that the chief fault is very high up and adroitly intimate that the centre of discipline was the Commander in Chief and that he could surrender his responsibility in this respect only with his office.

Judge Skinner[3] has been having interviews with the Pres' & Stanton of the most startling character. He has confidentially told me much of a most frightful and doleful import. As it was in the office of the Commission, I think I am justified in repeating in strict confidence, that the President has said that he was "under bonds" to let Halleck have his own way in everything in regard to the army: to make no appointments or removals even, without his advice or consent![4] The President goes about wringing his hands and whining. He can depend on nobody. He don't know what to think of anything. He has even groaned out with a sickly smile which showed that he was more than half in earnest but was too cowardly to acknowledge it—"It is now a fight for boundaries." Is this Halleck, or Seward?[5]

Straggling in action is half of it occasioned by want of an ambulance corps: the assistance of wounded comrads being an excuse for dropping out. Page[6] says he has seen five well men helping a man to the rear who had only a slight wound of the arm.

Beauregard decreed death to any man who left his place on the excuse of taking wounded off.[7] We must learn of our enemies, because they are in earnest. Is Halleck in earnest? He is a man without faith, an infidel, if faces are to be trusted.

The "radicals" are pitting Hooker[8] against McClellan. They are doing all they can again & even now, to bully down McC.

Yours Respectfully,

Fred. Law Olmsted.

The original is in box 641 of USSC-NYPL.

1. A reference to a letter about the importance of discipline which Bellows wished to send to President Lincoln. In this document Bellows argued that army regulations were excellent, and problems arose only because of a lack of enforcement. After stressing the hierarchical aspect of the army and the obedience owed by inferior to

superior officers, he strongly criticized the jealousies and quarrels among high-ranking army officers. As Olmsted suggested, the minister castigated the government for not ordering more courts-martial to be held. He also pointed out to Lincoln that he must take responsibility for instituting discipline; and if the secretary of war did not exact obedience among the generals, the president must discipline the secretary of war. Bellows then added, "Under any other govern't than ours, the mistakes, failures & mortifications of the alas! irresponsible men composing your Cabinet, would have long ago swept most of them out of place."

Bellows's letter did not mention the need for an ambulance corps but otherwise touched upon many of the points Olmsted had raised. On October 1 Bellows drafted the letter and informed Olmsted, "I have to-day written a paper addressed to the President, on the subject of discipline in the Army, which so puts the responsibility on *his Shoulders*, that I am almost afraid the Ex. Com. won't adopt it—at any rate—not without paring all its edges." Bellows's trepidations were correct; that day the Executive Committee decided not to send the letter to Lincoln or allow it to be published (HWB to FLO, Oct. 1, 1862, USSC-NYPL, box 745: 2377; HWB, "Draft of a letter to the President of the United States on Discipline," Oct. 1, 1862, USSC-NYPL, box 753: 4766).

2. Olmsted probably heard Halleck's private complaints about straggling during the September 17 meeting between the Sanitary Commission and the general. George Templeton Strong possibly alluded to this subject when he stated that Halleck "maundered about certain defects of discipline which he said prevented McClellan from moving more than five miles a day and [Gen. Don Carlos] Buell more than three—'when he moves at all, that is.'"

Olmsted's reference to McClellan's public confessions probably stemmed from the circular the general ordered on September 9, 1862, to be issued against straggling. In it McClellan blamed "inattention and carelessness on the part of those high in rank" for the "straggling and want of discipline which now obtain in the various corps." General Order number 155, also issued on September 9 at McClellan's direction, provided penalties against straggling (*Diary of the Civil War*, p. 258; O.R., ser. 1, vol. 19, pt. 2, pp. 225, 226-27).

3. Mark Skinner (1813-1887), as a prominent Republican from Chicago, Illinois, knew Lincoln well. A native of Vermont, Skinner studied law and moved to Chicago in 1836. He served as city attorney and U.S. district attorney and was elected to the state legislature as a Democrat in 1846. Five years later he won election as judge of the Cook County Court of Common Pleas but served only one term. Opposing the Kansas-Nebraska Act, he left the Democratic party in 1854. Instead of resuming his law practice, he became a financial adviser for corporations and nonresidents who wished to invest in Chicago real estate.

When in 1861 Chicago formed its own soldiers' aid organization (which soon became a branch of the U.S. Sanitary Commission), Skinner was chosen as the group's first president. He held this position until illness forced his resignation in 1864. The U.S. Sanitary Commission also elected him to membership in December 1861. During the quarrel between the Sanitary Commission and its Cincinnati branch, Skinner, though a Western member, threw his influence behind the national organization. He was also active in civic and charitable institutions such as the Chicago Home for the Friendless, the county hospital, and the Chicago Reform School (*Encyclopaedia of Biography of Illinois*, 3 vols. [Chicago, 1892-1902], 1: 31-34; *Biographical Sketches of the Leading Men of Chicago* . . . [Chicago, 1868], pp. 597-604; USSC, *Minutes*, p. 87).

4. Henry W. Halleck accepted the post of general-in-chief upon the stipulation that he possess authority to plan and supervise all army operations (T. Harry Williams, *Lincoln and His Generals* [New York, 1952], p. 139).

5. Probably a reference to Secretary of State William Henry Seward's reputed overea-

gerness to compromise with the South (Glyndon G. Van Deusen, *William Henry Seward* [New York, 1967], p. 341).

6. Jesse William Page (1820–1888) graduated from Bowdoin College, and received his medical degree from the University of Maryland in 1848. He entered the Commission's service in 1862 and by early 1863 was its inspector in New Bern, North Carolina. Page was a logical choice for that post since he had practiced medicine in eastern North Carolina for ten years. In 1864 the commissioners removed Page from his post because he had "repeatedly" failed to make reports, but they reinstated him in 1865. After the war Page served as a U.S. pension agent in North Carolina for over a year (Bowdoin College, *General Catalogue of Bowdoin College and the Medical School of Maine: A Biographical Record of Alumni and Officers, 1794–1950* [Brunswick, Me., 1950], p. 81; USSC, *Minutes*, p. 191; J. W. Page to John S. Blatchford, Oct. 12, 1866, USSC-NYPL, box 1086: 10).

7. Olmsted is referring to the section of the orders issued in March 1862 by Confederate general P. G. T. Beauregard that read: "To quit their standard on the pretence of removing or aiding the wounded will not be permitted. Anyone persisting in it will be shot on the spot" (Frank Moore, ed., *The Rebellion Record: A Diary of American Events . . .*, 11 vols. [New York, 1866], 4: 385).

8. Joseph Hooker (1814–1879) was promoted to major general of volunteers during the Peninsula campaign and commanded the V Corps of the Army of the Potomac at the battle of Antietam. He was a graduate of West Point and had fought in the Mexican War but had retired to civilian life prior to the outbreak of the Civil War. Although many army officers and civilians disliked and distrusted Hooker as a heavy drinker and an intriguer, the more radical antislavery Republicans strongly supported him. In January 1863 Hooker received command of the Army of the Potomac, which he held until June of that year (*DAB*; *War for the Union*, 2: 432–33).

To Mary Perkins Olmsted

Sanitary Commission,
Frederick city, Maryland
Septr. 26 1862.

Dear Wife,

I came yesterday to this place and shall go to Hd Quart's A.P.[1] tonight, if I can, that is to Sharpsburg, passing through all the battle-grounds, on the way. I find the hospitals here in admirable condition, under the circumstances, and our agent[2] a splendid fellow, quite taking the lead. The people are gloriously loyal, the women especially, and are working nobly among the wounded. Both armies have held the town which is a close built, modest, respectable old city, and there was a cavalry charge and battle in the main street. When McClellan rode in, at last,[3] there was a scene; the loyal who had been disgusted with the filthy, lousy secesh & who had shut themselves up closing their shutters &c. came into the streets crying with joy, and a beautiful, modest well bred girl, whom I conversed with yesterday in a hospital, in her excitement threw herself upon McClellan's horse's neck—(a beautiful thorough-bred, bay stallion, with that large affectionate eye and silky mane and pliant ears; it would make a good picture wouldn't it?) Every house was thrown open.

I don't know how soon I shall return to Washington—probably day after tomorrow unless I go on to Chambersbg,[4] or unless the army advances & a battle is eminent. Have heard nothing from you or of Vaux, since I last wrote.

Your affectionate husband

Fred. Law Olmsted.

1. That is, the headquarters of the Army of the Potomac.
2. Lewis H. Steiner, a native of Frederick (FLO to L. H. Steiner, Sept. 24, 1862, USSC-NYPL, box 835, 1: 89–92).
3. Union troops entered Frederick on September 12. McClellan rode into town the following day and received an enthusiastic welcome (George B. McClellan, *McClellan's Own Story: The War for the Union* . . . [New York, 1887], pp. 569–71).
4. Chambersburg is located in southern Pennsylvania, southeast of Gettysburg.

To CHARLES LORING BRACE

Private & Confidential

U.S. Sanitary Commission,
Adams' House, 244 F Street,
Washington, D.C., Septr 30th 1862.

My Dear Charley,

I enclose a paper which I wrote with the purpose of sending to the Tribune,[1] but upon reading it over, I concluded they wouldn't publish it, unless for the purpose of printing an insulting reply a la Greely, and that they wouldn't understand me. I am content therefore to limit its influence to what may result from your *private* perusal.

Since writing it, I have been to the battle fields of Northern Maryland and my favorable judgment of McClellan's military trustworthiness has risen. The dirty, paltry, narrow-minded talk that I now hear from

McClellan's enemies here, reduces my estimate of the average American intellect and rouses a deeper indignation than anything that has occurred in the war. Such ingratitude is astounding. In my life, nothing has more astonished me. There is a simpleton who one week runs away from Washington, tells me that our army was crowding into Alexandria in the utmost confusion, famished, sick, disgusted and demoralized, not to be depended upon for anything, and that the rebels with an overpowering force are already at Ball's Crossroads[2] and their videttes have been seen at Chain bridge, from which the planking has been removed;[3] further up they are crossing the river and will raise Maryland & sneak down on "our unprotected side"—(which thanks to Gnl McClellan's precaution last year, was not unprotected).[4] Genl McClellan was at this time acting as quarter master at Alexandria, with a force of 115 men all told, under his orders, everything having been done that was possible by his superiors to make it appear that he was an unsuccessful man, and to bring him into contempt with the army. Since then Lee and his whole army (nearly) have been on this side of the Potomac, threatening Washington, Baltimore & Philadelphia, in a rich agricultural region, and with every advantage that could be asked for a successful campaign. His pickets have been within a few miles of the Balt° & Washington R.R., he has held the Balt° & Ohio road, the northern turnpike & canal of Washington.[5] McClellan has in a week reorganized the defeated, disgusted, half starved, sick, weary and almost mutinous army; has led it by the most fatiguing marches against the enemy, driven him from the fertile plains to a high country having the greatest advantages for defence, has defeated him in a battle of the grandest magnitude, so that he has sneaked off in the night, leaving his wounded, and is now held at bay in a position from which he can neither advance or retreat except at great disadvantage to himself—a desperate position. And now I find my simpleton, $10,000 richer than he was a fortnight ago by the rise in stocks, back at Willard's, carping and indignant with government for allowing McClellan to command an army, because he has not done more! What would he have? He would have had the army immediately follow up its advantages of Thursday by a vigorous attack and advance on Friday. He would have had the various attacks so timed on Thursday that the enemy could never withdraw forces from one part of the field to reinforce another, and thus his retreat might have been cut off. Does the fool know how much ammunition, McClellan had left, after the great quantities Pope had blown up or given to the enemy, after forced marches, almost constant firing for several days and two grand actions, the last beginning before daylight and continuing without a moment's abatement of incessant firing till after nightfall? Does he know that half the force manning our artillery at the close of the day was drawn from the infantry and cavalry, that a large proportion of our artillery horses were dead, that next morning most of our men had been twenty four hours without food, and were so fatigued that they could hardly stand? Does he know that McClellan had been deprived of a large part of the staff of aids which he had trained & organized, that at 12 °'ck on the day of the battle, not one of his aids had a horse to carry him, that each lost or wore out completely two horses on that day & yet McC. was often standing alone without an aid to send for information or with orders, and this on a battlefield of hills, four miles in length of line?[6] He knows nothing, he cares nothing for this. McClellan should have taken the whole rebel army, and because he has not, he deserves to be kicked from his saddle, and another Pope put in his place. McClellan was called upon for the "defence of Washington". He was anxious and urgent that he might have a larger purpose; that he might be allowed to control Harper's Ferry. He made three general propositions with regard to Harper's ferry and was told to mind his business, which was the defence of Washington. The consequence of this want of confidence in him, was that the traitors had thirty more field pieces playing upon him than they otherwise would have done, were well supplied with ammunition, and were able to cross the river unopposed.[7] Just so, it has always been. For a year past, they have been going on in this way, and this noble people continues to be led to ruin by the meanest, weakest, most selfish, self-sufficient and altogether most contemptible peddling politicians that ever existed.

And you Charley Brace, having faith in their lies, simply[8] because they ride the antislavery horse, help those who egg them on to still greater depths of meanness.

Yours

Fred. Law Olmsted.

1. The article that Olmsted intended to send to Horace Greeley's *New-York Daily Tribune* has not survived.
2. Demoralized after the defeat at the second battle of Bull Run, Union troops straggled back to Alexandria and Washington in late August and early September. By September 5 reports circulated that rebel cavalry had raided Ball's Cross Roads in northern Virginia, approximately three miles south of the Potomac River (*Washington Evening Star*, Sept. 5, 1862, p. 2).
3. By September 4, Confederate sentries, or vedettes as Olmsted termed them, had been observed between Leesburg, Virginia, and the chain bridge, the bridge over the Potomac River approximately three miles northwest of Georgetown (*Washington National Intelligencer*, Sept. 4, 1862, p. 3).
4. In the fall of 1861 McClellan had ordered the building of a system of earthwork fortifications that would ring Washington. At that time the northern and western areas of the District of Columbia had neither soldiers nor fortifications to protect them (G. B. McClellan, *McClellan's Own Story*, p. 73).

5. By September 9 there were reports that the Confederates had cut the Chesapeake and Ohio Canal bank and destroyed canal boats and that their pickets had been sighted on the Baltimore turnpike near Frederick (*Washington National Intelligencer,* Sept. 9, 1862, p. 3).

6. McClellan believed his army too severely injured and disorganized to give battle on September 18. He also indicated that many of the "heaviest and most efficient batteries" had exhausted their stores of ammunition by the end of September 17, and that ammunition and provisions needed to be distributed to the infantry troops. He did not, however, cite a shortage of aides as a factor influencing his decision not to attack (G. B. McClellan, *McClellan's Own Story,* pp. 618–20).

7. Olmsted here is referring to the capture of Harper's Ferry by Thomas J. "Stonewall" Jackson's Confederate troops. McClellan had earlier suggested that the Union garrison be removed and combined with his forces, but his recommendations went unheeded. When the Confederates captured Harper's Ferry, they gained eleven thousand prisoners and over forty artillery guns, few of which had been "spiked" (William Jewett Tenney, *The Military and Naval History of the Rebellion in the United States* . . . [New York, 1865], pp. 269–71; O.R., ser. 1, vol. 19, pt. 1, pp. 546–48).

8. By a slip of the pen, Olmsted here wrote "simple."

To Henry Whitney Bellows

U.S. Sanitary Commission,
Adams' House, 244 F Street.
Washington, D.C., Septr 30th 1862.

My Dear Doctor,

You will be pleased to know that I receivd the first intimation of the Mayor's[1] intention to nominate me this afternoon, and immediately replied that I now found myself so absorbed in the work of the Commission that I could not but hope it would be rejected by the Aldermen and it is with great relief that I see tonight that [it] has been rejected by them.[2]

Douglas told me tonight that he could not stand the office work, and if I intended to keep him at it, he must resign. He said also that he thought we were working all our men to death, and urged that I should fix office-hours for them. I don't think this practicable, as it becomes us to be especially prepared for emergencies liable to occur at any hour. I shall try, however, to reduce the hours of necessary confinement.

We greatly need one or two more good gentlemen surgeons for camp inspectors.

Heintzleman[3] over the river is gathering an army. He has now 80,000 and one of the staff told us today that he said he would move when he had 100,000. When he moves, there will probably be business and we must be ready. There are large movements of troops northward. They are not arriving very fast.

Halleck is becoming known as a universally unpopular man. The agitation for Ambulance corps[4] is becoming strong, and we hear the hope and the expectation frequently expres[sed] that he can't last long. I attach some weight to it.

The neuralgia of which I was complaining yesterday was the butt end of a big cold, acquired at Sharpsburg, which is taking its course through me with unparalleled velocity, accelerated by Dr Alcorn's vapor bath. It has confined me but not kept me from the table—the writing table I mean.

We have had a visit from Dr Hosmer and Mrs Seymour[5]—several visits indeed; they go homeward to-morrow, quite astonished and most favorably impressed with our business. Their report will be valuable to us.

Weather hot at noon, cold at midnight; agreeable, but requiring inconveniently particular attention to our friend Quinia.[6]

1:30 A.M.: drunk coming (or going) thro' the avenue. Good night.

Yours Respectfully

Fred. Law Olmsted.

The original is in box 641 of USSC-NYPL.

1. George Opdyke, mayor of New York City.
2. On September 29, 1862, George Opdyke submitted Olmsted's nomination as street commissioner to the board of aldermen, which rejected it by a vote of 10 to 5. Both the New-York Times and the New-York Daily Tribune of September 30 reported the aldermen's decision (New-York Times, Sept. 30, 1862, p. 2; New-York Daily Tribune, Sept. 30, 1862, p. 8).
3. Samuel Peter Heintzelman (1805–1880), a brigadier general and graduate of West Point, commanded the III Corps of the Army of the Potomac in September 1862. Heintzelman's corps and other units under the command of Gen. Nathaniel P. Banks were stationed at Alexandria to defend the capital from attack. All these troops totaled only approximately 72,500 in September 1862. Olmsted's reference is unclear, but he appears to have been anticipating a battle south of Washington, D.C. (Warren W. Hassler, General George B. McClellan, Shield of the Union [Baton Rouge, La., 1957], pp. 234, 312; George Washington Cullum, Biographical Register of the Officers and Graduates of the U.S. Military Academy at West Point, N.Y. . . . , 3rd ed., 3 vols. [Boston, 1891], 1: 372–74).
4. Since the beginning of the Civil War, the Sanitary Commission had been attempting to improve ambulance service. Its first attempts were directed toward the Army of the Potomac. In October 1861 Olmsted warned McClellan that should a battle soon occur, "the present want of any organized ambulance system, would fix a just stain upon our National Character for humanity and providence of life." Olmsted also enclosed a report that criticized the two-wheeled "Finley" ambulances, most commonly used by the army, as particularly painful to the patients transported. This

report called the ambulance drivers "very careless and unskillful" as well as unreliable in times of danger. During the fall and winter of 1861 the commissioners in their meetings with McClellan vainly urged the creation of a separate, trained ambulance corps to replace the regimental band members and hospital attendants who were then assigned to ambulance duty. The only improvement made in 1861 came from the orders issued by Charles S. Tripler, then medical director of the Army of the Potomac, that bandsmen and other soldiers detailed for ambulance duty be drilled in the carrying of stretchers.

The Peninsula campaign and the second battle of Bull Run highlighted the inadequacies of existing ambulance service. Even before the second battle of Bull Run, Jonathan Letterman, the new medical director of the Army of the Potomac, had begun a reorganization of ambulance service. He removed ambulances from the regiments and organized a corps of ambulance workers commanded by a captain, with a first lieutenant for each regiment. Although the workers used under this plan were still soldiers detailed from line duty, they were chosen by the medical officers.

The Sanitary Commission approved of Letterman's measures but still hoped for a thorough reorganization that would include all the Union army. They joined forces with the surgeon general to try to achieve this end. On August 20 Hammond and Olmsted discussed the former's plan for an ambulance corps commanded by the medical officers. Most likely this was the plan for an ambulance corps made up solely of trained noncombatants that Hammond submitted to Stanton early in September. Not only did Stanton deem the plan too expensive, he also objected that noncombatants would further add to the confusion during battles. But the Sanitary Commission did not despair of convincing the War Department and the general-in-chief to accept an ambulance corps controlled by the Medical Bureau. In mid-September the commissioners met with Halleck in an unsuccessful attempt to overcome his opposition (FLO to G. B. McClellan, Oct. 3, 1861, USSC-NYPL, box 833, 1: 369½; FLO to HWB, Aug. 20, 1862, USSC-NYPL, box 641; George Worthington Adams, *Doctors in Blue: The Medical History of the Union Army in the Civil War* [New York, 1952], pp. 57–100; William Quentin Maxwell, *Lincoln's Fifth Wheel: The Political History of the United States Sanitary Commission* [New York, 1956], pp. 74–77, 176–79; Louis Caspar Duncan, *The Medical Department of the United States Army in the Civil War* [Washington, D.C., 1916], pp. 10–16).

5. Elizabeth Staats Seymour (1816–1876), the wife of Horatio Seymour, Jr., who was a prominent lawyer in Buffalo, New York. Active in charitable causes, she served as president of the Buffalo branch of the Sanitary Commission through the Civil War. According to John S. Newberry, her great enthusiasm and administrative ability placed her "in the front rank of that great army of noble women to whom we owe the success of the Supply Department of the Commission."

George W. Hosmer (1804–1881), the pastor of the First Unitarian Church of Buffalo. A member of Buffalo's army aid society, he wrote in the autumn of 1862 a report about his visit to military hospitals and Sanitary Commission agencies. Dr. Hosmer's report was as favorable as Olmsted predicted, and the Sanitary Commission arranged for ten thousand copies to be distributed (*Buffalo Commercial Advertiser*, March 16, 1876, p. 3; John Strong Newberry, *The U.S. Sanitary Commission in the Valley of the Mississippi, during the War of the Rebellion, 1861–1866* [Cleveland, Ohio, 1871], pp. 285–86; Henry W. Hill, ed., *The Municipality of Buffalo, New York: A History, 1720–1923*, 4 vols. [New York, 1923], 2: 617–18; FLO to Mrs. Joseph Follett, Oct. 21, 1862, USSC-NYPL, box 835, 1: 296–99).

6. Quinine, the remedy for malaria.

CHARLES LORING BRACE TO FREDERICK LAW OLMSTED

Hastings
Oct 1—[1862]

My dear Fred,

If I had seen your last long letter (about the Repub. politicians)[1] in print, I shd. have thought it one of the Herald's[2] editorials or of that sort. But coming from you, I am troubled & feel confirmed in an opinion fast growing in me—that our whole Northern system of politics has broken down—in men & administration—at home & abroad—in diplomacy, statesmanship & war—& that the South is far ahead of us. Yet I can hardly believe that *Wilson* is as bad as you paint him. Sumner[3] certainly is a statesman and patriot—Stanton & Chase I think may be what you picture. I don't agree with you in your estimate of Fremont. I see no evidence for it—& much to the contrary. The opinion of "army-officers" would not weigh much with me.

Pope, no one here believed in. But McClellan—here I get yours of the 30th, & must reply to it. I don't think the letter to the *Tribune* is really worth printing. But your "confidential" note to me contains strong facts, which I was ignorant of, & which justice to Gen McClellan requires should be known, so I shall extract from it for the *Times*—I think you can n't object.

Now for my answer, though you must have heard every point before.

I admit that Gen M^cC. is a "good stupid Christian," a conscientious loyal gentleman, a thorough disciplinarian—possibly a good organizer. But the faults which, I believe, have nearly ruined the nation, are *over-caution* which lets the golden moment slip by & *slowness*, both of mind & action: these faults too being soon known to the enemy & played upon by them.

I charge then (1) That it was Gen McClellan's fault that the Potomac was so long blockaded—he refused the 2000 men which the Navy Department wanted to clear Mathias Point. (This was Fox's testimony)[4] Cause—his over-caution. (2) That he should have attacked Manassas in December—the roads were good, the rebels only had then 30,000 or 40,000 men & the position not very strong (This is Hurlbert's[5] testimony & seems generally admitted).

Our men "were not thoroughly disciplined"—but were theirs? I doubt it—I doubt their superior discipline. The surgeons taken in Harper's Ferry, told me that the Southern officers boasted they never had a drill, that they couldn't even hold a dress-parade—all the orders they knew were *charge! & fire!*. They are more in earnest—that is all—& have better officers. Our superior numbers might have driven them, in Dec.

(3) The whole idea of the Peninsula campaign seems to me a gigantic blunder. Here was a point which the enemy had spent a year in fortifying: supported on one flank by the Merrimac[6] (considered then worth a corps of 30,000 men), whose attack necessitated the separation of our armies. Even if the plan had been carried out of putting McDowell with 40,000 at Urbanna to cut off the rebels' retreat, it would have been very dangerous strategy. Suppose they had left 10,000 in Yorktown, & had gobbled up McD. on their way! The campaign involved among its possibilities too, exposure to the most malarious region north of the Carolina-coast, as well as trench-work in that sickly country.

(4) He ought to have assaulted Yorktown at once. Rebel accounts now agree that they had only a small body of men there.[7] (I enclose evidence) He lost more in the trenches than he would have done in an assault, & gained none of the advantage of a surprise.

(5) He did not support Hooker properly in the Battle of Williamsburgh—and did not follow it up eagerly enough. Read Hooker's Report & enclosed extract.[8]

(6) He exposed a raw corps in the front, with a river between different parts of his army—& then utterly disorganized the corps by a hasty telegram. He did not follow up Fair Oaks with the fresh part of his army.[9]

(7) He waited too long—allowing the Richmond army to be heavily reinforced & Jackson at last to combine with them.[10] He was defeated by a massing of the enemy on his right when as the Princes[11] say "two brigades would have saved the day"—he not sending them & not turning the battle by attacking their weakened left.

In all his battles, he never gained anything by strategy or skill—but simply by the hard fighting & fearful sacrifice of his men. His battles have been slaughters with nothing gained. His trenches cost more lives than the bloodiest assault. His delays have cost hundreds of millions, the national honor, & universal discouragement. His action (till Antietam) has brought only disgrace and disaster.

As to South Mountain & Antietam, there is no especial strategy. He beats the enemy simply by weight—by superior physique & artillery. There is no manoeuvre—no skill. The rebels gain *their* point of strategy—to delay him, till they can take Harper's Ferry (the most disgraceful thing in the War to us). If it is correctly reported, he had Porter's division 25,000 & 15,000 reinforcements the day after the battle—fresh eager men.[12] Had they not ammunition? Could they not have interrupted the retreat? The enemy right under his nose, crossed 100,000 men, baggage & cannon & supplies over a river without losing a wagon or man.

Of course, such facts as you mention, may explain & excuse this—but coming in with all the others, they seem consistent—to be all fruits of Over-caution & Slowness. Harper's Ferry may not have been his fault. The recovering of the spirit of the army is very remarkable, and if due to their confidence in him, it is a great card for him.

I feel a profound, moral conviction that under Gen McClellan we shall not for two years more, drive out the rebels from Virginia—and *never* conquer them.

And yet I *know* of no proper General.

He seems a man, with too heavy a task for his powers & who fears to risk his reputation by trying anything.

You see how Europe regards him.[13]

But to another point—I am exceedingly anxious to get your views on the probable effect of the Proclamation[14] upon the slaves.

Will they rise—or run? Will they fight their old superiors? Are you not somewhat surprised at the success of experiments with the freed negroes—at Hilton Hd.[15] & elsewhere? I have the impression that you did not have the same confidence in their capacities, as most of the humanitarians.

Did you happen to notice a leader of mine in last Sunday's Times on the Proclamation.[16]

I took the ground that the negroes wd not rise but run—and that the South wd be much disturbed—that the slaves wd be armed—& a war of extermination wd. ensue &c &c.

Godkin[17] is here.

Are you to clean our streets? Heaven grant it!

Yours affectionately

C. L. Brace

Thursday

P.S. I don't know but I ought to speak more of your Article. We honestly believe McC. incapable of gaining us ultimate victory & would like another General, if one could be found. So long as he is General, we support him & do not backbite him, any farther than to check any false & unreasonable idolatry or idea of him.

The feelings of the Army are to be regarded—but even they are less than the life of the Nation. It is an injustice to the other brave officers, to exaggerate McC.

Facts on either side should always be published.

There is no use in Anti-Slavery men uniting by blinding their eyes & stopping up their ears—& then being dragged over the precipice.

1. See FLO to CLB, September 20, 1862, above.
2. The *New York Herald.*
3. Sen. Charles Sumner.
4. In his speech of July 16, 1862, Sen. Zachariah Chandler quoted testimony that Gustavus Vasa Fox, assistant secretary of the navy, had given before the Joint Committee on the Conduct of the War in February 1862. Fox stated that in 1861 McClellan failed to provide the four thousand soldiers necessary for a joint expedition to seize and fortify Mathias Point on the Potomac River below Washington. According to Fox, had Union forces been able to capture Mathias Point, they could have kept the Potomac open to navigation (Z. Chandler, *Conduct of the War,* pp. 8–10).
5. Brace is probably referring to statements made by the Southern-born literary man, William Henry Hurlbert (1827–1895). Imprisoned in Richmond in 1861, Hurlbert had escaped during the summer of 1862. Thus he could discuss Confederate estimates of their army's strength, but he does not appear to have testified before the Joint Committee on the Conduct of the War.

   Olmsted, who had been friendly with Hurlbert while they worked for *Putnam's Monthly Magazine* in the 1850s, saw the latter soon after his escape. Olmsted then wrote his wife that Hurlbert "said a good deal about the rebels but it was not very new & confirms my latest views of their condition & feeling" (FLO to MPO, Aug. 20, 1862; *DAB*).
6. The C.S.S. *Virginia,* formerly the U.S.S. *Merrimac,* had been rebuilt as an ironclad after the Confederate capture of the naval yard at Norfolk. Even after the drawn battle with the Union navy's ironclad, the U.S.S. *Monitor,* in March of 1862, the *Virginia* played a part in defending the James River and Richmond (*War for the Union,* 2: 50–56).
7. The Union army on the Peninsula in late April and early May of 1862 far outnumbered the Confederate defenders of Yorktown. At the end of April, McClellan's troops numbered approximately one hundred twelve thousand effectives while the Confederate garrison at Yorktown contained only about seventeen thousand men. A total of approximately fifty-five thousand Confederate soldiers were then stationed in the vicinity of Yorktown and Williamsburg (*O.R.,* ser. 1, vol. 11, pt. 3, pp. 130, 484).
8. Gen. Joseph Hooker, who commanded the 2nd Division of the III Corps at the battle of Williamsburg, wrote in his report of May 10, 1862:

   History will not be believed when it is told that the noble officers and men of my division were permitted to carry on this unequal struggle from morning until night unaided in the presence of more than 30,000 of their comrades with arms in their hands; nevertheless it is true. If we failed to capture the rebel army on the plains of Williamsburg it surely will not be ascribed to the want of conduct and courage in my command. (*O.R.,* ser. 1, vol. 11, pt. 1, p. 468.)

9. More than three weeks of little fighting followed the battle of Fair Oaks (Seven Pines) on May 31, 1862. At that battle, the Confederates had attacked Keyes's and Heintzelman's corps, separated from other Union troops in the area by the flooded Chickahominy River.
10. Brace is describing the Seven Days' battles of June 26–July 1, which occurred after Thomas J. "Stonewall" Jackson's army reinforced Lee.
11. François Ferdinand Philippe Louis Marie d'Orléans (1818–1900), Prince de Joinville; and his nephews, Louis Philippe Albert d'Orléans (1838–1894), comte de Paris, and Robert Philippe Louis Eugene Ferdinand d'Orléans (1840–1910), duc de Chartres. The Prince de Joinville, son of deposed French monarch Louis Philippe, and his nephews visited America in 1861–62, and the younger men served as aides-de-camp to McClellan during the Peninsula campaign. In October 1862 de Joinville, under a

pseudonym, published a report on the campaign in the *Revue des deux mondes*. In this article, he described the battle of Gaines' Mill: "The reserves are all engaged, there is not a disposable man left. It is six o'clock, the daylight is fast disappearing; if the federal army can hold out an hour longer the battle is won, for at every other point the enemy is repulsed, and Jackson, Hill, Lee and Longstreet will have urged up their troops in vain." De Joinville then related how the Confederate reserves broke the Union line, and the battle was lost. Although this publication (later translated into English by William Henry Hurlbert) had not appeared by the time Brace wrote this letter, he may have read similar comments elsewhere by the European visitors about the battle of Gaines' Mill (Prince de Joinville, *The Army of the Potomac: Its Organization, Its Commander, and Its Campaign*, trans. William Henry Hurlbert [New York, 1863], pp. 3, 89–90; *Webster's Biographical Dictionary* [Springfield, Mass., 1980]).

12. Excepting the artillery, most of Fitz-John Porter's V Corps was held in reserve during the battle of Antietam. His command then included far fewer men than Brace's estimate (O.R., ser. 1, vol. 19, pt. 1, pp. 338–39).

13. Perhaps Brace's notion of European opinion was influenced by the reports and editorials appearing in the *Times* of London. During the summer of 1862 that newspaper suggested that McClellan had accomplished little with an enormous army. It also attacked his veracity and accused him of describing his defeats as victories. Although not particularly hostile to McClellan during the autumn of 1862, the *Times* considered all the Union generals to be rather incompetent braggarts (*Times* [London], July 7, 1862, p. 11; July 16, 1862, p. 8; July 19, 1862, p. 5; July 21, 1862, p. 8; Aug. 1, 1862, p. 9; Sept. 19, 1862, p. 7).

14. The preliminary Emancipation Proclamation issued by President Lincoln on September 22, 1862, declared free the slaves in all states in rebellion on January 1, 1863 (excepting Tennessee and some areas already under Union control).

15. One of the southernmost South Carolina sea islands.

16. A reference to the editorial "The President's Proclamation," which was published in the *New-York Times* of September 28, 1862, on page 4.

17. Edwin Lawrence Godkin (1831–1902), an Anglo-Irish journalist who had immigrated to the United States and who had become a close friend of Brace and Olmsted, Godkin had traveled to Europe in the summer of 1860 to improve his health. He remained in France and Switzerland until September 1862. Upon his return, he resumed his position as correspondent for the *London Daily News*. Early in 1863 he and Olmsted began to lay plans to found a weekly paper. Although their efforts to secure the necessary funding failed during the summer of 1863, Godkin established such a journal, called the *Nation*, in July 1865 and served as its editor-in-chief (Edwin L. Godkin, *Life and Letters of E. L. Godkin*, ed. Rollo Ogden, 2 vols. [New York, 1907], 1: 188–89; NCAB).

To Henry Whitney Bellows

Private

U.S. Sanitary Commission,
Adams' House, 244 F Street,
Washington, D.C., Octr 3^d 1862.

My Dear Doctor,

I have had an intimation that the mayor knows what he is about and may very likely yet fetch me in. I don't want to tell him that I hope he won't, and if he appointed me, I should feel bound to accept, but I confess to you that I have found it impossible as yet to give up either the park or the Sanitary, both being labors of love to that degree with me, and I should groan to give up both.

I suspect that the mayor should personally about as soon have Smith,[1] and if you don't want him to take me, I wouldn't object to your telling him so, if it came in your way. I feel really grateful to him, and wouldn't like to have him think that I would stand back if he really wanted me.

I want to exterminate the Slaveholders—or rather slaveholding and the state of society founded on it. To that end I think I can work better here than anywhere else. After the war I want to be Supt of the Central Park in fact as well as name. But I am a soldier of the republic & will go where duty calls me. Perge modo.[2]

True the New York aldermen need to be fought quite as much as Lee[3] and Typhoid, but a fresh man would do for that saddle better than for this perhaps.

Yours faithfully and respectfully

Fred. Law Olmsted.

Dr Bellows.

The original is in the Henry Whitney Bellows Papers, Massachusetts Historical Society, Boston, Massachusetts.

1. Probably Thomas E. Smith, another of Mayor Opdyke's nominees for the post of street commissioner. The board of aldermen rejected Smith's appointment on October 1 (*New-York Times*, Oct. 2, 1862, p. 2).
2. "Just go ahead" or "do but fare on." Olmsted is quoting from Virgil's *Aeneid*, in which Venus tells her son Aeneas, who is then wandering in the desert:

perge modo atque hinc te reginae ad limina perfer.
(Do but fare on, press on from here to the queen's palace.)

(Virgil, *Aeneid*, trans. C. Day Lewis, bk. 1, l. 389.)

3. Confederate general Robert E. Lee.

To Henry Whitney Bellows

> U.S. Sanitary Commission,
> Adams' House, 244 F Street,
> Washington, D.C., 3ᵈ October 1862.
> *night*

My Dear Dʳ Bellows;

I now take up your letter of the 30ᵗʰ recev'd today and to which I replied en gros this P.M., to reply to it seriatim,[1] as you request.

1   As you advise both notices[2] to "go on", I have re-started them. They will appear in about a dozen leading papers daily for a month. We have evidence of their value, frequent reference being made to them. I am glad of the document but I trust you will also get something from Dunning. I have asked Collins to give me some notes of his observations. I had intended to have got something from Furness. Steiner writes that he is preparing his account of September observations in accordance with my instructions.[3]

2   With regard to Dʳ Tucker[4] and Registration I wrote you fully yesterday. Nothing important has transpired today, but we are promised the Hospital morning Returns, to-morrow morning.

3   *Hospital visitation*: I wrote Dʳ Van Buren fully this afternoon. I have nothing to add at present.[5]

4   *San Francisco Woman's Relief Fund.* I advised you this P.M. that that was all right, as you wished.[6]

Prof. Bache has not returned.

5   I also told all I knew of *Pierce*[7] *the ambulancier.*

6   I think it was the first practical thought with most of us on hearing of the St Francisco offering:[8] "We shall have need to scrutinize our expenses more carefully and to guard against any just ground of the charge of extravagance". Guard against the appearance of lavish and even the appearance of careless expenditure we can not. I have thought deeply upon this. I saw the difficulty of the case, as soon as I took up the business

of the Commission and I have sat up with it a good many nights since as it opened larger. Put any ordinary system of checks: Hold the Commission or hold its agents to the rigid accountability which would usually and in ordinary cases, rightly be imposed on trustees of funds charitable and patriotic; require the same parsimony of expenditure, impose the same checks upon waste, or upon channels of possible waste, and I am convinced you would greatly increase its expense or diminish its usefulness. Nay, more, this would be the case should you impose such checks, and attempt to secure as much exact accountability, as the large majority of your subscribers or patrons would themselves deem essential, and which if they were in your place they would demand. They have a right to demand it, why don't they? Nobody who reads the names of the Commissioners wants to go further. These are men with whom it is safe to deal on different terms from those which ordinary sagacity would prescribe in the case, were they, or the most of them, either stock-brokers or church dignitaries; professional money-makers, or professional philanthropists. Take another step. My Dear Doctor, how much do you think I have pocketed of the Commission's money? What is my salary? How much have I drawn of it & how much do you owe me? You know nothing about it. The fact is that when my personal account comes to be "rigidly investigated", it will have a queer look. The vouchers would hardly pass muster with my beloved Andrew H. Green, Comptroller of the Central Park. In fact, such a complete case of perfectly blind reliance on a man's honor was scarcely ever known before out of the records of Crim. Con. Jurisprudence.[9] Not only on his honor but on his judgment. Yes more than this—on the honorable exercise of his judgment, and the judicious use of your confidence in his honor.

I ought not to have referred to my own experience. It is hard for me to do so without an expression of feeling, which, without a knowledge of how I had been previously used would not seem very creditable to me. I once stood a full half hour before the whole Board of Commissioners of the Cent[l] Park under a cross-examination of Belmont[10] and Green about a bill of plumbing-work ordered by me in an emergency (pipes burst in a hard-frost, or something of that sort) the result of which was that the bill, amounting to forty dollars, being then more than a year due, was ordered to be paid by a Resolution of the Board which embodied a formal reproof to me, and yet which passed by a majority of one, only Green & Belmont voting against it, on the ground not that the work was not absolutely necessary or that the charge was unjustly large, but that it had not been specifically authorized in advance by the Board.[11] The same year the authorized expenditure for which I was responsible, was above a million and a half. Of course there continued to be such unauthorized expenditures, as that one for plumbing, and the Resolution which reproved me for letting them come to the knowledge of the Board, was equivalent to a reduction of my salary by so much as they amounted to. Five million dollars were expended on the park for which, as Superintendent of its final application, I was exclusively responsible, yet I was never intentionally or consciously put upon my honor for the right use of one cent by the Commission or the Treasurer. Belmont once said in exact terms that I was not to be dealt with as a gentleman. Now, I think, I need not be ashamed to tell you that I am something more than grateful to be dealt with as I am by the Commission—your Commission.

It was a constant fight on the Park between myself and Green, as to how the Engineers and draughtsmen and other officers proper should be dealt with. I wanted to put them, in certain matters, within certain limits, on their honor, to make our work—artists' work as it was with these very much—a labor of love. I perfectly succeeded. It naturally and inevitably became so with any man of ordinarily harmonious nature. But Green did all he could to prevent it, he forced me to do much which had directly the contrary tendency and he did all he could to make all these gentlemen understand that we regarded them from first to last as eye-servants and public-robbers. Whenever it was possible he required me to deal with them on his principles, when for instance, they were working fourteen and sixteen hours a day from pure love to keep our plans ahead of the field-work, he would oblige me to deal out drawing paper, pencils and india-rubber, as if it were whiskey to sailors. For these matters of cents he could control, the millions, he couldn't.

Now with all this pretence and form of accountability, I need not say it would have been almost as easy as not for me to have constructed various perfectly secure subterranean eddies whereby some faithful friend would now be holding for me enough to make me a magnifico, and that really after all, that Commission of the Park depended a thousand times more on my honor than upon all their pretence of watchfulness; that this was, in fact, a pure form and pretence, and except as it kept them right before the world and Albany,[12] was only calculated to suggest and stimulate eye-service, extravagance and peculation.

Excuse my garrulity, I'm not urging or explaining, I know, but only losing my temper. It's nine hours after office-hours[13] and you mustn't hold me too tight to the grindstone; if you do, I shall let up when your back is turned, tomorrow.

My explanation might have been shorter, but some explanation was necessary before I dare say that at 40, I have the continuous *delight* of a good boy, in the consciousness that you are worldly wise in dealing with *me* in just the *unbusiness-like* way you do. To save my life, I couldn't help giving you at any moment the best that was in me that moment. The great forbearance with which you all treat my confounded obstreperousness and uncontrollable eagerness in debate too, pays equally well, I hope. If I struggle with your purposes before they are determined, they go into my heart just as if I hadn't, the moment you commit them to me, finally & fully and, New England fashion, I'm sure that I'm the better servant for sitting at the same table with you and being allowed to talk more than my share,—your hired man always had the best appetite and took sugar and milk, a good deal of both, in his tea, and it paid, in fact, not to mind it.

Well—you can't have red-tape when your object is to get clear of red-tape. You can't have the ordinary securities here against waste and extravagance and petty peculation. You can't have your cake and eat it. Yet we must have some checks, some business forms and bars and limits. What, where to put them, when to use them, when to dispense with them? This all depends on the men and the circumstances from day to day. When to caution, when to stimulate or encourage or loosen finally depends, generally on the man you are dealing with; his training, habits, disposition. I don't say when to reprove, because really, when reproof proper, showing a loss of faith, is necessary, it will generally be better to part at once. For finally, what is your best security; rather, speaking officially I should ask, what is my best security, since the ordinary business methods of security are impracticable in my dealings with those subordinate to me? Precisely the same as yours with me. And if ever a set of men loved to do exactly what was wanted of them and to avoid what it was wanted they should avoid; it is this Sanitary Commission set. Their heart is in the economy as well as the work to be done. They love not only the work, but they love and honor the Commission and they never are persistently disposed to run into any other track than that the Commission wants to direct its expenditures. Their heart is in their duty and not only in their duty to the soldier as they may think it, but in their duty to the Commission.

This security must be nursed and humored and coaxed and cultivated. It has been & there are men who hadn't a bit of it when they came here, but have a good deal now, and it constantly grows with them. If it didn't, they wouldn't be here.

Instead of a lapse from good habits, or an increasing looseness, in the office, I think I see that there is much truer sailing as our purposes and limits become, by being produced in practice, better understood, more clearly and accurately defined, and as experience and reflection on experience makes their wisdom more acceptably evident.

There is an increasing faith that the Commission knows what it is about, and with it an increasing congruity and envelopment within the mantle of the Commission.

This is not an answer to your cautions, but is suggested by them, it is a pleasure to me to say it, & I trust it will be a pleasure to you to hear it, I mean the experience, the fact (if I am right about it), not the theory, which, of course is as old with you as it is with me.

As to your cautions practically, I believe I told you a day or two ago, I should have to sacrifice some of the elasticity of the office in order to secure more exact responsibilities. I'm doing it.

Concerning the sick-soldier's wife, Knapp promises some explanation; so of the three months back.[14] You may remember however, that I advised the Commission that my rule of monthly settlements had been disregarded and how it came to be so, in general, for some months past.[15]

As to your unanimous judgment in Ex. Com. of certain cases of special relief,[16] I am sorry to say I differ with you. I differed with you last winter in just the opposite way. I then thought these expenditures not strictly legitimate and that they must be incurred if at all only in the most extreme & urgent cases—with more caution than you, especially D[r] Agnew, were disposed to admit would be consistent with our anti red-tape platform. (I remember how he put me down with phrases very like those with which you shut Knapp's mouth in this same letter apropos de blankets: "We have but one duty, to help the sick and let our reputation take care of itself.") Now, however, if we give it up, we shall do so with the clear understanding as you say we ought, that the state agents will take it up. Now, I regard the state agents, and so do you, as a great evil, as encouraging and manifesting and keeping alive a very bad and dangerous spirit. I want to give them as little excuse as possible for staying here and appealing to state pride to furnish them with money. This is a national business not a state business and I would rather we did it than have it done as a state business.

You are singularly mistaken, however, if you suppose, as you seem to, that there has been recently a great increase in this class of expense. The February (1862) account was I remember particularly considered by the Board, Mr Knapp being present and laying it in detail before you. It was warmly approved by everyone except myself. It amounted to $353.20. The September account under the same head is—$114.30.

7   *Harris M.D. S.C.*[17]

I bow to D[r] Clark and Mr Binney.

8   *Economize the force at Washington.*

There are to-day no "*half-employed men*"; "*laggards*" or "*paid hangers on round*", here. There is not a single-man "*kept against emergencies.*"[18]

9   *Reply to Mr Knapp.* I have communicated it to him. I am fortunately situated between you for that purpose, as I don't think I quite agree with either.[19]

10   *Yours Cordially,*

ditto,[20] and with the truest respect

G[l] Secy, Fred. Law Olmsted.

445

At Knapp's request the $25.00 Bill is enclosed. Please return it, after it has been considered by the Committee.

The original is in box 951, USSC-NYPL.

1. That is, point by point.
2. Both Bellows's and Olmsted's references to these notices are vague, but they possibly mean the two articles published in late September in which the Commission described its activities after the battle of Antietam and called for new donations of supplies and money ("An Urgent Appeal from the Sanitary Commission," *New-York Times*, Sept. 25, 1862, p. 2; "What the Sanitary Commission is Doing," ibid., Sept. 26, 1862, p. 2).
3. Olmsted is referring to Sanitary Commission document number 48, an account of the organization's services to the wounded of the battle of Antietam. The persons mentioned were Sanitary Commission workers whose observations were not included in that report. Edwin J. Dunning and Lewis H. Steiner were inspectors, and Charles Collins and Horace Howard Furness served as volunteer assistants to the inspectors. At the time Olmsted wrote this letter, Steiner was probably preparing his own account of the Commission's work at Antietam, which was published later in 1862 (Lewis H. Steiner, *Report of Lewis H. Steiner, M.D., Inspector of the Sanitary Commission, Containing a Diary Kept during the Rebel Occupation of Frederick, Md., and an Account of the Operations of the U.S. Sanitary Commission during the Campaign in Maryland, September 1862* [New York, 1862]; doc. no. 48 in USSC, *Documents*; "Roster of Persons Employed by the Sanitary Commission," Oct. 1, 1862, USSC-NYPL, box 642).
4. Probably Carlos Phillips Tucker (b. 1822), a physician from New York City who had graduated from the College of Physicians and Surgeons there. Chosen by the New York members to oversee the hospital directory, Tucker did not favorably impress Olmsted. On October 1 he complained to Bellows: "I am afraid Tucker is not the right man. He has spent a week or more upon it, and I don't think he has yet suggested an original idea about it." Perhaps realizing the harshness of his criticism, Olmsted added: "In saying that Tucker is not the man, I mean not the ideal man. He will do I believe better than anyone else who has been suggested and is available." When the Executive Committee voted to carry out the registration project only if the government would at least partly finance it, Olmsted ordered Tucker to return to New York and report to the Executive Committee. Although the Commission by mid-October was forging ahead with its plans for a directory, John Bowne, not Dr. Tucker, then headed the project (John Shrady, ed., *The College of Physicians and Surgeons, New York, and Its Founders, Officers, Instructors, Benefactors, and Alumni: A History*, 2 vols. [New York, c. 1903–4], 2: 28–29; FLO to HWB, Oct. 1, 1862, USSC-NYPL, box 641; FLO to [C. P.] Tucker, Oct. 5, 1862; FLO to HWB, Oct. 13, 1862, USSC-NYPL, box 641).
5. In preparation for a special inspection of the military general hospitals sponsored by the Sanitary Commission, William Van Buren had prepared a circular to be sent to the distinguished civilian physicians who would be undertaking the inspection. On October 3 Olmsted recommended some changes in and additions to the suggested queries in the circular (later published as a part of Sanitary Commission document number 56). Generally he urged that the guidelines for the inspection should emphasize inquiry into and advice upon medical care and sanitary conditions (FLO to W. H. Van Buren, Oct. 3, 1862, USSC-NYPL, box 835, 1: 163–67; doc. no. 56 in USSC, *Documents*).

6. The ladies of San Francisco raised a soldiers' aid fund which they sent to President Lincoln in the fall of 1862. Upon the recommendation of Surgeon General Hammond, the contribution was turned over to the Sanitary Commission to be used in its work. Olmsted, in a letter begun on October 2, informed Bellows that Hammond had telegraphed his thanks to the women and that the Commission also had written them (HWB to FLO, Sept. 30, 1862, USSC-NYPL, box 745: 2354; FLO to HWB, Oct. 2, 1862, USSC-NYPL, box 641).

7. Henry Miller Pierce (1831–1902) was president of Rutgers Female Institute, later Rutgers Female College, located on Fifth Avenue in New York City. In the fall of 1862 he was in Washington to urge the creation of an independent ambulance corps. In a letter that Bellows had not yet received, Olmsted, who distrusted Pierce's motives, wrote: "Pierce—of Rutgers' Institute, has been here off and on for months. Hammond says he wants to be Colonel commanding the ambulance corps. He is supposed to have some friend at court and pushes the matter. Hammond is glad to use him and thinks he will do for the colonel—if he earns it." While Pierce's crusade for an ambulance corps coincided with that of the Sanitary Commission, he had no formal links to the Commission (FLO to HWB, Oct. 2, 1862, USSC-NYPL, box 641; HWB to FLO, Oct. 13, 1862, USSC-NYPL, box 746: 2463; *Medical and Surgical Reporter*, n.s., 9, no. 1 [Oct. 4, 1862]: 17).

8. Olmsted is referring to a gift of one hundred thousand dollars given to the Sanitary Commission by the citizens of San Francisco in September 1862. Bellows in his letter of September 30 had chided Olmsted about the increased expenses of the Washington office and had added, "Because we have a rich uncle in San Francisco, who sends us $100,000—we must not grow less careful what we do, than if we had only 10,000 in hand" (HWB to FLO, Sept. 30, 1862, USSC-NYPL, box 745: 2354).

9. *Crim. con.* was the standard abbreviation for *criminal conversation*, the Victorian term for illicit sexual intercourse. In England the criminal conversation suit was a civil action brought by an injured husband for damages against his wife's lover. From 1798 until 1857, success in such a suit was required for any husband who wished to receive a total divorce (allowing remarriage), which could be granted only by Parliament. Olmsted was jokingly alluding to the absence of safeguards against fraud and collusion in such suits. Collusion between the husband and the wife's alleged paramour was easy because the wife was not a party to the case and could neither testify nor call witnesses to defend her reputation. Moreover, standards of evidence to show that adultery had occurred were very loose, and the husband, not wishing to appear to be profiting financially from his wife's adultery, frequently did not collect the damages awarded him. The divorce bill that passed in 1857 abolished the suit for criminal conversation and set up stricter guidelines concerning the award of damages in cases of adultery (Judith Schneid Lewis, "The Problem of Criminal Conversation: A Study in Victorian Social Attitudes" [Unpublished paper, Johns Hopkins University, 1972], pp. 1–2, 12–17, 27–34).

10. August Belmont (1816–1890), a wealthy banker, prominent Democrat, and member of the Board of Commissioners of Central Park. Olmsted, as superintendent of Central Park, and Belmont, as a commissioner, had often been at loggerheads. In 1858 the banker had supported the amendments to Olmsted and Vaux's Greensward design that had been proposed by his fellow commissioner Robert J. Dillon. Olmsted had complained in 1861 that Belmont, from the time the Greensward plan had been adopted, had been doing his utmost to hinder and delay its implementation. Olmsted's dislike for Belmont stemmed not only from previous quarrels but also from a belief that the banker, an agent for the Rothschild family, represented the aristocratic pretensions of riches and a desire for a fixed, hereditary nobility in America. Furthermore, by the summer of 1863 Olmsted would view Belmont as a virulent Copperhead who was attempting to mislead the people (*DAB*; FLO to John

Bigelow, Feb. 9, 1861 [*Papers of FLO*, 3: 324–25]; FLO to Oliver W. Gibbs, Nov. 5, 1862, below; FLO to Edwin L. Godkin, July 15, 1863, below).

11. The editors have been unable to discover any other account of this incident.

12. Albany, as the capital of New York, is used here as a synonym for state government.

13. That is, 2:00 A.M.

14. Bellows, in his letter, complained about some of the expenditures that Knapp, as head of the Commission's special relief division, had authorized. According to Bellows, "The whole six items entered under Special Relief—amounts to $104.25 (& ending with $25. for clothes &[c]. for a sick-soldier's wife!!) we account irrelevant & unjustifiable." He further pointed out that expenses incurred by the soldiers' lodge operated by special relief had been allowed to accumulate for four months, even though the Commission's policy was to settle such accounts each month (HWB to FLO, Sept. 30, 1862, USSC-NYPL, box 745: 2354).

15. Most likely Olmsted is referring to the rule that in September 1862 read, "Before the fifth day of each month, an account of all claims against the Commission, for goods or services rendered to it during the previous month, will, as far as possible, be collected, approved, and paid, and the accounts of the Office will be audited by one of the Secretaries, assisted by an expert accountant, or if that is impracticable, by any two of the above-named Officers" ("Rules of the Central Office," doc. no. 53 in USSC, *Documents*).

16. According to Bellows, the Executive Committee unanimously opposed many of the expenses incurred in special relief for soldiers passing through Washington. The minister argued, "The state agents so numerous & with so little else to do, must now send their own men *Home*" (HWB to FLO, Sept. 30, 1862, USSC-NYPL, box 745: 2354).

17. Bellows reported the praise that Henry G. Clark, who was in charge of the special inspection of military hospitals, and Horace Binney, Jr., had given to Elisha Harris for usefulness and efficiency and added the further comment, "Our Ex. Com are always however very skeptical on that point let the evidence be as it will! and I share all their doubts" (ibid.).

18. Olmsted here is quoting from Bellows's advice on how to lessen the expenses of the Washington office (ibid.).

19. Knapp had argued that even when the Sanitary Commission urgently needed supplies, it should not ask the government for them. Bellows, in turn, asserted: "When we can use govt stores *better* than they can for the service of the sick, it is our duty to take them. We have but one duty, to help the sick & let our reputation take care of itself" (ibid.).

20. Olmsted is playfully repeating the closing of Bellows's letter as one more point needing a response and is adding to it a sentiment of his own.

To CHARLES LORING BRACE

> U.S. Sanitary Commission,
> Adams' House, 244 F Street,
> Washington, D.C., 4ᵗʰ Octʳ 1862.

My Dear Charley,

I am responsible for nothing to go before the public which I write as "private". You would do very wrong to publish information so obtained.

How do you know how or from whom or with what injunctions I got it? I don't know to what you refer, but if you have not carried out your intention, you must not. Private means private. I would give a great deal rather than risk a chance of having it published and shall feel very uneasy.

Now as to your *charges* and the *facts* upon which you rest them—I have time but for a few and but a word for them. First as to the Potomac, you *assume* that it was from fear of disaster or ill-success that it was not done. *I suppose you are mistaken.* I think it would have been a piece of stupid folly for a very different reason. Who told you the motive? What right have you to assume it?

Manassas: I say nothing as to the main question except that your "facts", which are not proven themselves, prove nothing. But I did not argue that time was wanted to discipline our army for the capture of the country Rail Road station at Manassas. *It was wanted before a steady, irresistible progress of our army thro' Virginia and Carolina could be calculated upon with reasonable confidence.* The talk of rebel surgeons about the value of raw troops, "charge and fire!" is all the most contemptible nonsense. You ought to be ashamed of yourself for introducing it in an argument.

"The whole idea of the Peninsula campaign seems a gigantic blunder." Where and how have you learned what it was? Only officially from a man whom I regard as a liar, a gambler in armies, who had bet heavily against Gen'l McClellan, who prays with clergymen and never ceases with Genl McClellan's subordinates of the army to call him "a God damnd fool."[1]

"He ought to have assaulted Yorktown at once. Rebel accounts agree that they had only a small body of men there." Your extract which you say is *"evidence"* was evidently prepared for your market in Richmond. It is simply notoriously false. It certainly is no more *evidence* than Mother Hubbard[2] is authority in astronomy.

I have seen Yorktown; seen the camps there and the works, and I never heard an officer or well-informed gentleman, on the ground, friend or enemy of McClellan, pretend for a moment that it would have been possible to take the works by assault without approaches and breaches, and I don't myself believe it would. I have heard that experienced European officers expressed doubt if it could have been taken after a month's cannonading, by assault, and I have heard old and new officers say that with 20,000 men it could be held interminably against a land force from the South, only.

"He lost more men in the trenches than he would have lost in an assault."

How many did he lose in the trenches? You don't know. Did he lose 10,000? Did he lose 1000? Did he lose 10?

I was on the ground during nearly the whole of the trench operations. I had a trusty, expert, experienced surgeon[3] who visited the hospitals
and the trenches daily. I don't believe he lost ten men in the trenches.

"His trenches have cost more lives than the bloodiest assault."

Again where is the evidence?

I beg you to consider this. Where is the evidence? I have followed
him as closely as it was possible for me, in person, in each campaign, and I
have had the best men I could get for love or money to study this very
question. All his trenching has cost no more life than Fremont's at St Louis
or Halleck's at Corinth, (Jackson's at New Orleans I might add).[4]

But you are sure that I am wrong? Where again, I say, is your
evidence?

I tell you my friend that the whole of that standard accusation is a
pure, unadulterated, stale lie, as much so as the Coup d'Etat.[5] There never
was the smallest ground of truth in it. It was a clean creation of our damnd
swindling, perjured Abolition politicians, in my judgment. So, don't assume it as granted again in argument with me, if you please.

There follow various statements from skedaddling newspaper reporters of the anti McC. party, and of rival, ambitious soldiers. They have
never been replied to by McC. His facts, and as head of the army he was
not unlikely to be as well informed as the rest, you haven't got. The
statements you refer to are purely ex parte, there is a motive against truth
in each; they *are not* evidence and they would prove nothing *essential* to
your case, if they were.

"In all his fighting he has gained nothing by strategy or skill but
simply by hard fighting and fearful sacrifice of his men."

This is the wickedly careless accusation of a highly prejudiced man
given over to believe a lie. It is precisely what Gates said of Washington.[6]

"His delays have cost hundreds of millions, the national honor &
universal discouragement."

Endless begging of the question. I assert that "his delays" have
never been his delays. That interference and arrest of his operations in the
interests of certain Presidential aspirants, and of John Pope, Fremont and
McDowell, have occasioned and necessitated these delays. I assert and
believe that these operations if not thus interfered with would have saved
hundreds of millions & all the rest. My assertions are as good as yours.
From the specimens you give of the grounds on which you make them, I
think better.

"Disgrace and disaster." (McClellan.)

Back again. (Stanton & Chase.)

Your statement of the conditions of South Mountain and Antietam I accept no more than that about the ditches.

Had they not ammunition? (What a question?) Their cartridge boxes full, I suppose.

"I feel a profound moral conviction that under Gen. McClellan we shall not for two years more drive out the rebels from Virginia, and never conquer them."

So do I, if Stanton & Chase rule and you and others who believe in their statements, instead of asking for the facts and drawing your own conclusions from them, continue to encourage them in their corner-grocery strategy.

"And yet I know of no proper General."

In one word, you give it up, then.

"You see how Europe regards him."

You see how Europe regards Davis.

You see how Europe regards Butler.

You see how Europe regards the Emancipation Proclamation.[7]

The more I investigate the grounds of the statements, upon which the whole of the war on McC. is based, the more disgraceful to our national education its success seems to me to be. Spirit rapping[8] is nothing to it. That was simply folly. This is wicked injustice and ingratitude. Without the smallest knowledge of facts, the most improbable theories are built with splendid stucco fronts, upon statements emanating from nobody knows who, which are in themselves such improbable conjectures that a school-boy ought to have ears pulled, for seriously presenting them as conjectures. And upon these theories, a large part of our writing and spouting population insist that plans shall be further erected, upon the success of which they are willing to stake the existence of the nation.

But I think I see gleams of returning sense, even from this cesspool of mischief. God grant it be not too late.

Part Second

Haven't I told you again & again the niggers can't combine—therefore *can't "rise"*?

"Will they run?" Yes, when they have something to run to. But they will not run to starvation. I sent my views of this to the Times & they were published sometime last winter, early.[9]

I never had the smallest confidence in the success of the dealings with negroes in South Carolina. I couldn't imagine a worse way of treating them & I told Chase so.

I saw your Sunday leader & in the main agree with it, but it will require something more than letting them alone. No, I'm wrong. I don't believe the slaves will be armed or a war of extermination (by them on their masters) ensue. They will never do it. Never fight against them except in our armies, led by white men.

Give my dearest love to Godkin. I would limp ten miles to talk an hour with him.

Now don't regard me as a devoted partisan of McClellan. He is treated with the most abominable, infernal injustice and when I cease to hate this & those who induce it, and who are so reckless of truth to induce it, when for an instant I cease to kick and struggle against this & them, I shall the next instant hate myself with the intensity of hell.

Yours affectionately

Fred. Law Olmsted.

1. Secretary of War Edwin M. Stanton (see FLO to HWB, July 13, 1862, above).
2. Presumably the nursery rhyme character.
3. Dr. William M. Chamberlain.
4. Gen. John C. Frémont and Gen. Henry W. Halleck in the Civil War, and Gen. Andrew Jackson in the War of 1812.
5. A reference to rumors that McClellan intended to overthrow the government and become dictator.
6. Olmsted's account of the famous quarrel in 1777–78 between American Revolutionary generals Horatio Gates (c. 1728/29–1806) and George Washington (1732–1799) is somewhat in error. Gates himself did not criticize Washington but permitted the circulation of a letter written to him that allegedly insulted Washington with the sentence, "Heaven had determined to save our country, or a weak general and bad counsellors would have ruined it" (Samuel White Patterson, *Horatio Gates: Defender of American Liberties* [New York, 1941], pp. 216–23).
7. Olmsted probably believed that the European reaction to Jefferson Davis had been favorable. Since Davis had served as a U.S. senator and a cabinet member, some English commentators tended to view him as more qualified than Lincoln to preside over a nation.

   European, especially English, opinion had run high against Union general Benjamin Butler after May 1862, when he issued his notorious "woman order," which authorized Union soldiers in occupied New Orleans to consider any female who insulted them to be a prostitute. Some commentators interpreted the order as allowing not only insult but actual physical abuse of these women.

   At the time Olmsted wrote this letter, the actual European reactions to Lincoln's preliminary Emancipation Proclamation, issued on September 22, had not been received and reprinted in the American newspapers. Yet some of the abuse that the North would receive for this step had been suggested in editorials in the *New York World* and *Tribune* that reported and commented upon earlier denunciations of such a plan by the *Economist*, *Saturday Review*, and the *Times* of London (Donaldson Jordan and Edwin Pratt, *Europe and the American Civil War* [New York, 1931], p. 104; Ephraim Douglass Adams, *Great Britain and the American Civil War*, 2 vols. [London, 1925], 1: 59, 81; *New-York Daily Tribune*, Oct. 1, 1862, p. 4).
8. A reference to the alleged communications from the spirit world received through knocking noises by mediums such as the Fox sisters who lived near Rochester, New York. In 1850, after the girls, Margaret and Kate, then sixteen and fourteen, began

hearing and translating these sounds, they went on tour; and a host of imitators sprang up. In 1888 one of the sisters confirmed the suspicions of many when she revealed that they themselves had created the sounds (*Notable American Women*).
9. See "How to Reason with the South," November 29, 1861, above.

To Henry Whitney Bellows

Private.

Sanitary Commission,
Adams' House, 244 F street,
Washington, D.C., Octr 7 1862.

My Dear Doctor,
    I received this evening your letter by Knapp and his gratifying verbal report. Also a copy of your letter to Mr. Teshmacher,[1] which I intend to return herewith.
    I had another of those protracted turns of vertigo which have troubled me lately, yesterday and hardly dare write again yet. (I call it vertigo, which it isn't, but it answers for an explanation. I always wonder when it comes surging thro' my brain, if it isn't apoplexy this time).[2]
    The state and individual relief operators are I fear doing us much harm, by spreading false reports of us. They seem to be very industrious at this, and we have got to head them off. It is no time to retrench. We had better cut a broad swarth for the next two battle-months, even if we have then to greatly close down. By that time the S. G['s] arrangements will be better than now, and the education he is giving the Surgeons will have become more effective. The small craft are annoying us very much. Our policy is to fire up strong, run them down and outsail them. When we have a tolerably clear sea again, we can measure our coals.
    We have no stores on hand and urgent calls. We have no reserve for battles—not the slightest.
    I am afraid that it was a mistake to give out material to make up,[3] unless you were prepared to do so on a very large scale, continuously.
    It has struck me in hearing Knapp talk tonight of his conversation with you, that you were almost certain to imbibe a somewhat erroneous impression of the effect on me of your letter. I was simply embarrassed by the uncertainty in which your letter left me as to how far you wished me to act on my judgment. It is not only perfectly just but perfectly natural and

453

commendable that, as the business of the Commission increases in importance, my *relative* responsibility sh'd lessen, but you ought, when you
resume a responsibility which I have for a time been allowed to exercise, to
notify me of it, otherwise it may place me in a very embarrassing position,
and the mere state of doubt as to what my responsibilities are, and as to
how much I am to depend on you, is unfavorable to good and decisive
judgment. Your action with regard to the West, of which you here advise
me, is a case in point.[4] I had previously done all that I thought necessary to
accomplish the very purposes you had in view, and I think I so informed
you. You have nevertheless felt it to be necessary to give orders for these
same purposes from the Exec. Com. It was either a mistake of mine, or it
was a mistake of yours, for such a course would of course lead soon, if it has
not in this instance, to complexity of instructions and contradictory requirements. Again, I observe that Newberry reports to you direct. (I have
not received a word from him)   You say that you will send his letter to me.
Is that the course you wish his reports to take in future? This is, in fact
gradually ceasing to be the Central Office of the Commission. I trust you
will fully believe me when I say that if this is your wish, I have not the
slightest objection, and that I should not regret it or be annoyed by it. But
any change of this kind ought not to be made in a slip-shod way. There
ought to be a clear understanding where responsibility finally rests. Upon
this point there never can be too much red-tape; beyond it, hardly too
little.

Excuse me if I seem to be assuming a didactic style; I merely wish
to establish a ground for asking in general for more specific definement of
my duty.

Is there not a vagueness in the duty taken by the Executive Committee? There are certainly two quite distinct classes of duties exercised by
it, and it seems to me that it would be better that they should be separated,
and that theoretically and on your records there should be two Committees; one to act (as a Vice Commission), chiefly if not solely on matters
referred to it from this office—matters too important to be decided here,
under ordinary circumstances, without the approval of the Executive
Committee, which would then assume the responsibility of them, before
the Board. The other the New York Committee, looking after local matters, such as purchases and shipments under advice from this office, or
instructions from the Executive Committee; inspection of local hospitals,
transports etc. The Medical Committee would still have distinct duties.

My opinion is that such an arrangment would practically save time
and do away with the necessity of a good deal of debate. A clear sense of
responsibility always begets decisive thought, and a defined and limited
range is necessary to a clear sense of responsibility.

THE EXECUTIVE COMMITTEE OF THE U.S. SANITARY COMMISSION

I have spent a good deal of thought and of talk and some ink upon the arrangment of supplies for McClellan's army, all of which would have been held in abeyance had I known that you had it in view to deal with Dunning. I shall welcome him most heartily and there will be no difficulty in readjusting arrangments to accommodate him, but I have been wasting my time nevertheless—and it ought not be the business of both the Executive Committee and of myself, at the same time, to be occupied independently with practical questions of this kind.

I think that either I should have no official responsibility with regard to the West, or that you should have no strictly official intercourse with Newberry—extraordinary occasions excepted—except through this office. For—as an illustration—I have also been wasting a good deal of thought upon that matter of the Western Council, and what may grow out of it, if your Committee is going to take the management of it directly. I have been slowly cogitating upon it and matters connected with it, for some time, and when I have nothing more immediately important, I shall have some suggestions to submit to you. You will remember that I intimated as much when I was in Walpole. Judge Hoadly's[5] suggestion of a

455

Western Executive Committee and the call for the Indianapolis meeting,[6] led me to propose to Newberry part of a crude idea, which I should have presented to the Commission in a mature and complete form, had not my illness interfered with all such intentions. I did not give it to Newberry, or propose that you should do so, in a positive form, because I did not think it had been deliberated enough upon, and I wanted him to feel his way for a time with it. For the present at least we should allow it to be merely an advisory Council. It should have no authority, positively, over our property or agents.

I shall make good use of Mrs Kirkland.[7] I am very glad to have her here.

Yours Respectfully,

Fred. Law Olmsted.

Rev. D[r] H. W. Bellows;
Chm[n] E. C.[8]

The original is in box 951 of USSC-NYPL.

1. Henry Frederick Teschemacher (or Teschemaker) (1823–1904), the German-born mayor of San Francisco for three terms, from 1859 until 1863. A resident of the city since 1842, Teschemacher was viewed as a champion of good government. He served as chairman of the San Francisco Committee of Thirteen (also known as the Central Committee of the Soldiers and Sailors' Relief Fund), which raised approximately four hundred thousand dollars for the Sanitary Commission in 1862 (Melvin G. Holli and Peter d'A. Jones, eds., *Biographical Dictionary of American Mayors, 1820–1980: Big City Mayors* [Westport, Conn., 1981], pp. 357–58; H. F. Teschemacher to HWB and GTS, Sept. 19, 1862, Henry Whitney Bellows Papers, Massachusetts Historical Society, Boston, Mass.).
2. Olmsted is referring to fainting and dizzy spells that had sometimes resulted from his overwork and exhaustion. During the autumn of 1845 such attacks had led him to give up attendance at scientific lectures at Yale College. In 1863 he described his symptoms during a similar attack as "causing me instinctively to sink to the floor," and he added, "I believe it to be a hesitation of the brain to perform its functions owing to deficient nutrition, or more immediately to a deficient flow of blood to the brain" (JO to FLO and John Hull Olmsted, Dec. 30, 1845; *Papers of FLO*, 1: 192, 225; FLO to MPO, July 20, 1863).
3. That is, dry goods to be made into needed hospital clothing for the soldiers by patriotic women belonging to the local societies. Apparently Olmsted convinced Bellows that the Commission should not take the supplying of such materials as one of its purposes. In a Sanitary Commission document of October 23, 1862, Bellows commented: "I regret to state that the Commission, after a short trial of the plan of furnishing material, finds it working so badly for its own interest, that it has been compelled to abandon it. We find that if we supply any Societies with material, we must supply *all*, and that to attempt this, would ruin our treasury in twenty days." The minister further argued that the resources of the Commission were needed for

its principal duties: the inspection of camps and hospitals, the collection and distribution of supplies, the preparation of helpful manuals for military officers, as well as battlefield relief, the care of convalescent soldiers, and the study of the condition and needs of the sick and wounded soldiers (doc. no. 54 in USSC, *Documents*).

4. In a letter of October 6 Bellows advised Olmsted, "I have written Dr. Newberry to establish his *Western* Council at once & to enter on active operations in view of recent & coming battles." Bellows later elaborated on this plan to Newberry: "As a council of advice with local and partial authority, subject to revision, and liable to orders from the Commission, it will be very useful. Beyond that, it must do harm." Such a Western council was, however, never put into operation (HWB to FLO, Oct. 6, 1862, USSC-NYPL, box 951; "The National Quality of the Commission" [HWB to JSN], Nov. 5, 1862, doc. M-6, Frederick Law Olmsted Collection, Rare Book Room, U.S. Army Military History Institute, Carlisle Barracks, Pa.).

5. George Hoadly (1826–1902), vice-president of the Cincinnati branch of the Sanitary Commission. Born in New England of distinguished lineage, Hoadly moved to Cleveland, Ohio, as a child. He attended college there and studied law at Harvard and in Salmon P. Chase's law office. Hoadly's marriage in 1855 to Robert W. Burnet's niece allied him to a prominent Cincinnati family. He served as judge of Cincinnati's superior court from 1851 until 1855 and was reelected to the post in 1859 and 1864. Hoadly began his political career as a Democrat, but his views on slavery, like those of his mentor Chase, led him to become a Republican. He returned to the Democratic party during Reconstruction and was elected governor of Ohio in 1883. At the close of his career, he was a successful corporation lawyer in New York City.

Hoadly's role in representing the Cincinnati branch's claims before the U.S. Sanitary Commission won him the dislike of Olmsted and the other commissioners. Olmsted particularly resented the manner he believed Hoadly had assumed toward the national Commission and declared himself astonished by "the utter recklessness of his assertions, the weakness of his arguments and the want of every quality which a judge or gentleman should evince in a discussion of this sort." Ten days later Olmsted suggested that Hoadly simulated anger in order to cloak what even the latter realized were unjustified claims and actions.

Not only did Olmsted deem Hoadly unscrupulous and ungentlemanly, but he also came to believe that the Cincinnatian contributed—even if unwittingly—to secessionist plots. In early January 1863 Olmsted told another member of the Sanitary Commission: "I feel that we are going to strike with some effect upon a matter of infinitely more importance than the health and comfort of our soldiers. I begin to have a suspicion that Hoadly, in this matter, has been the cat's paw of a bigger and deeper scoundrel than himself." Olmsted had heard rumors that a plot existed for "working off New England," that is, isolating and separating that section from the other loyal states. To the general secretary, the "secessionism" of Hoadly and the Cincinnati branch aided and abetted such plans for further splintering the Union (DAB; FLO to HWB, Dec. 10, 1862, below; FLO to Mark Skinner, Dec. 20, 1862; FLO to [HWB?], Jan. 3, 1863).

6. See FLO to JSN, November 5, 1862, note 1, below.

7. Caroline Matilda Stansbury Kirkland (1801–1864), author and close friend of Henry W. Bellows. During the eight years she lived in Michigan, she wrote two books about frontier life which received considerable critical acclaim. After the accidental death of her husband in 1846, Caroline Kirkland supported herself by a literary career. She edited *Sartain's Union Magazine* for several years, wrote short stories and a biography of George Washington, and compiled anthologies. She and Olmsted probably became acquainted in the 1850s while working on the *Schoolfellow Magazine*, which was published by Dix, Edwards & Company.

During October 1862 Henry W. Bellows employed Caroline Kirkland to work for the Sanitary Commission in Washington with the intention of having her explain the Commission's work and policies to the many women who called there. He told Olmsted, "You will find her strong & wise; able to meet these women with a will & a reason stronger than theirs'—& knowing the sex, as *we* cannot, she can stave off a good deal of impertinence that you cannot deal with." Olmsted, however, asked her to compile a narrative of the Commission's hospital transport service from letters written by him and other Sanitary Commission employees and volunteers. Unable to complete that task, she largely blamed working conditions at the Commission office, which totally lacked "the privacy and quiet necessary for any literary effort." Early in 1863 Olmsted reorganized and rewrote the manuscript which Caroline Kirkland had begun, and it was published that year as *Hospital Transports* (*Notable American Women*; *DAB*; *Papers of FLO*, 2: 374–75; C. M. Kirkland to FLO, Nov. 18, 1862; K. P. Wormeley to FLO, Oct. 15, 1862, and Feb. 28, 1863; HWB to FLO, Oct. 5, 1862, USSC-NYPL, box 746: 2405).

8. That is, the Executive Committee of the Sanitary Commission.

To Mary Perkins Olmsted

U.S. Sanitary Commission,
Adams' House, 244 F Street,
Washington, D.C., 11th Octob[r] 1862.

My Dear Wife,

Your three several letters, that written en route, and nos 1 & 2 from Holly Hill are receivd.[1]

It will be hardly possible for me to leave now before end of next week. It is obvious that the Sanitary business now requires my whole time and energy. It is peculiar, you see, in this, that if the war was on a scale of 25 prct less magnitude, every day's demand *of the present* would be felt as a great occasion, requiring the most energetic use of all the means in our power to meet it decently. Such in real truth is the case, and we can't be too wide awake and earnest when well-directed labor must be so well repaid in saving of human life and suffering. But from this plain rise constantly mountains of the steepest sort, and no sooner do I feel that I have got things prepared to overcome one than another arises overtopping it beyond. So, I never can begin to prepare to go to New York without seeing that it must be at the cost of neglecting something which in ordinary times would be felt to be of the gravest importance, demanding everything of a man.

You say you didn't know that you had reproached me. You hadn't; I was reproaching myself and arguing the case with you. Thank you for encouraging me—that I suppose is what I need.

As to your Vanderbilt landing project;[2] I think you may calculate thus: Fred will come to New-York in a few days, *to work on the park*. That is his object & his only justification for being away from Washington. He will need to give the greater part of every day to the park and of every night to the Sanitary Commission, which holds regular meetings two evenings in the week at about Madison Square & four times a week after three o'clk at 498 Broadway.[3] He will come short of this only from very constraining & important demand elsewhere or from fatigue amounting to illness. That is simply his duty as a man: Local and special family duties must rightly be arranged where they can on this stem, because if *the men* don't, as a rule, at this time so arrange their special family duties in relation to the larger communal-part of their family duties, there is the greatest possible danger of such an upsetting of the very frame of society, that it would have been better that our children had never been born. A rather dark prospect, but not as dark as most other folks's that I meet nowadays—and whether it is dark or not is simply a question of heroism. It is a day for heroes & we must be heroes along with the rest. I think that a vacation of a day or two at Holly Hill would be about as good a thing for me as anything else, especially if I don't have to fight Hadley.[4] Vanderbilt's landing is neither one thing nor the other—neither park nor vacation for me. It is the furthest point from the park to which I could go and not be out of town to it. Could we possibly go into Vaux's house temporarily?[5] Could we get decent furnished lodgings in town for a month? I shall need to have a horse boarded somewhere—probably can have him kept at the Arsenal[6]—if not, shall pay for it at a stable on 59th St. Is Jack or Sochques[7] at liberty?

I write coarsely of *my* convenience, not selfishly, but because I can set that forth & you can judge how much I ought to yield of it better than I can see yours which is far more complicated, being the retail department of the family business, and judge what I should demand of it. I can not tell you how much money I can furnish for it. I had to borrow $300 for the stable work you know (carpenter's bill) which I haven't yet paid.[8] The book-keeper, who has been working 12 to 14 hours a day for a long time, has not been able to clear up my account. Our old book-keeper left; we had an incompetent man here while I was on the Pamunkey.[9] My rules were disregarded, partly the fault of the Executive Committee, who helped to get things mixed up, and while I know that it's all right in a general way, I feel cautious about going on at random. I hope to have everything square soon & to begin November with no obligations and an income of $4000. This I mean is reasonable, but till then, I am inclined to move as slowly as possible, and on short tacks either way.

My present foresight is strong to your being in Washington this winter. The Sanitary is too large to be managed parenthetically. You might think that it seemed bad managment that I don't divide it off more &

throw it upon the others. My dear, good organizing talent (like mine) is the rarest thing to find(!) You can't get it under $4000 a year & this is a "charitable" establishment. Volunteer unpaid work even of good men, you know what it is. I believe that Bellows, Van Buren, Agnew & Gibbs give, each nearly as much as I, but they are not paid; they are not subordinate, except at intervals and temporarily, to me. I can't throw upon them any of my responsibility and I really have to do their work over again—most of it—that is, to judge of it & argue it over with them. See Bellows' letter enclosed.[10] Well, I think I have got to be normally in Washington for six months more pretty certainly—at least six months, don't you? Even if we are never so successful; the San. Com. will have to do for that much. Then I had better have you here all. We will be as frugal as we can, & San. Com. must pay me enough for it. I hope it won't be much more than at present. Knapp & Jenkins have both determined to have their families here.

I can only thus give you the elements. I will accommodate myself to your judgment on them. I really mean so & you will not be afraid, please.

I had a great little pleasure last night, in being able to telegraph back in answer to the enclosed notes from Portsmouth Grove:[11] "Be of good cheer!" In less than 40 hours from the time the letters were written, I had a letter back which would give that good soul Wormeley, a chance to sleep. I got the letters at 10 P.M. & sent a decisive favorable reply by the train at 6 A.M. following. I like to have the gratitude & friendship of such a high strung and thoroughbred woman, even at [a] small cost.

There are lots of "delegations" here from Boston & New York about ambulances &c.[12] and heavy business generally in our line. I have had to enlarge the office.

Yours lovingly,

Fred.

P.S. *I enclose letter from Vaux & check for $166.66* (just received).

1. Mary Perkins Olmsted and her children had traveled from Connecticut to Staten Island, where her grandmother, Abigail Smith Perkins, the widow of Dr. Cyrus Perkins, resided at a farm called Holly Hill (Laura Wood Roper, *FLO: A Biography of Frederick Law Olmsted* [Baltimore, 1973], p. 58; Edmund Janes Cleveland and Horace Gillette Cleveland, *The Genealogy of the Cleveland and Cleaveland Families* . . . , 3 vols. [Hartford, Conn., 1899], 1: 876).
2. Vanderbilt's Landing, the third and last stop on Staten Island of the ferry from New York City, was located on the Upper Bay. Mary Perkins Olmsted may have thought that this area's proximity to the ferry would make it a convenient place to stay while

Olmsted was working in New York City ([Selden C. Judson], *Illustrated Sketch Book of Staten Island, New York, Its Industries and Commerce* [New York, 1886], p. 108).

3. The most likely location of these meetings was Bellows's home, the parsonage of All Souls Church, on the corner of Fourth Avenue and 20th Street, approximately four blocks from Madison Square. The New York members of the Commission rented a loft at 498 Broadway in May 1862 but moved their office after mid-October to 823 Broadway (*Diary of the Civil War*, pp. 226, 265).

4. Andrew Hadley had been the Olmsteds' tenant on Tosomock, the family's farm on Staten Island, for over two and one-half years. The editors have found no reference to any quarrel between Olmsted and Hadley. The tenant, however, had often fallen behind in his rent payments, and Mary Perkins Olmsted considered him to be "a little shiftless" (MPO to JO, Feb. 16, 1862; FLO to JO, March 12, 1860; see also MPO to JO, July 17 and Dec. 19, 1861).

5. Apparently the residence of the Calvert Vaux family was still one of the buildings of the former convent of Mount St. Vincent in Central Park. During Vaux's illness, he and his wife had been staying with one of his physicians (FLO to MPO, Sept. 21, 1862, above; *Trow's New York City Directory . . . For the Year Ending May 1, 1863* [New York, 1862]).

6. The New York State Arsenal, located in the southeast corner of Central Park and acquired by the Central Park commission in 1858 (*Papers of FLO*, 3: 184, n. 21).

7. Jack and Sochques ("Socks") were Olmsted's horses (MPO to JO, July 9, 1861).

8. Olmsted had borrowed $300 from his father in August to build a stable at Tosomock, but had loaned $150 to Vaux during the latter's illness in September (FLO to JO, July 25 and Sept. 15, 1862).

9. While Olmsted was on the Peninsula, a Mr. Cave served as the Commission's bookkeeper. He did not apply for the position but rather was temporarily entrusted with those duties because of the Commission's pressing need. When his competency in the job was questioned in mid-July, Cave left and refused ever to return to the Commission (JFJ to HWB, May 4, 1862, USSC-NYPL, box 640; Alfred J. Bloor to FLO, July 30, 1862, USSC-NYPL, box 744: 2004).

10. Olmsted most likely enclosed the letter that Bellows had written to him on October 8 in reply to Olmsted's detailed letter of October 3, presented above. In it the minister had apologized for his recent letters expressing dismay over the large expenditures of the Washington office. Olmsted probably wished his wife to see Bellows's judgment of his own and the other commissioners' abilities in managing the affairs of the Sanitary Commission, which read:

> I am not a man of business, as you have doubtless found out. I wear the mask of one with some poor attempt at enacting the character—in all this the recent San. Com. life of mine, but it is a very shameful hypocrisy on my part, & you & every other Commissioner, must have seen how constantly the mask is dropped & how little of that sort, it covers!
>
> . . . You must allow me to prance about now and then, on my official-horse; & wink at the folly, without publickly laughing. I claim the privilege of being inconsistent, & of contradicting myself, and of ordering & counter-manding—as other Brig. Gen^{ls} of Volunteers do. I haven't the least disposition therefore to hold so much as a parasol up against the peltings of your gentle but piercing storm, as you unfold the policy of the Commission so truly, & show how inconsistent it is with my recent letters. . . .
>
> I won't attempt to explain how we came to our *panic* about money &c. We are all busy men—concerned half the day with other matters—& bringing our minds, spasmodically, to bear on Com^n business, at the set moments. Of course we don't, & can't, keep everything in mind. (HWB to FLO, Oct. 8, 1862, USSC-NYPL, box 746: 2434.)

461

11. Katharine P. Wormeley, then working as a lady superintendent of nurses at the military hospital at Portsmouth Grove, Rhode Island, had written three letters to Olmsted asking for his aid. Dr. Edwards, the surgeon at Portsmouth Grove, had been transferred to Washington, D.C., and she wished Olmsted to use his influence with the surgeon general to have that order revoked. Believing the transfer to be part of an attempt to place an unfit physician in Edwards's position, she complained, "If he goes, all the happy and confident hopes I have of this hospital and my future in it are crushed." Olmsted's allusion to giving her a chance to sleep refers to a sentence in her third letter in which she declared, "Do you know so deeply anxious am I that I did not sleep all night, & shall not till I hear that all is safe" (K. P. Wormeley to FLO, Oct. 8 [misdated Oct. 9] and Oct. 10, 1862).

12. A reference to the delegations, headed by Henry M. Pierce and Henry Ingersoll Bowditch (1808–1892), that were in Washington lobbying for an ambulance corps. In September 1862 the National War Committee of the Citizens of New York appointed a committee composed of Pierce, Charles Gould, and the political scientist Francis Lieber to recommend the formation of an independent ambulance corps to the president and the War Department. At about the same time the Boston Society for Medical Improvement chose Henry Ingersoll Bowditch, who was an eminent physician, professor at Harvard Medical School, and abolitionist, as its representative to present a plan for an ambulance corps to the secretary of war. Bowditch himself had brought the ambulance question before the society. His experience with ambulance drivers while he served as a volunteer physician after the second battle of Bull Run so shocked and horrified him that he vowed to devote himself to securing a trained corps. Unlike Pierce, Bowditch was closely connected to the Sanitary Commission. He participated in the Commission's special inspection of military general hospitals during the fall of 1862. When Bowditch wished to discuss the ambulance corps with Jonathan Letterman and General McClellan, Olmsted wrote a letter of introduction which indicated Bowditch would represent the Commission and its views (Vincent Y. Bowditch, *Life and Correspondence of Henry Ingersoll Bowditch*, 2 vols. [Boston and New York, 1902], 2: 8–17; *Boston Medical and Surgical Journal* 67 [Sept. 25, 1862]: 164–66; *DAB*; doc. no. 56 in USSC, *Documents*; FLO to Jonathan Letterman, Oct. 21, 1862; National War Committee of the Citizens of New York, *Report of the Committee Appointed to Examine a Plan to Provide for Greater Efficiency in Ambulance and Camp-Hospital Corps* [New York, 1862], pp. 1–4).

CHAPTER VII

THE QUEST FOR LOYALTY
AND UNION

In the Fall of 1862 gifts by citizens of California totaling over two hundred thousand dollars gave the U.S. Sanitary Commission the financial stability it had lacked, but the money also raised problems for the Commission. Aware that the Western Sanitary Commission had received fifty thousand dollars from that donation, the Cincinnati branch pressed its claim for a portion for itself. The letters in this chapter indicate Olmsted's reluctance to acknowledge Cincinnati's claim and his conception of the relationship between the national Sanitary Commission and its local branches. His writings also reveal his growing distrust of the representatives of the Cincinnati claim. Letters to John S. Newberry in October and November further illustrate that Olmsted viewed the problems with the Cincinnati branch as but one expression of the parochialism and particularism that everywhere hampered the work of the Sanitary Commission.

In addition to fighting the spirit of localism among soldiers' aid organizations, Olmsted also tried to combat it in social and political life. Letters to Wolcott Gibbs setting forth a rationale for the formation of the group that became the Union League Club of New York reveal Olmsted's conception of "loyalty." These letters also illustrate his hatred both of aristocratic ideals of social organization and of the states' rights doctrines that he believed had helped bring about the Civil War. Olmsted's impassioned defense of the Emancipation Proclamation presents an important statement of his war aims and shows his fervent desire that the war put an end to slavery. In his letter to William Henry Hurlbert, Olmsted reiterates his commitment to sustain the war and his belief that such steadfastness was becoming widespread.

While attempting to foster unity elsewhere, Olmsted faced growing rifts within the Sanitary Commission over his policies. The letters in
this chapter detail his worsening relations with the Executive Committee
and his unsuccessful attempts to retain his independence and discretionary powers. The letter of December 6 to George Templeton Strong employs both logic and ridicule to criticize what Olmsted viewed as an over-
emphasis upon procedure that threatened the flexibility of the Commission. The toll that these disagreements began to take on him can be
seen in his highly emotional letters of December 27, 1862, and January
1863. The conduct of the Commission's Western operations remained a
sore spot, and Olmsted's letter of February 4 presents his view of his
relations with John S. Newberry.

During this period Olmsted's ties with New York City began to
loosen. In his letter of November 13 he gives a humorous description of
the house he rented in order to bring his family to Washington, but the
letter of February 16 shows his dismay and sadness that his connection
with the Central Park was rapidly drawing to a close.

To JOHN STRONG NEWBERRY

U.S. Sanitary Commission,
Adams' House, 244 F Street,
Washington, D.C., 11th Octr 1862.

Dear Doctor,

I have received your favor of the 30th ulto enclosing roster and
newspaper report of the convention of "delegates of Sanitary Commissions" at Indianapolis.[1] I don't like this last as well as you do, probably
because I didn't apprehend as much. A charitable association for the relief
of Soldiers is not a Sanitary Commission. And the Sanitary Commission,
its dépôts and agents are all and each perfectly independent of any and all
other associations and organizations except that of the government of the
United States. The local societies are contributive to it—that is to say are
allowed the benefit of the agencies and arrangments which it establishes.
The "Branches" are chartered by it, to aid it *exclusively*, not on terms
which they, the branches, propose, but under rules which the Commission
establishes, not for the convenience or pleasure of the branches but for the
purpose of turning to the best account the benevolence of the country—
not of the branches in any peculiar manner.

Right or wrong; this is the theory of the Commission, and it must be stood by until the Commission changes it. The Commission is not a mere central benevolent committee. It is a sub-bureau of government under appointment from the President.

It seems to me that this was entirely misapprehended, if not by the delegates, at least by the reporter, and the misapprehension is very likely to lead to mischief by and by.

I think *you* make a mistake in having the smallest regard to localities or local prejudices in choosing our inspectors. It is impossible that anybody else can know anything, compared with you, of the qualifications required of inspectors—to please Cincinnati or Indiana it seems to me should be no part of the object in view in looking for them. You must be the judge of this, however, I only know that I should be afraid that it would induce a relation to & dependence upon these local societies which would eventually prove very inconvenient to me, if I were in your place.

I am hoping every hour to hear from you about the recent battles.[2] Remember that the more you do in every battle, the more you spend judiciously, the larger our income will surely be, the more we shall have to spend,—*provided* it is promptly and cleverly made known to the public at the moment of the public's interest in the other matters of the battle. So use the telegraph freely on all such occasions.

We are fighting the battle of the ambulance corps and independent transportation with all our might here, but will have to keep it up till Congress acts, I fear.[3] Fire up the West & act on members of Congress, when you can. I shall have the hospital Directory at work in a week, I think.

We are gaining ground greatly with the Surgeons.[4]

Your report of your organization—roster—is very satisfactory.

I propose to make your compensation $2500, and house-rent, with such allowance as you may find necessary or proper for certain classes of house-expenses, which it is probable that you will find it impracticable to separate clearly from office expenses. I mean the occasional entertainment of officers, surgeons and visitors from "Branches", with whom it will be economical of your time and facilitate business if you dine &c. either at your own house or at a hotel—the expense in either case being properly chargable to the Commission.

Yours Very Truly

Fred. Law Olmsted.

Dʳ Newberry.

The original is letter 147 in volume 1 of box 914 of USSC-NYPL.

1. Here Olmsted is referring to a convention that took place in Indianapolis, Indiana, on September 24, 1862, and that the local newspaper reported as a meeting of "delegates of the Sanitary Commissions of the West." Although the newspaper clipping that Newberry enclosed with his letter has not survived, it may have been an article in the *Indianapolis Daily Journal.* The writer of that news item assumed that the branch organizations in Chicago, Cleveland, and elsewhere were separate sanitary commissions and implied that each took independent, autonomous action (*Indianapolis Daily Journal*, Sept. 25, 1862, p. 2).
2. The Kentucky campaign that culminated in the battle of Perryville on October 8, 1862. Although Braxton Bragg's Confederate army defeated the Union troops, the Confederate position was untenable, and Bragg's forces retreated to Tennessee (*War for the Union*, 2: 284–89).
3. By mid-October 1862 some of the supporters of an ambulance corps despaired of obtaining it from the War Department and turned their attention to securing congressional action. On October 10 Hammond told Bellows that he believed Stanton would never institute such a corps. The experience of Henry Ingersoll Bowditch and Henry M. Pierce with General Halleck seemed to bear out such pessimism about the War Department. After having promised his assent to the corps if Pierce could obtain McClellan's endorsement, Halleck disregarded McClellan's statement and for a fourth time asked Pierce for a written description of such a corps. Although Dr. Bowditch indignantly began lobbying Congress, the ambulance bill that passed the House of Representatives early in 1863 was killed in the Senate. Henry Wilson, a senator from Bowditch's own state, pronounced it inexpedient. Only six weeks after the ambulance bill failed to pass, Bowditch learned that his eldest son, wounded in battle, had died after being left on the field until a fellow soldier transported him by horseback to a hospital. The Boston physician then redoubled his efforts, and in 1864 a bill, sponsored by Henry Wilson, extended Letterman's ambulance system to all the Union armies (W. A. Hammond to HWB, Oct. 10, 1862, USSC-NYPL, box 640; H. I. Bowditch to FLO, Nov. 5, 1862, USSC-NYPL, box 746: 2697; George Worthington Adams, *Doctors in Blue: The Medical History of the Union Army in the Civil War* [New York, 1952], pp. 78–89).
4. Perhaps a reference to the increased contact with and friendliness of the army surgeons. Following a suggestion made by Olmsted, the surgeon general and the other military medical officers stationed in Washington began during the fall of 1862 to meet with the physicians of the Sanitary Commission to discuss subjects of mutual interest. These conferences resulted in the formation of the Army Medical Society, which included Sanitary Commission workers as well as army doctors (doc. no. 56 in USSC, *Documents*).

To Oliver Wolcott Gibbs

New York, Nov 5th 1862.

My Dear Gibbs,

Your request can not be passed by, this direful day,[1] but I can only give it stolen time.

The method must be built up from the motive.

Of your motive I judge from our short conversation and the name you gave your suggestion—"Loyalists' Club."[2]

We regard ourselves as distinguished from some others by our loyalty to something, to which they, whatever they profess, whatever they may, even, believe of themselves, are not, in our estimation, loyal. We desire to recognize this distinction as a ground of a certain alliance, by which we may express our greater pleasure in the society of those who agree with us, and something more.

To what are we loyal and they not?

We agreed that Belmont and Stebbins[3] must be of the other sort. To what are they not loyal? Both will swear allegiance to the Constitution. Stebbins within a year has declared to me that slavery must & should be abolished and the rebels exterminated. Supposing him sincere I still could not suppose him to be sympathizing with what loyalty includes with me. I feel that Liberty and Union is not all. Neither Belmont nor Stebbins could with sincerity say, I believe, that they would not, if they could, have a priviledged class in our society, a legal aristocracy. Both, I believe, hold, in their hearts *European* views on this subject. Both regard our society as "a failure" because of the want of a legally priviledged class. Both feel something of contempt for a man—at least they feel themselves to be the natural superiors of a man who does not feel himself to belong to a class, which he thinks ought to be priviledged. I, on the other hand, feel a certain contempt or a sense of superiority to a man, who wants any such legal setting up. They sympathize with what has always been the prevailing sentiment of the aristocratic and cultivated class abroad, and avowedly of only a very vulgar, presuming and peculiarly snobbish class here. We sympathize with what has been a prevailing sentiment with the highest quality of men peculiarly in our own country, the men, too, who formed our country and gave it to our keeping. To their sentiment in this respect and to this quality given by them to our nationality, we are loyalists—they are renegades. We are the hereditary, natural aristocracy—they are parvenu's; we are rich, they are vulgar. Your club then would be a club of true American aristocracy, the legitimate descendants and arms-bearers of the old Dukes of our land, of our law-givers: Loyalists. Difference of opinion within this should be tolerated; we would only require that in this, our disposition, and sense of personal dignity, should not be braved or erased. We wish also to establish the fact that there is an "aristocratic class" in New-York, which in this respect, is not European—which shall not be felt by an English gentleman to be the mere ape and parrot of a European gentry.

To this end the foundation should be very securely and cautiously laid.

OLIVER WOLCOTT GIBBS

Let us begin with a club, clubbing to canvass for a club. The Ante-Club. Agnew, Van Buren & yourself say, the tripod of it. Calvinistic, Catholic and cautious, (Man with his savage energy and directness; man fraternated and deliberatized; man philosphized and re-led to nature). Now close the doors and let in no man who has not blue blood to your certain knowledge; no man who does not burn with the sacred fire. Get in 15 to 30 of this elite of the elite, all of whom must, in the nature of the case, be too much personally interested, not to be willing and able to help with serious deliberate exercise of judgment. Select them, one by one, with great caution. Then classify them, not by set numbers, but according to their peculiar geniuses, knowledge and habits of judgment, into committees, to consider different questions of organization. One of these upon the shibboleth or test question for loyalty; another upon other conditions desireable to be required of membership; another upon Constitution & Byelaws with a sub committee—or a subsequent—upon plans of operation; rooms etc.

Of the first point, I have indicated the direction my views take at first opening ground. Of the second: three classes should be regarded: *first*; men of substance and established high position socially. I mentioned Minturn & Brown[4] as first occurring to me, last night. Men of good stock or of notably high character, of legal reputation, would be desireable: Strong and Jay.[5] So men of established repute in letters or science. And especially those of old colonial names, well brought down, as old Col. Hamilton.[6] A larger proportion of this sort I should consider absolutely essential to success in the purpose I see. They must be in the centre. *Second*, clever men, especially of letters, wits and artists who have made their mark. *Third*, promising young men—quite *young* men, who should be sought for and drawn in and nursed and nourished with care, but especially those innocent rich young men of whom I see many now, who don't understand what their place can be in American society, gentlemen, in the European sense, in a society which has no place for "men of leisure"; they are greatly tempted to go over to the devil, (boss devil).[7] The older and abler established men ought to fraternize with them, to welcome and hold every true man of them in fraternity—so soon they may govern us if they will.

The question is: what can be offered each of these classes, and what shall be asked of them?

As to the first class, everything must be asked; can anything be offered but the satisfaction of a patriotic and Christian purpose? This with some, if it can be well presented, will go a great way. Can anything be added?

Of the second; it is only necessary to ask little. This is essential. Let me mention names: Kapp,[8] who knows more & talks better upon the vital cords of American history than any man I know. Cap Curtis, Col. Waring, Captn Worden; Col. Elliott[9]—all men who must live on their pay & all who must live carefully & feel every dollar. If these repeat the password, they ought to come in easily, for, once in, they will be the best working members. The fee should not be high then.

For the third class, good rooms with something to do, is alone essential (what else is needed, follows). Billiards & Reading and smoking at least. I should question if all that is necessary could not be got by arrangment with some Hotel or Restaurant of the better sort. A club suite of rooms opening out of, or by a side door into, the Maison Doree[10] for instance; at least to its kitchen and some of its service.

I have not considered the question, whether the club should be actively engaged in propagating the faith? From within the club the faith should be actively propagated outwardly, I think, and by reason of the club, but not by the club as a club, a sufficient objection being, that certain members would be forced to quit by the expense if it were to be; (there are others).

For this reason & for others it should be understood that those who join the club do so from other motives than those which usually influence gentlemen to join clubs, and that they will aid its purposes otherwise than by their fees and annual dues. A committee of correspondence and publication should be provided with a special fund by contributions of members, not assessment, for instance. (All propagative correspondence & publication to be in the name of members, not of the Club).

The club should be, *as a club*, quiet and as little as practicable known by people not its members. So far as known, it should be purely in its *social* quality: Absolute secrecy as to its inner purpose is perhaps not to be required, but I should think it might be best that no member should propose or suggest to anyone else that he should join the club until, after having in private obtained assurance of his "loyalty", he had been proposed in the club, considered, and his election provisionally assured. Such assurance by the by could be best obtained negatively: by the question, "Don't you *hate* such & so?" rather than: "don't you love such and so?" It is easier to profess true hate than true love.

These matters & much else having been well discussed and determined in your Ante-Club, I should then set all to work to cautiously and adroitly canvass for members, not admitting them to the Ante Club & not organizing the Club of the Club till a sufficiently large list of men unanimously regarded as desireable had been made tolerably sure of, as ripe enough in loyal spirit to join it heart & soul when asked. Then organize the Club proper, the members of the Ante Club being its first members and first officers; bring in the marked men in squads rapidly, but so that those of each may fully understand it & their part in it, and have their say about those proposed still to be added before the latter are addressed on the subject.

Yours very Cordially,

Fred. Law Olmsted.

Wolcott Gibbs Esq[r]

The original is in the archives of the Union League Club, New York City.

1. Olmsted's gloom stemmed from the election results of the previous day in New York, where Democrats had captured the principal offices and a majority of the congressional seats (*New-York Times*, Nov. 5, 1862, p. 4).
2. Olmsted's first reference to the organization that in February 1863 began its existence as the "Union League Club of New York."
3. Henry G. Stebbins (1811–1881), like August Belmont, was a banker, a Central Park commissioner, and a prominent Democrat. Both Stebbins and Belmont supported the North during the Civil War, but the former was an especially staunch War Democrat. Despite the objections Olmsted here voices, Stebbins apparently was later admitted to the Union League Club. Belmont, however, never became a member (*New-York Times*, Dec. 11, 1881, p. 2; ibid., Nov. 25, 1890, pp. 1–2).

4. Probably New York City merchant Robert B. Minturn and banker James Brown.

5. John Jay (1817–1894), a descendant of the Federalist statesman of the same name, was a lawyer active in the Republican party (*DAB*).

6. James Alexander Hamilton (1788–1878) was the son of Alexander Hamilton and the father of Olmsted's associates in Sanitary Commission work Eliza Hamilton Schuyler and Mary M. Hamilton. Long active in politics, Hamilton was a prominent Jacksonian before affiliating with the Whig party in 1840. Later a Republican, he urged emancipation as a war measure during the Civil War. Hamilton had aided Olmsted in the latter's plan to grow cotton using free labor in Texas and had also signed a petition urging Olmsted's appointment as superintendent of Central Park in 1857 (*DAB; Papers of FLO*, 2: 448, n. 5).

7. Olmsted probably intended his phrase to have a double meaning. In the autumn of 1862 Sanitary Commission members and employees had begun to refer to the spirit of localism as the "boss devil" or "old boss devil." Thus, Olmsted is suggesting that without the influence of a club emphasizing nationalism, rich young men might be tempted by the doctrines of states' rights and secessionism as well as by the snares of the better-known devil (see FLO to HWB, Nov. 24, 1862, n. 6, below).

8. Friedrich Kapp (1824–1884), a German-born lawyer who lived in New York City. He and Olmsted had worked closely in the free-soil movement. During the Civil War, Kapp introduced Olmsted to German officers in the Union army. Kapp returned to Germany in 1870 but retained his admiration for Olmsted. In 1879, during a visit to the United States, Kapp invited Olmsted to a dinner given for his American friends and called Olmsted "one of the best and oldest of them" (*Papers of FLO*, 2: 66–69; F. Kapp to FLO, Dec. 30, 1879).

9. Captain Curtis and Colonel Waring were Olmsted's former business associates Joseph B. Curtis and George E. Waring. Olmsted probably had not learned that Curtis, who was to die at the battle of Fredericksburg in December 1862, had been promoted in August from the rank of captain to that of lieutenant colonel in the 4th Rhode Island. Waring was colonel of the 4th Missouri Cavalry. Captain Worden may have been John Lorimer Worden (1818–1897), a native of Westchester County, New York. A career naval officer, he was not, however, promoted from commander to captain until February 1863. In March 1862 Worden, as commander of the U.S.S. *Monitor*, had been the hero of its engagement with the C.S.S. *Virginia*, formerly known as the *Merrimac*. Colonel Elliott probably was Henry Hill Elliott, Jr. (b. 1833), son of Henry Hill Elliott and nephew of Olmsted's friend Charles Wyllys Elliott. The younger Elliott was lieutenant colonel of the 1st Louisiana, a regiment of Union soldiers raised after the capture of New Orleans (*DAB*, s.v. "Worden, John Lorimer"; Wilimena Hannah [Eliot] Emerson, Ellsworth Eliot, and George Edwin Eliot, Jr., eds., *Genealogy of the Descendants of John Eliot, "Apostle to the Indians,"* 1598–1905, new ed. [New Haven, Conn., 1905], pp. 158–59, 190; see also FLO to MPO, June 28, 1861, n. 7, above, and FLO to JO, Aug. 3, 1861, n. 8, above).

10. A restaurant on 14th Street at Union Square in New York City which was patronized by the well-to-do (*Diary of the Civil War*, p. 168).

To John Strong Newberry

Private

New York,
Novr 5th 1862.

My Dear Newberry,

I have just received your letter of 1st inst.

A general letter of the President written today, at my request, and with my advice, in parts, answers better than I felt able to do myself, your previous letters.[1] I am an exceedingly labored and poor writer. I can not write what I have thought. Writing is a laborious *process* of judgment with me. I never know quite what I think until I act, or write action. I depart from my inclination and custom in replying at all to the unjust complaints of your letter of the 1st about the two dispatches: "one gives me an imperative order to do what I think should have been left to my judgment."

At a meeting of Exec Com., a letter from Evansville was read, upon which it was moved that Dr Newberry be instructed to immediately visit Evansville &c. The motion was at once put & would have been carried as a matter of course, when I protested; the matter was argued for fully twenty minutes with much warmth, I standing alone in maintaining the view which you take of it. I at length demanded, as it were, on personal grounds, that it should be referred to me with only general instructions. Even this would not have been done if Dr Bellows had not announced his intention (since chang'd) of visiting Evansville the next week. I prepared the telegram with all consideration for your responsibility which proper respect for the views of the Committee allowed.[2]

The second dispatch if I mistake not was written "by order of Exec. Com". It was, I'm pretty sure, dictated by the Committee. But if not, the printed circular of the President about *material* & his letter of today will satisfy you that I had no responsibility in the matter, except as a member of the Committee, acquiescing in an established policy. On an application by telegraph from Washington for $2000 to your credit, at your request, received there from Louisville, I immediately moved that $5000 be placed to your credit at Washington, which, as I telegraphed you, was ordered. This was *before* your letter was recvd, to *which* the President's is especially a reply, though only a few minutes. The telegrapham informing you of this & giving you general instructions for *liberal expenditures* was written before your letter to which the present is a reply, was received. This will satisfy you of the erroneous ground of the complaint in question.

As to your letters, reports and enclosures; *each one to which you refer has been duly forwarded to me from Washington & immediately read to the Exec. Committee* (without the loss of a single mail). They were not replied to sooner because I found myself on a difft scent from the Committee & I didn't wish to blow the trumpet to you with an uncertain sound. About all this, Dᴿ Bellows' letter will satisfy you, I presume.[3]

My enquiry about the Louisville office was a perfectly natural one and consistent with a full understanding of all you had previously written. You had gone to L. with the intention of establishing yourself there: you had made preliminary arrangements, but as I yet understand it, you had not, according to my advices receivd here or in Washington, until day before yesterday, definitely established yourself there. Your official address so far as I yet see, was, at the time the dispatch was dictated, Cleavland. At least you had not removed your family; you intended to do so, & it was not unlikely that you would be temporarily in Cleaveland for that purpose. It cost little more in time or money to take you by way of Cleaveland, and in doing so, the inquiry was a natural and just one.

I hate to refer to such matters, but here I will just add, though I don't like to have you get the slightest ground that I lay up and remember such things, that your letter to Dᴿ Bellows—the "mad" letter of last July,[4] in its whole drift & purport, as far as I am concerned, is wrong. I never did or said anything on which such a construction could be truly placed, as you then showed yourself to believe it just and right to suppose. I am not afraid to let your opinions of me take care of themselves, having considerable respect for the logic of facts, but I will just advise you that it is not unlikely that by and by when any gentleman tells you such a story about me as you repeat in that letter, you will be able to assure him that he does not know me as well as you do.

Now oblige me, by putting all this damd stuff behind the fender of your memory & no more of it. This is a private letter. As secretary I do not reprove or reply to reproofs. I instruct & advise when I think necessary, and I receive advice.

Since we broke ground I have had nothing from the West with so much pleasure as your letter recvd & read in Committee last night.[5] It is where I have wanted you to stand from the start. I haven't blamed you that you haven't been able to, or believed that you were able to if you could think so, but I have felt that you didn't have the desire to take that ground as much as I could wish, & that you didn't see as I did that you could have no sound footing till you were able to get to it.

Now I want you to get *early* to Washington without fail. Put a man at Louisville to answer for you in good time & don't let anything detain you.

Consider all your arrangements, as far as practicable, provisional, till you reach Washington because I have irons heating. If I hadn't I should come to you but I simply can not.

Send or bring in good time *exact* full estimated statement, if not statement from record, of goods put in *our* dépôts, subject to *our* order, from all the West, & distinct statements of what has been done by our Auxiliaries on their own hook or hook & hook with us. This for the year or for all time before Nov. 1ˢᵗ as full & complete as possible, but *estimate* full & complete at any rate. Please don't fail in this.

Buy freely, services & goods, so you don't let people feel that they have not got to buy for you. Use your money freely but not publickly. One thing I don't like in your letter, by the way, at all. Your beef soup factory belongs to the San Com, don't it, then what has Cleaveland & Louisville got to do with paying for it? This is all wrong.[6]

Now, excuse me for not before referring to your reiterated complaints about Western hospitals; your letters are all at Dʳ Bellows's office & he will reply I hope seriatim.[7] He is, on my motion, to address Meigs on the general subject, & Hammond.[8] I don't know that we can do anything more. I believe that you are most grossly and absurdly mistaken as to the disposition of the govt to favor Eastern armies. As to any such disposition or inclination on my part, or on the part of the Commission, it is so preposterous that I can not say anything about it. But as to the army of the Potomac upon which you say government is heaping its favors, I solemnly assure you, that to the best of my knowledge & belief, there is not one word of what you say of the cruel neglect of the Western armies, not one particular of that neglect as enumerated by you, in which the Army of the Potomac is not treated worse. At the last exact accounts that I had, considerable parts of the army were not only "without half tents enough", there were *no* tents for sick or well. For weeks in many regiments the sick call had not been sounded because the surgeons asserted that having no medicines, no tent, nothing by which they could do anything for the sick, it was mockery to call them. Three weeks after Antietam, Douglas[9] wrote after visiting field hospitals containing over 2,000 of the severest cases (not removeable) that he had seen in no hospital as much medicine as he could carry in his pocket & that the medical stores of the whole could be packed in a barrel.

What I say above with regard to armies isn't intended to apply to Gen'l hospitals—of which I can not speak with confidence. I certainly believe that the hospitals at Cincinnati & St Louis are better treated than those at Washington. I do so because Gnl Hammond & common report asserts it. Common report of surgeons who have served East & West, as I understand it, asserts the direct reverse of every assertion of your letter on this subject except only the single one about pavilions.[10] It is not a fortnight since for the third time, we succeeded after a deal of expostulation in having some hundred sick removed from pestilential warehouses, where according to our inspectors' repeated reports they were dying of suffocation. I suppose there are 10,000 sick & wounded in the district, Maryland & Virginia not a bit better off in any respect than those you tell of at Louisville.

I heard the enquiry put to the Surgn Genl just before I left Washington, "Why is it so much more difficult to secure their rights to the sick in Washington than anywhere else?" And the S.G. showed by his reply that he believed it to be undeniably true that Western surgeons were better treated than eastern. That is to say, Surgeons at a distance from Washington than those near Washington, for nobody but a "Western man", or a South Carolinian, could ever have got the other idea into his head.

Once for all, I am an utter & complete stranger, except through you & other Western friends of late, to all such ideas of East & West. They are as new to me as would be the same ideas with regard to St Lawrence States and Potomac States. I do not believe there is an Eastern man who entertains them or can comprehend them except he has caught the habit at the West. As I hope to be saved, there is not in my soul the seed of a greater difference of regard between New York & Illinois or Ohio than between New York and Maine or New Jersey. It never occurred that there could be, till you suggested it. The war experienced has opened my eyes to something at the West which I hate and don't want to have to do with, but I yet hate whatever it is that can let American citizens vote for Woods & Brooks & Seymour,[11] more, I believe, & want to get away from it. In fact I haven't seen a man with a pleasant face today that it hasn't cost me a strong effort to overcome the attraction of my walking-stick for his skull or my fist for his nose, or my boot for his coccyx.

(And this is Sanitary education).

E. Pluribus Unum, & we'll all go home together.

Yours affectionately

Fred. Law Olmsted.

MS. copies of my circular to Stayers at Home[12] & my letter about Furness &c.[13] were prepared for you before the first was printed or the last sent, but I held on to feel surer of the Exec. Committee before writing you about them.

The original is letter 268 in volume 1 of box 914 of USSC-NYPL.

1. Newberry's letter of November 1 survives only in a fragmentary letterpress copy, and only a published version of Bellows's letter to Newberry has been discovered

(JSN to FLO, Nov. 1, 1862, USSC-NYPL, box 918, 1: 288–90; "The National Qual-
ity of the Commission" [HWB to JSN], Nov. 5, 1862, doc. M-6, Frederick Law
Olmsted Collection, Rare Book Room, U.S. Army Military History Institute, Carlisle
Barracks, Pa.).

2. Olmsted refers here to his telegram of October 31 to Newberry, which read: "Aid
demanded at Evansville. Committee wish immediate inspection. What have we
done there, reply by telegraph. Is Louisville office established?" (FLO to JSN, Oct.
31, 1862, USSC-NYPL, box 914, 1: 178.)

3. According to Bellows, Olmsted successfully argued that the Sanitary Commission
was national and central in its scope, must cover the entire ground with its agents
and inspectors, and must defy any of its branches claiming independence ("The
National Quality of the Commission" [HWB to JSN], Nov. 5, 1862, doc. M-6, Frederick Law Olmsted Collection, Rare Book Room, U.S. Army Military History Institute, Carlisle Barracks, Pa.).

4. This letter apparently has not survived.

5. Probably a reference to the letter of October 24, 1862, which was later published as
part of Sanitary Commission document number 55, "Operations of the Sanitary
Commission at Perryville, Ky." In this letter Newberry called the condition of the
wounded in that battle "peculiarly distressing" and continued:

> No adequate provision had been made for their care. The stock of
> medicines and hospital stores in the hands of the surgeons was insignificant.
> They had almost no ambulances, no tents, no hospital furniture, and no proper
> food. In addition to this, the small village of Perryville afforded but very imper-
> fect means for the care of the great number of wounded concentrated there,
> either in the way of buildings to be used as hospitals, or resources and appliances
> of any other kind.

Disputing the assertion that such suffering inevitably accompanied all warfare,
Newberry fixed blame not upon the army medical men but upon a defective system
that neither provided a trained ambulance corps nor secured independent transportation for the medical officers' supplies (doc. no. 55 in USSC, *Documents*).

6. Late in 1862 the Sanitary Commission set up a factory in Cleveland to manufacture
concentrated beef from vegetables and beef supplied free of cost by local meat
packers. The cannery operation proved complicated, and the Commission turned
the business over to a private firm which then continued to supply a high-quality
article below market cost (John Strong Newberry, *The U.S. Sanitary Commission in
the Valley of the Mississippi, during the War of the Rebellion, 1861–1866* [Cleveland,
Ohio, 1871], pp. 323–35).

7. Bellows instructed Newberry that the Sanitary Commission intended to investigate
the supervision of military hospitals nationwide and would institute a special inspection by eminent physicians in the West as well as in the East. While the Commission
would sometimes furnish supplies to a hospital where one of its branches existed, it
would usually try to stimulate local support there. In particular, Bellows urged
Newberry to investigate conditions at the military hospital at Evansville ("The National Quality of the Commission" [HWB to JSN], Nov. 5, 1862, doc. M-6, Frederick
Law Olmsted Collection, Rare Book Room, U.S. Army Military History Institute,
Carlisle Barracks, Pa.).

8. The surgeon general, William A. Hammond, and the quartermaster general, Montgomery C. Meigs.

9. John H. Douglas.

10. That is, the Eastern theater of the war was better supplied with the new pavilion
hospitals, which consisted of either a group of detached buildings clustered together
or a central building with long wings radiating outward. The Sanitary Commission
urged the construction of pavilion hospitals because current medical theory held

that the dispersion and separation of patients would help prevent the creation of dangerous poisons and miasmas in the hospital (G. W. Adams, *Doctors in Blue*, pp. 9–11).

11. A reference to Democratic candidates who had just been elected to the U.S. House of Representatives from New York City: Fernando Wood (1812–1881), former mayor of New York City and a leader of the Mozart Hall machine; his brother Benjamin Wood (1820–1900), owner of the *New York Daily News*; and James Brooks (1810–1873), editor of the *New York Express*. Horatio Seymour (1810–1886) gained the state's gubernatorial chair (*DAB*; *BDAC*).

12. Olmsted's circular "What They Have to Do Who Stay at Home" explained and defended the Sanitary Commission's relief service. Olmsted argued that the stockpiling of supplies for emergency use after battles and the distribution of supplies to those soldiers most in need, regardless of their home state or city, were the most humane and efficient methods. Noting that recent battles had almost exhausted the Commission's stores, Olmsted called for contributions, either directly to the Commission or through its auxiliary societies (FLO, "What They Have to Do Who Stay at Home," Oct. 21, 1862).

13. Horace Howard Furness (1833–1912) was the son of William Henry Furness, an abolitionist and Unitarian minister of Philadelphia. After graduating from Harvard College in 1854, Horace had become a lawyer. Although increasing deafness made him unfit for military service, he was an accomplished public speaker. He became a traveling lecturer for the Sanitary Commission in the fall of 1862. His mission in New England was to encourage the formation of local organizations that would cooperate with and contribute to the Commission and also to counter the growing localism and parochialism of local groups. In October 1862 he explained the Commission's view to his wife as follows: "There is an evil threatening the Sanitary Commission & thereby the real good of our army, this is the organization of state societies, for the sole relief of soldiers of one particular state." Furness almost revered Olmsted, whom he called "the Master." Olmsted, in turn, was "delighted" with the younger man's volunteer service for the Commission at Antietam and pronounced him to be "discreet, large-hearted and sober." Olmsted's reference in the letter presented here probably is to his letter of October 14, which was written to inform Bellows that Furness had accepted the duty of traveling agent and "General Agent to visit societies and arrange correspondences, overruling and instructing local agents" (*DAB*; Horace Howard Furness, *The Letters of Horace Howard Furness*, ed. Horace Howard Furness, Jr., 2 vols. [Boston, 1922], 1: 110–11, 117–22; FLO to HWB, Oct. 14, 1862, USSC-NYPL, box 641).

To Oliver Wolcott Gibbs

New York 7th Nov. [1862]

My Dear Gibbs,

I take your note with good appetite and readily assimilate the whole. You both enlarge and compact the purpose or motive.[1] All the more, however, I feel it to be of the highest importance for success that the *general intentions* of my plan of the *process* of welding the club should be adopted from the start.

Almost everything depends upon your original foundations. Be careful to let nothing be done which shall prevent its being *easy* to follow a process of that kind. The plan should be thoroughly considered and deliberately matured by not more than seven representative men, before anyone gets a strong *set* about it, and before anyone beyond that seven(?) gets any claim in courtesy or policy to have an influence in it. It will save much time, discussion & some hard feeling to get the general scheme, plan, purpose and *limit of purpose*, well defined & mapped out, before it is to be talked about & men brought into it. It is so easy for men to carelessly form plans & start upon ideas, which it is more [or] less difficult to give up. It's much better to present the whole (a map of the whole) where the balance of parts and the consequent boundaries, are taken in at a glance, before any part is seen by itself and becomes of more importance than all the rest. Here as in everything else, (San. Com.) the first necessity of economy & efficiency is a clear limitation of what is to be undertaken.

(Sunday night will be the last chance for me on this subject for a month or two).

Yours cordially

Fred. Law Olmsted.

The original is in the archives of the Union League Club, New York City.

1. Upon receiving Olmsted's suggestions of November 5, Gibbs, in turn, sketched his own view of the areas the proposed organization would cover: "My central ideas are to instill and develop an intensely patriotic national feeling and to make politics an honorable and elevating pursuit by bringing back a class of men who have long since abandoned the subject in disgust." He then continued:

> I want to see the grandest and widest schemes of national advancement brought forward and urged by able writers as *national* schemes. I want a club with men in it big enough to originate and receive such ideas. You remember perhaps my suggestions as to National Agricultural and Acclimatization Societies. They will serve as illustrations of directions of labor and thought. . . . I don't mean to be purely material. I am only bringing forward what seem to me large ideas because they are large and therefore expand the mind that takes them in. Now I think a club of acute large active minds making such subjects topics for conversation, thought and labor and looking at them always from a truly national American point of view might do much intellectually.

Gibbs also argued that the club could improve social and political life by lending support to Olmsted's view of a "natural" rather than a hereditary aristocracy, by helping to make the *New York Evening Post* the nation's foremost newspaper, and by providing a forum for "the fullest, freest and frankest discussions of all great national topics" (O. W. Gibbs to FLO, Nov. 6, 1862).

To Mary Perkins Olmsted

Washg[n]   Nov 13th [1862]
I believe

My Dear Wife,

The house isn't so good as I thought it was. All the furniture is hideous. Captn Snow[1] was Commander of first class small potato steamboat, and the house was fitted up with what was left when she was worn out. I do hope you will bring things. I want the carpet covered with brown linen or hardware paper might do as it's a hard worn steamboat carpet of the largest pattern I ever saw. Spiders seen thro' Lord Rosse's[2] telescope with the rest under the mopboard. Yellow & blue, with green roses and red cauliflowers sticking up thro' the spiders' legs. There are ottomans made of it with the interior anatomy of a spider's eye running over three sides. Bring something nice for the baby to be educated on.

There is a little book-case, not very little, in the library. I particularly request you to have Mankite[3] pack up about five yards of books [of] all sorts. The next thing I want is curtains, drapery, tablecloths, everything of that kind you can hitch on, piano-covers and things that will hide pieces of chairs. We have got to live on pinewood fires chiefly, in fireplaces—hand irons & fenders will be wanted. But books & cloths & pictures—For these I beg.

Your affectionate fellow sufferer,

There's five hens & a cock and I've got a fresh egg. The cow is going & the milch runs clear. A black boy does it.

All the mahogany colored furniture is very sticky & keeps so. The chairs have been mended all through very much and stuck up thick without regard to expense or broadcloth. So—

Godkin[4] & I came as near heaven as we have either of us been for some time, today because a green servant made a fire of charcoal in the furnace stove downstairs, turned on the damper into the chimney & turned off that into the parlor. We managed to get to the window & open it in time, but have both been in a queer way ever since. Gitting all right.

Affectionately,

---

1. Charles C. Snow rented Olmsted his house at 332 G Street, with its furnishings, on a six-month lease, beginning November 10, 1862, for $750 (FLO, indenture with Charles C. Snow, Oct. 23, 1862, USSC-NYPL, box 748: 3266).
2. William Parsons (1800–1867), third earl of Rosse, was an astronomer who designed and constructed a reflecting telescope used for the observation of nebulae (DNB).

3. Unidentified.
4. Edwin L. Godkin.

To Henry Whitney Bellows   [November 24, 1862][1]

Monday, Nov[r] 2, [186]2

My dear Doctor,
        The number of women in attendance upon the Council[2] is six-
teen. It has necessarily occupied my attention almost exclusively since the
Commission adjourned. The objects in view have all been most successfully accomplished. After full discussions the judgment has been unanimous upon the various points upon which I wished advice. There were
three delegates from the West, one from Louisville and two from Chicago.[3]
The difference between our Western operations and our Eastern has been
fully brought out, and the Westerners seem to be fully convinced that ours
is a better and nobler way. I detained D[r] Newberry to take part in the
discussions, perceiving that it would have great advantages. The Chicago
ladies say that Judge Skinner told them that the California money ought all
to be used by the Central Society and if it was determind to divide it
among the branches, he should not be disposed to take any for Chicago,
believing that it would do more harm than good. After you left the other
day I had a very frank conversation with the Cincinnati men.[4] They tacitly
acknowledged that we were right, but as often as they were brought to this,
they retracted and gave me to understand that right or wrong the people of
Cincinnati had determined to have their share with St Louis of the bounty
of California,[5] and there was little use in reasoning about it. St. Louis was
their rival, and they were merchants & there was not much use in convincing them of what was right in the matter. The people thought they were
going to have $50,000 or more and they would be disappointed and angry if
they didn't get it. Finally, that was all there was about it. However they
gave me to understand and I thought intended to do so, that they would
resist the popular clamor, as far as they could without sacrifice of their
personal popularity, and do their best to prevent rash action. They left with
profuse and hearty expressions of gratitude and good feeling. You can
judge what they are worth. I think *they* are well disposed and rather
ashamed of their position as attorneys of the O.B.D.[6] They were commissioned to bully us, were rather surprised at their ill-success, and ashamed of
the attempt and not unwilling (if they saw how they could) to apologize for
it and give it up.

JANE CURRIE BLAIKIE HOGE

After full consideration Newberry declined to take any of the Eastern inspectors. The West is better supplied with Inspectors than the East and he has two new ones to come in. I give him the best of our Relief Agents and offered him any of the others, but he declined taking any more. Various arrangments are concocted between us, the final determination of them to be upon reports which he is to make as soon as he gets to Louisville and has conferred with Judge Skinner & others. I have given him some suggestions which, if he is able to act upon them, will, I think, give Cincinnati the opportunity of coming into line, gracefully.

Let me refer to the statement which you and others so often made that the greater part of our expenditures had been at the East. Goods & money coming to us come to a common stock. From that common stock, the wants of soldiers are to be everywhere supplied justly, equitably. No one says their wants at the West have been less attended to or not as well supplied as at the East. No one who knows anything about it: No one says it with truth. At the West certain advantages are secured from government more freely than at the East. Certain classes of stores fill our dépôts more readily and fully than at the East. The Cincinnati Branch & others at the West have foolishly chosen, instead of sending money to our treasury, to

481

MARY ASHTON RICE LIVERMORE

expend the money for themselves, *giving* us certain stores, which at the East *we* have purchased. This & this only is the foundation of the impression you have. And in the form in which it was frequently stated during the session, it is mistaken and unjust. It is utterly and completely false, first & last from beginning to end, that the Commission by accident or design favors the East or gives the East any advantage over the West, and I cannot allow the Commission to show the slightest appearance of entertaining that idea without protesting against it. I beg that nothing shall be done or said which shall seem in the slightest degree to intimate an admission that we entertain the charge or are affected by it. To do so will only confirm & establish the ignorant in their mistake, and the rascals in the belief that we can be bullied out of our well considered, just and honest arrangments.

My attention is at this moment called to a Resolution passed in my absence Saturday night, requiring me to submit to the Exec. Com. all augmentation of salaries. I don't think such a resolution should have been considered in my absence. I think it was unnecessary, will be very inconvenient and can do only harm. I have always referred my intentions in this respect in cases of any importance to you or the Exec. Com. if not to the Board. A request from you that I should do so would certainly have been all sufficient to correct any want of consideration in this respect. If I have ever refrained from it, it has been because I did not think you wished to be troubled in the case, that it was too unimportant—or because there were special causes for immediate decision. I think it impracticable to comply with this order without loss of efficiency, & request you to ask the Exec. Committee in my behalf, to direct its suspension.[7]

(The ladies are making arrangments to call on the President of the U.S.)![8]

Speaking of salaries, what was the action of the Exec. Committee upon my suggestions? There was some action. Mr Strong requested me to give formal shape to it for record. I did so, with an addition which was in harmony with the views expressed, by members, though not upon motion, but all the rest (in effect) was on motion. Was this adopted or rescinded, and just how does it stand now?[9]

Will you please direct that copies of proceedings of the Ex. Com. shall be transmitted to me daily?

I beg the Surgical Committee[10] to find me some good general inspectors.

Yours Respectfully,

Fred. Law Olmsted.

Rev[d] D[r] H. W. Bellows.
President.

The text is from a letterpress copy on pages 102–12 in Olmsted's private letterbook.

1. Olmsted dated this letter "November 2," but all evidence points to Monday, November 24, as the day that it was actually written. It was entered in the letterbook between letters dated November 14 and November 25. The Woman's Council to which Olmsted refers met from November 21 to November 24, and Olmsted's meeting with associate members of the Sanitary Commission from Cincinnati could have taken place only in late November. Most likely he wrote the numeral "2," planning to find out the day's exact date and place its second numeral after the "2," but forgot to make that addition.
2. The Woman's Council, a meeting of female representatives from the Sanitary Commission's auxiliary societies, convened on November 21 in Washington, D.C. The main purposes of the meeting were: to define more precisely the relationship of

483

these societies to the Commission; to systematize more fully the societies' activities; to assure the continued donation of needed hospital supplies; and, in general, to stimulate and strengthen patriotism and support for the war effort. Among the auxiliary organizations sending delegates were the Woman's Central Association of Relief, the New England Women's Auxiliary Association, and the Northwestern branch (Linus Pierpont Brockett and Mary C. Vaughan, *Woman's Work in the Civil War: A Record of Heroism, Patriotism, and Patience* [Boston, 1867], p. 531; Mary Ashton [Rice] Livermore, *My Story of the War: A Woman's Narrative of Four Years Personal Experience* . . . [Hartford, Conn., 1887], pp. 232–41; FLO to Henry B. Rogers, Nov. 22, 1862, USSC-NYPL, box 835, 1: 529–31; HWB to FLO, Dec. 9, 1862, USSC-NYPL, box 747: 2973).

3. The editors have been unable to identify the delegate from Louisville, but the Chicago representatives were Jane Currie Blaikie Hoge (1811–1890) and Mary Ashton Rice Livermore (1820–1905), two of the Sanitary Commission's best publicists and most tireless workers. Born in Philadelphia, Jane Blaikie married Abraham Hoge, a Pittsburgh merchant, in 1831 and became the mother of thirteen children. Mary Rice, before her marriage to Daniel Livermore, a Universalist minister, taught school in her native Massachusetts and was a governess in Virginia. As a wife and mother of four, she assisted her husband in the writing, editing, and management of the *New Covenant*, a religious periodical that he owned and published. The Hoge family moved to Chicago in 1848, the Livermores in 1858, and a common interest in benevolent reform soon brought the two women together.

From the beginning of the Civil War, Jane Hoge and Mary Livermore shared a desire to aid the soldiers, and both volunteered their services to the Chicago branch of the Sanitary Commission. In March 1862 they visited and reported upon military hospitals in such towns as Cairo, Mound City, Paducah, and St. Louis. Impressed by their talents and enthusiasm, Mark Skinner, president of the Chicago branch, proposed to Olmsted in late November 1862 that the Sanitary Commission employ them as salaried organizers and lecturers. Olmsted enthusiastically agreed and added, "I am sure that women like these under such general guidance as you could easily give them, could add to our resources for efficient, methodical and regular relief, the value of thousands of dollars weekly." In December 1862 Jane Hoge and Mary Livermore hired housekeepers to care for their families and began to devote all their time to the Sanitary Commission. They worked as a team and shared a monthly wage of fifty dollars (which was increased to seventy-five dollars in the summer of 1863). As directors of the women's auxiliary of the Chicago branch, they organized and roused to action thousands of tributary local relief societies in the Midwest. Individually each wrote numerous articles and circulars and undertook strenuous tours involving many speaking engagements. Early in 1863 they visited the sick and wounded of Grant's army near Vicksburg. That summer the two women organized the first of what was to be the single most effective fund-raising device for the aid societies: the sanitary fair, in which donated articles and services were sold and entertainment was provided.

Olmsted remained on good, though not particularly close, terms with both Jane Hoge and Mary Livermore. The payment of their salaries by the Washington office of the Commission at one point became erratic, and they appealed to Olmsted, who quickly straightened out the problem. Most likely he thought of them in terms similar to those used by George Templeton Strong, who declared, "They are fearful and wonderful women, whose horsepower is to be expressed in terms of droves of horses." Although Olmsted mailed a photograph of himself to the ladies in the summer of 1863, his relationship with them effectively ended with his resignation from the Sanitary Commission. When, in 1885, he again met Mary Livermore, who had by then become a noted speaker for temperance and women's rights, he did not remember her (*Notable American Women*; FLO to Mark Skinner, Nov. 25

and Dec. 20, 1862; FLO to M. A. Livermore, April 25, 1863, USSC-NYPL, box 835, 2: 530–31; M. A. Livermore to FLO, June 30, 1885; *Diary of the Civil War*, p. 562; J. C. Hoge to FLO, Jan. 11, 1865).

4. Samuel J. Broadwell (1832–1893) and Joshua Hall Bates (b. c. 1817), lawyers, members of the Cincinnati branch, and associate members of the Sanitary Commission. Broadwell, a Cincinnati native, participated in religious and benevolent organizations. Bates, born in Massachusetts, graduated from West Point and served five years in the army. In the spring of 1861 he, as a brigadier general, helped organize the volunteer troops from Ohio. In November 1862 both men were in Washington, D.C., to remonstrate against the view expressed in Olmsted's recent circular, "What They Have to Do Who Stay at Home," that the branch societies were intermediaries in the collection and forwarding of supplies from the people to the Sanitary Commission rather than independent organizations of collection and distribution (Charles T. Greve, *History of Cincinnati and Hamilton County, Ohio, Their Past and Present* [Cincinnati, Ohio, 1894], pp. 564–65; George Washington Cullum, *Biographical Register of Officers and Graduates of the U.S. Military Academy at West Point, N.Y. . . .*, 3rd ed., 3 vols. [Boston, 1891], 1: 683).

5. The San Francisco Committee of Thirteen, which contributed two gifts, each of one hundred thousand dollars, to the Sanitary Commission during September and October 1862, had noted in its first letter about the award that part of the money should be distributed to the groups in Cincinnati and St. Louis if they had separate organizations and treasuries. As it forwarded the second half of this contribution, the Committee expressly stipulated that fifty thousand dollars, one-fourth of the total, be given to the Western Sanitary Commission in St. Louis (Henry F. Teschemacher to HWB, Sept. 18, 1862, Henry Whitney Bellows Papers, Massachusetts Historical Society, Boston, Mass.; J. E. Yeatman to HWB, Oct. 4, 1862, USSC-NYPL, box 642).

6. An abbreviation for "Old Boss Devil," a term used by Sanitary Commission employees to designate the spirit of localism manifested by village and state societies that wished to care only for "their own soldiers" and opposed the centralized action represented by the Sanitary Commission. Horace H. Furness in early November 1862 described how, at a meeting with Olmsted and Bellows, the latter read a recently received letter "brim full of the boss devil, horns & tail, full & vigorous." Bellows himself boasted of how, at a public meeting in Brooklyn, his speech won the crowd over to the Sanitary Commission and "the *old boss* was killed & quartered on the spot" (H. H. Furness, *Letters*, 1: 122; HWB to FLO, Nov. 25, 1862, USSC-NYPL, box 747: 2854).

7. This first protest lodged by Olmsted against the Executive Committee's resolution limiting his discretionary power over salaries produced no change in position by the Committee. Bellows reported the Committee's adamant views and explained: "They are sensitive to every thing connected with their responsibility as to the expenditure of money, and they are perhaps as sensitive as their Secretary himself, as to any massing of the grave obligations of the Board in any one hand. The same deference which the Secretary requires of his agents & Secretaries, they think it their duty to exact from the Gen¹ Secretary" (HWB to FLO, Nov. 29, 1862, USSC-NYPL, box 747: 2886).

8. The women attending the Woman's Council requested and received an audience with President Lincoln on November 24 (H. H. Furness, *Letters*, 1: 125–27; Jane Currie [Blaikie] Hoge, *The Boys in Blue; or Heroes of the "Rank and File."* . . . [New York, 1867], pp. 81–82).

9. Olmsted's specific suggestions do not appear to have survived.

10. Possibly Olmsted meant the Commission's Medical Committee: William H. Van Buren, Cornelius R. Agnew, and Wolcott Gibbs, all of whom held medical degrees (doc. no. 56 in USSC, *Documents*).

To John Strong Newberry

U.S. Sanitary Commission,
Adams' House, 244 F Street,
Washington, D.C., Dec[r] 4th 1862.

My Dear Doctor,

I have just received your package of the 30th. It contains precisely what I wanted.[1] From Resolutions of last Thursday[2] I infer that Cincinnati is determined to run her own machine. It is obvious that there are and always have been two parties, and that the federal & Christian party theoretically, are cowards practically and therefore worse children of the devil than the other sort.

I am working with all my might & constantly upon the argument against them & it will be absolutely conclusive, and Judge Hoadly will have to write himself down a very poor lawyer if he don't give in.

I trust we shall be able to prove him also, in that case, as poor a politician as he is lawyer. That is for you to do. Do all you can to divide & conquer; get a party, however small, to stand by us in Cincinnati, but not to halfway stand by us; let it be strong in its convictions if not in numbers. If this can't be got, strengthen Columbus, if Columbus will hold fast to us. If not, then fall back on Cleaveland & send evangelists from C. thro' all Southern Ohio preaching in every church. Can't you get some rheumatic chaplains for this sort of work?

The Ex. Com. have stopped the $50,000 in effect.[3] I will write you after I better understand what they mean. Meantime spend money wherever you can with any certain advantage. Occupy the special fields of the Cincinnati branch especially. Buy waggons & horses & have [no care for expense. Go into] Missouri & Kansas as strongly as possible also. What is St Louis doing with its $50,000? Keep them at home. We are greatly wanting supplies here, more than you are, I judge, very much, but it would not pay to send your contributions here. From N. Orleans Blake[4] writes he is well supplied & has little to do. We send additional hands to Newbern today.[5] Have good accounts from the column at Suffolk.[6]

Please write often & send Inspectors' Reports weekly.

We greatly need a clear statement of our issues of hospital supplies—thro' our inspectors, clear of all side channels.

Yours Very Cordially

Fred. Law Olmsted.

The original is letter 289 in volume 1 of box 914 in USSC-NYPL.

1. On November 25 Olmsted had asked Newberry a series of questions about what documents and written instructions the Cincinnati associate members of the Sanitary Commission had received. In reply Newberry forwarded a copy of the circular he had sent the Cincinnatians and informed Olmsted that he had mailed a copy of all the Commission's published documents to them (FLO to JSN, Nov. 25, 1862, USSC-NYPL, box 914, 1: 255; JSN to FLO, Nov. 30, 1862, USSC-NYPL, box 918, 1: 305–8).

2. Olmsted appears to have been confused about the date in question and to have been referring to resolutions taken up on November 21 rather than 27. He was also mistaken about the same dates in the report he wrote in early December. The resolutions mentioned were those passed by the Cincinnati branch and presented to the U.S. Sanitary Commission. In short, the Cincinnatians argued that the U.S. Sanitary Commission had always undertaken the distribution of supplies in the Western theater of the war through its branches, and that it should not alter such a system. They also directed that their members who were designated to attend the U.S. Sanitary Commission's meeting insist that their branch receive a share of the California donation equal to the fifty thousand dollars given to the Western Sanitary Commission at St. Louis (doc. no. 60, pp. 3–6, in USSC, *Documents*).

3. The Sanitary Commission in its meeting of November 21 had approved a resolution, proposed by Olmsted, "that the Treasurer be instructed to meet Mr. Olmsted's draft for fifty thousand dollars, to be deposited at the West for the general purposes of the Commission." Olmsted probably intended to undercut the demands being made by the Cincinnati branch for a share of the California money by having Newberry expend this large sum in the Midwest. On December 1 Olmsted requested that Strong deposit the sum in the Washington office's bank account. By that time the Commission's Executive Committee had reconsidered the board's action and had decided that neither Olmsted nor Newberry should authorize expenditures of over one thousand dollars without its permission (USSC, *Minutes*, pp. 116–18; FLO to GTS, Dec. 1, 1862, USSC-NYPL, box 610: 968).

4. George Albert Blake (1828–1892), a physician and Sanitary Commission inspector in the Department of the Gulf. Born in New Hampshire, he graduated from Williams College and received his medical degree from Harvard. After briefly living in Iowa, he settled permanently in Walpole, New Hampshire. Blake served the Sanitary Commission from the fall of 1861 until 1867. During much of the war he was stationed at or near New Orleans. After the war he worked in the Commission's Army and Navy Claim Agency. Blake's connections with both Harvard University and Walpole suggest that Bellows or Knapp recruited him for the Sanitary Commission's staff (Calvin Durfee, *Williams Biographical Annals* [Boston, 1871], p. 584; Eben Burt Parsons, *Obituary Record of the Alumni of Williams College, 1891–92* [Williamstown, Mass., 1892], p. 157).

5. New Bern, North Carolina.

6. Suffolk, Virginia, the county seat of Nansemond County, is located approximately fifteen miles southwest of Portsmouth.

To George Templeton Strong [December 4, 1862][1]

4th Oc[t] [186]2.

My Dear Mr Strong,

I have just got yours of yesterday. I have Mr Allen's papers[2] but have not had time to look at them. I have also just got a package from Newberry which I see at a glance is conclusive as to instructions to Cincinnati associates—though I had got evidence enough to hang them on before.

My telegram[3] was, I believe, intended to convey this idea: The Cincinnati Committee did not raise the money question before the Commission; therefore Commission did not act upon it, (nor is Ex. Com. prepared at once to do so). The question however as put in Resolution of last Thursday seems to be a judicial question—a question of the meaning of terms and of evidence. If the Cincinnatians have a good *claim* to the $50,000 or any other sum, as a matter of contract, as they assert, they need be in no trouble or haste about it, for they can't suppose we can or would cheat them out of it. The Committee of Conference[4] will be able to decide this: being good lawyers. I fear precipitate action in a rage, for which there is no occasion, & think it best at all events that we should be right on the record, as doing all we could to avoid this. With this view, fearing my telegram to you would be too late, I wrote a personal letter last night to Judge Hoadly;[5] of which I will send you a copy.

Your resolution about the $50,000 seems to me to make the matter much harder (in the west) than if nothing had been done & exhibits a want of confidence in Newberry which entirely justifies Western secession.[6] Please explain the motive to me that I may not act indiscreetly upon it.

It seems to me you are still running upon the theory of two Executive offices for the same responsibility. If so, I warn you that we shall soon be on a rock. I shall trust to your caution & you to mine & between the two, there will be an oversight, and, crack! down we go.

I think I shall go to Phila. about next Monday to see Jun[r] Mr Binney & read my paper to him before final revisal.[7] Will you meet me there?

News from Blake, all right at N. Orleans; excellent medical service.
Yours Very Truly

Fred. Law Olmsted.

The text is from a letterpress copy on pages 137–40 of Olmsted's private letterbook.

1. Olmsted misdated this letter "4th Oct.," but its content and its placement among letters written in December in his letterbook reveal that it must have been written on December 4.
2. Olmsted had written to George F. Allen, secretary of the Woman's Central Association of Relief, to obtain a copy of the memorial that led to that association's becoming a branch of the Sanitary Commission. Olmsted wanted that document because, as he explained to Allen, "I wished to ascertain if there was any indication in it of an intention on your part to control the dépôt of the Commission at New York, independently of the Commission. Of course, I am confident that nothing of the kind would be found. It might be desirable, however, that I should be able to produce evidence that you had no such intention in taking the title of 'Branch'." Such information bore directly upon the contention of the Cincinnati Branch that it had always worked independently of the national Commission in its distribution as well as in the gathering of supplies (FLO to G. F. Allen, Dec. 4, 1862).
3. On December 2 Olmsted telegraphed the Executive Committee in New York: "Cincinnati Committee expressly stated they did not bring the money question before Commission. Whether yes or no depends on result of conference. A legal question. If independent their title is good to it. Send this to Mr Strong immediately if answer to Cincinnati has not gone" (FLO to USSC Executive Committee, Dec. 2, 1862, USSC-NYPL, box 835, 1: 590).
4. At the Sanitary Commission meeting of November 21, Mark Skinner and Horace Binney, Jr., both of whom were lawyers, were appointed to serve as a committee of reply to a report submitted by the Cincinnati branch and were instructed to confer with the Cincinnatians. In early December Olmsted apparently believed that this committee should actually resolve the dispute about whether the Cincinnati branch was entitled to a part of the California donation (ibid.; USSC, *Minutes*, pp. 118–19).
5. Olmsted in his letter attempted to conciliate Hoadly by noting that Cincinnati's remonstrances had been referred to a committee composed of Binney and Skinner, each of whom was president of a branch of the Sanitary Commission. Counseling moderation, Olmsted also assured Hoadly that Cincinnati's claims would receive "the most unprejudiced consideration":

> It has seemed to me that there were certain facts in the case which you have not been informed of, or have not fairly considered, and that in consequence, there was with some portion at least of your body, a feeling of something like resentment for what is supposed to be an unjust disposition on the part of the Commission.
> Knowing thoroughly well, as I do, how mistaken this is, and believing that it is only necessary that all the facts in the case should be well understood by both parties to bring them to a substantial agreement, I sincerely hope that no precipitate action will be taken in the premises by your branch. (FLO to George Hoadly, Dec. 3, 1862.)

6. See FLO to JSN, December 4, 1862, note 3, above.
7. The report that Olmsted was composing in reply to the Cincinnati branch. On December 1 he had told Strong, "I work night and day, upon the matter, dropping everything else." The final version of this report, 138 pages long in its printed form, was dated December 18, 1862, and was entitled "An Account of the Executive Organization of the United States Sanitary Commission" (FLO to GTS, Dec. 1, 1862; doc. no. 60 in USSC, *Documents*).

To George Templeton Strong

6th Dec. [186]2.

My Dear Mr Strong:

I have your letter of Dec. 5th.

I perfectly imagined the motives of your Resolution about the $50,000. The particular danger of the hour is in the other direction from that which you are suddenly changing your policy to guard, as I see it.[1] I stated my plan when I offered the Resolution or made the request to the Board which led to the passage of the Resolution. I stated that I should direct Dr Newberry to have his accounts audited monthly by a Committee of citizens of whom one must be an expert accountant.[2] The whole theory of our work is opposed to the control of expenditure, as you say, by a Wall St Committee or an Executive Committee on Wall St. We should be [s]lower to fill gaps than medical directors themselves for they have only to go to their major generals in the next tent, commonly, to find a power of the largest discretionary expenditure. Under your present theory, it would be necessary for Dr Smith[3] at Tallahatchie to satisfy Dr Prentiss[4] at Holly Springs, and for the latter to satisfy Dr Newberry at Louisville, or wherever he may be, and for the latter to satisfy and to make me able to satisfy you, and for you to consider the question (according to your explanation) of being able to satisfy all Wall Street and through Wall St, the public, before authority & means could be got to make an expenditure at our front on the enemy in Mississippi of a tenth part in cash of the cash expenditure which was made in a week lately sixty miles from Washington, without the smallest part of such caution. I say that this precaution then fully justifies the position of Cincinnati.[5]

You are right as to the money question with Cincinnati. I had forgotten the bearing of Mr Binney's Resolution on the point.[6]

Two assistants have been under orders for a fortnight past for Dr Page. The War Dpt order for their transportation was got yesterday and Mr Spaulding[7] left to join his colleague in New York. Dr Page will be reproved for troubling you in the matter.

We have an inspector at Suffolk and are in constant communication with him.

It is not possible to undertake the bulletin at present.[8]

Yours Respectfully

Fred. Law Olmsted.

Geo T. Strong, Esqr

The text is from a letterpress copy on pages 630–33 of volume 1 in box 835 of USSC-NYPL.

1. George Templeton Strong, in response to Olmsted's letter of December 4, urged him, "Do not suppose for a moment that the resolution of the Exec. Com. about the $50,000 deposit is founded on any want of confidence in Dʳ Newberry or in *any one*." Strong then outlined the Committee's reasoning:

   We are on the eve of a controversy with Cincinnati in which we shall be exposed to unfriendly criticism & attack on every vulnerable point, relevant or irrelevant. Independently of this we ought so to conduct our affairs that we can at any time invite a thorough overhauling of them. Reports to our prejudice may arise at any time that would make it necessary for us to ask some Committee of well known merchants to inspect our books and certify that all is right. Now the appropriation of so large a sum as fifty thousand dollars—nearly one fourth of our assets to be disbursed by an Executive officer without nominal supervision & control by the central Committee of the Board—would be thought by Wall St. an unbusiness-like slovenly reckless transaction. (GTS to FLO, Dec. 5, 1862, USSC-NYPL, box 747: 2944.)

2. Strong patiently replied to Olmsted's objections: "When Dʳ Newberry's 'western auditing committee' shall become a reality, we may be able to rescind our resolution, or so to modify it that our supervision shall be only nominal. Till then supervision in some way seems to us an absolute necessity. The question is how to exercise it so as to hamper you & Dʳ Newberry *least*" (GTS to FLO, Dec. 8, 1862, USSC-NYPL, box 747: 2965).

3. Thomas Blanch Smith (1835–1875), on the Tallahatchie River in Mississippi. Educated at Columbia College and the College of Physicians and Surgeons in New York, he was practicing medicine in his native Rockland County, New York, at the beginning of the Civil War. After duty as a Sanitary Commission inspector in 1862, he became the resident surgeon at "The Home," the Commission's shelter for sick and convalescent soldiers who were passing through Washington, and also served as a medical examiner of disabled soldiers seeking pensions. Smith resumed his private practice after the Civil War and was active in his local and state medical societies (Arthur S. Tompkins, ed., *Historical Record to the Close of the Nineteenth Century of Rockland County, New York* [Nyack, N.Y., 1902], pp. 202–3; doc. no. 77 in USSC, *Documents*).

4. Walter Mead Prentice (d. 1864), then stationed at Holly Springs in northern Mississippi, served as an inspector in the Western department of the Sanitary Commission from the fall of 1861 until early in 1863. He had graduated from Willoughby Medical College and had practiced medicine in Canfield and Cleveland, Ohio. Presumably his residence of over seven years in Cleveland had introduced him to John S. Newberry, who recruited him to work for the Sanitary Commission (biographical data courtesy of Glen Jenkins, the Cleveland Health Sciences Library of the Cleveland Medical Library Association and Case Western Reserve University, Cleveland, Ohio; *Cleave's Biographical Encyclopaedia of the State of Ohio. City of Cleveland and Cuyahoga County* [Philadelphia, 1875], pp. 107–8).

5. That is, the charges by the Cincinnati branch that the U.S. Sanitary Commission was an Eastern organization which had neither adequate knowledge of the needs of the Western army nor adequate means of distributing its supplies there (doc. no. 60 in USSC, *Documents*; George Hoadly to HWB, Nov. 5, 1862, USSC-NYPL, box 640).

6. In his letter of December 5 Strong pointed out, "Tho' the Cincinnatians did not raise the money question at our last meeting, we *decided* it, by adopting Mʳ Binney's resolutions." Strong was referring to the resolutions that stated that funds given to the Sanitary Commission were for the benefit of the entire army and that the Com-

mission could not entrust any of its funds to an organization not under its supervision (GTS to FLO, Dec. 5, 1862, USSC-NYPL, box 747: 2944; USSC, *Minutes*, p. 118).

7. H. B. Spaulding, the Commission's chief clerk during the autumn of 1862 ("Roster of persons employed by the Sanitary Commission," Oct. 1, 1862, USSC-NYPL, box 642).

8. The Executive Committee was desirous of having each of the offices of the Commission in Washington, Louisville, Boston, and elsewhere draw up a weekly bulletin about its current activities. In his letter of December 5 Strong queried Olmsted: "Cannot such a system be set in motion? Surely a brief outline of what has been done during the week could be noted on paper in ten minutes" (GTS to FLO, Dec. 5, 1862, USSC-NYPL, box 747: 2944).

To HENRY WHITNEY BELLOWS

Dr Bellows:

Washington   Dec 10./[18]62

My Dear Doctor,

I have just got your letter of 9th.

It has never occurred to me that there was "anything personal" in the Exec. Com. proceedings.[1] Nor do I object with any feeling to a radical change throughout in the policy of the Commission; on the contrary, if it is deliberately thought best to make a change of policy I will pull around with hearty good will, but I do object, and it is a personal wrong to me, although I know it is not thought to be, to interfere and reverse a single detail of a columnar policy. The reversal ought to be made on principle and to run through the whole. As it is, you knock one cog out of a wheel and say you do it because Wall St. might not like that kind of a wheel.

I do object however, to the Resolution as it stands on various other grounds; even if the policy was to be changed to meet the Wall St. demand, I should object to the Resolution. It is fundamentally wrong in principle, and all Wall St to the contrary notwithstanding, if Wall St knows no better, the plan and idea of the Resolution is wrong and wasteful; there is not and there never was a large business well done—as well done as it might have been and ought to have been—where that plan and idea had been adopted, and Mr. Strong is entirely mistaken in supposing that practical men insist upon it.[2] It is always held to be an open question and one to be decided by the nature of the service and the character of the men to be dealt with. I will demonstrate this by as good authority as any on the continent. The Resolution was a mistake and is calculated to bring the

GEORGE HOADLY

Commission into discredit and to injure the reputation of its secretary as a man of practical sagacity. I say is calculated to—I don't think it will, perceptibly, but I do not believe in playing fast and loose with anything which I think wrong essentially. I am sorry that the Committee can't and won't take the responsibility of getting round it, off from me.

As to the state & local B.d.[3] the less he is denounced and directly engaged with, the better. Our policy should be to strengthen ourselves positively not relatively. I say: "do what you think right for these, but remember the San. Com. reaches far beyond and over all; they may all die & the San. Com. is enough to do the work if it has the means. Let the San Com. die and they can't all together do the work. They are very well in their way but give the men of Gen'l Grant & Gen¹ Butler & Gen¹ Hunter[4] your aid as well and a fair share of it."

As for Judge Hoadly, the more I study the case, the more I am astonished by the utter recklessness of his assertions, the weakness of his arguments and the want of every quality which a judge or a gentleman should evince in a discussion of this sort.

Newberry writes of about half his strongest points: "this is a falsehood"—not a mistake.[5] I will treat him as tenderly as a brother, but I

493

will, as far as his argument is concerned, box him up in an air tight coffin. And if, oh! Domine, he does not apologize to you, he will stand before all the West, in the character of a shameless confidence-man and brazen hearted imposter, for a clearer attempt to come a stuffed wallet game over a respectable middle aged gentleman in a white-choker, was never shown up in the columns of the Police Gazette.[6] I shall assume that it was an accident, or rather a piece of eagerly reckless acquisitiveness, but if it was so, the Judge will admit that he has had a lesson in harsh judgments by which more than one scoundrel will profit in the future of his bench. Really tho', he must think us eastern people jolly green. Have you read the last edition, London, by Dutton Cook, I think, of "the Prodigal Son?"[7] Do you remember how Mr What'shisname René pulls the ear of the bad boy? I'm going to pull the Judge's ear, till he'll cry for Doctor Agnew to stop me, just so, and for the same reason.

I have another inspector engaged, and several lay agents, all I want or can manage to have in training very well at present.

Yours affectionately

FRED. LAW OLMSTED.

The original is in box 641 of USSC-NYPL.

1. Bellows in his letter explained the latest Executive Committee resolution—that no expenditure over one thousand dollars be made without permission from the Executive Committee. He attempted to smooth Olmsted's ruffled feathers by asserting:

    Our Committee seem to feel very anxiously their money responsibility. You must not misunderstand the restrictions they put on you, as in any way personal to you—but as essential to what they think business principles. My own imperfect acquaintance with these principles, makes me reluctant to oppose the convictions of men so shrewd & wise as Strong & Gibbs & Van Buren in matters of that sort. (HWB to FLO, Dec. 9, 1862, USSC-NYPL, box 747: 2973.)

2. Olmsted here is probably referring to a section of a letter by Strong that emphasized the necessity that the Commission's business dealings be above suspicion. Strong argued:

    Our doings are watched by solemn business men, & by rival agencies who would like to announce the discovery of any weak point in our system. We must adopt business like methods, & use a little caution, formality and red tape, not only for our own credit, but for the sake of the army which would suffer if business men were led to withdraw their confidence & their contributions. And I believe it would do us very serious mischief if it were said in Wall St. "That Sanitary Commission has become quite a big thing. It has received $____, it spends $____ a month, it employs _____ agents of one sort or another, but it don't settle their pay. There is one of its members who attends to all that, and pays them just what he thinks right. The Commission don't know anything about it. They have a treasurer, he don't know anything about it. He pays out money when it's called for & asks no questions."

The response would be "That's a very loose way of doing business. I sent them fifty dollars a month ago—but I don't think I shall send them any more." (GTS to FLO, Dec. 6, 1862, USSC-NYPL, box 747: 2951.)

3. "Boss devil" (see FLO to HWB, Nov. 24, 1862, n. 6, above).
4. The Army of the Tennessee, commanded by Ulysses Simpson Grant (1822–1885), the Army of the South, commanded by David Hunter (1802–1886), and the Army of the Gulf, commanded by Benjamin F. Butler. Olmsted probably did not realize that at this time Hunter had temporarily relinquished his command to serve on the court-martial of Fitz-John Porter (*DAB*; Frederick H. Dyer, *A Compendium of the War of the Rebellion . . .* , 3 vols. [1908; rpt. ed., New York, 1959], 1: 363–64, 486, 548).
5. Olmsted here is probably commenting on John S. Newberry's detailed statement about the remonstrance offered by the Cincinnati branch. This report, apparently written by George Hoadly, elaborated charges that Hoadly had made one week earlier in his letter to Bellows. At only one point did Newberry actually write, "The whole statement is a falsehood!" The assertion that drew such a strong response concerned a proposal to create a general Western sanitary commission which allegedly had been offered by William Greenleaf Eliot and defeated by Newberry at the Indianapolis convention. But on numerous other points, such as the work of distribution, his instruction of the Cincinnati branch, and the Commission's earlier approval of Cincinnati's labors, Newberry specifically disputed Hoadly's assertions ("Dr. Newberry's Notes on the Report by the Cincinnati Branch Made November 12, 1862," USSC-NYPL, box 753: 4791).
6. At this time the *National Police Gazette*, established by George Wilkes in 1845, was publishing crime news and sensational biographies of criminals that ostensibly would enable the respectable public to identify and beware of these villains (Frank Luther Mott, *A History of American Magazines . . .* , 5 vols. [Cambridge, Mass., 1938–68], 2: 324–39).
7. Edward Dutton Cook (1829–1883), British author, wrote the novel *A Prodigal Son*, which in 1862 was serialized by two magazines, *Once a Week* and *The Living Age*. The novel's plot centered upon the attempted blackmail of a young man who was trying to live down his youthful indiscretions, which included an ill-chosen marriage. In the episode to which Olmsted here refers, a French police inspector, René Isidor Philippe St. Just Lenoir, has just collared Alexis Pichot, a youthful hoodlum involved in the blackmail scheme, and is pulling his ear to make him listen and carry a message to his fellow conspirators (Dutton Cook, *A Prodigal Son* [London, 1863]).

To John Strong Newberry

Sanitary Commission,
Adams' House, 244 F street,
Washington, D.C., Dec 27th 1862.

My Dear Doctor,
    Eliot[1] has been here and obtained from the Secy of War a General order reestablishing the Westⁿ Sanitary Commission of Gen'l Fremont with all its original priviledges &c & extending its territory to all of the

GEORGE LAFFERTY ANDREW

army under the observation of Dr Wood—that is to say all your department.[2] This was a week ago Thursday, and he left the moment the order
was signed. It has been kept a secret, and I am informed of it confidentially; being forbidden to mention it by telegraph lest it should be known
that I had got wind of it at the War Office[3] (These are not my surmises or
precautions).

You can draw your own inferences—I have conferred with Prof^r
Bache & Mr Strong & they say drive ahead and occupy all the ground as
fast as possible.[4] It is especially desirable you should have an inspector at
once in Arkansas & Missouri. I mean to send you Andrew, our best man
for some purposes—most experienced & trustiest, and with important
influence in Indiana.[5] My advice is that you make him your Corresponding
Secretary in charge of Central office—for collecting and dépôt business &
Warriner[6] ditto, ditto, for field operations—but this is the barest suggestion. I think you should organize so as to have absolutely nothing vital
depending on yourself, so as to be free to travel and throw yourself in,
where most needed, week after week.

Prof[r] Bache is anxious you should strengthen at Nashville, thinking it looks like a great battle in that part of the field before long.[7]

Favorable accounts from all quarters (except yours). I have heard nothing from you since you were in New York.[8] I beg to have stated weekly reports from each inspector. I am never able to say what we *are doing* in the West, an enquiry almost daily made to me. It would be well [worth] fifty thousand dollars a year to us to be kept constantly well informed of what is going on in the West.

Yours Very Truly

Fred. Law Olmsted.

D[r] J. S. Newberry
Louisville, Ky.

The original is letter 320 in volume 1 of box 914 of USSC-NYPL.

1. William Greenleaf Eliot (1811–1887), Unitarian minister and a founder of the Western Sanitary Commission. Born in Massachusetts, he graduated from Columbian College in Washington, D.C., and Harvard Divinity School. Arriving in St. Louis in 1834, he organized the First Congregational Church (Unitarian) there and became active in the city's educational affairs. While serving on the city's school board, he supported the taxation necessary to support the public school system. He also founded Washington University and raised money for its support.

    A long-time critic of slavery and an advocate of gradual emancipation, Eliot strongly supported the Union. His concern for sick and wounded soldiers provided the impetus for the formation of the Western Sanitary Commission. Eliot was also an important representative of and propagandist for that organization. His efforts resulted in John C. Frémont's issuing a special order in September 1861 which recognized the Western Sanitary Commission. After Secretary of War Cameron ordered Frémont to revoke or modify his order, Eliot convinced the secretary to allow the St. Louis organization to remain independent of the U.S. Sanitary Commission. He similarly persuaded Stanton in December 1862 to reissue and affirm the Frémont order that had given recognition and special privileges to the Western Sanitary Commission. Eliot's ties to New England through his ancestry and education garnered much needed financial support from the East for his organization.

    Eliot's relations with the U.S. Sanitary Commission were never particularly smooth. The members resented his appeals to the East for aid, and they believed him to be sly and conniving. Olmsted most likely shared this distrust of Eliot (Charlotte C. Eliot, *William Greenleaf Eliot: Minister, Educator, Philanthropist* [Boston and New York, 1904], pp. 31, 73–77, 216–22; DAB; *Diary of the Civil War*, pp. 188–89).
2. On December 16, 1862, Stanton approved and extended John C. Frémont's order of September 1861, which originally had been disapproved by the then secretary of war, Simon Cameron. Stanton's action granted the Western Sanitary Commission the privilege "of extending its labors to the camps and hospitals of any of the Western armies, under the direction of the assistant surgeon-general, Col. R. C. Wood" (O.R., ser. 3, vol. 2, p. 947).

3. Olmsted learned of this order from Surgeon General Hammond on December 21. Fearing that Stanton would learn that he had leaked the information, the surgeon general asked Olmsted not to send the news by telegraph (FLO to GTS, Dec. 21, 1862).
4. In a letter of December 21 to Strong, Olmsted argued that the U.S. Sanitary Commission had not lost its privileges but would have to be prepared to divide funds in the West with the Western Sanitary Commission. He continued:

> We should be prepared to meet them with propositions which they will not expect, and in doing so have chiefly regard to preventing them from stealing a march upon us with our contributors in the East and California. . . . They must be left if possible with no false grounds of appeal for further assistance from the East. Then with the weight of Cleveland, Chicago and Louisville, we must try to effect an alliance and correspondence between them and ourselves by which the essential principles of our plan shall be saved from sacrifice.

Strong in his reply of December 24 countered:

> I don't see that our position is affected. Nor do I see the necessity of our dividing the California fund with St Louis—or ceasing to cry aloud for more money for general National purposes. I should push the Western campaign on *both* sides the Mississippi with all possible vigor. Coalition or alliance with St Louis is of course desirable, but I fear it cannot be done.

Olmsted agreed and was relaying this advice to Newberry (FLO to GTS, Dec. 21 and Dec. 26, 1862; GTS to FLO, Dec. 24, 1862, USSC-NYPL, box 748: 3117).
5. George L. Andrew had influential political connections in his home state of Indiana. Most important was Schuyler Colfax, his friend from neighboring South Bend, who had served as a U.S. congressman since 1855 and who became Speaker of the House of Representatives in 1863. Colfax was a Republican, but Andrew was also on good terms with Graham Newell Fitch, a physician and Democrat who had formerly been a U.S. senator from Indiana (G. L. Andrew to W. H. Van Buren, Sept. 8, 1861, USSC-NYPL, box 728: 513; *BDAC*).
6. Sanitary Commission inspector Henry A. Warriner.
7. Bache was anticipating the battle of Murfreesboro (Stones River), which occurred December 30, 1862–January 3, 1863 (*War for the Union*, 2: 375–77).
8. Olmsted had seen Newberry at meetings of the Sanitary Commission in New York City on December 15 through 17 (USSC, *Minutes*, pp. 121–26).

To Henry Whitney Bellows

Sanitary Commission,
Adams' House, 244 F street,
Washington, D.C., Dec. 27th 1862

My Dear Doctor,

I can not go on with the business with these daily orders from and this daily reporting to the Executive Committee. It is not a question of right or wrong, reason or folly; it is a question of constitution. My brain simply vomits all the business that I bring to it. I can lay hold of nothing right end foremost. I have my way of carrying on business, and it plainly is not your way. You do not comprehend me, and I feel that you won't and there's no use talking. What I mean is that there's no use *trying*. Somehow or other, you have taken all the energy out of me. I've lost command of my business; I can't get hold of it. The moment I take up a question and try to penetrate it, somebody shoves a slide before my eyes inscribed "Executive Committee", and it's all hazy and I turn sick. If Jenkins or Knapp ask me for instructions, instead of taking hold to answer them, I think, "What have the Committee said about that?" "How is that under the rule of the Committee?" "What will the Committee think about it?" "I don't know what the Committee may be doing about that." "Well, *I think* so & so, but if I say so, I shall get a gentle reminder from the Committee that I might as well have consulted them." "I *should* do so & so, but the Committee won't understand it & will fear something is wrong & then there will be some general instruction that will practically work out [to] the loss of the best part of my last month's work." In one way or another the devil jams the Committee on my brain, turn which way I will, and it's wrong for me to try to cover it up, though I perfectly know that you won't believe me, or rather, again, won't understand me & will think it's merely a whimpering way I have of nursing my self will and vanity. Be it so. Weaknesses are facts just as much as cannon-balls & you have to meet them and perhaps be bowled out by them. Honestly, I feel that my power of usefulness is gone, and that I ought to resign and that you ought to accept my resignation, but I know you won't think so, and would be angry with me if I did what you would regard as a wholly uncalled for thing, at a time when the Commission most needed my best service. The Commission can't get my best service, because it can not go through these doors, but you won't believe it, and I am too sincerely respectful to you to insist upon my own convictions. I know this will sound funnier than anything else, but again it's true, all the same. I do respect your judgment and the Committee's judgment from the bottom of my soul, however I rampage on it. Think of trying to preach a sermon seated on the desk with your back to the audience and your feet dangling under you, doctor, or think of trying to preach in the centre of a circle with your audience all around behind you, turn where you will, and you will know how I feel every day when I try to take hold of the business after reading yesterday's proceedings of the Exec. Com. (I mean any day's yesterday). My audience is always coughing behind me, and I have no appetite for anything but to write a ream to the Executive Committee; I feel always, there's the vital point, there's no use trimming sail when, for all I know, the rudder-ropes are just going to break.

You have got to the end of my capacity; I know you think well of me, and I need not be ashamed to tell you in advance that now, you are going to see me fail & disappoint you. I'm so much but that's all. You can't make as much of me as we would both be glad that you could. But when you find me out, don't call it by its wrong name. I'm a good man to work by the month or the quarter but a good for nothing to work by the day. I believe that it's neither vanity nor priggishness, but simply the place where God saw fit to put in my special stupidity. So I don't expect to repent of it, or be sorry for the consequences but take them along with baldness and decayed teeth and such-like blessings. I shall be glad if you can too—so it needn't make any difference in your friendship for me.

I don't mean to say anything more about it; I shall do my best to obey orders, but I can never remember four things at a time & shall soon fail in that, even, I fear. I really am an honest, faithful and in my way precise sort of servant to you, but my way is not your way of being precise and you will soon be thinking me very loose, and rather indifferent to my duty.

You know there's no use talking to a man when he gets a notion of this sort between his teeth. The best way is to say as little as you can decently, and let him run till you see what comes of it. So now I've treated my conscience to a burst, will say no more about it for the present.

The original is in box 641 of USSC-NYPL. Although this letter ends abruptly and is unsigned, it does not appear to be a fragment.

To Henry Whitney Bellows

[c. December 1862–February 1863]

My Dear Doctor,

Your playful remark that my idiosyncracies must be consulted, suggests this protest against any possible misunderstanding of Mr Olmsted's expression of judgment vs a member of the Executive Committee. Mr Secretary Olmsted asks no consideration of his *peculiar* idiosyncracies, Mr Committee-man Olmsted argues that the fact that *every man* has his idiosyncracies & consequently his own way of proceeding in the accomplishment of any purpose, is a sound reason for the rule that you should always give as much freedom to your agent of business as you dare.

Your business will be better done the more it is done free from unnecessary guidance. I, Committee-man Olmsted, don't think your business will be as well done as it might be if you now give, as has been proposed, peremptory orders to Mr Secy Olmsted, especially if you give peremptory orders to those for whose action you mean to hold him responsible, to do this or that, to go here or there, without reference to his deliberate judgment of what would be the quickest and surest way of taking hold of every handle of all the various classes of business you want him to presently have in hand.

If he is not, by reason of his idiosyncracies or otherwise, prepared at once to inform you about his deliberate judgment, it is his duty to advise or to ask a postponement of such action. And Committee-man Olmsted very justly urges the expediency of granting this favor, not in consideration of the peculiar idiosyncracies of the Secretary, but in consideration of the general rule—applying to Secretaries and not to Olmsteds—to which the undersigned has referred. In my judgment the Committee has made the Secy aware of its purposes; he should be allowed to ponder on the question of how best to carry them out—to feel the way a little before he is ordered how to carry them out—not as a matter of kindness or justice but of business expediency.

Inter al.[1]

F.L.O.

The original is in the Henry Whitney Bellows Papers, Massachusetts Historical Society, Boston, Massachusetts.

1. That is, between us.

To HENRY WHITNEY BELLOWS

Jan. 4th [186]3.

Dr Bellows
My Dear Doctor,
The Surgeon General hopes this week to be able to get a bill introduced into the Senate for a general improvement and enlargement of the Medical organization of the Army. He thinks that he has secured the

favor of the Senate Military Committee for it, and that it can be carried in the Senate. He would like to have you watch its progress, and, if convenient, so time the next meeting of the Commission here, that the influence of the members may be brought to bear personally in its favor, when it shall be hanging in the House.[1]

The Surgeon General has got wind of an intrigue against him in the Department, which he is prepared to meet boldly by suspending Perley[2]—the only question being as to the best moment for doing so.

If all signs did not fail in dry weather, I should say that it looked more and more as if Stanton must go out. Gen'l Butler is the darkest spot in the rising cloud.[3] May his reign soon refresh us![4]

Yours Respectfully,

Fred. Law Olmsted.
Gl Secy

The text is from a letterpress copy on pages 202–4 of Olmsted's private letterbook.

1. A reference to Senate Bill 470, which the Senate acted upon in late January 1863. This measure proposed to increase the number of medical personnel, mainly surgeons, who could be appointed to both the regular and volunteer armies, and to repeal the law requiring an assistant surgeon to serve five years before being promoted to surgeon. The bill would also have provided each army corps with a medical director and would have increased the rank of a department's chief medical director from major to colonel. Another section of Senate Bill 470 increased the rate at which military hospitals were paid for the commutation of a soldier's daily ration from eighteen cents to thirty cents. Many senators objected to the increased expenditures the bill would entail, and they struck out all its provisions except that adding 50 surgeons and 250 assistant surgeons to the volunteer forces. The House of Representatives took no action upon the measure, and thus it was never passed (*Congressional Globe*, 37th Cong., 3rd sess., 1862–63, 41: 446–51, 468–75, 523).
2. Thomas Flint Perley (1815–1889) graduated from Bowdoin College and studied medicine in Maine. Joining the army as a brigade surgeon of volunteers in 1861, he received an appointment as medical inspector general with the rank of colonel in June 1862. The Sanitary Commission believed Perley to be poorly qualified for that post and attributed his selection to the influence of Senator William P. Fessenden. Perley resigned in August 1863 and moved to Maine because of his wife's ill health. There he served as a surgeon of volunteers until 1865 (Guy V. Henry, *Military Record of Civilian Appointments in the United States Army*, 2 vols. [New York, 1870], 1: 104; Martin Van Buren Perley, *History and Genealogy of the Perley Family* [Salem, Mass., 1906], p. 221; William Quentin Maxwell, *Lincoln's Fifth Wheel: The Political History of the United States Sanitary Commission* [New York, 1956], p. 156).
3. Rumors abounded in Washington during December 1862 and January 1863 that Stanton might be removed from his post as secretary of war. Benjamin F. Butler was among those mentioned as his likely successor (Benjamin Franklin Butler, *Private and Official Correspondence of Gen. Benjamin F. Butler during the Period of the Civil War*, 5 vols. [n.p., 1917], 2: 589–90).
4. Olmsted probably is making a play upon the homophones "rain" and "reign."

To Henry Whitney Bellows

> Sanitary Commission,
> Adams' House, 244 F street,
> Washington, D.C., Jan. 13th 1863.

My Dear Doctor,

I read your letter of Jan. 12th with the deepest pain.[1] The members of the Executive Committee I regard as the best and dearest of friends. I know that I respect and love them & am grateful to them. I pray God with my whole soul to keep me truly dutiful to them while also dutiful to the trust they have given me, so long as I hold it.

Would to God, I had resigned it two months ago. I shall regard as one of the great misfortunes of my life that I did not.

I pledge you my honor that I take no step and write no word without a humble and earnest and careful effort, that it shall not widen the difference between myself & my friends, which since the last session has given me constant painful anxiety. My conscience and honor—or if you must think so, my diseased vanity—would not allow me to pass the action of the Committee referred to, in silence. I said what I thought my duty required as simply as possible. My motive I presume has been again misunderstood, as I am forced to think it has been by the members of the Committee, in nearly everything during the last two months. Is it not more likely that there has been something wrong with me.

The original is in box 641 of USSC-NYPL. Although this letter ends rather abruptly and is not signed, it appears to be complete.

1. The editors have been unable to locate this letter by Bellows, which apparently has not survived.

To George Templeton Strong

> Washington, Jan 29th 1863

My Dear Mr. Strong,

I thank you heartily for the intention of your note of the 28th.[1]

You have rightly conjectured the passage in your letters to me to which I referred in conversation with Dr Bellows. I regarded it as a frank expression (so far as frankness was possible) of an ill defined, uneasy apprehension that your affairs in my hands were very poorly or inadequately superintended and accounted for. Such a vague apprehension has been manifested in various ways, all infinitely more painful to me than the distinct statement of a distinct conviction would have been. Being vague, not being acknowledged even to yourselves in a distinct form, you were never ready to permit it to be uprooted in the only way in which it could possibly be removed, and yet it influenced your actions in a way which was calculated to seriously cripple my ability to meet my responsibility.

I beg you to believe me,—and I say this because experience teaches me that my friends do not always readily believe what is true of me in such cases—such an apprehension troubles me very little (give me sound bottom and stand clear of me & I will be able to remove it) but its vagueness and uncertainty as to influence upon you troubles me greatly, because of the uncertain, variable and unsymmetrical policy of action which it will induce.

The conversation which I had with you in the New York office after the Board adjourned removed any occasion for a subsequent reference to your note of Dec. 10th in which the passage referred to occurs.[2] I did not receive that note, although written previously to that conversation, until after my return to Washington. Had I received it before the New York meeting, it would only have led me to say what I did to you at the close of the session, at an earlier day, and as giving me ground for asserting the existence of such an apprehension and of the utter inadequacy of the way you were influenced to act by it to relieve you of it, I should have had occasion only to thank you for it.

Hence I thank you for the *intention* of your present favor, meaning that a disclaimer of any intention to hurt my feelings is wholly unnecessary. I could never suspect you of it—or of carelessness or unadroitness in that respect. My feelings are not thin skinned but any uncertainty as to what is required of me as a duty, and of my ability to meet it, is more irksome to me than perhaps is right. You know that I know and apprehend less than most men of my qualities in other respects of some of the ordinary pleasures of society—I have some peculiarity of that sort. I believe that I am also less susceptible than most men to the ordinary hurts of society. But I have my own weak points & sometimes when I wince, it is not at the hurt which is most readily supposed.

I can sleep on the floor very well, but I can't sleep on a bed with one sheet. Nor can I rest on any halfway about my business.

Very Sincerely & cordially,

Fred. Law Olmsted.

George T. Strong Esq[r]

The text is from a letterpress copy on pages 221–25 of Olmsted's private letterbook.

1. Strong's letter of January 28, 1863, which was intended to mollify Olmsted, apparently has not survived.
2. The editors have been unable to discover Strong's letter of December 10, 1862, to Olmsted expressing a lack of confidence in Olmsted's superintendence.

To Oliver Wolcott Gibbs

Washington, Jan. 31st 1863.

My Dear Gibbs,

Please let me know of your progress with the National.[1] Now is the time to drive that sort of thing it seems to me. It looks to me as if the question of popular doggedness of purpose in the war was soon to be determined and might be turned by a hair. It is only necessary that a certain number of men should commit themselves to go through with it whatever comes & whoever else drops out, to give no hearing to any suggestion of quitting it, come what will, to make final success sure. We have more of the brute force of persistent obstinacy in our Northern blood than the South has, if we can only get it in play, and it is plainly merely a question of who will hold out longest. The danger is that the politicians will get the idea that the people are tired of the war and begin to play for that disposition. We ought to have the means by organization in any crisis to create and manifest public sentiment against them. We ought to be able to bring evidence—such as by the continued contributions to the Sanitary Commission,—that the people are still ready to sacrifice of their property in the war—ready, willing and able. We ought to be able to have at every step backward like that of the Democrats in Indiana, a counter step like that of the Democratic officers from Indiana.[2] Such matters should not be trusted to take care of themselves. Be sure the traitors don't trust to mere spontaneous action of their sympathizers. The quiet substantial people are sound but quiet substantial people don't display themselves. Your league ought to be extended over the whole country before Congress adjourns & it ought to have something to do besides talk within itself.

Should a club or league be started in Washington of residents, like Bache? Can I be of use to suggest it? If not, please tell me why not—that is, why are you not ready to spread the movement? Are you discussing it?[3]

Do you want me as a member of the New York club? I don't want to pay to both. Shall you—should I, not quit the Century?[4] Will you oblige me by enquiring the next time you are at the Century whether I ought to be paying anything there. Is there not a provision by which non-resident members are relieved of their taxes?

Why do I not receive the Stillé pamphlets for distribution?[5] Is it not your intention to send them to the office for distribution through the country by our system? I want to do something for that. I will pay for a hundred or two of the pamphlet if nothing else, if you will let me.

I feel, you will see, as if our machinery for spreading Sanitary ideas thro' the country ought to be made use of for strengthening the Union otherwise, somehow, as this could be done at no cost & nobody the wiser, as to the Sanitary's having anything to do with it.

Why not get together three or four men in Phil[a] next week, meeting the Phila[da] leaguers & determine upon a form of pledge or instrument of linking together for the country. I like your printed statement better the oftener I read it—it is excellent & I should be glad to have you hold to it every word & without additions—as it originally stood. The Phil[a] don't mean enough. Any rogue could drive a four horse coach through it.[6] Everybody who has been in Fort Lafayette[7] could swear to it. Loyalty means lickspittle to save the Union with some men. On what terms would you take peace? that is what we want to know of men we are to associate with. On condition of unquestionable nationality based on Federalism and the annihilation of the dogma of States rights (as ever under any circumstances to be thought of as superior to it). That is the battle we have got to fight now or hereafter. I want to fight it now, when our hand is in. Avoid words which connect us with the old fight as much as you can, and use those & those allusions which make it a matter of today as much as possible; but do so in order to commit & establish the temper of the people for the struggle in the long future against Westernism and all other forms of breaking up. I like yours a great deal better than the Philad[a] heading, though it must, of course, take a different form, as a constitutional declaration.

But pray get it into that form & set it going.

Yours affectionately

Fred. Law Olmsted.

Prof[r] Gibbs.

The original is in the archives of the Union League Club, New York City.

1. During the embryonic stages of the Union League Club of New York, its founders often called it the National. In the letter presented here Olmsted was responding to the rough draft of a circular proposing the formation of the "National Club," which Gibbs drew up in mid-January. Olmsted probably also knew that an organizational

meeting had been planned for January 30 and wished to know what it had accomplished (*Diary of the Civil War*, pp. 276–88).

2. Olmsted is contrasting the actions of the Democratic legislators in Indiana with those of Democratic army officers from that state. When the Indiana state legislature met in early January 1863, some Democrats denounced the Emancipation Proclamation and vowed not to provide further levies of men and money for the war. Democratic officers of the Indiana regiments in the Army of the Cumberland met on January 22 and adopted a series of resolutions. They praised Republican governor Oliver P. Morton, criticized the Democratic legislators for disloyalty, and advocated a vigorous and unconditional prosecution of the war (*War for the Union*, 2: 390; *New-York Daily Tribune*, Jan. 24, 1863, p. 5).

3. Although Gibbs was trying to encourage the creation of similar clubs of loyalists in other cities such as Chicago, Boston, and Albany, he told Olmsted, "I do not think it yet worth while to start a league in Washington because there is no permanent material there but upon this point consult Bache after you receive the papers" (O. W. Gibbs to FLO, Feb. 8, 1863, USSC-NYPL, box 756: 357).

4. In 1859 Olmsted had become a member of the Century Club, which was composed of one hundred gentlemen interested or active in the fine arts. On February 8, 1863, Gibbs chided Olmsted for considering resignation from the club: "Do not think of resigning the Century. It has a great influence for good in this city & most of the members are hearty in their loyalty. . . . I will enquire about your dues at the Century but I think the rule is that absent members pay except when abroad" (ibid.; *Papers of FLO*, 2: 366; James Grant Wilson, ed., *The Memorial History of the City of New York, from Its First Settlement to the Year 1892*, 4 vols. [New York, 1892–93], 3: 428–29).

5. In 1862 Charles J. Stillé wrote a pamphlet entitled *How a Free People Conduct a Long War*. In this work he drew parallels between the Civil War and English wars, most notably the English Peninsular campaign during the Napoleonic Wars. Stillé focused upon the variability of public opinion and concluded that the English experience "proves quite clearly that in the support of public opinion, and in the means requisite to maintain a great army, those fundamental essentials of real military success, our Government is immeasurably stronger than the English ever was at any period of the war."

   Gibbs, in his reply to this letter, assured Olmsted that copies of Stillé's pamphlet had been mailed to him, and continued: "Of course they are to be distributed through our agents but not paid for with San. Comm. money. We have raised a private fund for that purpose" (Charles J. Stillé, *How a Free People Conduct a Long War: A Chapter From English History* [New York, 1863], p. 11; O. W. Gibbs to FLO, Feb. 8, 1863, USSC-NYPL, box 756: 357).

6. Here Olmsted is expressing his approval of the rough draft of a declaration of aims drawn up by Gibbs for the New York organization. This document has not survived, but it apparently explicitly denounced states' rights doctrines by pledging the members to oppose such dogmas "open or insidious." Olmsted found such a declaration far more acceptable than the articles of association of the Union League of Philadelphia, which made membership contingent upon only an "unqualified loyalty to the Government of the United States, and unwavering support of its efforts for the suppression of the Rebellion." Other potential members of the New York organization held reservations about such an open attack upon states' rights, and that section was deleted. The revised version of the New York circular required of potential members "uncompromising and unconditional loyalty to the Nation, and a complete subordination thereto of all other political ideas." This test, in Gibbs's opinion, did not demand enough, but he defended it to Olmsted on February 8: "I shall hope for your approbation of our plan of organization though it does not come up to my temperature which is full white heat. I wanted it to sound like a trumpet but find that it was necessary to begin with a whistle."

When the Union League Club of New York met on February 21, 1863, it adopted a suggestion put forward by Henry W. Bellows that the requirement for membership be only "absolute and unqualified loyalty" and "unwavering support" of the war. George Templeton Strong, who agreed with the conception that Gibbs and Olmsted shared of the club, told the latter, "I cannot refrain from expressing my pain, disgust and wrath at the fact that at a meeting *here* last Saturday night (about 30 or 40 present) our rather masculine and straight-out platform had all the oak timber taken out of it, and the vague generalities of the Philadelphia paper substituted for it." To these men, the new platform was too narrowly conceived, since it addressed only the war aims of the government, not the philosophical roots of the rebellion (Guy Gibson, "Lincoln's League: The Union League Movement during the Civil War" [Ph.D. diss., University of Illinois, 1958], pp. 37, 60–65; Henry W. Bellows, *Historical Sketch of the Union League Club of New York, Its Origin, Organization, and Work, 1863–1879* . . . [New York, 1879], pp. 22–26; O. W. Gibbs to FLO, Feb, 8, 1863, USSC-NYPL, box 756: 357; GTS to FLO, Feb. 25, 1863).

7. Numerous prisoners suspected of disloyalty were detained at Fort Lafayette in the New York harbor under the presidential suspension of the writ of habeas corpus (*War for the Union*, 2: 312).

To William Henry Hurlbert

Jany 31st [186]3.

My Dear Hurlbert,

I have been led to see that people of good general education, themselves politicians and administrators, here in Washington, have exceedingly vague ideas of administration, of the relations of authority and responsibility, of assignments of duty, and accountability with reference to given assignments, and that the words administrative and executive are commonly used as synonymous and so on. It is plain that the alphabet of administration is unknown to the Secretary of War, and to many others who are assigned by superior administration to administrative responsibilities of the gravest importance. It is surprising to me that their unfitness, or unfittedness from want of knowledge and skill in administration, for their offices, is not more clearly seen and remarked upon; equally so that the exceptions in this respect, among whom I reckon Wells, Meigs, Shiras & Hammond[1] (Commissary & Surgn-Genl) are not more clearly recognized. And this leads me to ask you whether there is not a Euclid of Administrative Science, whether there are not established axiomatic truths, and propositions acknowledged to be demonstrated from them. Is it nowhere laid down, for instance, "As is the measure of free-will so is the measure of responsibility,"? and the corollary, "In proportion as free will (authority or discretion) is restrained, responsibility is reduced,"?

Are there not authorities on the abstract science of administration? If so, can you tell me what they are, and if not, what come nearest to it?[2]

Then, can you tell me where I can find an account of the history and of the recent net results and conclusions of the English examinations for civil appointments?[3]

As to the temper of the people—the people 'way back—the contributions to the Sanitary Commission afford no bad test. I suppose the relative value to the contributors of goods now given is piece for piece fully tenfold greater than when, about 16 months ago, the superfluous old shirts &c. were gathered up. Contributions of this kind costing little were at one time very large. This was not long in any given locality. After the superfluity was exhausted in a household, its contributions were very small; then there were jolting periods of sentimental enthusiasm, and again a fall. Then as the cost and difficulty and discouragement of the war increased, it was clear that certain people were taking hold of it in a different spirit; contributions became steadier and more carefully considered. Except for a short period of enthusiasm more than a year ago, contributions—household contributions, have never been as large as at present; the volume is ever slowly and steadily increasing. Its value is not far from $3000 a day, which, recollect, is wholly a free-will offering of households, about two thirds of it being a money expenditure, the fathers of families, the remainder being the labor of women & children. It is an interesting question how much it is an expression of patriotism and how much of pity. The general tenor of the letters from contributors shows that it is mainly patriotism, devotion to what the writers suppose to be the end for which the soldiers suffer, which inspires the gifts, Union and emancipation being generally associated.

I can not doubt that the respectable middle-class people of the country are gradually setting their teeth in the old revolutionary way. Seven years, if necessary, and the gallows in every town, if necessary, but the business is to be done. (I don't want the above facts published until I can be more accurate about them.)

Yours Sincerely

Fred. Law Olmsted.

The text is from a letterpress copy on pages 226–32 of Olmsted's private letterbook.

1. Gideon Welles, secretary of the navy; Montgomery C. Meigs, quartermaster general of the army; Alexander E. Shiras, assistant to the commissary general; and William A. Hammond, surgeon general.

2. Hurlbert, in his reply of February 6, cited a manual that he believed to be written by the marquis de Turgot, a French peer and former ambassador to Spain, as the best book on the science of administration (W. H. Hurlbert to FLO, Feb. 6, 1863).

3. Hurlbert suggested that Olmsted consult a report, published in 1860, by a parliamentary select committee on civil service appointments (ibid.).

To Henry Whitney Bellows

Unofficial.

U.S. Sanitary Commission,
Adams' House, 244 F Street,
Washington, D.C., Feby 4th 1863.

My Dear Doctor,

I send you a printed copy of the General order about the Exec. Service.[1] I have changed in proof the first ¶ partly in order to avoid the use of the designation West, & so that no distinction may appear historically, as of an organic character, between West & East. What I understand to be the truth is recognized. Prof Bache was not quite satisfied with the original in this respect when he saw it in print.

I have also substituted for Western Secretary the phrase Assistant General Secretary, which seems to me to be more accurate. Please telegraph if you object.

I propose to leave next week for the West if nothing comes to prevent. That I can do good at the West or obtain the means of doing good, I don't doubt. That in order that I may go to the West, many matters will be forgotten, neglected, delayed & much sacrificed, I know, and I believe that my going to the West will cost more than it will be worth a great deal, though as this will only be in the absence of results which would otherwise be secured, and nobody knows what these are, it will never appear to be so.

I have made a great mistake in the whole organization of the Commission's Executive service, if there is a necessity that I should go anywhere. There is an officer appointed to do what is wanted of me now at the West. I know that to acknowledge & manifest that it is necessary that I should supplant him, that the Commission thinks that he is incompetent, that he needs or ought to have a reserved force of this kind behind him, that the Commission can not depend on him, but must take a superior officer away from his post and proper duty to satisfy them on the point of duty belonging to the subordinate—to do this by a formal order, without dismissing the subordinate is a very unjust and radically bad piece of business. And glad as I shall be—never having been in the Northwest at all (north of the Ohio & west of Buffalo)—to have the opportunity of travelling there with the Commission's introduction & at the Commission's expense, as a matter of personal profit, as Secretary of the Sanitary Commission, I shall go under protest & compulsion. I believe [it] to be wrong—just as sinful as lying or stealing—except as it is a mistake. But of course, I am not responsible, and if you say so, I go. I assume that you do & am arranging accordingly.

Now what do I go for? Must I say it again? I can not do other people's business. I do not believe in scolding (except one's superiors). When I find an agent whom I am convinced can't or won't meet his responsibility, I know of but one thing to do with him—drop him.

The Commission has no right to place me in a position where I must either reprove or discharge one of its own members. It is an absurdity. I would not, I do not & I will not assume such a duty. If he is not competent for the duty given him by the Commission, the Commission must find it out for itself and must act therein as seemeth to it good. As Secretary in the service of the Commission, I shall express no opinion on the subject, adversely to the judgment of the Commission. I believe that he is competent, that he knows his business better than I do, and that any constraint used upon him by me can only be harmful to his sense of responsibility and thus to that instinctive action on which his efficiency entirely depends. His desire that I should come into his shop, his desire that the Commission should come into his department, thus mixing up his business with the Commission's business—as if the Commission could possibly help him, could do anything but obstruct and embarrass and derange all his work, by coming into his shop—is the worst thing I know of him, and the way to remedy it is not for me to be sent to the West. It is to tell him to mind his business & if it's too much for him, to ask authority to employ assistants & money to pay them till he gets enough & good enough. Give me money & law enough & I can be as good a general as McClellan, better, because with money and law enough I can buy McClellan & put Stanton, Gurowski[2] & Co. in Fort Lafayette. I know enough to take McClellan's ideas if they are worth taking & to let him go ahead if there's any go ahead in him. If there is not, no power under heaven will ever put it there. Judgment goes with freedom & with self-dependence. Constrain a man or relieve him of his responsibility, by so much as you do so, you annihilate his capacity. Newberry wants to be relieved indirectly of a responsibility which you want him—which your system requires, that he should be equal to. Hereafter who is to be to blame for what is wrong in the West? Not I, not Newberry. I have taken, and I will take upon me no duty that can not be better performed at Washington, which could not be as well or better performed in Timbuctoo[3] with sufficient telegraphic, speaking tube and atmospheric railway advantages. The further (i.e. the more distinctly) removed an administrator is from pure execution the better. I am the Commission's executive, but with reference to my executives, I am a pure administrator, and it is just as absurd & as fatal for me to take my executives' business, or if you please, other executives' of the Commission's business, out of their hands as it is for the Exec. Com. to take my business out of my hands. I know what the effect is on me, and I know what is wrong if it does not have the same effect on them. Their business is too big for them. The remedy is to cut down their business by wholesale, not piece-meal. That will work harm & only harm continually.

Well, in the absence of instructions, I go west for personal recreation, and to organize the new adjutant's department,[4] so, by wholesale, reducing Newberry's duty, (though he won't see it so), and to cultivate a friendly feeling amongst all concerned by a little white lying, and also to demonstrate the fact that we are not obstinate mules and are willing to give way to people's mistakes & to pretend that we don't think them mistakes, when we want their confidence & this is necessary thereto.

I should like to go to Cairo, & I suppose it will be best to do so, to satisfy Judge Skinner, & I shall go to Chicago & be there several days. In fact there & then, I expect to really do the most. I shall stop at Cleaveland just to set Miss _____ right about Federal relations & come back by Erie road to New York, if you have no objections. That will take three weeks. Do you want me to go to St. Louis? If so, what for? I should like to go there, if you can give me an excuse, but I can't see that it would pay. I would like to go to Sault St Mary or Slave lake,[5] for that matter. Could Detroit, Montreal, Quebeck and some icebergs be brought in anyhow? May I go down the great river to the "cut-off," or to Memphis? If they happen to have taken Port Hudson, may I go on & see my brother?[6] I have long had a curiosity to see Westn Arkansas, and I think there is a mystery about the Commission's agency in Kansas that possibly might be investigated with advantage on the ground. Prof^r Bache is preparing a new map of Eastern Tennessee, I have long felt a great interest in that region. In truth the only country I don't care a durn for out west is that around about and below Nashville. But if you say it, I shall even go there. For any good purpose, it will, I think, add a fortnight.

How long are you willing I should be absent from Washington? Congress will have adjourned or be close upon it, before I get back—at the shortest.

Prof^r Bache promises to be Act^g Genl Secy in my absence.

The Prof[r] by the way agrees with me that you should give notice that on account of my intended visit to the West, the March quarterly meeting will be postponed till a date to be fixed upon my return. I shall want three weeks to settle & prepare my report.[7]

I expect to leave here Tuesday or Wednesday next.[8]

I pray you not to tell me I must not go now, when I am so docile. (Did you ever hear Chas Elliott's[9] docile story?) about a man named Hoadly in Cincinnati!)

I am, my dear doctor,
Yours devotedly,

Fred. Law Olmsted.

Rev[d] D[r] Bellows.

The original is in box 951 of USSC-NYPL.

1. A reference to the "General Order of the Sanitary Commission for Its Executive Service," written by Olmsted, dated January 27, 1863, and published as Sanitary Commission document number 61. The section of the first paragraph to which Olmsted refers was the provision that the Commission have a central office located near the central office of the U.S. War Department and also "a branch of the Central Office at a point where communication can best be commanded with the chief sources of supply of goods contributed by the public for this service which are at the greatest distance from the Central Office, and with those portions of the army which will be best served therefrom." This distant subdivision would be called the associate general secretary's department rather than the Western department.

   Olmsted's paper set forth the executive organization and responsibilities of both departments of the Commission. It charged the associate general secretary and his branch to send copies of all official papers, all important information about the branch's operations, and quarterly reports of its property, expenditures, and personnel to the central office. The associate general secretary would assume responsibility for all goods received and disbursed and for the appointment, control, and dismissal of the agents in his department. The central office would be responsible for keeping records and preparing reports for all the executive operations of the Sanitary Commission (doc. no. 61 in USSC, *Documents*).

2. Adam Gurowski (1805–1866), a Polish aristocrat who early opposed Russian domination of Poland. Active in the revolution of 1830, he escaped to France and his property was confiscated. By 1835 his advocacy of Pan-Slavism under Russian leadership removed Russian opposition to him and he was allowed to return to his native land. In 1849 Gurowski immigrated to the United States, where he wrote articles, pamphlets, books, and newspaper columns. During the Civil War he was sympathetic to the Radical Republicans and often severely criticized Lincoln's administration. Olmsted probably was familiar with the praise of Stanton and the violent censure of McClellan in Gurowski's published diary, which appeared late in 1862.

   Olmsted probably first encountered Gurowski personally during his years in New York's "literary republic" in the mid-1850s. The two men may have met, but Olmsted certainly had heard about Gurowski from his friend Charles A. Dana, who published the Pole's letters in the *New-York Daily Tribune*. Dana also allowed Gurowski to read articles on Russia and the Slavs prepared for the *Tribune* by Karl Marx and Friedrich Engels. Gurowski actually rewrote two of the pieces, changing their tone from anti- to pro-Pan-Slavism, and he convinced Dana to reject other articles by Marx and Engels. Olmsted, on business in London for *Putnam's Magazine* in the fall of 1856, met with Marx and confidentially told him about Gurowski's role in the rejection of the articles. At that time Olmsted mistakenly believed Gurowski to be secretly in the pay of the Russian government (LeRoy Henry Fischer, *Lincoln's Gadfly, Adam Gurowski* [Norman, Okla., 1964], pp. 63–66, 91–96, 127–29; NCAB).

3. Timbuktu, a major trading center of West Africa and the proverbial distant place, located in modern-day Mali.

4. A reference to the provision of the "General Order" that created an "Assistant Secretary for the Branch Central Office," who like a military adjutant would be in charge of record keeping and correspondence. He was to be accountable to the central office in that respect but otherwise would be the deputy of the associate general secretary (doc. no. 61 in USSC, *Documents*).

5. Sault Sainte Marie, two adjacent towns—one in Michigan, the other in Ontario, Canada—each located at the lower outlet of Lake Superior. Great Slave Lake lies in the Canadian Northwest Territories between Hudson Bay and the Yukon.

6. At this time Olmsted's half-brother, Albert Henry Olmsted, who had enlisted in the 25th Connecticut in August 1862, was stationed in or near Baton Rouge, Louisiana, and only fifteen or twenty miles from Port Hudson, a Red River garrison held by a large Confederate force. Port Hudson surrendered to Union troops after the fall of Vicksburg in July 1863 (Connecticut, Adjutant General's Office, *Record of Service of Connecticut Men in the Army and Navy during the War of the Rebellion* [Hartford, Conn., 1889], p. 793; William Augustus Croffut and John M. Morris, *The Military and Civil History of Connecticut during the War of 1861-65 . . .*, rev. ed. [New York, 1868], p. 319; *War for the Union*, 3: 50–51, 73).

7. The next meeting of the Sanitary Commission did not take place until June 1863 (USSC, *Minutes*, p. 135).

8. Olmsted left Washington on February 18 rather than February 10 or 11 as he here predicted (Bloor Diary, Feb. 18, 1863).

9. Charles Wyllys Elliott (1817–1883), one of Olmsted's friends who was an author and landscape gardener. A member of the Board of Commissioners of the Central Park from 1857 through 1860, Elliott had urged Olmsted to apply for the position of superintendent of Central Park in 1857. During the eight years Elliott spent in Cincinnati, he probably met George Hoadly, who was then a law clerk in the office of Salmon P. Chase (*Papers of FLO*, 1: 384, n. 2; ibid., 3: 83).

To Calvert Vaux

Feb'y 16th [186]3.

My Dear Vaux,

I think your uppermost notions on such matters[1] are sound and healthy, quite as much so as mine—probably more—and I am willing to trust them. It will probably be a question of degree, of accumulation; when it gets so bad you can't stand it, you will resign gracefully. I shall be content that it is the best thing to be done under the circumstances.

All the same, I can't help exceedingly regretting the circumstances. For myself, I would sacrifice anything but honor and a fair reputation to maintain a position of considerable influence upon the management of the park. I would drop the Sanitary Commission instantly, and everything else, to secure it with moderate means of livelihood—say $3000 a year, but I don't much hope that this can be grown into now. The reason I left the Park was, I think, because, I was likely to have more influence in the direction in which I wanted to use it when absent than when present, because of the evident antagonistic disposition, jealousy and resistance of Green[2] to me personally. It was not, it certainly was not *merely* because it was so uncomfortable and harassing to me, and it was not merely because I could work to some better end, here, though it has turned out so. As far as my disposition is concerned, I am devoted to the park. With my own judgment of my abilities, and of the possible influence of the park, I think this disposition is reasonable and just.

There is some little disagreement of old standing between us on this point. I recur to it simply in justice to my feelings, when I say that I shall heartily go with you in any action you may think it necessary to take. I shall quit, whenever I do, completely quit my hold with regret, and probably not without a dull hope that Green will yet be floored, Green and the Green influences, and that I shall come to my own again—my own by right of essential qualifications and by the superior value which I can give it. It will continue to be just beyond my highest hope of fortune, to be allowed to superintend the park with a reasonable degree of freedom from Greenism.

I suppose this disposition of mine, intangible as it is, is entitled to just the slightest possible weight, if not in your main decision, then perhaps in the manner of acting upon it—possibly it will happen so. Otherwise you wouldn't have written for my consent. But that is absolutely all [that] needs to be respected on my side, and I shall be thoroughly satisfied that what you think is best, is best.

Yours affectionately,

Fred. Law Olmsted.

The text is from a letterpress copy on pages 249–52 of Olmsted's private letterbook.

1. That is, relations with the Board of Commissioners of the Central Park. Since the firm Olmsted & Vaux had become architects to the park in the spring of 1862, Vaux had assumed most of the responsibility of superintending the finishing work and

dealing with the board and the tight-fisted comptroller, Andrew H. Green. By 1863 Vaux was fighting an unsuccessful battle to retain the firm's preeminence on the park by preventing the commissioners from consulting other architects concerning designs for gates at the 59th Street entrances. Most likely the action of the commissioners on January 26, 1863, in referring plans for the gates submitted by Green to a committee with instructions "to consult such architects in relation thereto, as they may deem proper," prompted an anguished protest by Vaux to Olmsted, to which the letter presented here is a reply (*Papers of FLO*, 3: 38).

2. Andrew H. Green.

To Charles Janeway Stillé[1]

Altoona,[2] Feb'y 25th 1863.

My Dear Mr Stillé,

I have read "Northern Interests and Southern Independence"[3] with the greatest interest and pleasure. I regard it as being of the highest value to the nation and have a renewed sense and enlarged sense of the great indebtedness in which we are all placed to you. I disagree with you in opinion as to the proclamation and regret, deeply regret, that you were compelled to express the views given in the pamphlet. I do not even agree with you as to the disastrous results which it has produced.[4] It has served to unmask the traitors in our midst, I do not believe it has made one. I do not believe that the administration or the war has one intelligent opponent which it had not before, though both have many more active and open enemies. Of its effects on the army it is yet too early to judge. The public reports from Louisiana are unfavorable, but I have received today a letter from my brother who is camped side by side with a negro regiment at Baton Rouge, and all he says about it is in the highest degree commendatory and encouraging.[5] My brother is not an abolitionist, or was not. The proclamation has been made the excuse or cover for a great deal that is exasperating and its results seem to be bad among ourselves, but recollect that Seymour of Connecticut[6] and every other man of real prominence opposed the war, opposed the administration quite as decidedly (and with greater real courage) a year ago, as now. But whatever evil it has done at home is in my judgment far more than compensated by the advantage it has given us abroad. Neither the French nor the English government will as willingly as before, face the consequences of directly aiding to establish a slave-holding nation; of making a legally free people slaves. The danger of recognition, or of the encouragement of recognition, in England has been completely removed. England is today on our side; her influence is on our side. It was not before the Proclamation. The favor of Germany is ten times as strong as it was before emancipation, and France must proceed with more hesitation than she otherwise would to work against us.[7] This is all known and felt & must be acted upon at the South. Davis's[8] hope of creating a cry of indignation is all gone. The world is with us, is against him, and he and they know it.

And I for one, would rather the war never stopped, would rather suffer the deep humiliation of a peace with the certainty that it was but a mockery and would be but a short and ill-kept truce, I would rather go through the farce of acknowledging Southern independence, than have the Union ever again as it was. Slavery and republican liberty can not exist together. I do not wish to call Alabama my country when the law will neither protect my life there nor attempt to punish my assassinators. I wish that my children may be free to travel safely throughout my country and yet I wish them to be free to form the opinion that slavery is not right, or expedient. I have never said that it was not right, I have never said that emancipation was expedient before the proclamation, but having written calmly of what I have seen, my books have been burned, my property injured, my reputation vilified, I have been libelled and slandered, and my life threatened publickly.[9] I don't want my children to be subject to this without redress in their own country. I don't mean they shall be. I opposed the proclamation until it was issued. I shall stand by it now as long as I live, and I shall try to bring up my children to make it good. I shall be for continual war, or for Southern independence rather than go back one step from it. There is but one way in which I believe prolonged peace to be practicable—it is called extermination.

I seldom express these opinions; I have never expressed them so strongly before. Perhaps I have never held them so clearly. This is the result of my reflections upon your argument—that portion of it addressed to those who think with me. I feel that when I tell you how greatly I value your pamphlet as a whole, I should not be honest to hold this difference back.

I trust [it] may be as largely circulated as the previous one has been and do as much good. I hope especially that it may be sent to any democrat who can read, in Connecticut, and to every member of the next Congress (who can read).

I am, dear Sir, gratefully yours

Fred. Law Olmsted.

C. J. Stillé Esqr

The original is in the Charles Janeway Stillé Papers, Historical Society of Pennsylvania, Philadelphia, Pennsylvania.

1. Charles Janeway Stillé (1819–1899) belonged to a wealthy Philadelphia merchant family. He graduated from Yale College in 1839, studied law, and though admitted to the bar, did not practice it. During the Civil War, Stillé sought ways to aid the Union effort. As an associate member of the Sanitary Commission, he worked energetically in the Philadelphia branch organization. Early in 1864 the Sanitary Commission elected him to full membership and that October chose him to serve on the Executive Committee. He also became well known for his patriotic pamphlets, especially *How a Free People Conduct a Long War*. In 1866 the Sanitary Commission published his authorized history of its activities during the war. After the war Stillé taught at the University of Pennsylvania and served as its provost from 1868 until 1880.

   Olmsted and Stillé frequently corresponded about Sanitary Commission business during 1862 and 1863, but they never developed a personal relationship. Although he admired Stillé's writings, Olmsted was uncomfortable with the former's conservative Democratic politics. After the war the two men corresponded only once: in 1891, when Olmsted was gathering photographs and documents for a collection of Sanitary Commission materials to be given to the Massachusetts Order of the Loyal Legion. Stillé then praised Olmsted's efforts to preserve the Commission's history and sadly wrote:

   > As I have grown older many of my early illusions have disappeared, among others the strong faith I once held that the American people would never forget what they owed to the Sanitary Commission, and especially to the work of Dr Bellows & yourself in its management. Every now & then there seems to be a revival of the interest felt in the affairs of the war, but I have been painfully impressed with the feeling that all the humanity & especially *all the science* (of which we used to be so proud) so abundantly displayed for the relief of the soldiers have been absolutely forgotten.

   (*DAB*; USSC, *Minutes*, pp. 173, 204; C. J. Stillé to FLO, June 1, 1891.)

2. Olmsted wrote this letter at Altoona, Pennsylvania, en route to Pittsburgh to meet with a branch association of the Sanitary Commission.

3. Stillé's pamphlet, *Northern Interests and Southern Independence*, published in 1863, argued that the North's security and well-being demanded that an end be put to the South's determined quest for independence. Stillé focused upon what he called the "four great pillars which support the whole edifice of northern prosperity": "the free navigation of the rivers,—the security of our foreign commerce,—unrestricted inland communication and intercourse,—and safety against foreign invasion." According to him, Southern independence would weaken all the nation's supports. The loss of control over the Mississippi River and the Gulf of Mexico would interrupt trade and communications and threaten foreign commerce, while the existence of a fifteen-hundred-mile border with the South would invite foreign invasion.

   Stillé gave Olmsted a copy of *Northern Interests and Southern Independence* on February 24 when the latter was in Philadelphia to attend a lecture by Henry W. Bellows at the Academy of Music (Charles Janeway Stillé, *Northern Interests and Southern Independence: A Plea for United Action* [Philadelphia, 1863]).

4. In his pamphlet, Stillé did not specifically mention the Emancipation Proclamation nor did he directly argue that it had produced "disastrous results." At several points in his narrative, however, he was generally critical of the government's measures and actions. The passage that Olmsted probably believed to be the strongest attack upon the Proclamation ran:

   > There are some whose scruples it is impossible not to respect, who are lukewarm in the support of the war, because they think they see in certain acts of

violence done to those principles of constitutional restraint which lie at the basis of our system, a tendency which, if carried out, would destroy our barriers against despotic power. . . . No one who has been brought up to revere the great principles of constitutional liberty can regard with favour what is called "military necessity," or *raison d'état*, still it is clear, that there are rare contingencies in which, like the law of self-preservation, it must be invoked and irregularly applied. . . . After all, however we must never forget that in this unhappy condition of things our choice is reduced to a choice of evils. Shall we submit to a temporary despotism now, in order that we may be saved from one tenfold more fearful in the future? (Ibid., pp. 46–47.)

5. On February 2, 1863, Albert Henry Olmsted wrote his father (in a letter that probably was forwarded to Olmsted): "We have one negro regt here: the 3ʳᵈ La. Vols. It is commanded by Jack Nelson who used to keep the gymnasium in Hartford. It is said to be very well drilled. I shall try to see them as soon as I get a chance" (A. H. Olmsted to JO, Feb. 2, 1863).
6. Thomas Hart Seymour (1807–1868) of Hartford, Connecticut, consistently opposed military coercion of the South during the Civil War and was Connecticut's most prominent Peace Democrat. Although he had fought in the Mexican War and had served as Connecticut's governor, as a U.S. congressman, and as minister to Russia, he was defeated in his 1863 bid for Connecticut's governorship (*BDAC*; George Dudley Seymour and Donald Lines Jacobus, *A History of the Seymour Family: Descendants of Richard Seymour of Hartford, Connecticut* . . . [New Haven, Conn., 1939], pp. 364–67).
7. Olmsted no doubt had noted the recent outpourings of pro-Northern opinion among the English, especially among the religious middle classes and the industrial workers, in response to the Emancipation Proclamation. While from the beginning of the war these groups tended to side with the North, in 1863 their support became more pronounced and stronger. French public opinion, distinctly more favorable to the South, probably changed little. The German states, especially Prussia, observed strict neutrality, but the sympathies of both the leaders and the people lay with the North even before the Proclamation (Donaldson Jordan and Edwin J. Pratt, *Europe and the American Civil War* [Boston and New York, 1931], pp. 147–57; Harold M. Hyman, ed., *Heard Round the World: The Impact Abroad of the Civil War* [New York, 1969], pp. 102–4, 151–54).
8. Jefferson Davis.
9. See FLO to Alfred T. Field, July 31, 1861, notes 2 and 3, above.

To Mary Olmsted

Altoona, Pa.   Feby 25ᵗʰ 1863

My Dear Mary,

I received the enclosed this morning at Philaᵈᵃ, just as it is.[1] (Came to Philᵃ yesterday afternoon and assisted last night at a glorious meeting at the Academy of Music.[2] Dʳ Bellows's address was very fine. I want very much that it should be repeated in every county in Connecticut now—

before you get so excited that it will be denounced as a political lecture, which it certainly is. I am writing to all my friends who I think can help to bring any influence to bear in Connecticut urging and entreating them to do their utmost. It would be a fearful calamity if Seymour[3] should be elected. I would rather Washington should be taken by the enemy and I would give more to make sure of a sound republican victory in Connecticut than to take Charleston or Richmond. I think every thread of influence which can possibly be used in any quarter in any way, should be strained to the utmost. These traitors amongst us are worse than those of the South. I would draw the line as sharply as possible; as sharply as between decent people and rogues—not that they are rogues any more than the enemy in the South individually but dangerous and disgusting madmen and women they are. Run up your flag, fly your ribbons, wear and show every possible badge and pledge of Nationalism; stamp under foot every speck of "states' rights." Up with the blue and down with the black,[4] and make all your friends do so. Have no friends who will not.

If mother wants more of the Rosecrans' letter,[5] Pittsburg address &c than she gets (we are printing them now), she can, or you can for her, write to D[r] Jenkins, Mr Bloor, or simply "Sanitary Commission, Washington" & call for just as many as you think you can use to advantage—from one to five thousand, mentioning that I said you could have them, for asking, for distribution in Connecticut. They will also send you, if you ask for it, fifty of Stillé's first pamphlet—"Free People Long War." The second one is better for Democrats (it is just out, Stillé gave me the first copy last night.) but it is strongly against the Proclamation & favorable to a restoration of slaves and I am for fighting to the last moment for the proclamation. If Seymour is in great danger of being elected, I don't know but the last moment has come in which we can fight for it, but am not willing to give it up yet.

I am off at last for the West. Hope to see Rosecrans,[6] God bless him. Knapp goes to take care of me, & I am going to take it easy. I had to leave Washington & spend four days in Balto. to clear off business that as long as I staid in Washington I could not do; as it was, Jenkins came on twice to see me while there. The knapsack[7] went by Express about a week after you left W,[8] it is just exactly what he wants, was filled mostly with chockolate, sweet, eatable coffee condensed with sugar and cream, condensed milk, and a few cans of soup and mutton chops. Love to father & mother.

Affectionately

Fred. Law Olmsted.

The original is in the possession of Terry Niles Smith.

1. Olmsted's enclosure has not survived.
2. On February 24, 1863, Henry W. Bellows gave an untitled speech at the Academy of Music in Philadelphia about the objectives and activities of the Sanitary Commission. The necessity for such a commission sprang, he argued, from the enormous expansion of the army, which in turn created problems of hygiene and medicine that were beyond the immediate capacity of the Medical Bureau to solve. Moreover, the size of the army in the field meant that even though the Medical Bureau was spending far larger sums, contributions from the public would continue to be vital in relieving the suffering among sick and wounded soldiers. Describing the army's medical officers as competent and dedicated, Bellows called for the people to aid them rather than criticize the "red tape" necessary to the system. He also detailed the work of the Sanitary Commission in inspecting camps, giving advice, amassing statistics, and organizing the nation's benevolence.

    Most likely Olmsted believed that the following call for national unity was the "political" aspect of Bellows's speech:

    > We all have our municipal pride. We all have a love for our individual States; and to overcome this love to some extent, for the time, in favor of a broader affection, was a part of our mission. In ordinary times, it is well to trim the lamp of domestic affection; to feed the fire of municipal pride; to tend the larger altar of State rights. But at a time like this, we ought to bring every particle of patriotic fuel we can, to make that central flame which our fathers kindled on the Federal altar, burn brighter, so that the nations of the world, who are watching with jealous eyes from every headland of Europe to see its glory eclipsed, may find it surging up with a double splendor, and shedding an immortal radiance upon the whole horizon of humanity.

    (U.S. Sanitary Commission, Philadelphia Agency, *Speech of the Rev. Dr. Bellows, President of the United States Sanitary Commission, Made at the Academy of Music, Philadelphia, Tuesday Evening, Feb. 24, 1863* [Philadelphia, 1863], pp. 21–22.)
3. Thomas Hart Seymour (see FLO to Charles J. Stillé, Feb. 25, 1863, n. 6, above).
4. Olmsted may have been suggesting that the South, with its privateers, operated under the black flag that commonly denoted piracy and death.
5. An open letter written by Gen. William S. Rosecrans on February 2, 1863. In this letter, which was published by the newspapers, Rosecrans praised the Sanitary Commission:

    > Experience has demonstrated the importance of system and impartiality as well as judgment and economy, in the forwarding and distribution of these supplies. In all these respects the United States Sanitary Commission stands unrivalled. Its organization, experience, and large facilities for the work are such that the General does not hesitate to recommend, in the most urgent manner, all those who desire to send sanitary supplies to confide them to the care of this Commission.

    The Sanitary Commission reprinted this article as a flyer for use in raising funds ("Major General Rosecrans on Contributions for the Sick and Wounded," Feb. 2, 1863).
6. William Starke Rosecrans (1819–1898), major general of volunteers and commander of the Army of the Cumberland. A graduate of West Point, he spent ten years in the army before resigning to become a civil engineer. As a brigadier general of volunteers in 1861, he built upon McClellan's early successes to push the Confederates out of northwestern Virginia. Transferred to Mississippi in May 1862, he commanded at the indecisive battle of Iuka and the Union victory at Corinth. In command of the newly organized Army of the Cumberland, he advanced on Braxton Bragg's Confederate

troops at Murfreesboro in late December 1862 and brought about the battle that ended in Bragg's retreat. Despite repeated urgings from his superiors in Washington, Rosecrans did not advance again until August 1863. His defeat at the bloody battle of Chickamauga led to his removal from command that October. He headed the Department of the Missouri in 1864.

Although in the spring of 1863 Olmsted greatly admired Rosecrans, his later acquaintance with the old soldier was not so pleasant. Rosecrans served in the U.S. House of Representatives as a Democrat from California from 1881 until 1885. During his second term the two men were often at odds over the construction of the terrace that Olmsted proposed for the West Front of the U.S. Capitol. Apparently interested in obtaining the post of Architect of the Capitol, Rosecrans put forward his own plan for the terrace and criticized Edward Clark, the long-time Architect of the Capitol. Rosecrans also criticized Olmsted to his face for his plan for the West Front terrace. As Olmsted recounted in early 1884: "I had a queer interview with Rosecrantz yesterday. He ridiculed and denounced my work so violently and absurdly, (urging me to abandon it & support his plan) that I feel pretty sure that if he talks in the same way to others, and especially if he makes a speech in the House, as he evidently intends, of corresponding character, he will provoke a counter-sentiment, and we shall gain by it." In 1885 Rosecrans sought to convince labor unions to support his own appointment by promising them more favorable wage agreements, and his accusations against Clark sparked a congressional investigation of the latter. These efforts were unsuccessful, and Rosecrans had to content himself with another governmental post—that of register of the treasury, which he held from June 1885 until 1893 (*DAB*; William Mathias Lamers, *The Edge of Glory: A Biography of William S. Rosecrans, U.S.A.* [New York, 1961], p. 250; G. W. Cullum, *Biographical Register*, 2: 115–16; FLO to John C. Olmsted, Feb. 26, 1884, and Edward Clark to FLO, March 24 and April 2, 1885, Olmsted Associates Records, Library of Congress, Washington, D.C.).

7. That is, Olmsted had prepared a knapsack of food to send to his half-brother, Albert Henry Olmsted, who was then stationed in Louisiana (see FLO to HWB, Feb. 4, 1863, n. 6, above).

8. Mary Olmsted had been visiting in Philadelphia and Washington. She traveled to New York on December 16 and arrived home on February 17. The length of her stay with the Olmsteds in Washington is unclear, but she was there by February 1 (Bloor Diary, Feb. 1, 1863; JO Journal, Dec. 16, 1862, and Feb. 17, 1863).

CHAPTER VIII

JOURNEY IN THE WEST

THE LETTERS AND WRITINGS presented in this chapter provide a rich collection of Olmsted's views on a number of subjects that he had long believed important. These pieces also show him to be a perceptive observer of American manners and mores. The writings that stemmed from his journey in the "West" (actually the Midwest and South) indicate his continuing interest in civilization in America. His portraits of a "palatial hotel" in Cincinnati, the cabin of an Illinois frontiersman, and Euclid Street in Cleveland all illustrate the significance he attached to domestic amenities. Olmsted's descriptions of St. Louis and Chicago identify an obsession with business which was leading the "best men" there to neglect civic affairs and improvements such as parks. His observations on white Southerners, slaves, and slavery, while expressing views similar to those in his books on the South, also form important additions to those earlier accounts.

Although Olmsted's travel accounts reflect his earlier concerns, his writings of this period also show his intense interest in the progress of the war and in the men engaged in it. His descriptions of Cincinnati reveal his admiration for loyalty and patriotism, while his vignettes of campaigning with the armies of Rosecrans and Grant give his most idyllic pictures of army life. Olmsted also provides vivid accounts of his meetings with those two generals, and his frank letter to Edwin L. Godkin assesses Western generals and their strategy.

523

JOURNEY IN THE WEST

Spring 1863

INTRODUCTION

CINCINNATI

Diary, March 1st 1863.
At the Burnet House, Cincinnati.[1]

A house for travellers having the architectural pretensions of a palace (see cut). The exterior and the common parts of the interior, the halls, parlor dining room, stately & splendid, there being marble floors, stained glass, gilding, mirrors, height and space. There is even an enormous painting "The last man, by Beard"[2] with a printed description in the sublime romantic style. If the describer's estimate is just, it will probably be better known to thee, O Carl, student of the centuries to come[3] [to] whom I commend this scroll, greeting, than it is to me, who saw it at great disadvantage of gloom, crosslights and distracting influences of porters hustling baggage under it. The palatial spirit is more practically shown in the conspicuously hung "Rules for Office boys"—in which "gentlemanly deportment" is insisted upon. The boys of the 1st watch are to rise at 4 A.M. and go on duty at 5 A.M. They remain on duty with intervals for breakfast, dinner and supper, till 12:30 P.M. There is also a period after they "go into the dining room" which is unexplained. Two of the boys (lads of fifteen), questioned apart, said that they got about three hours off duty, (besides mealtime, perhaps), between morning and night, thus catching a good nap. I trust my good Carl that even poor Irish boys are to be better taken care of than this, with you.

We waited, I think, five minutes, after entering our names on the office register, last night, before anyone paid the slightest attention to us. Then a portly clerk, with an habitual smile of self complacency and an occasional smile of good fellowship for those with whom he associated with familiarity, came with a leisurely air to the other side of the counter, and without saluting us, or looking in our faces asked—"Want a room together, you two?"

"Two connecting rooms, if possible."

"Can't do that; give you two beds in a room, if you want."

"Very well."

"Go up now?"

"Yes, if you please."

THE BURNET HOUSE IN CINCINNATI

"Show the gentlemen to 145. Key."

"Here is the card for our baggage," putting it in his hand.

He *threw* it back on the counter towards us, "Keep that," turning away as he spoke.

"Here Sir! Please to take this and send up our baggage when it comes, and let us have a fire in our room."

"Fire in 145. You'll have to pick out your baggage for yourself when it comes."

"This card gives the numbers on the baggage. We don't want to come down. We want you to have it picked out and sent up." But he was engaged in a laughing conversation with someone else and made no reply.[4]

We had not sat at a table since yesterday and it being now night wanted dinner. So in lack of our baggage, in the cold room, we washed off the dust of travel and came down to the stately dining room, which looks well, spacious, and not crowded—a large number of tables for small parties—waiters in white jackets. The head waiter, in black, wants us to join a party of strangers—taking tea at one of these tables. "No, we want dinner and to sit by ourselves, if you please." We get our table, but can have no dinner except what is on the bill of fare for tea. (Yet the principal R.R. train from all the East has just arrived, and many passengers must come here daily, in just our predicament. How different from the Lord Warden at Dover.)[5]

525

Well, the tea bill includes beef steak and fried potatoes, and we get a pint of "Saunders' private stock" sparkling Ohio wine, cheap at 50 cts and excellent, which is more than can be said of anything else—the fried potatoes are greasy with grease, not quite sweet—the coffee is queer, "hain't got no hot milk"—fine sugar without sugar spoon, and stained with the coffee of the last man's spoon who used it. Waiters come three at a time, when the wine is opened, their white jackets creased with soot; hands dirty; tones nonchalant; action defiantly lazy; noisy. Presently, one after another, four newcomers are marshalled to our table; then for a period no waiter near us and three of the newcomers wait, sullenly. We were talking of matters not of public interest so with the accessions to the table, we stop talking and, feeling a little annoyed, are silent and no man speaks to another, till the others having got their tea go out, leaving K[6] & I to resume our conversation still liable to interruption, with our coffee.[7]

The office boys of gentlemanly deportment are Irish lads who ought to be at school, with rough chopped hair, dirty, unbroken street boys, just as they land from the ship, except that they wear greasy castoff cloth coats. Our room is kept tolerably clean as far as sweeping and dusting goes, but is comfortless, two French beds with dirty counterpanes, a small battered pine bureau and table, two chairs with a spittoon, washstand & crockery to match.[8] There is a carpet, its original color all lost in dye of tobacco and soot. Not a particle of curtain, tablecloth or other drapery— the ceiling is stained with a leak from the story above. And yet this room is the very nicest part of the house which I have seen. Some parts look as if not the slightest work of repair or cleansing had been done upon them since the house was built, twenty years ago, I guess. Though pretty well built originally, there are multifold signs of dilapidation. The halls have been for hours cluttered up with heaps of dirt swept from the sleeping rooms and the chambermaids' utensils; these girls loiter and cluster together outside our door and talk loudly. Having waited this morning more than half an hour for a fire, when it was at last made, I said to the fireman,—an Irish laborer, as dirty as a chimney sweep—"I want you to come in again and look after this fire by and by, and to keep up a little fire here steadily, as long as we stay."

"You'll just ring the bell when you'll be after wanting me."

"That's just what I don't want to do. I shall be going out again, and I don't want to wait half an hour, whenever I come in, for a fire to be made."

"Then ye'll tell them at the office when ye's goes down."

"Not at all. I want you to come in now and then & keep the fire alive."

"I can't do it then."

"Why not?"

526

"That's what I'm toold. I'm toold not to touch a fire in the house, never, unless I gets an order to do it from the office, each time."

"Then leave some coal here on the hearth, and I will put it on."

"I moostn't, devil a spoonful. 'Twould be as much as my head 'ould be worth. It's agin the rool of the house. Ye's got yer allooance—that's a pail-ful's, a pail-ful's what they alloo ye's, an ye'll not get any moore."

"Is that a pail-ful?"

"Well, it's not just a pail-ful, but it's what they alloo for one order. Ye may call it a pail-ful if ye's likes. Ye'll get no more till ye's orders it to the office begorrt."

"You positively can not give me a fire that will last more than one hour."

"I can. Upon an ordre."

After a while I went down to dinner and said: "I will trouble you to have my fire freshened up, if you please."

"All right. Fire in 145."

"I only want it freshened."

"All right." And this freshening was charged at half a dollar in the bill, and insisted upon, as "our rule".

Shall I mention the dirty thumb of the careless waiter sticking into the soup which he dashes under my nose at dinner though I haven't asked for it and don't want the vile slop—the difficulty of getting towels enough which when got are but half the size of my handkerchief. I speak literally; the old gravel walks of the central court, now covered with oyster shells which appear to have been pitched out of the kitchen windows with dishcloths and broken plates, the piece of wretched sign painting representing a German Beer garden, in a great gilt frame on the mantel-piece of the "Gentlemen's sitting room". What else is necessary to justify the assertion that the palatial hotel is the dreariest of all American humbugs, and that neither by Russell,[9] by Trollope,[10] nor by Lord Vane Tempest,[11] has the half of its vileness been told? But this is the American hotel at its worst estate.

The hotel is a continual speculation you must understand, O! Carl, the play thereof being in this wise: first to make for it a great reputation as a palace, and to this end, grandeur, marble, stained glass, brocade, Wilton,[12] French cook, drill-mastered waiters, spacious terrace, cool walks, fragrant Havanas, receptions, hops, splendid this, splendid that, "splendid" everything; and when all the world echoes it, change of proprietors, reduce expenses one half; keep up the prices and heap up the charges[13] till after half a dozen pretences of resuscitation perhaps, patching, whitewashing and certain new furniture to be advertised, it gets to be so bad that there is a chance to try the game over again with the public at the same point with a new palace crammed with all the latest modern conveniences, but still with never the smallest chance for a short breath of sound, quiet, homely comfort—such as the poorest traveller can command in every village in England. Yes I say that after a recent experience of the Continental in Philadelphia,[14] much the highest attainment in palatial hotels which we have reached.

If dreariness could be added to the Burnet House by anything this rainy day, it would be by this Sunday newspaper,[15] full not only of sneaking sedition but with the meanest effort to play in the interest of treason upon the lowest and most dangerous prejudices of the poor Irish. Cincinnati, I'm told, abounds with Secessionists—open and avowed. The pirate Semmes's[16] family are here; his daughter is a belle and is actually received in the houses of Union men. Contempt for the Eastern armies, a "Western spirit" growing; flippant criticisms from every knot of loungers in the halls, upon matters that they know nothing at all about. Dreary, dreary.

So far, are you justified, O, Englishmen.

But could you never after such a dark day, catch the lights of the picture as I did at night?

At a fireside as glowing, as tasteful, as full of the spirit of true art and the highest civilization, as any you have in England even.[17] So far as our skill and knowledge has attained, I verily believe, oh student of history to be born, that you will know nothing better. But better yet is that we have found tonight in Cincinnati: the cheerful, true hearted, sustained, unfaltering, more than Roman-Christian courage, faith and patriotism of two American mothers,[18] whose boys—one a corporal with Rosecrans, the other a private with Grant—are fighting for that fireside, for those mothers, as they have been, oft disabled and oft returning, for nearly two years and who write always "in such good spirits". God be thanked for such mothers and such boys, and for the nation and the laws under which they have grown. Whatever you have, oh student, better mothers, better boys, you will not have.

The present population of Cincinnati and suburbs is about 200,000,[19] and it is a better built city on an average than Paris or London— better for the convenient life of the people on an average. I am astonished with its improvement in this respect since I was here last, ten years ago.[20] There are buildings by scores, grand, solid, substantial, and of good architecture. Cincinnati, it strikes me, is a more respectable town as seen in its streets than New York, Boston or Philadelphia. A not very badly built town of nearly two hundred thousand souls, yet have I a friend living,[21] who saw the shantees of the earliest settlers here, and the surveyors staking out the first street lines.

After attending an address given by Henry W. Bellows at the Philadelphia Academy of Music on February 24, Olmsted began his journey. He arrived in Altoona, Pennsylvania, on the 25th. The following day he traveled to Pittsburgh, where he addressed the local branch of the Sanitary Commission. At two o'clock on the morning of February 28, he boarded the train to Cincinnati, arriving there that evening (FLO to MPO, Feb. 25 and 28, 1863).

1. The Burnet House, located on Third and Vine streets, was "Bracketed Italian" in its architecture, and its six stories contained 340 rooms. Built approximately fifteen years before Olmsted's visit, it was described in 1851 by a local author as "undoubtedly the most spacious, and probably the best, hotel in its interior and domestic arrangements, of any in the world" (Charles Cist, *Sketches and Statistics of Cincinnati in 1851* [Cincinnati, Ohio, 1851], p. 164).

2. Possibly James Henry Beard (1812–1893), an artist who grew to maturity in Ohio and worked in Cincinnati until 1870. Although best known for his pictures of life among the poor, Beard also painted more traditional scenes and portraits (*The Britannica Encyclopedia of American Art* [New York, 1976]).

3. Olmsted must have deliberately chosen the proper name "Carl" for his imaginary reader because of its connotations. The origin of the name lay in the term "carl," or "carle," signifying a man of the people, a countryman or husbandman. As a variant of the pseudonym "yeoman," which Olmsted himself frequently used, this name further stressed his interest in the common man. Olmsted's direct reference here also plays upon education; his greeting mimics the traditional opening lines of a college diploma. In the St. Louis and Chicago section of "Journey in the West," Olmsted originally gave his historical student the surname "Grubber," which also suggests a common laborer, possibly one who worked on the land, but deleted those references when he rewrote the section.

4. Here Olmsted inserted a note to himself, "1st (note explains baggage transfer arrangement)." Most likely he meant to explain in a footnote the arrangements by which the baggage would be transferred from the train to the hotel.

5. The Lord Warden was a hotel in Dover, England, where Olmsted had probably stayed in early November 1859 when a gale delayed for a day his crossing of the English Channel (Ivan Green, *The Book of Dover: Cinque Port, Port of the Passage, Gateway to England* [Chesham, 1978], pp. 88–89; *Papers of FLO*, 3: 234).

6. Olmsted's traveling companion, Frederick N. Knapp.

7. Here Olmsted began a new paragraph: "Two major generals in uniform, with families at an adjoining table, the waiters said were Buell and Crittenden. Plenty of minor officers about the house." He then lined through both sentences and resumed his description of the Burnet House. Later he completely dropped the idea of mentioning Don Carlos Buell and Thomas L. Crittenden. On the back of the last page of the Cincinnati section of "Journey in the West," he wrote: "March 2d— Major Generals Buell and Crittenden we see at the public tables of the hotel and last night we met Gen'l Wallace at a friend's house. This is almost as bad as at Washington, where someone complained that he could not spit out of his window without hitting a brigadier." Olmsted crossed out these sentences and did not replace them.

8. In his first draft Olmsted exclaimed, *"This is the whole of the furniture."* He later lined through this sentence.

9. Early in 1863 British reporter William Howard Russell published *My Diary North and South*, a volume of impressions and reminiscences from his 1861–62 sojourn in the United States. Although Russell's criticisms of American hotels generally focused on the crudeness of those in the South, he, like Olmsted, was dismayed at the lack of comfort in the so-called palatial hotels. Russell described Willard's City Hotel in Washington:

> The tumult, the miscellaneous nature of the company—my friends the prizefighters are already in possession of the doorway—the heated, muggy rooms, not

to speak of the great abominableness of the passages and halls, despite a most liberal provision of spittoons, conduce to render these institutions by no means agreeable to a European. (William H. Russell, *My Diary North and South* [Boston, 1863], p. 34.)

10. Anthony Trollope (1815–1882), an English novelist, who by 1863 had received recognition for his works *Barchester Towers* and *Framley Parsonage*. Trollope traveled in the United States and Canada from August 1861 until March 1862 and published *North America*, an account of his American experiences, in the fall of 1862. Generally a good-humored observer of American mores, Trollope was also sympathetic to the American experiment in democracy and disapproving of secession. In all his writings on the United States, he tried to be scrupulously fair and to avoid the harsh criticisms that had characterized the travel account written by his mother, Frances Trollope, in 1832.

Trollope, however, was not fond of the American hotel, which he called "an institution apart, and a thing of itself," different from hotels elsewhere in the world. He believed that the American innkeeper's main goal was to have a magnificent building: "A commanding exterior, and a certain interior dignity of demeanour is more essential than comfort or civility." Trollope was especially offended by the meals served at "palatial hotels" and noted disgustedly, "How I did learn to hate those little dishes and their greasy contents!" Summing up his opinion, he wrote, "I do not like the American hotels, but I must say in their favour that they afford an immense amount of accommodation" (Anthony Trollope, *North America*, ed. Donald Smalley and Bradford Allen Booth [New York, 1951], pp. vi-xxvi, xxxii, 483, 485, 490, 492; *DNB*).

11. Adolphus Frederick Charles William Vane-Tempest (1825–1864), younger son of Charles William Stewart, earl of Vane and third marquess of Londonderry, and of his second wife, Lady Frances Ann Vane-Tempest. Arriving in Washington, D.C., in August 1861, Vane-Tempest voiced his criticism of American hotels to William Howard Russell, who related it in his own book. When Vane-Tempest protested to the clerk at Willard's Hotel against being lodged in room 125, saying that he could not "go up so high," the clerk sneeringly informed him, "I can put you at twice as high—I'll give you No. 250 if I like." The English nobleman then found another lodging (Peter Townend, ed., *Burke's Genealogical and Heraldic History of the Peerage, Baronetage and Knightage*, 105th ed. [London, 1970], p. 1642; W. H. Russell, *My Diary North and South*, p. 513).

12. Probably Wilton carpets, which typically were a deep, cut velvet pile and which were named after the English city where they were manufactured (*OED*).

13. Olmsted originally drafted this section: "keep up the prices and heap up the charges and half a dozen rail-roads can be built out of the profits." He later crossed out the last phrase.

14. A 600-room luxury hotel that had opened in February 1860. Olmsted may have visited it at the beginning of his Western journey (A. Trollope, *North America*, p. 290n).

15. Probably the *Cincinnati Enquirer*, a Democratic newspaper owned by Washington McLean and James J. Farran. The efforts to play upon poor Irishmen's prejudices to which Olmsted alludes were probably the *Enquirer's* criticisms of the war as benefiting only the Negro and those with government contracts (Robert S. Harper, "The Ohio Press in the Civil War," *Civil War History* 3 [Sept. 1957]: 224, 233–34).

16. Raphael Semmes (1809–1877), naval officer and privateer. He served in the U.S. Navy from 1826 until 1861, when he resigned to join the Confederate Navy. Semmes took command of the C.S.S. *Sumter*, a privateer harassing Northern ships. Transferred in August 1862 to command of the *Alabama*, a British-built man-of-war, he continued his successful forays against United States trading vessels until the

Alabama was sunk off the coast of France in 1864. Semmes eluded capture and returned to the Confederate States in January 1865.

In 1837 Semmes had married Anne Elizabeth Spencer of Cincinnati, Ohio. In early 1863 she and her younger children were visiting her brother there. The daughter who was a belle was probably Catherine Middleton Semmes (b. 1845) or possibly Ann Elizabeth Semmes (b. 1847). In the spring of 1863 Anne Spencer Semmes and her children were allowed to cross Union lines to return to the South (Raphael Thomas Semmes, *The Semmes and Allied Families* [Baltimore, 1918], pp. 74–75; Walter Adolphus Roberts, *Semmes of the Alabama* [Indianapolis, Ind., 1938], pp. 35–36, 117, 223; *DAB*).

17. Following this sentence, Olmsted wrote:

> I will even confess that I think there is a delicacy and refinement almost beyond what you have allowed to it, my good friends Trollope and Russell—your civilization has not gone one step beyond it, and that you would admit I'm sure. And I came back to this dreary public pig stye refreshed and greatly encouraged, set up by the cheerful, true hearted, sustained, unfaltering, more than Roman-Christian courage, faith and patriotism of two American mothers.

He later lined through the entire first sentence of this passage and replaced the first half of the second sentence with the phrase presented in the text here.

18. Sarah Hart Elliott Perkins (1814–1885) and another woman, whom Olmsted elsewhere identified only as Mrs. Walker. Sarah Perkins, widow of a Cincinnati clergyman, was the older sister of Olmsted's friend Charles Wyllys Elliott. In 1862 she and Olmsted had corresponded briefly about the progress of the war. Her son, then serving in the Union army, was probably William Channing Perkins (1842–1884) or possibly Edward Cranch Perkins (b. 1844) (Wilimena Hannah Emerson, Ellsworth Eliot, and George Edwin Eliot, Jr., eds., . . . *Genealogy of the Descendants of John Eliot: "Apostle to the Indians," 1598–1905* . . . [New Haven, Conn., 1905], pp. 120–24; FLO to MPO, March 2, 1863, below).

19. Cincinnati's population in 1860 was approximately 160,000 (U.S. Department of the Interior, Customs Office, *Preliminary Report on the Eighth Census* [Washington, D.C., 1862]).

20. Olmsted had visited Cincinnati for one or two days in November 1853 at the beginning of his second journey through the South. His view of the city then was that "bricks, hurry, and a muddy roar make up the whole impression" (Frederick Law Olmsted, *A Journey Through Texas; Or, a Saddle-Trip on the Southwestern Frontier* [New York, 1857], p. 8; *Papers of FLO*, 2: 472).

21. Because Cincinnati was first settled in the late eighteenth century, this statement probably is quite exaggerated. Olmsted possibly is referring to his friend Charles Pinckney James, who was born in Cincinnati in 1818. James spent his childhood in a town that was not only increasing in size but also taking on the social and cultural aspects of other older urban centers (Richard C. Wade, *The Urban Frontier: The Rise of Western Cities, 1790–1830* [Cambridge, Mass., 1959], pp. 22–27, 102–5; FLO to MPO, March 2, 1863, n. 3, below).

.

To Mary Perkins Olmsted

> On a steamboat from Cincinnati
> to Louisville,
> March 2[d] 1863.

Dear Wife,

I sent you a note on arriving at Cincinnati. There are a great many fine buildings in Cincinnati. I should think that Idlitz[1] had been there. The better class of dwellings while not often pretending, look substantial and very comfortable and the town was not very dirty, though gloomy from the weather, smoke and soot. The great Burnet House, a palace in appearance, abominable. Two pleasant experiences relieved the gloom of our visit. First a visit to Mrs Perkins,[2] Chas Elliott's sister, who lives delightfully in a cottage in pleasant, spacious grounds four miles out. There was another widow with her, both have boys in the army, and two of her younger sons were now ill at home, with scarlet fever; but it was as nice a little home as you ever saw, and Mrs P. (at 48, Knapp says) is very pretty, with that fresh Elliott complexion, and as vivacious as a girl, *running* ahead to open the gate for our carriage, just like a child in exuberant health.

This morning we breakfasted with Judge James[3] who once visited us at the island. Before his fire as we came in, stretched out in a lounging chair, was a great, tawny, Kentucky [*giant*] lion, grand with mane thrown back and flowing tossing flaxy beard, hawk nose, and—human eye. "My friend, Colonel Anderson,"[4] upon which he gathered himself up and gave me his great hand, warmly and said with a strong kind voice. "I'm very glad to meet you, Mr Olmsted; the Judge and I talked over you a good deal a few years ago. I am a good deal indebted to you—though I don't know as it's turned out now, whether I am glad of it. Yes, I am. 'Twas your book,[5] which the Judge put in my hands, that first put me up to going to Texas. I chased up a good many of your friends there. You remember Dagener.[6] I spent a good deal of time with him. He is a very noble man, poor fellow, I don't know what will have become of him."

"Then I have heard from them since you have. Dagener is in jail in San Antonio. For some reason they don't hang him. His wife died. His two sons escaped to the mountains, were hunted up and shot. When they came to tell the father" &c. and so we went on. There was not a man I had known in Texas, that he did not know all about. Dresel[7] is keeping a toy shop in Monterey. Ulrich[8] is there; Theissen[9] had gone to Costa Rica to marry Miss Riotte[10] &c. I told him Pitkin's[11] story about the matches & the lieutenants clearing off the Northerners. He had not heard it, but said it was very probable. He had been in Dallas and had investigated the business for himself, was perfectly satisfied the fires were accidental.[12] Some

CHARLES ANDERSON

people had got a mania for hanging men. He knew of a man with such a mania at San Antonio, a Methodist, who pursued Ulrich vindictively when the trouble came because Ulrich had started a story of him, which was generally believed, that at a prayer meeting where he wanted to pull out a handkerchief to wipe his weeping eyes, he brought out instead a rope, which he had been getting ready to hang a man with.

Well—we got upon the war at last. He had been at Murfreesboro[13] and fought it over again for us. It was sheer obstinate pluck on our part & finally, a mistake of the enemy, who thought from our holding out that we must have got reinforcements & that it would be safe to retreat—only this that saved us from the God Almightiest whipping that ever men got. He gives a poor impression of the discipline of Rosecrans' army, or of the possibility of disciplining our volunteer army at present. He don't care what becomes of slavery, and is a[s] thorough a Union man as I have seen. It turned out, that we were one and all thorough converts to Federalism[14] except James who says he was never anything else. We agreed that it was not unlikely we should have to come to a fight among ourselves about that yet, and that, if it came to the worst, we must fight. We could not suffer "States Rights" to accomplish secession. There was a good deal of quiet,

533

unconscious heroic spirit, evident in all the party—a closer sympathy and concurrent progress with what I found at Philadelphia than I had expected in Cincinnati. Secesh is very strong there. The folly of the people unaccountable. Well known & avowed Secessionists live comfortably. The pirate Semmes'[15] family among the rest. Mrs Perkins said his daughter was the belle at a party lately at a house which she had formerly visited.

This will go from Louisville, I am well.

Your affectionate husband,

Fred. Law Olmsted.

Olmsted wrote this letter on Sanitary Commission stationery but lined through the printed heading.

1. Leopold Eidlitz (1823–1908), a European-born architect who, after immigrating to New York in 1843, designed numerous churches and public buildings there. Eidlitz's favorite style was German Gothic (*DAB*).

2. Sarah Hart Elliott Perkins. Her younger sons, then ill with scarlet fever, probably were Henry Hill Perkins (b. 1845) and James Handasyd Perkins (1848–1889) (W. H. Emerson, *Genealogy of the Descendants of John Eliot*, p. 124; see also "Journey in the West, Cincinnati," March 1, 1863, n. 18, above).

3. Charles Pinckney James (1818–1899), lawyer and jurist. A graduate of Harvard College, he practiced law in his native city of Cincinnati and served on the state supreme court. In 1863 he moved to Washington, D.C., where later he was appointed as a justice of the Supreme Court of the District of Columbia (Ophia D. Smith, "The Family of Levi James and Its Alliances," *Bulletin of the Historical and Philosophical Society of Ohio* 8 [July 1950]: 198–200; Harvard University, *Quinquennial Catalogue of the Officers and Graduates of Harvard University, 1636–1900* [Cambridge, Mass., 1900], p. 159).

4. Charles Anderson (1814–1895). Born in Louisville to a distinguished Kentucky family, he was the brother of Robert Anderson, the Union army commander at Fort Sumter in April 1861. Charles Anderson practiced law in Dayton and Cincinnati and in 1844 won election to the state senate, where he supported increased civil rights for blacks. In 1859 he moved to Texas but he returned to Dayton during the Civil War. Commissioned colonel of the 93rd Ohio in the summer of 1862, he was seriously wounded at the battle of Murfreesboro and resigned from the service in February 1863. He was elected lieutenant governor of Ohio in 1863 and briefly served as governor after the death of Governor John Brough (Robert Sobel and John Raimo, eds., *Biographical Directory of the Governors of the United States, 1789–1978*, 4 vols. [Westport, Conn., 1978], 3: 1210–11; J. Fletcher Brennan, ed., *A Biographical Cyclopaedia and Portrait Gallery of Distinguished Men . . .* [Cincinnati, Ohio, 1879], pp. 78–79).

5. Olmsted's book *A Journey Through Texas*, published in 1857.

6. Edouard Degener (1809–1890), a well-born German political refugee who lived in Sisterdale, Texas. In February 1854 Olmsted spent several days with Degener, his wife, and their two sons, Hugo and Hilmar. In 1862 Degener was imprisoned for his Unionist sentiments, and his sons were killed at the battle of the Nueces in August of that year.

The sentence that Olmsted did not complete in his letter to Mary probably concerned Degener's reaction to the news of the battle's outcome. According to
Olmsted's friend Friedrich Kapp, when the imprisoned Degener "was informed by
his friends, who did not dare to reveal to him the whole truth, that one of his sons
was killed, he said incredulously: 'No that cannot be, they are either both living or
both dead, for the one would not forsake the other'" (*Papers of FLO*, 2: 276–77, 280;
Friedrich Kapp to FLO, Nov. 20, 1862).

7. Julius Dresel (1816–1891?), a German immigrant to Texas and a staunch supporter
   of free-soil colonization. Before the war, he worked a farm and operated a store in
   San Antonio. Anderson's reference to Monterrey probably meant Monterrey in the
   state of Nuevo Leon, Mexico (*Papers of FLO*, 2: 436–42; *An Illustrated History of
   Sonoma County, California* . . . [Chicago, 1889], p. 506).

8. Joseph Ulrich, a native of Pennsylvania who ran a general store in San Antonio and
   who had assisted Adolf Douai in editing the antislavery *San Antonio Zeitung* (*Papers
   of FLO*, 2: 400–404).

9. Gustave Theissen, the German farmer living near Sisterdale with whom Olmsted
   had stayed overnight during his journey through Texas (ibid., pp. 475–76).

10. Probably one of the daughters of Charles N. Riotte (b. 1814), a Prussian-born lawyer
    whom Olmsted had met in West Texas. Olmsted helped Riotte secure the post of
    U.S. minister to Costa Rica in 1861. After his removal from that office in 1867,
    Riotte was appointed U.S. minister to Nicaragua (ibid., pp. 18, 25, 75–77).

11. The editors have been unable to identify this informant. He may have been a
    distant relative, since Olmsted's grandmother's name was Content Pitkin.

12. A reference to the great fire of July 8, 1860, which raged through the business
    district and destroyed much of Dallas, Texas. Local whites, alarmed by reports of
    other fires in the vicinity, believed that their slaves, with abolitionist aid, had deliber-
    ately started the fire. Three slaves were hanged, and two white men from Iowa were
    publicly whipped and ordered to leave the county (John William Rogers, *The Lusty
    Texans of Dallas* [New York, 1951], pp. 89–95).

13. In the battle of Murfreesboro (Stones River), Tennessee, on December 30, 1862–
    January 3, 1863, the Union Army of the Cumberland, advancing from Nashville
    under the command of William S. Rosecrans, attacked Confederate forces com-
    manded by Gen. Braxton Bragg. The fighting was bloody but indecisive. Bragg
    retreated from middle Tennessee, but Union forces there did not advance during
    the next six months (*War for the Union*, 2: 375–77).

14. That is, a strong central government.

15. Raphael Semmes (see "Journey in the West, Cincinnati," March 1, 1863, n. 16,
    above).

535

JOURNEY IN THE WEST

Spring 1863

Nashville to Murfreesboro
with Rosecrans

(Murfreesboro')[1] March 7th 1863

At midnight, we went to the office of the hotel to arrange for leaving in the morning: the clerk informed us that the train left at 7 o'clk, we should be called at 5¼.; bkfast at 6 and leave by an omnibus at 6:15 for the R.R. Station.

"There's no need of calling us so early—call us at 5:45."

"Can't do that."

"Why not?"

"Our rule is 5:15."

"I don't care for your rule. We wish to be called at 5:45."

"Can't do it."

"Certainly you can send a servant to rap at our door at any hour, can't you? We take the risk of being late, if that is what you mean."

"Well, 'twouldn't be safe. It might be forgotten; I couldn't undertake to remember it."

"But put it on your memorandum."

"Reckon, I might forget to look at it if I did."

And all persuasion, expostulation and argument was in vain. It is the custom of the country for the public to accommodate itself to the convenience of the great hotel keepers, to the Rail Road and steamboat men, and individual non-conformists will not be tolerated. So we were visited at 5:15; had fried beef steak and coffee without milk, and slapjacks, in the dining room before the fires were lighted, at 6, and ten minutes after we took our seats were told that the omnibus was ready. We packed into it, and were furiously driven, as if the time were short, to the station, where we waited again nearly three quarters of an hour. The omnibus following us, driven as if the occasion for speed were still more desperate, capsized upon one of the rocks in the road and a lady and gentlemen badly bruised were lifted out and led to the station.

Again the ladies' car [was] sternly guarded, and we were driven into a steerage, close and filthy. The atmosphere high, stove-heated, dense, rank, pipe-tobacco-smoke, the cushions of the seats damp, the floor everywhere sole-deep with a shine of tobacco spittle, clay tracked in, pipe ashes, bread, cake and apples, left by yesterday's passengers. These things make some people sick but not the large mass of the travelling public, when women and men who travel with them and Major Generals, (for I observe that Major Genl Mitchell,[2] Commander of the Post of Nashville, goes in with the women) are withdrawn. It is not agreeable to us and we would keep the window open, but K.[3] has a cold, and it rains and is raw and gusty. On the whole, the majority of those in the car probably like it rather better for not having been cleaned. There is not a shadow of choice where any man shall spit or empty his pipe or drop his apple cores and parings, and at least nineteen in twenty of the passengers are smoking pipes, or chewing tobacco or apples. Don't suppose, however, that conversation is suspended. I think our English friends give a rather exaggerated idea of our taciturnity.[4] As we leave the town and K. asks: "What are those earthworks?" an answer comes from before and behind, and this leads to conversation and frank relations of personal experience with the army & the people hereabouts. And this is our universal experience—the people one meets by chance are directly approachable, obliging, communicative and accommodating: much more so than in England, according to my experience.[5] There they are obliging in a different way, with formality and consciousness. Here, no one thinks of saying thank you for being accommodated with roadside information. A man asks: "What place is this? How far is it from Murfreesboro'?" of the company at large within hearing. He does not acknowledge an answer as a courtesy by so much as a look. He feels illused, if nobody answers, and so, someone says: "Must be about fifteen miles. I never was here before, looks like they had had a scrimmage here. There's two bullet-holes through the target of that switch-handle. There was a little dépôt building that they burnt there."

The rail-road had been very thoroughly demolished by the enemy; for many miles there was a continuous series of the remains of fires made from the wooden ties and sleepers, with the iron rails laid on them and when thus heated, bent so as to be useless. As on the road from Louisville to Nashville, every bridge had been destroyed. But our army had completely rebuilt everything except the station-houses and the new bridges were always protected by guards, having stockades and rifle-pits, and sometimes more complete earth-works of defence. Burnt farm-houses were frequently seen and near those which remained the absence was notable of all domestic animals except horses mounted by soldiers or attached to army waggons. The devastation was worse than on the other side of Nashville. We were glad to be assured that the rebels had left not much of this sad work to be done by our men. Not a few planters' houses remained uninjured: yet the track of war could generally be traced in broken fences, campfire-brands in their door-yards or recent waggon roads run through them. Very few of the inhabitants, white or black, were to be seen.

The Rail Road runs through nearly the centre of the field of the battle of _____ before Murfreesboro' (battle of Stones River),[6] and the ground was at once recognizable by the clusters of fresh graves, generally a few dozen together, once or twice several hundred, rarely one isolated. Scores of dead horses lay still unburied.

Having arrived at Murfreesboro', we were guided by a fellow passenger with a major's shoulder-straps, along deeply mired roads crowded with army waggons and soldiers, horse and foot, to the square of the village, at a corner of which was a relief station of the Sanitary Commission, after visiting which and looking into a few of the village stores, long, narrow rooms, occupied as hospitals for the wounded, who seem to be doing well and were neatly cared for, we proceeded to call on General Rosecrans.[7] He occupied the most comfortable house of the town, a short distance from the square. There were lounging sentries—that is to say, "American citizens", wearing army clothing and holding muskets on their shoulders or resting upon them, but completely free from any uniformity of appearance one with another or from any resemblance to the European idea of a soldier in carriage, manner, or style of wearing their dress. They looked at us as we passed them and entered the front-door of the Head Quarters house but said nothing. Officers, orderlys and citizens were standing in conversation or moving through the hall. As it seemed to be the function of no one present to advise or direct strangers, we opened a door into a side room, where we found a number of young officers, all busy writing at desks. Evidently the aids, young fellows, at once seen to be of a superior class—selected men, refined, intelligent and giving promise of promptness and courtesy. One immediately stepped from his desk to receive us. "Is Col _____ here?"

"He is out at this moment."

"We have letters to Gen'l Rosecrans to whom we wish to pay our respects when it will be convenient for him to receive us."

"The General is just now at breakfast; if you will come with me, I will take you to General Garfield,[8] his Chief of Staff."

Going into another room, we found Gen'l Garfield, who, knowing nothing of us except from our statement that we were of the Sanitary Commission, made us at home in the midst of his business, in the simplest and heartiest and most good humored way possible, talking and writing, soon making familiar friends of us, on the ground of our knowing one and another of his old friends.[9] Presently we found an old acquaintance in one of the staff[10] who came in with papers, and then while we were talking, a man walked in rapidly, saying: "Did you see that statement of the Chicago Times,[11] Garfield? That must be stopped. Write a peremptory contradiction of it."

"Will you show about what you want it to be on paper. Here it is. Take my chair. These gentlemen have letters to you from Bache of the

WILLIAM STARKE ROSECRANS

Coast Survey and D[r] Bell of Louisville.[12] Mr Olmsted, Mr. Knapp. General Rosecrans."

"I'm glad to see you Sir. I am glad to see you Sir. Keep your seats"; and he gives us his hand, fixing his eye, searchingly but with a pleasant twinkle, upon us for a moment, and then turning to the desk, where he writes carefully, with pauses, paying no attention to those who come in until he has written three or four lines. "There, something in that way, Garfield. When have you seen Prof[r] Bache, Mr Olmsted? What a nice little hand he always writes." and then he opens the letters. While he is reading them, a telegraphic dispatch is brought in, Genl Garfield reads it and says: "_____ telegraphs that he hears heavy guns to the Southward."

Genl Rosecrans lifts his head, holding Prof[r] Bache's letter still: "That must be Sheridan.[13] Telegraph _____ & _____ to see if they have heard firing today?"

"I have already done so," said Captain Bond.

"Anything from Davis?"[14]

"Nothing; he no doubt moved two brigades to Salem this morning."

"He should have three days' rations."

539

"He has."

"Let's look at the map." and he rose and walked with Garfield & Bond into the next room. Presently coming back, he was saying: "Let them all have three days' cooked rations."

"They are all about ready. Could move in half an hour."

"That's right." and he took his seat by the desk and read the letters through; then rose, and said: "Come into my room, gentlemen," and we walked into a room with a large four post bed; a silk ensign hanging over it. "Take seats, take seats. Have a cigar? Mr. Knapp: have a cigar? Your association has done a heap of good here. There is a great deal of benevolence in our people, but benevolence is very often misdirected and wasted so that it does more harm than good. You have done just what [was] wanted to be done in giving system and order to it. It was a capital good thing for us."

"I am glad you so regard it. Let me thank you for your assistance to the purpose of the Commission. Your letter[15] was not only very gratifying to the Commission, but it has been of great value in getting the popular attention directed to the mistake of schemes for aiding the army which have state or local limits. I must say, General, that I think the Sanitary Commission has more claims upon the gratitude of the country for what it has done in a quiet, unaggressive way to lead the people out of their old narrow state and local bounds of interest and sympathy and to foster a purely national exercise of patriotic sentiment, than for the assistance which it has been able to bring to the Medical department in relieving the sick and wounded. Your letter helps greatly to establish precisely that conviction which the Commission has been constantly endeavoring to carry to every fireside in the loyal states, since the war commenced."

"I am glad if it will help at all in that. It's hard when people are bent on doing something for the relief of soldiers from their own district, to check them, and tell them it is not their soldiers but the soldiers of the country they are to help. It looks almost unkind, but it is the only real Kindness and certainly the only real patriotism. It would have been better that some of the sick and wounded should have suffered and died from want, than that anything should have been allowed which would encourage that very spirit at the North which we are fighting against at the South. We have got to conquer it and trample it out, or it will destroy us. They are so set upon being little nigger aristocrats that they will sacrifice everything else to it. What is their spirit of chivalry? It's the same spirit which loves to bully niggers. And it grows out of that. It's contemptible meanness. They boast of their honor. Their honor! What does it amount to? They reverence it just so long as it keeps ahead of their self interest and passions, but as soon as their passions or selfish interest come in play, honor falls behind. They are honorable just so far as it jumps with their convenience and pleasure to be honorable. Beyond that they are the meanest men in the world, full of miserable pride, violent and uncontrollable in their selfishness. That's my experience with them, here and everywhere. We've a great work before us here. Please God, we'll do it. My only hope is" (here he paused, turned in his chair, took his cigar from his mouth and threw his head forward looking at us, first one and then the other, keenly in the eyes and after a pause nodding two or three times, I nodded in response. He nodded again, significantly, and his eyes gleamed.) "My only hope is—that God is just." (pausing again) "We were not a war-like people. I wish that we had been a virtuous people. But we have a wonderful patriotism standing opposed to the selfish pride of those little nigger-tyrants. I have studied history with some care but I don't believe, I do not believe that as much pure patriotism—pure patriotism, without mixture of self interest—was ever found in the common run of any people on the earth before. Men, common men in the ranks deliberately make offering of their lives for the sake of the nation. Selfishness has not as deep a root as usual in men who really do that, really, without any humbug. I saw a man the other day: He was mortally wounded and he knew that he could not live more than a few hours. 'It's all right,' said he, 'all right,' as cheerfully as I can say it now. 'I made up my mind when I listed,' said he, 'that I would give up my life for the country, and now it's all right. I have nothing to say against it. It's all right, General.'"

We referred to Garasche,[16] whom we had known and loved in Washington. "Garesche," said the General, "gave his life to save this nation as fully, as truly and as simply as ever any man gave his life to any cause. He expected to be killed in that battle. He fully prepared himself for it. He asked my leave to retire for a short time half an hour before he was killed. I know what he retired for. He was all ready to meet death. I never saw anything finer in my life than his face when he drew his sword. You would have thought it the happiest moment of his life. He knew where he was going."

This is a poor report of the opening of our conversation. I perceive that I have failed to catch the style of General Rosecrans's language, which was in the highest degree direct, forcible and plain, boldly idiomatic and with frequent unhesitating reference to fundamental religious principles, but I have followed my memory of his very words as precisely as possible. We remained in the bed-room two hours and a half, the General twice insisting upon our remaining when we rose to go. He discoursed to us during more than half of this time and always in much the same tone; manifesting the strongest devotion to our nationality; the strongest aversion to everything of a disintegrating tendency. He hated the policy of politicians. Justice must save us—nothing less. Justice is our policy. What is the most truly and permanently just, that is best. The just policy is the wisest policy, and in the end it will take with the people. Politicians make the greatest mistake about that. They would hit the favor of the people a great deal easier, oftener and better, if they would go right straight ahead as they thought absolutely just, and not ask what the people want. In the end the people will find out and hold fast by a just man. He referred to the evils growing out of the interests of Governors and other elective officers controlling appointments and promotions[17] as one of the grandest difficulties which the army had to struggle with but readily and emphatically assented when I [said] evils of this kind were not peculiar to American armies.

Further advices by telegraph coming in, a consultation of Generals was held, in the midst of which a parcel which had come by our train was opened, and found to contain maps, sent from the Coast Survey office, one being of Eastern Tennessee. This and others were studied, and various surmises canvassed of the intention of the enemy in the movements of which symptoms were reported. (Three regiments of ours had been taken prisoners by Van Dorn's cavalry the day before.)[18] Among the Generals present was Jeff. C. Davis, who invited us to visit him in his camp. He did not remain long, and left with orders to have everything in readiness to move instantly upon an order, the intention being to move his division, seventeen miles to the right that night, upon a certain anticipated contingency.

Before leaving, we expressed a wish to look at the army in its camps, and were advised to visit a part of Davis's division which was only two miles out, and which might be in movement by the time we reached them. "I should like to have you see them on the march," said the General. A verbal order was given to provide us with two horses and an orderly. As an indication of the character, not of General Rosecrans, but of our army and people, I cannot omit to mention that my horse appeared never to have known a curry comb and to have lain the last night and for many nights in mud; the bridle had been plainly stomped under foot in clay, it was knotted at the end, where the buckle had been torn loose, and clods of fresh clay were still attached to it; the saddle, the regulation dragoons' saddle—a McClellan frame[19] strapped upon a ragged blanket—was equally rude and dirty. I had some difficulty in mounting and the orderly did not offer me the slightest assistance, obliging me to step out in the deep mud of the street while he kept his seat. Once mounted, the horse proved an excellent one; active, spirited, plucky, untiring, and perfectly well-trained as a saddle-horse, and the orderly proved a remarkably intelligent, patriotic and obliging man, a very pleasant leader and companion, for our excursion.

We galloped out upon a road dangerously crowded with army waggons, the empty ones driven recklessly, the six mules to each waggon not unfrequently disobeying orders when at full speed and by some eccentric action, when attempting to turn out, suddenly throwing the waggon into the ditch, giving occasion for a frightful expenditure of oaths and lashes, from the rude fellows who drove postilion fashion,[20] with a single line to the leaders.

Genl Davis's quarters were pointed out to us at a small dilapidated house, without furniture, in heavily wooded low ground; mud and water fetlock deep to the door, before which there was a rude rack at which horses were hitched. There were a few scattered tents before it, and among them, a camp forge, with the blacksmiths shoeing horses. There were sentries and officers about the door, but they paid no attention to us, and we walked in and found Gen'l Davis alone writing at a rude table, the room containing two chests, a case of maps, a camp-bed and some personal equipments.

Olmsted went from Cincinnati to Louisville, Kentucky, by steamboat on March 2 and stayed there through March 4. He traveled to Nashville, Tennessee, probably by rail, remained there at least one night, and proceeded to Murfreesboro by train on March 7 (FLO to MPO, March 2, 1863; FLO to USSC, March 4, 1863, USSC-NYPL, box 757: 657; HWB, "Notes of Olmsted's Talk," April 16, 1863, USSC-NYPL, box 641).

1. Although this section is headed Murfreesboro, its opening scene takes place in the hotel where Olmsted stayed in Nashville.
2. Robert Byington Mitchell (1823–1882), brigadier general and chief of cavalry in the Union Army of the Cumberland in 1863 (DAB).
3. Olmsted's companion, Frederick N. Knapp.
4. A reference to descriptions of taciturn Americans by British visitors such as Anthony Trollope, who wrote about his fellow travelers in the West: "If addressed, they answered me. If application was made by me for any special information, trouble was taken to give it me. But I found no aptitude, no wish for conversation; nay, even a disinclination to converse. . . . I have done my very best to break through this ice, and have always failed" (A. Trollope, North America, p. 143; see also "Journey in the West, Louisville toward Cairo," March 13, 1863, nn. 2 and 3, below).
5. During the 1850s Olmsted had visited England on three different occasions. In 1850 he, his younger brother John Hull Olmsted, and their friend Charles Loring Brace walked from Liverpool to London. After touring in London and on the continent, they proceeded through the midlands to Scotland. From April through October 1856 Olmsted again traveled in Great Britain. In October and November of 1859 he visited parks in the London area and in the midlands (Papers of FLO, 1: 354–55, 394; ibid., 2: 484; ibid., 3: 234–39]).
6. Olmsted appears not to have known that the battle of Murfreesboro (Stones River) occurred from December 30, 1862, until January 3, 1863.
7. William Starke Rosecrans (see FLO to Mary Olmsted, Feb. 25, 1863, n. 6, above).
8. James Abram Garfield (1831–1881), soldier, congressman, and twentieth president of the United States. By 1861 Garfield had been a teacher, president of Hiram College, and an Ohio state senator. At the outbreak of the Civil War, he helped raise the 42nd Ohio and served first as its lieutenant colonel, then as its colonel. Promoted to the rank of brigadier general of volunteers in January 1862 after a successful battle in Kentucky, he also fought at Shiloh. Poor health then removed him from the field until early 1863, when he became Rosecrans's chief of staff. After the battle of Chickamauga, Garfield was promoted to major general. He then left the army to

serve in the U.S. House of Representatives (*DAB*; William Mathias Lamers, *The Edge of Glory: A Biography of William S. Rosecrans, U.S.A.* [New York, 1961], p. 250).

9. Here Olmsted crossed out the remainder of the sentence, which read, "especially Dr Newberry of the Commission, who was a townsman for whom he expressed a warm regard."

10. Probably Frank Stuart Bond (1830–1911), a native of Massachusetts who grew up in Connecticut. Although appointed a first lieutenant in the 10th Connecticut, Bond never served with that regiment. In December 1862 he became Rosecrans's aide-de-camp and was promoted to the rank of major after the battle of Murfreesboro ([John Fitch], *Annals of the Army of the Cumberland*... [Philadelphia, 1863], pp. 51–52).

11. Probably Rosecrans had just read in the *Chicago Times*, a newspaper strongly opposed to the Emancipation Proclamation, a letter purportedly by a private in the Army of the Cumberland. This soldier alleged that the Proclamation had destroyed support for the war among his fellows, even those like himself who had voted for Lincoln, and he added, "I have not seen one here that is anxious for a fight" (*Chicago Times*, March 6, 1863, p. 1; Wood Gray, *The Hidden Civil War: The Story of the Copperheads* [New York, 1942], pp. 98–99).

12. Theodore Stout Bell (1807–1884), president of the Kentucky branch of the Sanitary Commission. Trained as a tailor, Bell sought a higher education and graduated from the university medical school in Louisville in 1832. He pursued a medical practice there and edited the *Louisville Medical Journal* (which became the *Western Journal of Medicine and Surgery*). In 1857 Bell was appointed to a chair in the university medical school at Louisville. He also participated in humanitarian and civic organizations and was a frequent contributor to George D. Prentice's newspaper, the *Louisville Daily Journal*.

Bell impressed Olmsted very favorably. When Charles Loring Brace was planning a Western trip, Olmsted gave him a letter of introduction to Bell and described the Kentuckian as a "physician, naturalist, politician, philanthropist and humble Christian of the Plymouth bretheren style. A real triumph of a Kentuckian, true a[s] steel & hot as fire." Olmsted saw Bell as "magnificent," but warned the abolitionist Brace, "He don't care for slavery, but is not an abolitionist by conviction, I think."

Bell seems to have reciprocated Olmsted's regard. In the letter delivered by Olmsted to Rosecrans, the physician declared that it was Olmsted's "creative genius that endowed the Central Park, in the City of New York with those elements of beauty and taste that will ultimately make it one of the gems of this Continent." Moreover, he credited Olmsted with having built up the Sanitary Commission. "There is not one Sanitary deed of kindness, mercy, philanthropy rendered to the loyal soldiers," continued Bell, "that may not claim Mr. Olmsted as its chief author. . . . You will find him all in heart and mental power, you could wish a man to be" (*History of the Ohio Falls Counties* [Cleveland, Ohio, 1882], pp. 442–45; FLO to CLB, July 19, 1863; Theodore S. Bell to William S. Rosecrans, March 4, 1863, from USSC-NYPL, courtesy of William Quentin Maxwell).

13. Philip Henry Sheridan (1831–1888), a West Point graduate and career army officer who had been promoted to major general of volunteers on December 31, 1862. Participating in the battles of Perryville, Murfreesboro, and Chickamauga, Sheridan was given command of the cavalry in the Army of the Potomac in 1864 (*DAB*).

14. Jefferson Columbus Davis (1828–1879), Union soldier. Born in Indiana, Davis enlisted to serve in the Mexican War. He remained in the army, receiving promotions to the rank of captain by 1861. Appointed colonel of the 22nd Indiana Infantry in August 1861, Davis became a brigadier general that year. Like Rosecrans and Garfield, he saw early service in the Western theater of the war by participating in the battles of Pea Ridge and Corinth as well as those of Murfreesboro and Chickamauga. In the autumn of 1862 Davis, upset over a reprimand, shot and killed his

commanding officer, Gen. William Nelson, in a Louisville, Kentucky, hotel. Although Davis was never brought to trial for that homicide, he received no further promotions (DAB).

15. That is, the open letter by Rosecrans praising the work of the Sanitary Commission. See FLO to Mary Olmsted, February 25, 1863, note 5, above.

16. Julius Peter Garesché (1821–1862), a graduate of the United States Military Academy and a career army officer who served with distinction in the Mexican War. In 1855 an appointment as assistant adjutant general stationed him in Washington, where he probably met Olmsted in 1861 or 1862. Garesché became Rosecrans's chief of staff in November 1862 and was killed on December 31, 1862, during the battle of Murfreesboro while attempting to rally a brigade (Appleton's Cyc. Am. Biog.; W. M. Lamers, Edge of Glory, pp. 193, 232–33; George Washington Cullum, Biographical Register of the Officers and Graduates of the U.S. Military Academy at West Point, N.Y. . . . , 3rd ed., 3 vols. [Boston, 1891], 2: 81–82).

17. The governor of a state providing a volunteer regiment controlled the appointments and promotions of that regiment's officers from the rank of captain through that of colonel. Thus an officer's appointment or promotion might depend more upon his political influence than upon his military experience or ability (War for the Union, 1: 227–35).

18. During an engagement at Thompson's Station, Tennessee, on March 5, 1863, Confederate cavalrymen in the Army of Mississippi, under the command of chief of cavalry Gen. Earl Van Dorn (1820–1863), captured over one thousand Union soldiers (Jon L. Wakelyn, Biographical Dictionary of the Confederacy [Westport, Conn., 1977]; Robert G. Hartje, Van Dorn: The Life and Times of a Confederate General [Nashville, Tenn., 1967], pp. 279–89; Frederick H. Dyer, A Compendium of the War of the Rebellion . . . , 3 vols. [1908; rpt. ed., New York, 1959], 2: 854).

19. A saddle designed by George B. McClellan and adopted by the U.S. Army in 1859. The most prominent feature of the McClellan saddle was its sparing use of leather—it had an open seat, and a single skirt protected both rider and horse (Randy Steffen, United States Military Saddles, 1812–1943 [Norman, Okla., 1973], pp. 63–65).

20. Although "postilion" usually refers to the rider of the left-hand leader horse, Olmsted here appears to describe a slightly different arrangement, probably that in which the drover rode the last left-hand mule.

To Mary Perkins Olmsted

Nashville, Sunday,
March 8th 1863.

My Dear Wife,

We returned tonight from the Army of the Cumberland—about Murfreesboro'. We were three hours yesterday with Rosecrans, whom I found as open, frank and down-right a man as I ever saw. We saw his way of doing business too, being in his bedroom, when telegraphic dispatches of demonstrations of the enemy arrived, and the maps consulted and a small council held, and the army ordered to be ready to move with three days' rations. We were furnished with horses and rode with an orderly two miles out to Gen Jef. C. Davis's Hd Q. Saw one of his brigades and were then invited to go out with him for the night, which we did; taking a company of cavalry and riding through the woods after dark four miles: three of which was outside of our pickets and where several men had been shot during the day by the enemy. Our advance guard reported seeing a small party of horsemen, supposed to be of the enemy. At four miles out we came to three brigades of infantry and a battery in bivouac, and after a few enquiries, rode up to a great plantation house. "Let Company B bivouac along this fence till 2 o'ck, then make a reconnaissance up the crossroad, with good flankers out all the time."

The brigade commanders were sent for and we went in and had a bit of plantation life. Master was an officer in rebel army, visitor a widow, husband killed in rebel army at Fort Donaldson,[1] house burned at battle of Murfreesboro' and all the people pretty badly used—60 niggers, belonged on the plantation, all but 16 gone. Council of war among the brigadiers; orders to have the whole force under arms an hour before the dawn of day. After this we went out and in a gathering thunder storm with some dropping sat by a camp-fire, while Mingo[2] fried ham and made coffee. After three hours yarning, went back to the house where we—the general and staff—slept on the floor and in feather beds. Turned out at five A.M., bluebirds and others making night hideous, and breakfasted or pretended to breakfast, and then waited orders till 9 o'ck when, no orders arriving and the enemy not having been seen, the general took the cavalry company and a large staff and first visited three of the regiments of his division who were with him in the battle of Pea-Ridge of which today was the anniversary.[3] One of them was his own old regiment, _____ Illinois,[4] which when they saw us coming, ran together and formed on parade. So the general made them a speech and I don't think I was ever more taken aback in my life than when he closed with: "Men! We have some friends here from the East. From the Army of the Potomac, Mr Olmsted and Mr Knapp. They will be glad to give you a few words of greeting!" Then trotting round to my rear with a wink. Unfortunately Knapp was in my rear, and there I stood, when they had done cheering the general, on a little horse, with 350 heroes who had marched 5000 miles since the war began and had fought three of the hardest fought battles of the war, Pea Ridge (Corinth) Perryville and Stones River,[5] waiting for me to talk to them. I waited a minute and then rose in my stirrups and said:—just sixteen words, whereupon a fellow called three cheers for Mr Olmsted, and they came and next thing I knew I heard the General say: "I had rather lead them through ten battles than make one speech to them," and found it was all over, and we were on the war-path. Cavalry before and behind and flanking parties, galloping off to look over each rising ground right and left. We rode over several large cotton plantations, cotton of last crop remaining unpicked in many cases. Finally heard heavy guns on the left. There was a halt and a talk. "They are pushing Sheridan at Triune"[6] was the conclusion, and the brigade commander with us, took a small escort and went back to have everything ready for an instant move in support of Sheridan, if it should be required. We rode on and came at length to the extreme right of our line of battle before the enemy entrenched before Murfreesboro'. Davis' division was the second from the right. He went over the whole ground of the first day's battle. There were scores of dead horses—hundreds in all the field & thousands of fresh graves. "Just here I lost a thousand men from one of my brigades, before we gave an inch." The trees were shattered. One small tree had twenty seven musket balls in it. One white oak two feet thick, a round-shot hole clear thro' the middle. Many considerable trees were prostrated.

We rode all along the line to the centre, and then in to Murfreesboro' where we had another short interview with the Gen'l and then hurried to the train by which we returned here.

All well, but I can hardly walk from the bed to the table, my leg so stiff.

A nice bit of amateur campaigning, eh?

We propose to go to Mammouth Cave[7] tomorrow & next day to Louisville, and then after a day or two to Cairo, & then to Vicsburg and a market.

The army looks rougher than in the East, but hardy, tough, cheerful, ready and good natured.

No letter yet from Charley.

No letter from Charlotte.

Dada.[8]

Mrs. Olmsted

1. The battle of Fort Donelson, culminating in the Union army's capture of the fort, took place on February 12–16, 1862.
2. Unidentified, perhaps a slave on the plantation.
3. The battle of Pea Ridge occurred in northwestern Arkansas on March 6–8, 1862.
4. Olmsted here meant the 22nd Indiana Infantry, the regiment of which Jefferson C. Davis had been colonel in 1861 (DAB).
5. By mistake Olmsted actually referred to four different battles of 1862: Pea Ridge, Arkansas (March 6–8), Corinth, Mississippi (October 3–4), Perryville, Kentucky (Oc-

tober 8), and Murfreesboro (December 30, 1862–January 3, 1863). The 22nd Indiana fought at Pea Ridge, Perryville, and Murfreesboro (F. H. Dyer, *Compendium of the War of the Rebellion*, 2: 675, 733, 773–74, 851–52).
6. Triune, Tennessee, located in eastern Williamson County, approximately ten to fifteen miles from Murfreesboro.
7. Mammoth Cave is the large underground network of passages and caverns located in south-central Kentucky, approximately ninety miles north of Nashville, Tennessee.
8. Olmsted's joking reference to himself in relation to his stepchildren John Charles and Charlotte Olmsted.

JOURNEY IN THE WEST

Spring 1863

Louisville toward Cairo

Cairo, supra Mississippi,
March 13ᵗʰ 1863.

By a fracture of the promises of the Ohio and Mississippi Rail Road Company, we were yesterday thrown upon our resources for twelve hours, at a small way station, in the midst of the great prairie region of Illinois, just as Mr Trollope was at Centralia.[1] There were a score of men besides ourselves and some women left in the lurch with us. I walked the length of the railway platform several times during the day, to see if I could find the [*typical*] American, as seen in numbers, and described by Mr Trollope at Centralia under similar circumstances.[2] There were individuals "walking the deck" and smoking solitarily and silently, but never did I find twice the same man thus engaged, nor of the score was there more than one who was not during the greater part of the day joined to one of the several groups which I invariably found engaged in conversation or playing euchre. The one solitary man who answered to Mr Trollope's description of the American with twelve hours on his hand[s] at a rail-road station in the far West, was an American Indian, who did exhibit precisely that taciturn, self-wrapped and stolidly self-sufficient aspect in which Mr Trollope saw so many of his fellow-detained white men. I thought when I read Mr Trollope's book that this description was very clever and true, though it was mysterious to me, how it could be so and I have often since [*asked myself what it meant*].[3] I spoke of it to gentlemen at Cincinnati and Louisville and they were decidedly of the opinion that it was a mere accident of the occasion from which Mr Trollope had generalized carelessly. They, who had travelled much in the West and a little in Europe, were quite sure that men were more ready to converse, more likely to be quickly on familiar terms with each other in America—in the West especially—than in Europe, than in England particularly.

This accords with my experience yet I recognized something familiar in Mr Trollope's picture. It reproduced sensations of my Southern experience.[4] I think this is true: that the American is more content to be solitary and silent upon occasion, than the European; that though this Indian habit is not constant with him, it sits more naturally upon him when he lacks satisfactory opportunity for social life, than, under similar circumstances, it does upon the European. Mr Trollope is an exception to his countrymen, if, under the circumstances described, he was not unusually morose, not to say crabbed and quarrelsome, while forced by the mismanagement of the railway company to wait twelve hours on a miserable railway junction platform, with not the smallest object of interest to him in the neighborhood and no better dinner to be had than was to have been expected at a prairie hamlet in Illinois. I thought yesterday, supposing twenty Englishmen averaging first, second and third class railway travellers had been set down here in this way without even a decent ale-house or skittle yard to resort to, or a fine bit of scenery or of architecture to regale their eyes upon—only this dreary prairie to the monotonous horizon—how would they have talked? The whole day would have been consumed in selecting associates to grumble with and in grumbling. I think that of our twenty Yankees, ten gave vent to their disappointment at the moment they discovered how we were situated, in one or two sound oaths and imprecations upon the Ohio and Mississippi Rail Road Company. The remainder acted precisely as if they had expected it and bargained for it, and after one minute of swearing, I did not hear a word on the subject during the day.[5] It is a misfortune and a fault of our national character that we bear evils too patiently and carelessly.[6] If every American traveller was made crabbed for a day by every rail-road company's or inn-keeper's mismanagement that he suffered from, if some one of every twenty would write for the Times, or even, as I do, once in ten thousand cases, complain, in a book,[7] of these things, our progress in civilization would be more sure.

Nothing was more unsatisfactory to me in Mr Russell's book than his picture of the American on the prairies of Illinois.[8] I knew that it must be incomplete and untrue in its incompleteness from the mere statistics of Illinois,[9] but I thought that there must have been more that was disagreeable and unpromising in the condition of our prairie population than I had before supposed and less that would be agreeable to see than I had imagined, or that so keen, careful and generally good humored an observer as Mr Russell would not have failed to see it. Yesterday was my first day on the prairies of the free states. I am glad to be obliged to think that either

Mr Russell was very unfortunate, or that I was very fortunate in my experience. And yet I saw some of the most disagreeable people and one of the most tiresome landscapes that I ever met with. I saw all that Mr Russell describes so graphically and most of it was as hateful to me as it was to him. But I saw a good deal that he did not see and which would have made his first day on the Illinois Central Rail Road much pleasanter if he had seen it.

I will describe some things that I saw.

First; two small, low, very rude, log-cabins, connected by a roof so as to make a third apartment open to the weather and the road on one side; by the side of it a log corn-crib, both standing in the midst of a small (for the prairies) corn-field, in which stood a number of very poor horses and cattle. A man and woman and a number of children were sitting, lounging or moving listlessly in the roofed space or before it. They were ill-dressed, perhaps ragged; dirty and forlorn looking. The picture was very familiar to me and I have described it before.[10] I could swear that man moved to "The Illineyes" from the slave states many years ago; that he has got corn and hogs more than enough, sells enough to buy tobacco, molasses and store-goods, and to warrant not a few visits to one of the dram-shops of which so many were seen by Mr Russell;[11] that he thinks it's getting too close settled round here, but don't want to go north, and don't want to go back to "a nigger state" and don't find any place in Southern Illinois that is not getting too close settled up to suit him to begin on, so he can't be induced to sell out to his neighbors who would gladly unite to pay him twice the market value of his property to get him to move away from them.[12] I could swear that he has never written a letter in his life; that he takes no newspaper,[13] that he thinks the Vice President is a mulatto, that the President is a despot, that he means to resist the execution of the Conscription Act and to refuse to pay any war taxes; that he thinks Northern and Southern Illinois ought to be two states, and that he hates a Yankee "worse than a nigger"; that he is in short a poor white of the South out of place.[14] There are many such in Southern Indiana and Illinois. He has his good qualities. He helped to drive the Indians away from here, as well as the panthers and wolves. And much as I pity him and his children, if I was obliged to live here on the prairie, I would rather live under his roof than in a wigwam, I would rather be him than to be the savage that I have seen.[15] He has done some work by which others have benefitted as well as himself. He has not the smallest particle of servility; I should not be surprised if he were a member of some church and meant to do God's will, according to his light; and on the whole, I must say that I think that the average English agricultural laborer[16] leads even a less enviable life than this poor man on the prairies. He never had any fear that he could not get food for his children or that he might have to come on the parish.[17]

1. After leaving Murfreesboro, Olmsted returned to Louisville, Kentucky, and took a train north to the Ohio and Mississippi Railroad, which crossed the southern Midwest from Cincinnati to St. Louis. At Odin, Illinois, where he was to transfer to the Illinois Central Railroad for the journey into Cairo, Olmsted missed the train and, like Anthony Trollope had been, was forced to wait in a prairie station. Trollope's layovers—each of four hours—took place at Seymour, Indiana, on the Ohio and Mississippi Railroad, and at Crossline, Ohio, rather than at Centralia, Illinois, as Olmsted reported. Olmsted probably confused Trollope's railroad itinerary with that of William H. Russell, who passed through Centralia, located only fifteen miles from Odin (FLO to JFJ, March 12, 1863, USSC-NYPL, box 757: 753; FLO to JSN, March 13, 1863, USSC-NYPL, box 914, 2: 218; W. H. Russell, *My Diary North and South*, p. 350; A. Trollope, *North America*, p. 447).
2. In this sentence, Olmsted lined through the word "typical." According to Anthony Trollope, his fellow passengers at Crossline, Ohio, sat idly and contentedly in silence near a stove for hours. He described the typical "western American" thus:

   > He balances himself on the back legs of an arm-chair, and remains so, without speaking, drinking, or smoking for an hour at a stretch; and while he is doing so he looks as though he had all that he desired. I believe that he is happy, and that he has all that he wants for such an occasion;—an arm-chair in which to sit, and a stove on which he can put his feet, and by which he can make himself warm. (A. Trollope, *North America*, p. 450.)

3. Olmsted crossed out the last five words of this last phrase but neglected to line through the first five words.
4. During his first journey in the South, Olmsted had complained to his friend Charles Loring Brace, "You can't imagine how hard it is to get hold of a conversable man." On the second journey, which took him through the back country, Olmsted found many—gentlemen as well as overseers and poor farmers—unwilling to give him more than monosyllabic replies (FLO to CLB, Feb. 23, 1853 [*Papers of FLO*, 2: 210]; BC, pp. 11–15, 17, 42–43, 126, 174–75, 229–30).
5. Following this sentence, Olmsted originally wrote, "If there was an Englishman there, I am sure that he went about growling for hours, making himself disagreeable, thereby, to the Americans, but I confess that I did not have the misfortune to meet him." He crossed out this criticism and did not replace it.
6. Olmsted's and Trollope's descriptions of the American traveler reached one similar conclusion: that he bore delays more patiently than his English counterpart. Trollope observed that

   > an Englishman, if he be kept waiting by a train in some forlorn station in which he can find no enjoyment, curses his fate and all that has led to his present misfortune with an energy which tells the story of his deep and thorough misery. Such, I confess, is my state of existence under such circumstances.

   But the novelist saw little of such impatience among Americans:

   > I should have expected to see them angry when robbed of their time, and irritable under the stress of such grievances as railway delays; but they are never irritable under such circumstances as I have attempted to describe, nor, indeed, are they a people prone to irritation under any grievances.

   (A. Trollope, *North America*, pp. 449–50.)
7. From 1852 to 1854 Olmsted had complained about inns and transportation facilities in letters first published by the *New-York Daily Times*. He then included many of these observations in his books.

8. William H. Russell described his journey on the Illinois Central Railroad from Cairo to Chicago. While he admitted that "it would be very wrong to judge of the condition of a people from the windows of a railway carriage," he analyzed the villages he had seen in just that manner:

> The external aspect of the settlements along the line, far superior to that of slave hamlets, does not equal my expectations. We all know the aspect of a wood in a gentleman's park; which is submitting to the axe, and has been partially cleared, how raw and bleak the stumps look, and how dreary is the naked land not yet turned into arable. Take such a patch, and fancy four or five houses made of pine planks, sometimes not painted, lighted by windows in which there is, or has been, glass, each guarded by a paling around a piece of vegetable garden, a pig house, and poultry box; let one be a grocery, which means a whiskey shop, another the post-office, and a third the store where "cash is given for produce." Multiply these groups, if you desire a larger settlement, and place a wooden church with a Brobdignag spire and Lilliputian body out in a waste, to be approached only by a causeway of planks; before each grocery let there be a gathering of tall men in sombre clothing, of whom the majority have small newspapers, and all of whom are chewing tobacco; near the stores let there be some light-wheeled carts and ragged horses, around which are knots of unmistakably German women; then see the deep tracks which lead off to similar settlements in the forest or prairie, and you have a notion, if your imagination is strong enough, of one of these civilizing centres which the Americans assert to be the homes of the most cultivated and intelligent communities in the world.

Russell also surmised that few distinctions existed between the highest and lowest classes in these villages: "The highest of the bourgeois who leads the mass at meeting and prayer, has but little to distinguish him from the very lowest member of the same body politic" (W. H. Russell, *My Diary North and South*, pp. 349, 350–51).

9. The "statistics of Illinois" probably refers to items enumerated by the federal census and illustrative to Olmsted of an area's progress toward civilization. Examples would include population as well as the number of towns, churches, libraries, and newspapers.

10. This description does closely resemble Olmsted's earlier accounts of Southern non-slaveholders. For instance, he wrote in 1854:

> They build a small cabin or shanty, of logs, upon the ground, in which to live with the simplest housekeeping utensils. They raise swine in the forest, and generally own a horse or a pair of cattle, and perhaps a cow—all of the meanest description. They raise on their clearing a meagre crop of corn and a few potatoes, and this, with the game they shoot, furnishes them with food. . . . They are very seldom observed at work, but are often seen, like young Rip Van Winkle, lounging at the door of a grocery, or sauntering, with a gun and a dog, in the woods. ("The South" no. 47, *New-York Daily Times*, Jan. 26, 1854 [*Papers of FLO*, 2: 253].)

11. Russell emphasized the ubiquitousness of dramshops in the Midwest when he noted that many of the railroad towns were "formed by accretions of small stores and drinking places, called magazines, round the original shed wherein live the station master and his assistants" (W. H. Russell, *My Diary North and South*, p. 349).

12. This statement echoes comments reported by Olmsted during his Southern journeys. The nonslaveholding whites whose land bordered Meredith Calhoun's huge Red River cotton plantation had "a standing offer of much more than the intrinsic value of their land . . . to induce them to move away." Mr. R. (Richard Taylor) so disliked the proximity of poor Acadians that "he was willing to pay two or three times as much as their property was actually worth, to get them to move off"

(Frederick Law Olmsted, *A Journey in the Seaboard Slave States, with Remarks on their Economy* . . . [New York, 1857], p. 673; *BC*, p. 75; see *Papers of FLO*, 2: 214, 222–23, for the identification of Calhoun and Taylor).

13. Olmsted originally phrased the first part of his description, "I could swear that he can't write," a comment reflecting his view that illiteracy was widespread among those of Southern background.

Olmsted's political references are to beliefs which were commonly held or promulgated by Democrats with Southern sympathies. During the 1860 presidential campaign, secessionist Robert Barnwell Rhett had called Hannibal Hamlin, the swarthy Republican vice-presidential candidate, a mulatto; and this false charge undoubtedly found some believers. Many Democrats considered President Lincoln a despot because of his suspension of the privilege of the writ of habeas corpus, an executive action that allowed detentions without the filing of formal charges. The various conscription laws and war taxes, such as the direct tax of 1861 and the personal income tax, also were unpopular among Democrats. The separation of northern and southern Illinois into two states and the hatred of Yankees—that is, New Englanders—probably refers to Democratic agitation to place southern Illinois, Ohio, and Indiana in the Confederacy or in a separate Northwest Confederacy which would exclude New England ("The South" no. 47 [*Papers of FLO*, 2: 252–53]; Harry Draper Hunt, *Hannibal Hamlin of Maine: Lincoln's First Vice President* [Syracuse, N.Y., 1962], pp. 121–22; James G. Randall, *Constitutional Problems under Lincoln*, rev. ed. [Urbana, Ill., 1951], pp. 147–68; *War for the Union*, 2: 190–91; W. Gray, *Hidden Civil War*, pp. 45–46, 134–35).

14. Olmsted first wrote, "that he is in short what they call in this part of the country an Egyptian of pure stock, uncontaminated." Southern Illinois was often called Egypt, and many of its inhabitants had immigrated there from the South or were the descendants of such immigrants.

15. Olmsted had earlier written about his visit in 1854 to an Indian camp in Texas:

> Here, at least, was nothing but the most miserable squalor, foul obscenity, and disgusting brutishness, if there be excepted the occasional evidence of a sly and impish keenness. We could not find even one man of dignity; the universal expression towards us was either a silly leer or a stupid indifference. (F. L. Olmsted, *A Journey Through Texas*, p. 289.)

16. The impoverished condition of English agricultural laborers had struck Olmsted during his walking tour in 1850. He noted that one laborer took it for granted that his family would often have only dry bread to eat. Although Olmsted then believed that the lot of agricultural workers in England had improved during the past ten years, he still found it to be deplorable ([Frederick Law Olmsted], *Walks and Talks of an American Farmer in England*, 2 vols. [New York, 1852], 2: 99–104, 108).

17. Olmsted here began a new paragraph, "Came to the next." Then in pencil he scribbled, "It was a good house a Pennsylvanian—built upon a cabin—." He then circled this entire addition in pencil. He probably intended to write a paragraph that would contrast the house of the Southern-stock "poor white" with that belonging to his neighbor from Pennsylvania.

At the end of this section, Olmsted scrawled in pencil, "Different classes—all improving English family sending for mother & brother." This note indicated subjects that he intended to address in subsequent drafts, but these were never written.

JOURNEY IN THE WEST

Spring 1863

Memphis to Young's Point

March 16 to 24   1863

At the Gayoso House,[1] the waiters were civil and willing at their duties. There were not half enough of them and they were slow, particularly when out of sight. One being asked, said they had been slaves; he did not know whether they were free now or not. Some said they were; some that they were not, but they were paid wages regularly now and no grumbling. The head-waiter, (a fine looking mulatto) did not take wages but he always got pretty much what he wanted. He was a son of the proprietor, who was also his owner and who had owned most of the servants. They were well-treated, nothing to grumble at. The same man, having thrown off his coat in an endeavor to get our door open, came back to put it on, after he had got some way off, going downstairs to get another key, and said: "D'ole man catch me widout my coat, he give me hell." Nor was there in any way the slightest evidence of insubordination or failure of discipline. So easy is the transit from Slavery to Freedom. These slaves could easily have gone to a free state,—some had gone—but were quite content to remain with their owner on wages. They were of the most intelligent class and could read—indicating that education is not dangerous if followed by a just remuneration for service.[2]

18th

At the invitation of Brig. Gen'l Webster,[3] who still wears the shoulder straps of a Col. of Artillery, we spent the evening at a very pleasant country-house with interesting Southern trees about it, which is occupied by a mess of staff officers, two of whom have their wives with them. Gnl W. is superintendent of Military R.R. of the Dpt. having formerly been Chf. of Staff of Gnl Grant & acting Engineer. He acknowledged that the pilfering, peculation and smuggling on the R.R. was extensive and that it was more than he could do to prevent it.[4] He said that the treachery, trickery, falsehood, disregard of obligations, of solemn engagements and of the oath of allegiance met with in the planters of the country was hardly conceivable. Planters who talked very well & had all the air of sober, honest, highminded men, when put to test, proved perfectly shameless; acted like professional rogues. This was even more the case with the women who would lie, as to the concealment of goods in their dresses for instance, with the utmost appearance of simplicity, and who would meet exposure of their falsehood without blushing. It was altogether out of the usual experience of people of ordinarily honest lives. It seemed as if they had acquired a habit of virtue in certain lines of life, a familiarity with deceit and a habit of hardness and boldness in certain other lines of life, the two lines running parallel & contiguous and the mind reverting from one to the other with no consciousness of the enormity of the transition. I have heard several officers engaged in Quarter Master and Provost Marshal duties which led them to constant dealings with the inhabitants, endeavor to describe a similar experience. Said one, "I have learned to hate a man at sight when he is called high-toned.[5] It is a phrase in constant use here, and I have had daily applications from men who bring bundles of testimonials, always describing them as 'high-toned gentlemen', and nine tenths of them turn out infernal scoundrels, no more to be trusted on their word, than so many men taken out of a city jail."

Making every allowance for prejudice, from the frequency with which statements of this kind of experience are made, by men of the character of Genl Rosecranz and Gen[l] Webster (I could quote others both in the Army and Navy, of notably cautious and charitable habits of mind), a conviction of the shallow character of the honor and chivalry boasted of as the best fruit of slavery must be establishing itself very generally in the minds of our officers. On another point of character, an officer said to me, "A short time before the war, I showed a Virginia friend, your account of your adventures in search of hospitality in Virginia,[6] and asked him what he thought of it. It made him very angry, and he declared that it was a pure fiction. There was no possibility of its being true. I confess to you, as I knew nothing of you then, I regarded your statements as incredible, but since I have come in contact with these planters on their own ground, and have seen how mean, dishonest and treacherous to friend and foe, they can be, upon the slightest temptation of selfishness, nothing is more incredible to me than the old romance of their hospitality."

Another officer, having an important cavalry command said, "We had an amusing confirmation of your observations while we were stationed on _____ river. There are some fine large plantations there, and on one or two of them there were some very pretty young women. We had to protect them, of course, and after a little war-like severity, they seemed to come to the conclusion that Yankees were not to be hated under all circumstances and our fellows used to ride with them, always supplying them with horses, for theirs had all gone off with Van Dorn.[7] By and by they got so that whenever they wanted a ride, they would send a servant over to some [of] us to borrow horses. They looked to us, of course, for many other favors, for the country was all in our hands and under military law. At length, some of the young men, getting back after a ride with them, late in the evening, just as a thunderstorm was coming over, were invited to spend the night, and when they [were] leaving the next morning, the overseer remarked that he reckoned they had forgot to pay for their lodging. To be sure they had, they said, and asked how much they should pay. The overseer reckoned it would be a dollar a piece for the two officers and the orderly, and two levies a piece for the five horses. They paid him and came over to camp and told the story, and as it gave a good deal of amusement, the experiment was tried again and after that several times by different officers and pay was always taken, sometimes by the young ladies themselves. I heard a good many say that they never believed your account before."[8]

Called on Major Gnl. Hurlburt,[9] commanding the Post. He is much denounced as drunken, unapproachable and inefficient, if not purposely neglectful of the crimes with which his subordinate officers are charged. He met us, however, with a clear eye, a good voice and a frank manner; and his request that we would if possible, make a careful inspection of his old brigade and his evident confidence and pride in the excellence of its administration, its good police, its bread and baking arrangments, and other characteristics which are only acquired by volunteers under an efficient and paternal command, led me to believe that his recent promotion had not been owing to altogether unjustifiable political favoritism, as is much reported.

I requested Genl Hurlbert to issue a special order to prevent frauds which we had discovered to be practiced under pretence of bringing goods into the department for gratuitous distribution to the hospitals. He saw the matter clearly, took hold of it promptly and promised that the order should be issued. A more comprehensive order, however, subsequently obtained from Genl Grant,[10] commanding the department, superceded the necessity for action by Genl Hurlbert. He repeated with emphasis the common charges of treachery, promise-breaking and perjury against the rebel population of the town and its vicinity.

Met Asst Surgn Genl Wood;[11] Dr Irwin,[12] Chief Surgeon of the Hospitals at Memphis, and a number of the surgeons in charge of the hospitals, this evening. Struck by the youthful, almost boyish, appearance of some of the latter. The hospitals we find in good order, though hardly as good as those of Louisville or Washington. Hotels and other buildings are used for hospitals, none of them being well adapted to the purpose. Two very excellent Northern ladies, one the widow of the late Governor [*Harvey of Wisconsin*],[13] who lost his life, by an accident, while looking after the comfort of the wounded at Pittsburg Landing, and Mrs [*Canfield*],[14] widow of Colonel [*Canfield*] of the Ohio Volunteers who was killed in the same battle, devote themselves to the assistance of the convalescent, permanently disabled, and discharged men, at Memphis; the former visiting the hospitals generally; the latter limiting her duty to the convalescent camp, which contains at this time 1500 patients. Both are women of unusual beauty, discreet, resolute, modest and thorough-bred and are working in a spirit of holy devotion to the cause which cost them their husbands. We were particularly impressed with the common sense evinced in the operations of Mrs _____ and I felt that the Commission was honored in her acceptance of a responsibility in its service.

K. had an interview with the mayor,[15] to make arrangments for the establishment of temporary accommodations for discharged invalids. Subsequently going to keep an engagement with him, he found him addressing a large and enthusiastic club of Union citizens. A spirit of hatred of the rebels, far stronger than exists anywhere at the North, was evinced by this assembly.

20th

Steamboat South Wester was advertized to leave for Young's Point at 4 P.M. of yesterday. We came on board, took our state-rooms, and then went on shore for the evening. She failed by only fourteen hours to keep the promises of the advertisement, leaving at six this morning, disappointing two of our friends who accustomed to the commercial customs of the west, and not making enough allowance for the gradual improvement effected by military influences in favor of punctuality, thought that they were safe to breakfast on shore and so were left behind. There was a nearer approach to the customs of civilization in the table than at any public table I have yet seen at the West, except that of the Galt House at Louisville.[16] K and I slept the first night on the cabin floor (the berths being all full) and were turned out at daylight to make room for the breakfast table. As there was no unoccupied room elsewhere, we were obliged to walk the deck for three hours. It is not agreeable to do so on a cold, malarious, gusty March morning, for a man who don't smoke. Fortunately, K had been able to make friends with the cook and so we got a private coffee.

There were not nearly as many very disagreeable people on this boat, as we have before had with us on the rivers, passes being refused just now with considerable approach to determination to keep away people whose visits are not supposed to be for the public interest. Still I heard men telling how they had been able to get a pass by persevering effort, and changing the point of approach, after it had been once or twice peremptorily refused them. A majority of the passengers were military and medical officers. There was a surgeon of the rebel army, who had been up the river with prisoners. We were not aware of it till the last afternoon when we found him in earnest but good natured discussion with a man who described himself as a real Massachusetts Copperhead. The latter did his best to impress upon the Surgeon that the United States would give the rebels anything they would ask if they would only come back into the Union, but would never cease fighting them until they gave up the project of independence. The rebel on the other hand did his best to convince the Copperhead that his party would do anything and everything for peace which could be wished by a sincere hater of negroes and Abolitionists, which the Copperhead boasted himself to be, except acknowledge allegiance to the flag of the United States. This they now hated with more than mortal hatred. And upon these ideas they were eloquent by turns, hour after hour, never making the smallest progress except in illustrating and enforcing them. They agreed in one thing: idolatry for Judge Taney's version of the Constitution[17] and contempt for the Declaration of American Independence.[18]

March 21st [1863]

About 100 passengers (below Helena)[19] chiefly Military, officers & privates with some civilians with special passes for business with the army. Three ladies of the family of one of the Major Generals, and of precisely that queenly type of beauty which Russell(?)[20] says is not seen in America. A much more agreeable company than we have had before. There is a Lt. Col. of the regular army; his parents were Virginians and he has been a slave owner. In the course of conversation, he said: "The Southerners can not comprehend the moral question of this war; it is natural with you to see a man in a negro; a Southerner can not. He sees a brute. He can not feel that a negro is entitled to the rights of a man. I never realized it myself until lately." He then related an occurrence of revolting treatment of a negro girl too horrible to be described or imagined—I never heard anything more disgusting—for which friends of his, whom he had associated with as gentlemen, had been directly responsible. They had spoken of it with some regret and some acknowledgment of shame, but with scarcely more than if the girl had been a brute; nor had he ever till this moment felt the full horror of it. Yet he had always thought slavery a bad thing and wished it could be done away with. But it had only been of late that he had felt what a wicked thing it was and had got to hate it. He had always hated the abolitionists before; now he was as strong and deep an abolitionist as Garrison[21] himself. I asked what had produced so sudden and complete a change? "I hardly know: the President's proclamation[22] came upon me like a wet blanket. It shocked and frightened me. I felt for a time as if I had no country; that the President had destroyed it. But I suppose it made me reflect more deeply than I had done before. It seems now as if scales had fallen from my eyes. Words have a new meaning to me. I see that a Negro is a man, in a sense that is new to me. I see that Slavery is wrong, that it is the

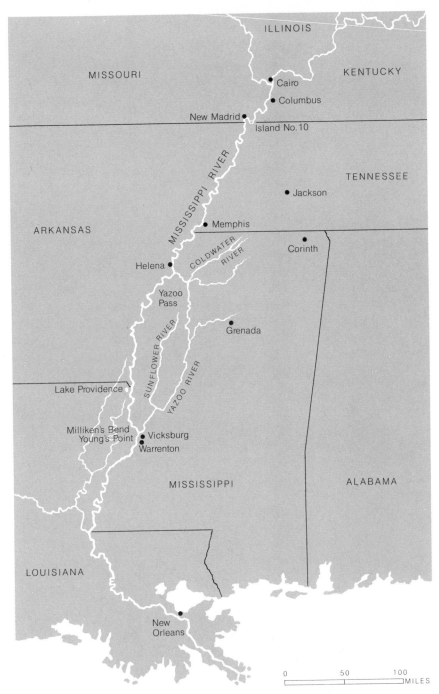

THE SOUTHERN VALLEY OF THE MISSISSIPPI, 1863

cause of the war a long way back. I believe that God is leading us; that we needed all our reverses to bring us to the proclamation. They talk of setting it aside, but that can never be done. It stands, and the government may do what it will, there are people who will carry on this war as long as Slavery exists in the land. I am one of them. We have no government, it is a mockery to call anything a government that attempts to govern this land leaving any men in it slaves."

23ᵈ (Sunday?)[23]

We passed during the afternoon several points where the levees had been cut and the water was rushing from the Mississippi over the plantations on the Louisiana side. At length we came to the village of Lake Providence, where we landed. There a canal had been constructed through the village with the lake in its rear, and a torrent was rushing into it through a crevasse of the levee about 200 feet wide. The village was inundated north of the canal, the water being above the pew-tops of the church, and two or three small houses falling over. On the South side, negroes were at work throwing up and strengthening a slight levee upon which the water was pressing hard. A regiment of our forces was stationed here, and we walked along the little levee, where the negroes were at work, through a graveyard, where billets of wood marked with the initials of Union volunteers thus: /J.P./1ˢᵗ Wis. Bat./March 10ᵗʰ/ stood among the mossy marble tablets and obelisks of the old residents of the village, and so came to the Head Quarters of the Post, a cottage in a garden full of the most delicious fragrance of spring, and with a variety of flowering plants and foliage, which we keep in glasshouses at the North. The fragrance all came however from the humble violet. Upon the levee where we landed, there were two hundred bales of cotton, with the mark of the rebel Confederacy upon them. Upon these were two aged negro men, in queerly, much be-patched clothing. One said that he was eighty two, the other that he was seventy six years old.

"You look older than that."

"Some depends on what kine of a master a man has, how ole he looks," promptly replied one.

"Where is your master?"

"Done gone."

"Gone and left you behind?"

"Yes, Master, done gone and took all der likely hans and leff de ole men and women and some older chilren and no 'count, broken-down fellers, and tells us to take kar of ourselves. We hain't got no right to take kar of ourselves now."

"Deh was tree likely fellas," said the other, "dey did reckon wot was gwine to happen, and dey did get off in de swamp and he doan git dem; not dat time, he doan. I reckon dey be free men, now massa, all dah lives, doan't they?"

"I hope so."

"Dey's got a right to take kar of dairselves; dey's right smart likely hands."

There were some young men also leaning on the cotton bales. One of these told us to whom he belonged. He spoke of his owner not unkindly, and said he took good care of his negroes on the front plantation; but he had three plantations. "If I'd been on dat front plantation, I wouldn' hev come away."

"What did you come away for?"

"Well I was on one of de back plantation."

"Why didn't you stay on it?"

"We had a cruel overseah, an I didn' see for why I wans stay dah to be whipd to death, and amost starved and no clothes this year at all; thought I might come out heah and see 'f I couldn' git some work and take kar o' myself."

At ten o'clock of a dark rainy night, the boat stopped again, and going on deck I found that we were in the centre of a semicircle of camp-fires; the drums beating the tattoo. Morning disclosed the tents of Mc-Clernand's Corps d'Armée[24] encamped on the Louisiana shore at Milli-ken's Bend—Head Quarters in a planter's house near us.

23^d Monday

Heavy rain, and the deep mud ashore prevented a visit to the camps or to Head Quarters, from which, however, we received a splendid festoon of yellow jasmine vine, in full flower. At noon we shifted our quarters to the Sanitary Commission's storeboat the Omaha, visited the hospital boat D. A. January, Dr Rush, in charge, which we found admirable in all her fittings and very well managed.[25]

Near her was an old wharf-boat, or flatboat with a shantee built upon it, which was used as an asylum for negroes unfit for work. The occupants were chiefly women and children with some old men; the boat had apparently been captured by a foraging party, and loaded with corn in the husk; the negroes had husked the corn and on a heap of the husks at one end of the boat reposed five women with little babies. Two of these had this morning made their way here, having waded through four miles of water, during the night, with their babies on their back. The water is all but ice cold; we saw a large cake of ice floating past this morning. Six others came with them. They gave the name of their late owner and said that he had six plantations. He had sometime before taken off all the best working hands from those near the river.

In the afternoon, we ran down the river ten miles further to Young's Point, where General Grant, commanding the department has his head Quarters on the steamboat Magnolia, and where Sherman's[26] Corps d'Armée is encamped.

The point is chosen, no doubt, because the bank is more elevated than any other within twenty miles northwardly of Vicksburg. There is no land in sight up or down the river, from the landing; the forest-trees rising from the water on both banks of the river, except upon a space just here, three or four hundred yards in length, where there is a clearing held in dispute by land and water. There is a levee, seen through trees, a hundred yards back, and between the shore and the trees, the clearing, several acres in extent, half covered with puddles of water, and penetrated by some shallow bays. Two or three hundred mules with a few horses are picketed, very fine, fat, sleek, mules, and a few horses also good and in good condition. There are a few tents and booths and army waggons and a couple of siege guns, and through the trees over the levee, other tent-tops can be discerned. There is a small house with shade trees and a hospital flag at the upper end of the clearing and just back of the little ridge of the levee, which bends to the river bank, there. Opposite this, with her head pushed diagonally up on the bank is the Magnolia, and then a line of a dozen boats in irregular echelon. Upon the hull of one of these is a large house two hundred feet long and two stories high, occupied as a warehouse by the Commissary Department. Opposite us is the mouth of the Yazoo, defined by an opening of the young growth of forest trees of the submerged shore disclosing a sylvan perspective, a quarter of mile in depth, closed by a curve of the stream. Crowded against the trees which define the Yazoo, there are three or four black hulls of the navy, and just at the mouth two large river steamboats, one the flag-ship of Admiral Porter,[27] the other the hospital of the squadron. About two miles down the river on this, the Louisiana, side, there are several more steamboats and beyond them, a large iron-clad. The Mississippi curves in that direction. Vicksburg is at the next turn—in plain sight a quarter of a mile below, Head Quarters is just screened from it by the trees opposite.

Rounding too, we pushed our nose between two of the boats two hundred yards below the Magnolia, and shoved it upon the bank. The two boats on our right form floating barracks for our engineer regiment. The boats on our left are ordnance boats; common Mississippi steamboats, the deck of the broad hull about a foot out of water, a second deck supported on stanchions fifteen feet above this; upon this second deck the cabin, and on the roof of this a small house, being the third story above the hold, which contains the quarters of the officers of the boat, and the pilot room or wheel house. The boiler with its furnaces and the engine stand on the lower deck; the kitchen, shut in by a slight wooden partition, is attached to the starboard paddle box, a coal-fire is kept alive in the furnaces, so that steam may be got up quickly if required, and I can see another coal-fire sputtering in the kitchen stove. Between the kitchen and the furnaces and within ten feet of both, and all along this open deck from stern to stem, so far as I can see, stands a pile of several hundred cases of musket cartridges. From the window of my state-room, I could throw a cigar clear over the pile upon the coal beyond, from which the furnace-fires are fed. I suppose the hold is full of artillery ammunition. Along side of this on the other side is another similar ordnance boat. During four days that we lay here, I saw no precautions against fire taken on these boats. Other boats, with their furnace doors open and fires blazing, sparks drifting in gusty weather from their chimneys, rounded too, as our own boat had done, against them, ran into them, and made fast to them; the ammunition in wooden boxes, piled ten feet high, entirely exposed at the sides. There was a volunteer with a musket generally sitting on a hawser coil near the gang-way, who was probably called the guard, but I never saw him in the exercise of any duty except that of nursing a musket. People, strangers, in and out of uniform, went on board, and travelled across the ordnance boats, as a common highway. I have done so myself when our boat lay outside of them. I called the attention of our captain to the circumstance. He took the idea that I thought it dangerous, and said: "Them boxes is very tight."

"But suppose some of that dry kindling stuff over the furnace should happen by accident to get on fire; what would become of all these boats?" The captain was lighting a fresh cigar so I answered myself, "Chips?"

"Yes, I expect there wouldn't be much else," said the captain, recovering breath. "That's what I'm afraid on,—fire. I ain't afraid of anything else on a steamboat, but I'm always keerful about fire."

"It wouldn't leave a man alive from here to the Magnolia."

"Expect not."

"I thought that I had a pretty good idea of the shiftless way in which our war-business was being done, but I never conceived that such carelessness as this could be possible. I have heard people grumble because Rosecrans exposed himself unnecessarily in battle, but here is Grant quartered alongside of a wooden powder magazine with two fires burning in it, and half a dozen other fires within fifty feet of it."

"But you see them boxes is very tight. There ain't no danger if they are keerful. I've carried powder in that way on this boat; that's the

THE HEADQUARTERS OF GRANT'S ARMY, NEAR VICKSBURG, 1863

way we always carry it. They wanted me to take some on, that time I took a load of wounded, but I had a hospital flag and they had no right to put it on a hospital boat."

The next day some clothing which had been put out on the roof of the ordnance boat to dry, took fire, probably catching from sparks drifting from the chimney, and the crew had lively work stamping it out.

"Lucky they see it 'fore it took the wood," remarked the captain, who was timid about fire, and then he lighted another cigar, and presently walked through the ordnance-boats (stooping with the cigar in his mouth, to get over the piles of ammunition), so as to look out at their stern and see where he could work in to get alongside one of the coal-boats, of which there were a dozen lying on shore, just beyond them. Once I noticed some negroes making a fire on the ground ashore within twenty feet of the ammunition. Within a hundred feet there were several open camp fires of the quartermasters' men and sutlers—loose hay lay all about among them. On the last night of our stay, we were awakened by a crash, which brought all our company into the cabin in night clothing.

"What's the matter?"

"Nothing, only the Commissaries' wharf-boat [floating warehouse][28] got adrift and dragged off three steamboats with her, and one of them has drifted foul of us," and so we lay grinding between the astray and the ordnance boat till the former drifted past us. The steam-boats got up steam as soon as possible and then laid hold of the wharf-boat and towed her back to her berth.

So, accidents will happen, and it's best to be careful about fire, as the captain reasonably observes.

24th

Genl Grant sent one of his aids to accompany us on a visit to the canal;[29] by which it has been supposed that he intended to pass below Vicksburg. The work upon it is at present abandoned, partly because of the high water, partly because the enemy has erected a battery which completely enfilades it. The men working on the dredges, though these were never struck, when they found that they were within range, refused to work, saying they did not agree to be shot at. They were not enlisted men, and it was not in their contract that they should work under fire.

The canal was a much smaller affair than it had been represented to be by the newspaper correspondents. We ran within long range of the Vicksburg batteries, near enough to set our watches by the town-clock, reading the figures with a glass, and to see negroes shovelling upon the earth-works, under a white overseer. The army desires to attempt a direct assault upon the batteries, approaching them by boats, and most of the young officers we meet share in this desire. To me, it seems that the attempt would be one of extreme folly.

24th[30]

Made a tour of the camps of Sherman's corps today, with Dr Hewit,[31] who has just been relieved of duty as Medical Director of the Department. We were furnished with good horses, well groomed and well-equipped, from Head Quarters—the staff horses are kept on the boat. Our road was on the levee, (except for a short distance where we crossed a mirey cotton-field on a corduroy road), to a distance of about two miles which brought us to the canal, where we turned upon a new levee formed by the earth thrown out of the canal which we followed to the embankment of a rail-road, from which the superstructure had been removed. The water was up to within about three feet of the top of the levee on the river side; on the other, the flat ground of the cotton fields was about fourteen feet below its top, the camps stretched for two miles or more through these fields in a line parallel with the levee.

The tents of one battery which had been previously camped on lower ground, from which they had been drowned out, were pitched in terraces upon the slope of the levee. There had been some apprehension that the whole corps would be obliged to come to this resort—the tents had consequently been pitched as closely as practicable and the scene was grotesquely picturesque. Elsewhere the slope of the levee was lined with graves, and we came upon a funeral escort burying the remains of a captain. They can not bury elsewhere, because of what is called the seepage-water—the water which filters through or under the levee and though gradually draining to the swamp in the rear, at once fills any cavity of the surface. It is partly owing to the impression produced by this long line of graves upon the levee, which must be seen by anyone who visits the army, that exaggerated reports from inconsiderate persons, of the mortality of this army have reached the public.

The editors have here omitted a page of notes preceding this section in the original manuscript. These notes, made by Olmsted during his journey, obviously formed the basis for his accounts of his sojourns in Memphis and at Young's Point, and the material is presented here only in its more finished form. Also omitted is Olmsted's account of his journey from New York to San Francisco in September 1863, which was filed with the "Journey in the West" and will be published in volume five of the Olmsted Papers.

1. The white-columned Gayoso House, with its scenic view of the Mississippi River, had been built in the mid-1840s by Memphis entrepreneur and planter Robertson Topp. A prewar Unionist active in Whig politics, Topp had owned many slaves and large amounts of real estate in Memphis, but the Civil War wrecked his fortune (Shields McIlwaine, *Memphis down in Dixie* [New York, 1948], pp. 84–85, 113, 144–45; John McLeod Keating, *History of the City of Memphis and Shelby County, Tennessee . . .*, 2 vols. [Syracuse, N.Y., 1888], 2: 223–26).

2. A reference to white Southerners' fears that education for blacks would encourage insubordination or rebellion. Most ante-bellum Southern states proscribed teaching slaves to read and write, and some also banned schools for free blacks (Kenneth M. Stampp, *The Peculiar Institution: Slavery in the Ante-Bellum South* [New York, 1956], p. 208; Ira Berlin, *Slaves without Masters: The Free Negro in the Antebellum South* [New York, 1974], pp. 285–86).

3. Joseph Dana Webster (1811–1876), soldier and businessman. Webster, who had served in the army from 1838 until 1854, oversaw the construction of Civil War fortifications at Cairo, Illinois, and Paducah, Kentucky. Commissioned colonel of the 1st Illinois Artillery in February 1862, he then served as Grant's chief of staff until October 1862. Promoted to brigadier general in November 1862, he was appointed military governor of Memphis and superintendent of military railroads. Later in the war, he served as chief of staff for Sherman (*Appleton's Cyc. Am. Biog.*).

4. A brisk illegal commerce began in Memphis after its capture by Union troops in June 1862. Numerous Northern speculators attempted to buy Southern staple crops, and, to obtain cotton, some were willing to sell or exchange contraband articles such as medicine and shoes, which were then smuggled behind Confederate lines to aid that army (*War for the Union*, 2: 103–5; Gerald M. Capers, Jr., *The Biography of a River Town: Memphis, Its Heroic Age* [Chapel Hill, N.C., 1939], pp. 152–58).

5. A meeting with Samuel Perkins Allison in Nashville, Tennessee, in December 1853 had then led Olmsted to a great deal of reflection about Southern, "high-toned" gentlemen. He noted such virtues as bravery, generosity, and courtesy among South-

erners, but he concluded that even the finest of them lacked the moral earnestness he so much admired among his Northern friends and acquaintances. Summarizing his view of Southern gentlemen, he wrote: "They do not seem to have a fundamental sense of right. Their moving power and the only motives which they can comprehend are materialistic or Heavenalistic—regard for good (to themselves or others or to God) in this world or in another." Olmsted believed that the best Southern gentlemen did not attain his ideal, but he was far more contemptuous of other well-to-do men there:

> Everywhere you meet them, well dressed and spending money freely, constantly drinking, smoking and chewing; card-playing and betting; and unable to converse upon anything that is not either grossly sensual or exciting, such as street encounters, filibustering schemes, or projects of disunion or war. These persons are, however, gentlemen, in the sense that they are familiar with the forms and usages of the best society, that they are deferential to women, and that (except in money matters) their word is to be implicitly relied upon.

(FLO to CLB, Dec. 1, 1853 [*Papers of FLO*, 2: 235]; "The South" no. 46 [*Papers of FLO*, 2: 242–45].)

6. Olmsted is referring here to an incident illustrating his view of Southern hospitality that he had recounted in *Back Country*. Becoming ill outside Lynchburg, Virginia, he sought and was refused shelter at six different houses over a period of several hours, even though he told the owners about his weak condition. Only after ten o'clock in the evening did he finally succeed in gaining lodging at a small store (*BC*, pp. 400–404).

7. From October through December 1862 Gen. Earl Van Dorn had conducted Confederate cavalry operations in northern Mississippi and western Tennessee (R. G. Hartje, *Van Dorn*, pp. 250–51, 266–67).

8. In a section of *Back Country* that took issue with Southern polemicist J. D. B. DeBow's views of Southern hospitality, Olmsted wrote: "Only twice, in a journey of four thousand miles, made independently of public conveyances, did I receive a night's lodging or a repast from a native southerner, without having the exact price in money which I was expected to pay for it stated to me by those at whose hands I received it" (*BC*, p. 407).

9. Stephen Augustus Hurlbut (1815–1882), the older half-brother of Olmsted's friend William Henry Hurlbert (who had changed the spelling of his surname). In 1845 Hurlbut migrated from his native South Carolina to Illinois, where he practiced law and was active in state politics. Commissioned a brigadier general of volunteers in May 1861, he was promoted to major general in September 1862 and received command of the XVI Corps at Memphis that December. Hurlbut, who had served two terms in the Illinois legislature in the 1850s, was again elected to the state legislature in 1867 and to the U.S. Congress in 1872 and 1874. He also served as minister to Colombia, 1869–72, and as minister to Peru, 1881–82. After 1863 numerous charges of drunkenness and corruption were leveled against Hurlbut (*DAB*; *BDAC*).

10. Special Order number 88, issued on March 29, 1863, provided free transportation for U.S. Sanitary Commission stores. To prevent goods directed to individual soldiers or intended for resale from being included in those shipments, all packages were to be inspected by a Sanitary Commission agent or to have an invoice. That agent would also give an inventory of each shipment and a weekly report of supplies issued and recipients to the department's medical director (*O.R.*, ser. 1, vol. 24, pp. 153–54).

11. Since his appointment as assistant surgeon general in June 1862, Robert C. Wood had been stationed in the West.

12. Bernard John Dowling Irwin (d. 1917), major and surgeon in the U.S. Army. After

the battle of Shiloh, Irwin, who was a career officer, set up the first American tent hospital (Francis Bernard Heitman, *Historical Register and Dictionary of the United States Army . . .* , 2 vols. [Washington, D.C., 1903], 1: 564; *Infantry Journal* 23 [April 1928]: 368–75; George Worthington Adams, *Doctors in Blue: The Medical History of the Union Army in the Civil War* [New York, 1952], p. 82).

13. Cornelia Adelaid Perrine Harvey, widow of Louis Harvey (1820–1862), governor of Wisconsin, whom she had married in 1847. Prominent in Whig and later in Republican politics, Louis Harvey had served in the state legislature before his election as governor in 1861. He took great interest in the welfare of Wisconsin's soldiers and organized a relief expedition after the battle of Shiloh in April 1862, but was accidentally drowned there. Cornelia Harvey, widowed and childless, received permission to visit Mississippi River hospitals as an agent of the state. She was especially active in St. Louis, Cape Girardeau, and Memphis. After a few weeks at Young's Point in April 1863, she became seriously ill and had to return home. Later she persuaded Union authorities to set up a general hospital in Madison, Wisconsin, to serve soldiers not convalescing well in the South. After the war she helped establish an orphanage in Wisconsin for children left fatherless by the war.

In this manuscript Olmsted lined through the names Cornelia Harvey and Martha Canfield and replaced them with blanks (Linus Pierpont Brockett and Mary C. Vaughan, *Woman's Work in the Civil War: A Record of Heroism, Patriotism, and Patience* [Boston, 1867], pp. 260–68; R. Sobel and J. Raimo, eds., *Biographical Directory of the Governors*, 4: 1724–25).

14. S. A. Martha Canfield, who had accompanied her husband, Herman Canfield, colonel of the 71st Ohio, to war. After his death in the battle of Shiloh, Martha Canfield nursed in the hospitals of the XVI Corps of the Union Army of the Mississippi in and near Memphis in 1863. She also took an interest in the freed slaves of that area and helped found an orphanage for black children in Memphis (L. P. Brockett and M. C. Vaughn, *Woman's Work in the Civil War*, p. 495).

15. John Park became mayor of Memphis in July 1861 and retained that position after the federal occupation of Memphis in 1862. He may have been a Unionist, but it seems unlikely that his loyalty was as fervent as Olmsted depicts it. In 1864 Gen. C. C. Washburne did not except Park in a denunciation of the "disloyal character" of the Memphis municipal government and "its want of sympathy for the government of the United States." Washburne removed all the city's officials, including Mayor Park, who later resumed that office and served through 1866 (John Preston Young, *Standard History of Memphis, Tennessee . . .* [Knoxville, Tenn., 1912], pp. 125, 148–49; J. M. Keating, *History of the City of Memphis*, 2: 28–29).

16. The Galt House, in Louisville, Kentucky, was a well-known luxury hotel that served food of high quality. It had been built in the mid-1830s, and Olmsted may have stayed there during his second journey to the South (Isabel McLennan McMeekin, *Louisville: The Gateway City* [New York, 1946], pp. 91–93; F. L. Olmsted, *Journey Through Texas*, p. 22).

17. This linking of Taney's version of the Constitution to a contempt for the Declaration of Independence suggests that Olmsted was thinking of the opinion that Supreme Court Chief Justice Roger B. Taney (1777–1864) wrote in the famous Dred Scott case in 1857. Ruling that Scott, a black who asserted that residence with his master north of the Missouri Compromise line had freed him, was still a slave and that Congress had no power to exclude slavery from the territories, Taney also declared that native-born blacks were not and could not be citizens of the United States. His opinion on black citizenship was based on the condition of blacks at the time the Constitution was adopted: "They had for more than a century before been regarded as beings of an inferior order; and altogether unfit to associate with the white race, either in social or political relations; and so far inferior that they had no rights which the white man was bound to respect." Thus Taney found it "impossible

to believe" that citizenship had been extended to this group. Olmsted probably believed that this decision conflicted with the assertion in the Declaration of Independence that "all men are created equal, that they are endowed by their Creator with certain unalienable Rights" (*DAB*; Vincent J. Hopkins, *Dred Scott's Case* [New York, 1951], pp. 61–79; Henry Steele Commager, ed., *Documents of American History*, 5th ed. [New York, 1949], pp. 100, 342).

18. Olmsted probably meant to lengthen this section by rewriting parts of the journal he had kept. He scrawled at the end of this passage: "(See note-book, acct of Helena & Yazoo Pass excerpt.)."

19. In the notes that Olmsted made in a small journal, he described Helena, Arkansas, as "a wretched town, nearly submerged, levee broken in, water running up the streets from river" (FLO, "Journal, 1863").

20. Olmsted appears to have been uncertain about whether to attribute this comment to William Howard Russell. Although the British newspaperman had remarked that the beauty of women in New York was "prettiness rather than fineness," Olmsted possibly was thinking of the observation made by an earlier British visitor, James Silk Buckingham, that, at a New York party, "There were no 'fine women' in the English sense of that term, comprehending the requisites of tall, full, and commanding figures, bold and striking as well as beautiful features, rosy colour, expressive eyes, and the noble air and carriage of a lofty and dignified rank" (W. H. Russell, *My Diary North and South*, p. 22; James Silk Buckingham, *America, Historical, Statistic, and Descriptive*, 3 vols. [London, 1841], 1: 57).

21. The noted American abolitionist William Lloyd Garrison (1805–1879).

22. That is, the Emancipation Proclamation.

23. Olmsted misdated this section. The correct date was Sunday, March 22.

24. John Alexander McClernand (1812–1900), Union general. A lawyer and Democrat from Illinois, he had served five terms in the U.S. House of Representatives by 1861. He was commissioned a brigadier general in 1861 and was promoted to major general by the spring of 1862. In the autumn of 1862 he recruited and organized an expedition to open the Mississippi River and captured Arkansas Post on the Arkansas River in January 1863. However, Grant, then commander of the Army of the Tennessee, decided to assume command of the expedition and ordered McClernand to Milliken's Bend to command the XIII Corps there. Grant and McClernand had been at loggerheads since the battle of Shiloh in 1862, and Grant's criticism of the Arkansas Post maneuver and his takeover of McClernand's expedition only increased tensions. In June 1863 Grant ordered McClernand back to Illinois. Although McClernand regained command of the XIII Corps early in 1864, ill health soon forced his return to civilian life (*DAB*; *War for the Union*, 2: 377–88).

25. The 500-bed *D. A. January* transported sick soldiers to hospitals in Memphis, St. Louis, Mound City, Keokuk, and other cities. Jane C. Hoge visited the boat in 1863 and later described it: "The 'D. A. January' seemed almost faultless in its arrangements; cleaner beds, cleaner patients, purer air, better cooked food, or more watchful and tender nursing, one could hardly desire" (Jane Currie [Blaikie] Hoge, *The Boys in Blue; Or, Heroes of the "Rank and File."* . . . [New York, 1867], p. 277).

26. William Tecumseh Sherman (1820–1891) was major general of volunteers in 1863 and commanded the XV Corps. He had been transferred west after the battle of Bull Run and served with Grant at the battles of Shiloh and Corinth as well as at the siege of Vicksburg. When Grant received command of the western armies, Sherman was elevated to command of the Army of the Tennessee (*DAB*).

27. David Dixon Porter (1813–1891), commander of the Mississippi Squadron. During the Civil War he participated in the expedition that captured New Orleans and was promoted to the rank of acting rear admiral in the fall of 1862. Porter helped capture Arkansas Post in January 1863 and played an important role at the siege of Vicksburg (*DAB*).

28. Olmsted's brackets.
29. A reference to the canal built at Young's Point in an attempt to create a new channel for the Mississippi River, by-passing Vicksburg, which lay in a hairpin curve of the river. On March 8, 1863, a break in the canal's dam stopped all work on it. Olmsted was justifiedly skeptical of its possibility of success and told his wife, "It may be put to some small use but will never turn the Mississippi or be a ship canal." The canal proved too shallow for most vessels in the Union fleet (*War for the Union*, 2: 412–14; FLO to MPO, March 31, 1863).
30. Olmsted again misdated a section. The correct date was March 25 (see FLO to JO, April 1, 1863, below).
31. Henry Stewart Hewit (1825–1873), physician. A graduate of Yale, Hewit studied medicine in New York and served in the army for four years. From 1852 until the Civil War he practiced medicine, first in San Francisco, later in New York City. In 1861 he reentered the army as a brigade surgeon of volunteers and rose to be medical director of Grant's army at Shiloh and Vicksburg (*Appleton's Cyc. Am. Biog.*).

To John Olmsted

Sanitary Store Boat, "Dunleith",
on the Mississippi, above Memphis;
April 1ˢᵗ 1863.

Dear Father,

We are returning from a visit to the army before Vicksburg, which we reached on the 22ᵈ. General Grant's command consists of four army corps: one under Gen'l Hurlbert is in Tennessee; there being detachments at Columbus; Isᵈ No 10; New Madrid, Jackson, Helena, and considerable bodies at Corinth and Memphis. A second corps is amphibious between Helena and New Providence, under Gen'l McPherson;[1] a third, having been recently drowned out of camp at Young's Point, near the canal across the neck, is now at Milliken's bend, ten miles above; Sherman's corps alone remains in direct observation of Vicksburg. It is camped on a series of plantations, from one to two miles above the canal. Head quarters is on the steamboat Magnolia, which lies, nose up, on the only ground which I saw, above water, outside the levee below Milliken's bend. There were a dozen large steamboats at the same place, two being quarters of Col. Bissell's[2] Western Engineer Regiment; two ordnance boats, (loaded with ammunition) one medical store-boat; one hospital boat, several transports and forage boats, and one immense floating ware-house containing Commissary stores; also a score or two of flatboats loaded with coal. The space of ground out of water is about 1000 feet in length. At the other end of

Sherman's encampment, there are half a dozen more Commissary boats. There are near here also three or four iron-clads and rams, and in the mouth of the Yazoo, which is just opposite Hd. Q., the flag boat of Admiral Porter, half a dozen mortar boats, another iron-clad, and some more rams and a naval hospital boat. Most of the Squadron, and considerable force from each army-corps were absent on the Sunflower and Blackwater expeditions,[3] from which they were getting back as we left; the sternwheel transports, wonderfully knocked to pieces; their smoke-stacks all down, so that the black coal-smoke was thrown directly upon the hurricane decks, which were necessarily crowded with men, who must have been nearly suffocated by it.

The day after our arrival Gen'l Grant sent an aid on board our boat to take us [as] near to Vicksburg as it would be safe to go. It was near enough to set our watches by the town-clock and to see negroes shovelling earth upon the breast-works. Bissell was building a case-mate battery for two 30 lb[r] Parrotts,[4] concealed from the enemy by the levee, at the point nearest the town; from which it was intended to open fire upon their R.R. station and Commissary storehouse, the morning after we left. The next

day we went with Medical Director Hewit, to look at the camps, riding on the levee, and across one plantation on a corduroy road. The ground inside the levee even, is elsewhere impassible, the ground being all soaked, where it is not flooded, with the "seepage-water" straining through and under the levees. The camps are near the levee; the tents being furnished with bedsteads made of saplings, lifting the men a few inches off the ground; the men of one battery, having been flooded out elsewhere, had pitched their tents on terraces cut in the slope of the levee; forming a very picturesque camp; the levee is here about 14 ft. high. A part of McPherson's men whom we visited opposite Yazoo pass were camped on a strip of the forest left above water, not more than fifty feet wide; the water so nearly over it, that the swell caused by our boat rolled into one of the tents. The water had risen an inch and a half during the night, and you would say it was about the most dismal place and the most dismal prospect upon which an army could be put. So here of Sherman's corps: the ground all asoak and water backing up on them in every direction except where the levee [re]strained it. The levee itself was lined with graves; there being no other place where the dead could be buried, on account of the water, which at once fills every cavity. These graves, which must be seen by everyone, there being no other road to travel near the camps, have helped, I suppose, to give the impression that Grant's army was in a terribly diseased state. I suppose country people would get the impression that a fearful epidemic was prevailing if they should see the burials daily occurring in any town of 40,000 inhabitants, or if they should see all the graves made within a month placed in two lines, head to foot, as they are for this army, on the levee.

In fact the health of the army, tho' not quite as good as that of the army in general, is amazingly good. You can not conceive how well and happy the men in general looked. They are mostly now well broken in, and know how to take care of themselves. Considering that they were living athletically and robustly, with plentiful air; I don't know anything that they wanted. I have enough of the Bedouin nature in my composition to envy them. I never saw men looking healthier or happier. The food is abundant, varied and most excellent in quality. I don't believe that one in fifty ever lived as well before. They were well-clothed and well-shod. If I were young and sound, I would like nothing so well as to be one of them.

We dined at Sherman's Head Quarters, which are in a planter's house in a little grove of willow oaks and Pride of China, just greened out, but dinner was served in a tent. Here I met Captain Janney,[5] Sherman's staff-engineer, with whom I rode a couple of hours in the afternoon and whose talk I enjoyed greatly. He has had a half artist education in Paris and was warm on parks, pictures, architects, engineers and artists. Reminiscences of Cranch and Fontainbleau; of student-life at the Politechnique and Centrale, discussions of the decoration of the Louvre,[6] had a peculiar zest in the midst of raw upper Louisiana plantation, where nature's usual work is but half-done; looking across the River into tree-tops hung with the weird Spanish-moss, vultures floating above; shouts and turmoil of a gang of contrabands tearing down the gin-house of the plantation—Captain Janney wants the material for bridges—the drums beating and bugles sounding for evening parade behind and the distant boom of Farragut's big guns on the Hartford,[7] pitching shells at intervals into my quondam host's, Dick Taylor's,[8] rebel batteries at Warrenton. Another excellent fellow here was Sherman's Medical Director, McMillan,[9] whom I have known before; indeed have met often since the war began. He was Stoneman's[10] Medical Director on the Peninsula. He was grossly abused by the Herald's correspondent, for "entire neglect to make any provision for the wounded" at the battle of Chickasaw bluffs,[11] whereas his arrangments were really the most complete that have ever been formed before a battle, with perhaps a single exception, and he is one of the most humane, industrious, enlightened and efficient surgeons in the Army. It is oftener than otherwise that the really good surgeons are maligned and held up to public execration, and the surgeons who always fail in an emergency pass for the best.

McMillan & Janney rode with us to call on Gen'l Steele,[12] living in a large room of a planter's house, which had been half finished years ago, and since inhabited in its unfinished state. There were school-classics left behind on the mantel-piece. From Gen'l Steele's we rode to Gen'l Blair's[13] also quartered in a planter's house. (The boat shakes so, it is scarcely possible to write legibly—but a pencil can be better managed).[14]

Janney, by the way, who has charge of the Young's Point Canal and employs several hundred contrabands, and who also employed a large number while Sherman's corps was at Memphis, speaks well of the negroes as industrious, disciplinable, grateful and docile. They have less vigor and endurance than whites, can not do as much hard work and seem generally to be of weak constitution. A remarkable proportion of them are deformed or mutilated, apparently from injuries in childhood. Nearly all bear the marks of injuries which they are unable to explain. You know that I have contended that the negro race in slavery was constantly growing in the mass less and less qualified for self dependence; the instinct of self-preservation being more and more worked out, and the habit of letting "master take care of his nigger" bred in to the race.[15] Janney believes that slave children while more precocious than white, suffer more from accidents than the children of the poor with us. The most valuable negroes, who are also, as a rule, the cleverest, have generally been taken away from the plantations by their owners, the least enterprising and those who would be most bewildered in trying to look out for themselves, and who are worth least for army purposes, being left as they are always told to "look after things" on the plantations. Wonderfully little it is they have to look after, however. A good many who are taken away, however, contrive to escape and return to the plantation or to their relatives and friends who follow the Union army. They often show strong attachments in this way, not to their owners but to localities and to their families. Among the company which was working under him at Memphis, Captain Janney said that there was one very active, sharp, industrious and faithful fellow, who had left a plantation about twenty miles off. Soon after his good qualities had attracted Janney's attention, his owner—a rank rebel, came as they often do, with complete assurance, to ask that he should be given up to him. Janney assured him that the country needed his services and it could not be thought of at present. Some weeks after this the same negro came one morning to Janney's tent and said: "Here's a right good fowling-piece, Captain, and I want to gib it to you."

"Where did you get it?"

"Got him ob my old massa, Sah."

"How is that? What did he give you his fowling piece for?"

"Did'n gib'm me, Sah; I took 'em."

"When?"

"Last night."

"Has your master been here again?"

"No Sah, I been down dar, to de old place, myself lass night, and I see de gun, dah, and I tort he was a rebel and he ortn't to be let hab a gun, and I ort to take 'em away, tort dat wus right, Captain, wasn't it? He ain't no business wid a gun, has he? Only to shoot our teamsters wid it."

"What sent you out there?"

"Well, I went dah, Sah, for to get my wife and chile dat was dah. I tried to get 'em nodder way but I was cheated, and I had to go myself."

"What other way did you try?"

"I'll tell ou, Sah; I want my wife and chile: dey was down dah on de ole plantation. Last Sunday when we'd got our pay, I seen a white man dat libs ober dah, and he tell me if I gib him my money he get my wife for me. I had thirty dollars Sah, and I gib it to him, but my wife did'n come. So I went myself. My wife, house servant, Sah, and I creep up to de house and look into de windah: de windah was open and I heah de ole man and de ole woman dere snorin in de corner, and I put my head in and dah I see de gun standing by de fi' place. I jumped rig[ht] in and cotch up de gun, and turn roun' and hold em so. Says I, 'Master, I want my wife.' 'You can take her,' says he, and he didn say another word, nor move a bit, nor Missis eider. My wife she heerd me, and she come down wid de chile and we just walk out ob de door; but I tort, I'd take de gun. He ain't no Union man and he ortn't to hab a gun, Captain. You'll take it, Sah, won't you?"

"Yes, I'll turn it in for you."

Returning to the Magnolia, we took tea with Gen'l Grant. He told me of the return of Admiral Porter and the failure of the "Sunflower" expedition. He said there seemed to be no way open to attack Vicksburg but by direct assault in front and an attempt to take it in this way would involve a frightful loss of life. He was obviously full of grave thought and concern and I avoided keeping his attention at all. He lives in the ladies' cabin of the boat, there is a sentry, or an apology for one, at the boat's gangway, but he stops no one from going on board, and there is free range in the cabin for anyone to and beyond the table, which the General, with others, writes upon, near the stern. He is more approachable and liable to interruptions than a merchant or lawyer generally allows himself to be in his office, and in my observation, citizens who had been allowed to come to the army to remove bodies of the dead for their friends; or on other pretexts, several times came in and introduced themselves to him; one man saying, "I hain't got no business with you, General, but I just wanted to have a little talk with you because folks will ask me if I did." The General had just received a number of Vicksburg papers by a deserter, which he invited me to look over. He was reading these and writing during most of the evening, while I was conversing with the gentlemen of the staff; when I rose to go, he got up and said: "I wish you would be in as much as convenient while you stay, I am not always as much occupied, as I am tonight, and whenever you see that I am not, understand that I shall be glad to talk with you." The next night I went in and had an hour's conversation with him. He is one of the most engaging men I ever saw. Small, quiet, gentle, modest—extremely, even uncomfortably, modest—frank, confiding and of an exceedingly kind disposition. He gives you the impression of a man of strong will, however, and of capacity, underlying these feminine traits. As a general, I should think his quality was that of quick common-sense judgments, unobstructed by prejudices, and deep abiding quiet resolution. He confided to me in a comic, plaintive, half humorous, half indignant way, the annoyances, obstructions, embarrassments and hindrances to which the Governors of the various Western states constantly subjected him, and keenly reviewed their various methods. The Governors of Iowa and Wisconsin[16] were moderate in their inflictions and seemed to have some appreciation of his situation. He must do them the credit to say that they were forbearing and thoroughly patriotic. The Governor of Illinois[17] was an amiable and weak man. He seemed to think it his business to help any citizen of Illinois to anything he wanted. "He must be in the habit of signing papers without reading them, and the quantities of letters he writes me urging me to grant favors to people who come here with them, is appalling. Favors too, which he ought to know that I have no right to grant—no more than you would have. It's very hard [on me], especially when he sends women here, to get favors for their sons. It's a pastime to face a battery compared with facing a woman begging for her son, you know. These letters from the Governor of Illinois being all open letters, are written in the most earnest tone of personal and official anxiety. "He could not be more in earnest if he were pleading for his own son. And yet there are so many of them, they can't mean anything. I've been expecting a letter from him to tell me that he did not want me to pay any attention to them. It's different with the Governor of Indiana.[18] He is perfectly cold-hearted. He seems to think, because I have some Indiana regiments, that he has a right to demand my assistance in any way he chooses, to carry out his state political arrangments. By the way, doctor,[19] there's a lady from _____ on the _____ which arrived this afternoon, who has a great many favors to ask. I've seen her; I can't see her again. You must answer her. It's easier for you to say no to a woman than 'tis for me. Some things she wants, can be granted; some can't; you'll see how it is, when you talk with her. But don't leave it necessary for me to see her again."[20]

I had some suggestions to make to the General; he heard me patiently, met me quickly, almost eagerly, adopted and advanced upon my views, allowed me to prepare a draft for an order in accordance with them, which next day he adopted adding one clinching sentence, and handed over to his adjutant General,[21] who at once gave it the form of an order, signed, copied, printed and issued it.[22] The openness of mind, directness, simplicity and rapidity of reasoning and clearness, with consequent confidence, of conclusion, of Gen[l] Grant is very delightful. Those about him become deeply attached to him. Towards Sherman there is more than attachment, something of veneration, universally expressed, most by those who know him most intimately, from which I suspect that he has more genius than Grant.

We spent one day chiefly among the iron-clads and gun-boats. Admiral Porter is a gentlemanly, straight forward and resolute sort of man. Breese[23] his flag-captain a smiling, cheerful and most obliging and agreeable man. He assumes friendship from the start, but, with all this, one gets an impression of strong will & great certainty that when the time comes for boarding or cutting out, he will bear his part with the same ingenuous ease and grace. Some of the new men of the navy whom we saw did not strike us so favorably. Scurvy was threatening the squadron and we put on 200 barrels of potatoes and onions on the flag-boat.

April 3[d]   Cairo.

We have just arrived here, all quite well.
Expect to go to St. Louis this evening.
Your affectionate Son,

Fred. Law Olmsted.

John Olmsted, Esq[r]
Hartford, C[t]

(Please send this to Washington.)

1. James Birdseye McPherson (1828–1864), a West Pointer and career army officer. Serving in the Western campaigns of the Civil War, he was promoted to major general after the battle of Corinth. In March 1863 he commanded the XVII Corps. A popular and capable officer, McPherson was killed during the Atlanta campaign (*DAB*).
2. Josiah Wolcott Bissell (b. 1818), colonel of the volunteer regiment known as Bissell's Missouri Engineers, had supervised construction of a canal that contributed to the Union capture of Island Number Ten (*Appleton's Cyc. Am. Biog.*).
3. A reference to the joint Union army-navy operations of February-March 1863 that sought alternative water routes by which to attack Vicksburg. By "Blackwater" Olmsted probably meant the Yazoo Pass expedition, which attempted to use an old inlet of the Mississippi River opposite Helena, Arkansas, as a route to the Yazoo River via the Coldwater and Tallahatchie rivers. The levee was cut on February 3, but obstructions in the channel prevented the gunboat expedition from entering Yazoo Pass until February 25. The delay allowed the Confederates to erect Fort Pemberton on the Tallahatchie near its confluence with the Yalobusha into the

Yazoo. Attempts by the Yazoo Pass expedition to subdue the fort in mid-March were unsuccessful. On March 17 the Union troops retreated and although reinforcements arrived, no further challenge was mounted. Although it did not return to base until early April, the expedition's effectiveness was ended by late March.

What Olmsted described as the "Sunflower" expedition was an attempt in mid-March to traverse the bayous near Vicksburg to the Sunflower and Yazoo rivers. Admiral David D. Porter commanded the expedition, and by March 19 his ironclads had met numerous obstructions near Deer Creek and were in danger of being cut off from their land support by the Confederates. Although Sherman's troops joined Porter's forces on March 21, the admiral believed their numbers insufficient. By March 28 his battered boats had returned to Young's Point (Fletcher Pratt, *Civil War on Western Waters* [New York, 1956], pp. 146–54; U.S. Department of the Navy, Naval History Division, *Civil War Naval Chronology, 1861–1865*, 5 vols. [Washington, D.C., 1961–65], 3: 22–54; John G. Milligan, *Gunboats down the Mississippi* [Annapolis, Md., 1965], pp. 130–41).

4. Parrott guns were cast-iron, muzzle-loading rifled cannons with reinforced breeches, designed by American inventor Robert Parker Parrott. Available in various calibers, the Parrott guns were frequently used by Union troops and were known for their durability (*DAB*).

5. William LeBaron Jenney (1832–1907), a Massachusetts native who studied at Phillips Andover Academy, Harvard's Lawrence Scientific School, and the Ecole Centrale des Arts et Manufactures in Paris. Enlisting in the army in August 1861, he served as an engineer on Grant's staff and became Sherman's chief engineer. In December 1865, as Jenney was preparing to resign from the army, he wrote to Olmsted requesting his aid in securing work in New York on either Central Park or what would become Prospect Park in Brooklyn. Jenney desired a position that would combine his interests in architecture, gardening, and engineering. Although Olmsted encouraged Jenney and requested more information about his engineering experience, he apparently was not able to offer a suitable post. After the war Jenney moved to Chicago, where he worked as an architect, engineer, and landscape architect. In 1883 he designed the Home Insurance Building in Chicago and pioneered the principle of skeleton construction central to the erection of skyscrapers. Jenney also designed numerous houses and commercial buildings in Riverside, the planned community laid out by Olmsted and Vaux near Chicago. In the 1870s he drew up plans for the West Parks in Chicago (*DAB*; W. L. B. Jenney to FLO, Dec. 2 and Dec. 16, 1865; Theodore Turak, "William LeBaron Jenney: Pioneer of Chicago's West Parks," *Inland Architect* 25 [March 1981]: 38–45).

6. A reference to the subjects covered in Olmsted and Jenney's discussion of Paris. Olmsted knew and admired Christopher Pearse Cranch (1813–1892), a Unitarian minister, poet, painter, and critic, who lived in Paris from 1853 until 1863. Fontainebleau, a small town approximately forty miles southeast of Paris, is known for its large, beautiful forest and for its royal palace, erected by Francis I and enlarged and renovated by his successors, including Napoleon I and Napoleon III. The Louvre is the national art museum of France, which Olmsted had visited during a European journey. The schools mentioned were two of the prestigious *grandes écoles* of France. The renowned Ecole Polytechnique, founded in 1794, prepared young men for public service and educated the governing elite of France. The Ecole Centrale des Arts et Manufactures, founded in 1829, taught "industrial science" and trained engineers, producing approximately three thousand during its first forty years (*Papers of FLO*, 2: 341–42, 345–46; Antoine Prost, *Histoire de l'enseignement en France, 1800–1967* [Paris, 1968], pp. 224, 300–304).

7. The U.S.S. *Hartford* was the flagship of David Glasgow Farragut (1801–1870), rear admiral of the U.S. Navy and commander of the expedition that had captured New Orleans in 1862 (*DAB*).

8. Richard Taylor (1826–1879), Confederate major general and commander of the District of West Louisiana. In 1853, during his first journey in the South, Olmsted had visited Taylor's sugar plantation, Fashion, twenty miles west of New Orleans. Taylor, the son of former president Zachary Taylor, was originally a Whig, but became a Democrat during the 1850s and was elected to the Louisiana state senate. He was a delegate to the state's secession convention in 1861 and voted for secession. During the war, Taylor served in the East until he received the command in Louisiana in July 1862 (*DAB*; Jackson Beauregard Davis, "The Life of Richard Taylor," *Louisiana Historical Quarterly* 24 [Jan. 1941]: 52–61; *Papers of FLO*, 2: 213, 214).

9. Charles McMillan (c. 1825–1890), who joined the 71st Regiment, New York State Militia, in April 1861 and was appointed major and surgeon in the summer of 1861. He served in the army until October 1865 (Frederick Phisterer, comp., *New York in the War of the Rebellion, 1861–1865*, 3rd ed., 6 vols. [Albany, N.Y., 1912], 1: 690–91, 696; F. B. Heitman, *Historical Register and Dictionary*, 1: 677).

10. George Stoneman (1822–1894) was chief of cavalry of the Army of the Potomac and also commanded a division under McClellan (*DAB*).

11. Apparently a correspondent for the *New York Herald* had criticized McMillan's care of the wounded after the assault on Chickasaw Bluffs, Mississippi, produced almost eighteen hundred Union casualties on December 29, 1862 (F. H. Dyer, *Compendium of the War of the Rebellion*, 2: 775).

12. Frederick Steele (1819–1868), a West Point graduate and career army officer who had fought in the Mexican War. After serving in Missouri and Arkansas, he was promoted to major general of volunteers in November 1862 (*DAB*).

13. Francis P. Blair, Jr., resigned from the U.S. House of Representatives in July 1862 to join the Union army. He was reelected to Congress that fall but did not leave the army to take his seat until January 1864. During the Vicksburg campaign, Blair was promoted to major general (*DAB*; Elbert B. Smith, *Francis Preston Blair* [New York, 1980], pp. 334–35).

14. Olmsted wrote this sentence and the remainder of the letter in pencil.

15. Perhaps Olmsted's clearest statement of his belief in the debilitating effect of slavery on blacks appeared in his "The South" series of newspaper letters published by the *New-York Daily Times*. In one of them he contended:

> *The mind and higher faculties of the negro are less disciplined and improved in slavery than in the original barbarism of the race*, because in the latter state he has at least to exercise them under the necessity of contriving to procure food, raiment, and habitation; in providing for his offspring, in the consequently necessary acquisition of property, exciting cautious enterprise, having reference to the chances of the future, and in the defence of personal liberty. I do not believe there is a body of men in the world that have so stupid, unmanly, and animal an existence as the *rank and file plantation negroes* of our Southern States. (Frederick Law Olmsted, "The South" no. 26, June 21, 1853 [*Papers of FLO*, 2: 166].)

16. Samuel Jordan Kirkwood (1813–1894), a Republican who served as governor of Iowa from 1860 to 1864; and Edward Salomon (1828–1909), a Prussian emigrant who succeeded to the gubernatorial office in Wisconsin after the accidental drowning of Governor Harvey in 1862 (R. Sobel and J. Raimo, *Biographical Directory of the Governors*, 2: 432–33, 4: 1725–26).

17. Richard Yates (1818–1873), a Republican and a loyal supporter of Lincoln, was governor of Illinois from 1861 until 1865. Yates later served in the U.S. Senate (ibid., 1: 374).

18. Oliver Perry Morton (1823–1877), governor of Indiana from 1861 until 1867, one of

the organizers of the Republican party there, and U.S. senator from 1867 until his death (ibid., 1: 405; *DAB*).

19. That is, Henry Stewart Hewit, medical director of Grant's army (see "Journey in the West, Memphis to Young's Point," March 18–24, 1863, n. 31, above).

20. In 1868 when Grant was being considered as a candidate for the presidency, his drinking habits became an issue. Olmsted, in an open letter to the *Nation*, defended him and gave an account of his first meeting with Grant in 1863 which is slightly different and far more detailed than that presented here. According to Olmsted, Grant had been reviewing the progress of the Vicksburg campaign for him and Knapp when they were suddenly interrupted:

> A moment before we could not have imagined that there was a woman within many miles of us; but, turning my eyes, I saw one who had just parted the screen, comely, well-dressed, and with the air and manner of a gentlewoman. She had just arrived by a steamboat from Memphis, and came to present General Grant with a memorial or petition. In a few words she made known her purpose, and offered to give in detail certain facts, of which she stated that she was cognizant, bearing upon her object. The General stood listening to her in an attitude of the most deferential attention, his hand still upon his chair, which was half in front of him as he had turned to face her, and slightly nodding his head as an expression of assent at almost every sentence she uttered. When she had completed her statement, he said, speaking very low, and with an appearance of reluctance: "I shall be compelled to consult my medical director, and to obtain a report from him before I can meet your wishes. If agreeable to you, I will ask him to call upon you to-morrow; shall I say at eleven o'clock?" The lady bowed and withdrew; the General took a long breath, resumed his cigar and his seat, said that he was inclined to think her proposition a reasonable and humane one, and then went on with the interrupted review.

Olmsted then described a meeting between Knapp and the lady a week or so later "upriver." When he contradicted her assertion that a man of Grant's "deplorable habits" should not command an army,

> she then described her recent interview with General Grant, and it appeared that, from her point of view, the General was engaged in a carouse with one or two boon companions when she came unexpectedly upon him; that he rose to his feet with difficulty, could not stand without staggering, and was obliged to support himself with a chair; that he was evidently conscious that he was in an unfit condition to attend to business, and wanted to put her off till the next day; that his voice was thick, he spoke incoherently, and she was so much shocked that she was obliged to withdraw almost immediately. The next day, being ashamed to see her himself, he sent his doctor to find out what she wanted.
>
> Mr. Knapp then told her that, having been one of the boon companions whom she had observed with the General on that occasion, and that having dined with him and been face to face with him for fully three hours, he not only knew that he was under the influence of no drink stronger than the unqualified mud of the Mississippi, but he could assure her that he had never seen a man who appeared to him more thoroughly sober and clear-headed than General Grant at the moment of her entrance.
>
> Notwithstanding his assurances, the lady repeated that she could not doubt the evidence of her own senses, and I suppose that to this day Mr. Knapp and myself rank, equally with General Grant, in her mind as confirmed drunkards.

(Frederick Law Olmsted, "The Genesis of a Rumor," *Nation*, April 23, 1868, pp. 329–30.)

21. John Aaron Rawlins (1831–1869), assistant adjutant-general, issued the order. A successful lawyer and Grant's neighbor in Galena, Illinois, he became the latter's intimate friend while serving on his staff during the Civil War. Grant sometimes drank to excess during periods of loneliness and depression, but Rawlins convinced him to give up alcoholic beverages. During the Civil War, Grant's few binges of drinking seem to have occurred during Rawlins's absence. Rawlins served as secretary of war during Grant's presidency (*DAB*; William S. McFeely, *Grant: A Biography* [New York, 1981], pp. 84–87, 133–36).

22. A reference to a discussion with Grant about the transportation of donated supplies to soldiers in the Mississippi River valley and to the special order issued at Olmsted's recommendation. The "clinching sentence" which Grant added was probably the concluding one: "All orders from these headquarters authorizing the free transportation of sanitary stores from Cairo south on boats other than the one herein assigned for that exclusive purpose are hereby rescinded." Apparently Grant mistakenly believed that the Western Sanitary Commission possessed its own independent transportation. When the Western Commission protested this order, Olmsted asked Grant to modify it (FLO to U. S. Grant, April 21, 1863; see "Journey in the West, Memphis to Young's Point," March 18–24, 1863, n. 10, above).

23. Kidder Randolph Breese (1831–1881) participated in the Mississippi River expeditions of 1862 and was promoted that July to lieutenant commander. In 1863 he commanded the flagship *Black Hawk* in Porter's squadron (*DAB*).

To Edwin Lawrence Godkin[1]

St. Louis, Mo.   April 4th 1863

My Dear Godkin,

I arrived here this morning just a week from Young's Point, leaving there as the Sunflower expedition was returning, the boats all looking as if they had been through a terrible hurricane. I went near enough to Vicsburg to see the guns and sentries, and darkies still throwing earth on the fortifications. I saw a good deal of Grant & Sherman's staff and conversed with Grant and with Admiral Porter, also with Gen'l Hurlbert, Genl Blair, and Gen Steele, and Gen'l Webster. I got no facts from any of them which are not public, I presume, but putting what I saw and heard together, I formed some judgments not agreeing with the public's ideas. I could not get any solid ground whatever for the general confidence that we should be in Vicksburg in three to thirty days, that the enemy were evacuating V. &c. &c. I believe Vicsburg to be impregnable from the river side. I do not believe that Grant ever expected to accomplish much by the canal—or canals—and I do not believe that he now expects to take Vicksburg from the river. I expect to see Farragut's two vessels in some way strengthened and supported;[2] a post established with a garrison of a few thousand men in observation of Vicsburg, and some sort of semi aquatic force—possibly a musquito fleet able to work till last of June through the crevasses into streams running into Red River, the whole answering the purpose of keeping a respectable force of the enemy in men, artillery and garrison stores for a siege employed on the defences from above Vicsburg to Port Hudson, and cutting off supplies and hindering communications from the West.

Both Grant & Porter looked to me like disappointed and anxious men, at a loss what to do. It will surprise me to find that my instinct in this respect was at fault. Yet if it were not for this, I should be inclined to think that Grant never had counted upon getting into Vicksburg at this time, from the river, but had always expected in due time to suddenly bring his army up the river again. He has at this moment a larger number of light-draft stern-wheel boats than ever before, more this week than last. This all looks as if he intended to continue operations in the Yazoo country. There is but one move that way that does not look to me impracticable—Look at the map—I mean a move on Grenada. That might do. South of that, I hardly think that anything could be done. It is possible they may hit upon some plan of a combined attack from the South side, but the water is over all the country up to the bluffs, and the bluffs are lined with entrenchments. It is wooded (swamp) below the bluffs so there is no navigation.

I expect to see Grant's army back at Corinth on the whole and I do not think his operations before Vicksburgh will have been a waste of time. The fact is it is a very tough job and if he has succeeded in cutting off supplies permanently from the West, he has made half his siege.

But I have been thinking of another operation: whether that old rascal Halleck[3] has thought of it before, judge you. I could never see yet, what his brains were doing except blundering and bullying. Look at our situation at the West. One strong army at Murfreesboro', soon to be dependent on maintaining a long line of rail-road with many bridges through a hostile population; then no force of consequence till you reach the Potomac on the right and Vicsburg on the left. There are three small rattle-trap gun-boats on the Tennessee, I believe. Land-forces lately withdrawn & sent to Helena & below, leaving only a few weak garrisons north of Corinth. Ashboth[4] is at Columbus with a few regiments of raw infantry; no cavalry and I saw recruiting bills and Confederate Conscript Notices which had been taken down from houses a few miles from him. On the triangle of Corinth, Jackson (Tenn.), Memphis, there is the best part of a corps; a good defensive force. Then we string along down the river. Where does the enemy need to be strong to resist us. We threaten him at two points West of Richmond only. Tullahoma (Chattanooga)[5] and Vicsburg. He is strongly fortified at both points. Ten or twenty thousand men will leave Vicsburg perfectly secure against any attack of the force on the river, (while on the river). Is there not thus offered to the enemy a great inducement to make a bold push into Kentucky—perhaps into Ohio or Illinois? It is a favored policy and he might be forced into it by popular outcry. How should we be situated if he attempted it? Rosecrans, when I was at Murfreesboro a month ago, was well advanced with two very large works. I take it, he has by this time two strongly entrenched camps with stores which would keep his army some weeks, if the enemy got in his rear. The same is the case, I believe at Corinth where we have been adding to and strengthening the works during the winter.

Rosecrans' army consists mainly of the best marching men. So large a force was never before so mobile. If the enemy is forc'd to a grand invasion of Kentucky as a desperate move, Rosecrans is in a position to go at him in flank and rear, neglecting his communications till a great battle is fought with his veterans, the newer troops holding the dépôt at Murfrees-boro', and Grant is in a position to move simultaneously from his present positions by way of Corinth, either upon Tullahoma or the rear of Vicks-burg. The enemy will be sure to have left one or the other, or both, with a much weaker force than they otherwise would have. Looking over the ground again with this idea, I see that Grant's force is disposed thus; 1st a strong garrison at Corinth; 2d a strong rail-road guard and (to be) rear guard at Jackson, Tenn. and Memphis. 3d an advance-guard ready to move, now at Memphis; 4th a division at Helena with transportation to Memphis by boat and to Corinth by rail, reaching there as soon as the (3d) can be moved out from there. 5th a corps now in small boats apparently for operations in the Yazoo swamps, but which could be got to Memphis as soon as (4) could be got out of the way. 6th another corps at least, probably more, (to be spared from "before Vicksburg") which could be steamed up to Memphis by the time 5 was sailed away. Thus he has it in his power to move in strong force from Corinth, within a much shorter space of time than could, without consideration of all these facts, be reasonably antici-pated. Looking at the detail I find it favorable to such a movement. The dépôts &c. are all right for it as far as I can see.

In Grant, Sherman & Rosecrans, we have three who may well be great Generals. I suspect that Sherman has the most genius. Grant is, par excellence, a *gentleman*, a modest, good hearted, self-sacrificing, resolute common-sense gentleman. In whatever you write, treat Grant with great respect. He seems to me to have a poor staff. Sherman, relatively, as a corps-commander, a better one; McPherson can be depended upon, and his corps is in the highest condition. McClernand is a miserable, squab-bling, mean intriguing politician; flay him alive at the first chance. You can't do him wrong, on the whole. Steele is just a first rate steady fighting man; no general except for a division in a corps. Hurlbert promises better than I had been led to suppose. He manages at any rate to have his force well-taken care of and well-disciplined, and he is quick and decisive in intellect.

Rosecrans is quick of comprehension, fertile & quick in expedients; not, I think, a deep plotter and arranger, but excellent—none better in the midst of active operations. His head holds calmly a great deal of stir, the thicker and faster it comes, the clearer & more decisive he is. He is ambitious; over confident; enthusiastic, vain, religious and healthily patriotic and angry with rebels. He is the only General I have seen in the West who fights with this sort of religious enthusiasm in his cause. Jeff C. Davis is first rate in his place, but fit for nothing larger. He is a full blooded Copperhead.

Both armies are in the finest conceivable moral and physical condition. They are well clothed, well-shod, well-armed and are living like fighting cocks. They want for nothing in these respects. Parts of them are really well-disciplined. The mass is not, but is improving—poor officers gradually working out, and, on the whole, good officers working into the higher places, though there are too many exceptions. The Generals suffer more than those at the East from the state-politicians—Governors especially—Grant is, in his good nature, nearly driven crazy by them. "The lobby" is as regularly a part of the Western Armies, as it is of Congress and the Legislatures. Governors and governors' personal friends, appointed to do something for Governors' regiments, can't be forced out. You see what Fremont caught by trying it.[6] Oh, no, it wouldn't be democratic—it certainly wouldn't be Western, if a General should shut himself up. He must treat everybody civilly and not attempt to be exclusive. Apparently there's no help for it. There is no guard—nothing when you are once in the post lines, to prevent you, Tom, Dick, & Harry, from going right into the General's inner office, among his maps & papers, and holding him for an hour by the button, telling him what you think about the advantage of getting your son made a captain or Brig. General. Even women do it, I have seen them, before Vicsburg. How do they get there? Somebody asks somebody to ask the Governor to help them and he must do it, or take the consequences. The Governors can't pass, but can request passes—if necessary can request them from Secy of War, & get their requests backed by Senators; and in various ways can make Generals suffer if their requests are not regarded.

It is the state organizations, the state appointments, and the fear of offending state governments, at Washington, that stands in the way of our making our army what it needs to be, more than anything else.

I leave for Chicago, on the 6th and expect to reach Washington on the 15th.

I am ready to go into a paper with you at a month's notice, whenever you call.[7]

With kind regards to your wife,[8]
Yours faithfully

Fred. Law Olmsted.

E. L. Godkin, Esq[r]

I think that Grant, Sherman & Hurlbert all believe in fighting negroes—but the Army is unquestionably very strongly against it, violently so.[9] The army is excessivly over-confident in itself & contemptuous of the enemy. They all want to assault Vicksburg from the river.

The original is in the Edwin Lawrence Godkin Papers, Houghton Library, Harvard University, Cambridge, Massachusetts. Olmsted wrote this letter on Sanitary Commission stationery bearing the address of the central office in Washington, but that heading is not reproduced here.

1. At the time this letter was written, Edwin L. Godkin was a special correspondent of the *London Daily News* and also wrote for the *New-York Daily Times*. In this letter and the two written from Gettysburg in July, Olmsted sought to provide information for articles (William M. Armstrong, *E. L. Godkin: A Biography* [Albany, N.Y., 1978], p. 62; see also FLO to Edwin L. Godkin, July 15 and July 19, 1863, below).
2. In mid-March 1863 David Glasgow Farragut ran the *Hartford*, and its gunboat, the *Albatross*, up the Mississippi River past the batteries at Port Hudson and Grand Gulf and anchored them at Warrenton. Farragut then returned downriver to blockade the entrance to the Red River. Olmsted's reference to a mosquito fleet meant a group of comparatively small vessels (U.S. Department of the Navy, Naval History Division, *Civil War Naval Chronology*, 3: 48–49).
3. Henry W. Halleck, general-in-chief of the U.S. Army, was familiarly known as "Old Brains" (*DAB*).
4. Alexander Sandor Asboth (1811–1868), a civil engineer and Hungarian soldier exiled with Lajos Kossuth. A friend of Olmsted, Asboth had worked in 1860 with the firm Olmsted & Vaux to survey the area north of 155th Street in Manhattan for a state-appointed commission empowered to lay out the street system of that area. In 1861 Asboth had joined the Union army and had been promoted to brigadier general of volunteers after his service in the battle of Pea Ridge in 1862. He commanded at Columbus, Kentucky, in 1863 (*DAB*; *Papers of FLO*, 3: 256–57; A. S. Asboth to MPO, Aug. 17, 1860).
5. Tullahoma, Tennessee, lay on the Nashville and Chattanooga Railroad line, approximately sixty miles northwest of Chattanooga. After Confederate general Braxton Bragg retreated from Murfreesboro, he made his headquarters at Tullahoma until forced out in late June 1863 (Thomas Lawrence Connelly, *Army of the Heartland: The Army of Tennessee, 1861–1862* [Baton Rouge, La., 1967], pp. 80, 85).
6. John Charles Frémont lost his post as commander of the Department of the West in October 1861. Although Lincoln had several reasons for removing Frémont, Olmsted here is referring to the problems caused by the general's disagreements with the politically powerful Blair family over the awarding of contracts and military appointments in Missouri (*War for the Union*, 1: 324–27; see FLO to CLB, Nov. 8, 1861, n. 13, above).

7. The paper project that, after several false starts, became the *Nation*, under the editorship of Godkin in 1865.
8. Frances Elizabeth Foote Godkin (1837–1875) of New Haven, Connecticut, had married Edwin L. Godkin in 1859 (*Papers of FLO*, 3: 83).
9. Although the Lincoln administration had earlier withheld official approval of blacks as soldiers, by 1863 it had come to favor the recruitment and use of Negro troops. Olmsted was probably correct that Grant, Sherman, and Hurlbut were willing to use black soldiers in April 1863. Neither Sherman nor Grant was, however, in the vanguard of that effort. Sherman has been called the commander least sympathetic to blacks as soldiers. Although Grant in February 1863 had excluded blacks from the area occupied by his troops, a rebuke from Halleck changed his conduct. A general order issued by Grant in April called for his commanders to aid not only in organizing black regiments but also in "removing prejudice against them" (Dudley Taylor Cornish, *The Sable Arm: Negro Troops in the Union Army, 1861–1865* [New York, 1956], pp. 121–23, 174).

JOURNEY IN THE WEST

Spring 1863

St. Louis, Chicago

St Louis.
[April 4–11, 1863]

In the general street aspect of St Louis there is nothing peculiarly Western. It is substantially built—more so than most Eastern towns—more so than New York on an average. There are few buildings of notable character, many which are respectable. The same is true of the town socially, I judge. We dined one day at a small villa.[1] The people—well-bred and neither genteel nor stylish—were chiefly of Southern birth and of modified Southern manners. I should probably have said Western, if I had not become familiar with those which are Southern. The wines were nearly the same as at a Charleston dinner of similar scale, the talk about them was a playfully held but natural remnant of the serious Charleston habit of wine-talk.[2] There were some good paintings and an exquisite small statue by an Italian sculptor; the grounds had a plantation rudeness, inequality of keeping and untidiness. The family, hot and strong Unionists, hating the rebels and zealous with newly emancipated repugnance to Slavery, had nevertheless an obvious, though unconfessed and probably unconscious pride in being Southern. But this they would, if it had been demonstrated to them, have themselves regarded as a weakness, possibly; what they never thought of concealing or suppressing or restraining from its utmost outpouring was their satisfaction in being St Louisians. No subject was talked of that did not give occasion for some new method, (always used confidently and with certainty that it was kindness to do so) for trumpeting St Louis. It was the same with every man & woman we met in St Louis. The devout dwellers in Mecca do not worship the holy city more than every child of St Louis, his city. It happened that I was enough interested to enjoy this. It was what I wanted. And the most notable thing I learned of St Louis was the pleasure of the people to talk about it—what it had been, what it would be.

The two things which interested me most, after the poorly contrived barracks of immense extent,[3] and the military hospitals,[4] were the Mercantile Library[5] and the Botanic gardens of Mr. _____[6] promised by him to be given at his death to the city. The Botanic Garden greatly disappointed me—simply because I had sometime before read an account of it in the Western advertising style in which it was magnified by adjective force, many hundredfold. It's a very noble affair for Mr _____ a man who came here from England, poor & who has been working very hard for the best part of a long life to be able to be munificent, but it's a dwarfish & paltry affair for a town like St Louis and with its prospects. The next generation will be by no means satisfied, I hope, with such a baby-house sort of public garden. I doubt not the plan will have been simplified a great deal before you see it. Mr. _____, it is said, has lately proposed to enlarge his gift by presenting the city with ground for a park.[7] There are several hundred acres of land in his possession about the Botanic garden, having at present a majestic simplicity of surface. A park of noble breadth and delicious repose of character could be made here. Such a gift would be of ten thousand times the value of the garden, even for educational purposes.

There is a danger that the bad qualities of the New York Central Park, growing out of natural limitations of the site not to be overcome, will lead to a fashion of cheap park-planning, in which a sentiment will reign the reverse of that which is characteristic of nature on the continent and of that which, except for fashion, would be most agreeable to the people.[8] The craving, and incoherent cry of the people of St Louis even now for a pleasure-ground and for rural-recreations is to be detected in various ways, most demonstratedly to the capitalist by the experience of a company who lately established in the suburbs an Agricultural Fair-Ground. On the occasions when it has been open to the public, on payment of admission fees, more than forty thousand persons a day have visited it; on one day, when the Prince of Wales took part in the performances, above eighty thousand.[9] This number was pretty well established, I was told, though in part only by the admission-fees, the gates and fences having been carried away in the press. One of the treasured utterances of the Prince on the occasion, after having been cheered by several acres of close packed men, was: "I suppose there are more than a thousand people here." At least thirty thousand must have been looking him in the face at that moment, it is said. The investment of the company in the grounds, buildings and otherwise is supposed to be about one hundred thousand dollars; its receipts during a cattle-show and agricultural festival of one week have been sufficient to justify a prize-list of twenty thousand dollars. This for the sake of amusement, not for acquisition of valuable information or other hope of pecuniary return. And this in a town west of the Mississippi, nearly one third of the population of which have been brought across the Atlantic from Germany, as steerage-passengers,[10] and every man in which, of the rich as well as the poor, seems enslaved to a habit of incessant activity and labor to enlarge the supply, at St Louis, of the material wants of men. The tide of commerce incessantly flows through every man's brain. You perceive it as strongly in those of the quieter callings—the teachers, preachers, physicians, as in others. All are busy with the foundation-laying of civilization. Some stones for the super-structure are being set but they are so let in to the foundations that the sense of commercial speculation is never wholly lost.

Out of domestic life, the Mercantile Library was the most respectable matter that I came in contact with in St. Louis. A very large hall with a goodly number of men and women, boys and girls, reading books, and looking at statues and paintings. These were not all very good, but enough to feed that part of a man's nature through which works of art do him good, better than one man in a million is fed by unassociated reachings out for such aliment. Even the Mercantile Library, however, is mercantile and, as I inferred from some account of its rent transactions, would hardly exist—certainly would not be what it is—had not the plan for it possessed a certain element of good trading. I think it was, in some way or other, apropos of the Mercantile Library that a gentleman said to me: "People here like very much to associate all their benevolence with business. Almost any benevolent enterprise will be taken hold of liberally here, if you can show that it carries a business advantage to our city with it. We are all very fond of feeling that we are driving business and philanthropy harnessed together in the same team." An enormous building designed for a hotel but not occupied, was pointed out to us.

"Why is it not occupied?"

"It really is not needed as a hotel. It would not pay expenses, I suppose, if it were opened, now."

"Why was it built then?"

"The capital was supplied for it by the property owners in this part of the city because they thought it would have a favorable influence upon the value of property. They have in effect, for this reason, given a bonus of several hundred thousand dollars in order to get the finest hotel in the city established where it will help to bring their lots and buildings more into public view. That is a kind of advertising which is very much resorted to here. Our churches are built, in that way, a great deal."

I was glad to notice that the public schools were an object of pride with the citizens. The buildings are large. I did not enter them nor meet any of the teachers.

In passing through a part of the town occupied almost exclusively by Germans, on a warm Sunday when the windows were generally open, I noticed much new and smart furniture and that the women were nearly all smartly dressed. I saw no squalid poverty except among negroes & fugitives from the seat of war, I did not see a beggar in St. Louis. I do not recollect that I saw a policeman, though I did more than once see and experience the need of one. It is certainly from no action of the law or good regulations or public provision for paupers that no beggar & so little poverty is seen. Yet St Louis, it is generally supposed, suffers much more than any other considerable town out of the rebel states from the war. Its growth had been recently very rapid until it was arrested by the war. I asked an old resident,[11] distinguished for his interest in the poor & needy, and who had been a mayor of the city, "How generally have poor, laboring men and families been found, in your observation, to improve their condition, after they have moved to St Louis?"

He answered, "invariably," meaning, no doubt, that any exceptions were of a plainly accidental character.

"Can you see that the children of those who came here longest ago are now generally fit for higher social duties and of a higher rank as men than their fathers?"

"Universally so; with the Germans especially; they become Americans, with all the American characteristics."

There are probably a larger number of men of what would be considered moderate wealth in the middle class of England, in St Louis, than in any town of its size in Europe. I asked my friend, the ex-mayor, "How many of these came to St Louis comparatively poor men?"

"There is scarcely one that did not begin here by sweeping out his employer's store or office, and that is true of most of our very wealthiest men also—our bankers and capitalists. We nearly all began here with nothing but our heads and hands."

This being the case it is really more marvelous how well the people live within their own houses than how very poorly they live out of their own houses.

In going from St Louis to Chicago, we had to cross the Mississippi in a steam ferry-boat, and this was our leave-taking of the Mississippi and its steamboat business. There are two lines of railroad to Chicago. In purchasing tickets for one of them, we were assured that the train upon it would reach Chicago two hours sooner than that leaving at the same hour by the other road, and this statement was confirmed by a gentleman who appeared to be accidentally present, and who said that he had often travelled by both roads. We should have chosen the road we did all the same, if the exact truth had been told us, which was that we should be two hours longer upon it than upon the other. The usual method was practiced of causing a panic among the passengers leaving the hotel in an omnibus, by an appearance of great impatience over the last man to come out and of reckless haste in driving, so that all but the very old travellers were greatly relieved when it was ascertained that the ferry-boat for the train had not left. On that ferry-boat however, we remained at the hither landing three quarters of an hour, being detained twenty minutes past the proper time of starting by the arrival of a large herd of swine. Swine are hard to drive upon a ferry-boat. Sometimes when they were coming nicely, slowly and methodically over the gang-plank, it would seem as if instantaneously the devil entered into all of them, their heads were reversed and they were leaping frantically away from the boat. The dropping of a gate in the boat's rail prevented those already on board from taking part in this stampede, but nothing could stop those outside till they found themselves on the other side of their drivers, when they would, for the most part, stop and stand quietly till the cordon was again drawn round them. The last of these stampedes occurred at the moment when all but two of the hogs had been got inside of the gate. One stopped as usual and was brought back; the other, finding himself alone, after doubling two or three times, took an up-river course and ran straight out of sight. To my surprise, the captain refused to wait for him and so the Great Eastern Mail and passengers for "Chicago, Cincinnati and the East," were generously allowed to leave St Louis, only twenty minutes behind time. I am sorry to say that the trains waited for them. Fare thee well, Father of Waters, who art also Father of Lies to us. May thy tide be[12] clearer and less eddying to my friend, the student of the next century.

We visited in succession after St Louis, Chicago, Cincinnati (again), Cleaveland and Buffalo[13]—all cities of the West, though Buffalo is in an Atlantic state, and all having certain grand characteristics in common. Of these, unquestionably the most noteworthy is the great number of pleasing, detached family residences. Cleaveland, the smallest of the five towns, having a population of 70,000(?),[14] has been built the most deliberately and is most remarkable in this respect. Buffalo but little less so, Cincinnati least. I believe that every family that is fairly at home in this town (Cleaveland)[15]—a town as large as _____, lives in its own separate house and has its own trees or plants. I did not see a block of buildings, except for warehouses and shops. We drove out on one street a mile and then back on another; every house on both was a villa, in a garden, and every one looked comfortable, as if inhabited by a fore-handed man, with a family of sociable habits and some impulses of taste.

Among them all there was not one that would fairly rank as a mansion in England or a chateau in France, but there were many that were really fine small family houses, well designed architecturally of beautifully-tinted lime-stone, and of faithful construction. Euclid Street in Cleaveland is a much finer street than Fifth Avenue. It is a thousand-fold more a distinctively American sight. There is a great deal of real elegance and some respectable magnificence on Fifth Avenue, but Euclid Street displays, on an average (though there are some instances of the following of ridiculous fashions), on the whole, better architecture and better taste in all respects. There is comparatively little that is atrociously bad—less than you would find attending as many villas about London. There is a prettier flower garden and a prettier fernery on Euclid Street than is to be found, to my knowledge, on New York island. That which gratified me most of all at Cleaveland, I am not at liberty to describe. It was a social exposition which would not have suggested to Mr Russell's mind, the reflections to which the reception at the house of Monsieur B. of Fifth Avenue, gave rise,—not even those upon the prettyness of the women.[16] I am sure that I saw as *fine*-looking a woman in Cleaveland as ever I saw in London. And I met with evidence of a cheerful, quiet, deep, patient religious patriotism in certain women of Cleaveland which placed more, under the circumstances, to the credit of American women than would suffice to balance many sins of the rich, silly & incompetent competitors with aristocratic magnificence who so readily come under the observation of English travellers.

I have thus told of Cleaveland because I saw more there in one day of what seemed to me to be purely American in character,—American, without being local, provincial, Eastern or Western, rich or poor, and American without savor of modern foreign influences but of that which exhibited American dispositions and taste developed with unusual freedom and luxuriance, than I have ever seen in any other considerable town. I saw matters which I might ridicule or criticise, communal matters especially, which showed that gentlemen were scarcer than gentlewomen in Cleaveland, but these were not as distinct as the same class of matters elsewhere, and I shall take other illustrations of them as showing national defects of character.

There is too much of the Aladdin's lamp character about the town of Chicago, for me to speak of it analytically. Driven rapidly through a broad street to my hotel—a street lined with grand houses of marble or a stone of greater beauty and equal splendor—in gaslight, I had a sensation when I first entered the town almost like that of first passing at night through the boulevard l'Italien.[17] The next day, standing in this street, a middle-aged gentleman[18] said: "When I first brought my family here to live, there was not a human sign to be seen looking inland from where we now stand, except a few deep-worn Indian trails parting the prairie-grass." There were now, literally, miles of buildings stretching out in that direction.

It seems useless to describe Chicago. What it was when I saw it, it will not be by the time this is read. They are hardly beginning except in a few streets, even to lay the foundations of the future town. Many hundred houses are building today, in the midst of the war, but the most of them are of wood, handy to tear down or move away, as the owners become richer and have capital to put into stone and brick. But although temporary and slightly built houses for the most part, the same general characteristics prevail in them, as in the dwellings of Cleaveland. That they are on an average smaller and less strikingly comfortable, is readily accounted for by the more deliberate building of the slower-growing city. Half the present population of Chicago came to it "looking for a job of work," within ten? years. It can hardly be considered to have as yet a fixed population, so lately was the greater part of it adrift. Seldom, nevertheless—doubtful if ever—has a town's population been so firmly anchored to the ground as that of Chicago. There are scarcely any rented houses or house-lots. Every man owns that whereon and wherein he lives.[19]

Everybody believes that the town is to continue enlarging. "We do a larger corn and pork business today than is done in any other town in the world, and yet for want of facilities for handling it and carrying it from these prairies which have really but just begun to be cultivated, millions of acres [are] lying untouched—thousands of bushels of corn of last year's crop still remain behind. Thousands of bushels have indeed actually been used for fuel this year, being cheaper than coal, although coal can be dug out on most farms from within six feet of the surface. Chicago must soon double again."

It is sad to see with how little forethought the town is nevertheless suffered to enlarge. It is only a multiplication of parallelograms upon a flat surface. "Outside his own house, no man thinks of anything but his private business" it is said. It is not strictly true, as the history of the war will show, but also it is confessed that good impulses, hastily and carelessly followed, have sometimes led to results not altogether desirable or honorable to the town, even in its war business. The demand for talent in making the enormous exchanges required by commerce to be effected at Chicago, is in fact so constantly beyond the supply, that no valuable exercise of judgment can be spared to anything else.

Individuals are found making some attempt to resist the tide, but such attempts do not affect the community. In all affairs of the community, you see evidence of inconsiderateness and temporizing, make-shift expediency. A gentleman was solicited to be a candidate for the mayoralty of the town. He laughed at the supposition that he could find time from more important business for attending to the mayor's duties. Almost anybody could manage the mayor's office. A bad man would let the taxes be increased a good deal while a good manager might continue to improve the condition of the town without increasing them. But what would the difference amount to when distributed among all this prosperous community? A few dollars more or less in taxes, a little more dust and mud, an infinitesimal variation in insurance dividends, etc. That is all the difference which would be felt by most men. Look now at the thousands of comfortable dwellings which men have built for their families here within a few years. Consider that these men came here for the most part, poor, and that these dwellings measure the demand of Commerce for the application of talent to the exchange of produce and manufactures, and it can be better understood why the mayor's office should go a-begging among men of more than ordinary talent. Looking back upon it from the next century, the fallacy of Chicago, in this, will be obvious and its results will be deplored probably. A few churches recently built may possibly yet remain for the comfort of [*my friend the historical student Grubber*] the next century. One of them I hope will contain a tablet perpetuating the name of the projector and engineer of the elevation of the street grades now going on piece-meal and (distrustfully) timidly.[20] But when I ask myself, what are the people of Chicago doing for their successors, I confess that I think of nothing of consequence, except their loyal labor in exchanging the farmer's wheat for that which if it were wanting to the farmers, would make them less resolute in their support of the government in its struggle with Slavery. But a Chicagonian might ask me: "Do you think our public schools of no consequence—to the number of which we add one yearly, each giving instruction at the expense of the community to a thousand scholars, on an average?"

I will supply the omission for so much as it is. Four hundred of these boys in each school are soon to be voters; four hundred of the girls, the wives and mothers of voters [*one, perhaps, to be the grandmother of my friend Grubber to come.*] Of how much consequence does the Chicago community think it to be that good judgment, patience, zeal and satisfaction of healthy ambition should be found in the education of these? The same goods disposable in law, or medicine, or banking bring a rent of from five to ten thousand dollars a year in hundreds of instances. The Chicago Market pays for them in Rail Road Superintendents, six thousand; a good lot held by a steamboat pilot readily commands three thousand. One thousand, or at the most, twelve hundred dollars a year gets all which the city demands in the heads of this educational business. I saw bankers and lawyers and doctors and railroad men, who looked like well-to-do gentlemen. I saw teachers who looked like sickly and over-wrought peasants in the castoff clothes of gentlemen, and I was not surprised to find that it was a matter of pride and boasting that trees and flowers had been allowed to grow unmolested in the courtyard of a school of over a thousand scholars. That enough disciplinary force and administrative ability to effect this triumph could have been bought in Chicago, for a hundred dollars a month, is somewhat surprising. I should have thought it would have been worth more in Railroad, or steamboat or hackney-coach business.

Yet that the people love their children and take considerable interest in their public schools, there is no doubt. They speak of them with apparent pride, as if they thought that their policy toward them was a wise and liberal one. Perhaps it is, as compared with that of other civic interests, but as compared with the policy which rules the management of commercial interests in Chicago, it seems to me to be careless and unwise.

A lawyer told me that some years ago he was asked and consented to take an important Judgeship at Chicago.[21] He held the seat two years; the responsibility was enormous, and the mere routine of duty exceedingly severe. He rose at eight o'clock and at ten minutes before nine entered the court-room, where he commonly sat, with an intermission of one hour for dinner, till after night-fall. Then he came home with notes and papers to be studied at night. Finding that he was no longer able to discharge his cases from his mind during sleep, that his eyes were failing, and that his brain was getting into a morbid condition, he surrendered the office, greatly to the disappointment of the profession and the public. His salary was fifteen hundred dollars. The private business which he sacrificed in taking the office was worth at least five thousand dollars. The Clerk of the Court, for duties involving no grave personal responsibility and no talent whatever, received as his fees in the cases tried, five thousand dollars a year—(at the same time the Judge received $1500.) I have been assured by many persons that no man in all the Northwestern States has, equally with this gentleman, the confidence of the people, as a man possessing all the qualities of a sagacious, well-read and upright Judge. No man has larger or more delicate trusts placed upon him in the way of business. The work of that judgeship remains undivided and the pay for it remains the same. It may be that the business pretended thus to be provided for, is well-done, but if it is, it is in defiance of every law of nature which the citizens of Chicago regard in their commercial business before it comes into court.

I met with several illustrations of this political vice at Chicago and St. Louis. I had been advised some years before of an intention to form a city park at Chicago. I asked what had come of the project. It was not well received by the people: the first difficulty had been local jealousies; every householder had been afraid that it would benefit some other part of the town to the disparagement of that in which he was interested. This, with the general apprehension of being taxed without a certainty of being benefitted in property, quenched the movement. "Still," said my informant,[22] "if any man of ability had been able to take the trouble to study the matter carefully and devote himself for a month to setting it forth in a well defined scheme, so that the people could easily give it a fair consideration, I have no doubt it could have been carried out. There is not a city in the world where something of the kind is really so much wanted or in which the people would be more grateful for it or would more willingly pay for it, if they could once realize what it would be."

I was strikingly reminded by this of a conversation I once had with a gentleman living near a considerable Midland town of England.[23] He was speaking of a plan for the Sanitary improvement of the town, the failure of which he demonstrated to me cost many lives yearly and which he considered to perpetuate a serious danger to his own family. "Why can it not be accomplished?" I asked.

"Because we live under mob-law, Sir. Because we are governed here by a body of thick-headed, beer-swilling house-holders, who think that any plan for improvement is a conspiracy of the gentry to rob them in the shape of taxes, and not to be listened to for a moment. There is not a publican in the town who has not more power of life and death over us than all the gentlemen in the county."

My English friend, saying this, sat in his library looking out upon his garden. My Illinois friend sat in his library, looking out upon his garden. Their tastes were identical. The latter was a man of considerably greater wealth. Had he been in England, he would have followed his tastes with more freedom. The Englishman [*a man of liberal politics too*] had no confidence in the capacity of the people to be convinced by a fair argument addressed to their own interests, because of their prejudices founded upon a political distinction of classes. The Western man had confidence that his project would be adopted by the people, if anyone would take the trouble to fairly understand the advantages which it promised them and fairly advertise these to them. The real difficulty was thus confessed to be not with the people, not to result from the legal conditions of society, but to rest with—himself. Why should it rest with him—a Christian gentleman, to all appearance? I determined to push my study further, if he would excuse a personal inquiry.

"You are blessed with a liberal and more than usually enlightened education. Your tastes are unusually sound and healthy. You appreciate the use of trees and greensward for yourself and your children, as is proved by the unusual expenditure you have made to connect them with your house, and your care to provide inducements to athletic amusements in connection with them for your children. You have experienced in your own sensations and you have seen evidence in the appearance of the people when using the public pleasure grounds of Europe, of the influences favorable to health in body, mind and soul which are exerted by such grounds. You know that there is not a town in Christendom, where the people, from the excessive and exciting demand of commerce upon them, and from the monotony and unattractiveness of the natural landscape about them, would receive as much benefit from the tranquilizing amusements into which a well managed park would persuade them, as in this very town. You know and you demonstrate by the arrangments you have avowed that you make for that purpose for your own children, that you consider that such amusements are the best antagonists of the ordinary temptations to vice of a great city. You know that the park which could now be secured to the people who will live here even twenty years hence at an expense equal to the value of two days' labor each month for a year of the present population, will be then unattainable by them by any expenditure. You know that if it should be provided for them, they would most willingly pay what it will cost as a debt transmitted to them. You know that if the work had been done & the debt incurred ten years ago which would have then been necessary to have secured a park to Chicago, you now and all the tax-payers now, would not lose the possession of it, for ten times its cost. All this you appreciate. And you tell me that if a well considered project for a park were properly brought before the people, it could be carried at any time. Why don't *you* give consideration to such a project and why don't *you* bring it properly before the people?"

"I could not do it, without too much neglecting my business."

"Why should you have a business so engrossing?"

"I will tell you. Five years ago, when I returned from Europe with my family, I brought with me books, pictures, statues, which I had carefully selected for my own enjoyment, as you see. I brought them to my house here, with a resolute determination that I would enjoy them; that I would live as gentlemen do in Europe. I saw what a useful and even essential part, those whom we would call here idle men, play in the sum of business of every well-established community, doing, in fact, just such work as you now propose to me to do, and which is, unfortunately for us and our children, left undone here for want of them. But I had certain legal trusts resting on me, which I had no right to neglect. These obliged me to have an office in the town. I intended to spend an hour or two every day at the office, merely to superintend this necessary legal business. I was deter-mined that I would employ clerks for every bit of the work which did not require the exercise of my own judgment and my actual presence. But first I found that the trust was already much larger than I had left it and had calculated upon finding it; secondly it rapidly grew larger and more compli-cated upon my hands; finally I found it impossible to leave any business of the least consequence to a clerk. I have never been able to retain a clerk or any man for a clerk's duties, for more than six months, who had any

595

respectable discretionary ability. Such a man, if he is honest, can not possibly remain engaged in any subordinate employment in Chicago. I could point you out hundreds of instances in which this has been illustrated. If a man has any ability to be useful in a large way, and can be trusted, he is absolutely sure to be found out and, in one way or another, made accessible to everybody. I am willing to pay large salaries to my clerks, but that is not enough. Money will not hold them to subordinate duties. Money will not buy the services of a man who is fit to be trusted comprehensively in Chicago, in any subordinate capacity.

I began by occasionally telling my wife to take her morning drive without me; then by giving it up altogether; then I had breakfast served earlier and would sometimes have dinner served later to accommodate an exigency that detained me at the office; then I got to sending word to my wife not to wait dinner for me. Then I had my dinner hour altered to conform to the customs of businessmen here. Then I got to snatching a dinner sometimes in the midst of business at some place in town and letting my family dine without me. My wife complains now that she and the children never see me until night, when I am usually so fagged out that I fall asleep in my chair. Of course I don't mean to have this continue, but at present I can't help it.

Today, I arranged everything to leave my office early to come and dine with you. I have a case in hand to be carried into court. It was necessary for this purpose to have a certain notice recorded at the Court House. I directed my clerk to attend to it. The simplest thing possible you would think, but as I drove past the Court House in coming home, I did not quite feel as if I had done my duty in leaving that to my clerk. I determined to go in & make sure that it was all right. It would detain me from you but five minutes at most. I found that, whether owing to my clerk or the clerk of the records, I don't know, the notice was not properly recorded, and I stayed long enough to make it right. It would have postponed the settlement of a very unpleasant business, and given great anxiety and annoyance to certain friends and clients of mine, had I trusted my clerk. I could better have given a week to the business than have suffered what I should, had I done so.

You see how it is. No man of any ability for affairs of public moment can be allowed to withdraw himself from the immediate commercial necessities of our city. Just think of it. Here, in the midst of this war, the business & the profits of business are greater than ever before. A single one of our grain elevators has given its owner a profit of a thousand dollars a day the year through. How can you expect us to attend to parks and water-works & libraries? I feel their importance as much as you do, but is it not more important that those starving men in Lancashire[24] should be fed? And here is the corn with us trodden under foot. Almost literally as cheap as dirt, quite as cheap as dirt six feet from the surface. I don't directly deal in corn to be sure, but somehow or other I am a part of this great corn exchanging machinery of Illinois, and if you will take the vote of Lancashire upon it, I will be bound, that for the present, I can't be spared from it. I'm sure I wish I could."

"So do I," said his wife, with a sigh.[25]

[*It is not quite the same at St. Louis, "We had here," said a gentleman of St Louis, "an opportunity of getting almost without cost, within our city, a finer Park than is possessed by any city in the world", and he convinced me by going over the ground, that the statement was scarcely extravagant. Even now, a very fine park could be secured at a cost which a few years hence would probably be considered to have been inconsiderable. But the prosperity of St Louis is arrested by the war and slaves are yet bought & sold in St Louis. For thinking men therefore the question of emancipation leaves little time for any less momentous matter of concern.*]

Scarcely anything is done publickly in Chicago entirely free from the current of business interests. As at St. Louis, a church steeple will be built higher than it otherwise would be because the neighboring lot-holders regard it as an advertisement of their property. There is nothing done in Chicago that is not regarded as an advertisement of Chicago. Chicago's reputation for liberality is regarded in subscriptions to every benevolent enterprise. It would be a mistake to suppose that the people were excessively sordid and penurious. They acquire wealth rapidly; they are not indisposed to use it freely—even carelessly. They subscribe to benevolent enterprises not merely with an advertising purpose. They build churches not merely to improve the value of house-lots. A portrait painter who ranks high among the first dozen in the world[26] is maintained in Chicago. Chicago has drawn to herself preachers and doctors and engineers and editors whom old Eastern communities would have gladly retained—has drawn them by overbidding older communities. I suppose it is the same with her teachers. The older communities are still stupider in respect of teachers. The people are willing to pay the full market-price for every commodity required for public use, but, individually, no man is willing to give much of his own personal concern to the work of public affairs. He prefers to yield to the demand of commerce. There are no men who have no part in business. Let a man develop and make manifest considerable talents, such as would be required for any duty of statesmanship, the demand of commerce seizes and disposes of him. You say that he is wanted for a certain office. Who want him? The people. How much do the people want him? The salary of the office is $2000. He is more wanted by the people in his regular business then, for attending to which a profit is offered him of $10000.[27] But is he to count serving his fellow citizens at nothing? Serving his fellow citizens? Do you not beg the real question?

Where is the evidence that as Judge or Mayor, or School Commissioner, he will be doing more for his fellow citizens than in giving all his talents to business? What is business? The business of Chicago merchants is just now in part, the reduction of the cost of suppressing the Slaveholders' rebellion by cheapening the cost of supplying bread to the soldiers and sailors, oats to the horses, copper for the field-pieces, lead for the bullets, and so on; in part, the supplying of food to the factory operatives in the East and in Europe, many of whom, but for their exertions, would otherwise have been the victim of this Slaveholders' rebellion. Is it certain that they are wrong in neglecting what are called public affairs so much as they do? Take any one man; see what he is doing where he is—measure what people are willing to pay him for what he is doing, by his profits, and you will admit, I think, that it is a question whether he can be better employed for the public interests, just at present. But there are a large number of good businessmen who are not so well-paid. So? Why are they not? What is the evidence that they are good businessmen? Why are others paid better than they? Only because the public believe them to be better businessmen, is it not? There are several grades between the best businessmen of Chicago and those whom they employ in their public offices.

The conclusion which all this would seem to justify is that what is called public business is of comparatively small consequence in a town like Chicago. That it is of much more consequence than it is generally supposed to be, and that in their haste the people of Chicago make much waste, by their carelessness in public business, I don't doubt, but I think it is clear that the importance of applying talent & honesty to public business is much less relatively to its importance for private business, in the condition of Chicago, than in the condition of Leeds or Lyons.[28]

1. Probably a dinner at the home of James E. Yeatman. On April 4, 1863, after arriving from Young's Point via Memphis and Cairo, Olmsted wrote John S. Newberry, "I am going to call on Mr Yeatman as soon as I have closed this." James E. Yeatman was a staunch Unionist from a well-to-do Tennessee family. John Bell, a presidential candidate in 1860 and a former U.S. senator, was his stepfather (James Cox, *Old and New St. Louis: A Concise History . . . With a Biographical Appendix . . .* [St. Louis, Mo., 1894], pp. 188–89).
2. Olmsted most likely gained this impression of the "Charleston habit of wine talk" during his first journey through the South in 1853, when he stayed in that city for almost one week. Neither in his published writings nor in his private letters, however, did he mention any social engagements in Charleston (*Papers of FLO*, 2: 469).
3. Benton Barracks, erected near the St. Louis fairgrounds in 1861 by Gen. John C. Frémont and named in honor of his father-in-law, Thomas Hart Benton. In 1862 Anthony Trollope described the soldiers' quarters at Benton Barracks as overcrowded and incredibly dirty and fetid (Ernest Kirschten, *Catfish and Crystal: The*

Bicentenary Edition of the St. Louis Story [Garden City, N.Y., 1965], p. 216; A. Trollope, *North America*, pp. 392–93).

4. There were approximately fifteen military hospitals located in the St. Louis area in 1863 (Jacob Gilbert Forman, *The Western Sanitary Commission; A Sketch of Its Origins, History* . . . [St. Louis, Mo., 1864], pp. 6–10, 45, 73–74, 86–87; E. Kirschten, *Catfish and Crystal*, p. 216).

5. The St. Louis Mercantile Library Association was formed early in 1846, and its library opened in 1847. The library moved in 1855 from rented quarters to its own building on the southwest corner of 5th and Locust streets. Although voting membership in the Library Association was limited to dues-paying merchants and clerks, other citizens could, by payment of the dues, become entitled to use the library reading room and to borrow books (St. Louis, Mercantile Library Association, *Catalogue, Systematic and Analytical of the Books of the Saint Louis Mercantile Library Association* . . . [St. Louis, Mo., 1858], pp. iv–vii; idem, *Mercantile Library Association of St. Louis* [New York?, 1889?], p. 1; *Campbell & Richardson's St. Louis Business Directory for 1863* . . . [St. Louis, Mo., 1863]).

6. A reference to the Missouri Botanical Garden established by Henry Shaw (1800–1889), a St. Louis philanthropist. An English immigrant, Shaw opened a store in St. Louis in 1818 and retired in 1840 with a sizable fortune. A visit in 1851 to Chatsworth, the estate of the Duke of Devonshire, inspired Shaw to begin his own botanical garden. In 1857 he gathered suggestions about laying out the garden from eminent botanists and gardeners such as Asa Gray, professor of natural history at Harvard College, and William Hooker, director of the Royal Botanical Gardens at Kew. That year preparatory work was begun on the grounds, and in 1858–59 a library and museum building was erected there (NCAB; St. Louis, Missouri Botanical Garden, *First Annual Report, 1889* [St. Louis, Mo., 1890], pp. 12–14).

7. Probably the 276 acres that Henry Shaw later gave to form Tower Grove Park, adjoining the Missouri Botanical Garden. Work began on the park in 1866, and between 1867 and 1890 over twenty thousand trees were planted there (St. Louis, Missouri Botanical Garden, *First Annual Report*, pp. 23–24).

8. Here Olmsted presumably is referring to the extreme ruggedness of the Central Park site, especially of the lower park below the Old Croton Receiving Reservoir at 79th Street, which made it impossible to achieve the "breadth" of effect and of treatment that was the preferred kind of park scenery and which, in fact, the terrain did allow in the lesser-used upper park. The lower park tended to consist of a series of small set pieces of scenery rather than the broad "passages of scenery" that Olmsted highly valued.

9. Albert Edward (1841–1910), then Prince of Wales, later Edward VII of England, arrived in St. Louis on September 26, 1860. The following day he visited the agricultural fair (Nicholas Augustus Woods, *The Prince of Wales in Canada and the United States* [London, 1861], pp. 319–21; [Pierre Joseph Olivier Chauveau], *The Visit of His Royal Highness the Prince of Wales to America* . . . [Montreal, 1860], p. 97).

10. In 1860 over 50,000 Germans—almost one-third of the city's population of 160,000—lived in St. Louis (Walter B. Stevens, *St. Louis: The Fourth City, 1764–1911*, 2 vols. [St. Louis, Mo., 1911], 2: 687; U.S. Census Office, 8th Census, *Preliminary Report on the Eighth Census, 1860* . . . [Washington, D.C., 1862], p. 244).

11. The editors have been unable to identify Olmsted's informant.

12. "By" in the original.

13. Olmsted left St. Louis on April 6 for Chicago and probably remained there until April 11. His return trip included only a brief stopover in Cincinnati, where he conferred with John S. Newberry. He stayed one night in Cleveland and another in Buffalo and arrived back in Washington, D.C., on April 14 (FLO to Edwin L. Godkin, April 4, 1863, above; FLO to JSN, April 4, 1863, USSC-NYPL, box 914, 1: 326; FLO to Mark Skinner, April 24, 1863; Bloor Diary, April 14, 1863).

14. Olmsted obviously was uncertain about Cleveland's population, which the 1860 federal census reported to be forty-three thousand (U.S. Census Office, 8th Census, *Preliminary Report*, p. 242).

15. Here Olmsted affixed an asterisk and scribbled at the bottom of the page, "Remark of driver of hackny coach who took me from Hartford to Litchfield, 1863—about society in Cleaveland go anywhere." He probably intended to add an anecdote to his final draft.

16. William Howard Russell devoted part of a chapter in *My Diary North and South* to a description of the reception at the elegant New York City home of "Monsieur B." (probably August Belmont), "the representative of European millions." Then Russell mused over what he saw as a difference between New York gentlemen and "their less effective and showy" counterparts elsewhere in the world, and he used an extended metaphor to compare them:

> When a man looks at a suit of armor made to order by the first blacksmith in Europe, he observes that the finish of the joints and hinges is much higher than in the old iron clothes of former time. Possibly the metal is better, and the chasings and garniture as good as the work of Milan, but the observer is not for a moment led to imagine that the fabric has stood proof of blows, or that it smacks of ancient watch-fire.

The perception of a similar lack of proven quality, or substance and solidity, in Americans was perhaps what motivated Russell to decide that in Monsieur B.'s soirée, "there was something wanting—not in host or hostess, or company, or house—where was it?—which was conspicuous by its absence." Russell then voiced a similar opinion of the beauty of American women: "It is prettiness rather than fineness; regular, intelligent, wax-like faces, graceful little figures; none of the grandiose Roman type which Von Raumer recognized in London, as in the Holy City, a quarter of a century ago" (W. H. Russell, *My Diary North and South*, p. 22).

17. The Boulevard des Italiens, a large, tree-lined street with magnificent buildings, had long been popular with fashionable Parisians, who thronged its streets in the evenings (John Scott and M. P. B. de la Boissiere, *Picturesque Views of the City of Paris and its Environs . . .* [London, 1823], [p. 5]).

18. Probably Mark Skinner, president of the Chicago branch of the U.S. Sanitary Commission, who had moved to Chicago in 1836 from his native Vermont (*Encyclopedia of Biography of Illinois*, 3 vols. [Chicago, 1892–1902], 1: 31–32).

19. Olmsted then began a new paragraph:

> "It is very difficult to carry any scheme of public improvement here," said a wealthy gentleman, "because the greater part of the voters are small property-holders—each man owning his own house and the ground about it— and they will always vote against anything that promises to increase the taxes, unless its advantages to them can be very easily and clearly seen. And then every man here is too much absorbed in his own personal affairs of business to spare time to give careful attention to civic affairs much less to undertake to enlighten others about them."

He then crossed through this section and did not replace it.

20. Olmsted is referring to the regrading of the streets which had been proceeding since the 1850s in an attempt to lift them above the water level and improve drainage. Olmsted later commented upon this process when he was working on the World's Columbian Exposition in Chicago:

> The manner in which the site of the Exposition will be built up out of a swamp will add to this characteristic interest of the city. It is all in keeping with the entire building of the city that, in order to gain the esthetic value of a view over

the Lake, the difficulties and cost and horticultural disadvantages of building up a site out of swamp divided by barren sand dunes should have been disregarded. The boldness of the proposition is quite in line with that so successfully carried out of screwing up thousands of houses in order to get their front doors above a satisfactory level for streets.

(Bessie Louise Pierce, *A History of Chicago*, 3 vols. [New York, 1940], 2: 317–18; FLO to Clarence Pullen, Jan. 7, 1891, Olmsted Associates Records, Library of Congress, Washington, D.C.)

21. Mark Skinner was the sole judge of the Cook County Court of Common Pleas from 1851 to 1853. Pleading poor health, he did not seek reelection (*Encyclopedia of Biography of Illinois*, 1: 32–33).

22. Probably Ezra Butler McCagg (1825–1908), a Chicago lawyer and Mark Skinner's successor as president of the Chicago branch of the U.S. Sanitary Commission. Several characteristics point to McCagg as Olmsted's informant. McCagg had received a classical education in his native New York State. Like the informant, he had visited Europe approximately five years before Olmsted's visit to Chicago. McCagg also possessed the cultured tastes and appreciation of natural beauty that Olmsted ascribed to his informant. The McCagg house had attached greenhouses and was usually full of flowers. McCagg himself was a Shakespearean scholar and possessed a valuable art collection and a private library of English manuscripts. In wealth and business responsibilities McCagg further resembled the informant. He served as the principal legal adviser of the wealthy Ogden family and married widowed Caroline Ogden Jones. The management of his stepchildren's enormous legacies consumed much of his time. Indeed, Olmsted's account of McCagg's workday in 1871 echoed the description presented here: "Mr McCagg attends regularly to his law business, going into the business quarter of the city every morning & spending the day as ever you or I have done. He is like all Chicago men of business excessively held to it."

Perhaps prodded to action by the conversation related here and by his continuing friendship with Olmsted, McCagg became a leader in the park movement in Chicago after the war. In 1867 he drafted the first of several bills to establish a large park on the south side of the city. He was also elected president of the Lincoln Park Commission, established in 1869 by a state law later declared invalid. McCagg did not serve on the new commission appointed in 1871, and Olmsted and Vaux did not design Lincoln Park. However, Chicago's South Park Commission did hire them to design the 1,055–acre South Park, now known as Washington Park, Jackson Park, and the Midway Plaisance (*Appleton's Cyc. Am. Biog.*; John Moses and Joseph Kirkland, *History of Chicago*, 2 vols. [New York, 1895], 2: 169–71; E. B. McCagg to Olmsted, Vaux & Withers, May 1, 1869; Olmsted, Vaux & Co., *Report Accompanying Plan for Laying Out the South Park* [Chicago, 1871]; Andreas Simon, ed., *Chicago the Garden City* [Chicago, 1893], p. 40; FLO to A. T. Field, April 11, 1871).

23. Probably Alfred T. Field, Olmsted's English friend who in 1863 lived in the midlands near Birmingham. Olmsted had visited Field's home during his European trip in the autumn of 1859. Olmsted thought that Field and Ezra McCagg possessed such similar tastes that he wrote Field a long letter introducing McCagg when the latter was planning a trip to England in 1871 (*Papers of FLO*, 1: 342; Charlotte Field to FLO, Nov. 18, 1859; FLO to A. T. Field, April 11, 1871).

24. Olmsted's informant is referring to the great suffering among unemployed textile mill workers in Lancashire, England, during the Civil War. By 1863 the North's blockade of Southern ports had created a "cotton famine" in England; and cotton mills, for the most part concentrated in Lancashire, had laid off the majority of their employees or closed. In the northern United States, considerable sympathy existed for the English cotton mill workers who, despite the economic hardships they were

undergoing, generally supported the North (Joseph H. Park, "The English Working-men and the American Civil War," *Political Science Quarterly* 39 [Sept. 1924]: 432–57; William O. Henderson, *The Lancashire Cotton Famine, 1861–1865* [Manchester, 1934], pp. 7–12, 42–118).

25. After this paragraph, Olmsted scrawled "Foundation of wealth—humus—how gradually developed" and drew a box around these words, probably to remind himself to make additions on those subjects.

26. Probably George Peter Alexander Healy (1813–1894), an artist who studied in Paris and painted Louis Philippe and numerous other renowned figures of the day. His most famous work was "Webster Replying to Hayne." Healy moved to Chicago in 1855 (*DAB*; Alfred Theodore Andreas, *History of Chicago*, 3 vols. [Chicago, 1885], 2: 559–60).

27. In the arrangement of the Olmsted Papers in the Library of Congress, the following pages of "Journey in the West," along with part of a speech presented in Chicago, precede the "St. Louis, Chicago" section. Since these pages appear to summarize points made in that section, the editors have moved them to its conclusion. They have omitted the fragment of the speech and Olmsted's account of a journey made from Washington to New York in May 1863, since neither forms an integral part of Olmsted's Midwestern journey.

28. Leeds, England, and Lyons, France.

CHAPTER IX

OLD PROBLEMS AND NEW PROJECTS

THE SPRING AND SUMMER of 1863 marked a difficult period in Olmsted's life. He found his position with the Sanitary Commission increasingly unsatisfactory as disagreements with members of the Executive Committee became more frequent and more difficult to resolve. His correspondence shows his unsuccessful attempts to design a new organizational structure for the Commission that would be acceptable both to himself and the other commissioners. Letters to Henry W. Bellows in April, July, and August also indicate some of the philosophical and practical differences that separated Olmsted from other members of the Commission, most notably Cornelius R. Agnew and John S. Newberry. Letters to John S. Blatchford and to the Executive Committee express Olmsted's disapproval of the activities of the U.S. Christian Commission, while the letter of July 25 reproves Bellows for an overly generous notice of that group. The letters of August 15 and 16 emotionally sum up Olmsted's service with the Sanitary Commission, while the letter of resignation of September 1 more formally weighs his achievements and failures.

The increasing likelihood that Olmsted would soon resign from his post at the Sanitary Commission contributed to other difficulties. His letters of April and May 1863 cast light upon a painful quarrel with his usually patient and supportive father. These letters also express Olmsted's regret that his role in shaping Central Park was rapidly drawing to a close. Moreover, they evaluate the alternative careers open to him and candidly assess his abilities—a stock-taking in which he again engaged during August. During the summer Olmsted's letters and the prospectus that he wrote with Edwin L. Godkin trace his part in planning a weekly journal and in securing funding for it. Although the editorship of the paper that in 1865 began publication as the *Nation* seemed Olmsted's most promising prospect for employment, a new opportunity suddenly appeared in August 1863—the superintendency of the Mariposa Estate in California and its gold mines. These writings indicate the considerations that would lead him to accept this position.

Amid the uncertainties of his professional and personal life, Olmsted remained intensely interested in the future position of Southern blacks and the military progress of the war. His testimony before the Freedmen's Inquiry Commission and his letter to Charles Eliot Norton illustrate his faith in the ability of former slaves to be good soldiers. The letter to Norton also indicates Olmsted's determination that the war bring an end to slavery and the social and political systems it had nourished. His letter of July 4 discusses the "national instinct" of the people which Bellows had attempted to plumb in a sermon. Other letters written in July give Olmsted's reaction to the draft riots in New York City, describe the battlefield at Gettysburg, and assess Gen. George G. Meade as commander of the Army of the Potomac.

To John Olmsted

Private

U.S. Sanitary Commission,
Adams' House, 244 F Street,
Washington, D.C., April 18th 1863.

Dear Father,

Your very generous proposition and offer[1] is received with abundant gratitude. This only is to be said: While I am in the service of the Sanitary Commission, I can lay up no money. I take for services, $2500. If necessary, I draw upon the Commission beyond that amount for official expenses, chiefly travelling expenses.[2] I still get $100 a month from the park,[3] (out of which Weidenmann[4] has been paid) though I expect any day to hear that this is stopped.[5] With the general rise in prices, I find myself constantly dropping a little behindhand, not that we have standing debts unpaid, but that in order to prevent this, some additional restriction upon expenditure becomes from month to month necessary. But I never find myself quite square up. So that if I should leave the Commission Sanitary, as I am liable to do at any moment, I should be obliged to call on you to tide me over to the next berth. Under these circumstances, I can not undertake with much confidence to pay off $2000. If I set about it, I shall probably be led to some change. But seeing how other men are paid—the Assistant Secretaries of War and the Inspectors General for instance get less than I do[6]—it seems hardly reasonable for me to hope that I can do better. It is much more likely that for a time I may be forced to do worse. The Commissioners blunder so in their business, whenever I am away, or not able to point out their misunderstandings of it, that I am constantly holding myself ready to jump off. That you may not think me impracticable in this, I will simply say that I always have Prof[r] Bache—a shrewd and just old public functionary—in confidence and that he says the Commission will at once break to pieces whenever I leave it, and that he will resign whenever I do. That is to say I do not contemplate resigning except upon a necessity which he recognizes to be imperative. You know that clergymen & doctors are intolerable men of business. The amount of labor and vigilance and anxiety to prevent the funds and powers of the Commission from being ill-used—greatly and scandalously—may get to be beyond my capacity. In which case, the Commissioners must either submit to a system and discipline in their own transactions, which they hitherto refuse, or I must be relieved of responsibility. If they will not relieve me otherwise, I must relieve myself. I am practically relieved of all general responsibility at this moment, and I shall refuse to resume it except upon better conditions of personal security than before.[7] I could probably at once take the business of editing the Loyal League's publications[8]—doubtful if it would pay. If I should be led to this or in this direction, I should try to establish a high-class weekly paper, getting the League men to guarantee its expenses for a year—or something of that sort. I think that I am well fitted for a newspaper manager. There is only one business I would prefer to this—that is the management of a large Negro colony. I want to demonstrate the feasibility of the plan which I advocated in one of the Georgia chapters of Seaboard Slave States, of navigating our ship out of Slavery.[9] For when we have subjugated the rebels, we have still the nation of half savage Africans to the South of us, to deal with.

On one tack or another, I don't fear that I can not find business to which I am suited, in which I can work with a will and earn the livlihood of my family. But none of these doors seem to open anything better than that. I couldn't help speculating for accumulation at Chicago.[10] There is such an obvious want of a pleasure-ground there, I think that by a small admission fee, a handsome interest on a large expenditure of capital, could be got. But even to talk it up would require time & capital which I have not got. (If by rents and admissions, season-tickets &c, expenses, taxes & interest could be met, and the land held; of course the rise upon it would be the accumulation of capital.)

But I am accumulating nothing, and see the opportunity of accumulating nothing—by which I could hope to pay $2000 in a year or two. It is hardly just to my prudence to say that I am accumulating nothing. I am accumulating capital of reputation, by which businessmen regard me as a man of unusual capacity & good judgment in certain respects, and there are some matters which it is getting to be thought I can handle better than anybody else in the country. This is a moderate property sure, unless I break down in health, and may lead to something better than that. Besides which—besides what appears—I have been for some time accumulating notes and materials for a book which I think, if I can ever put six months of library-work upon it, will [*be worth*] more to the world, and [. . .] otherwise [. . .][11] Bushnell's sermon on the Tendency of emigration to Barbarism).[12]

I will do whatever you advise of course, but you can't reckon upon my being able to pay $1000 a year at present, I think. Probably the better way would be to mortgage for it.

The farm is going to the dogs & no help for it, that I can see. Its value for sale would be very small now—which shows what speculators think of it. It is a great drag on my comfort. An elephant to carry about.

We are all very well. Baby walking into childhood & Charly into a young man with a music-teacher and conceptions of pocket-money. I am much better for my Western scrabble, weigh more than I have in fifteen years, having gained [*half a*] pound.

---

1. John Olmsted's letter has not survived, so his proposition to his son cannot be clearly ascertained. Most likely, however, it was an offer to lend money for capital improvements to Tosomock, the Staten Island farm originally bought for Olmsted but at this time technically the property of his stepchildren, John Hull Olmsted's children. In July 1862 Olmsted had suggested "a scheme of comprehensive and steady improvement" that he believed would add at least one hundred dollars per acre to the farm's value. He told his father:

   I think that $3000 would be required to improve buildings, fences, tools, survey & surveyor's service in laying out, $1000 for trees, hedge-plants & manure. For service one good gardener & one laborer, with a pair of horses &, perhaps a boy, half the time. This force, I mean, on an average should be added to what the farm would employ, without expense, in merely farming purposes. Call it $600 a year. I think this would provide for the progressive improvement and maintenance of ornamental planting, roads, &c. on a scale which it would be worth my while to attend to, and it is as much as I should feel justified in expending on the property as a speculation, under present circumstances.

   Olmsted's reference to the generosity of his father's offer suggests that the elder Olmsted was requesting only partial repayment—to a maximum of two thousand dollars—of the loan (FLO to JO, July 25, 1862).

2. On November 21, 1862, the Sanitary Commission had approved a resolution that Olmsted's annual salary should be increased from twenty-five hundred to five thousand dollars as of October 1, 1862, because he had been "devoting his whole time to the service of the Commission." Olmsted, however, chose to regard this increment only as a supplement for his expense account. In December he told George Templeton Strong, "I wish you to understand that it is my intention to draw only the same actual compensation for services as heretofore, to wit, $2500. per annum, but to avoid the necessity of a careful discrimination between expenses incurred clearly on account of the Commission and expenses which are more or less of a personal character, I shall regard the action of the Committee as relieving me from accounting for the additional sum of $2500" (USSC, *Minutes*, p. 119; FLO to GTS, Dec. 22, 1862).

3. On April 10, 1862, the Central Park commission appointed Olmsted and Vaux to be "Landscape Architects to the Board" at a joint salary of forty-five hundred dollars annually. Calvert Vaux apparently suggested that Olmsted take twenty-five hundred dollars of this sum; in August 1862 Olmsted told him, "I don't know exactly what is right under the circumstances but it certainly is not right that you should do all the work and give me more than half the pay and was never intended by me." Olmsted argued that two thousand dollars was fully his fair share and added, "Whenever your own necessities require that you should take more than $2500. from the park, or whenever it seems necessary that our joint compensation from the park should be reduced, let me know and I will endeavor to make arrangements to get on with less than $2000." Possibly Vaux's illness during the fall of 1862 had by the spring of 1863 led to the reduction of Olmsted's share of the salary to twelve hundred dollars (New York City, Board of Commissioners of the Central Park, *Minutes of Proceedings of the Board of Commissioners of the Central Park* [New York, 1858–69], April 10, 1862, p. 111; FLO to CV, Aug. 23, 1862; see also FLO to MPO, Sept. 21, 1862, n. 1, above).

4. Jacob Weidenmann (1829–1893), who was then superintending the execution of plans prepared by Olmsted and Vaux for the grounds of the Hartford Retreat for the Insane. Born at Winterthur, Switzerland, Weidenmann studied architecture in Zurich before immigrating to the United States in 1856. After studying landscape gardening and working in collaboration with Eugene A. Baumann, he moved to Hartford, Connecticut, in 1859 to prepare designs for that city's public park (now known as Bushnell Park).

   Olmsted and Vaux had begun work on plans for the Retreat for the Insane in the summer of 1860, and by June 6, 1861, they had hired Weidenmann to direct the operations. During the next two decades and particularly after the dissolution of his partnership with Vaux, Olmsted continued to rely on Weidenmann's skills as draftsman and landscape architect. Together they prepared plans for Congress Park in Saratoga Springs, New York (John S. Butler to FLO, June 6, 1861; Jacob Weidenmann, *Victorian Landscape Gardening: A Facsimile of Jacob Weidenmann's Beautifying Country Homes. With a New Introduction by David Schuyler* (Watkins Glen, N.Y., 1978).

5. A reference to the likelihood that Vaux would resign from Central Park, which he did less than a month later (see FLO to CV, Feb. 16, 1863, above).

6. These appointees received considerably less than Olmsted's total annual income (thirty-seven hundred dollars from Central Park and the Sanitary Commission combined). The inspector general of the Medical Bureau was paid an annual salary of approximately twenty-seven hundred dollars; medical inspectors, approximately twenty-four hundred dollars; and assistant secretaries of war, three thousand dollars (John Scroggs Poland, *A Digest of the Military Laws of the United States . . .* [Boston, 1868], pp. 58, 216).

7. Probably Olmsted considered himself relieved from general responsibility because he had just returned from a journey on April 14 and had not resumed the position of

general secretary, which had been filled in his absence by J. Foster Jenkins (see FLO to HWB, April 25, 1863, below; Bloor Diary, April 14, 1863).

8. In the spring of 1863 two loyal leagues, the Loyal League of Union Citizens, headed by conservative merchant Prosper M. Wetmore, and the Loyal National League, under the aegis of John Austin Stevens, Jr., a Republican, were formed to enlist the support of people from a wide range of occupations and incomes. Olmsted is probably referring to neither of these groups, but rather to the Loyal Publication Society of New York, formed in February 1863 and closely linked to the Union League Club of New York and the Loyal National League (Guy Gibson, "Lincoln's League: The Union League Movement during the Civil War" [Ph.D. diss., University of Illinois, 1957], pp. 204–5, 217; Frank Freidel, "The Loyal Publication Society: A Pro-Union Propaganda Agency," *Mississippi Valley Historical Review* 26 [1939–40]: 359–62).

9. See FLO to JO, February 24, 1862, note 2, above.

10. The editors have been unable to discover any purchases of land or any correspondence by Olmsted that is related to the possible establishment of a park in Chicago in 1863. His account of a conversation with Ezra B. McCagg does, however, indicate his deep interest in such a project (see "Journey in the West, St. Louis, Chicago," April 4–11, 1863, above).

11. This passage was obliterated when someone, probably Mary Bull Olmsted, cut out Olmsted's signature on the back of this page of the letter. In 1864 she gave "about a 1/2 dozen" of Olmsted's autographs to a "Baltimore lady who would not take no for an answer." Olmsted, upon learning that his signature had been removed from letters for an autograph seeker, lined through his signature at the end of the letter that he was writing to his father and added: "I don't like signatures to private letters going to the public & the autograph enterprises disgust me. I beg you never give my autograph to anybody. Take them back if you can" (JO to FLO, April 14, 1864; FLO to JO, March 11, 1864).

12. A reference to the sermon "Barbarism the First Danger. A Discourse for Home Missions," by Horace Bushnell (1802–1876), the renowned Congregational minister who was the pastor of Olmsted's family in Hartford. Bushnell, whose views had long influenced Olmsted, had written this sermon in 1847. In it the minister pointed out a decline toward barbarism that he believed always accompanied emigration into the wilderness. Olmsted's recent journey through the Midwest and Southwest probably reminded him of Bushnell's sermon and led him to ask his half-sister Mary for a copy of it. While in California Olmsted again attempted to obtain the sermon for his own use and complained: "I have often requested Mary O to get me a copy of Dr Bushnell's Discourse of *Barbarism the First Danger*—I think that's the title. If you can't get it otherwise, ask the Doctor, & then advertise. I would give $10 or $20 for a copy, if necessary" (FLO to JO, March 11, 1864; *Papers of FLO*, 1: 72–74).

Testimony of
Fred. Law Olmstead, Esqr
Sec^y of Sanitary Com^n
before the
Special Inquiry Commission[1]

April 22, '63.

Fred. Law Olmstead:
Secretary Sanitary Commission.
Recently returned from the South West.—

Q. To what states did you go?
A. I went into the valley of the Mississippi, & passed through parts of the
   states of Tenn., Ky., La. and Miss.
Q. As far as you were thrown among the freedmen, did there seem to be
   any method of organization?
A. I did not discover any general uniform organization. Any theoretical
   organization was very poorly carried out.
[Q. *Did there appear to be any plan, designed to furnish the contrabands
   with work?*]
A. [*None whatever.*] I saw several instances where they were employed in
   the Quarter Master's Dep't., and I made inquiries of officers with
   reference to their efficiency, and in every case, the report was favorable, where anything like a painstaking method had been adopted and
   pursued. It appeared [*exceedingly*] easy to control them; they were as
   industrious as any class in similar circumstances; [*and the experiment
   was always successful, where they took proper working men and women.
   The engineering officer of Gen. Sherman's staff*[2] *employed many of
   these men on the work of filling a crevasse in the canal opposite Vicksburg; and he said they worked better than the whites.*]
      [*Rev. Mr. Patten*[3] *& Rev. Mr. Alexander*[4] *of Chicago had been
   making an examination into the condition of things at Cairo. There was
   said to be a bad state of things there; whether caused by the inefficiency
   or indifference of the officers in charge.*]
Q. Do you think, from what you saw & heard, that the able-bodied men
   feel disposed to enlist?
A. That depends entirely on circumstances; on the inducements which
   are offered. If the government arms & equips them as it does white
   soldiers; pays them as it does white soldiers; and pledges them its
   protection in all the rights of prisoners of war, as it does white soldiers,[5]
   I think that large numbers would feel disposed to enlist. But I think

this enlistment of the blacks may be begun in the wrong way or under the wrong officers, so that it would do more harm than good. It may easily be commenced in such a way that it will be sure to fail [*and everybody will be discouraged*].

Q. What do you think would be the effect on the slaves in the Rebel States, of the U.S. arming and well-treating any considerable number of them?

A. I think such a policy, carried out, would tend directly to the still further disorganization of plantation discipline which is equivalent to the disintegration of the peculiar structure of society at the South.

An officer at New Madrid said to me that he believed a Regiment could be raised at that point in a fortnight composed of runaways from plantations of disloyal men. The slightest encouragement would bring them.

The general sentiment of the officers in the Western Army, seems to be,—unexpectedly to myself—favorable to the enterprise. They are inclined to try it, but fear that their men will not be willing to serve in cooperation with negroes. My own opinion is that a single engagement in which a negro regiment has come to the support of a white regiment, or has stood side by side with it in trying circumstances will set that all right.

As to the capacity of the negro to be a soldier, I have no doubt. I have myself seen them manifest every quality asked for in a soldier. I believe many of them are capable of making military heroes. It is perhaps more necessary than with the white Americans that they should be adroitly handled. I think, however, that one eminently good quality of the negro soldiers will prove to be their faithfulness.

I saw collections of slaves at various points—depots arranged for their reception. One [*very*] large crowd opposite Vicksburg—many women and children among them, almost without any protection or support. [*A little corn was thrown to them, or something of that kind, but no care or any systematic attention bestowed.*] I think better treatment, and some organized reception and distribution, by which they would be able to support themselves by compensated labor, would add largely to the number of fugitives from the Rebel states.

Q. Do you think there is any system of communication by which the slaves can send back word of their treatment?

A. I have little doubt of it. I think there should be established large depots—places of reception & distribution—cities of Refuge, so to speak, where they would be absolutely protected from insult and injury until they could obtain employment.

Q. What agency should the Government exercise towards the freedmen who are arriving?

A. I think it should establish these depots or colonies of refuge, and then place the freedmen on confiscated plantations, in a condition as much as practicable assimilating that to which they have been accustomed, except that it should insure them as far as practicable against abuse and give them wages proportionate to their capacities and industry. [*These colonies I think should be placed in the charge of honest and devoted Superintendents, who have faith in the capacity of the colored race.*]

Q. Do you think that the demand for compensated labor, would absorb the supply of those escaping from Slavery?

A. I think the labor market of the United States *would* do so—at least for the present—perhaps to the end, if many of them should be employed in the working of confiscated plantations. But I am not sure of it. [*It is an experiment.*] If they were treated with systematic kindness and humanity, so that large numbers should be induced to come out, I doubt if the balance of demand and supply in open market of the north would adjust itself with sufficient rapidity to prevent much suffering unless government provided for a part upon the abandoned plantations.

Q. Do you believe the Colonization of Colored People would be Practicable?

A. To some extent, for exceptional cases. I think Government should encourage the hiring of negroes (hitherto slaves,) by their masters. The one important duty of government at present, however, seems to me to be to establish in some way, a responsible guardianship of the contrabands. They should be registered and classified, and so divided and superintended that someone could always be held accountable for an honest and humane guardianship of every man, woman & child among them. This is not required merely from considerations of benevolence and justice to the negroes, but of economy in prosecuting the war.

The text is taken from a draft version of testimony before the American Freedmen's Inquiry Commission that is in the American Freedmen's Inquiry Commission Papers, Houghton Library, Harvard University, Cambridge, Massachusetts. This draft is by a copyist but includes emendations and additions in Olmsted's hand. The editors have indicated in bracketed italics substantive material that was later lined through. A final, shortened manuscript version of the testimony is in Record Group 94, Records of the Office of Adjutant General, Entry 12, Letters Received, folder 7, pages 171–74 (328-0-1863), National Archives and Records Service, Washington, D.C.

1. In March 1863 Secretary of War Edwin M. Stanton appointed three well-known antislavery men and reformers as the American Freedmen's Inquiry Commission to investigate the condition of Southern blacks within the Union lines and to suggest

"practical measures for placing them in a state of self-support and self-defense, with the least possible disturbance to the great industrial interest of the country and of rendering their services efficient in the present war." The three commissioners— Samuel Gridley Howe, Robert Dale Owen, and James Morrison McKaye— immediately began to gather testimony and in June 1863 issued a preliminary report. In its final report of 1864 the Commission advocated the creation of a temporary freedmen's bureau. The commissioners generally recommended giving short-term aid to the freedmen, securing their civil rights, protecting them from a restoration of any form of slavery, and then leaving them to care for themselves (E. M. Stanton to R. D. Owen, J. M. McKaye, and S. G. Howe, March 16, 1863, in O.R., ser. 3, vol. 3, pp. 73–74; "Preliminary Report of A.F.I.C.," June 30, 1863, ibid., pp. 430–54; "Final Report of A.F.I.C.," May 15, 1864, ibid., vol. 4, pp. 289–382).

2. William LeBaron Jenney (see FLO to JO, April 1, 1863, above).
3. William Weston Patton (1821–1889), an antislavery Congregational clergyman and an associate member of the U.S. Sanitary Commission. Olmsted had probably first met Patton during the latter's eleven-year pastorate at the Fourth Congregational Church in Hartford, Connecticut. In 1857 Patton became minister of the First Congregational Church in Chicago. He was a vigorous supporter of the Sanitary Commission and from 1864 served as vice-president of the Chicago branch. That year Patton also wrote a pamphlet defending the Commission's reliance upon paid rather than volunteer workers. After the Civil War, the minister edited a religious journal and in 1877 was selected as president of Howard University, a post he held until his death (Charles Robson, ed., *The Biographical Encyclopedia of Illinois of the Nineteenth Century* [Philadelphia, 1875], pp. 181–82; New York University, *General Alumni Catalogue of New York University, 1833–1905. College, Applied Science and Honorary Alumni* [New York, 1906], p. 9).
4. Possibly Alexis Alexander, secretary (1857–63) and former pastor of the B'nai Sholom Jewish congregation in Chicago. Not a fully ordained rabbi, Reverend Alexander had organized and was teaching the congregation's school in 1863 (Morton M. Berman, *Our First Century, 1852–1952: Temple Isaiah Israel, The United Congregations of B'nai Sholom, Temple Israel and Isaiah Temple, 5612–5712* [Chicago, 1952], pp. 11–14; information courtesy of Linda J. Evans, Chicago Historical Society, Chicago, Ill.).
5. Black soldiers faced difficulties in obtaining equal treatment in all three of the areas mentioned by Olmsted. More frequently than their white counterparts, Negro soldiers were issued obsolescent flintlock muskets or other inferior firearms. Until 1864 they also received six dollars less each month in pay than did white volunteers. In addition, the black soldier's lot in battle was more dangerous than his white comrade's. The Confederacy in April 1863 decided that captured black soldiers would not be considered prisoners of war and thus could be put to death as insurrectionary slaves or sold into slavery. Although the General Order 100 promulgated by the Northern government that same month declared black soldiers to possess all the rights of belligerents, gaining the South's compliance with this order was difficult. After the storming of Fort Wagner near Charleston, South Carolina, in July 1863, in which numerous black soldiers were killed or captured, President Lincoln proclaimed that the North would follow a policy of retaliation, putting to death one Confederate prisoner for each black soldier executed by the Confederates and setting to work at hard labor one Confederate for each black soldier sold into slavery. Although Lincoln's order brought some protection to the captured black soldier, the North was never able to force the South to exchange captured black prisoners. In fact, the exchange of prisoners between the two governments foundered primarily on this issue (Benjamin Quarles, *Lincoln and the Negro* [New York, 1962], pp. 167–78; Dudley Taylor Cornish, *The Sable Arm: Negro Troops in the Union Army, 1861–1865* [New York, 1956], pp. 162–69, 184–86).

To JOHN OLMSTED

Washington, April 25th 1863

Dear Father,

I have just received your note of the 24th.

I am sorry you are not willing to enter into the case a little. I want to do what you would wish me to if you completely understood the circumstances.

Why do you tell me that I ought to have held on to my "salary of $5000," and that the citizens of New York would have sustained me?[1] I do not understand the reason of your so frequently repeating this to me. I think that I am willing to *do* anything that you advise and always have been. I think that I went upon your theory of the case to the utmost. I worked myself almost to death's door to save the place. There was nothing that I would not have done to save it. You can not possibly have regarded it with half the earnestness that I did. Not merely my pecuniary interests but my ambition and pride and more than that—affection for my work and—moral obligation to do all that it was possible for me to do to control so valuable an agency of civilization—all combined to urge me to do that which you apparently reproach me for not doing, merely on the ground of pecuniary interest. There was never a day when I would not gladly have held my place on the park at half the salary. I would as gladly today retake it as ever, and I never for a moment felt otherwise. Under these circumstances, do you suppose that I did not try what could be done to save me through public opinion. It would take me a week to tell you what I did in this way. You seem to me to give yourself unnecessary annoyance by adding to your regret that I was no longer able to keep the post, regret for my incompetence, weakness & folly. I gained the post by my own wholly unaided exertions. If I had a friend in the Commission, he only struck me back.[2] The same qualities, and judgment and skill in their use by which I gained it, I used with far greater effort and persistence to retain it. You have formed some theory about it based on a misconception of the facts. No man familiar with the circumstances from observation holds your view, not one. Try Vaux, Dana, Raymond.[3] It pains me that you should have the misfortune of supposing me to be so much less respectable a man than I am.

As for the farm—my time is worth more in fifty ways I could use to earn money, than it could be worth to manage it more closely. The difference between the best practicable management, and the worst, is comparatively small. It has been for sale, and known to be for a year or two past. Mr Aspinwall[4] has been solicited to buy it. I spent some time there last summer[5] and made enquiries about the sale of property; I have done so since. If I know nothing about it, it is the fault of my intellectual capacity, not of any carelessness or prejudice. Please not to hold such an idea. You can easily satisfy yourself whether Mr Aspinwall will meet your view, and won't you feel enough better to have your mind set at rest, as to my mistakes about it, to make it pay to take that trouble?

With your understanding of me, is it not easier to understand how I got off the park than how I got on? or than how I got on so well with this Sanitary Commission? It's a poor rule that won't work both ways. You have no right to demand of me invariable success in everything. Some matters must be sacrificed to others. I act always on certain, plain, simple principles of management. Generally they carry me through. Once or twice they have failed. Where is the man whose management never does fail. I say that my way, generally carries me through the storms, when most other men's ways wouldn't. Instead of losing, I gain confidence by experience in my principles; I think that, on the whole, facts justify them & that they are entitled to your respect & confidence also.

As to the $2000, I don't want to pretend that I have confidence that I can pay you that or any other sum of money, when I may not unlikely fail & disappoint you. I did not say what you assume that I said. That would have been ungrateful and unconfidential. I told you candidly and fairly and as fully and truly as I could, the grounds upon which I had to make up a judgment. Knowing those grounds, if you would still think that I should be justified in undertaking what, without knowing them, you proposed that I should undertake, I was disposed to do it, and if this didn't appear from my letter, I'm sorry for it and want to make amendment.

Although the signature was cut from this letter, probably by Mary Bull Olmsted, the letter appears to be complete.

1. John Olmsted's letter has not survived, but apparently he reproached his son for not fighting to retain his position as architect-in-chief and superintendent of Central Park with an annual salary of five thousand dollars. Although in 1863 Olmsted's connection with the park was rapidly drawing to a close, John may have been referring to events that had significantly diminished Olmsted's position and power two years earlier. In January 1861 he had tendered his resignation to the Central Park commission in an unsuccessful attempt to regain authority over expenditures, which had passed to Andrew H. Green. Again, in March 1861, Olmsted informed the board that if he did not receive greater independence in hiring, he wished to be relieved of responsibility for supervising the construction of the park. In June 1861 the commissioners granted him a small measure of independence in purchasing but relieved him of all responsibility for superintending construction except the finishing operations necessary to carry out his design. Possibly John Olmsted meant that his son should then have publicized his difficulties with the commissioners and looked to the public for support of his position (*Papers of FLO*, 3: 34–39).

2. Charles Wyllys Elliott was the friend who was serving on the Central Park commission in 1857 and who encouraged Olmsted to seek the post of superintendent of the park. It is unclear whether Olmsted in this allusion to Elliott's having "struck me back" referred to the position of superintendent of the park, which he received in 1857, or to the post of architect-in-chief, to which he was named in May 1858 after his and Vaux's "Greensward" design was chosen for the park. Although Olmsted asserted that he disliked the title "Architect-in-Chief," he may have resented a proposal by Elliott in December 1858 to change his title to "Superintendent of the Park," to name Vaux "Architect of the Park," and to transfer authority over architectural design and construction to the latter. Although the board gave Vaux the title "Consulting Architect" in January 1859, it did not alter Olmsted's title until May 1859, when he was named "Architect-in-Chief and Superintendent" (ibid., pp. 14, 27–28).
3. Calvert Vaux, Charles A. Dana, and Henry J. Raymond.
4. Presumably the wealthy New York merchant William Henry Aspinwall, who at one time lived in New Dorp on Staten Island. He and Olmsted were acquainted through Sanitary Commission affairs (Ira K. Morris, *Morris's Memorial History of Staten Island, New York* . . . , 2 vols. [New York, 1898–1900], 2: 237; FLO to Bertha Olmsted, Jan. 28, 1862, above).
5. After his arrival back in New York City from the Virginia Peninsula, Olmsted traveled to the family's farm, Tosomock, on July 18, 1862, and remained there approximately one week (FLO to JFJ, [July] 18, 1862, USSC-NYPL, box 743: 1570; FLO to JO, July 25, 1862).

To Henry Whitney Bellows

Private

Sanitary Commission,
Central Office, 244 F street,
Washington, D.C., April 25th 1863.

My Dear Doctor,
Enclosed you will find an official note,[1] which I want you to bring before the Executive Committee, to make sure there is no misunderstanding about my duty. I positively can not have any responsibility for the general management at present. If they should refuse to allow it on the ground I have named, then I beg that you will recommend that leave of absence be given me for a month.

Agnew gives me the severest task in averages that I ever had. He writes me a hasty letter[2] (and gives me the promise of more) which is the purest kindness and friendship in its candor and carelessness of self-presentation. I couldn't ask more of my wife. But it is just as careless in its injustice. Satan himself could not be as indifferent to a man's rights with-

615

OLMSTED'S CRITICS: JOHN STRONG NEWBERRY,
GEORGE TEMPLETON STRONG, AND CORNELIUS REA AGNEW

out consciousness of self-reproach. If I were a member of the Executive
Committee and another man—I don't care who—was General Secretary,
and any other member should say what Agnew writes to me, I should not
allow the Committee to adjourn before one of these three acts were
passed:

I. The suspension of the General Secry;

II. The expulsion of that member; or

III. The withdrawal of Mr Olmsted from the Committee.

The letter in fact proves to me that my worst anticipations, expressed to you some time ago, of what would result, from the complication
of responsibility between the Exec. Com. & the Genl Sec'y, are realized
and are irremediable. In other words, I feel that my professional reputation
is under the feet of the careless, good natured, self-opinionated Executive
Committee. Where is the court that I can claim a fair trial before? Who is

going to take the trouble to investigate the questions between Agnew and myself? They are not a whit less complicated or difficult to go fairly, honestly, justly to the bottom of, than were their popular impressions about McDowell. McDowell had for his professional vindication a dozen men at work for a month.[3] Agnew himself wouldn't give an hour's patient study to this business to save my life. He can't do it. It's not in him. And because it is not in him, he is no more fit to be an Executive Officer than I am to be an orator. Now I should die at the stake before I would treat another man as Agnew, in perfect unconsciousness of injustice, indolence or of the slightest swerving from the obligations of friendship, with in fact, unquestionably the opposite of all this, treats me. You may not be able to agree with me in the least—or to understand what I mean—but, you got me into the scrape and I hope you won't be impatient if I do claim a priviledge which I know that you don't concede to any other man. This therefore is outside of the Sanitary Commission, and I am

Very gratefully Yours

Fred. Law Olmsted.

The original is in box 641 of USSC-NYPL.

1. In this note, Olmsted asked Bellows to notify the Executive Committee of his intention, already approved by Bellows, not to resume immediately the supervision of Sanitary Commission affairs. Olmsted explained his reason to Bellows: "My journey to the West necessarily creates a hiatus, and in order to make legitimate use of that journey I am obliged to prolong it, after my actual return to Washington." Thus Olmsted intended to consider the Commission's organization in light of his recent journey. Until he resumed the post of general secretary, Jenkins would act in that capacity (FLO to HWB, April 25, 1863, USSC-NYPL, box 641).

2. On April 24 Agnew complained to Olmsted about the Sanitary Commission employees stationed with the Army of the Potomac. With information that he probably received from Sanitary Commission inspector Isaac Kerlin, Agnew denounced four employees—Charles S. Clampitt, Waldo F. Hayward, George Walter, and Gershom Bradford—for character flaws ranging from "oafishness" to "beastly drunkenness" and declared they should be "dismissed from the service at once and forever." He continued: "Our functions are of too important a character to justify us in keeping an Institute for the reform of immoral persons. It will take six months for us to regain what we have lost in the Army and we never shall obtain the hold that the Christian Commission has."

   While Olmsted found this demand for the summary dismissal of employees upon unproven charges to be unfair, he no doubt was also insulted and irritated by other sections of Agnew's letter which conflicted with his notions of how businesses should be conducted. The physician argued that the Commission's dependence upon employees' reports of their own conduct was "radically wrong" and added, "All men need to be watched and I shall hereafter be more strenuous than ever, in insisting upon your visiting our fields of operations." Such close supervision would completely reverse Olmsted's policy, which was to hire the "best men" and put them upon their own honor to perform their tasks conscientiously. Agnew was even more directly critical of Olmsted's management of the Commission. "I believe, as I have always believed, that you should be a Locomotive Secretary, instead of spending so much time in office work upon theoretical plans of organization," he chided. "While we are theorizing in Washington about organization our agencies in the Potomac Army are rotting from neglect."

Olmsted in his reply to Agnew thanked him for his candor and transferred responsibility for management to members of the Executive Committee:

> When we differ in judgment, as I now understand the case, it is your duty to control, not merely to advise me, and I am and have been as loyal to duty as you could ask me to be, when it is distinctly set before me. For whatever is wrong in the management, remember that you are responsible, and act accordingly.

(C. R. Agnew to FLO, April 24, 1863; FLO to C. R. Agnew, April 25, 1863; see also FLO to HWB, Oct. 3, 1862, above, and July 25, 1863, below.)

3. A reference to the military court of inquiry which Gen. Irvin McDowell requested in the fall of 1862 in response to rumors of his disloyalty and drunkenness. The dozen men presumably were the clerks that McDowell used to gather and transcribe information for his defense. In February 1863 the four-man court held all the imputations against McDowell to be unfounded (O.R., ser. 1, vol. 12, pt. 1, pp. 36, 323–32).

To Charles Eliot Norton

Washington, April 30th 1863.

My Dear Sir,

I am truly obliged to you for your favor of the 22[d] in reply to my note to Mr Forbes.[1]

The slip enterprise[2] is certainly a most effective measure for good, and if I should be able, at any time, to contribute to it, I shall gladly avail myself of your invitation.

To establish our nationality on a firm and permanently firm basis, it will be necessary that we have no dealings with slaveholders and rebels or disaffected people at the South, except as with criminals who have no civil rights, who have—as such—no property; as with men to whom nothing can be conceded, who can have nothing to give us but submission, and with whom consequently all idea of compromise is out of the question. As Mr Seward said the other day, whenever the people have made up their minds to a long war, the war is at an end.[3] That is to say, as soon as it is known that we will never give up, that we want no peace and will have no peace with traitors, no one can doubt—no one at the South can doubt, what the result will be. It is simply a question [of] whose resources will hold out longest. Everyone at the South must see that [as] the nation's will. Every man then who would not prefer death to submission, will be under a constant temptation to ask: "If I have got to submit, might I not as well submit now?" This would not at once or soon bring resistance to an end but would only make that end sure—the result sure. To reach it the leaders and desperate men, and those whom they could control, would keep together as armies as long as they could, afterwards as bands in the mountains and swamps, and a large part of the population would continue, while nominally submissive, to give them all the aid, and the civil officers of the nation, all the embarrassment possible. Probably for many years, in parts, no considerable part of the population will take part in elections or hold civil office, and those who do take office will be in danger of assassination and all manner of underhanded annoyance and obstruction. War will then continue for years as civil war, having the more common characteristics of civil war. Practically, therefore, what we need of the people is that they should say no more, ever, of peace with the South. Peace is to be come at by a gradual process, not by a treaty of peace, not by any act of Congress, least of all by any compromise, but by the gradual wearing out, dying off and killing off—extermination of the rebels.

Now I think the great work of those who are in a position to lead the people, is that of familiarizing them with this idea, of rooting out of their minds the idea that the war is to be ended by an event—the Tribune idea,[4] the sensational idea. I think an appetite for sensations is clearly not as strong as it was and yet I fear that the promise of a peace, jubilee-holiday with fire-works and a grand inflation of business, would reconcile a good many of us to the prospect of having Southern gentlemen back again in Washington society. It is this danger we need to fortify the people's mind against now.

At the West, especially in the Southern part of the Western states and in the large towns, not only is Copperheadism and hatred of New England and a hankering after the nobility of the South very strong, but with loyal men to a great extent, the passion of money-making, especially by land speculation, constantly struggles with patriotism. Patriotism will lose a great advantage in this struggle when the Mississippi shall be opened. There will from that time be a strong and constantly increasing disposition throughout the West, but especially in the Western large towns, to make some arrangement with the rebels—no matter what, so the Mississippi trade can be resumed.

Hence I hope that you will do all you can to propagate the resolution that peace shall be gained in Alabama only as it has been, partially, in Maryland and Western Virginia and Kentucky and Missouri. That the rebels are to be exterminated, and the process of extermination is likely to continue for years.

619

That is the spirit of the unconditional Union men of the border states. Let us insist upon it that that is the spirit of loyal men everywhere.

I really think, however, if we can manage to keep the war along only one year more, get a hundred thousand negroes habituated to working only for wages, and have a few regiments of them stand up well, side by side, with the white ones, in some great battles, the disintegration of Southern Society—of the Slave Social System—will be permanently established.

Thank God, we live so close upon it. It is more than I had expected a hundred years would bring the world to.

I do not know enough of Genl Banks' arrangment[5] to judge fairly of it. But if he can get a quarter part of the slaves who were in Louisiana to work for money-wages, I think he will have struck the heaviest blow at Slavery that it has yet received. My impression is that you overestimate the danger to be apprehended from any intermediate state between Slavery and Freedom. Men who have been accustomed to manage negroes as slaves, will not be able to do anything with them in any condition which closely resembles but is not slavery. It will be easier for them to deal with them as free-men than as apprentices. The contradictions of Slavery itself are an intolerable embarrassment. The self control which would be required by an apprenticeship would be impossible. They could never help taking the aims of an owner and getting themselves into trouble thereby.

A year more of war and slave-holders will be mere lingering survivors of a nearly extinct class of mankind. They are out of place in the world.

With sincere respect, I am cordially Yours

Fred. Law Olmsted.

Chas. Eliot Norton Esq[r]

The original is in the Charles Eliot Norton Papers, Houghton Library, Harvard University, Cambridge, Massachusetts.

1. Olmsted's letter of March 11, 1863, to John Murray Forbes has not survived, but according to Norton, Olmsted wrote about "an alarming amount of prejudice and falsehood afloat about New England" in the Midwest (C. E. Norton to FLO, April 22, 1863).
2. A reference to the first activities of the New England Loyal Publication Society, sponsored by John Murray Forbes with Norton as his chief editor of publications. On April 22 Norton wrote Olmsted that because the Loyal League and other patriotic societies had been publishing pamphlets, "We determined that the best mode of affecting public opinion left open to us was through the circulation of 'slips' to the loyal press throughout the country. We are now, therefore, so far as we have been

able to obtain lists of newspapers, sending slips, generally three a week to the press in all the loyal states." Norton then solicited any writing that Olmsted might be able to undertake for the society:

> If at any time you should wish to bring any special topic connected with public affairs, before the country, it will give us great satisfaction to circulate anything you may write or may select for the purpose. I trust that you may have leisure enough to write from time to time a brief article which can be sent out either with or without your name as you prefer.

(Ibid.; see also George Winston Smith, "Broadsides for Freedom: Civil War Propaganda in New England," *New England Quarterly* 21 [Sept. 1948]: 292–97.)

3. The editors have found no evidence that Secretary of State William H. Seward made a public pronouncement to this effect. Olmsted probably learned of this remark from Bellows, who reported that during a dinner with him Seward had said: "The moment the people were thoroughly ready for a long war, perfectly made up to it—the war would wholly cease. That is, absolute unity of purpose in a determination to fight out every obstacle to success, would present a front before which Rebeldom would quail & fade away at once" (HWB to Eliza Bellows, April 23, 1863, Henry Whitney Bellows Papers, Massachusetts Historical Society, Boston, Mass.).

4. The *New-York Daily Tribune*.

5. Nathaniel Prentiss Banks (1816–1894), Massachusetts politician and after December 1862 commander of the Department of the Gulf. Olmsted is referring to the contract labor system that Banks had instituted in Union-occupied parts of Louisiana through General Order 12 of January 30, 1863. Banks's policy encouraged blacks to return to the plantations and agree to one-year contracts that provided food, clothing, and compensation, either as monthly wages or as a small share of the crop, at the end of the period. The quartermaster's department operated abandoned plantations on a similar contract basis.

In his letter of April 22 Norton had commented upon this system:

> I am not satisfied with the state of things in regard to slavery in New Orleans. It is very important that what is done there should be done well, and the labor system that General Banks is introducing seems to be full of danger if taken as a model for other places. It will not do for the United States to engage in a system of apprenticeship, or to guarantee labor to its employers. It seems to me plain that the only safe system is the purely voluntary one. Under any modified system of slavery or apprenticeship the risk of tyranny on the part of masters, or the continuance of servile qualities among the slaves is very great. The slaves may have to learn the value of independence and self-dependence through much misery, but it is better that they should thus learn it than be subjected any longer to the will of a master sustained as in this case it is by the power of the United States.

Norton was objecting to aspects of Banks's policy that left blacks in a condition similar to slavery. The regulations provided that "the officers of the Government will induce the slaves to return to the plantations where they belong, with their families," a clause that was sometimes interpreted to mean that blacks had to work for their former owners. Although one of Banks's subordinates urged him to recognize explicitly the right of blacks to choose their employers, he refused to do so. The contracts also included a provision that such a contract would not "imply the surrender of any right of property in the slave or other right of the owner" (C. E. Norton to FLO, April 22, 1863; Peyton McCrary, *Abraham Lincoln and Reconstruction: The Louisiana Experiment* [Princeton, 1978], pp. 115–22, 135–37, 149–54; C. Peter Ripley, *Slaves and Freedmen in Civil War Louisiana* [Baton Rouge, La., 1976], pp. 47–53).

To John Olmsted

Sanitary Commission,
Central Office 244 F street,
Washington, D.C., May 2ᵈ 1863.

Dear Father,

I wanted the benefit of your judgment. I don't know what you mean by asking my pardon, but I know that I never gave you occasion to keep up that style of dealing with me. Now I should like to know what you would advise me or what you wish me, to do, fairly considering the facts I have laid before you. If you think I am wrong in my view I want to know it & where & how. You did write as if you thought me wrong. If I am wrong, I want to be right. Why not give me a chance?

I am very glad Ally[1] is back and not wholly broken down. Give my congratulations & love to him.

I am going to New York tomorrow night.

You characterize my letter[2] as "unkind". I am sure that the intentioₙ was nothing but kindness—an effort to remove the grounds of false and uncomfortable suppositions which you had expressed about your son. It will take more than one night's sleep to make me content to rest or to allow you to rest with such impressions. I deal with you as I hope my children will deal with me. I don't want them to be indifferent to my judgment of them or to lazily let me set them down as unwise and obstinate in their own wisdom. However wanting in sagacity I may be, I am obstinate only in honest dutifulness. You ought to know that I will never quietly acquiesce in being put in an undutiful position.

Your affectionate Son,

Fred. Law Olmsted.

1. Olmsted's half-brother, Albert Henry Olmsted, was discharged from the 25th Connecticut because of poor health on April 8, 1863. He had become seriously ill late in January and had only partly recovered. Probably he arrived in New York from New Orleans in late April (Connecticut, Adjutant General's Office, *Record of Service of Connecticut Men in the Army and Navy* . . . [Hartford, Conn., 1889], p. 793; A. H. Olmsted to Bertha Olmsted Niles, April 1, 1863; A. H. Olmsted to JO, April 13, 1863).
2. See FLO to JO, April 25, 1863, above.

To John Olmsted

Washington,
May 22ᵈ 1863.

Dear Father,
    I enclose a note written a month ago or so and since lying perdu[1] in my pocket. I have not heard anything of Ally since his arrival at New York.
    Vaux has been finally badgered off the park and my relations with it are finally closed. He couldn't bear it even as *consulting* architect. They wound it up with a very innocent complimentary resolution.[2]
    I have been engaged in preparing some schemes of reorganization for the San. Com.[3] I refused to return to the duty of General Secretary—as central Executive officer—on my return from the West, but have been very hard at work. The Board meets, second Tuesday of June, &, I hope, in New York.
    We shall go on next week, and I think that I shall stay and work in New York till the meeting. It is very hot and noisome here, but we are all pretty well. Charley learning to fiddle, Owen to climb over the house, and Marion to say "dada". She is uncommonly backward and only half pint pot size, but lively and clever enough.
    Your affecᵗᵉ son

Fred. Law Olmsted.

1. *Perdu* is a French participle meaning lost. Olmsted is probably referring to his letter of May 2 (see FLO to JO, May 2, 1863, above).
2. On May 12, 1863, Calvert Vaux sent Olmsted a copy of his letter of resignation from the post of "Landscape Architects to the Board," which he and Olmsted had held jointly since April 1862. Vaux deemed the resignation "the best thing to be done now" and told Olmsted: "I look forward with satisfaction to the time when I shall again be a free agent. This has been a dead weight to me ever since you left & for some time before." Two events probably triggered Vaux's action: the commissioners' decision in January 1863 to consult outside architects about structures to be built in the park, and the securing of an extension of the park to 110th Street. Vaux resented the possible hiring of outside architects, and once the plan for the extension had been accepted, he no longer felt an obligation to remain associated with the park. In the resignation that he drew up, Vaux gave the excuse that it would be impracticable for either Olmsted or himself "to give a continuous personal attention to the park operations during the ensuing summer."
    During its meeting of May 14, 1863, the Central Park commission accepted Olmsted and Vaux's resignation. The "very innocent complimentary resolution" to which Olmsted refers read, in part: "The Board takes pleasure in expressing its high

esteem for them personally, and its unabated confidence in their high artistic taste, and in their superior professional abilities" (CV to FLO, May 12, 1863; CV and FLO to the Board of Commissioners of the Central Park, May 12, 1863; *Papers of FLO*, 3: 37–38; New York City, Board of Commissioners of the Central Park, *Minutes of Proceedings*, April 10, 1862, p. 111; ibid., May 14, 1863, p.6).
3. See FLO to MPO, June 26, 1863, note 1, below.

To Mary Bull Olmsted

Sanitary Commission,
Central Office, 244 F street,
Washington, D.C., May 22[d] 1863.

Dear Mother,

I duly received your letter of the 16th and this morning one from Miss Schuyler[1] on the same subject.[2] I think you have taken the wise course. I have only one thing to suggest. It is better that no goods should come than that soreness, distrusts and divisions should arise among loyal people through a strong rivalry of competing philanthropists. I hope you will say as little as possible, think as little as possible, of the differences between you and Mrs Cowen[3] and make light of them. At any rate, let them say what they will, make our friends understand that our rule is not to disparage others, or to be tempted to do so. There are various ways of helping the country. Patience, cordiality and a spirit of conciliation and union, sacrificing nothing essential, is what is most wanted to be fostered, and the sick and wounded can suffer a good deal rather than we can afford to do anything counteractive to that spirit.

Neither your "circular" nor Mr Hale's[4] Sermon have reached me. I will enquire about Stillé's pamphlet.[5] How many do you want? I could send a hundred I suppose.

One expression of yours rather shocked me—I don't expect and don't want a short war. We are at the beginning of our work. Above all things don't encourage the idea that the war is to be soon over or that it is ever to be ended by a blow. Our only hope, as far as I can see, of eradicating Slavery is to keep our armies moving through the South for years. Above all I hope that we shall never have a treaty of peace or a declaration of peace with the rebels. We are to reestablish the supremacy of the laws of the Union, by force of arms everywhere, little by little, and let peace grow up after that, under our armed protection to those who choose peace for

LOUISA LEE SCHUYLER

themselves. That from the start has been my theory. Dr Bellows has just got it well beaten out in his fast-day sermon.[6]

I propose to bring Mary & all, round by sea to New York next week. She will make a short visit to the island & then call on you in Hartford on her way to Litchfield.[7] I hope to see you at that time also. I will try, but don't expect to succeed, to get Dr Bellows to "address" you.

Affectionately,

Fred.

The original is in the possession of Terry Niles Smith.

1. Louisa Lee Schuyler (1837–1926), chairman of the Committee of Correspondence of the Woman's Central Association of Relief. A descendant of Alexander Hamilton and Revolutionary War general Philip Schuyler, she was born to wealth and social prominence. Her parents, George Lee and Eliza Hamilton Schuyler, were members of Bellows's congregation at All Souls Church and supporters of Charles Loring Brace's Children's Aid Society, in whose industrial schools Louisa served as a sewing instructor before the Civil War.

During the Civil War the Woman's Central Association of Relief in New York became an important first step in Louisa Schuyler's career of public service. Then only twenty-three years old, she had no important role in the W.C.A.R. at the time of its formation, but her mother was a member of its Executive Committee and Henry W. Bellows personally asked Louisa to work in the organization. Her tireless energy, organizational skill, and tactful yet firm diplomacy in relations with the

W.C.A.R.'s local tributary societies steadily increased her importance and power. As chairman of the Committee on Correspondence (first formed in 1862 as a subcommittee), she tried to ensure a steady stream of needed supplies and to foster a spirit of nationalism that would override state and local concerns.

Louisa Schuyler and Olmsted probably first met when Charles Loring Brace introduced Olmsted to the Schuyler family in 1855, but it was their wartime work that created a strong bond of sympathy between them. Louisa Schuyler thoroughly understood and shared Olmsted's conception of the Commission's mission during the war. Upon his resignation, she wrote him:

> I have never been able to impress upon others the *magnitude* of the work, to make them see what it was capable of, to look outside and beyond the boxes and bales into the hearts of the people, and to feel that our greatest work was not merely in results which might be handled, but in the patriotic education of the people. . . . And through it all, without a word on either side, I *know* how you looked upon the work in the same light and how you felt the responsibility of it, and were putting your highest powers and your whole heart into it.

She also believed that Olmsted had been "always looking ahead, ready to sieze [sic] every opportunity, able to comprehend a whole and gifted with the power of bringing this *whole* down to *working* details."

At the end of the war Louisa Schuyler collapsed physically and remained almost an invalid for six years, but her interest in philanthropic causes remained. In 1869 she began to plan for a voluntary private organization that would oversee and supplement the efforts of the state institutions of correction and charity. This body, which became the State Charities Aid Association, was composed of local committees which regularly inspected and advised hospitals, asylums, almshouses, jails, and schools of correction. Believing Olmsted to have special ability for conceptualizing both far-sighted schemes and the practical plans for their operation, she early asked his opinion of her proposal: "I have so much more confidence in your Judgement than that of any one else, that I should hesitate to bring forward any plan of work that you believed to be unadvisable or not feasible." As Louisa Schuyler organized the constituent parts of the S.C.A.A., she continued to consider Olmsted's aid and opinions important. She sent her organizational drafts for his "sharpest criticisms" and also recruited his participation. In 1877 he wrote a handbook for the inspection of poorhouses which she considered to be "perhaps the most valuable document" her organization had published.

Olmsted's collaboration with Louisa Schuyler continued until his move to Brookline in 1881. She remained an active organizer for benevolent causes. In 1907 she became one of the first trustees of the newly formed Russell Sage Foundation, and she was a great influence upon the founding in 1915 of the National Committee for the Prevention of Blindness (Robert D. Cross, "The Philanthropic Contribution of Lousia Lee Schuyler," *Social Service Review* 35 [Sept. 1961]: 290–301; *Notable American Women*; L. L. Schuyler to FLO, Sept. 1, 1863, Aug. 27, 1869, Dec. 11, 1875, and Feb. 12, [1877]).

2. A reference to the dissension in the Hartford Soldiers' Aid Society over the question of reserving at least part of its contributions solely for soldiers from Connecticut. Olmsted had convinced his stepmother that the Sanitary Commission's policy of providing needed supplies to soldiers regardless of state origin was the wisest course. But some of her fellow managers of the Hartford society, especially Sarah S. Cowen, disagreed. While the quarrel was in large part over policy, an element of personal rivalry also existed. When the society in 1863 again selected Sarah Cowen as its secretary, Mary Bull Olmsted and three other women resigned.

Louisa Schuyler visited Hartford in May 1863 to assess the problem but decided the rift was too large to be bridged. At their meeting, Sarah Cowen reiterated the Hartford society's new position: that it would forward two-thirds of its contributions to the Sanitary Commission but distribute the remainder to Connecticut soldiers. She agreed to allow the Sanitary Commission to canvass the towns and countryside around Hartford, and Louisa Schuyler encouraged Mary Bull Olmsted to undertake that activity (L. L. Schuyler to FLO, May 20, 1863, USSC-NYPL, box 955: 1631; L. L. Schuyler to MBO, May 11, 1863, USSC-NYPL, box 667: 87–88; *Hartford Daily Courant*, June 15, 1863, p. 2).

3. Sarah S. Cowen, secretary of the Hartford Soldiers' Aid Society in 1862 and 1863 and an advocate of reserving at least a part of the supplies raised by that organization for the sole benefit of regiments from Connecticut. Horace Howard Furness considered her to be the main proponent of the spirit of localism in Hartford and described her at his lecture there in January 1863: "The horns of the boss devil were plainly prominent protruding from the head of Mrs. Cowen on the front bench" (H. H. Furness to FLO, Jan. 29, 1863).

4. Edward Everett Hale (1822–1909) was a Unitarian clergyman and the pastor of Boston's South Congregational Church. Active in the New England Emigrant Aid Company in the 1850s, Hale had collaborated with Olmsted in aiding the free-state settlers in Kansas and encouraging free-labor emigration to Texas. The sermon to which Olmsted here refers was probably "The Desert and the Promised Land," published in 1863, in which Hale compared Northern disaffection with the war to the murmurings of the Israelites after their flight from Egypt (*DAB*; *Papers of FLO*, 2: 64–65; "The Desert and Promised Land. A Sermon," in Frank Freidel, ed., *Union Pamphlets of the Civil War, 1861–1865*, 2 vols. [Cambridge, Mass., 1967], 1: 503–11).

5. Probably *How a Free People Conduct a Long War* (see FLO to Oliver W. Gibbs, Jan. 31, 1863, above).

6. On April 30, 1863, the day proclaimed by President Lincoln as a national day of prayer, fasting, and humiliation, Henry W. Bellows preached a sermon entitled "The War to End Only When Rebellion Ceases," which attacked what he believed to be a degeneration of the American character caused by materialism, westward migration, and, most important, slavery. To Bellows, slavery had caused the Civil War by undermining the morality of the country—by creating a moral stupor and political apathy in the North and by breeding a "suicidal recklessness" that led to secession in the South. But, Bellows argued, secession had in fact planted the seeds for the nation's regeneration. The peace movement in the North and the army's experience with Southern blacks as soldiers and allies had confirmed the North in an antislavery policy as well as in a determination to win the war. According to Bellows, "The question for loyal men, is not *when*, but only *how* the war is to end, and they have no question that the war is to end, only when the Rebellion stops, be it one year, five years, or our natural lives."

The part of Bellows's sermon to which Olmsted probably refers reads as follows:

The longer our forces are in the field, the more obstinately they are resisted, the larger the force we are compelled to bring to the war, the more completely we are driven to overrun every acre of the enemy's area—the more thoroughly and completely do we disintegrate his country, saturate his barbarous civilization with ours, carry our customs, our people, our temper, and our industry into his territory, and take moral possession of his soil. His stout resistance, successful skirmishes, do but familiarize us the more with him and him with us. I can not even regret that his stubborness is continued—for if he bent before our blast, we should have passed over him with less effect. The war is by its duration, and its thoroughness preparing the South to make a possible part of a free country. You can not plough the yielding sand nor plant it; but the tough marl may be broken up, spite of all resistance, if only oxen enough are put to the yoke! We have oxen enough, and by the grace of God, we mean to plough the Southern cotton-fields with the heifers of freedom and sow it with Northern wheat. War is the only culture our Southern waste admits of. By no other tillage can it be added to the area of cultivated American civilization.

(Henry W. Bellows, *The War to End Only When Rebellion Ceases* [New York, 1863], pp. 7, 13–15.)

7. Litchfield, Connecticut, where Mary Perkins Olmsted spent part of August 1862 and much of the summer in 1863 (FLO to MPO, Aug. 12, 1862, n. 7, above; FLO to MPO, July 27, 1863).

Prospectus for a Weekly Journal

[c. June 25, 1863]

This Pamphlet is printed for private circulation only,
and it is requested that it may be returned to the Trustees.

It is proposed to establish a weekly journal, the main object of which would be to secure a more careful, accurate and elaborate discussion of political, economical and commercial topics, than is possible in the columns of the daily press, and a more candid and honest discussion of them than the constitution of the daily press admits of. The way in which the latter treats the questions of the day, is necessarily imperfect, slip-shod and inaccurate, if for no other reason, for the mere want of time of its writers to do better. Each topic has to be handled on the very day on which it comes up, and, let the writer who takes hold of it be ever so conscientious or pains-taking, he is compelled to dispose of it by the aid of such knowledge as he happens to command at the moment, and in most cases with the aid of scarcely any reflection. The result is, in appearance, an essay, but in reality an extemporaneous speech, containing simply a first impression, delivered as hastily as the pen can be made to move over the paper. It would, consequently, possess little value, even if there was a positive certainty that the article was the product of sincere and unbiased conviction. But this is not likely to be the case, owing to the fact that nearly all the daily newspapers of influence and importance, are either the organs of men who seek political prominence, and who make them subservient to the advancement of their personal fortunes, or else are compelled, owing to the smallness of their price as compared with the weight of their expenses, to follow that course which will secure the largest circulation. A

628

sufficiently large circulation can only be secured by bending to the demand of a portion of the public not the most intelligent, by reflecting its prejudices, and by endeavoring to solve every problem in legislation or political economy in the manner which will be agreeable to it. The result is that every event of the day is colored so as to make it serve either the purposes of the editor, or of the party to which he belongs, or in a manner to commend itself to minds which are not given to a consideration of fundamental principles.

Before the present convulsion in our affairs, these defects of the press, though by no means unnoticed, were not seriously felt. It did not much matter to many educated men, how things were publicly discussed, about which their own minds were not deeply occupied. Since the commencement of the rebellion there has been a wide change in this respect. Questions of the most momentous importance come up daily, and exact grave consideration from all. The experience of most persons will confirm the assertion that the manner in which the daily newspapers deal with these questions is most defective and unsatisfactory. Their false prophecies, their abandonment of all attempt to sift evidence—often unavoidable, it is true—their constant sacrifice of the truth to the demand for startling effects, the factious, flippant and reckless way in which many of them deal with the most serious topics, constantly remind their more intelligent readers that they are prepared to suit the requirements of the greatest number, but not by any means the best qualified, of those whose judgment goes to make up that force in human affairs called public opinion.

A weekly journal, of the kind contemplated, would not be open to these objections. There would be time for the deliberate preparation of its articles. The public would look to it for careful rather than early comments on subjects of interest. The editor could, therefore, exact from his contributors all the accuracy, completeness and finish which his space would admit of, and the readers would find in it the matured views of competent authorities, instead of the first impression of writers not always possessing special qualifications for their task. It would be its place to lead public opinion rather than to follow it.

If this purpose should, at first thought, be considered quixotic, it must be remembered that while, four years ago, intelligent men could avoid giving much consideration to questions of government and legislation, this is no longer the case; henceforward they *must* give consideration to these questions or prepare themselves to accept the destruction of their country. There is nothing clearer than that the time in which anybody was competent to administer our affairs is forever gone by. Whatever may happen, we have before us a future of standing armies, of large navies, and of complicated foreign relations, and we shall have to add to these, the grave task of reducing a disaffected population of four millions into order and submission, and of raising the same number of degraded slaves into the ranks of industrious citizens.[1] A government which has problems of such magnitude to work out must be aided and supported by men more thoughtful, more far-seeing, more attentive to remote consequences than those whose demand establishes the character of our present daily press. It is a necessity of the country that studious men should take hold of public affairs, and be felt as a power; it is important that they should come closer and more constantly together—should be organized and possess means which they have not hitherto had of making themselves heard and their influence felt. It should be remembered, however, that even if it were practicable to obtain such articles daily as ought properly to appear in a paper which would answer this purpose, people would not pay for such a mass of erudition and ability every day, and, if they did, could not, in a society like ours, read and digest it. Even such a paper as the London *Times* can not be read as our daily newspapers are mostly read—as, for instance, in the street cars. But at some time in the course of every week many men can find an opportunity, and will have the inclination, to deliberately read three or four articles in which real thought and study are brought to bear upon matters of public interest.

The strongest objection that is raised against the establishment of such a paper is the difficulty which, it is alleged, would be experienced in finding writers. There is, however, very little doubt that this would be mainly a question of money, though partly a question of the amount of influence which would be exercised by the paper. In all the professions, as well as outside of them, there are men of high attainments, to be found, who would be willing to write upon their special subjects, if paid well enough, and if the place in which their articles were to appear would command for them consideration and influence. And a weekly paper would be exempt from the disadvantage, under which the daily papers labor, of being compelled to seek its contributors in the place of publication. The editor of the latter is forced to depend, for the most part, on men attached to his office. Even on political topics, the editor of a weekly paper might collect his articles over an area of five hundred miles, and as regards the purely economical, commercial, literary, and social articles, they might be written in any part of the Union. This is, of course, an uncommon advantage, as it gives the whole country for a field of selection, and there are undoubtedly a large number of skilled writers, who, writing poorly every day, would write once a week very well, and still a larger number who, utterly unable to write every day, would produce once a fortnight, or once a month, contributions of great value. That many of this latter class would be brought to light by the existence of a periodical anxious to get their articles, and willing to pay well for them, there is no doubt.

It is obvious, however, that a publication of this kind could not, under the most favorable circumstances, rely upon a circulation so large as to make it possible to keep the price very low. The most careful writing on any subject is not, even in a periodical form, either read or appreciated by very large numbers, and those who are interested in seeing thought and study applied to politics, necessarily form in every community a comparatively small minority. The same thing may be said of those who really desire and appreciate careful and conscientious criticism in science, art and literature; so that it is not anticipated that such a paper as is proposed could be sold at much less than ten dollars a year.

This raises, what is, without doubt, the most serious question of all: whether at this price, such a periodical would find purchasers in sufficient numbers to make it successful. Are there, in short, in the loyal States several thousand persons of sufficient taste and education to make them desire to have on their tables, every week, a periodical, professedly critical, and not merely popular or partizan? The answer to this must, of course, be mainly conjectural, but the following are some reasons for giving it in the affirmative:

That there is such a class, that it already is not small, and that it is increasing, is proved by the sale of many high class works of all kinds, native and foreign. There is no country, except England perhaps, in which books which require a good deal of previous culture for the enjoyment of them, are so widely diffused as in America at this moment. An illustration of this may be found in the fact, that more than two thousand copies of such a book as Mill "On Liberty,"[2] which is very abstract in its subject and style, and not by any means popular in its opinions, have actually been sold here within a few months. Moreover, the number of authors in all departments whose claims to places in the front rank is everywhere acknowledged, is increasing every year. This could not happen unless the class which has the wealth, taste and culture to enable them to appreciate their works were also increasing, for, from this, writers as well as readers must come. Readers are the soil from which writers spring. It is also proved by the increasing interest in, and love of art, as shown by the large and growing production of pictures of a high order, and which find ready sales at high prices. There is hardly a doubt that those who are interested in books and pictures, are also interested in having competent, careful, and impartial critiques upon them, and these are things which, at present, are not to be found in the newspaper press, and which it would be one of the main objects of the proposed journal to supply. So it may be said, that there is some basis to start upon, and a fair prospect of a circulation which would increase in the direct ratio of the progress of the country in every direction.

It must not be forgotten, too, that such a paper would have no rival. There is nothing in the field which, in the least, resembles what is now proposed.[3] It would at once gather to itself all the materials for success which actually exist, and would have the best chance of appropriating those still to be created. It would, however, have to depend mainly for success on the power and accuracy of its writing rather than on advertizing. It could not be puffed into circulation. So that at least one year, and perhaps two, might be expected to elapse before it would be established on a firm commercial basis. Consequently it would not be prudent to attempt to start it with less capital than would be sufficient to cover its entire expenses for a year.

No one should be asked to subscribe to its stock merely for the ordinary purposes of commercial speculation, but it is thought that in the present condition of public affairs, motives may be found which will appeal no less powerfully to many than purely commercial ones. The federal system is at this moment in greater peril than it has ever been in since the Union was formed. The rebellion has shaken the popular faith in its strength if not in its value, and on this faith, its durability must be greatly dependent. A convulsion has occurred which even the authors of the *Federalist* pronounced all but impossible,[4] and, rousing the people suddenly from dreams of peace and security, it has thrown them into a state of doubt, of which malcontents and demagogues are eagerly availing themselves. The very same doctrines, uttered in almost the same language, which formed the main impediments to the formation of the government, are now used to aid in its overthrow. The people are urged to leave it to its fate, by the same arguments by which their fathers, eighty years ago, were urged not to establish it. The dangers of concentrated power, and of standing armies, are painted in frightful colors,—the overwhelming importance of local interests is energetically and insidiously preached. One of our most powerful demagogues has even gone so far as to propose the separation of the town from the State, for the advantage of the local politicians,—a point far beyond the wildest theorizing of the earlier enemies of the Union.[5] A Union resting on the mere inclination of the members of it, is declared to be the only Union possible; although this is the very kind of Union which was tried under the old confederacy, and found worthless. The necessary inconveniences of the Union as it is, are made to wear the appearance of wrongs or calamities, while the possible advantages of separation are constantly hinted at. The State is held up as our real mother and protector, as something entitled to the devotion and affection of all its citizens, while the Federation is represented as a mere machine, to be maintained as long as it runs well, but not worth very great sacrifices for its preservation. All these devices were encountered by the founders of the government, but they are more formidable now than they were then, because the independence of the State organization was, at that day, associated in the popular mind with dissension, repudiation and stagnation at home, and with weakness and contempt abroad. The people had tried it and found it wanting. Now, however, it is the Union which is presented in association with evil and misfortune. It is for the perpetuation of the federal system, and the propagation of the federal idea, that the country is passing through its present throes, and it is consequently a comparatively easy task for the enemies of both to cheat the ignorant, the unreflecting or the timid into the belief that the remedy for what we are now suffering, lies in the relaxation of the federal bond, and the exaltation above all else of the individual States. War and heavy taxation have come in the Union, and it is, therefore, easy to persuade many that peace and security might be found outside of it. The worst and greatest dangers that can befall us, threaten us, they are told, from such an alleged augmentation of its strength as is necessary to carry on a war with its enemies in arms, while our dearest blessings might survive its overthrow, were it destroyed to-morrow.

There is amongst us, also, a large body of sympathizers with Southern theories of government, who, under the pretence of sustaining the States' rights doctrine, are intentionally laboring for the maintenance of Slavery and the overthrow of popular government. They zealously ascribe our troubles to the very nature of our popular institutions, and lose no opportunity of drawing unfavorable contrasts between the administration of our affairs, and that of monarchical or aristocratic societies. They have, it cannot be denied, already achieved a good deal of success among the men of property of our eastern cities. It only remains for them to win over the education and cultivation of the nation to insure the triumph of their ideas. With property and intelligence lost to popular government, it is easy to see that it might become so intolerable for all, that we should take refuge in the only refuge which would be left us, sheer absolutism. For nothing can be more certain than that for a society such as ours, based on an equality of conditions, there is no resting place between broad democracy and pure despotism. We have neither the men nor the manners for a mixed system, and if we acknowledge that the people cannot manage their own affairs, we have no resource but to surrender them into the hands of one able and energetic ruler.

It is, for all these reasons, more necessary than it has been at any period of our history, that there should be some publication, largely devoted to the task of holding up to the eyes of those who should be the leaders of public sentiment, the now forgotten perils and inconveniences of petty sovereignties, the innumerable dangers to our prosperity, and even to our civilization itself, of such a state of things as we should certainly drift into, if the so-called rights of States became the paramount consideration in our politics. From whatever point of view we look at it, there is nothing so essential to the future peace and happiness of our country, as a general and clear perception of the relations which exist between events of constant occurrence and the fundamental principles of our national as distinguished from our State and commercial existence. But to keep the attention of the people fixed upon the remote consequences of apparently insignificant occurrences, the daily press is too superficial, while the monthly and quarterly magazines necessarily lag behind the period of popular interest in the various events of which they treat.

For these reasons, it is believed, that there is no way in which capital can be so well invested, regard being had to the overruling interests of all, as in the promotion through the instrumentality of such a publication as is proposed, of careful, candid and conscientious study of the deeper nature and remoter bearings of the leading events of each passing week.

The proposed paper would somewhat resemble the London *Spectator*,[6] in appearance, and arrangement, as well as in character, though less heavy and less elaborate, both in the selection of subjects and in the treatment of them. It would be made up—

1. Of three pages of short comments on the principal occurrences of note, legal, social, commercial and political—of the preceding week.

2. Of three or four carefully prepared articles on the leading topics of the day.

3. Of about the same number on questions of social, economical, literary or scientific importance—including under the term "scientific," jurisprudence, political economy, agriculture and manufactures.

4. Thoroughly careful and impartial critiques on the books, pictures, and theatrical and musical performances of all the leading cities.

5. Correspondence from Paris and London giving a popular summary of all that is most interesting in the literary, social, and political world in England and on the Continent: amongst other things, a condensed account of the most noteworthy discoveries and inventions made in Europe and elsewhere.

It is intended that all those articles shall be marked by such an amount of research and accuracy as shall give the publication a value in this respect, peculiar to itself.

For the fund to be contributed to establish the paper above proposed, the undersigned have consented to act as Trustees, and subscriptions to the said fund may be made to them.

> Howard Potter,
> George T. Strong,
> William J. Hoppin.[7]

The text presented here is taken from an untitled printed version in the Olmsted Papers.

1. The slave population of the states of the Confederacy had in 1860 totaled slightly over 3.5 million, but the white population then was almost 5.5 million.

2. *On Liberty*, by noted English utilitarian philosopher John Stuart Mill (1806–1873), was first published in 1859 (*DNB*).

3. Olmsted is correct that none of the journals of the day resembled this proposed periodical. Serious journals such as the *Atlantic Monthly* or the newly revitalized *North American Review* were published quarterly or monthly. Weekly journals tended to be miscellanies that lacked the analytical rigor Olmsted and Godkin desired. *Harper's Weekly*, the highest quality weekly paper, was best known for its excellent engraved illustrations and its serialized fiction by noted English authors. Moreover, in its political editorials, *Harper's Weekly* had been decidedly Democratic and conciliatory to the South. Only in 1862, as Olmsted's friend George William Curtis began to write its political editorials and Thomas Nast began to draw its political cartoons, did *Harper's* begin to support the war enthusiastically (Frank Luther Mott, *A History of American Magazines* . . . , 5 vols. [Cambridge, Mass., 1938–68], 2: 27–45, 469–75).

4. *The Federalist* was a series of articles written by Alexander Hamilton, John Jay, and James Madison in 1787 and 1788 in support of the proposed federal constitution. In number 7 Hamilton discussed possible causes of war among the states, such as boundary disputes and competition over commerce, which he believed a union of states would be able to remove. He also stated, in number 9, that "a firm Union will be of the utmost moment to the peace and liberty of the States, as a barrier against domestic faction and insurrection." In number 10 Madison argued that the proposed union of states would be better able to overcome the ill effects of disputes among contending interests:

> The influence of factious leaders may kindle a flame within their particular States, but will be unable to spread a general conflagration through the other States. A religious sect may degenerate into a political faction in a part of the Confederacy; but the variety of sects dispersed over the entire face of it must secure the national councils against any danger from that source. A rage for paper money, for abolition of debts, for an equal division of property, or for any other improper or wicked project, will be less apt to pervade the whole body of the Union than a particular member of it; in the same proportion as such a malady is more likely to taint a particular county or district, than an entire State.

(Alexander Hamilton, John Jay, and James Madison, *The Federalist: A Commentary on the Constitution of the United States* . . . , ed. Benjamin Fletcher Wright [Cambridge, Mass., 1961], nos. 7, 9, and 10.)

5. A reference to Fernando Wood's proposal of January 1861 advocating the establishment of New York City as a sovereign state or "Free City." Wood argued that this status would allow the city to escape the tyranny exercised over it by the state government at Albany and would also enable it to retain commercial ties with the Southern confederacy then forming. Attracting little support, this proposal passed from public notice at the beginning of the Civil War (Samuel Augustus Pleasants, *Fernando Wood of New York* [New York, 1948], pp. 113–17).

6. *The Spectator: A Weekly Review of Politics, Literature, Theology, and Art* was established in London in 1828 by Robert Stephen Rintoul. In the 1860s the journal consisted primarily of thoughtful analyses of the week's events, commentaries on current events, occasional articles on the fine arts and religion, and reviews of books. *The Spectator* steered an independent course in politics but generally supported reform and reformers (*DNB*; Henry Richard Fox Bourne, *English Newspapers: Chapters in the History of Journalism*, 2 vols. [London, 1887], 2: 46–47, 249–50, 345).

7. William Jones Hoppin (1813–1895) attended Yale College and graduated from Middlebury College. One of the original members of the Century Club in New York, he authored several plays and frequently wrote art criticism. He was also a founding member and the first treasurer of the Union League Club of New York. From 1876 through 1886, he served as secretary to the U.S. legation in London (*Yale Obit. Rec.*, 4th ser., 6 [June 1896]: 357–58; *NCAB*).

To Mary Perkins Olmsted

New York, June 26th 1863.

Dear Wife,

I yesterday received yours of 24th.

I am in great perplexity and trouble. Newberry telegraphs that he shall resign if the new plan is persisted in, and our people think that resignation means Western rebellion. If that were all, I believe that I could screw them up to dare it, but, this morning, Judge Skinner telegraphs that the Chicago men don't like it, for quite other reasons than Newberry's—reverse reasons—they will not unite with St. Louis. I have had the greatest difficulty in holding onto Douglas, who will resign the moment he hears the new plan is given up.[1]

I tell you this, only that you may see that it would not do for me to leave New York. I can manage the Exec. Com. while here, very well but they would put the fat in the fire as soon as I left them.

On account of the interesting state of things on the border[2] too, I ought not to go further off. I never felt so near taking a musket myself. I can't see what has become of the manliness of able bodied men who stay at home and grumble at the government, at such a time as this.

Go to Litchfield. I will visit you there as soon as you would rather have me than not—all considered. I find it very lonely here.

Meantime, I am not without hope of having a real home in New York next winter. We had a meeting at the Clubrooms[3] last night, half a dozen or more gentlemen, but one "capitalist" amongst them, Geo Griswold Jr.[4] and he said, I have not time &c. but if you get up a subscription, will you please put me down for $1000? We appointed Howard Potter, Geo. T Strong, & W[m] J Hoppin, *Trustees*, & resolved to go ahead. The paper I read prepared by Godk & myself was much liked and is printing.[5] I can only say that so far, the enterprise is initiated as I could wish in all respects. We meet about it on Tuesday night and shall then go ahead for subscriptions. The thing starts so favorably, I shall go into it strong, meaning to succeed.

I enclose draft for $150.

Your affectionate man

Fred Law Olmsted.

1. Here Olmsted is referring to the new plan of organization for the U.S. Sanitary Commission drawn up by him and approved by the board in June 1863. A full description of this proposed reorganization has not survived, but Olmsted apparently envisioned separating the business of supply from other functions, such as inspection. The supply department would consist of the Atlantic, Eastern Central, Western Central, and Mississippi sections, each with an appointed committee which could draw up applicable rules. Each section would be accountable to a secretary for supply, John S. Newberry. The Commission would also consist of a department of inquiry and advice, which would include sections for inspection and statistical studies, and a department of ways and means.

Newberry objected to the reorganization as a radical change that was unnecessary because the present system was functioning quite adequately. He also disliked the idea of a separate supply department and argued that the inspectors for the Commission should be overseeing the distribution of supplies. Newberry further objected that the plan would increase his responsibilities while decreasing his power. Members of the Chicago branch, however, apparently objected to cooperating with the Western Sanitary Commission (in the proposed Mississippi section) and disliked the leeway given to localism. The reorganization was never put into effect (John H. Heywood to HWB, June 23, 1863, USSC-NYPL, box 640; HWB to JSN, June 24, 1863, USSC-NYPL, box 710, 1: 10–17; FLO, "Minutes of Special Committee on Organization," June 15, 1863; FLO to JO, June 14, 1863; William Quentin Maxwell, *Lincoln's Fifth Wheel: The Political History of the United States Sanitary Commission* [New York, 1956], pp. 217–19).

2. The "border" was that between the United States and the Confederate States of America, and the "interesting state of things" referred to the Confederate invasion of Maryland and Pennsylvania. By June 27 Richard S. Ewell's Confederate troops were at Carlisle, Pennsylvania (*War for the Union*, 3: 79–81).

3. In the spring of 1863 the Union League Club of New York rented as its clubhouse the house belonging to the Parish family at 26 East 17th Street overlooking Union Square (*Diary of the Civil War*, pp. 304, 307).

4. George Griswold, Jr. (1819–1884), was a wealthy New York merchant and partner in the firm of N. L. & G. Griswold. His father had been very successful in the China trade and the import-export trade with the West Indies. Griswold was also one of the original members of the Union League Club (*New-York Times*, April 27, 1884, p. 14).

5. See FLO and Edwin L. Godkin, "Prospectus for a Weekly Journal," [c. June 25, 1863], above.

To Henry Whitney Bellows

New York, July 4ᵗʰ [1863]
(1 A.M.)

My Dear Doctor,
Your "pilot" discourse[1] is a profoundly suggestive one, and hangs weightily upon me. I wish the philosophical part of it, the philosophical drift of it, could be strengthened, elucidated and established, without the expressions of conviction [upon] questions which unquestionably still are questions, and questions either of practical judgment or of fact dependent on evidence still to be brought forward (under the editorship of Mr Marble).[2] As to this latter, by the way, as respects McClellan, the bitterest, most relentless, most assured and confident enemy McClellan has ever had or has is the Spirit of the Times,[3] a paper the circulation of which is almost wholly among men of the Democratic class of the most robust kind, horsemen, sportsmen and publicans. In the last week's number you may see evidence of this. If Mead[4] is whipped, the administration may have to recall McClellan to make peace with the Copperheads; no one will ever suspect it of doing so from conviction, for nothing will have occurred to change the opinion which was the ground of his removal, and as this is an executive question, I would rather see the war prolonged a year and Washington taken, than that anything further should be done to establish the rule that the people are to be consulted on executive questions. I have no doubt at all that a monarchy is a better form of government than such a democracy would be. What we want is more executive skill, not less, in our Executive. Make the President a mere agent, or let him adopt the principle that he is a mere agent of the will of the people in executive matters and it's all up with the republic. For this reason, while I think that we sorely need a man of greater executive ability, and not a mere blunderer upon good things, in the place of Bully Stanton, I would never countenance anything like a demand upon the President for his removal. The Sec'y of War is a sub-executive and such appointments should be regarded wholly from the point of the President's responsibility. If he suits *him*, it's nobody's business till the time comes for turning *him* out. Not that we should not have and express an opinion, as a landsman may & should upon the profanity and brutality of a ship's mate while he would never think of advising the captain to disrate[5] him. It was on that ground I first hated and still hate Greeley[6] & Cᵒ with regard to McClellan. I think the injustice of the attacks on McClellan before he was removed and the dillydallying with him of the President, account for much [of] the popular outcry for him, so far as there is one which is not mere copper demagogueism.[7] A large share, however, is readily traced to the feeling which I fully shared of the whole

Army of the Potomac during the peninsula campaign, that the enemies of McClellan were its enemies, were working for its division, for the strengthening of Pope and McDowell at its expense, and, so, for its defeat. I felt perfectly sure at that time that these enemies of McClellan were taking the best course they possibly could to establish a strong party devoted to McClellan, from a sentiment of hatred of injustice, there being 120,000 men, at least, all busily engaged, with an impulse of self-preservation and self-glory added to a conviction of truth, in repelling the calumnies against McClellan with which the leading republican papers were then teeming and in crying him up as a man to be loved and hurrahed for. This began long before he had done anything. Each man writing to his father, brother or friend; writing from camp, writing from the side of McClellan. Think of the influence of these (say) 200,000 letters a week, under the circumstances: consider the reflex influence on the Army, and then the influence of men who having axes to grind, know of this power and want to use it, and to nurse and sustain it for their use: Consider that most of the more influential officers of the Army of the Potomac owed their promotion to McClellan and had got into a habit of considering their fortunes bound up with his. Then consider the weakly wicked conduct of his (these) friends, which I suppose there is now no doubt led to the recall of McClellan and the enormous advantage in satisfaction of sensational appetite and romance which this gave him.[8]

I don't think you need look to any popular instinct to account for whatever demand there may have been for the restoration of M'c the little.[9] It is simply an imposition upon the understanding of the people taken unwittingly by the impolitic and over-eager, impatient and incautious, and unwise opponents of McClellan. I saw plainly that this would be the effect of it, and warned Dana and Godwin[10] of it, long before he was removed. Nothing but the same stupid folly, forcing Burnside & Hooker to attack under circumstances where success was not to be calculated on,[11] has prevented the popular instinct from remanding McClellan to obscurity. He has able—the very ablest—politicians of the country to nurse the sentiment, established so strongly by his enemies in his favor, and they have managed him with the greatest skill, but they have scarcely succeeded. I believe that in spite of all the fortuitous circumstances which have combined to favor him, he has not half the popularity he had the day he was removed—that the popular conviction is *settling* against him. If Mead is defeated, there is no more reason for the restoration of McClellan than there was the day he was removed—not even in the instincts of the people, in my judgment. To prevent a revolution, in the rage of anger with another defeat, the administration may be weak enough to recall him, and he may, if circumstances favor, do well, for there is no doubt that he has some highly valuable qualities, but I am sure that he is no more to be compared with such men as Rosecrans and Grant, for handling an American army in the wilderness of the South than Miss Dix is to be compared with Miss Nightingale in the work of reforming military hospitals.[12] [*Both are popular heroes, both are great at beginnings and in promises and hopes.*] I think if there is anybody Lincoln ought to know, and his instinct to be trusted upon, it is McClellan; when he decided against him, he had a right to demand that his decision should be acquiesced in. And I believe, that Fitz John Porter needs hanging as much as any other criminal who remains unhung—not that he is a bad man for social purposes—but because he was the worst possible soldier, and in a volunteer army his crime is the most dangerous one and most insidious one possible.[13] It is of the utmost consequence that nothing should be done to increase the temptations to it; that nothing should be said which should seem to indirectly justify it. Your remarks on McClellan had not this bearing but the talk of most of those with whom this discourse if pronounced publickly would rank you, has, and McClellan still treats Fitz-J. Porter as his warmest friend, appears with him at his side, in welcoming regiments of his old army, encourages the suggestion that he will again fight with him and in all this, McClellan himself, it seems to me, is guilty of a grave military offence, an unsoldierly and an ungentlemanly insult to the government and the law—to military law. If the sentence of such a court-martial as Porter had is not to be considered as final (in the absence of additional evidence) what in military authority, in government and law, is ever entitled to be so considered, what is to be respected? McClellan may have a private conviction in favor of his friend—but considering what the offence of his friend was, it would be indelicate in him to express this conviction publickly, and to express it in his official capacity, before soldiers—to treat Fitz Jn. Porter otherwise than as a disgraced officer, if not as a disgraced man, a criminal, as he does, should destroy all confidence in him as a soldier by instinct—a military genius. It has mine, completely. Nothing he can ever do hereafter, will wholly satisfy me that he is a man to be safely trusted with great military power. If he can act as he has done during the last six months under the influence of personal disappointment, personal friendship and personal flexibility, he would be a very dangerous successful general. How could such a man be saved from his friends. Belmont[14] and Barlow[15] would be rulers of the United States, and the greater their crimes, so they were true to him, or he thought them so, the greater would be their power.

I am sure that there is something to be drawn from the root of your discourse which we are all possessed of in our convictions and are aching to have enunciated—I am, and long have been—and I have been trying for two hours tonight to get hold of it right end foremost, but I can't. I feel sure, however that your view of McClellan is not the true product of it. Further—consider that the popular instinct gave us Pierce and Buchanan;[16] the vox populi of New York is as strong for Wood[17]—considering time and circumstances, far stronger than for McClellan. How often the vox populi turns upon its idols in sudden hatred—consider Cromwell & Louis Philippe[18] and thousands other. I am sure the popular instinct is not to be consulted in choice of executive agents—nothing is more fallacious, more deceptive, more contradictory. It is fickle as the winds and as inconsequential. I doubt if we understand the popular instinct which we denominate "for the Union"; that may be its cry, but its impulse [is] deeper. No man knows, by looking inward, what it is; no man tells you; why should you think that the most common outcry was the truest expression of it? I doubt if it is. What are the phenomena which lead to your attempt to analyze this instinct? Is it anything more than this, that the war goes on, when if the people did not wish it to go on, it would surely cease? (And that the strength of the people's will in this respect is such as to carry on the war, over all the obstacles which the want of faith in them and all other blunderings of their servants have raised to its successful prosecution?) This at any rate is the great fact. The question then is why do they will to go on with the war? Now it seems to me that the measure of our regard for the Union is very largely a matter of calculation and reasoning, as Mr Seward has illustrated,[19] but love of locality, love of neighborhood & pride of possessions & conse[quent] rivalship, hatred & contempt of other localities, neighborhoods, sections, countries & states, is more instinctive—less a matter of calculation—therefore states-rights and sectionalism is more truly instinctive than our love for the Union.[20] Hatred of oppression, of injustice, is another instinctive sentiment; reason may cover it in individuals—reason acting under impulse of overweening selfishness, jealousy & small pride, but may not the instinct thus apparently destroyed for a time in the individual, contribute to the instinctive will of the commonwealth against slavery? This is the wildest sort of hypothesis, I know, and I don't even say that I believe it. I would at most say, that I seem to be conscious that there is an analogy in the working of my own instinctive inclinations to forget self in the consciousness of an unselfish purpose to be aided by going with the tide of men. It would be very natural that I should deceive myself by giving it a wrong name.

But there are other instincts, revenge—the instinct to punish what we regard as a wrongdoing—which often overcomes selfishness, in its commoner manifestations—and, again, the mere desire to succeed in what we have once undertaken—& other simpler instincts common with individuals in private affairs—both combine to constantly reestablish the disappointed will to put down the rebellion—the rebels.

Doubtless there are others. Probably all exist with most of us, perhaps all exist with all, but of course in very variable proportions, the hatred of oppression stronger with you and I, desire for revenge with

Scripture Dick,[21] all however combining in the resultant force—the will of the people. It will be an awful disappointment to me, I trust that I shall die rather than experience it, if civil war ends here without having accomplished the practical dissolution of Southern Society. If I understood you, I feel that I differ with your statement of your supposed views about this and about Slavery most deeply.[22] I don't want, and I suspect that very few do want, what you may mean by an immediate, complete abolition of slavery; but I do want the dissolution of Southern Society and I mean, as one part of the people, to have it. I believe it to be practicable, ten times as practicable as peace and Union without it will ever be. The Southern instinct is not stronger than mine in this respect; the Union can never be reestablished with that people. As a people it must and my instinct, I am sure, says it shall be destroyed, or I shall. I would rather die than live with the possibility of an attempted Union with that people again. I know that they are my enemies, until I have them thoroughly conquered, subdued and dethroned as joint sovereigns of this land of ours from St Laurence to the Gulf. Down with them, damn them! till they submit and acknowledge that as a separate people they are a conquered people; then, if they can make themselves of us again, very well; if they can't, they must perish as other peoples have. I am very sure that that is my instinct. I hate them, with what I flatter myself is to some extent a righteous hatred but, at any rate, I hate them, & when you talk seriously of the war's ending without their being thoroughly subjugated and destroyed as a peculiar form of society—more peculiar than Cape Cod Society is, in comparison with Pennsylvania Society—the bitter feeling that comes upon me, is proof that this hatred is tremendously deep & quiet, but also tremendously strong instinct. I verily believe it is stronger than my love of life, though variably and intermittently manifesting itself at all distinctly or consciously.

This is, I am much inclined to think, the truer explanation of the instinct which carries on the war. I think that I could find interest underlying this instinct, not my interest, nor this Northern people's now, but the interest of the race which is to occupy the land here—our stock. It will be better for man here, that one or the other of these types of Society should be violently disarranged, disturbed, so that it never can be itself again. If it is so too, it is my interest now that it shall be the Southern one, and so again I nurse and comfort myself in my grim resolution.

Let the War go on!

Yours Affectionately

Fred. Law Olmsted.

Dʳ Bellows:

The original is in box 641 of USSC-NYPL. Substantive material lined through by Olmsted has been included in italics within brackets.

1. On July 2 and 3 Henry W. Bellows composed an address, which he later called "The National Instinct Our Guide Through the War," and read it to Olmsted. The manuscript of the version that Olmsted heard has not survived, but a later, published version appears to be essentially the same. Bellows discussed the course of the war and argued that the South's willingness to set aside states' rights for centralization explained its successes. After positing that the government of the North was and should be controlled by popular opinion, he speculated that the strongest "national instinct" among the common people was devotion to the Union and unwillingness to see the country divided. He interpreted this Unionism to be more widespread than opposition to slavery. Despite his own dislike of slavery and his desire for emancipation, he argued that only the idea of union could rally the people behind the government: "the great mass of the people feel it in their bones that the Nation must be maintained, and is to be saved, let the conditions be what they may—with slavery or without slavery. They mean to fight for the National integrity, the universal area, and a common and political existence, a country, and the same country!" He then suggested that "it is the duty of the thoughtfulness, the educated mind and heart and will of this country, to study the National instincts, and respect them as the voice of God; and that nothing short of this can extricate us from our National difficulties."

    The entire letter presented here constitutes Olmsted's critical response to Bellows's address. Temporarily swayed by these reservations, the minister put aside the speech and in late July told Olmsted, "I am very glad I had the wisdom to go no further with the paper I read you." But that was not the last of the speech. In November 1863 Bellows did not prepare a Thanksgiving sermon; but discovering this undelivered address among his papers, he decided to present it. His congregation was aghast; according to Bellows, "I never met a more chilled and recalcitrant audience!" His parishioners viewed the speech as an attack upon the policy of emancipation and as a defense of McClellan and the Democratic party. No doubt the draft riots that had occurred between the writing of the paper and its delivery made Bellows's emphasis upon the sacredness of the "national instinct" of the people less acceptable. One critic in the *Evening Post* even argued that Bellows was unsuitable for the presidency of the Sanitary Commission (Henry W. Bellows, *The National Instinct Our Guide Through the War: An Address Given on Occasion of the National Thanksgiving, November 26, 1863* [New York, 1863], the Department of Rare Books and Special Collections, Princeton University Library, Princeton, N.J.; HWB to FLO, July 23, 1863; HWB to Charles J. Stillé, Dec. 8, 1863, Charles Janeway Stillé Papers, Historical Society of Pennsylvania, Philadelphia, Pa.).

2. A sardonic reference to Manton M. Marble, editor and publisher of the *New York World* and a prominent defender of McClellan.

3. The *Spirit of the Times*, sometimes known as *Wilkes' Spirit of the Times*, was founded in 1859 by George Wilkes, who also owned the *National Police Gazette* and had been an editor for an earlier magazine called *Porter's Spirit of the Times*. Like its predecessor, *Wilkes' Spirit* concentrated upon racing, the theater, and sports (F. L. Mott, *History of American Magazines*, 1: 480–81; 2: 203–4).

4. On June 28, 1863, George Gordon Meade (1815–1872) accepted command of the Army of the Potomac after Joseph Hooker asked to be relieved of command. Hooker's resignation resulted from clashes with Henry W. Halleck, general-in-chief (*DAB*; *War for the Union*, 3: 91–95).

5. To reduce to a lower rank.

6. Horace Greeley.

7. By "copper demagogueism," Olmsted means demagoguery by Copperheads, Northerners who sympathized with the South. The epithet "Copperhead" was used as

early as July 1861 to associate disloyal and pacifist Northerners with the snake, which was believed to strike its victims from a place of concealment and without warning (Wood Gray, *The Hidden Civil War: The Story of the Copperheads* [New York, 1942], pp. 140–41).

8. Many of the officers of the Army of the Potomac were strong supporters of McClellan. Among the corps and division commanders who greatly admired him were Fitz-John Porter, William B. Franklin, John Sedgwick, William F. "Baldy" Smith, Winfield S. Hancock, Darius N. Couch, and John F. Reynolds. Olmsted's reference to "weakly wicked conduct" suggests that he was focusing upon Franklin and Porter, whose slowness to reinforce John Pope at the second battle of Bull Run was believed by many to have contributed to the Union defeat in that battle and the subsequent dismissal of Pope and recall of McClellan.

9. Bellows in his address argued that the removal of McClellan, "the idol of the soldiers and of the commmon people," from command of the Army of the Potomac was "against the popular instinct of the country, and therefore a mistake." Citing political reasons as the cause of McClellan's dismissal, Bellows himself claimed not to like the general's political views or associates, but protested that McClellan "is a thoroughbred soldier, and has the confidence of the soldiers of this country who have fought under him. Those most influential in ousting him have not done better than he did" (H. W. Bellows, *National Instinct*, pp. 24–25).

10. Olmsted's friends Charles A. Dana, a former editor of the *New-York Daily Tribune*, and Parke Godwin, an editor of the *New York Evening Post*.

11. Ambrose E. Burnside and Joseph Hooker had in turn commanded the Army of the Potomac during two recent defeats, the battle of Fredericksburg on December 13, 1862, and that of Chancellorsville on May 2–4, 1863.

12. An unfavorable comparison of Dorothea Dix, the superintendent of army nurses in the United States, to Florence Nightingale (1820–1910), the noted English nurse and hospital reformer whose work during the Crimean War had received much acclaim (*DNB*).

13. Fitz-John Porter (1822–1901) was a graduate of West Point and a career military officer. As commander of the V Corps of the Army of the Potomac from May 1862 until his removal and court-martial in November 1862, Porter had performed well during the Seven Days' battles. In January 1863 the court-martial found him guilty of misconduct in the face of the enemy and disobedience to a superior officer's orders. Although these charges stemmed from his slowness to reinforce John Pope during the second battle of Bull Run, Porter's conservative Democratic politics and his pronounced and ill-concealed contempt for Pope probably played a large part in securing the verdict that he had disobeyed orders. Olmsted's judgment of Porter as "the worst possible soldier" and his "crime" as the "most dangerous" and "most insidious" offense for a volunteer army stemmed from a belief in the necessity for strict subordination to those of higher rank as part of military discipline.

    Porter, who believed himself the victim of a Radical Republican plot, fought for years to have his case reopened. In 1878 he procured a rehearing before a presidentially appointed military board, which then set aside the verdict of his court-martial. In 1885 the U.S. Congress officially reinstated Porter into the army at his former rank (*DAB*; Henry Gabler, "The Fitz John Porter Case: Politics and Military Justice" [Ph.D. diss., City University of New York, 1979], pp. 209–15, 282–97, 315–21, 415, 467).

14. August Belmont.

15. Samuel Latham Mitchill Barlow (1826–1889), a lawyer and prominent New York City Democrat. Barlow was a close friend and political adviser of McClellan (*DAB*).

16. Former Democratic presidents Franklin Pierce and James Buchanan.

17. Former New York City mayor Fernando Wood, who was then a member of the U.S. House of Representatives.

18. Oliver Cromwell (1599–1658), who ruled as lord protector of Britain after the execution of King Charles I in 1649, became increasingly unpopular before his death. Louis Philippe (1773–1850) became the "citizen-king" of France after the abdication of Charles X during the July Revolution of 1830. Louis Philippe was deposed during the Revolution of 1848.

19. It is not clear whether Olmsted is alluding to Seward's own political career as illustrating a calculation of the value of the Union or is referring to Seward's beliefs on the subject. Although Seward during the 1850s had warned that slavery was giving rise to "an irrepressible conflict" between opposing forces, he had assumed a Unionist stance which was conciliatory toward the South while he was seeking the Republican presidential nomination in 1860 and during the secession crisis in 1860–61. In 1863, however, in a speech given shortly after the surrender of Vicksburg to Union forces, the secretary of state argued, "We have reached, I think, the culminating point at last; we have ascertained the amount of sacrifice which is necessary to save the Union, and the country is prepared to make it" (David M. Potter, *Lincoln and His Party in the Secession Crisis* [1942; rpt. ed., New Haven, Conn., 1971], pp. 23–35, 81–88, 160–76, 303–14, 336–67; William Henry Seward, *The Works of William H. Seward*, ed. George E. Baker, 2nd ed., 5 vols. [Boston, 1884], 5: 487).

20. Over fifteen years earlier Olmsted had discussed his own "instincts" toward sectionalism and nationalism. He told his friend Frederick Kingsbury, "You've no sort of sectional feeling—I have the strongest in the world." But Olmsted then also believed himself "tremendously patriotic," perhaps instinctively so, and declared: "It's the strongest principle in my nature, if it is a natural instinct. It's stronger than love, hatred, selfishness or even I do confess religion or the love of life itself" (FLO to F. J. Kingsbury, Sept. 23, 1847 [*Papers of FLO*, 1: 303–4]).

21. The editors have been unable to identify this person or character.

22. Here and in the remainder of this section, Olmsted was taking issue with Bellows's statements about slavery and the ending of the war. In his sermon the minister discussed how thoroughly slavery had become a part of the Southern social system, and he argued:

> I have but one expectation left me with these views. Southern society must either be essentially *exterminated*, or we must adopt sooner or later some gradual scheme of emancipation. If the war goes on, upon the principle of utter immediate destruction of slavery in its economic form, it is also the utter destruction of Southern society. That may possibly be inevitable. But I think not—and therefore, I think the instincts of the Nation will see their way to some scheme by which, the political power of slavery being broken, its economic and social status can be borne with under some conditions of gradual disappearance, similar to, though not so favorable, as those which have just been adopted by the State of Missouri.

Bellows also wrote in this document,

> But the instinct of the people, nationally considered, does not, I fear and regret, make the extinction of slavery an end to the war, or a means to that end; and my own frank opinion is that the war will cease successfully for us long before the Southern people are exterminated, leaving slavery a broken and declining, but still a large and protected, interest—no longer a source of fear and dread, but remanded to the position it had when our Nation was formed, a temporary, a perishing, a recognizedly evil institution, without political importance, but still a social and serious moral plague and curse.

In Olmsted's view, as expressed here, social as well as political change at the South would be necessary for a reconstructed nation (H. W. Bellows, *National Instinct*, pp. 12–13, 21).

To Mary Perkins Olmsted

Sanitary Commission,
Baltimore
July 7th 1863.

My Dear Wife,

I left New York Saturday night, spent Sunday in Philadelphia, where I got the first conclusive and circumstantial account of the victory of Mead,[1] came here by Sunday night train bringing Knapp. Here at the Eutaw[2] we have a score of slightly wounded officers, mostly Massachusetts men. While in Phil[a] we bought several tons of fresh eggs, butter, mutton, chickens, fruit, milk, &c. which were delivered Monday morning to a refrigerating car (with a ton of ice) which we chartered for the purpose. Coming here ahead of it we bought a lot of large camp-meeting tents, and a large lot of miscellaneous furniture, loading another car, last night got one ice-car over to the Northern Central Road,[3] and both cars attached to the first train through to Gettysburg after the battle. Mr Bullard[4] and seven men[5] went with them to establish a Home and Relief Station. Several others, with Mrs & Miss Woolsey,[6] and another car-full of stores went up this evening. We had fifteen men there before with waggons running from Westminster and Frederick.[7] Douglas also went up last night, to draw off most of our regular force and some of the waggons to Frederick. Our regular waggon force was on the ground during the battle, and the waggons visited all the field-hospitals as fast as they were established and hours before they received supplies from other quarters. We have today purchased four pairs of horses and four sutlers' waggons, which will start tomorrow for Frederick. I shall also go tomorrow to Frederick, and there load the waggons and send them scouring all the country where we have been skirmishing. I have arranged to receive and take care of about forty tons of supplies a day, for the present, if the people supply them, as I think they will.

The 14th Connecticut is a glorious regiment; the sooner Connecticut sends another like it, the better.[8]

I am pretty well tired with day and night work, but not ill.

You ought to get fat on the news of the week. Lee is not routed by a good deal and our army, when the battle was over, had hardly a breath in it. It was but a hair's breadth from a terrible defeat for fully half an hour. A single additional gun with the enemy might have broke our line and all would have been gone. But our men never behaved so well and I believe they fought better than the enemy—they were cool and steady and showed every good quality of veterans, and it was I suppose the best

THE U.S. SANITARY COMMISSION AT GETTYSBURG, JULY 1863

fought field of the war. Its moral effect is incalculable, taken with Vicksburg and Tullahoma,[9] and what is better than all, if true, the report of the President's draft of 300,000,[10] (only I wish it had been larger) it would compensate for a lifetime of struggling with blue-devils.

I think we can hold our heads up with a good conscience again.

Yours affectionately,

Fred. Law Olmsted.

Olmsted wrote this letter on Sanitary Commission stationery, lining through the Washington address of the central office.

1. That is, the Union army's victory at the battle of Gettysburg, which occurred on July 1–3, 1863.

2. The Eutaw House, a hotel in Baltimore (John Thomas Scharf, *History of Baltimore City and County* . . . [Philadelphia, 1881], p. 516).
3. The North Central Railroad, which ran from Baltimore to York, Pennsylvania.
4. Oliver Crosby Bullard (1822–1890), a brother-in-law of Henry Ward Beecher, had been in business, had operated a boys' school, and had superintended farms before he entered the Sanitary Commission's service in December 1862. He became an assistant special relief agent in February 1863 and organized special relief services at Baltimore and after the battle of Gettysburg. Continuing to work for the Sanitary Commission, he headed special relief at New Orleans for almost two years. Olmsted's relations with Bullard continued after the war as the careers of both focused on landscape architecture. As park inspector of Prospect Park in Brooklyn during the 1870s, Bullard oversaw planting and managed the force of keepers in the park. In the mid-1880s he became superintendent of parks in Bridgeport, Connecticut, a post he held until his death. There he oversaw construction of Beardsley Park, designed by Olmsted in the 1880s (*Bridgeport Daily Standard*, Oct. 27, 1890, p. 4, courtesy of David W. Palmquist, Bridgeport Public Library, Bridgeport, Conn.; O. C. Bullard to John S. Blatchford, Oct. 20, 1866, USSC-NYPL, box 1086: 27; William Sumner Barton, *A Genealogical Sketch of Dr. Artemas Bullard of Sutton, and His Descendants* [Worcester, Mass., 1878], p. 21).
5. The seven men included Edmund Mills Barton (1838–1918) from Worcester, Massachusetts; Nicholas Murray (1842–1918) of Elizabeth, New Jersey; and two unidentified Germans. Both Barton and Murray, the sons respectively of a prominent judge and of a Presbyterian clergyman, served as relief agents for the Sanitary Commission with the Army of the Potomac in 1863. In later life both men became librarians—Barton at the American Antiquarian Society and Murray at the Johns Hopkins University (*Boston Evening Transcript*, April 15, 1918, p. 12; information on Barton courtesy of the American Antiquarian Society, Worcester, Mass.; "Nicholas Murray," *New York Times*, Dec. 10, 1918, p. 13; Williams College, *Fiftieth Anniversary Report of the Williams College Class of '62* [Lancaster, Pa., 1913], pp. 74–75).
6. Georgeanna Woolsey and her widowed mother, Jane Eliza Newton Woolsey (1801–1874). The Woolseys had gone to Gettysburg because a telegram from Olmsted had given them the mistaken impression that Charles W. Woolsey, then a soldier in the Army of the Potomac, had been wounded. The Woolsey women remained in Gettysburg and worked at the Sanitary Commission's lodge for wounded soldiers who were awaiting transportation. Georgeanna Woolsey wrote a short account of their labors entitled *Three Weeks at Gettysburg*, which was first privately printed, then published and distributed by the Sanitary Commission (*Notable American Women*; Anne L. Austin, *The Woolsey Sisters of New York: A Family's Involvement in the Civil War and a New Profession [1860–1900]* [Philadelphia, 1971], pp. 93–94; Georgeanna Muirson [Woolsey] Bacon and Eliza Newton [Woolsey] Howland, eds., *Letters of a Family during the War for the Union, 1861–1865*, 2 vols. [New Haven, Conn., 1899], 2: 527–29).
7. Westminster and Frederick in western Maryland were, respectively, stations of the Western Maryland Railroad and the Baltimore and Ohio Railroad, which were near Gettysburg and still open. The fifteen Sanitary Commission workers at Gettysburg probably included inspectors Lewis H. Steiner and Gordon Winslow; relief agents J. Warner Johnson, William A. Hovey, and James Gall; storekeepers H. P. Dechert, Sanford Hoag, George C. Edgerly, J. C. Bush, and Samuel Bacon; and two other workers identified only as Mr. Paige and Mr. Biddle ("Report on the Operations of the Sanitary Commission during and after the Battles at Gettysburg, July 1st, 2d, and 3d, 1863," doc. no. 71 in USSC, *Documents*).
8. The 14th Connecticut, a veteran regiment reduced to less than two hundred men, showed great determination and heroism at Gettysburg. Several companies of the regiment were ordered on July 3 to capture and hold the Bliss house and barn, then

used by Confederate sharpshooters. The Connecticut soldiers successfully stormed and held the buildings until they were allowed to burn them. That day the regiment also formed a part of the Union line that repelled the famous charge of Confederate general George E. Pickett. In this fighting the 14th Connecticut captured five Confederate regimental battle flags (Charles D. Page, *History of the Fourteenth Regiment, Connecticut Vol. Infantry* [Meriden, Conn., 1906], pp. 143–56).

9. On July 4, 1863, Vicksburg, Mississippi, surrendered to Ulysses S. Grant's forces after a siege which had begun on May 18. Meanwhile, in Tennessee, William S. Rosecrans had moved his Army of the Cumberland against Braxton Bragg's troops. The Confederates abandoned their fortified base at Tullahoma, northwest of Chattanooga, on June 30 (*War for the Union*, 3: 65–72, 189–93).

10. A reference to reports that President Lincoln would call up a new army of three hundred thousand under the draft law that had been enacted during the spring of 1863 (*New-York Times*, July 9, 1863, p. 4, and July 10, 1863, p. 4).

To the Executive Committee
of the United States Sanitary Commission

Frederick, July 9th 1863.
night

To the Exec. Com.

I observe in the newspapers of Philadelphia and Boston a great many excited, sensational appeals from the Christian Commission and various one horse societies, founded on their alledged grand operations at Gettysburg. I am informed that fathers of the Christn Commission have stated that they were at Gettysburg before us and that their operations were much larger than ours.[1] It is sometime since we have advertised much, for reasons, and I have had many enquiries. I send draft of advertisement[2] which I request may now be published a few times, largely and prominently, *heavily leaded throughout,* in the prominent papers of New York, Boston and Philadelphia. It should be so leaded as to occupy a column, with no display lines or other trick except large type and leads. This might possibly cost $1000. I think it might be worth $100,000. It is striking for steady cooperation, when the iron is hot and small fry frantic.

I now anticipate a great battle tomorrow or next day, twenty or thirty miles west of here. There were, this morning, fifteen long R.R. trains of rations, forage, ammunition &c. waiting their turn three to five miles back from here. A lot of ice ordered some time ago for the hospitals has been four days on the road from Baltimore here. Such things as stretchers were all left behind at Gettysburg and have yet to arrive here by rail. The town is crammed with waggons waiting to be loaded. There is admirable order, but it is inevitable that the troops gone forward should be but poorly supplied: if there are waggons & horses enough, there is not road-room to get up all they need. The Army Corps which passed thro' here today marched 28 miles yesterday on short rations, the men in fine spirits and willing. Considering the weather, such continued hard marching is unequalled. Of course everything will be dropped that is possible to leave behind. Of Medical & Surgical stores and appliances, and of proper supplies for the wounded, I fear that scarcely any can have gone forward. Forty surgeons called at this office of the Commission this morning, nearly all enquired for chloroform. I have telegraphed for a supply. Fifty surgeons came from the Washington hospitals today & have been sent forward tonight in army waggons.

If a battle is fought, the demand upon the Commission will be ten times greater than ever before, I fear, notwithstanding the Surgn General is here and everything will be done that is possible, but when it is medicines or gunpowder that must be left behind, it will of course be medicines.

Let no high toned appeals be made, but every woman should be at her post and kept there. You must of course expect strong calls on the Treasury. I suggest that my advertisement down to the last complete sentence on page 4 be transmitted to California by telegraph—"To the Associated Press the following statement is published here of the operations of the Sanity Commis[n] in connection with the recent battles."

Let Mr Collins[3]—(or, one of you) call on the newspapers and get them to print this in the style & type of leading articles, paying whatever is necessary, and getting editorial call of attention to it, if possible.

P.S. Col. Sawtelle[4] has just read me one line from a telegram from his chief, Genl Ingalls.[5] "Come up; I think we shall begin in the morning." We have 4 waggons, (bought & loaded with field supplies last night in Bal[to] & Washington) which arrived tonight & two saddle-horses, 4 more saddle-horses & saddle bags were bought in Bal[to] today & will reach here tomorrow at 1 P.M. by rail, also chloroform. Brink[6] & three relief agents are here. I shall drive everything possible (buying up the stock of tin cups, morphine, crackers &c. of the town-shops), send our train under Hoag[7] toward Boonsboro' early in the morning, and when the horses arrive, probably go on with Steiner myself to the field. I have telegraphed to Buffalo, Boston & Philadelphia, orders for supplies.

Yours Respectfully,

Olmsted.

A WAGON OF THE U.S. SANITARY COMMISSION

The original is letter 2270 in box 955 of USSC-NYPL.

1. A reference to numerous appeals for contributions by the U.S. Christian Commission and various local relief societies. The Christian Commission, founded by the Young Men's Christian Association in November 1861, stated its purpose to be the "spiritual and temporal welfare" of the soldier. Although it saw its distinctive work as the saving of souls, the Christian Commission believed that the distribution of supplies and battlefield relief aided its religious purpose by opening "the hearts of those who receive them to the glad reception of the Gospel." Relatively inactive until the autumn of 1862, the Christian Commission had become a formidable fund-raising rival to the Sanitary Commission by the summer of 1863.

   After the battle of Gettysburg, the Christian Commission and local societies were, indeed, issuing urgent appeals for aid. One such notice by the Christian Commission, published in the *Philadelphia Daily News*, declared: "Send all the stores of every kind possible; there is great want of most kinds of hospital stores, shirts and drawers especially, and delicacies. Please publish: *the necessity is very great that everything should be hurried on*." However, the editors have found no reports published by July 9 in which the Christian Commission claimed to be first or to have the largest operations at Gettysburg. Other groups soliciting supplies included the Fifth Baptist Church, the Ladies Aid Society of St. Paul's Episcopal Church, the Cincinnati Society, and volunteer workers from the Adams Express Company (*Philadelphia Daily News*, July 9, 1863, p. 1; *Boston Evening Transcript*, July 6, 1863, p. 2; *Philadelphia Inquirer*, July 9, 1863, pp. 2, 8; United States Christian Commission, *Facts, Principles and Progress* [Philadelphia, 1863], pp. 7–13).

2. Olmsted probably enclosed a copy of the item, written by him and entitled "For the Wounded," that appeared in numerous newspapers with the dateline "Frederick City, July 9, 1863." In the article he described the magnitude of the Commission's work not only at Gettysburg but also with the Union armies in the West and South. Olmsted's intent of "striking for steady cooperation" can be most clearly discerned in the following section:

651

At this moment the Commission is issuing goods to the value of at least twenty thousand dollars ($20,000) a day. A work of this character and magnitude can only be sustained by the constant, systematic cooperation of a great number of auxiliary societies, and by frequent contributions from all who appreciate its beneficence. . . . It is only asked that the present occasion may be taken to establish a more complete adoption of the system of the Commission by the connection of individuals with existing societies cooperating with the Commission, by enforcing more steady, regular and systematic methods of collecting and transmitting contributions, and by establishing a conviction of the folly of spasmodic efforts in a work of this kind. Hundreds will owe their lives this week to those who did not hold their hand when there was no special public excitement, by which the Commission had stores ready at Frederick, Baltimore and Washington, and reserves at Philadelphia, New-York and Boston. . . . A momentary enthusiasm is not desired, but the Commission offers its agency to all who wish to steadily contribute to the relief of the sick and wounded, and to the comfort of the army, by such means and methods as experience leads it to adopt, until the rebels are conquered, and the volunteer army disbanded, which last, under no circumstances, can possibly occur for a long time to come. Let those who have not begun to work systematically for the army begin now. Let those who have been working steadily become more steadfast and orderly in their work. ("For the Wounded," New-York Times, July 16, 1863, p. 5.)

3. Benjamin Collins, superintendent of the New York office of the Sanitary Commission.
4. Charles G. Sawtelle, who had served in the quartermaster's department during the Peninsula campaign and had been promoted to lieutenant colonel in August 1862 (Francis Bernard Heitman, *Historical Register and Dictionary of the United States Army* . . . , 2 vols. [Washington, D.C., 1903], 1: 862).
5. Rufus Ingalls (1819–1893), a West Point graduate and career officer, served as chief quartermaster of the Army of the Potomac from July 1862 until June 1864, when he became chief quartermaster of the armies attempting to capture Richmond. Remaining in the army after the war, Ingalls was named quartermaster general in 1882 and retired in 1883 after forty years' service.

Olmsted knew and admired Ingalls's work during the Peninsula campaign. In the book *Hospital Transports*, Olmsted described Ingalls as "kind, prompt, and decisive." In September 1862 the Commission passed a resolution thanking the soldier for his "many favors." Olmsted in the draft letter he prepared to notify Ingalls of this honor added, "[I] beg you to receive also the assurance of my personal gratitude and respect" (George Washington Cullum, *Biographical Register of the Officers and Graduates of the U.S. Military Academy at West Point, N.Y.* . . . , 3rd ed., 3 vols. [Boston, 1891], 2: 185–86; *Hospital Transports*, p. 21; FLO to Rufus Ingalls, Sept. 20, 1862, USSC-NYPL, box 835, 1: 68; U.S. Military Academy, West Point, Association of Graduates, *Annual Reunion, 1893* [Newburgh, N.Y., 1893], 24: 81–86).
6. Charles Wesley Brink, a physician and Sanitary Commission inspector. A graduate of the College of Physicians and Surgeons in New York, Brink joined the Commission in July 1862. He served in the field at the second battle of Bull Run as well as at the battles of Cedar Mountain, Antietam, Fredericksburg, and Gettysburg.

Opinions about Brink's value to the Commission varied. In the autumn of 1862 Cornelius R. Agnew told Olmsted that "Brink is weak & not to be trusted when energy & snap are required." He continued, "I hope we will be able to replace Brink with a man of more force; his manner is so hesitating & so deficient in demonstrative energy that for anything like quick, widespread effort he is next to useless." Olmsted himself admitted Brink to be "slow and a little eccentric" but declared that he also "turns up a trump in an emergency. He shrinks at nothing and is never wearied" (C. R. Agnew to FLO, Sept. 30, 1862, USSC-NYPL, box 745: 2350; FLO to GTS, Dec. 26, 1862; C. W. Brink to John S. Blatchford, Oct. 23, 1866, USSC-NYPL, box 1086: 8; Columbia University, *Catalogue of Officers and Graduates of Columbia University* . . . [New York, 1906], p. 214).

7. Sanford Hoag, a storekeeper for the Sanitary Commission (USSC, *Minutes*, p. 164).

To Edwin Lawrence Godkin

Sanitary Commission,
Frederick, July 15ᵗʰ 1863.

My Dear Godkin,

I spent two days and nights at Head Quarters on Beaver Creek near Williamsport.[1] I saw Genˡ Meade a few hours after the escape of Lee was established.[2] He is tall, thin, stooping, but has a most soldierly and veteran-like appearance; a grave, stern countenance—somewhat Oriental in its dignified expression, yet American in its race-horse gauntness. He is simple, direct, deliberate and thoughtful in manner of speech and general address. On the whole he impressed me very favorably. He is a gentleman and an old soldier. He expressed disappointment at the escape of Lee, but said: "With the information that I had yesterday, I could not on the whole have been justified in—[hesitating][3]—saying that if we attacked yesterday there were sufficient grounds for a conviction that we should not get the worst of it."

"I had ordered an attack this morning. I was myself rather disposed to try it yesterday, but all my corps commanders except one were decidedly against it, and my own conviction was not strong enough to warrant me in acting against theirs."

"We are not as strong as we are supposed to be. I dare not say how weak we are." Reinforcements were constantly arriving; it was raining hard, the Potomac was rising. I suppose that we were by reinforcements and improvement of position ten thousand stronger on Tuesday than on Monday morning. I think Meade somewhat hoped that Lee would be tempted to attack on Monday. I went out on Monday P.M. Our line had been advanced during the day nearly a mile, and was advanced quarter of a mile while I was with it; the men & batteries all in line of battle and with slight entrenchments, which they seemed to construct almost of their own accord or as a matter of course. In the woods or behind woods as soon as

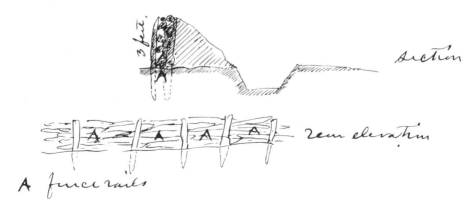

the line was formed, they began felling timber, so that it would answer the purpose of abatis. I went through the line and advanced to the outermost skirmishers who were driving the rebel skirmishers slowly back from tree to tree in the woods. I crept up with General Crawford[4] amongst them to a point where with a glass we could see through the wood and caught a glimpse of an earthwork before us and could see the dirt thrown (throwing) up from the ditch upon it.

I believe that in my estimate sent you a week or more ago[5] of the forces at Gettysburg, I overstated ours. I had a hint that nobody was allowed to know how small it was, & I could see that those who knew best were not willing that I should believe some parts of the Army to be as weak as I know they are. All who were likely to be well informed, unquestionably believe that Lee outnumbered us.[6] They say we could not possibly have held out fifteen minutes longer and for half an hour the chances were felt to be evenly balanced. We could not spare a man, and it seemed as if the slightest additional force on the part of the enemy would have broke us.

The old army of the Potomac is in fine condition, marches twenty or thirty miles a day & accepts what comes to it without hesitation—its chief discouragement arises from the smallness of the regiments, many being as low as 200 men. Many who were brigade commanders at Antietam and are now division commanders have fewer men under them now than then. The statement made by Wilson Senator, before the riots,[7] that the draft was to be immediately enforced & the drafted men used to fill up the old regiments,[8] was received with prolonged cheering. It is what all want—want more than anything else.

I enclose a note about the position from one of our inspectors, written on *Monday*. ("The hermaphrodite Medico", means "Miss Walker

M.D.", "Doctoress Walker," "Walker M.D. on the war-path,"[9] as one of ours describes her).

I bruited the matter of the Weekly to the Surgeon General, who received it in the warmest manner possible. He said that he would do everything he could for it. I asked if he could recommend any writers in the Army. "I will write for it, I will write on Sanitary and Social Science[10] all you want." He told me who was the best man in the army on projectiles, & said that he thought he could be got & he would introduce me to him in Washington. We discussed others.

I have heard nothing from New York—of the subscriptions. Nothing had been done when I left. Bellows & Agnew have been absent. Our operations have been on a much larger scale than ever before.[11] I will send you some notes in a few days showing their magnitude. The immediate movement of the Army after the battle, taking its administrative offices, left the necessity for our aid, peculiar[ly] at Gettysburg. The Army trains are astounding. The daily consumption of forage by the Army (before the recent reinforcements) was 1000,000 lbs of oats (at 3½ cents) 300,000 lbs. of hay (at 1½ c.) 150,000 lbs of corn, (at 2 cents).

I don't think the riots will harm our enterprise. How I wish it was started & we could pitch in! I think you should take the ground that the most dangerous foes of the republic are in New York City, that the government has now the right and duty to put them down; that from this moment to the end of the war, government should deal with New York and other insurrectionary towns & districts, as it does with Baltimore & Nashville and New Orleans. Let Barlow & Bennett & Brooks and Belmont & Barnard & the Woods & Andrews and Clancey[12] be hung if that be possible. Stir the govt up to it. I didn't mean to omit Seymour.[13]

Our inspector who has arrived this moment from Berlin[14] says there is no intention of crossing for *three days*. I can't understand it. He says he thinks there was an apprehension that the enemy would resist the crossing. We have two pontoon bridges laid below Harper's ferry—and hold both sides at Harper's ferry—though not in force on the Virg[a] side.

When Meade telegraphed that the enemy had gone, Halleck replied that he must acquit himself for allowing him to escape by his energy in pursuit of him &c.[15] the tone being regarded by Meade as insolent. Genl Ingalls came into the tent as he was reading it & Meade said: "Ingalls don't you want to take command of this army?"

"No, I thank you. It's too big an elephant for me."

"Well, it's too big for me, too, read that." and then he immediately wrote in reply that his resignation was at the service of the Department. Two hours afterwards he received for answer to his reply that neither the President nor the General in Chief wished to be understood as blaming General Meade for the escape of the rebel army.[16] This I know to be true, but as I can't mention my authority, it should not be made public except in general terms. I was at Hd Q at the time.

Yours Very Truly

Fred. Law Olmsted.

The original is in the Edwin Lawrence Godkin Papers, Houghton Library, Harvard University, Cambridge, Massachusetts.

1. Williamsport and Beaver Creek are located in western Maryland, near Hagerstown. Olmsted probably arrived there on Sunday, July 12, and left Tuesday, July 14.
2. Olmsted met with Meade on the afternoon of Tuesday, July 14. At eleven o'clock that morning Meade had telegraphed Henry W. Halleck that his forces had discovered that Lee's lines had been evacuated (O.R., ser. 1, vol. 27, p. 92).
3. These brackets were used by Olmsted.
4. Samuel Wylie Crawford (1829–1892), a career army officer who was a brigadier general of volunteers. He commanded the 3rd Division of the V Corps of the Army of the Potomac at the battle of Gettysburg (NCAB).
5. Godkin never received this letter, which appears to have been irretrievably lost.
6. Olmsted was mistaken about the relative strength of the armies. Union forces of approximately eighty-three thousand at the battle outnumbered the Confederate army of approximately seventy-five thousand (Thomas Leonard Livermore, Numbers and Losses in the Civil War in America, 1861–65, 2nd ed. [Boston, 1909], pp. 102–3).
7. Riots against the draft raged through New York City from July 13 until July 17, 1863, after the selection of men for military duty had begun by lottery on July 11. The rioters, who were protesting both conscription and the section of the law that allowed men to evade military service by procuring a substitute or paying three hundred dollars, directed much of their violence against blacks and prominent Republicans, both of whom were blamed for the continuance of the war. The mobs looted and burned numerous homes and businesses as well as a Negro orphanage and attacked or harassed numerous black New Yorkers. Over one hundred rioters and their victims were killed (Adrian Cook, The Armies of the Streets: The New York Draft Riots of 1863 [Lexington, Ky., 1974], pp. 55, 188–206).
8. The editors have not been able to trace this statement to Senator Henry Wilson. On July 11, 1863, the New-York Times declared that it had learned by a "special dispatch" from Washington that the troops raised under the draft would fill vacancies in existing regiments rather than form new regiments. This course, however, was not followed (New-York Times, July 11, 1863, p. 4).
9. Mary Edwards Walker (1832–1919), a physician and feminist who received her medical training at Syracuse Medical College. She was committed to dress reform, and her "bloomer" costume probably prompted some of the remarks that Olmsted here recorded. After receiving an appointment as an assistant surgeon in the fall of 1863, Dr. Walker served with the Army of the Cumberland. In 1865 she received the Congressional Medal of Honor for Meritorious Service, an honor that was withdrawn in 1917 when a federal board of review revoked a large number of Civil War citations (Notable American Women; Charles McCool Snyder, Dr. Mary Walker: The Little Lady in Pants [New York, 1962], pp. 16, 155).
10. To a nineteenth-century man such as Olmsted, the term "social science" meant the study of relationships in society, especially the study of social problems and the

means to combat them. Thus Olmsted probably expected Hammond, who had published a book in 1863 on hygiene, to write about topics relating to public health (Thomas L. Haskell, *The Emergence of Professional Social Science: The American Social Science Association and the Nineteenth-Century Crisis of Authority* [Urbana, Ill., 1977], pp. 87, 100–105).

11. As Olmsted pointed out in a report written on July 23, 1863, the Sanitary Commission had been very active before and after the battle of Gettysburg. It distributed two wagonloads of medical supplies before the battle, and two more arrived there on July 3 as the battle was ending. Despite the capture of one wagon, the Sanitary Commission then sent eleven wagonloads of supplies from Westminster, Maryland, before the railroad into Gettysburg was repaired on July 6. At the same time as it began forwarding supplies by rail, the Commission set up a relief station at the railroad to feed and shelter wounded soldiers who were awaiting transportation to hospitals in Eastern cities. Later the relief station was moved into town. In addition to providing hospital clothing for ten thousand men, the Commission distributed over sixty tons of perishable items, including eleven thousand pounds of poultry and mutton, twenty thousand pounds of ice, six thousand pounds of butter, and ten thousand loaves of bread (Frederick Law Olmsted, "Preliminary Report of the Operations of the Sanitary Commission with the Army of the Potomac, During the Campaign of June and July, 1863," *New-York Times*, July 31, 1863, p. 3).

12. Olmsted is listing those (primarily prominent Democrats) whom he believed had encouraged and abetted the riots through criticism of the draft and of the Lincoln administration. His references are to S. L. M. Barlow; James Gordon Bennett (1795–1872), publisher of the *New York Herald*; Congressman James Brooks; August Belmont; George Gardner Barnard (1829–1879), a Tammany Hall–supported judge of the New York Supreme Court from 1860 until his impeachment in 1872; Fernando and Benjamin Wood; John U. Andrews (1825–1883), a Virginia-born lawyer and self-proclaimed "states' rights" Democrat; and John Clancy (1830–1864), editor of the *New York Leader.*

　　　　Most of this group had little actual connection with the riots. On July 13 Judge Barnard reportedly helped dissuade a group of rioters from attacking the home of Mayor George Opdyke. In that speech Barnard denounced the draft and Lincoln's administration but argued that the people could and should depend upon the courts rather than violence to protect their rights. Andrews appears to be the only person here named who gave active support to the riots. On July 13, while standing in front of a burning draft office, he incited the crowd there to open opposition to the draft. Prosecuted in federal court for conspiring to levy war against the United States and resisting the execution of its laws, Andrews was sentenced to three years' imprisonment at hard labor (*DAB*; Alexander B. Callow, Jr., *The Tweed Ring* [New York, 1966], pp. 135–38; A. Cook, *Armies of the Streets*, pp. 60–61, 73–74, 184–87, 285–87, 309; *New-York Times*, July 2, 1864, p. 4; "The Leader of the Riots Dead," ibid., Dec. 8, 1883, p. 2).

13. Horatio Seymour, governor of New York. A Democrat in politics, he had become an important leader of the opposition to the Lincoln administration and had denounced both the draft and the Emancipation Proclamation as unconstitutional. At this time, Olmsted's anger against Seymour was probably particularly intense because of the latter's speech outside City Hall in New York City during the second day of the draft riots. In his speech, Seymour called for peace and order and reminded the crowd that the courts would decide the constitutionality of the draft. Republican critics charged that Seymour had addressed the crowd as "my friends" and was far too conciliatory in his remarks (*DAB*; A. Cook, *Armies of the Streets*, pp. 104–6).

14. Berlin, Maryland, on the Potomac River approximately ten miles east of Harper's Ferry.

657

15. Urging that "the enemy should be pursued and cut up, wherever he may have gone," Henry W. Halleck closed his message at one o'clock in the afternoon on July 14: "I need hardly say to you that the escape of Lee's army without another battle has created great dissatisfaction in the mind of the President, and it will require an active and energetic pursuit on your part to remove the impression that it has not been sufficiently active heretofore" (O.R., ser. 1, vol. 27, p. 92).

16. Olmsted's account of these events is essentially correct. At 2:30 P.M. on July 14, Meade telegraphed Halleck, "Having performed my duty conscientiously and to the best of my ability, the censure of the President conveyed in your dispatch of 1 P.M. this day, is, in my judgment, so undeserved that I feel compelled most respectfully to ask to be immediately relieved from the command of this army." At 4:30 P.M. Halleck replied to Meade: "My telegram, stating the disappointment of the President at the escape of Lee's army, was not intended as a censure, but as a stimulus to an active pursuit. It is not deemed a sufficient cause for your application to be relieved" (ibid., pp. 93–94).

To Edwin Lawrence Godkin

Sanitary Commission,
Baltimore, July 19th 1863

My Dear Godkin,

I arrived here this morning from Frederick via Gettysburg, and found here yours of the 11th—I don't remember much of the missing letter. It was written while we knew little of the Gettysburg battle & contained such information as I could pick up from officers wounded and en route home, at this house. I was led to think that the forces engaged were very nearly equal. I now think that our force was considerably the smaller. I was all over the ground yesterday. The field and all distances are much larger than I had supposed. The hills, except on the extreme left of our line, are gentle elevations. If the Hillhouse hill in New Haven[1] were cleared of wood, it would bear some resemblance to them. Artillery could be galloped easily anywhere except on the extreme left and right, where there is a very rugged, rocky and wooded region. Here on the second day Longstreet[2] made a desperate attempt to outflank us, and at some points, where the ground was taken and retaken, I found plenty of evidence of terrible fighting. On one elevation a few rods square I saw a dozen or more exploded shells, and quite a number of knapsacks and caps with shot-holes through them, both Federal and confederate, with other equipments. The roads for miles about the town, as well as the course of the federal lines, are still strewn with wrecks of equipments, muskets, bayonets, caissons, and baggage waggons with broken wheels, although the provost marshal[3] has had parties engaged in collecting them ever since the battle and much must have been carried off by the country people. Ten miles off I met two farmers on horseback, each carrying three or four muskets, with some other things. The dead men are all buried and a great business is being done in disinterring bodies for embalming and shipment north. There are half a dozen difft embalmers competing for it. The Governor of Pennsylvania,[4] I believe, pays for the removal of all Pennsylvania dead to their friends. The horses are mostly half covered with earth or partially burned, but the stench remains and pervades the town.

The hills on which the rebels formed of which you read,[5] are unnoticeable swells of ground parallel to the lines of the federal force and about half a mile distant. They are generally wooded on the rear slope and in some parts on the front. They completely screen all movements in the rear of their crest. The valley between the two elevations is smooth, generally with a turf surface, with some ploughed ground, standing wheat and orchards. The fields are large. There were some stone fences on the federal hill[6] and rail fences in the valley. There were also plenty of loose stones throughout the federal position. These were got together at night and a slight breast work formed of them—simply by laying them one against and upon another. Here and there some little earth had been thrown against them. They are not more than three feet high and are just like the slightest kind of stone fence of our New England sheep-pastures. A tree-trunk, fence rails, a broken waggon and sometimes a dead-horse had been laid in when it came handy. The rebels wherever they advanced their lines, with any hope of holding them, which was the case only where woods and orchards partially covered them, had thrown up more complete works, chiefly of fence rails, occasionally with a ditch, as I sketched the plan of ours before Williamsport the other day. They had also barricaded the roads on their flanks.

I should think that a true estimate of the battle lay just about midway between the accounts of the New-York and the Richmond papers. Lee's loss must have been much greater than ours.[7] Both sides fought with great confidence and determination, to the last. Our side was not whipped, and, considering the first day as skirmishing, lost no ground except temporarily. The rebels did not generally consider themselves whipped, I imagine, and probably expected to have another day of it. While their loss was the greater, their disorganization was less, chiefly because their bodies are all more numerous than ours. I presume their corps, brigades, divisions, regiments & companies, would all number fifty per cent more than ours. I have no doubt that Lee's army is better, man for man, than ours, today, solely because of its better organization.

I came here last night from Gettysburg, being twelve hours on the way, most of the time in a dirty hog-car with a lot of dead Pennsylvanians

659

and wounded rebels. These latter did not talk much but one said about Vicksburg, "It would have been better for us, if they had got the whole of Lee's army." They did not appear to have a thought of the end of the war, expressed surprise at the kindness with which they were treated when they came as invaders, and were as usual peevish, childish and exacting among themselves about their wounds and pains.[8]

I shall be in New York, in course of the week & hope I may be able to come to Litchfield next week. I have heard nothing from any of the Committee[9] and presume the riots have knocked the project out of their heads, if so I shall try to put it in again. I wish we could fix upon a name.[10] Saturday, The Result, The Equation, The Statesman, The Politician, The Gist, The Civilian, The Householder, The Welcome, The Arbitrator, The Attestor, The Harvester, The Garner, The Cultivator, The Supporter, The Support, The Maintainer, The Retriever, The Holdfast, The Gentleman's Weekly Review, The Weekly Review, The Gentleman's Review, The New Review, The Exchange, The Comprehensive, The Comprehensive Review, The Front, The Review of the Week, Scribner's Review, Toucey's Review, Rodman's Review,[11] The Yeoman, The Yeoman's Review, Yeoman's Weekly, The Week's Work, The Work of the Week, The History, The Historian, The Week, The Topic, Topics of the Week, The Loyalist, The Loyal Review, The Loyalist's Review, The Loyal Observer &c.

The Loyalist wears better than other[s] with me, and it would be [a] name associated with the time of its origin, if it should live.

Yours Very Truly

Fred. Law Olmsted.

E. L. Godkin, Esq[r]

Sanitary Commission,
July 19th Bal[to] 186[3]

P.S. A Surgeon who left Harper's ferry this morning, tells me that the last corps was crossing this morning but it is known not to be the intention to pursue the enemy. Reason, the army is too much fatigued and worn down, man & horse, to undertake forced marches. This is the conclusion of a medical survey. It is thought they will move six miles a day only—taking it easy, while they guard against inroads from Lee, through the mountains. The Quarter Master is making arrangements to ship stores to Warrenton.[12]

The following are among the corps and division generals which the Army of the Potomac has lost since its organization, including some of those transferred to other commands: Sumner, F. J. Porter, W. F. Smith, Franklin, And. Porter, Hooker, Burnside, Hancock, Couch, Siegel, Reynolds, Dana, Hartsoff, Park, McClellan.[13] Its old Quarter M. Genl. whose name, I can't recall,[14] is another important head gone, though the present, Gen'l Ingalls is a better one.

There are but 1500 men of the regular army in the Army of the Potomac, at present. In ten of the regiments of regulars there are today but 1,000 men—or 100 men to a regiment on an average. The largest regular regiment in the army is, I believe, the 8th now in New York, numbering 600 men.[15] The full force of these regiments is over 1500, each.

A wounded Mass. officer told me that when his regiment went into action at Gettysburg, it had but forty of the original 1040 privates who enlisted in it two years ago. As it had the very hottest place on the left centre, he supposed that not one now remained. This was the third time he had been disabled and he had been six months of the war a prisoner.

You will see that all the public reports make a different statement of the vote of the Council of War on Monday from that which I gave you a few days ago from Meade.[16] I may have misunderstood or misrecollected what he said, but I should think not. Possibly he used a general term— speaking of the sentiment of his corps commanders as a body, but if so, he certainly gave me to understand that it was against attack on that day. I think that I *was* mistaken in putting the phrase: "I dare not say how weak we are," into Meade's mouth. It was Ingalls who said that, I conclude.

F.L.O.

The original is in the Edwin Lawrence Godkin Papers, Houghton Library, Harvard University, Cambridge, Massachusetts.

1. The location of Sachem's Wood, the mansion of the Hillhouse family, on the hill at the head of Hillhouse Avenue in New Haven, Connecticut (Richard Hegel and Floyd Shumway, eds., *New Haven: An Illustrated History* [Woodland Hills, Ca., 1981], pp. 134–35).
2. James Longstreet (1821–1904) commanded the I Corps of the Army of Northern Virginia. On the afternoon of July 2 Longstreet's Confederates attacked the extreme left of the Union line, where Daniel Sickles's III Corps had assumed an advanced and exposed position. In the desperate fighting that followed at the Peach Orchard, the "Devil's Den," and the "Valley of the Shadow of Death," the Union forces successfully held the important hilltops called Little and Big Round Top (*War for the Union*, 3: 99–105).
3. Marsena Rudolph Patrick (1811–1888), a West Point graduate, served as provost-marshal general of the Army of the Potomac from October 1862 until March 1865. In his diary entry of July 5, 1863, Patrick recorded that General Meade had ordered him to arrange for the burial of the dead and "the securing of property on the battlefield" (G. W. Cullum, *Biographical Register*, 1: 622–23; Marsena Rudolph Patrick, *Inside Lincoln's Army: The Diary of Marsena Rudolph Patrick, Provost Marshal General, Army of the Potomac*, ed. David S. Sparks [New York, 1964], p. 268).

4. Andrew Gregg Curtin (1815?-1894), the Republican governor of Pennsylvania from 1861 until 1867 (*DAB*).

5. Seminary Ridge.

6. Cemetery Ridge.

7. Although estimates of the casualties at the battle of Gettysburg vary, the Confederates probably lost as many and very likely more soldiers than the Union army. One careful scholar has suggested that the number of killed, wounded, or missing among the Union forces exceeded twenty-three thousand, while the Confederates lost over twenty-eight thousand (T. L. Livermore, *Numbers and Losses*, pp. 102–3).

8. Olmsted told his wife that for four hours on his trip from Hanover Junction to Baltimore, he lay "upon the floor of a car which yesterday carried hogs & had not been cleaned, and was now occupied with wounded rebels and a dead Pennsylvanian, the whole producing the most sickening stench I ever endured."

Olmsted's remark about the Confederate prisoners indicates no change in opinion during the year that had elapsed since he, on the Virginia Peninsula, had written: "Naturally enough, the prisoners do not 'bear up' as well as our own men. There is not only more whimpering, but more fretfulness and bitterness of spirit, evinced chiefly in want of regard one for another" (FLO to MPO, July 20, 1863; *Hospital Transports*, p. 120).

9. A committee of gentlemen, which included Henry W. Bellows, had been chosen at the meeting in late June to obtain the necessary financial backing for the proposed weekly journal (HWB to "Dear Sir," July 4, 1863, Henry Whitney Bellows Papers, Massachusetts Historical Society, Boston, Mass.; FLO to MPO, June 26, 1863, above).

10. For several weeks Olmsted had been casting about for a name for the proposed journal. While asking his wife's aid in early July, he listed a number of possible titles: "Help me to a name for the project—Comment, Examiner, Reviser, Inspector, Tide, Key, Scrutiny, National, Faggot, Yeoman" (FLO to MPO, July 2, 1863).

11. Here Olmsted appears to have interjected three titles as jokes. He probably intended "Scribner's Review" to refer to the publishing house headed by Charles Scribner (1821–1871), which was then renowned for publishing the works of well-known theologians and Biblical "higher criticism" by German scholars. "Toucey's Review" was a facetious mention of Isaac Toucey (1796–1869), a prominent Connecticut Democratic politician and secretary of the navy during Buchanan's administration. Olmsted had opposed Toucey's election as governor of Connecticut in 1846 and probably considered him a Southern sympathizer. "Rodman's Review" may have been Olmsted's playful antidote to "Toucey's Review." Thomas Jackson Rodman (1815–1871), inventor of an improved process for casting cannon, was head of the U.S. arsenal at Watertown, Massachusetts (*DAB*; "The History of a Publishing House, 1846–1894," *Scribner's Magazine* 16, no. 6 [Dec. 1894]: 793–96).

12. That is, Rufus Ingalls was making arrangements to ship stores to Warrenton, Virginia, approximately fifty miles southwest of Washington, D.C.

13. Twelve of the generals Olmsted lists here were former division or corps commanders in the Army of the Potomac during McClellan's command in 1861–62 and no longer serving in it at the time this letter was written. John Fulton Reynolds had been killed at the battle of Gettysburg, during which Winfield Scott Hancock had been seriously wounded. Edwin Vose Sumner and Franz Sigel had resigned their commissions, while Fitz-John Porter had been removed from command and cashiered (and his friend George B. McClellan had been removed from command of the army). William Farrar Smith, Joseph Hooker, Ambrose E. Burnside, Darius Nash Couch, and John Grubb Parke had been transferred to brigade or higher commands in other departments, and William Buel Franklin and Andrew Porter had been given other duties. Two of the officers on Olmsted's list, Napoleon Jackson Tecumseh Dana and George Lucas Hartsuff, had held only brigade commands in the Army of the Poto-

mac; both had been wounded at the battle of Antietam and thereafter received assignments in other departments (*DAB*; Frederick H. Dyer, *Compendium of the War of the Rebellion . . .* , 3 vols. [1908; rpt. ed., New York, 1959], vol. 1).

14. Stewart Van Vliet, whom Olmsted had known during the Peninsula campaign.
15. The U.S. 8th Infantry, then serving with the Army of the Potomac, was ordered to New York City on July 15, 1863 (*O.R.*, ser. 1, vol. 27, pt. 3, p. 704).
16. Although Olmsted had written that all but one of Meade's corps commanders advised against attack, the newspapers described a more equal division. On July 16 the *New-York Times* reported that only four of Meade's officers opposed an attack; according to the *Tribune*, seven of the twelve officers present at the council of war opposed, and only Meade and four other generals favored, an attack (*New-York Times*, July 16, 1863, p. 8; *New-York Daily Tribune*, July 16, 1863, p. 1).

To Henry Whitney Bellows

Personal, Very.

Sanitary Commission,
Central Office, 244 F street,
Washington, D.C., July 25th 1863.

My Dear Doctor,
I have just received your favor of the 23d at the close of which is this enquiry:
"How did Haywood and Clampitt[1] get back? I thought they were dismissed on grounds of unfitness in important respects. I can't say that the advice of the President and Dr Agnew has met with any superfluous respect in this case."
The General Secretary has no longer any rights, duties or responsibilities except those he has in common with the other members of the Executive Committee, and except as they may be committed to him from time to time, the only difference being that, whereas it is optional with other members of the Committee to undertake any special service when requested to do so, the General Secretary can not decline and must hold his judgment in subjection to that [of] any other member of the Committee who addresses him in his capacity of a paid officer, from the standpoint of a quorum of the Committee. My private opinion is that such a complicated arrangment thrown upon the simple organization under which I originally engaged to serve the Sanitary Commission with the title of Secretary is quite sure to involve constant misunderstandings, mistakes and misfortunes. I believe the Commission is not one tenth part as useful as it

663

would be if the original plan of organization had been maintained.[2] I am as certain that the Commission can not exist long with its present arrangments as I am that I should not exist if I tried and succeeded in making my heart and brain interchange duties. It sickens me daily to see the mischief resulting from it. My self respect and my sense of truth and justice revolt at the task which I prescribe myself. Nevertheless receiving the money of the Commission, and the continued respect and kind intention of its members, I do require of myself constantly to perform as far as my imagination, sympathy and skill enable me to appreciate it, *the will of the Commission.*

D[r] Agnew and yourself went to Acquia Creek & Falmouth and spent a few days.[3] You were ill; you nevertheless saw a great deal; you returned, and I had several hours conversation with you about what you saw. You did not, nor did Agnew, tell me that you saw one single thing for yourself unfavorable with regard to Haywood & Clampitt. I do not remember that you ever said one word to me about them. Agnew did not; but *he wrote* me that they were drunkards, not that he saw them drunk, but that he was told that they were so.[4] At the same time he told me other things which I knew to be not true. The authority he gave was D[r] Kerlin.[5] D[r] Kerlin had been repeatedly ordered to report any and every man whom he had reason to believe to be unfit for the duties in which he was engaged. He had officially in writing endorsed Haywood & Clampitt as suitable persons for the duties assigned them. He had distinctly said that they did not drink to harm them. D[r] Kerlin was a man of intensely strong and easily excited prejudices against persons not of a certain class or habit. He told a good man that he must give up *smoking* or leave the service of the Commission, but when the man refused to refrain from smoking (at a proper time and place) he relented or backed down. This man was mentioned with Haywood & Clampitt, *as a drunkard.*[6] I protested directly, against what I deemed to be the wicked carelessness of D[r] Agnew—I believe, as D[r] Agnew does not, in "degrees of sin", and I believe that his sin was a very much deeper one, involving far greater injury to the service of the *Commission's purpose* than that which he recklessly assumed Clampitt, Haywood and Bradford to be guilty of. But considering his statement to be endorsed by you and to be addressed to me *as the servant of the Commission,* I advised D[r] Jenkins that *the Commission* must be assumed to have tried and found guilty these three men and that it was his duty to remove them. He did so.

The evidence against the men as I understood, and understand, rested wholly on the statements of D[r] Kerlin. D[r] Kerlin, after he had offered me his resignation, acknowledged that he had spoken of them and declared that he had considered them to be drunkards. He could give no satisfactory explanation of the inconsistency of this statement with previous statements, nor could he give the smallest *grounds for the opinion* last expressed. He had no facts. He had nothing but the indefensible opinion of a prejudiced mind to justify the libel. I had not seen these men. It had cost me nothing but a word of advice to Dr Jenkins to remove them, I had no prejudice to be gratified by their vindication except a prejudice of justice, but the result of a half hour's free conversation with Dr Kerlin, was to convince me that his opinion was of no more value than a child's, and that for all he *knew*, Dr Bellows, Dr Agnew, and himself had consumed more intoxicating drink, while at Acquia Creek, than the three men whom he had accused. I verily believe, today, and I have spent a good many hours in enquiring of the *facts*, that these men are no more guilty of drunkenness—were no nearer being drunk at any time, on any single occasion while in the service of the Commission, than on certain occasions, Dr Kerlin, himself. An unprejudiced person—whom I could trust, and whom I employed confidentially—going to Acquia, had reported to me that he had seen Dr Kerlin when he appeared to be, and when he thought he was, excited by liquor. I have never found the slightest evidence of that kind against Haywood, Clampitt or Bradford.

When Dr Kerlin left, Dr Douglas was acting General Secretary. I don't know how far he was acquainted with the facts of the removal of Clampitt, but he had been personally associated with Clampitt for some time, in the field & knew him well. Dr Douglas had to appoint someone at once to succeed Kerlin. The enemy was threatening an attack, and the engagement of the cavalry at Brandy Station was likely to bring on a general engagement.[7] Six of our experienced men had left and Dr Kerlin reported the rest demoralized, and our relations with the Medical Director[8] to be as bad as possible. It was imperatively necessary that some man should go there of comprehensive executive capacity. Dr Douglas requested Dr Steiner to go. Dr Steiner made certain conditions, of which one was that he could have Clampitt as his aid or chief Executive Assistant. He had not known of his dismissal. Dr Douglas informed [him] of it, and of the grounds of it. Dr Steiner said, "it is impossible! I had him under my eye constantly for six months, he lived most of the time at my table, slept in the same room with me; he had every temptation and opportunity to drink; liquor & wine were constantly open to him and I never saw the slightest sign of weakness that way. He will do more work and do it better and make less trouble and be surer of coming out right than any man I have met in the service of the Commission or anywhere else. You must let me have him for I know that I can depend upon him, and he is the only man I could get whom I could depend upon equally: *I will answer for his perfect sobriety."* Dr Douglas authorized Steiner to send for him to employ him. I told Douglas when I heard of it that I was sorry for it and told him how strongly Dr Agnew felt. Dr Douglas repeated to me what Dr Steiner had said, and added, "Why *I know* it's so, myself. Clampitt was with me at

665

Harper's ferry for more than a month and I never saw him out of temper, I never heard an uncivil or coarse word from him, and I never heard him accused by anyone of anything which would indicate that he had any bad habits. There is not a more correct man in the Commission's service."

To this I had my own observation to add. I was with Clampitt for a week, living intimately with him and I had never the slightest reason to suspect him of a habit of over-drinking. His appearance and manner was not attractive to me—chiefly from reserve and gravity—but he was energetic, industrious and discreet, obviously enough—I mean, markedly so. So I could not but believe Steiner & Douglas and Jenkins (and Andrews)[9]—all of whom had lived closely and intimately with him, rather than Kerlin who had not, but had at intervals visited him. There is no doubt at all that Clampitt smokes, after dinner, when he has no active work to do. Upon my honor, I believe the accusation against him has no other foundation than this; Dr Kerlin's zealous imagination acting upon it. I believe that it was a greater wrong, a greater unjust injury to remove him than it would be to remove me or to cause your removal from your church, *on the same grounds.*

What was my duty? As a member of the Executive Committee to order his re-removal or as a member of the Committee to reconsider the judgment, ("on appeal,") of yourself and Dr Agnew, in the light of new evidence?

I did and said *nothing* except in expression of my regret, but I intended to state the facts to the Executive Committee, to which I reported in person the next day. Other matters, more important, crowded it out of my mind, and I forgot it entirely till Agnew reminded me at Frederick. I then stated to him the simple fact of Steiner's making it a condition of accepting a duty of importance, at a time when his services could not be dispensed with without throwing away the whole value of the Commission to the Army of the Potomac.

Here I want to say a word—making a clean breast of this part of my troubles—about another man. Kerlin was appointed to the A. of the P. with especial reference to hunting out indiscretions and weak and improper persons. He was especially, strongly and repeatedly charged with this duty. He reported, after a full investigation of affairs at Acquia, that one man had been drunk, and according to standing orders this man[10] was sent up, and considered himself dismissed. Jenkins & Knapp each saw him, privately, without suggestion from me. They had no interest in him, except as in any stranger. They both independently came to the conclusion that he had given way to an extraordinary temptation and that he was deeply and sincerely repentant of it. The man supposed that he was dismissed, did not ask to be restored or forgiven; asked no favor, but said that it was what he deserved. Knapp came to Jenkins to ask and urge that he should not be turned adrift, and Jenkins having independently adopted the same idea of him, offered him a situation, under his own eye in Washington, which he accepted with great thankfulness.

Mr Harris (Rev'd.)[11] wrote to Dr Agnew complaining of this. Dr Agnew wrote a severe note to me. I replied stating the facts and reasons of Jenkins's action, and Agnew replied that he thought Jesus Christ would have done the same thing and he thanked Dr Jenkins for it. After your visit to Acquia, however, Dr Agnew again wrote me, complaining in still more severe terms than before of my keeping a drunken beast in the service of the Commission when good Dr Kerlin had personally requested his removal.[12] Dr Kerlin had *not* requested his removal but had approved of the action of Dr Jenkins,—or had said that he did so. Dr Agnew's heat and style and his ignorance of the matter was such that after our previous correspondence on the subject, and as I had then fully resolved on presenting my resignation at the next meeting of the Commission, I did not think it necessary to reply in detail. (Dr Agnew's letter was a private one). It is right that I should tell you that the man still remains in the service of the Commission and has a very responsible duty which he performs far better than it has ever been performed by anyone except himself. I have known him slightly, before. He was, ten years ago, Assist^t Secretary of the Kansas Aid Society and I then saw a good deal of him. He brought excellent testimonials of character to us. No one believes that he has taken a drop of strong drink, though it passes daily through his hands, in the last six months. The evidence that he ever was drunk in our service, so far as I am informed, is less than I have that the Revd Mr. Harris himself was drunk while in it. (He resigned from it sometime ago, and I don't mean to say he was a drunkard, by any means).

As to Haywood, he was employed by Knapp, for a few days only, in extra service, at Baltimore, it is true, with my consent. If Haywood had been employed regularly and there was evidence that he was a common drunkard, unfit to be trusted with business, it hardly seems to me there would have been occasion to assume that your and Dr Agnew's advice had not been treated with dutiful respect until enquiry had been made—as you evidently have in your own mind assumed—evidently, from the form of your enquiry. Mr Haywood is a respectable professional man. He was employed in my office, and in connection with the transport service, under my personal observation for more than a year. I don't believe there is any more ground for the accusation of drunkenness against him than there is against Dr Jenkins, Dr Douglas, Mr Knapp or myself. But under your advice he was dismissed upon that disgraceful ground, greatly to the inconvenience and injury of the service in this department and he has never been restored to the regular service. The reason for his being employed by Mr Knapp temporarily, he can best tell you. I can only say that the promptness and completeness with which Mr Knapp was able to meet my calls upon him after I left Balt° astonished me. I never have seen as large an amount of business so well done. Mr Knapp credits much of it to Haywood whom at his special request, I approved of his calling to his aid, when I found it necessary to leave him myself.

Now, my dear and most revered friend, I know that you will be annoyed that I take the trouble to write you a long letter of explanation about such a matter as this. You ought to know that I never would spend a minute upon it as a mere matter for self defence, for I know that whatever you say offhandedly, you don't believe that I am disposed to treat your advice without respect. Nor do I want to reproach you for the worst form of injustice—contemptuous indifference to justice—the root of Slavery. But I want to show you—at least I want to do some justice to my own desire that you should understand, why I can not do business in the way the Commission wishes. It is not my business to blame you or to point out to you where my judgment differs with yours, when you *decide* a question. You have a right to *decide officially*, and it is my duty officially to accept your decision—The responsibility is yours, if it is wrong, and I have no right to be troubled about it, officially. You and the Executive Committee do a great deal which for me to do, would be as morally wrong as picking a pocket or receiving a bribe. I think that you have no more right to do business in the free and easy, careless hasty inconsiderate way you do, than you have to leave your butcher's bills unpaid or to drop your lighted cigar-end in the straw of a stable-door. That is not the way that business is done successfully. Everything must, in one way or another, by one method or another, be thoroughly done, or trouble comes of it. Your business, if you had any with the Acquia Creek cases *in detail*, was to see that they were thoroughly investigated. Neither you nor I could have made such an investigation *personally* without an absurd waste of time, but either you or I could have reviewed such an investigation—or could have appointed somebody in whose just and thorough judgment we could reasonably confide to make such an investigation, and then could have acted justly, honestly, prudently and economically. The little false economy of saving the trouble of doing so, has already cost the Commission a hundred times what such a thorough study of the case would have cost at the time. And so it is always with your hasty decisions. And now it costs me this letter, as being cheaper to me than to let it be unwritten. I can't neglect to take trouble about a question like that you put to me, because it is a question of justice; and if you neglect such a question, the whole foundation of your business is falling out. I don't speak in the smallest degree from the moral point of view, nor, *now*, from the point of view of self-respect, but from that of the instinct of a business manager. A pirate-captain or a leading politician would have the same feeling about his dealings with his crew or his lobby-agents. I have fallen upon an exceedingly small and unimportant and not by any means a conclusive example, of the sort of thing which I refer to in the business of the Commission which makes it so hateful to me—not in the least morally, but scientifically. You can not have the small-est conception, I fear, of the perfect tempest of feeling, which I have to bear up against, when I read such a piece of stupid, savage folly as New-berry's letter to Carpenter.[13] It is partly personal, the sense of personal insult, for it gives the lie to half the writing which has [been] done in this office, (*in my name*), during the last two years—gives the lie to letters which I have written today, which I wrote yesterday, with my own hand. But I don't think I should feel much for that. But here is a business for which I have some sort of responsibility—an undertaking in which I have a part, in which it is partly my duty to be successful. And here is a man who acting partly for me (i.e. in the name of *our* Commission) deliberately, publickly and formally takes pains to give the public precisely the impres-sion which it is a distinct part of that undertaking—if I know anything about it—to prevent, who directly avows and advertises that we—(I) do not do that which we have daily, for the last two years, with a thousand tongues declared that we undertake to do. (Literally and precisely so—only substituting sheets or advertisements for tongues). The whole success of the Sanitary Commission has been gained by steadily ramming it in to the convictions of the people, by every means which we could possibly con-trive to use that such a condition of things as Newberry takes pleasure in setting forth to Carpenter would not ever exist, at least, if our honor, and business ability, could be trusted. The wickedness, the injustice, the devil-ish scoundrelism of such a state of things as he sets forth, is bad enough, when one is made to feel himself a part of it, but—is it not enough to drive a common man mad, when it is proclaimed from the house-top, as if it were a nice thing to do? What should I think if I had no personal interest in the Sanitary Commission, on reading that letter? What—perhaps it is bet-ter to ask—must such a man as Sydney Gay, who read Mrs Swisshelm's[14] letter about soldiers dying in Washington, by scores daily, for want of lemons, and who believed it, and roused the country on the subject, and had a mind to publicly denounce the Sanitary Commission because it had not bestirred itself about it, think about it. (I suppose you remember what Gibbs told us of his conversation.) Gay's intellect may be a little peculiar, but he is not more likely to be carried away by such a letter than 9/10[ths] of our subscribers & contributors. Suppose he reads that letter of Newberry's & is in earnest, & thinks about it, being about to give $5000 for the relief of soldiers & wishing to give it rightly? He reads that the Secretary of the Sanitary Commission, especially charged with a comprehensive oversight of its Western duties, on a certain date knew that the Army at Vicksburg was ten times as badly off for lemons as that at Washington. The men there were ten times as badly off (in wounds) as Mrs Swisshelm's in Washington and it was ten times as hot there—(or ten degrees hotter). Now what does the Secretary thus responsible for the Sanitary Commission do? He scours the whole Western country and finds only ten boxes of lemons—that is all he can do—to send those ten boxes of Western dried lemons. Poor fellows! he must let them die; he has done all *he* can do. And that very day, Dr Bellows, you were assuring Mr Carpenter that there was an abundance of lemons, other things were more wanted, very much, there was an *over* abundance of lemons, in the stores of the Sanitary Commission; people had been made by false statements, over liberal in that article, *and, that "the Sanitary Commission, at its Central Office was constantly informed of the wants of the army everywhere, and looked out equally well to supply the wants of every part of it."* You told me that you so told Mr Carpenter; I wondered how you dared tell him so, in a private and confidential way. I say it, through Bloor, and otherwise, many times every day. I suppose it has been said under my name, with your endorsement, more than a million times; and literally every time *it was a lie,* unless we meant to say that that was what we *undertook* to do, *only* as far as the means were placed in our power. I can answer for my part that that was what I meant—I meant it in earnest expecting to take some trouble & bear some unpleasantness to make it good, steadily and continuously, however. But to return to Mr Gay. What does he see? The Sanitary Commission with $255,000 lying idle in bank at New York, with lemons poured in upon it to an amount that led its president to discourage the further contribution of them; with the free use of telegraph and "special facilities of transportation," could not send a single lemon beyond the ten boxes which Dr Newberry's researches brought out in the West. The Sanitary Commission is bankrupt, spite of its $255 thousand in bank & all the rest: the poor fellows must die for all it can do for them. In fact the President of the San. Com. hasn't an idea *there is any want* of lemons there—no information has reached *him* on the subject; however, it may be at the Central Office. But, thank God! the policemen of New York are equal to the emergency. Just in the nick of time, in this terrible extremity, they direct Mr Carpenter to send 50 boxes of fresh lemons; bought with money *especially contributed for the purpose,* in New York to Vicksburg. They don't wait for information "through the Central Office," but in confidence in the inevitable failure of every big organization like this humbugging Sanitary Commission to do what it pretends, they guess the poor fellows who have fallen before the hell-fire of Vicksburg will not have been provided for, and they do it, and, *vide* Dr Newberry or Dr Warriner, great is their glory! It was a "welcome"—nay "a *priceless*", a "*munificent* donation" ($250,000 in bank) "at that moment doubly valuable *because no lemons could be procured*—at the West"—by the Sanitary Commission. If it had not been for the singular wisdom of the Metropoli-

tan police & the singular energy which overcame, in its struggle for humanity, even the Alleghany mountains, there was no earthly hope for
lemons with Dr Newberry & Dr Warriner. Now, to whom does Dr Newberry's letter invite Mr Gay to give his $5000 for the relief of the wounded
of the Army of the Union? To that lying, cheating, humbugging, swindling,
assuming, pretentious "organization", called the Sanitary Commission—or
to the far sighted and truly humane Metropolitan police-force? Good
Heavens, doctor, don't you feel the insult to your understanding of all this?
Will you tell me again that it is an idiosyncracy—a monomaniacal sensitive-
ness that makes me sore to it? I could bear the lie—my part in it, but the
worst of it is, *I was in earnest*, I did not mean it should be a lie. I had really
undertaken it, and I had rather be roasted alive than to make such a
miserable failure in my undertaking! This seems to me to be an aggravated
specimen, rather, of Newberry's malice, or whatever it is, for I can't believe
him such a complete ass as he must be if it is a mere blunder—but something of the sort is coming every week. I assure you I had rather a friend
should post me as a liar, I would rather walk up the whole length of
Broadway arm in arm with Gurowski[15] talking of McClellan, than to read a
copy of Newberry's paper.[16] I never see it without reddening. My dear
Doctor, between you and I, I mean every word I say, my face flushes, and a
real tempest of mortification and shame passes through the fibre of my
brain. How can I bear it? What can I do, then? Quit the damned thing?
What possible ground can I have the face to do that upon? Shouldn't I be a
pretty pharisee to go to you and say, "Doctor, I am too good to sail in your
boat any longer, you must let me get out, I can't stand your lying." I know
perfectly well that can't be the reason. You love truth and you love success,
quite as much as I do, and your intellectual striking power is ten times
mine. Why, then, do I feel it, and you don't? I can only see that it is my real
business, my responsibility in the matter, is different from yours. I am paid
for it, I live by it, it is my duty to devote myself to it *thoroughly* and
comprehensively. I must take hold of it in that spirit, or I am stealing to
keep my wife from starving. I don't believe that you would deal with your
servants or your sexton, as you did with Haywood & the other fellows. I
don't believe Agnew deals so with his patients; I don't believe Gibbs deals
so with his pupils, nor Strong with his clients. And if any man deals with
his partner as you deal with your Western Branches & with Newberry, all I
can say is, woe be to that House!

If you did not see all this, my dear doctor, at the outset—see that it
would be impossible to carry on the undertaking as you have been trying to
do it for the last year and a half, if it was not most distinctly determined
that it should never be liable to the miserable, dilettanti good fellows picnic
club-style of management, but that it should be put on business principles—that is to say should possess the power which carries the energy

of individual interest, individual pecuniary interest—then I never more thoroughly misapprehended an hour's talk of any man in my life. I would no more have touched the infernal business if I had not supposed that you gave me your assurance that I should have absolute control of the Executive management—that there should be no interference or complication of authority, even by recommendations and advice, with my selection and government of the employees; I would as soon have accepted an invitation to undertake a course of experiments in arsenick eating. I hate nothing in the world so much as this which I have endured the last year. There was no way in which you could have proposed that I should torture myself, equal to it. How you and the rest bear it, is the greatest mystery in the world to me.

There are piles of letters to be answered. As an honorable man, I can no longer answer them as I have been accustomed to do. Your letter about the Christian Commission[17] and Newberry's letter about the lemons directly contradicts the stereotyped answers. The only other answer that can be made is "I confess that the Sanitary Commission is a cheat—an imposition. Send your goods to the Christian Commission & the Metropolitan Police force of New York."

I am sorry that I have blundered into the Christian Commission business. I didn't mean & don't mean to discuss it with you. I never have said a word against the Christian Commission, but I will confess to you that giving, I hope, all respectful consideration to your statements, I believe that the Christian Commission did more harm than good, at Gettysburg. I have been on the ground and studied it for myself and this after hearing Agnew talk, unchecked and unopposed by me, for a week, about it. But I don't mean to discuss it, because I have not the ability to fully explain the grounds of my convictions, without a month's study, and you would never have the patience to read the volume I should have to write. Take my opinion for what it's worth and forgive my assurance. I only hope that you will not, as Agnew does, assume that any one of us, who thinks you are mistaken in your supposed facts, is led so to think from a mere prejudice and bigotry of partisanship. I am not a partisan, in my brain, of the Sanitary Commission but I am a partisan of the principles which the Sanitary Commission has commonly professed to be governed upon and which the Christian Commission disregards even more than the Sanitary Commission in practice.

Doctor! whose business was it to see that if there was a deficiency of lemons at the West, while the Sanitary Commission had plenty at the East, that deficiency was supplied? Who is responsible to the good men and women who have contributed four million dollars to the Sanitary Commission to relieve suffering among the sick & wounded of the Union

Army that the suffering of the poor men of Vicksburg which made the paltry gift of fifty boxes of lemons, one of priceless value, while the Commission had in New York what was equal to fifty thousand boxes of lemons, on its hands? Who is officially responsible? That question is asked, today, doctor, by many good women and some men in half the villages of New England and New York, and all those who have been in correspondence with this office or its branches; who have read your publications and taken pains to so inform themselves of the plan of the San. Com. that they could defend it and advocate, and who by their intelligent advocacy have gained or carried to our stores these millions—every one of these is explaining that this neglect—the state of things poetically described by Newberry— could not have existed if Mr Olmsted, the General Secretary, had been equal to his duty, had done what he had undertaken to do, had kept his promises. You have told them so, and I have told them so, a great many times.

My dear Doctor, has the Commission treated me justly, in forcing me to stand in this shameful position.

As I understood it, the Commission made a certain engagement with me, upon which engagement I pledged my honor and reputation that if certain money was entrusted to the Commission, certain results should follow. Those results don't follow. What do I know about Vicksburg, about Port Hudson, about Tullahoma? What has it been in my power to do for the sufferers there? Do you suppose they would have been without lemons at Vicksburg, if you had kept your promises with me? letting me manage the business for which you—even so late as the last meeting but one of the Commission's—formally declared and insisted that I was responsible?[18] Before the siege of Vicksburg commenced, I was brooding over the demand there would be there—in that hot climate—for acid drinks, and I even mentioned a crude suggestion to the Exec. Com. to supply them direct from the West Indies, by New Orleans.[19] But I had no power to act, no rights where I had—so your nonsensical resolutions say—responsibilities. Not your resolutions, only, but your public declarations of all kinds—your advertisements—the letters which Bloor, down below, is writing this minute. I fully believe that the interferences of the Exec. Committee, encouraging and sustaining the little vanities and jealousies of Dr Newberry & the Western branches, has cost hundreds of lives. I don't care for the lives or the suffering. I do care for the broken promises, for the false pretences, of this business.

I end as I began. It sickens me, daily, to see the mischief resulting from it. My self respect and my sense of justice and truth revolt at the task which I prescribe myself. Nevertheless, receiving the money of the Commission and the continued respect and kind intention of the members of the Commission, I do require of myself constantly to perform, as far as my imagination, sympathy and skill enable me to appreciate it—*the will of the Commission.*

I ask you, doctor of divinity, whether I am right, to do so? I know your answer. "Do you suppose that Strong and Gibbs and Van Buren and Agnew and I, love truth and hate falsehood and injustice less than you?"

I do not, but I believe that corporations have no souls, and I believe that business done without a soul, is damned, if the corporation is not.

I have hoisted a flood-gate and let run a pent up stream. No doubt it is muddy truth that has run, but, after all, is it not truth? Say it is exaggerated, that it is morbid—but there is truth in it, too. I feel sure there is, and that this truth has not had the weight with you that it should. I know that there must be something in the intense and continued feeling that I have, that you have not yet seen, and which you ought to see.

Now that you have more freedom, if not leisure, more quietness & solitude, I beg for our business's sake, for our friendship's sake, and for our country's sake, that you will really weigh these wild ideas that I have let pour out today, once more, and remembering that though you don't often see them, they abide with me and have been abiding with me, for nearly a year. Weigh them and see if there be not something in them, as I think there must be, which deserves a different treatment from any which it has yet received.

If there is a wrong in what we are doing or leaving undone—are responsible for—that wrong ought not to be merely covered nicely up, or slid along from month to month and year to year.

Yours, steadfastly, whether or no,

Fred. Law Olmsted.

The original is in box 641 of USSC-NYPL.

1. Waldo F. Hayward and Charles S. Clampitt were Sanitary Commission employees whose dismissal Cornelius R. Agnew had demanded in April 1863. Hayward, who had been employed by the Commission for approximately a year, helped transport the sick and wounded from the Virginia Peninsula. The Commission probably first employed Clampitt late in the summer of 1862; he was a quartermaster during the Antietam campaign. After the battle of Fredericksburg, both Hayward and Clampitt served as relief agents with the Army of the Potomac until they lost their jobs in the spring of 1863. Hayward thereafter appears to have worked only briefly for the Commission, when Knapp was forwarding supplies from Baltimore to Gettysburg early in July. Clampitt, however, was rehired and by the fall of 1863 had become the Commission's dispatcher for the Army of the Potomac. In August 1864 he was its chief storekeeper with that army (FLO to Alfred J. Bloor, July __, 1862, USSC-

NYPL, box 744: 2017; "Report on the Operations of the Inspectors and Relief Agents . . . after the Battle of Fredericksburg . . . ," doc. no. 57 in USSC, *Documents*; USSC, *Minutes*, p. 164).

2. Olmsted is referring to the description of the secretary in the plan of organization drawn up for the Sanitary Commission in June 1861, which called him "a gentleman of special competency, charged with the chief executive duties of the Commission." Olmsted believed that the creation of the Executive Committee in October 1861 and the subsequent enlargement of its functions had usurped executive duties belonging to the secretary ("Plan of Organization . . . ," doc. no. 3 in USSC, *Documents*).

3. Bellows and Agnew visited the Sanitary Commission's posts with the Army of the Potomac at Acquia Creek and at Falmouth on April 17 and 18, 1863. It seems likely that Bellows, upon his return, criticized Sanitary Commission employees to Olmsted. The minister in a letter of April 19 to his wife and daughter characterized the agents as "good, bad, and indifferent" and specified that Hayward was "heavy, cold & not in place" and that Clampitt and another employee named Gershom Bradford were "poor." At that time Bellows believed that the Commission's posts with the Army of the Potomac needed "radical reform" (HWB to Eliza and Anna Bellows, April 19, 1863, Henry Whitney Bellows Papers, Massachusetts Historical Society, Boston, Mass.).

4. Olmsted is somewhat misrepresenting Agnew's letter and its criticisms of Hayward and Clampitt. Agnew did not accuse the two employees of drunkenness but vaguely called them unsuitable and of "bad character." He also charged, "Clampart [*sic*] is entirely unfit by reason of his habits and rough, loaferish appearance. Hayward is brusque and unfaithful." Agnew then recommended that these men and two other employees "be dismissed from the service at once and forever" (C. R. Agnew to FLO, April 24, 1863).

5. Isaac Newton Kerlin (1834–1893), a New Jersey–born physician who in late 1862 entered the employ of the Sanitary Commission and in 1863 became chief inspector responsible for the Commission's agents and inspectors stationed with the Army of the Potomac. Kerlin had studied medicine at the University of Pennsylvania and in 1858 had been appointed assistant superintendent of the Pennsylvania Training School for Feeble-Minded Children, then under the direction of his former medical instructor Dr. Joseph Parrish, who undoubtedly also recommended him to the Sanitary Commission.

   Kerlin's work at first pleased Olmsted, who in December 1862 remarked, "Little Kerlin is on the whole the best general we have this side the Alleghanies." Problems arose, however, in the spring of 1863. Rather than directly criticizing or even asking for the dismissal of several of his subordinates, Kerlin apparently complained secretly about them to Agnew and prompted his demands of April 24. Kerlin was also unable to work well with Jonathan Letterman, the medical director of the Army of the Potomac. On May 8 Kerlin resigned his position and explained his actions to Olmsted: "My reasons for so doing are of a mixed character—I am dissatisfied with myself, and disappointed in my realization of the work of the Commission. Knowing my incompetency, I cannot honorably continue in the position I occupy."

   The Executive Committee was shocked by Kerlin's resignation, and Bellows immediately sought an explanation from Olmsted. After an interview with Kerlin on May 21, Olmsted reported that the physician felt discontented, demoralized, and incompetent. Olmsted's own opinion was that Kerlin was not the man for the position, "though a most excellent man for some duties, I am sure." He explained that Kerlin "plainly was incompetent, and it was a mistake to place him in a place of superintendence, with an army, chiefly I think owing to a peculiar class of very strong prejudices which he has, and to a special failing. The former I am

675

inclined to attribute to his Quaker associations—of which I have had no experience. The failing is a special liability to misjudge men. He is a very poor judge of character, working wholly by rule from symptoms, not at all by intuition from sympathy."

Kerlin became superintendent of the Pennsylvania Training School in 1864 and spent the remainder of his life there. He retained an admiration for Olmsted and in 1880 sent him a copy of one of his own monographs "only to indicate that you are held by me in the most respectful remembrance, & that I wish you to know the line of my present work" (FLO to GTS, Dec. 26, 1862; I. N. Kerlin to FLO, May 8, 1863, USSC-NYPL, box 759: 1473; HWB to FLO, May 12, 1863, USSC-NYPL, box 759: 1523; FLO to HWB, May 21, 1863, Henry Whitney Bellows Papers, Massachusetts Historical Society, Boston, Mass.; I. N. Kerlin to FLO, Oct. 15, 1880; Henry W. Ashmead, *History of Delaware County, Pennsylvania* [Philadelphia, 1884], p. 627; *Transactions of the Medical Society of the State of Pennsylvania* . . . 25 [1894]: 386–87).

6. Gershom Bradford (b. 1838), a Sanitary Commission employee and the brother-in-law of Frederick N. Knapp. Agnew did not specifically accuse Bradford of drunkenness but argued that "Bradford is not possessed of a single quality that we need in our employees." Bradford does not appear ever to have worked for the Sanitary Commission after his discharge late in April of 1863 (Horace Standish Bradford, "Descendants of Gov. William Bradford" [ms. at New England Historical Genealogical Society, Boston, Mass.]; C. R. Agnew to FLO, April 24, 1863).

7. A reference to the engagement of June 9, 1863, in which Union cavalrymen commanded by Alfred Pleasanton successfully attacked J. E. B. Stuart's Confederate cavalry at Brandy Station, Virginia (*War for the Union*, 3: 79–80; F. H. Dyer, *Compendium of the War of the Rebellion*, 2: 918).

8. Relations between the Sanitary Commission and Jonathan Letterman, medical director of the Army of the Potomac, deteriorated during the spring of 1863. Although Letterman enforced rules of hygiene and diet that the Sanitary Commission had long advocated, he also discouraged the Commission's aid. Rather than allowing the Commission's relief agents to transport their own stores, he ordered that such supplies be sent with those of the medical officers (W. Q. Maxwell, *Lincoln's Fifth Wheel*, pp. 203–4; Bennett A. Clements, *Memoir of Jonathan Letterman* . . . [New York, 1883], p. 13).

9. George L. Andrew.

10. George Walter, who became an employee of the Sanitary Commission late in 1862. During the 1850s he had served as general superintendent of both the New York Kansas League and the American Settlement Company, two free-soil organizations interested in planting colonies of Northern antislavery settlers in Kansas. In January 1863, while Walter was stationed at Acquia Creek, his superior Isaac N. Kerlin recommended his discharge and told J. Foster Jenkins, "Walters [*sic*] is utterly unfit for any position in which he can be sufficiently authoritative to become insulting, while his habitual drinking will account for the large number of empty whiskey bottles in the rear of the store-house." In Washington, Jenkins and Knapp decided that Walter deserved another chance and gave him a position in the Commission's central storehouse. Late in 1863 he remained there as receiving storekeeper (Ralph Volney Harlow, "The Rise and Fall of the Kansas Aid Movement," *American Historical Review* 41 [Oct. 1935]: 2; I. N. Kerlin to JFJ, Jan. 24, 1863, USSC-NYPL, box 755: 218; USSC, *Minutes*, p. 163).

11. William C. Harris, a Presbyterian clergyman who served as a relief agent for the Sanitary Commission with the Army of the Potomac from January through June 1863. He had been the chaplain of the 106th Pennsylvania from October 1861 through October 1862. Bellows believed him "fussy and conceited, but high-toned and devoted." Harris may have been a protégé of Agnew, since the two shared an evangelical outlook. Resigning from the Commission because of poor health, Harris

later became pastor of the Towanda Presbyterian Church in Towanda, Pennsylvania, and organized a Christian reading room and a chapter of the Young Men's Christian Association there (HWB to Eliza and Anna Bellows, April 19, 1863, Henry Whitney Bellows Papers, Massachusetts Historical Society, Boston, Mass.; W. C. Harris to John S. Blatchford, Dec. 31, 1866, USSC-NYPL, box 1086; David Craft, *History of Bradford County, Pennsylvania* . . . [Philadelphia, 1878], pp. 162, 175, 231).

12. Olmsted's account of his correspondence with Agnew in February and April 1863 is essentially correct. Although Agnew told Olmsted in February, "I honor you for the Christian magnanimity displayed in the case of Walters," he was writing by late April that "Walters nearly ruined the interest of the Commission by his beastly drunkenness" and that he should be immediately dismissed (C. R. Agnew to FLO, Feb. 15 and April 24, 1863).

13. Olmsted is referring to a letter written by John S. Newberry to Daniel S. Carpenter, inspector of New York's metropolitan police, and published in the *New-York Daily Tribune* of July 23, 1863. Newberry effusively thanked Carpenter for the police force's donation of fifty boxes of lemons for sick and wounded soldiers at Vicksburg and called the gift "most welcome" and "priceless." Newberry continued: "The munificent donation chanced at that time to be doubly valuable, from the fact that though generally needed, no lemons could be procured anywhere at the West. I had exhausted the markets in all our Western cities, and had only been able to procure some ten boxes for Rosecrans's and Grant's armies, when several hundreds were imperatively demanded." This letter infuriated Olmsted because it contradicted the Sanitary Commission's stated goals and methods. Newberry was endorsing sporadic, special donations shipped long distances, a practice the Sanitary Commission had consistently disparaged as wasteful. Moreover, according to the Sanitary Commission's system, if Newberry needed lemons and could not obtain them in the West, he should already have requested them from the central office (*New-York Daily Tribune*, July 23, 1863, p. 8).

14. Jane Grey Cannon Swisshelm (1815–1884), journalist and antislavery and women's rights reformer. From 1848 until 1857 she edited the *Saturday Visiter* [sic], an abolitionist journal, in Pittsburgh, Pennsylvania. Her marriage of twenty-one years had long been troubled, and in 1857 she left her husband and moved to St. Cloud, Minnesota, where she began another antislavery journal. In 1863 she returned to the East and became a nurse that spring in the military hospitals in Washington, D.C. Olmsted is probably referring to a letter by Jane Swisshelm that appeared in the *New-York Daily Tribune*, whose managing editor was Sydney H. Gay. Her article recorded a conversation with a wounded soldier in a Washington hospital who asked only for "something to quench thirst." When she remonstrated that Dorothea Dix had said that the government supplied all that the surgeons allowed the patients to drink, the soldier replied that during long, hot days he became tired of drinking only water. A chorus of other voices then reiterated his request for something "sour" such as lemonade to quench thirst. Jane Swisshelm ended her story with a plea for "thirstquenching" supplies to be sent to her Washington address (*Notable American Women*; *New-York Daily Tribune*, May 13, 1863, p. 1).

15. Adam Gurowski was well known in Washington for his careless dress, eccentric, abrupt manners, and the tirades of abuse that he directed against political enemies such as McClellan (LeRoy Henry Fischer, *Lincoln's Gadfly, Adam Gurowski* [Norman, Okla., 1964], pp. 95–97, 135–42; see also FLO to HWB, Feb. 4, 1863, n. 2, above).

16. The *Sanitary Reporter*, which was published by the Western department of the Sanitary Commission and whose first issue was dated May 15, 1863.

17. Olmsted is referring to a letter written by Bellows to the editor of the *New-York Times*. In his description of the condition of the wounded at Gettysburg, the minister included the following tribute to the Christian Commission:

The farmers and townfolk sent large supplies to the Christian Commission, in addition to their own copious stores, which, by the aid of a force of two hundred volunteers, chiefly ministers, were rapidly and efficiently distributed. Some thousands of tired and hungry soldiers were fed at their saloon of refreshments. The wounded men had letters written for them home, and received religious counsel and support to a most gratifying extent. I desire to give the strongest expression to my own sense of the enterprise, zeal, and blessedness of the labors of this sister institution on the battle-field of Gettysburgh.

Olmsted objected to this glowing praise because he thought it unwarranted and the Christian Commission's course unwise. He disapproved of its policy of using only short-term, unpaid volunteer agents, because he believed it harder to gain systematic, steady effort from them. Olmsted doubtless also disliked the manner in which the Christian Commission mixed evangelizing with the care of the sick and wounded, for he believed good care to be a basic right of the soldier (Henry W. Bellows, "The Field of Gettysburgh," *New-York Times*, July 16, 1863, p. 3).

18. A reference to the resolution proposed by Bellows and passed by the Sanitary Commission on January 24, 1863, that held Olmsted responsible for the Western department, ordered him to visit it, and further stated that "having once surveyed it, he shall coordinate the Western Department with the Central Office, holding the Western Secretary responsible for weekly reports to him." The resolution also called for Newberry to be "instructed to hold direct official communication only with the General Secretary." Another resolution, approved at the same time, however, stated that the "peculiarities of the Western Department require more flexibility in the arrangements than are found necessary in the East," and the Commission also commended Newberry for his management of the Western department (USSC, *Minutes*, p. 134).

19. On May 22 Olmsted gave Bellows some "floating ideas" about projects the Commission might undertake in the Southwest. "Of course, in the absence of reports," added Olmsted, "we are all in the dark as to what is wanting there, and can only conjecture." He then suggested, "If there should be a couple of big battles in the West next week, I think you might spend a few thousand dollars profitably in a wholesale purchase of lemons, tamarinds, bay-water, cologne water, etc. shipping direct to Cairo and Louisville." Olmsted also discussed military hospitals at the Southwest and speculated that a large one might be established south of Vicksburg. He offered, "If this should be the case, might we not charter a schooner and run her from the West Indies, with tropical fruits, there?" (FLO to HWB, May 22, 1863.)

To John Samuel Blatchford[1]

Sanitary Commission,
Central Office, 244 F Street,
Washington, D.C., July 27th 1863.

My Dear Sir,

Absence from Washington has prevented me sooner giving a personal answer to your favor of the 15th.[2]

I do not approve the course pursued by the Christian Commission for reasons which have repeatedly been set forth in printed papers; I enclose one of these of which some fifty thousand have been distributed in a circular form, this year.[3] We undertake to provide beforehand for the necessities of the wounded. On the ground that we do so—that it will not do to wait for a battle to occur before providing for it—we constantly urge steady work and a continued flow of contributions of all kinds. We undertake, so far as our advice is taken and our plan is successful, to be ready for battles: to have goods always within our reach. If then we should issue sensational bulletins of the character of those of which you send copies,[4] startling, harrowing and exaggerated, we could undoubtedly get large contributions to our Treasury upon the occasion, but, having begged our friends, in effect, not to put us to the necessity of depending upon such means, obviously inadequate for prompt relief, it seems to me neither right nor expedient to resort to them.

The advertisement, written at Frederick and published in the New York, Philadelphia & Baltimore, (and, I presume, Boston)[5] papers, during the second week after the battle of Gettysburg, was intended to enforce the lesson of preparative industry, and liberality. It must be constantly kept in mind, that, notwithstanding the magnificent contributions of California made wholly in money, and the large money contributions of Boston and New York, more than two thirds of all the relief which the Sanitary Commission is able to render in the form of supplies comes from little country societies, composed of people of little wealth. It is the steady labor of these people that we want. We can afford to do nothing which will tend to cause its remission.

I suppose that in spite of all the telegrams and excited appeals made to the citizens of Boston, ignoring all other means of aid to the wounded of Gettysburg, except what should go through the hands of the Christian Commission, there was ten times the real value of supplies sent from and through Boston to the wounded there, by means of the Sanitary Commission, that there was by the Christian Commission.

I am, dear Sir,
Yours Very Respectfully,

Fred. Law Olmsted.
Genl. Sec.

Jno. S. Blatchford Esq[r]
Boston, N.E. Branch, Sanitary Commission

The original is in box 54 of USSC-NYPL.

1. John Samuel Blatchford (b. 1831), secretary of the Boston branch of the Sanitary Commission, eventually became Olmsted's successor: he began to serve as the last general secretary of the Sanitary Commission in April 1865 (W. Q. Maxwell, *Lincoln's Fifth Wheel*, p. 286; Eliphalet Wickes Blatchford, comp., *Blatchford Memorial II: A Genealogical Record of the Family of Rev. Samuel Blatchford, D.D.* . . . [Chicago, 1912], pp. 69–70).
2. In this letter, which was accompanied by clippings about the Christian Commission from the Boston newspapers, Blatchford argued that the way the Sanitary Commission publicized its activities allowed the Christian Commission to be more successful at fund raising. He believed that public interest in the care of wounded soldiers was most intense at the time great battles occurred and that the Commission reported its activities too long after battles, when interest had flagged. Outlining an alternative approach, he wrote,

   > A brief official despatch relating to the operation of the Commission upon the [field], transmitted with the news of an Engagement, for the press, must necessarily commend the Commission to the attention and sympathies of the public, more than the most elaborate and valuable report of its operations, weeks or months after the occurrences have transpired.

   Blatchford also suggested that the Commission publish in the newspaper press articles from its own publications which clearly set forth its principles and operations (J. S. Blatchford to FLO, July 15, 1863, USSC-NYPL, box 955: 2669).
3. Olmsted's enclosure has not survived, but he probably included a circular such as "What They Have to Do Who Stay at Home," which urged the importance of sustained work and giving to soldiers' aid societies.
4. No doubt, the urgent appeals in the Boston newspapers for contributions of money and supplies by George H. Stuart of the U.S. Christian Commission (see *Boston Morning Journal*, July 4, 1863, p. 4; ibid., July 9, 1863, p. 4; *Boston Evening Transcript*, July 10, 1863, p. 3).
5. Olmsted's item "For the Wounded" (see FLO to Exec. Comm., USSC, July 9, 1863, n. 2, above).

To Henry Whitney Bellows

Philadelphia,[1] July 28th 1863

My Dear Doctor.

I hope that you will pardon me for leaving the kind letter I got from you a day ago, unanswered, while I ran off on a spree of ill-nature. I am really oppressed beyond endurance by my grief that the grand purposes which I have had at heart in the Commission should appear to me to be sacrificed to little personal whims and good purposes of a narrow and ambiguous kind. I think the Commission has been wheedled and soft soaped and swindled. I know that I have. Promise after promise, made in the most solemn and imposing manner, has been broken with me, and all with pretence of religion & love & friendship. The worst of it is, I can't now see any way out of it, we have let ourselves be caught and fettered and now we must be led about, whether we will or no. Accordingly, I chafe and fume like a caged lion. Give me credit for prudence, however. When the exhibition is open, you know that I play my part as gently as a sucking dove.

I am on my way, I hope to Walpole, and there, you can chloroform me or beat me blue and silent.

I can't agree with you about the Brooklyn Daily.[2] The enterprise I have in mind, seems to me as different from a daily newspaper, as a daily newspaper is different from a pamphlet. I am encouraged that three out of four came down with their quota.[3] If all do as well, the capital can be raised in New York alone, which is more than I expect. But I do hope that nothing will be postponed till September. It is of very great importance that the business should get its foundation before September. It is not essential, but it is very important. What a pity it is not in existence now. Never was there so favorable a season for planting good seed, especially in New York. There is a tide in the affairs of men. There are tides & there is tide up now, higher & stronger than ever before. The Times, by the way, has had excellent articles on the riots.[4] I agree with you, I think, about them, but a great deal depends on what is not yet decided.[5] The opportunity for revolutionizing New York is a grand one.

I broached the matter of the Review to the Surgeon General. He took what seemed to me the most extravagantly sanguine view of its success, as a power in the land. He at once volunteered to write for it all that would be taken on his specialties of Social Science. This without being asked. He also without being asked, said that if there was difficulty about capital, he would be responsible for $3000, to be collected in $500 sums among his friends.

Crane[6] has arrived from New Orleans. There is nothing of special interest in his reports. I think they did wrong to reduce our force there so much & shall, if I can, send an early reinforcement. Their theory was that the Banks' expedition was at an end, & they enlisted for that. The larger part of the troops in that department are on their way home, to be paid out.[7]

Yours affectionately

Fred. Law Olmsted.

Dr Bellows.

The original is in the Henry Whitney Bellows Papers, Massachusetts Historical Society, Boston, Massachusetts.

1. Olmsted was in Philadelphia en route to New York City and Walpole.
2. Bellows was urging Olmsted to become editor of a daily newspaper in Brooklyn. When the minister asked the merchant A. A. Low for a contribution for the journal proposed by Olmsted and Godkin, Low "declined on the score, that he & Mr. Chittenden had just subscribed $10,000 cash! to start a daily newspaper in Brooklyn, designed to correct & purify public opinion there—& that a larger fund was to be raised—and that they were to look up *an editor*." "It immediately occurred to me," Bellows continued, "could not these two things somehow be made *one*?" (HWB to FLO, July 23, 1863.)
3. That is, three of the four gentlemen who answered Bellows's request had pledged five hundred dollars in cash to help start a weekly paper. Bellows had not received a reply from six other men to whom he had written, and he speculated that they would do little before September (ibid.).
4. Since the second day of the draft riots, the *New-York Times* had been publishing articles and editorials critical of the rioters and demanding that the riots be suppressed and the draft enforced.
5. Bellows believed that the time that had been required to suppress the riots was not unduly long, given the fact that they had broken out unexpectedly in a city whose militia had gone to help repel the Confederate invasion of Pennsylvania. He also argued:

> The effect of the *emeute* will be good. It has developed the power and determination of property-holders—united three quarters of the city in solid phalanx—aroused a needed jealousy of Irish & Catholic manoeuvres, & so weakened the Democratic party, always flattering that clique. Moreover, it came at a right time, when there is no scruple about shedding blood. A mob was never less safe than in a time when bloodletting is familiar. It was a lucky time for us—also—because we had great victories & tall news to keep up our spirits in the face of such domestic mortification & appalling evil.

Bellows added: "The treatment of the negroes by the Irish is one of the most humiliating & disgusting events in Modern History. I think it will make thousands of anti-slavery men—& do the race immense good in the end" (HWB to FLO, July 23, 1863).
6. Edward Augustus Crane (1832–1906), physician and inspector of the Sanitary Commission. A Massachusetts native, Crane was a graduate of Amherst College and Harvard Medical School. Before the Civil War, he practiced medicine in Providence, Rhode Island.

   Crane joined the Sanitary Commission in 1862 and worked in southern Pennsylvania during the Antietam campaign. His later assignments took him to the Department of the Gulf in Louisiana and to the Department of the South in South Carolina. After the war he moved to Paris, France, where he remained for most of his life. In 1870 he played an important role in the formation of the American Association for the Relief of the Misery of Battlefields, which was active during the Franco-Prussian War (Amherst College, *Biographical Record of the Graduates and Non-Graduates*, ed. William J. Newlin, rev. ed. [Amherst, Mass., 1939], p. 92).
7. The Banks expedition, though popularly believed at its inception to be an invasion force against Texas, had been besieging the Confederate garrison at Port Hudson, Louisiana, during the spring and early summer of 1863. Port Hudson surrendered to Union forces on July 7, 1863 (George Winston Smith, "The Banks Expedition of 1862," *Louisiana Historical Quarterly* 26 [April 1943]: 341–60; Fred Harvey Harrington, *Fighting Politician: Major General N. P. Banks* [Philadelphia, 1948], pp. 118–24).

To Mary Perkins Olmsted

New York, July 29th [1863]

My Dear Wife,

I arrived here last night. This morning I receive yours of 26th.

My conscience reproaches me about father. I shall go to him as soon as I can—probably first of next week. I suppose him to be at Sachem's Head.[1] Write if he is, or is not, please, immediately. If I can, I will leave here on Saturday.

I saw the Prof^r[2] yesterday. He spoke with obvious satisfaction of your visit & the pleasure of Mrs Bache[3] in overhauling flowers with you and that sort of thing. He is very well. Is to be here tonight on his way to Wolcott.[4] He spoke of Frank[5] as a smart and diligent boy.

About the church, I prefer that you should follow your inclinations. You know that I have very little choice, but so far as I have, your argument does not weigh against it. I would much prefer that the children never heard a sermon, if they could attend worship of a decorous character without it. And, among Sermons, the duller and least impressive, the better. I crave and value worshipfulness, but I detest and dread theology & formalized ethics. My experience is too, that Episcopalians are better men than Presbyterians. These are crude, general propositions. Individual men & manners and thoughts & ways of thinking are likely, of course, to override them.

I can't tell you how much it rejoices me to hear that you feel relieved of care & grow calmer, smoother & cheerfuller.

Not the least progress, unless it be backward, in my plans & enterprises. I don't feel as if I could stand the San. Com. any longer. Prof^r Bache said yesterday that he should quit, whether I did or not, if Newberry was allowed his way.

Yours affectionately,

Fred.

Make the most of Litchfield & make yourself unwilling to think of coming away.

1. A rocky point of land overlooking the ocean in Guilford, Connecticut, the town in which Olmsted had in 1847 operated a farm purchased for him by his father. Probably Olmsted thought his father was staying at the Sachem's Head House, a large hotel and popular summer resort there (Bernard Christian Steiner, *History of Guilford and*

Madison, Connecticut [1897; rpt. ed., Guilford, Conn., 1975], pp. 204–5, 209; *Papers of FLO*, 1: 227, 282–83, 297–98).

2. Alexander Dallas Bache.
3. Nancy Clarke Fowler Bache, the wife of Alexander Dallas Bache.
4. Probably a reference to the small hill town near Waterbury in western Connecticut.
5. Francis Walley Perkins (b. 1844), the son of Francis and Miriam Walley Perkins, was the first cousin of Mary Perkins Olmsted. Probably Bache had met Perkins while the latter was visiting the Olmsteds (Edmund Janes Cleveland and Horace Gillette Cleveland, *The Genealogy of the Cleveland and Cleaveland Families . . .* , 3 vols. [Hartford, Conn., 1899], 2: 1612).

To Robert Morton Lewis[1]

U.S. Sanitary Commission,
New-York Agency, 823 Broadway.
New York, July 30th 1863.

My Dear Sir,

Dr Weir Mitchell,[2] who is engaged in an inspection of the prisoners' dépôt at Fort Delaware,[3] has represented to us that the hospital there is in a disgraceful condition. He has been informed that requisitions upon the Commission, endorsed by him, will be met from the dépôt in Philadelphia. Please make return to the office at Washington of any goods which may be issued for this purpose, and with your return, please send the original requisitions with Dr Mitchell's endorsement.

I do not suppose the demand will be a large one, but if it should occasion remark and there should be a doubt about issuing goods to surgeons when it is known that they are to be used almost wholly for the benefit of rebels, it may be well to say that the Commission proceeds upon the ground that every rebel whose life is saved will increase the inducement presented to the rebel authorities to treat carefully all Union men who fall into their hands. Every Union man whose life is saved by them buys back to them a man of their own, whose life we have saved. Of course, the more rebel-lives we can have to deal with, the more valuable we make to them the lives of the Union men whom they may take prisoners.

Yours Respectfully

Fred. Law Olmsted.
Genl Secy

R. M. Lewis Esqr
Phila

The original is letter 378 in box 591 of USSC-NYPL.

1. Robert Morton Lewis, Jr. (c. 1828–1899), a Philadelphia merchant who was a graduate of the University of Pennsylvania. At the end of 1862 Lewis assumed general superintendence of the Philadelphia branch of the Sanitary Commission, replacing his college classmate William Platt, Jr., who had died suddenly. Lewis held this position until the end of the war and also served as secretary of the Women's Pennsylvania Branch of the Sanitary Commission (*Philadelphia Inquirer*, Dec. 31, 1899, sec. 2, p. 6; University of Pennsylvania, General Alumni Society, *General Alumni Catalogue of the University of Pennsylvania* [Philadelphia, 1917], p. 45; *McElroy's Philadelphia City Directory for 1863* . . . , 26th ed. [Philadelphia, 1863]; U.S. Sanitary Commission, Philadelphia Branch, *Report of the General Superintendent of the Philadelphia Branch of the U.S. Sanitary Commission to the Executive Committee, January 1st, 1865* [Philadelphia, 1865]).
2. Silas Weir Mitchell (1829–1914), physician. Mitchell, who later became a noted neurologist and the author of numerous books of prose and poetry, received his medical degree from Jefferson Medical College. During the Civil War he worked at military hospitals and was sympathetic to the aims of the Sanitary Commission (Howard A. Kelly and Walter L. Burrage, *Dictionary of American Medical Biography: Lives of Eminent Physicians of the United States and Canada* . . . [New York, 1928], pp. 854–57).
3. Fort Delaware, located on Pea Patch Island in the Delaware River approximately forty-five miles from Philadelphia, became a regular prison depot in 1863. Swampy and overcrowded, it had an alarmingly high death rate and was one of the prisons most feared by captured Confederate soldiers (William Best Hesseltine, *Civil War Prisons: A Study in War Psychology* [Columbus, Ohio, 1930], pp. 180–88; Hedwig Friederike Lesser, "Civil War Prisons: A Study of the Conditions under Which They Operated" [Ph.D. diss., University of Alabama, 1968], pp. 193–94).

To Edwin Lawrence Godkin

Sanitary Commission,
Central Office   244 F street,
Washington, D.C., August 1st 1863

My Dear Godkin,
Nothing has been done by any of our "committee"—not a step made. Reason—the riots knocked it out of their heads. All the people they were to see have gone out of town, and are difficult to get at. Bellows alone took the lazy way of writing to them, (breaking his promises) with the result which I reported—which is therefore encouraging.[1] I have tried to set them going again, but I don't believe anything will be done till the town returns. I have done all I decently could to avoid this postponement— perhaps a little more than I should. But having made up my mind that not much would be done *here* at present, I have commissioned Knapp to visit

685

Boston and apply personally to twenty men there whom he knows, which he will begin doing in a fortnight if nothing prevents.

I believe the money will be got. I caught Dana[2] today & talked to him about it. He said: "I don't believe it will succeed—but I am not sure, and I shall be glad to have it tried." He thought that I could get the money. I had quite a full talk but got little that was new from him. He did not like "the Week",[3] nor do I, nor anything else.

I should have left here today, but am ill. I hardly ever suffered so much from the heat. I don't know what to make of it. I shall get to Litchfield early in the week. Write me there & come over if convenient. I shall go on to Walpole.

Yours affectionately,

F.L.O.

The original is in the Edwin Lawrence Godkin Papers, Houghton Library, Harvard University, Cambridge, Massachusetts.

1. See FLO to HWB, July 28, 1863, note 3, above.
2. Charles A. Dana, assistant secretary of war and a former editor of the *New-York Daily Tribune*.
3. That is, as a name for the proposed weekly journal.

To JOHN OLMSTED

New York. Aug. 10th [1863]
Monday

Dear Father,

I telegraphed you that I had been called unexpectedly to New York by the Mayor.[1] He has offered me the Superintendency of the Mariposa estate in California, now owned by a company in New York. It is a whole county 5 x 40 miles,[2] with a tenant population of 7000, entirely owned with everything on it by the Company.

The only inducement to accept it would be the compensation, which is not fixed but would be liberal, the Mayor said. He added that he should be willing to make it $10,000 a year with some small contingent dividend. It is 200 miles from the coast and dreary, I have no doubt.

He wants an immediate decision & that I should start in a month.

I suppose that I shall have to decide before I can see you, but I wish that you would write me what you think about it. I am rather disposed to decline it chiefly, or partly, because I think it might be too much for me. I should have complete, entire, uncontrolled management. There are seven mines[3] opened besides a large amount of Chinese placer mining,[4] a rail-road[5] & more to be laid out, and a great commercial business established. Please write immediately.

Your affectionate son

Fred. Law Olmsted.[x]

[x]Brevoort House[6]

1. George Opdyke.
2. Olmsted's information was incorrect. The Mariposa Estate covered about seventy square miles, only a small part of the one thousand square miles of Mariposa County (*The Mariposa Estate: Its Past, Present and Future* . . . [New York, 1868], p. 5; Owen C. Coy, *California County Boundaries* [Berkeley, Ca., 1923], pp. 160–65).
3. The mines on the estate were the Princeton, Mariposa, Green Gulch, Oso, Mount Ophir, New Britain, Pine Tree, and Josephine. The last two were adjacent and were often considered to be a single mine (FLO to James Hoy, Oct. 19, 1863).
4. Placer miners used pans or other simple hydraulic means to wash gold from the deposits or formations in which it occurred.
5. A four-mile gravity railroad that carried ore from the Pine Tree and Josephine mines down to Benton Mills on the Merced River, where it was processed (Shirley Sargent, ed., *Mother Lode Narratives: By Jessie Benton Frémont* [Ashland, Ore., 1970], p. 155).
6. A hotel at Fifth Avenue and Clinton Place, near Washington Square, in New York City. Olmsted used the "x" by his signature to indicate that he was staying at the Brevoort House.

To Mary Perkins Olmsted

New York, August 12th 1863

My Dear Wife,

I think that I shall make up my mind tonight, and *if the result of enquiries today* is favorable, shall decide to go.

The case stands thus: The company is controlled by respectable, steady, careful capitalists.[1] It is this point only that I am not yet satisfied about. They are very anxious to get me—this anxiety has been increased and developed today. They have, at present, abundance of capital unemployed. Consequently there is every reason why they should be willing to pay me all that it would be reasonable to wish. If I don't go there, so far as remuneration commercially of my services [is concerned], it will be because I estimate my value unreasonably high.

Setting aside the commercial question then, as to my family: The question should be not one of inclination & satisfaction, but: for the ultimate welfare of my family, what is best?

Finally, general benevolence or religious duty. It is at least doubtful if my part in the Sanitary Commission, for good is not ended. The paper project & my general chance of usefulness in the settlement of the war questions: This weighs upon me the most. But it is absolutely intangible, prospective and speculative. I am in danger of estimating too highly the value of my judgment, and my ability to make it operative with the public. On the other hand, there is a much more certain, tangible & immediate prospect of exercising a powerful & within certain limits controlling influence favorable to religion, good order & civilization in the field to which I am invited. As the clergymen say when a rich parish bids for them against a poorer: I think the call to California is a *clear* one, if not as loud as that to the battle here.

If I go, it will be almost immediately, as soon as in any manner, I can get off.

I think therefore, you had better be considering what you want me to do for you—where & how you will live, etc.

A letter from father, just received, decidedly advises me to go. All the friends whom I have consulted, concur. I mean that they think, much against their inclination, that it is a plain, man's duty, & I can't help it—for instance, Strong, Jenkins, Howard Potter. Dudley Field is a large stockholder[2] & is very anxious I should go. I don't count his, as advice, therefore.

Meantime, don't think that I fail to see the immense labor, anxieties and—heroisms, which acceptance will impose upon me. I hate the wilderness & wild, tempestuous, gambling men, such as I shall have to master, & shrink from undertaking to encounter them, as few men would.

Your affectionate husband

Fred. Law Olmsted.

---

1. The officers of the Mariposa Company were: James Hoy, president; George Farlee, vice-president; Morris Ketchum, treasurer; and John Watt, secretary. The board of

directors included Frederick Billings, John Frémont, George Opdyke, and Trenor Park (JO Journal, Oct. 1863).
2. David Dudley Field (1805–1894), noted lawyer, had received two thousand shares of Mariposa Company stock from John Frémont as payment for legal services (*DAB*; Charles G. Crampton, "The Opening of the Mariposa Mining Region, 1849–1859, With Particular Reference to the Mexican Land Grant of John Charles Frémont" [Ph.D. diss., University of California at Berkeley, 1941], pp. 269–70).

To SAMUEL GRIDLEY HOWE

New York, August 13th 1863.

My Dear Doctor:
I yesterday received your note of the 8th & immediately called at some of the Insurance companies to obtain the specific information you wish.[1]

The only company in New York which has taken slave risks at all extensively is the Knickerbocker.[2] They have insured only for the period of a year and chiefly on the lives of house-servants, mechanics & steamboat men, (waiters, barbers & deck-hands), a class in which there is a large proportion of yellow men. They have invariably taken careful descriptions as to color, hair &c. The number of lives, I could not learn, but the amount insured was $150,000 to $200,000 a year, during three years before the rebellion. The President[3] seemed to have carefully studied the question whether the risk was greater with yellow than with black men and to have come quite decidedly to the conclusion that it was not. Neither the Knickerbocker nor any other Life Insurance Company of New York discriminates in its rates in favor of the pure black.

The Life Insurance of plantation negroes is almost wholly with local companies at the South, principally at New Orleans and Charleston (or Columbia) S.C. It is not known that they favor black risks. It is presumed that they do not.

I made enquiry of practical men everywhere as I travelled through the South—managers, overseers, small planters, & plantation physicians & nurses—the result was a complete change in the opinion with which I entered upon the enquiry and the conclusion that there was no solid ground for the common assertion of the physical debility of the yellow people, so far as ordinary plantation experience is concerned. There is a more complete statement of my information somewhere in my books.[4]

I don't mean to express a decided difference with you in this opinion which you express, but merely that I do not consider it, by any means, a settled question, even at the South. It is a mere guess that you hear, and not a soundly established judgment, from those who are most ready to express an opinion at the South. The balance of *facts*, as far as I could learn them, was anything but conclusively in favor of the popular theory.

Yours Very Respectfully

Fred. Law Olmsted.

Dr S. G. Howe,
Freedmen's Enquiry Coms^n

The original is in the American Freedmen's Inquiry Commission Papers, Houghton Library, Harvard University, Cambridge, Massachusetts.

1. In a letter of August 5 (which Olmsted misread as August 8) Howe asked for information and Olmsted's own views of the question of whether differences in fertility, morbidity, and mortality existed between American blacks and mulattoes. Considering one of the most important issues facing the American Freedmen's Inquiry Commission to be the "probable persistency of the coloured population in the U.S.," Howe in particular requested vital statistics for the two groups. He also inquired whether insurance companies and the marketplace tended to favor blacks over mulattoes.

   Howe clearly was influenced by the "American school" of anthropologists, which theorized that blacks and whites were two separate species and that the mulatto was a hybrid, weaker than either and doomed to extinction. In the letter of August 5 he told Olmsted, "In the north, as it seems to me, the mulatto, though not a mule, is far less fertile than the white; & his progeny is feeble & often scrofulous." Postulating that emancipation would bring a greater amalgamation of races, Howe questioned, "Will not the dilution of pure african blood go on; a weaker & a weaker blood follow, until at last the type will disappear?" This interest in the mulatto led him to interrogate not only Olmsted but also the noted scientist Louis Agassiz, a defender of the theory of separate species. Agassiz assured Howe that the adaptation of races to climate meant that Southern whites would migrate to the North, pure Negroes would remain in the South, and mulattoes would gradually die out (S. G. Howe to FLO, Aug. 5, 1863; William Stanton, *The Leopard's Spots: Scientific Attitudes toward Race in America, 1815–59* [Chicago, 1960], pp. 66–68, 76–79, 152, 189–96).
2. The Knickerbocker Life Insurance Company, which was founded in 1850 and whose office in 1863 was located on Broadway in New York City (J. Owen Stalson, *Marketing Life Insurance: Its History in America* [Bryn Mawr, Pa., 1969], p. 785; *Trow's New York City Directory . . . For the Year Ending May 1, 1864* [New York, 1863], p. 23).
3. Erastus Lyman (*Trow's New York City Directory*, p. 24).
4. Olmsted had included two sections about the health and vigor of mulattoes in his books about the South. In these discussions, he reported the testimony of Southerners and indicated that the more knowledgeable observers found no significant differences in health between mulattoes and blacks. At Meredith Calhoun's enormous Red

River plantation, Olmsted questioned the overseers, the manager, and the head of the slave nursery about mulatto weakness and infertility—a theory they generally disputed. The manager thought that mulattoes

did not stand excessive heat as well as the pure negroes, but that, from their greater activity and willingness, they would do more work. He believed they were equally strong, and no more liable to illness; had never had reason to think them of weaker constitution. They often had large families and he had not noticed that their children were weaker or more subject to disease than others.

When Olmsted asked the slave nurse to show him the healthiest and the sickliest children under her care, she indicated both mulattoes and blacks among the healthy group but no mulattoes among the weak ones; and she replied to his direct question, "Well, dey do say, master, dat de yellow ones is de sickliest, but I can't tell for true dat I ever see as dey was." He also discussed the free mulattoes of Cane River, Louisiana, with several people, including some residents of the area. Although one man told him that the mulattoes "had sore eyes, and lost their teeth early, and had few children, and showed other scrofulous symptoms, and evidences of a weak constitution," Olmsted came to doubt this testimony and wrote:

I think this gentleman must have read De Bow's *Review*, and taken these facts for granted, without personal knowledge; for neither my own observation, nor any information that I could obtain from others, at all confirmed his statement. Two merchants, to whom I had letters of introduction, and to whom I repeated them, assured me that they were entirely imaginary. They had extensive dealings with the colored planters, and were confident that they enjoyed better health than the whites living in their vicinity. They could not recollect a single instance of those indications of weak constitution which had been mentioned to me. The colored planters, within their knowledge, had large and healthy families.

Olmsted also noted that other planters, businessmen, and a free mulatto of the area seconded the merchants' opinions (*BC*, pp. 90–92; Frederick Law Olmsted, *A Journey in the Seaboard Slave States, With Remarks on their Economy* . . . [New York, 1856], pp. 630–42; *Papers of FLO*, 2: 222–23, 227).

To Henry Whitney Bellows

U.S. Sanitary Commission,
New-York Agency, 823 Broadway.
New York, Aug 15th 1863.

My Dear Doctor,

I have received your letter of the 13th and will give the most respectful consideration to it.

I believe, and I think that I could demonstrate to you, that you overstate, very much, my position & prospects here.[1]

Commercial supply & demand is not a perfect criterion of real *value*, but it is in a degree indicative of value. Now the facts are that I am much poorer than when I first came to New York. I mean that if I fell sick and broke down, or went blind, or broke the other leg, I have nothing whatever that I have a right to fall back upon. If I should die, my wife & children would be in absolute poverty. I don't mean that my father wouldn't keep them out of the poor house, but I have no right to look to him again. Yielding once before to just such arguments as you address me, I sank more than he could conveniently spare. I have debts of say $12000,[2] which though the sheriff is not likely to trouble me about, my self-respect is. My family & myself must live if we live at all, not abstemiously. What are my prospects—what is my solid pay? Not enough to keep me square with the world. I am running out (suffering to run out) (slowly & imperceptibly) the little property of my brother's children,[3] because I do not feel able to take care of it. And what I get, has been taken against the protests, formal and insinuated, of a respectable portion of my employers. For my personal satisfaction—aside from the considerations you urge—patriotism & purposes of unselfish nature—I would gladly accept a clerkship in Wall Street on $3000 a year, for the rest of my life. I would "sell out" for that tomorrow, if I could save a few hours a day for study & miscellaneous work of that character which don't bring pay representable by dollars.

That is the measure of the commercial value of my services in the world's market where I am & where you wish me to be—where you urge that I should remain, on the ground that my services are of more value than they can be in California. When I ask what I have really lately accomplished and have a clear field to accomplish in the immediate future, I don't think this pay is bad by any means. I think it above rather than below the market-rates for such services. As to the San. Com., my dear Doctor—I think it has been decided again & again that I am not wanted. Not in so many words, not in the logical and distinctly conscious conclusions of *my friends*, but in the deliberately vetoing—obstructing, condemning, upsetting and disusing all that I regard to be of any value in my work of the last two years. So, I say again, that the facts—hard experience—don't bear out your estimate of the value of my services—nor, I think, does your own common-sense as evinced in deeds that speak more truly than words. Commerce, I say, tells me that the real value of my marketable (available) talents in this market is not above $3000 per annum (in legal tender paper).

Now Commerce tells me—I use the estimate, or interpretation, of Howard Potter which is not the highest—that in California my services are worth, for five years, at least $15000 a year—in gold.[4] You may take necessarily increased expenses & call it $10,000 in gold if you like.

You won't tell me that there is no field for patriotism & religion in California. I won't say that it is presumptuous to set a higher value on what I may do here—but I will say that you don't know anything about the irksomeness of the fetters which bind me here & which cramp & paralyze half my powers. I don't want to claim a special exemption from the auri sacra fames,[5] but you must know that I would not be drawn away from here now by any amount of wealth, for my personal comfort's sake. Nor does fear for the means of educating my children control me, though I don't see how I am to secure them what you say is all that I ought to wish.[6] (If I saw even that tolerably sure, I would not hesitate.)

If the newspaper was absolutely sure, on a strong basis, I think I should stay, but you know & admit that it is not. In short I would & will contract to give the services you value so highly, at one half or even one third what commerce offers me, in hard cash, as the measure, of the value of my services, in California for the next five years.

The above was written on the spur of the moment—after coming downtown, with the intention of calling on the company and presenting them a provisional conclusion to go. I have hesitated—I can't tell you how reluctant I am to give up what my heart is so much in here. I have finally telegraph'd you, as you will know.[7]

I think I am right—I am more nearly content to let it be decided in this way than any other that has occurred to me. Unfortunately Potter & Strong & Hoppin, & everybody else is out of town.

This, I only want to add. I think it right, under the present circumstances, to relieve myself of the obligation, which before would have rested in my mind, to pay back the $40,000, when I could.[8] There is a small chance that the paper will become a property—it is really of no tangible market value, but such as it is, I think I shall be entitled to claim to have it.

I understand, of course, that I am to be my own judge of how the contract proposed is to be carried out. I shall be under obligations to nobody, but in sacrificing this California offer, give what is a fair share with others toward a common end.

I—you may see—feel pretty confident that you will take the responsibility necessary, considering that there can be no doubt that if you undertake to collect the money upon this basis—your undertaking & the reason of it being stated—you will be successful.

If your answer is favorable, I shall go right at the paper as I think there is no time to be lost.

Yours affectionately

Fred. Law Olmsted.

693

The original is in the Henry Whitney Bellows Papers, Massachusetts Historical Society, Boston, Massachusetts.

1. Bellows, in his letter of August 13, extolled Olmsted's merits. To the minister, the recent Union victories at Gettysburg and Vicksburg heralded the approach of a complete Union triumph and, in its wake, the necessity for reconstructing the social and political order of the nation. Bellows believed that at such a time Olmsted's talents—like his own—would be indispensable, and he wrote:

   > I think you are gradually but surely gaining a place of confidence and respect as a man of statesmanlike mind and character: that you have already become known in a way to give your future words and works, great efficacy. I don't know a half-dozen men in the whole North, whose influence in the next five years I should think more critically important to the Nation. I don't know how it is to come in— whether by means of the Newspaper (which I think can be made to go) or by means of public office—but I am sure it is to be largely felt. . . . I think the faith of many, already pinned unconsciously to you, would fail and grow cold, if you should quit the field under what would seem to be a pecuniary temptation. There is a feeling that you are one among very few, *superior* to money attractions. You never *will* be rich, and I am inclined to think you never *ought* to be. It is because I am so sure of your disinterestedness and elevation of purpose, your thorough and high-paced patriotism, your willingness to agonize in thought for the truth of things, and to say it fearlessly, yet prudently, that I am so reluctant to give the least countenance to your tempting scheme. (HWB to FLO, Aug. 13, 1863.)

2. Olmsted probably refers here to money lost through the failure of the publishing house of Miller & Curtis in 1857. On August 11, 1863, after learning that Olmsted was considering the position offered by the Mariposa Company, George Templeton Strong commented, "Olmsted has not a mercenary nerve in his moral organization, but he has a wife & children to provide for—and he wants the luxury of paying certain debts of the old Putnam's Magazine concern with which he was connected, for which debts he was never legally liable nor morally liable, so far as I can make out." Five thousand dollars of the total that Olmsted gives probably was the money that his father had advanced in 1855 for him to become a partner in Dix, Edwards & Company, the firm that published *Putnam's Magazine* and that later became Miller & Curtis. Not only was this initial investment lost, but Francis George Shaw, George W. Curtis's wealthy father-in-law, who had been attempting to keep the business solvent, became legally liable for fifty thousand dollars of its debts. Shaw estimated in 1860 that these debts could be settled for twenty-four thousand dollars, and Olmsted's share was calculated to be eight thousand dollars, which was reduced to seventy-five hundred dollars when Olmsted transferred the copyright of his book *Back Country* to Shaw (*Papers of FLO*, 2: 20, 54–55; ibid., 3: 82, 105; George Templeton Strong Manuscript Diary, Aug. 11, 1863, New-York Historical Society, New York City; William Emerson to MPO, July 31, 1860).

3. That is, Olmsted was allowing Tosomock, the Staten Island farm of his stepchildren, to fall into disrepair (see FLO to JO, April 18, 1863, n. 1, above).

4. Here Olmsted cites Howard Potter's opinion because the latter's position as a director of the Pacific Mail Company provided knowledge about California and business affairs there (FLO to MPO, Aug. 11, 1863).

5. Part of the following quotation from Virgil's *Aeneid*:

   > Quid non mortalia pectora cogis
   > Auri sacra fames!
   > (To what lengths is the heart of man driven
   > By this cursed craving for gold!)

(Virgil, *Aeneid*, trans. C. Day Lewis, bk. 3, ll. 56–57.)

6. Olmsted first began this sentence "Nor do I fear much for." He lined through the last three words but inadvertently did not cross out "do I."

7. Olmsted's telegram has not survived, but Bellows's response indicates that Olmsted asked him to raise the forty thousand dollars necessary to begin publication of the weekly journal (HWB to FLO, [Aug. 16, 1863], Henry Whitney Bellows Papers, Massachusetts Historical Society, Boston, Mass.).

8. The letter that Bellows was circulating to raise funds for the proposed weekly journal indicates that Olmsted and Godkin had earlier intended to return the principal to the subscribers in two or three years if the paper should prove successful (HWB to "Dear Sir," July 4, 1863, Henry Whitney Bellows Papers, Massachusetts Historical Society, Boston, Mass.).

To Henry Whitney Bellows

U.S. Sanitary Commission,
New-York Agency, 823 Broadway.
New York, 16th Aug. 1863   Sunday.

My Dear Doctor,

Before replying to the body of your letter of the 13th let me tell you what Mr Strong forgot to do. I think that your letter to D[r] Newberry[1] was not sent from here. It reached here just at the time that I advised Mr Strong (sitting as the Executive Committee) that I was considering the proposition to go to California, and he concluded that until that was decided, it was best not to stir up the business with Newberry.

I should like to think, doctor, that a tenth part of what you say of me was true, or that you really and practically believed it to be true.[2] I have very strong, positive convictions of a practical character, with regard to the relations of the states and the government, the people and the army, the army & the government, the slaves and the people and the slaves & the government. I have been living two years in Washington, nominally in confidential relations with the War department. Now if I was entitled to one tenth the influence which you claim, is it possible that I should not have made this felt in some way in the government? Certainly I have not been obtrusive, impertinent, disrespectful; nor have I been lazy or careless, but from no person or body of influence and importance have I or my endeavors to serve the country been received otherwise than with contempt. The Secretary of the Treasury and the Secrety of War have put me out of the way with falsehoods.[3] The Sec. of War has paid me more respect than anybody else in Washington by expressions indicating that he hated

695

me, but in general, I do not stand nearly as high, in my own estimation of the respect in which I am held by the nation, as when I went to Washington, two years & more ago. I never, anywhere in the world, have been so completely snubbed & set down and made of no account—leaving positive insults out of thought—as continuously, as I have been in Washington. My books, my views, my practical suggestions, are better known in the British parliament, and by French & German Political Economists than by anyone in, or having influence upon, our own government. A foreign minister is the only man in Washington who has ever taken the trouble to call upon me on account of the five years' hard study I gave to the practical difficulties of Slavery.[4] And I have had three times as many letters from Europe, as from my own country, called out by what I have written. I don't know a single native American, who has shown me that he has really carefully read and understood and appreciated what I have written, where I know a dozen foreigners. There are plenty of other ways in which my ambition is more than satisfied, and what I have described is no failure, because I have not sought for satisfaction in those directions. I am not disappointed; I certainly am not soured, but I draw inevitably conclusions from what has thus *happened* [to] me (incidentally) which are inconsistent with your propositions and your expectations for me. If I were what you think, while living two years at Washington, without ambitious effort or lobbying or courtiership, some wave would have lifted me into indubitable influence upon public affairs. Men who have not a tythe of my practical sagacity are constantly so lifted.

I think my experience with the Commission further illustrates your practical error. I have labored with all my brains & blood to conservate and make practical, certain convictions with which I entered upon the business of the Commission, and which I supposed were as strongly fixed in the minds of its members as my own—which I supposed to be the very root of the Commission. What is the result? So far from conserving and making practical those principles, the Executive business of the Commission is conducted in complete antagonism to them—not merely in disregard of them but in antagonism to them, conserving and establishing the opposite principles, and rendering it impossible for its original or my original principles to be respected in practice. So far as I have had an object at heart in the work of the Commission, that object has not only failed to be realized, but the Commission has worked directly against it.[5] I have worked with all my might, I have given the most careful and complete study of which I was capable, to prevent just that which my dearest friends, those—who, if my influence was of any practical value, would most surely yield to it—have deliberately, persistently and resolutely accomplished. For practical purposes, I have stood alone and have fallen alone, in the Commission. As far as the Sanitary Commission is concerned, my life in the last two years is as complete a failure as Jeff Davis's—more so—for he has yet a chance of success. What then? I neither give up my convictions nor my courage. I have made a mistake, the nature of which I don't comprehend—the whole *course* of the Commission being absolutely incomprehensible to me—but this is clear enough: that I have been working at disadvantage—was out of my place. I am very little if at all chagrined by it, but I mean honestly, and healthily, to take the lesson.

Now, if I differ with your estimate of my abilities, it is not from humility altogether. I believe—as far as it can be said of anything, I *know* that I have unusual abilities, unusual, far reaching sagacity. I know that certain matters appear very different to my mind's eye than to that of the members of the Sanitary Commission, certain other matters very different to my mind's eye to that of the directors of the Mariposa estate. Very different indeed. Yet I think that I am right; I look at them again & again & try to see them as they do and I can't. Is it self-conceit that prevents me? In my inmost convictions, I am sure that I think not, on the contrary I fall back on my experience, and I find myself saying these are matters in which my mind's eye sees clearer than usual. I can trust it better than I can trust other men—taking them as they come—until they are proved. Therefore I am confident, I can't help being confident. If the Sanitary Commission had trusted me as it originally proposed to do, it would have accomplished infinitely more than it has done. I can't expect them to believe it, & it's bad taste to claim it. I won't claim it, but it's a fact in my mind nevertheless.

So the Mariposa business has been shamefully mismanaged heretofore; its managers have not seen certain aspects of it which I see, and the present directors, though they see that there must have been great mistakes, don't really see the case, as I do. If they will really put the management in my hands as they propose, for two or three years, I know (humanly speaking) that I can astonish them. That I can double their estimate of their wealth in it. I could set twenty millions more of gold afloat than will be got out with their present ideas of managing it—penny-wise, pound foolish—held doubtingly in New York and not likely to resist the gradual pressure of accumulating practical results from California.

So it is not from humility, or any disposition to underrate my practical sagacity that I say that I can't subscribe to a tenth part of what you say of my powers of usefulness. I see what ought to be done but I can't get other men to see it. (This is a very incomplete statement).

I accept your view of my duty.[6] Please understand this. When you say that I can't be and ought not to be wealthy, you practically admit that I can't be and it isn't best I should be a materialist or mere capitalist. I don't ask anything better for myself or my children than you say I should be content with. I am a long way from having secured so much, but never mind that. You say I ought to be a public leader or educator. What is the way to take for that? I say that I have missed it during the last two years. I have done nothing—nothing commensurate with your estimate of my abilities, or with my hard work—the direct results of my work are nil. You and the Commission have knocked down faster than I have built up, that which I have been trying to build. I have done a good deal *with* you, but it was not what I wanted to do. My purposes have failed. I have led nothing, to nothing. I have followed & helped you to lead to something that I care very little for.[7] I feel that I have been on the wrong road. I want to get on the right road. Suppose I went to California and succeeded as I think I should, and came back in five years with $50,000, well invested. I think there would be two results: first: I should not be under temptation to work for purposes which my own convictions did not approve, as I am now, second: people—capitalists & men controlling capital—would have some real confidence in my practical sagacity, in my judgment of matters of business. The very offer from Mariposa is evidence you may say that capitalists have that confidence now. True, and so had the Sanitary Commission two years ago. They have confidence in me; but when it comes to matters of action, no man has as much confidence in me as in himself—when he can get anybody else to agree with him. You yourself invariably set my judgment aside most decisively, no matter with how much careful labor it has been formed, when any impression of yours, no matter how carelessly formed, is confirmed by Dr Agnew's or Dr Newberry's. The grand inducement to me to go to California is that when I shall have returned, I may not be wholly dependent for the means of making my abilities for patriotic and philanthropic labor, available, on completely satisfying and conquering the judgment of a number of other men.

For this, experience teaches me, is what I never can depend on doing—or rather that, in practical affairs, it does not answer to depend on my ability to do this. For I have apparently carried the convictions of the San Commission completely a number of times and been led to go in with measures of a comprehensive kind in consequence, and then had them nipped, twisted, turned about or fairly emasculated, because I did not know how to hold those convictions fast till they were clinched by results. I see more & more, every year of my life, that the best policy, pursued haltingly and faithlessly and inconsistently is not half as good as an indifferent policy pursued boldly, strenuously, completely. I don't want to live in a continual struggle with my friends for leave to do a good thing so poorly that it had better not have been done at all, any more.

(I think the Sanitary Commission has done a great deal of good, but I think it may have done more harm in this; that it has prevented others from doing or another method of accomplishing what it originally undertook to do and has since refused to do).[8]

People do have faith in a man who is able and has proved himself able to do well for himself. A poor man is considered a failure and can not command deep confidence in his undertakings for public ends.

You see the conclusive reason which will send me to California (if I go). It is so strong with me that if I were perfectly satisfied of what, if I go at all, I shall make myself satisfied, I should feel as if I had done wrong in the proposition I made you by telegraph.

The opinion of my prospective influence which your letter expresses, I hold to be enormously extravagant. I don't believe that it is established & abiding with you. Nevertheless it has influence with me. I have confidence in my convictions—in my convictions of means to ends in matters of administration, but I have not confidence that I possess or can use the necessary means of making those convictions useful to the public, here and now. Let me make money and I shall have. Not that, even with money & the prestige of a money-maker, I think I could take the position to which you even now invite me; but I could go steadily along to the sure advancement of *some* results intended, while now I never know that I am not rowing in just the opposite direction to that I desire to follow.

But my proposition is consistent with this. Give me the newspaper, untrammelled by obligations to yield my judgment to that of others, in matters in which I think that I am wisest, or best informed, and I am content to stay. If others, men of money, can be got to accept a very small percent of your convictions of the public advantage to be got from my staying here, the history of the Sanitary Commission proves that it will not be a difficult matter to secure that advantage. I only want that it should be distinctly understood that they buy me as I am. I shall make the paper what I think it ought to be. But enough of that.

I wanted to refer to one or two points of your letter by themselves.

"The final history of the San. Com.":[9] I must honestly say that at present I have no inclination to touch it: perhaps I shall have more, when my present immediate disappointment is further in the background. But I honestly confess that I think I made my final effort to save the Commission from shipwreck at the last meeting, and when it turned out that I had missed my calculations about Chicago, my heart sank within me.[10] The Sanitary Commission may continue to exist in name, but its voyage is over. Between you and I, there should be no disguise. I know that you differ with me. You don't understand me, I don't understand you, in this matter. We agreed to differ eight or nine months ago.[11] Differing with you, arguing with you and against you, in every way I knew how, in season & out of season—I yet have loyally worked on your plan, and, to save the ship, on any plan, all I possibly could. Neither you nor I, now command the crew. Dr Newberry does.

As to your reference to your letter to Dr Newberry: Your view comprehends but one point—a plain, tangible point. It leaves entirely out of view what is of infinitely more influence on my convictions—the constant manners and language of friendly confidence and Christian & manly truthfulness, concealing purposes & plans which he knew to be revolutionary.

I am willing and earnestly anxious, doctor, to do anything I can for the Sanitary Commission, but, hereafter, it must be inevitable that where I show my hand in its affairs, there will be friction and scandal. You have yet great means of usefulness in the Commission and you should make the best use of them. It is not best for this purpose you should have a row before the public, or with any considerable portion of those who have been your friends. If I stay with you officially, I think that this is inevitable. I must go strongly against the West, must rouse its anger by confessing my convictions, and so lead to a division of the Commission and general row and breakup and scandal and injury to the cause of the country; or I must quit it, quietly. I know you won't see it so, but you have seen very little of what I have seen in the business of the Commission during the last year. I don't say that I will not again yield to your judgment, if you insist upon it, but if I do, it must be understood that it is your judgment and not mine, that rules. You are the President and head of the Executive Committee and I am under your government, but my convictions are an element in the question of what had best be done with me; and my conviction is: drop me and then you can make Newberry responsible to somebody, or if it proves that you can't, throw him overboard. I will have nothing more to do with him. It is not possible that I can have more to do with him except fighting. That conviction is so strong with me, doctor, that I think that I have a right to insist that you shall pay me so much practical respect as to accept it. Your letter to Newberry is blank cartridge to a mob in my judgment—for instance—you make him understand that you think that all I want or have wanted is reports from him—but reports are nothing of consequence in themselves,—his persistent refusal is of consequence, of great consequence, as a sign of a *disposition* not to be correspondent subordinately to the Commission. You narrow it to a technicality almost. It is the disease & not the symptom that destroys. And the disease has destroyed, past recovery for anything I care for. I gave you plenty of other symptoms, you must remember.[12] The one you mention, anybody can see—suppress that, and if the disease is there, as my conviction is that it is, and you only aggravate it in other & more vital quarters. I don't say there is no question about the disease. It *is* a question whether he can not be subordinate *to the Commission*—it is no question whether he can not be subordinate to me as the representative of the Commission. I have suspended judgment on the latter question two years. It is no longer suspended, and if you think my judgment of men worth anything, I must claim that you respect it in this. At all events, don't expect me to act on the contrary supposition or to pretend to. I can not allow myself to be assumed to be in the most remote degree responsible for [the] affairs between which and myself D[r] Newberry stands, now or hereafter. With all possible respect, I must be allowed to say that I will not be.

Joining you for a trip on Monday week.[13]

I have been consistently trying to arrange for a meeting of the Committee on Organization.[14] The first day on which every member would probably be able to meet at Walpole is that day or the day following, and I have been reckoning on that for some days past: What now shall be done? The members can be got, I think all, to meet you anywhere in New-England any day that (next) week. There should be several days, of course, for a careful consideration of the affairs of the Commission. Whether I go to California or not, I shall expect some instructions for winding up my official affairs. The old arrangments are dead and no new ones substituted. As I said at the last meeting, my office as General Secretary no longer exists for practical purposes. A great deal of business is constantly post-poned, at a wicked loss, until a general plan of business can be established. I have presented, one after another, three different plans;[15] each has been set aside. Each has cost me a great deal of hard study—for which I have got nothing but Agnew's sneer at "organization" and Newberry's more practi-cal expressions of contempt and now, I must confess that my resources are exhausted. I see no way of carrying on the business. It is too late to revert to the old—the last plan. It required for its success what it evidently can not get, a hearty cooperation of all parties.

I never was so entirely at a loss as to a plan for accomplishing any desirable result. But this is partly owing to my peculiar notions of the nature of the trust of the Sanitary Commission, I suppose. I must confess that so far as I can see that has been irretrievably sacrificed. I must also confess, and you know that I do it with great pain and only in the spirit of complete frankness that you have always commanded from me, that with it, my interest in the Sanitary Commission has ceased. I need not say that I mean solely in the institution; I never felt more attached to the men.

Most Affectionately Yours

Fred. Law Olmsted.

The original is in box 641 of USSC-NYPL. Bellows apparently filed with this letter his handwritten draft of resolutions to the board upon Olmsted's resignation.

1. A letter of August 10, 1863, in which Henry W. Bellows reproved John S. Newberry for his persistent failure to submit weekly reports to the central office of the Sani-tary Commission (HWB to JSN, Aug. 10, 1863, USSC-NYPL, box 955).
2. See FLO to HWB, August 15, 1863, note 1, above.

3. Primarily a reference to his experiences with Salmon P. Chase and Edwin M. Stanton during the spring of 1862, when Olmsted wished to be given superintendence of slaves on the captured plantations at Port Royal. Stanton also frequently clashed with the Sanitary Commission. Although the editors have found no specific statement indicating Stanton's hatred of Olmsted, the secretary of war's dislike of the Sanitary Commission was well known and no doubt extended to Olmsted.

4. Possibly Rudolf Schleiden (1815–1895), the foreign minister from the German free city of Bremen. Born in Schleswig-Holstein, he had served in Washington since 1853. As a representative of a shipping power, Schleiden was especially interested in averting the Civil War; and at William H. Seward's request, he served as an unofficial mediator between the North and South late in April 1861.

Schleiden's background, interests, and temperament all make it plausible that he would have called upon Olmsted. As a German liberal who had been a delegate to the Frankfurt parliament in 1848, Schleiden probably was acquainted with some of Olmsted's German émigré friends, such as Friedrich Kapp and Edouard Degener. Moreover, Schleiden was a close student of American culture and society and was likely to have read Olmsted's travel accounts about the South. The minister from Bremen was also quite friendly and sociable (*Enciclopedia universal ilustrada europeo-americana* [Madrid, 1927]; Ralph Haswell Lutz, "Rudolf Schleiden and the Visit to Richmond, April 25, 1861," *Annual Report of the American Historical Association for the Year 1915* [Washington, D.C., 1917], pp. 209–16.

5. Olmsted is referring to his difficulties with John S. Newberry and the Western branches of the Sanitary Commission. Olmsted believed that these societies' excessive local pride and their interest in caring for soldiers from their own localities resembled the states' rights doctrines of the Southern secessionists. He also thought that his goal of creating a truly national organization had been thwarted by the autonomy of action and exemption from rules that the Executive Committee had been willing to grant to Newberry. It was this belief that led Olmsted late in May 1863 to complain to Bellows:

> I have considered myself a Central and not an Eastern officer of the Commission, and have not been and am not disposed to require of its Eastern Secretaries what the Commission does not wish me to require of the Western, nor to enforce with them what I cannot enforce with the Western Secretary. It would be a useless expense to require exactness of returns and accounts at the East, so long as they cannot be procured at the West. (FLO to HWB, May 25, 1863.)

6. Bellows argued that Olmsted's duty lay in leading the American people at a critical stage in the country's development:

> *The country can not spare you at such a juncture.* I think *you* must *feel this in your bones.* I don't think you can make up your mind to become the agent of a set of money-makers on the Pacific Coast—let them offer you a fortune or no, while Providence is holding out the splendid opportunity of usefulness in the Nation and to Humanity—at the most critical and serious lustre of its history! You are not the man not to see this—and seeing it, you are not the man to throw away your duty and your reward at once, into the Mariposa claim. (HWB to FLO, Aug. 13, 1863.)

7. Olmsted meant that he had helped Bellows build an organization that had primarily solicited large donations from the public and distributed them among the soldiers. Much of his indifference to this aspect of the Sanitary Commission stemmed from his belief that the people, even without the stimulus of the Commission, would be aiding the soldiers. In May 1863 Olmsted summed up those objections:

> The Commission hasn't made the people liberal. I have studied this pretty carefully and I fully believe the Commission does more to hinder than it does to

promote supplies to the sick and wounded. Separate the liberality of the people from the Commission at this moment, and what is there to give you satisfaction in its work? We talk of nothing but the amount that is given us and that passes through our hands. That is not the Commission's doing; it is the liberality of the confiding people. And if the Commission is not actually doing nothing, where is the evidence of it? (FLO to HWB, May 25, 1863.)

8. Most likely Olmsted is referring to the Commission's original objects of scientific inquiry and advice in relation to preserving the health of the Union soldier. Although the Commission continued to sponsor projects such as the special inspections of hospitals, Olmsted probably believed that more of its resources should be turned to such ends.

9. In his letter of August 13 Bellows asked Olmsted to consider writing the history of the Sanitary Commission and stressed the importance of that work:

> I have had an impression, that the telling of the History of the Sanitary Commission would afford one of the best themes for political instruction to the people, ever afforded anyone, that you would one day do this, and that about our work, you would crystallize all the large, rich and varied experience you have had in this *vast sea* of our National Life.

In 1866 Charles J. Stillé published the authorized history of the Commission (HWB to FLO, Aug. 13, 1863).

10. See FLO to MPO, June 26, 1863, note 1, above.

11. Olmsted is referring to differences of opinion with the Executive Committee about the powers of the central office and the general secretary, especially in relation to the Western secretary. By December 1862 these differences had become difficult to resolve.

12. An example of Olmsted's complaints about Newberry's lack of subordination can be found in a letter of May 25, 1863, to Bellows. Olmsted described in detail how Newberry had thoroughly disregarded plans for a bulletin to be published regularly by the central office. Early in 1863 Olmsted had begun arrangements, had given Newberry specific instructions about the kind of information needed, and had received the promise that it would be supplied. Olmsted later recounted Newberry's actions:

> While in Louisville Mr Civil, a bookseller, referred incidentally to a project of a Louisville Sanitary bulletin. I mentioned this to Dr Newberry and he said that it could not and would not be carried out. He had never heard of it and wouldn't entertain it for a moment. Nevertheless he now writes me that the Western bulletin will be published in a few days and he thinks will do great good. Not the slightest attention has as yet—three months afterwards—been paid to my request and instructions, and the Central bulletin of the Sanitary Commission is as far off as ever. (FLO to HWB, May 25, 1863.)

13. On August 13 Bellows invited Olmsted to visit at Walpole and join him and his children on a trip to the White Mountains (HWB to FLO, Aug. 13, 1863).

14. In the summer of 1863 the Committee on Organization apparently consisted of Olmsted, Bellows, A. D. Bache, Wolcott Gibbs, and newly elected Sanitary Commission member J. Huntington Wolcott ("Memo on Special Committee on Organization," June 15, 1863; FLO to JO, Aug. 2, 1863; USSC, *Minutes*, p. 137).

15. It is unclear whether Olmsted here is referring only to variants (which have not survived) of the plan of organization that he put forward in June 1863 or means also to include the executive reorganization that he proposed in January 1863 (see FLO to HWB, Feb. 4, 1863, nn. 1 and 4, above).

To Henry Whitney Bellows

New York, September 1ˢᵗ 1863.

To the Reverend H. W. Bellows, D.D.
President of the Sanitary Commission:
Sir,

[*In accordance with the purpose verbally announced at the last meeting of the Board,*[1] *I now resign the office of General Secretary of the Sanitary Commission.*]

I have [*earnestly and*] faithfully striven to accomplish the ends had in view by the Commission when in June 1861, you requested me to undertake a certain part in its plan of serving the country.

This part included the organization of an Executive service which should possess, among other properties, the following:

1ˢᵗ   That of securing to the Commission exact and trustworthy information at frequent intervals, by a uniform method and with uniform scales of measurement, with regard to the health and disease and the conditions of health and disease, of all portions of the army, equally, at all places, at all times, under all circumstances.

2ᵈ   That of presenting to the Commission means for communicating sanitary advice to the army, in all its portions, under all circumstances, at any time, by a uniform method.

3ᵈ   That of presenting to societies proposing to aid the army by gifts of sanitary articles and supplementary hospital supplies, a system for the distribution of these, uniform in its general methods, business-like in accountability, completely and unfailingly subordinate and auxiliary to the essential means, methods, offices and discipline, established to secure the efficiency of the army for its great purpose of fighting, and giving to every part of the army, at all places, at all times, under all circumstances, its fair share, relatively to the degree of its need, of the common stock of these gifts.

The duty thus assigned me was one beset with obvious difficulties. The Commission, after conference with the military authorities had, however, determined that it was practicable to overcome these, and, relying upon the assurances of confidence, and patience, and the promises of Executive freedom and support which I received from yourself and the members of the Commission, I gratefully accepted the honorable task assigned to me, [*and came under obligation to accomplish the purpose designed by the Commission in establishing my office.*]

It was not to be expected that entirely satisfactory arrangments should at once be perfected. The uncertainty of being able to sustain the requisite expenditure was a sufficient bar to the employment of the necessary agents of a complete system at the outset. The great enlargement of the army commencing two months after I entered upon my duty, extended the period of this embarrassment, and it was not completely removed until after the close of the first year, when the great gifts of California to the Treasury of the Commission began.

Nor was it to be supposed that all difficulties could be perfectly foreseen and a method of dealing with them forecast so perfect as to be incapable of improvement. A time of trial, of adjustment, accommodation and discipline was to [be] assumed. Yet as the Commission was made for this war, such period of probation could not be expected to be indefinitely prolonged.

At the last meeting of the Commission, two years had elapsed since I entered upon my task and I had not yet been able to make a general report showing the successful operation with all parts of the Army of the system which I had undertaken to form. I had never yet been able to give the information required of me from any part of the Western Department; [in fact,] I had never been able to report that either of the other above-stated conditions of the system existed in the Western Department; I had, under instructions from the Commission, officially visited the Western Department and ascertained by personal observation that they did not exist. Nor could I report that the system had been perfected in the other Departments. Its complete adjustment [and final perfection] at the East necessarily waited upon the promise of a final success of all parts in the West. It would have been absurd to give it a longer period of probation. Several modifications and adjustments which I had from time [to time] proposed to adopt to meet alledged special difficulties existing in the Western Department had been pronounced by the under Secretary for the Western Department appointed by the Commission, to be impracticable, and the Commission had adopted his opinion.[2] It was full time therefore that the scheme should be abandoned, or that I should cease to be in any manner responsible for any further attempt or pretence of going on with it. I was thus driven to state before the Commission at its last meeting that I must either be definitely relieved of further responsibility for its executive service or a new scheme must be adopted. I presented a new scheme for consideration. It was [fully] considered by a special Committee and unanimously recommended to the Commission for adoption. It was considered by the Commission as a Board, and unanimously adopted. Since then you have seen fit to suspend its operation. The considerations which led you to the determination to do so are of a permanent nature. I am compelled to acknowledge the wisdom of your determination and consequently to acquiesce in the abandonment of the scheme, and to adopt for myself the alternative of retirement from the position in which I have failed to accomplish the duty assigned me.

705

It is unnecessary to enquire whether my failure has been due to a bad plan; to a want of cooperation which I had a right to depend upon the Commission for securing me, or to an inherent impracticability of the purpose which I was sub-commissioned to accomplish. [*I believe that the purpose was originally a good and practicable purpose, and that I have failed to perform the duty of accomplishing it which was assigned to the office of the General Secretary of the Commission. I have no reason to believe that I shall hereafter succeed in accomplishing it. It is but just, therefore, that I should be allowed to vacate that office. I have been disappointed in the expectations with which I accepted the office of General Secretary and*] Whatever the causes of my disappointment, I think [it] right that I should be allowed, after two years ineffectual struggling with them, to be my own judge of the duty of holding out longer against them [*when further struggling with them is hopeless*]. I do not believe that the Commission will, upon reflection, regard me as having been practically wanting in patience or perseverance. The constant evidences which have met me of the personal respect, and friendship and of confidence carried in some respects to a neglect of precaution against error which my own judgment does not justify, has left it impossible for me to regard any action of the Commission which has disappointed me, otherwise than as I should regard a well established difference of judgment upon any question in which I had no special occasion for personal interest. Only because it was impossible for me to doubt this [*extreme*] good will of the Commission, and because I believed that my resignation would be received with regret, have I refrained to this time from presenting it. I was about to offer it to you in January last, but was prevented by the earnest request of the Vice President,[3] at whose suggestion I subsequently proposed a modification of the relations between the Western Department and the Central office, which met with your approval and received the authoritative endorsement of the Board, but in attempting to carry out which, I failed to receive the necessary cooperation of the Western Secretary. I do not know how it would be possible for me to do more than I have done to bend all my personal dispositions to my best judgment and understanding of the wishes of the Board, through a continuous failure of what I have supposed to be my reasonable expectations for more than a year past. If after all it should not be deemed by the Commission, as you have intimated to me is your opinion, that I am justified in withdrawing from my office, it must be because of a sound difference of judgment between the Commission and myself, and I can only hope that I shall be excused for acting in accordance with my own long-deliberated convictions [*of duty*]. [*The duty of the General Secretary, and of the whole Executive service, both wherein it has been partly successful and wherein it has failed to be accomplished, is one of very minor importance.*]

During the period in which I have held the office of General Secretary, goods have been conveyed in trust to the Executive department, for which I have been officially responsible before the public, for a large part of which I am unable to account. I estimate the total value of them at $3000,000. Goods to the amount of about $2000,000 have been conveyed in trust to that portion of the Executive Department which I have had the means of controlling. For reasons already indicated, I am unable to render an exact account of the disposition of these; [*general*] reports have from time to time been made to the Commission which account in a loose way for them, and I can now only add that I have been possessed of means of information which I think justify me in reporting that, with a loss of less than the hundredth part of one per centum of their value, caused by mismanagement, unfaithfulness and dishonesty of agents for the selection and control of which I am responsible, these goods have been disposed of in accordance with the intentions of those who entrusted them to the Commission, except only in the failure of an equitable distribution, arising from imperfect information of the condition and wants of different parts of the army. The expense of the Executive Department solely incurred for the distribution of these goods, has been as nearly as can be ascertained, not more than three per centum of their value. Instructions were once given me to insure all goods in dépôt, but at my request, I was subsequently permitted to use my discretion in this respect. I have not insured for reasons heretofore explained but have relied for the safety of the goods in store upon the faithful watchfulness of the agents whom I have employed. The loss of goods in consequence [*by fire and thieves*] has amounted to less than 1 per centum of what insurance would have cost.

I have from time to time presented my account of money expenditures, with vouchers, but the Commission has never made provision for auditing it since early in the first year. The total amount of money for which requisition has been made or receipts given the Treasurer with my sanction or authority is, according to my account, ____$.[4] This statement, I am informed by the Superintendent of the New York office, agrees with the Treasurer's books. Full book accounts for the expenditure of this amount of money in the service of the Commission will be found in the Central Office. Vouchers for the whole amount are also filed at the Central Office. In the failure of a proper official auditing of these, I have deemed it a proper precaution to submit them to an examination and comparison with the book accounts by special boards of persons whose honesty and competence for the duty I could presume to be known to the Commission. The following named persons have at different times acted in this capacity, and all the vouchers and accounts for the whole sum of [____] have been examined and approved by two or more of them.[5]

Since I determined upon resigning the office of General Secretary,

I have made engagements which will prevent me from performing any of the peculiar duties of a member of the Commission. I therefore also resign at this time, the seat to which I am entitled on the Board.[6]

Notwithstanding the shortcomings of the special Executive department of the Commission under my headship, a great deal has been accomplished with it. I do not think it right to credit it with the distribution of the goods contributed through its agency by the people to the army, for it can not be known that had this agency not been offered the people, one really accomplishing a distribution more equitable and better accounted for and consequently entitled to and securing the more complete confidence of the people would not have been organized by others. But, on the other hand, it is certain that the evils which have been seen to arise from local partisanship, prejudice and favoritism, from the attempts of demagogues and swindlers to turn the patriotism and humanity of the people to their private advantage, from the difficulty of harmonizing the attempts of the people to aid the army [directly], with the necessities of discipline, from the jealousy of an authorized interference with or intrusion upon their business felt by the medical officers of the army, and the consequent antagonism between these officers and many humane and patriotic people, from unfounded and exaggerated reports of the Sanitary condition of the army and of the [medical] treatment of the sick and wounded, tending to make an unnecessary dread [and hatred] of the necessary liabilities of army-life, and thus to make military service more unpopular, and the draft more hateful;—it is certain that all these evils would have been vastly increased had no attempt been made to establish a federal and equitable method of distribution of the gifts of the people based upon a complete system of information and a thoroughly comprehensive provision of agents with all parts of the army. The arguments which have been used to bring the people to adopt and cooperate with the means provided for this purpose, to sustain and assist the Commission in its purpose of instructing the Army in Sanitary knowledge, in improving the Medical Department, in encouraging a more rigid discipline and in urging the timely recruiting of the existing organizations of the army by draft and otherwise, the value of the service which the Commission has rendered the nation in its influence upon public opinion in these respects, I believe to be far greater than any direct value of its Executive service with the Army, and it is true that the advantage it has had for affecting public opinion in all these respects has all rested upon what it has attempted to do and been supposed to have done with its Executive service. The [direct value of the] instruction given the Army, and the influence exercised by the Commission upon the Army favorable to Sanitary precautions, has been wholly by means of its Executive Service. This has been of immeasurable value and I do not know that for this purpose any essential improvement upon the means adopted could have been made. A more complete system and greater painstaking in this direction might have excited jealousy and created annoyance to a degree which would have been subversive of its purpose.

But I regard the whole duty of the Executive Service, both wherein it has been successfully undertaken and wherein it has failed to be strenuously pursued and consequently to be accomplished, as a part of the service of the Commission of very small importance relative to the great benefaction of which it laid the foundation, independently in the main, of its Executive department. I refer to the reform and enlargement, and to the popular support of the reform and enlargement of the Medical Department of the Army and to the wonderful suppression which, in the midst of this period of intense popular excitement, we have witnessed, of Quackery, Pedantry and the conservatism of ignorance.[7] When I attempt to foregather the results of a really true, liberal and worshipful love and devotion to pure science, which is the truth of God's laws, acting upon and through the Medical Department of these great popular armies, and gaining for itself the respect, admiration and confidence of all the loyal people of the land by reason of its sincerity, its simplicity of faith, its generosity and its boldness of generosity, I hardly dare refer to the apparently feeble means employed by the Sanitary Commission in its desire to elevate [and] advance, the Medical Department in this direction, yet it is impossible not to remember the hopes and the fears with which labors have been directed to this end under your leadership, and in which hopes and fears I have had the honor to share.

Looking then, at the whole field of the present, the disappointment and failure in my special official department is of small moment and the grounds of satisfaction preponderate so largely that [*had it not seemed to me to be required for truth's sake, I could in presenting my resignation, have omitted all mention of the reasons for it, and*] I must regard the time during which I have been connected with the Commission as the most fortunate period of my life. I close that period with hearty congratulations and deep gratitude.

The text of this document, which may have been presented orally, was taken from a rough draft in box 951 of USSC-NYPL. The editors have presented in bracketed italics substantive material that Olmsted crossed out and did not replace.

1. The last formal meeting of the Sanitary Commission was held from June 10 to June 13, 1863. Here Olmsted may be referring to a session of the Executive Committee in New York during late August 1863 (USSC, *Minutes*, pp. 135–41).
2. See FLO to MPO, June 26, 1863, note 1, above.
3. Alexander Dallas Bache.

4. Here Olmsted probably was unsure of the exact amount and planned to supply the figures before submitting the letter.
5. Olmsted did not include these names in this draft.
6. The Sanitary Commission did not accept Olmsted's proferred resignation from the board. In October 1863 the commissioners accepted Olmsted's resignation from the post of general secretary with "profound regret" and further resolved:

> That from the beginning of our enterprise, the organizing genius of Mr. Olmsted, trained by rich experience in other large and successful undertakings, has been a chief source of whatever merit has characterized the operations of the Sanitary Commission; and that we find our consolation in the loss of his personal services, in the fact that his plans and ideas are so ineffacably stamped on our work, that we shall continue to enjoy the benefit of his talents and the inspiration of his character, as long as the Commission lasts.

The board also directed that Bellows send the resolutions to Olmsted in California "with a letter expressive of our warm personal attachment, and an earnest expression of our wish, that he will withdraw his resignation as a member of the Board."

That December, Olmsted replied to Bellows, "As the members of the Commission must have been aware at the time of passing these Resolutions that it would be impossible for me to attend their future meetings or to perform any of the peculiar duties of a member, I am proud to accept the honorary position offered me in the request to withdraw my resignation as a member of the Board" (HWB to FLO, Oct. 17, 1863; FLO to HWB, Dec. 25, 1863, USSC-NYPL, box 616: 3317).
7. Olmsted first gave an alternative ending to this sentence "and to the wonderful resistance which during this period of intense popular excitement, true Science, Medical, Sanitary and Social Science in the broadest sense, has made against Quackery, while it has been marching on and extending its heavenly influence with and control over the masses of the people at an unexampled rate of progress."

APPENDIXES

I

CHRONOLOGY OF FREDERICK LAW OLMSTED

1861–1863

1861
April 12   Confederate attack on Fort Sumter.

June 13   President Lincoln signs order creating USSC.

June 20   Appointed resident secretary (later general secretary) of USSC.

June 28   Arrives in Washington to assume duties.

July 21   Confederate troops defeat Union soldiers at battle of Bull Run.

September 5   Presents report on the demoralization of the volunteer soldiers during battle of Bull Run.

November 7   Union combined army-naval expedition captures sea islands of South Carolina.

November–December   *Cotton Kingdom* is published.

December 10   Bill to reform Medical Bureau is introduced in Congress.

1862
February 13   Receives offer from Salmon P. Chase to work with plantation blacks as representative of Treasury Department in South Carolina sea islands and at the same time is

	offered position of street commissioner of New York City by Mayor George Opdyke.
April 13	Meets with Secretary of War Stanton to ask for position superintending blacks in the sea islands.
April 16	President Lincoln signs into law the bill reorganizing the Medical Bureau.
April 25	U.S. Senate confirms appointment of William A. Hammond as surgeon general.
April 29	Goes with Sanitary Commission workers to Virginia Peninsula to direct operation of hospital ships.
May 30–31	Battle of Fair Oaks (Seven Pines).
June 25–July 1	Seven Days' Battles.
July 17	Leaves Virginia Peninsula and returns to New York City.
August 29–30	Union troops are defeated at second battle of Bull Run.
August 30– September 11	Visits Saratoga Springs, N.Y., for reasons of health.
September 17	Battle of Antietam.
September– October	Large donations to the Sanitary Commission are received from California.
November– December	Cincinnati branch of USSC threatens to become independent unless it is given a portion of donation from California.
November 22– December 8	Olmsted's power to disburse funds and award salary increases is limited by Executive Committee of USSC.

1863

February 21	Union League Club of New York meets for the first time.
February 25– April	Undertakes "Journey in the West," with stops in Altoona, Pittsburgh, Cincinnati, Louisville, Nashville, Murfreesboro, Memphis, Helena, Young's Point, Cairo, St. Louis, Chicago, and Buffalo.
April 14	Returns to Washington.
April 25	Refuses to resume general superintendence of USSC.
June 25	Holds organizational meeting to secure funding for proposed weekly newspaper.

July 1–3	Union forces turn back Confederate invasion at battle of Gettysburg.
c. July	*Hospital Transports* is published.
August 10	Is offered position of superintendent of Mariposa Estate in California.
September 1	Resigns as general secretary of USSC.
September 14	Sails for California.

LIST OF TEXTUAL ALTERATIONS

Each entry in the list gives the page and line number of the altered text, followed by the original form of the text. For documents beginning after the first line of a page, lines are counted from the addressee line or from the first line of the title of the document. Alterations of text in the endnotes of a document are identified by page, note, and line number.

BIOGRAPHICAL DIRECTORY

79: 5   unintentional in

114: 17   life nothing

CHAPTER I

To Henry Whitney Bellows, June 1, 1861
118: 12   confession my

To John Olmsted, June 26, 1861
120: 7   apprehend be

120: 19   affctn

To Mary Perkins Olmsted, June 28, 1861
121: 14   wood a
122: 2   Bat° just
122: 2   outskirts a
122: 3   sleevs
122: 4   arms: hospital
123: 4   stop a

123: 8   coved
123: 17   trowsers strolls
123: 32   up tell
123: 33   lines shoot
123: 34   over fire

To Mary Perkins Olmsted, July 2, 1861
126: 1–2   4ᵗʰ probably

CHAPTER II

To Mary Perkins Olmsted, July 29, 1861
131: 11–12   God McIntee

To William Cullen Bryant, July 31, 1861
133: 22   officers, did   *134: 14*   Respctfly
134: 6   improvemt

To Alfred Field, July 31, 1861
136: 8   How with   *136: 8*   had could

To John Olmsted, August 3, 1861
138: 10   animals there   *138: 40–41*   shirts sheets
138: 31   army will

To Louis Henry Steiner, August 12, 1861
143: 1   reckord   *144: 4*   occasion you

To Henry Whitney Bellows, August 15, 1861
147: 1   throughly

To Henry Whitney Bellows, August 16, 1861
148: 14   from, day   *149: 3*   well thank
148: 31   necessary tell

"Report on the Demoralization of the Volunteers," September 5, 1861
163: 19   forces which   *165: 9*   spoke it
163: 20   approaching to   *174: 23*   all there

To John Olmsted, September 12, 1861
195: 7   appeared with   *196: 19*   Wednesday—baggage
195: 35   hand) We   *196: 24*   bivouc
195: 40   force) His   *196: 27–28*   it two
196: 1   indispensble   *196: 38*   N.Y. 2ᵈ
196: 6   drove some   *197: 6*   circumlocution was
196: 8   it the   *197: 25*   affection

CHAPTER III

To Henry Whitney Bellows, September 25, 1861
200: 14–15   office you   *202: 28–29*   them. Miss Dix
200: 18   place taken   *203: 5*   bring
201: 5   recevd   *203: 16*   generalization the
201: 15   o'ck   *203: 21–22*   swing. Hoping

To Mary Perkins Olmsted, September 28, 1861
207: 16–17   Ecce homo! I   208: 7   on
207: 18   equisitely

To Henry Whitney Bellows, September 29, 1861
209: 7   me I   210: 18   told will
210: 11   strength spirit

To Mary Perkins Olmsted, October 19, 1861
213: 12   us Mr   213: 29   o ck

To Mary Olmsted, November 6, 1861
218: 13   you refer   219: 4   so the
218: 19   them he   219: 33   gneral
218: 35–36   field those

To Charles Loring Brace, November 8, 1861
224: 16   entirely the

To Charles Handy Russell, November 12, 1861
226: 13   skillfully carefully   227: 8   taste judgment
227: 1   Board, for   227: 31   Respy

To John Strong Newberry, November 16, 1861
229: 8   trouble the   229: 12   trouble for
229: 9   out we   229: 14   out we

To Sarah Blake Sturgis Shaw, November 29, 1861
231: 11   surgeons Every   232: 12–13   one-hundreth

"How to Reason with the South," November 29, 1861
233: 18   imperfect it   237: 2   discontented of
236: 38   imperative, for

To John Murray Forbes, December 15, 1861
240: 10   continues I

To Henry Whitney Bellows, December 20, 1861
242: 16   inefficient let   242: 18   precisly

To Henry Whitney Bellows, December 21, 1861
246: 8   out there   246: 13   made we

To James Russell Lowell, January 12, 1862
248: 13   not it

To John Strong Newberry, January 15, 1862
250: 10   Prest   250: 16   issud

To Henry Whitney Bellows, January 18, 1862
252: 11   friends instead   254: 20   Prest

To Bertha Olmsted, January 28, 1862

256: 21 judgment, McC.	258: 9 overwhlmd
257: 10 Comsn	258: 15 hand grows
258: 9 much he	258: 16 quaint ready

To George Frederic Magoun, February 6, 1862

261: 11 Virginia in	263: 30 Expeditions a
261: 11 manner, ravaged	263: 32 Missouri they
261: 11 War furnishes	264: 12 have that
261: 15–16 state sufficient	264: 14 Union come
261: 38 low Iowa	264: 17 contribution there
262: 31 one to	265: 24 report supply
262: 37 Commission is	265: 25 organization: sixth
263: 5 known how	265: 26 St Louis: eighth

To Henry Whitney Bellows, February 7, 1862
268: 10 them to

CHAPTER IV

To Henry Whitney Bellows, February 15, 1862

272: 11 shally disjointed	272: 27 fair steady

To James Reed Spalding, February 15, 1862

275: 26 12000	276: 1 temporizing penny

To Manton Malone Marble, February 16, 1862
278: 10 function, is

To John Strong Newberry, February 24, 1862
279: 15 myself approved

To Charles Eliot Norton, March 3, 1862
284: 11 deposit he

To Abraham Lincoln, March 3, 1862

286: 20 charity, second	287: 13 points the
286: 21 obligations, third	287: 26 failure otherwise
286: 27 are they	287: 27 it, will

To John Olmsted, March 25, 1862

291: 13 made without	291: 26 Washton

To Edwin McMasters Stanton, April 13, 1862

292: 3 slavery there	293: 24 what, to
293: 8 hard unrequited	293: 42 heal
293: 8–9 crude monotonous	294: 15 government nothing
293: 22 African	294: 25 demonstrate what

295: 36 Slavery will	299: 16 matter to
297: 21 rights; to	300: 6 attention, it
298: 15 men women	300: 13 government the
298: 17 alone what	300: 21 because, I
298: 23 them; Can	301: 10 recvd
298: 39 As	301: 11 suffg
298: 41 districts.	301: 12 sufict
299: 10 therefor I	301: 20 suptdce

To James Erwin Yeatman, April 17, 1862
307: 7 St. Louis why

To John Strong Newberry, April 18, 1862
308: 26 are compared

To John Olmsted, April 19, 1862

309: 9 receved	310: 7–8 again at
309: 11 matter, did	310: 19 who this
310: 3 Commission our	311: 15 soed

CHAPTER V

To Henry Whitney Bellows, May 7, 1862

320: 25 avergg	322: 11–12 industry
320: 29 ordred	self-possession
320: 35 assst	322: 18 arrivg
321: 5 circumstances satisfactory	322: 31 Respy
322: 11 unting	

"Labors of the Sanitary Commission," May 15, 1862

327: 13–14 Wmsbg	327: 22 sake give
329: 10 hospital the	330: 6 outside to
329: 17 it only	330: 9 way a

John Foster Jenkins, May 18, 1862

334: 15 me it	334: 38 justice that
334: 24 placed there	336: 7 receivg
334: 28 friends; is	336: 9 ladis

To John Foster Jenkins, May 20, 1862

338: 12 him handed	340: 32 lead
340: 24 practicable not	341: 22 Gl Sy

To John Foster Jenkins, May 21, 1862

343: 20 distant, and	345: 6 Dpt
344: 19 advancing anything	345: 21–22 men there

345: 43   North, shall
346: 7   tons, at

346: 35   night-fall though
348: *n. 12, l. 4*   entrance shelter

To John Foster Jenkins, May 29, 1862
352: 8   Mr Rogers we
353: 3   been since
353: 3–4   sailed trying
353: 17   dumb foundered
353: 25   arrived not
353: 35   out as
353: 41   surgeons twenty
353: 43   nurses I
354: 7   rest the

354: 10   Vanderbilt) equip
354: 10   us; put
354: 16   but
354: 17   Gnl is
354: 39–40   here on
354: 40   arrival about
355: 9   San. Com. credit
355: 12   governors there
355: 17   them best

To Henry Whitney Bellows, June 3, 1862
357: 27   up she
357: 37   fireing
358: 13   this he
360: 3   Dr Smith, not
360: 11–13   required. I
360: 39   need from
361: 23   hobbld
361: 31   circumstances the

361: 36   orders, of
361: 37–38   pantleoons
362: 29–30   hospital might
362: 31   useing
364: 12   Sawtelle at
364: 23   them, had
364: 42   Syracuse and
366: *n. 10, l. 25*   time perform

To Mary Perkins Olmsted, June 11, 1862
368: 30   lonely are

368: 39   untireing

To Henry Whitney Bellows, June 13, 1862
370: 38   responsibility, orders

To Henry Whitney Bellows, June 17, 1862
373: 4   War) 2
373: 29   time) my

373: 36   Commission I

To Henry Whitney Bellows, June 18, 1862
374: 9   this send
375: 1   not that

376: 37   expressed have

To Henry Whitney Bellows, June 22, 1862
379: 13   condition that
379: 38   soldierly orderly

380: 33   Associations and
380: 35   men; we

To Charles Loring Brace, June 29, 1862
382: 6   general, I

To Mary Perkins Olmsted, July 3, 1862
385: 7   hill artillery
385: 18–19   shell the

385: 20   intensity; then

To Henry Whitney Bellows, July 4, 1862

388: *12*	do to	391: *16*	sickness and
389: *30*	enemy again	391: *16*	list, will
389: *30*	repulsed reforms	391: *18-19*	requirements the
390: *5*	holding with	392: *4*	30,000 our
390: *6*	of, the	392: *22*	Gl. Sy.

To Abraham Lincoln, July 6, 1862

394: *3*   Gl. Sec'y

To Henry Whitney Bellows, July 7, 1862

396: *3*   anticipated no   396: *23*   Respy

To Preston King, July 9, 1862

397: *13*   watchful wiley   397: *15*   another government

To Sydney Howard Gay, July 12, 1862

399: *38*   judge a   400: *17*   comes he
400: *16-17*   that when

To Henry Whitney Bellows, July 13, 1862

402: *7*   place do

To Henry Whitney Bellows, July 13, 1862

404: *5*   service, no

CHAPTER VI

To Mary Perkins Olmsted, August 12, 1862

408: *6-7*   morning breakfasted   409: *21*   proffesnl
409: *8*   Knapp's a

To John Strong Newberry, August 25, 1862

411: *37*   Septer

To Charles Loring Brace, August 25, 1862

413: *16*   (McClellan's) I   413: *33-34*   Stanton. We

Charles Loring Brace to Frederick Law Olmsted, September 12, 1862

415: *29*   through to   416: *14*   health
416: *13*   Colonel Letitia   416: *15*   affly

To Charles Loring Brace, September 21, 1862

418: *11-12*   else you   420: *29*   affectly
420: *1*   Horton M.C.

To Mary Perkins Olmsted, September 21, 1862

422: *20*	swore, so	423: *18*	not do
422: *31*	aftwds	423: *33*	regardg
422: *41*	New York sent	424: *2*	St rent
423: *3*	govmt		

To Henry Whitney Bellows, September 22, 1862
426: 27   Beuregard

To Mary Perkins Olmsted, September 26, 1862
428: 3   Mryld   429: 10   affecte

To Charles Loring Brace, September 30, 1862
430: 20   R.R. he   431: 8   nothing he
431: 4   organized that   431: 10   not he

Charles Loring Brace to Frederick Law Olmsted, October 1, 1862
435: 26   which I   437: 27   affly
436: 1–2   officers Our

To Henry Whitney Bellows, October 3, 1862
440: 26   resply

To Henry Whitney Bellows, October 3, 1862
442: 10   patrons, would   444: 36   acceptibly
443: 28   all that   444: 42   it) not
443: 28   Park, depended   444: 42   theory which
443: 35   grindstone, if   445: 13   Agnew were
444: 17   rather speaking   445: 19   agents and

To Charles Loring Brace, October 4, 1862
449: 2–3   intention you   452: 6   abominable infernal
450: 17   me if   452: 6   infernal, injustice
450: 33   John Pope Fremont   452: 10   affectly
450: 37   specemins

To Henry Whitney Bellows, October 7, 1862
453: 14   operators, are   455: 7–8   indepently
454: 3   exercise to

To Mary Perkins Olmsted, October 11, 1862
458: 11   magnitude every   460: 14   determed
460: 8   is to   460: 20   written I

CHAPTER VII

To John Strong Newberry, October 11, 1862
464: 16   branches propose,

To Oliver Wolcott Gibbs, November 5, 1862
468: 4   reled   470: 16   admitg

To John Strong Newberry, November 5, 1862
472: 6   recevd   473: 30   recive

474: 12   reitrerated
474: 21   knowlege

475: 4   district Maryland

To MARY PERKINS OLMSTED, NOVEMBER 13, 1862
479: 15   book-case not
479: 22   affecte

To HENRY WHITNEY BELLOWS, NOVEMBER 24, 1862
482: 4   false first
483: 2   it it

To JOHN STRONG NEWBERRY, DECEMBER 4, 1862
486: 6   recevd
486: 15   case as
486: 20   not then
486: 29   are I

486: 29   judge very
486: 32   colum
486: 36   Cordly

To GEORGE TEMPLETON STRONG, DECEMBER 4, 1862
488: 12   so) The
488: 24   west than

To GEORGE TEMPLETON STRONG, DECEMBER 6, 1862
490: 12   say by
490: 16   theory it

490: 20   accordg
490: 21   public before

To HENRY WHITNEY BELLOWS, DECEMBER 10, 1862
492: 3   Washgn
493: 7   with the
494: 7   aquisitiveness
494: 8   so the

494: 15   agents all
494: 17   affectly
494: *n. 2, l. 6*   caution formality
494: *n. 2, l. 10* $____ it

To JOHN STRONG NEWBERRY, DECEMBER 27, 1862
496: 14   do, do
497: 1–2   Nashville thinking

497: 3   yours) I

To HENRY WHITNEY BELLOWS, DECEMBER 27, 1862
499: 19   brain turn
499: 32   same I

499: 35   danging
499: 36   you turn

To GEORGE TEMPLETON STRONG, JANUARY 29, 1863
504: 12   cases, such
504: 12   little—give
504: 13   it—but

504: 20–21   conversation until
504: 22   meeting it
504: 31   it is

To OLIVER WOLCOTT GIBBS, JANUARY 31, 1863
505: 19   ready willing
505: 28   not please
505: 28–29   is why

506: 3   recive
506: 31   affctly

To WILLIAM HENRY HURLBERT, JANUARY 31, 1863
508: 9   synonimous

To Henry Whitney Bellows, February 4, 1863
510: 18   West many   511: 27   him—could
511: 3   Buffalo) to   511: 28   shop, is

To Calvert Vaux, February 16, 1863
515: 11   disposition jealousy   515: 34   affectly
515: 15   concerned I

To Charles Janeway Stillé, February 25, 1863
516: 37   recognition or   519: n. 5, l. 2   here the
517: 19   seen my   519: n. 5, l. 3   Hfd

To Mary Olmsted, February 25, 1863
519: 4   recived   520: 33   do, as
519: 6   Acady   520: 39   Affecty
520: 13   ribbons wear

CHAPTER VIII

Journey in the West, Cincinnati, March 1, 1863
524: 12   just it   527: 9   yes
524: 13   thee O   527: 19–20   rule" Shall
524: 13   Carl student   527: 30   Trollope nor
524: 21–22   fifteen) questioned 528: 24   boys one
526: 9   another four   528: 36   Cincinnati it
526: 12   and feeling   528: 36   me is
526: 32   sweep—I   529: n. 7, l. 2   adjing
526: 37   in for   531: n. 17, l. 3   it my

To Mary Perkins Olmsted, March 2, 1863
532: 35   father &c

Journey in the West, Nashville to Murfreesboro, March 7, 1863
536: 8   ombus   538: 7   foot to
536: 8   6.15   538: 32   who knowing
536: 10   There's   539: 2   Rosecrans.
536: 10   5.45   540: 3   back; he
536: 13   5.15   540: 7   room gentlemen
536: 14   5.45   540: 41   play honor
536: 16–17   hour can't   541: 7   gleamed. "My
536: 26   5.15   542: 25   An
537: 5   cold and   542: 32   blanket, was
537: 10   however that   542: 35   mounted the
537: 31   Nashville every   542: 41–42   excentric

To Mary Perkins Olmsted, March 8, 1863
546: 25   when no

Journey in the West, Louisville toward Cairo, March 13, 1863

549: 10 than under	549: 13 morose not
549: 12 if under	549: 13 quarrelsome while

Journey in the West, Memphis to Young's Point, March 16–24, 1863

554: 16 said "D'ole	560: 13 rear and
554: 16 nor	560: 26–27 landed there
554: 25 evng	561: 1 fellas, said
554: 28 supdt	561: 1 other, dey
554: 29 ackndgd	561: 11 plantation I
555: 13 high-toned gentlemen	561: 12 away.
555: 15 jail.	561: 20 again and
555: 40 ride they	562: 5 commandg
556: 4 said and	562: 9 that
556: 12 commandg	562: 17 fat sleek
556: 16 manner and	562: 31 Porter the
556: 28 commandg	563: 10 state-room I
557: 3 resolute modest	563: 13 boat. (During
557: 25 floor the	564: 19 Nothing only
557: 25 full and	565: 24 relived
558: 21 conversation he	565: 33 other the
558: 21 The	
560: 5 government it	

To John Olmsted, April 1, 1863

570: 3 Missippi	574: 3 gun has
571: 3 Hd. Q. the	574: 4 there?
571: 11–12 it. The	574: 28 one at
572: 5 army tho'	574: 41 go he
572: 6 general is	575: 2–3 quiet gentle
572: 14 sound I	575: 5 will however,
572: 14–15 them. We	575: 9 obstructions
572: 20 parks pictures	embarrassments
572: 22 Louvre had	575: 26 them they
572: 40–41 best. McMillan	575: 36–37 again." I
573: 3–4 managed). Janney	576: 9 but with all this one
573: 7 disciplinable grateful	576: 11 out he
573: 23 after however	

To Edwin Lawrence Godkin, April 4, 1863

580: 11 together I	582: 17 both with
580: 17 canals and	582: 27 more, to
581: 10 this I	582: 30 could without
581: 17 that I	583: 6 comes the
582: 4 Rosecrans when	

Journey in the West, St. Louis, Chicago, April 4–11, 1863

587: 26   transactions would
587: 27   is, had
588: 15   supposed suffers
588: 20   found in
588: 32   How
588: 32   men?
588: 43   them we
589: 14   nicely slowly
589: 20   would for
589: 25   surprise the
590: 10   average, though
590: 11   fashions, on
590: 41   splendor in
591: 2   live there
591: 4–6   direction. It
591: 12   part the
591: 37   town even
591: 42–43   community you
592: 8   mud; an
592: 9   dividends etc.
592: 15   a begging

592: 27   me: Do
593: 29   States, has equally
593: 31   sagacious well-read
594: 11   town the
594: 24   England he
594: 43   of, the
595: 4–5   them would
596: 1   man if
596: 9–10   capacity. I
596: 20–21   it. Today
596: 32   mine had
596: 34   should had
596: 34–35   so. You
597: 8   St Louis, *an*
598: 8   whom but
598: 13   admit I
598: 13   think that
598: 19–20   offices. The
600: *n. 15, l. 2*   H^d
601: *n.22, ll. 14–15*   business going

CHAPTER IX

To John Olmsted, April 18, 1863
604: 15   this some

To John Olmsted, April 25, 1863
614: 7   me is
614: 22   could the

614: 24   what without knowing
them you

To Henry Whitney Bellows, April 25, 1863
617: 12   mean, but

To Charles Eliot Norton, April 30, 1863
618: 17   up that
618: 18   traitors no one
619: 6   control would
619: 18   all, by

619: 31   strong but
619: 32   money-making especially
620: 12   were, in
621: *n. 3, l. 5*   is absolute

To Mary Bull Olmsted, May 22, 1863
624: 11   possible of

625: 6   try but

"Prospectus for a Weekly Journal," June 25, 1863
630: 39   and a still a
632: 22   doctrines uttered

633: 12   than
633: 41   itself of

To MARY PERKINS OLMSTED, JUNE 26, 1863

636: 4   recved
636: 7   all I
636: 23   night half

636: 25   said I
636: 25–26   subscription will

To HENRY WHITNEY BELLOWS, JULY 4, 1863

638: 13   Times a
638: 17   Copperheads, no
638: 24   less in
639: 8   truth in
640: 6   upon it
640: 28   criminal as

641: 2   circumstances far
641: 16   prosecution? This
641: 22   neighborhoods sections
642: 7   want what
642: 17   Gulf Down
642: 29   think the

To MARY PERKINS OLMSTED, JULY 7, 1863

646: 35   army when

646: 35   over had

To THE EXECUTIVE COMMITTEE, JULY 9, 1863

650: 10   fifty
650: 13   fought the
650: 33   town-shops) send

650: 35   Buffalo Boston
652: n. 6, l. 6   wen

To EDWIN LAWRENCE GODKIN, JULY 15, 1863

654: 3   formed they
654: 19   condition marches

654: 21   regiments many
655: 1   M. D." "Doctoress

To EDWIN LAWRENCE GODKIN, JULY 19, 1863

658: 14   wood it
659: 35   rebels, did
660: 11   Equation The
660: 22   Loyalist, wears

660: 38–39   W. F. Smith Franklin
660: 39–661: 1   Reynolds Dana
Hartsoff

To HENRY WHITNEY BELLOWS, JULY 25, 1863

665: 7   Bellows D^r
666: 26   till, Agnew
667: 25   informed is
669: 25   ability could
671: 14   specemin
671: 20   word, I
671: 29   yours, I
671: 37   wo

672: 6   advice with
672: 7   employees,—I
672: 31   not as
673: 26   Commission's formally
673: 27   commenced I
678: n. 17, l. 3   ministers were
678: n. 19, l. 9   case might

To JOHN SAMUEL BLATCHFORD, JULY 27, 1863

679: 16–17   New York Philadelphia
679: 22   New York more

679: 29   Gettysburg except

To HENRY WHITNEY BELLOWS, JULY 28, 1863

681: 21   you I think about

To MARY PERKINS OLMSTED, JULY 29, 1863

683: 27   not if

To Edwin Lawrence Godkin, August 1, 1863
686: *12*   affectly

To John Olmsted, August 10, 1863
686: *11*   liberal the   687: *9*   affection
687: *2*   you but

To Mary Perkins Olmsted, August 12, 1863
688: *10*   Finally general   688: *22*   go it
688: *17-18*   limits, controlling   688: *27*   think much

To Samuel Gridley Howe, August 13, 1863
689: *9*   house-servants mechanics   690: *7*   Respectly

To Henry Whitney Bellows, August 15, 1863
691: *6*   recevd   692: *27*   Com. my
692: *4*   die my   693: *21-22*   circumstances to
692: *7-8*   me I   693: *23*   mind to

To Henry Whitney Bellows, August 16, 1863
695: *21*   impertinent disrespectful   698: *27*   me is
696: *36*   Commission that   699: *35*   I there
696: *43*   concerned my   699: *36*   me I
697: *26*   directors though   701: *9*   got I
698: *16*   True and   701: *14*   meeting my

To Henry Whitney Bellows, September 1, 1863
704: *24*   these uniform   706: *30*   which I
705: *12*   Commission two   707: *7*   indicated I
706: *12*   them to   707: *32*   office agrees
706: *24*   regret have   709: *9*   foundation independently

INDEX

Italic numbers indicate illustrations.

731